Shepherd's Notes
NEW TESTAMENT

One Volume Commentary

HOLMAN®
REFERENCE
BRENTWOOD, TENNESSEE

Shepherd's Notes on the New Testament

The interior was typeset by TF Designs, Greenbrier, TN.

Binding	ISBN
Hardcover	979-8-3845-2351-2

Printed in China
1 2 3 4 5 — 28 27 26 25
AP FT1617201

CONTENTS

HOW TO USE THIS BOOK

DESIGNED FOR THE BUSY USER

Shepherd's Notes on the New Testament is designed to provide an easy-to-use tool for getting a quick handle on the New Testament Bible books important features, and for gaining an understanding of their messages. Information available in more difficult-to-use reference works has been incorporated into the *Shepherd's Notes* on the New Testament format. This provides you with the benefits of many advanced and expensive works packed into one compact volume.

Shepherd's Notes on the New Testament are for laymen, pastors, teachers, small-group leaders and participants, as well as the classroom student. Enrich your personal study or quiet time. Shorten your class or small-group preparation time as you gain valuable insights into the truths of God's Word that you can pass along to your students or group members.

DESIGNED FOR QUICK ACCESS

Bible students with time constraints will especially appreciate the time-saving features built into the *Shepherd's Notes format*. All features are intended to aid a quick and concise encounter with the heart of the messages of the New Testament books.

Concise Commentary. The New Testament books are filled with stories about characters who respond to God's call in their lives. Short sections provide quick "snapshots" of the narrative and themes of these books, highlighting important points and other information.

Outlined Text. Comprehensive outlines cover the entire texts of the books. This is a valuable feature for following each narrative's flow, allowing for a quick, easy way to locate a particular passage.

Section Summary. These summary statements or capsule thoughts appear at the close of every key section of the narratives. While functioning in part as a quick summary, they also deliver the essence of the message presented in the sections which they cover.

Sidebars and Charts. These specially selected features provide additional background information to your study or preparation. Charts offer a quick overview of important subjects. Sidebars are used throughout each book calling your attention to historical-cultural information, Old Testament and New Testament references, word pictures, and personal application for everyday life.

Maps. These are placed at appropriate places in the book to aid your understanding and study of a text or passage.

Questions to Guide Your Study. These thought-provoking questions and discussion starters are designed to encourage interaction with the truth and principles of God's Word.

DESIGNED TO WORK FOR YOU

Personal Study. Using the Shepherd's Notes with a passage of Scripture can enlighten your study and take it a new level. At your fingertips is information that would require searching several volumes to find. In addition, many points of application occur throughout the volume, contributing to personal growth.

ABBREVIATIONS IN CSB BIBLES

AD	In the year of our Lord
BC	before Christ
c.	century
ca	circa
chap(s).	chapter(s)
cp.	compare
DSS	Dead Sea Scrolls
e.g.	for example
Eng	English
etc.	et cetera
Gk	Greek
Hb	Hebrew
i.e.	that is
Lat	Latin
lit	literal(ly)
LXX	Septuagint—an ancient translation of the Old Testament into Greek
MT	Masoretic Text
NT	New Testament
ms(s)	manuscript(s)
OT	Old Testament
pl.	plural
Ps(s)	Psalm(s)
Sam	Samaritan Pentateuch
sg.	singular
Sym	Symmachus
Syr	Syriac
Tg	Targum
Theod	Theodotian
v./vv.	verse, verses
Vg	Vulgate—an ancient translation of the Bible into Latin
vol(s).	volume(s)

Matthew

INTRODUCTION

The Gospel of Matthew has likely influenced more people than any other Christian book. Its role of influence probably began with its acceptance by Antioch, a great early Christian center. The greater use of Matthew comes in part from its first-place position in the New Testament. Also, only Matthew contains the Sermon on the Mount (Matt 5–7).

AUTHOR

Early in the first century AD, a Christian writer wrote this account of Jesus's life and teachings. This Gospel, like all four canonical Gospels, is anonymous. Nowhere in the Gospel does it disclose its author. Early tradition, however, attributed the work to Matthew, one of Jesus's twelve apostles.

AUDIENCE

Early church tradition meshes with the style and contents of the Gospel to suggest that Matthew wrote to a Jewish-Christian audience. It is difficult to narrow down the destination any further. A few ancient sources favored Palestine, perhaps Jerusalem. Modern scholars often propose Syria, particularly Antioch.

PURPOSE

Matthew most likely wrote his Gospel for several reasons: (1) he wanted to convince non-Christian Jews of the truth of Christianity; (2) he sought to explain to Christians how their religion is the fulfillment of God's promises and patterns of activity in the Old Testament; (3) he wanted to give young believers basic instruction in Christian living; (4) he wanted to encourage his church in the midst of persecution from hostile authorities in both Jewish and Roman circles; and (5) he desired to deepen Christian faith by supplying more details about Jesus's words and works.

DATE AND PLACE OF WRITING

Hostility between the Jews and Jesus's followers on the pages of the Gospel has suggested to many that Matthew's Jewish-Christian church had decisively broken from the (non-Christian) synagogue. This often leads to dating the Gospel to the mid-80s or later, after the synagogues allegedly introduced a curse on heretics (including Christians) into their liturgy of prayers. Quotations from the apostolic fathers suggests an upper limit for the dating around AD 100. As a result, most Bible scholars believe Matthew's Gospel was written around AD 80 and 90.

DISTINCTIVES IN MATTHEW'S GOSPEL

Several distinctive characteristics are evident in Matthew.

- Because of its position, it is the most widely read book in the New Testament and has exerted the greatest influence on the world.
- Ten parables appear in Matthew that are not found in the other Gospels: the wheat and the weeds (13:24–30), the hidden treasure (13:44), the pearl of great price (13:45–46), the dragnet (13:47–50), the unforgiving servant (18:23–35), the laborers in the vineyard (20:1–16), the two sons (21:28–32), the wedding banquet (22:1–14), the ten virgins (25:1–13), and the talents (25:14–30).
- The only two parables recorded involving money are found in Matthew's Gospel: the unforgiving servant (13:21–35) and the laborers in the vineyard (20:1–16).
- Of the four Gospels, only Matthew's makes specific mention of the Church (16:18; 18:17).
- Matthew stressed "last things," the coming of the end time (e.g., 24:1–25:46).

WORD PICTURE

Matthew's Titles for Jesus

Christ. The Greek transliteration of the Hebrew term *Messiah*, which means "the anointed one."

Son of David. Points to the Messiah's link to Israel's most honored king and the fact that he is to be of royal blood.

Son of Abraham. Traces Jesus's lineage back to the founding father of the nation of Israel.

MATTHEW 1

HEADING (1:1)

This heading introduces the main character of Matthew's Gospel and describes his identity in terms of his Jewish heritage. The titles "Christ," "Son of David," and "Son of Abraham" held high significance for Matthew's audience.

RECORD OF JESUS'S ANCESTRY (1:2–17)

Purpose of Matthew's Record

Many people skip over the genealogies of the Bible. After all, lists of obscure, long-dead people are not very interesting. But Matthew had a definite purpose in starting his Gospel with Jesus's genealogy. The *linear genealogy*, which Matthew uses, seeks to show that the final person listed has a legitimate right to the position of honor the person occupies. Matthew wanted to establish Jesus as a legitimate descendant of David and rightful candidate for the messianic throne.

Structure of the Record

He divides the genealogy into three general sections (of fourteen entries), each covering a phase of Jewish history. The first section spans Abraham to David, the greatest king of Israel (vv. 2–6). The second section covers Jewish history from the time of David's son Solomon to the Babylonian exile (vv. 7–11). The third section includes the time until the coming of Jesus, the Savior of all people (vv. 12–18).

Special Features of the Record

Matthew's genealogy contains several points of special interest.

Mention of Four Women. Contrary to Jewish tradition, Matthew includes four women in his genealogy. Moreover, these were not women one might expect to be included. Tamar was an adulteress (v. 3). Ruth, a Moabitess, was not a Jew (v. 5). Rahab was a harlot (v. 5), and Bathsheba, the wife of Uriah, had been wrongfully taken by David (v. 6). The factor that clearly applies to all four is that suspicions of illegitimacy surrounded their sexual activity and childbearing.

This suspicion fits perfectly with the circumstances that surrounded Mary, so Matthew immediately takes pains to refute it. In fact, the grammar of verse 16 makes clear that Joseph was not the human father of Jesus. The pronoun *whom* is feminine and therefore can refer only to Mary as the human parent of the Christ child.

Joseph as Jesus's Legal Father. Matthew, true to Jewish custom, traces Jesus's descent through Joseph, even though Joseph was not Jesus's real father. According to Jewish Law, however, Joseph, as Mary's husband, was Jesus's *legal* father.

THE BIRTH OF JESUS THE MESSIAH (1:18–25)

Matthew begins his Gospel by recounting selected events surrounding Jesus's birth (about 4–6 BC). The rest of Matthew's "infancy narrative" is comprised of five quotations from the Old Testament and the stories

PERSONAL APPLICATION

The inclusion of four women in Jesus's genealogy shows that: (1) God can use all kinds of people, even those who are conspicuously imperfect, in the carrying out of his plan, and (2) we see the solidarity of Jesus with sinful humanity. Jesus came to sinful human beings to break down barriers between God and human beings, Jew and Gentile, male and female, and the righteous and the unrighteous.

OLD TESTAMENT REFERENCE

Virgin Birth

The virgin birth of Jesus is a fulfillment of Old Testament prophecy. Isaiah 7:14 tells us: "Therefore, the Lord himself will give you a sign: See, the virgin will conceive, have a son, and name him Immanuel."

HISTORICAL BACKGROUND

Magi were wise men, priests, and astrologers who were students of the heavens and interpreters of dreams. Joseph and Mary received a visit from magi whose interpretation of the stars led them to Palestine to find and honor the newborn King. They may have come from Babylon, Persia, or the Arabian desert.

that illustrate five ways those texts were fulfilled in Jesus (1:18–2:23). The first of these fulfillments is the virginal conception of Jesus. Matthew's account of Jesus's birth is written from Joseph's viewpoint. In contrast, Luke's Gospel narrates the event from Mary's point of view.

OLD TESTAMENT REFERENCE

The Magi

Verses 4–6 contain the second of Matthew's five fulfillment quotations of prophecy: "Bethlehem Ephrathah, you are small among the clans of Judah; one will come from you to be ruler over Israel for me. His origin is from antiquity, from ancient times." (Mic 5:2)

Section Summary

Matthew sees in the coming of Jesus the complete fulfillment of Isa 7:14. That prophecy calls the son who would be born "Immanuel," meaning "God with us."

QUESTIONS TO GUIDE YOUR STUDY

1. What is the value of Matthew's genealogical record to us?
2. What do the record's special features reveal?
3. How do Old Testament prophecies support Jesus's birth as that of the Messiah?

HISTORICAL BACKGROUND

Dreams in the Bible

In the ancient Near Eastern world, dreams had great significance. In some cases, they provided information about the future and were used to show the dreamer the right decision to make. The dreams of common people were important to them, but the dreams of kings and holy men or women were important on a national or international scale. As Matthew's narrative shows, God used dreams as a vehicle of revelation in the birth and early days of Jesus.

MATTHEW 2

Matthew opens this chapter by providing the time and place of Jesus's birth, which took place approximately five miles south of Jerusalem, at the time when Herod was king.

VISIT FROM THE WISE MEN (2:1–12)

A group of wise men, or magi, journeyed from the East to pay homage to the newborn Jewish king. We don't know how many were in the group. The traditional idea that there were three stems from the mention of three kinds of gifts.

This unusual event occurred close to the time of Jesus's birth, but its exact time is unknown. These men studied the heavens and saw a new star which they interpreted as heralding the birth of the long-hoped-for Messiah of the Jews.

When Herod learned that the wise men were searching for the Jewish king, he became deeply troubled. He was jealous of any threat to his throne. Herod implemented a plan to murder all male infants in an effort to make sure he killed the new Jewish king. In a dream, God warned the wise men not to go back to Herod. They obeyed God's warning and returned by another route to their home country.

OLD TESTAMENT REFERENCE

From the fact that Jesus's family stayed in Egypt until Herod died, Matthew sees fulfillment of the words of the prophet Hosea: "When Israel was a child, I loved him, and out of Egypt I called my son" (11:1). Matthew looks deeper and sees Jesus repeating the experience of the Israelites by being called out of Egypt.

Section Summary

This event shows God's intention to bless Gentiles as well as Jews through his Son. The openness and obedience of these Gentiles stand in sharp contrast to the hostility toward Jesus on the part of Herod.

JOSEPH AND MARY'S ESCAPE FROM KING HEROD (2:13–18)

Herod did not take lightly the failure of the magi to return to him. His order to kill all the male children two years of age and under put Jesus in danger.

But God intervened. In a dream, he warned Joseph to leave Bethlehem quickly, taking Jesus and Mary with him. Joseph obeyed at once, and they fled to Egypt, a Roman province not under Herod's rule. There they found safe haven from Herod and his murderous schemes. Joseph and his family remained in Egypt until Herod's death.

Section Summary

Although Bethlehem became a place of death and sorrow, Jesus's birth signals the promise of future restoration and life.

JOSEPH AND MARY'S RETURN TO NAZARETH (2:19–23)

After Herod the Great died and the danger to Jesus was past, God once again sent an angel to give instructions to Joseph in a dream. Joseph, Mary, and Jesus were to return to Israel. As before, Joseph obeyed without questioning.

Section Summary

Jesus's residence in the despised city Nazareth, following his birth in a humble village, speaks greatly of his humility. This was, however, completely in line with his character as revealed in Phil 2:5–13.

QUESTIONS TO GUIDE YOUR STUDY

1. Note how God used the Old Testament Scriptures to convince Herod where Jesus was born. Does God still use Scripture to convince his people?
2. What events of Matthew 2 point to Jesus as the Messiah?
3. What part did dreams play in the birth and infancy of Jesus?

HISTORICAL BACKGROUND

The place-name *Nazareth* means "branch." It was located in the hill country of lower Galilee about halfway between the Sea of Galilee and the Mediterranean Sea. It was a small village in Jesus's day and did not enjoy prominence until its association with Jesus. To some, Nazareth was a despised city (cp. John 1:46).

OLD TESTAMENT REFERENCE

Matthew sees Jesus's residence in Nazareth as a fulfillment of the prophets' words that the Messiah would be known as a Nazarene. Matthew's statement is somewhat difficult to interpret because no mention of Nazareth can be found in the Old Testament. One explanation, however, may shed some light on Matthew's possible meaning. Isaiah prophesied that people would despise the Servant of the Lord. Some of the contempt shown for Jesus can be seen in the words of Nathanael who, when told about Jesus, asked, "Can anything good come out of Nazareth?" (John 1:46).

MATTHEW 3

In this chapter Matthew jumps abruptly from the events surrounding Jesus's birth to the time of his adult life. He begins this section with the sudden appearance of John the Baptist in the Judean wilderness.

OLD TESTAMENT REFERENCE

"Prepare the way of the LORD in the wilderness make a straight highway for our God in the desert." (Isa 40:3)

THE PREACHING OF JOHN THE BAPTIST (3:1–6)

His Preaching

John's preaching called for the people to repent as he announced the nearness of the "kingdom of heaven" (v. 2). That phrase has the same meaning as the "kingdom of God" and refers to God's kingly rule.

The most important component of John's message concerned his relationship to the Messiah. John preached a coming judgment that the Messiah would carry out. The unusual fact about John's preaching and baptism was that he called Jews to baptism and repentance. In contrast, the Jews believed it was the Gentiles who needed to repent and be baptized.

WORD PICTURE

Repentance is one of the most often mistranslated, and often misunderstood, words of the Bible. The language of the New Testament has a word for *repent* and a different word for *sorry*. The tragedy of it is that we do not have an English word that reproduces exactly the meaning of the Greek word *metanoeō*, "to repent." Too often readers take the word *repent* to mean "to be sorry again." John did not call on the people to be sorry but to change their ways. The word Matthew uses here is a change of mind or attitude that issues in a change of action. A person who truly repents turns from sin and submits his or her life to God's rule.

His Purpose

The people considered John's appearance as the fulfillment of Isaiah's prophecy: The passage in Isaiah speaks of God's coming to lead his people out of their exile in Babylon. It mentions a voice that cried out for a way to be made for the coming of the Lord. Matthew sees John the Baptist as that voice preparing the hearts of the people for the coming of the Messiah, who would lead them out of sin's exile.

John's ministry accomplished three purposes:

1. He prepared for the Messiah's coming by raising expectations and calling for repentance (v. 2).
2. He explained the nature of the Messiah's mission (v. 11; Luke 3:16).
3. He inaugurated the Messiah's ministry by baptizing Jesus (vv. 13–17; Mark 1:9–11; Luke 3:21–23).

Section Summary

God sent John the Baptist as a voice to prepare the hearts of the people for the coming of the Messiah. John clearly taught that one's faith is a matter of personal commitment, not a reliance on ancestral pedigree.

JOHN'S CONFRONTATION WITH THE PHARISEES AND SADDUCEES (3:7–12)

Two groups of Jewish leaders appeared on the scene in Matthew's narrative: the Pharisees and Sadducees. These parties represented two of the main religious sects of Jesus's day. Most of the Jewish supreme court, the Sanhedrin, belonged to one of these two groups.

John's View of the Jewish Leaders (vv. 7–10)

Members of both groups came to John for baptism, either out of curiosity or for public show. John compared them to snakes fleeing a grass fire, calling them a "brood of vipers!" The term *vipers* is in reference to their shrewdness and to the danger they posed to others. John's reaction indicates that he doubted their genuineness and did not heartily welcome them as prospective converts.

John's Baptism (vv. 11–12)

John described his baptism as one for "repentance" (v. 11). He looked ahead to the One who would appear after him who would baptize "with the Holy Spirit and fire."

HISTORICAL BACKGROUND

John the Baptist

John the Baptist was a prophet from a priestly family. He preached a message of repentance, announced the coming of the Messiah, baptized Jesus, and was beheaded by Herod Antipas. John's clothing reminded the people of the ancient prophet Elijah (cf. 2 Kgs 1:8). It was generally believed that Elijah would return just before the Messiah made his appearance. John wore camel hair clothing with a leather girdle. His diet would be considered repulsive to most Westerners. He lived off the land, eating insects (such as locusts, an excellent source of protein) and wild honey (Matt 3:4).

JEWISH GROUPS IN JESUS'S DAY

GROUP	MEANING OF THE NAME	BELIEFS	ACTIVITIES
Pharisees	"The separated ones"	Viewed entire OT as their authority; accepted oral law	Established and controlled synagogues
Sadducees	"The righteous ones"	Viewed only the Torah (Law) as their authority; opposed oral law	In charge of the temple and its services
Essenes	Unknown origin	Considered other literature as authoritative; held to very strict ascetics	Copied and studied manuscripts of the Law
Zealots	Refers to their religious zeal	Similar to Pharisees but believed God had the right to rule over the Jews	Extremely opposed to Roman rule over Palestine
Herodians	Based on their support of the Herodian rulers	A political group comprised of representatives of varied theological perspectives	Supported Herod and the Herodian dynasty

Section Summary

Christians in every age must heed the same warning John gave to the Pharisees and Sadducees. It isn't enough to trust in one's memberships or associations. Without the evidence of a changed life and perseverance of faith, all such grounds of trust prove futile.

THE BAPTISM OF JESUS (3:13–17)

Because baptism implies that a person has repented, John balked at baptizing Jesus. Jesus nevertheless requested baptism for a different reason, "to fulfill all righteousness." That is, his baptism would be doing God's will. John baptized Jesus by immersing him in the water. His rising up from the water provided a picture of his death, burial, and resurrection. Here we have the three persons of the Trinity represented: The Son is baptized, the Spirit descends upon the Son as a dove, and the Father announces his approval from heaven.

Section Summary

The baptism of Jesus marked his entrance into public ministry and confirmed him as the Son of God. The Holy Spirit came to anoint and empower him for the mission that lay ahead.

PERSONAL APPLICATION

Temptation

The word *tempt*, as used here, means "to solicit to sin." Both the Old and New Testaments make clear that God does not entice persons to sin, but both Testaments indicate that God allows human beings to be tempted. The Bible refers to the temptation as coming from the "tempter," "devil," or "Satan." James 1:14 also tells us that "each person is tempted when he is drawn away and enticed by his own evil desire." Persons are thus tempted by the tempter or from within themselves.

QUESTIONS TO GUIDE YOUR STUDY

1. Describe John the Baptist's mission. What did he accomplish?
2. What does it mean to repent?
3. Why was it so important that Jesus be baptized?

MATTHEW 4

JESUS'S TEMPTATIONS IN THE WILDERNESS (4:1–11)

Immediately after Jesus's baptism, the Holy Spirit orchestrated the circumstances that permitted the devil to test Jesus's understanding of his sonship. The Spirit led Jesus into the wilderness where he fasted forty days and forty nights before the temptations took place.

The First Temptation: To Win the World with Bread (vv. 2–4)

This temptation was twofold. First, Jesus had just spent forty days fasting in the wilderness, and he must have been very hungry! Second, the devil used that hunger to suggest a way for Jesus to use his powers. Jesus responds to each temptation with a quote from the Old Testament.

The Second Temptation: To Win the World with Amazing Feats (vv. 5–7)

Having failed with the first temptation, the devil tried again. He took Jesus to the highest portion of the temple and told Jesus to throw himself off. The devil quoted Psalm 91:11–12 to Jesus, which promised God's protection for those who put their trust in him. But Jesus realized that deliberately placing oneself in danger to force God's protection would be presumptuous.

The Third Temptation: To Win the World with Satan's Methods (vv. 8–10)

The devil tried yet a third time. He showed Jesus "all the kingdoms of the world." He proposed to give Jesus all of it if Jesus would only bow down and worship him. Here Satan was implying that the good result (dominion over the world) would justify the evil means used to attain it.

The devil left defeated, his attempts to sway Jesus having failed. He would, however, try to tempt Jesus many times during his forthcoming ministry.

Section Summary

Adam, the first man, gave in to Satan's testing, wanting to be like God himself. But Jesus, who was God's Son, chose the way of service to his Father, wherever that way might lead.

JESUS'S MINISTRY IN GALILEE (4:12–16)

Jesus settled in a new town, Capernaum, which became the headquarters for his Galilean ministry. It was larger and more significant than Nazareth, and it was strategic because of its lakeside setting on the northwest shore of the Sea of Galilee. With this event, Matthew sees the fulfillment of Isa 9:1–2. Here Jesus began preaching.

Verse 12 alludes to the fate of John the Baptist, which will be discussed in more detail in chapter 11.

Section Summary

Jesus begins his earthly ministry. In Jesus the kingdom of God was no longer future but had now become present tense.

OLD TESTAMENT REFERENCE

The Devil

The word *devil* in Greek, the language of the New Testament, means "accuser," as does the Hebrew word translated "Satan" in the Old Testament. Scripture teaches that Satan was a created being, an archangel, and the leader of the rebellious angels who became forever opposed to God and whose ultimate doom Christ's death ensured (e.g., Job 1–2; Zech 3:1–2; 1 Chr 21:1; Luke 10:18; Rev 20).

PERSONAL APPLICATION

God has promised believers the power to overcome temptation. First Corinthians 10:13 promises, "No temptation has come upon you except what is common to humanity. But God is faithful; he will not allow you to be tempted beyond what you are able, but with the temptation he will also provide the way out so that you may be able to bear it."

PERSONAL APPLICATION

The English word *gospel* is from the New Testament Greek word *euangelion*, which means "good news." Prior to the second century, it always referred to oral communication.

THE BEGINNING OF JESUS'S MINISTRY (4:17–22)

A Summary Statement of Jesus's Preaching (v. 17)

Matthew introduces Jesus's public ministry with a statement of the message of his preaching and teaching: "Repent, because the kingdom of heaven has come near."

Jesus Calls His First Disciples (vv. 18–22)

Jesus chose a close group of followers who could share in his work. So early on he called four men to be his disciples. The first two, fishermen, were brothers named Andrew and Simon Peter. We know from John's Gospel that Jesus was already acquainted with these two during the ministry of John the Baptist (John 1:40–42). Two other brothers, James and John, received Jesus's call. They, too, were fishermen and may also have known Jesus earlier.

PROPHECIES FULLFILLED BY JESUS IN MATTHEW

His virgin birth and role as God with us	Matt 1:18,22–23	Isa 7:14
His birth in Bethlehem and shepherd role	Matt 2:4–6	Mic 5:2
His refugee years in Egypt and role as God's Son	Matt 2:14–15	Hos 11:1
His upbringing in Nazareth and messianic role (the Hebrew term for *branch* is *nezer*)	Matt 2:23	Isa 11:1
His preaching ministry in Galilee and role as Light to the Gentiles	Matt 4:12–16	Isa 9:1–2
His healing ministry and role as God's Servant	Matt 8:16–17	Isa 53:4
His reluctance to attract attention and his role as God's chosen and loved Servant	Matt 12:16–21	Isa 42:1–4
His teaching in parables and his role in proclaiming God's sovereign rule	Matt 13:34–35	Ps 78:2
His humble entry into Jerusalem and role as King	Matt 21:1–5	Zech 9:9
His betrayal, arrest, and death and role as Suffering Servant	Matt 26:50,56	The prophetic writings as a whole

JESUS'S TEACHING, PREACHING, AND HEALING (4:23–25)

These three verses amount to a summary statement of Jesus's public ministry. His travels throughout Galilee were characterized by preaching the gospel to open-air crowds as well as in local synagogues. Jesus's preaching was accompanied by mighty acts of healing.

Section Summary

Jesus's invitation to repent, receive the good news, and become citizens of God's kingdom will have significant implications for the attitudes and behavior of those who respond. We see the details of kingdom living in what follows.

QUESTIONS TO GUIDE YOUR STUDY

1. How did Jesus's three temptations differ?
2. What can we learn from the way Jesus resisted and defended himself against these attacks from the devil?
3. How will Jesus help you deal with temptations in your life?

MATTHEW 5

This chapter begins Jesus's first of five discourses in Matthew. This discourse, known as the Sermon on the Mount, covers 5:3–7:27.

PERSONAL APPLICATION

Jesus presents his hearers with nine beatitudes. These beatitudes instruct followers of Jesus in how to have real and lasting happiness. The word *blessed* refers to those who are, and will be, happy because of God's response to their behavior or situation.

THE SETTING (5:1–2)

This sermon likely took place on a plateau in a hilly area near the Sea of Galilee.

THE BEATITUDES (5:3–12)

***"Blessed are the poor in spirit, for the kingdom of heaven is theirs"* (v. 3)**

These are people who realize their own spiritual poverty. They put all their trust in God's ability to supply their spiritual need.

***"Blessed are those who mourn, for they will be comforted"* (v. 4)**

Those who feel sorrowful because of their own sins and failure and because of the world's evil will ultimately be comforted.

OLD TESTAMENT REFERENCE

"But the humble will inherit the land and will enjoy abundant prosperity." (Ps 37:11)

"Blessed are the humble, for they will inherit the earth" (v. 5)

The humble person has "a gentle strength" (Robertson). God gave a promised land to his people in the Old Testament. The new land of promise will be inherited by those who manifest this characteristic.

"Blessed are those who hunger and thirst for righteousness, for they will be filled" (v. 6)

These are people who want, more than anything else, to see the world's evil (including what is wrong in their own lives) overcome by God's righteousness. Jesus promises these people that God's righteousness will prevail and their desire for it will be satisfied.

"Blessed are the merciful, for they will be shown mercy" (v. 7)

Merciful people realize their own need for God's pardon. Having known God's grace in their own lives, they want to forgive and help others.

"Blessed are the pure in heart, for they will see God" (v. 8)

The pure in heart are those who serve God with single-minded devotion and unmixed motives.

NEW TESTAMENT REFERENCE

"Pursue peace with everyone, and holiness—without it no one will see the Lord." (Heb 12:14)

"Blessed are the peacemakers, for they will be called sons of God" (v. 9)

Jesus promises this blessing not to those who remained neutral or to those who simply love peace but to those who are actively involved in making peace. Christ himself was the "Prince of Peace" (Isa 9:6). He came to bring reconciliation between God and mankind and between individuals. Those who, through him, are at peace with God can join him in his work of reconciliation.

"Blessed are those who are persecuted because of righteousness, for the kingdom of heaven is theirs" (v. 10)

Jesus declares that the kingdom of heaven belongs to those who are persecuted for upholding God's standards of justice, truth, and goodness.

"You are blessed when they insult you and persecute you and falsely say every kind of evil against you because of me" (v. 11)

This is an expansion of the preceding beatitude and is often included with it. Here Jesus tells the disciples that the consequences of following him might result in persecution for righteousness's sake.

Section Summary

Humanity's self-centeredness seeks personal security and survival above the good of others. The Beatitudes, the kingdom blessings, are an inversion of that attitude and its accompanying worldly value system.

SALT AND LIGHT (5:13–16)

Jesus teaches his disciples that their functions in the world are like those of salt and light.

"You are the salt of the earth" (vv. 13–14)

Salt was important in the ancient world because it kept food from spoiling. Like food, society needs an antidote for its corruption. The disciples are to be this antidote.

"You are the light of the world" (vv. 14–16)

Jesus himself is the "true light" (John 1:9) and the "light of the world" (John 8:12). He also called the disciples "the light of the world." Just as the lights of a city situated on a hilltop cannot be hidden, so the disciples radiate the light that comes from Jesus.

PERSONAL APPLICATION

Salt is different from the food into which it is put. When a Christian stops being different from the world and no longer works against the forces of decay, that person stops being salt to the earth. Such a Christian will have no positive influence in the world.

PERSONAL APPLICATION

A lamp that is hidden provides no benefit. Christians sometimes try to hide their light from the world's darkness. Instead, they are to shine in the darkness, dispelling the darkness with loving service. They are to make their influence as Christians felt in the world. Their motive is not to draw attention to themselves but to lead people to give glory to God, who is the source of their works.

Section Summary

Both metaphors Jesus uses in this section raise important questions about Christian involvement in society. We are not called to control secular power structures. But we must remain active preservative agents in calling the world to heed God's standards.

THE PLACE OF THE JEWISH LAW (5:17–20)

Jesus tells his listeners that he has not come "to abolish the Law or the Prophets." Rather, he has come to fulfill them. Jesus goes on to describe the kind of righteousness he requires of his followers by means of six illustrations seen in verses 21–48.

Section Summary

Jesus came not to abolish the Law and the Prophets but to fulfill them and to make it possible for his followers to fulfill them.

A NEW LOOK AT THE LAW AGAINST MURDER (5:21–26)

After reminding his listeners that the Ten Commandments forbade murder, Jesus goes on to deepen the requirements of that commandment. He points out the attitudes of hatred, anger, and contempt that lay behind the act of murder. He considers those attitudes so wrong that he suggests they should be punishable as the actual act of murder.

One who has contempt for another sees that person as less than completely human. Murder grows out of that attitude. Jesus provided two illustrations: (1) leaving a gift at the altar to reconcile with one's brother or sister, and (2) reaching a settlement quickly with one's adversary.

Section Summary

We are all on our way to God's court. Christians should settle any differences with others in this life. Reconciliation with others shows a right relationship with God.

HISTORICAL BACKGROUND

Two Rabbinical Sayings

1. "The eye and the heart are two brokers of sin."

2. "Passion lodges only in him who sees."

Quoted in A. T. Robertson, *Word Pictures in the Greek New Testament*, 6 vols. (Broadman Press, 1932), 1:46.

THE PROBLEMS OF ADULTERY AND DIVORCE (5:27–32)

The Problem of Adultery (vv. 27–30)

Jesus next reinterprets the commandment forbidding adultery. He teaches that it is not enough to refrain from the act of adultery. Lust, too, is sinful and is the beginning point for committing adultery.

The Problem of Divorce (vv. 31–32)

According to Jewish law, a man could divorce his wife, but a wife could not divorce her husband. To give some protection to wives, the biblical law required a husband to provide the wife he was divorcing a "written notice of divorce" (Matt 19:7).

PERSONAL APPLICATION

Jesus has a more exacting standard for his followers than what the Jewish law demands. Jesus opposed divorce completely, except in the case of adultery.

Section Summary

Jesus's words about marriage and divorce are meant to reveal God's ideal standard—marriage is a solemn, lifelong covenant between a man and a woman.

OATH TAKING (5:33–37)

An oath that made use of God's name was considered absolutely binding. For fear of not being able to keep a promise, a person might swear by something less than God's name, such as Jerusalem or the earth, for example. Jesus completely rejected this practice.

Jesus declared that everything was connected to God, and he told his followers not to take oaths. A person of integrity, one whose word can be trusted, has no need for oaths.

HOW TO OVERCOME EVIL (5:38–42)

Jesus quotes part of the Old Testament law of retaliation (Lev 24:17–20). But he teaches that his followers are to live by a higher standard than that. They are not to "resist" evil with evil. Instead, if they are struck on one cheek, they are to "turn the other cheek." Turning the other cheek could mean to act in a positive way for the good of the one who has given the insult.

Section Summary

Jesus teaches his disciples to let generosity, not the desire for revenge, rule their relationships with others. A Christian should be willing to do more than forced to do.

HOW TO TREAT AN ENEMY (5:43–48)

Jesus opposes an attitude of hatred for one's enemies. He calls for love for one's enemies and prayer for one's persecutors. To act in such a way would be to exhibit some of the same characteristics of God himself.

There is nothing unusual about loving someone who loves us back. But it takes grace to love those who hate us. Jesus's followers must demonstrate this higher moral standard.

PERSONAL APPLICATION

In dealing with others, Jesus teaches that his followers should be willing to give more than the Law requires. If forced to walk one mile by someone, a Christian ought to travel voluntarily *two* miles with that person.

Section Summary

Christians are to be good to all people, including their enemies.

QUESTIONS TO GUIDE YOUR STUDY

1. What was the significance of the Sermon on the Mount? Does it have a present-day application?
2. Jesus used salt and light to describe how his disciples should function in the world. In what ways do his disciples function as salt and light?
3. What was Jesus's position on divorce? How does society's standard measure up to his standard?

MATTHEW 6

This chapter is a continuation of the Sermon on the Mount.

FIRST EXAMPLE: HOW TO GIVE GIFTS (6:2–4)

Almsgiving was the practice of giving charitable gifts. Because Jewish law did not require almsgiving, it was considered especially praiseworthy. "Sound[ing] a trumpet" was a figurative way of saying that the people of Jesus's day found ways of calling others' attention to what they were doing.

Section Summary

Jesus does not want his disciples to do good works in order to bring attention to themselves. God sees all gifts, even those given in secret.

SECOND EXAMPLE: THE MODEL PRAYER (6:6–15)

Its Purpose and Structure

In teaching the disciples about prayer, Jesus contrasts the insincere prayers of hypocrites with the proper way to pray. So he provides them with a model prayer. This prayer is also known as thete Lord's Prayer or the Disciples' Prayer. It is a model prayer because it contains the components and attitudes Jesus's disciples should exhibit and incorporate into their lives. The first half of this prayer focuses exclusively on God and his agenda as believers adore, worship, and submit to his will before they introduce their own personal petitions.

Its Petitions

WORD PICTURE

Father

Jesus addressed God as "Father," which translates the Aramaic word *Abba*. It is an intimate term, and its use in this way was unparalleled in first-century Judaism. God is as accessible as the most loving human parent.

"Our Father in heaven" (v. 9)

Jesus knew God as his Father, and he taught the disciples to trust him as their Father. The phrase "in heaven" balances this intimacy with an affirmation of God's sovereignty and majesty.

"Your name be honored as holy" (v. 9)

In Hebrew thought, one's name represented that person's personality, character, and authority. This first petition is a plea that all people may come to regard God as holy. We should treat all that God has created as holy and honored because of his perfection and goodness.

"Your kingdom come. Your will be done" (v. 10)

These two petitions are closely related and have almost the same meaning. They express the desire that the acknowledgment of God's reign and the accomplishment of his purposes take place in the world even as they already do in heaven. This request is that victory over evil will become a reality.

"Give us today our daily bread" (v. 11)

WORD PICTURE

Daily

"The meaning . . . seems to be 'for the coming day.'" A. T. Robertson, *WPNT*, 1:53.

From this point on, the prayer's petitions have to do with people's needs. Jesus recognizes that his followers need food and other essentials. "Daily" means that which is necessary for existence for the immediate future, perhaps for the coming day. This part of the prayer acknowledges our ultimate dependence on God's generosity for all our needs. Christians, therefore, should pray daily for the next day's provision of life's essentials as they recognize that all sustenance for life comes from God.

"Forgive us our debts, as we also have forgiven our debtors" (v. 12)

His petition sees us as debtors before God because of our sins. It is a plea for continued forgiveness, requesting the restoration of fellowship with God. At the same time it acknowledges that we cannot expect to receive God's forgiveness unless we show forgiveness toward those who have wronged us.

"Do not bring us not into temptation, but deliver us from the evil one" (v. 13)

Whereas the previous petition asked forgiveness for sins one has committed, this petition asks for strength *not* to commit future sins. We must be careful not to misunderstand this request to mean that God brings us to the place of temptation. The best way we should take these words is, "Don't let us succumb to temptation," or "Don't abandon us to temptation." The second part of this petition is a plea for deliverance from the "evil one," Satan, from whom all evil ultimately comes.

AN ADDITIONAL NOTE (6:14–15)

These two verses contain an explanation of prayer for forgiveness of sins and describes the negative consequences of failure to forgive others. The person who does not forgive will not be forgiven.

Section Summary

The Lord's Prayer contains the components and attitudes that Jesus's disciples should exhibit and incorporate into their lives.

THIRD EXAMPLE: FASTING (6:16–18)

Fasting, or abstinence from food for a period of time, is the third religious practice Jesus warned about. Like almsgiving and prayer, fasting must come from the right motive, or it loses its value. Jesus declares that the hypocrites made a conspicuous production of their fasting. They did so to gain praise from people rather than from God.

Jesus wants his disciples to behave differently. They are to behave normally when they fast, knowing that God alone would know about their secret act of devotion.

Section Summary

Fasting was the third religious practice Jesus warned his disciples about. The key to the religious practice of fasting is doing it with the right motive.

TRUE AND LASTING RICHES (6:19–21)

Jesus wanted people to have life's material necessities. But he knew the dangers of making the accumulation of material possessions the goal of one's life. He taught that there is no final security in earthly possessions. People need, instead, to devote their attention to acquiring "treasures in heaven."

NEW TESTAMENT REFERENCE

Temptation

"No one undergoing a trial should say, 'I am being tempted by God,' since God is not tempted by evil, and he himself doesn't tempt anyone." (Jas 1:13)

HISTORICAL BACKGROUND

Fasting

Fasting is the laying aside of food for a period of time when a believer is seeking to know God in a deeper experience. The Bible describes three main forms of fasting: (1) the normal fast—abstinence from food; (2) the absolute fast—abstinence from both food and water; and (3) the partial fast—a restriction of diet rather than complete abstinence.

PERSONAL APPLICATION

Treasures in Heaven

This phrase can be defined broadly as holiness of character, obedience to all of God's commands, service to God, and merciful deeds done to others. In this context, however, storing up spiritual treasures focuses particularly on the compassionate use of material resources to meet the physical and spiritual needs of others, in keeping with kingdom priorities.

Section Summary

Rather than accumulating material wealth, Jesus's followers will work for spiritual riches that are invulnerable to loss and death.

THE LAMP AND THE BODY (6:22–23)

Jesus draws a spiritual analogy from the physical realm. The physical eye brings light or darkness into the body, depending on the eye's state of health. A person's inner being, too, has an eye—a spiritual eye that is focused on God. If that eye is sound, it brings God's light into the person's being. However, if the eye tries to focus on both God and worldly values at the same time, it becomes unsound. Spiritual vision then becomes blurred, and spiritual darkness instead of light will fill the person.

Section Summary

The health of one's spiritual eye determines one's overall well-being.

THE CHOICE OF A MASTER (6:24)

Jesus teaches that no one can be a slave to two masters. *Mammon* is the Aramaic word meaning "money" or "material resources." Many perceptive observers have sensed that the greatest danger to Western Christianity is not prevailing ideologies or philosophies but the all-pervasive materialism of our affluent culture.

Section Summary

Serving God demands full allegiance. The pursuit of wealth can be all-absorbing, leaving no room for God in our lives.

PERSONAL APPLICATION

Worry is the key word of this section, as it occurs six times. Certainly, Christians must plan for the future, but they need not be anxious. Jesus illustrates his point by discussing the basic provisions of food and clothing. God provides for the birds of the air and the lilies of the field. In view of God's provision, anxiety over food, clothing, and the future is adopting a pagan mindset, one that does not trust in God.

THE FUTILITY OF WORRY (6:25–33)

Section Summary

Those who make service to God their life's goal need not worry about material provisions.

QUESTIONS TO GUIDE YOUR STUDY

1. Name the three illustrations of piety Jesus used. What point was he making with these?
2. How can we best make use of the model prayer?
3. What is the danger of focusing on acquiring material possessions in this life?

MATTHEW 7

JUDGMENT AND DISCERNMENT (7:1–6)

Jesus warns that his disciples are not to be characterized by judgmental attitudes. Certainly, some kinds of judgment are necessary, but Jesus warns against unloving, condemning criticism of another person. On those occasions when we render a negative evaluation of others, our purposes should be constructive and not retributive.

PERSONAL APPLICATION

Judge

This word can imply "to analyze or evaluate" as well as "to condemn or avenge." The former senses are clearly commended to believers (e.g., 1 Cor 5:5; 1 John 4:1), but the latter are reserved for God. In this passage, the word is used to forbid an action already taking place and can be translated as "stop judging."

PRAYER: ASKING, SEEKING, KNOCKING (7:7–12)

Persistence in Prayer (vv. 7–11)

Jesus teaches that his disciples should pray persistently. The verbs *ask*, *seek*, and *knock* are present imperative forms that stress the need for persistence, often over a period of time. This persistence is an indication of our seriousness in making the request and of our confidence that God will answer. It is petitioning God with an expectant attitude. A key theme here is God's generosity. Jesus says that if human parents who are sinful know how to give good gifts to their children, how much more will God, who is perfect, give good gifts to those who ask.

Section Summary

Persistent prayer brings an answer. God is generous and gives only good gifts to those who come to him in prayer.

The Golden Rule (v. 12)

"Therefore, whatever you want others to do for you, do also the same for them." This saying has become known as the Golden Rule because of its central role in Christian ethics. It was known to the Jews in a negative form, but Jesus gave it a positive turn. Note that this rule is meant for those under the rule of God, not for the world at large. Only a person whose will is submitted to God can care as much about another's welfare as his own.

HISTORICAL BACKGROUND

The Golden Rule

This name is usually given to the command of Jesus recorded here and in Luke 6:31. The designation "Golden Rule" does not appear in the Bible, and its origin in English is difficult to trace. The principle of the Golden Rule can be found in many religions, but Jesus's wording of it was original and unique.

Section Summary

In view of God's generosity to us, treating others in the manner we would like to be treated ourselves is the least we can do.

The rest of the Sermon on the Mount offers no new commandments but encourages obedience to those already given while warning against disobedience. The following three illustrations by Jesus make plain that there are ultimately only two categories of people in the world: (1) those who hear, obey, and are saved and (2) those who only hear and so are destroyed. In each case, the consequences are eternal.

WORD PICTURE

Narrow—Broad

The word *narrow* comes from a verb meaning "to experience trouble or difficulty"; *broad* can have overtones of "prosperous."

THE WIDE AND NARROW GATES (7:13–14)

This first illustration contrasts those who select the narrow rather than the wide gate. Jesus teaches that there are two differing paths a person may follow, as seen in Psalm 1. Most people, with little thought, enter the wide gate and follow the easy, wide way. It takes a definite, conscious act of the will to choose the narrow gate and follow the difficult, narrow way. The hard, narrow way leads, in the end, to life for the few who find it.

THE TRUE AND THE FALSE (7:15–23)

The second illustration contrasts those who bear good fruit with those who bear bad fruit. Jesus knew that, at times, his Church would be influenced by false prophets. His followers needed to be able to distinguish between the true and the false. Jesus gave only one criterion: fruit.

HISTORICAL BACKGROUND

A wise person building in the Judean desert would erect a dwelling on a secure rock to protect the house from flash floods.

THE PARABLE OF THE TWO BUILDERS (7:24–27)

The third illustration contrasts those who build their homes on solid rock with those who build on shifting sand. The foolish person would build directly on the sand and have no protection against the devastation of the elements.

Section Summary

It is not enough simply to hear Jesus's call or even to respond with a flurry of good deeds. Rather, we must build a solid foundation that combines authentic commitment to Christ with persevering obedience.

THE CROWD'S RESPONSE TO JESUS (7:28–29)

Jesus spoke with a power and authority that commanded the attention and respect of his listeners. The crowds marveled and contrasted Jesus's teaching with that of the scribes. For the people, the difference was one of authority.

QUESTIONS TO GUIDE YOUR STUDY

1. What principles of prayer did Jesus teach?
2. What are some ways we might apply the Golden Rule in our everyday lives?
3. What lessons can we draw from Jesus's three illustrations about disobedience?

JESUS'S DISCOURSES IN MATTHEW

Scripture	Key Section	Narrative Purpose
Matthew 1–4	Opening Narrative	The Introduction
Jesus's Discourses (Sermon Teaching), *Matthew 5–25*	Sermon on the Mount *Matthew 5–7*	The Kingdom Constitution
	Commission of the Twelve *Matthew 10*	The Kingdom's Foundational Leaders
	Kingdom Parables *Matthew 13*	The Pursuit of the Kingdom (in the King's Absence)
	Teaching on the Church *Matthew 18*	The Relational Principles in the Kingdom
	Olivet Discourse *Matthew 24–25*	The Kingdom's Future
Matthew 26–28	Closing Narrative	The Climax

MATTHEW 8

JESUS'S HEALING OF A LEPER (8:1–4)

Following the Sermon on the Mount, as Jesus descended the mountain, a leper came and knelt before him and said, "Lord, if you are willing, you can make me clean." This was an opportunity for Jesus to show how he viewed the law. The leper's coming to Jesus was a violation of the law of Moses, since lepers were considered unclean. Jesus reached out and touched the leper, healing him immediately. Because the law forbade touching a leper, this gesture proved at least as shocking as the leper's original approach and request. Yet, the touch of Jesus does not violate the law as the healing is instantaneous. Jesus's touch makes clean what was unclean. Of interest is the fact that Jesus sent the man to the priest in accordance with the requirements of Lev 14:1–32. Jesus honors the law of Moses, teaches others to do so, but gives a glimpse, in this healing, of what it means to fulfill the law.

HISTORICAL BACKGROUND

Leprosy

Leprosy was a generic term applied to a variety of skin disorders, ranging from psoriasis to leprosy. Its symptoms ranged from white patches on the skin to running sores to the loss of fingers and toes. For the Hebrews, it was a dreaded malady that rendered its victims ceremonially unclean—unfit to worship God. In addition, anyone who came in contact with a leper was considered unclean.

THE HEALING OF THE CENTURION'S SERVANT (8:5–13)

As Jesus reached Capernaum, the headquarters for his Galilean ministry, a centurion met him, asking for help. This centurion was a Gentile officer in the Roman army. He explained to Jesus that his servant was paralyzed and "in terrible agony." Orthodox Jews would have considered the centurion unclean because of his race and would have despised him all the more as a symbol of Roman oppression.

The centurion's faith in Jesus was strong: "But just say the word, and my servant will be healed." Jesus was amazed at his faith. It even exceeded the faith he had found among God's own people, the Jews. In response to the centurion's faith, Jesus told the man that his request was answered. At that moment the centurion's servant was healed.

THE HEALING OF SIMON PETER'S MOTHER-IN-LAW (8:14–15)

OLD TESTAMENT REFERENCE

Matthew wrote that these healings fulfilled Isaiah's prophecy in Isa 53:4: "He himself bore our sicknesses, and he carried our pains."

Simon Peter had a house in Capernaum. When Jesus visited Peter's home, he saw that Peter's mother-in-law was "lying in bed with a fever." Jesus healed the woman by touching her hand. Her fever left and her strength returned immediately. She began serving Jesus, who was a guest in the house.

This small miracle highlights at least three important points:

1. It shows Jesus healing a woman.
2. The healing was a private miracle.
3. It shows that a person who has been touched by Jesus, whether physically or spiritually, will want to serve him.

OTHER HEALINGS (8:16–17)

That same night, Jesus healed many others who were brought to him.

Section Summary

The three miracles recorded in this chapter demonstrate Jesus's compassion to heal many who were demon possessed and sick. By doing so, Jesus fulfilled Isa 53:4.

TWO WHO WANTED TO FOLLOW JESUS (8:18–22)

As Jesus planned to cross to the other side of the Sea of Galilee and escape the crowds, two would-be followers spoke to him.

The Scribe (vv. 18–20)

The scribe was overly eager to become a disciple. He assured Jesus that he would follow him anywhere he might go. Jesus recognized that in his confident enthusiasm, the scribe failed to grasp what following Jesus might involve. In Jesus's response to the scribe, he refers to himself as the Son of Man whose "dominion is an everlasting dominion" (see Dan 7:13–14).

A Would-Be Disciple (vv. 21–22)

Whereas the scribe was overly eager, this man was hesitant. He wanted to follow Jesus but only after he had taken care of other obligations. He was not ready to follow Jesus, as other priorities came before discipleship.

Section Summary

Discipleship involves commitment and sacrifice. Those who would be disciples need to count the cost.

HISTORICAL BACKGROUND

Storms on the Sea of Galilee

Such storms are the result of two simple facts:

1. Water retains its warmth longer than the surrounding land.

2. The warm air above the lake tends to rise whereas cold air sinks. When the sides of the lake are steep, this movement of the air is exaggerated. The cold air pours down the hillside like a flood, suddenly displacing the warmer air, which is forced upward. (Denis Baly)

JESUS'S CALMING OF THE STORM (8:23–27)

Jesus and his disciples boarded a boat for the trip across the Sea of Galilee. Jesus slept during the crossing. A sudden storm arose, and the waves began to engulf the boat. Lives were at risk! Amazingly, Jesus remained so calm that he continued to sleep. His frightened disciples awakened him, begging him to save them from the storm's danger. Jesus chided them for their fear and lack of belief. Then he stood and calmed the waves and wind. The disciples wondered aloud about the identity of the Man: "What kind of man is this? Even the winds and the sea obey him."

Section Summary

Jesus demonstrated power over the destructive forces of nature, which were under the devil's sway. Such a Person is worthy of worship.

HISTORICAL BACKGROUND

"The whole subject of demonology is difficult. Some hold that it is only the ancient way of describing disease. But that does not explain the situation here. Jesus is represented as treating the demons as really existing as separate from the human personality." A. T. Robertson, *WPNT*, 1:69.

JESUS'S HEALING OF TWO DEMON-POSSESSED MEN (8:28–34)

Here Matthew's narrative illustrates Jesus's ministry of exorcism. When Jesus and his disciples arrived on the eastern side of the Sea of Galilee, they were met by two demon-possessed men who lived in tombs, or burial caves, in the side of a mountain. These men were so violent that no one would go near them.

The demons possessing these men recognized Jesus and his power to destroy them. When they realized that Jesus intended to cast them out of the men, they asked to be sent to a herd of pigs nearby. Swine, like tombs, were sources of defilement according to the law of Moses. Jesus agreed to their request.

When the demons entered the pigs, the entire herd rushed down the steep bank and drowned in the Sea of Galilee. This demonstrated Jesus's authority over the forces of evil. The local farmers and townsfolk asked Jesus to leave, as his presence made them uncomfortable.

Section Summary

Jesus demonstrated his authority over the powers of evil. The local people asked Jesus to leave their area. Sinful people often recoil in the presence of holiness because it highlights their own shortcomings and, in this case, had negative economic implications.

WORD PICTURE

Son of Man

Matthew uses this term to express the deity of Jesus, the unique Son of God. His references point to some aspect of Jesus's earthly ministry, such as his authority to forgive sins and to interpret the meaning of the Sabbath. Three categories of "Son of Man" sayings in the Gospels are generally recognized: (1) those that present him in his earthly role, (2) those that highlight his suffering, and (3) those that point to his glory. The background for this title is likely Dan 7:13–14.

QUESTIONS TO GUIDE YOUR STUDY

1. Jesus's miracles in this chapter demonstrate his authority. What was significant about each miracle with regard to the positioning of the Jewish law?
2. What does Jesus require of those who follow him?
3. Have you had experiences that prompted you to express awe at the character or attributes of God?

MATTHEW 9

A PARALYTIC'S FORGIVENESS AND HEALING (9:1–8)

After Jesus returned to Capernaum, a group of men brought a paralytic to Jesus for healing. Surprisingly, Jesus declared the man's sins forgiven. Apparently, Jesus decided that such forgiveness was necessary before the paralytic could be healed. In response to the faith of those who brought this man, Jesus both forgave the man's sins and healed him. The crowd was amazed at Jesus, with a combination of terror and awe, and they gave glory to God for what he had done.

Section Summary

This miracle caused people to give glory to God because he had delegated such authority to Jesus. His works of healing and forgiving were signs that God's kingdom was dawning.

THE CALL OF MATTHEW (9:9–13)

Matthew Becomes a Disciple (v. 9)

Passing by the customs house (toll station) in Capernaum, Jesus saw Matthew, a Jewish tax collector. Tax collectors were an especially despised group of people, with corruption widespread in their ranks. Matthew gives no indication of any prior exposure to Jesus's person or preaching. When Jesus called Matthew to follow him as a disciple, Matthew responded immediately.

Matthew Throws a Party (vv. 10–11)

On a later occasion, Matthew threw a party for Jesus. Many of Matthew's colleagues, fellow tax collectors, and other "sinners" joined him.

The Pharisees' Criticism (vv. 11–13)

The Pharisees could not understand why Jesus would eat with the kinds of people who attended Matthew's party. Contact with "sinners" was forbidden by their laws. Consequently, they questioned the disciples about Jesus's behavior. Jesus, however, heard their questioning and answered them himself. He replied, "It is not those who are well who need a doctor, but those who are sick." He had come to call sinners, not the righteous. He suggested that the Pharisees study Hos 6:6: "I desire faithful love and not sacrifice." The Pharisees had become so intent on the perfect keeping of their rituals that they neglected showing mercy to others.

HISTORICAL BACKGROUND

Matthew

Matthew means "the gift of God." He was a tax collector called by Jesus to be an apostle. Why did Jesus call Matthew? Because Matthew had the gifts to be trained as a disciple to share with others, could keep meticulous records, and was a potential recorder-author of the Gospel of Matthew. From the earliest times, Christians have affirmed that Matthew wrote the Gospel that bears his name.

WORD PICTURE

The word "sinners" was used in at least two special senses. Here the term refers to the most criminal and disreputable kinds of people in society.

Section Summary

Jesus's fraternizing with disreputable people provided an example for his disciples. We would do well to reevaluate regularly our efforts to reach those in need and those considered outcasts in our society.

A QUESTION ABOUT FASTING (9:14–17)

John's Disciples Raise the Question (v. 14)

Some disciples of John the Baptist came to Jesus with a question. Both they and the Pharisees fasted, but Jesus and his disciples did not make a practice of doing so. John's disciples wanted to know why.

Jesus had no objections to fasting and at times fasted himself (Matt 4:2). He believed, however, that a person should fast only when the occasion warranted it and not as a mechanical ritual.

Jesus's Answer (vv. 15–16)

Jesus provided an illustration of the fact that existing religious structures of his day could not contain the new wine of his gospel.

OLD TESTAMENT REFERENCE

In the Old Testament, fasting was usually a spontaneous expression of mourning, repentance, or supplication in a time of crisis. Jesus used this opportunity to refer to his coming death. "Will be taken away" perhaps alludes to Isa 53:8 and is a foreshadowing of Jesus's crucifixion. At that point, fasting and mourning will be appropriate.

Illustration of New Wine into Old Wineskins (vv. 16–17)

Jesus reinforced his point of the parable by illustrating the incompatibility of the old and the new ages. A person would be foolish to place an unshrunk patch of cloth on an old garment. It would pull and tear at the garment. Nor would someone pour new wine into a brittle old wineskin. The fermenting of the wine would eventually cause the wineskin to burst. A person should use new containers that are flexible.

Judaism's emphasis on legalism and rituals was incompatible with Jesus's gospel.

FOUR DIFFERENT MIRACLES (9:18–34)

Matthew's narrative now presents a group of four healings. Jesus's activities are beginning to attract the opposition of Jewish leaders.

A Request to Raise a Daughter (vv. 18–19)

A ruler of the synagogue asked Jesus to heal his daughter, who "just died." From the accounts of Mark and Luke (Mark 5:22–43; Luke 8:41–56), we know this ruler's name was Jairus. This man believed strongly in Jesus's power over death. Jesus and his disciples went with Jairus.

Miracle 1. The Healing of a Woman with a Long-Term Illness (vv. 20–22)

On their way to Jairus's house, a woman came behind Jesus and touched the edge of his cloak. She experienced hemorrhaging for twelve years and believed she could be healed if only she could touch Jesus's clothing. At that moment Jesus turned, looked at the woman, and declared that her faith had brought healing.

Miracle 2. The Raising of the Ruler's Daughter (vv. 23–26)

Jesus then completed his trip to Jairus's house. Upon arriving, he ordered the musicians and professional mourners to leave. Jesus viewed the girl's death as temporary. He took the girl's hand, lifted her up, and brought her back to life. The news of this miracle spread like wildfire.

Miracle 3. The Restoring of Two Blind Men's Sight (vv. 27–31)

Jesus next demonstrated his healing power over blindness. Two blind men called out to him and begged for healing. Jesus first made certain they believed he could heal them. He told them, "Let it be done for you according to your faith." In response to their faith, he gave them their sight.

WORD PICTURE

According to Your Faith

This phrase means "in response to," not "in proportion to" their faith.

Miracle 4. The Healing of a Mute (vv. 32–34)

A demon-possessed man who couldn't talk was brought to Jesus for healing. This man's illness cut him off from society. Jesus cast out the demon, and to the amazement of the onlookers, the man was able to speak.

Section Summary

These miracles show the relationship between faith and miracles.

JESUS'S REASON FOR MINISTRY (9:35–38)

Jesus had deep compassion for the crowds. He likened them to sheep without a shepherd and as a vast crop of ripe grain in need of harvesters. He decided it was time to send out laborers to gather the harvest. In this section, Matthew lists the twelve disciples called to join Jesus in his mission.

QUESTIONS TO GUIDE YOUR STUDY

1. Explain the significance of fasting. What are its benefits? How should one practice fasting?
2. Why couldn't the Pharisees' religion receive Jesus's gospel?
3. What was the driving force behind Jesus's ministry?

MATTHEW 10

A LISTING OF THE TWELVE (10:1–4)

Jesus called twelve men to be his apostles. Their number calls to mind the twelve tribes of Israel and suggests that Jesus was building a community of followers in conscious opposition to the current leadership of Israel.

Section Summary

The twelve men Jesus chose to represent him were not likely the kind we would have chosen for an important mission. Yet Jesus granted them authority to do miracles and relied on them to be his first laborers in the field.

THE APOSTLES' ASSIGNMENT (10:5–15)

Jesus sent the twelve disciples on a special mission. According to Mark's Gospel, he sent them out in pairs. This mission included preaching the gospel, healing the sick, and exorcising demons. He told the Twelve to

HISTORICAL BACKGROUND

The Twelve Apostles

Name	*Meaning*
Simon	"hearing" (Hebrew)
Andrew	"manliness" (Greek)
James	"Jacob" (Hebrew)
John	"the Lord is gracious" (Hebrew)
Philip	"horse lover" (Greek)
Bar-tholomew	"son of Talmai" (Hebrew)
Thomas	"twin" (Hebrew)
Matthew	"God has given" (Hebrew)
James "the younger"	"Jacob" (Hebrew); "the small one"
Thaddaeus	from "breast" and "heart" (Hebrew)
Simon the Zealot	"zealous one" (Greek)
Judas Iscariot	"man of Keri-oth" (Hebrew)

concentrate on the "lost sheep of the house of Israel." Jesus provided specific instructions for carrying out the mission.

Section Summary

Israel would be the first to receive the gospel message.

WARNINGS AND ASSURANCES ABOUT PERSECUTION (10:16–33)

Jesus Warns Them of Possible Persecution (vv. 16–28)

WORD PICTURE

Apostle

Apostles were persons sent to accomplish a mission, especially the twelve apostles Jesus commissioned to follow him. An apostle represents the one sending and has authority to represent the sender in business, political, or educational situations.

Jesus declared that he was sending out his apostles as "sheep among wolves" (v. 16). They would be faced with possible persecution from civil and religious authorities for representing Jesus. However, their proper response was to fear God, not people.

Verses 22 and 23 are two of Jesus's most difficult sayings to interpret. Their meanings are not certain.

Saying 1. "The one who endures to the end will be saved." He could have meant that a person dying for Christ or denying him would be vindicated by God if he chose to be loyal unto death.

Saying 2. "You will not have gone through the towns of Israel before the Son of Man comes." Jesus was referring to something other than the final appearing of the Son of Man at the end of the age. The transfiguration of Jesus is one possibility. Or he may have been speaking of the times he would appear after his resurrection.

Jesus Reassures Them of God's Love (vv. 29–33)

God even counted the hairs on their heads! The disciples were of great value to God. Those who would acknowledge Jesus before others would receive acknowledgment by Jesus to God the Father. To "acknowledge" Jesus means to declare one's allegiance to him. It carries the sense of "confess" or "trust in."

Section Summary

The disciples would be faced with possible persecution from civil and religious authorities for representing Jesus. He taught them that their proper response was to fear God, not people.

PUTTING GOD ABOVE FAMILY (10:34–39)

Jesus declared that anyone who loved a family member more than him was not worthy of him. Jesus must take first place in the life of a follower, who must "take up his cross and follow" Jesus. To carry one's cross means a willingness to die for Jesus.

Section Summary

Jesus was on the way to a cross, and his followers had to be ready to share his death, if necessary.

REWARDS FOR RECEIVING GOD'S MESSENGERS (10:40–11:1)

The people's reception of the apostles would correspond to their reception of Jesus. Those who received the apostles would be receiving Jesus and the Father. Those who received any messenger of Jesus would be rewarded.

Jesus's instructions to the twelve apostles about their mission was now complete. He closed his discourse on an optimistic note in hopes of a positive response.

QUESTIONS TO GUIDE YOUR STUDY

1. Describe your initial impressions about the twelve men Jesus called to be his apostles. How do they complement one another? What potential personnel management issues might Jesus face?
2. What was the purpose of Jesus's assignment for the disciples?
3. Explain Jesus's insistence on placing the importance of discipleship above that of the family.

MATTHEW 11

Verse 1 can be taken as a conclusion to the previous sermon in chapter 10 or as a transitional verse. At this time, Jesus carried on his ministry of teaching and preaching in the towns and villages of Galilee.

A QUESTION FROM JOHN THE BAPTIST (11:2–6)

John the Baptist abruptly reappears in the narrative. He was in prison during Jesus's Galilean ministry.

WORD PICTURE

Even the most courageous and faithful of God's servants may experience doubt. Confessing our doubts to God and asking for his help are good first steps of faith.

John's Question about Jesus's Messiahship (vv. 2–3)

While in prison, John heard some puzzling information about Jesus's ministry. Apparently, he was seeing no signs of the imminent judgment of the wicked that Jesus promised (Matt 3:10). John was beginning to have doubts about whether Jesus was the Messiah. As a result, he sent some of his disciples to question Jesus about his identity.

HISTORICAL BACKGROUND

According to Jewish historian Josephus, Herod Antipas had John imprisoned in the fortress of Machaerus, near the Dead Sea.

Jesus's Reply (vv. 4–6)

Jesus answered John's question by itemizing his works that authenticated his messiahship. He then encouraged John to remain faithful to him, no matter what might come.

Section Summary

John was beginning to doubt Jesus's identity. His messiahship unfolded much differently than most people expected it would—even the most faithful. Most anticipated a political leader who would overthrow the oppressive Roman rule. Jesus assured John that he was the Messiah and, in spite of appearances to the contrary, he encouraged John to remain faithful to him.

JESUS'S TESTIMONY ABOUT JOHN (11:7–15)

After answering John's question, Jesus talked to the crowds about John. He supported the legitimacy of John's ministry by posing two rhetorical questions:

1. Did they expect to see "a reed swaying in the wind"?
2. Did they expect to see a "man dressed in soft clothes"? Jesus assured the crowd that John was God's messenger and that no person ever born was greater than John.

Section Summary

Jesus confirmed the validity of John the Baptist's ministry and of John's greatness.

THE CROWDS' REACTION TO JESUS AND JOHN THE BAPTIST (11:16–19)

Jesus compared his own generation to children who criticized their friends for not playing games *their* way. He then contrasted himself with John. They were opposites in attitude and lifestyle, but both were necessary to God's plan.

HISTORICAL BACKGROUND

Capernaum

Capernaum appears in the biblical record only in the Gospels, where it is mentioned 16 times. Jesus chose Capernaum as his base of operations when he began his ministry (Mark 1:21; 2:1).

JUDGMENT ON UNBELIEVING TOWNS (11:20–24)

Although Jesus's mission was not to act primarily as a judge, he showed that judgment was part of his role. He functioned as judge when he condemned the cities that had rejected him. He would judge a few cities more severely because they had received more immediate, dramatic, and straightforward revelation. He had special words of condemnation for Capernaum, where he had lived during his Galilean ministry.

AN INVITATION FROM JESUS (11:25–30)

Jesus closed this time with the crowd with three important statements concerning the mystery of God's revelation, the source of his own authority, and an invitation to respond to the revelation they had so far received.

The Mystery of God's Revelation (vv. 25–26)

These verses are apparently a public prayer. Jesus contrasted the "wise and intelligent" and the "infants." Infants were those who responded to God and saw him at work in the ministry of Jesus. The wise and intelligent were people like the scribes and Pharisees who felt secure in their own knowledge and so failed to see God revealed in Jesus.

The Source of Jesus's Authority (v. 27)

Jesus declared that God committed "all things" to him. God, therefore, was the source of his authority. The word used for "know" involves the most intimate and fullest acquaintance.

The Invitation (vv. 28–30)

Jesus then appealed for a response to his revelation. It is an invitation to all who hurt or who recognize their spiritual need. He assured them that his "yoke is easy" and his "burden is light." Jesus's requirements for righteousness were no less stringent than those of the Jewish leaders, but they could be accomplished more readily through the strength Christ provides through the Holy Spirit.

Jesus equated the Christian life with rest. This rest would not be a life free from effort or sorrow. It would be a life of peace in the midst of life's trials and struggles. To illustrate this point, Jesus used an illustration from farming. Like the yoke that couples oxen together, discipleship does not exempt one from work but makes it manageable.

HISTORICAL BACKGROUND

Yoke

A yoke was a wooden frame placed on draft animals to make them pull in tandem. Simple yokes consisted of a bar with two loops, either of rope or wood, which went around the animals' necks. In the Bible, the word *yoke* is most often used to speak of slavery, bondage, and hardship. Positive usages include the yoke of Christ (Matt 11:29–30) and the joint nature of the Church's work (Phil 4:3).

Section Summary

Jesus delivered three commands in his invitation: come, take, and learn. The first two commands are in response to a crisis, but the third is a response to "learn" and begins a lifelong process of knowing God.

QUESTIONS TO GUIDE YOUR STUDY

1. John the Baptist had prepared the way for Jesus. What circumstances now caused him to question Jesus's identity?
2. Although they were quite different individuals, how did John the Baptist and Jesus complement each other? What did each uniquely accomplish?

3. What truths might we derive from Jesus's actions against the cities that rejected him?

MATTHEW 12

WORD PICTURE

The Sabbath is the day of rest, considered holy to God. Humans are to rest as God rested on the seventh day following the creation of the universe. It was viewed as a sign of the covenant relation between God and his people and of the eternal rest he promised them. Jesus's habit was to observe the Sabbath as a day of worship in the synagogues, but his failure to comply with the minute restrictions of the Jewish leaders brought conflict with the religious leaders of his day.

Sabbath observance was one of the three most important and distinctive badges of Jewish life (the other two were circumcision and dietary law).

"REAPING" AND "THRESHING" ON THE SABBATH (12:1–8)

According to the laws of the scribes and Pharisees, it was lawful to satisfy one's hunger from a neighbor's grain field, but it was not lawful to do so on the Sabbath. The Pharisees observed what Jesus did and reminded him that his actions violated the law. They viewed plucking grain as "reaping" and rubbing off the husks as "threshing." They classified these actions as "work."

Jesus responded to their objections by quoting examples from the Old Testament that showed human need was allowed to take precedence over religious regulations. Jesus climaxed the dialogue by stating, "The Son of Man is the Lord of the Sabbath" (v. 8). Jesus's sovereign authority would determine how the Sabbath is fulfilled in the kingdom age.

HEALING ON THE SABBATH (12:9–14)

On the same day, Jesus went into a synagogue where he met a man with a shriveled hand. Taking the initiative to stir up controversy, the Pharisees posed this question to Jesus: "Is it lawful to heal on the Sabbath?" (v. 10).

Jesus first answered with a short parable about rescuing a sheep that had fallen into a pit. Sheep were valuable resources, and exceptions were made for working to rescue sheep on a Sabbath. With one statement Jesus indicted the Pharisees' scale of values: "A person is worth far more than a sheep." His conclusion was, "So it is lawful to do what is good on the Sabbath" (v. 12). Jesus then healed the disabled man.

The Pharisees' power and influence came from the scrupulous keeping of the oral traditions. Jesus was a threat to all they stood for. For the first time in Matthew's Gospel, we are told that the Pharisees began to plot Jesus's death.

Section Summary

As Messiah, the inaugurator of God's new age, Jesus had the right to reinterpret the Sabbath's meaning and requirements.

JESUS WITHDRAWS FROM HOSTILITY (12:15–21)

Realizing that the Pharisees were plotting against him, Jesus withdrew from the area of greatest danger.

Section Summary

Jesus's time to die had not yet come. He continued his ministry of teaching and healing.

THE UNPARDONABLE SIN (12:22–37)

Jesus healed two men, one mute and the other blind. However, the Pharisees made their familiar claim that Jesus's exorcising of demons was really the work of Beelzebul, the prince of demons. Jesus then illustrated the correct interpretation of his exorcisms with a short parable. No one can attack a well-guarded home without first rendering the guard powerless. The point of the parable is that Jesus's exorcisms demonstrate that God through Christ is decisively defeating the devil.

Jesus then explained to his accusers about the one sin for which there is no forgiveness. Forgiveness is possible for all kinds of sins when a person repents, but blasphemy against the Holy Spirit is the unpardonable sin. He asked his audience of Pharisees to come clean, calling them a "brood of vipers" (v. 34), echoing John the Baptist's words in Matt 3:7.

WORD PICTURE

The Unpardonable Sin

The unpardonable sin involves setting one's mind against the Holy Spirit and crediting Satan with what is God's work. It is also to deny the work of the Holy Spirit who testifies about the finished work of the Lord Jesus. To do so is to blaspheme against the Holy Spirit and reject the message of the gospel. To "blaspheme" means to speak an insult against someone so as to defame that person's reputation and character.

Section Summary

The unpardonable sin is not restricted to Jesus's day. It happens today when a person sees a work that is without question God's work but claims it is Satan's.

THE DEMAND FOR A SIGN (12:38–45)

Some of the scribes and Pharisees asked Jesus to give them a sign to prove his identity. To ask for a sign was evidence of unbelief, and Jesus viewed their demand as such.

Jesus told them they would receive a sign but that it would not come on their demand. He used Jonah as an analogy. Just as Jonah's message was God's sign to the Ninevites and Solomon represented God's wisdom to the Queen of Sheba, Jesus was God's sign to the Jews.

The unbelief of the Jews caused them to demand a sign. Jesus offered only the "sign of Jonah."

OLD TESTAMENT REFERENCE

Jesus's sign would be the "sign of the prophet Jonah." Just as Jonah spent three days and nights inside a big fish, Jesus would spend three days and nights in the realm of the dead before coming forth resurrected from death, as Jonah emerged from the big fish.

JESUS'S TRUE FAMILY (12:46–50)

Before Jesus was finished speaking with the scribes and Pharisees, his brothers and mother came to him. Despite the growing rejection of

Jesus, his mother and brothers had been wanting to get through the crowd to speak to him.

After he became aware that his family was present, Jesus pointed to his disciples and said, "Here are my mother and my brothers." He was willing to put God's will above the will of his beloved family.

Section Summary

Believers as people should care for one another as if they were family members. How powerful a witness to the world would be a display of family-like unity in every church!

QUESTIONS TO GUIDE YOUR STUDY

1. What was the significance of Jonah's sign?
2. What was Jesus's point in referring to his disciples as "my mother and my brothers"?

MATTHEW 13

This section of Matthew begins the third major block of Jesus's teaching, which is an entire sermon comprised of a series of seven interrelated parables and an added eighth. These parables comprise a dazzling array of stories in which the nature of the kingdom, or the rule of God, is explained.

THE PARABLE OF THE SOWER (13:1–9)

WORD PICTURE

Parable

Parable means "a putting alongside for purposes of comparison and new understanding." Parables use pictures such as metaphors or similes and frequently extend them into a brief story to make a point or disclosure.

The Parable (vv. 1–8)

Jesus told the crowd about a farmer who sowed his field. The sower's seed fell on four different kinds of soil:

1. Some seed fell on the hard pathways in the field. Birds came and ate that seed.
2. Some seed fell on soil thinly covering a layer of rock. Warmth caused those seeds to germinate quickly. But the sun caused the seeds to wither and die since they could not take root.
3. Some seed fell on deeper soil that contained thorns. The seeds grew for a while, but the thorns choked them out.
4. Fortunately, some seed fell on good soil. Those seeds grew, and the harvest of grain was abundant.

The Challenge (v. 9)

Jesus ended this parable with a challenge to those who heard him: "Let anyone who has ears listen." He was telling the crowd to be like the good soil, letting the seed of the gospel produce an abundant harvest in them.

JESUS'S REASON FOR TEACHING IN PARABLES (13:10–17)

The disciples asked Jesus why he spoke in parables. Although Jesus's answer is difficult to interpret, the reason points to a principle involving human response. He tells them that because of their receptivity, they were able to understand his parables. The crowds, for the most part, lacked this receptivity. Those who were already receptive would be given increased understanding. Those closed to the truth would become even more blind and deaf to it.

Section Summary

Of the four kinds of soil in the parable, only one is good. Only true believers will bear the proper spiritual fruit.

THE PARABLE OF THE WHEAT AND THE WEEDS (13:24–30)

This parable speaks of two different kinds of seeds sown by two different people, a farmer and his enemy. Weeds (*darnel*), at first, are often indistinguishable from wheat. Upon discovering weeds among his grain, the patient farmer decides not to risk pulling the weeds before the harvest, as some of the wheat might be lost in the process. When harvesttime comes, he will have the reapers first gather and then destroy the weeds. Jesus later explains this parable in verses 36–43.

Section Summary

Where there are genuine Christians, there are also counterfeits. Discovering and completely rooting out counterfeits may not be possible given our limited knowledge.

NEW TESTAMENT REFERENCE

Counterfeits

Satan employs many counterfeits for the things of God. He uses counterfeit Christians (2 Cor 11:26) and a counterfeit gospel (Gal 1:6–9). He encourages a counterfeit righteousness (Rom 10:1–3) and has a counterfeit church (Rev 2:9). And, at the end of the age, he will produce a counterfeit Christ (2 Thess 2:1–12).

PERSONAL APPLICATION

Main Point: God permits the righteous and wicked to coexist in this age, but eventually he will separate the wicked, then judge and destroy them.

THE PARABLES OF THE MUSTARD SEED AND THE LEAVEN (13:31–33)

The Mustard Seed (vv. 31–32)

Jesus told a pair of parables about the growth of God's kingdom. He first compared God's kingdom to what happens when a tiny mustard seed is sown. That little seed grows into a treelike plant as high as ten feet—large enough for birds to nest in its branches.

The Leaven (v. 33)

He then compared God's kingdom to what happens when a little leaven is added to a batch of meal. Only a small amount of leaven is required to make dough rise. The increase in size brought about by leaven is one of Jesus's points.

Section Summary

Small beginnings lead to great results. Like leaven, the kingdom will be an unseen but powerful force working within the world to bring about transformation.

THE PARABLES OF THE HIDDEN TREASURES AND THE PEARL OF GREAT PRICE (13:44–45)

The Hidden Treasure (v. 44)

Jesus compared a person who enters the kingdom to a man who sells everything he owns to buy a field containing a treasure that will more than compensate for his sacrifice.

The Pearl of Great Price (v. 45)

Jesus makes the same point by describing a merchant who purchases a costly pearl. Again, the man gives up everything to obtain his treasure.

Jesus was using these parables to call his readers to a choice. He was offering them an opportunity to live under God's rule.

THE PARABLE OF THE DRAGNET (13:47–50)

This parable concerns a net used in fishing. Jesus reminds his hearers how a net, when thrown into the water, gathers in all kinds of fish. Then, after returning to the shore, the fishermen separate the good fish from the bad. "Bad" fish were those inedible according to Jewish law.

This parable points to the mixed character of the Church. At the end of the age, God will separate the righteous from the wicked, sending the wicked ones into the "blazing furnace" (v. 50).

THE PARABLE OF THE SCRIBE TRAINED FOR THE KINGDOM (13:51–52)

Jesus compares his disciples to a householder who uses both his old and new possessions and goods to care for the needs of his family and guests. Jesus's disciples will combine their knowledge of God's past revelation in the Old Testament with their growing knowledge of a new, fuller revelation in Jesus.

Section Summary

Only by relating the old to the new could the disciples meet the needs of those to whom they will minister.

JESUS'S REJECTION IN HIS OWN HOMETOWN (13:52–58)

Jesus briefly returned to his hometown, Nazareth, to teach in the synagogue. It turned out that the people knew him as the son of Joseph, the carpenter. They were too familiar with Jesus and his family to believe he was anyone out of the ordinary. Matthew records that the people took offense at him. Jesus found curiosity, jealousy, and outright hatred in Nazareth; but he found very little faith.

HISTORICAL BACKGROUND

"A prophet is not without honor except in his hometown and in his household" (13:57). This saying is found in Jewish, Greek, and Roman writings.

QUESTIONS TO GUIDE YOUR STUDY

1. What are parables?
2. Why did Jesus teach in parables?
3. Which of the kingdom parables especially grabs your attention? Why?

MATTHEW 14

THE DEATH OF JOHN THE BAPTIST (14:1–12)

Herod Antipas, a son of Herod the Great, ruled Galilee at the time. He imprisoned John because of John's denunciation of his marriage to Herodias. Divorcing his own wife, Herod married Herodias. John the Baptist openly criticized the marriage as unlawful and, therefore, adultery.

Jewish law did not permit a person to be executed without a trial. Neither did it allow beheading as a form of execution. Yet Herod put to death his hated critic without a trial.

THE FEEDING OF MORE THAN FIVE THOUSAND (14:13–21)

After hearing of John the Baptist's death, Jesus withdrew to an unpopulated area east of Galilee. The crowds, however, would not leave Jesus alone. Jesus had compassion for them and performed healings. Evening came, and no provision was made for food. A survey of available food turned up five loaves and two fishes. Using these limited supplies, Jesus miraculously multiplied the food and fed the entire crowd with twelve full baskets of food left over.

Section Summary

The miraculous feeding of the five thousand, then and now, assures us that whatever our needs may be, God has more than adequate resources to meet them.

HISTORICAL BACKGROUND

Sea of Galilee

Also called Lake of Gennesaret. *Galilee* means "circle." A freshwater lake nestled in the hills of northern Palestine. It is 13 miles long and eight miles wide. In the first century, the Sea of Galilee was of major commercial significance. The fishing industry flourished there.

MIRACLES ON THE SEA OF GALILEE (14:22–34)

The Storm (vv. 22–24)

After the feeding of the crowd, Jesus made his disciples get into a boat to go to the other side of the Sea of Galilee.

When the crowd and the disciples were gone, Jesus went into the hills by himself to pray. Meanwhile, the disciples, about halfway across the Sea of Galilee, were battling a storm.

Jesus Walks on Water (vv. 25–27)

In the midst of the storm, Jesus came walking toward them on the water. At first, the disciples, caught up in their circumstances, thought they were seeing a ghost.

Section Summary

Jesus told them to take courage. It is interesting to note that Jesus's statement, "It is I," is literally "I am." This is a conscious echo of the divine name of Yahweh (Exod 3:14).

Peter Walks on the Water (vv. 28–31)

WORD PICTURE

Doubt

The Greek word translated "doubt" suggests the idea of going two different directions at once.

Upon seeing Jesus walking on the water, Peter asked Jesus to enable him to do the same thing. We do not know Peter's motive for wanting to do so. Jesus agreed and enabled Peter to start walking toward him. Before he reached Jesus, Peter became afraid of the wind and conditions. Peter began to doubt his ability to continue. Peter was more focused on the surrounding storm than on the Lord. As a result, Peter began to sink and needed to be rescued.

When Jesus and Peter stepped into the boat, the wind stopped blowing. Then the disciples had the assurance they needed. As a result, they worshiped Jesus as the Son of God.

The disciples landed at Gennesaret, where many sick people were brought to Jesus. All who touched even the fringe of his garment were healed.

Section Summary

In the midst of the storm, Jesus went to the disciples and saved them. It is interesting to note that the very waves that were frightening the disciples were the waves that brought Jesus to them.

QUESTIONS TO GUIDE YOUR STUDY

1. What aspect of the feeding of the five thousand impacted you the most?
2. Describe the circumstances of the storm that threatened the disciples. What encouragement can we gain from this account of Jesus calming the storm?
3. What feelings and thoughts do you believe Peter was experiencing after Jesus rescued him from sinking and as they walked into the boat?

MATTHEW 15

CONFLICT WITH THE PHARISEES AND SCRIBES (15:1–20)

A group of Pharisees and scribes came to see Jesus. They were on a fact-finding mission to investigate his activities and teachings. They began by asking him why his disciples didn't wash their hands before eating.

OLD TESTAMENT REFERENCE

"These people approach me with their speeches to honor me with lip-service, yet their hearts are far from me." (Isa 29:13)

A Question about Handwashing (vv. 1–9)

This question had nothing to do with hygiene; it was strictly a matter of ritual. The group accused Jesus of violating rabbinic tradition by eating bread with hands not washed in the proper rabbinic tradition.

What Defiles a Person (vv. 10–20)

Jesus answered his accusers by employing a standard rabbinic technique of replying directly with a counterquestion. He used a quote from Isa 29:13 to describe their behavior.

Jesus taught that a person is not defiled by what he puts into his mouth. The primary source of evil is internal, from the evil of the human heart.

Jesus called the Pharisees "blind guides" (v. 13) because they failed to see the truth of his identity and teaching. The equally blind people they led would fall with them.

Section Summary

Moral purity and the keeping of God's Word begins within a person's heart—one's thoughts and will.

A CANAANITE WOMAN'S FAITH (15:21–28)

This woman was a Gentile. "Canaanite" was a general term for the pagan inhabitants of the promised land whom Israel was told to conquer in Joshua's day. She pleaded for Jesus to heal her demon-possessed daughter. She was persistent in her plea and had a tenacious faith. Jesus marveled at her faith. It was in stark contrast to the lack of faith exhibited by the religious leaders. Jesus responded to this woman's faith and granted her request. From a distance, he healed her daughter immediately.

THE FEEDING OF MORE THAN FOUR THOUSAND (15:29–39)

This feeding contains too many differences to be a variant account of the same incident.

As before, Jesus asked about the available resources. This time there were seven loaves and some small fish. Taking, blessing, and breaking the food, Jesus gave it to the disciples for distribution to the crowd. After all the people were fed, seven baskets of food remained.

Section Summary

This second feeding miracle emphasized the fact that although his primary mission was to Jews, Jesus could act on behalf of the Gentiles as well.

QUESTIONS TO GUIDE YOUR STUDY

1. Jesus taught that the primary source of defilement came from the heart. What examples of "heart defilement" might believers want to avoid?
2. What about the Canaanite woman's faith impressed Jesus?

MATTHEW 16

A DEMAND FROM THE RELIGIOUS AUTHORITIES FOR A SIGN (16:1–12)

The Pharisees and Sadducees demanded a sign from Jesus that proved the divine origin of Jesus's exorcisms. Their purpose was to test him and possibly diminish his influence with the people.

SIMON PETER'S RECOGNITION OF JESUS'S IDENTITY (16:13–20)

Jesus posed a question to the disciples: "Who do people say that the Son of Man is?" (v. 13). The disciples responded with several opinions. Peter acted as spokesman for the group, saying, "You are the Messiah, the Son of the living God" (v. 16). This is the first time in Matthew that anyone in Jesus's audience has acknowledged him as the "Messiah."

Jesus praised Simon for his confession of faith. He declared that this insight came from God, not from human sources. He gave Simon a new name—Peter, which means "rock." The rock on which the Church is built is the faith shown by Peter in making his confession.

WORD PICTURE

On this Rock

This phrase denotes a ledge or cliff or rock like that referred to in Matt 7:24 on which the wise man built his house. *Petros*, the Greek word for Peter, refers to a smaller detachment of a massive ledge. But A. T. Robertson says, "Too much must not be made of this point since Jesus probably spoke Aramaic to Peter which draws no such distinction." *WPNT*, 1:131.

Section Summary

The recognition of Jesus's messiahship marked an important step in the disciples' understanding of Jesus. However, he was not to be the kind of Messiah the Jews expected.

THE PATH OF CHRIST AND HIS FOLLOWERS (16:21–28)

Building on Peter's confession, Jesus began to teach his disciples what his messiahship actually involved. He would be a suffering Messiah, not a military warrior or a political leader. The disciples would follow Jesus along the same path, many becoming martyrs for their faith.

Section Summary

Following Christ is a life of self-denial. It means to give oneself wholly to Christ and to share in his rejection, shame, suffering, and death. As with Jesus, his followers' suffering will lead to glory.

QUESTIONS TO GUIDE YOUR STUDY

1. The Jewish authorities demanded a sign from Jesus. What might have been their proper approach to Jesus?
2. To follow Christ is a commitment to self-denial. What does self-denial involve?
3. What was the disciples' understanding of Jesus's messiahship at this point in Matthew's narrative?

OLD TESTAMENT REFERENCE

In this picture, Moses symbolized the Law while Elijah stood for the Prophets. Jesus came to fulfill both. Both Moses and Elijah were connected in Old Testament writings with the age of the Messiah. Their appearance with Jesus meant in part that he was the prophet whom Moses foretold in Deut 18:15 and the Messiah whom Elijah would precede, as foreseen in Mal 4:5.

MATTHEW 17

THE TRANSFIGURATION (17:1–13)

Jesus took the three inner-circle disciples—Peter, James, and John—with him up on a high mountain. Some have suggested Mount Tabor;

WORD PICTURE

Transfiguration

The word *transfigured,* in more common English, is translated "transformed." The Greek word used is *metamorphoō,* from which we get the English word *metamorphosis.*

others, Mount Hermon. There the disciples saw Jesus transfigured before their eyes. For that brief moment, they saw Jesus as the heavenly Lord. His personal appearance and that of his garments were changed. His skin and clothes shone with dazzling brilliance and whiteness, suggesting glory, sovereignty, and purity. This event was a foreshadowing of Jesus's future glory.

As the disciples watched, Moses and Elijah appeared and spoke with Jesus.

Evidently Peter, not understanding what was happening, wanted to prolong the vision. He began to speak about setting up shelters for Jesus, Moses, and Elijah so they could stay longer. Then a bright cloud overshadowed them. The voice of God spoke from the cloud and said, "This is my beloved Son, with whom I am well-pleased. Listen to him!" (v. 5).

The awestruck disciples "fell facedown and were terrified" (v. 6). Based on the Greek word Matthew used, the disciples' fear was more terror than reverence, although their posture may have suggested an element of worship.

Section Summary

The transfiguration was a foreshadowing of Jesus's resurrection and return.

WORD PICTURE

Little Faith

One of Matthew's favorite adjectives is a word translated "little faith." Matthew uses it five times in his Gospel (6:30; 8:26; 14:31; 16:8; 17:20). The word is really a combination of two words: meaning "a small amount" and "faith." Jesus spoke this word as a tender rebuke during the disciples' times of anxiety.

THE DISCIPLES' LACK OF FAITH (17:14–21)

The overwhelming experience on the mountain soon gave way to everyday reality. Jesus and the three disciples returned from the mountain. While they were away, a crowd gathered with the nine remaining disciples. During Jesus's absence, the nine disciples tried to heal an epileptic boy but without success.

The disciples asked Jesus why they were not able to heal the boy. (After all, he gave them the authority to heal the sick.) Jesus blamed their failure on their lack of faith or, better, minuscule faith.

Section Summary

It is important to cultivate faith. Faith "the size of a mustard seed" suggests not only little faith but also life and growth.

NEW TESTAMENT REFERENCE

From Luke's account, we know their conversation with Jesus concerned his coming death.

MORE WORDS FORETELLING JESUS'S DEATH (17:22–23)

In these two verses Jesus tried to prepare the disciples for what to expect on their coming visit to Jerusalem. He explained that he would be arrested and killed. Yet he would be raised on the third day after his death. The disciples were "deeply distressed" (v. 23). Although they were becoming accustomed to the fact of Jesus's coming death, they were finding the idea very troublesome.

A QUESTION ABOUT TAXES (17:24–27)

Poll-tax collectors came to Peter and asked him whether Jesus paid the annual half-shekel tax that Jewish males were required to pay for temple upkeep.

Jesus took the opportunity to teach an important lesson. As sons of the kingdom, he and his disciples should be exempt from having to pay the temple tax. So as not to offend the Jews he was trying to reach, however, he would pay the tax. He then gave instructions to Peter to catch a fish. The first fish he would catch would have a shekel in its mouth. With that shekel, Peter was to pay the tax for himself and Jesus.

If Jesus and his followers failed to pay this religious tax, most likely others would have misunderstood. The loving thing for Jesus and his disciples to do was to take into account their influence on others and pay the tax. Concern for others is a valid reason for not always exercising one's rights.

QUESTIONS TO GUIDE YOUR STUDY

1. What was the significance of the transfiguration?
2. What steps might we take to resolve "little faith"?
3. Considering Jesus's other miracles, what is different about his healing of the boy with a demon?

HISTORICAL BACKGROUND

Taxes in Jesus's Day

In the New Testament era, Herod the Great levied a tax on the produce of the field and a tax on items bought and sold. Other duties paid to foreign powers were:

- a land tax
- a poll tax
- a kind of progressive income tax
- a personal property tax
- a house tax levied in Jerusalem

Taxes were paid directly to Roman authorities. The Israelites resented most deeply the duties paid to the occupying powers. Many zealous Jews considered it treason to God to pay taxes to Rome. When questioned about paying the poll tax, Jesus surprised his questioners by saying that the law should be obeyed.

MATTHEW 18

GREATNESS IN THE KINGDOM (18:1–4)

The Disciple's Question (v. 1)

The disciples came to Jesus with a question. "So who is the greatest in the kingdom of heaven?"

Asking the question, however, revealed a serious misunderstanding on their part about the nature of God's kingdom. And, in light of Jesus's recent and repeated predictions of his own death and teaching on self-denial, the question seemed highly inappropriate.

How to Enter the Kingdom (vv. 2–3)

Jesus called a child to himself and told the disciples they must "turn and become like little children" (v. 3) or they would never enter God's kingdom.

NEW TESTAMENT REFERENCE

In his Gospel, Mark tells us the disciples had been discussing this question among themselves. Luke tells us they even reached the point of arguing about it (Luke 9:46).

The Greatest in the Kingdom (v. 4)

The greatest person in the kingdom is one who "humbles himself like this child" (v. 4). This is a question every follower of Jesus should ask regularly in retrospect: Is my confidence like that of a child who trusts the goodness of the Father, or is my confidence in myself?

Section Summary

Too often we concern ourselves with our status here and now. Jesus represented a reversal of the world's values. He counted humility as the mark of greatness.

PERSONAL APPLICATION

Jesus emphasized the seriousness of causing a weaker Christian to sin. Better to have a large millstone hung around one's neck and be cast into the sea than to cause a little one to sin.

RESPONSIBILITIES TOWARD LITTLE ONES (18:5–6)

Jesus identified himself with children and the lowly people whom the world ignored or rejected. To receive a child or a child in faith (a new or immature Christian) in Jesus's name, as his representative, is to receive Jesus himself.

Section Summary

As representatives of Jesus Christ, we need to be examples to others in the faith.

WORD PICTURE

Temptation

The Greek word is *skandalon,* which can also mean stumbling block, hindrance, trap, snare, or something that causes us to fall.

WHAT TO DO ABOUT TEMPTATION (18:7–9)

Jesus goes on to teach his disciples more about the problem of temptations. He makes an important point that we must be careful not to tempt others to sin. We need to exercise the kind of self-discipline that will rid our lives of whatever is causing a temptation to sin.

Section Summary

Faithful dependence on God, regardless of how others treat us, makes us great in God's eyes.

THE LOST SHEEP (18:10–14)

Jesus stressed the untold value God places on every person, regardless of that person's status by earthly standards. To illustrate this, Jesus told a parable about a lost sheep. Jesus declares that the shepherd will not be content until all the sheep are safe. He will leave the flock to look for that lost sheep until he finds it.

Section Summary

We should humble ourselves and never cause others to sin. God never despises his people but is always concerned to go to great lengths to preserve them. God does all he can to make certain that none of them will perish.

DISCIPLINE WITHIN THE CHURCH (18:15–17)

In his Sermon on the Mount, Jesus taught the necessity for making things right with a brother whom one offended before bringing an offering to God. He placed responsibility on the wrongdoer for bringing about reconciliation. In this passage, Jesus describes a four-step procedure for dealing with the problem of being wronged by a brother. Those steps are outlined on this page.

Section Summary

Discipline within the church is necessary to avoid compromising the unity and testimony of God's people. Jesus taught that complaints between believers must be reconciled and relationships restored.

THE AUTHORITY OF THE CHURCH (18:18–20)

Earlier, Jesus promised Peter the authority to "bind" and "loose" (cf. 16:19). Here the church's authority seems to apply also to the right to accept or expel members. The church's loosing and binding—forgiving or refusing to forgive—carries the authority of God. The church's actions, however, are to conform to Jesus's teaching and not be arbitrary. The church has the responsibility of obtaining God's guidance in decision-making.

God promised to be with any two or three believers who come together to pray in his name. God, of course, is omnipresent, but he is uniquely present in every Christian gathering as his Spirit indwells believers.

Section Summary

The Jews believed God's divine presence was with those engaged in studying the Law. Jesus promised to be that divine presence in the midst of those gathered to seek his will.

A PARABLE ABOUT FORGIVENESS (18:21–35)

Here is the fifth and last of the uniquely Matthean accounts involving Peter.

PERSONAL APPLICATION

Steps to Reconciliation between Two Believers

1. Confront the fellow believer. Ideally, the two should resolve the problem without involving anyone else.
2. If the first step fails, the offended believer is to take two or three other believers with him. The other believers can observe the attitudes and motives of the two and attempt to bring reconciliation.
3. If step 2 fails, the matter should be brought before the assembled church. Here, restoration and reconciliation are to be the goals.
4. If the church fails to bring harmony, the church is to exclude the erring believer from the fellowship because of his or her unwillingness to overcome the barrier with the offended believer.

WORD PICTURE

Where Two or Three Are Gathered

"For where there are two or three who have been joined together into my Name with the result that I am the common object of their faith, there I am in their midst." Kenneth S. Wuest, *The New Testament: An Expanded Translation*, p. 47.

HISTORICAL BACKGROUND

Seventy-seven times can also be translated seventy times seven. *Seven* came to symbolize completeness and perfection. So we are to forgive not merely seven times (already a gracious number of forgiveness), but seventy times seven (limitless forgiveness, beyond keeping count).

A Question and an Answer (vv. 21–22)

Peter, probably acting as spokesman for the group, asked Jesus how often it was necessary to forgive a fellow believer. He generously proposed seven times, which went beyond the rabbinic maxim for forgiving three times. But Jesus tells Peter he should be ready to forgive seventy-seven times!

A Parable (vv. 23–34)

Jesus told a parable found only here in Matthew's Gospel. The parable teaches the importance of forgiveness. A king decided to "settle accounts" with his servants. One of the servants owed the king 10,000 talents (estimates range from several million to 1 trillion dollars), but he had no way of repaying the debt. The king ordered the debtor and his family sold, along with all his possessions.

Falling to his knees, the indebted servant promised to repay all he owed if the king would not carry out the intended punishment. The king took pity on the servant and canceled his enormous debt.

But as the servant was leaving the king's presence, he met a fellow servant who owed him a small sum. You might expect the servant to forgive gladly the small debt since he just had his enormous debt canceled by the king. Instead, the servant grabbed the man by the throat and demanded payment, refusing to listen to the man's pleas for mercy, and threw him into prison.

Upon hearing what the servant did, the king ordered him imprisoned until he could pay the debt.

PERSONAL APPLICATION

1. God takes the initiative to go to great lengths to bring to him those who have strayed.
2. Reclaiming such people should lead to joyous celebration.
3. The faithfulness of the majority should never excuse us for ignoring anyone who remains distant from God.

The Parable's Application (v. 35)

Jesus applied this parable to the lives of his hearers. No forgiveness we might show can compare to the forgiveness already shown us by God. If we are not willing to forgive a fellow believer from the heart, we will find no forgiveness from God. An unforgiving person is incapable of receiving God's forgiveness.

Section Summary

Three themes emerge from this parable: (1) God's boundless grace, (2) the absurdity of spurning that grace, and (3) the frightful fate awaiting the unforgiving.

QUESTIONS TO GUIDE YOUR STUDY

1. What should be our attitude toward a new or weaker believer in the faith?

2. Jesus spoke strongly about the problem of temptation. What preventive steps might we take to prepare for times when temptations come?
3. Describe Jesus's qualities as Shepherd. In what ways have you benefited from his shepherding in your life?

MATTHEW 19

TEACHINGS ABOUT DIVORCE (19:1–12)

The Question (v. 3)

This time the Pharisees asked Jesus a question about divorce to test him. They asked whether it was lawful for a man to divorce his wife for any reason.

Back to the Beginning (v. 4)

Jesus quoted from Genesis 2:24 and pointed out that the marriage covenant has two parts: "leave . . . and be united." That means "to transfer one's fundamental allegiance from parents to spouse."

The Pharisees' Counterquestion (vv. 7–9)

The Pharisees countered with a question about Moses's statement that a man could divorce his wife by giving her "divorce papers." The Pharisees' counterquestion raised the obvious objection: Why did God permit divorce in Old Testament times if he categorically opposed it?

In his reply, Jesus went beyond both competing schools of Pharisaic thought—the Hillelites, who granted divorce "for any good cause," and the Shammaites, who limited it to adultery. Jesus emphasized the permanence of marriage as God's original design.

The Disciples' Reaction and Jesus's Reply (vv. 10–12)

The disciples were amazed at Jesus's teaching. They declared that it might be better for a man not to marry at all if God's ideal for marriage was so high.

Section Summary

God's provision for divorce was temporary, based on the rebellion of fallen humanity.

BLESSING THE CHILDREN (19:13–15)

In this section Jesus dealt with his disciples' impatience at certain individuals who asked him to bless their children. Jesus overruled his disciples and invited the children to come to him.

HISTORICAL BACKGROUND

In Jesus's day, the rabbinic school of Hillel held that divorce was lawful for almost any cause. According to this school, a man was justified in divorcing his wife for burning his dinner! The school of Shammai, in contrast, held that only the wife's adultery was a lawful reason for divorce. The wording of the text reflects only a man's perspective, since women were rarely, if ever, able to divorce in ancient Judaism.

OLD TESTAMENT REFERENCE

From early times provision was made for divorce among the Israelites (Deut 24:1–4). Presumably prior to this decree, a wife could be put out of the home at the pleasure of her husband. Now he was required to write out "divorce papers" and give them to his wife as proof he was divorcing her. This gave some dignity and protection to the divorced woman.

HISTORICAL BACKGROUND

A Psychological Paradox

The young man claims to have kept all these commandments and yet he was not satisfied. He had an uneasy conscience and Jesus called him to something he did not have. A. T. Robertson, *WPNT,* 1:157.

DEMANDS OF THE KINGDOM (19:16–26)

The Young Man's Question (vv. 16–22)

A man came to Jesus and wanted to know what he must do to gain eternal life. Jesus was not satisfied with the young man's obvious Jewish answer to his question. The man wanted to limit what he had to do. Jesus diverted the young man's attention from his inadequate criteria of entering into life and focusing on the standard of divine goodness.

Section Summary

Three lessons from this event touch all of us:

1. ***One can be interested in eternal life without possessing it (v. 17).***
2. ***Many who claim to have obeyed God have done so only in a superficial way (v. 20).***
3. ***The young man lacked eternal life because he rejected Jesus's call for repentance (v. 22).***

WORD PICTURE

Needle

Matthew uses the word for an ordinary needle, whereas Luke (18:25) uses the term for a surgical needle.

The Danger in Riches (vv. 23–26)

Jesus now begins a dialogue with his disciples. He says it's easier for a camel to pass through the eye of a needle than for a rich man to enter the kingdom of God.

PERSONAL APPLICATION

Many who are first will be last, and many who are last will be first. Many who apparently accomplished much and so seemed to deserve much will be surprised to find themselves last in the kingdom. Many who assumed they would be last will, in reality, be first.

THE REWARDS FOR CHRIST'S DISCIPLES (19:27–30)

In contrast to the young man who would not sacrifice his wealth to follow Jesus, the disciples gave up a great deal of earthly security to follow him. Peter reminded Jesus of this and asked him what kind of reward they might receive. Jesus assured them that in the world to come, they would receive a hundred times what they sacrificed, together with eternal life.

Section Summary

In God's kingdom, earthly values will be reversed. The hundredfold compensation Jesus promised his followers will be more wonderful than anything this earth has to offer.

QUESTIONS TO GUIDE YOUR STUDY

1. How did Jesus answer the Pharisees' question about divorce?
2. Why did Jesus have a special concern for children?
3. What prevented the young man from following Jesus?

MATTHEW 20

THE PARABLE OF THE VINEYARD WORKERS (20:1–16)

Jesus pictured harvesttime, during which a farmer hired a certain number of seasonal workers each day according to his needs. He went to the marketplace, the center of town, at about six o'clock in the morning and hired a group of laborers for one day's work. At about nine o'clock, seeing others who needed work standing in the marketplace, he hired yet another group. Then, at about noon and at three o'clock he hired more laborers. Finally at five o'clock, with only an hour left in the workday, he hired a few more workers.

At six o'clock in the evening, the farmer instructed his steward to pay the workers, beginning with those hired last and ending with those he hired first (at six o'clock in the morning).

Surprisingly, those who worked only one hour received a full day's pay, just as those who worked long and hard for twelve hours. Those who worked all day complained to the farmer. They couldn't deny that he kept his part of the bargain, as he paid them what he promised. They were jealous of those who were paid as much as they after so little work, and they became angry because they did not receive a bonus.

PERSONAL APPLICATION

MAIN POINT: God's grace does not contradict standards of fairness but exceeds them.

NEW TESTAMENT REFERENCE

Twice before he tried to explain these coming events to them, but they did not understand (16:21–23; 17:22–23). Now Jesus tells them what will happen in greater detail than before.

Section Summary

This parable emphasizes a right attitude in service. God is generous and will always give us better than we deserve.

JESUS'S THIRD STATEMENT ABOUT HIS DEATH (20:17–19)

On the way to Jerusalem, Jesus again tells his disciples what will happen there. He will be delivered to his enemies, the scribes and chief priests. The religious leader will condemn him. They will then deliver him to the Romans (Gentiles) for mockery, scourging, and execution by crucifixion. But, on the third day, he will be raised from death.

Section Summary

The exalted Son of God must first become God's Suffering Servant and die. Few, including the twelve disciples, are ready for this.

MORE ABOUT GREATNESS (20:20–28)

The mother of James and John came with them to make a special request of Jesus. Kneeling before him, she asked that her two sons be given special places of honor in his kingdom, one at his right hand, one at his left. It is almost certain that James and John had their mother make this request for them.

Jesus explained to these two close disciples that they didn't really know what they were asking. He was talking about his coming death, while they were thinking about their "proper place" in the kingdom. He then redirected their attention to his coming suffering. His question, "Are you able to drink the cup that I am about to drink?" (v. 22), was really asking if they were ready to die with him.

WORD PICTURE

James would be the first of the Twelve to face martyrdom (Acts 12:1–2).

Jesus assured them that they *would* drink his cup.

Verse 28 stands among the most valuable in Matthew's Gospel. In it, Jesus declares that he came to serve rather than to be served. He came to give his life as a ransom for many. The word *many* (v. 28) refers to all who accept Jesus's offer of forgiveness, made possible by his death, and who commit their lives to him in discipleship.

WORD PICTURE

Ransom

This word is one commonly employed as the price for a slave who is then set free by the one who bought him. Jesus gave his own life as the price of freedom for the slaves of sin. A. T. Robertson, *WPNT* I, p. 163.

Section Summary

Jesus declared that the decision as to who would have positions of honor in his kingdom was not his to make. Only the Father himself knew who would occupy the places of honor.

THE HEALING OF THE TWO BLIND MEN (20:29–34)

Jesus and his disciples left Jericho, followed by a large crowd. As they traveled, they came upon two blind men sitting beside the crowd. Hearing that Jesus was passing that way, the two men cried out to him for mercy, using the messianic title "Son of David" (v. 30). The crowd tried to quiet the men. Perhaps the crowd feared trouble from the authorities if Jesus were publicly called the Messiah.

But Jesus heard the repeated cries of the blind men and asked what they wanted. At their request, out of compassion, he healed them both. The men were so grateful for their healing that they became Jesus's followers.

HISTORICAL BACKGROUND

Jericho

In Jesus's day Jericho was a prominent city of Judea, strategically located on the route from Galilee to Jerusalem. It was the last major city one passed through before climbing the treacherous road to Jerusalem. Because it was a wealthy city, it attracted beggars.

QUESTIONS TO GUIDE YOUR STUDY

1. Why were the vineyard farmer's payments for labor fair to all the workers?
2. What is the lesson of the parable of the vineyard?
3. Why was it so difficult for the disciples to accept a Suffering Servant as the Messiah?

MATTHEW 21

ROYAL ENTRY INTO JERUSALEM (21:1–11)

Jesus was nearing Jerusalem and the last days of his earthly life. He planned to make a dramatic entry into the city to make himself known as the Messiah, but not the kind of Messiah the people were expecting.

The significance of this event for the New Testament writers is obvious since all four Gospels record it. It was Passover, and one estimate has about two and one-half million people present in Jerusalem for the celebration. Jesus could have chosen no better time for symbolically presenting himself to his people. Yet he was fully aware that the minds of the religious leaders were already set against him. He could expect nothing but hostility from them. Because of the prevailing circumstances, this account is often misnamed the "triumphal entry."

OLD TESTAMENT REFERENCE

"Rejoice greatly, Daughter Zion! Shout in triumph, Daughter Jerusalem! Look, your King is coming to you; he is righteous and victorious, humble and riding on a donkey, on a colt, the foal of a donkey." (Zech 9:9)

Preparation for the Entry (vv. 1–7)

It seems that Jesus already made plans for a donkey (Zech 9:9) and its colt to be ready for him. Matthew makes it a point to mention that the colt had never been ridden.

OLD TESTAMENT REFERENCE

"He who comes in the name of the LORD is blessed. From the house of the LORD we bless you." (Ps 118:26)

The Crowd's Response (vv. 8–11)

Although he was riding a donkey, the crowd gave Jesus the kind of greeting they would have given a king. Most laid garments down in his path. Others spread tree branches along the roadside.

The crowds shouted words to Jesus from Ps 118:26. This is one of the *hallel* psalms used to greet pilgrims who came to Jerusalem at feast times.

Section Summary

As Jesus entered Jerusalem, he received a king's welcome. The procession had a powerful impact on the inhabitants of the city. Added to the cries of "Hosanna" was the title "Son of David."

JESUS CLEARS OUT THE TEMPLE (21:12–17)

All four Gospels include the incident of Jesus's cleansing the temple. He found it busy with the activity of money changers and sellers of sacrificial birds and animals. Since sacrificial birds and animals had to be officially certified and unblemished, it was helpful to purchase them at the temple. Evidently, the selling and money changing had become a means of cheating and exploiting the people. Jesus became angry at what he saw. He drove out the merchants and overturned their tables. Instead of attacking the political base of Roman rule, as most would have hoped, Jesus's attack threatened the center of Judaism itself.

OLD TESTAMENT REFERENCE

The rationale for Jesus's behavior is in fact scriptural. As he cleared the area of the various commercial transactions, Jesus began to fulfill the prophecy that a day would come when no "merchant" or "Canaanite" would remain in the house of God (Zech 14:21). Jesus then quoted portions of Isa 56:7 and Jer 7:11. God's house was to be a house of prayer.

Section Summary

Jesus's cleansing the temple of the money changers fulfilled Old Testament prophecy.

HISTORICAL BACKGROUND

Fig Tree

The common fig tree has a short stout trunk and thick branches and twigs bearing coarsely lobed rough leaves. Rounded fruits ripen during the summer. Figs dry well and were stored as cakes for future use.

THE FRUITLESS FIG TREE (21:18–22)

On the following morning, as he returned to Jerusalem from Bethany, Jesus was hungry. He saw a fig tree by the road and thought he would eat some figs from it. Upon closer inspection, however, he found that the tree had only leaves and no fruit.

Seeing the tree was barren, Jesus declared that the tree would never again bear fruit. The tree immediately withered. Why would Jesus work this destructive miracle? He used the fig tree and its destruction to symbolize Israel's coming fate. To all outward appearances, Israel was full of the promise of spiritual fruit. In reality, Israel was fruitless. Like the fig tree, it would be destroyed because of its barrenness and indict them for their lack of belief in John. If they claimed John's source of authority was a merely human one, they would anger the people. The people believed John was a prophet, a messenger from God.

WORD PICTURE

Regretted

Literally means "to be sorry afterwards." A. T. Robertson says, "Here the boy got sorry for his stubborn refusal to obey his father and went and obeyed. Godly sorrow leads to repentance, but mere sorrow is not repentance." A. T. Robertson, *WPNT*, 1:170.

It was a no-win scenario for the authorities. Neither answer was safe. The authorities decided to claim ignorance: "We don't know." Because the leaders did not answer his question, Jesus insisted that he would not answer theirs.

Section Summary

In a scheme to trap Jesus, the temple authorities trapped themselves and could only answer him with an expression of ignorance. Since they could not judge John, they could not fairly judge Jesus.

After Jesus refused to answer the leaders' question about his source of authority, he told three parables: the two sons, the wicked tenants, and the marriage feast of the king's son. All three parables were directed against the Jewish leaders, echoing the spiritual failure of official Israel.

JESUS'S PARABLE ABOUT TWO SONS (21:28–32)

In the parable of the two sons, a man told one of his sons to work in his vineyard, but one son refused his father's request. Later that day, however, the son was sorry he refused and did go to work. The other son said he would go to work, but he did not go.

The son who refused and later changed his mind represented the irreligious Jews, such as publicans and sinners, who were flocking to Jesus. The son who said, "I will, sir" (v. 30), and did not go to work represented the Jewish religious leaders who failed to recognize God's saving actions in the ministry of Jesus. Jesus commended the irreligious Jews who were repenting but gave a firm rebuke to the self-righteous Jewish leaders.

Section Summary

Like the second son in the parable, the Jewish authorities promised they would do God's will. Yet, they did not believe John the Baptist, who brought them God's demand for repentance. God demands real obedience, not simply lip service.

JESUS'S PARABLE ABOUT A VINEYARD'S FARMERS (21:33–41)

The Story (vv. 33–39)

A man planted a vineyard, equipping it with a hedge for protection from animals, a watch tower, and a winepress. Then he went abroad and left the vineyard in charge of tenants who agreed to pay their rent in the form of part of the yearly crop. When the time came for the grapes to be ready, the owner sent some of his servants to get his share. Instead of giving the servants the fruit, however, the tenants attacked them. One was beaten, one was stoned, and one was murdered. A second group of servants sent by the owner received the same treatment. Finally, the owner sent his son to get the fruit, thinking the tenants would surely respect him. But the servants did not respect the son and killed him instead.

A Question and an Answer (vv. 40–41)

After delivering the parable, Jesus asked a question of the authorities. His question was, "When the owner of the vineyard comes, what will he do to those farmers?" (v. 40). They answered by saying that the owner would naturally put them to death and give management of the vineyard to new farmers who would give him the fruit he was due. As before, the authorities condemned themselves with their own words.

The Parable's Symbolism

In this parable, the owner represents God, and the vineyard represents the Jewish nation (Isa 5:1–7). The farmers who rented the vineyard are the Jewish leaders, and the servants beaten and killed refer to the Old Testament prophets. The son who was murdered represents Jesus. The destruction of the husbandman points to the utter overthrow of the Jewish religious leaders in Jerusalem in AD 70. Giving the vineyard to others suggests the transfer of God's kingdom to "a people for [God's] possession," who would be redeemed Jews and Gentiles (1 Pet 2:9). Just as the owner expected fruit from the husbandman, God expected fruit from the nation of Israel. Their fruitlessness led to judgment.

OLD TESTAMENT REFERENCE

Jesus quoted from Ps 118:22–23 to warn the leaders about the consequences of rejecting him. That passage speaks of a stone rejected by builders but finally made "the cornerstone."

HISTORICAL BACKGROUND

Cornerstone

The stone laid at the corner to bind two walls together and to strengthen them. Used as a symbol of strength and prominence.

THE CORNERSTONE (21:42–43)

Section Summary

The kingdom would be taken from the leaders who had not been faithful to God's will.

QUESTIONS TO GUIDE YOUR STUDY

1. When Jesus rode into Jerusalem on a donkey, how were the people receiving him? What were they anticipating?
2. Jesus cleared the temple of the money changers. What drove him to take such decisive and strong measures?
3. What is the lesson of the fruitless fig tree?

MATTHEW 22

INVITATIONS TO A WEDDING BANQUET (22:1–14)

HISTORICAL BACKGROUND

Banquet

An elaborate meal, sometimes called a feast, and prominent in sealing friendships and celebrating victories. This latter purpose is seen in Jesus's reference to the messianic banquet.

Refusals (vv. 1–7)

Jesus told a story about a king who was planning a wedding banquet for his son. In accordance with Near Eastern custom, the king first sent out servants to give a general invitation to those he wanted to invite. Those who were invited refused the invitations.

When the banquet was prepared, the king again sent out invitations to the same guests, giving them another chance. This time the message declared that the banquet was ready. Most of those invited made excuses for not going. And, incredibly, the rest killed the servants who brought them the invitation. To refuse an invitation was to reject the king's authority. To kill the king's servant was an offense requiring severe punishment. The angry king sent troops to destroy and burn their city.

The Banquet Guests (vv. 8–10)

Determined to fill the hall for his son's wedding feast, the king sent his servants to bring in all kinds of people, good and bad, from the streets. These became the king's banquet guests.

In this story, Jesus was speaking about the Jewish leaders. They should have been overjoyed to receive an invitation to God's banquet table. Yet, they were hostile or indifferent to the invitation when it came through Jesus. For that reason, God opened the doors of his kingdom to all kinds of people. That is why Jesus's ministry extended to "sinners" and outcasts.

The Guest without a Wedding Garment (vv. 11–14)

One member of the group appeared without the proper wedding clothes. When questioned why he was not dressed for the occasion, the man offered no excuse. The king had him bound and thrown outside the lighted banquet hall into the darkness. There he could regret what he had done. Jesus concluded the parable by saying, "For many are invited, but few are chosen."

Section Summary

God, in his grace, has called many people to receive his salvation. But those who accept God's salvation must accept it on his terms.

IS IT RIGHT TO PAY TAXES? (22:15–22)

The Controversial Question (vv. 16–18)

Evidently the three parables Jesus just delivered enraged the religious authorities, for Matthew tells us they met to decide how best to trap Jesus. They decided to do so with a political question: "Is it lawful to pay taxes to Caesar or not?"

Jesus's Answer (vv. 19–22)

They chose a highly controversial question. Whatever Jesus's answer, he was certain to displease some of the people. Jesus at once saw through the ruse. Calling his questioners hypocrites, he asked for one of the coins with which the tax was to be paid. He then asked them whose image was on the coin, and they answered, "Caesar's."

When Jesus told them, "Give, then, to Caesar the things that are Caesar's, and to God the things that are God's" (v. 21), they marveled at his answer and had no argument.

Section Summary

The emperor had the responsibility for minting and circulating the coins bearing his image. So the coins actually belonged to him. If he requested their return in the form of taxes, the people should give back what belonged to him. But they must also give back to God what belongs to God. Each person bears God's image, and God wants each person given back to him in total allegiance.

HISTORICAL BACKGROUND

Saddducees

Small in number, they were a wealthy, aristocratic, and priestly party. This Jewish sect refused to believe in any doctrine that could not be established from the Law, the five books of Moses.

Consequently, they did not believe in resurrection from the dead, angels, or oral tradition.

THE SADDUCEES' QUESTION (22:23–33)

The Question (vv. 23–28)

OLD TESTAMENT REFERENCE

"I am the God of your father, the God of Abraham, the God of Isaac, and the God of Jacob." (Exod 3:6)

The Sadducees took the stage next. They ridiculed the notion of resurrection by means of a worst-case scenario. They used a deliberately exaggerated example, hoping Jesus would discredit himself before the people. Their question was based on Moses's teaching in Deut 25:4–6.

Moses taught that if brothers lived together, and one died childless, his brother should marry the widow to provide an heir for the dead brother. Suppose, they asked Jesus, seven brothers in turn married the woman, each dying without leaving a child. After his own death, whose wife would the woman be in the resurrection?

Jesus's Answer (vv. 29–32)

OLD TESTAMENT REFERENCE

This is the first controversy in which Jesus gave a straight answer to a question. Without hesitation, Jesus quoted Deut 6:5, a verse repeated daily by devout Jews. He went on to quote a related commandment from Lev 19:18, which commanded that a person should love his neighbor as he loved himself.

Jesus declared the Sadducees were doubly wrong. First, they assumed any future life would have to be a continuation of this present material life. They did not realize God's power to create a whole new order in the life to come. Second, Jesus told them their denial of the resurrection proved they did not even understand the Scriptures. He then quoted from Exod 3:6, part of the Scripture they accepted and claimed to understand.

The People's Reaction (v. 33)

Jesus's response was unanswerable. In spite of the Sadducees' attempt to hurt Jesus, the crowds "were astonished at his teaching."

Section Summary

Answers to questions about the future must rest on the authority of God's Word. The Sadducees were not only foolish but also ignorant of the Old Testament Scriptures. Jesus had so completely answered them that they were "silenced."

THE TWO GREATEST COMMANDMENTS (22:34–40)

HISTORICAL BACKGROUND

The Pharisees recognized 613 laws; 365 were negative commandments, and 248 were positive.

To this point, the Pharisees sent their disciples and others to trap Jesus. Now they came themselves. A lawyer, an expert in the Law, posed the next question.

The Lawyer's Question (vv. 34–36)

The lawyer asked Jesus what he considered to be the greatest of the Law's commandments.

Jesus's Answer (vv. 37–40)

Jesus's point was that a person could not love God without also loving his neighbor. Neither could a person really love his neighbor unless he first loved God.

Section Summary

If a person loves God with all his being and loves his fellow people as he loves himself, he will keep all of God's commandments.

OLD TESTAMENT REFERENCE

Jesus based his argument on Ps 110:1, assuming with the Judaism of his time the accuracy of the Davidic superscription and the inspiration of the actual text itself, which would imply its truthfulness. Jewish tradition recognized Ps 110 as messianic in nature. It referred to the Messiah as a transcendent being who would sit at God's right hand, not as a military leader.

A QUESTION FOR THE PHARISEES (22:41–46)

Having answered the questions of the Pharisees and Sadducees, it was now Jesus's turn to do the questioning. Facing the gathered Pharisees, he asked their opinion about "the Messiah." "Whose son is he?" (v. 41), he asked.

They replied, "David's." The Pharisees' answer set up Jesus's real question from Ps 110:1: If the Messiah is merely the human offspring of David, why does David himself speak of him as "Lord"—a master or sovereign above the one who is king of Israel and the highest human authority in the land?

Matthew tells us that no one dared ask him questions from that time on.

Section Summary

The Pharisees' concept of the Messiah was too limited. They needed to see that the Messiah could be the transcendent, heavenly Lord as well as the human descendant of David.

QUESTIONS TO GUIDE YOUR STUDY

1. What is the point of the parable of the wedding feast?
2. Jesus answered questions about paying taxes to Caesar. Is his answer applicable to our present-day tax obligations?
3. Why are the "two greatest commandments" so important to God?

MATTHEW 23

Chapter 23 begins Jesus's final discourse that takes place in two parts. This chapter is the first part.

CRITICISM OF THE SCRIBES AND PHARISEES (23:1–12)

Speaking to his disciples and to the gathered crowd, Jesus exposed the faults of some of the scribes and Pharisees.

A Warning (vv. 2–3)

Jesus told his audience to pay attention to the teachings of these religious leaders. After all, they sat in "the chair of Moses," the chair in the synagogue from which the Law's meaning was interpreted. But these leaders did not always practice what they preached.

Faults of the Leaders (vv. 4–10)

Several other characteristics of the scribes and Pharisees disturbed Jesus. For instance, they loved to show off their piety. They had to have an audience for everything they did.

What Makes a Person Great (vv. 11–12)

Once again Jesus repeated the principle he often taught before. The truly great person is one who serves others.

A SERIES OF ACCUSATIONS (23:13–36)

In the following series of seven accusations, each preceded by "woe to you," Jesus continued to criticize the hypocrisy he saw in the lives of the scribes and Pharisees. These "woes" were expressions of grief and sorrow uttered out of concern for the wrongs these religious leaders were doing to other people and for the punishment they were about to bring on themselves.

Shutting People Out of the Kingdom (v. 13)

Jesus first accused the leaders of shutting people out of God's kingdom. They refused to accept Jesus's invitation to enter the kingdom by faith and repentance, and they kept others from doing so as well.

The Problem of Proselytes (v. 15)

In Jesus's day, Judaism had a missionary dimension. Jesus said the scribes and Pharisees would "travel over land and sea to make one convert." But then they would weigh down that convert under their law, making him twice as legalistic as themselves.

Insincere Oaths (vv. 16–22)

The leaders, in a sense, made perjury legal with their teachings on oaths. For example, if a person swore by the temple, he did not have to keep his oath. Jesus recognized that no matter what a person might swear by, all belonged to God; therefore, the person who swore was calling God as a witness to his promise and was bound by the oath.

NEW TESTAMENT REFERENCE

Oaths

Jesus raised the oath to a new level of understanding. See Matt 5:33–37. At his trial before Caiaphas, Jesus was silent to the questions until a binding oath was placed upon him. See Matt 26:63–65. Jesus did not condemn oaths, only the abuse of God's name in the taking of oaths.

Tithing the Little; Neglecting the Great (vv. 23–24)

While meticulously tithing these tiny herbs, the scribes neglected the truly important aspects of the law such as justice, mercy, and faithfulness (v. 23).

Only Clean on the Outside (vv. 25–26)

Jesus compared the Jewish leaders to cups and plates that are clean on the outside but dirty on the inside.

Like Whitewashed Tombs (vv. 27–28)

Jesus saw that the scribes and Pharisees were like those whitewashed tombs. On the outside all appeared to be well. Inside, however, they were full of decay.

HISTORICAL BACKGROUND

Before Passover, tombs were whitewashed not only to beautify them but also so pilgrims could see them easily and not be defiled by walking on them.

Completing the Work of Their Fathers (vv. 29–36)

Now Jesus's judgment on the leaders reached its zenith. The ancestors of the Jewish leaders killed the prophets God sent to them. But they were about to complete their fathers' work by killing Jesus and others who would come in his name.

Section Summary

The seven "woes" (accusations) by Jesus were a collective criticism of the hypocrisy of Israel's Jewish leaders. His accusations reach a climax as he shows a solidarity between the current Jewish leaders and their predecessors who murdered the prophets of God.

A LAMENT FOR JERUSALEM (23:37–39)

Knowledge of Jerusalem's approaching destruction filled Jesus with the deepest sorrow. Jesus hoped to take the children of Israel under his wing and nurture them like a mother hen does her baby chicks. But they were not willing and so would face their judgment.

Section Summary

God never imposes his love by overriding human will. Unbelieving Israel had chosen its own destiny.

QUESTIONS TO GUIDE YOUR STUDY

1. What plagued the scribes and Pharisees to cause them to be so consistently hypocritical?
2. Describe a great person according to verses 11–12. What are some examples of great people?

3. Where do Pharisaical attitudes surface in today's church? What is our best response toward hypocrisy?

MATTHEW 24

A PREDICTION AND TWO QUESTIONS (24:1–3)

Jesus's Prediction (v. 1)

As they left the temple, Jesus's followers marveled at its grandeur (cp. Luke 21:5). Jesus predicted what might have seemed inconceivable at the time—the temple would soon be destroyed.

HISTORICAL BACKGROUND

In AD 70 during the siege and fall of Jerusalem, the commanding Roman general Titus tried to save the temple. He gave orders "to club down anyone who disobeyed his orders, but the soldiers, driven by their hatred of the Jews and the hope of finding riches in the temple, were not to be restrained." Cleon L. Rogers Jr. in *The Topical Josephus* (Zondervan, 1992), 195.

The Disciples' Questions (vv. 2–3)

During their conversation, two questions surfaced regarding Jesus's coming and the end of the age.

Question 1. When they rested on the hillside, the disciples naturally questioned when such a catastrophe would occur. "Tell us, when will these things happen?" (v. 3).

Question 2. "And what is the sign of your coming and of the end of the age?" (v. 3).

Section Summary

Jesus will make clear that the destruction of the temple and the end of the age are two separate events. Because the disciples could scarcely imagine that one could occur without the other, they considered both questions one and the same.

A WARNING NOT TO MISREAD EVENTS (24:4–14)

Jesus's answer to the disciples' questions first addressed the question about the sign of the end of the age. He warned his disciples not to allow themselves to be led astray by the many false messiahs that would come.

The time between Jesus's earthly life and the earth's end time would be marked also by sufferings in the church. Persecutions and executions of Christians would occur. Partly because of these, many within the church would lose faith and love and be misled by false prophets.

Section Summary

The period of time before Christ's return will be characterized by a growing polarization between good and evil. God's people will increase in power, witness, and impact in the world, even as persecution and hostility intensify and global conditions deteriorate. The end will come only after the gospel is "proclaimed in all the whole world as a testimony to all nations" (v. 14).

ABOUT JERUSALEM'S COMING DESTRUCTION (24:15–28)

The Destruction of the Temple (vv. 15–20)

Not yet having answered the disciples' second question, Jesus next launched into an explanation about the coming destruction of Jerusalem. He spoke of the *desolating sacrilege* as a sign that it was time to flee the city. This event is commonly known as the "abomination of desolation." The only advance notice of this event Jesus gave involves an event that will profane the temple, fulfilling the prophecy of Dan 9:27.

Tribulation (vv. 21–28)

Escape will become all-important, for Jerusalem's destruction will be associated with great tribulation. Destruction will arrive so quickly that believers must waste no time fleeing from the city.

Section Summary

Jesus predicted the coming destruction of Jerusalem. The temple itself would be profaned and then destroyed.

SIGNS OF CHRIST'S SECOND COMING (24:29–31)

Jesus warned his disciples against believing that wars, earthquakes, and famines were signs of the end. But he did tell them the signs that would announce his coming at the end of the age. Jesus portrayed his return in the imagery of cosmic upheaval. The universe will no longer continue as it has. His imagery may well point to overthrow of the cosmic and demonic powers often associated in paganism with the sun, moon, and stars.

THE FIG TREE'S LESSON (24:32–35)

Jesus used the fig tree as an illustration of a sign pointing to a coming event. He reminded his disciples that the appearance of leaves on a fig tree means "that summer is near" (v. 32). In a similar way, he told them

HISTORICAL BACKGROUND

Herod's Temple

Herod's temple was the third one built in Jerusalem. Solomon's was first; Zerubbabel's second. Construction on Herod's temple began around 20 BC. The main structure was completed within ten years. The decoration and finishing continued until AD 64, more than thirty years after Jesus's crucifixion.

WORD PICTURE

Tribulation

The word *tribulation* refers to a particular time of suffering associated with events of the end time. It will surpass any trouble yet experienced in human history (Matt 24:21).

WORD PICTURE

"It is useless to set the day and hour for Christ's coming. It is folly to neglect it. This figure of the thief will also be used by Paul concerning the unexpectedness of Christ's second coming." A. T. Robertson *WPNT*, 1:195.

WORD PICTURE

Abomination of Desolation

This term dates back to the Old Testament. It refers to that which is detestable to God and is particularly related to idolatry. The English word *abomination* translates four Hebrew words and one Greek word. Those words mean "stinking, rotten," "a detested thing," and "offensive, detestable." It is a special term used in the books of Daniel, Matthew, Mark, Luke, and Revelation. In Daniel, the word for "desolation" is *shomem*, which has two root meanings. One meaning is "to be desolated, ravaged," and the second is "to be appalled, astounded." The original passage in Daniel serves as the textual and historical precedent for later applications. The passages in the Gospels and Revelation point ahead to the destruction of Jerusalem in AD 69–70.

the occurrence of "these things" would mean his coming is near—"at the door" (v. 33). This is a difficult text to interpret.

WATCH AND BE READY! (24:36–44)

Jesus told his disciples that the exact hour and day of his second coming were known only to God the Father. Even he, God's Son, did not share the knowledge of the time of the end.

Section Summary

We do not know when Christ will return. It is imperative then that we remain prepared for his coming.

A CHALLENGE TO FAITHFULNESS (24:45–51)

Jesus illustrated his point about preparedness with a detailed, three-pronged parable. This parable contrasts a faithful servant with a wicked servant.

Section Summary

The faithful servant was rewarded, and the unfaithful servant was punished. God has commanded all individuals to be good stewards of his creation and therefore holds us all accountable.

QUESTIONS TO GUIDE YOUR STUDY

1. What would signal the destruction of the temple?
2. How will Christ's second coming differ from his first?
3. What should be the attitude of believers toward Jesus's return?

MATTHEW 25

This chapter presents a collection of three parables.

NEW TESTAMENT REFERENCE

"For the Lord himself will descend from heaven with a shout, with the archangel's voice, and with the trumpet of God, and the dead in Christ will rise first." (1 Thess 4:16)

THE PARABLE OF THE WISE AND THE FOOLISH MAIDENS (25:1–13)

Jesus used a parable about a wedding to emphasize the need for preparation for his return. The main characters in this parable are ten maidens awaiting the arrival of the bridegroom. All ten carried lamps since the festivities were taking place at night. The imagery of the parable accurately reflects typical customs of first-century Palestinian wedding festivities.

But the bridegroom did not come when expected. Because of the delay, the maidens slept. At midnight, however, they were awakened by the news that the bridegroom was finally coming. Little oil was left in the maidens' lamps after the long wait. This was no problem for five of the maidens, who wisely brought flasks of oil. But the other five were not prepared for a possible delay and had no extra oil.

The five who had extra oil had only enough for themselves. They told the others to go and buy more. Although it was midnight, it was possible that all the villagers were out for the wedding celebration and some merchant might have been willing to sell them oil. By the time these five maidens returned from buying oil, the bridegroom had already come. He and his procession were already gone to the marriage feast, and the door was closed. The bridegroom refused to let latecomers come in.

Section Summary

This parable emphasizes that each believer has a personal responsibility to remain faithful to God and to prepare for his return.

THE PARABLE OF THE TALENTS (25:14–30)

Jesus told another parable to emphasize the importance of responsibly using one's God-given gifts in the time before Christ's return. He spoke of a man who was getting ready for a journey. Before he left, the man turned his assets over to three of his servants for management in his absence. These assets were given in the form of "talents," which were a measure of weight of money in silver or gold. Today, we call a person's abilities "talents" because of this parable.

This master gave his most capable servant five talents to manage. The second most capable servant received two talents. And the third received one talent. The servant with five talents used his money so well that he doubled it. The servant with two talents did the same. But the servant with one talent, fearful of losing the money, buried it in the ground.

When the master returned after a long absence, he called in the three servants for an accounting. He praised the first two servants, who doubled their talents. They handled their assets so capably that he rewarded them with even greater responsibility. The third servant tried to excuse his failure to use the master's money productively. His reason for fear of investing came from his knowledge that the master was "a harsh man" (v. 24). The master had nothing but condemnation for this servant. He took that servant's one talent and gave it to the servant who had ten.

PERSONAL APPLICATION

Jesus's advice to his followers was to "be alert" (v. 42). That is, be prepared for his coming, since they could not know the time of his return.

HISTORICAL BACKGROUND

Sheep and Goats

Sheep were the prominent animals in the sacrificial system of Israel. They were also a valuable source of food and clothing.

Goats are extremely destructive to vegetation and contribute to erosion, as they tear plants out of the soil.

Sheep and goats grazed in the same pasture and freely mingled. From a distance, they often looked similar in appearance. But it was necessary for Palestinian shepherds to separate the herds because male goats were often hostile toward the sheep.

Jesus contrasted sheep and goats. In his parable of the sheep and goats (Matt 25:31–46), sheep symbolize God's righteous people, and goats symbolize the unrighteous.

PERSONAL APPLICATION

Those who make use of what they have will receive even more; those who fail to use what they have will lose what they have.

Section Summary

Each individual is responsible for the use of only those gifts and abilities that God has given him or her.

THE PARABLE OF THE SHEEP AND THE GOATS (25:31–46)

This is the last of Jesus's parables in Matthew's narrative. It is a parable about the final judgment.

The parable pictures Jesus as the heavenly Son of Man, seated on the throne, surrounded by angels. In the parable, Jesus is described as Judge, King, and Shepherd. As the people of all nations stand before him, Jesus will make a separation. He will act as a shepherd in separating the goats from the sheep. In this parable, sheep symbolize God's righteous people, and goats symbolize the unrighteous.

In the last judgment, Jesus will put the sheep at his right hand, the place of favor. The goats will be at his left. He will invite the sheep to share in his Father's kingdom because of their ministry to him on earth. He will declare that they fed him, quenched his thirst, and welcomed him when he was a stranger. The righteous will be totally surprised. When, they will ask, had they ever done these things for Jesus? He will tell them that in performing acts of kindness for those in need, they performed them for him.

For the goats on the left, the verdict is different, although the criterion for judgment is the same. They are to have the "eternal fire" because they did not care for Jesus when he was suffering. These, too, will question Jesus. They will not remember seeing Jesus sick, needy, thirsty, or hungry. Jesus will tell them that he was present in all the suffering people they encountered. By not ministering to them, they failed to minister to him.

PERSONAL APPLICATION

God will one day judge the entire world based on their response to the gospel.

Section Summary

There are two kinds of people in the world who will be distinguished based on their response to the gospel and its emissaries. Proper responses are rewarded; improper responses lead to eternal punishment.

QUESTIONS TO GUIDE YOUR STUDY

1. The parable of the ten maidens holds what lesson for us?
2. The parable of the talents is well known. What important lessons emerge from this parable?
3. Contrast sheep and goats. What is the main point of the parable of the sheep and goats?

MATTHEW 26

This chapter begins Matthew's final block of narrative. The key elements in this part of the narrative are the passion and crucifixion (26:1–27:66) and Jesus's resurrection (28:1–20).

A PREDICTION AND A PLOT (26:1–5)

The Prediction (vv. 1–2)

At the end of Jesus's teaching on the Mount of Olives, he predicted for the fourth time (according to Matthew's record) that he would soon die. This time he added something new to his prediction. His death by crucifixion would take place during Passover, only two days away.

> **HISTORICAL BACKGROUND**
>
> **Passover**
>
> The first of three annual Hebrew festivals. It commemorated the final plague on Egypt when the firstborn of the Egyptians died and the Israelites were spared because of the blood smeared on the doorposts (Exod 12).

The Plot (vv. 3–5)

Meanwhile, the elders and chief priests, members of the Sanhedrin (the Jewish high court), were plotting Jesus's death. They met at the palace of Caiaphas, who was then high priest. These religious leaders were agreed on the necessity of putting Jesus to death, but the timing was a problem for them.

Section Summary

Feeling more and more threatened by Jesus, the religious leaders took bolder steps. They decided to meet so they could plot Jesus's death.

AN ANOINTING AT BETHANY (26:6–13)

At Bethany, Jesus was at the home of a man called Simon the leper. No doubt Simon was a former leper, cured perhaps by Jesus. During the meal at Simon's house, a woman took an alabaster flask of perfume (likely her most valuable possession) and poured it on Jesus's head. From John's account (John 12:1–8), we know this woman was Mary of Bethany.

> **HISTORICAL BACKGROUND**
>
> **Bethany**
>
> Located on the Mount of Olives' eastern slope, Bethany was about two miles southeast of Jerusalem. Bethany was the last stop before Jerusalem just off the main east-west road coming from Jericho.

Section Summary

Mary's loving, generous act was a ministry to Jesus. It possibly was her last opportunity to minister to Jesus before his death. Her attitude was in contrast to the critical attitude of the disciples.

JUDAS'S OFFER OF BETRAYAL (26:14–16)

The religious authorities were looking for an opportunity to arrest Jesus without creating a disturbance among the people. Their objective became unexpectedly easier when Judas came to the chief priests with an offer to betray Jesus. The chief priests agreed to pay Judas thirty shekels,

HISTORICAL BACKGROUND

Passover Meal

The lamb for the meal (if this was a complete Passover dinner) had to be slaughtered that afternoon at the temple. The meal would begin at six o'clock that evening.

OLD TESTAMENT REFERENCE

Jesus went on to say that he would fulfill the role of which the prophets wrote. He would be the Suffering Servant and Shepherd dying for his sheep (see Isa 53:3–8 and Zech 13:7). Although he was fulfilling his role, he lamented the fate of his betrayer.

the price of a slave. Matthew writes that from that time on, Judas looked for a chance to betray Jesus.

Section Summary

For a bribe of thirty shekels, the price of a slave, Judas agreed to betray Jesus and turn him over to the religious authorities.

PREPARATIONS FOR THE PASSOVER MEAL (26:17–19)

The disciples asked Jesus for instructions about preparing the Passover meal. This meal had to be eaten within the city of Jerusalem. Because space was at a premium, guests who traveled to the city for the feast had to borrow rooms from residents.

Section Summary

The disciples plan a Passover meal, which will be Jesus's and the disciples' final hours together. This "Last Supper" takes place in a large upper room of a house.

A FORETELLING OF BETRAYAL (26:20–25)

That night Jesus and his disciples shared the Passover meal. As they ate, Jesus solemnly told his disciples that one of them would betray him. Judas kept his plans secret from the other disciples, but Jesus knew his heart. This news greatly upset the disciples. Except for Judas, each asked Jesus, "Surely not I, Lord?" (v. 22).

Although Jesus did not identify his betrayer, he did say that one who dipped food into the dish with him would betray him. No doubt several of them had already done so by this time.

At this point Judas asked, "Surely not I, Rabbi?" Jesus replied, "You have said it" (v. 25).

Section Summary

Judas is revealed as the one who will betray Jesus to the religious authorities. With full knowledge that Jesus is aware of what is about to happen, Judas proceeds with his plan.

THE BREAD AND THE CUP (26:26–29)

After sundown on Thursday, Jesus and his disciples relaxed to enjoy the Passover meal. During the meal, Jesus took, blessed, and broke bread. As he gave it to his disciples, he told them to eat the bread. It represented his body. Soon that body would be given for them in death. After the disciples said a prayer of thanksgiving, he gave the cup to his disciples, telling them all to drink from it. The cup represented Jesus's "blood of the covenant" (v. 28), which would soon be "poured out for many for the forgiveness of sins."

Jesus saw this meal as a foretaste of the meal he would someday share with his followers in the kingdom of his Father.

This last meal, meanwhile, was a pledge of the certainty of the kingdom's establishment and their sharing together in it.

Section Summary

The celebration of the Lord's Supper signaled two important points, one of which looks backward while the other looks forward: (1) As we look back, we commemorate Jesus's redemptive death; (2) as we look ahead, we anticipate his return with all the redeemed.

A PREDICTION OF DENIAL (26:30–35)

After Jesus and the disciples finished the Passover meal, they sang a hymn, probably taken from Pss 115–118, which formed part of the Passover liturgy.

Jesus then prophesied that the disciples would be scattered. Peter confirmed his loyalty to Jesus, protesting that he would never fall away. But Jesus knew better. Jesus told him that during the night, before the rooster crowed in the morning, Peter would deny him three times. The others voiced their loyalty as well. John's Gospel tells us that Judas had left the group during the Passover meal.

Section Summary

Peter would have likely fought and died for Jesus that night if Jesus had declared himself a military Messiah and ordered a revolt against Rome. But Peter would find himself unequal to testing when it came in an unexpected form.

A TIME OF AGONIZING PRAYER (26:36–46)

The Scene at Gethsemane (vv. 36–38)

Jesus went with his disciples to Gethsemane, probably a garden on the Mount of Olives. Jesus wanted to pray and instructed his disciples to stay outside, but he took his three closest disciples—Peter, James, and John—with him.

HISTORICAL BACKGROUND

The Lord's Supper

The terms *eucharist, thanksgiving*, and *Communion* are often applied to the Lord's Supper, and each highlights a specific aspect of this ordinance. "The Lord's Supper" appears more satisfactory for the overall designation, reminding Christians that they share the loaf and cup at his table, not their own.

Paul emphasized the memorial aspect of the supper: "Do this in remembrance of me." Christians were to remember that the body of Christ was broken (bread) and his blood shed (cup) for them. As the Passover was a symbol of the old covenant, the Lord's Supper is a symbol of the new. Christians remember the sacrifice provided for their deliverance from bondage and look forward to the ultimate consummation in the land of promise, the kingdom of God.

NEW TESTAMENT REFERENCE

"During his earthly life, he offered prayers and appeals with loud cries and tears to the one who was able to save him from death, and he was heard because of his reverence." (Heb 5:7)

Jesus's Prayers and the Disciples' Weakness (vv. 39–44)

Walking a short distance from the three, Jesus fell prostrate to the ground. His prayer, in summary, asked his Father if there was any other way to accomplish the mission he was sent to accomplish. Certainly on his mind was the gruesome method of execution awaiting him. His greater agony was the anticipation of bearing the world's sins.

NEW TESTAMENT REFERENCE

Jesus told them about the anguish he was experiencing. He was overwhelmed with sorrow and described it as being as great as death's sorrow. Jesus wanted these disciples' human sympathy and support to help him through his ordeal, so he asked them to watch with him.

The Meaning of This Time of Prayer (vv. 45–46)

No other recorded experience of Jesus reveals his human side so vividly. It is only because he endured such human agony and testing that he can strengthen us in our times of sorrow and temptation and sympathize with us.

Section Summary

Many of Matthew's underlying themes converge here at the garden. God is in control of all these events, however tragic they may seem to others. Jesus is the Son of God who is suffering and dying. His death is humiliating but voluntary, an act of obedience fulfilling God's will.

ARREST IN THE GARDEN (26:47–56)

Judas arrived at the garden with an armed crowd ready to arrest Jesus. The crowd evidently consisted of the temple guard and servants of the high priest. Because those who came to make the arrest did not know Jesus, Judas agreed to identify Jesus with a sign. He would kiss Jesus, as was customary for a disciple greeting his master.

OLD TESTAMENT REFERENCE

"He willingly submitted to death, and was counted among the rebels; yet he bore the sin of many and interceded for the rebels." (Isa 53:12b)

Even in the face of Judas's treachery, Jesus reacted with sadness instead of anger. He called Judas "friend," still holding open the door of repentance. However, Jesus had no intention of resisting arrest. He saw it as fulfilling Isa 53:12.

Confronted with Jesus's failure to resist and his refusal to let them fight for him, all the disciples fled. Jesus would have to face his ordeal alone.

Section Summary

Jesus's obvious submission to his arrest emphasizes his sovereignty and the voluntary submission to his death.

HISTORICAL BACKGROUND

Caiaphas

Son-in-law of Annas, who was high priest from AD 6 to 15. Caiaphas was appointed around AD 18 and removed about AD 36.

AT CAIAPHAS'S PALACE (26:57–68)

Matthew now describes the illegal hearing Jesus received at the palace of the high priest, Caiaphas. Peter, having fled with the rest of the disciples, now returned to see what was happening. He remained in the high priest's courtyard.

The high priest put Jesus under oath and demanded that Jesus tell the council whether he was "the Messiah, the Son of God" (v. 63).

Jesus's response was, "You have said it" (v. 64). To the high priest, these were words of blasphemy.

He tore his clothes as an indication that he was hearing blasphemy. Jesus equated himself with God.

Those present then blindfolded Jesus and followed with a round of abuse. They spat in his face (a serious insult) and hit him and said, "Prophesy to us, Messiah! Who was it that hit you?" (v. 68). In this experience, Matthew explains that Jesus fulfilled the prophecy of Isa 50:6.

OLD TESTAMENT REFERENCE

"I gave my back to those who beat me, and my cheeks to those who tore out my beard. I did not hide my face from scorn and spitting." (Isa 50:6)

Section Summary

The illegal council meeting accomplished its purpose. The Jewish leaders had their "charge" against Jesus. They could now take the trial to the next level.

PETER'S DENIAL (26:69–75)

Jesus was tried inside the high priest's palace, but outside Peter was going through a painful trial of his own. As Peter sat in the high priest's courtyard, a servant girl approached him. She remarked that Peter had been with Jesus. Peter denied her statement to all in the courtyard. He then remained in the courtyard.

Later, another servant girl told bystanders that Peter had been with Jesus. This time Peter swore an oath that he did not even know Jesus.

Still later, a bystander accused Peter of being a follower of Jesus. With even greater intensity, Peter swore that he did not know Jesus. Immediately a rooster crowed. Peter remembered Jesus's prediction of denial. Overwhelmed at his disloyalty, he "wept bitterly" (v. 75).

Section Summary

While Jesus holds up under life-threatening conditions, Peter fails miserably under less-threatening conditions.

QUESTIONS TO GUIDE YOUR STUDY

1. Why was there controversy about Mary's anointing of Jesus? What was Jesus's attitude about it?
2. Why was the Gethsemane experience so agonizing for Jesus? What made this time necessary?
3. What are the signs that Jesus voluntarily submitted to the events which led to his death?

MATTHEW 27

JESUS'S SENTENCING BY THE JEWS (27:1–2)

Early the next morning, the Sanhedrin met again, this time officially and legally. The meeting seems to have been for the purpose of deciding what charge to bring against Jesus so the Romans would put him to death.

At this point, Matthew interjects a section about Judas's death before continuing his account of Jesus's appearance coming before Pontius Pilate, the Roman governor.

OLD TESTAMENT REFERENCE

Sanhedrin

The highest Jewish council in the first century. The council had seventy-one members and was presided over by the high priest. Both Sadducees and Pharisees were members of this council.

At this time, the Sanhedrin lacked the power to put a person to death (see John 18:31). But Rome would never execute a person on a charge of blasphemy because that charge pertained only to Jewish law.

Section Summary

The religious leaders officially meet to decide what charges to bring against Jesus. The Sanhedrin decides to bring Jesus before Pontius Pilate, the Roman governor of the region.

JUDAS'S TRAGIC END (27:3–10)

Realizing that Jesus had been condemned, Judas felt remorse for his act of betrayal. He returned the thirty silver shekels to the elders and chief priests. He confessed to them that Jesus was innocent and that, in betraying him, he sinned.

When Judas realized the religious authorities were not going to reconsider their actions against Jesus, in anger and despair he threw the money down in the temple and left. Seeing no relief for his guilt, Judas committed suicide by hanging himself.

OLD TESTAMENT REFERENCE

The chief priests collected the coins but refused to keep the money because they considered it "blood money" and unclean. They finally agreed to use the money to buy a field for the burial of strangers who might die while in Jerusalem. Matthew saw this as fulfilling Old Testament Scripture (see Jer 32:7–8 and Zech 11:12–13).

Section Summary

Judas acknowledged his remorse to the chief priest for his betrayal of Jesus, admitting that Jesus was an innocent man. Filled with guilt, Judas hanged himself. Refusing to ask forgiveness from God, his guilt became more than he could bear.

JESUS BEFORE PILATE (27:11–26)

Matthew now resumes the narrative where he left off in verse 2. Pilate, the Roman governor of Judea, was in Jerusalem at the time, although his official residence was in Caesarea. The religious leaders then delivered Jesus to him.

Questions from Pilate (vv. 11–14)

Pilate's first question: "Are you the king of the Jews?" (v. 11). Pilate's only concern was whether Jesus had broken Roman law.

OLD TESTAMENT REFERENCE

Jesus's silence fulfilled the prophecy in Isa 53:7, which says in speaking of the Suffering Servant, "He was oppressed and afflicted, yet he did not open his mouth."

Jesus answered, "You say so" (v. 11). After his answer, the religious authorities hurled their accusations at Jesus. But he refused to reply to their charges.

Pilate's second question was, "Don't you hear how much they are testifying against you?" Jesus remained silent, which surprised Pilate.

Jesus or Barabbas (vv. 15–23)

Evidently, Pilate remained unimpressed with the case against Jesus. He saw no evidence of treason. At Passover, it was customary for the governor to release a prisoner for the people. Pilate took advantage of this custom to try to win the crowd's approval for Jesus's release. A man named Barabbas was in prison on charges of murder and insurrection. Pilate offered the crowd a choice to release either Jesus or Barabbas.

During this proceeding, a message reached Pilate from his wife. She had a dream about Jesus that greatly disturbed her. She warned her husband not to prosecute this innocent man.

Pilate's Decision (vv. 24–26)

Pilate found himself in a quandary. He had a potentially serious riot on his hands if he went ahead and released Jesus. He needed to keep the peace in Jerusalem if he wanted to retain his position as governor. And he needed the support of the religious leaders who were urging Jesus's crucifixion. Yet Pilate must have realized the sentencing of an innocent man to death was a betrayal of Roman justice.

Pilate, however, was too insecure to uphold principles of Roman law or follow his wife's intuition. When Pilate asked the crowd what he should do with Jesus, the people cried out for his death by crucifixion: "Crucify him!"

Pilate literally "washed his hands" of the matter, using this Jewish custom to proclaim his innocence.

HISTORICAL BACKGROUND

The Phases of Jesus's Illegal Trial

1. The religious leaders already passed a death sentence for Jesus before the trial began (John 11:50; Mark 14:1).
2. The leaders used false witnesses to testify against Jesus (Matt 26:59).
3. No defense for Jesus was allowed (Luke 22:67–71).
4. The trial took place at night, a violation of Jewish laws (Mark 14:53–65; 15:1).
5. The high priest put Jesus under oath but then incriminated him for what he said (Matt 26:63–66).
6. Serious charges were to be tried only in the high council's regular meeting place, not in the high priest's palace (Mark 14:53–65).

Section Summary

Pilate let the crowd make the choice: Jesus or Barabbas? They chose to free a murderer rather than the One who came to save them from sin. Jesus would be executed for the crime for which Barabbas was guilty.

MOCKING BY ROMAN SOLDIERS (27:27–31)

At this point, Pilate's soldiers took Jesus into the governor's palace, where he faced more mocking and ridicule. They were then ready to take Jesus to the site of his crucifixion.

THE EXECUTION OF JESUS AT GOLGOTHA (27:32–44)

A convicted criminal was expected to carry the horizontal beam for his own cross to the site of the crucifixion, where the vertical beam was already in the ground. Apparently, Jesus was too weak and injured from his flogging to carry it very far. The soldiers had Simon of Cyrene help carry the crossbeam.

The crucifixion took place at Golgotha, meaning "Place of the Skull." There, Jesus's hands and feet were nailed to the cross between two robbers, who may have been followers of Barabbas. Over Jesus's head was placed a wooden placard reading, "THIS IS JESUS, THE KING OF THE JEWS" (v. 37). While he hung on the cross, Jesus was offered a pain-killing drink, but he refused it, allowing him to maintain a clear and fully conscious mind.

While on the cross, during his greatest physical agony, Jesus faced ridicule from three different groups: passersby, religious leaders, and the two robbers beside him. One of the taunts from the crowd was, "If you are the Son of God" (v. 40)—an exact reproduction of Satan's catcall in Matt 4:3, during Jesus's temptations in the wilderness.

OLD TESTAMENT REFERENCE

The soldiers followed the usual custom of casting lots (perhaps variously marked pebbles) for Jesus's clothes. This fulfilled the words of Ps 22:18, "They divided my garments among themselves, and they cast lots for my clothing."

HISTORICAL BACKGROUND

Death by Crucifixion

The method the Romans used to execute Christ was the most painful and degrading form of capital punishment in the ancient world. A person crucified in Jesus's day was first beaten with a whip consisting of thongs with embedded pieces of metal. This scourging was designed to hasten death and lessen the terrible ordeal. After the beating, the victim carried the crossbeam to signify that life was over and to break his will to live. A tablet detailing the crime was often placed around the criminal's neck. At the site, the prisoner was tied (normal method) or nailed (if a quicker death was desired) to the crossbeam.

Section Summary

Jesus endured extreme pain and ridicule from the soldiers, the religious leaders, and the crowd. He willingly submitted to this abuse as part of his mission.

THE DEATH OF JESUS (27:45–50)

At Jesus's death, three unusual events took place: unnatural darkness, the rending of the temple veil, and the resurrection of the saints.

Darkness (vv. 45–46)

From noon until three o'clock in the afternoon, the land was covered in darkness. This is the first of three remarkable events in nature associated with his death and reflecting its cosmic significance. Perhaps this darkness was symbolic of God's judgment upon those who rejected his Son. It isn't surprising that nature reacted with darkness during the hours when the Creator hung dying on the cross.

Jesus Gives Up His Spirit (vv. 47–50)

At about three o'clock, Jesus cried out the words of Ps 22:1: "My God, my God, why have you abandoned me?" This cry of Jesus is the only one of Jesus's sayings from the cross preserved by Matthew and Mark. Others are recorded by Luke's and John's Gospels. God the Father was there in this entire event, using it to reconcile the world to himself. But

Jesus was bearing the sin of the world. The One who had been totally free from sin was now bearing the world's sin.

Then, after a loud cry, Jesus yielded his spirit. Luke records, "Father, into your hands I entrust my spirit" (23:46). John records, "It is finished" (19:30).

ACCOMPANYING EVENTS (27:51–56)

Rending of the Temple Veil (v. 51)

The veil at the entrance to the holy of holies was split "from top to bottom" (v. 51). This rending of the temple curtain can symbolize the opening of direct access to God because of Jesus's death.

Tombs Opened by an Earthquake (vv. 52–53)

An earthquake split rocks and caused tombs to open. Matthew wrote that after Jesus was raised from the dead, the bodies of many of God's people buried near Jerusalem were raised.

Witnesses to the Events (vv. 54–56)

Matthew listed followers who witnessed the events of the cross. These included Mary Magdalene and Mary the mother of James and John. Matthew apparently believed these women deserved credit for their faithfulness by their presence during Jesus's greatest trial and suffering.

HISTORICAL BACKGROUND

Temple Veil

This curtain separated the most holy place from the holy place (2 Chr 3:14). Only the high priest was able to pass through the veil and then only on the Day of Atonement (Lev 16:2).

Section Summary

Events within the world of nature testified to the monumental significance of the crucifixion.

BURIAL IN JOSEPH OF ARIMATHEA'S TOMB (27:57–61)

The Jewish law required that the body of an executed person be buried the same day death occurred. Jesus died about three o'clock on Friday afternoon. It was necessary that he be buried before the Sabbath began at sunset.

Joseph of Arimathea, called a "rich man" by Matthew (v. 57), asked for and received permission from Pilate to take the body of Jesus for burial. At least two of Jesus's women followers from Galilee watched as Joseph laid Jesus's body in the tomb and sealed it. These were two of the women, Mary Magdalene and the "other Mary" (v. 61), who saw the crucifixion from a distance (see John 19:39–40 for additional details about Jesus's burial).

OLD TESTAMENT REFERENCE

"If anyone is found guilty of an offense deserving the death penalty and is executed, and you hang his body on a tree, you are not to leave his corpse on the tree overnight but are to bury him that day, for anyone hung on a tree is under God's curse. You must not defile the land the LORD your God is giving you as an inheritance." (Deut 21:22–23)

HISTORICAL BACKGROUND

The Jews believed that death was irrevocable after a person had been dead three days, since by then the spirit had left the body.

Section Summary

Jesus's body is finally laid to rest in a stone tomb. His burial is witnessed by others, and the tomb is sealed.

THE GUARD (27:62–66)

Only Matthew left a record of an action taken by the Jewish authorities after Jesus's death.

On the Sabbath, the day after Jesus died, the Pharisees and chief priests went to Pilate with a request. They told Pilate that Jesus promised to rise from the dead three days after his death. They feared Jesus's disciples would steal his body and then claim that he had risen. That fraud, they declared, would be even worse than Jesus's fraudulent claim to be the Messiah.

They asked that Pilate make the tomb secure until Jesus had been dead three days. Pilate agreed to the religious leaders' request. He gave them a group of soldiers to guard the tomb, and the stone at the tomb's entrance was sealed.

WORD PICTURE

The Resurrected Body

Those raised from death have a bodily existence. The earthly body of lowliness will be renewed like the glorious body of the resurrected Jesus, becoming a heavenly body. Resurrection does not mean the personality dissolves into a larger whole. Rather, it means the total transformation of flesh and blood into a spiritual body, that is, a personality created and formed anew by God's Spirit. The resurrection body is new and unimaginably superior to the earthly body, while it maintains some continuity with life as lived before death and resurrection.

Section Summary

The religious authorities took special measures to guard against a "fraudulent resurrection" of Jesus. In the end, their actions only served to add evidence to the event of Jesus's resurrection.

QUESTIONS TO GUIDE YOUR STUDY

1. What are your impressions of Jesus's trial? Why didn't Jesus defend himself?
2. What Old Testament prophecies did Jesus's trial and death fulfill?
3. What was the significance of the natural events that took place at the time of Jesus's death.

MATTHEW 28

RESURRECTION! (28:1–7)

Early on Sunday morning, Mary Magdalene and Mary the mother of James and Joseph went back to Jesus's tomb.

The women were greeted by something very different from what they had expected. Either just before or at the time of their arrival at the tomb, "there was a violent earthquake" (v. 2). An angel appeared, rolled the stone away from the entrance, and, in triumph, sat on the stone.

NEW TESTAMENT REFERENCE

According to Mark's and Luke's Gospels, they were bringing spices to anoint Jesus's body (see Mark 16:1; Luke 24:1).

Section Summary

As he had predicted he would, Jesus rose from the grave on the third day after his death. Jesus had conquered death!

A MEETING WITH JESUS (28:8–10)

The women quickly left the tomb to carry out the angel's instructions. Fear mingled with the joy they felt as they ran to tell the eleven remaining disciples the news of the resurrection.

As they went, Jesus himself met them. This meeting was not merely a vision. The women were able to grasp his feet in an act of worship. He was the Jesus they remembered. But now they recognized him as deserving worship belonging to God alone.

Jesus repeated the instructions the angel gave the women (v. 7). There was an important change, however. He called his disciples "my brothers" (v. 10). They failed him completely in his time of greatest trial, but Jesus forgave them and looked ahead to what they would be as they served him in the future.

Section Summary

Jesus was raised from the grave! The response of the women is worship.

A COVER-UP OF THE TRUTH (28:11–15)

Some of the Roman soldiers told the chief priests about the supernatural events that occurred.

The chief priests decided their best course of action was to bribe the soldiers to cover up the truth. The soldiers accepted the payment and agreed to say they had fallen asleep while on guard, and Jesus's disciples had stolen the body.

Of the four Gospels, only Matthew tells us how the religious authorities answered the fact of the empty tomb. No one denied that the tomb was empty and that Jesus's body could not be found. Matthew declared that even when he was writing his Gospel, this falsehood was still being circulated to explain Jesus's resurrection.

Section Summary

The chief priests learned the truth about the supernatural events surrounding Jesus's resurrection. They resorted to bribery to fabricate a lie to explain what happened.

A WORLDWIDE MISSION (28:16–20)

Jesus's Great Commission (vv. 18–19)

Jesus's commission to his disciples is sandwiched between a truth and a promise—which taken together more than equip disciples for carrying out the commission.

The truth is that (v. 28) all authority in both heaven and earth was given to Jesus. The promise (v. 30) is that this One who has all authority is with his disciples—not only now but until the end of the age.

WORD PICTURE

Disciple

In the Greek world, the word *disciple* normally referred to an adherent of a particular teacher or religious-philosophical school. It was the task of the disciple to learn, study, and pass along the sayings and teachings of the master.

Section Summary

The Great Commission, like the rest of Matthew, defines evangelism as making disciples who are baptized and who obey all of the commandments of Jesus.

QUESTIONS TO GUIDE YOUR STUDY

1. What evidence does Matthew present that Jesus has risen from the grave?
2. What is to be the main activity of the Great Commission?
3. What implications does Jesus's promise, "I am with you," have for us as we carry out his Great Commission?

Mark

INTRODUCTION

The Gospel of Mark is the shortest of the four accounts of the life and teaching of Jesus. Many scholars believe it was the first Gospel written.

GOSPEL OF MARK IN A "NUTSHELL"

Purpose:	To preserve the story of Jesus after the passing of first-generation Christians
Theme:	Kingdom of God
Major Doctrine:	Discipleship
Other Doctrines:	Doctrine of Christ, doctrine of the last days

HISTORICAL BACKGROUND

Papias, bishop of Hierapolis, who lived from about AD 60 to 130, is one of the earliest sources to mention the Gospel of Mark. Eusebius quoted Papias: "Mark was the interpreter of Peter and wrote accurately but not in order of whatever he remembered about the things which were said or done by the Lord" (*Church History* 3.39.15).

AUTHOR

The title "according to Mark" was added to this Gospel by scribes who produced the earliest copies of the Gospel. According to early church tradition, Mark recorded and arranged the "memories" of Peter, thereby producing a Gospel based on apostolic witness. Peter was undoubtedly the source for most of Mark's Gospel. Besides the content that came from Peter, there is indication of Mark's own narrative and the inclusion of gospel truths that were spoken by others and were put into writing. Mark himself was likely an eyewitness to part of what he wrote. Regardless of his sources, the Holy Spirit used Mark's own personality in the writing.

Mark became an important assistant for both Paul and Peter, preaching the good news to Gentiles and preserving the gospel message for later Christians. Some traditions maintain that Mark died a martyr's death.

WORD PICTURE

Although Mark was a common Roman name, the Gospel writer was probably John Mark.

WORD PICTURE

Mark's Gospel contains many terms borrowed from Latin and written in Greek, including "plotting" (3:6), "Legion" (5:9), "taxes" (12:14), and "flogged" (15:15).

AUDIENCE

Mark wrote his Gospel for Gentile Christians. He explained Jewish customs in detail for the benefit of readers unfamiliar with Judaism (7:3–4; 12:18). Mark translated several Aramaic expressions for a Greek-speaking audience (5:41; 7:11,34; 15:22). Gentiles would have especially appreciated Mark's interpretation of the saying of Jesus which declared all foods clean (7:19; cp. with Matt 15:17–20). Mark's Gentile audience may explain his omission of the genealogy of Jesus. Perhaps these Gentile readers were Roman Christians.

Early Christian tradition places Mark in Rome preserving the words of Peter for Roman Christians shortly before the apostle's death (see 1 Pet 5:13). According to tradition, Peter was martyred in Rome during the Neronian persecution, which would place the date of Mark's Gospel about AD 64 to 68. Such a hostile environment motivated Mark to couch his account of the life of Jesus in terms that would comfort Christians suffering for their faith. The theme of persecution dominates the Gospel of Mark (10:30; cp. Matt 19:29; Luke 18:29). Jesus's messianic suffering is emphasized to inspire Christians to follow the same path of servanthood (10:42–45). Roman Christians would be encouraged, knowing that Jesus anticipated that "everyone will be salted with fire" (9:49; 13:9–13). Dying for the gospel would be equivalent to dying for Jesus (8:35; Matt 16:25; Luke 9:24).

PURPOSE FOR WRITING

The concerns Mark addressed were typical of Christians of his generation and are pertinent to ours. Mark wrote to preserve the story of Jesus after the deaths of first-generation Christians such as Peter. Mark, however, was not a mere archivist, for he used the story of Jesus for pastoral purposes.

Mark wrote to encourage Christians to persist in faithful discipleship, particularly in the crisis of persecution. Sometimes Mark used Jesus's sayings to encourage perseverance (8:34–38; 13:11). More often he encouraged faithful discipleship through the examples of his characters:

1. Jesus, who by his exorcisms and healings triumphed over evil but who committed himself to a life of humble service, suffering, and death.

    - John the Baptizer, who was Jesus's forerunner in proclamation and death.
    - Those first disciples, who left all to follow Jesus but often lacked faith and understanding and failed Jesus through their rebuke, betrayal, denial, and abandonment.

- The women, who anointed Jesus for his death, who accepted the suffering, dying Christ of the cross and tomb.
- Bartimaeus, who once was blind but then through the mercy of the Son of David saw and followed Jesus in the way of the cross.

2. Mark encouraged Christians to courageous witness. The call of the first disciples included Jesus's promise to make them "fish for people" (1:17; cp. 6:6b–13). Mark encouraged witness in the face of Jewish opposition through the thirteen "conflict stories" illustrating Jesus's authority (2:1–3:6; 3:20–35; 7:1–23; 10:1–12; 11:27–12:37). Mark likewise encouraged witness through the example of his characters: the friends of the paralytic who brought him to Jesus, the former demoniac who proclaimed how much Jesus did for him, the Syrophoenician women who envisioned a gospel that reached the Gentiles, the people of Bethsaida who brought a blind man to Jesus for healing, those who brought their children to Jesus, and ultimately Jesus before the Sanhedrin (14:62; see 13:11).
3. Mark encouraged Christians to hope in the promises of Jesus. Mark might be termed "the Gospel of loose ends." Mark often pointed ahead to promises that were only fulfilled *outside* his story. For example, John promised one who "will baptize . . . with the Holy Spirit" (1:8); Jesus promised that God's "mustard seed" of a kingdom would become a large plant (4:30–32) and that disciples would be given grace to share Jesus's cup of suffering and baptism of death (10:39). Also, Jesus promised that the Spirit would enable disciples to withstand persecution and witness boldly (13:9–13) and that Jesus would meet his disciples in Galilee after the resurrection (14:28; 16:7). Mark doubtless knew traditions such as those Luke incorporated in Acts that related the fulfillment of such promises.

PERSONAL APPLICATION

The oldest manuscripts of Mark end with the fear and silence of the women in 16:8. This puzzling ending reminds contemporary disciples that the Jesus story is unfinished until we share the message boldly with our generation.

PERSONAL APPLICATION

That Mark left "loose ends" suggests that for Mark the "Jesus story" is not finished until it is finished through the bold witness and costly discipleship of his followers.

HISTORICAL BACKGROUND

Matthew has the essence of more than 90 percent of Mark's verses, and Luke has the essence of more than 50 percent of Mark's verses. The two Gospels often use Mark's actual words as they see things together with Mark. (Matthew, Mark, and Luke are known as the Synoptic Gospels, which means "to see together"). Only one-third of Mark's verses do not appear somewhere in Matthew or Luke. John's Gospel may well have benefitted from acquaintance with Mark.

DATE OF WRITING

Precisely how early Mark wrote his Gospel is not certain, but some leading scholars hold that AD 50 is probable (A. T. Robertson, *Word Pictures in the New Testament*, "Matthew and Mark," 1:249).

THE PLACE OF MARK'S GOSPEL

The Gospel of Mark was, more or less, neglected among the Gospels until relatively recent times. When it became widely held that Mark was the first and primary Gospel, it was then moved front and center of attention. Matthew and Luke obviously had great appreciation for Mark from the beginning.

LITERARY STYLE

Good storytellers captivate audiences by using everyday language that provokes strong imagery. Mark's language is simple, direct, and understandable.

LITERARY FORM

Upon first reading, the Gospel of Mark appears to be an arbitrary collection of stories about Jesus. However, upon closer inspection, it becomes apparent to the observant reader that Mark arranges the material in a more sophisticated fashion to convey truth on a higher level.

Mark tells the story of Jesus as a whole. Mark develops the unifying plot of the gospel story by unveiling the hidden identity of Jesus. The messianic secret is part of the mystery of the kingdom of God, understood only by insiders—"to those on the outside everything is said in parables" (4:11,33–34). Mark uses the messianic secret to organize his story around the progressive revelation of Christ and the faith pilgrimage of his disciples.

The literary form of Mark's Gospel is no accident. The arrangement of the Gospel material gives every indication that a skilled literary craftsman has been at work.

QUESTIONS TO GUIDE YOUR STUDY

1. What did Mark wish to accomplish with his Gospel?
2. What features distinguish Mark's Gospel account from Matthew, Luke, and John?
3. What are the key themes of Mark's Gospel?
4. Based on this introduction, what are we to gain from a study of Mark's Gospel?

Israel in the Time of Jesus

MARK 1

Mark begins his account by focusing on the source and content of the good news of Jesus Christ. He then gives attention to Jesus's baptism and wilderness temptation before moving on to begin his story of Jesus's ministry.

WORD PICTURE

The word *gospel* refers to the proclamation of the good news, not its prediction. To this point, the gospel had been anticipated; now it becomes a present event.

THE BEGINNING OF THE GOOD NEWS (1:1)

Mark's first verse offers the theme and summary of the book. "Beginning of the gospel" sums up the entire book and its events.

The source of the good news: Jesus Christ. *Jesus* was a common Hebrew name equivalent to *Joshua,* which means "Yahweh saves." *Christos* is the Greek translation for the Hebrew word that means "messiah" or "anointed one."

Mark completes the title of his book with the term "Son of God," which points to Jesus's divinity.

ANNOUNCING THE GOOD NEWS (1:2–3)

Mark begins his story by combining the God-inspired promises of the prophets Malachi and Isaiah (cp. Mal 3:1 and Isa 40:3 with Mark 1:2–3).

PICTURING THE GOOD NEWS IN SYMBOL (1:4–5)

When John the Baptist appears as the appointed messenger, his work is laid out for him. He is to make a road for the Lord, use preaching as his method, and tell people to prepare themselves for the Lord's coming.

When a king traveled in those days, he sent workers to smooth the road and announce his coming. That was John's job for the King of kings.

According to Luke's Gospel, John the Baptist began his ministry around the Jordan River in the fifteenth year of the reign of Tiberias Caesar (Luke 3:1–3), which must have been AD 26 or 27. John's preaching emphasized the coming judgment, the need for repentance, and the coming of the Messiah. He lived an austere existence. He wore the dress of a prophet—camel hair and a leather belt (Matt 3:4; Mark 1:6). He was beheaded by Herod Antipas.

John preached a message of repentance. He baptized those people who repented in the Jordan River.

Verse 5, "The whole Judean countryside and all the people of Jerusalem were going out to him," means that all kinds of people, in great numbers, came to John for baptism.

FULFILLING PROPHECY (1:6–8)

John the Baptist further fulfilled prophecy by arriving on the scene like the Old Testament prophet Elijah. John's food was locusts and wild honey.

John drew a sharp contrast between his water baptism and Jesus's Holy Spirit baptism. John's water immersion was momentary, and it pictured the purified life of repentance. Jesus's Holy Spirit immersion will be eternal in nature, and it will purify. Jesus will saturate his followers with his Holy Spirit.

WORD PICTURE

Repentance

In the New Testament, the word *repentance* means "coming to one's senses; a change of mind that shows up in a person's life through his beliefs, commitments, attitudes, and behavior."

THE BAPTISM AND TEMPTATION OF JESUS (1:9–13)

Baptism—Jesus Enters the Ministry (vv. 9–11)

Jesus presented himself for John's baptism even though Jesus was sinless and needed no baptism to picture his repentance. Then why was he baptized? Jesus counted himself a human and made a point to do everything God expected a human to do. Moreover, Jesus identified himself with the sinful people he came to save.

Jesus was baptized by John in the Jordan River. The Spirit of God descended as Jesus came up out of the water. John the Baptist saw the Spirit's descent (John 1:32), and the voice of God the Father was audible (Mark 1:11). Spirit, Son, and Father—all three persons of the Trinity were present.

Temptation—Jesus Overcomes the Adversary (vv. 12–13)

After the awesome and unique experience of his baptism, the Holy Spirit sent Jesus into the wilderness to be tempted by Satan for forty days. That would test his purposes and methods. Verse 13 tells that Jesus and Satan battled in the deepest wilderness.

In that day, a wilderness was generally regarded as the home of evil powers and a stronghold of the devil. The temptation probably took place in the Judean wilderness.

PERSONAL APPLICATION

Satan tempted Jesus to make him fall, and he tempts Christians today for the same reason. As in the case of Jesus, God allows temptation to strengthen believers, not make them fall. The same Holy Spirit who gave Jesus the power to win will give believers power to win over temptation today. Although temptation is a lifetime battle, believers can resist sin by standing firm in the Lord Jesus, trusting that what he offers is far better.

PREACHING IN GALILEE (1:14–15)

After John the Baptist's arrest, Jesus began his Galilean ministry, preaching the good news that came from God. The world has waited and hungered for the words of verse 15:

"The time is fulfilled, and the kingdom of God has come near. Repent and believe the good news!"

The phrase "kingdom of God" refers to the kingly rule of God. At that time the rule of God is to be internal rather than external, over the hearts of people rather than over the military powers of the day. In a unique way, the kingdom is both present (Luke 7:18–23; 10:23–24) and yet to come (Mark 14:25; Luke 11:2).

The news demanded a response of repentance and belief in the gospel (Mark 1:15). "Believe" is the word of response that answers the question of how to receive the good news—how to enter the kingdom. Belief is more than intellectual assent. It is trust of a person's entire being to the good news.

CALLING FOR DISCIPLESHIP (1:16–20)

There is a lapse of time between the incidents recorded in verse 15 and those recorded in verses 16–20. The context of repenting and believing is immediately succeeded by the context of leaving and following.

WORD PICTURE

Disciple

One who learns from a master or teacher.

Jesus commanded two sets of brothers, Simon Peter and Andrew and James and John, to follow him. The brothers followed Jesus earlier (John 1:35–42), but this call was to continuous discipleship. Immediately, they left their business and followed Jesus.

PERSONAL APPLICATION

The timeless good news appeared when Jesus entered his public ministry. Now, as then, it demands a verdict from the listener. Answering yes to Jesus calls for a willingness to leave and risk everything.

JESUS'S PUBLIC MINISTRY (1:21–28)

Authoritative Teaching (vv. 21–22)

On a Sabbath day, Jesus went to the synagogue and taught (v. 21). The people were dumbfounded at the teaching of Jesus. He taught with authority rather than citing a string of footnotes as the rabbis generally did.

Technically, the Jewish Sabbath began at sunset on Friday and ended at sunset on Saturday, but Saturday was considered the Sabbath day.

Powerful Healing (vv. 23–28)

Authoritative teaching was accompanied by powerful action. A man with an unclean spirit was in the synagogue. The demon cried out through the man, "What do you have to do with us, Jesus of Nazareth?"

Jesus responded to the man with a simple, authoritative command: "Be silent, and come out of him!" The evil spirit left like a storm, with a thunderous shriek and a discharge of power that floored the man (v. 26).

The people were amazed and responded with the question, "What is this?" (v. 27). The people were familiar with rituals for casting out demons, but they never witnessed this kind of authority. As a result of this event, Jesus's fame began to spread quickly.

HEALINGS AT PETER'S HOUSE (1:29–34)

After they left the synagogue, Jesus and his four disciples (Andrew, Peter, James, and John) went directly to Peter's house.

Peter's mother-in-law was sick with a high fever. When Jesus was made aware of this, he healed her. She gave evidence of complete healing and showed her gratitude by ministering to Jesus and his disciples.

Mark then tells us that a steady stream of suffering humanity flooded the door of Peter's house.

They waited until sundown—the time when the Sabbath was over—when they could carry their sick friends and family members to Jesus without violating rabbinic law.

HISTORICAL BACKGROUND

Peter lived in Capernaum, a city on the northwest shore of the Sea of Galilee. Jesus made his headquarters there for his ministry throughout Galilee (2:1; 3:19; 9:33; 10:10).

A DOUBLE PURSUIT (1:35–39)

Jesus rose early in the morning to pray. His disciples went to look for him and remind him that he was now in great demand. Jesus told them he had work to do not only in Capernaum but throughout the region of Galilee.

JESUS CURES THE INCURABLE (1:40–45)

People did not consider leprosy a sin, but they did think leprosy could be an act of judgment from God against someone (Num 12:10). They also believed the Messiah would be able to heal leprosy (Matt 11:5; Luke 4:27). The Mosaic law prescribed ceremonial cleansing for anyone whose leprosy happened to go away (which was considered a miracle of God's grace). The cleansing Jesus speaks of in Mark 1:44 is detailed in Lev 14:1–32. The leper had confidence Jesus could heal him if he chose. Jesus expressed his willingness and then simply commanded the leper to be clean.

Jesus sternly charged the healed leper not to tell who healed him, then sent the man out to the priest to have his healing officially confirmed (vv. 43–44). But the healed leper couldn't keep silent about the source of his healing.

HISTORICAL BACKGROUND

Leprosy

Leprosy is a generic term generally applied to a variety of skin disorders from psoriasis to true leprosy. Its symptoms ranged from white patches on the skin to running sores to the loss of fingers and toes. It was terminal, but it seemed interminable because it sometimes lasted for as long as 30 years. Its suffering went beyond the physical, for its victims also suffered psychologically. Heartbreaking loneliness accompanied the leper's physical pain and mental anguish.

Section Summary

Mark's Gospel's is fast-paced and action oriented. It opens with Jesus's baptism, temptation, the call of the four disciples, and the early ministry in Galilee. The kingdom of God, a major theme of the Gospel, is much in evidence as Jesus delivered people from diseases, including leprosy, and demons.

QUESTIONS TO GUIDE YOUR STUDY

1. What was John the Baptist's role? What was the content of his message?
2. What is significant about Jesus's baptism? Why did he insist on receiving it?
3. Why was it so important for Jesus to experience the temptation in the wilderness?

HISTORICAL BACKGROUND

Most Jewish exorcists used much magic and many words when trying to cast out a demon.

4. From the account of the many people who sought Jesus's healing help, what do we learn about the character of Jesus?

MARK 2

WHICH IS EASIER? (2:1–12)

Jesus was back in Capernaum, apparently teaching at Peter's house. Four men brought a friend who was paralyzed for Jesus to heal. They couldn't get in the house because of the crowd. So they took their friend up on the roof, made a hole in the roof, and lowered their friend down in the presence of Jesus.

Jesus had compassion on the man and told him that his sins were forgiven. This statement brought a strongly negative response in the minds of the scribes who were looking on. They didn't say anything, but Jesus knew what they were thinking.

HISTORICAL BACKGROUND

The Typical House in Jesus's Day

The homes of the poor were small and modest, generally consisting of one to four rooms, and almost always including a courtyard on the east of the house so the prevailing westerly winds would blow the smoke away from the house. The only ways of escape from the dim, cramped interior of the house were the courtyard and especially the flat roof.

The roof was supported by beams laid across the tops of narrow rooms, which were then covered by brush and packed with mud to a firm and smooth surface. The paralytic at Capernaum was let down to Jesus through a hole dug out of such a roof (Mark 2:4). It was covered with clay tiles (Luke 5:19).

The scribes were the grammatical and editorial nitpickers of their day. Although they were laymen with another occupation to make their living, it was their job to copy the biblical texts, keep them pure, and expound their meaning. We owe a lot to good grammarians and editors, but it is easy to see how these first-century scribes would find it hard to accept change. Later the scribes would be joined in their criticism and opposition to Jesus by Pharisees, elders, priests, Sadducees, and Herodians as well as the fickle crowds and the spineless Roman rulers.

Jesus asked them whether it was easier to tell a person his sins were forgiven or to command a paralyzed person to stand up and walk. Jesus then commanded the man to walk. He did, and the crowd was amazed.

SUDDEN SURRENDER (2:13–17)

Jesus next called a tax collector named Levi (commonly known as Matthew) as a disciple. Levi not only responded positively to Jesus's call; he gave a party and invited his friends to meet Jesus. The religious leaders criticized Jesus for keeping company with these men. Jesus said he had not come to call good people but sinners.

HISTORICAL BACKGROUND

Capernaum was a customs center where Levi worked. He was an unlikely prospect for discipleship because he bore the stigma of having sold out to Rome. His job was to collect taxes for a foreign people who occupied the country, and he also lived off of those taxes.

FASTING (2:18–22)

Jesus's critics found two practices that were out of step with their traditions: fasting and observance of the Sabbath.

Those who followed John the Baptist and those who followed the way of the Pharisees may have fasted for different reasons, but fasting was a part of the religious observance of both groups. However, the Old Testament commanded fasting only once a year: on the Day of Atonement (Exod 20:10; Lev 16:1–4; 23:26–32; 25:9; Num 29:9–11). By the New Testament era, Pharisees were fasting regularly on Mondays and Thursdays and seemingly making quite a show of it. Fasting could accompany repentance, or it could serve as a sign of mourning. Except for the Day of Atonement, though, fasting was a matter of choice that had become a tradition.

Jesus answered the question about fasting by saying that fasting is a practice done in connection with funerals and grieving but is completely out of place at a wedding. Jesus pictured himself as the bridegroom and his disciples as the wedding guests. The principle he set forth is that circumstances should dictate the time of fasting.

Verses 21–22 contain two brief parables.

Parable 1. The Unshrunk Cloth. The unshrunk cloth of the new covenant cannot be patched onto the worn-out garment of Judaism (v. 21).

Parable 2. Old and New Wineskins. Likewise, the covenant wine cannot be kept in the rigid, old wineskin of Judaism. Fresh wine should be put in unused wineskins, which are flexible enough to expand without bursting.

The point of these two parables is that Jesus knew his message called for dramatic change and that only those who were flexible enough to receive new truth could make the transition.

PERSONAL APPLICATION

Tradition has its place, but it also has its time. When the time is up, it is right to change and move forward under God's guidance.

PRECEDENT AND PRIORITY (2:23–28)

Time and again the religious leaders accused Jesus of breaking the Sabbath. The Pharisees had things reversed; they had forgotten that the Sabbath is made for man and not man for the Sabbath (v. 27).

In this particular case, Jesus did not deny the charge of the Pharisees but defended the behavior of his disciples with a precedent from the life of David (see Mark 2:25–26; 1 Sam 21:1–6). The Pharisees faced a dilemma: If they condemned the disciples, they would also have to condemn David. David had also broken the ceremonial law when it became necessary. So the precedent introduces the principle of verse 27: Man's emergency needs have priority over the Sabbath law of complete rest.

Jesus restored the Sabbath to its original place of serving people rather than enslaving them.

JESUS'S SELF-REVELATION IN MARK 2

STATEMENT OF SELF-REVELATION	VERSE
"The Son of Man has authority on earth to forgive sins"	v. 10
"The groom" of the Church	vv. 19–20
"The Son of Man is Lord even of the Sabbath."	v. 28

WORD PICTURE

Son of Man

Jesus's statements of self-revelation point to aspects of his earthly ministry, such as his authority to forgive sins and to interpret the meaning of the Sabbath. Three categories of "Son of Man" sayings in the Gospels are generally recognized: those that present him in his earthly role, those that highlight his suffering, and those that point to his glory (Dan 7:13–14). In general, the title "Son of Man" focuses more on Christ's divinity than his humanity. It should be viewed as pointing to Jesus's special role. He is the one who has authority to forgive sins (Matt 9:6; Mark 2:10; Luke 5:24).

Section Summary

Jesus's exercise of authority and his friendship with sinners quickly got the attention of the religious leaders, leading to their opposition.

QUESTIONS TO GUIDE YOUR STUDY

1. The paralytic's friends sought Jesus to heal the man's physical problem. What did Jesus do?
2. This chapter introduces the element of conflict in response to Jesus's ministry. What kinds of conflicts did he encounter?
3. Mark records two parables in this chapter: the parable of the unshrunk cloth and the parable of the old and new wineskins. What point do these parables make?
4. Through his ministry, Jesus reveals who he is. What statements of self-revelation do we see in this chapter?

MARK 3

In this chapter the theme of controversy is again prominent. The religious leaders clashed with Jesus about their ideas of what may be done on the Sabbath and over the source of Jesus's power to exorcise evil spirits. Other major themes include the choosing of twelve disciples (vv. 13–19) and the sin of blasphemy of the Holy Spirit (vv. 28–30).

HISTORICAL BACKGROUND

The Herodians

The Herodians catered to the Romans. They are mentioned in only three places in the New Testament (Matt 22:16; Mark 3:6; 12:13).

RELIGIOUS RIGOR MORTIS (3:1–6)

Jesus entered a synagogue and encountered a man with a shriveled hand, and Jesus restored the hand. A number of Pharisees watched intently. These Pharisees went from this occasion to conspire with the Herodians to put Jesus to death.

The sick people literally threw themselves against Jesus in their belief that mere contact would bring a cure (v. 10). Jesus did not mind touching or being touched by the untouchables (Mark 1:40–41), but the crowd was about to crush him. Jesus told his disciples to keep a boat ready in case he needed to move out into the water.

Section Summary

Jesus felt both anger and grief at the reaction of the Pharisees to his healing a man on the Sabbath.

CONTROVERSY STORIES IN MARK

CONTROVERSY	REFERENCE IN MARK
Over Jesus's right to forgive sins	2:1–12
Over Jesus's fellowship with tax collectors and "sinners"	2:13–17
Over the disciples' freedom from fasting	2:18–22
Over the disciples' picking grain on the Sabbath	2:23–27
Over Jesus's right to do good on the Sabbath	3:1–6
Over the nature of Jesus's family	3:20–21,31–35
Over the source of Jesus's power to exorcise	3:22–30
Over the disciples' eating with unwashed hands	7:1–5,14–23
Over the Pharisees' and teachers' of the law setting aside the commands of God in order to observe their own tradition	7:6–13
Over the legality of divorce and God's intention for marriage	10:1–12
Over Jesus's authority to cleanse the temple and John's authority to baptize	11:27–33
Over paying taxes to Caesar and giving God his due	12:13–17
Over marriage at the resurrection, the power of God, and the witness of Scripture	12:18–27
Over the most important commandment	12:28–34
Over the nature of the Messiah—son of David or David's Lord	12:35–37

MINISTERING AND BEING MISUNDERSTOOD (3:7–35)

Jesus continued his Galilean ministry, which now enters a new phase. It changes location, attracts a more varied congregation, and includes the calling of twelve special disciples.

A Seaside Retreat (vv. 7–12)

Jesus and his disciples retreated to the seaside. Wherever Jesus went, he was pursued by the crowds, not only from Galilee but in the regions northwest, south, and east of Galilee.

A Mountaintop Experience (vv. 13–19a)

From the seaside, Jesus hiked to a mountaintop experience. From the multitude he selected a choice group to gather before him on the hillside (v. 13). And from that group Jesus formally appointed the Twelve who would serve as his disciples and apostles (see "The Twelve Apostles" on page 27).

Section Summary

From the multitude of followers, Jesus selected a choice group of twelve disciples.

Mistaken Concern about Jesus (vv. 19b–27)

Jesus returned home to eat and rest (perhaps in Simon Peter's home). While speaking to the teachers of the law who came down from Jerusalem, Jesus's family arrived to "restrain" him, for they believed he was "out of his mind." From their point of view, Jesus was taking imprudent risks and was not getting the food and rest he needed.

HISTORICAL BACKGROUND

One of the prevailing beliefs of that culture was that stronger demons had power over weaker demons.

The teachers of the law, with whom Jesus was talking, explained Jesus's effectiveness in casting out demons by saying that he did so through the power of Beelzebul—the prince of demons.

Jesus answered the scribes' charge by questioning whether Satan would cast out Satan: "How can Satan drive out Satan?" (v. 23). His point was that a kingdom that is divided against itself cannot stand.

PERSONAL APPLICATION

Many commentators have wisely suggested that fear of having committed the unpardonable sin is the best assurance a person can have that he is not yet guilty. Coming to know the saving grace of God through Jesus Christ is the only way to be assured of never committing the unpardonable sin.

A Permanent Sin (vv. 28–30)

At this point, Jesus gave one of the gravest warnings ever given to human beings. Blasphemy against the Holy Spirit is a unique sin. It is the only sin for which there is no forgiveness.

People who blaspheme the Holy Spirit reveal a spiritual condition that is incapable of the one condition of forgiveness: that is, repentance. Many biblical scholars say blasphemy of the Holy Spirit is an enduring condition, not a temporary act of sin. In a manner of speaking, when the optic nerve of the soul becomes severed, a person lacks moral discernment, and he may judge that holy acts come from an unholy spirit rather than from the Holy Spirit of God.

OLD TESTAMENT REFERENCE

Jesus knew from Scripture that commitment to God must have priority when choosing between God and family (Exod 32:25–29; Deut 33:8–9).

Proof of Spiritual Kinship (vv. 31–35)

Jesus's family arrived. They wanted to take Jesus home with them. But Jesus told them that commitment to God must have priority—even over family.

Section Summary

From the multitude of followers, Jesus selected a choice group of twelve disciples. Opposition to Jesus grew stronger. His enemies said that Beelzebul was behind his mighty acts of casting out demons.

QUESTIONS TO GUIDE YOUR STUDY

1. What was the issue behind Jesus's healing of the man with the shriveled hand? What lesson did Jesus teach from this encounter?
2. What is the difference between an apostle and a disciple? What does a disciple do?
3. What is the sin of blasphemy against the Holy Spirit? Why is it unforgivable?
4. Why did Jesus refuse to listen to the pleas of his family and friends and go on preaching?

MARK 4

JESUS TEACHES IN PARABLES (4:1–32)

Mark 4 gives an account of Jesus's teaching in parables. In this setting, Jesus taught from a boat anchored just offshore while the crowd was on the shore. The water provided the amplification needed to communicate with the crowd.

HISTORICAL BACKGROUND

The Purpose of Parables

Parables were simple stories from everyday life that shed light on profound spiritual truths. Parables helped make abstract teachings concrete and meaningful, moving from the known to the unknown. Parables left men and women wondering and thinking for themselves rather than dismissing and forgetting truths that were beyond their understanding.

THE KINGDOM PARABLES OF MARK 4

PARABLE	THEME	MAIN TRUTH
Parable of the Sower	Response of God's Word	Only "good soil" hearers will receive the Word and bear fruit.
Parable of the Lamp	Responsibility of those in the kingdom	Each Christian is like a lamp, lighted for the one purpose of illuminating the good news.
Parable of the Seed Growing	Certainty of growth in the kingdom	The kingdom's growth is certain when the seed and the right soil get together, for God assures its growth.
Parable of the Mustard Seed	Completion of the kingdom	When time ends and the kingdom is complete, God's rule and authority will be complete.

HISTORICAL BACKGROUND

The trip from Capernaum on the northwestern shore to the eastern shore of the Sea of Galilee is about six miles.

PARABLE EPILOGUE (4:33–34)

Jesus spoke to the crowds in parables. He gave more extensive explanations of his teachings to his disciples.

JESUS'S POWER OVER NATURE (4:35–41)

As the disciples got halfway across the Sea of Galilee on their way to Gadara, they got caught in the middle of a dangerous storm. Fearing for their lives, they awoke Jesus, who was sleeping through the ordeal. He calmed the disciples and commanded the winds and seas to "Silence! Be still!" The storm immediately disappeared. In the calming of the wind and sea, God in Christ overruled the disorder of nature (Ps 107:23–32).

Section Summary

Jesus taught in parables. The theme of his teaching was the kingdom of God. Jesus demonstrated his lordship over nature when he calmed a storm on the Sea of Galilee.

QUESTIONS TO GUIDE YOUR STUDY

1. What is the "kingdom of God"?
2. Why did Jesus choose to teach by using parables?
3. Mark records four parables of Jesus in this chapter. What is the main point of each? What do we learn collectively from these truths?
4. What is the lesson of Jesus's calming of the storm? How might that lesson apply to believers today?

HISTORICAL BACKGROUND

Today some would say that this man whom Jesus healed was demon possessed, while others would say he was mentally ill. The Bible often speaks of demons as literal beings and offers no apology or detailed explanation.

PERSONAL APPLICATION

The man, now whole, wanted to come with Jesus. But Jesus told him to go back home and tell people what God had done for him.

MARK 5

JESUS'S POWER OVER DEMONS (5:1–20)

Upon arriving at Gadara, Jesus met a demon-possessed man. Knowing that Jesus would expel them from the man, the demons begged Jesus to let them go into the 2,000 hogs nearby. Jesus granted them their request, and the evil spirits left the man and entered the pigs. The herd rushed down the steep bank into the lake and were drowned.

JESUS'S DISPLAYS OF POWER IN MARK 5

MIRACLE	PASSAGE	SIGNIFICANCE
Jesus heals the demoniac	vv. 1–20	Jesus's power over demons
Jesus heals the woman with a disease	vv. 21–34	Jesus's power over disease
Jesus raises Jarius's daughter from the dead	vv. 35–43	Jesus's power over death

JESUS'S POWER OVER DISEASE (5:21–34)

Once again Jesus crossed the sea and met a crowd. This time the crowd included a synagogue ruler (or administrator) named Jairus. Jairus's little daughter lay near death. So he forgot both his personal pride and the dignity of his office as he fell at Jesus's feet and begged Jesus to come and heal his daughter. Jairus's request was urgent, and Jesus's response was immediate: He started to Jairus's home, and the crowd followed (vv. 21–24).

On the way to Jairus's home, a woman who suffered with a disease for twelve years silently pushed through the crowd, hoping to steal a miracle from Jesus. She touched the hem of Jesus's garment with the faith that she would be healed. Instantly, after twelve years of misery, she was healed.

HISTORICAL BACKGROUND

Her condition was desperate. She was poor, weak, ceremonially unclean (Lev 15:25–27). Undoubtedly, the woman had tried all of the eleven cures prescribed in the Talmud (a book of Jewish writings).

JESUS'S POWER OVER DEATH (5:35–43)

In the meantime, Jairus's daughter died, and his messengers saw no need for Jairus to bother Jesus anymore. Jesus told Jairus to stop being afraid and to keep on believing. Jesus went to Jairus's house and told the girl to "get up." Immediately the girl stood up and walked around.

Section Summary

Jesus showed his power over demons, incurable disease, and even death. He replaced fear with faith.

QUESTIONS TO GUIDE YOUR STUDY

1. What is Mark's focus in this chapter?
2. Why do you believe Jesus allowed the demons to inhabit the 2,000 hogs, only to have them drown in the lake?
3. What was the response of the healed demonic?
4. What lessons might we, as modern believers, learn from the events of this chapter?

PERSONAL APPLICATION

All the people touched by Jesus's power in Mark 4:35–6:6 accent the nature of his power: power over nature, power over demons, power over disease, power over death. But this picture ends in discord, for there was no power he could exercise over unbelief.

MARK 6

In this chapter Mark provides accounts of some of the best-known events in the Gospels: the sending out of the Twelve; the beheading of John the Baptist; Jesus's feeding of the five thousand; and Jesus walking on the water.

NO POWER OVER UNBELIEF (6:1–6)

Jesus and his disciples returned to Nazareth of Galilee, where the people refused to accept Jesus for who he was—the Messiah. Their unbelief was a barrier to the exercise of Jesus's power, so he did no powerful work there.

HISTORICAL BACKGROUND

Jewish custom and Scripture required that there be two witnesses to attest a truth (Num 35:30; Deut 17:6).

TRAINED FOR SERVICE (6:7–13)

Jesus called the disciples to be with him for training so they could go out and serve him. Jesus divided the Twelve into twos and gave them power for the work that lay ahead. The disciples had the authority of the One who sent them. They healed the sick, drove out demons, and called their hearers to repent.

A COMMISSION FULFILLED (6:14–29)

Herod feared that Jesus was John the Baptist resurrected. At this point Mark chooses to flashback to give an account of John the Baptist's unjust arrest and murder by Herod.

NEW TESTAMENT REFERENCE

Outside of the resurrection, this miracle of the feeding of the 5,000 is the only miracle found in all four Gospels.

JESUS FEEDS FIVE THOUSAND (6:30–56)

The apostles returned from their mission. Because of the disciples' fatigue and the pressing crowds, Jesus suggested a retreat. So they set sail for a quiet, restful place across the lake.

The only rest Jesus and the disciples got, however, was on the boat during the crossing. When Jesus and his disciples got off the boat, they were met by the fleet-footed crowd who beat them to their place of retreat.

It is about a four-mile voyage across the lake (where Jesus and the disciples crossed) and about 10 miles around the lake on foot.

Jesus taught the crowds until the afternoon grew late, and then startled the disciples by saying, "You give them something to eat." The disciples objected because of the cost of such an undertaking. The disciples forgot that Jesus could use and multiply whatever they had for whatever need existed. They found five barley loaves and two fish. Jesus blessed the food, broke it, and gave it to his disciples for distribution. Miraculously, there was enough food for everyone, with 12 baskets of food left over.

Following the miracle of the feeding of the 5,000 Jesus quickly ordered the disciples to sail while he dismissed the crowd. After retreating to a hillside to pray, Jesus saw that the disciples' boat was caught in a storm on the sea. Jesus walked on the water to their boat and got in the boat with them. The sea immediately calmed down. The experience left the disciples dumbfounded.

As Jesus's boat drew near the western shore of the Sea of Galilee, the crowds immediately recognized him. He ministered to many who needed healing. His tireless, selfless service is a lesson for his followers.

Section Summary

Jesus continued to show his lordship over every dimension of life. He empowered his disciples for multiplying his work in the towns and villages of Galilee.

QUESTIONS TO GUIDE YOUR STUDY

1. What was the response of Jesus's hometown and his relatives? Why did the people view him as they did?
2. Describe the sending out of the Twelve. What was Jesus's goal with this mission?
3. What lesson did the disciples learn from the feeding of the 5,000?
4. What did the disciples learn (and what can we learn) from Jesus's rescue of the disciples in the storm?

MARK 7

A MAN-MADE RELIGION (7:1–8)

The Pharisees and scribes condemned Jesus and his disciples for breaking "the tradition of the elders" because they failed to observe ritual handwashing before they ate. In their efforts to be separate, the religious leaders failed to understand that the condition of a person's heart toward God and man is the basis for God to judge a person as being holy.

A RELIGIOUS TRAVESTY (7:9–23)

Jesus continued his attack against man-made rules that contradict the command of God. Exodus 20:12 and 21:17 clearly show that a person is responsible for his parents (Mark 7:10). Yet, the religious lawyers had invented a mythical loophole for commandment evasion. Jesus answered the religious leaders by condemning their hypocrisy.

Jesus explained to the crowd, and later in greater detail to his disciples, that it was not a man's eating habits that made him "unclean." The body's natural process is to take anything that enters the stomach and pass it out of the body. But a person's spiritual condition is revealed by that which is within the heart. If the heart is unclean, then evil words and deeds will be the result.

WORD PICTURE

The title Pharisees means "separated ones."

HISTORICAL BACKGROUND

Corban was a Hebrew word that was used in the last centuries BC and the first century AD in a dedication formula. The word was used in the Old Testament to indicate a gift to God. During Jesus's earthly ministry, *corban* was used by the Pharisees and scribes and their followers to indicate the setting aside of something as a gift to God or as a temple gift.

NEW TESTAMENT REFERENCE

John's Gospel explains this quick dismissal of the crowd. They were about to make him king. The crowd's expectations of Jesus ran counter to God's will for him.

FAITH THAT BRINGS A RESPONSE (7:24–37)

For all practical purposes, Jesus's Galilean ministry is over, and he traveled to the region of Tyre and Sidon. This withdrawal begins an extensive circular journey that is Jesus's longest recorded trip.

A Mother's Faith (vv. 24–30)

A woman whose daughter was possessed by an unclean spirit or demon believed Jesus had the power to heal her daughter. Jesus tested the mother's faith, and she persisted in recognizing Jesus as Lord. Jesus pronounced the daughter healed because of the woman's expression of faith. What made the woman's faith unique was that she would not take no for an answer. Her faith was real.

OLD TESTAMENT REFERENCE

Those familiar with the Old Testament saw the miracle as a reminder of Isa 35:4–6, which gives a preview of the Messiah's healing actions.

Faithful Friends (vv. 31–37)

Friends of a man who was deaf and had a speech impediment wanted Jesus to lay his hands on the man for blessing or healing. Jesus took the man aside and privately communicated with divine sign language the healing that would take place. After Jesus touched the man's ears and placed the saliva on his tongue, Jesus prayed, "Be opened!" Instantly, the man heard and spoke clearly.

Section Summary

Jesus exposed the hypocrisy of religion that is so focused on externals that it loses touch with matters that most concern God.

QUESTIONS TO GUIDE YOUR STUDY

1. Why did the religious leaders condemn the disciples? What was Jesus's response to the leaders?
2. What was the religious leaders' "tradition of the elders"? What did Jesus have to say to them? What lesson did he give to the crowd that had gathered?
3. Jesus healed a woman's daughter who was possessed by an unclean spirit or demon. Jesus rewarded her faith. What lessons might we learn from this woman about the nature of genuine faith?
4. In verses 31–35, Jesus healed a man who could not hear or speak. How did Jesus heal the man?

MARK 8

PERSONAL APPLICATION

Jesus can do great things with small resources.

FAITH AT WORK (8:1–10)

Mark's next account pictures 4,000 hungry people in the desert with no food to eat. Because Jesus's followers were with him for three days, they ran out of provisions. As he fed the 5,000 earlier (6:30–44), Jesus now also feeds the 4,000.

A FAITHLESS REQUEST (8:11–13)

Some Pharisees challenged Jesus to give them a sign to prove his messiahship or authority. It is obvious that their motive was not a desire to believe in Jesus but a desire to discredit him. His life and ministry are enough for those who really want to believe. The only sign he will give will be the sign of Jonah (Matt 12:39–40).

The Old Testament prophet Jonah was in the stomach of the fish three days and nights. Jesus will die, be buried, and rise from death on the third day.

BEWARE OF THE YEAST (8:14–21)

The disciples became concerned when they discovered they had only one loaf of bread with them in the boat. Jesus cautioned his disciples to guard against the yeast of the Pharisees and the yeast of Herod.

Yeast was leaven. It symbolized moral influence—whether good or bad. However, more often than not, it stood for bad (Matt 16:6; Luke 12:1), and it stands for evil in verse 15.

Jesus did not want the evil thinking of the Pharisees to contaminate their faith. They witnessed Jesus's miraculous feeding of 5,000 people and then 4,000 people. Being in Jesus's presence, how could they be concerned about having just one loaf of bread?

A RESPONSE TO FAITH (8:22–26)

After so many examples of spiritual blindness, Jesus healed a man who was physically blind. This miracle was done in private, and saliva was used, but it is unique in that the healing came gradually in two stages instead of happening instantly. This partial healing represented the disciples who were unable to understand fully who Jesus was.

WORD PICTURE

The title *Christ* was Greek, and *Messiah* was Hebrew for "the Anointed One."

TURNING POINT (8:27)

Mark 8:27 divides the book of Mark. Up to this point in the book, the emphasis has been on Jesus's ministry. From Mark 8:27 onward, the emphasis is on Jesus's approaching suffering, death, and resurrection.

THE DISCIPLES' UNDERSTANDING TESTED (8:27–33)

From Bethsaida, Jesus and his disciples went north about 25 miles to the villages around Caesarea Philippi. The city itself was named after Caesar, and it was an area where Caesar was looked upon as lord.

In this passage Jesus questioned the disciples about his identity by asking them who other people said he was. Jesus then asked the disciples, "Who do you say that I am?" Like a rifle shot, Peter answered, "You are the Messiah." Because Jesus was not ready to reveal his messiahship, he commanded their silence concerning this matter.

The prevailing Jewish idea of how the Messiah would establish his kingdom included military violence that would be destructive and a nationalistic spirit that would be vengeful (cp. 2 Sam 7:14–16 and Jer 23:5–6 with Isa 53:3–5).

Jesus reeducated the disciples about the meaning of *discipleship*. Jesus referred to himself as "the Son of Man" who must suffer, be rejected, die, and rise again. Messiah is a suffering servant. The disciples' gladness turned to sadness when Jesus began to reveal more fully what it meant to be Messiah.

WORD PICTURE

Most scholars believe that "the kingdom of God come in power" (9:1) refers to one or more of the following:

- the transfiguration
- the resurrection of Jesus
- the gift of the Spirit at Pentecost
- the expansion of the early church. (See Matt 16:27–28 and Rom 1:4 for related texts.)

THE COST OF DISCIPLESHIP (8:34–9:1)

After telling what price he would pay for man's redemption, Jesus revealed what it would cost a person who really *wanted* to follow him. Verse 34 sets forth three conditions of discipleship: denying oneself, taking up a daily cross, and continual loyalty to Jesus.

Mark's early readers were enduring persecution, and the words of Jesus must have been an encouraging challenge to continue the Christian life in the face of death.

Section Summary

Jesus took his disciples on a retreat. In that setting, Peter confessed Jesus was the Messiah. Jesus began to explain the implications of his being Messiah—both for him and for his disciples.

QUESTIONS TO GUIDE YOUR STUDY

1. As Jesus had fed the 5,000 (6:30–44), he now also fed the 4,000. What truths about Jesus does this story teach us?
2. Why did Jesus rebuke the disciples in verses 17–21? What did he specifically say to them?
3. What were the marks of Jesus's messiahship? Why did the disciples have a difficult time accepting these?
4. What is the cost of discipleship, as revealed by Jesus himself?

MARK 9

THE TRANSFIGURATION (9:2–8)

As a preparation for the difficult road ahead, Jesus took Peter, James, and John up on a high mountain. There for a brief time, God allowed them to see the glory of Jesus. He was transfigured before their eyes. Moses and Elijah appeared and talked with Jesus. Moses represents the Law and Elijah the Prophets. Jesus is the fulfillment of all that is written in the Law and the Prophets.

HISTORICAL BACKGROUND

This event occurred most likely on Mount Hermon (elevation 9,100 ft.). Its name means "devoted mountain," and it stands at the northern boundary of Israel.

GOD'S PLAN OF REDEMPTION (9:9–13)

With Elijah's image fresh in their minds, the disciples wanted Jesus to explain the teachings about Elijah's return before the coming of the Messiah. Jesus explained that John fulfilled the role of Elijah in the sense that he had turned people back to God in repentance and forgiveness.

HISTORICAL BACKGROUND

Transfiguration

Every Christian has the promise of a future transfiguration. Interestingly, the Greek word for *transfigured* or *transformed* (used in v. 2) is applied in Rom 12:1–2 and 2 Cor 3:18 to obedient Christians who let God transform their lives.

FAITH'S QUALITY (9:14–29)

After descending from the mountain, Jesus was greeted by powerless disciples, arguing scribes, and a brokenhearted father with an epileptic son. The debate was focused on the epileptic boy. The disciples failed to cast out from the boy the evil spirit endangering his life.

The father asked Jesus to help the boy if he could. "If you can?" Jesus replied, assuring the father that all things are possible to those who believe.

The father cried out to the Lord, "I do believe; help my unbelief!"

Jesus healed the boy.

Privately, the disciples asked why they weren't able to cast out the demon. Jesus explained that this kind of demon could be driven out only by prayers of faith (vv. 19, 29; the best Greek manuscripts do not include fasting as a requirement for casting out demons).

A PROPHETIC PROMISE (9:30–32)

Jesus wanted to be alone with his disciples to teach them further about his messiahship. He tried to impress upon them the price and promise of redemption. They found it difficult to grasp Jesus's kingship and his certainty of resurrection.

MISPLACED COMMITMENT (9:33–37)

On the way to Capernaum, Jesus taught his disciples about greatness. They were confusing greatness with grandness and were still committed to selfish goals. Jesus explained that if they wanted to be first and great, they must be last and least.

MOTIVE, NOT METHOD, IS WHAT COUNTS (9:38–41)

John and the other disciples did not want anyone to use Jesus's name authoritatively to cast out demons unless he was a part of Jesus's company. Jesus told the disciples to test a person's commitment by his motive, not his method.

NEW TESTAMENT REFERENCE

Both the New International Version and the New Revised Standard Version omit verses 44 and 46, as do the most ancient manuscripts. But those verses are identical with verse 48, which depicts the awfulness of hell.

TOTAL COMMITMENT (9:42–50)

Jesus warned his disciples that it would be tragic for anyone to cause any of his children who tried to follow him to stumble in sin. Causing others to stumble into sin is a serious offense. He emphasized that the cost of discipleship is great, teaching that believers are to have purity, zeal, and fellowship.

Section Summary

Three of the disciples witnessed the transfiguration of Jesus. In spite of this experience, some of these same disciples argued over who was the greatest, showing that they did not understand what Jesus's kingdom was all about.

HISTORICAL BACKGROUND

Rabbinic Teachings on Divorce

Deuteronomy 24:1 was generally accepted as a statement of legal procedure for divorce, but there were two rabbinic schools that held opposite and extreme views on reasons for divorce. The school of Hillel believed a man could divorce his wife for almost any reason: spoiling the food, dancing in the streets, talking with a strange man, letting her husband hear her speak disrespectfully about her in-laws, being a loud-mouthed, brawling woman. One rabbi even extended the reason for divorce as being adequate if the husband should find someone he liked better than his wife. In contrast, the school of Shammai gave adultery as the only reason for divorce.

QUESTIONS TO GUIDE YOUR STUDY

1. Describe Mark's account of the transfiguration. What was its significance?
2. What lesson did Jesus teach with the healing of the demon-possessed boy?
3. Why were the disciples arguing about greatness? What lesson did Jesus teach them about true greatness?
4. What do we learn from verses 42–50 about the commitment to discipleship?

MARK 10

Mark 8:27–9:50 focuses on Jesus's teaching about his messiahship and what it means to follow the Messiah. In Mark 10 Jesus seems to turn on one light after another until he has illuminated the full meaning of discipleship.

Mark 9 formally ends Jesus's Galilean ministry. Mark 10–15 records the Judean ministry. However, from the turning point of Mark 8:27 onward, there is a sense in which only the name *Jerusalem* is significant. Everything will eventually come to a climax in Jerusalem.

JESUS'S MINISTRY IN MARK

REGION OF MINISTRY	PASSAGE IN MARK
Galilee (Early)	1:14–3:6
Galilee (Later)	3:7–6:13
Judea	10:1–15
Ideals—Not Ideas	10:1–12

THE PHARISEES' UNDERSTANDING OF DIVORCE (10:1–4)

Once again Jesus was surrounded by crowds and, as usual, he taught them. The "all-knowing" Pharisees who came to Jesus were just the opposite of learners. They did not come to receive knowledge from Jesus but to trap him with a question. They asked him: "Is it lawful for a man to divorce his wife?" (Mark 10:2).

Of course, any answer Jesus gave would put him in conflict with one of the pharisaic ideas about divorce (see Matt 19:1–9). As the parallel account in Matthew reveals (19:3–12), the basic question is not whether divorce was permitted but for what reasons it might be permitted.

JESUS'S CLARIFICATION OF THE TEACHING ON DIVORCE (10:5–12)

The Pharisees tried to trap Jesus with the question: "Is it lawful for a man to divorce his wife?" Jesus changed the question and turned it back on the Pharisees, asking them what Moses commanded. Jesus showed the Pharisees that God intended for a man and woman to marry, leave their parents, become one, and discipline themselves to live together for life.

THE ESSENTIAL QUALITIES OF DISCIPLESHIP (10:13–16)

Using children as an object lesson, Jesus taught about kingdom citizenship. Disciples are to portray the same traits as these children: trust, humility, and obedience.

ONE WAY TO DISCIPLESHIP (10:17–22)

A rich young ruler came to Jesus and asked what he could do to inherit eternal life, thinking he could perform some act to inherit it. Jesus gave him the formula for discipleship: go, sell, give, come, and follow me. Because the ruler could not surrender his possessions, he went away in despair.

THE ABSOLUTE GRACE OF GOD (10:23–27)

Jesus commented to his disciples that it is hard for the wealthy to enter the kingdom of God. It is easier for a camel to go through the eye of a

HISTORICAL BACKGROUND

Divorce and the Law in Jesus's Day

According to Jewish law, a man could not be charged with adultery against his own wife, but she could be charged with adultery against her husband (Deut 22:13–30). However, the husband could he charged with adultery against another man's wife. Under Roman law, a woman could divorce her husband, but under Jewish law a woman could not divorce her husband, technically speaking. Under Jewish law the act of divorce remained as the husband's act, but the wife could claim various reasons as justification for divorce. Some examples were: denial of sexual rights, impotence, leprosy, entrance into a disgusting trade, and other select reasons. Under Jewish law the woman was discriminated against.

WORD PICTURE

"The Eye of a Needle"

The word for *eye* means "hole, perforation, opening." The needle's eye was considered the smallest opening. The camel was the largest animal that came to mind. However, twice in the Talmud (Jewish writings), there is reference to the impossibility of an elephant's passing through the eye of a needle. In the picturesque language of the Hebrews, impossible comparisons were often used to make a point.

needle than for a rich man to enter the kingdom of God. The disciples were amazed, for Jewish people equated wealth with the special favor of God.

THE DIVIDENDS OF DISCIPLESHIP (10:28–31)

Peter told Jesus that he and the other disciples had left all to follow Jesus. His implication was that they had done what Jesus commanded: "What are we going to get in return?" Jesus answered Peter with three prophetic promises: (1) one hundred times as much as a disciple gives up for the sake of Christ and the gospel, (2) the challenge of persecutions, and (3) the fulfillment of eternal life, which has already begun for those who trust Jesus.

DISCIPLES UNTO DEATH (10:32–44)

On the way to Jerusalem, Jesus paused along the way to give his disciples a third major prophecy about his approaching death and resurrection. He announced that he would be betrayed, condemned, mocked, flogged, and killed.

We can see this increasing vividness in prophecy in chart form:

PREDICTIONS OF CHRIST'S PASSION*

EVENTS PROPHESIED ABOUT CHRIST	MARK 8:31	MARK 9:31	MARK 10:33–34	SUFFERING NARRATIVE
1. Betrayed/delivered to chief priests and scribes	✓	✓	✓	14:53
2. Rejected/condemned by chief priests and scribes	✓	—	✓	14:64
3. Handed over to Romans (Gentiles)	—	—	✓	15:1
4. Humiliated and beaten	—	—	✓	14:65; 15:1–20
5. Executed	✓	✓	✓	15:24
6. Resurrected	✓	✓	✓	16:9

*(This chart is adapted from commentaries by Vincent Taylor, *The Gospel According to St. Mark* [New York: St. Martin's Press, 1959]; and William L. Lane, *Commentary on the Gospel of Mark*, New International Commentary on the New Testament [Grand Rapids: Eerdmans, 1974], as published in Johnnie C. Godwin, Mark, *Layman's Bible Book Commentary* [Nashville: Broadman & Holman Publishers, 1979], p. 88.)

STANDARDS FOR GREATNESS (10:35–45)

There are a lot of standards for judging greatness, but two standards stand in stark contrast to each other.

Worldly Standards (vv. 35–40)

In spite of all Jesus's teachings, James and John still had worldly dreams of occupying the highest positions in Jesus's kingdom. They and their mother still misunderstood the nature of the kingdom of God (Matt 20:20–21; but see 27:56). "Right hand" and "left hand" were Jewish terms for being next to the king in honor. Jesus graciously told the disciples they did not know what they were asking. In fact, if Jesus had literally fulfilled James and John's request, they would have occupied the other two crosses on Golgotha; for it was on Golgotha that Christ was lifted up, then glorified by the Father.

Heavenly Standards (vv. 41–45)

Jesus taught that the heavenly standard is that whoever wants to be great must be a servant, and whoever wants to be the greatest of all must be the slave of all.

WORD PICTURE

Ransom

For the first time in the book of Mark, Jesus interpreted the purpose of his life. He came to die in our place (v. 45). He came as a ransom to free those who were kidnapped by sin. This word for *ransom* is used only here and in Matt 20:28 in the New Testament. But related words that talk about "ransom," "redeem," or "redemption" appear in several places (see Luke 1:68; 2:38; 24:21; Titus 2:14; Heb 9:12; 1 Pet 1:18). The text does not press the terminology to say who receives the ransom, nor should that be as important as the deliverance of captives by the life of Christ (see Isa 53:10–12 for the fact of Christ's death taking the place of sinful humanity).

SIGHT AND DISCIPLESHIP (10:46–52)

Jesus passed a blind man, Bartimaeus, who begged Jesus to have mercy on him. Bartimaeus needed his sight, and Jesus announced that Bartimaeus' faith had made him well.

Section Summary

Jesus proceeded to Jerusalem, ministering and teaching as he went.

QUESTIONS TO GUIDE YOUR STUDY

1. What question did the Pharisees use to try to trap Jesus? What lessons did he teach from this encounter?
2. What are the essential qualities of Jesus's disciples?
3. What is the lesson of the account of the rich young ruler?
4. The disciples would often argue about who would receive the highest positions in the kingdom. What did Jesus say about standards of greatness?

MARK 11

Throughout Mark's Gospel, Jesus forcefully revealed his messiahship through authoritative teachings and actions. From this point on, the events occur in and around Jerusalem. There are quiet times, but there are also times of stormy conflict. In scene after scene, Jesus emerges as the undisputed Master Teacher. However, with every clash with the Jewish leaders, Jesus comes one step closer to the cross.

THE PEOPLE ACCLAIM JESUS'S AUTHORITY (11:1–11)

It was the time of Passover. The Jewish expectations for messianic deliverance were at their highest. Jesus entered Jerusalem riding a donkey, and the crowds received him as the Messiah. They spread their outer garments and leafy branches in the road, shouting, "Hosanna! Blessed is he who comes in the name of the Lord!" Contrary to the hopes of the crowd, he was a king of peace, not a military conqueror who promised to rescue them from Roman occupation.

POWER WITH PURPOSE (11:12–14)

On his way to Jerusalem, Jesus became hungry and saw a fig tree with leaves but no fruit. With a word, Jesus caused the tree to wither. Symbolically, this mysterious event may represent Israel's unfruitfulness and approaching doom.

AUTHORITATIVE ACTION (11:15–19)

When Jesus arrived at the temple in Jerusalem, he found that the temple was an unholy cattle market where worshipers were cheated out of their money. With explosive force he ended it all, driving the money changers out of the temple.

Money changers were present at the temple to exchange Roman or other moneys for Jewish money acceptable in the temple worship. Worshipers could also purchase birds and animals used for sacrifice. Since sacrificial birds and animals had to be officially certified and unblemished, it was helpful to purchase them at the temple. Some exchangers profited greatly and loaned their money. Their interest rates ranged from 20 to 300 percent per year. Evidently, the selling and money changing became a means of cheating and exploiting the people. In anger at this corruption of the purpose of the temple, Jesus turned over the tables of the money changers and drove them and the sellers of animals out of the temple court.

Jesus's actions amazed the scribes and chief priests and struck fear in them.

ACCESS TO AUTHORITY (11:20–26)

Once again Jesus and his disciples passed the dried-up fig tree that was "withered from the roots up." Jesus used this opportunity to teach his disciples the power of faith—faith that moves mountains.

A STALEMATE (11:27–33)

A religious delegation asked Jesus for his religious credentials. Jesus met the opening question with a paralyzing and defeating counterquestion: Is the authority of John the Baptist from heaven or from man? To admit that John's authority was divine would be a self-condemnation for the religious leaders, and it would be an admission that Jesus was the Messiah. They were beaten. The religious leaders gave the only answer left to them: "We don't know" (v. 33).

Section Summary

Jesus entered Jerusalem riding a colt in what has come to be called the triumphal entry. Once in Jerusalem, he cleansed the temple, cursed a fig tree, and was questioned by the religious leaders.

QUESTIONS TO GUIDE YOUR STUDY

1. What is the significance of Jesus entering Jerusalem on a donkey at Passover? What were the people's expectations?
2. What is the lesson of the dried-up fig tree? What does it symbolize?
3. Jesus contrasted doubt and faith. What points did he make?
4. Jesus outmaneuvered the religious leaders who questioned his authority. How did he respond? What was their dilemma?

MARK 12

This chapter continues the events of the previous chapter, with Jesus following up on his discussion with the religious leaders.

THE PARABLE OF THE TENANTS (12:1–12)

Jesus followed the unanswered questions of the religious leaders with the parable of the tenants. The following chart indicates the symbolism of the parable.

HISTORICAL BACKGROUND

The destruction of the tenants undoubtedly looked ahead to the destruction of Jerusalem that would occur in AD 70 when the Romans destroyed Jerusalem.

PARABLE OF THE TENANTS

SYMBOL	COUNTERPART IN REALITY
The vineyard	Israel
The owner	God
The tenants	Jewish leaders
The servants	The prophets
The son	Christ

HISTORICAL BACKGROUND

The Pharisees thought of themselves as the purist representatives of God, who also represented the best interests of the Jewish people. The Herodians were a political party of Jews who supported Herod Antipas and, consequently, supported Rome. These two groups wanted to bait Jesus and catch him like a fish.

HISTORICAL BACKGROUND

In those days people held that coinage was a sign of a king's power over his conquered land.

Jesus concluded the parable by asking and then answering his own question about the ultimate fate of the tenants (v. 9). The religious leaders saw that the parable was directed at them. They looked for a way to arrest Jesus.

TO PAY OR NOT TO PAY? (12:13–17)

The Pharisees and Herodians, although natural enemies, united to trap Jesus. They asked Jesus if it was lawful to pay taxes to Caesar. Beyond the question of legality, they were asking whether they ought to pay or were permitted to pay the tribute. Knowing his questioners' evil motive, Jesus asked for a tax coin. By asking whose image and name were on the coin, Jesus caused his questioners to tear apart their carefully built dilemma, for they had to answer "Caesar's."

TWO DIFFERENT WORLDS (12:18–27)

The Sadducees now confronted Jesus. Their far-fetched and absurd example of seven brothers, one wife, and no children stemmed from what was called levirate marriage (Deut 25:5–10; Ruth 4:5; Mark 12:19–22; *levir* is Latin for "brother-in-law"). If a brother died without any children, it was the duty of his brother to take the widow as his wife. The Sadducees used it to question Jesus and ridicule belief in the resurrection. They intended to put down Jesus as a teacher and imply that life beyond the grave would include polygamy. Jesus informed the Sadducees that they were wrong and used Old Testament Scriptures to prove his point.

The Sadducees were priests of the temple and came from aristocratic families of Jerusalem. The Sadducees looked to the first five books of the Bible (the Pentateuch) for their doctrinal beliefs, and they did not believe in resurrection from the dead, angels, demons, spirits, or Jesus (see Acts 23:8). The Pharisees did believe in the resurrection from the dead, angels, demons, and spirits.

AUTHORITY AND PRIORITY (12:28–34)

Jesus's response to the Sadducees impressed a scribe who wanted to know which commandment had priority over all others. Jesus told him that loving God completely is the first commandment. And, when a person gives God first love, that person will also love his or her neighbor.

SONSHIP AND LORDSHIP (12:35–37)

Jesus did not wait for questions to continue his teaching. He went to the temple and asked questions that needed to be answered and provoked thought.

Although a descendant of David by birth, the Messiah was much more than a mere human descendant of David. His was also David's Lord by divine nature.

MISUSED AUTHORITY (12:38–40)

The scribes were seen as people of authority, for they were experts at explaining the law of Moses. But Jesus cautioned the people against following so-called experts when they misused their authority by calling attention to it.

PERSONAL APPLICATION

Jesus did not condemn all religious leaders, but he did condemn those who were guilty of hypocrisy, self-righteousness, and covetousness. Their self-centered attitudes led them to misuse authority. The need for Jesus's caution does not end with those who hear him.

SPIRITUAL SCALES (12:41–44)

As Jesus watched the crowd put their money into the temple treasury, he noticed a widow who gave all she had—two mites. This offering seemed meager compared to the large offerings the rich people were giving. He pointed out that from God's perspective, the greatest gift is that which costs the giver the most.

Section Summary

Jesus taught in Jerusalem. His parable of the tenants reinforced the intention of the religious leaders to arrest him.

QUESTIONS TO GUIDE YOUR STUDY

1. Describe the parable of the tenants. What is its main point?
2. Jesus's enemies asked him if it was lawful to pay taxes to Caesar. What was their motive in asking this question? What was Jesus's answer?
3. What was the Sadducees' question? What was Jesus's skillful response? What was the scribe's question and Jesus's response to him?
4. What lesson can we learn from the widow who gave two mites?

MARK 13

If Mark wrote his Gospel about AD 65, he wrote in the middle of a chaotic decade. Christians in Rome were having to deal with Nero and his persecution. Christians in Jerusalem faced the turmoil that would come from AD 66 to 70 and would result in the destruction of Jerusalem in AD 70.

Mark 13 is an assurance chapter punctuated with commands on how to face the future. Its writing is prophecy and is steeped in Jewish thought and terminology about the day of the Lord.

WORD PICTURE

Hosanna is a Hebrew word that means "save, we pray!" (see Ps 118:25–26).

HISTORICAL BACKGROUND

The Temple in Jerusalem

Solomon's temple was the first temple. It was built about 960–950 BC. The Babylonians destroyed that temple in 581 BC. Zerubbabel led in the building of a second temple on the same site, and it was completed about 515 BC. The second temple was not bad, despite what some writers have written about it. In fact, that temple stood for almost five hundred years, a longer time than either Solomon's temple or Herod's temple existed.

THE BEGINNING OF THE END FOR JERUSALEM (13:1–2)

As Jesus and the disciples left the temple, his disciples commented on the grandeur of the temple complex. For nearly a thousand years, the temple site in Jerusalem had been a place of religious importance for all Jews, but it had become unholy. Jesus announced its impending destruction.

A VIEW TO THE FUTURE (13:3–8)

On the Mount of Olives, across from the temple, the disciples wanted to know more about Jesus's prophecy of the temple's destruction. He taught them about the specific time between the present and the destruction of Jerusalem and the general time between the present and Jesus's second coming.

THE DIFFICULT WAY OF DISCIPLESHIP (13:9–13)

Jesus taught the disciples about the high cost of discipleship. A characteristic of true disciples is that they endure whatever persecution comes their way, and they do not abandon their faithful following of Christ.

HISTORICAL BACKGROUND

The temple was on a hill that was 2,470 feet above sea level. The temple faced the east where the sun rises over Mount Olivet, which is 200 feet higher than the temple hill. From that vantage point, the original four disciples (Peter, James, John, and Andrew, 1:16–20) were with Jesus, who was seated in a customary teaching position.

HOPE BEFORE THE RUINS (13:14–23)

In this section, Jesus shared the sign that will appear before Jerusalem's destruction and offer hope of escape for those who recognize the sign and leave Judea. The disciples were to be on their "guard" and watch for the signs of the impending destruction of Jerusalem.

SIGNS OF THE SAVIOR (13:24–27)

These verses refer to the second coming of Christ and the signs of the coming Savior. To communicate with his readers, Mark uses poetic language drawn from Old Testament background about the day of the Lord.

A PARABLE OF PROMISE (13:28–31)

Jesus taught the disciples a lesson with a parable from nature. As the twigs of a fig tree get tender and the leaves come out, one knows that summer is near. Jesus told them that when they saw "these things happening," they would know that "he is near," that is, the destruction of Jerusalem.

PERSONAL APPLICATION

We are to live in such a way that whether the Lord comes during the night watches or during the day, we will be ready for his return.

CERTAINTIES IN UNCERTAIN TIMES (13:32–37)

No one knows when the day of the Lord, the second coming of Christ, will arrive. God the Father alone knows when this event will take place.

Section Summary

Jesus taught regarding the near-term future as well as events of the long-term future.

QUESTIONS TO GUIDE YOUR STUDY

1. What is the setting for Mark 13? What three future events are associated with this chapter?
2. Why was Jerusalem to be destroyed? What was the sign of the destruction of Jerusalem? What attitude are believers to assume, and what are they to do when they see the sign? Will Jerusalem's destruction be final?
3. What are characteristics of true disciples?
4. From what we read in this chapter, what are the signs of Jesus's second coming? What do we know about the time of his coming? What should the believer's attitude be with regard to Jesus's imminent return?

HISTORICAL BACKGROUND

The Jewish historian Josephus has given a fuller description of this destruction in his writings called *The Wars*.

MARK 14

Mark 14 begins what is known as the "passion narrative." *Passion* basically means suffering. From this point on, Mark dealt with the events that led up to the death of Christ.

NEW TESTAMENT REFERENCE

One cannot be dogmatic about the exact chronological order of time and events of the story. The Romans kept time one way, and the Jews kept time another way. However, we do know the crucial steps of the story; and we can gain insights by studying parallel passages from the other Gospels (see Matt 26; Luke 22; John 12:1–18:1; also see 1 Cor 11:23–26).

THE RELIGIOUS LEADERS PLOT TO MURDER JESUS (14:1–2)

Two days before the Passover, the chief priests were looking for the best way to end Jesus's life. The religious leaders decided to arrest Jesus privately to avoid creating a riot.

MARY ANOINTS JESUS (14:3–9)

While Jesus was eating a meal with friends at Bethany, Mary suddenly broke a vial of costly perfume and anointed Jesus's head and feet with it, and then she wiped his feet with her hair. Judas and the other disciples at first silently resented what they considered a waste of 300 *denarii* worth of perfume (see Matt 26:8; John 12:4–5).

Jesus's response to those who rebuked Mary was, "She has anointed my body in advance for burial."

HISTORICAL BACKGROUND

A denarius was what a laboring man earned for one day's work.

JUDAS SELLS OUT FOR MONEY (14:10–11)

Judas betrayed Jesus, selling him out for the price of a slave (thirty pieces of silver). He conspired with the priests and scribes to find Jesus and arrest him.

NEW TESTAMENT REFERENCE

Even my friend in whom I trusted, one who ate my bread, has raised his heel against me. (Ps 41:9)

THE DISCIPLES PREPARE FOR THE PASSOVER (14:12–16)

Jesus wanted his disciples to prepare for the Passover meal. Jesus secured a room where the disciples would be his guests for this meal.

OLD TESTAMENT REFERENCE

The Passover meal was a time to remember God's deliverance of Israel from Egypt.

JESUS EXPOSES THE TRAITOR (14:17–21)

During the Passover meal, Jesus announced that one of the Twelve would betray him. Each disciple was sad, expressing the hope that he was not the betrayer.

BEGINNING A MEMORIAL (14:22–25)

During this Passover observance, Jesus began the memorial we know as the Lord's Supper. The broken bread symbolized Jesus's broken body. The fruit of the vine was a picture of Jesus's blood "poured out for many." The Passover meal customarily ended with the singing of hymns of praise from the latter part of Pss 113–118. This group of psalms is known as Hallel Psalms (or we might say Hallelujah Psalms).

NEW TESTAMENT REFERENCE

Comparing Gospel Accounts

For the reader to supplement Mark's brief, quick-moving account, it is especially important to study the other Gospels for details and helpful insights. Mark 14:43–15:41 parallels the following passages from the other three Gospel accounts:

Matthew 26:47–27:56

Luke 22:47–23:49

John 18:2–19:30

Those passages move from the betrayal of Jesus, through the trials and crucifixion, to Jesus's victorious death.

PREDICTING DESERTION AND DENIAL (14:26–31)

Jesus announced that all the disciples would desert him. In fact, Peter would not only desert him, but he would also deny him three times that night. Despite Jesus's prediction, the disciples did not consider it possible for them to desert or deny him.

WILLING GOD'S WILL (14:32–42)

The garden of Gethsemane, located at the foot of the Mount of Olives, became a scene of agony and victory, for here Jesus faced the alternative of avoiding death. Jesus prayed that if it were possible, he might be delivered from the cup of suffering. However, he affirmed his preference for the Father's will.

A COWARDLY ARREST (14:43–52)

Judas entered the garden of Gethsemane and led the Sanhedrin guard to seize Jesus. Jesus voluntarily placed himself in the custody of the mob. While Jesus remained calm, the disciples panicked and ran. Jesus foretold this (Mark 14:27), as did Zechariah (13:7). Verses 51–52 tell of a young disciple who may have been the last to run away and was nearly caught. If this is the case, it is Mark's humble way of saying, "I was there, and I also deserted him."

A JUDICIAL FARCE (14:53–65)

Jesus had two trials with three stages each, according to the collective Gospel records: a religious trial and a civil trial. This passage focuses on the religious trial.

The Sanhedrin was made up of the high priest, former high priests (chief priests), and others who were called elders and scribes. This Jewish supreme court had access to a temple police force that could act within certain limitations under Roman law.

A Kangaroo Court (vv. 53–54)

To try Jesus, the Sanhedrin broke its own rules. It could not meet legally until sunrise, nor could the court meet during any of the great feasts. They broke these rules and others. It is clear that the court's interest was not justice.

Lying Witnesses (vv. 55–59)

The court had trouble finding a charge that condemned Jesus to death. The false witnesses didn't give a consistent testimony.

OLD TESTAMENT REFERENCE

According to law, at least two witnesses were needed to agree on a specific charge to make an accusation stick (Num 35:30; Deut 17:6; 19:15).

A Blinding Truth (vv. 60–65)

Not getting anywhere with the false witnesses, the high priest asked Jesus if he was the Messiah, the Son of God. Jesus answered simply, "I am."

This response greatly angered the high priest, who tore his clothes. He charged Jesus with blasphemy, a crime punishable by death under Jewish law.

PETER: A DISCIPLE IN DENIAL (14:66–72)

In the courtyard below Jesus's trial, Peter denied his association with Jesus three times, as Jesus had predicted. Realizing what he did, Peter wept bitterly.

Section Summary

Jesus hosted the Passover meal for his disciples and initiated the Lord's Supper. He was then arrested and taken first to a religious trial.

QUESTIONS TO GUIDE YOUR STUDY

1. Why were the religious leaders determined to murder Jesus?

2. What was the cup Jesus asked the Father to deliver from him? What did he accomplish in the garden of Gethsemane?
3. What kind of religious trial did Jesus receive? What details does Mark provide?
4. With what crime did the leaders charge Jesus? How serious was the charge?

MARK 15

This chapter gives a detailed account of Jesus's trial, crucifixion, and death.

Since only the Romans could impose the death penalty, the Jewish leaders decided to take Jesus from their religious court to Pilate's civil court, probably about 6:00 a.m.

CHANGING COURTS AND CHARGES (15:1–5)

To the Roman government, the charge of blasphemy, which the Jews had pronounced, did not merit a death sentence from the civil court. So the Sanhedrin downplayed blasphemy and charged Jesus with treason.

NEW TESTAMENT REFERENCE

When Pilate, the Roman governor, heard that Jesus was a Galilean, he sent him to Herod Antipas, the Galilean ruler (Luke 23:5–12).

The accusing leaders made four specific charges against Jesus:

1. Stirring up people against Rome,
2. Prohibiting the poll tax,
3. Claiming to be a king, and
4. Claiming to be the Son of God (Luke 23:2; John 19:7).

The first two charges were false, and the last two charges were unrecognized truths about Jesus.

A CONDEMNING CROWD (15:6–15)

At Passover, it was customary for the Roman governor to release any *one* prisoner the people wanted released. When Pilate offered Jesus, the crowd instead chose Barabbas, a known murderer, thief, and insurrectionist. The crowd cried for crucifixion, and Pilate agreed to give them what they wanted. Pilate faced a dilemma. He wanted a clear conscience, and at the same time he tried to appease the crowd.

A REDEEMING DEATH (15:16–41)

After enduring cruel and brutal mockery, Jesus was crucified. Along with Jesus, two other men were crucified. They occupied the places James and John had naively asked for (Mark 10:35–38).

Crucifixion was a cruel death on a cross. It involved the pain of a body torn by nails, exposure to the weather, and—if the person lasted long enough—hunger and thirst.

Unexplainable darkness came at noon and lasted until 3:00 p.m. Jesus cried out the words of Ps 22:1, "*Eloi, Eloi, lemá sabachtháni?*" ("My God, my God, why have you abandoned me?") (v. 34). Some bystanders thought he was calling on Elijah to deliver him from the cross (v. 35). Jesus then cried out and breathed his last.

At the moment Jesus died, the curtain of the temple split from top to bottom (Mark 15:38; Matt 27:51). There were two curtains or veils in the temple: one at the entrance to the temple itself and one that hung between the holy place and the holy of holies. If the curtain that split was the one that led to the holy of holies, it is symbolic of Jesus's gift of direct access to God. For up until that time only the high priest was to go into the holy of holies, and that was only on the Day of Atonement (see Lev 16). Jesus provides direct access to God for every worshiper. If the curtain that split was the one at the entrance to the temple, it foreshadows the destruction of the temple. Either way, Jesus's death and the splitting of the curtain announced that things would never be the same again. There is a new day of faith and a new covenant!

HISTORICAL BACKGROUND

Golgotha was the site of the crucifixion. It is an Aramaic word for "Place of the Skull." "Calvary" is the Latin translation of Golgotha, and it means "a bare skull."

BURYING THE MESSIAH (15:42–47)

Critical Timing (v. 42)

Jesus died about 3:00 p.m. on Friday afternoon, the day of preparation for the Sabbath. Because the Jewish Sabbath began at 6:00 p.m. on Friday evening, Jesus's burial presented a time problem for anyone who wanted to give him a proper burial. Furthermore, touching a dead body made a Jew ceremonially unclean for seven days; so to bury Jesus on the Sabbath puts those friends of Jesus in a position of being unable to take part in the Sabbath or the religious festivities that would begin in a few hours.

OLD TESTAMENT REFERENCE

Although the Romans crucified Jesus, it was the Jews who demanded the crucifixion. The Romans did not care how long a body hung on a cross. However, by Moses's law, an executed criminal was not supposed to remain on a tree (or cross) overnight (Deut 21:22–23). This explains why the Jewish leaders wanted to speed up the death of Jesus and the other two men on the crosses (John 19:31).

Belated Bravery (vv. 43–46)

Technically, Jesus's body belonged to the Roman government, as did the bodies of all executed criminals. The Romans usually left a body to decay on the cross unless friends or relatives asked for burial permission.

Joseph of Arimathea asked Pilate for the privilege of burying Jesus's body. When Pilate was convinced that Jesus was dead, he granted Jesus's body to Joseph for burial. Jesus was then laid in an unused tomb, which was sealed by a huge rock resembling a grindstone that is rolled downhill into its place at the entrance of the tomb.

Burdened Planning (v. 47)

Faithful women followed Jesus from the trial to Golgotha to the tomb. These women, with their deep love for Jesus, were still there when everyone else had gone. Mary Magdalene and Mary, the mother of Joses, watched to see where Jesus was buried.

Section Summary

Jesus was brought to Pilate the Roman governor, who reluctantly sentenced him to death.

QUESTIONS TO GUIDE YOUR STUDY

1. What were the charges against Jesus? How valid were they?
2. Did Jesus receive a fair trial? Describe Mark's account of the civil and legal proceedings.
3. The crowd chose to free Barabbas rather than Jesus. What was the cruel irony of their choice?
4. What is the significance of the rending of the curtain of the temple?

MARK 16

HE IS RISEN! (16:1–8)

At sunrise, on the first day after the Sabbath, Mary Magdalene, Mary the mother of James, and Salome brought spices to anoint the body of Jesus. They were concerned because they did not know who would roll away the stone that guarded the tomb's entrance. The women were shocked to find the stone rolled away when they arrived. Inside was an angel who announced to the women that "he has risen!" The angel then commanded the women to tell the disciples about the resurrection. Terrified, the women fled, speaking to no one, "since they were afraid" (v. 8).

EPILOGUE (16:9–20)

"Afraid" (v. 8) does not appear to be a good word to end an account of good news, and though the oldest and best manuscripts do end with Mark 16:8, vv. 9–20 and another ending began to show up very early in other manuscripts. Scholars differ on whether Mark intended to stop at 16:8, but they largely agree that what we have in 16:9–20 was not written by Mark. Five viewpoints summarize most thinking about the ending of the Gospel of Mark:

- Mark completed his Gospel with 16:8 even though the ending is abrupt.

- The original ending of Mark's Gospel may have been torn off at the end of the scroll.
- Mark could have been interrupted and was not able to finish all he wanted to write in the inspired record.
- Verses 9–20 are considered by some scholars to be part of the original Mark's Gospel.
- Verse 8 could have had a different ending as indicated in the New English Bible: "And they delivered all these instructions briefly to Peter and his companions. Afterwards Jesus himself sent out by them from east to west the sacred and imperishable message of eternal salvation."

Because we are almost 2,000 years removed from the original writing, no one knows exactly how Mark ended his book. We do know that Jesus's tomb was empty and that Jesus appeared to his disciples on several occasions after his resurrection. Paul most concisely speaks about resurrection appearances and the meaning of the whole Christ event (in 1 Cor 15:3–8).

PAUL'S ACCOUNT OF JESUS'S POST-RESURRECTION APPEARANCES

APPEARANCE	PASSAGE
1. Peter	Luke 24:34; Mark 16:7; John 21:1–14
2. The Eleven	Matt 28:16–20; Luke 24:36–49; John 20:19–25
3. Five hundred believers	1 Cor 15:6
4. James	1 Cor 15:7
5. The apostles	1 Cor 15:7
6. Paul	1 Cor 15:8

Regardless of whether the verses originally appeared in the Gospel of Mark, it is still important to take a summary look at Mark 16:9–20. Most of the content in these verses appears elsewhere in the Gospels or in Acts. The breakdown of verses 9–20 and their possible counterparts elsewhere may be helpful:

- Verses 9–11: Appearance to Mary Magdalene (see Luke 24:10–11,22–24; John 20:11–18; and possibly John 20:1–2).
- Verses 12–13: Appearance to the two travelers (see Luke 24:13–35).
- Verses 14–18: Appearance to the Eleven (see Luke 24:36–49; Matt 28:16–20; and parts of the book of Acts).

- Verses 19–20: Ascension and continued activity (see Acts 1:9–11).

Scholars see other parallels in addition to these, but the heart of Mark 16:9–20 is reflected in the passages cited above. Readers will share different concerns about the verses that likely were not in Mark's original Gospel and which may not have support elsewhere in the New Testament. For example, with regard to drinking something deadly or picking up serpents (v. 18), it is not wise to build a theological position on these verses alone.

We now come to the end of Mark's record about Jesus. But the end of that story is only a beginning for those who turn from their sin and put their trust in Jesus as Lord and Savior. Mark's Gospel is not a biography. It is good news that calls for every person to decide what he or she will do personally with Jesus Christ. The essential truth is this: *Jesus Christ is God's good news for mankind, and Jesus alone is the way to eternal life.* Outside of Christ there is only spiritual death. So life's crucial question to all who read this Gospel is: What will you do with Jesus?

PERSONAL APPLICATION

Verses 9–20 call Christians to preach and minister in the power of the resurrected Christ, who did not leave his disciples alone to continue his work.

Section Summary

Mary Magdalene, Mary mother of James, and Salome came to the tomb to anoint the body of Jesus. They found the tomb empty and a young man who told them Jesus had risen from the grave. The messenger told the women to tell this to the disciples, who were to go to Galilee where Jesus would meet them.

QUESTIONS TO GUIDE YOUR STUDY

1. When the women arrived at the tomb, what were they expecting to see? Describe what happened.
2. What makes the resurrection so important to the Christian faith?
3. What does the resurrection of Jesus mean to you?
4. Why are verses 9–20 of Mark 16 controversial? How is this passage viewed by most believers? What is your view?
5. How would you summarize the importance of Mark's Gospel to your understanding and Christian experience?

Luke

INTRODUCTION

Luke's Gospel is the longest single book of the New Testament. Luke wrote as a Christian historian. He intended that his Gospel and Acts serve as a single volume dealing with the beginning and growth of the early church.

AUTHOR

The authorship of Luke was never disputed until the second half of the nineteenth century. Yet it should be observed that Luke and Acts are two of the nine books in the New Testament that are anonymous. Neither Acts nor Luke names its author; but since the second century, church tradition has identified Luke as the author of Luke-Acts.

AUDIENCE

Luke was explicitly written to Theophilus (1:1–4). Theophilus appears to have had some exposure to the faith, as Luke's introduction makes clear. In fact, it is likely that Theophilus was a Gentile believer struggling with his association in a movement that had Jewish origins.

PURPOSE

Luke wrote his Gospel for a variety of reasons that include the following:

1. Luke wanted to confirm the message of God's promise and salvation through Jesus.
2. He wished to portray God's faithfulness both to Israel and to all persons while explaining why so many in Israel tragically rejected Jesus.
3. He wanted to lay the foundation in Luke for his defense in Acts of the full membership of Gentiles as part of God's people and promise.

WORD PICTURE

The Gospel of Luke and the Book of Acts were both addressed to Theophilus (Acts 1:1), whose name means "friend of God." All we know about Theophilus is found in these two verses. The words "most honorable" suggest that he was a person of authority, perhaps a government official. Theophilus may have been a convert who was taught many things about Christ, or he may have been an open-minded seeker who heard these things. Luke wrote so that Theophilus would know the truth and certainty of the Christian gospel.

HISTORICAL BACKGROUND

Paul referred to Luke as "the dearly loved physician" (Col 4:14). During Paul's last imprisonment in Rome, he wrote to Timothy: "Only Luke is with me" (2 Tim 4:11).

4. He wished to offer a word of reconciliation and explanation to Jews by showing how responding to Jesus was the natural fulfillment of God's promises to Israel.
5. He wished to show that God's promise extends to all people by showing the variety of social classes and people who responded to Jesus.

HISTORICAL BACKGROUND

"We can be fairly certain of the circumstances in which Luke learned of these events. Having come to Jerusalem with Paul just before the latter was arrested and being on hand to accompany him again when he was eventually sent away from Caesarea on the voyage to Rome, Luke presumably stayed in Palestine for the two-year period of his friend's imprisonment and without doubt used the opportunity to gather material for his Gospel. Behind chapters 1 and 2 in particular, there must surely lie long conversations between him and Mary."

Michael Wilcock, Savior of the World: The Message of Luke's Gospel *(Leicester: Inter-Varsity Press, 1979), 42.*

DATE AND PLACE OF WRITING

Date. The date Luke was written cannot be established with certainty. Luke wrote his own introduction (1:1–4), which indicates that he was not the first to make a written record of God's revelation in Christ. Most biblical scholars believe that both Luke and Matthew drew on Mark's Gospel in writing theirs. It seems likely that Luke was written before Acts, since Acts is part 2 of Luke.

Acts ends before the outcome of Paul's appeal to Caesar is known. This would have been in the early 60s. On this view, Luke would have been written prior to 60 and thus Mark all the earlier.

Place of Writing. The most probable origin of Luke is Rome. Luke reached Rome in Paul's company and was in Rome when Paul wrote Colossians and Philemon during Paul's first Roman imprisonment (AD 59–62). The circumstances would have allowed time for the composition of Luke-Acts.

LITERARY FORM

Luke is a Gospel, a form unique to the Bible. The account operates like a narrative. It is more than a biography because it is selective and has a theological message to convey. It is a history but only a selective history. We are told nothing about the details of Jesus's childhood. Rather, we move from Jesus's birth directly to his ministry with only one incident from the age of 12 and the ministry of John the Baptist intervening briefly. A Gospel is a theological, pastoral explanation of the significance and impact of Jesus's life, death, and resurrection. So characters, setting, movements of time and location, mood, and the arrangement of events are all a part of telling the account of Jesus's ministry.

BASIC OUTLINE OF LUKE'S GOSPEL

I. John the Baptist and Jesus (1:1–2:52)
II. Preparation for Ministry (3:1–4:13)
III. Galilean Ministry (4:14–9:50)
IV. Jerusalem Journey (9:51–19:44)
V. Final Ministry in Jerusalem (19:45–24:53)

QUESTIONS TO GUIDE YOUR STUDY

1. Why did Luke write his Gospel?
2. Where did Luke get his material for writing his Gospel? Explain the relationship between Luke and Acts.
3. What are some of the distinctives and unique themes of Luke's Gospel?

LUKE 1

PROLOGUE (1:1–4)

Luke's main purpose for the prologue was to establish his credibility as a historian. He sought to do this in 1:3 by compounding terms that reveal his care and expertise in writing.

The Period in Which the Gospels Were Written (vv. 1–2)

Verse 1 reveals that Luke was not the first to write about what God in Christ had caused to be accomplished among the believers.

Very likely many of the writings were not what might be called complete accounts of the coming, teachings, ministry, death, and resurrection of Jesus. Many of the early writings probably were about only one or perhaps a few aspects of the gospel.

The Writing of Luke's Gospel (vv. 3–4)

Luke did not include everything about Jesus in his Gospel. He, like other Gospel writers, was selective in what he recorded. He was a writer and witness, not just a compiler. Everything he found in his careful research did not become part of his book, only what fitted his purpose.

HISTORICAL BACKGROUND

Luke's Gospel begins with a literary prologue that ranks among the best Greek literature of the first century. Numerous parallels of such a prologue exist in the Jewish and Hellenistic literature of that period.

SUMMARY

Luke's main purpose for writing the prologue was to establish his credibility. It was the first step to accomplishing his goal for writing his Gospel, which was to help his readers become certain of the truthfulness of the gospel teachings the readers had been taught. Although a careful historian, Luke made no secret of his faith and of his purpose to seek to persuade others to have faith in Christ.

NEW TESTAMENT REFERENCE

Mark's Gospel was probably one of the writings that preceded Luke. The essence of over 50 percent of the verses in Mark is found in Luke. The percentage of Mark in Matthew is even higher—about 90 percent.

JOHN THE BAPTIST'S BIRTH ANNOUNCED (1:5–25)

Luke moves from prologue to two important birth announcements. Zechariah and Elizabeth, the parents of John the Baptist, represent the true piety that existed in Israel. They were righteous in the best sense of the word. They believed in and practiced prayer; they hoped for the coming of the Messiah.

Zechariah was offering incense in the temple when the angel appeared to him. Zechariah responded to the angel with a question reminiscent of Abraham's words under similar circumstances (v. 18; Gen 15:8), but he lacked Abraham's faith. The angel's prophecy must have seemed too good to be true, as he responded with the question, "How can I know this?" Because of his unbelief, Zechariah was unable to speak until John's birth. Elizabeth viewed her childlessness as a stigma; therefore, she rejoiced when she realized she was pregnant. She already was experiencing, in anticipation, the joy and gladness of which Gabriel spoke.

Section Summary

Gabriel announced to Zechariah that he would be the father of the prophet who would call people to repentance before the coming of the Lord.

JESUS'S BIRTH ANNOUNCED (1:26–38)

Having just described the announcement of John the Baptist's birth, Luke proceeds with a description of the announcement of Jesus's birth.

An angel appeared to Mary, a virgin, and announced that she would give birth to Jesus. Unlike Zechariah, she responds with trust and submission to God's will.

This account of Jesus's birth has a number of parallels with John's birth: the mention of the sixth month and two of the main characters, the angel Gabriel and Elizabeth.

Section Summary

The mighty work God did in John the Baptist's conception would be surpassed by an even greater miracle in the virginal conception of Jesus. In addition, the mighty work God foretold he would do through John the Baptist's ministry would be surpassed by an even greater work through his Son's ministry.

THE MEETING OF JOHN THE BAPTIST AND JESUS (1:39–56)

Elizabeth's Prophecy (vv. 39–45)

Mary hastened to visit her relative Elizabeth. As soon as Mary greeted her, Elizabeth was filled with the Spirit and spoke as a prophet. She referred to Mary as "the mother of my Lord" (v. 43) and blessed her for believing God's word. This scene thus reinforced the theme of superiority of Mary's son to Elizabeth's son.

Elizabeth's words in verse 42, like Gabriel's in verse 28, were used in later centuries to exalt Mary to a divine-like role of her own. This

ANGELIC ANNOUNCEMENTS IN LUKE

PASSAGE	ANGEL	RECIPIENT(S)	SUMMARY	RESPONSE
Luke 1:5–25	Gabriel	Zechariah	The angel informed Zechariah that he and his wife, Elizabeth, would have a child in their old age.	Zechariah was overcome with fear, doubt, and questioning. "'How can I know this?' Zechariah asked the angel. 'For I am an old man, and my wife is well along in years'" (v. 18). As a result of his faithless response, Zechariah became mute until after the birth of his son, John the Baptist.
Luke 1:26–38	Gabriel	Mary	The angel told the Virgin Mary that she would give birth to a son who would be "the Son of God" (v. 35).	"'I am the Lord's servant,' said Mary. 'May it happen to me as you have said.' Then the angel left her" (v. 38).
Luke 2:8–20	An angel of the Lord	The shepherds	A proclamation that the Savior of the world was born	"Let's go straight to Bethlehem and see what has happened, which the Lord has made known to us" (v. 15).
Luke 24:5–7	Two men in dazzling clothes	Women at the tomb	Proclamation of Jesus's resurrection and call to remember Jesus's promises about his resurrection	Remembered Jesus's promises, found the Eleven, and told them what they discovered (vv. 8–9)

misses the point not only of these passages but also of the whole New Testament. Mary was the recipient of grace, not a source of grace. Her blessedness was the blessedness of one who became a willing channel of divine blessings to others.

Mary's Song (vv. 46–56)

Mary's response in verses 46–55 reflects humble trust. This passage is a kind of hymnlike poem—often called the Magnificat.

Mary understands the significance of Gabriel's proclamation that was affirmed by Elizabeth (vv. 42–45) and she responds in song (cp. 1 Sam 2:2–11). Historically this section has been called "The Magnificant" (Latin for "My soul magnifies the Lord") as it is Mary's reflection on what the Lord has done for her (vv. 46–49) and for future generations (vv. 50–55). It is also a song of thanksgiving, praising God for both provision and deliverance.

Section Summary

In this passage we see several of Luke's major emphases. First is the theme of reversal. The humble are exalted, and the arrogant are brought low. Second, we see the fulfillment of prophecy and the divine promises. Third, we gain an understanding of Mary's offspring. The child born of Mary was clearly greater than the child born of Elizabeth.

HISTORICAL BACKGROUND

Naming of Children

In biblical tradition, the task of naming a child generally fell to the mother (Gen 29:31–30:24; 1 Sam 1:20), but could be performed by the father, and in exceptional cases by nonparental figures. The biblical concept of naming was rooted in the ancient world's understanding that a name expressed essence. To know the name of a person was to know that person's total character and nature. Revealing character and destiny, personal names might express hopes for the child's future. Changing of names could occur at divine or human initiative, revealing a transformation in character or destiny.

THE BIRTH OF JOHN THE BAPTIST (1:57–80)

His Name Is John (vv. 57–66)

Neighbors and relatives assumed the child of Elizabeth and Zechariah would be named for his father, but Zechariah and Elizabeth remembered the angel's words and named him John. All of this was done in such a way that everyone who heard it was impressed. They wondered what special destiny awaited this child: "What then will this child become?"

Light in the Darkness (vv. 67–79)

Now Zechariah was filled with the Spirit and prophesied of the new day about to dawn. His poem or song is often called the Benedictus. The first half of the song (vv. 68–75) wove together several Old Testament promises (e.g., 1 Sam 2:1,10; Ps 89:3; Ezk 34:23–24) that stand fulfilled in the Messiah's coming.

In the Wilderness (v. 80)

Luke summed up John's childhood in this single verse. The last part of the verse is laden with anticipation. John went into the wilderness. Later the word of the Lord would come to him in the wilderness, and he would begin his call for repentance.

Section Summary

Luke wanted his readers to understand Zechariah's divinely inspired hymn as praising God for fulfilling his promises to his people and describing the roles of John the Baptist and especially the Messiah.

QUESTIONS TO GUIDE YOUR STUDY

1. Describe Luke's prologue. How does it relate to his goals for writing his Gospel?
2. Compare the births of John and Jesus. What parallels do we see? What contrasts does Luke make?
3. What is the significance of Mary's song?
4. What truths does Zechariah's hymn present? Why would its message be significant to the people of Israel?

HISTORICAL BACKGROUND

Augustus Caesar ruled as emperor over most of the civilized world. He was honored as a great benefactor. Under his reign the world enjoyed a period of peace. This passage in Luke told of the coming one who would offer the kind of peace that lay beyond the power of the most powerful man on earth.

LUKE 2

THE BIRTH OF JESUS (2:1–20)

Next follows Luke's narrative of Jesus's birth.

The Fullness of Time (vv. 1–7)

Luke's purpose in mentioning Caesar Augustus's decree probably was to show that God moves in the affairs of nations to accomplish his purposes. The Caesars appeared to be in control of human destiny, but God was at work through all these events, working out his eternal purposes.

Heaven Touches Earth (vv. 8–14)

At many points in Luke 1:5–2:52, signs herald the divine intervention into history, but none is more dramatic than the angels' announcement to the shepherds on the night of Jesus's birth. Three verses focus on the significance of this unique event: 10, 11, and 14.

Verse 10 is the angels' announcement of "good news of great joy that will be for all people." This was the first public announcement of the good news of Jesus's birth.

Verse 11 focuses on the one whose coming was heralded. Each of the three titles—Savior, Christ, and Lord—has significant meaning:

Verse 14 has been translated various ways. A paraphrase of this passage might be, "Peace to people who are the objects of God's good will" (Robert J. Dean, *Luke*, Broadman & Holman, p. 27).

HISTORICAL BACKGROUND

Savior, Christ, Lord

Luke used three titles to describe Jesus. Each was steeped in Old Testament Scriptures and rich in meaning for Luke's readers.

Savior means "healer, deliverer, benefactor." Christ means "Messiah," the anointed one to rule as king in fulfillment of God's promises to David. *Lord* speaks of the divine nature of the One who was born.

These three titles also appear together in Phil 3:20.

Witnesses of the Good News (vv. 15–20)

The shepherds were not only the first to hear the proclamation of the good news, but they were the first humans to tell others.

Section Summary

By conveying the historical setting and circumstances of Jesus's birth, Luke reinforced two of his themes: (1) that Jesus was the fulfillment of the Jewish messianic hopes, and (2) God's sovereignty over history.

OLD TESTAMENT REFERENCE

Mary and Joseph performed three ceremonies prescribed by the law: (1) they circumcised their eight-day-old Son (Gen 17:9–14); (2) Mary went to the temple for purification as prescribed in Lev 12:22–24; and (3) they presented Jesus in the temple following the instructions in Exod 13:2, 12–15.

An important aspect of this passage is that it reveals Jesus was born into a home of modest means but a home of deep loyalty to the religion of the Old Testament.

LIGHT TO THE GENTILES AND GLORY TO ISRAEL (2:21–39)

The temple was central in Israel's worship and hopes. We find it prominent in this chapter of Luke's narrative (vv. 22–38,41–51). In this particular section, Luke 2:22–38 tells how Jesus was presented in the temple as an infant.

According to the Law (vv. 21–24)

Five times in this episode Luke mentions that Mary and Joseph acted according to the law (vv. 22, 23, 24, 27, 39).

The Shadow of the Cross (vv. 25–39)

Three times the passage refers to the Spirit's influence on Simeon, a devout man living in Jerusalem at the time of Jesus's birth. Simeon was seeking the fulfillment of messianic prophecy when Israel would be restored. God promised Simeon that he would not die before seeing the Christ. When Joseph and Mary brought Jesus to the temple for purification rites, Simeon blessed God for allowing him to see God's salvation. This salvation would be not only glory for Israel but also light for the revelation to the Gentiles.

Simeon warned that Jesus would cause both the "falling" and "rising" of many in Israel.

A prophetess, Anna, also recognized Jesus as the Messiah and thanked God for him.

HISTORICAL BACKGROUND

Feast of the Passover

Passover was one of the three annual festivals Jewish men were required to celebrate in Jerusalem (Deut 16:16). Passover itself was the opening feast of the seven-day (or eight-day by another reckoning) festival called the Feast of Unleavened Bread and was celebrated on the fifteenth day of Nisan. The entire feast, however, was popularly called the Feast of Passover. Passover commemorated God's deliverance or exodus of his people out of Egypt and the death angel's passing over Israel's firstborn.

Section Summary

Simeon's prediction (vv. 34–35) is the first connection in Luke between Jesus's mission and suffering. For the first time, the shadow of the cross fell across Jesus's life. Jesus is the salvation of God, but in the midst of hope is the reality that fulfillment comes mixed with pain and suffering.

THE BOY JESUS IN THE TEMPLE (2:40–52)

Apart from the summary statements about Jesus's growth in 2:40 and 2:52, the only knowledge of Jesus's childhood comes from the episode recorded in 2:41–51.

Mary and Joseph attended the Feast of the Passover every year. When Jesus was 12 years of age, they brought him along to the feast.

When they returned home, the boy Jesus remained behind. When a concerned Mary and Joseph returned to Jerusalem looking for the missing boy, they were astonished to find him in the temple sitting among the teachers.

The teachers at the temple were amazed at the careful attention, insightful questions, and wise answers of the boy from Nazareth.

Mary's anxious question and Jesus's answer are the heart of the passage. Jesus revealed an awareness of his unique relationship with his heavenly Father: "Didn't you know that it was necessary for me to be in my Father's house?"

As an obedient son, Jesus dutifully returned to Nazareth with his parents. In verse 52 Luke chronicles the development of Jesus intellectually ("in wisdom"), physically ("in stature"), spiritually ("favor with God"), and socially ("and with people").

Section Summary

This section, dominated by Old Testament allusions, opens Luke's Gospel with notes of fulfillment and indications of God's direction. The brief glimpse of Jesus as a child that Luke provided forms a kind of bridge between the events connected with his birth and the account of his adult ministry.

QUESTIONS TO GUIDE YOUR STUDY

1. What unique aspects about Jesus's birth does Luke reveal with his infancy narrative?
2. What is significant about the prophecies of Simeon and Anna?
3. Luke is the only Gospel that records an event from Jesus's childhood. What insights about Jesus's growth and development can we glean from this brief account? Why do you think Luke included this passage?

LUKE 3

JOHN THE BAPTIST, A MAN WHOSE TIME HAD COME (3:1–6)

As in 2:1, Luke opened this account by tying the opening events of Jesus's ministry to contemporary history.

Part of Luke's purpose for writing his Gospel was to help his readers date the events. He was writing a Gospel about a Savior for all people. He wanted Theophilus and other Gentile readers to see the events narrated as part of the fabric of a world shared by Jews and Gentiles alike.

NEW TESTAMENT REFERENCE

In 1:5 Luke began with the words "In the days of King Herod of Judea." Luke 2:12 mentions Caesar Augustus and Quirinius, the governor of Syria. Luke 3:1 dates the following events "in the fifteenth year of the reign of Tiberius Caesar."

Luke 3:2b brings John back into the picture after noting in 1:80 that he went to live in the wilderness.

John not only preached repentance before the Lord's coming; he also signified this message with baptism. The Old Testament prophets used various kinds of prophetic symbolism. John's prophetic sign was baptism. This was a way of signifying repentance and forgiveness.

HISTORICAL BACKGROUND

Baptism of Repentance

Several New Testament texts refer to repentance, baptism, and forgiveness (see Acts 2:38). "Repentance" here literally means a change of mind but refers more broadly to the human involvement in the experience of conversion.

THE MISSION OF JOHN THE BAPTIST (3:7–20)

In this section Luke gives us three examples of John the Baptist's preaching.

Example 1. Baptism and Repentance (vv. 7–9)

John's message was repentance; baptism was its sign. The crowd came for baptism but needed forgiveness. John called some of them "a brood of vipers" and refused to baptize them because he saw no evidence of repentance. Without a change of heart, baptism would have been a farce. It was meaningful only as a sign of genuine repentance. Repentance, not baptism, is what brings forgiveness.

Example 2. Changing How We Live (vv. 10–14)

There is a striking contrast between the people in verses 7–9 and those of verses 10–14. The former group presumed on their ancestry and did not repent. The latter group was typical of those who earnestly heeded John's call for repentance.

Example 3. The Spirit and Fire (vv. 15–20)

Because John's activity aroused great interest and speculation, it was only natural that some wondered whether he was the Messiah. John quickly denied this. In his day, one of the duties of a slave was to remove his master's shoes.

Thus, John saw himself as a slave in comparison to the Messiah.

Section Summary

Alfred Plummer says of John the Baptist: "The whole man was a sermon" (Gospel According to St. Luke, ***p. 86). Luke 3:1–20 shows how John was consumed with his awesome mission. Luke tells of his prophetic call, his message, his words about the Messiah, and his arrest.***

OLD TESTAMENT REFERENCE

The phrases "from heaven" and "with you I am well-pleased" are possible allusions to Ps 2:7 and Isa 42:1.

JESUS'S BAPTISM (3:21–22)

Luke's account of Jesus's baptism emphasized that it happened when all the people were being baptized. This showed his intent to identify with those he came to serve and save.

LUKE'S GENEALOGY (3:23–38)

This genealogy contains 77 ancestors. The exact arrangement of generations, in contrast to what we find in Matthew, is uncertain.

It's likely that if all the facts were known, it would be clear why the two genealogies are different.

Section Summary

This section is a prelude to Jesus's public ministry. It shows Jesus committing himself to a mission of service and sacrifice. His genealogy emphasizes his ties not only to Israel but also to all humanity.

QUESTIONS TO GUIDE YOUR STUDY

1. What is repentance? What must one do to truly repent?
2. Describe the universal nature of the gospel? Why was this a revolutionary concept among John's listeners?
3. What characterized the message of John's preaching?

HISTORICAL BACKGROUND

When a Gentile became a Jew, one of the requirements was a kind of baptism. The Gentile immersed himself in water as a part of his entrance rites into Judaism as a proselyte. John's baptism was different from the proselyte baptism in at least two ways. First, John did the baptism himself. Second, and more important, John's baptism had a strong moral and universal basis. Proselyte baptism assumed Gentiles were outsiders who needed to be baptized to become insiders. John's baptism assumed that everyone needed repentance to be an insider.

LUKE 4

TEMPTED AS WE ARE (4:1–13)

Jesus's temptations were like ours in that they were real, but his experience with temptation was unique in two ways:

1. He resisted temptation and did not sin.
2. He met temptation on the field of battle and emerged victorious.

The temptations themselves came from external sources, and in all three Jesus was obedient to God's will. The temptations were all messianic in nature and thus should be seen as a parallel to 1 John 2:16.

NEW TESTAMENT REFERENCE

Hebrews 4:15 said of Jesus that he was "tempted in every way as we are, yet without sin." This statement underscores the reality of Jesus's temptations.

The First Temptation: Physical Needs (vv. 3–4)

Jesus was tempted to use his power to meet physical needs. This was more than a temptation to feed himself miraculously; it was a temptation to embark on a mission to feed hungry people.

He resisted by quoting Deut 8:3.

The Second Temptation: Power (vv. 5–8)

Jesus's second temptation was to seek the power of a world ruler. The subtle appeal of the temptation—like the other two—was that it matched popular expectations about the Messiah.

Again, Jesus resisted by quoting Deut 6:13.

OLD TESTAMENT REFERENCE

"He humbled you by letting you go hungry; then he gave you manna to eat, which you and your ancestors had not known, so that you might learn that man does not live on bread alone but on every word that comes from the mouth of the LORD." (Deut 8:3) "You must revere the LORD your God, serve him, and take oaths using only his name" (Deut 6:13)

"You must not put the LORD your God to the test as you did at Massah." (Deut 6:16)

The Third Temptation: Popularity (vv. 9–12)

The third temptation was to perform a dazzling miracle in the temple. Many people were anxiously awaiting a Messiah who would perform spectacular signs.

Once again Jesus quoted Scripture, this time Deut 6:16.

Section Summary

Throughout his temptations, Jesus found his answers in the Scriptures. He was armed with the "sword of the Spirit" (Eph 6:17) for his battle with the devil. His being "full of the Holy Spirit" is a model for the believer.

OLD TESTAMENT REFERENCE

"The Spirit of the Sovereign LORD is upon me, because the LORD has chosen me. He has commissioned me to encourage the poor, to help the brokenhearted, to decree the release of captives, and the freeing of prisoners, to announce the year when the Lord will show his favor, the day when our God will seek vengeance, to console all who mourn." (Isa 61:1–2)

JESUS'S MINISTRY IN GALILEE IN MINIATURE (4:14–30)

A Good Start (vv. 14–15)

Luke began his portrayal of Jesus's ministry with the account of Jesus's first sermon, and in it Luke provided his readers with Jesus's own description of his mission and ministry.

A Mission to the People (vv. 16–21)

This is one of the earliest records of what took place in a Jewish synagogue service. As was the custom, Jesus stood to read the Scriptures and sat to teach.

His Own Received him Not (vv. 22–30)

The initial reaction of Jesus's hearers was favorable. But as he continued, they began to wonder and raise questions in their minds. They wondered at the discrepancy between the man and his message.

Jesus, sensing their skepticism, used two proverbs to illustrate their feelings:

1. "Doctor, heal yourself."
2. "No prophet is accepted in his hometown."

These proverbs were Jesus's way of responding to their demand for signs among his own neighbors. His ministry, which was as broad as human need, could not be confined to his hometown or even to his own nation. They became so angry that they ran Jesus out of town and even tried to kill him.

WORD PICTURE

Proverbs

This word is translated from the Greek term *parabolē*, which has a broad range of meaning from story and example parables, allegories, similitudes, and metaphors to proverbs. This particular proverb has numerous parallels both in form and in context. For context, see Luke 23:35. For form, we find in Greek literature, "Physician, physician heal thine own limp!" Here as elsewhere (Luke 5:22; 6:8; 7:40; 9:47; 11:17), Jesus possessed a unique awareness of others' thoughts.

Section Summary

Luke records the earliest days of Jesus's Galilean ministry, which centered in the synagogues of Galilee. Initially, Jesus was popular and well received by his audience. But soon he was greeted with skepticism.

THE POWER OF THE AUTHORITATIVE WORD (4:31–44)

Luke records four incidents in this section that take place in Capernaum, a kind of home base for his Galilean ministry. Here Jesus shows his power over demons and physical diseases.

Section Summary

Two major themes of Luke emerge in this section. First, Jesus performed miracles that were examples of his power and authority. Second, Luke clarifies for his readers how Jesus's self-proclaimed messianic mission is to be interpreted.

WORD PICTURE

Kingdom of God

Verse 43 is the first occurrence of the expression "kingdom of God" in Luke. As he anticipated that his readers already possessed some understanding of its meaning, Luke made no attempt to define the expression.

QUESTIONS TO GUIDE YOUR STUDY

1. Why is Jesus's victory over temptation such an encouragement for the believer? In what ways was his temptation different from ours? What steps or precautions might believers take to equip themselves for resisting temptation?
2. Describe Jesus's mission as he began his Galilean ministry? How was he received?
3. What is a parable? Why did Jesus use them in his teaching?
4. What message did the miracles of Jesus convey to those who witnessed them?

LUKE 5

BASIC STEPS IN FOLLOWING JESUS (5:1–11)

Obedience (vv. 1–5)

Simon Peter already had some kind of relationship with Jesus, but until this incident he was basically a fisherman. He fished as a business, not as a hobby, and he was good at it. He and his partners, James and John, were owners of a fishing business.

Jesus's command in verse 4 probably took Peter by surprise. His answer was typical of Peter's later responses to Jesus. He said what he thought but ended up doing as Jesus commanded.

HISTORICAL BACKGROUND

"Fishermen made a better-than-average income (even if they had a bad night . . .), so leaving their job is an act of radical commitment that they would expect to adversely affect them economically."

Craig S. Keener, The Bible Background Commentary: New Testament *(Downers Grove: InterVarsity Press, 1993), 201.*

Confession (vv. 6–8)

The miracle of the great shoal of fish overwhelmed not only Peter's nets and boats but also Peter himself. Peter asked Jesus to depart from him.

Commitment (vv. 9–11)

Fortunately for Peter, Jesus did not go away. Instead, he spoke words of comfort and challenge. He dealt kindly with Peter's fear and agitated spirit. He then called Peter to become a different kind of fisherman. No longer was he to catch fish; now he was to catch human beings.

Peter's response was total commitment. Giving up his business to follow Jesus was not easy, but his experience with Jesus brought him to the point of commitment. He cut his ties with the past. From now on he would follow Jesus.

HISTORICAL BACKGROUND

Pharisees

The teachers of the Law who opposed Jesus were comprised primarily of the Pharisees. They were the most influential of the three major Jewish sects (the other two being the Sadducees and Essenes). We first read of them in the second century BC.

They believed in a strict keeping of the law, as interpreted in their own traditions. They were separatists who sought to avoid contact with unclean things and unclean people. The "teachers of the law," or scribes, were professional students of the Law, and most of them were Pharisees.

Section Summary

Those who would follow Jesus must embrace three basic steps: (1) obedience, (2) confession, and(3) commitment. When Peter cut his ties to the past, it was the first step in his pilgrimage as a disciple. There can be no pilgrimage without a beginning.

JESUS HEALS A LEPER (5:12–16)

No group in ancient society was more pitiful than lepers. Their disease was a slow, lingering death. They died inch by inch. To make matters worse, lepers were cut off from the rest of society, including their families. Nothing but a corpse was worse than a leper. Yet Jesus dared to touch the leper and to speak the authoritative word that caused him to be cured.

BLASPHEMY (5:17–26)

A Delegation of Dignitaries (v. 17)

Pharisees and teachers of the law showed up to hear and observe Jesus. They came from all over Galilee and Judea, including Jerusalem itself. Luke mentions no sinister intent, but these religious leaders became Jesus's severest critics.

Sins Forgiven (vv. 18–20)

A paralytic was brought to Jesus for healing. To bypass the crowd surrounding Jesus, the men who brought the paralytic went onto the roof and lowered him through the tiles into the middle of the crowd in front of Jesus. He forgave the paralytic of his sins and then healed him.

Blasphemer or Savior? (vv. 21–26)

The scribes and Pharisees began accusing Jesus of blasphemy. He was claiming to do something only God can do—forgive sins.

The people who witnessed the miracle responded with praise for God's grace for the paralytic. "Awe" or fear is a common response by those who witness God's power.

Section Summary

The testimony of the New Testament is that Jesus was without sin. His opponents, however, accused him of several "sins." Because Jesus claimed to do something only God can do (forgive a man's sins), the scribes and Pharisees accused him of blasphemy. In contrast to the religious leaders, the crowd was amazed at Jesus's miracle of healing and gave praise to God.

HISTORICAL BACKGROUND

The tax collectors were outcasts from respectable society. They were collaborators with a foreign government. They had daily contact with all kinds of other "unclean" people. The word "sinners" here (v. 30) means the common people who paid little heed to the religious scruples of the Pharisees.

ASSOCIATING WITH SINNERS (5:27–32)

Luke presents Jesus as the friend of sinners. Jesus freely associated with all kinds of people, which placed him on a collision course with the Pharisees.

In response to his critics, Jesus used the analogy of the physician who went where the sick people were.

Section Summary

True Christianity has always broken down economic, social, ethnic, and racial barriers.

HISTORICAL BACKGROUND

Wineskins

Wine making has always been a major industry in Syria-Palestine. In Old Testament times, the presses for making wine were usually cut or hewed out of rock and were connected to channels to lower rock-cut vats where the juice was allowed to collect. The juice was then poured into jars or wineskins. Wineskins were dehaired skins of small animals such as goats, which were sewn together to hold milk and wine. The point of Jesus's parable is the incompatibility of the old wineskin with the new wine. New wine, if placed in old wineskins, will destroy both skins and wine because as the new wine ferments, the old wineskin is not sufficiently pliable and will thus burst, spilling the wine.

NEGLECTING RELIGIOUS DISCIPLINES (5:33–39)

Fast or Feast? (vv. 33–35)

Pious Pharisees fasted twice each week. They apparently viewed fasting as a mark of special commitment and dedication. They criticized Jesus's disciples for not fasting.

Jesus explained that fasting during a wedding is inappropriate. The Bible refers to the messianic age as a wedding feast.

The Old and the New (vv. 36–39)

Jesus broadened his application with another analogy, which Luke calls a parable. The issue was the relationship between the new way of Jesus and the old way of Judaism. Jesus's way simply cannot be "patched" onto Judaism like a piece of cloth.

Section Summary

The human response to the gospel is one of Luke's strong emphases. Jesus's mission included several calls: (1) a call for sinners to repent; (2) a call to follow Jesus; and (3) a call that addressed the outcasts.

QUESTIONS TO GUIDE YOUR STUDY

1. Jesus freely associated with the outcasts of his day. What are some ways we might implement his example in our society?

2. What was Jesus's point regarding fasting? Why did the Pharisees take issue with him?
3. Consider Jesus's parable of the old and the new wine. What made Judaism so inadequate to contain the new way of the gospel?

LUKE 6

BREAKING THE SABBATH (6:1–11)

Lord of the Sabbath (vv. 1–5)

Keeping the Sabbath was near the top of the list of Pharisaic virtues. As in other areas, the Pharisees had their own rigid definitions and requirements. They were determined to avoid even the appearance of working on the Sabbath.

Jesus kept the Sabbath as the Old Testament had intended, but he made no effort to conform to the rigid scruples of the Pharisees. He referred his critics to the example of David. When David was desperately hungry, he broke the law by eating the bread of the presence (vv. 3–4). If David could do this, how much more could the Son of David?

NEW TESTAMENT REFERENCE

Jesus on occasion fasted, and he often spent time in prayer. However, he did not make fasting into a prescribed ritual. The kind of fasting he practiced was a natural fasting that resulted from preoccupation with more important matters (see John 4:31–34).

Doing Good on the Sabbath (vv. 6–11)

The original intent of the Sabbath was to provide a day of rest that would free people from the tyranny of a life of unending toil. God, therefore, instituted the Sabbath for the good of humanity.

Verse 11 describes the deep fury of Jesus's critics. They felt humiliated. Now they were more than critics; they were enemies.

HISTORICAL BACKGROUND

Sabbath

The Sabbath is the day of rest, considered holy to God. It derives from God's rest on the seventh day following his creation of the universe. It was viewed as a sign of the covenant relation between God and his people and of the eternal rest which he promised them. The habit of Jesus was to observe the Sabbath as a day of worship in the synagogues, but his failure to comply with the minute restrictions of the Pharisaic observance of the law brought conflict and confrontation with the religious leaders of his day.

Section Summary

In this section Jesus claimed that he, as Son of Man, was Lord of the Sabbath. He also manifested this authority by healing a man on the Sabbath.

DISCIPLESHIP AS A WAY OF LIFE (6:12–49)

In this section, Jesus selected his closest followers and instructed them and his other disciples. Verses 20–49 make up what is sometimes called the Sermon on the Plain.

CHOOSING OF THE TWELVE DISCIPLES (6:12–19)

Luke's account of the choosing of the Twelve emphasizes the all-night prayer that preceded the choice. The selection of the Twelve signified the new Israel that Jesus was creating. The 12 apostles corresponded to the 12 tribes of Israel.

LISTS OF DISCIPLES IN THE NEW TESTAMENT

1. Matthew 10:2–4
2. Mark 3:16–19
3. Luke 6:12–16
4. Acts 1:13

HISTORICAL BACKGROUND

The word "disciples" (v. 13) means "learners" or "followers" and refers to the larger group of Jesus's followers. The word "apostles" means "messengers sent out under the authority of another." The word was most often used later of those whom the risen Christ sent out as witnesses of his resurrection. The Twelve formed the core of these special witnesses. Luke noted that after Judas's death a replacement was chosen.

THE SERMON ON THE PLAIN (6:20–49)

Beatitudes and Woes (vv. 20–26)

Luke now introduces us to Jesus's second sermon (the first was recorded in 4:16–30).

Whereas his first was addressed to "crowds," this sermon he addressed to his disciples.

Beatitudes. The word "blessed" means "happy" or "fortunate." Jesus pronounced as blessed the poor, the hungry, the sad, and the persecuted.

Woes. Jesus also pronounced woes on the counterparts of the blessed: the rich, the well fed, the merry, and the popular.

Here we find one of Luke's major emphases, which is the great reversal the kingdom brings. His list of beatitudes and woes are exact opposites. Jesus turns everything upside down to make an important point: the kingdom of God is the ultimate good.

Love of One's Enemies (vv. 27–36)

Love is the heart of Jesus's teachings, and these verses are crucial to understanding what he meant. Jesus defined love as action, not emotion. Whatever we feel about our enemies, we are to act for good on their behalf.

The Golden Rule (v. 31)

This rule sums up Jesus's main point. Notice that Jesus stated the rule positively, not negatively. The Golden Rule calls on followers of Jesus to take the initiative. How do you want others to treat you? Treat them that way. Do the good for them that you want done for you.

HISTORICAL BACKGROUND

The Golden Rule is also stated in Matt 7:12. The designation, Golden Rule, doesn't appear in the Bible, and its origin in English is difficult to trace. The principle of the Golden Rule is found in many religions, but Jesus's wording of it was original and unique.

Judging Others (vv. 37–42)

There is nothing unusual or difficult about liking people who like us or doing good to those who do good to us. This is how most people act.

Jesus calls us to God's kind of love. Those who practice this kind of love are recognized as sons of God.

Tests of Goodness (vv. 43–49)

The Fruit Test (vv. 43–45). A person's character is revealed by what he or she says and does. Trees are known by their fruits. Likewise, both good people and evil people reveal their inner attitudes and values by their actions and words.

The Obedience Test (vv. 46–49). Those who call Jesus "Lord" are not really his unless they practice what he tells them to do. What they profess should match what they practice.

HISTORICAL BACKGROUND

A centurion was a Roman officer who commanded about 100 men. We get a uniformly favorable impression of centurions who are mentioned in the New Testament. Centurions were usually career soldiers, and they formed the backbone of the Roman military force.

Section Summary

Luke's emphasis on love for one's enemies is seen most clearly when one compares his expanded account with the parallel in Matthew.

QUESTIONS TO GUIDE YOUR STUDY

1. What sparked confrontation between Jesus and the religious leaders?
2. What does it mean to be "blessed"? How do poverty, hunger, and distress transform into blessing?
3. The Golden Rule is a commonly used teaching today. What is the point of the Golden Rule?

LUKE 7

JESUS HEALS THE CENTURION'S SERVANT (7:1–10)

Jesus responded to the faith of a Roman centurion by healing his servant. Similar accounts are also found in Matt 8:5–13 and John 4:46–53. Jesus marveled at the faith of this Gentile—a faith greater than he had found in all of Israel.

NEW TESTAMENT REFERENCE

The Gospels record three specific instances of Jesus restoring the dead: (1) Jairus's daughter (Matt 9:18–26; Mark 5:21–43; Luke 8:40–56); (2) the son of the widow of Nain (Luke 7:11), and (3) Lazarus (John 11:1–44). These people were restored to life, but later they died. Jesus's power over death in their lives, however, points to his own unique resurrection. He was raised as the conqueror of death, never again to die (Rom 6:9).

JESUS RAISES THE WIDOW OF NAIN'S SON (7:11–17)

Part of Jesus's ministry involved restoring the dead to life.

Jesus restored the son of a widow at Nain. This young man was her only son. She was dependent on him for support, protection, and companionship. "Fear came over everyone" who saw this, "and they glorified God."

Section Summary

In this section we find Jesus responding to people in various ways. He was amazed at the faith of the centurion and healed his servant. In another account, he responded with compassion to the needs of the widow and then brought her son back to life.

JESUS REVEALS HIMSELF TO JOHN THE BAPTIST (7:18–30)

A Question (vv. 18–20)

John the Baptist was imprisoned because he boldly spoke the truth. While John was in prison, his disciples brought him word of what Jesus was doing. John then sent two disciples to Jesus with this question, "Are you the one who is to come, or should we expect someone else?"

An Answer (vv. 21–23)

John's earlier statements show that he thought of the Messiah's work primarily in terms of judgment on evil. John apparently was perplexed because Jesus was not acting as he expected.

Jesus's answer to John supports this interpretation of John's perplexity. Jesus continued his ministry of helping and healing in the presence of John's disciples. Then he sent them back with this answer to John's question: "Go and report to John what you have seen and heard: The blind receive their sight, the lame walk, those who have leprosy are cleansed, the deaf hear, the dead are raised, and the poor are told the good news."

Jesus Bears Witness to John the Baptist as His Forerunner (vv. 24–30)

After the messengers of John left, Jesus delivered a powerful and lyrical tribute to John. He portrayed John as a bold, courageous prophet.

Section Summary

When John the Baptist questioned whether Jesus was really the Messiah, Jesus provided an answer that highlighted six of his works that fulfilled Old Testament messianic promises. Jesus clearly bore witness that John the Baptist was his forerunner.

JESUS EXPERIENCES REJECTION (7:31–35)

Some accused Jesus of the sins of the people whom he associated with. Although they rejected the austere John and his message, they also rejected the sociable Jesus and his message. Despite the differences between John and Jesus, their message was the same.

JESUS FORGIVES SINS (7:36–50)

Just as Jesus sometimes ate with tax collectors and sinners, so he sometimes ate with Pharisees. Therefore, when Simon the Pharisee invited Jesus to dinner, Jesus accepted.

It was not uncommon for people from the street to come in and observe such festivities. But Simon was shocked to see a sinful woman come in and proceed to anoint Jesus's feet as described in verse 38.

HISTORICAL BACKGROUND

In an account that parallels the New Testament closely, the Jewish historian Josephus stated that Herod Antipas arrested John and subsequently executed him at Macharaeus because "he feared that John's so extensive influence over people might lead to an uprising." (*Antiquities*, 18.5.2)

OLD TESTAMENT REFERENCE

What Jesus told John shows that Jesus's work was a fulfillment of a number of prophecies in Isaiah: "On that day the deaf will hear the words of a document, and out of a deep darkness the eyes of the blind will see. The humble will have joy after joy in the LORD, and the poor people will rejoice in the Holy One of Israel." (Isa 29:18–19)

WORD PICTURE

Sinners

The character of this woman is important due to Luke 7:39,47. This woman could have been a sinner because of her occupation. Tax collectors, tanners, camel drivers, and customs collectors, among others, were considered ceremonially impure because of their occupations and could be labeled "sinners." In this instance, however, this woman's sinfulness involved moral, not ceremonial, matters.

Simon quickly formed his own conclusion based on what he saw. He assumed two things about a prophet: (1) a prophet would have special insight into a person's character, and (2) a prophet would not knowingly let an immoral woman anoint his feet. He therefore concluded that Jesus was not a prophet.

WORD PICTURE

The point of Jesus's parable is that regarding forgiveness of sins, each of us has been forgiven a debt none of us could pay. The degree of our love and gratitude depends on our own estimate of the amount of that debt and of the grace of God in forgiving us. A person, therefore, does not have to be a sinful reprobate in order to appreciate the love of God.

To show his true prophetic insight by reading the thoughts of Simon, Jesus told the parable of the two debtors. The debtors owed a debt they could not pay. The creditor forgave them both. Each should have been grateful. Differences between what each was forgiven are relative. Each should have been grateful based on what he had been forgiven, not based on comparing his debt with the debts of others.

In response to this woman's act of worship, Jesus claimed to forgive her sins: "Your faith has saved you. Go in peace." Notice that Jesus did not say, "God forgives you." Instead, he exercised his divine prerogative and personally announced that her sins were forgiven. This claim once again irritated his critics.

Section Summary

We see Luke's theme of the great reversal in this passage. Once again the one expected to have the inside track to forgiveness and salvation—a religious leader—is found outside of God's kingdom. On the other hand, the outcast—a woman who was a sinner and despised by religious leaders such as Simon—found forgiveness. Again, the last have become the first and the first last.

QUESTIONS TO GUIDE YOUR STUDY

1. What prompted John to question Jesus's messiahship? What was significant about Jesus's response to John?
2. The same people who rejected John's message also rejected Jesus's message. What about this message caused the people to reject it?
3. What was the point of Jesus's parable of the two debtors?

HISTORICAL BACKGROUND

Luke 8:1–3 signified the higher plane to which Jesus lifted women. In his day it was a man's world. Only males participated fully in synagogue services. Jesus treated women as persons in their own right. He not only liberated them from what afflicted them but also included them among his followers. The latter relationship was reciprocal; it included not only his help for them but also the help they could give to him and the others.

LUKE 8

A SUMMARY OF JESUS'S MINISTRY (8:1–3)

At this point in his narrative, Luke summarizes Jesus's ministry of proclaiming the good news of the gospel of God's kingdom and ministry of healing. This summary is like the one in 4:40–44, but here Luke mentions the Twelve and "some women" and even names the latter three—Mary Magdalene, Joanna, and Susanna. These women had been healed of evil spirits and other infirmities.

THE PARABLE OF THE SOILS (8:4–15)

Jesus told the parable of four kinds of soils. They are as follows:

Hard Ground. As in the case of the sower's seed, some of Jesus's words fell on hard ground. These people included his enemies who closed their eyes to the light and their ears to the truth.

Shallow Soil. Some seed fell on shallow soil; and some of Jesus's words were heard by superficial followers, whose early enthusiasm faded and disappeared in times of trouble.

Weed-Filled Soil. Still other seed fell in the weed-filled corners of the field. Some of Jesus's words gained a sympathetic hearing but never bore fruit because the hearers allowed cares and pleasures to predominate.

Good Soil. Fortunately, some seed fell on good soil and yielded much fruit, and some of his words were heard by genuine followers whose lives testified to the reality of their faith.

PARABLE OF THE LAMP (8:16–18)

These three verses are found elsewhere in Luke in three separate places (11:33; 12:2; 19:26). Luke uses them here to reinforce the message of the parable of the soils. Those who heard the word with faith and commitment have the light, and the light is for sharing that others may see. God intends that the light be seen, not hidden. Each person, therefore, should be careful to hear as God intends. Hearing involves a twofold responsibility—to receive and share the light.

JESUS'S TRUE FAMILY (8:19–21)

This incident further reinforced the lesson about hearing. Jesus taught here that the members of his larger family are those who hear the Word of God and do it. The occasion for this lesson was the coming of Jesus's mother and brothers.

Section Summary

This section of Luke's narrative concerns Jesus's teaching about the hearing of God's Word and, in particular, hearing God's Word in Jesus's parables. Luke informs his readers that belonging to Jesus's family is not a matter of physical kinship but of hearing and doing God's Word.

JESUS CALMS THE SEA (8:22–25)

As the disciples were crossing the Sea of Galilee, Jesus fell asleep in the boat. Suddenly, a squall descended upon the sea. The winds and raging waters placed the boat in great danger. Fearing for their lives, the disciples awakened Jesus who got up and commanded the elements to stop.

WORD PICTURE

Lesson: Response is determined by the kind of soil on which the word of the gospel falls. The seed of truth will grow only in "receptive" soil.

As followers of Christ, we must let the seed of God's Word take root in our lives so we will bear fruit.

NEW TESTAMENT REFERENCE

Mark's account of this incident reveals that Jesus's family had come to try to take him home because they thought he was losing his mind. This is understandable, for John 7:5 states that his brothers did not believe in him. Jesus was everything a brother and a son should be, but when family interests threatened his mission, he put the will of his Father first.

NEW TESTAMENT REFERENCE

Miracle Stories in the Gospels

Jesus's calming of the sea is a typical account of a miracle story. These stories normally contain three elements:

1. A description of the need (e.g., 8:23: they "were in danger"),
2. The miracle itself (e.g., 8:24: "He . . . rebuked the wind and the raging waves . . . and there was a calm."), and
3. The reaction to the miracle (e.g., 8:25: "Who then is this?").

WORD PICTURE

Although God does not always shield us from the destructiveness of all life's storms, he can always be trusted to be there in the storm with us.

In this case, likely Luke wanted his readers to understand how Jesus's power and might related to their own situation. He wanted them to recognize that because of their Lord's power there was no need to fear. Jesus's power was greater than their needs. Therefore, they should not doubt or fear but only believe, for their Lord can and will calm the storms that rage against them.

"Where is your faith?" was Jesus's rebuke of his disciples for their lack of faith. They failed to trust God to watch them as they went about doing his will.

The disciples' fear of the storm was replaced with a different fear. After Jesus's demonstration of power, they felt fear and amazement in the presence of one who could command obedience from the winds and water: "Who then is this?"

JESUS HEALS A DEMON-POSSESSED MAN (8:26–39)

Next, Jesus and his disciples encountered a demon-possessed man. Society tried to restrain him in chains, but he had broken these and was living among the tombs.

Jesus exorcised the demons and allowed them to enter a nearby herd of pigs.

The sad part of this story was the people's reaction. They asked Jesus to leave. Luke mentioned their great fear as the reason. This kind of superstitious fear rejects Jesus and the help he offers.

The man healed of the demons begged Jesus to let him accompany him. Jesus told the man to return home and tell others what God had done. This man, probably a Gentile, became the first witness for Jesus in Gentile territory.

JESUS HEALS THE HEMORRHAGING WOMAN (8:40–48)

When Jesus returned to Galilee, he found the crowds waiting. As he pressed through the crowd, a woman who was ill for 12 years with an incurable malady touched his garment, believing that doing so would heal her. Upon touching his garment, she was immediately healed. Jesus responded to her by saying, "Your faith has saved you."

WORD PICTURE

At least two themes are prominent in the account of these events. First, with these two miracles, Luke showed his readers that two of the effects of the fall—disease and death—are subject to Jesus. Second, salvation comes through faith, and the woman and Jairus revealed the kind of faith Jesus seeks. The big lesson of this portion of Luke's narrative is that Jesus can be trusted.

JESUS RAISES JAIRUS'S DAUGHTER (8:49–56)

While Jesus was still speaking, Jairus, the synagogue leader, received word that his daughter died. Hearing this news, Jesus said to him, "Don't be afraid. Only believe, and she will be saved." Jesus went to Jairus's house and commanded the child to "get up!" Her spirit returned to her, and she stood up.

Section Summary

These four miracles of Jesus show God's grace and power in four areas that threaten human life and welfare: (1) nature's sometimes destructive force; (2) the enslavement resulting from the power of evil; (3) the pain and helplessness of lingering illness; and (4) the fearful reality of bereavement and death.

QUESTIONS TO GUIDE YOUR STUDY

1. What is the point of the parable of the soils? What kind of soil are you?
2. What do the four miracles of 8:22–56 tell us about Jesus?
3. What point was Luke making for his readers in his accounts of the healing of the woman with a hemorrhage and the raising of Jairus's daughter?

LUKE 9

THE MISSION OF THE TWELVE (9:1–6)

The disciples were with Jesus during much of his Galilean ministry. Now Jesus sent them out to do what they saw him do.

HEROD'S QUESTION ABOUT JESUS (9:7–9)

Herod Antipas heard reports of what Jesus and the Twelve were doing. He was aware of three explanations about who Jesus was: (1) some thought Jesus was John the Baptist raised from the dead; (2) others thought he was Elijah; and (3) still others believed that one of the ancient prophets was brought back from the dead.

The report that perplexed Herod was the one about John the Baptist, whom Herod ordered beheaded. Perhaps there was a certain amount of guilt in Herod's heart. Luke records that Herod wanted to see Jesus, perhaps to reassure himself that Jesus was not John. Luke 23:6–12 records the sad scene when Jesus and Herod finally met.

HISTORICAL BACKGROUND

Herod Antipas was the son of Herod the Great. He was tetrarch of Galilee and Perea (4 BC–AD 39). Jesus referred to him as "that fox" (Luke 13:32).

THE FEEDING OF THE FIVE THOUSAND (9:10–17)

This miracle is the only one in all four Gospels that occurred in Galilee, and the only one that is recorded in all four.

After the Twelve returned from their mission, they reported to Jesus. He and the Twelve withdrew to a remote place. However, the crowds heard of it and followed.

Although the disciples wanted to dismiss the crowd, Jesus commanded them to feed the crowd. The crowd numbered about 5,000, and the disciples had only five loaves of bread and two fish. Taking the loaves, Jesus gave thanks and then broke the bread. He performed a miraculous multiplication of the available food and provided an abundance that was more than enough nourishment for the crowd. Luke records that the disciples gathered 12 basketfuls of leftovers.

WORD PICTURE

Disciple

The basic meaning of the word *disciple* is "learner" or "pupil." Normally it referred to the adherent of a particular teacher or religious/philosophical school. Disciples of the rabbis could select their teachers. Jesus often demanded extreme levels of personal renunciation (loss of family, property, etc.). He asked for lifelong allegiance as the essential means of doing the will of God.

Section Summary

The feeding of the 5,000 was a turning point in Jesus's ministry. After this event, his popularity with the masses declined, and he devoted more of his time to instructing the disciples.

PETER'S CONFESSION (9:18–22)

Each of the Synoptic Gospels records the confession of Peter (Matt 16:13–33; Mark 8:27–33), but only Luke places it in the context of Jesus's prayer life.

Peter declared Jesus to be God's promised Messiah. His confession that Jesus is "God's Messiah" is significant at this point in Luke's Gospel.

At this stage of their understanding, however, the disciples saw Jesus as the Messiah of popular Jewish expectations.

JESUS'S TEACHING ON THE PASSION AND DISCIPLESHIP (9:23–27)

Jesus explained that he would be crucified and that those who follow him would need to take up their cross.

WORD PICTURE

The word "transfigured," in more common English, is translated "transformed." The Greek word used is *metamorphoō*, from which we get the English word *metamorphosis*.

OLD TESTAMENT REFERENCE

In the transfiguration, Moses symbolizes the Law, while Elijah stands for the Prophets. Jesus had come to fulfill both. In Old Testament writings, these two men were also connected with the age of the Messiah. Their appearance with Jesus meant in part that he was the prophet Moses foretold (Deut 18:15) and the Messiah whom Elijah would precede (Mal 4:5).

THE TRANSFIGURATION (9:28–36)

Each of the Synoptic Gospels records the transfiguration, but only Luke tells us that it took place while Jesus was praying.

Jesus took the three inner-circle disciples (Peter, James, and John) with him to a high mountain, likely Mount Hermon. There they witnessed Jesus transfigured before their eyes. For that brief moment, they observed him as the heavenly Lord. His personal appearance and that of his garments changed.

Joining Jesus and the disciples were Moses and Elijah. Luke is the only one who records what Moses, Elijah, and Jesus spoke about: "His departure, which he was about to accomplish in Jerusalem." A cloud enveloped the group, and a voice came from the cloud challenging Peter, James, and John to listen to Jesus when he told them about what the future held.

Section Summary

The transfiguration was an open display for the disciples of the glory Jesus had before the incarnation. It was also a foreshadowing of Jesus's resurrection and return.

THE HEALING OF THE BOY WITH AN UNCLEAN SPIRIT (9:37–43A)

After Jesus and the disciples descended the mountain, they met the crowds and a desperate situation. The disciples were unable to heal a boy with an evil spirit.

In bringing deliverance, Jesus challenged both the father and the disciples to greater faith and ardent prayer. The father's confession of the emptiness of his faith made contact with the riches of Christ's grace. Jesus's healing of the boy left the people astonished.

THE SECOND PASSION ANNOUNCEMENT (9:43B–45)

Jesus spoke again to his disciples about what lay ahead for him. Jesus's second prediction of his passion reminded the disciples that he was a suffering Messiah rather than a conquering Messiah. They still did not grasp what he was saying.

WHAT MAKES A PERSON GREAT? (9:46–50)

Jesus now presented instructions about discipleship and humility in order to spotlight the self-seeking strife erupting among the disciples.

Section Summary

The disciples were arguing about who among them was the greatest. Jesus used this as an opportunity to teach them about the way of the cross. A humble, childlike trust and a tolerant spirit toward others are the marks of followers of Jesus.

HISTORICAL BACKGROUND

James and John were called Boanerges, which means "sons of thunder." The name may be indicative of the thunderous temperament these brothers apparently possessed. It is interesting to note that James would be the first apostle to give his life in the service of Christ. John would later be called the "apostle of love."

THE MISSION TO SAMARIA (9:51–56)

This is the first mention of the Samaritans in Luke's Gospel. The people of a Samaritan village refused to welcome Jesus because he was a Jew on his way to Jerusalem. The response of James and John in verse 54 shows how far they were from sharing Jesus's commitment to the way of the cross. Wanting to call down fire on those who rejected them is an understandable reaction, but Jesus rebuked them.

TEACHINGS ON DISCIPLESHIP (9:57–62)

Luke has the most complete account of Jesus's contact with three prospective disciples who lacked commitment.

HISTORICAL BACKGROUND

Interestingly, 70 Gentile nations are mentioned in Gen 10.

Section Summary

Discipleship is not a frivolous decision. Jesus demands unqualified commitment of his disciples. Those who will be his disciples must first count the cost before making such a commitment.

QUESTIONS TO GUIDE YOUR STUDY

1. What lessons did the feeding of the 5,000 teach the disciples? What does this event teach us about Jesus?
2. Review the Gospel accounts of the transfiguration (Matt 16:27–17:8; Mark 8:38–9:8; Luke 9:26–36). What was its purpose? Why were Elijah and Moses present?
3. What was the disciples' understanding of Jesus's messiahship? Why was Peter's confession significant?

HISTORICAL BACKGROUND

Samaria and Samaritans

In the days of Christ, the relationship between the Jews and the Samaritans was greatly strained. The animosity was so great that the Jews bypassed Samaria as they traveled between Galilee and Judea. They went an extra distance through the barren land of Perea on the eastern side of the Jordan River to avoid going through Samaria. Jesus forbade this animosity. He rebuked his disciples for their hostility to the Samaritans (Luke 9:55–56), healed a Samaritan leper (Luke 17:16), honored a Samaritan for his neighborliness (Luke 10:30–37), praised a Samaritan for his gratitude (Luke 17:11–18), asked a drink of a Samaritan woman (John 4:7), and preached to the Samaritans. Then in Acts 1:8 Jesus challenged his disciples to witness in Samaria. Philip, a deacon, opened a mission in Samaria (Acts 8:5). A small Samaritan community continues to this day to follow the traditional worship near Shechem.

LUKE 10

THE TRAINING OF THE SEVENTY-TWO FOR MISSIONARY SERVICE (10:1–16)

At this point Luke records the mission of the 72, which is similar to the mission of the Twelve in 9:1–6. Luke provides more fully Jesus's instruction here than he did for the earlier sending of the Twelve.

Section Summary

Jesus appointed 72 missionaries who were to go ahead of him to every town and place he was about to go. They were "sent ones" who would proclaim the gospel message and prepare the villages for Jesus's spiritual coming and resurrection.

CAUSE FOR REJOICING (10:17–24)

The Return of the Seventy-Two (vv. 17–20)

The words *joy* and *rejoice* are the keys to this passage. The 72 returned with joy after their successful mission. Jesus shared their joy but reminded them to rejoice primarily not in being empowered for service but in having been saved by grace.

The Blessedness of the Disciples (vv. 21–24)

These verses complete the description of the responsibilities and privileges of discipleship begun in 9:51.

Section Summary

The 72 who were appointed and sent to proclaim the gospel returned rejoicing over a successful mission. Jesus told them they were privileged to see and hear what the kings and prophets of the old order had yearned to see and hear.

THE PARABLE OF THE GOOD SAMARITAN (10:25–37)

A lawyer asked Jesus two questions. The first question was, "What must I do to inherit eternal life?" Jesus responded by telling the lawyer the answer was written in the law. The lawyer correctly identified Deut 6:5 and Lev 19:18 as the answer. This led to the second question, "And who is my neighbor?" Jesus answered with the parable of the good Samaritan. This parable is unique to Luke and does not appear to be linked chronologically to the preceding or following incidents. Probably no parable has been allegorized more often than this one.

On the road between Jerusalem and Jericho, a Jewish traveler was assaulted by violent men, who robbed him and left him for dead. Both a priest and a Levite who passed by refused to help their injured countryman because they would incur expensive and inconvenient ceremonial defilement by contact with someone who might be dead. Jesus shocked his audience by suddenly introducing a hated Samaritan who showed compassion by dressing the victim's wounds, letting the man ride the donkey through dangerous territory while he walked, and paying money to an innkeeper for an extended convalescence for the injured man. The Samaritan even promised credit for the additional funds if they were needed.

HISTORICAL BACKGROUND

The 17-mile road from Jerusalem to Jericho drops more than 1,000 feet. It is wild country with many places for robbers to hide.

WORD PICTURE

Jesus deliberately chose an outsider, and a hated one at that, for his hero to indicate that being a neighbor is not a matter of nationality or race. He used the parable to show the lawyer that he had asked the wrong question. The question should not be, "Who is my neighbor?" but "To whom can I be a neighbor?"

Section Summary

The Samaritan showed by his actions what love is. The reality of his compassion is seen in what he did to help the man. Christian love is acting for the good of the other persons—whoever they are, whatever the cost, and however we feel.

MARTHA AND MARY (10:38–42)

Luke alone records this incident. The story emphasizes that quiet dependence on Jesus is more important than bustling service.

Section Summary

Within this short passage is a clear emphasis on the importance of hearing Jesus's word. To listen to Jesus as Mary did is the best thing one can do, even better than serving.

QUESTIONS TO GUIDE YOUR STUDY

1. Why does Luke provide such a strong emphasis on the mission of the 72?
2. Describe the mission of the 72. Were they successful? How were the 72 "blessed"?
3. Contrast the attitudes of Mary and Martha. What was Jesus's response to each?

HISTORICAL BACKGROUND

Disciples of the rabbis often asked for instruction on specific practices. In view of all the disciples had seen Jesus do, it is interesting that they asked him to teach them to pray.

WORD PICTURE

"Bread" is an example of a figure of speech known as synecdoche, in which a part (bread) represents the whole (food). Bread, therefore, is a request for the basic necessities of life, not for luxuries.

WORD PICTURE

We learn to pray by praying. The one who prays out of a sense of need is the one who truly learns to pray. Jesus insisted that perseverance with a God-honored request will bring a positive result. It is important to keep in mind that the context makes clear that our persistence does not pressure a reluctant God into responding to our requests; rather, he examines our motives to determine the presence of genuine desire.

LUKE 11

JESUS'S TEACHING ON PRAYER (11:1–13)

The Model Prayer (vv. 1–4)

Luke's Gospel emphasizes Jesus's prayer life. The disciples' awareness of this caused them to make their request. He answered them first by giving them a model prayer.

The prayer includes several petitions.

"Your name be honored as holy." This first petition asks God to cause his name to be honored as holy, or "glorified." "Name" refers to God's reputation and thus his honor.

"Your kingdom come." Although the kingdom had already come in Jesus's ministry, its final consummation will be in the future.

"Give us each day our daily bread." There is confusion about what the word *daily* means. Suggested meanings are: (1) bread that is essential for existence, (2) bread of the coming day, or (3) bread for the present day.

"Forgive us our sins." The Model Prayer assumes the regular need for confessing sin, even as 1 John 1:9 does. The issue is not one of salvation but the regular cleansing from sin that each believer needs.

"Do not bring us into temptation." Helpful paraphrases of this idea might include, "Do not allow us to enter into temptation that could destroy us" or "Keep us from yielding to temptation."

Section Summary

The Model Prayer contains the components and attitudes that Jesus's disciples should exhibit and incorporate into their lives. The first half of this prayer focuses Godward while the second half focuses usward. It's an example of the kind of prayer God hears and honors.

The Need to Pray (vv. 5–8)

After teaching the disciples how to pray, Jesus turned to a more difficult task—teaching them the need to pray. Jesus reinforced the Model Prayer with the parable of the persistent friend.

The Encouragement to Pray (vv. 9–13)

Verse 9 is an encouragement to continue in praying, whereas verse 10 is a promise to those who do.

The progression of commands—ask, seek, knock—is an example of the figure of speech called synonymous parallelism, in which the same basic thought is repeated rhythmically.

Section Summary

The person who prays out of a sense of need is the one who truly learns to pray.

THE BEELZEBUL CONTROVERSY (11:14–23)

Beelzebul is a name used for Satan in the New Testament. On more than one occasion, Jesus's opponents accused him of being linked with the devil. Here he answered them by using language reminiscent of Exod 8:19 to point to the irresistible conclusion that God's power was at work. God was using the casting out of demons to press his sovereign claims on those who saw these signs.

HISTORICAL BACKGROUND

"'This is the finger of God,' the magicians said to Pharaoh. But Pharaoh's heart was hard, and he would not listen to them, as the LORD had said." (Exod 8:19).

THE RETURN OF THE UNCLEAN SPIRIT AND TRUE BLESSEDNESS (11:24–28)

Jesus's concluding warning shows that a person who expelled the spirit of evil (that is, a demon) must replace it with a more powerful source of strength. The kingdom of God can bring a full and complete victory over evil.

WORD PICTURE

Woe

The word *woe* is an interjection of grief or denunciation and is often rendered "alas!" Jesus used the word *woe* here not as a curse but as an expression of deep regret. Jesus's purpose for these woes was to expose the sins of the Pharisees and lawyers to try to help them and the people adversely influenced by them.

THE SIGN OF JONAH (11:29–32)

At this point, Luke answers the request for a sign in 11:16 by linking it to the tradition concerning the present generation's desire for a sign.

Signs do not produce faith. Even the greatest sign, the resurrection, will not produce faith in an unwilling heart.

SAYINGS ABOUT LIGHT (11:33–36)

A lamp is made to shine. The eye is like a lamp for the body: good eyes illumine, but diseased eyes distort and darken.

A DENUNCIATION OF THE PHARISEES AND SCRIBES (11:37–54)

After Jesus spoke, he accepted an invitation from a Pharisee to have lunch. When Jesus failed to follow rabbinic tradition for handwashing before eating, his host was astonished. Jesus sensed his host's displeasure and warned the Pharisee of the danger of emphasizing the external over the internal. What follows is a series of six woes: three against the Pharisees (vv. 42–44) and three against the lawyers, or scribes (vv. 42–52).

WORD PICTURE

All Greed

Greed is an insatiable desire and lust for more and more. It is all-consuming, so that all of life becomes focused on the accumulation of wealth. There is no room for anything, not even God. This is why it is so hard for a rich person to enter God's kingdom.

This uncontrolled behavior often is the reason for damaged or destroyed relationships as it is a grasping after the most and the best without regard for others.

Section Summary

With a series of woes, Jesus strongly denounced the Pharisees' and lawyers' practices that emphasized the outward over the inward, thus allowing their hypocrisy to remain unchanged.

QUESTIONS TO GUIDE YOUR STUDY

1. What encouragements to pray does Jesus give us?
2. What was the sign of Jonah? Why did Jesus give the people this sign?
3. Why did Jesus denounce the Pharisees and lawyers? How relevant are Jesus's woes when applied to today's religious systems?

LUKE 12

This chapter consists primarily of teachings Jesus addressed to his followers. The chapter's three main themes are: (1) courageous confession, (2) the proper perspective on possessions, and (3) faithful stewardship.

WARNINGS AND EXHORTATIONS (12:1–12)

Beware Hypocrisy (vv. 1–3)

Hypocrites try to hide the truth by pretending to be something they are not. Jesus charged the Pharisees with hypocrisy because they tried to hide what they really were behind masks of outward religious practices.

PERSONAL APPLICATION

"By the fear of the Lord, men depart from evil; by the fear of man, they run themselves into evil."

John Flavel

Fear and Trust (vv. 4–7)

Verses 4–12 clearly refer to a persecution situation. In such a time, disciples will be tempted to fear their persecutors. Why should they fear when all that persecutors can do is kill them? The Bible consistently declares that the fear of God is the only fear that is justified. If people fear God, they need be afraid of nothing else.

Speaking Up for Christ (vv. 8–12)

In situations when believers are tempted to deny Christ, they must be on their guard against denying him in word or deed.

This passage does warn about a sin for which there is no forgiveness. The person who persists in rejecting light and truth stands in danger of becoming so hardened that he or she attributes the work of the Spirit to Satan (cp. Matt 12:24–32). This is more than a personal affront against Jesus; it is a hardening of the heart against every attempt by God's Spirit to bring mercy, grace, and truth. Only people who refuse forgiveness are unforgivable.

WORD PICTURE

The Unpardonable Sin

The unpardonable sin involves setting one's mind against the Holy Spirit and crediting Satan with what is God's work. To do this is to blaspheme against the Holy Spirit. To "blaspheme" means to speak an insult against someone to defame a person's reputation and character.

The unpardonable sin is not restricted to Jesus's day. It happens today when a person sees a work that is without question God's work but claims it is Satan's work.

Section Summary

Having denounced (with the six woes) the glaring inconsistency of the Pharisees' behavior, Jesus's warning against their hypocrisy makes a fitting conclusion. Jesus also warns believers about fear, confession, and the unpardonable sin, but he assures them of God's presence and the Spirit's guidance in times of persecution.

THE PARABLE OF THE RICH FOOL (12:13–21)

Jesus refused to act as a judge in a family dispute about inheritance. He chose instead to deal with the moral issue involved in the dispute: covetousness. Covetousness is a combination of greed and envy. It is the desire for more and more, which often is activated by wanting what someone else has.

Section Summary

The parable of the rich fool is about greed and the folly of one's reliance on wealth. Jesus warned his followers against all forms of greed.

CARE AND ANXIETY (12:22–34)

Having given a negative example of the principle in verse 15 with the parable of the rich fool, Luke provides a corrective to the believer's relationship to possessions. Whereas covetousness is the desire for more and more but never getting enough, anxiety is the crippling fear that there may not be enough.

The catchword in this section is *worry*. Jesus told his disciples that they need not worry for daily bread or clothing. In his sovereign care of his creation, God feeds the ravens and clothes the lilies. How much more, then, will he care for his children.

HISTORICAL BACKGROUND

"The lilies Jesus spoke of were the scarlet anemones. After one of the infrequent showers of summer rain, the mountain side would be scarlet with them; they bloomed one day and died."

William Barclay, The Gospel of Luke, *165.*

Section Summary

If all of nature trusts God to meet its needs, God's children should trust him to meet their needs. Rather than worry about "things" or use them as substitutes for life, believers should concentrate on the concerns of the kingdom.

THE WATCHFUL SERVANTS (12:35–48)

Whereas stewardship of possessions is implicit in the previous section, the rest of this chapter deals with stewardship of life and service. It does so in connection with the Lord's coming. The three parables on vigilance that follow emphasize the need for his followers to be ready for his coming.

JESUS—THE GREAT DIVIDER (12:49–53)

Jesus saw that the outcome of his mission would be a crisis out of which would come judgment and division. Jesus came to bring peace. His ultimate intent is not to bring the kind of division described in verses 51–53, but such division is inevitable when some choose to follow Christ and others reject him.

SIGNS OF THE TIME AND SETTLING WITH ONE'S OPPONENTS (12:54–59)

The multitudes to which Jesus spoke had an amazing lack of awareness of what was going on around them. They could read nature's signs, but they did not read the signs of the times in which they lived.

Section Summary

As believers, we must see that nothing keeps us from serving God faithfully, whether it be the seeming delay of Jesus's coming, persecution, or the unbelieving attitude of the world.

QUESTIONS TO GUIDE YOUR STUDY

1. What was the nature of the Pharisees' hypocrisy? What was sinful about it?
2. What is the unpardonable sin? Why is it unforgivable?
3. What is the relationship between our stewardship of life and service and the Lord's coming? What should be the believer's stance regarding his return?

LUKE 13

THE NEED TO REPENT (13:1–9)

Lessons from Tragedy (vv. 1–5)

The controversy story (vv. 1–5) and parable (vv. 6–9) in this passage are unique to Luke's Gospel. Verses 1–3 refer to a recent incident in which Pontius Pilate had several Galileans killed while they were offering sacrifices in the temple. Verses 4–5 recount another tragedy, the collapse of the Tower of Siloam, which killed 18 residents of Jerusalem.

The self-righteousness of reporters of the incident at the temple assumed the Galileans got what they deserved. Also, many assumed the construction accident at the tower was a divine judgment on workers willing to be paid with divine money. Jesus points out that in both incidents the victims of these tragedies were not especially evil. The lesson Jesus drew from these examples was the audience's need to repent.

Parable of the Barren Fig Tree (vv. 6–9)

This parable complements the teaching in verses 1–5. A tree that received special treatment from its owner had not borne fruit. The owner of the fig tree had every right to expect fruit after three years. He ordered it cut down, not only because it was useless but also because it exhausted the soil.

The vinedresser, however, interceded to give the tree one last opportunity. If the tree did not bear fruit in the coming year after additional care and treatment, it would then be cut down. The parable's point is that although God is patient and forbearing, continued refusal to repent spells certain doom.

Section Summary

Jesus's main lesson to his audience was the need to repent while there is opportunity.

THE HEALING OF THE CRIPPLED WOMAN ON THE SABBATH (13:10–17)

The debate over the proper use of the Sabbath caused ongoing controversy between Jesus and his opponents. Here Jesus took the initiative. He used his authority and power by healing on the Sabbath a woman who, for 18 years, had been incapable of walking erectly. The action annoyed the synagogue leader, who said to the crowd, "There are six days when work should be done; therefore come on those days and be healed and not on the Sabbath day."

HISTORICAL BACKGROUND

"The incident is recorded nowhere else, but is in entire harmony with Pilate's record for outrages. These Galileans at the feast in Jerusalem may have been involved in some insurrection against the Roman government, the leaders of whom Pilate had slain right in the temple courts where the sacrifices were going on. Jesus commented on the incident, but not as the reporters had expected. Instead of denunciation of Pilate, he turned it into a parable for their own conduct in the uncertainty of life."

A. T. Robertson, Word Pictures in the New Testament, *2:185.*

PERSONAL APPLICATION

Although the immediate application of this entire section (Luke 12:54–13:9) was to Israel, the principles apply to persons and groups in every generation. No issue is more urgent than the need to repent; the alternative is inevitable judgment.

Jesus denounced the leader's hypocrisy by showing that Jewish legalists violated the Sabbath in feeding their animals. The result was that while the people rejoiced in this display of God's glory and power, the ruler and Jesus's other adversaries were humiliated.

WORD PICTURE

Commenting on the point of these two parables, scholar I. Howard Marshall notes, "The stress is not so much on the idea of growth in itself as on the certainty that what appears tiny and insignificant will prove to have been the beginning of a mighty kingdom."

I. Howard Marshall, The Gospel of Luke *(Grand Rapids: Eerdmans, 1978), 561.*

THE PARABLES OF THE MUSTARD SEED AND LEAVEN (13:18–21)

The Mustard Seed (vv. 18–19)

Jesus first compared God's kingdom to what happens when a tiny mustard seed is sown. That little seed grows into a treelike plant as high as 10 feet—large enough for birds to nest in its branches.

The Leaven (vv. 20–21)

He then compared God's kingdom to what happens when a little leaven is added to a batch of flour. Only a small amount of leaven is required to make dough rise. The increase in size brought about by leaven was one of Jesus's points.

Section Summary

Jesus told the parables of the mustard seed and the leaven to affirm the certainty of God's purpose. The mustard seed grows into a tree large enough for many nesting birds. Even so will the kingdom's influence extend like a tree to encompass many.

WORD PICTURE

That Fox

Why did Jesus call Herod a "fox"? He may have referred to a fox's renowned cunning. If so, he was discounting Herod's death threat as a strategy to try to frighten Jesus away. In that day, "fox" also meant an insignificant person, as contrasted to a "lion," a person of true greatness.

THE NARROW DOOR (13:22–30)

Luke begins the second part of his travel narrative by mentioning Jesus's journey toward Jerusalem. Someone from the crowd asked Jesus the question, "Lord, . . . are only a few people going to be saved?" He did not answer the question directly. In essence, he asked another question, Are you among the saved?

The door of salvation stood open to any who would enter. The "many" who "will try to enter and won't be able" to are those who wait until the door is closed before trying to enter. No amount of effort or excuses will avail once the door is closed.

Section Summary

Jesus is the one who controls the destiny of humanity. He possesses the keys of the kingdom and as a result also of death and Hades. A person's ultimate destiny is determined by whether Jesus will say on the final day, "I know you."

WARNING ABOUT HEROD AND THE LAMENT OVER JERUSALEM (13:31–35)

We are not told why the Pharisees reported Herod's death threat to Jesus. He directed his reply to Herod; therefore, he accepted the report as accurate.

QUESTIONS TO GUIDE YOUR STUDY

1. What is the point of the parable of the barren fig tree? How does it apply to all generations?
2. Why were the Jewish leaders of Jesus's day at odds with him about the Sabbath?
3. What are Jesus's warnings in the "narrow door" passage (vv. 22–30)? What is the point we all need to heed?

LUKE 14

In this chapter Luke brought together a block of three episodes critical of the Pharisees. All three episodes center on eating, and they illustrate the hostility that official Judaism displayed toward Jesus and his gospel.

HEALING OF THE MAN WHOSE BODY WAS SWOLLEN WITH FLUID (14:1–6)

Luke highlighted the distorted values of the Pharisees, who showed no concern for the sick man. Under the guise of piety, they sought to censure Jesus for his Sabbath behavior. Jesus showed compassion for the man, healed him, and then silenced his opponents.

SAYINGS CONCERNING BANQUET BEHAVIOR (14:7–14)

In the context of Jesus's dining with a Pharisee, Luke introduces two unique sets of ethical teachings that illustrate Christian attitudes and behavior.

Seeking the Chief Places (vv. 7–11)

The first set of teachings is called a "parable," which is somewhat surprising, for what follows does not appear to be what is traditionally thought of as a parable. The instructions could be taken literally, of course, but they also teach a general attitude toward self and others which is appropriate for members of God's kingdom.

Making a Guest List (vv. 12–14)

This second set of sayings turned to the case of a host who was self-seeking in his selection of guests. Hosts were challenged not to invite guests

HISTORICAL BACKGROUND

The chief seats were the first reclining places at the table. A. T. Robertson notes, "On a couch holding three the middle place was the chief one. . . . The place next to the host on the right was then, as now, the post of honour."

A. T. Robertson, WPNT, 2:*195.*

who were able to reciprocate. One should, instead, use the banquet as an opportunity to help those who cannot reciprocate. Four groups are mentioned: the poor, the maimed, the lame, and the blind.

Section Summary

Luke highlighted the distorted values of the Pharisees, who showed no concern for the sick man (14:1–6), maneuvered for status (vv. 7–11), and lacked compassion for the poor and needy (vv. 12–14). In contrast to the behavior of the Pharisees, Jesus called his hearers to display humility (v. 11) and mercy (v. 12).

THE PARABLE OF THE GREAT BANQUET (14:15–24)

Jesus viewed God's kingdom as a joyful, sumptuous feast to which God issues a gracious invitation. Verse 16 refers to an initial invitation, whereas verse 17 refers to a later announcement when the feast is ready.

Making Excuses (vv. 18–20)

HISTORICAL BACKGROUND

In many parts of the Middle East, both then and now, to refuse a second summons was a serious breach of etiquette.

Presumably all the guests accepted the initial invitation; but when the slave announced the feast, they joined in what appears to be a conspiracy of excuses. The three excuses given are examples of the lame excuses given by the entire group.

There Is Still Room (vv. 21–24)

The clear teaching of the Scriptures is that God's intent from the beginning has been to include all people in the invitation. No one is excluded except those who refuse to accept the invitation.

Section Summary

The rejection of Jesus and the kingdom by official Judaism precipitated the inclusion of Israel's outcasts and the Gentiles. The great reversal has taken place. This parable also contains an emphasis on God's providential rule of history. The rejection of the gospel by Israel's leadership will not thwart God's plan. The kingdom has come, the banquet room will be filled, and God's plan will be accomplished.

THE CONDITIONS OF DISCIPLESHIP (14:25–35)

After the parable of the great banquet, Luke relates several of Jesus's teachings that set forth three conditions of discipleship:

Condition 1. Hate (v. 26). Jesus's statement in verse 26 referred to those times when family loyalty comes in conflict with one's commitment to Christ.

Condition 2. Cross Bearing (v. 27). To bear a cross in Jesus's day meant to be willing to die a martyr's death. Jesus used this challenge earlier in calling his disciples to deny self in total commitment to him and his way. In this context, hating one's life means a willingness to give one's life for Christ's sake.

Condition 3. Total Commitment (vv. 28–33). A disciple must relinquish everything.

WORD PICTURE

Hate is "the language of exaggerated contrast, it is true, but it must not be watered down till the point is gone."

A. T. Robertson, WPNT.

Section Summary

Salvation is free, but it is not cheap. It involves repentance, commitment, and renunciation of anything that stands in the way of the abundant life to which Christ calls his disciples.

HISTORICAL BACKGROUND

The coin was a drachma, representing about a day's wage for an average worker.

QUESTIONS TO GUIDE YOUR STUDY

1. What truths is Jesus conveying with his ethical teachings about banquet behavior?
2. What is the point of the parable of the great banquet?
3. Read erse 26. When becoming a disciple of Jesus, what does it mean to hate one's family?

LUKE 15

Luke 15 is among the most famous chapters in the Bible. The most familiar part is the story of the prodigal son.

The following three parables are connected by a theme—the joy of the lost being found.

HISTORICAL BACKGROUND

"Edersheim quotes a Jewish saying, 'There is joy before God when those who provoke him perish from the earth.' But Jesus has a very difference concept of God. He rejoices over the returning penitent more than over many safely in the fold."

Leon Morris, The Gospel According to St. Luke *(Grand Rapids: Eerdmans, 1974), 238.*

PARABLE OF THE LOST SHEEP (15:3–17)

The story is of a shepherd who had a hundred sheep and lost one of them. He looked for the lost sheep until he found it. Placing it on his shoulders, he brought it home. What follows is a time of rejoicing.

Section Summary

This parable focuses on the shepherd's concern for one lost sheep, his diligence in seeking it, and his joy in finding it. Jesus teaches that these are God's attitudes toward sinners.

PARABLE OF THE LOST COIN (15:8–10)

A woman was concerned over the loss of one coin. She diligently sought it and rejoiced when she found it. Jesus spelled out the parable's lesson: "I tell you, in the same way, there is joy in the presence of God's angels over one sinner who repents."

PARABLE OF THE PRODIGAL SON (15:11–32)

This parable might better be titled the parable of the gracious father, for that is the true focus of its teaching.

The Prodigal's Plight (vv. 11–16)

HISTORICAL BACKGROUND

According to the Jewish principles of inheritance, the older son would receive two-thirds of the estate and the younger brother one-third.

From a human point of view, the prodigal son can be faulted primarily for disregarding his responsibilities as a son toward his father. Insofar as his actions typify sinners, he shows the folly of misusing God-given freedom to seek freedom from a responsible relationship to God. Sinners squander God's gifts in a futile search for life and fulfillment on their own terms.

The Prodigal's Decision (vv. 17–19)

The previous two parables focused on the seeking love of God, but they did not show the sinner's response to that love. When a shepherd finds a lost sheep, he needs only to pick it up. The same is true of a lost coin. But a lost person is different. When a person is lost, the person must choose to receive God's forgiving love.

Jesus said that the prodigal "came to his senses." Like someone awakening from a dream, he came to grips with reality. He saw himself as he was and remembered his father's house. Yet, he felt no hope of restoration to sonship. He dared to hope only that his father would hire him as a servant. He knew his father treated his servants much better than his current employer treated him.

The Father's Welcome (vv. 20–24)

Just as the shepherd and the woman rejoiced over finding the sheep and the coin, the father rejoiced over finding the son.

The waiting father rushed to welcome his son. Before the prodigal could finish his carefully rehearsed confession, the father gave orders to bring out the best robe for his son and to put a ring on his finger and sandals on his feet. He then called for a fatted calf to be killed and a feast to begin.

HISTORICAL BACKGROUND

"The calf would be enough to feed the whole village; this would be a big party! Aristocratic families often invited the whole town to a banquet when a son attained adulthood (about thirteen years old) or a child married."

Craig S. Keener in The Bible Background Commentary, *233.*

The Older Brother's Complaints (vv. 25–30)

The older brother's complaints about the father's treatment of the prodigal match the Pharisees' complaint about Jesus's treatment of sinners.

The Father's Entreaty (vv. 31–32)

The father's response was patient and gracious. The proud son complained that he was reduced to the status of a slave. If so, the father implied, this was by his own choice, not the father's. As far as the father was concerned, all the privileges of sonship were his if he would but recognize it. The father entreated his older son to share in the joy of the restoration of the younger son and brother.

At this point, Jesus left the story open-ended. The curtain fell without hearing the older son's response to this father's entreaty. These parables in this passage emphasize God's love and grace for outcasts. God accepts all repentant sinners, no matter how outcast they may be.

QUESTIONS TO GUIDE YOUR STUDY

1. In the parable of the prodigal son, who and what do the key fictional characters represent in the real world?
2. What is the main point of the parable of the prodigal son?
3. From the three parables in this chapter, what do we learn about the character and attributes of God the Father?

LUKE 16

The proper use of money is one of the themes of Luke's Gospel. All of chapter 16 is devoted to it.

THE PARABLE OF THE DISHONEST MANAGER (16:1–8A)

A manager oversaw a rich man's estate. He was accused of wasting his employer's possessions. This wastefulness may have resulted from incompetence or dishonesty or both. His employer told him to turn over the records of the estate as part of giving up his position as manager.

Aware that he was soon to be unemployed, the manager began to plan for his future needs. He hit on a scheme to use his present position to make friends who would care for him when times got bad. He called his employer's debtors and, one by one, reduced their debts.

Outsiders who heard about the cancellation of the interest would have assumed the rich man authorized this action because of his religious scruples. The rich man, therefore, did not want to lose his new reputation as a man who put principle above property. It was in this spirit that the rich man commended the shrewdness of the dishonest manager.

Section Summary

Someday money and possessions will be useless. However, money can be used now in ways that create an eternal fellowship. When life comes to an end, the wisdom of lasting investments will become clear.

WORD PICTURE

Shrewdly

Shrewdly is a morally neutral term. Here it refers to the keen foresight with which the manager prepared himself for being fired. This adverb comes from the Greek word for "mind," the discerning intellect. Synonyms include "discreetly" and "prudently."

"The lord does not absolve the steward from guilt and he was apparently dismissed from his service. His shrewdness consisted in finding a place to go by his shrewdness. He remained the steward of unrighteousness even though his shrewdness was commended."

A. T. Robertson, "Luke," WPNT, 2: *217.*

SAYINGS ON STEWARDSHIP (16:8B–18)

A Lesson for Sons of Light (vv. 8b–9)

The latter half of verse 8 begins Jesus's observations about the parable. The rich man in the story commended the shrewd scoundrel, and Jesus observed that the sons of light can learn a lesson from this son of darkness. Jesus did not commend the manager's dishonesty, but he did point to the manager's initiative and foresight in planning for the future.

Money—the Acid Test (vv. 10–12)

A wealthy father may entrust his son with a small amount of responsibility before the son comes of age. The son's faithfulness with a little shows he also will be faithful over all that ultimately will be entrusted to him.

Money—Possession or Possessor? (v. 13)

A person can serve only one God. If a person's attitudes and actions are preoccupied with money, money becomes that person's master.

PERSONAL APPLICATION

"As the shrewd steward used the mammon of unrighteousness (or riches) to insure a welcome into the houses of those who benefited from his evil deed, so the followers of Christ should use this mammon of unrighteousness (or riches) to insure that they will be welcomed into heaven. Not that this will insure their going to heaven. As children of light they are already going there. The point is that upon arrival they will be welcomed by those who are already there as the result of the children's proper use of their stewardship."

Herschel H. Hobbs, An Exposition of the Four Gospels *(Grand Rapids: Baker, 1966), 3:240.*

Contrasting Views About Money (vv. 14–15)

When the Pharisees heard what Jesus said about money, they scoffed at him. They viewed money differently. They saw money as evidence of God's favor, not as a false god threatening to take God's place.

The Danger of Self-Justification (vv. 16–18)

The Pharisees prided themselves on their careful observation of the law and often accused Jesus of disregarding their laws and traditions. In verse 17 Jesus affirmed the lasting importance of the moral truth in the law. He then touched on an issue about divorce.

THE PARABLE OF THE RICH MAN AND LAZARUS (16:19–31)

This parable is unusual in that it is the only parable in which a character is named.

When Lazarus died, he was carried away by angels. (Lazarus's name means "God has helped.") The rich man (sometimes called "Dives" from the Latin word for "rich") died and was buried, no doubt with a lavish funeral and many eloquent eulogies. However, there were no ministering angels to take him to heaven. Instead, he found himself in Hades. He urged "Father Abraham" to send Lazarus to his five brothers, but Abraham said they have Moses and the Prophets; that is, they should read and listen to the Bible. All that is needed for salvation and doing good to others can be found there. This parable also points forward to the resurrection of the Lord Jesus.

The parable's lessons come in two parts. It illustrates the blessedness of the poor believer (v. 20) and the woe of the unbelieving rich (v. 24).

WORD PICTURE

"Little ones" (v. 2) are not only children but also persons of immature faith. The bad example of a Christian, especially a Christian leader, has a disastrous impact on those who are looking for an example of what a Christian should be.

Section Summary

Jesus taught that money and possessions are gifts and trusts from God. God lends us these with the expectation that we will use them to help others. When we do, we are drawn closer to God and to those who are helped.

QUESTIONS TO GUIDE YOUR STUDY

1. What is the point of the parable of the dishonest manager? About what was he dishonest?
2. How should the believer view money? What is the danger of placing one's trust in money?
3. What lessons do we learn from the parable of the rich man and Lazarus?

LUKE 17

TEACHINGS ADDRESSED TO THE DISCIPLES (17:1–10)

This is a collection of four of Jesus's sayings.

Beware Leading Others Astray (vv. 1–2)

Jesus warned his disciples against doing anything that would cause others to fall into sin.

When Your Brother Sins Against You (vv. 3–4)

The word "brother" shows the close ties that bind members of the family of faith. Verses 1–2 warn against offending a brother. And verses 3–4 tell us what to do when a brother or sister has sinned against us: "Rebuke him, and if he repents, forgive him." Verse 4 shows that no limits are to be placed on this forgiveness.

God absorbed the hurt of our sin on the cross and offers us forgiveness and reconciliation.

Increase Your Faith (vv. 5–6)

The demands of discipleship are great. The disciples recognized they needed divine help to fulfill such demands. Therefore, they said to Jesus, "Increase our faith."

Jesus's answer clarified the nature of true faith. The issue is not a need for greater faith—if by that we mean something we can do. Even faith as small as a tiny mustard seed opens the way for God to act out of his limitless resources.

WORD PICTURE

Faith that Moves Mountains

Jesus spoke of faith that can uproot a tree and plant it in the sea. Matthew's parallel involves moving a mountain from one place to another. These hyperbolic expressions describe what faith can do. But in practice, Jesus was not speaking of a faith that stages a miraculous event but of a faith that facilitates healing (Luke 7:9; 8:48; 18:42; Acts 14:9), that understands the need of Christ to suffer (Luke 24:25–26), that has confidence in God's providential care (8:25), that will not fall away (8:13; 22:32) but will endure (Acts 14:22), and that will believe God and grow (Acts 6:5; Luke 1:45 with 1:20).

Beware Pride (vv. 7–10)

Pride is among the greatest dangers we face as believers. Jesus used a parable to illustrate his point. The parable of the unprofitable servant is directed to the human tendency to say, "What a great person I am" rather than "How great is God!" Believers are like servants who, when they have done all that was demanded of them, can at best confess that they are unworthy and have only fulfilled their obligations.

Section Summary

Luke provides a collection of sayings about discipleship with respect to believers' relationships to their neighbors and their personal relationships with God.

THE GRATEFUL SAMARITAN (17:11–19)

This account of the grateful Samaritan begins with Jesus's healing of 10 lepers at a distance. Jesus didn't touch them. He didn't even declare they were healed. He simply commanded them to go and show themselves to the priests. As they proceeded to the priests, they were healed. One of the lepers, upon observing his healing, returned to give thanks to Jesus. Luke then pointed out that this leper was a Samaritan.

Section Summary

This healing account provides another example of Jesus's power. Luke presents a key truth for his readers: One can experience God's work of grace yet fall short of receiving salvation.

THE COMING OF THE KINGDOM OF GOD (17:20–37)

The Kingdom Has Come (vv. 20–21)

The time of the kingdom's coming was a subject of great interest to the Pharisees. However, their understanding of the nature of the kingdom caused them to miss its present reality. Jesus taught that the kingdom was already among them: "The kingdom of God is in your midst."

The Kingdom Is Coming (vv. 22–24)

The term "kingdom," as used by Jesus, means reign, not realm. It is the reign of God as King. God has always been sovereign, but many people have not acknowledged God as their Lord. The sovereignty of God was declared in a new and powerful way in the life and ministry of Jesus.

First Comes the Cross (v. 25)

The cross is the heart of God's purpose and the key to his kingdom.

The Time of His Coming (vv. 26–30)

Jesus consistently taught the certainty of his coming but the uncertainty of the time.

Effect on Present Actions (vv. 31–33)

The hope of the future coming affects present actions and values.

Coming Judgment (vv. 34–37)

The future coming will involve judgment. Verses 34–35 refer to the separation of persons with close earthly ties but with different ultimate allegiances.

Section Summary

God's kingdom would not be preceded by signs that could be calculated and observed. On the contrary, the kingdom was already present in the coming of Jesus Christ. As for the Son of Man's coming, it will be unexpected, and people will be unprepared.

QUESTIONS TO GUIDE YOUR STUDY

1. As followers of Christ, how are we to deal with brothers and sisters who sin against us?
2. What is the nature of true faith? What does Jesus mean by needing the faith of a mustard seed?
3. What effect should the fact of Jesus's imminent return have on us today?

LUKE 18

THE PARABLE OF THE UNJUST JUDGE (18:1–8)

This parable is closely connected to the preceding material by theme and audience, and it continues Jesus's teaching of the disciples. In the parable, two characters make up the picture: a persistent woman and an unjust judge. The woman is a widow who represents the needy, helpless, poor, and oppressed. She wanted help against an adversary. The judge finally agreed to vindicate her against her adversary. She annoyed him into granting her request. He reached the stage where he would do anything to get her out of his hair.

The point of the parable is this: If the unjust judge finally grants the persistent widow's request, how much more will a just God hear and grant the petitions of his followers who pray to him day and night?

HISTORICAL BACKGROUND

"This judge was one of the paid magistrates appointed either by Herod or the Romans. Such judges were notorious. Unless a plaintiff had influence and money to bribe his way to a verdict, he had no hope of ever getting his case settled."

William Barclay, The Gospel of Luke, *222.*

The last question of the parable is somewhat puzzling. The intent of the question is not to raise doubts but to serve as a challenge from Jesus to his followers to persevere in faith in the difficult times ahead.

PERSONAL APPLICATION

"If I felt my heart as hard as a stone; if I did not love God, or man, or woman, or little child, I would yet say to God in my heart, 'O God, see how I trust Thee, because Thou art perfect, and not changeable like me. I do not love Thee. I love nobody. I am not even sorry for it. Thou seest how much I need Thee to come close to me, to put Thy arm round me, to say to me, my child: for the worse my state, the greater my need of my Father who loves me. Come to me, and my day will dawn; my love will come back, and, oh! how I shall love Thee, my God! and know that my love is Thy love, my blessedness Thy being.'"

George MacDonald, In Between Heaven and Earth, *ed. Ken Gire (San Francisco: HarperCollins, 1997), 111–12.*

Section Summary

We do not need to "wear down" God until he acts on our behalf. As a Father, he is sensitive to our every need and ready to answer our prayers.

THE PARABLE OF THE PHARISEE AND THE TAX COLLECTOR (18:9–14)

Within this parable we encounter a self-righteous Pharisee whose prayer in the temple was essentially a self-eulogy. He thanked God that he was not like the others. In itself, the prayer could have been acceptable if the Pharisee was thanking God for protecting him from circumstances that might have led him to become a thief or adulterer. However, the Pharisee saw his not succumbing to such sins as purely his own doing. There was no thanks for what God had done but rather a long list of personal achievements (note the *I*'s!).

In contrast, the tax collector demonstrated his attitude even by his physical stance. He stood "far off." His prayer sought God's mercy and forgiveness just like the psalmist (Ps 51:1). The result, which would have been shocking for many of Jesus's listeners, was that the sinner who sought God's mercy left justified, not the Pharisee.

Section Summary

In the parable of the Pharisee and the tax collector, the Pharisee was so busy priding himself on his performance that he failed to realize he lacked the essential requirement of a right attitude. God relates to those people who have lost their pride and humbled themselves in repentance.

WORD PICTURE

Eye of a Needle

Attempts to understand this saying as involving a camel going through a small city gate (no evidence exists of a gate named Eye of the Needle) or as a mistranslation ("camel" as a mistranslation of the word "cable") lose sight of the hyperbolic nature of Jesus's words. There is a rabbinic analogy that speaks of an elephant going through the eye of a needle, which is an example of the hyperbolic nature of Jesus's saying in verse 25.

JESUS'S BLESSING OF THE CHILDREN (18:15–17)

Jesus teaches that one must receive God's kingdom like a little child. Jesus says the kingdom belongs to "such as these." Little children possess humility because they lack anything to boast of and can make no claim on God.

THE RICH RULER (18:18–30)

We find the story of the rich young ruler in all three Synoptic Gospels, but only Matthew states that he was young. This ruler's concern was "to inherit eternal life."

Jesus saw that this man's whole life was wrapped up in his prosperity. He realized that only a complete renunciation would free this man to follow him in the way of life that was abundant and eternal.

The rich man rejected the gospel, as he loved his possessions more than God and his neighbor.

Riches and the Kingdom (vv. 24–27)

The ruler's rejection of the gospel was the occasion for Jesus's statement about the difficulty of a rich man entering the kingdom. The disciples were shocked at what Jesus said. The theology of the day interpreted wealth as a sign of God's favor.

Forsaking All for the Kingdom's Sake (vv. 28–30)

Following the ruler's refusal to forsake all and follow Christ, Peter pointed out that he and the other disciples had done just that. Jesus assured Peter and the others that any sacrifice for the sake of the kingdom would be more than repaid.

Section Summary

The rich ruler's life was wrapped up in his prosperity. The Bible is clear that all of us are in a plight from which we can be saved only by the grace and power of God.

PERSONAL APPLICATION

Three lessons from this event touch our lives:

1. One can be interested in eternal life without possessing it.
2. Many who claim to have obeyed God have done so only in a superficial sense.
3. The rich ruler lacked eternal life because he rejected Jesus's call for repentance.

THE THIRD PASSION ANNOUNCEMENT (18:31–34)

This account involves Jesus's third passion prediction.

The disciples still do not comprehend what Jesus is saying.

THE HEALING OF THE BLIND MAN AT JERICHO (18:35–43)

As Jesus approached Jerusalem, a blind man called out to Jesus from the roadside, "Jesus, Son of David, have mercy on me!" Others tried to silence him, but he refused to be quiet. Jesus heard his prayer and restored the blind man's sight.

PERSONAL APPLICATION

Bartimaeus is an example of faith that refuses to give up. He showed great faith by responding to what he heard, persisting in his request for help, and standing to his feet when Jesus summoned him. Bartimaeus then followed Jesus.

QUESTIONS TO GUIDE YOUR STUDY

1. What is the point of the parable of the unjust judge?
2. What is it about childlike faith that Jesus commends? In what ways do we often complicate the matter of faith in our busy and complex lives?
3. The rich ruler rejected the gospel of Jesus Christ. What was his struggle? What might we learn from this tragic story?

LUKE 19

ZACCHAEUS, THE TAX COLLECTOR (19:1–10)

As Jesus passed through Jericho, the chief tax collector, Zacchaeus, sought to catch a glimpse of him. Because of his short stature, he climbed a tree. To his surprise, Jesus called him by name to come down, and together they went to Zacchaeus's home. Luke doesn't tell us the conversation, but Zacchaeus emerged a changed man. He made two promises: (1) to give half of his possessions to the poor, and (2) to pay back four times in cases where he had defrauded someone.

Section Summary

Zacchaeus showed the same determination to contact Jesus as Bartimaeus. He did not come to Jesus out of mere curiosity or with any skepticism but with an openness to Jesus's message. His spontaneous act of repentance revealed the work of grace in his heart and proved that he was now a son of Abraham.

HISTORICAL BACKGROUND

Jericho was 17 miles east-northeast of Jerusalem. In Jesus's day it was famous for its balm (an aromatic gum known for its medicinal qualities). This, along with its being the winter capital, made it a wealthy city.

WORD PICTURE

Mina

The shekel was the basic unit of weight in the Hebrew system. Multiples of the shekel were the mina and the talent. A talent is estimated to have been about 3,000 shekels and a mina about 50 shekels. Although a mina was worth only about one-sixtieth of a talent, 10 minas was still a significant amount as it represented about three months' wages.

OLD TESTAMENT REFERENCE

Zacchaeus's restitution was far greater than it needed to be. "When a man or woman commits any sin against another, that person acts unfaithfully toward the Lord and is guilty. The person is to confess the sin he has committed. He is to pay full compensation, add a fifth of its value to it, and give it to the individual he has wronged." (Num 5:6–7)

THE PARABLE OF THE TEN MINAS (19:11–27)

The parable of the 10 minas is also known as the parable of the pounds and is similar to the parable of the talents (Matt 25:14–30). In the parable a noble man, about to be appointed king, gave 10 servants each 10 minas, which they were to "put to work" until the noble man returned as king. Luke's readers would have understood the noble man's absence to represent the time between the ascension and the second coming of Christ.

When the noble man returned as king, he sent for the servants to learn what each had gained with his 10 minas. He rewarded those who had been faithful and judged those who had been unfaithful.

Section Summary

God entrusts believers with the gospel, and he wants them to multiply his message so the entire world will hear it. It is the obligation of believers to be faithful stewards of the message he has entrusted to us until Jesus comes.

THE MESSIANIC ENTRY INTO JERUSALEM (19:28–40)

Jesus now entered Jerusalem, his city of destiny.

He entered as the Messiah, but not as the Messiah whom many of his countrymen were seeking.

As Jesus approached Jerusalem, his following grew. As the procession reached a point where the city came into view, "the whole crowd of the disciples began to praise God joyfully with a loud voice for all the miracles they had seen." While Jesus was welcomed by many, he was criticized by the religious leaders.

OLD TESTAMENT REFERENCE

"Rejoice greatly, Daughter Zion! Shout in triumph, Daughter Jerusalem! Look, your King is coming to you; he is righteous and victorious, humble and riding on a donkey, on a colt, the foal of a donkey." (Zech 9:9)

JESUS'S LAMENT OVER JERUSALEM (19:41–44)

As Jesus approached Jerusalem, he wept over it, knowing the judgment would come in AD 70 when the Romans would destroy Jerusalem and the temple.

Section Summary

Official Israel failed to submit to God's rule. This could only result in a visitation of divine judgment, and Jesus wept for Jerusalem.

THE CLEANSING OF THE TEMPLE (19:45–48)

Jesus's cleansing of the temple was an act of prophetic symbolism, not a sudden outburst of righteous indignation.

Jesus not only drove out the agents of the high priest, but he also proceeded to make the temple court into the place for his daily teaching of the people.

OLD TESTAMENT REFERENCE

"'See, I am going to send my messenger, and he will clear the way before me. Then the Lord you seek will suddenly come to his temple, the Messenger of the covenant you delight in—see, he is coming,' says the LORD of Armies. But who can endure the day of his coming? And who will be able to stand when he appears? For he will be like a refiner's fire and like launderer's bleach." (Mal 3:1–2)

QUESTIONS TO GUIDE YOUR STUDY

1. What lessons do we learn from the conversion of Zacchaeus?
2. What lessons about stewardship do we find in the parable of the 10 minas? What can we do to be faithful stewards?
3. Why did Jesus choose to enter Jerusalem as he did?
4. What was Jesus's larger purpose in driving out the people who were selling animals in the temple?

LUKE 20

A QUESTION OF JESUS'S AUTHORITY (20:1–8)

The religious leaders asked Jesus the source of authority for what he was doing. Their hope was that his answer would get him into trouble with the Roman authorities.

Jesus refused to take the bait. Instead, he asked them a question: "Tell me, was the baptism of John from heaven or of human origin?" If they pleased the crowd by saying John was from God, the people would ask them why they did not believe John when he was alive. If they were to give their honest opinion that John was not a true prophet, the people might stone them.

Section Summary

Hoping to trap Jesus, Jewish leaders questioned his authority for cleansing the temple. Jesus refused to answer the question of the Jewish leaders, and by doing so he showed that their problem was not ignorance but intentional opposition to God's will.

THE PARABLE OF THE VINEYARD OWNER (20:9–19)

A man planted a vineyard and leased it to tenant farmers. At harvest time, he sent servants, on three successive occasions, to collect some of the produce. The tenants beat the servants. Finally, the owner sent his own son. The tenants killed him.

Jesus asked his audience what the owner would do with the tenants and then answered his question by saying that the owner would kill the tenants and give the vineyard to others.

The teachers of the law and chief priests sought to arrest Jesus because they knew the tenants in the parable represented them. However, they were kept from carrying out their desire because of the people, who were supportive of Jesus.

OLD TESTAMENT REFERENCE

The parable concludes with a quotation from Ps 118:22 in which Jesus declares that he was God's foundation stone. God will establish his kingdom on him, and he will be the focal point of judgment.

Section Summary

In the midst of the controversy regarding Jesus's authority, he told a parable and asked a question that gave an overview of God's plan. They revealed God's commitment to his Son despite Jewish rejection. The nation's rejection would cost them. The kingdom would go to new tenants.

A QUESTION ABOUT TRIBUTE TO CAESAR (20:20–26)

Some of the religious leaders approached Jesus and attempted to set him up, first by flattery and then by asking him a double-edged question. "Is it lawful for us to pay taxes to Caesar or not?"

Jesus knew that affirming the lawfulness of paying tribute to the Romans would alienate him from the Jews. Denying the lawfulness of the tax would bring Roman wrath upon him.

His answer sliced through the horns of the dilemma. When the Jewish leaders produced a coin in response to Jesus's request, they were undercutting their objection to the tax. Their use of the coin suggested a tacit acceptance of the emperor's authority. Jesus's logic was that the coin belonged to Caesar, and they should return to him his due.

HISTORICAL BACKGROUND

The tribute was an annual poll tax, which the Romans had begun to levy in AD 6. The imposition of this tax led to a Jewish rebellion under Judas the Galilean (see Acts 5:37). Romans required the payment of the tax with a special coin imprinted with a likeness of the emperor. Use of this special coin angered the Jews. Normal business activities used a copper coin without the image of the emperor.

Section Summary

Christians must accept the state as ordained by God and render respect and obedience to the governments. When a conflict arises between our allegiance to the state and our allegiance to God, we must be true to God.

A QUESTION ABOUT THE RESURRECTION (20:27–40)

Luke now reports a second and final attempt by the leaders to confound Jesus in argument. This time the Sadducees, who are only mentioned here in Luke's Gospel, raise a far-fetched example.

Telling a story of a woman who was married successively to seven siblings after each previous sibling spouse had died, the Sadducees asked Jesus, "In the resurrection, therefore, whose wife will the woman be? For all seven had married her." Their intent was to make the idea of the resurrection a joke.

In his response, Jesus presented two objections to their question.

They failed to understand the Scriptures and the power of God. Those who share in the resurrection will not marry.

HISTORICAL BACKGROUND

Sadducees

"The Sadducees are mentioned here only in this Gospel. None of the Sadducee writings have survived so our information about the sect is fragmentary and we see the Sadducees only through the eyes of their opponents. . . . They were the conservative, aristocratic, high-priestly party, worldly-minded and very ready to cooperate with the Romans, which, of course, enabled them to maintain their privileged position."

Leon Morris, The Gospel According to Saint Luke, *289–90.*

Section Summary

Jesus's answer to the Sadducees' question revealed his unsurpassed wisdom and knowledge. In contrast, the Sadducees failed to understand the Scriptures. Jesus's opponents were forced to commend him and decided to cease further attempts to entrap him with his words.

A QUESTION ABOUT DAVID (20:41–44)

After his critics decided to ask no further questions, Jesus took the offensive and asked them a question about their designation of Messiah as the Son of David. He referred them to Ps 110:1, the most frequently quoted Old Testament text in the New Testament, to show that the use of the title was inadequate and perhaps misleading as a guide to the Messiah's identity. Jesus pointed out that the Messiah was not a mere earthly replica of David but rather was David's Lord. He emphasized that the Messiah was divine as well as human.

HISTORICAL BACKGROUND

"This is the declaration of the LORD to my Lord: 'Sit at my right hand until I make your enemies your footstool.'" *(Ps 110:1)*

WARNINGS CONCERNING THE SCRIBES (20:45–47)

These verses describe religion at its worst. These leaders were using their religion to advance their own personal ambitions and to feed their pride.

QUESTIONS TO GUIDE YOUR STUDY

1. What gave Jesus the authority to cleanse the temple of those who were defiling it?
2. What is the lesson of the parable of the wicked tenant farmers?
3. Jesus strongly denounced the hypocrisy of the scribes and Pharisees. What are parallels in today's religious structure that we as believers need to be aware of and quick to denounce?

LUKE 21

THE WIDOW'S OFFERING (21:1–4)

The widow in the temple is the epitome of true religion, just as the scribes are the epitome of false religion.

The wealthy gave out of their abundance and, as a result, did not even miss it. By contrast, the widow gave all she had.

PERSONAL APPLICATION

"God's estimate of benevolence takes in not only what is given, but what is reserved."

George R. Bliss, Commentary on the Gospel of Luke *(Philadelphia: American Baptist Publication Society, 1884), 299.*

Section Summary

God measures the gifts of his people not based on their size but on the basis of how much remains.

THE DESTRUCTION OF THE TEMPLE (21:5–6)

As Jeremiah had prophesied the destruction of Solomon's temple, so Jesus foretold the destruction of Herod's temple. Many people in Jeremiah's day and in Jesus's day assumed that God would never allow his temple to be destroyed or his people judged.

The Babylonians destroyed Solomon's temple in 587 BC. When Roman armies besieged Jerusalem in AD 70, the last fanatical defenders took refuge in the temple. Eventually, the Romans overwhelmed them and leveled the temple, as Jesus predicted.

SIGNS BEFORE THE END (21:7–11)

The disciples' questions (v. 7) focused on how they could know when the temple would be destroyed. This event was associated in their minds with the end of the old order and the establishment of God's final kingdom. But Jesus taught them that the "end won't come right away."

Jesus taught here that signs prior to the end include false teachers, a worsening world political situation, international crises, worldwide calamities, persecutions, and the preaching of the gospel.

WORD PICTURE

Redemption

The word *redemption* occurs only this time in Luke-Acts. For Luke, this probably means the consummation of the hopes and promises for God's people. His readers would no doubt think of this redemption as involving salvation in its fullest sense.

Redemption is the reason Christians can "stand up and lift [their] heads." In the last days, they can be even more encouraged because their redemption is coming.

THE COMING PERSECUTION OF THE DISCIPLES (21:12–19)

Jesus predicted a time of intense persecution before the temple would fall. He challenged his followers to see hostility not as a threat but as an opportunity for bearing testimony.

JESUS'S DISCOURSE IN LUKE 21:7–36

SECTION (VERSES)	TOPIC	KEY POINT
7–11	Signs before the end	Observable events will signal the coming judgment
12–19	Persecution of disciples	Many will suffer for their faith
20–24	Jerusalem's desolation	God will judge Jerusalem for its rejection of his purpose
25–28	Coming of the Son of Man	Christ's glorious return and the redemption of believers
29–33	Parable of the fig tree	Duty of watching for Christ's appearance
34–36	Exhortation to vigilance	Being prepared for his coming

THE DESOLATION COMING UPON JERUSALEM (21:20–24)

These verses refer to the fall of Jerusalem, not the final coming of Christ. Having described what must take place before the destruction, Luke now describes the destruction itself.

THE COMING OF THE SON OF MAN (21:25–28)

The vivid language of verses 25–26 symbolizes the giving way of the old order of creation to the new order of Christ's eternal kingdom. Jesus emphasized, however, not the signs themselves but the effect of these signs on humanity unprepared for Christ's coming.

Section Summary

The mustard seed has become a tree (13:19); the yeast has leavened the whole dough (13:21). The longings of Luke's readers are now realized to the fullest.

THE PARABLE OF THE FIG TREE (21:29–33)

This parable serves as a reassuring word for the preceding section about the Son of Man's coming. Even as the leafing of a fig tree announces the coming of summer, so the signs of 21:25–26 will announce and guarantee the Son of Man's coming.

The certainty of all this is assured by two emphatic elements:

1. The statement, "Truly I tell you" (v. 32).
2. The fact that the coming of the Son of Man is a more enduring promise than the existence of heaven and earth. The latter will pass away, but not Jesus's words.

OLD TESTAMENT REFERENCE

Verse 27 refers to the fulfillment of Dan 7:13–14, 27. Jesus often referred to Himself as the Son of Man. Daniel describes how God would give the Son of Man sovereignty over all things. In a sense, this happened in connection with Jesus's life, death, and resurrection. In this sense, the kingdom is already a reality. In another sense, however, the present reality of the kingdom is recognized only through the eyes of faith. At Christ's future coming, the domination of godless nations will end, and all people will become aware of the sovereignty of the Son of Man (Phil 2:9–11).

In Luke, the events of the fall of Jerusalem are largely in view from verses 5–24. But those events are like those of the end.

EXHORTATION TO VIGILANCE (21:34–36)

Since that day will come unexpectedly, disciples are to watch and be faithful. The events of AD 70 are a guarantee that the end will also come, since one set of events pictures the other.

WORD PICTURE

Jesus's followers are to "be alert at all times" and "praying." Grammatically, this phrase is best understood as revealing the means by which one can be watchful: Be always watchful by praying.

THE MINISTRY OF JESUS IN THE TEMPLE (21:37–38)

These verses form a concluding summary for the entire section on Jesus's ministry in Jerusalem.

Section Summary

The Son of Man's return is guaranteed. Disciples of Jesus are to watch and pray and to be faithful. In this way they can prepare for his coming.

QUESTIONS TO GUIDE YOUR STUDY

1. What is the key lesson of the story of the widow's offering in the temple?
2. Why did God allow the destruction of the temple and the fall of Jerusalem? Might God still allow this kind of judgment today?
3. What is the point of the parable of the fig tree? What does the phrase "this generation" mean?

LUKE 22

At this point, Luke's narrative shifts to his account of Jesus's passion. We have shifts in both scene (temple to city) and content (teachings of Jesus to stories of Jesus). The passion consists of three parts, each containing unique events.

LUKE'S PASSION NARRATIVE

EVENT	PASSAGE
Part 1	
Plot to betray and kill Jesus	22:1–6
The Last Supper	22:7–23
Teachings of Jesus	22:34–38
Part 2	
Jesus's arrest	22:39–53

EVENT	PASSAGE
Jesus's trial	22:54–23:25
The crucifixion	23:26–49
Jesus's burial	23:50–56
Part 3	
The resurrection and ascension of Jesus	24:1–53

THE PLOT TO KILL JESUS (22:1–6)

The religious leaders already plotted to kill Jesus. The plot became easier when one of his disciples offered to make him available to the priests. Judas's willingness to betray Jesus simplified the task of the Sadducean priests. Fearing an arrest during the Passover feast might provoke a public revolt, they looked for an opportunity to make an arrest in secret.

THE LAST SUPPER (22:7–38)

The Preparation of the Passover Meal (vv. 7–23)

Luke portrays Jesus as an obedient Jew who kept the law and celebrated the Passover. When the day arrived, Jesus sent Peter and John to prepare the Passover meal. Because Jesus was aware of Judas's plan to betray him, he kept secret the place of the meal. Even Peter and John did not know where it was to be held until they arrived.

The Passover—Lord's Supper (vv. 14–20)

In connection with his last Passover meal with the apostles, Jesus instituted the Lord's Supper, which like the Passover commemorated a divine deliverance and looked forward to the future consummation of God's kingdom. His words in verses 15–18 show that he saw this as his last meal with his followers before his suffering and death.

JESUS'S FAREWELL DISCOURSE

SECTION	PASSAGE
Judas's betrayal of Jesus	22:21–23
Selfish desire for greatness	22:24–30
Peter's denial foretold	22:31–34
Misunderstanding of the nature of the kingdom	22:35–38

Jesus's Betrayal Foretold (vv. 21–23)

From God's point of view, the death of Jesus was God's plan for human redemption. However, those who were responsible for his death are held

WORD PICTURE

Satan Entered Judas

"That Satan entered into Judas, means that the devil, to accomplish his malignant purposes against our Lord, took advantage of the wickedness of Judas, to direct him as a serviceable tool. Many other psychological explanations of the act of the traitor have been ingeniously attempted; but to carry them through without the supposition of Satanic agency has proved a sea of difficulty in which all have floundered—not swum."

George R. Bliss, Commentary on the Gospel of Luke *(Philadelphia: American Baptist Publication Society, 1884), 309.*

HISTORICAL BACKGROUND

Their sign of the location was a man carrying a water jar, which was unusual since carrying water was considered women's work.

HISTORICAL BACKGROUND

The Passover celebrated a past deliverance—God's deliverance of Israel from Egyptian bondage. Over the centuries it also came to be an anticipation of God's coming kingdom.

accountable for what they did. Judas was not a helpless pawn in a divine drama, or Jesus would not have pronounced judgment on him for his betrayal.

WORD PICTURE

Betray

Jesus's words of prediction at the Lord's Supper hold more meaning than a simple prediction of betrayal. The tense of the phrase is active and forward moving in its meaning. Grammatically, this phrase is a "present active participle," which means that the one betraying was "actually engaged in doing it." A. T. Robertson, "Luke," WPNT, 268.

A literal translation would be "him who is in the process of betraying." The betrayal had already begun (22:3–6).

Greatness in the Kingdom (vv. 24–30)

A dispute over who was to be considered the greatest among the disciples become an occasion for Jesus to teach about true greatness in God's kingdom. Jesus contrasts the attitudes and values of the world with what it means to be great in God's kingdom.

Peter's Denial Foretold (vv. 31–34)

All four Gospels predict Peter's coming threefold denial. Luke alone refers to Satan's role in Peter's downfall. Even though Peter would experience great trials, Jesus indicated that he had prayed for Peter's faith to hold firm. Peter's answer showed that he comprehended neither the serious events fast approaching nor the reality of his own weakness.

Two Swords (vv. 35–38)

This last account in Jesus's farewell discourse is not found in any of the other Gospels. Jesus contrasted the past mission of the disciples with the changed situation that was about to take place. On their early mission the disciples went out without provisions and depended entirely on the hospitality of their hearers. In the new situation brought about by Jesus's death, they must go equipped and be prepared to face hostility and persecution.

This involved their purchasing a "sword" because what the Scriptures said about the death of God's Son was about to be fulfilled. The opposition to Jesus that had been mounting was about to come to its culmination, and the end was near. To Jesus's frustration, however, the disciples failed to grasp his meaning in the use of the sword metaphor, and he concluded the conversation.

WORD PICTURE

Take This Cup Away from Me

"Cup" is a metaphor for Jesus's suffering (Mark 10:38–39; Matt 20:22–23). It is a metaphor in this passage not for physical death in general but for the particular death Jesus would suffer. "As He stood on the very brink of this awful experience his holy soul drew back from the horror of becoming the very essence of sin. If there were any other way by which man could be saved—but, if not, then He was ready for God's will to be done."

Herschel H. Hobbs, An Exposition of the Gospel of Luke, *312.*

Section Summary

Jesus used his Last Supper with the disciples as an occasion to deliver his farewell discourse. Although the disciples gained from his teaching, they failed to grasp fully his explanation of what was about to happen.

JESUS'S ARREST (22:39–71)

Luke now directs his narrative to events surrounding Jesus's trial and crucifixion. The scene is now the Mount of Olives.

PERSONAL APPLICATION

"So, whoever thinks he stands must be careful not to fall" (1 Cor 10:12).

The Prayer of Jesus (vv. 39–46)

The opening account in this new section involves Jesus's prayer on the Mount of Olives. He taught the disciples that they needed to pray so their faith would not fail. They needed to pray, "Do not bring us not into temptation" (11:4). Their lack of prayer at this crucial time would help Luke's readers understand Peter's failure in the temptation that was to follow.

Luke's readers are again reminded that Jesus's suffering is at the heart of God's plan. His prayer clearly revealed that despite his own personal desire, he was submitting to the divine will, which involved the necessity of his death. His prayer served as a pattern for Luke's readers who might have to walk in the footsteps of their Lord.

The Arrest of Jesus (vv. 47–53)

A crowd including Judas, the chief priests, and officers of the temple guard approached Jesus to arrest him. John's account includes Roman soldiers as part of the crowd.

Before Jesus could stop him, one of his disciples cut off the ear of a servant of the high priest. Jesus rebuked his disciples and healed the servant.

Jesus then rebuked his opponents for their cowardice in not arresting him openly while he taught in the temple: "Have you come out with swords and clubs as if I were a criminal? Every day while I was with you in the temple, you never laid a hand on me."

He also pointed out that this was the last desperate attempt of the power of darkness to thwart God's plan. What was taking place involved a far deeper opposition than that between the Jewish leaders and Jesus. It involved the cosmic opposition between Satan, the ruler of this age, and God. But God had permitted the opponents of his Son this hour. The power of darkness would be allowed to do what it wanted with Jesus. And so Jesus submitted to the will of the Father.

Peter's Denial of Jesus (vv. 54–62)

When Jesus was led away, Peter followed at a distance and then on into the courtyard of the high priest. While in the courtyard, he was asked on three occasions whether he knew Jesus. Each time Peter denied that he knew Jesus. Then he remembered what Jesus predicted. He then "went outside and wept bitterly."

PERSONAL APPLICATION

Although Peter's fall was lamentable, his repentance and subsequent service to Christ as recorded in Acts provides hope for all Christians.

The Mocking of Jesus (vv. 63–65)

After his arrest, Jesus was mocked and suffered just as he predicted. Because he was acknowledged as a prophet by other people, he was blindfolded and asked to identify who beat him. The account ends with Jesus receiving further insults from his captors.

Jesus Before the Sanhedrin (vv. 66–71)

Jesus was next taken before the Sanhedrin.

The morning meeting was an attempt to legitimize what they already decided to do. The Sanhedrin could not conduct a trial on a capital case at night. Also, this was not a trial at which evidence was being considered. The verdict was predetermined.

HISTORICAL BACKGROUND

The Sanhedrin was a Jewish court of 70 members plus the high priest. They exercised authority over the religious life of the Jewish people. They also operated under the jurisdiction of the Roman authorities.

Looking to officially charge him with blasphemy, the Sanhedrin tried to get Jesus to admit that he was the Messiah. "Are you, then, the Son of God?" they asked.

Jesus's reply was, "You say that I am."

The leaders took Jesus's answer to their question as an affirmation and a claim to be the Christ, the Son of God. "We've heard it ourselves from his mouth." As far as Jesus's opponents were concerned, their purpose had now been achieved. It did not matter to them that Jesus was convicted on the basis of his own testimony, a patently illegal procedure.

Section Summary

Jesus's betrayal and arrest were the result of a plot carried out illegally by the religious authority. What was taking place involved a far deeper opposition than that between the Jewish leaders and Jesus. It involved the cosmic opposition between Satan, the ruler of this age, and God. And so Jesus submitted to the will of the Father.

QUESTIONS TO GUIDE YOUR STUDY

1. What is the significance of the Lord's Supper to present-day believers?
2. Review the message of Jesus's farewell discourse at the Last Supper. What was the disciples' attitude and response to his teaching? Which of Jesus's points did the disciples fail to grasp?
3. As you read Luke's account of Jesus agonizing in prayer before his arrest, what human emotions do you see? What does the account reveal about his relationship with the Father?

LUKE 23

JESUS'S TRIAL (23:1–25)

Jesus Before Pilate (vv. 1–5)

The entire Sanhedrin brought Jesus to Pilate. The Sanhedrin condemned Jesus for the sin of blasphemy. However, this was not a crime in the eyes of Rome.

A CHRONOLOGY OF THE EVENTS OF JESUS'S ARREST AND TRIAL

EVENT	SOURCES WITHIN THE GOSPELS
1. Jesus is arrested.	Mark-Matthew, Luke, John
2. Jesus appears before Caiaphas.	John
3. Jesus is "tried" by the Sanhedrin led by Caiaphas.	Mark-Matthew, Luke, John
4. The Sanhedrin meets a second time to draw up official charges against Jesus to be presented before Pilate.	Mark-Matthew
5. Jesus is led to Pilate.	Mark-Matthew, Luke, John

Verse 2 spells out the accusations against Jesus: (1) subverting a nation; (2) opposing the payment of taxes to Caesar; and (3) claiming to be Messiah, that is, a king.

Focusing on only the third accusation, Pilate asked Jesus, "Are you the king of the Jews?"

Jesus responded, "You say so."

Pilate's verdict in verse 4 shows that he believed Jesus was innocent: "I find no grounds for charging this man." (The information in verses 4–5 is unique to Luke.) This should have been the official verdict, and the charges should have been dismissed. But the enemies were insistent, and Pilate did not act decisively. When Pilate learned that Jesus was from Galilee, he tried to solve his dilemma by sending Jesus to Herod Antipas, tetrarch of Galilee and Perea.

HISTORICAL BACKGROUND

Pontius Pilate was the Roman governor of Judea from AD 26 to 37. His tenure as governor or prefect consisted of one provocation of Jewish sensibilities after another. In view of his record, it is a little surprising that Pilate allowed himself to be pressured by Jewish leaders to crucify Jesus. One possible explanation is that he already felt his position was in jeopardy.

Jesus Before Herod (vv. 6–12)

The account of Jesus's appearance before Herod is unique to Luke. This was the Herod who imprisoned and killed John the Baptist. Herod was thrilled at the prospect of seeing Jesus perform some sign, but Jesus refused to dignify him with any kind of reply. The evil ruler reacted by subjecting Jesus to cruel and humiliating mockery. He then sent Jesus back to Pilate without passing any sentence on his guilt or innocence.

Luke's purpose in recording this event is to provide a second ruler's testimony to Jesus's innocence.

Pilate's Sentence (vv. 13–16)

Pilate interpreted Herod's actions to mean that Herod found Jesus innocent. Neither of these men, however, escaped guilt for their involvement in this shameful miscarriage of justice (Acts 4:27). Luke's readers are clearly told that two rulers—the Roman governor Pontius Pilate and the tetrarch of Galilee, Herod Antipas—found Jesus innocent and wanted to release him. Therefore, Jesus's crucifixion had nothing to do with personal guilt or culpability.

Pilate continued to seek Jesus's release. This time he sought to do so by allowing the people to choose, according to the custom, which "criminal" they wanted released. Pilate issued another strong statement about Jesus's innocence and then offered to have him released. Roman law allowed for a prisoner to be beaten as a kind of warning for the future. Pilate hoped this compromise would satisfy Jesus's accusers.

Jesus Delivered to Be Crucified (vv. 18–25)

To Pilate's dismay, the Jewish leaders and the people cried instead for the release of Barabbas. For the third time Pilate pronounced Jesus as innocent and sought to release him. The crowd kept shouting, "Crucify! Crucify him!" Pilate was now intimidated by the Jewish leaders and the crowd. Finally, he passed judgment on Jesus. He released Barabbas to the people and handed over Jesus to their will.

HISTORICAL BACKGROUND

Death by Crucifixion

Crucifixion was the method the Romans used to execute Christ. It was the most painful and degrading form of capital punishment in the ancient world. A person crucified in Jesus's day was first beaten with a whip consisting of thongs with pieces of metal attached to the end. This scourging was designed to hasten death and lessen the terrible ordeal. After the beating, the victim carried the crossbeam to signify that life was over and to break his will to live. A tablet detailing the crime was often placed around the criminal's neck. At the site, the prisoner was tied (normal method) or nailed (if a quicker death was desired) to the crossbeam. The nail would be driven through the wrist rather than the palm, since the smaller bones of the hand could not support the weight of the body. Pins or a small wooden block were placed halfway up the stake to provide a seat for the body lest the nails tear open the wounds or the ropes force the arms from their sockets.

Section Summary

In spite of repeated pronouncements of his innocence, Jesus was sentenced to die by crucifixion. Jesus's opponents preferred the release of a revolutionary and a murderer rather than the one who "went about doing good and healing" (Acts 10:38).

THE WAY TO THE CROSS (22:26–32)

Jesus was now led away from the presence of Pilate to the place of execution. On the way, Simon of Cyrene was commandeered to carry Jesus's cross. As they proceeded, a great multitude of people followed. Among them were women, mourning and weeping over what was happening.

Jesus used this opportunity to pronounce that such mourning should not be directed toward him but reserved for themselves. This incident, recorded only in Luke, points to the judgment coming on Jerusalem. A most terrible time of tribulation was coming upon them. In this poignant scene Jesus uttered a final prophetic warning of the judgment coming upon Israel.

Section Summary

Being a disciple means to take up a cross and follow Jesus. Simon of Cyrene was, so to speak, the first person to take up his cross and follow Jesus.

THE CRUCIFIXION (23:33–49)

The Romans reserved the horrors of crucifixion for criminals and slaves. This method of capital punishment was the first-century counterpart to firing squads and electric chairs.

THE SEVEN SAYINGS OF JESUS ON THE CROSS

SAYING	PASSAGE	EXPLANATION
1. "Father, forgive them, because they do not know what they are doing."	Luke 23:34	Jesus asked forgiveness for his enemies.
2. "Truly I tell you, today you will be with me in paradise."	Luke 23:43	Jesus offered paradise to the repentant thief on the cross.
3. "Woman, here is your son" and "Here is your mother."	John 19:27	Jesus committed the care of Mary to his disciple John.
4. "My God, my God, why have you abandoned me?"	Matt 27:46	Jesus was aware of his present alienation from God.
5. "I'm thirsty."	John 19:28	Jesus expressed agony due to the torture of crucifixion.
6. "It is finished."	John 19:30	A cry of victory, expressing that he had paid the debt of sin.
7. "Father, into your hands I entrust my spirit."	Luke 23:46	An expressed confidence in the triumphant restored fellowship with the Father after death.

THE TWO CRIMINALS (23:39–43)

Jesus Crucified (vv. 33–38)

After Jesus arrived at Golgotha, "The Skull," he was crucified between two thieves. Crucifixion was a method of execution designed to torture and humiliate the victim. The Gospels do not focus on the torment Jesus endured but on the significance of his death.

As he was crucified, Jesus prayed for the forgiveness of his opponents. Lots were cast and Jesus's garments were divided. While the people watched, the rulers taunted Jesus, repeating some of his claims as being the Messiah.

The Gospels record seven sayings of Jesus on the cross. Two of Luke's sayings are prayers. As he was being crucified, he kept praying, "Father, forgive them, because they do not know what they are doing" (v. 34), and "Father, into your hands I entrust my spirit" (v. 46).

The incident of the two criminals raises the question of why some people believe and some don't. Both criminals apparently were exposed to the same sights and sounds; yet one joined in the mockery of Jesus, and the other believed. The one who believed asked to be remembered in Christ's coming kingdom. Jesus promised him that he would be with Jesus in paradise on that very day.

OLD TESTAMENT REFERENCE

Two other men, both criminals, were led out with Jesus. This fulfilled the prophecy of Isa 53:12, which says of the suffering Savior, he "was counted among the rebels; yet he bore the sin of many."

The Death of Jesus (vv. 44–49)

The eerie darkness of Jesus's final hours pointed to the cosmic significance of his dying. The cry recorded by Matthew (27:46) and Mark (15:34) showed that the forces of darkness did their worst to Jesus during that time. The prayer in verse 46 showed that Jesus had won the victory. At the time the disciples did not realize this, but after the resurrection they saw the cross in a totally new light.

The tearing of the temple curtain signified that the death of Christ opened the way for all people into the presence of God. Knowing that he completed his departure, Jesus committed his spirit into his Father's hands: "Father, into your hands I entrust my spirit." And then he breathed his last breath.

The response of the Roman centurion is the account's high point, serving as the final witness to Jesus's innocence. The centurion was convinced that Jesus was innocent and praised God.

WORD PICTURE

Paradise

This is an old Persian term meaning literally "enclosure" or "wooded park." All three New Testament references, including this one, refer to the abode of the righteous dead. Over the years, it came to refer to heaven.

The dead in Christ share with the living this hope of the final consummation of God's redemptive purpose.

Section Summary

Even in his crucifixion Jesus was in control of all that was taking place. All was happening in accordance with the fulfillment of his teachings and plans. No one took his life from him. He gave it freely.

THE BURIAL OF JESUS (23:50–56)

Joseph of Arimathea (vv. 50–53)

Joseph's act was a sign of hope. As a member of the Sanhedrin, he opposed what that group had done. Now he acted with faith and courage to provide a tomb for the body of Jesus.

The Women (vv. 54–56)

These verses bridge the gap between Luke's accounts of the crucifixion and resurrection of Jesus. These loyal women had ministered to him in life. They were determined to do what they could for him after he was dead.

QUESTIONS TO GUIDE YOUR STUDY

1. Throughout his trial, Jesus was seen as innocent by the authorities; yet he allowed himself to be sentenced and executed. Why did he not contest these proceedings?
2. Evaluate the character of Pontius Pilate as presented in Luke's account. What were his convictions? What ultimately drove his decision making?

3. What is the significance of the suffering Christ endured on the cross? What do his death and resurrection mean to those who believe on him?

LUKE 24

This chapter deals with the resurrection and ascension of Jesus. In this section, we find the culmination of all that has gone before. Luke divides this section into five accounts. None of the Gospels records all the resurrection appearances of Jesus. Each evangelist tells of the resurrection in light of his distinctive purpose. Luke emphasizes the reality of the resurrection and the difference it made in the lives of the disciples.

THE WOMEN AT THE EMPTY TOMB (24:1–12)

Carrying spices they prepared, Mary Magdalene, Joanna, and Mary the mother of James went to visit the tomb of Jesus. They were greeted with a shock. They found the stone rolled away and the tomb empty. In their perplexity they heard two angels announce that Jesus was not dead but alive! However, when they reported this to the apostles, they did not believe them. Some of the men went to the tomb and found it empty.

The angels reminded the women that Jesus predicted his death and resurrection. How could the disciples have heard those predictions and not be expecting Jesus to be raised from the dead? Apparently, they heard only what they expected to hear.

HISTORICAL BACKGROUND

Emmaus

"Emmaus" means "hot baths." It was a village about seven miles from Jerusalem. As many as four sites have been proposed as the location of Emmaus, but certainty isn't possible.

JESUS'S APPEARANCE ON THE ROAD TO EMMAUS (24:13–35)

Only Luke records this appearance of Jesus to two of his followers on the road to Emmaus. In fact, this is one of three accounts of post-resurrection appearances unique to Luke.

These men on their way to Emmaus spoke frankly with Jesus but did not recognize him. Their conversation revealed how Jesus's friends were feeling before they became aware of his resurrection. They revealed their feelings not only by their words but also by how they looked: "They stopped walking and looked discouraged" (v. 17).

Jesus then led the two into a discussion. Many people of Jesus's day were diligent students of the Scriptures, but most missed the central message. They focused their attention on the passages that presented the Messiah as a glorious King, but they missed the passages that spoke of suffering as God's way of dealing with evil. The risen Lord, still unrecognized by the two Emmaus disciples, proceeded to show them how this theme runs through the Old Testament (v. 27). He showed them that the suffering of the cross is the way of triumph.

The day was almost over when the two men recognized Jesus. He then miraculously disappeared from their sight. Their certainty in knowing Jesus came in the sharing of Scripture and the "breaking of the bread." They now knew why their hearts burned within them as they walked along the way.

HISTORICAL BACKGROUND

Jesus's Resurrection Body

The exact nature of Jesus's resurrection body remains a mystery. He appeared to the disciples from time to time, usually suddenly. On the other hand, he had a body that could be seen and touched, and the disciples recognized the body as Jesus's body. The resurrection of Jesus, therefore, means more than that Jesus's spirit survived death. It points to two great truths of Christianity: (1) the tomb was empty; and (2) people saw Jesus alive in bodily form.

JESUS'S APPEARANCE TO THE DISCIPLES IN JERUSALEM (24:36–43)

The disciples, fearing persecution from the authorities, had met behind locked doors.

Jesus suddenly and supernaturally appeared to them. If the disciples believed Jesus was risen, why were they startled and frightened when Jesus appeared to them? Hearing Peter's testimony was one thing, but suddenly being confronted by the Lord was something else. Jesus challenged them to look carefully and to touch him. He even ate a piece of fish to show them he was not a ghost.

Even as Jesus spoke to them, the disciples "still were amazed and in disbelief because of their joy" (v. 41).

NEW TESTAMENT REFERENCE

The disciples were to be Jesus's witnesses, and they were to proclaim what they themselves had seen and heard. First, however, they were to wait in Jerusalem until Jesus sent the promise of his Father so they would be divinely empowered to fulfill this mission. In two other Gospels, as well as in the longer ending of Mark, there exists some form of a final commissioning scene (Matt 28:19–20; John 20:21–23; Mark 16:15–16).

JESUS'S COMMISSION TO THE DISCIPLES (24:44–49)

Having assured the disciples of his physical resurrection, Jesus then gave them his final instructions. As with the two disciples on the road to Emmaus, he explained to them what is written in the Scriptures. To fulfill the Scriptures, something else must be accomplished. It involved the preaching in Jesus's name of repentance for the forgiveness of sins to all the world, beginning in Jerusalem.

Section Summary

This entire chapter has focused on the disciples' role as eyewitnesses of Jesus's ministry, death, and resurrection. They were directed to share their personal experience of the risen Christ.

THE ASCENSION (24:50–53)

These verses are a short account of the ascension, which is also described in Acts 1:9–11.

Leaving Jerusalem, Jesus led the disciples to Bethany on the Mount of Olives. After bestowing upon them his parting blessing, he was taken up into heaven. The striking part of this account is what happened after Jesus left the disciples. Having worshiped Jesus, the disciples returned with great joy to Jerusalem.

Earlier, when Jesus was taken from them by death, they were completely demoralized. But now, after being assured of his resurrection, they were able to rejoice even though he had departed from them. What better could show the difference made by their confidence in the resurrection of Jesus Christ from the dead!

Section Summary

The question "Who is Jesus?" is now fully answered. The disciples' worshiping Jesus was an acknowledgment of his divinity.

QUESTIONS TO GUIDE YOUR STUDY

1. What was the scene at the tomb of Jesus when the women arrived? What was the reaction of the women? What would have been your reaction?
2. When the two disciples on the road to Emmaus finally recognized who Jesus was, what confirmed his identity? What lessons might we draw from this event?
3. For what reasons did Jesus make his several post-resurrection appearances? In what ways does his ministry continue?
4. Jesus's disciples carried out their commission having been eyewitnesses of Jesus's ministry, death, and resurrection. On what basis do his followers today carry on the Great Commission?

HISTORICAL BACKGROUND

The Significance of the Ascension of Christ

The ascension concluded Jesus's earthly ministry. It allowed eyewitnesses to see both the risen Christ on earth and victorious and also the eternal Christ returning to heaven to minister at the right hand of the Father. Moreover, the ascension expanded Christ's ministry from its geographically limited earthly dimensions to its universal heavenly dimensions.

John

INTRODUCTION

The Gospel of John is perhaps the most intriguing of the four accounts of the life and teaching of Jesus. In recording more than a theological treatise, John put the challenge of the incarnation before his readers—God in human flesh.

GOSPEL OF JOHN IN A "NUTSHELL"

Purpose:	"But these are written so that you may believe that Jesus is the Messiah, the Son of God, and that by believing you may have life in his name." (John 20:31)
Major Doctrine:	Salvation
Key Passages:	John 1:14; 3:16–21
Other Key Doctrines:	The Person and Work of Christ The Holy Spirit

AUTHOR

The authorship of the Gospel of John has been traditionally ascribed to the apostle John, the son of Zebedee and the brother of James. The Gospel itself, however, does not name its author. This has made authorship a much-debated issue among interpreters. The only reference to the author is the "disciple Jesus loved" (21:20, 24).

The apostle John is usually seen as the author because the Gospel exhibits many marks that suggest it was written by one who was an eyewitness to the life and ministry of Jesus.

PURPOSE FOR WRITING

John included a more precise statement of purpose in his Gospel than did the other Gospel writers. From his statement in 20:31, we can see:

1. He *was selective*. His Gospel suggests that much more could have been written regarding Jesus, but only selected events are recorded.
2. His *Gospel is evangelistic*. John wanted others to believe in Jesus Christ and receive eternal life.
3. His *gospel focuses strongly on the identity of Jesus*. Jesus is not only Israel's Messiah; he is the Word of God—the Son of God.

HISTORICAL BACKGROUND

The Jews of the dispersion were scattered in various parts of the world. The Diaspora took place over several centuries beginning in the eighth century before Christ. By the time John was written, as many Jews lived outside of Palestine as within it.

DATE OF WRITING

Most interpreters have concluded that John's was the last of the four Gospels to be written, most likely between AD 85 and 95.

AUDIENCE

It is not completely clear who John's audience was. Some believe he wrote his Gospel to Jewish Christians. Others find it addressed to Jews of the dispersion.

John's Gospel could have addressed early Christians as they worshiped and witnessed. Others think that it was addressed to no one in particular but to the world at large.

Therefore, looking at all three possible target audiences—Jewish, Gentile, and Christian—and all three time frames—past, present, and future—the Gospel of John was sent out into the world to convince people that Jesus Christ was God's Son, the Savior, and to challenge them to faith in him.

WORD PICTURE

Gospel

The word *gospel* comes from the Anglo-Saxon word *godspell*, which literally means "good news." It is a narrative of the good news of Jesus Christ. Within the New Testament, the word *euangelion*—which is translated "gospel"—always refers to oral communication, never to a document or piece of literature. Not until the beginning of the second century and the writings of the church fathers do references to Gospels—written documents—occur.

LITERARY FORM

The literary form of John's Gospel is just that—a gospel.

John made use of many features of Hebrew poetry. His Gospel does not contain parables of the kind included in Matthew, Mark, and Luke but rather brings forth the many allegories Jesus used in his teaching.

KEY FEATURES IN JOHN'S GOSPEL

An Emphasis on Signs. In John's Gospel a miracle is a sign. These supernatural events point to Jesus's divine origin and are witness to his deity.

An Emphasis on Jesus's Attendance at Feasts. Within his Gospel John mentioned three Passovers, the Feast of Tabernacles, and the Feast of Dedication.

An Emphasis on Jesus's Judean Ministry. John's Gospel provides us with the fullest account of Jesus's ministry in Judea. John's narrative supplements the information we find in the Synoptic Gospels regarding Jesus's ministry in Judea.

Many Lengthy Discourses. These discourses are replete with key questions, profound answers, and dialogue. It is likely that John paraphrased Jesus's words and summarized the discourses in his own words.

THEOLOGICAL SIGNIFICANCE OF JOHN'S GOSPEL

From this Gospel we learn much about God as Father. Contemporary believers are indebted to John for their habit of referring to God simply as "the Father."

The Gospel of John focuses on Jesus Christ. It is clear in John's Gospel that God in Christ has revealed himself (1:1–18). God is active in Christ, the Savior of the world, bringing about the salvation he has planned (4:42).

John's Gospel tells us more about the Holy Spirit than the other Gospels. The Spirit is active at the start of Jesus's ministry (1:32), but the Spirit's full work was to begin at the consummation of Jesus's own ministry (7:37–39). The Spirit brings life (3:1–8), a life of the highest quality (10:10), and leads believers in the way of truth (16:13). In this way, the Spirit multiplies Jesus's ministry for and through Christians of all ages.

HISTORICAL BACKGROUND

Matthew, Mark, and Luke are called the Synoptic Gospels because their view of Jesus is similar. They share much of the same content, order, and wording while having marked differences.

ETHICAL SIGNIFICANCE OF JOHN'S GOSPEL

In response to the work of God in their lives, Christians are to be characterized by love (13:34–35). They owe all they have to the love of God, and it is proper they respond to that love by loving God and other people.

BASIC OUTLINE OF JOHN

I. Introduction (1:1–2:11)
II. Jesus's Public Ministry (2:12–4:54)
III. Opposition to Christ (5:1–12:50)
IV. Final Words and Deeds of Christ (13:1–21:25)

QUESTIONS TO GUIDE YOUR STUDY

1. What did John want to accomplish with his Gospel?
2. Matthew, Mark, and Luke are known as the Synoptic Gospels. Why is John's Gospel different from these three Gospels?
3. What are the key themes of John's Gospel?
4. Based on this introduction, what are we to gain from a study of John's Gospel?

TITLES FOR JESUS IN JOHN		
TITLE	**SIGNIFICANCE**	**REFERENCE**
Bread of Life	The one essential food	6:35
Good Shepherd	Gives guidance and protection	10:11
Lamb of God	Offered his life as a sacrifice for sins	1:29
Light of the World	One who brings hope and gives guidance	9:5
Rabbi/Teacher	A title of respect for one who taught the Scriptures	3:2
Son of God	A title of deity signifying Jesus's unique and special intimacy with the Father	20:31
Word	Eternal God who supremely reveals God	1:1

JOHN 1

John opens his Gospel with an eloquent prologue: "In the beginning was the Word." The first eighteen verses introduce themes that John elaborates on in the rest of his Gospel.

THE PROLOGUE (1:1–18)

MEANING OF THE TERM *WORD* TO JOHN'S FIRST READERS

AUDIENCE	MEANING
1. Jews	Power—the Word of God that "spoke" the world into being
2. Greeks	Principle—the rational principle or rational mind that rules the universe
3. Christians	Proclamation—the preaching of the gospel

"The Word was God" (vv. 1–3).

No other book in the Bible has a prologue as overtly theological as does the Gospel of John. First, John references Gen 1 and makes a clear and decisive statement regarding the nature of Jesus: "The Word was God." John wanted it known that Jesus Christ is fully God in human form.

THREE BASIC AFFIRMATIONS OF CHRISTIAN DOCTRINE IN JOHN 1:1

AFFIRMATION	SIGNIFICANCE
1. "In the beginning was the Word"	The Word existed *before* creation
2. "The Word was with God"	The personal relationship of the Word to God
3. "The Word was God"	The Word is true deity

HISTORICAL BACKGROUND

John the Apostle

John was the son of Zebedee and the brother of James. John is always mentioned in the first four lists of the twelve apostles. He is also among the "inner three" who were with Jesus on special occasions. Five books of the New Testament are attributed to John: this Gospel, three epistles (1, 2, 3 John), and Revelation. In each case, the traditional view that the apostle was the author of this Gospel can be traced to the following second-century writers: Irenaeus, Clement of Alexandria, and Tertullian. Neither the Gospel nor the epistles identify their author by name.

And yet John makes clear that while he equates the Word with God, the Word is distinct from the Father.

The Purpose of the Word (vv. 4–5)

Christ, the Word, brings life, a life that serves as the "light" for all people. The life that Christ offers is not temporal; it is eternal. It is of God. The questions and concerns of this world that find no ultimate answers are met by the Light that pierces all darkness with the brilliance of truth, yet this truth has been rejected.

John expresses two purposes with the concepts of *light* and *life*: (1) Jesus Christ came into the world to reveal the person and character of God; and (2) Christ came to redeem people.

Section Summary

The Word that existed prior to creation has now become human in a person, Jesus Christ of Nazareth. The Word is now dwelling among mankind, displaying the glory of God and shining the Light of life in a dark, sinful world.

POINTS OF CONTRAST BETWEEN LIGHT AND DARKNESS IN JOHN'S WRITINGS

LIGHT	DARKNESS
God	Satan
Truth	Lies
Holiness	Sin
Life	Death

THE WORLD AND THE WORD (1:6–18)

Jesus as the Light. The Word has come into the world as a Person. The witness to that Person will be given by another person. That witness is a man sent by God—John the Baptist. His purpose is to lead people to believe in the Light, who is Jesus (1:35–37). Jesus's light is a witness to all people. Those who respond to his witness will become children of God by divine creation (1:12–13).

The Word becomes flesh. In verse14 we have one of the most profound statements in all history. The Word who created everything became a human being—lived in a particular place and time in history. This Word dwelled among us.

WORD PICTURE

Word

The term *logos* was probably chosen for several reasons: (1) its meaning in the Old Testament, (2) its use in Greek, and (3) its use in contemporary Hebrew literature, where the concepts of *wisdom* and *word* were being spoken of as essential attributes of God. John saw that the same agent of God who created the universe was at work in a new creation inaugurated by Jesus's coming. The creative Word of God became flesh—showing forth the glory of God (John 1:14).

HISTORICAL BACKGROUND

"The *Logos* here is more than reason, more than word; it is more than wisdom personified. The term designates a Person, distinct from and yet co-eternal and identical in essence with God—'all that God is the Logos is.'"

G. Turner and Jesus Mantey, *The Gospel According to John*, 54.

Section Summary

In one of the most profound statements in all history, the Word took the form of a person and entered the human race. The Word has now pitched his tent among people.

OLD TESTAMENT REFERENCE

The Jews used a lamb as a sacrifice for the Passover Feast, which celebrated Israel's deliverance from bondage in Egypt. Isaiah offered the idea of the Suffering Servant in terms of a sacrificial lamb (Isa 53). John is declaring that Jesus is the true sacrificial lamb for the Passover; his death would now serve as the deliverance of God's people from their sins. As Paul wrote in his letter to the church at Corinth, "Christ our Passover lamb has been sacrificed" (1 Cor 5:7).

JOHN THE BAPTIST'S ROLE (1:19–28)

John's narrative now shifts from poetry to prose. He explains the relationship between John the Baptist and Jesus Christ. John the Baptist was sent from God (1:6), but John was not himself the Light (v. 8). He came as a witness to Christ (vv. 7,15).

Section Summary

John the Baptist offered the words of the prophet Isaiah about the nature of his identity: "a voice of one crying out in the wilderness: Make straight the way of the Lord" (1:23; see Isa 40:3). John denied being either Isaiah or Elijah, as some proposed. What was at hand in Jesus's mind was how John became a fulfillment of the prophecy recorded in Mal 4:5.

In this Gospel we see a threefold purpose for John's testimony:

1. To fulfill the prophecy of Isa 40:3.
2. To call people to repentance.
3. To draw people's attention to the coming of the Messiah, Jesus Christ.

Section Summary

John the Baptist had a distinct role as forerunner to the Messiah's coming. His purpose, rooted in a prophecy of Isaiah, was to call people to repentance and point them to the coming Messiah.

WORD PICTURE

Son of Man

The term *Son of Man* is a messianic term that has its roots in the Old Testament. It is the term Jesus used most often to identify himself. The term went beyond classifying Jesus as a human. It also pointed to his heavenly origin and his glory. It spoke of his lowliness and humility in showing God to others through his suffering.

THE LAMB OF GOD (1:29–34)

John the Baptist's confession upon seeing Jesus—that here was "the Lamb of God, who takes away the sin of the world" (v. 29)—was of great significance.

John the Baptist then gave testimony that he "saw the Spirit descending from heaven like a dove, and he rested on" Jesus (v. 32). This confirmed to John that Jesus was the Messiah. Then he declared: "I have seen and testified that this is the Son of God" (v. 34).

Section Summary

Jesus is the true sacrificial lamb; his death would serve as the deliverance of God's people from their sins.

JESUS CALLS HIS DISCIPLES (1:35–51)

Andrew and Another Disciple (vv. 35–42)

The calling of Andrew, Simon Peter's brother, was the direct result of John the Baptist's testimony about Jesus as the Lamb of God. John did not name the second disciple mentioned in the narrative, but some believe it was the apostle John himself.

After spending an evening with Jesus, Andrew found his brother and made a startling announcement: "We have found the Messiah" (v. 41). He then brought Simon to Jesus.

Upon encountering Simon, Jesus gave him a new nickname, Cephas.

Philip and Nathanael (vv. 43–51)

Jesus took the initiative in calling Philip. His simple invitation was, "Follow me" (v. 43). Philip then shared his experience with Christ with another, Nathanael. He gave testimony to Nathanael that the One to whom the Scriptures gave witness is here. At first Nathanael was skeptical, but upon meeting Jesus he turned from his skepticism to faith.

Section Summary

Jesus began to choose his disciples. Included in this first group of four was Simon, to whom Jesus gave a new name—Cephas, meaning "rock."

WORD PICTURE

Cephas/Peter

The names "Cephas" (Aramaic) and "Peter" (Greek) both mean "rock." That Peter would be given this name is interesting because he was anything but rock-like. Peter was impulsive and undisciplined in spirit, a rough-hewn man of raw emotion. Yet Christ called those whom he would develop, and Peter would indeed become the pillar of the church, the "rock" upon which the early church would depend (Matt 19:16; Acts 2).

QUESTIONS TO GUIDE YOUR STUDY

1. What meaning was John trying to convey to his readers with the term *Word?*
2. What is the significance of the Word becoming flesh?
3. What was John the Baptist's role in relation to the Messiah?
4. What themes did John introduce in this first chapter?

JOHN 2

This chapter begins a major division of John's Gospel that deals with the signs Jesus used to point beyond himself to a truth about God. The eleven chapters of this section have to do with Jesus's public ministry.

WORD PICTURE

Sign

The Gospel of John uses the word *sign* rather than *miracle*. Signs served as authentication for Jesus's nature and mission. Further, a sign points beyond itself to a major truth about God made known through Jesus Christ. Throughout the section of John's Gospel that deals with Jesus's signs, a miracle is always a sign that points beyond the event of the miracle to a greater truth.

TURNING WATER INTO WINE (2:1–11)

The Sign (vv. 1–10)

Jesus's first miracle was at a wedding at Cana of Galilee.

During the wedding festivities, the wine ran out unexpectedly. Not only was this an embarrassing situation for the wedding family, but it

WORD PICTURE

Cana

Cana was about eight miles north of Jesus's hometown, Nazareth.

THE FIRST SIGN:
CHANGING WATER TO WINE

SIGN	CHARACTERISTIC OF JESUS'S POWER	RESULT OR RESPONSE
Jesus causes water to change into wine.	Creative	The disciples believed in Jesus.

could also expose them to legal liability. Mary informed Jesus that the wine supply was exhausted. At the proper time, Jesus instructed servants to fill several stone waterpots with water. He then had them draw out some water and take it to the steward of the feast. The steward, upon tasting the wine, remarked that the quality of the wine was better than before.

PERSONAL APPLICATION

With Jesus there is full and complete revelation of God. He brings new joy into life. When the old life has gone flat, Jesus introduces a new joy and vitality.

The Meaning of the Sign (v. 11)

Numbers often have a symbolic meaning in the Bible. Seven is the number of completion, whereas the number six indicates something just short of completion. Six waterpots were used, which are connected to Jewish ritual observances. The knowledge the Jews had of God and their relationship to him through the Jewish law was incomplete. *One* was needed to make it complete—Jesus.

THE SEVEN SIGNS IN JOHN

SIGN	REFERENCE	CENTRAL TRUTH
1. Changing water to wine	2:1–11	Points to Jesus as the source of all the blessings of God's future (see Isa 25:6–8; Jer 31:11–12; Amos 9:13–14)
2. Healing the official's son	4:43–54	Points to Jesus as the Giver of life
3. Healing the invalid at Bethesda	5:1–15	Points to Jesus as the Father's coworker
4. Feeding the five thousand	6:1–15,25–69	Points to Jesus as the life-giving Bread from heaven
5. Walking on water	6:16–21	Points to Jesus as the divine I AM
6. Healing the man born blind	9:1–41	Points to Jesus as the Giver of spiritual sight
7. Raising Lazarus	11:1–44	Points to Jesus as the Resurrection and the Life

Section Summary

The water, used for purification, is replaced with wine, which would come to symbolize the blood of Christ. The blood of Christ did indeed supplant the Jewish ceremonial system in regard to the problem of sin and a holy God's demand for righteousness. Jesus performed his first miracle by turning water into wine. It was symbolic. As the complete revelation of God, Jesus brings new joy into life.

JESUS CLEARS OUT THE TEMPLE (2:12–25)

All four Gospels include the incident of Jesus's cleansing the temple. In this act, Jesus brought forth God's standards of right and wrong.

It was Passover, the time of remembering how God delivered Israel from bondage in Egypt. Jesus encountered individuals who were profiteering from the religious festival.

Jesus saw these merchants taking advantage of the pilgrims to Jerusalem. He was incensed by what he saw and made a whip out of cords. Jesus then overturned the tables of the money changers and chased them and their animals from the temple. He then charged the money changers with making the house of God a house of trade.

This spectacle aroused the indignation of the Jews. Their concern was not the moral issue of whether the sellers and money changers should have been there but rather on what grounds Jesus took it upon himself to expel them. When the Jews called for a "sign," Jesus responded, "Destroy this temple, and I will raise it up in three days" (v. 18). Jesus was referring to the temple of his body.

A result of this cleansing of the temple was that Jesus introduced a new kind of worship. Whereas the money changers substituted convenience for compassion and sacrifice for submission, Jesus showed that the Father demands instead sincerity and truth in worship.

HISTORICAL BACKGROUND

Money Changing in the Temple

Money changers were present at the temple to exchange Roman or other money for Jewish money acceptable in the temple worship. Worshipers could also purchase birds and animals used for sacrifice. Since sacrificial birds and animals had to be officially certified and unblemished, it was helpful to purchase them at the temple. Some exchangers profited greatly by loaning their money. Their interest rates ranged from 20 to 300 percent per year. Evidently, the selling and money changing became a means of cheating and exploiting the people. In anger at this corruption of the purpose of the temple, Jesus turned over the tables of the money changers and drove them and the sellers of animals out of the temple court.

Section Summary

Incensed at what was taking place at the temple, Jesus used a whip and drove the money changers from the temple. Although the Jewish authorities were indignant, Jesus succeeded in showing that the Father demands sincerity and truth in worship.

QUESTIONS TO GUIDE YOUR STUDY

1. John's Gospel presents seven signs, the first of which appears in this chapter. What is a sign, and what is its purpose?
2. Who were the money changers, and what were they doing in the temple?

HISTORICAL BACKGROUND

Nicodemus

His name means "conqueror of the people." John identified Nicodemus as a Pharisee and a member of the Sanhedrin, the Jewish ruling council. He was a "teacher of Israel," that is, an authority on the interpretation of the Hebrew Scriptures. The reference to Nicodemus's initial coming at night to see Jesus highlights his later public participation in Jesus's burial (John 19:39–41). His contribution was aloes and spices, enough to prepare a king for burial.

WORD PICTURE

Water and the Spirit

There is some debate about the meaning of *water*. Because the Pharisees were aware of John the Baptist's baptism, Jesus could have been alluding to John's baptism for repentance. His baptism suggested repentance from the former manner of life. The meaning of *Spirit* is clear, as it was a reference to the spiritual rebirth—regeneration—brought about by the activity of the Holy Spirit in a human life.

"Born of water" could also refer to physical birth. Jesus contrasted this with being born of the Spirit. "Unless someone is born of water and the Spirit, he cannot enter the kingdom of God. Whatever is born of the flesh is flesh, and whatever is born of the Spirit is spirit" (John 3:5–6).

3. Why did Jesus clear the temple? What resulted from this incident?
4. What did Jesus mean with his statement, "Destroy this temple, and I will raise it up in three days"?

JOHN 3

This chapter deals with the theme of the new birth and contains perhaps the most familiar verse in the Bible: John 3:16. This verse is often referred to as "the Bible in miniature."

GOD'S SAVING LOVE (3:1–21)

Nicodemus Learns of the New Birth (vv. 1–15)

Nicodemus had everything: power, prestige, and position. He was a member of the Sanhedrin, a council of seventy elders—a group that was most interested in following the law precisely. Yet he decided to visit Jesus at night. In spite of all he had, he wanted to know more about Jesus's teaching. This conversation between Nicodemus and Jesus is the first discourse John recorded in his Gospel.

Nicodemus opened the conversation with Jesus with a compliment by calling him "Rabbi." *Rabbi* means "teacher." Although Nicodemus knew that Jesus was not formally trained, he apparently observed that God was a part of what Jesus had been doing.

Jesus got to the heart of the matter and his message: "Unless someone is born again, he cannot see the kingdom of God" (v. 3). A startling statement indeed to Nicodemus! He began to interpret it literally and questioned the possibility of being physically reborn. Rephrasing his statement, Jesus asserted that unless one is born of both "water and the Spirit" a person cannot enter the kingdom of God. Jesus clarified that he was speaking about a spiritual rebirth, not a physical one.

The Good News of Jesus Christ (vv. 16–21)

There can be little doubt that this section of John's narrative is the most familiar in all of Scripture, with verse 16 serving as the most familiar single verse in all the Bible. There is good reason, for John 3:16 presents the clearest, simplest statement of the good news of Jesus Christ.

There are three key aspects to the good news:

1. God loves us.
2. God's love is so great that he sent his only Son to tell the world about God's love.
3. Anyone who believes in God's Son will never die but will live forever with God.

Belief means far more than intellectual assent to the claims of Christ. It means placing one's life and trust in complete surrender to the one in whom we believe.

Section Summary

To enter the kingdom of God, one must be "born again." Because of his love for us, God sent his only Son into the world to save us. The good news of Jesus Christ is that by believing in him we can be born again and receive eternal life.

JESUS, THE DISCIPLER (3:22–36)

When students of the life of Christ list the priorities of his ministry, many items come to mind: the miracles, the teaching of the multitudes, the crucifixion, and the resurrection. But one of Jesus's top priorities was discipling twelve men. This required time, and he took the time (v. 22) to prepare these men for the time when he would no longer be visibly present.

During this time, an argument developed between some of John's disciples and the Jewish leaders over ceremonial cleansing. The appropriate means of achieving ceremonial cleansing of their bodies and eating utensils was of great interest to the Jewish community. When the matter was brought to John, the question of Jesus's ministry in relation to John's ministry surfaced. The loyalty of these disciples to their master, John, is evident as they allowed envy to enter into their thinking about Jesus. John's reply affirmed his previous testimony about Jesus. It also provided an important insight into John's character.

Knowing a teachable moment had presented itself, John informed his students that "no one can receive anything unless it has been given to him from heaven" (v. 27).

John knew that he was "from the earth," whereas Jesus, as God's Son, was "from heaven" (v. 31). John taught his disciples that their relationship with God's Son had eternal consequence.

Those who believe in and obey Jesus have eternal life. Those who don't believe and obey are in sin and have the abiding wrath of God on them.

Section Summary

This section is a clarification of the question of the followers of John the Baptist. It also answers the controversy that might arise between the followers of John and the church. Jesus is the new Master. John had simply pointed the way.

WORD PICTURE

Wrath

The Greek word for *wrath* is *orgē*, which denotes God's abiding opposition to sin.

HISTORICAL BACKGROUND

John the Baptist

John the Baptist was a prophet from a priestly family. He preached a message of repentance, announced the coming of the Messiah, baptized Jesus, and was beheaded by Herod Antipas. John's clothing reminded the people of the ancient prophet Elijah (cp. 2 Kgs 1:8). It was generally believed that Elijah would return just before the Messiah made his appearance. John wore camel-hair clothing with a leather girdle. His diet would be considered repulsive by most Westerners. He lived off the land, eating insects (such as locusts, an excellent source of protein) and wild honey (Matt 3:4).

PERSONAL APPLICATION

The point of this affirmation is clear. Knowing God has given everything, one who loves God will not envy another person's gifts, abilities, or accomplishments. John understood his role in relation to Jesus as that of the best man to the groom at a wedding. John instructed those who had supported and followed his ministry that Jesus must become greater, while he, John, "must decrease" (v. 30).

JESUS'S DISCOURSES IN JOHN

REFERENCE	WHERE DELIVERED	STYLE	TO WHOM	LESSON
3:1–21	Jerusalem	Conversation	Nicodemus	We must be "born of water and the Spirit" to enter the kingdom of God.
4:1–30	Jacob's Well	Conversation	Samaritan Woman	"God is Spirit" and must be worshiped in Spirit and truth.
4:31–38	Jacob's Well	Conversation	The Disciples	Our food is to do his will.
5:1–47	Bethesda—a Pool	Conversation	The Jews	To hear him and believe on him is to have everlasting life.
6:22–71	Capernaum	Sermon	The Multitude	Christ as the Bread of life.
7:11–40	Temple—Jerusalem	Instruction	The Jews	Judge not according to outward appearance.
8:12–59	Temple—Jerusalem	Instruction	The Jews	To follow Christ is to walk in light.
10:1–21	Jerusalem	Instruction	The Jews	Christ is the door; he knows his sheep; he gives his life for them.
12:20–50	Jerusalem	Exhortation	The People	Death or life; way of eternal life.
13:1–20	Jerusalem	Exhortation	The Disciples	The lesson of humility and service.
14–16	Jerusalem	Exhortation	The Disciples	The proof of discipleship: that he will come again.

QUESTIONS TO GUIDE YOUR STUDY

1. What do we know about Nicodemus? Why was he interested in what Jesus had to say?
2. The "new birth" is the heart of Jesus's message. What does it mean to be "born again"?
3. In referring to the new birth, what did Jesus mean when he said that those who are born again are born of "water and the Spirit"?
4. What question did John's disciples ask concerning Jesus? What was John's reply?

JOHN 4

The key event of this chapter is Jesus's encounter with the Samaritan woman. This account provides us with an excellent model for considering the nature and strategy of evangelistic outreach.

HISTORICAL BACKGROUND

Samaritans were rejected by Jews primarily because of their mixed Gentile blood and their differing style of worship, which centered on Mount Gerizim. On this mountain the Samaritans had built a temple that rivaled the Jewish temple in Jerusalem. Samaritans insisted on worshiping at Mount Gerizim even after their temple was destroyed.

JESUS THE SOURCE OF LIFE (4:1–26)

Not wanting to be seen in competition with John's ministry, Jesus returned to Galilee. On that journey he passed through Samaria. Most Jews went out of their way to avoid Samaria. Not Jesus. Samaria was a part of his mission. The division between the Jews and the Samaritans was legendary and one that Jesus refused to recognize.

Jesus's excursion into Samaria resulted in one of the most fascinating dialogues recorded in all of Scripture. Resting near a well, Jesus encountered a Samaritan woman who was living a life of habitual immorality. Their conversation proceeded on two levels, the spiritual and the temporal, with the woman constantly finding excuses to counter Jesus's probing of her life.

Her first shock was that Jesus would even speak to her, a Samaritan woman, considering the animosity between Jews and Samaritans. Jesus responded not to her questions but to her needs, offering her the opportunity to receive "living water" (v. 10).

Here we see much regarding the intent of Jesus's ministry, which was to bring people to a realization of the state of their life to lead them to repentance and a new life in him. In their new lives they honor and worship God in spirit and truth daily. In his answer, Jesus freed worship from the limitations of place. The location of worship is not important, but the object of worship is!

Section Summary

In his encounter with the Samaritan woman at the well, we see much regarding the intent of Jesus's ministry, which was to bring people to a realization of the state of their lives that leads them to repentance and a new life in him.

PERSONAL APPLICATION

"Both for perplexity and for dulled conscience the remedy is the same: sincere and spiritual worship. For worship is the submission of all our nature to God. It is the quickening of conscience by His holiness; the nourishment of mind with His truth; the purifying of imagination by His beauty; the opening of the heart to His love; the surrender of will to His purpose—and all of this gathered up in adoration, the most selfless emotion of which our nature is capable and therefore the chief remedy for that self-centeredness which is our original sin that is the source of all actual sin."

J. Temple, *Readings in St. John's Gospel*, 68.

THE MESSIAH'S MISSION (4:27–38)

When the disciples rejoined Jesus, they did not dare ask him about his conversation with the Samaritan woman but rather inquired about his physical well-being. Perhaps they thought hunger had deprived him of his senses, as he should have known better than to talk with such a woman. Jesus then continued the disciples' education, instructing them that his "food" was to "do the will of him who sent me and to finish his work" (v. 34).

Section Summary

As Messiah, Jesus's mission was to confront all people with the saving, liberating truth of himself.

JESUS AS THE SAVIOR OF THE WORLD (4:39–42)

Jesus's encounter with the woman at the well and her subsequent sharing of that conversation resulted in many Samaritans believing in Jesus. After they met Jesus themselves, they believed not because of what the woman said but because they came to believe themselves "that this really is the Savior of the world" (v. 42). This confession of the Samaritan believers—that Jesus is the Savior—is found only here and in 1 John 4:14. Only through Jesus is the world able to be saved, and this salvation is indeed for everyone in the world.

MIRACLES OF JESUS IN THE GOSPEL OF JOHN

MIRACLE	PASSAGE
Water turned to wine	2:1
Healing of a royal official's son	4:46
Healing of a lame man at Bethesda	5:1
Feeding of five thousand	6:1
Walking on the sea	6:16
Healing of the blind man	9:1
Raising of Lazarus	11:38
A miraculous catch of fish	21:1

THE HEALING OF THE OFFICIAL'S SON (4:43–54)

After his time in Samaria, Jesus returned to Galilee. There he met a royal official whose child was near death. Jesus commented how the belief of the Galileans was tied to his production of miraculous signs

THE SECOND SIGN: THE HEALING OF THE OFFICIAL'S SON

MIRACLE PERFORMED	CHARACTERISTIC OF JESUS'S POWER	RESULT OR RESPONSE TO THE SIGN
Jesus heals a boy from a great distance by his word.	Master of *distance, space*	The official believed in Jesus.

and wonders. This provided an interesting contrast, for the Samaritans believed "because of what he said" (v. 41), while the Jews believed because of "signs and wonders" (v. 48). As Jesus would later say to Thomas following his resurrection, "Blessed are those who have not seen and yet believe" (John 20:29).

PERSONAL APPLICATION

Jesus was clearly on a mission, one that was God informed and God directed. What was that mission? To confront people—all people, as the Samaritan woman demonstrated—with the truth of himself. Jesus told them that the fields were "ready for harvest" (v. 35) and that in entering the field for work it made no difference whether one plants the seed or brings in the crop. This is an important truth, for there should never be competition among Christians regarding differing fields of service. All should share in the joy of seeing the kingdom of God expanded.

Section Summary

Jesus's second sign was a miracle of healing the official's son, who had become ill. This sign demonstrated his mastery over the limitations of distance or space.

QUESTIONS TO GUIDE YOUR STUDY

1. Why was it considered so strange for Jesus to speak to the Samaritan woman?
2. What did John mean by the phrase "living water" in describing this story?
3. What was the Messiah's mission?
4. Jesus's second sign was the healing of the official's son. What does this sign show us?

JOHN 5

Starting with this section of John's narrative, we see an increasing reaction to Jesus's ministry. Each incident of controversy is set within the context of a Jewish festival, which serves to heighten the dramatic effect of the religious leaders' opposition to Jesus. Also, John uses the third sign to develop the theme of unbelief.

HISTORICAL BACKGROUND

The name of this feast is not mentioned, but it was probably one of the three pilgrimage feasts that all Jewish males were expected to attend: Passover, Pentecost, or Tabernacles.

JESUS HEALS AN INVALID (5:1–5)

THE THIRD SIGN: THE HEALING OF THE INVALID AT BETHESDA

MIRACLE PERFORMED	CHARACTERISTIC OF JESUS'S POWER	RESULT OR RESPONSE TO THE SIGN
Jesus heals a man who has been ill for thirty-eight years.	Master of time	The Jews begin persecuting Jesus.

After an unspecified period of time, Jesus traveled to Jerusalem for a "Jewish festival" (v. 1).

Jesus passed by the Bethesda pool, where several invalids had placed themselves. The waters, when stirred, supposedly had miraculous powers of healing. Jesus asked a man who had been there for thirty-eight years an interesting question: "Do you want to get well?" (v. 6). In Jesus's day, many people depended on their unfortunate condition for financial support given by healthy individuals out of pity.

Another possible reason for Jesus's question relates to the man's spirit. Many who have experienced prolonged pain or misfortune have surrendered even the will to attempt to overcome their situation in life. When the invalid shared with Jesus his difficulty of getting into the pool for healing, Jesus proclaimed: "Get up, . . . pick up your mat and walk" (v. 8). The man was healed instantly.

This healing took place on a Sabbath. The Jewish leader's response was not joy over the man's healing but concern that he was violating the Sabbath by carrying his mat!

The law of Moses did not forbid such a practice; only the Jewish *interpretation* of the law of Moses forbade it. Jesus found the healed man and, as with the Samaritan woman at the well, addressed the deeper condition of the man's relationship with God. Jesus's words are interesting: "Do not sin anymore, so that something worse doesn't happen to you" (v. 14).

HISTORICAL BACKGROUND

"'The Jews' of verse 10 must have been Pharisees. They stopped him to charge him with being a lawbreaker, 'It is not lawful for you to carry your pallet.' Doubtless they had in mind Exodus 20:10, 'You shall not do any work' on the sabbath. How much work is there in carrying a krabbatos (poor-man's pallet) across town? Not much, and it was not the kind of labor prohibited by the Exodus law anyway. But the Pharisees would not even lift saliva from their mouth to rub on their sore eyes on the sabbath because it meant carrying a burden." R. Summers, *Behold the Lamb*, 88.

Section Summary

Jesus's third sign of his power, the healing of an invalid, showed his mastery over time. With the healing, Jesus emphasized that the consequences of sin are far more serious than any form of physical illness we might have.

THE SON OF GOD (5:16–30)

John now informs his readers that because of this healing on the Sabbath, the Jews began to persecute Jesus. This is the first recorded hostility toward Jesus in John's narrative. Jesus's view of God ran counter to that of the religious leaders.

Jesus then rebuked the leaders for their response. This rebuke outraged the Jews because "he was even calling God his own Father, making himself equal to God" (v. 18). The Jews did not object to the idea of God as Father. They were concerned that Jesus somehow was in a special relationship to God as his Father, thus intimating that Jesus was equal with God.

Jesus then gave a clearly defined, seven-point response about the relationship between the Father (God) and the Son (himself).

1. The Son can do nothing without the Father (vv. 19,30).
2. The Father loves the Son and reveals everything to him (v. 20).
3. The power to bestow life itself is shared by the Father and the Son (v. 21).
4. God has given all judgment over to the Son (v. 22).
5. The Father and the Son share equal honor (v. 23).

PERSONAL APPLICATION

"In gratitude of this divine gift the man was enjoined to sin no more . . . he should not let the bitter memory of 38 tragic years continue to separate him from God. Bad as it had been to lie on a mat for most of his life, it would be even worse to be spiritually deformed, for God does not judge sickness, but he does judge sin." William Hull, *The Broadman Bible Commentary*, vol. 9, 263.

6. Belief in the words of the Son result in eternal life (v. 24).
7. The consummation of the age will be by and through the Son (vv. 25–30).

The Jews objected to Jesus's answer because of their staunch monotheism (belief in one God). Christians are monotheists as well yet maintain that the nature of the one true God is that he is triune—three persons (Father, Son, and Holy Spirit), one God.

To the Jewish mind, Jesus's claim to be God was blasphemous because it suggested the idea of two gods. Of course, nothing of the sort was in mind with Jesus's self-declaration as the Son of God. Rather, Jesus proclaimed that he was God in human form, the second Person of the Trinity.

PERSONAL APPLICATION

Legalism is a dreadful distortion of God's will for those whom he created to live in fellowship with him. The attitudes of the heart, not just outer deeds, matter to God. When the inner world is ordered so as to give first place to God and his will, the outer world will exhibit holiness—a holiness seen in the life and ministry of Jesus.

Section Summary

Jesus made the bold claim that he was the Son of God. Interpreting it correctly as his claim to be equal with God, the Jews were incensed.

TESTIMONY TO JESUS (5:31–47)

Throughout his narrative, John links the theme of *witness* to the theme of belief. Jesus's defense statement included five witnesses that give testimony to his claim to be the Son of Man. These include John the Baptist (v. 33), the works of Jesus (v. 36), God himself (v. 37), the Scriptures (v. 39), and Moses (v. 46).

The Witness of John the Baptist (vv. 31–35)

It was John the Baptist who first declared that Jesus was "the Lamb of God, who takes away the sin of the world" (1:29).

The Witness of Works of Jesus (v. 36)

These were the powerful acts of Jesus done on earth in cooperation with the Father (cp. 5:20; 9:4; 10:25,32,37–38; 14:10–11; 15:24).

The Witness of the Father (v. 37)

Three times the Father's witness came verbally during Jesus's ministry (Luke 3:22; 9:35; John 12:28–30).

The Witness of the Scriptures (vv. 39–44)

The Scriptures were the foundation of his opponents. What they sought in their studies of the Scriptures could only be found in Jesus. But the leaders would not accept his witness or his claims based on the Scriptures. Included in the Old Testament Scriptures was the witness of Moses (vv. 45–47).

With these witnesses, Jesus clearly distinguished the worth of human testimony from God's testimony (vv. 34,41,44).

Section Summary

Witness and belief are two key themes that John links in his Gospel. In his defense statement to the Jews, Jesus included five witnesses that give testimony to his claim to be the Son of Man.

QUESTIONS TO GUIDE YOUR STUDY

1. What was significant about Jesus's third sign?
2. Why did Jesus's healing of the invalid cause a controversy with the religious leaders?
3. The first recorded hostility toward Jesus in John's narrative has to do with Jesus's view that he is the Son of God. Why did this cause such a furor among the Jewish leaders?
4. What witnesses gave testimony to Jesus's claim to be the Son of man?

JOHN 6

This chapter contains several of Jesus's divine acts, including two of the seven signs. It also shows this period to be a time of testing for the disciples. In these verses they faced three tests as they dealt with the needs and reactions of the crowds: (1) addressing the hunger of the five thousand, (2) dealing with Jesus's popularity with the crowd, and (3) their choice to follow the crowd or remain with Jesus.

FEEDING THE FIVE THOUSAND (6:1–15)

THE FOURTH SIGN: THE FEEDING OF THE FIVE THOUSAND

MIRACLE PERFORMED	CHARACTERISTIC OF JESUS'S POWER	RESULT OR RESPONSE TO THE SIGN
Jesus multiplies the bread and fish to feed the crowd.	Master of *quantity*	The crowd wanted to make Jesus king.

The feeding of the five thousand is the one miracle, apart from the resurrection, that occurs in all four Gospels. The number of people fed was actually far greater than five thousand, for this figure referred only to the men, since women and children were not counted (Matt 14:21). At a time of human hopelessness, Jesus took over. He had the disciples seat the people in a grassy area. Then Jesus took bread and fish given to him by a boy, blessed the food, and gave it to the people. There was enough to satisfy the hunger of all the people. What seemed to be a hopeless situation was turned into a scene of hope by the power of God working through Jesus.

This sign pointed to the divine nature of Jesus, demonstrated by his power and authority over the natural, created world. The crowds seemed more interested in Jesus's signs than in his truth. This miracle led the people to try to make Jesus king by force. God's design was not that Jesus manifest himself as an earthly king but as the Suffering Servant who would give his life as a ransom for many (Mark 10:45). The result of this miracle was that some people began to believe that Jesus was indeed the prophet greater than Moses that the Scriptures prophesied.

PERSONAL APPLICATION

Not only did Jesus meet the needs of the people, but he also supplied them with more than enough. This was a lesson to the people, and to us today as well, that God through Jesus Christ provides more than is adequate for human needs.

Section Summary

The fourth sign was Jesus's miracle of the feeding of the five thousand. His provision was more than sufficient. In meeting the need of the crowd, not only did Jesus show his power over the natural, created world; he also showed that he was the master of quantity.

HISTORICAL BACKGROUND

Sea of Galilee

The place-name means "circle." The sea is a freshwater lake nestled in the hills of northern Palestine. Its surface is nearly seven hundred feet below the level of the Mediterranean Sea, which is some thirty miles west. It is fed mainly by the Jordan River. The nearby hills of Galilee are about fifteen hundred feet above sea level. The lake is thirteen miles long and eight miles wide at its greatest east-west distance. Because of its location, it is subject to sudden and violent storms of short duration.

"I AM" SAYINGS IN THE GOSPEL OF JOHN

SAYING	REFERENCE
"I am the bread of life."	6:35
"I am the light of the world."	8:12
"I am the gate for the sheep."	10:7
"I am the good shepherd."	10:11,14
"I am the resurrection and the life."	11:25
"I am the way, the truth, and the life."	14:6
"I am the true vine."	15:1,5
"I'm a king."	18:37

JESUS WALKS ON THE WATER (6:16–21)

Jesus dismissed the crowd and sent his disciples to cross the Sea of Galilee without him. Sensing that the crowd wanted to make him king, Jesus retreated to the hills to be alone. The crowd was more interested in a Messiah who healed the sick and fed the hungry. But Jesus's kingdom would be spiritual rather than political.

As the disciples rowed across the lake, .the winds picked up and a storm arose. As the disciples approached the halfway point across (about three or four miles), they saw Jesus walking toward them on the water. Not recognizing that it was Jesus, the disciples were terrified. In another situation of human hopelessness and fear, Jesus gave hope and assurance: "It is I. Don't be afraid" (v. 20). Other Gospel accounts of this event tell

THE FIFTH SIGN: JESUS'S WALKING ON WATER

MIRACLE PERFORMED	CHARACTERISTIC OF JESUS'S POWER	RESULT OR RESPONSE TO THE SIGN
Jesus walks on the wind-whipped waves to meet the disciples' boat.	Master over *natural law*	Matthew tells us that the disciples worshiped Jesus as the Son of God

us that Jesus calmed the wind and waves. According to John's account, the boat immediately reached its destination at the other shore.

Section Summary

By walking on the water, Jesus showed his mastery over nature. Through their experiences with Jesus, they learned much about who Jesus is and about the nature of God's kingdom.

THE BREAD OF LIFE (6:22–59)

After the feeding of many thousands, it is not surprising that these same people sought Jesus again. When they found him, Jesus read their hearts and confronted them with their motive: "You are looking for me, not because you saw the signs, but because you ate the loaves and were filled" (v. 26). Jesus then encouraged them not to devote themselves to such pursuits but rather to seek "food that lasts for eternal life" (v. 27).

"I AM" SAYING: THE BREAD OF LIFE (V. 35)

STATEMENT	SIGNIFICANCE
"I am the bread of life." (v. 35)	Jesus satisfies our deepest spiritual needs.

He reminded them of their forefathers during the years of wilderness wandering and how God provided them with manna to meet their physical needs: "He gave them bread from heaven to eat" (v. 31). Jesus then compared the Israelites' physical needs to the spiritual needs of his audience. "I am the bread of life. . . . No one who comes to me will ever be hungry, and no one who believes in me will ever be thirsty again. . . . I am the bread that came down from heaven" (vv. 35,41). This the first of seven "I am" statements recorded in John's Gospel.

WORD PICTURE

Truly I Tell You

This phrase, translated by the CSB as "Truly I tell you," begins with "amen, amen" in the Greek text. The NRSVUE translates this text as "Truly, truly I say to you." This formula is a teaching technique that indicated a crucial idea from Jesus. It occurs in verses 26,32,47, and 53.

COMPARISON BETWEEN MANNA AND JESUS: THE BREAD OF LIFE

MANNA	JESUS
Came at night	Came when men were in darkness

MANNA	JESUS
Met physical need	Meets spiritual needs
A gift from God	God's gift to the world
Had to be picked up and eaten	Must be received and appropriated

In his bread of life discourse, Jesus made several bold statements:

1. No one can come to the Father through Christ except as the Father wills (v. 44).
2. To be in a relationship with God is to be in a relationship with Jesus (v. 45).
3. Only the Son, Jesus, has seen the Father (v. 46).
4. The Bread of life came down from heaven. Only by eating that bread can eternal life be gained.

Section Summary

Jesus is the Bread of life, and only he can satisfy the deep spiritual needs of people. One may appropriate eternal life only by receiving Jesus Christ as Savior.

THE HOLY ONE OF GOD (6:60–71)

Some Disciples Abandon Jesus (vv. 60–69)

Jesus's bread of life discourse was not well received by all of his followers: "This teaching is hard. Who can accept it?" (v. 60). Many followers grumbled and turned their backs on Jesus. When Jesus asked the Twelve if they also wanted to depart, they remained with their Master. Peter responded for them all: "Lord, to whom will we go? You have the words of eternal life. We have come to believe and know that you are the Holy One of God" (vv. 68–69).

The Holy One to Be Betrayed (vv. 70–71)

But all was not well. Jesus knew from the beginning which disciple would eventually betray him. Jesus informed the Twelve that "one of you is a devil" (v. 70), referring to Judas.

Section Summary

Recognizing Jesus to be "the Holy One of God," the Twelve chose not to follow the crowd but to remain with him.

WORD PICTURE

No Longer Accompanied Him

The word for *accompany* is a term composed of two words in the Greek language: *alongside* and *walk*. Those disciples who abandoned Jesus were no longer willing to walk beside him. They were no longer committed to him and his mission. This word (*peripatoun*) is used to epitomize discipleship.

QUESTIONS TO GUIDE YOUR STUDY

1. What does the miracle of feeding the five thousand teach us?
2. What lessons might the disciples have learned from their experience in the storm on the Sea of Galilee? What principles from this passage might we apply to the "storms" we face in our own lives?
3. What did Jesus mean when he claimed to be the Bread of life? What does that mean to you?
4. Why was it so difficult for some disciples to continue following Jesus? What made Jesus's discourse on the bread of life a hard teaching to them?

JOHN 7

This chapter begins the section some call "the period of conflict." The religious leaders, having witnessed Jesus's signs and miracles and listened to his sermons, now began to oppose him.

GOD'S TIME (7:1–13)

Some might wonder why Jesus would stay away from Judea because the Jews there were waiting to take his life, especially because Jesus willingly went to death at the time of his crucifixion. Simply put, it was not his time (vv. 6–8). The time for surrendering his life would come but not now; God desired more to be accomplished through Jesus's life. All would transpire at the moment God intended.

HISTORICAL BACKGROUND

The Feast of Tabernacles

The Feast of Tabernacles was observed in the fall. It consisted of celebration and thanksgiving for the fall harvest, especially the grape harvest, and commemoration of the wilderness wanderings. One of the three feasts that Jewish men were required to attend, it got its name from the use of temporary booths or tabernacles erected in the vineyards during the harvest to guard the fields. Lasting a full week—eight days with a Sabbath added at the end, it was a popular festival among the people.

AN AUTHORITATIVE TEACHER (7:14–24)

At the appropriate time, halfway through the Feast of Tabernacles, Jesus revealed himself and began to teach. The crowds were surprised that Jesus did not study under any of the noted Jewish scholars. Jesus responded to their amazement. His teaching was not his own, but it came "from the one who sent me" (v. 16).

Jesus provided three lines of support for his teaching:

1. *His Authority*. It was rooted in the Father who sent him.
2. *His Selfless Ministry*. What he had done was not for self-glorification.
3. *The Place of the Law*. The Jews cherished the law of Moses but did not keep it.

Section Summary

Jesus's authoritative teaching astonished the festival crowd. Jesus responded by providing authoritative support for his teaching.

THE SPIRIT PROMISED (7:25–44)

Many people believed that no one would know the origin or birthplace of the Messiah. Therefore, since they knew of Jesus's origins, he could not be the Messiah (v. 27), according to their perspective. As a result, they tried to seize Jesus, but they were unable to lay a hand on him because "his hour had not yet come" (v. 30).

One of the features of the Feast of Tabernacles was carrying a jar of water from the pool of Siloam to the temple each day. Each morning a procession of priests carried the water, which was poured into a bowl at the altar while the trumpet sounded and the people shouted. Against this symbolic background, Jesus showed up at the feast on the last day.

Section Summary

For those who believed in him, Jesus promised to satisfy their spiritual thirst by providing "streams of living water." This "living water" represented the Holy Spirit, who would be poured out on believers on the day of Pentecost.

A PROPHET FROM GALILEE? (7:45–52)

The temple guards sent to arrest Jesus exclaimed, "No man ever spoke like this!" (v. 46). The Pharisees dismissed the guards as deceived, arguing that since none of the Pharisees had expressed belief in Jesus, then he was not to be accepted. The Pharisees elevated their own sense of learning and understanding. In so doing, they exaggerated the ignorance of the average person. This produced a spiritual pride that led them to believe true understanding existed in their teachings.

Then Nicodemus, who spoke with Jesus earlier (3:1–21), reminded them that no one was to be judged without a hearing. They responded with the firm conviction that no prophet could come from Galilee.

A SINLESS JUDGE (7:53–8:11)

The teachers of the law and the Pharisees brought to Jesus a woman who had been caught in adultery. They wanted him to pronounce proper judgment upon her. The Pharisees' purpose was to trap Jesus. If he neglected to suggest a stoning, as the law required, he could be charged with being a lawbreaker. If, however, Jesus did advocate stoning, then he would bring the wrath of the Roman government upon himself. How

PERSONAL APPLICATION

"Jesus claimed that in Him might be found the fulfillment of all which this ritual represented. In addition, those who slaked their spiritual thirst at this spring would become fountains for the spiritual refreshment of others. . . . He who trusts in Christ not only receives the water of life that springs up to eternal life but becomes the source of that gift to others. For no one can possess (or, rather, be indwelt by) the Spirit of God and keep that Spirit to himself. Where the Spirit is, He flows forth; if there is not flowing forth, He is not there." William E. Temple, *Readings in St. John's Gospel*, 130.

HISTORICAL BACKGROUND

Over the years, this passage has been viewed differently, as some scholars have raised questions about its authenticity. Key reasons for this are that the text appears out of place and it differs from John's writing style. For the most part, however, Protestants and Roman Catholics alike regard this passage as authentic Scripture, even though it has been understood by textual scholars for centuries to be out of place.

This little story captures magnificently both the gracious, forgiving spirit of Jesus and his firm call to the transformation life. Gerald L. Borchert, *John 1–11* New American Commentary 25A, 369–76.

did Jesus handle this dilemma? "The one without sin among you should be the first to throw a stone at her" (v. 7).

Jesus didn't break the law, yet he ensured that the woman wouldn't be stoned. When everyone left, Jesus addressed the woman's two greatest needs: self-esteem and a new life. For her self-esteem, he assured her that he, who was without sin, did not condemn her. For her deepest need, a new life, Jesus said, "Go, and from now on do not sin anymore" (v. 11).

Section Summary

The story of the woman caught in adultery captures both the gracious, forgiving spirit of Jesus and his firm call to the transformation life. Jesus addressed the woman's two greatest needs: her self-esteem and a new life.

QUESTIONS TO GUIDE YOUR STUDY

1. What authority did Jesus claim to have to back up his teaching?
2. What is the point of Jesus's teaching about the "streams of living water"? How did the crowd respond to this teaching?
3. Prior to his crucifixion, Jesus avoided attempts on his life. Why were his enemies repeatedly unsuccessful?
4. What was the purpose of the Pharisees' bringing the woman who had committed adultery to Jesus? What lessons can we gain from this event?

JOHN 8

PERSONAL APPLICATION

Jesus's assertion that if people knew him, they would know his Father is one of the most striking in all the New Testament. He was speaking to some of the most educated, most religious people who have ever lived. They were confident they knew God and understood his ways. But their rejection of Jesus shows they didn't know God. They knew only their own ideas about God.

Because John 7:53–8:11 is a unit of Scripture, 8:1–11 is included with the treatment of the preceding chapter.

THE LIGHT OF THE WORLD (8:12–30)

"I AM" SAYING: THE LIGHT OF THE WORLD (V 12)

STATEMENT	SIGNIFICANCE
"I am the light of the world." (v. 12)	To know Jesus is to know God.

Verses 12–18 constitute Jesus's fourth public discourse in John's Gospel. Here, the second of Jesus's "I am" statements occurs: "I am the light of the world" (v. 12). The relationship between Jesus and his Father is such that Jesus could say, "If you knew me, you would also know my Father" (v. 19).

Teaching about his identity and nature, Jesus revealed that he was from above and not of this world (v. 23). Further, " if you do not believe that I am he, you will die in your sins" (v. 24). This statement elicited a shocked, "Who are you?" (v. 25). Jesus answered that he was who he had always claimed to be—the one sent from the Father, the Son of Man.

Section Summary

Jesus claims to be the "light of the world." His relationship with the Father of is such a nature that Jesus can say, "If you knew me, you would also know my father" (v. 19).

PERSONAL APPLICATION

Many have wondered how a loving God can condemn persons to hell. The proper response is that he does nothing of the sort. Individual persons condemn themselves by choosing to reject Jesus Christ and the truth he came to share with the world.

PERSONAL APPLICATION

Truth is not assent to a proposition but trust in Jesus, who said, "I am the way, the truth, and the life." He is the one who liberates.

TRUTH THAT SETS ONE FREE (8:31–41)

Jesus emphasized that holding to his teachings is essential in order to claim to be one of his disciples. "If you continue in my word, you really are my disciples. You will know the truth, and the truth will set you free" (vv. 31–32). Further, his teachings should be accepted as absolute truth. This truth, and no other, has the power to set a person free (v. 32). Many philosophies and ideologies claim to be based on truth, but all truth is God's truth. All claims to truth must be judged in light of God's revealed truth and knowledge. To adhere to a false view of reality is to be held captive by ignorance. The truth of Jesus sets persons free from all such bondage (v. 34).

Notice that Jesus's promise that his disciples would know the truth and find deliverance in the truth is conditional. It hinges on the words "if . . . then." The condition is that disciples must "continue" in His teaching.

This "if . . . then" construction (v. 31) speaks of a condition and its consequences. The following chart reveals the structure of this passage.

The Pharisees refused to listen to the truth of Jesus, insisting instead on clinging to their own understandings. The idea of being free was too much for their pride: "'We are descendants of Abraham,' they answered him, 'and we have never been enslaved to anyone. How can you say, "You will become free"?'" (v. 33). Perhaps the most telling verse is when Jesus stated that they had "no place" for his word (v. 37).

WORD PICTURE

Continue In

This is a characteristic word in John's Gospel. *Continue in* is a verb that means to "abide," "hold to." Here it is used of continuing in Jesus's teachings. This is an active, not a passive, activity. To "continue in" the word means not only knowing the truth but *living* it. "Continuance in the word (teaching) proves the sincerity or insincerity of the profession. It is the acid test." A. T. Robertson, "The Fourth Gospel," *Word Pictures in the New Testament*, vol. 5, 149.

JESUS'S PROMISE OF TRUTH AND FREEDOM

CONDITION	CONSEQUENCES	PROMISED BENEFIT
	1. You are my disciples.	Discipline
"If you continue in my word"	2. You will know the truth.	Discernment
	3. The truth will set you free.	Deliverance

Section Summary

To those who continue in his Word, Jesus promises knowledge of the truth and freedom from bondage to sin. The Jewish leaders, however, found "no place" for Jesus's teaching.

WHO IS YOUR FATHER? (8:42–47)

If God was their Father, then they would love him. Jesus made clear that his origin was divine, his mission was God planned, and his purpose was God willed.

People cannot hear what God has to say if they do not belong to God (v. 47). If people choose to listen to evil, then they close out the voice of God. The basic disposition of Satan is that of a liar, a perverter of truth, one who deceives everyone who allows him to direct their lives and thoughts.

THE ETERNAL "I AM" (8:48–59)

Desperate to discredit Jesus, the Jews accused him of being a Samaritan as well as demon possessed (v. 48). Jesus denied the charge and immediately resumed his charge that they were living apart from God (v. 49). He added that if anyone kept his word, he would "never see death" (v. 51). The Jews were outraged. They saw Jesus as placing himself above even Abraham. With one voice they asked in indignation, "Who do you claim to be?" (v. 53).

Jesus replied that God glorified him, that he knew God, and that he kept God's Word. Further, Abraham "rejoiced to see my day; he saw it and was glad" (v. 56). This brought utter amazement to the crowd. They challenged him, for Jesus, a young man, was claiming to have seen Abraham.

Jesus gave one of the most important answers to any question posed to him in the entire Gospel of John: "Truly I tell you, before Abraham was, I am."

Jesus then hid and slipped away from the temple grounds. The timing of Jesus's death was not for the crowd to decide.

WORD PICTURE

The only other time the phrase "I am" was used to describe someone was in Exod 3:14, where God claimed that name for himself. No identity statement could be clearer. Jesus claimed to be God himself in human form. The Jews did not respond with words but picked up stones to kill him for blasphemy. This is a "vivid picture of a mob ready to kill Jesus, already beginning to do so."

A. T. Robertson, "The Fourth Gospel," vol. 5, 159.

Section Summary

Jesus identified himself with the eternal "I am," meaning that Jesus claimed an eternal existence with God. Reacting to Jesus's claim, the religious Jews sought to kill him.

QUESTIONS TO GUIDE YOUR STUDY

1. In what sense is Jesus the "light of the world"? What truths does this statement convey?

2. Why are people who do not respond to the light condemned to hell?
3. Jesus said the condition for one's knowing the truth and being set free by it is "continu[ing] in" his teaching. What did he mean by this?
4. What were the implications of Jesus's claim to be the eternal "I AM"?

JOHN 9

John continues his theme of *light*, which he introduced in 8:12. The sixth sign of Jesus's deity, the healing of the man born blind, occurs in this chapter.

SIN AND SICKNESS (9:1–12)

THE SIXTH SIGN: JESUS'S HEALING OF THE MAN BORN BLIND

MIRACLE PERFORMED	CHARACTERISTIC OF JESUS'S POWER	RESULT OR RESPONSE TO THE SIGN
Jesus heals a man blind from birth.	Master over *misfortune*	The Jewish leaders investigate the man's healing.

Jesus saw a man who was blind from birth. His disciples, reflecting a common belief of the day, wanted to know who sinned and caused this man to be blind. Was it his parents or the man himself?

Refuting this entire system of thought, Jesus proclaimed that "neither this man nor his parents sinned" (v. 3). Instead, this man was there at that moment for God to work in his life in order to glorify Jesus.

Jesus spat on the ground, making a mud mixture of dirt and saliva, and placed the mud on the blind man's eyes. He then instructed the man to wash his eyes in the pool of Siloam. The man did so and returned, seeing! The mud exercise was not medicinal but served as a means for the blind man to express his faith in Jesus's words. This sign pointed to Jesus as the Giver of spiritual sight.

Jesus suggested a time would come when the work of the kingdom of God would not be able to continue. That time was not the end of his life, as the "we" in verse 4 suggests, but when the consummation of the age takes place. Until that day, God's people must do all they can to combat evil and do good in the name of Christ.

OLD TESTAMENT REFERENCE

Jesus performed more miracles related to giving sight to the blind than any other miracle. Such an activity was forecast in prophecy as a messianic act (Isa 29:18; 35:5; 42:7). Jesus came to restore the sight of human beings who had become blinded to the things of God.

HISTORICAL BACKGROUND

The rabbis taught that no one died unless there had been sin. Even a child could sin in the womb, they suggested, or even in the preexistent state prior to conception.

Section Summary

Jesus's healing of the man blind from birth was the sixth sign witnessing to his deity. This sign pointed to Jesus as the Giver of spiritual sight.

THE POWER OF PERSONAL TESTIMONY (9:13–34)

The man who was healed testified that he believed Jesus was a prophet (v. 17b). This was not the answer the Pharisees wanted to hear. Questioned again, the healed man said, "One thing I do know: I was blind, and now I can see!" (v. 25). This simple testimony has been the undeniable evidence for the Christian faith for centuries. His final words carry the greatest sting: "If this man were not from God, he wouldn't be able to do anything" (v. 33). The Pharisees became enraged, accused the man of being a sinner, and had him removed from their presence.

THE HEALED MAN'S CONFESSION (9:35–41)

After hearing that the man he healed was removed from the synagogue, Jesus looked for him. He offered one decisive question, "Do you believe in the Son of Man?" (v. 35). The man responded, "I believe, Lord!" and worshiped Jesus.

The healing of this blind man took place on two levels: (1) at the physical level his sight was restored; and (2) on the spiritual level he came to faith in Christ. This man served as a model for Jesus's entire ministry. The Pharisees who witnessed this event responded only in indignation that Jesus would suggest they were blind (v. 40). Jesus responded that if they were truly blind they would be guiltless, but since they claimed sight, their guilt remained (v. 41).

PERSONAL APPLICATION

Now as then, some people claim to see but are spiritually blind. And others admit their blindness and ask Christ to restore their sight.

Section Summary

Jesus's miracle of healing caused two different responses. The healed man confessed his faith in Jesus, while the Jewish leaders did not believe and remained blind in their sin. It is not possible to remain neutral before Jesus.

QUESTIONS TO GUIDE YOUR STUDY

1. Why did the disciples and others assume the blind man's condition was the direct result of sin in the family?
2. What great lesson does Jesus's healing of this blind man teach us?
3. What was the effect of the healed man's testimony on the Jewish leaders? Why did they respond as they did?

4. What lessons can we apply from this passage of Scripture to our human condition today?

JOHN 10

In chapter 10, John introduces the picture of the relationship between the sheep and their Shepherd. In covering this material, it might be helpful to keep in mind Old Testament passages that refer to rulers and leaders as shepherds: Ezek 34; Isa 56:9–12; Ps 23.

JESUS IS THE "GATE" FOR HIS SHEEP (10:1–10)

"I AM" SAYING: THE GATE FOR THE SHEEP (V 7)

STATEMENT	SIGNIFICANCE
"I am the gate for the sheep." (v. 7)	Jesus is the only entrance into the family of God.

Jesus used this parable to explain his role as the gate to the kingdom of God. Shepherds regulated the coming and going of sheep between the sheep pen and the pasture. As the gate, Jesus decides who enters the family of God. He gives salvation, security, and satisfaction to all who come into the family of God through faith in him.

HISTORICAL BACKGROUND

The Sheep Pen

Shepherding was a part of life in Judea, and people were familiar with the sheep pen. A sheep pen could take many forms: a pen constructed of rocks and limbs, and often a cave. Sometimes it stood in front of the shepherd's home, and its entrance was also the entrance to the house. A gatekeeper might be employed to stand watch over the sheep pen at night.

Section Summary

Jesus characterized himself as the gate through which the sheep enter the sheep pen. Only through Jesus can one enter into the family of God.

PICTURES OF JESUS IN THE GOSPEL OF JOHN

PICTURE	LESSON TAUGHT	REFERENCE
The good Shepherd	Christ the only way to God	10:1–26
The vine and the branches	The need to abide in Christ	15:1–6

JESUS IS THE "GOOD SHEPHERD" (10:11–21)

"I AM" SAYING: THE GOOD SHEPHERD (VV. 11, 14)

STATEMENT	SIGNIFICANCE
"I am the good shepherd." (vv. 11,14)	The good Shepherd has personal concern for the sheep or persons in his flock.

One of the great images of Jesus is as the "good shepherd" (v. 11). Jesus pointed to three dimensions of the shepherd-sheep relationship to communicate his relationship to believers.

1. He is the gate to the sheep pen, meaning that no one can enter the fold through any other means than Jesus himself (vv. 1, 7–9). Only through Jesus Christ can anyone be made right with God and find eternal life.
2. Jesus leads his sheep. No other voice is the true voice of leadership (vv. 3b–5).
3. As the good Shepherd, Jesus protects his flock—even to the point of death (v. 11).

Unlike someone who watches sheep for employment, Jesus is a good Shepherd motivated by love for his sheep (vv. 12–13).

As the good Shepherd, Jesus mentioned that there are other sheep who will listen to his voice and will one day be brought into the fold. More than likely, what he had in mind were the Gentiles who would come to believe in Christ. The idea is not that of many shepherds with many flocks but of one Shepherd joining together one flock (v. 16; cp. Eph. 2:16). Jesus was not forced into being the good Shepherd; He willingly took the role upon himself, and for this God loves him (vv. 17–18).

WORD PICTURE

Good Shepherd

John used an unusual term for *good*. It means "good, beautiful." It has the connotation of a winsome, attractive, and virtuous person. We might use this word in the sense of a model of perfection. Few portraits of Jesus have more appeal than his role of Shepherd. The "goodness" of this Shepherd abides in the fact that he does not spare himself in looking after the sheep. The good Shepherd willingly lays down his life for his sheep. This, in fact, is exactly what Jesus did.

Section Summary

Jesus is the good Shepherd. In this role, he has personal concern for the individuals in his flock. The sheep have his leadership and protection. The good Shepherd's love for his sheep is so great that he would willingly lay down his life to protect the sheep.

HISTORICAL BACKGROUND

This section of chapter 10 takes place two or three months later at the Feast of Dedication. This feast celebrated the dedication and reopening of the temple by Judas Maccabeus in December of 165 BC, after it had been desecrated by the Syrian ruler Antiochus Epiphanes in 168 BC (cp. Dan 11:31). This event is commonly referred to as "Hanukkah," or the Feast of Lights.

DEDICATION, JESUS, AND HIS SHEEP (10:22–42)

The Relationship Between the Sheep and Their Shepherd (vv. 22–29)

These verses cover several key truths presented by John.

1. *The sheep hear the Shepherd's voice* (v. 27). Those who are Jesus's followers respond to his teaching.
2. *The sheep know the Shepherd* (vv. 14,27). Jesus's followers have a relationship with him and are completely committed to him.
3. *The sheep follow the Shepherd* (v. 27). Followers of Jesus are persistent in obeying the teachings of Jesus and his Word.
4. *The sheep have eternal life* (v. 28). Jesus's followers are secure in the strong, protective hand of God.

Jesus also declared that "I and the Father are one" (v. 30). Jesus and God are not, according to the Christian doctrine of the Trinity, identical persons but separate persons who are of identical nature.

The Jews Attempt to Stone Jesus (vv. 30–42)

The Jews picked up stones to kill Jesus. They considered it blasphemous for a person to claim to be God (v. 33). Jesus responded to their anger by pointing back to the Old Testament where, in accord with the worldview of the ancient Near East, rulers and judges, as emissaries of the heavenly King, could be granted the honorary title "god" (Ps 82). If they could accept that title for those to whom the Word of God came, how much more they should accept the idea that God's anointed should be called God (vv. 34–37). Jesus went on to say that if they did not believe his testimony, they could look at the works he did (vv. 37–39). However, this argument did not persuade his enemies, and they tried again to seize Jesus for execution.

Section Summary

The relationship of the sheep to the Shepherd is based on the sheep's belief in the Shepherd. It is one of commitment and obedience on the part of the sheep. The good Shepherd loves and protects his sheep.

QUESTIONS TO GUIDE YOUR STUDY

1. What did Jesus mean by claiming to be the "gate for the sheep"?
2. Describe the relationship between the sheep and the Shepherd. What makes Jesus a "good" Shepherd?
3. Describe the relationship between the sheep and the Shepherd. What key truths are associated with this relationship?
4. Why did the Jewish leaders want to stone Jesus? What resulted?

JOHN 11

The key event in this passage is Jesus's miracle of raising Lazarus from the dead. Although Lazarus's sisters, Mary and Martha, appear in the Synoptic Gospels (Matthew, Mark, and Luke), it is John who places so much emphasis on the raising of Lazarus from the dead.

LAZARUS DIES (11:1–16)

The sisters of Lazarus sent word to Jesus that Lazarus was ill. Jesus assured them that Lazarus's condition would not result in death. Jesus delayed going to Lazarus for two days after receiving the message about his death.

HISTORICAL BACKGROUND

Lazarus

The name *Lazarus* means "one whom God helps." Lazarus was a personal friend of Jesus and the brother of Mary and Martha.

His disciples urged Jesus not to go, for there were individuals who wanted to kill him. Thomas, often called "the doubter," revealed the depth of his commitment to Jesus when he said to his fellow disciples: "Let's go too so that we may die with him" (v. 16).

JESUS'S EMOTIONS (11:17–37)

One of the most moving scenes in the life of Jesus is at the tomb of Lazarus. Here we see not only the power of Jesus to raise the dead but also the emotions of Jesus moved by the grief of those around him.

Martha's faith was evident as she approached Jesus, four days after the death of Lazarus, professing belief that he could have saved her dead brother. When Mary came as well and Jesus saw her grief and the grief of those with her, he was "deeply moved in his spirit and troubled" (v. 33). Then "Jesus wept" (v. 35). He wept because of his deep love and affection for Lazarus and his sisters.

PERSONAL APPLICATION

What could testify more to the divine nature of Jesus than to exhibit the power needed to raise a person from the dead? Note that the raising of Lazarus serves as a foreshadowing of the power of God to resurrect all believers one day to fellowship and eternal life in Christ. Unlike Lazarus, who was raised only to die again, Christians will be raised to eternal life.

Section Summary

Lazarus, whom Jesus loved, fell ill and died. Jesus, moved by the grief around him, showed his human nature by weeping.

JESUS: THE RESURRECTION AND THE ALIGN WITH JESUS (11:38–44)

THE SEVENTH SIGN: THE RAISING OF LAZARUS

MIRACLE PERFORMED	CHARACTERISTIC OF JESUS'S POWER	RESULT OR RESPONSE TO THE SIGN
Jesus raises Lazarus from the dead.	He is master of *death.*	Many put their faith in Jesus.

In a loud voice Jesus called out to Lazarus, "Lazarus, come out!" Still bound in his graveclothes, Lazarus came forth.

HISTORICAL BACKGROUND

The Jewish people believed the spirit of a dead person hovered over the body for three days before departing on the fourth day. The fourth day was when the process of decomposition began. Because of this, there would be no doubt for those who witnessed this miracle that Lazarus was dead.

Section Summary

Physical death may overtake the believer, but spiritual death has no power over the believer. A person who believes in Jesus Christ personally shall continue to live. Although death stands as the last and strongest enemy, it is defeated through belief in Jesus Christ. Jesus is both the resurrection and the life.

THE SANHEDRIN REACTS (11:45–54)

The resurrection of Lazarus caused many people to place their faith in Jesus. It also led to a meeting of the Sanhedrin, the Jewish council. The Sanhedrin was concerned about the growing influence of Jesus with the people. They acknowledged his miracles and feared that these would create such a following that even Rome would feel threatened. Rome might take away the authority of the Sanhedrin and do away with Israel as a nation.

Caiaphas, the high priest for that year, said it would be better if one man died than that the entire nation be removed. So, from that point on, Jesus and the Sanhedrin were on a collision course.

HISTORICAL BACKGROUND

Mary of Bethany

Mary was the sister of Martha and Lazarus. All three were apparently part of an inner circle of Jesus's associates. John, in his Gospel, placed an emphasis on their status. Mary played a primary role in the episode of Lazarus's resurrection from the dead (John 11). In John 12, she anointed Jesus's feet with precious oil. This served as an important confessional function of anticipating his death. Given the sequence in John's Gospel, Mary is portrayed as a follower who was well acquainted with Jesus's ultimate destiny.

JESUS PREPARES FOR THE PASSOVER (11:55–57)

The religious authorities put out an order for people to report Jesus's presence so they might arrest him. Jesus, aware of the Passover plot on his life, withdrew from Jerusalem to a wilderness area about twelve to fifteen miles away from the city. He stayed there with his disciples until the Passover season.

Section Summary

Attending to their own interests and security rather than the welfare of others and the kingdom of God, the religious authorities plotted to kill Jesus.

QUESTIONS TO GUIDE YOUR STUDY

1. Jesus delayed coming to Lazarus while he was ill. What might have been his reason?
2. What significance does the sign of the raising of Lazarus hold?
3. Why did the Sanhedrin react so decisively toward Jesus's miracle of raising Lazarus?
4. Jesus avoided further confrontations with the religious leaders after learning of their plot to kill him. What was his purpose in withdrawing?

HISTORICAL BACKGROUND

The Sanhedrin

The Sanhedrin was the high court of the Jews. In the New Testament period, it was comprised of three groups: the chief priests, the elders, and the teachers of the law. Its membership reached seventy-one, including the high priest, who served as the presiding officer. Under Roman jurisdiction, the Sanhedrin was given great power, but it could not impose capital punishment (John 18:31).

JOHN 12

DEVOTION OR DEATH? (12:1–11)

This portion of John's Gospel contains a host of important elements, including Mary's devotion to Jesus, the deceit and corruption of Judas, and the judgment of Jesus on both Mary and the poor.

The Devotion of Mary (vv. 1–3)

The perfume Mary used to anoint Jesus's feet was expensive, a luxury item for herself, selflessly given in devotion to Jesus. She poured it on the feet of Jesus in an act of humility; attending to the feet of another person was the work of a servant. Wiping the oil with her hair was also unusual, for respectable women did not unbraid their hair in public. Mary exhibited unrestrained love and devotion to Jesus that went beyond personal cost and concern for the opinion of others.

PERSONAL APPLICATION

Individuals are often able to deceive others about their relationship to God, but never is God deceived, since he sees into the heart of every person.

Judas's Deceit (vv. 4–6)

This is the sole passage in the Gospels that reveals the wicked character of Judas before his betrayal of Jesus. While John related Judas's dishonesty in hindsight, at the time Judas must have been highly esteemed by the Twelve because he was trusted with caring for the money bag.

PERSONAL APPLICATION

Through the centuries, this statement of Jesus has been misinterpreted as an excuse to neglect the poor. The point Jesus made was that Mary's devotion at this particular time and place was worthy of the cost.

Jesus's Judgment of Mary and the Poor (vv. 7–11)

Jesus affirmed Mary's act of devotion and linked it to his own burial. Mary did not intend for this to be the significance of her act, but Jesus interpreted it this way.

Jesus defended what Mary had done against the charge of the disciples that she should have sold the perfume and given the money to the poor. "You always have the poor with you" (v. 8), he declared.

Section Summary

In a show of love and devotion for Jesus, Mary of Bethany anointed Jesus's feet with an expensive oil. Because of his approaching death, he linked this act to the preparation of his body for burial.

HISTORICAL BACKGROUND

The palm branches the crowd had were symbolic; they were used in celebrations of victory.

PRAISING THE KING (12:12–19)

Jesus's triumphal entry into Jerusalem coincided with the Passover Feast.

The crowds responded to Jesus with shouts of "Hosanna!" and "Blessed is he who comes in the name of the Lord—the King of Israel!" as he entered Jerusalem.

The Gospel of John emphasizes the royalty of Jesus. Only John's Gospel records that the people also shouted, "Blessed is he who comes in the name of the Lord—the King of Israel !" (v. 13). The crowd's exultation, as well as Jesus's riding a colt, was not seen as the fulfillment of prophecy (v. 16) by the disciples until after his death, burial, and resurrection. This moment was perhaps the high mark of Jesus's popularity and influence. In only a matter of days, however, these "Hosannas!" would turn to "Crucify him!" (19:15).

WORD PICTURE

Hosanna!

Hosanna is a Hebrew or Aramaic word that is best translated as a prayer: "save *now*," or "save." It was an expression of praise.

Section Summary

Jesus entered Jerusalem as the Passover Feast was being celebrated. The crowd welcomed him with shouts of "Hosanna!" How the crowd's attitude would change in a few short days!

THE HOUR HAS COME (12:20–36)

The request of some Greeks to interview Jesus brought a lengthy response from Jesus regarding the path before him. Throughout the Gospel of John, Jesus avoided situations that would hasten his death. But now the "hour" arrived for "the Son of Man to be glorified" (v. 23). His death and subsequent resurrection are what Jesus had in mind with the term *glorified*.

At this point Jesus restated what he said earlier—that death is a condition of life at its fullest.

Jesus understood that his death would bring life to many people (v. 24). Nevertheless, Jesus's heart was "troubled," which is all that John writes in relation to the Gethsemane passages of Jesus's final hours recorded in the other three Gospels. Jesus's troubled heart likely was the result of his bearing the weight of the sin of the world as a sinless being. This went beyond the physical and emotional agony that awaited him. While he contemplated praying to God for deliverance, he remained on the course toward what God had willed for him.

The cross would achieve salvation for those who believed, bring judgment upon the world for their refusal to believe, and defeat Satan's rebellion once for all. The lifting of Jesus on the cross would be the beacon that would draw all people—regardless of sex, race, social status, or nationality—to himself for deliverance from sin (v. 32).

Verses 35–36 are the last words of Jesus's public ministry. They were a warning to the Jews to embrace salvation while there was still time.

NEW TESTAMENT REFERENCE

Jesus often used observations from nature to illustrate spiritual realities (Mark 4:3–12). Earlier he compared the kingdom of God with a sower scattering seed. "Now He speaks of what happens to the seed that bears fruit. It must first die. It must lose its own identity, that the new plant may spring up."

William E. Temple, *Readings in St. John's Gospel*, 195.

Section Summary

The time had come for the "Son of Man to be glorified" (v. 23). His work of public ministry was finished. Jesus found the weight of bearing all the sin of the world troubling, yet he obeyed the will of the Father and stayed his course.

THE JEWS' REFUSAL TO BELIEVE JESUS (12:37–50)

They could not believe, not because their freedom of choice was removed from them but because they purposely rejected God and chose evil. Thus, God turned them over to their own choice.

OLD TESTAMENT REFERENCE

The Jews witnessed so many signs and other miraculous deeds of Jesus that it is difficult to understand why they refused to believe. The answer is found in prophecy. Quoting Isa 53:1 and 6:10, John showed that the people were fulfilling what their own Scriptures had predicted (vv. 38–40). The Jews would not and could not believe.

In verses 44–50, Jesus summarized the theme of his teaching. This is likely a summary statement from the Gospel writer as Jesus closed his public ministry.

WORD PICTURE

Last Day

There is a difference in meaning between the phrase "last day" (v. 48) and the much-used phrase "last days." The latter refers to the current period of time, begun when Christ entered the world (Acts 2:17; Heb 1:2; 1 Pet 1:20; Jude 18). The *last day* (singular), however, refers to the consummation of time and history when the great resurrection and judgment of all persons will occur (1 John 2:18).

Section Summary

In spite of all the signs they had witnessed, the Jews refused to believe Jesus. Quoting Isa 53:1 and 6:10, John showed that the people were fulfilling what their own Scriptures had predicted. They had rejected God and chosen evil.

QUESTIONS TO GUIDE YOUR STUDY

1. What prompted Mary to anoint Jesus's feet with oil? How did he interpret this act?
2. What does the term *hosanna* mean? Why was the crowd shouting this as they greeted Jesus? What were they expecting from him?
3. As Jesus prayed in the garden of Gethsemane, why was he "troubled"? What was his attitude toward the Father's will?
4. Isaiah predicted that the Jews would reject the Messiah. Why did the Jews reject Jesus and his teaching?

PERSONAL APPLICATION

Jesus was able to perform this act of utter humility because of his keen understanding of who he was, where he had come from, and where he was going (v. 3). This is a key to humility in all persons—a healthy and balanced understanding of who they are.

JOHN 13

Jesus's public ministry has drawn to a close. Beginning with this chapter, Jesus emphasized his ministry to those who had responded to the gospel.

JESUS, THE HUMBLE SERVANT (13:1–17)

We see the love of Jesus for his disciples as well as those who would come to be his disciples in the washing of the disciples' feet. The servant motif, so prevalent in the Gospel of Mark (10:45), is revealed here as well. Servanthood is love at work (v. 1).

Jesus's washing of the disciples' feet had both an ethical and a symbolic sense. The ethical sense is emphasized in John 13:14–15, where Jesus presented himself as the example of humble, loving service (cp. Luke 22:27). The command to do for one another what Christ had done for them was not to be confined to washing feet.

HISTORICAL BACKGROUND

Foot Washing in the Bible

Foot washing was an act necessary for comfort and cleanliness for any who had walked on dusty Palestinian roads in their sandals.

Section Summary

We see the love of Jesus for his disciples in his washing of their feet. The servant motif so prevalent in the Gospel of Mark (10:45) is revealed here as well. Servanthood is an expression of love.

PERSONAL APPLICATION

If Jesus, Lord and Teacher, washes our feet, how much more should we wash one another's feet (v. 14).

SATAN AND THE BETRAYER (13:18–30)

Betrayal is bad enough, but to do so after sharing a meal makes it even more heinous. At the moment Jesus identified Judas as his betrayer, Scripture tells us that "Satan entered him"; and Jesus said, "What you're doing, do quickly" (v. 27). This is the only use of the name *Satan* in John's Gospel, and it is unclear whether Jesus meant possession by Satan or the motivation from Satan to evil. Judas's fellow disciples, however, did not realize what Jesus was referring to, thinking that it had something to do with Judas's responsibilities as keeper of the money bag (v. 28). Jesus had to be betrayed, but Judas did not have to be that betrayer. It has been said that the difference between Judas and Peter—one of whom betrayed Jesus and the other who denied him—is that Peter sought forgiveness, but Judas did not.

OLD TESTAMENT REFERENCE

"The one who eats my bread has raised his heel against me" is a quotation of Ps 41:9.

Section Summary

Jesus identified his betrayer, Judas Iscariot. John tells us that Satan then entered into Judas.

THE MARK OF DISCIPLESHIP (13:31–38)

After Judas's departure, Jesus made clear that his time with the disciples was short (v. 33). The heart of this passage is found in vv. 34–35: "I give you a new command: Love one another. Just as I have loved you, you are also to love one another. By this everyone will know that you are my disciples, if you love one another."

Section Summary

The mark of the Christian is the love he or she exercises toward others. This love is not centered upon one's own interest but rather upon the welfare of others. It is the kind of love God extends to us.

HISTORICAL BACKGROUND

"There is a tradition that when John was an old man his pupils would set him in their midst, and he would say, 'Little children, love one another.' So the words which Jesus spoke in this tender scene stayed with him to the end of his life."

H. H. Hobbs, *An Exposition of the Gospel of John*, 216.

QUESTIONS TO GUIDE YOUR STUDY

1. What was the significance of Jesus's washing the disciples' feet?
2. What were Judas's motivations for betraying Jesus?
3. The mark of a disciple of Jesus is love. What are the characteristics of love?
4. What makes Christian love unique?

JOHN 14

The disciples had troubled hearts for several reasons: Jesus informed them of his impending departure, he revealed that a traitor was among them, and he predicted that Peter would fail him before all this was over. In this chapter, Jesus takes time to exhort the disciples and quiet their hearts.

THE REMEDY FOR ANXIETY (14:1–4)

Jesus urged his disciples to continue in their belief in him and not let their hearts be troubled by what was to follow. Such words from Jesus regarding his upcoming departure cast a net of depression upon the meal. Then came the words of comfort from Jesus: "Don't let your heart be troubled. Believe in God; believe also in me" (v. 1). Trust in God is the one true remedy for anxiety. Jesus completed the remedy for their concern by painting a beautiful portrait of the life that awaited them upon their reunion (vv. 2–4). The "many rooms" (v. 2) were "dwelling places" or "abiding places." These words indicated the permanency of the heavenly home of believers.

WORD PICTURE

Heart

The heart is the center of the physical, mental, and spiritual life of humans. It is the "seat of spiritual life . . . the center of feeling and faith."

A. T. Robertson, "The Fourth Gospel," Word Pictures in the New Testament" *WPNT*, vol. 5, 248.

Section Summary

Jesus's message in these verses is for his disciples to continue in their belief in him so as not to let their hearts be troubled by what would follow—his death and departure.

THE WAY, TRUTH, AND LIFE (14:5–14)

Jesus responded that a life given in belief and faith in him would pave the way to eternal fellowship with him (v. 6). Jesus's claim to be the way, the truth, and the life is of great importance. Jesus is not one of many ways to God but *the* only way.

That Jesus embodies and proclaims the truth is a major theme throughout John's Gospel. Jesus also offers life itself, life through God the Father, the Creator and Giver of all life.

"I AM" SAYING: THE WAY, THE TRUTH, AND LIFE (V 6)

STATEMENT	SIGNIFICANCE
"I am the way, the truth, and the life" (v. 6).	To the lost sinner who is ignorant and spiritually dead, Jesus is the way, the truth, and the life.

The last verse in this section has been widely debated as to its proper interpretation and application: "If you ask me anything in my name, I will do it" (v. 14). Was Jesus saying that we have unlimited power over God in determining what he will or will not do for us if we simply pray in Jesus's name? Clearly not, for this would be out of accord with the rest of the teaching of Scripture.

Section Summary

There is only one way to God, and this is through Jesus. To the lost sinner who is ignorant and spiritually dead, Jesus is the way, the truth, and the life.

THE COUNSELOR (14:15–31)

John's Gospel pays much attention to the Holy Spirit. In fact, of the four Gospels, his Gospel has more to say about the activity of the Spirit. Here Jesus referred to the Holy Spirit as the "Counselor." Note that Jesus called the Spirit "another" Counselor, suggesting that the work of the Holy Spirit would take over Jesus's roles in the lives of the disciples.

SPECIAL NAMES
FOR THE HOLY SPIRIT IN JOHN 14

NAME	MEANING
Counselor (v. 16)	He stands alongside, ministering to God's people.
Spirit of truth (v. 17)	He communicates and testifies to God's truth through conviction.

The Holy Spirit is also the "Spirit of truth" (v. 17). The Spirit testifies to the truth of God in Christ and brings people toward that truth through conviction which leads to repentance and faith. Jesus's bottom line here is that the Spirit will continue to bring the presence of Christ into the lives of the disciples (vv. 16–18, 20).

Jesus also dealt in this passage with the relationship between love and obedience. To love Jesus is to obey Jesus (vv. 15,23). If one does not obey Jesus, he doesn't love him (v. 24).

Section Summary

Jesus promised to send the disciples another "Counselor" (the Holy Spirit) whose work would take the place of his role in their lives. As the "Spirit of truth," this Counselor would also communicate and testify to God's truth.

QUESTIONS TO GUIDE YOUR STUDY

1. How is Jesus "the way, the truth, and the life"? (v. 6).

PERSONAL APPLICATION

God is sovereign over all and subject to none. We are to pray in accordance with the will of God—as exhibited in the life and teaching of Jesus. When Christians pray in that manner, their prayers will surely be answered. To pray in Jesus's name is to pray in accord with his will and mission.

PERSONAL APPLICATION

The role of the Holy Spirit as the one who "reminds" the disciples of what Jesus said and taught should not be overlooked as it relates: (1) to the writing of the New Testament and (2) to the ongoing life of the church. The church can expect this same ministry as it lives according to the teaching and encouragement of the Word of God.

2. What does Jesus's statement, "If you ask me anything in my name, I will do it" (v. 14) mean? How does this shape the prayers of believers?
3. Jesus told the disciples that he would send them the "Counselor" who was also the "Spirit of truth." What do these titles mean?
4. When it comes to following Jesus, what is the relationship between love and obedience?
5. How does the Spirit's ministry of "reminding" believers apply to believers today?

JOHN 15

Although John's Gospel does not have as many parables of Jesus as the other Gospels, John in this chapter records the parable of the vine and the branches.

THE TRUE VINE (15:1–17)

"I AM" SAYING: THE TRUE VINE (V. 1)

STATEMENT	SIGNIFICANCE
"I am the true vine." (v. 1)	To be a productive "branch," the believer must abide in Christ, the true vine.

Here Jesus puts forth another of his "I am" statements. In this saying, Jesus asserted that he was the "true vine" and that God was the gardener (v. 1). With this symbolism, we can see two scenarios that are representative of the Christian life:

1. The one who is on the vine and producing fruit (Matt 3:8; 7:16–20.
2. The one on the vine who is *not* producing fruit

The productive vine was pruned for greater production, while the non-productive vine was cut off for destruction. The key to producing fruits is one's relationship to the vine, to "remain in" the vine (vv. 4–5,7). Apart from Christ, nothing can be accomplished (v. 5).

Branches that abide in the vine experience growth and, as a result, fruitfulness. Jesus suggested a threefold progression of spiritual productivity, as the following chart shows.

HISTORICAL BACKGROUND

The Vine in the Old Testament

"The vine is one of the Old Testament figures used to illustrate the people of Israel. In Psalm 80: 8–19 Israel is the vine which God brought out of Egypt and planted in the ground which he has cleared to make room for it. The psalmist bewails the fact that it flourishes no longer, that its defenses are demolished and it is ravaged by marauders."

F. F. Bruce, *The Gospel of John*, 308.

WORD PICTURE

Remain

This word means "to stay, abide." Remaining in the vine is not a static or passive activity. In John 15:5, this word is in the present tense, which indicates continuous action. It is the branch that remains and continues to remain in the vine that produces fruit.

THE GROWTH AND PRODUCTION OF THE BRANCHES

ACTION	RESULT
Abiding (v. 1)	Fruit (v. 2)
Pruning (v. 2)	More fruit (v. 2)
Continued abiding (v. 5)	Much fruit (v. 5)

Section Summary of the Parable of the Vine and Branches

Metaphor used: Branches growing on a vine
Lesson: The believer's need to abide in Christ
Application: The main point is fellowship between the believer and Christ. To produce fruit, the believer must abide in Christ.

NEW TESTAMENT REFERENCE

Jesus did not indicate the nature of the fruit, but Gal 5:22–23 tells us that "the fruit of the Spirit is love, joy, peace, patience, kindness, goodness, faithfulness, gentleness, and self-control."

Section Summary

Jesus presented the parable of the vine and branches. The lesson of this teaching is the need of the branches (believers) to abide, or remain in, the vine (Jesus). Only by abiding in the true vine can the branches bear fruit.

PLANTED IN CHRIST (15:18–16:4)

What is the result of a life that remains firmly planted in Christ? Jesus suggested that such a person would be hated by the world (v. 19). Christ himself was hated and rejected because of the conviction that pierced the heart of every person he encountered. The Psalms predicted that Jesus would be hated without a cause (Pss 35:19; 69:4). Because of the life and teaching of Christ, people know the truth and have no excuse for their choices that deny God's rule (v. 24).

This conviction will not end with the life and ministry of Jesus, for the Counselor, or Holy Spirit, will continue to testify to the hearts and minds of person about the truth and claims of Christ (v. 26)—as Jesus's disciples give verbal witness to him (v. 27).

Why did Jesus share this with his disciples? He told them these truths "to keep you from stumbling" (16:1). Jesus prepared his disciples for the reality of the cross which they would also bear because of his name.

Section Summary

Jesus was rejected and hated. The disciples would also live in an atmosphere of persecution, hatred, and rejection following Jesus's departure. Those who remain firmly in Christ can expect the same kind of reception the world gave Jesus.

QUESTIONS TO GUIDE YOUR STUDY

1. What are the two scenarios we can see in the parable of the vine and branches? What is the parable's main lesson?
2. How do the branches of the vine produce fruit?
3. What kind of fruit do Christians produce?
4. What kind of reception can the believer who remains in the vine expect from the world?

JOHN 16

Because 16:1–4 is part of the discussion of the last section of chapter 15, those verses are treated with that chapter.

THE WORK OF THE SPIRIT (16:5–16)

In Convicting the World (vv. 5–11)

The main line of defense the disciples would have in the coming period of persecution would be the power of the Spirit in their lives. In a carefully detailed statement, Jesus outlined the convicting work of the Holy Spirit, all related to the work and person of Christ.

1. The Spirit will convict the world in the area of sin that results from disbelief in Jesus (v. 9).
2. The Spirit will convict the world in the area of righteousness in light of the life of Jesus (v. 10).
3. The Spirit will convict the world in the area of judgment because Jesus defeated the prince of the world (Satan) who now stands condemned (v. 11).

The conviction of judgment is the result of God's judgment on Satan by the cross (v. 11). Although Satan had been "ruler" of the world, God showed himself to be the true ruler of the world when he destroyed the power of Satan through Jesus's work on the cross.

WORD PICTURE

Convict

The word translated *convict* (v. 8) means "to expose, to convict, to cross-examine for the purpose of convicting or refuting an opponent, especially used of legal proceedings." F. Rienecker and C. Rogers, ed., *Linguistic Key to the Greek New Testament*, 254.

According to A. T. Robertson, this is "an old word for confuting, convicting by proof already in 3:29; 8:46." "The Fourth Gospel," *WPNT*, vol. 5, 266.

Guiding the Believer (vv. 12–15)

Only through the Spirit can an individual be brought to repentance which leads to faith. It is not good works that elevate our status before God but the finished work of Christ on the cross. The Holy Spirit makes effective in the heart of the believer what Christ has done.

The Spirit performs these ministries:

1. He guides believers "into all the truth" (v. 13).
2. He glorifies Jesus (v. 15).

The Holy Spirit, the Spirit of truth, will guide disciples into all truth (v. 13). His purpose is to reveal Christ. The mark of the work of the Spirit, then, is whether Christ is made central and glorified in a believer's life.

Section Summary

Jesus announced that he would send the Counselor (the Holy Spirit) to be with the disciples and to minister to their spiritual needs. Jesus then discussed the convicting work of the Holy Spirit, all related to the work and person of Christ.

"I HAVE CONQUERED THE WORLD" (16:17–33)

The disciples experienced understandable anxiety and confusion regarding all that Jesus shared with them. They were reluctant or unable to frame the question that was bothering them. But Jesus knew what they were thinking and spoke to their concerns (v. 19).

Jesus spoke directly with the disciples. He told them they were about to go through a time of deep grief while the world around them rejoiced—making their pain all the more intense.

Jesus didn't speak in abstractions. He told them that what they were about to go through was like a woman giving birth to a child. He promised them that on the other side of their grief, they would forget their pain—like the woman who embraces her newborn child. The joy they would experience on the other side of their grief would be something that no one could take from them.

Jesus told the disciples they would abandon him, but he wouldn't be alone. His Father would be with him.

His words of comfort were paramount with his passionate pleas to "Be courageous! I have conquered the world" (v. 33).

WORD PICTURE

I Have Conquered

The verb John used here means to "overcome." The force of this verb indicates a continuing victory. Jesus's words, "I have conquered the world," were not so much a promise as a statement of fact. His victory also applies to us today. Through him we are also able to overcome the world. First John 5:1–5 teaches that those who believe in him will be overcomers.

Section Summary

Victory over the forces and circumstances that invade our human lives are attainable through Jesus because he has overcome the world by his work on the cross.

QUESTIONS TO GUIDE YOUR STUDY

1. Why was it necessary for Jesus to send the Counselor? What would his role be?
2. Jesus described the convicting work of the coming Counselor. What is the nature of his work?
3. Why is the work of the Spirit so important in the life of a believer?

4. On what basis did Jesus declare that he had overcome the world? What does that mean to those who believe in him?

JOHN 17

Jesus ended his farewell discourse with a prayer—often called the "high priestly prayer."

WORD PICTURE

That

The Greek word *hina* translates into the English word *that* or the phrase "in order that." Sometimes *that* signals the content of what is being said. Usually, however, a clause that begins with the word *that* speaks of purpose. We can see that Jesus's prayer was full of purpose as the word *that* occurred nineteen times in his prayer.

INTRODUCTION TO JESUS'S INTERCESSORY PRAYER

Jesus's Requests. His prayer included many requests on behalf of himself, his disciples, and other believers (the church).

Jesus's Motives. Behind many of his specific requests we can often see his motive or purposes. Clearly, Jesus's motives were unselfish, as his dominant motive was that God would be glorified in the coming events of his death and resurrection.

JESUS PRAYS FOR HIMSELF (17:1–5)

PRAYER FOR HIMSELF THEME:
JESUS'S FINISHED WORK OF SALVATION
("THE HOUR HAS COME")

REQUEST	MOTIVE OR PURPOSE
1. "Glorify your Son" (vv. 1,5)	1. That God may be glorified
2. Restoration of Jesus's former status (v. 5)	2. That believers might have eternal life
	3. Jesus's earthly ministry was finished

Here we have the beginning of the longest recorded prayer of Jesus (17:1–26). In this first section of the prayer, Jesus noted that the cross would bring glory to himself, for it was the will of God and the means of salvation for all who would believe.

Section Summary

Jesus prayed for himself. His requests were that he would be glorified and that he might be restored to his former status. The key theme of this section of his prayer was his ministry: The work of salvation was finished.

JESUS PRAYS FOR THE DISCIPLES (17:6–19)

Most of this section of Jesus's prayer was devoted to the welfare of the disciples. Jesus prayed specifically for their protection in the area of unity

PRAYER FOR THE DISCIPLES THEME: SANCTIFICATION ("SANCTIFY THEM BY THE TRUTH")	
REQUEST	**MOTIVE OR PURPOSE**
1. Protection (v. 11)	1. That they be kept from sin and in fellowship with God
2. Unity (v. 11)	2. That they be united in purpose
3. Joy (v. 13)	3. That the joy of the Lord might be their strength
4. Sanctify them (v. 17)	4. That truth may liberate them from sin

(v. 11), emphasizing again the importance of the unity of the body of Christ, the church. This is not organizational unity but interpersonal, relational unity. Jesus also prayed that they would be protected from the evil one, or Satan, who is more than active in the world and bitterly opposed to the things of God (1 John 5:19). Finally, Jesus prayed that God would sanctify the disciples through the word of truth (v. 17). Sanctification is the divine process whereby God molds us according to his holiness. It is bringing to bear upon our lives the moral absolutes of the living God in such a way that they affect how we live and think. Sanctification and revelation are directly related. Without God's revelatory word to our life, the process of sanctification cannot begin.

WORD PICTURE

Sanctification

Sanctification is the process of being made holy, which results in a changed lifestyle for the believer. Christ's crucifixion makes possible the moving of the sinner from the profane to the holy so the believer can become a part of the temple where God dwells and is worshiped.

Section Summary

Jesus prayed for his disciples. The key theme of this section of his prayer was their sanctification.

JESUS PRAYS FOR THE CHURCH (17:20–26)

PRAYER FOR ALL BELIEVERS THEME: GLORIFICATION

REQUEST	MOTIVE OR PURPOSE
Unity (vv. 21,22,23)	That the Father's name might be known

Here Jesus's prayer turned specifically to those who would come to believe in him through the disciples' message and testimony. He prayed for unity among his followers.

Father and Son are inseparably one—the Father in the Son and the Son in the Father. Jesus prayed that his followers will be in both the Father and the Son in order to show to the world the oneness that comes from being rooted in God.

Section Summary

Jesus prayed for all believers (the church). The key theme of this section of his prayer was the glorification of believers.

QUESTIONS TO GUIDE YOUR STUDY

1. What makes this prayer of Jesus unique? What are its elements?
2. Sanctification is an important concept in Jesus's prayer. What is the doctrine of sanctification? Why was it so important to Jesus in this prayer?
3. In this prayer, what do we learn about the relationship between the Son and the Father?
4. How did Jesus pray for himself? For his disciples? For the church?

NEW TESTAMENT REFERENCE

The Synoptic Gospels (Matthew, Mark, and Luke) record that Judas betrayed Jesus with a kiss, the common gesture of greeting among friends. John's is the only Gospel that records that the attack on the servant of the chief priest was carried out by Simon Peter on a man named Malchus (v. 10). Luke records Jesus's healing of the man's wound (Luke 22:51).

JOHN 18

In this chapter, the countdown to the cross quickens. The events leading up to Jesus's crucifixion begin: his arrest, Peter's denial, and his religious and civil trials.

JESUS'S ARREST (18:1–14)

While in the garden of Gethsemane, Jesus and the disciples were confronted by a band of soldiers, accompanied by Pharisees as well as Judas, Jesus's betrayer. We are not told the number of arresting officers and soldiers, but the usual size of a Roman cohort was six hundred men. This would not seem necessary for arresting one unarmed man and a handful of followers. Is it possible the authorities feared that Jesus had a secret army ready to spring to his defense or that others sympathetic to Jesus would come to his aid?

Jesus's concern for his disciples at the moment of his arrest is evident (v. 8). Jesus rebuked Peter's effort at defending Jesus. In spite of Peter's good intentions, the "cup" that was before Jesus had to be embraced.

WORD PICTURE

Cup

The word *cup* is a metaphor for Jesus's suffering (Mark 10:38–39; Matt 20:22–23). It is a metaphor here not for physical death in general but for the particular death Jesus would suffer. In the Old Testament, the "cup" was often used for suffering (Ps 75:8; Ezek 23:31–34), as well as the wrath of God (Isa 51:17, 22; Jer 25:15; see also Rev 14:10; 16:19).

Section Summary

While in the garden of Gethsemane with his disciples, Jesus was approached by Judas and a band of soldiers. They arrested Jesus to bring him before the high priests.

JESUS BEFORE THE JEWISH AUTHORITIES (18:15–27)

Peter's First Denial (vv. 15–18)

The two interrogations may have been carried out by the religious authorities to give the sentence the semblance of a fair trial. Peter's first denial, all four Gospels report, came as the result of the challenge of a slave girl. She asked Peter if he was one of the disciples of Jesus, which Peter promptly denied (v. 17).

Jesus Before the High Priests (vv. 19–24)

Jesus was brought before Annas and Caiaphas. Annas was actually a former high priest, but he conducted the first interrogation before sending Jesus on to Caiaphas. The interrogations of Jesus by Annas and Caiaphas brought Jesus's response that he taught publicly and that he taught nothing in private that was not openly said to the crowds. This brought a blow to his face as if such a reply was improper when answering the high priest (v. 22). This blow was illegal in such questionings. Jesus's reply was the truth, and it should not have been rejected or reacted to with such violence. Note that John treated the Jewish trial with great brevity, devoting the majority of his narrative to the Roman trial.

HISTORICAL BACKGROUND

Annas served as high priest from AD 6 to 15. He still carried a lot of influence. Five of his sons served as priests, and the present high priest, Caiaphas, was his son-in-law.

The Drama of Betrayal (vv. 25–27)

Peter's second and third denials, followed by the prophesied crow of the rooster, are recorded just before the account of Jesus's interaction with Pilate (v. 38). John's narrative reveals two simultaneous plots:

- Peter's denials
- Jesus's interrogations and mock trial

Both of those constitute a drama of betrayal: one by the people who should have received Christ as King and one by a person who should have remained loyal to Christ as King.

HISTORICAL BACKGROUND

Jesus's appearance before Annas and Caiaphas was anything but legal. John records several of the illegal aspects of Jesus's religious trial:

- It was held at night.
- Jesus was *assumed* guilty and proven guilty.
- The court hired false witnesses to testify against Jesus.
- Jesus was mistreated while bound.
- The authorities did not allow Jesus a defense.

Section Summary

The arresting soldiers brought Jesus before Annas, the former high priest, and Caiaphas, the acting high priest. His trial before the religious leaders was illegal. During the course of these proceedings, Peter denied his Lord three times.

JESUS'S CIVIL TRIAL (18:28–40)

The Accusation to Pilate (vv. 28–32)

Next the Jewish leaders took Jesus to the palace of Pilate, the Roman governor. There is profound irony here. Their purpose was to have an innocent man put to death, yet they wanted to avoid becoming ceremonially unclean by going into the palace of the Roman governor.

"I AM" SAYING: THE KING (V. 37)

STATEMENT	SIGNIFICANCE
"I'm a king." (v. 37)	Jesus's kingdom is a kingdom of truth.

The Questioning by Pilate (vv. 33–38a)

Pilate's first question was perfunctory—almost a leading question in order to investigate the nature of the Jewish complaint. Jesus's answer was disarming, bringing a transparent reply from Pilate about the political tensions that had led Jesus to Pilate. Speaking in terms Pilate would understand, Jesus admitted being a King, but a King of far more than an earthly, temporal realm. Many people throughout Christian history have misinterpreted the kingdom of God in earthly terms.

As was his custom, Jesus then turned the discussion toward his mission. He informed Pilate that his kingly role was identified with testifying "to the truth. Everyone who is of truth listens to my voice" (v. 37). Pilate's response was legendary: "What is truth?" (v. 38). Was it a serious question or a sarcastic response? We simply do not know.

Pilate's Offer of Release (vv. 38b–40)

Pilate went to the Jews and discussed their charges against Jesus. He announced that he found Jesus guilty of no crime. He decided to offer Jesus's release in celebration of the Passover. The Jews, however, demanded the release of Barabbas, an insurrectionist and a murderer (Luke 23:19). This was a twist that apparently Pilate did not anticipate. Honoring the crowd's choice, he sentenced Jesus to death.

New Testament Reference

The Gospel of John records three major conversations between Jesus and persons who were confronted with the truth and the claims of the gospel. Nicodemus was a religious man who sought Jesus in order to pursue his spiritual questions (see John 3). The Samaritan woman was neither religious nor a skeptic but one who represented worldliness in its most common form. She was indifferent to the spiritual, living a life of moral self-indulgence (see John 4). Pilate, however, represents the modern secularist. Hardened to what would speak to his soul, he was neither open to nor inquisitive about the gospel.

Section Summary

After questioning Jesus, Pilate was convinced that Jesus committed no crime. In an attempt to free Jesus, Pilate offered to release Jesus as part of the Passover celebration, but the crowd insisted on the release of Barabbas instead.

QUESTIONS TO GUIDE YOUR STUDY

1. What did Jesus mean by "drink[ing] the cup"?
2. Jesus's religious trial was plagued by many irregularities. What were these? Why did the high priests take the steps they did to have Jesus killed?
3. Pilate's question, "What is truth?" has been much debated. Was Pilate being sincere or sarcastic?

JOHN 19

Christ's suffering, death, and burial are the key events of this chapter.

THE SOURCE OF POWER (19:1–16A)

The physical and emotional torture Jesus suffered is beyond description. He was not only physically beaten but was also ridiculed and mocked. Perhaps as one last effort to have Jesus released, Pilate presented him to the crowd after he was beaten to see if they could accept his liberation (v. 4). The Jews, however, insisted on his death because Jesus claimed to be the Son of God (v. 7).

Pilate's assertion that he had the power to free or crucify Jesus brought the following response from Jesus: "You would have no authority over me at all . . . if it hadn't been given you from above. This is why the one who handed me over to you has the greater sin" (v. 11). While Pilate was not the initiator of the death of Jesus, he was not without sin in the matter.

Section Summary

In preparation for his crucifixion, Jesus was flogged, mocked, and ridiculed. In spite of his innocence, the Jews insisted on his death. Pilate complied.

THE HOUR HAS COME (19:16B–27)

Every word of John's Gospel leads to this moment, for the "hour" had finally come. In one last effort to cleanse himself from guilt, Pilate had the title "JESUS OF NAZARETH, THE KING OF THE JEWS" fastened to his cross. It was written in three languages: Latin, Aramaic, and Greek (v. 19). To this point, every prophecy regarding the Messiah—even to the gambling for his clothes—was fulfilled (v. 24; cp. Ps 22:18).

Present at Jesus's crucifixion were his mother, his mother's sister, Mary the wife of Clopas, and Mary Magdalene. Also present was the author of this Gospel, John, whom Jesus instructed to care for his mother (v. 27).

Section Summary

Jesus was executed by crucifixion, the most painful and degrading form of capital punishment in the ancient world. John, the author of this Gospel, was present at the crucifixion.

HISTORICAL BACKGROUND

Death by Crucifixion

Crucifixion was the method the Romans used to execute Christ. It was the most painful and degrading form of capital punishment in the ancient world. A person crucified in Jesus's day was first beaten with a whip consisting of thongs with embedded pieces of metal. This scourging was designed to hasten death and lessen the terrible ordeal. After the beating, the victim carried the crossbeam to signify that life was over and to break his will to live. A tablet detailing the crime was often placed around the criminal's neck. At the site, the prisoner was tied (normal method) or nailed (if a quicker death was desired) to the crossbeam. The nails were driven through the wrist rather than the palm, since the smaller bones of the hand would not support the weight of the body.

THE SEVEN SAYINGS OF JESUS ON THE CROSS

SAYING	PASSAGE	EXPLANATION
1. "Father, forgive them, because they do not know what they are doing."	Luke 23:34	Jesus asked forgiveness for his enemies.
2. "Truly I tell you, today you will be with me in paradise."	Luke 23:43	Jesus offered paradise to the repentant thief on the cross.
3. "Woman, here is your son" and "Here is your mother."	John 19:26–27	Jesus committed the care of Mary to his disciple John.
4. "My God, my God, why have you abandoned me?"	Matt 27:46	Jesus was aware of his alienation from God.
5. "I'm thirsty."	John 19:28	Jesus expressed agony because of the torture of crucifixion.
6. "It is finished"	John 19:30	A cry of victory, expressing that He had paid the debt of sin.
7. "Father, into your hands I entrust my spirit"	Luke 23:46	An expressed confidence in the triumphant restoration of fellowship with the Father after death.

IT IS FINISHED: THE DEATH OF JESUS (19:28–37)

The actual death of Jesus was preceded with words fitting the narrative of John: "It is finished" (v. 30). What did Jesus mean by *finished?* The mission of Jesus, Son of God, was to die a substitutionary death for sinful persons. As a result of his death on our behalf, our sin was atoned, and eternal life through Jesus became attainable through a trusting faith.

With these final words, Jesus bowed his head and gave up "his spirit" (v. 30). This unusual way of describing a person's death suggests that Jesus died voluntarily as an act of the will. After his death, a soldier pierced his side, "and at once blood and water came out " (v. 34). From a medical standpoint, the mixture of blood and water from the spear's thrust was the result of piercing the sac that surrounds the heart (the pericardium) as well as the heart itself.

WORD PICTURE

It Is Finished

This is one word (*tetelestai*) in the Greek text. It carries the idea of completion. The words *It is finished* mean that "the debt of our sin is all paid!" It is "a cry of victory in the hour of defeat." (A. T. Robertson, "The Fourth Gospel," *WPNT* vol. 5, 304.) Of particular significance is that the Greek perfect tense is used, which indicates a completed action that has continuing results. This word could also be translated, "It is accomplished."

Section Summary

When Jesus finished his substitutionary work on the cross, he willingly and deliberately gave up his life. With the words, "It is finished," he gave up his spirit.

THE BURIAL OF JESUS (19:38–42)

After the death of Jesus, most of the disciples were nowhere to be found. But two persons who had been afraid to declare their allegiance up to this point came forward boldly to care for the body of Christ. These two were Nicodemus (John 4) and Joseph of Arimathea, a rich member of the Sanhedrin who had agreed to the condemnation of Jesus (Matt 27:57; Luke 23:50–51). Jesus was laid in a tomb following a traditional Jewish preparation.

QUESTIONS TO GUIDE YOUR STUDY

1. Why did the Jews insist on Jesus's death? In their view, what crime had he committed?
2. Read the account of Jesus's death and crucifixion in John 19. What physical suffering did Jesus endure? How do you think this suffering might compare to that of his bearing the weight of the world's sin?
3. What does the phrase "it is finished" convey?
4. What were the circumstances of Jesus's burial? Following Jesus's death, what was the apparent state of affairs among the disciples?

OLD TESTAMENT REFERENCE

The author of this Gospel, the apostle John, then offered his testimony that he was a witness to the crucifixion and that even to the final moment every detail fulfilled the prophecies concerning the Messiah (vv. 35–37; cp. Exod 12:46; Num 9:12; Ps 34:20; Zech 12:10).

JOHN 20

The resurrection accounts differ in each of the Gospels, with each presenting its unique emphases of the event. In this chapter, John records three post-resurrection appearances by Jesus, each of which has a dramatic effect on those he encountered.

THE RESURRECTION OF JESUS (20:1–18)

An Empty Tomb (vv. 1–10)

Mary Magdalene was the first person to arrive at the tomb of Jesus. Upon seeing the stone removed from the tomb, she ran to Peter and John, exclaiming that they had taken Jesus's body from the tomb. Peter and John ran to the tomb, finding only the strips of Jesus's burial clothes. Peter and John, as did Mary, failed to understand that the resurrection had occurred (v. 9).

A Risen Lord! (vv. 10–18)

After all the others left the empty tomb, Mary stood alone weeping. Two angels appeared to her and asked her why she was expressing such grief. She said that someone had taken her Lord and she was trying to find him. At that point Mary turned and saw Jesus.

The tenderness of the moment when he said, "Mary" and her recognition of him and cry of "*Rabboni!*" (meaning "Teacher") is one of the

PERSONAL APPLICATION

"Robertson renders Jesus's prohibition as 'Cease clinging to me.' And since the verb form is a present tense this seem to be a good translation. She was not to continue clinging to Him, but was to bear His message to the apostles. This is suggestive to us. We are not simply to linger about the shrine of the resurrection, but are to go declaring the fact of it."

H. H. Hobbs, *An Exposition of the Gospel of John*, 283.

emotional highlights of the entire Gospel of John. Jesus warned Mary not to "cling" to him, for he had "not yet ascended to the Father" (v. 17).

Section Summary

Jesus had risen from the grave! His first appearance was to Mary. His address to her, "Mary," and her recognition of him and cry of "Rabboni!" is one of the emotional highlights of John's Gospel.

PERSONAL APPLICATION

"What he commits to the disciples and to us is the power and privilege of giving assurance of the forgiveness of sins by God and correctly announcing the terms of forgiveness. There is no proof that he actually transferred to the apostles or their successors the power in and of themselves to forgive sin."

A. T. Robertson, "The Fourth Gospel," *WPNT*, vol. 5, 315.

God's forgiveness does not depend on human forgiveness, but rather forgiveness is extended by God as a result of individual response to the proclamation of the gospel by fellow human beings.

THE FORGIVENESS OF SINS (20:19–23)

Jesus encountered a group of frightened disciples behind locked doors, and he gave them what they needed most—himself. He showed them his hands and his side in order to dispel any doubt that they were seeing anything but their crucified Lord. As with the Great Commission recorded in Matt 28, Jesus decisively gave his followers the command to go into all the world and continue his ministry.

He breathed on them (v. 22) and commanded them to receive the Holy Spirit, who would be poured out upon them in fullness fifty days later, during the festival of Pentecost.

Jesus stated that if the disciples forgave anyone, they were forgiven, and if they did not forgive others their sins, they would not be forgiven. At first glance this is a remarkable statement that seems out of step with the role and authority of the disciples. It was not the disciples who could forgive sins but Jesus. The literal reading from the Greek text is clearer, stating, "Those whose sins you forgive have already been forgiven; those whose sins you do not forgive have not been forgiven."

Section Summary

John's second recorded post-resurrection appearance by Jesus was to his disciples. He appeared to them behind their locked doors. They rejoiced at seeing him and received peace and the spiritual power from him to complete their commission.

PERSONAL APPLICATION

Thomas's doubt was the same as that of many in the modern world. Unless he could see, taste, touch, and hear what was being presented as reality, he would not accept it as the truth. As Jesus noted, however, "Blessed are those who have not seen and yet believe" (v. 29).

THOMAS BELIEVES (20:24–30)

Thomas was not easily convinced of something that seemed impossible. Jesus directly addressed Thomas and instructed him to place his fingers in the nail prints in his hands and the spear wound in his side. Then Jesus declared, "Don't be faithless, but believe." As long as Thomas doubted, he remained faithless and useless.

Whether Thomas actually placed his fingers in the nail prints and side wound, we do not know. It appears that all demands for proof were forgotten, as he responded, "My Lord and my God!"

Section Summary

Unless Thomas could see, taste, touch, and hear what was being presented as reality, he would not accept it as the truth. That he demanded proof—and then believed—reinforces even more the credibility of the accounts of Jesus's resurrection.

JOHN'S PURPOSE FOR WRITING HIS GOSPEL (20:31)

John's purpose statement is included here, following the resurrection, in order that the reader might know the reason for this carefully detailed narrative of the life and teaching of Jesus. He desired that his readers:

- Might come to believe that Jesus Christ is the Messiah
- That through believing they might have eternal life

The purpose of the Gospel of John was to present Jesus as God in human form and that through faith in Jesus individuals would embrace salvation to eternal life.

WORD PICTURE

You May Believe

The force to the verb "believe" here is present tense. The idea John is trying to convey here is that those who believe *may keep on believing*. John's Gospel has had precisely that effect of continuous and successive confirmation of faith in Jesus Christ through the ages.

A. T. Robertson, "The Fourth Gospel," *WPNT*, vol. 5, 317.

QUESTIONS TO GUIDE YOUR STUDY

1. What caused Mary to recognize Jesus? What spiritual implications and lessons might we draw from this account of Mary's encounter with the Lord?
2. What were the results of Jesus's encounter with the disciples? Are there implications from the results of that encounter that apply to believers today?
3. How was Thomas typical of many nonbelievers today? What was the value of John's including the account about Thomas?
4. What was John's stated purpose for his Gospel?

JOHN 21

John's Gospel begins with a prologue and ends with an epilogue. A particular benefit of this epilogue is that we learn what happened between Simon Peter and Jesus and how Peter's denial of Jesus eventually concluded.

WORD PICTURE

153 Fish

Some have found significance in the number of fish the disciples caught, citing the belief of the ancients that there were 153 kinds of fish. This would indicate that the gospel would include all persons and that the net of the kingdom of God would be strong enough to hold all without breaking. Clearly the gospel is for all, and the kingdom of God holds everyone.

MIRACLES CONTINUE (21:1–14)

A Night of Failure (vv. 1–3)

Peter decided to return to his previous trade—fishing. He announced to the other disciples that he was going fishing, and six others joined him. Although nighttime was the usual time for fishing, the disciples fished all night without a catch.

A Morning of Success (vv. 4–14)

At daybreak, Jesus was watching from the shore of the lake. He shouted a question to them across the water, asking how they had fared during the night. At this point, they did not recognize him. Jesus then instructed them to cast the net on the other side of the boat. Desperate to try anything, they did so and caught fish! Then one of the disciples recognized Jesus. Then they joined him for breakfast.

The miraculous catch of fish and Jesus's fellowship with the disciples constitutes the third recorded appearance of Jesus following his resurrection. Here Jesus demonstrated again his power over the natural world.

PERSONAL APPLICATION

Jesus restored Peter before his peers. None of those present could ever forget this expression of mercy and forgiveness. This was a defining moment in how the Lord deals with his own when they stumble and fall.

Section Summary

Peter and six other disciples went fishing throughout the night, but by morning they had nothing to show for their work. Following Jesus's instruction, they cast their nets on the other side of the boat, catching 153 large fish. Jesus used this experience to drive home many lessons for the disciples.

DO YOU LOVE ME? (21:15–25)

Following their breakfast on the shores of the Sea of Tiberias (Sea of Galilee), Jesus turned to Peter and asked him three times if he loved Jesus. By the third time, Peter was grieved that Jesus continued to ask him. He confessed that Jesus knew all things—that he knew Peter's heart.

It's no accident that Jesus asked Peter three times concerning his love. Peter had denied the Lord three times.

HISTORICAL BACKGROUND

"There is an early tradition that Peter suffered martyrdom by crucifixion. The first mention of such is by Tertullian who makes reference to John 21:18. Later Origen said he was crucified head downwards. This was said to be at Peter's own request, since, having denied his Lord, he did not deserve to die as He did with his head upwards."

H. H. Hobbs, *An Exposition of the Gospel of John*, 294.

Following each affirmation of love, Jesus gave Peter a commission:

- "Feed my lambs."
- "Shepherd my sheep."
- "Feed my sheep."

Jesus then told the kind of death Peter would die to glorify God.

The final words of the Gospel of John change from firsthand narrative to a plural perspective. Not everything from the life of Christ was recorded but only those things the author felt supported the goal of leading individuals to belief in Jesus as the Son of God, who came to take away the sins of the world.

The Gospel of John concludes with a verification of the testimony contained in it: "We know that his testimony is true. And there are also many other things that Jesus did, which, if every one of them were written down, I suppose not even the world itself could contain the books that would be written" (vv. 24b–25).

Section Summary

Peter's three denials of Jesus were answered in three affirmations of love and service. He declared his love and loyalty, and Jesus accepted his confession and gave him a ministering responsibility. Peter was to shepherd the sheep of Christ's fold.

QUESTIONS TO GUIDE YOUR STUDY

1. What has been suggested as the significance of the miracle of the catch of 153 fish?
2. What was significant about Jesus's examination of Peter's love for him? What was Jesus trying to accomplish with his interrogation of Peter?
3. Drawing from the closing verses of this chapter, what was the author's strategy for developing and presenting his account of the gospel? What unrecorded aspect of Jesus's life would you wish to learn about?
4. This final chapter serves as an epilogue to John's Gospel. What unique information do we learn from it?

Acts

INTRODUCTION

The church happened. That is the fact of the matter. No human *person* set out to create the church.

The basic purpose of the book of Acts is to show the unimpeded spread of the church throughout the Roman world. Underlying that obvious purpose is Luke's aim to show that this spread took place in the power of the Holy Spirit as the gospel penetrated geographical, social, racial, and religious barriers. This narrative is Luke's account of how the Holy Spirit worked through men and women to proclaim and live out the news of God's coming for all the peoples of the world.

HISTORICAL BACKGROUND

Acceptance of Luke as author of the book of Acts was generally followed without serious question in the early church. Early Christian leaders such as Irenaeus, Clement of Alexandria, and Eusebius provide evidence for the Lukan authorship of Acts. The Muratorian Canon (AD 190) listed Luke as the author of Acts.

AUTHOR

Luke is author of both the book of Acts and the Gospel of Luke. He was a close friend and traveling companion of Paul. Many scholars believe Luke wrote his Gospel and Acts in Rome with Paul during the apostle's first Roman imprisonment. Apparently, Luke remained nearby or with Paul during that time, for Paul wrote in 2 Tim 4:11, "Only Luke is with me."

Lukan authorship of Acts remained relatively unchallenged until critical approaches to the New Testament developed. Despite some modern objections to Luke as the author of Acts, the ancient view of the early church still carries weight.

LUKE THE PERSON

Luke was probably a Gentile. Paul's reference to Luke in Col 4:14 indicates that Luke was a physician. No other certain information about Luke's background exists. However, the anti-Marcionite prologue to Luke's Gospel, dating from the second century AD, states that he was a native of Antioch, Syria, never married, and died in Boeotia at the age of eighty-four.

AUDIENCE

Where was Luke when he wrote Acts, and to whom did he write? These questions probably are unanswerable. Luke dedicated his book to Theophilus, which is a Greek name. Did Luke write primarily to Gentiles? If so, why did he concern himself so much with Jewish questions? Why the elaborate messianic proofs of Peter's sermons in Acts 2 and 3 if not to provide his readers with a pattern for witness to the Jews? The most likely answer is that Luke intended his work for Christian communities that included both Jews and Gentiles—mixed congregations such as those we encounter frequently in Paul's epistles.

WORD PICTURE

Theophilus

Some hold that his name is simply a generalization like "dear reader." Others prefer to think of him as a real person and as a pillar of some church. The name *Theophilus* means "loved by God."

PURPOSE

Luke's statement in the first two verses of Acts contrasts the purpose of the third Gospel, Luke, with the purpose of Acts. The Gospel of Luke was an account of what Jesus began to do and to teach up to the ascension. Acts is an account of the continuation of Jesus's work through the Holy Spirit at work in the early church. Luke traced the gospel from its beginning in Jerusalem into the center of power in the empire, the city of Rome.

DATE OF WRITING

The date for the writing of Acts is linked to the date for the writing of Luke. Both books have the same author, and Luke's Gospel is the first volume of a two-volume work. The date for Luke's Gospel is likely set in the early sixties. The most significant factor contributing to this date is the abrupt ending of Acts. The most cogent explanation of why Luke ended Acts with Paul still imprisoned is that Paul's imprisonment was still unresolved. The fact that Paul spent two years (Acts 28:30) in a Roman prison at the conclusion of Acts provides help in dating Acts in the early sixties. At the conclusion of Acts, Paul was still awaiting trial. The emperor Nero had not yet turned against the Christians as he did in AD 64. Therefore, Luke wrote Acts at some time in the early sixties.

STRUCTURE

Acts falls into two divisions: the mission of the Jerusalem church (Acts 1–12) and the mission of Paul (Acts 13–28). Each may be subdivided into two main sections. In the Jerusalem portion, chapters 1–5 treat the early church in Jerusalem, and chapters 6–12 treat the outreach beyond Jerusalem. In the Pauline portion, 13:1–21:16 relates the three major missions of Paul, and 21:27–28:31 deals with Paul's defense of his ministry.

LITERARY FORM

Acts is a history written with a purpose in view. Luke was not interested in outlining each facet of the development of the early church. Rather, he focused on how the gospel spread from Jerusalem to Rome. He also paid close attention to the work and ministry of Paul. Although Luke had a theological purpose for writing, we must understand that Acts contains reliable, trustworthy historical information.

BASIC OUTLINE OF ACTS

I. Peter: Missionary to the Jews (1:1–12:24)
  A. The Early Church in Jerusalem (1:1–5:42)
  B. The Outreach Beyond Jerusalem (6:1–12:24)
II. Paul: Missionary to the Gentiles (12:25–28:31)
III. The Three Major Missions of Paul (13:1–21:16)
IV. Paul's Defense of His Ministry (21:27–28:31)

ACTS 1

PROLOGUE (1:1–5)

Literary Prologue (vv. 1–2)

Clearly, the book of Acts is a continuation of Luke's Gospel, which Luke refers to as his "former book." As with his Gospel, Luke writes this letter to Theophilus.

Luke provides an interesting summary of his Gospel and its relationship to Acts. His Gospel contained "all that Jesus began to do and teach." This may imply that the work was unfinished. Indeed, the work and words of Jesus continue throughout Acts in the ministry of the apostles and other faithful witnesses. And that work still goes on in the work of the church today.

As with any good two-volume work, there is careful overlapping so that readers can get their bearings. The connecting overlap between Luke and Acts is the ascension of Jesus. Before Jesus went back to the Father, he gave instructions to his disciples (see Luke 24:44–49). The ministry of the Holy Spirit soon became a reality in the lives of the apostles. The Holy Spirit would enable and empower them in their newly commissioned tasks.

Instructions Prior to Pentecost (vv. 3–5)

For forty of the most unusual days this earth has experienced, the risen Christ presented himself alive. Hundreds, maybe thousands, saw Jesus die. To refute his detractors—but even more, to undergird his disciples—the resurrected Jesus conducted a ministry of personal appearances.

He came to the disciples to give them courage to for their mission. By his words and visibility Jesus assured them that the same God who snatched him from the clutches of death would be with them as they lived out their commission to go into all the world and make disciples of the nations.

WORD PICTURE

Many Convincing Proofs

During these forty days Jesus gave "many convincing proofs" that he was alive. The Greek word for "proofs" comes from logic and means "demonstrative proof or evidence."

Section Summary

For forty days after the resurrection, Jesus appeared personally to the disciples on many occasions. His instructions gave them courage and assured them of his presence and power in the days ahead.

CHRIST'S LEGACY: THE CALL TO WITNESS (1:6–8)

The disciples asked Jesus about when the kingdom would be restored to Israel. Jesus turned aside their speculation. The "times or periods" of such things were matters within God's own purposes and authority. Instead, he directed the disciples toward their task, which was to be his witnesses. Jesus promised them power for this world-sized task. Verse 8 provides a rough geographical scope of their mission: to "Jerusalem, in all Judea and Samaria, and to the ends of the earth."

THE ASCENSION OF CHRIST (1:9–11)

The ascension concluded Jesus's earthly ministry. It allowed eyewitnesses to see both the risen Christ on earth and victorious and the eternal Christ returning to heaven to minister at the right hand of the Father.

Contrasted to Christ's act of humbling himself to move from heaven to earth, and especially to the cross, is God's act of exalting Jesus.

Section Summary

The ascension of Jesus expanded Christ's ministry from its geographically limited earthly dimensions to its universal heavenly dimensions. He now occupies the highest position in the universe, in charge of everything that exists and all that happens.

WORD PICTURE

Who Were Together

This phrase (one word in the Greek language) is a favorite adverb of Luke's—"together." It is a word that means "with one mind." Luke uses it ten times in Acts. It expresses unity of purpose and particularly applies to the "one heart and mind" (4:32) of Christian fellowship (1:14; 2:1; 4:24; 5:12; 15:25).

PREPARATION IN THE UPPER ROOM (1:12–14)

The disciples returned to Jerusalem from the Mount of Olives to wait as Jesus commanded them. They gathered in an upper room of a large Palestinian house. Those present included the eleven disciples, "the women," including Mary the mother Jesus, and Jesus's brothers. Their primary activity was prayer. The time before Pentecost was a time of waiting, a time spent in prayer undoubtedly for the promised Spirit and for the power to witness.

RESTORATION OF THE APOSTOLIC CIRCLE (1:15–26)

During the period of prayer and waiting, an essential item of business was to restore the apostolic circle of the Twelve. Peter, clearly having become the leader of the group, addressed the assembly.

Judas's Defection (vv. 15–20)

Judas's defection from the ranks of the Twelve sparked the need to find a replacement. Peter referred to the Old Testament Scriptures for direction. He quoted Ps 109:8 as a prophecy foretelling Jesus's betrayal by a friend. He also quoted from Ps 69:25, which he saw as pointing to the desertion of Judas's place among the apostles. He saw that psalm as already fulfilled.

Matthias's Installation (vv. 21–26)

The qualifications for Judas's replacement were: (1) he witnessed Jesus's entire ministry, from his baptism by John to his ascension; and above all, (2) he witnessed the resurrection. The assembly put forward the names of two candidates: Joseph and Matthias. To select Judas's successor, they prayed for God's guidance and then cast lots. The lot fell to Matthias, and so he joined the eleven. Matthias receives no further mention in Scripture.

OLD TESTAMENT REFERENCE

"Let his days be few; let another take over his position." (Ps 109:8)

"Make their fortification desolate; may no one live in their tents." (Ps 69:25)

Section Summary

The assembly of apostles chose a replacement for Judas, betrayer of Jesus. After praying and casting lots, the group selected Matthias as the new apostle.

WORD PICTURE

Matthias

Matthias means "gift of God."

QUESTIONS TO GUIDE YOUR STUDY

1. What is the relationship between the book of Acts and the Gospel of Luke?
2. In what ways did the ascension change Jesus's ministry?
3. The disciples asked about when the kingdom of God would be realized. What did the restoration of the kingdom involve?

WORD PICTURE

Pentecost

Pentecost is one of the feasts of ancient Judaism that had its roots in Lev 23:15–21. Through the years it was variously called the Feast of Weeks or the Feast of Firstfruits. And it was scheduled to begin at the close of harvesttime. It is called Pentecost because it began on the fiftieth day from the first Sunday after Passover.

ACTS 2

The events in chapter 1 were a preparation for the outpouring of the Spirit on the praying band of believers during the Jewish festival known as Pentecost. In this chapter, their prayer was answered in a mighty way.

THE MIRACLE AT PENTECOST (2:1–13)

The miracle at Pentecost has been referred to as "the birth of the church." A significant parallel between Pentecost and Luke's infancy narrative is the prominent role of the Spirit in both.

The Gift of the Holy Spirit (vv. 1–4)

Luke describes the coming of the Spirit in three carefully constructed parallel statements, each pointing to an aspect of the event.

The result of the Spirit's coming is that those in the upper room were "filled with the Holy Spirit." From this point on in Acts, the gift of the Spirit became a normal experience upon becoming a Christian. In this event:

- "A sound . . . came . . . , and it filled the whole house." (v. 2)
- "Tongues like flames of fire separated and rested on one each of them." (v. 3)
- "They . . . began to speak in different tongues." (v. 4)

The event was audible and visible, and it manifested itself in an outward demonstration of inspired and understandable speech. The audible part is described as a violent, mighty wind.

OLD TESTAMENT REFERENCE

These events evoked Old Testament images. The violent wind and tongues of fire were familiar signs of the presence of God, especially connected with Mount Sinai. The miracle of communication in many languages reversed the curse of Babel.

The Witness to the Spirit (vv. 5–13)

Gathered were "devout people from every nation under heaven." Likely these were Diaspora Jews who returned from other nations to Jerusalem to live. Luke lists the names of the various nationalities present. It encompassed the Roman world, spanning what is present-day Iran, the Middle East, Turkey, North Africa, and west to Rome.

The crowd responded in two different ways to the wonders of God they just saw. Some made fun of them, while others were amazed and asked, "What does this mean?"

HISTORICAL BACKGROUND

Ability to Speak in Different Languages

At Pentecost the church received the gift to communicate the gospel in foreign languages (Acts 2; cp. 10:44–46; 19:6). The apostles spoke in foreign languages they had not previously studied. Jews from every Diaspora nation were amazed that the Galileans were able to speak in their languages. God gave his Spirit to all his people to witness and prophesy.

Section Summary

God gave the church the gift of the Holy Spirit. The Spirit's arrival was audible, visible, and manifested itself in an outward demonstration of inspired speech. The event of Pentecost meant that the gospel was now able to reach the world through the power of the Spirit.

PETER'S SERMON AT PENTECOST (2:14–41)

Peter's sermon is the first of many sermons and speeches in Acts. Luke recorded both the content and tone of these sermons. Peter's sermon is the heart of this chapter. The controversial and exciting nature of the Pentecostal experience attracted significant attention. The true focus of the chapter, however, is the beginning of Christian evangelism.

TEN MAJOR SERMONS IN ACTS

REFERENCE IN ACTS	AUDIENCE	CENTRAL TRUTHS
Peter's Mission Sermons 1. Acts 2:14–41	An international group of God-fearing Jews in Jerusalem for Pentecost	The gift of the Holy Spirit proves now is the age of salvation. Jesus's resurrection validates his role as Messiah.
2. Acts 3:11–26	A Jewish crowd in the Jerusalem temple	The healing power of Jesus's name proves that he is alive and at work. Those who rejected the Messiah in ignorance can still repent.
3. Acts 10:27–48	The Gentile Cornelius and his household	God accepts persons of all races who respond in faith to the gospel message.
Stephen's Sermon 4. Acts 7:1–60	The Sanhedrin	God revealed himself outside the Holy Land. God's people capped a history of rejecting the leaders he sent them by killing the Messiah.
Paul's Mission Sermons 5. Acts 13 6. Acts 17 7. Acts 20	Jews in the synagogue in Pisidian Antioch Pagan Greeks at the Areopagus in Athens Christian leaders of the Ephesian church	Paul's mission sermons illustrate the changing foci of the early Christian mission work: first Jewish evangelism, second Gentile evangelism, third development of Christian leaders.
Paul's Defense Sermons 8. Acts 22:1–21 9. Acts 24:10–21 10. Acts 26	Temple crowd in Jerusalem The Roman Governor Felix The Jewish King Agrippa II	Paul's defense sermons emphasize that Paul was innocent of any breach of Roman law. Paul was on trial for his conviction that Jesus was raised from the dead and commissioned him as a missionary to the Gentiles.

Two Themes Run Through the Sermon

Peter's primary theme is that Jesus's life, death, and resurrection happened according to God's plan. A second theme is the Jewish responsibility for Jesus's death.

The sermon evoked a response in the form of a question: "Brothers, what should we do?" Peter's answer was an offer to repent and be baptized. The response to Peter's invitation was overwhelming. About three thousand people "accepted his message" and were baptized.

Section Summary

Peter delivered the first Christian apology (defense) in the history of the church on the day of Pentecost. His address expanded on two simple themes: Repentance and baptism are to be done in the name of Jesus Christ.

THE FLAVOR OF THE FIRST NEW COMMUNITY (2:42–47)

This first summary provides a snapshot of the church immediately after its beginnings. The picture is one of maturing discipleship. The new converts were taught, continued to worship in the temple, and were unified economically and spiritually. Finally, "every day the Lord added to their number." The church was not only surviving, but it was also growing.

QUESTIONS TO GUIDE YOUR STUDY

1. What events took place at Pentecost? Describe the significance of each.
2. What two themes ran through Peter's sermon at Pentecost?
3. In his narrative, Luke provides several summaries about the progress of the church. How might your church's growth parallel that of the early church?

ACTS 3

THE FIRST RECORDED HEALING (3:1–10)

Peter and John were going up to the temple at the time of prayer. When they arrived at one of the temple's gates, a "man who was lame from birth" was in the process of being carried and placed there to beg for alms from those entering the temple. Those who entered the temple for the evening sacrifice and prayer would be particularly disposed to practice their piety by generously giving alms to a lame beggar. Almsgiving was one of the main ways to show kindness and thus was considered a major expression of a person's devotion to God.

When Peter and John encountered the lame man, Peter told the man to look at them. They did in the name of Jesus what Jesus himself had done so many times. Peter said to the lame man, "I don't have silver or gold, but what I do have, I give you: In the name of Jesus Christ of Nazareth, get up and walk!" (v. 6). Instantly the man's feet and ankles became strong. He jumped, walked, and leaped, calling attention to himself as he accompanied Peter and John into the temple courts. Verse 6 is the heart of the message, the one detail that sets this story apart from the usual narrative. Some things are more precious than silver or gold.

HISTORICAL BACKGROUND

Almsgiving

Although the Hebrew language had no technical term to refer to "alms" or "almsgiving," the practice of charitable giving—especially to the poor—became an important belief and practice within Judaism.

NEW TESTAMENT REFERENCE

Of the many miracles recounted in Acts, none has more formal resemblance to the miracles of Jesus in the Gospels than this one. The major difference is that while Jesus healed by his own authority, Peter healed by the "name" of Jesus. Peter's ability to heal was indeed by Jesus's authority at work through the agency of the apostles.

Section Summary

Those who were unworthy for worship in the old religion of Israel found full acceptance in the name of Jesus. The healing of the lame man amazed those who witnessed it and prepared them for Peter's explanation.

PETER'S SERMON IN THE TEMPLE (3:11–26)

The scene of Peter's next speech was Solomon's Colonnade, probably a covered area located on the eastern side of the temple, within the temple walls. As in the case of Pentecost, an apostolic action raised questions that gave Peter an opportunity to preach.

A comparison of this sermon and Peter's Pentecost sermon reveals that it is remarkably like his first sermon in both organization and content. Peter noted the will of God in the life, death, and resurrection of Jesus. He also emphasized the power of God to raise Jesus and gave a softer treatment of the Jewish responsibility for Jesus's death.

The two sermons contain significant differences as well. For example, the scriptural proofs in the Pentecost sermon aim at establishing the messianic status of Jesus. Those in this sermon are aimed at the need for the Jews to repent and accept Jesus as the one sent from God.

Peter gave the threefold result of repentance: (1) their sins would be forgiven, (2) the "seasons of refreshing" would come upon them, and (3) God would send the Messiah whom he appointed for them.

OLD TESTAMENT REFERENCE

Peter quoted Moses as one of the earliest Hebrew prophets to announce the coming of Messiah: "The LORD your God will raise up for you a prophet like me from among your own brothers. You must listen to him" (Deut 18:15).

Section Summary

Peter delivered a stirring speech at the temple. He noted the will of God in the life, death, and resurrection of Jesus. He included scriptural proofs in his sermon aimed at the need for the Jews to repent and accept Jesus as the one sent from God.

QUESTIONS TO GUIDE YOUR STUDY

1. By whose authority and power did Peter heal the lame man at the temple?
2. Why was almsgiving so important to the Jews? Do we have any modern-day counterparts to that practice?
3. What were the key points of Peter's sermon at the temple?

ACTS 4

To this point in Acts, there has been no resistance to the Christians on the part of the Jewish leaders. In fact, the picture was that of general acceptance and favor accorded the early believers by the people. It was the officials, however, who turned against them. The primary enemy was the priestly Sadducean aristocracy for whom the Christians were a serious threat to the status quo.

THE FIRST ARREST (4:1–31)

The Arrest and Interrogation (vv. 1–12)

Peter's sermon at the temple was suddenly interrupted by an official group of priests, the captain of the temple guard, and Sadducees.

The Sadducees likely feared reaction from the governing Roman rulers. Peter and John were arrested and placed in jail overnight.

The two were then ordered to appear before the Sanhedrin and account for their actions. They were probably in as much trouble for Peter's message in the temple as they were for healing the lame man. The question from the Sanhedrin was, "By what power or in what name have you done this?"

Peter answered them through the power of the Spirit. His testimony was, in many ways, a condensed form of his address at the temple. Peter explained that the power by which the lame man was healed was that of Jesus of Nazareth. Not only that, but Peter accused the Sanhedrin of responsibility for rejecting and killing Christ. He also proclaimed God's power in raising Jesus from the dead.

HISTORICAL BACKGROUND

The Sanhedrin

The Sanhedrin was the highest Jewish council in the first century. The word *Sanhedrin* is usually translated "council" in English versions of the Bible. The council had seventy-one members over which a high priest presided. The Sanhedrin included both of the main Jewish parties among its membership. Since the high priest presided, the Sadducean priestly party seems to have been predominant, but some leading Pharisees also were members.

Warning and Release (vv. 13–22)

In contrast to the apostles' boldness and freedom, the council sat in stony silence. After asking the apostles to leave the courtroom, the council assessed the evidence. It was hardly a clear-cut case. The council's response was a political one. Although they were unable to deny the apostolic miracle, they felt compelled to curtail the apostolic preaching. Peter and John were warned no longer to speak "in this name." The council had no alternative but to threaten the apostles and then release them.

The Prayer of the Community (vv. 23–31)

These verses give us a glimpse into the life of the Christians in Jerusalem. It is a report of the church's prayer of gratitude for God's deliverance of the apostles from the Jewish authorities. In response to their prayer for power and strength, their meeting place was shaken with the presence of the Spirit.

Section Summary

Through the power of his Spirit, God delivered the apostles from the Jewish authorities. God's Spirit shook the meeting place of the Christians who gathered to pray for the apostles. The result of the Spirit's presence was a renewed boldness by the church in proclaiming the gospel.

THE COMMON LIFE OF THE COMMUNITY (4:32–37)

This second summary amplifies the idea of common possessions among the community of believers. The Christians were living in harmony and unity. The proof of their unity was their willingness to share resources with one another. Through the charity of wealthier members, like Barnabas, those who were poor received enough. As a result, no one among them was "needy" (v. 34).

WORD PICTURE

Barnabas

Barnabas means "son of encouragement." This is the name given to Joseph, a Levite from Cyprus.

QUESTIONS TO GUIDE YOUR STUDY

1. How was the early church initially received by the Jewish authorities?
2. What annoyed and angered the Sanhedrin about Peter's and John's preaching?
3. The early church was a praying church. How did they pray? What might we learn from their example?

ACTS 5

ANANIAS AND SAPPHIRA (5:1–11)

Like Barnabas, Ananias and Sapphira sold property and gave the proceeds to the church. Unlike Barnabas, they agreed to lie about their profit from the sale. No doubt they were glad to be part of the movement and were serious about their involvement. Ananias and Sapphira were not as secure as Barnabas. Whereas Barnabas could freely and with no strings attached give his money to the church and brush aside the flattery, Ananias and his wife craved the adulation but could not bring themselves to part with all their goods. They would go after the best of both worlds: sell the property and make a show of giving it to the church but keep part of the proceeds hidden.

Peter saw through the attempt. He questioned the man, "Ananias, . . . why has Satan filled your heart to lie to the Holy Spirit and keep back part of the proceeds of the land?"

Ananias violated his own integrity, perjured the Spirit of God who now lived in his life, and made a mockery of the Holy Spirit's activity in his soul. Peter declared to Ananias, "You have not lied to people but to God." With that, he fell down and died.

Three hours later Sapphira arrived. When the apostle confronted her with the joint sin, she too fell dead. The same people who buried Ananias prepared her body for burial and placed her beside her husband.

This event had a powerful effect on the church. God's quick and decisive punishment created great fear in the church. Its members were terrified—a natural response to witnessing the power of God. This event

WORD PICTURE

Church

The word for "church" (Greek word *ekklēsia*) is first used in Acts 5:11. It meant "a free assembly of people." The Christian church was old and new: new in that it gave testimony to the life, death, resurrection, and ongoing ministry of Jesus; and old because the idea of the assembly reached back to the people of God created in the Exodus.

PERSONAL APPLICATION

Such immediate and radical judgment is not the usual way God deals with believers today. However, judgment, punishment for sin, and retribution are part of God's way of running a balanced moral universe. We need to get the message that we do not go on sinning with impunity, thinking that we won't have to reckon with God and others for our misdeeds.

HISTORICAL BACKGROUND

Apostolic Preaching

In their public preaching, the apostles directed their message to the unconverted. They stressed the gospel of Christ and preached for conversions. The apostles' message had several essential elements in common:

1. They proclaimed that Scripture was fulfilled.
2. The fulfillment came in the person of Jesus, whom they claimed as Messiah.
3. Salvation comes through the death, burial, and resurrection of Jesus, who ascended to the right hand of God, from where he will come again to judge the world.
4. Salvation consists in the forgiveness of sins and the gift of the Holy Spirit. When sin is taken away and the Holy Spirit comes in, a person has received eternal life.
5. The appropriate response to this gospel is repentance toward God and faith in the Lord Jesus.

has little to do with the amount a person gives. The importance lies with one's attitude. Ananias and Sapphira gave their offering to impress the congregation. The fact that they held back money and claimed they gave the entire sale price reflected a self-serving attitude, not one that served God.

Section Summary

Ananias and Sapphira, like Barnabas, sold some property and gave the proceeds to the church. They held back some of the proceeds but asserted that they gave the entire sale price. God's judgment was immediate death. The sin of Ananias and Sapphira was not that they kept some of the profit. Their sin was in lying to God and to the apostles by misrepresenting their act of giving.

Luke's second section summary and story of Ananias and Sapphira provided an interlude within the larger story of the conflict between the apostles and the Jewish authorities.

THE MIRACLES WORKED BY THE APOSTLES (5:12–16)

This is the third section summary statement in Acts. It emphasizes the healing ministry of the apostles and bears out the divine response to their prayer for signs and wonders. This passage, with its focus on the healing ministry and growing acclaim of the people, prepared for the renewed concern of the Sadducees and their arrest of the apostles.

THE APOSTLES BEFORE THE COUNCIL (5:17–42)

In the previous section (3:1–4:31), the Sanhedrin instructed the apostles not to teach and preach the gospel. With the growing success of the Christian witness came a heightened reaction on the part of the Jewish authorities. As before, the Sadducees were enraged by the apostles' preaching.

Arrest, Escape, and Rearrest (vv. 17–26)

An angel of the Lord appeared to the imprisoned apostles at night, opened the prison doors, and led them out. The angel then gave them God's instructions. They were to return to the temple and "tell the people all about this life." That is, they were to resume their witness and preach the message of salvation.

The Second Appearance Before the Sanhedrin (vv. 27–40)

Whereas the first meeting with the Sanhedrin involved only Peter and John, in this second appearance, all the apostles stood before the council.

Interestingly, the high priest made no reference to the apostles' escape, perhaps out of embarrassment. However, formal charges were brought this time. The apostles were duly warned by the court no longer to continue their witness, and they ignored the warning. They were accused not only of speaking and preaching but also of disobeying the Sanhedrin's specific order.

In response, the apostles echoed Acts 4:19: "We must obey God rather than people." Again, Peter accused the Jews of murdering Jesus, and then he proclaimed Jesus's resurrection. Peter's words were met with murderous anger. Some members of the council even called for the death penalty.

At this point Gamaliel, identified as a Pharisee, intervened. He was the voice of moderation. He urged the Sanhedrin to spare the apostles, appealing to the history of other messianic movements. Persuaded by Gamaliel's speech, the Sanhedrin decided to spare the apostles.

HISTORICAL BACKGROUND

Gamaliel

Gamaliel was a highly regarded Pharisee who was a member of the Sanhedrin. He squelched a plan by the Sanhedrin to kill the apostles by reminding the members that interference with what the apostles were doing might prove to be opposition to God. If the work of the apostles was a purely human work, Gamaliel said, it would come to nothing anyway. According to Acts 22:3, this Gamaliel was Paul's teacher. He was the grandson of the great Rabbi Hillel. He died about AD 52.

Release and Witness (vv. 41–42)

Again, the apostles were released but this time with a flogging. Likely, each received thirty-nine lashes. The flogging was a warning not to persist in their offense.

The apostles, however, were not persuaded. They would continue to obey God rather than men.

Section Summary

The apostles were brought before the Sanhedrin for a second time because of their witness for Christ. Although their lives were spared, they were flogged for their "offense." Undaunted by their punishment, the apostles continued to preach and worship, praising God for being able to suffer for the name of Christ.

END OF THE FIRST SECTION OF ACTS

This ends the first major section of Acts. Luke's two major themes are skillfully interwoven throughout these narratives. The gospel, through God's power, overcame the barriers of language and persecution. The Spirit was poured out on the church, empowering it to minister and grow. The Christian church was portrayed as a group of devout Jews who wanted nothing more than to be able to worship and minister without obstruction. The Jewish authorities, however, were unwilling to allow free rein to those who confessed Jesus as Messiah. And so a process of separation begins within Judaism. Out of this separation the church will emerge.

QUESTIONS TO GUIDE YOUR STUDY

1. What was the sin of Ananias and Sapphira? Why was God so decisive in his punishment?
2. What were the elements of apostolic preaching?
3. What was the attitude of the apostles at their second appearance before the Sanhedrin? What were the results of their trial?

HISTORICAL BACKGROUND

Hellenists

Those whose language and culture was Greek, even though they may not have been Greek by race. The word is derived from *hellas*, which is the Greek word for *Greece*.

ACTS 6

The church now faces a problem and finds a way of solving it.

APPOINTMENT OF THE SEVEN (6:1–7)

The Problem (v. 1–2)

For the first time a major division confronted the church. Conflicts arose between the Hellenists (Grecian Jews) and Hebraists (Aramaic-speaking Jews). The conflict came to a head because a large number of Hellenistic widows needed assistance. One of the ministries of the synagogue (and the church) was to provide food and assistance to those widows and children not supported by relatives. Perhaps most of the widows who needed help were Hellenistic widows, and a conflict arose over the proper distribution of food.

HISTORICAL BACKGROUND

Stephen

Stephen became the first Christian martyr. He was the central member of the Seven chosen to bring peace to the quarreling church (Acts 6:1–7). He was so mighty in the Scriptures that his Jewish opponents could not refute him as he argued that Jesus was the Messiah (Acts 6:10). Saul of Tarsus heard Stephen's speech to the Jewish Sanhedrin, which accused the Jewish leaders of rejecting God's way as had their forefathers. Saul held the clothes of those who stoned Stephen to death but saw Stephen die a victorious death. Stephen may have been the human agency that God used to conquer Saul, who became the great Christian missionary.

The Solution (vv. 3–4)

The apostles proposed a solution that pleased the entire community. That solution involved selecting a group of men to administer this assistance to widows. Like the apostles, these men were chosen for their wisdom and their spirituality.

Selection and Installation (vv. 5–6)

The church selected their ministers and set the Seven apart for their ministry. Stephen is named first, and he became the primary character in the following narrative. He is followed by Philip, who would become a major figure in the expanding Christian witness. The other five—Procorus, Nicanor, Timon, Parmenas, and Nicolas from Antioch—play no further role in Acts.

The church presented these men to the apostles, who confirmed the church's decision by praying and laying hands on the Seven.

Section Summary

Conflict within the community was resolved by choosing seven men who would administer the church's welfare system. By selecting the Seven, the apostles were free to carry out their primary responsibilities of preaching and bearing witness to Christ.

Transition (v. 7)

The narrative about Stephen is a major turning point in Acts. It ends a series of three trials before the Sanhedrin. The Stephen episode is the culmination in the witness to the Jews of Jerusalem.

STEPHEN'S ARREST (6:8–12)

Stephen's role in Acts is foreshadowed by the way Luke introduces him in 6:5, "a man full of faith and the Holy Spirit." Stephen was acting more like an apostle than a deacon. He was doing miracles, and none of the Hellenistic Jews could win an argument with him.

Stephen's Debate with the Hellenist Synagogue (vv. 8–10)

Members from the Freedmen's Synagogue were disturbed by Stephen's preaching and ministry. (Their name, *Freedmen,* may have referred to their identity as former slaves or descendants of captives taken from Palestine during the Diaspora.)

The Frame-Up (vv. 11–12)

Unable to resist Stephen's persuasive power and his logic, the Hellenist Jews resorted to underhanded methods. Their plan to stop Stephen included conspiracy, perjury, and mob psychology. They charged Stephen with blasphemy against the temple and the law. They then seized him and brought him before the Sanhedrin.

THE TRIAL BEGINS (6:13–7:1)

The trial provided a forum for Stephen to speak with passion and persuasion in the triumph of the Spirit. Before he spoke, Luke reminded us of the Spirit's power. As the charges were brought against him, all attention turned to Stephen to see how he would respond. His face looked like that of an angel, a true sign of God's presence.

As the trial began, the high priest asked Stephen, "Are these things true?" In our present-day court system that question would translate into, "How do you plead, guilty or innocent?"

Section Summary

Disturbed at Stephen's preaching and teaching, Hellenist Jews charged Stephen with blasphemy against the temple and the law. He was arrested and brought before the Sanhedrin.

QUESTIONS TO GUIDE YOUR STUDY

1. Describe the division that confronted the new church. What solution was reached?
2. Why were the Hellenist Jews at odds with Stephen?
3. What was Stephen's role in the growth of the early church?

ACTS 7

STEPHEN'S SPEECH BEFORE THE SANHEDRIN (7:2–53)

Overview

Stephen expressed three main ideas in his speech. The first was the Jewish reverence for the Holy Land. Most Jews were convinced that the land was God's greatest gift to them, and they considered Palestine to be the place where God lived and worked.

Second, Stephen showed that Moses, the one venerated by the Jews as the great giver of the law, was constantly disobeyed by the Jews. Finally, Stephen noted that God allowed Solomon to build the temple because the Jews demanded it. God himself was satisfied with the nomadic life of the tabernacle.

OLD TESTAMENT REFERENCE

"This is what the LORD says:
Heaven is my throne,
and earth is my footstool.
Where could you possibly
build a house for me?
And where would my resting
place be?" (Isa 66:1)

Stephen began his speech with great deference to his hearers, reminding them they were his fellow Jewish "brothers," and he showed respect to the elders of the Sanhedrin by referring to them as "fathers."

Stephen denied that God was tied to any land, recounting the history of the patriarchs and showing that God worked in their lives much more outside the promised land than within. It was to a landless Abraham that God gave the promises to Israel.

Stephen's speech climaxed in strong words toward the Jewish leaders. He termed them "stiff-necked" and accused them of denying God's prophets, Spirit, and Messiah. In response to the charge of blasphemy against the temple, Stephen accused the Jews of failing to obey the law of which they were so proud.

Section Summary

Stephen's speech is important in understanding the way in which the gospel moved from its Jewish beginnings to a Gentile world. That the Jews rejected the gospel should be no surprise. Stephen asserted that they had rejected the will of God throughout their history as God's chosen people.

STEPHEN'S MARTYRDOM (7:54–8:1a)

Whether Stephen intended to give a direct appeal for his hearers to repent, we will never know, for they abruptly broke him off. They were livid at his placing them on trial. Luke described them as "enraged." Swiftly, before the Roman soldiers could be alerted, Stephen was dragged, kicked, and tossed outside the city gates, thrown into the stoning pit, and quickly bludgeoned to death.

In his final gasps, pain was supplanted by God's gift of vision. Stephen declared, "Look, I see the heavens opened and the Son of Man standing at the right hand of God!" Jesus spoke similar words at his appearance before the Sanhedrin. The vision confirmed Stephen's testimony. One can understand the furious response in the Sanhedrin at Stephen's testimony to his vision. They stood condemned by his words. "Lord Jesus, receive my spirit!" echoed what Jesus prayed from the cross. Stephen died not in fear and despair but in victory.

Section Summary

Stephen's death was not the end. To the contrary, his death was another phase in the beginning of a new community that God was bringing into existence.

QUESTIONS TO GUIDE YOUR STUDY

1. What key points did Stephen drive home in his speech before the Sanhedrin?
2. What did Stephen say to the Sanhedrin that so angered them? What part did they play in Stephen's death?
3. What happened in the wake of Stephen's death?

ACTS 8

ENTER: SAUL OF TARSUS (8:1a)

It was no accident that young Saul of Tarsus witnessed the death of Stephen. He got frantically busy, trying to shake off the experience. Unable or unwilling to admit his feelings, he vented all his fears and frustrations on the believers. With the fury of a summer storm, he burst on the church, determined to stamp out this insidious movement. But all he succeeded in doing was furthering the spread of the gospel.

THE GOSPEL IN SAMARIA (8:1b)

Fleeing Jerusalem, new converts went to the outer region of Judea and even into Samaria.

It is of lasting credit to the early Christians that they pushed through their prejudices not only to live with the Samaritans but to present them with the gospel.

HISTORICAL BACKGROUND

Saul the Persecutor

Paul's Jewish name was Saul, given at birth after his father or some near kinsman, or even after the famous Old Testament King Saul, who like Paul was from the tribe of Benjamin. Being born in a Roman city and claiming Roman citizenship, Paul was his official Roman name. Tarsus, the place of Paul's birth (Acts 22:3), is still a bustling city a few miles from the Mediterranean Sea on Turkey's southern shore. Paul eventually went to Jerusalem to study under the famous rabbi, Gamaliel. At that time, he was probably thirteen to eighteen years old. Paul became zealous for the traditions and teachings of his people (Gal 1:14). He was a Pharisee (Phil 3:5). This zealous commitment to the study of the Old Testament laws and traditions is the background of Paul's persecution of his Jewish brothers who believed Jesus was the Messiah. Stephen's sermon before the Sanhedrin apparently stimulated Paul's persecution of the church.

STEPHEN IS BURIED (8:2)

The regulations of the Jews permitted burial for a criminal who was stoned to death but prohibited any lamentation over him. Stephen's friends, however, disobeyed the rules and buried him with much lamentation and mourning.

THE LION OF GOD (8:3)

Venting his anger, Saul went tearing through the city and its environs, seeking converts, disrupting worship services, and hauling men and women off to prison. Such "holy" crusades quickly lose all bounds of reason. Saul's vendetta was no different. Although Luke's account is sparse, the picture is one of midnight raids, good people poorly treated, and human rights disregarded in the name of religion—for the sake of God.

UNDAUNTED PREACHERS (8:4)

In the face of the persecution following Stephen's death, the Christians were scattered. Ripped from homes and families, hounded out of town, fleeing under cover of darkness, followers of the Way ran in every direction. But they remained undaunted, counting themselves blessed to be able to suffer persecution for their Lord. As they spread throughout the area, they also spread the gospel.

Section Summary

Following Stephen's death, Saul, the persecutor of Christians, tore through the city of Jerusalem to carry on his vendetta. In the face of this persecution, the Christians were scattered. As they spread throughout the area, they also spread the gospel.

PHILIP INVESTIGATES (8:5–8)

Philip, one of the Seven, found his way into Samaria. As with Stephen, the power of the Spirit was present in Philip's work. He preached and performed signs and wonders, such as healing and exorcising unclean spirits.

SIMON THE MAGICIAN BELIEVES (8:9–13)

Simon the magician (sometimes called Simon Magus) stands in contrast to Philip and his works. Magic was a significant form of religious expression in the ancient world. As a result of Philip's ministry, many Samaritans came to faith, including Simon.

PETER INVESTIGATES SAMARIA AND MEETS SIMON (8:14–25)

No one had told the Samaritans about the Spirit. That dimension of Christian experience was missing from the group. But when Peter, who experienced the Spirit, informed them of the grand possibility, they eagerly opened the windows of their souls to receive God's gift of the Holy Spirit.

Simon the magician could not believe his eyes. When Peter prayed and laid hands on people, they received the Holy Spirit. Simon thought that if he could have that power, his act would be a real winner. His shallow commitment to Christ became abundantly clear. He saw the invoking of the Spirit as a way to enhance his magic show. He had the audacity to offer to buy the gift from Peter.

Peter informed the startled charlatan that he never really had an experience with Jesus and that he would never receive the Spirit with this attitude. Peter answered him with, "Repent of this wickedness of yours, and pray to the Lord that, if possible, your heart's intent may be forgiven. For I see you are poisoned by bitterness and bound by wickedness."

Terrified, Simon begged Peter to pray that no ill consequences would fall on him.

THE WITNESS TO THE ETHIOPIAN TREASURER (8:26–40)

Philip's evangelistic activity did not end with Samaria. He was also chosen to participate in an advance of the gospel beyond Jerusalem, Judea, and Samaria. In response to the prompting of an angel, Philip went to a certain road in the desert and met an Ethiopian traveling home from a visit to Jerusalem. Philip was offered the opportunity to explain Scripture to the Ethiopian, to witness to him about Jesus, and to baptize him before being transported to another region by the power of the Spirit.

The conversion of the Ethiopian is placed in Luke's account between Philip's work in Samaria (in which one racial barrier is overcome) and the conversion of Cornelius in Acts 10. From a literary standpoint, we

HISTORICAL BACKGROUND

Philip

Philip was a respected member of the church at Jerusalem who was chosen as one of the Seven—the first "deacons" (Acts 6:5). Following Stephen's martyrdom, Philip took the gospel to Samaria, where his ministry was blessed. Subsequently, he was led south to the Jerusalem-Gaza road, where he introduced the Ethiopian eunuch to Christ and baptized him (Acts 8:26–38). He was then transported by the Spirit to Azotus (Ashdod) and from there conducted an itinerant ministry until he took up residence in Caesarea. Then, for twenty years, we lose sight of him. He is last seen in Scripture when Paul lodged in his home on his journey to Jerusalem (Acts 21:8). He had four unmarried daughters who were prophetesses.

HISTORICAL BACKGROUND

Simon

Luke does not mention Simon again, but the magician earned his negative place in history by giving his name to the practice of buying or selling a church office (simony).

would assume that these stories serve as steps in the gospel's transition from Jews to Gentiles.

Section Summary

The Spirit, having broken down the racial barrier that denied Samaritans religious access to God, now breaks down a physical barrier to faith as well. None would be judged based on racial or physical characteristics. Entry into the kingdom would depend solely on spiritual relationship with God.

QUESTIONS TO GUIDE YOUR STUDY

1. How do you think Saul's experience of watching Stephen being stoned to death affected him?
2. What was the result of Saul's persecution which scattered the Christians to other communities?
3. What landmark truth did the conversion of the Ethiopian treasurer convey?

HISTORICAL BACKGROUND

Damascus

Capital of Syria with close historical ties to Israel. It would have taken Saul at least six days to travel from Jerusalem to Damascus. This shows how far the Way had spread and how strongly Saul was motivated to stomp it out.

ACTS 9

GOD CALLS SAUL (9:1–30)

The first half of Saul's conversion account divides into three main sections: the appearance on the Damascus Road (vv. 1–9), the ministry of Ananias to Saul (vv. 10–18a), and the final confirmation of Saul's conversion through his bold witness in the Jewish synagogues of Damascus (vv. 18b–22).

NEW TESTAMENT REFERENCE

Saul's Conversion

Saul's conversion to the Christian faith is one of the most significant and far-reaching events in the history of the early church. There are three detailed accounts of this remarkable experience given in the New Testament. Luke records it here as historical fact, and Paul gives two accounts in his own words (Acts 22:6–11; 26:12–19).

The Appearance on the Damascus Road (vv. 1–9)

As Saul approached the gates of Damascus, suddenly a great light from heaven flashed around him. The light must have been intense, for the time of the occurrence was "about noon" (Acts 22:6). At the sight, Saul fell to the ground—a reaction found in the Old Testament from those who experienced a similar divine visitation. Then a voice came from heaven, "Saul, Saul, why are you persecuting me?"

Saul answered, "Who are you, Lord?"

The response from heaven was: "I am Jesus, the one you are persecuting." Now Saul beheld Jesus and the undeniable proof that he both lived and reigned in glory. Saul was completely broken. The raging persecutor was brought to his knees. For three days he remained blinded and neither ate nor drank.

The Ministry of Ananias to Saul (vv. 10–18a)

In Damascus lived a disciple named Ananias. The Lord appeared to Ananias in a vision with instructions to seek out Saul at the house of Judas. At first Ananias protested the commission. He knew who Saul was and was afraid of him. But Ananias obeyed and went to Saul, laying hands on him so he might recover his sight. Ananias acted as God's agent in healing and baptizing Saul.

The scene in Judas's house concluded with Saul's receiving nourishment and recovering his strength.

Saul's Bold Witness in Damascus (vv. 18b–22)

Immediately Saul began to preach in the synagogues, serving the gospel with all the zeal he formerly used to persecute it. He proclaimed Jesus as the "Son of God." Naturally, all who heard him were amazed that this noted enemy of the Way was now preaching Christ. Paul developed rapidly and "grew stronger." He soon became more than a match for the Jews with whom he debated.

Saul the Persecuted (vv. 23–31)

Saul was so successful in his witness that the Jews in Damascus plotted to kill him. This forced him to escape over the city wall and go to Jerusalem. The believers in Jerusalem were still afraid of him until Barnabas, acting as an encourager, vouched for Saul's sincerity and effectiveness in Damascus.

Section Summary

In a dramatic conversion experience, God called Saul to be his witness. Full of energy and zeal, Saul immediately began to preach and proclaim Jesus as the Son of God. The result of Saul's conversion was Christianity's most bitter enemy becoming its most ardent supporter.

PETER PERFORMS MIRACLES (9:32–43)

With Saul home in Tarsus, the narrative focuses once more on Peter. He last appeared in connection with the Samaritan mission (8:14–25). Now he participates in the greater Judean mission, evangelizing the coastal cities.

The Healing of Aeneas (vv. 32–35)]

Peter stopped at Lydda to visit the believers there. He found a paralytic by the name of Aeneas, who was bedridden for eight years. Peter took the initiative to heal Aeneas without any request, much as Jesus did on occasion. This healing was accomplished by a healing word, calling on the name of Jesus.

PAUL'S MISSION TRAVELS AND LETTERS

BOOK OF ACTS	ACTIVITY	APPROXIMATE DATE	WRITING
9:1–9	Paul's conversion	34–35	
9:26–29	Visit to Jerusalem	37–38	
11:27–30	Second visit to Jerusalem	48	
13–14	First mission (Cyprus and Galatia)	48–50	Galatians
15	Jerusalem Council	50	
16:1–18:22	Second mission (Galatia, Macedonia, Greece)	51–53	1, 2 Thessalonians
18:23–21:4	Third mission (Ephesus, Macedonia, Greece)	54–57	1, 2 Corinthians, Romans
21:15–26:32	Arrest in Jerusalem, trials and imprisonment in Caesarea	58–60	
27–28	Voyage to Rome, Roman imprisonment	60–63	Philemon, Colossians, Ephesians, Philippians
27–28	Release, further work, final imprisonment, and death	60–63	1 Timothy, Titus, 2 Timothy

The Raising of Dorcas (vv. 36–43)

Joppa was the main port city of Judea, located on the Philistine coast. Here lived a female disciple named Tabitha. In his narrative, Luke provides the translation "Dorcas" for his Greek readers. Tabitha had become sick and died. Knowing that Peter was close by—a distance of three hours journey by foot—the Christians at Joppa sent two men to Lydda to urge Peter to hasten to Joppa without delay.

When Peter arrived, he was taken to the upper room where Tabitha was placed. After dismissing the mourners, Peter knelt by her bed, fully aware that healing would not come from him but only through him in the power of Christ. After praying, Peter ordered her to open her eyes. She did so and immediately got up from her bed. There was much rejoicing and no little fear and awe when the crowd saw Tabitha walk out with Peter. More people believed in Jesus and attached themselves to local communities of faith because of this mighty act of God.

HISTORICAL BACKGROUND

Lydda

During the NT era, it was the district capital of Samaria. Christianity became a strong influence in Lydda by the second century.

Section Summary

Peter participated in the greater Judean mission, evangelizing the coastal cities. Luke records two key events from this mission: the healing of the paralytic and the raising of Dorcas from the dead.

QUESTIONS TO GUIDE YOUR STUDY

1. Saul had a dramatic conversion experience. What is especially striking to you about it?
2. Describe Ananias's feelings about helping Saul the persecutor. What might we learn from Ananias's response?
3. God turned Christianity's most bitter enemy into its most ardent supporter. What is your evaluation of the impact of this event on church members?

ACTS 10

Chapter 10 marks a high point in the church's expanding mission. God led Peter to witness to the Gentile Cornelius. Through that experience Peter became fully convinced of God's purpose to reach all peoples and hence became one of the greatest advocates of the mission to the Gentiles.

CORNELIUS THE CENTURION (10:1–2)

This section begins by introducing its first main character. His name was Cornelius, a centurion of the Italian Regiment who resided in Caesarea. Each detail of that statement is significant. That he was mentioned by name perhaps indicates that he was well known in the early Christian communities for which Luke wrote. He was a military man with the rank of centurion, which placed him in command of one hundred soldiers.

CORNELIUS'S VISION (10:3–8)

Cornelius saw a vision in which an angel from God appeared to him. His initial terror was eased when the angel called him by name and assured Cornelius that he found favor with God because of his prayers and generosity to others. The angel instructed Cornelius to send a message to Joppa, to the house of Simon, a tanner, requesting Simon Peter to come to Caesarea. Accustomed to giving and obeying orders, the centurion sent immediately for three of his men. He told them of the vision, gave them directions, and asked them to hurry.

HISTORICAL BACKGROUND

Cornelius

A centurion in the Roman army who lived at Caesarea. Although he was a Gentile, he was a worshiper of the one true God. He also treated the Jewish people with kindness and generosity. After an angel appeared to this pious soldier, he sent to Joppa for Simon Peter, who came to him with the message of forgiveness of sins through faith in the crucified and risen Christ. Cornelius became a Christian as a result of this incident. His conversion marked the beginning of the church's missionary activity among Gentiles. It also helped set the stage for an important early controversy in the church, for it raised the question of the possibility of salvation for non-Jews.

PETER'S VISION (10:9–16)

At noon the next day, Peter retreated to his host's house for prayer, rest, and food. On the roof of the house, while the meal was being prepared downstairs, Peter prayed and fell into a trance.

The heavens opened, and something like a huge sheet was let down. On the sheet were all kinds of animals and birds, ritually clean and unclean. A voice from heaven commanded Peter to rise, kill from among the animals, and satisfy his hunger. Peter was perplexed by the vision and protested vigorously. What the voice requested was strictly against the law.

Peter's reply was, "No, Lord! . . . For I have never eaten anything impure and ritually unclean." Why didn't Peter kill one of the clean animals? Because the clean animals were defiled by coming into contact with unclean creatures. Then came the clincher from God. "What God has made clean, do not call impure." Peter saw this vision three times, and then the sheet was taken back to heaven.

By this stage in his ministry, Peter's prejudices were being dealt with one by one. Already he experienced many startling encounters with Samaritans, Hellenist Jews, and even some Gentiles. Those whom he met, who came to faith in Christ, gave undeniable evidence of a life-changing experience with Jesus—the same kind of experience that Peter was realizing. So Peter was making progress in working through his prejudices, but he was far from liberated. The fisherman would need all the spiritual help he could get as he dealt with Cornelius.

Section Summary

God was preparing Peter for his meeting with Cornelius, a Gentile. Jews and Gentiles rarely ate together because Gentiles could not be relied upon to eat only those foods that were "clean." Peter's vision denied any distinction between "clean" and "unclean."

PETER'S VISIT WITH CORNELIUS'S MESSENGERS (10:17–23)

Peter no sooner woke from his vision than the messengers arrived to request his visit to Cornelius. He welcomed his guests and provided lodging for them.

Section Summary

This passage affirms the power of God to break down even the strongest barriers of prejudice.

OLD TESTAMENT REFERENCE

Clean and Unclean Animals

In Lev 11, Moses and Aaron give both principles and specific instructions concerning animals which can be eaten and which can't. One such principle is: Whatever has a divided hoof and chews its cud can be eaten. A rock badger chews its cud but doesn't have a divided hoof, so it couldn't be eaten. A pig, on the other hand, has a divided hoof but doesn't chew its cud, so for that reason it wasn't to be eaten.

HISTORICAL BACKGROUND

Caesarea

Located on the Mediterranean Sea twenty-three miles south of Mount Carmel is the city of Caesarea. It is also known as Caesarea of Judea. After AD 6 it became the official home of the Roman procurators. Hostilities between the Jewish and Gentile populations apparently had been a way of life in this city. The city appears in the book of Acts as a place of witness, travel, and the seat of government. Philip, having witnessed to the Ethiopian eunuch, is mentioned as arriving at Caesarea after a preaching mission. Peter led a centurion, Cornelius, who was stationed there to become a Christian. Paul had several reported contacts with the city as a port, and perhaps as a place of imprisonment and trial. Herod Agrippa I had a residence there and died there.

PETER TRAVELS TO CAESAREA (10:23–33)

The next morning Peter, the messengers from Cornelius, and several Jewish Christians from Joppa set out for Caesarea.

After telling his story, Cornelius then requested Peter to bear witness to the gospel before the gathering of Gentiles.

PETER'S WITNESS AT CAESAREA (10:34–43)

Peter declared that "God doesn't show favoritism" in that he offers himself to all men who will fear God and do what is right.

In line with other examples of apostolic preaching, Peter told his Gentile audience that even though Jesus did good and was well beloved, the Jewish leaders killed him by hanging him on a tree. But he did not stay dead because God raised him from death.

Peter closed with his personal affirmation of Jesus as judge of the living and the dead and the one about whom all the prophets had been speaking for centuries.

Section Summary

Peter's sermon focused on his role as apostolic witness to the entire ministry of Jesus—above all to his death and resurrection. His key point was that God accepts people of all races who respond in faith to the gospel message.

PERSONAL APPLICATION

Peter already showed his own hesitancy to reach out to the Gentiles. More conservative elements in Jerusalem would be even more hesitant. Only an undeniable demonstration of divine power could overrule all objections, and God provided precisely that in Cornelius's house. Peter called for the baptism of the Gentiles and their full inclusion into the Christian community. This event illustrates a salvation truth: We cannot separate a Christian's confession of faith from the reception of the Spirit. The only valid salvation experience must include both.

THE IMPARTIALITY OF THE SPIRIT (10:44–48)

Peter's preaching, coupled with the willingness of the Gentiles, opened the way for the Spirit of God to come to Cornelius and his company. As they listened to Peter's words about forgiveness for everyone who believes in Christ, the Holy Spirit suddenly descended on all the Gentiles assembled in Cornelius's house. It was an audible, visible, objective demonstration of the Spirit's coming upon them. The Jewish Christians who had come from Joppa to witness the encounter were amazed to see the manifestation of the Spirit among these Romans.

Peter spent several days with his new Christian brothers and sisters in Caesarea. This inevitably involved table fellowship, but that now presented no problem for Peter. It would, however, constitute a major difficulty for more conservative Christians of Jewish background in Jerusalem.

Section Summary

The gift of the Spirit had now been given to the Gentiles in what has often been described as the "Gentile Pentecost." This was a revelation to Peter, who now accepted Gentiles as part of the Christian community.

HISTORICAL BACKGROUND

Peter's Argument

1. The Holy Spirit came on the Gentiles just as he did on us.
2. Jesus said that John baptized with water but you will be baptized by means of the Holy Spirit.
3. Therefore, since God has given the Gentiles the same gift as he gave us, "How could I possibly hinder God?" (Wuest).

QUESTIONS TO GUIDE YOUR STUDY

1. What did the conversion of Cornelius signify?
2. Why did God give Peter the vision in verses 9–16? How did the vision impact Peter?
3. What was the key point of Peter's sermon at Cornelius's house?

ACTS 11

The events in Caesarea were soon reported to the Jerusalem church. The Jewish Christians accused Peter not of preaching improperly but of going into the house of "uncircumcised men" and eating with them.

PETER'S REPORT (11:1–18)

Peter responded by recounting the events surrounding the conversion of Cornelius, including his vision and the presence of the Spirit. The testimony of Peter and his six companions convinced those in Jerusalem. They rejoiced that God was calling the Gentiles to repentance and life.

Section Summary

Luke's message with this narrative of Peter's report to Jerusalem is that no one can oppose God or the spread of his gospel.

ANTIOCH'S WITNESS TO GENTILES (11:19–30)

Chapter 11 is devoted to the foundational events in the Gentile mission of the church. Two different churches play the primary roles. One was the Jerusalem church, led by the apostles and comprised mainly of Aramaic-speaking Jewish Christians. It recognized the divine leading in Peter's witness to Cornelius and concluded that God intended to lead the Gentiles to repentance and life.

The second was the Antioch church, established by Hellenists, those Greek-speaking Jewish Christians who had to flee Jerusalem after the martyrdom of Stephen. This church began to take to heart Peter's work and reach out to the Gentile population.

HISTORICAL BACKGROUND

Antioch of Syria

Antioch was the third-largest city in the Roman Empire—after Rome and Alexandria. It was founded on the Orontes River around 300 BC by Seleucus Nicator. From the beginning it was a bustling maritime city with its own seaport. It was located nearly three hundred miles north of Jerusalem and became home for many Jews of the Diaspora. Many of Antioch's Gentiles were attracted to Judaism.

Advance at Antioch (vv. 19–21)

By cooperating with the Lord, hundreds of people in Antioch came to faith in Jesus Christ and formed themselves into a strong church. Indeed, the Antioch church quickly became the great beachhead for launching the mission to the Gentiles. Further along in Luke's narrative, we find Paul adopting the Antioch church as his spiritual home.

Barnabas Sent to Antioch (vv. 22–24)

The Jerusalem church sent Barnabas to investigate reports of the overwhelming success of the gospel in Antioch. No doubt he eagerly accepted the assignment to investigate the Antioch church, rejoicing when he saw God living in the believers in Antioch. While he was in Antioch, he exhorted the church members to be faithful. Because of his preaching, even more people came to faith.

Barnabas Enlists Saul (vv. 25–26)

With the growing missionary success in Antioch, Barnabas needed help, and Paul immediately came to mind. Paul was in the area of his native Cilicia, to which he departed after his first visit to Jerusalem following his conversion. When Barnabas finally located Paul, he brought him back to Antioch, where the two were heavily occupied in preaching and teaching "large numbers."

Sending Famine Relief to Jerusalem (vv. 27–30)

One of the gifts of the Spirit to the church was that of prophecy. Perhaps men who felt this gift banded together into a school of prophets reminiscent of such groups in the Old Testament. A group of these men came to Antioch.

One of these men, Agabus, predicted a famine, which did occur. The church in Antioch, evidently spared the worst of the famine, collected funds to send to the mother church in Jerusalem for relief of suffering.

HISTORICAL BACKGROUND

Famine in Jerusalem

Luke dated the famine in Jerusalem squarely within the chronology of the Roman Empire. In fact, Luke's dating of this empire-wide famine within the reign of Claudius is confirmed by a number of other ancient sources, including the Roman historian Suetonius. Luke's main reason for mentioning the famine, though, was to show that the Gentile Christians in Antioch participated in the famine relief effort.

Section Summary

The church at Antioch represented another step in the movement of the gospel beyond Judea and Syria. In Antioch the disciples were first called Christians.

QUESTIONS TO GUIDE YOUR STUDY

1. When Peter reported to the Jerusalem Christians, what was their response?
2. What were the characteristics of the church at Antioch? How did they respond to the inclusion of Gentiles into the church?
3. Describe the ministry of Barnabas. What was his role in the early church?

HISTORICAL BACKGROUND

Herod Agrippa I

Herod was the name given to the family which ruled Palestine immediately before and to some degree during the first half of the first Christian century. Their family was complex, and what information has come down is frequently meager, conflicting, and difficult to harmonize. The chief sources are New Testament references, the Jewish historian Flavius Josephus, and a few obscure references by Roman historians such as Dio Cassius, Plutarch, and Strabo. Herod Agrippa I was the son of Aristobulus and grandson of Herod. He ruled with the title of king from AD 41 to 44.

ACTS 12

HEROD AGRIPPA'S PERSECUTION OF THE APOSTLES (12:1–5)

About the time the Antioch church was preparing its relief offering for the Jerusalem church, Herod began another round of persecution. This time the persecution of Christians was as much political as religious, since Herod was hardly a religious man. Such a persecution could have had religious motivations, though, if only for the political attempt to please the Jewish authorities. James, the brother of John, and one of the pillars of the Jerusalem church, was executed. Peter was arrested. Luke tells about the martyrdom of James with the utmost brevity. He apparently did not want to dwell on it but used the incident to set the stage for his main emphasis—God's deliverance of Peter.

Section Summary

Herod Agrippa initiated a round of persecution of the apostles, with significant results. James, the brother of John, was executed, and Peter was arrested and imprisoned.

PETER'S MIRACULOUS DELIVERANCE FROM PRISON (12:6–19a)

Peter was anticipating a fate similar to that of James as he awaited his trial. Herod commanded that Peter be guarded by four squads of four soldiers each. Herod's plans, however, were thwarted by God's deliverance of Peter from prison.

Suddenly an angel of the Lord appeared, and a flash of heavenly light filled the cell. Peter was fast asleep, and the angel forcefully roused him. Not fully alert, Peter did not know what was happening. The angel told him to put on his coat and sandals. Peter was totally passive throughout the entire incident. His escape was truly a *deliverance*.

The scene shifts to the Christian community that was praying fervently for Peter. He arrived at the house of Mary, mother of John Mark, and knocked on the door. Rhoda, a servant girl, answered and excitedly announced that Peter was at the door. Ironically, no one in this story was able to believe that Peter had been delivered from prison. Those gathered at the house of Mary and John Mark were unwilling to believe that Peter had escaped, even though their purpose for gathering had been to pray for Peter's release.

Verse 17 provides us with three important pieces of information: (1) Peter's report of his miraculous deliverance, (2) his instruction to tell the news to James, and (3) his departure to "another place," where he would find refuge from the wrath of Agrippa.

The guards who were watching Peter could not have prevented his release. But Herod, in his madness, had them executed when told of the escape.

Section Summary

The fervent prayer of the church led to Peter's miraculous release from prison. Ironically, they were surprised that Peter was delivered.

HEROD'S DEATH (12:19b–23)

There are two climaxes to the account of Herod's persecution. One is Peter's escape from his clutches. The other is Herod's own grisly fate. Chronologically, his death came anywhere from several months to a year after Peter's escape. Christians viewed it as a divine retribution for what they had suffered under the king.

The quarreling cities of Tyre and Sidon were celebrating the restoration of their relations. A festival was declared. Herod wore a garment made of silver that glistened in the morning sun. As Herod, in all his glory, turned and addressed the people, they shouted, "It's the voice of a god and not of a man!" Immediately he was struck down by the angel of the Lord and was eaten by worms.

Section Summary

This first major section of Luke ends with the death of Herod Agrippa I. Luke implied that Herod's death was related to his persecution of Jewish Christians.

A PEACE FOR THE CHURCH (12:24–25)

With Agrippa's sudden removal, the persecution of the church ended, and once more the word of God flourished.

QUESTIONS TO GUIDE YOUR STUDY

1. Describe the political climate of Herod Agrippa's reign. How did the church react to his persecution?
2. How did the praying Christians respond to the news that Peter had been delivered from prison? What lessons might we draw from this story?
3. Why did God strike down Herod Agrippa?

ACTS 13

Chapters 13 and 14 begin the story of the mission to the "ends of the earth." The Gentile mission, Paul's first missionary journey, started with Paul and Barnabas's work in Cyprus and in the Roman province of Galatia.

PAUL AND BARNABAS COMMISSIONED (13:1–3)

Acts portrays Paul as the great missionary, blazing trails for Christianity in areas that had never heard the gospel. Antioch served as a base from which Paul's journeys began, and he maintained close ties to the believers there throughout his missionary career.

The missionary call came to Paul and Barnabas while they worshiped with the church. The revelation that came was interpreted as being directly from the Spirit. The congregation responded in faith. The Spirit's command to call and commission Paul and Barnabas was quickly obeyed.

HISTORICAL BACKGROUND

Barnabas

Barnabas was a Levite and a native of the island of Cyprus. His name was Joseph before the disciples called him Barnabas. The name *Barnabas* means "son of encouragement," and he lived up to his name. He was an active participant in the spread of the gospel. He sold his property and gave the proceeds to the Jerusalem church (Acts 4:36–37). He introduced Saul of Tarsus to the Jerusalem church (9:26–27).

Section Summary

Paul and Barnabas were at church when they heard their call, and the congregation became a part of the total experience. To show their approval as well as to give their blessing, the congregation laid hands on these believers and sent them out on their mission.

SERGIUS PAULUS CONVERTED ON CYPRUS (13:4–12)

The evangelization of Cyprus paralleled that of Samaria. Paul and the gospel had to overcome opposition from practitioners of magic. Elymas the sorcerer was as formidable an opponent for Paul as Simon Magnus had been for Peter. In Elymas, Paul faced not only the threat of magic but that of Jewish opposition as well. Paul's triumph in this event showed the power of the gospel (and the Spirit) to deal with any opposition, especially that of magic. This event also resulted in faith on the part of the Roman proconsul, Sergius Paulus. Finally, almost as a footnote, Luke mentions that Saul's other name was Paul. (Saul apparently Latinized his name to Paul, by which he is called throughout the rest of his life.) Up to this point, Luke referred to Paul by his Hebrew name Saul, without any indication of Paul's social status. As Paul moved closer to the center of the Roman Empire, Luke switched names.

A SHORT CHRONOLOGY OF PAUL AND BEYOND

DATE	EVENT
Summer 44	Paul returned to Antioch
Spring 45	First missionary journey begun
Summer 47	First missionary journey ended
48	Jerusalem Council
Summer 49	Second missionary journey begun
Spring 53	Paul before Gallio
Late fall 53	Second missionary journey ended
Spring 54	Third missionary journey begun
Late summer 54	Paul's arrival in Ephesus
Summer 57	Paul's departure from Ephesus
November 57	Paul's arrival in Corinth
February 58	Paul's departure from Corinth
Late April 58	Paul's departure from Philippi
Late summer 58	Paul's arrival in Jerusalem, third missionary journey ended, Paul arrested
Summer 60	Paul before Festus
Late summer 60	Paul sailed for Rome
Late October 60	Shipwrecked on Malta
Late January 61	Paul sailed for Italy
Early Spring 61	Paul arrived in Rome
63	Paul's imprisonment ended

Section Summary

Paul's triumph in showing the power of the gospel to deal with opposition, especially magic, resulted in faith on the part of the Roman proconsul, Sergius Paulus.

The Setting (vv. 13–16a)

The remainder of Acts 13 is set primarily in Pisidian Antioch. It consists of three main parts: (1) Paul's journey to Antioch and the setting of the stage for Paul's speech in the synagogue, (2) Paul's address to the synagogue, and (3) the final response of the Jews and Gentiles on a second visit to the synagogue in Antioch.

Paul's Address to the Synagogue at Pisidian Antioch (13:16–41)

This is Paul's first recorded sermon. It has much in common with Peter's speeches—the emphasis on the Jewish leaders' responsibility for Jesus's death, the contrast between the death on the cross and the triumph of the resurrection, the apostolic witness, and the proofs from Scripture

HISTORICAL BACKGROUND

Paul's First Missionary Journey

Paul's first penetration into the Gentile world began in Antioch in Syria and took him to the island of Cyprus and the mainland cities of Perga, Antioch in Pisidia, Iconium, Lystra, and Derbe. After reaching Derbe, Paul reversed his travels, returning through the cities he just visited, and finally departing from the port of Attalia for the return to Antioch of Syria.

Paul's missionary policy involved entering a city, establishing a foundation among the residents who responded to his preaching, and moving to another city under pressure from local authorities or other evident signs of divine leadership. Barnabas accompanied Paul throughout this first journey, and John Mark served as a coworker for a portion of the trip. (See map of "Paul's First Missionary Journey" on p. 269) (even some of the same texts). This sermon has a feature in common also with Stephen's speech, namely, the introductory sketch of Jewish history. Whereas Stephen used Old Testament history to depict the rebellion of the Jews toward divinely appointed leaders, Paul used it to show God's faithfulness to his promises for Israel—promises that were ultimately fulfilled in Christ.

Paul addressed the men of Israel and the God-fearers (CSB: "devout converts to Judaism").

HISTORICAL BACKGROUND

"God-fearers" were Gentile believers in God, practitioners of Judaism, but not full-fledged converts. Paul emphasized that the Jews were chosen people, not because of their merit but because of God's grace.

Section Summary

Paul's presentation was designed to prove that Jesus was the Messiah who was promised in the Old Testament, that Jesus was crucified and raised from the dead, and that forgiveness of sins was offered through Christ.

THE SERMON'S AFTERMATH (13:42–52)

Paul's synagogue audience was at first favorably impressed by what he had to say. He was so effective, in fact, that many "followed Paul and Barnabas" and "almost the whole town" returned to hear him on the next Sabbath. The Jewish leaders responded to Paul's popularity with jealousy and abuse. Because the Jews rejected the gospel, Paul and Barnabas made clear that the gospel would be given to the Gentiles.

Section Summary

Paul and the Christian church often struggled to convince people their worship was different from other religious ceremonies. Therefore, when the Jews incited God-fearing women and leading men of the city, that posed a serious problem for Paul and Barnabas.

QUESTIONS TO GUIDE YOUR STUDY

1. What did overcoming Elymas the sorcerer show the people of Cyprus?
2. What was the point of Paul's address to the Jews at Pisidian Antioch?
3. Describe how the Jewish crowd responded to Paul's sermon?

ACTS 14

ACCEPTANCE AND REJECTION AT ICONIUM (14:1–7)

Paul and Barnabas left Antioch of Pisidia to go eastward to Iconium. They began their work in the synagogue, but opposition grew. Again, the Jews tried to stir up the Gentiles to have Paul and Barnabas stoned.

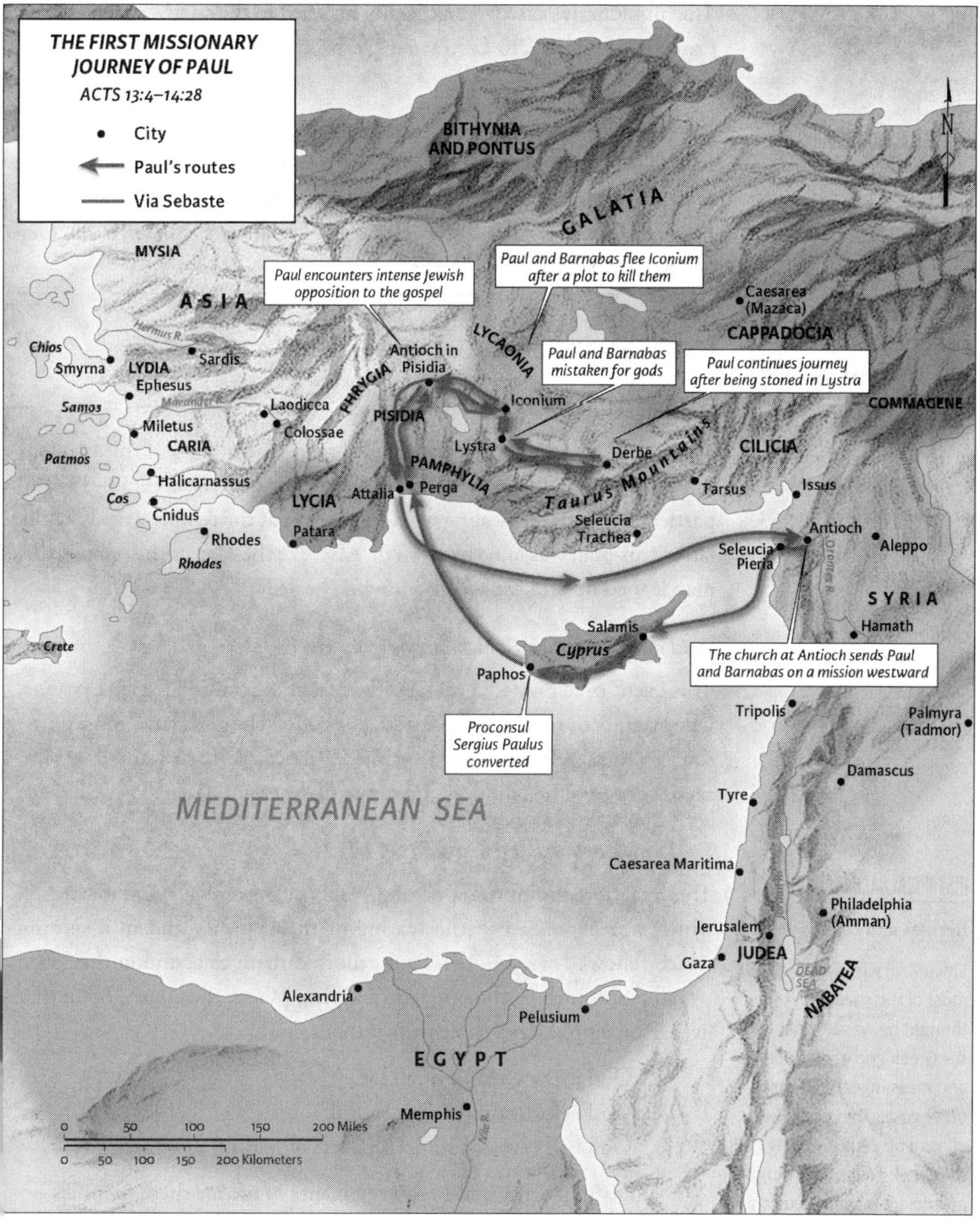

The First Missionary Journey of Paul

The missionaries discovered the plot and fled to the southern part of the province of Galatia, to Lystra and Derbe.

HISTORICAL BACKGROUND

Iconium

Iconium was a city in Asia Minor. Paul endured suffering and persecution at Iconium (2 Tim 3:11). Its location is that of the modern Turkish provincial capital of Konya. Iconium was mentioned for the first time in the fourth century BC by the historian Xenophon. In New Testament times it was considered part of the Roman province of Galatia. Evidently it has retained a continuous existence since its founding.

Section Summary

Paul followed the pattern of establishing a witness in the major population centers. While in Iconium, Paul and Barnabas took their message to both Jews and Gentiles. After discovering a plot by authorities to kill them, they fled to nearby Lystra and Derbe.

PREACHING TO PAGANS AT LYSTRA (14:8–21a)

A Lame Man Healed (vv. 8–10)

While at Lystra, Paul healed a crippled man. The healing of this man has many features in common with Peter's healing of Aeneas (9:32–35) and particularly with his healing of the lame man at the temple gate. Like the latter, this man was lame from birth. Also like the man at the temple, this man leaped up and walked about when healed.

Paul and Barnabas Paid Homage (vv. 11–13)

This event precipitated a remarkable reaction from the native Lystrans, who attempted to honor the apostles as gods. "The gods have come down to us in human form!" they exclaimed. The crowd then wanted to offer sacrifices to them—thinking Paul was Hermes and Barnabas was Zeus.

HISTORICAL BACKGROUND

Hermes and Zeus

Since Paul was doing most of the speaking, they thought he was Hermes—the Greek god of eloquence and messenger of all the other gods. They took Barnabas to be Zeus, the king of the Greek gods. According to an ancient legend, Zeus and Hermes once came to earth as humans. Archaeologists have discovered inscriptions in this region dedicated to Zeus and Hermes.

Paul and Barnabas Dismayed (vv. 14–18)

This reaction prompted a strong response from Paul and Barnabas, which was expressed in the tearing of their clothes and in a sermon which followed (vv. 14–18). Paul exhorted them to abandon their vain worship and turn to the one true and living God, the source of all that lives. Paul emphasized three things about God:

1. God is the Creator of all life.
2. God is forbearing and merciful.
3. God had revealed himself in acts of natural providence.

Paul begins with well-known elements of life for these Gentiles—

1. Rain from heaven
2. Crops in their season
3. Abundance of food that gives joy

He then says, in effect, let me tell you about the One who provides all of this for you. In spite of this effort, Luke says that Paul and Barnabas had difficulty keeping the crowd from sacrificing to them.

Paul and Barnabas Rejected (vv. 19–20a)

Ironically, the ministry at Lystra concluded when the crowd turned against Paul and tried to stone him to death. Jews from Antioch and Iconium, having followed Paul to Lystra, stirred up the crowd, who then stoned Paul and left him for dead.

Luke's matter-of-fact narration observes that other believers surrounded Paul to form a hedge around him as they returned to the city. This must have been a great encouragement to the believers and a great surprise to those who thought they killed Paul.

Paul and Barnabas did not linger in Lystra, as it was no longer safe. The next morning they set out for Derbe.

Section Summary

The fickle crowds, filled with propaganda from Jews who arrived in Lystra from Antioch and Iconium, turned against Paul and apparently joined in stoning him. Paul, left for dead by the vengeful mob, revived, returned to Lystra, and departed to preach in Derbe, over fifty miles from Lystra.

THE MINISTRY AT DERBE (14:20b–21a)

Luke provides only the essential details that a successful witness took place at Derbe and that many disciples were won to the Lord. Derbe was the easternmost church established on this mission by Paul and Barnabas.

THE MISSIONARIES RETURN TO ANTIOCH (14:21*B*–28)

Paul and Barnabas ended their mission work by retracing their steps to visit all the churches that had been established. Importantly, they "appointed elders" for each of the churches.

Section Summary

The missionary journey ended where it began, at Antioch of Syria. Paul and Barnabas reported all that had happened in Asia Minor, with special emphasis on the way God "had opened the door of faith to the Gentiles."

QUESTIONS TO GUIDE YOUR STUDY

1. How did the people of Iconium treat Paul and Barnabas? What was usually at the core of Jewish opposition?
2. What were the three main truths in Paul's sermon to the pagans at Lystra?
3. As Paul and Barnabas completed their mission, they retraced their steps on the return trip. What did they do to help

HISTORICAL BACKGROUND

Derbe

Derbe was an important city in the region of Lycaonia in the province of Galatia in Asia Minor. It was apparently near what is modern Kerti Huyuk. The residents of Derbe and Lystra spoke a different language from the people to the north in Iconium. Paul visited Derbe on his first missionary journey, fleeing from Iconium. Persecution in Lystra led to a successful preaching mission in Derbe. On the second missionary journey, Paul returned to Derbe. He apparently visited again on the third journey. Paul's fellow minister Gaius was from Derbe.

strengthen church leadership when they revisited the various churches?

ACTS 15

Acts 15:1–35 stands at the center of the book of Acts. Not only is this the midpoint in the narrative, but it is also central in the development of the narrative's total plot. The first half of Acts focused on the Jewish community, particularly the influential Jerusalem church. The Christian witness began there. Believers took all the preliminary steps for a major effort to reach the Gentile world. The stage was now set for Paul's mission to the heart of the Greco-Roman world as *the* missionary to the Gentiles.

DEBATE IN JERUSALEM OVER ACCEPTANCE OF THE GENTILES (15:1–35)

This section falls into four natural parts: the introduction, the debate in Jerusalem, the final solution, and the debate's conclusion.

The Criticism from the Circumcision Party (vv. 1–5)

There were many Gentiles in the church at Antioch. There is no indication that they were circumcised when they joined the Christian fellowship. This was disturbing to some Jewish Christians who came from Judea and insisted that circumcision was necessary for salvation.

The Debate in Jerusalem (vv. 6–21)

There were two major witnesses, both in defense of the view that the Gentiles should not be burdened by circumcision and the law. Peter spoke first, followed by James. Luke precedes both speeches with brief summaries that set the context of the conference.

Peter's speech reminded the group of the work of the Spirit in the conversion of the first Gentile, Cornelius. Paul and Barnabas also referred to the miraculous work of God in their experiences with the Gentiles. To James was left the final statement.

NEW TESTAMENT REFERENCE

Jesus's Brothers

During Jesus's ministry the brothers of Jesus were not believers. Paul specifically mentioned a resurrection appearance by Jesus to James (1 Cor 15:7). After the resurrection and ascension, Jesus's brothers are said to have been with the Twelve and the other believers in Jerusalem (Acts 1:14).

The Decision in Jerusalem (vv. 22–29)

James, the half brother of Jesus, was recognized as the leader of the church in Jerusalem. After the debate and testimonies, James gave his decision, which was subsequently ratified by the assembly. James, speaking courageously and against the prevailing spirit of the Jerusalem church, maintained that Gentile Christians should not be weighed down with Jewish customs. But, rather, for their own souls' good health, they should abstain from food offered to idols, avoid all sexual unchastity, and eat nothing strangled. The dietary regulations are attempts at compromise. It is as if James said, "We have freed you from circumcision. Help us save face a bit by observing these basic, painless food restrictions."

The decision pleased them all, and by common consent the council and Jerusalem congregation selected emissaries who would travel to the Gentile churches to give word of liberation.

Section Summary

James's decision stated that Gentiles would not be hindered from becoming Christians; they would not be required to undergo circumcision. Practically, however, the council requested that Gentile Christians refrain from practices that would put a strain on their relationship with Jewish Christians.

The Decision Reported to Antioch (vv. 30–35)

Antioch was the first recorded stop on the good news tour. Silas and Barsabbas, who were appointed by the Jerusalem church, read the letter and gave details of the decision. Amid much rejoicing, the Antioch group received the good news.

The Jerusalem Council marks the culmination of the first missionary journey and serves as the catalyst for the second missionary journey. The impetus for the second journey was the reading of the apostolic letter prepared by the Jerusalem Council to the churches in Asia Minor. If Paul needed a reason to strike again, the urgency to deliver the letter and interpret its intentions was all that was necessary.

See "Paul's Missionary Journeys Harmonized with the Pauline Epistles" on p. 308 for Section Summary information about Paul's first missionary journey.

PAUL PARTS COMPANY WITH BARNABAS (15:36–41)

Paul Proposes Another Trip (v. 36)

"After some time had passed," Paul suggested to Barnabas that they revisit "every town" where they established churches on their first mission. The imprecise time expression is perhaps significant as Luke's way of marking a major new division in the narrative.

Disagreement over John Mark (vv. 37–38)

Paul and Barnabas agreed to part ways. The reason for their going separate ways was not a happy one and involved a major disagreement between them. John Mark was the center of contention. He was Barnabas's cousin, and Barnabas had suggested that he accompany them as he had on their first mission (13:5). Paul did not think this a wise move

HISTORICAL BACKGROUND

John Mark

John Mark was an early missionary and church leader. He is the author of the Gospel of Mark. He was the son of Mary in whose home the Jerusalem believers met to pray when Peter was imprisoned by Herod Agrippa I (Acts 12:12). Mark was sometimes called by his Jewish name, John, and sometimes by his Roman name, Mark. He was a cousin of Barnabas (Col 4:10). After Barnabas and Paul completed a relief mission to Jerusalem, they took Mark with them when they returned to Antioch. When Barnabas and Paul went as missionaries, they took Mark to help. They went from Antioch to Cyprus and then on to Pamphylia, where Mark left them and returned to Jerusalem (13:13). The most likely reason for his leaving was because Paul became dominant and was taking the gospel to the Gentiles.

NEW TESTAMENT REFERENCE

Paul and John Mark Reconciled

When Paul wrote Philemon, Mark was one of Paul's fellow workers who sent greetings. Paul wrote to the Colossians to receive Mark should he came to them (Col 4:10). When Paul wrote his final letter to Timothy, he asked Timothy to bring Mark with him because Paul considered Mark a useful helper.

since Mark abandoned them on that occasion (v. 13). There may also have been a personality clash between Paul and John Mark.

For whatever reason, Paul and Barnabas were in sharp disagreement. Failing to resolve both the issue and their feelings, their only course of action was to separate.

Paul and Silas (vv. 39–41)

Paul needed a suitable replacement for a traveling companion and chose Silas. Paul and Silas headed north from Antioch by foot and visited the churches of Syria and Cilicia along the way.

HISTORICAL BACKGROUND

Silas

Silas was a leader in the early Jerusalem church. He accompanied both Peter and Paul on separate missionary journeys. One of his first missions was to carry news of the Jerusalem conference to the believers in Antioch.

Section Summary

After a disagreement on traveling companions, Paul and Barnabas parted company. As a result, Barnabas and Mark decided to travel to Cyprus, and Paul and Silas were to begin the second journey through Asia Minor and Greece.

QUESTIONS TO GUIDE YOUR STUDY

1. Describe the debate that took place in Jerusalem. What was the issue that needed a resolution?
2. How did James resolve the issue? How did the assembly respond to his decision?
3. Why did Paul and Barnabas part ways? Do you think this split helped or hurt the church's missionary efforts?

HISTORICAL BACKGROUND

Timothy

Personal name meaning "honoring God." When he was a child, his mother Eunice and his grandmother Lois taught him the Scriptures. A native of Lystra, he may have been converted on Paul's first missionary journey. By the time Paul came back to Lystra, Timothy became so well respected that Paul invited him to accompany him. Since Timothy's father was Greek, Timothy was not circumcised at birth.

ACTS 16

REVISITING DERBE, LYSTRA, AND ICONIUM (16:1–5)

Paul's first evangelistic tour went as far as Lystra and Derbe. When Paul and Barnabas left that area of Asia Minor, on their first trip, the Jews were so opposed to their ministry that the missionaries were forced to leave hurriedly. Paul's stated purpose for this trip was to strengthen the churches that were established in the earlier journey. The focus of his visit to Lystra, however, was on Timothy, a young disciple who came to faith in Christ on Paul's first visit there.

Paul accepted the recommendation of the believers in the area and took Timothy as a companion. Paul circumcised Timothy to make Timothy acceptable to Jewish Christians.

Section Summary

Paul's first evangelistic tour went as far as Lystra and Derbe. Paul's stated purpose for this trip was to strengthen the churches that were established in the earlier journey.

CALLED TO MACEDONIA (16:6–10)

Paul, Silas, and Timothy now headed north, probably from Pisidian Antioch through Phrygia and Galatia. But God had other plans for the missionaries. The Spirit prevented them from entering the Roman province called Asia. Unable to preach in Asia, the small company prepared to go into Bithynia, but once again they were prevented by the Spirit.

God sent a vision to Paul, perhaps a dream in the middle of the night. A man of Macedonia appeared, begging him to come and witness to the Macedonians. Paul realized this vision was God's way of calling him to a mission in Macedonia.

Section Summary

Twice the Spirit guided the movement of the gospel. Rather than moving toward the northern part of Asia Minor, as Paul desired, the gospel was pointed toward the Western world.

THE "WE" PASSAGES

At this point (16:10), the narrative changes from third person to first person. This begins one of the "we" passages in Acts that begins and ends with Philippi. The second "we" section begins when the missionaries return to Philippi (20:5–15). One possible explanation for this is that Luke was part of Paul's vision and a resident of Philippi.

WITNESSING IN PHILIPPI (16:11–40)

The remainder of this chapter concerns Paul's work in Philippi. It falls into four separate scenes.

Founding a Church with Lydia (vv. 11–15)

Philippi had such a small Jewish population that the city lacked the ten Jewish men necessary to build a synagogue. Among the women who gathered for prayer, Lydia, a businesswoman from Thyatira, was the one responsive to the gospel. Her offer of hospitality to Paul and his missionary team demonstrated the reality of her conversion. She did not just open her home to the missionaries; she also allowed it to become the gathering place for the entire Christian community.

HISTORICAL BACKGROUND

Lydia

Thyatira was a center of the purple dye business. Since purple goods were expensive, Lydia was likely a wealthy person and one who had traveled far more than most women of her day.

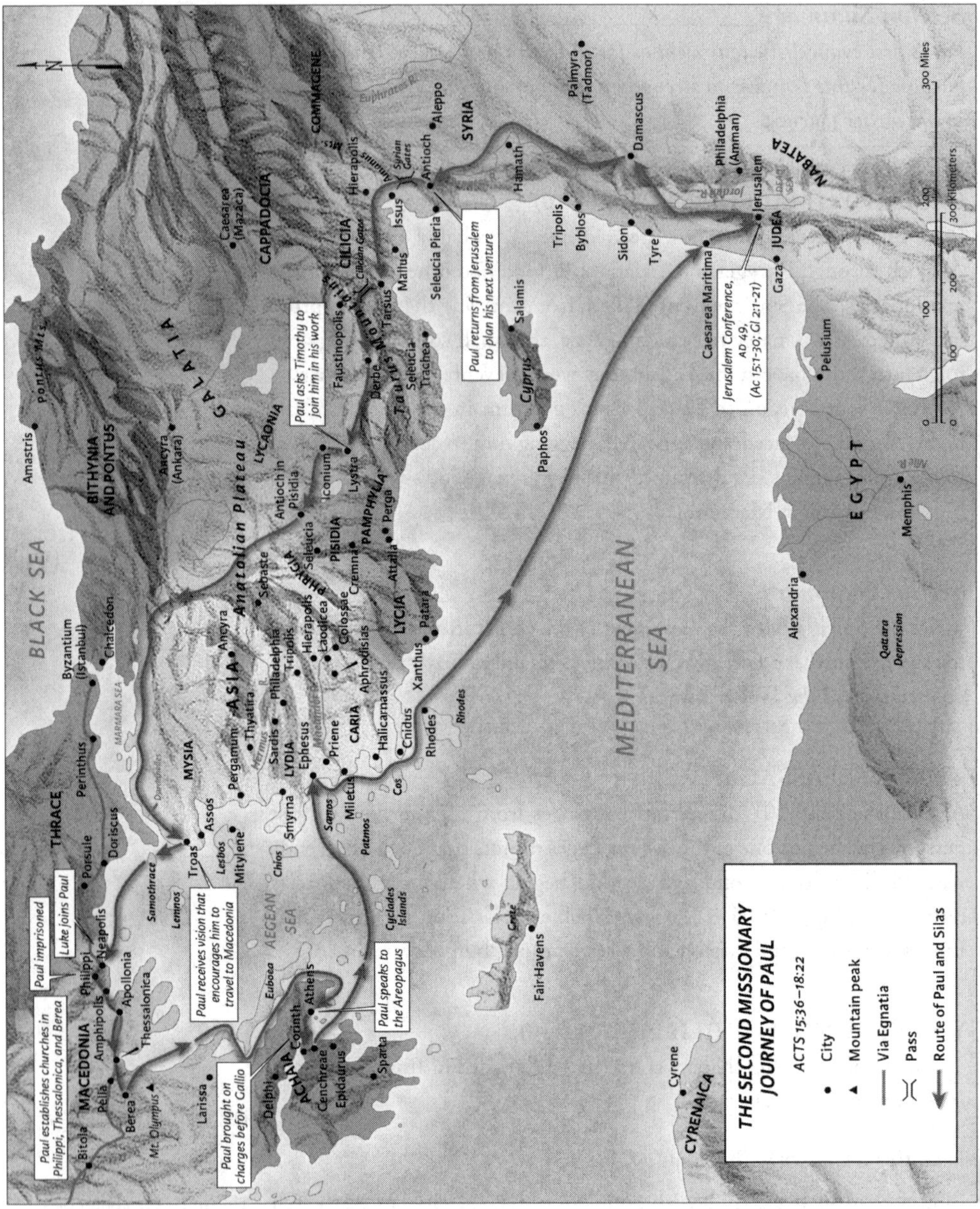

The Second Missionary Journey of Paul

Healing a Possessed Servant Girl (vv. 16–24)

Verse 16 opens a new scene but connects with the previous one to make a new narrative. On one of the occasions when the four missionaries were going outside the city to the place of prayer, they were encountered by a slave girl with a spirit by which she predicted the future.

Like the demoniacs during Jesus's ministry, the possessed girl was evidently able to see into the true nature of Paul's preaching, particularly into the reality of the God he proclaimed. She constantly followed the missionaries about, shouting that they were servants of the "Most High God" "who are proclaiming to you a way of salvation." Paul, in a form reminiscent of Jesus's exorcisms, commanded the spirit to leave the girl. The spirit did so immediately.

NEW TESTAMENT REFERENCE

The first-person narrative stops at verse 17 and does not reappear in Acts until Paul's return to Philippi in 20:6.

But her masters, who exploited her condition, lost their source of income and became furious at Paul. Seeing their young fortune teller well and whole, they dragged Paul and Silas before the magistrates who judged the city in the name of the Roman emperor.

Apparently, with little or no judicial hearing, Paul and Silas were stripped and beaten and then delivered to a prison keeper, who clapped them in stocks and locked them in a cell in the town dungeon.

Converting a Prison Keeper's Household (vv. 25–34)

This event falls into two divisions. The first relates to Paul and Silas's deliverance from prison. The second concerns the prison keeper and his household.

The Deliverance. It was the middle of the night. Paul and Silas were singing hymns of praise to God. As they sang and prayed, an earthquake shook the jail. The bars and doors flew open. Everyone's chains came loose. The chains, perhaps attached to the walls, were wrenched loose by the quake's violence.

HISTORICAL BACKGROUND

Prison keepers and guards were personally responsible for their prisoners and in some instances were executed for allowing them to escape.

The jailer was aroused by the earthquake and spotted the open door. Supposing the prisoners had already escaped, he drew his sword to kill himself, preferring death by his own hand rather than by Roman justice.

When Paul saw what the jailer was about to do, he shouted for him to stop, assuring him they were in their cell. The miraculous release did not lead to their escape but to a far more significant event—the jailer's conversion.

The Witness. Calling for lamps and torches, the jailer rushed in and fell at the feet of Paul and Silas. Paul had saved his life, and Paul's God—who in an instant made ineffective all his efforts at prison security—was obviously the one to be respected. The jailer's response was, "Sirs, what must I do to be saved?"

The missionaries' response was, "Believe in the Lord Jesus, and you will be saved—you and your household." At some point, the prison keeper's household entered the scene. The whole family came to faith in God.

Humbling the City Magistrates (vv. 35–40)

The next day the magistrates decided that Paul and Silas had sufficiently paid for the crime of disturbing the peace. So, quite casually, they issued an order for their release. After all, they were beaten and locked in the dungeon overnight—and all of that without a trial. It was strictly an illegal procedure. They scourged and imprisoned two Roman citizens with no formal condemnation, and that was beyond their authority.

When the magistrates learned they improperly treated and wrongly imprisoned Roman citizens, they became fearful. The magistrates who condemned Paul and Silas now found themselves genuine lawbreakers.

Paul insisted that the magistrates personally come to the prison and escort them out. The nervous magistrates entered the prison, escorted the prisoners out, and told them to leave town. Paul and Silas did leave, but only after they had spent some time with Lydia and other new converts in the city.

HISTORICAL BACKGROUND

Paul's Roman Citizenship

Paul was not only "a Hebrew born of Hebrews" (Phil 3:5) but a Roman citizen. Paul's rights as a Roman citizen come to the fore not only here but in Acts 22:24–29 when he was about to be beaten and in Acts 25:10–12 when he exercised his right to appeal to the emperor.

Section Summary

Part of the significance of the conversion of the Philippian jailer is that this is the first recorded episode of a person with no prior exposure to Judaism—an out-and-out pagan—becoming a believer in Jesus Christ.

QUESTIONS TO GUIDE YOUR STUDY

1. From the events of this chapter, describe how the Holy Spirit guided the movement of the gospel message.
2. Who was Lydia? How did she help the spread of Christianity into her community?
3. What was the result of Paul and Silas's witness to the prison keeper?

ACTS 17

ESTABLISHING CHURCHES IN THESSALONICA AND BEREA (17:1–15)

Acceptance and Rejection in Thessalonica (vv. 1–9)

Paul, Silas, and Timothy proceeded from Philippi to the major seaport city of Thessalonica, sixty-two miles away. Thessalonica was then (as now) the second-largest city in Greece. Here Paul resumed the missionary pattern established in the first missionary journey. Again, his ministry in the synagogue led to saving faith on the part of many Jews and Gentiles and opposition from leading Jewish citizens. As in Philippi, Paul and Silas were accused of insurrection, but they were released and asked to leave the city rather than being jailed.

Witness in Berea (vv. 10–15)

From Thessalonica the three missionaries went to Berea. Luke describes the Jews of Berea as being of "more noble character" than the Thessalonians. These people were open, tolerant, and generous. They took Paul's scriptural exposition seriously. They examined the Scriptures to see if they really did point to the death and resurrection of the Messiah as Paul claimed. They met daily to search the Scriptures. It is no wonder so many contemporary Bible study groups call themselves "Bereans."

This ideal situation did not last forever. Although their reception initially was more favorable than at Thessalonica, Paul again was forced to leave because of opposition aroused by the Jews who had come from Thessalonica. Leaving Silas and Timothy behind, Paul headed south to Athens.

Perhaps the most interesting part of this passage is that in Berea, Greek men as well as women believed.

Section Summary

Despite opposition from local Jews, the missionary team of Paul, Silas, and Timothy established churches in the Greek cities of Thessalonica and Berea.

WITNESSING TO THE ATHENIAN INTELLECTUALS (17:16–34)

The Athenians' Curiosity (vv. 16–21)

In Athens, Paul reasoned with the Jews at the synagogue. He also bore his witness in the Agora, the famous marketplace and hub of Athenian life. There he got his most pronounced response, especially from some of the philosophers.

The philosophers called Paul an "ignorant show-off." They did not understand Paul's concept of resurrection. Epicureans did not believe in any existence after death, and Stoics believed that only the soul, the divine spark, survived death. Their response to Paul's idea of resurrection was, "He seems to be a preacher of foreign deities."

HISTORICAL BACKGROUND

Success in Thessalonica

Paul later wrote to the Thessalonians, "In spite of severe persecution, you welcomed the message with joy from the Holy Spirit. As a result, you became an example to all the believers in Macedonia and Achaia. For the word of the Lord rang out from you, not only in Macedonia and Achaia, but in every place that your faith in God has gone out" (1 Thess 1:6–8).

HISTORICAL BACKGROUND

In Paul's day, Athens was only a shadow of its former glory in its golden age in the fourth and fifth centuries BC. Even the native population of Athens had dwindled, estimated at five thousand voting citizens. That number was, however, considerably augmented by artists, students, and tourists in the city. It was still considered the cultural and intellectual center of the Roman Empire.

HISTORICAL BACKGROUND

Ignorant Show-Off

When the philosophers dubbed Paul an "ignorant show-off," they were not using a complimentary term. They used a colorful word *(spermologos)* meaning "seed-picker," which evokes images of a bird pecking indiscriminately at seeds in a barnyard. It referred to someone who picked up scraps of ideas here and there and passed them off as profound truth with no depth of understanding.

Paul's Testimony before the Areopagus (vv. 22–31)

Paul's speech on the Areopagus was an attempt to present the gospel in a setting different from any Luke had described before. This speech is a masterpiece of Hellenistic rhetoric. Paul did not begin with the Old Testament; his starting point was Greek philosophy and literature. Paul had observed in the city an altar with the inscription: "To an Unknown God." This gave him the perfect launchpad for his presentation.

Paul presented four God-centered themes in his speech:

The Creator God. Paul referred to God as the maker of the "world," a term familiar to every Greek. Once granted the premise that God is Creator, two things follow. First, God "does not live in shrines made by hands." Second, God is totally self-sufficient and totally without need.

HISTORICAL BACKGROUND

Areopagus

The Areopagus was the site of Paul's speech to the Epicurean and Stoic philosophers of Athens, Greece. It was a rocky hill about 370 feet high, not far from the acropolis and the agora (marketplace). The word was also used to refer to the council that originally met on this hill. The name probably was derived from Ares, the Greek name for the god of war known to the Romans as Mars.

The Providential God. The verses of this section form the center of the speech. They contain two emphases: (1) God's providence over humanity and (2) human responsibility to God.

The Worship of God. This section is the basis for Paul's critique of idolatrous worship, and it provides the scriptural base for the speech. Scripture would have been meaningless to the Greeks, so Paul addressed them as much as possible in their own terms—just as he did the citizens of Lystra (14:15–17). If the Greeks genuinely accepted Paul's major premise that God is Creator, then they must also acknowledge their own idolatry and need for repentance.

The Judgment of God. Paul concluded that all people must ultimately stand before God and give an account of their relationship to him. The clincher that brought Paul's discourse to an abrupt halt was the resurrection of the dead. With the mention of the resurrection, the jeering started. The party broke up on that statement.

The Mixed Response (vv. 32–34)

Some of the Greeks scoffed, while others wanted to hear Paul again. A few people responded in faith. One who did believe was a member of the inner circle of Areopagites, a man named Dionysius. Another convert is mentioned by name—Damaris, a woman.

Section Summary

Paul's speech was unique in its appeal to Greek philosophical thought. Paul held his own, even in the midst of cynical intellectualism. The result was that some people who heard Paul were moved to salvation.

QUESTIONS TO GUIDE YOUR STUDY

1. How did the Bereans receive Paul and Silas? What did they accomplish there?

2. What was Paul's message to the Greek pagans? What was their response?
3. Women were prominent in Paul's Greek congregations. What instances can you cite where women were instrumental in the spread of the gospel?

ACTS 18

ESTABLISHING A CHURCH IN CORINTH (18:1–17)

From Athens, Paul next traveled to Corinth, a major commercial center. In Paul's day, Corinth was the largest and most cosmopolitan city of Greece.

The Mission to Corinth (vv. 1–11)

From Luke's narrative, we know that Paul ministered here for about eighteen months. Three things about this passage are noteworthy. First is Paul's encounter with Aquila and Priscilla. In these Jewish Christians Paul found company and encouragement when he needed both. They, like him, were tentmakers.

Second, Paul went to the Jewish community in Corinth. They rejected his witness and became abusive. Paul shook out his clothes in protest and told them he fulfilled his responsibility to them and they would have to live with the consequences of their guilt.

At Corinth Paul was able to witness freely, not just on Sabbaths. Second Corinthians 11:8–10 and Philippians 4:15–17 speak of the support of other churches while Paul ministered in Corinth. (See page 308, "Paul's Missionary Journeys Harmonized with the Pauline Epistles.")

The Accusation Before Gallio (vv. 12–17)

As a result of intensified attacks from some of the Jews in Corinth, Paul was brought before Gallio, the proconsul and charged with "persuading people to worship God in ways contrary to the law." Paul's appearance before Gallio is important in two respects. First, it established a precedent for the manner in which the Roman leaders should consider charges against Christians brought before them. Second, the mention of Gallio is an important reference point for determining the date of Paul's work in Corinth and for establishing the entire Pauline chronology.

Section Summary

Certain Jews, seeking to get Roman punishment of Paul charged him with advocating an unlawful religion. However, Gallio considered Christianity to be part of Judaism and granted it all the rights and privileges enjoyed by the Jewish religion in the Roman Empire.

HISTORICAL BACKGROUND

Corinth

Corinth was located on the southwest end of the isthmus that joined the southern part of the Greek peninsula with the mainland to the north. Corinth was an important city long before it became a Roman colony in 44 BC. In addition to the extant works of early writers, modern archaeology has contributed to knowledge of ancient Corinth. Corinth in Paul's day was a cosmopolitan city composed of people from varying cultural backgrounds. Being near the site of the Isthmian games held every two years, the Corinthians enjoyed the pleasures of these games and the wealth which visitors brought to the city. Sailors would come to the city to spend their money on the pleasures of Corinth, which was especially known for its licentious lifestyle.

HISTORICAL BACKGROUND

Corinth was one of the four prominent centers in the New Testament account of the early church, the other three being Jerusalem, Antioch of Syria, and Ephesus. Paul's first extended ministry at one city was at Corinth. After he visited Corinth for the first time, he decided to remain here for at least eighteen months. Paul's three longest letters are associated with Corinth.

RETURNING TO ANTIOCH (18:18–23)

This passage provides a transition between Paul's second and third missions. Capitalizing on the favorable judgment on the part of Gallio, Paul remained in Corinth for several more months, working day and night for the cause of Christ.

After his eighteen-month ministry at Corinth was completed, Paul and his companions (including Aquila and Priscilla) traveled to Ephesus. Paul left Aquila and Priscilla there while he returned to his home base, Antioch of Syria.

HISTORICAL BACKGROUND

Gallio, as Roman provincial governor of Achaia, was headquartered in Corinth. Certain Jews brought Paul before Gallio, seeking to have him punished. They charged that Paul advocated an unlawful religion. Gallio considered Christianity to be part of Judaism, with all the rights and privileges the Jewish religion enjoyed in the Roman Empire. In fact, Gallio refused to take jurisdiction over the dispute.

Section Summary

With Paul's return to Antioch, the stage was set for his third missionary journey. Aquila and Priscilla would carry on the witness in Ephesus until his return.

APOLLOS IN EPHESUS (18:24–28)

In 18:24–28 Luke mentions the arrival in Ephesus of Apollos, an eloquent Jew from Alexandria.

Apollos had a thorough knowledge of Scripture and spoke with fervor; however, he only knew of the baptism of John. After Priscilla and Aquila instructed him on this issue, Apollos traveled to the province of Achaia and the city of Corinth, where he provided significant help to those who had believed and refuted unbelieving Jews.

HISTORICAL BACKGROUND

Apollos

An educated man, Apollos handled Old Testament Scriptures with forcefulness. However, he lacked a full understanding of the way of God, so Priscilla and Aquila instructed him. Apollos became even more successful in his ministry. He greatly strengthened believers by using the Scriptures to demonstrate that Jesus was the Christ.

Section Summary

Paul launched his third missionary journey. Meanwhile, in Ephesus, a young Alexandrian Jew named Apollos, well educated in the Old Testament Scriptures, became a key figure in the spread of the gospel in the province of Achaia.

HISTORICAL BACKGROUND

Apollos in Corinth

Some New Testament references compare Apollos with Paul or Peter (1 Cor 1:12; 3:4–6, 22). In 1 Cor 4:6, Paul placed Apollos on the same level as himself. He also referred to Apollos as his brother (1 Cor 16:12). They both sought to defeat the arrogance and superiority that comes from being self-centered rather than Christ-centered. Because of Apollos's knowledge of the Old Testament, Luther suggested that Apollos might be the writer of the book of Hebrews.

QUESTIONS TO GUIDE YOUR STUDY

1. Describe the setting at Corinth. Why would many in this city oppose Paul's gospel message?
2. What strengths did Apollos bring to the leadership of the early church?
3. Describe the spread of the gospel to this point in Acts. Comment on how God orchestrated the varying personalities and events that contributed to its growth.

ACTS 19

Paul's third missionary journey parallels Jesus's passion narrative. Like Jesus, Paul turned his face to Jerusalem, where he was captured, taken before Jewish and Roman officials, and placed in Roman hands.

PAUL'S WITNESS TO THE DISCIPLES OF JOHN THE BAPTIST (19:1–7)

When Paul arrived at Ephesus, he encountered some disciples of John the Baptist.

Paul's interrogation of these followers of John revealed their lack of advancement beyond John the Baptist's initial preaching of repentance, which was in preparation for the coming of the Messiah. In fact, they were unaware of the events of Pentecost. Paul asked them if they received the Spirit. Their reply was, "We haven't even heard that there is a Holy Spirit."

After prayer and the laying on of hands, the Spirit came to these disciples. They spoke in tongues and prophesied. As throughout Acts, there was no set pattern in the way this gift was bestowed. The Spirit came at various times and in various ways.

OCCASIONS OF THE SPIRIT'S COMING IN ACTS

OCCASION	PASSAGE
The first Jewish believers	2:1–13
The Samaritans	8:14–17
The Gentiles	10:44–48
The partially taught disciples in Ephesus	19:3–7

Section Summary

Paul encountered disciples of John the Baptist who were unaware of the events of Pentecost. When Paul explained the fullness of Jesus's baptism, the disciples requested a new baptism. Paul laid hands on them, and they received the Spirit.

PAUL'S PREACHING IN EPHESUS (19:8–12)

For two years Paul preached the gospel in Ephesus and throughout the province so that "all the residents of Asia, both Jews and Greeks, heard the word of the Lord."

Another aspect of Paul's ministry in Ephesus involved the miracles of God. Luke described these as being "extraordinary," which is something of an understatement. The people would take cloths that Paul had touched and carry them to the sick for healing. The people believed that

HISTORICAL BACKGROUND

Paul's Third Missionary Journey

Paul began his third missionary journey from Antioch. He traveled through Galatia and Phrygia, provinces he visited on his previous missionary journeys. One of the key aims of this journey was to strengthen all the believers. Paul's third journey concluded with his arrival in Jerusalem in Acts 21:17.

HISTORICAL BACKGROUND

Ephesus

One of the largest and most impressive cities in the ancient world and capital of the Roman province of Asia during the reign of Hadrian. The city played a significant role in the expansion of Christianity. At the time of Paul, Ephesus was probably the fourth-largest city in the world with a population of 250,000.

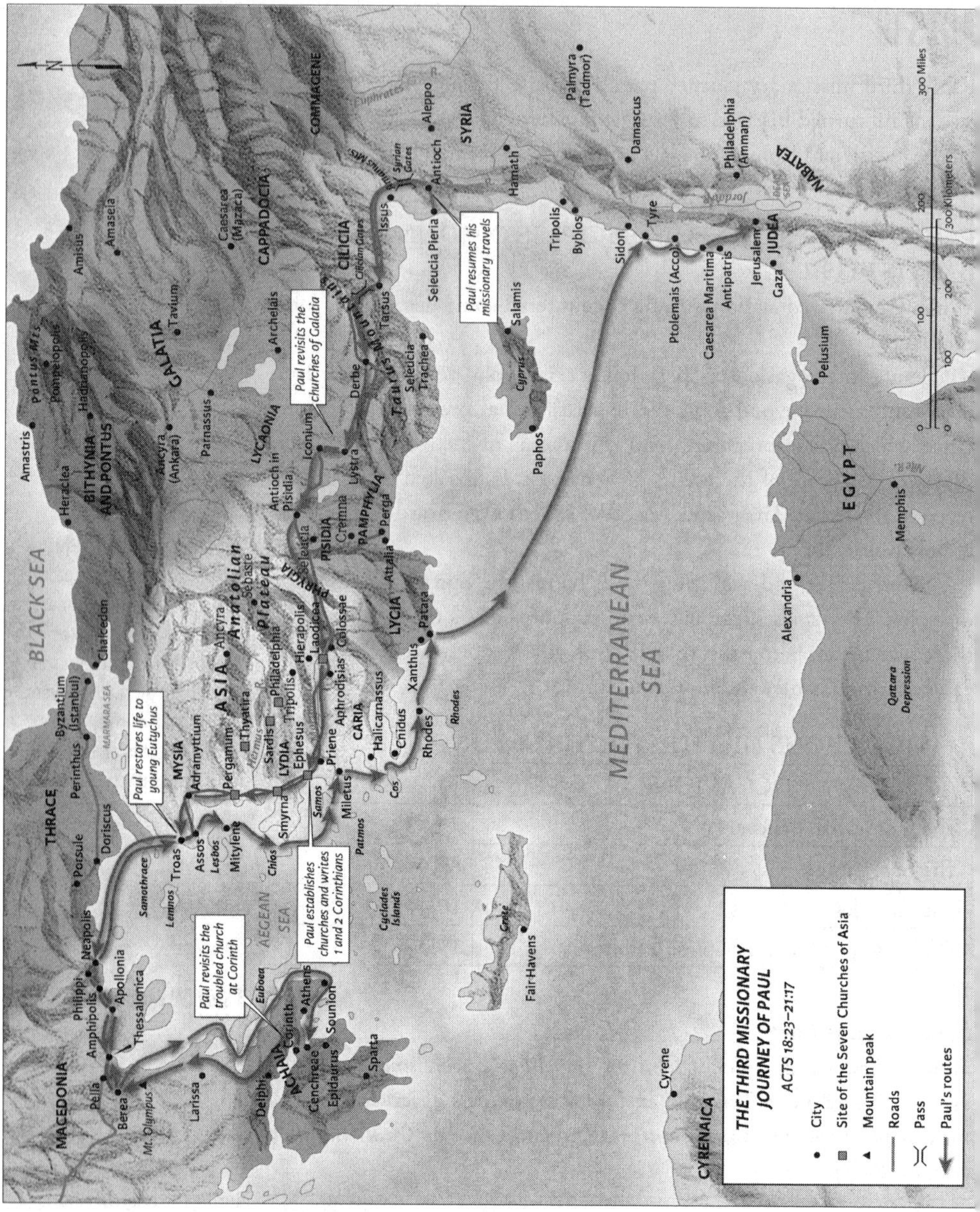

The Third Missionary Journey of Paul

cloths that touched the apostle's body had healing efficiency, and Luke indicated that such was indeed the case.

This break with the synagogue in Ephesus marks a painful phase in the development of the church. From this point on, the break between Jews and Christians, between synagogue and church, widened rapidly.

HISTORICAL BACKGROUND

There is one other aspect of Paul's Ephesian ministry that Luke did not elaborate on but that can be gleaned from Paul's letters. This was a period of extensive interaction with the churches which he established elsewhere. It was from Ephesus that Paul wrote his first letter to the Corinthians.

Section Summary

For three months Paul pleaded and argued with the Ephesian Jews about the kingdom of God. However, they refused to believe Paul's message. For two more years, Paul preached the gospel in Ephesus and throughout the province of Asia.

PAUL'S ENCOUNTER WITH FALSE RELIGION IN EPHESUS (19:13–20)

The example of Paul's genuine miracle working is followed by two episodes that involve false attempts to accomplish the miraculous.

HISTORICAL BACKGROUND

Ephesus was noted as a center of magic. The famous statue of Artemis, the centerpiece of her temple, was noted for the mysterious terms engraved on the crown, girdle, and feet of the image. Referred to as the "Ephesian scripts," this magical gibberish was considered to have great power.

Jewish Exorcists (vv. 13–16)

A group of fake exorcists who claimed to be sons of one Sceva, whom they declared to be a high priest (no such high priest ever existed, according to the best records), traveled around the empire, purportedly casting out demons. They watched Paul work and heard him casting out demons and do healing in "the name of the Lord Jesus."

They reasoned that if this worked for Paul, it would for them. The next time they confronted a man who seemed to be possessed by demons, they commanded the tormenting devils to come out "by the Jesus that Paul preaches."

The evil spirit answered them, "I know Jesus, and I recognize Paul—but who are you?" Suddenly the possessed man leaped upon the seven scoundrels, beat them with superhuman strength, tore their clothes from their bodies, and sent them reeling naked into the streets of Ephesus.

PERSONAL APPLICATION

Two lessons emerge from this story. First, Christianity has nothing to do with magic. The name of Jesus is no magical incantation. The power of Jesus drives out the demonic, and his Spirit only works through those who, like Paul, confess him and are committed to him. Second, the demon did acknowledge the power of Jesus over him.

Overcoming Magic (vv. 17–20)

This episode shows the triumph of the gospel over magic and the occult. To celebrate further the victory of Christian faith over magic, Luke recorded the memorable scene when many citizens of Ephesus who practiced magic and soothsaying burned their books and completely forsook their attempts at the magical arts. Books were expensive items in those days, but books of magic commanded a particularly handsome price. Luke estimated the value of those burned in Ephesus at fifty thousand pieces of silver.

PAUL'S DETERMINATION TO GO TO JERUSALEM (19:21–22)

Toward the end of his Ephesian ministry, Paul made a major decision. He determined to conclude his mission in the eastern provinces, go to Jerusalem, and then on to Rome.

HISTORICAL BACKGROUND

The Greek Goddess Artemis

Artemis was the Greek goddess of the moon. She was the daughter of Zeus and Leto, whose worship was threatened by Paul's preaching of the gospel. Artemis was the goddess who watched over nature for both humans and animals. She was considered the great mother image who gave fertility to humankind. In the Greek homeland she was usually portrayed by the statues as a young, attractive virgin with her hair pulled back on her head wearing a short tunic. In Ephesus and Asia Minor she was portrayed as a more mature woman. Her robe was draped in such a way as to expose her bosom, which was covered with multiple breasts, depicting her gift of fertility and nurture.

OPPOSITION TO PAUL BY THE CRAFTSMAN OF EPHESUS (19:23–41)

Instigation of a Riot by Demetrius (vv. 23–27)

Paul and his friends were so effective in the campaign to win the Roman province of Asia for Christ that many people became believers, forsaking Artemis and her craftsmen in the process. Demetrius, apparently a leader among the silversmiths, became so agitated over the financial threat that he inflamed others in the craftsman's guild to a riotous protest against Paul and other Christian leaders.

Uproar in the Theater (vv. 28–34)

Demetrius's appeal had the desired effect, with all the craftsmen running forth and shouting, "Great is Artemis of the Ephesians!" (Note that it was his appeal to religious and civic pride that was picked up.) A crowd quickly formed. Two of Paul's traveling companions from Macedonia were seized.

The mob then rushed into the theater, the largest public building in Ephesus. It was an open-air amphitheater, 495 feet in diameter, built into the western slope of Mount Pion. Its seating capacity has been estimated at 24,500.

A man named Alexander moved before the crowd and motioned for silence to make a defense before the people.

HISTORICAL BACKGROUND

The city clerk was the chief administrative officer of the city. He presided over both the council of city magistrates and the public assembly. In addition, he was the liaison officer between the city and the Roman provincial administration. The city clerk's main concern was that the disturbance would make an adverse impression on the Roman officials.

Pacification by the City Clerk (vv. 35–41)

Alexander was not able to gain the crowd's attention. The city clerk, however, had no difficulty quieting the commotion.

He outlined the two primary legal avenues Demetrius and his fellow craftsman could follow if they had any grievances against the Christians. One was the provincial court conducted by the Roman proconsul on specific days. The other was the regular town assembly.

The clerk then clinched his argument. He told the Ephesians that they were running the danger of being charged with insurrection, since they really had no legally valid basis for their unruly behavior. The clerk's counsel carried the day. He dismissed the gathering and the crowd disappeared.

Section Summary

This event indicates that Christians were not seen as a threat to the state and that they should be treated with tolerance in a religiously pluralistic society. After the trouble ceased, Paul left Ephesus for Macedonia.

QUESTIONS TO GUIDE YOUR STUDY

1. What were the disciples of John lacking? How did Paul rectify the situation?
2. What lesson can we learn from the story about the sons of Sceva?
3. How did Paul escape the mob incited by Demetrius the silversmith? What evidences are there that God was in control of the events in Paul's life?

ACTS 20

PAUL'S FINAL MINISTRY IN MACEDONIA AND GREECE (20:1–6)

A Productive Visit to Greece (vv. 1–3a)

After traveling around in Greece (Achaia) for some months, he settled in Corinth for the winter months. Many scholars believe it was during these cold days of winter (AD 56–57) that Paul wrote his great epistle to the Romans, preparing the way for what he hoped would be a pastoral visit to the capital city of the Roman Empire.

While strengthening the church or churches in Corinth and doing his writing, Paul also coordinated the collection of the offering he wanted to take to Jerusalem to relieve the suffering of the Christians there.

Paul Eludes a Plot (vv. 3b–4)

Just as he was about to board what may have been a ship filled with Jewish pilgrims headed for worship in Jerusalem, Paul and his friends uncovered a plot on the apostle's life. Indications are that once at sea, Paul would have been murdered. So Paul changed his plans. He journeyed by land to Macedonia and sailed from there to Jerusalem.

The Rendezvous in Troas (vv. 5–6)

His traveling companions went ahead of Paul to wait for him in Troas. Paul, who was joined by Luke, remained in Philippi until after the Passover before setting sail for Troas.

After the season of Passover, Paul and Luke sailed for Troas where they stayed seven days in final preparation for the trip to Jerusalem, which the resolute apostle felt compelled to make.

HISTORICAL BACKGROUND

Paul's Companions

At this point, Paul was fortunate to have with him companions from a number of cities where he had ministered: Sopater from Berea, Aristarchus and Secundus from Thessalonica, Gaius from Derbe, Timothy from Lystra, Tychicus and Trophimus from Asia.

Section Summary

Paul left Ephesus for a final swing through Greece, back to Asia Minor, and finally to Jerusalem. After eluding a plot on his life, Paul caught up with his traveling companions in Troas.

RESTORATION OF EUTYCHUS (20:7–12)

On their last day in Troas (a Sunday), Paul met with Christians for worship. This meeting is one of the earliest references to Christians meeting for worship on Sunday.

Since he was leaving the next morning by ship, Paul spent all the time he could with the Christians in Troas, talking far into the night. Eutychus, a young believer, perhaps even a slave, sat listening in the window of the upper chamber in which Paul was speaking.

Eutychus probably took refuge in the window to catch a breath of fresh air to fight drowsiness. That effort, however, brought disastrous results. He fell asleep and tumbled from the third story to the ground.

The congregation rushed outside. The boy died from the fall ("he . . . was picked up dead"; v. 9). But when Paul went and embraced him, Paul said, "Don't be alarmed, because he's alive." To everyone's amazement, the boy was brought back to live.

Section Summary

As Paul preached into the wee hours of the morning, Eutychus, a young believer, sat listening in a window of the upper chamber. He fell asleep and tumbled from the third story to the ground.

HISTORICAL BACKGROUND

This is an unusual passage (vv. 18–35) in that it is the only recorded address that Paul made to Christians. His other sermons were delivered either to Jews or Gentiles. This sermon contains both exhortation in the faith as well as defense (apology) of the faith. The sermon sounds much like some of Paul's letters. It's likely that Luke actually heard the sermon, was deeply impressed by it, and in later years reconstructed the speech when he compiled Acts.

VOYAGE TO MILETUS (20:13–16)

At Assos, Paul boarded the coastal ship that skirted the rugged shoreline, putting in at major towns and cities along the route—a sort of "commuter" boat. Since he was attempting to reach Jerusalem by Pentecost, he decided not to go all the way to Ephesus. Instead, when the boat made port at Miletus, about thirty miles from Ephesus, he sent word to the city asking the leaders of the Christian community to come to Miletus.

PAUL'S FAREWELL ADDRESS TO THE EPHESIAN ELDERS (20:17–35)

Paul begins by reminding the Ephesians of his conduct, style of ministry, and devotion while he was among them.

Paul could honestly say that he did not value his life above the calling God had given him. What really mattered to him was to do the will of God, to answer his call to the fullest extent, and to do what the heavenly Father prepared him to do. To sum up his speech, Paul said, in effect, "I've done all I can for you. Now it's up to you."

Tucked away in this passage is a challenging statement. Paul could honestly say, "I did not avoid declaring to you the whole plan of God." Christian teachers must deliver the whole Word of God, the positive and the negative, the soothing and the corrective.

Verse 32 is a beautiful benediction. Paul commended his Ephesian friends to God and to the word of his grace, which was able to build them up and to bestow their full inheritance as members of the Christian community.

Section Summary

Paul reported to the church about his missionary activity. His Miletus address is his third and final speech in Acts during the course of his missionary work.

PAUL'S MISSIONARY SPEECHES IN ACTS

LOCATION	MISSION	PASSAGE	AUDIENCE
Pisidian Antioch (synagogue)	First journey	13:16–41	Jews
Athens, Greece (Areopagus)	Second journey	17:22–31	Gentiles
Miletus	Third journey	20:17–35	Christians

FINAL LEAVE-TAKING (20:36–38)

For all his brave talk about marching steadfastly to Jerusalem, when the final moment of parting came, Paul and the elders were overcome with sadness. Grown men knelt by the seashore, joined hands, prayed to their heavenly Father, and wept. Then, spent by years yet profoundly encouraged by his words and example, those stalwart Ephesian leaders escorted Paul to his ship. With one more round of desperate, clinging embraces, they put him on board and watched him sail away.

Section Summary

This section concludes Paul's Ephesian ministry with its final farewell to the leaders of the church. From this point on, the focus will be Rome.

QUESTIONS TO GUIDE YOUR STUDY

1. What did the resurrection of Eutychus mean to the Christians who witnessed this event?

2. In the opening statement of his farewell to the Ephesian elders, Paul offered a model for ministry. What are the elements of the model, and how might we apply them to our present-day church ministries?
3. What are the key points of Paul's complete address to the Ephesian elders?

ACTS 21

VOYAGE TO JERUSALEM (21:1–16)

After the parting scene at Miletus, Paul resumed his final voyage to Jerusalem.

Warning at Tyre (vv. 1–6)

At Tyre, Paul and his traveling companions found the Christian community. Most likely it was established by the Hellenist mission to Phoenicia mentioned in Acts 11:19. During his visit, the Tyrian Christians "through the Spirit" urged Paul not to go to Jerusalem.

Warning of Agabus (vv. 7–14)

Paul's next stopping point was Ptolemais, some twenty-five miles south of Tyre, the most southerly of the Phoenician ports.

Here, Agabus reenters Luke's narrative (see 11:27–30). In a symbolic act much like the acted-out prophecies of the Old Testament prophets, Agabus predicted Paul's coming arrest in Jerusalem. He took Paul's girdle, the long cloth wound several times around his waist, and bound his hands and feet with it. Then he gave the interpretation of the act. The prophecy was that Paul would be bound by the Jews of Jerusalem and handed over to the Gentiles.

HISTORICAL BACKGROUND

Agabus

Prophet in Jerusalem who visited the church at Antioch and predicted a universal famine. His prophecy was fulfilled about ten years later during the reign of Claudius Caesar.

Paul's Arrival in Jerusalem (vv. 15–16)

Paul's journey was now nearly complete. There remained only the final sixty-four miles between Caesarea and Jerusalem. The Caesarean Christians had made housing arrangements for Paul with a man named Mnason. The Christian community at Jerusalem gladly welcomed Paul and his colleagues.

En route to Jerusalem, Paul received warnings of the imprisonment and hardships that awaited him in Jerusalem.

THE PLAN OF THE JERUSALEM ELDERS (21:17–26)

After greeting the respected leaders of the church, Paul proceeded to tell them about all that God did through him for the Gentiles. Paul did not owe these elders a report, but out of respect for their positions and the importance of the Jerusalem church, Paul was willing and eager to relate to them his experience as a missionary to the Gentiles.

Success was his problem. The elders rejoiced over his success—a genuine rejoicing, no doubt. They then shared their misgivings. Paul's success stirred up some animosity among Jews in Jerusalem. In addition, lies had been spread about his work and regarding his views on Gentiles and circumcision, dietary laws, and the relinquishing of ancient Jewish traditions.

To offset the lies and to assure the orthodox Jews of Paul's Jewishness, the Christian elders devised a plan. Paul would accompany to the temple four Jewish men who had taken a vow of purification and rededication. Paul would go through the same ritual of restoration they did and then pay the temple tax for them and himself. The process would take seven days. In this way the Jewish elders hoped the resentment among the orthodox Jews toward Paul would subside.

Paul agreed to this plan. He felt no inner need to go through the temple rituals. However, if it would keep peace in Jerusalem and give him further opportunity to preach to his Jewish brothers, he would attempt the reconciliation.

HISTORICAL BACKGROUND

Paul's Purification

It was customary for Jews returning to Jerusalem from Gentile territories to undergo a purification ritual that lasted seven days. This demonstrated full loyalty to the Torah. Paul underwent this purification and bore the heavy expense of doing so. He did not see his allegiance to Jesus as Messiah as at odds with his loyalty to the Torah.

Section Summary

Paul's successful missionary work stirred up animosity among the orthodox Jews in Jerusalem. To attempt a reconciliation with those Jews and assure them of his Jewishness, Paul agreed to the elders' plan.

THE RIOT AND PAUL'S ARREST IN THE TEMPLE AREA (21:27–36)

It was apparently the last day of the agreed-to plan of the elders when some Jews from Asia Minor screamed that Paul brought Gentiles into the inner court of the temple and, by doing so, defiled it. This false claim arose from the fact that Paul was seen in Jerusalem with a believer from Ephesus—Trophimus. The result of this was that the city was aroused. Immediately the crowd seized Paul, dragged him out of the temple area, and began to beat him. Meanwhile, word spread to the commander of the Roman forces in Jerusalem that the entire city was in confusion. The commander promptly moved to the eye of the storm with soldiers and officers. When the crowd saw the Romans approaching, they stopped beating Paul.

The Romans bound Paul with chains and pulled him away from the hostile crowd. The soldiers scurried up the steps into the fortress, dragging Paul with them.

HISTORICAL BACKGROUND

Tower of Antonio

Roman soldiers were stationed at the Tower of Antonio, a fortress along the northwest corner of the wall that surrounded the temple complex.

Section Summary

Jews from Asia Minor falsely accused Paul of bringing a Gentile into the inner court of the temple area and thereby incited a riot.

PAUL'S REQUEST TO ADDRESS THE CROWD (21:37–40)

As the soldiers whisked Paul away, he, in the Greek language, asked permission to address the tribune. Astonished that his prisoner knew Greek, the tribune (commander) demanded, "Aren't you the Egyptian who started a revolt some time ago and led four thousand men of the Assassins into the wilderness?"

Paul answered, "I am a Jewish man from Tarsus of Cilicia, a citizen of an important city. Now I ask you, let me speak to the people." Taken aback for a moment, the tribune motioned the crowd to be quiet and let Paul stand before them.

QUESTIONS TO GUIDE YOUR STUDY

1. What did Agabus's warning mean?
2. What plan did the Jerusalem Christians devise to reconcile Paul with the orthodox Jews. Why would it work?
3. Of what was Paul falsely accused? Why did this incident kill the elders' plan?

ACTS 22

PAUL'S SPEECH BEFORE THE TEMPLE CROWD (22:1–21)

When Paul spoke in Hebrew, the crowd grew even quieter to hear everything he said. Paul began his speech by closely identifying with the Jews. Although not of Judah but a Jew nonetheless, Paul was educated under the esteemed Gamaliel, reared in the most orthodox manner. And Paul vigorously attacked the new Christian movement when it appeared to be a threat to the ancient religion. Skillfully he retold his conversion experience on the Damascus Road. In the next phase of his sermon, he told of his command from the Lord to go to the Gentiles. With the mention of the Gentiles, the mob began to throw off their coats and toss dust in the air, shouting and calling for Paul's death.

Section Summary

Paul began his defense by identifying himself with his Jewish crowd. He told of his days as a persecutor, then spoke of his conversion and command to take the gospel to the Gentiles. Before he could finish, he was cut off by the Jewish mob.

THE ATTEMPTED EXAMINATION BY THE TRIBUNE (22:22–29)

The narrative following Paul's address is extremely dramatic and filled with suspense. At first it looked as though Paul might be torn to shreds by the Jewish mob, but he was once again rescued by Lysias, the Roman tribune (commander), and taken safely into the barracks. But the tide turned against Paul again as the tribune decided to examine him by the cruel Roman method of scourging. He was determined to flog Paul into some kind of confession. Again, Paul was rescued—this time by an appeal to his Roman citizenship.

The tribune asked Paul, "Are you a Roman citizen?"

Paul answered, "Yes." Those who were about to question Paul withdrew from him immediately. The tribune himself became alarmed when he realized that he placed Paul, a Roman citizen, in chains. The tribune abandoned his plans to scourge Paul and decided to involve the Jewish authorities to help settle the issue.

Section Summary

As Paul was being prepared for flogging and questioning, he appealed to his Roman citizenship. His questioners could not lawfully harm a citizen of the Roman Empire. Instead, the tribune decided to involve the Jewish authorities to settle the matter.

QUESTIONS TO GUIDE YOUR STUDY

1. What was Paul's message to the temple crowd? What particularly incited them?
2. How was Paul able to evade a flogging by claiming Roman citizenship?
3. Lysias, the Roman tribune, again saved Paul from the mob. What kind of impact do you believe Paul had on the life of this Roman commander?

ACTS 23

PAUL BEFORE THE SANHEDRIN (22:30–23:11)

Determined to know why the Jews would attack one of their own who was also a Roman citizen, the tribune arranged to have the Sanhedrin convene to hear Paul's case. Evidently, Rome's philosophy of governing her far-flung empire allowed each country to run its own affairs. Only in emergencies did Roman officials step in to have the final word. Lysias, the tribune, would have been content for the Jews to settle with Paul themselves so long as they did not violate his rights as a Roman citizen.

HISTORICAL BACKGROUND

Claudius Lysias

Claudius Lysias was the Roman tribune or army captain who protected Paul from Jews who wanted to assassinate him. He helped Paul escape the Jews so he could appear before Felix, the governor.

HISTORICAL BACKGROUND

Roman Citizenship

Roman citizenship rights were first formulated in the Valerian Law at the founding of the Roman Republic in 509 BC, but citizenship rights changed as Roman governments changed. In New Testament times the definition of citizenship came in the Julian Law passed near 23 BC. Roman citizenship could be gained in several ways: birth to Roman parents, including birth to a Roman woman without regards to the identity of the father; retirement from the army; being freed from slavery by a Roman master; buying freedom from slavery; being given citizenship by a Roman general or emperor as an individual or as part of a political unit; purchase of citizenship. Paul was a born citizen, but how his family gained citizenship we do not know.

The Sanhedrin was an august body of influential Jews, but Paul was not intimidated by them. After all, he likely knew many of them from his days as a student of Gamaliel and his days as a persecutor of Christians. He did not hesitate to address the body as "brothers." But Paul's familiarity on the part of the accused along with his poise probably infuriated the high priest, Ananias. The high priest immediately ordered that Paul be struck on the mouth for blasphemy.

Paul's response is understandable: "God is going to strike you, you whitewashed wall!"

When reprimanded for his insult, Paul said, "I did not know, brothers, that he was the high priest." Paul may have said this with a tone of irony. In effect, Paul was saying, "He didn't act like a high priest; how could I recognize him as such when he was so totally out of character?"

At verse 6 the proceeding takes a radical turn. Paul saw the makeup of the group to be conservative Pharisees and liberal Sadducees, and he aligned himself with the Pharisees. He then stated what he saw as the real reason for the trial—his "hope of the resurrection of the dead." Immediately both factions, always spoiling for a fight, began arguing vociferously. The dispute became so violent that the tribune became fearful for Paul's life. He commanded his officers to take Paul away.

The following night Paul was exhausted and fell into an uneasy sleep. Then came a sustaining vision of reassurance. Verse 11 says that "the Lord stood by him and said, 'Have courage! For as you have testified about me in Jerusalem, so it is necessary for you to testify in Rome.'" Now the visit to Jerusalem had received the Lord's endorsement.

Many of Paul's troubles the past two years had derived from his testifying to Christ before the Jews. Now his trip to Rome and all the legal hassle in between would be a testimony.

HISTORICAL BACKGROUND

Ananias the High Priest

Ananias was the high priest of the Jewish court known as the Sanhedrin. This is the court that tried Paul in Acts 23. As was typical of high priests who belonged to the aristocratic Jewish group known as the Sadducees, he was concerned to appease Roman authorities and representatives. This desire may have prompted Ananias to take such a personal interest in Paul's case, especially since some Roman authorities suspected the apostle of sedition against Rome. Because of Ananias's pro-Roman sentiments, he was assassinated by anti-Roman Jewish revolutionaries at the outbreak of the first great Jewish revolt against Rome in AD 66.

Section Summary

In the course of Paul's defense before the Sanhedrin, this body erupted into a violent discussion on the resurrection issue. The resurrection was the issue that separated Paul from the rest of the Jews. It was the real issue behind his trials, and in his subsequent defense speeches Paul constantly insisted on that fact.

THE PLOT TO AMBUSH PAUL (23:12–22)

Paul had little rest. Forty or more fanatical Jewish zealots bound themselves by an oath neither to eat nor drink until Paul was dead. These vigilantes took the measure of their religious leaders and quickly decided their "spiritual mentors" would cooperate with the plot. The rulers were told to ask the tribune to bring Paul once again to the Sanhedrin so the case could be settled. But they planned to ambush Paul and the guard before they arrived to address the Sanhedrin.

But God was in control (vv. 16–22). At considerable personal risk, Paul's young nephew, who had learned of the plot secretly, informed Paul and ultimately the Roman tribune of the plot.

Section Summary

Paul's nephew uncovered a Jewish plot to kill Paul. This plot involved at least forty men and the Sanhedrin. Lysias, the tribune, was informed of the plot.

PAUL IS HUSTLED TO CAESAREA (23:23–35)

Determined not to lose his Roman-citizen prisoner at the hands of an assassination team, the tribune immediately called for two of his centurions. He ordered them to muster a large force of men to escort Paul out of the city under the cover of darkness. About nine o'clock at night Paul and his large escort set out for the seacoast town of Caesarea.

Because of Paul's rank as a citizen and his reputation as a religious leader, Felix gave comfortable quarters within the palace, assuring him that the case would be heard as soon as possible.

Section Summary

Lysias, the tribune, had Paul escorted out of the city of Jerusalem under the cover of darkness. Paul was delivered to Felix, the governor in Caesarea, for trial.

QUESTIONS TO GUIDE YOUR STUDY

1. What was the significance of Paul's remark that Ananias the high priest was a "whitewashed wall"?
2. How does the story of the plot to ambush Paul show that God was in control of the events of Paul's life? To this point in Acts, how often did God use Roman officials to help or rescue Paul?
3. What kind of administrator was the Roman governor, Felix? How did he handle Paul's case?

HISTORICAL BACKGROUND

Felix the Procurator

Antonius Felix was the procurator of Judea when Paul the apostle visited Jerusalem for the last time and was arrested there. He remained in office until AD 60, when the emperor Nero recalled him. He was accused of poor administration. Felix is depicted as a man who listened with interest to Paul's defense, but he failed to make any decision with regard to the case or to the personal implications of Paul's message. Rather, he hoped Paul would pay him a bribe. Contemporary historians paint Felix as a brutal, incompetent politician who was finally replaced.

ACTS 24

Structurally, Acts 24–26 is built around the three major political figures before whom Paul appeared—the procurators Felix and Festus and the Jewish King Agrippa II. In between comes the pivotal event of Paul's appeal to Caesar.

THE TRIAL IN CAESAREA (24:1–23)

The Charges (vv. 1–9)

With due ceremony, the high priest and some of his colleagues, accompanied by a professional prosecutor named Tertullus, arrived five days later. After attempting to ingratiate himself with the governor, Tertullus leveled three charges at Paul.

Members of the Sanhedrin all concurred in these charges.

Paul's Rebuttal (vv. 10–21)

HISTORICAL BACKGROUND

Three Charges Against Paul

1. Paul was a pest in the empire who stirred up trouble everywhere.
2. He was a leader in the dangerous Nazarene sect.
3. He was a desecrater of the temple in Jerusalem.

Paul then answered the charges against him. In his rebuttal he insisted he had not profaned the temple. Rather, he was quietly going through a process of purification when Jews from Asia Minor falsely accused him of defiling the temple. In fact, his behavior in Jerusalem was an example of true Jewish piety.

Paul did not deny, however, his involvement in the work of Christ. To the contrary, he gave a spirited testimony of the Way that grew out of the Jewish religion. He insisted that he did not repudiate his commitment to the religion of his forebears when he took up the cause of Christ.

Felix's Indecision (vv. 22–23)

Felix quickly perceived that Paul did nothing wrong, certainly nothing worthy of Roman punishment. But he knew that if he summarily acquitted Paul, the Jewish leaders would stir up a riot and possibly murder Paul in the process. Under the guise of waiting to talk with the tribune, Lysias, Felix postponed a decision, thanked the Jewish rulers for their time, and ordered Paul placed under a rather loose house arrest.

Section Summary

Paul's trial before Felix ended on an uncertain note. Felix kept Paul in prison until the end of his term of office.

PAUL AND FELIX IN PRIVATE (24:24–27)

This concluding portion of Luke's treatment of Felix provides a glimpse into the procurator's personal life.

Why did Felix persist in calling in Paul for private conversations with him and his Jewish wife Drusilla? Obviously, Paul made both uncomfortable as he talked about justice, self-control, and future judgment. Still, they invited him on several occasions. It is true that Felix hoped for a bribe, but there must have been something in Paul's message that both attracted and repelled the regal couple.

Section Summary

Although Felix and his wife met privately with Paul on several occasions, they never fully believed his message of the gospel.

QUESTIONS TO GUIDE YOUR STUDY

1. Tertullus the Jewish prosecutor leveled what three charges at Paul?
2. After hearing the charges brought against Paul, what decision did Felix render on the case?
3. Why do you think Felix was persistent in calling in Paul for private conversations with him and his Jewish wife Drusilla?

ACTS 25

FESTUS PRESSURED BY THE JEWS (25:1–5)

As a direct result of Jewish unrest, Felix was recalled to Rome and replaced by Porcius Festus. No sooner had he come to town than the Sanhedrin rulers began to apply pressure on the governor to let Paul come to Jerusalem for trial. These wily elders sought to take advantage of the inexperienced governor.

Perhaps Felix briefed Festus on the Paul issue, or Festus may simply have refused to be stampeded into any action he would later regret. Instead, he invited a representative group to accompany him back to Caesarea, where together they would confront Paul and attempt disposition of the case.

HISTORICAL BACKGROUND

Festus

Assumed his office at Nero's appointment in AD 60. He held the office until his death in 62.

Section Summary

Recalled to Rome after an unsuccessful stint as procurator, Felix was replaced by Porcius Festus. Immediately the Sanhedrin rulers began pressuring Festus to bring Paul to Jerusalem for trial. Instead, Festus invited the officials to return with him to Caesarea.

PAUL'S APPEAL TO CAESAR (25:6–12)

The entire case had to be reopened to brief the new governor. Once again, the spokesman for the Sanhedrin hurled his empty charges at Paul while offering no proof for their validity. Paul calmly refuted every accusation.

Then the new governor gave the situation an unexpected (and providential) turn. Attempting to gain favor with the Jews, Festus asked Paul if he would be willing to go to Jerusalem for a full trial before the Sanhedrin. Paul knew he would have a better chance in a den of hungry lions than in Jerusalem.

Paul's response: "I appeal to Caesar!"

HISTORICAL BACKGROUND

This appeal was the right of every Roman citizen, although by no means did every citizen in trouble with local law get the privilege of journeying to Rome for a hearing.

With Paul's appeal, Festus was suddenly off the hook.

"You have appealed to Caesar; to Caesar you will go," declared Festus.

Section Summary

Realizing he would receive fairer treatment before the emperor in Rome than before the Sanhedrin in Jerusalem, Paul exercised his right as a Roman citizen and appealed to Caesar. Happy to be rid of Paul, Festus granted Paul's appeal.

FESTUS'S CONVERSATION WITH AGRIPPA (25:13–22)

Within days of Paul's appeal, Festus received a visit from the Jewish King Agrippa II and his sister Bernice. Likely this was an official visit to establish relationships with the new procurator upon his assumption of office. As king of the Jews, Festus felt that King Agrippa was in a unique position to assist him in the matter of Paul's appeal.

He told Agrippa that the Jews raised none of the charges he "was expecting." This most likely meant that the Jews were not able to charge Paul with treason or any crime under Roman law. Festus concluded his account by informing Agrippa of Paul's appeal. He was now holding Paul until he could arrange his transmittal to Caesar. In courteous language, Agrippa replied he would like to hear Paul himself. Festus granted his request.

HISTORICAL BACKGROUND

Agrippa II

Son of Agrippa I and brother of Drusilla and Bernice. With Agrippa II's death the Herodian dynasty came to an end in title as well as in fact.

Section Summary

Festus felt that King Agrippa could assist him in the matter of Paul's appeal. He needed to formulate an official report of the charges against Paul to be sent with the appeal.

PAUL BEFORE AGRIPPA: THE SETTING (25:23–27)

Festus set forth the immediate agenda, which was something definite he could place in his report to the emperor. He himself was at a loss for any specific charges they could level against Paul. He considered sending a prisoner to Rome without charges "unreasonable." He asked for Agrippa's assistance because the king was more familiar with Jewish matters.

WORD PICTURE

Unreasonable

The Greek word literally means "senseless." The charges against Paul were completely without foundation.

Section Summary

The importance of Paul's coming address is underlined by all the pageantry of the notables parading into the audience chamber. Because there were no specific charges against Paul, he called on King Agrippa for assistance. As it turned out, Festus was not a sterling example of Roman justice.

QUESTIONS TO GUIDE YOUR STUDY

1. How did the new governor, Festus, attempt to handle Paul's case?
2. What conclusions did Festus and Agrippa come to as a result of their conversation?
3. Why did Festus request Agrippa's assistance?

ACTS 26

Paul's speech before Agrippa is the culmination of Paul's defense in chapters 21–26. It brings together in final form all the themes of the previous five chapters.

PAUL'S ADDRESS BEFORE AGRIPPA (26:1–23)

This speech before Agrippa is strikingly parallel to Paul's speech before the temple mob. On both occasions Paul gave a testimony of his personal experience in Christ: (1) his Jewish upbringing, (2) his persecution of the Jews, (3) his conversion, and (4) his commission from the risen Lord.

With great ceremony and pageantry, the lords and ladies of the city gathered in the courtroom with Festus, King Agrippa and his sister Bernice, and certain Jewish leaders to hear Paul's defense. When Festus had done his sonorous intoning, Agrippa gave Paul permission to speak.

Once again Paul retold his conversion experience on the Damascus Road. Notice that each time Paul tells the story (or Luke records the telling) different shades of the narrative appear, but always there is the consistent theme: his determination to harass Christians, the great light, the voice, the blindness, and the total redirection of Paul's life.

Paul closed by saying that he had been obedient to his vision of Christ. He closed by testifying that his life had been a witness for Christ.

HISTORICAL BACKGROUND

Paul declared he was glad for the opportunity to state his case before the knowledgeable king. Although always pro-Roman, Agrippa had a Jewish background that probably gave him some acquaintance with Jewish religious and political maneuverings. Thus, he could listen with some appreciation to Paul's defense.

Section Summary

Paul once again appeared before a Roman official—this time King Agrippa. Again he emphasized his innocence of any breach of Roman law. Each of his trials brought him a step closer to Rome, and with each step he presented his testimony of Jesus.

PAUL'S APPEAL TO AGRIPPA (26:24–29)

Paul's talk about the Jewish Scripture and his references to the resurrection became too much for the Roman procurator. Festus interrupted Paul's address with, "You're out of your mind, Paul! Too much study is driving you mad." Although showing a popular prejudice often directed toward scholars, Festus did show genuine respect for Paul's learning.

Respectfully, Paul asserted he was in possession of his faculties. Then he directed an appeal to the king: "King Agrippa, do you believe the prophets? I know you believe." In effect, Paul was saying, "King, you know what I am talking about; you are alert. These marvelous events have not taken place in a tiny corner. The gospel is exploding all over the empire, especially in your kingdom." Suddenly the king was the defendant!

Agrippa protested with alarm. "Are you going to persuade me to become a Christian so easily? ?"

In a final burst of testimony, Paul declared, "I wish before God . . . that whether easily or with difficulty, not only you but all who listen to me today might become as I am—except for these chains." As a follower of Jesus Christ, Paul considered himself a free man despite the chains he was wearing.

WORD PICTURE

In a Corner

What had taken place was not done in secret, as was sometimes charged, but was done in the open, a matter of public knowledge.

PAUL'S INNOCENCE DECLARED BY GOVERNOR AND KING (26:30–32)

All this was too much for the royal inquisitors. Quickly the king and his sister, along with the governor, swept out of the courtroom. Safely in the governor's chambers, the king and Festus agreed there was no legitimate charge against Paul. If he had not appealed to Caesar, he could have been freed. But history's question to them is, in the face of Jewish opposition, *would* they have freed Paul?

Section Summary

After speaking to Paul, even Agrippa declared his innocence. In all, three times Paul appeared before Roman officials; each time no official verdict was rendered. Paul was about to realize his desire to preach the gospel in Rome.

QUESTIONS TO GUIDE YOUR STUDY

1. What did Paul's defense sermons emphasize?
2. Describe Paul's appeal to King Agrippa. What can we make of Agrippa's response?
3. What did the governor and the king declare about Paul's guilt or innocence?

ACTS 27

Most of the concluding two chapters of Acts is devoted to an extensive narrative of Paul's journey by sea from Caesarea to Rome to appear before Caesar. The account has much in common with ancient sea narratives and has provoked a lively discussion among scholars. The route followed, the landmarks passed, and the time lapsed are all given considerable detail. Likewise, there is a heavy use of technical seafaring terminology, and the account is considered a valuable source for ancient sailing techniques by scholars of the history of navigation.

The extensive travel narrative is one long, continuous story, and any division is somewhat arbitrary. The structure, however, does seem to involve an interplay with scenes that focus on Paul.

PAUL'S JOURNEY TO FAIR HAVENS (27:1–8)

As soon as Festus agreed to Paul's appeal to Caesar, arrangements were made for Paul and some other prisoners to be transported to Rome under the supervision of a centurion of the select Augustan Cohort. Luke accompanied Paul on this voyage. From the seaport of Caesarea, the band of prisoners, their guards, and other passengers took passage on a coastal ship that would put in at the small harbors along the way. The centurion's aim was to sail on this smaller vessel until he could arrange booking on a trans-Mediterranean ship.

After several weeks of slow travel, the desired passage was secured, and the centurion and his group boarded what was probably a large grain ship headed for Rome. The sailing season was getting shorter. The most advantageous time for sailing was late spring and summer. Indications are that it was early fall, which always brought uncertain winds making for slow, erratic sailing. In a harbor of Crete called Fair Havens, a shipboard conference was held with the centurion, the shipowner-captain, and Paul attending. Should they put in here for the winter or attempt to reach a more desirable harbor? Paul, from his years of experience as a traveler, urged them to stop where they were. The centurion and captain, however, wanted to push on to a safer harbor. Paul predicted that the voyage would be dangerous to both ship and life, but his warning was not heeded.

HISTORICAL BACKGROUND

Paul's Journey to Rome

Note the appearance again of the "we" sections of Acts. Luke, the author of Acts, joined Paul for this trip to Rome and remained with him until Paul was delivered into the custody of soldiers in Rome (28:16). The journey to Rome involved typical navigational practices and patterns of the first century. Due to dangerous weather conditions, no sailing occurred in the Mediterranean Sea during the period from mid-November to early March. Paul's voyage was near the beginning of this dangerous period, and the trip to Rome was interrupted by the advent of a sudden storm known as the "Euraquilo," a term for the northwest wind. The gale blew the ship for two weeks before it struck a reef at the island of Malta and broke apart.

Section Summary

Paul and some other prisoners were to be transported to Rome under the supervision of a centurion of the select Augustan Cohort. In a harbor of Crete called Fair Havens, the centurion in charge and the vessel's sailing professionals decided to push on to a safer harbor in spite of Paul's prediction that the voyage would be dangerous.

THE DECISION TO SAIL ON (27:9–12)

Although the decision to sail was made, Paul and his party still had to wait for a favorable wind, that was not long in coming. No doubt with lumps in their throats, the crew headed the ship for the open sea. For a short time, all went well, but suddenly a devastating northeastern wind came roaring upon them without warning. Since it was impossible to sail into the wind, the captain was forced to let the ship scud before the gale. After days of this kind of maddening sailing, they managed to put into a harbor of sorts at Clauda where they lashed the ship with cables to strengthen the hull. Back into the sea they were driven by the winds, but the storm did not abate. The ship's cargo and gear were gradually thrown overboard in an effort to make the ship more stable in the tossing sea. After days in the storm, the crew and passengers began to despair of coming through alive.

HISTORICAL BACKGROUND

Undergirders

Ancient ships had as part of their ordinary gear undergirders, which were simply ropes for passing round the hull of a ship. This practice helped prevent leaking when the ship was tossed in a storm.

Section Summary

The ship encountered a northeastern wind that made sailing nearly impossible. Despite the crew's efforts, the ship lost time, the conditions worsened, and sailing became more dangerous. Those aboard began to fear for their lives.

PAUL'S WORD OF ASSURANCE (27:21–26)

During all these days and nights no one had eaten anything. Who could even think of food while they fought every minute just to stay alive? Then one morning, Paul stood up, clung to a mast or a line, and declared: "You men should have followed my advice not to sail from Crete. . . . Now I urge you to take courage, because there will be no loss of any of your lives, but only of the ship." Paul told them that he had a dream the previous night and was assured that even though the ship and cargo were in danger, there would be no loss of life.

HISTORICAL BACKGROUND

"Anchors were used as brakes and were normally cast from the bow. Here they are cast from the stern, as was occasionally done if the events would otherwise blow the ship around."

Craig S. Keener, *The IVP Bible Background Commentary* (Downers Grove: InterVarsity Press, 1993), 403.

THE PROSPECT OF LANDING (27:27–32)

On the fourteenth night of this incredible journey, the sailors sensed they were nearing land. Soundings proved them right. They were drifting toward some unknown island. To slow down the drift, they put out stern anchors. Under the pretense of laying out anchors, some of the ship's crew tried to get into the lifeboat, but Paul warned the centurion, "Unless these men stay in the ship, you cannot be saved." The soldiers promptly cut the rope that tethered the small dinghy to the ship. They were now literally "all in the same boat."

PAUL'S' FURTHER ENCOURAGEMENT (27:33–38)

At the height of the storm, when spirits were at their lowest ebb, Paul spoke words of reassurance. With the thwarted attempt of the sailors, a ship badly battered by the storm, and no assurance they could get it safely to shore, Paul again rose to encourage the shaky voyagers.

It was just before the break of day, and daylight would bring the rescue attempt. He urged everyone to eat some food, as they would need all the physical stamina they could muster just to survive. He reassured all aboard that none of them would "lose a hair" from their heads. He then gave thanks before they ate.

Section Summary

Paul further reassured the ship's crew and passengers that they would survive their ordeal at sea.

THE DELIVERANCE OF ALL (27:39–44)

Final preparations for beaching the ship were made, only to have their plans dashed when it ran aground at her bow, leaving the stern exposed to the battering of the waves. The ship began to break up.

On instinct, the guards drew their swords to kill the prisoners lest they escape, but the centurion stopped them and allowed all the people, prisoners included, to get to shore the best way they could. By clinging to floating debris or swimming valiantly, everyone made it to safety, fulfilling Paul's prediction.

Section Summary

Paul's presence was in no sense responsible for the storm. If his advice was followed, the ship would never have encountered the storm in the first place. On the contrary, Paul's presence was responsible for their deliverance from the storm. His God was with him, and because he was with the apostle, all were saved.

QUESTIONS TO GUIDE YOUR STUDY

1. Discuss the "we" sections that have appeared throughout Acts. What might Luke have tried to convey with these sections?
2. From their experience sailing with Paul during the voyage to Rome, what might the ship's crew and passengers have learned?
3. In the midst of a storm that lasted for days, Paul remained an encouragement to those around him. How might we apply this attitude to the "storms" we face in our own lives?

ACTS 28

WINTERING IN MALTA (28:1–10)

In the dawn's early light, natives on the island looked out to the tossing sea and were surprised to see the ship breaking up with its frightened crew jumping overboard, swimming, clinging to planks, struggling toward land. By the time the shivering, bedraggled men stumbled to the beach, a big fire was blazing. They hovered around it, shaking from fear and cold. The island was Malta, off the southern coast of Italy. Luke remembered with deep appreciation the hospitality of the residents of that place.

HISTORICAL BACKGROUND

"St. Paul's Bay, in Malta with its little island creek and two seas meeting, fulfills all the conditions of Luke's narrative."

A. T. Robertson, *Epochs in the Life of Paul, 263.*

Paul's Deliverance from the Viper (vv. 1–6)

To keep the fire going, and probably to get his own circulation moving, Paul stirred around the beach, gathering wood to toss on the fire. Evidently, he picked up a snake, a viper, in some brush, and the fire jarred the snake into activity. To the horror of all bystanders (and probably Paul), the poisonous snake suddenly struck Paul's hand. The natives concluded that Paul was a murderer who was being punished by the gods for his evil deeds. But to their amazement Paul suffered no ill effects. After shaking the snake into the fire, he went about seeing to the ship's company. The natives' fear quickly turned to awe as the supposed criminal turned out to be a "god."

WORD PICTURE

Viper

Luke used a word for snake that is the term for "viper." The viper is a poisonous snake, but it has been pointed out that there are no poisonous snakes on Malta today. The poisonous snake in this passage has provoked much discussion among scholars. The current situation on the island would have little to say about conditions there in the first century. Obviously, the inhabitants of Malta recognized the viper as poisonous; otherwise they wouldn't have reacted as they did.

The Hospitality of Publius (vv. 7–10)

The governor of the island, a man named Publius, invited Paul, the ship's captain, the centurion, and others among the group to his home. There he entertained them for three days. During the visit, Paul was able to heal Publius's father of fever and dysentery as well as help many others on the island. After three months, the weather grew dependable enough for the group to continue their journey to Rome. Before they left, however, the people of Malta, out of gratitude for their healing and preaching, showered Paul, Luke, and the others with gifts for their voyage.

Section Summary

After shipwrecking on Malta, Paul and his group spent the next three months with the people of that island. Paul was able to minister to them by healing the governor's father and others.

ROME AT LAST! (28:11–16)

In early February, passage was booked on a grain ship that had wintered in Malta. They sailed first to the port of Syracuse on the island of Sicily, then on to Rhegium in Italy, and finally to Puteoli in the Bay of Naples.

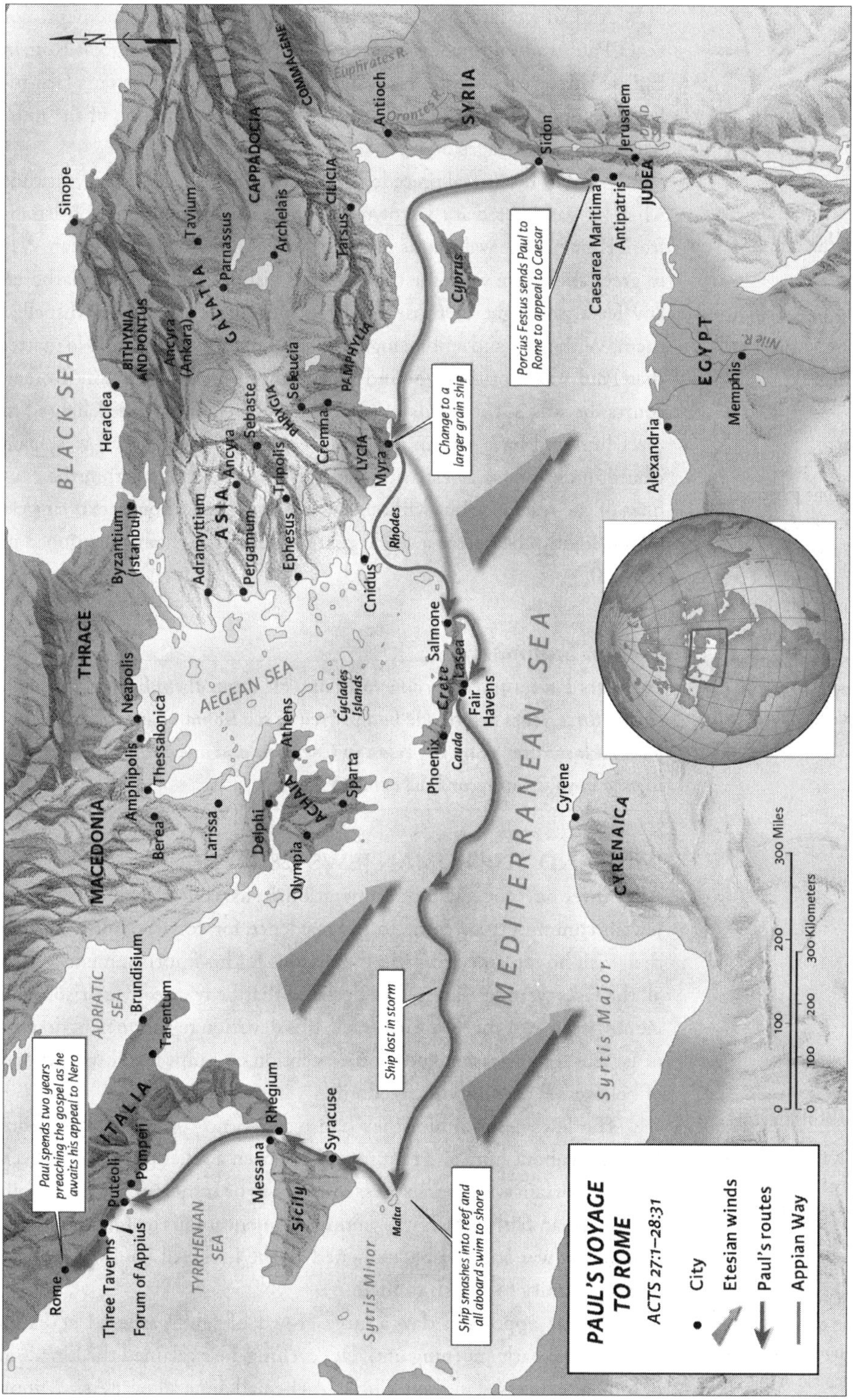

Paul's Journey to Rome

"And so we came to Rome" (v. 14)! What an understatement! For years Paul wanted to come to Rome. He wrote them his great Roman Epistle three years before. He prayed to see Roman Christians face-to-face. At long last, after years in prison in Caesarea and one of the most harrowing sea voyages on record, he came to Rome.

Word of his arrival preceded Paul. Imagine his delight and gratitude when he was greeted at two towns along the way by groups of Christians from Rome, some walking as much as forty miles down the Appian Way to greet and make welcome their famous visitor. If the apostle harbored any fears, the sight of those brethren must have completely dispelled them. With tears and embracing, Paul and Luke greeted them. No matter that Paul was a prisoner bound for an uncertain future before Roman courts; he was in the hands of God, and the believers were delighted to meet him and have him in their midst. Once in Rome, Paul was again placed under house arrest with freedom to move about within the confines of the residence but without the liberty to leave. Some texts suggest he was lightly chained to a single guard—hence the chains mentioned in verse 20.

HISTORICAL BACKGROUND

Puteoli

Puteoli, from its trade with Alexandria and the East must have had a colony of Jews who were related to the Jews in Rome. Also, they had a Christian community.

For some reason, the centurion allowed Paul (probably with a guard) to remain in Puteoli for seven days, during which he and the Christian community there became fast friends and enjoyed a time of mutual deepening of faith.

Section Summary

For years Paul wanted to come to Rome. He wrote them his great Roman epistle three years before. He had prayed to see Roman Christians face-to-face. At last, after years in prison in Caesarea and one of the most harrowing sea voyages on record, he came to Rome.

PAUL AND THE ROMAN JEWS (28:17–29)

After three days for rest and recuperation, he asked leaders of the Roman Jewish community to come to his residence for conversations. During their visit he explained to them the reasons for his imprisonment. When all the facts were considered, he declared that he was really a prisoner in Rome because of the "hope of Israel." His devotion to the ancient dreams of Israel—of a Messiah and God's intention of a universal brotherhood of believers—cost him his freedom.

The Jews assured him they had received no communication from Jerusalem about him, and that must have been a relief to Paul. But even more important was their expressed desire to hear more from Paul about the Christian faith, which was gaining momentum in the Gentile world, although it was still terribly maligned by the Jews. All Paul wanted was an opportunity to preach to them.

NEW TESTAMENT REFERENCE

"And now I stand on trial because of the hope in what God promised to our ancestors, the promise our twelve tribes hope to reach as they earnestly serve him night and day. King Agrippa, I am being accused by the Jews because of this hope." (Acts 26:6–7)

On the appointed day, a large crowd of Jews gathered at Paul's house. From early morning until late evening, he explained the kingdom of God as expressed in Jesus Christ. As he had done all over Asia Minor, he attempted to convince them that Christianity was not a competitor with but a fulfillment of Judaism. The response was typical—some believed, and some did not. Apparently to set the record straight, the apostle told the crowd that he was not surprised at the mixed response because the prophet Isaiah long ago had foretold that many of those to whom the Messiah would be sent would reject him. But that would not be the end of the matter. God's salvation had been sent also to the Gentiles, and they would listen.

AN EPILOGUE WITHOUT A CONCLUSION (28:30–31)

For two years, at his own expense, Paul lived and preached in Rome, welcoming all who came to him. Acts comes to a rather abrupt ending. We ache to have a definitive answer about what happened to Paul after the two years. Was he executed? Was he freed? Did he make the trip to Spain that he had envisioned? We do not know. Whatever may have been the outcome of Paul's Roman imprisonment, Luke seems to have deliberately chosen to end the story in this abrupt way.

But of this we are sure: Paul preached the unsearchable riches of Jesus Christ openly and unhindered. During those years he wrote his famous Prison Epistles, always concerned for persons and churches that were trying to live out the meaning of their faith in Christ. The content of Paul's message forms the conclusion to the book of Acts. He preached "the kingdom of God" and taught about "the Lord Jesus Christ." The two belong together: The good news of the kingdom is the good news about Christ.

The book of Acts ends as though there would be a sequel, and that has always been the spirit of the church and the gospel. Thanks be unto God—the story has no end but moves on "without hindrance."

OLD TESTAMENT REFERENCE

"And he replied: Go! Say to these people: Keep listening, but do not understand; keep looking, but do not perceive. Make the minds of these people dull; deafen their ears and blind their eyes; otherwise they might see with their eyes and hear with their ears, understand with their minds, turn back, and be healed." (Isa 6:9–10)

Section Summary

For two years, at his own expense, Paul lived and preached in Rome, welcoming all who wanted to come to him. Then Acts comes to a rather abrupt ending. We do not know the outcome of Paul's Roman imprisonment. We do know that he preached the message of Jesus Christ openly and unhindered, and during those years he wrote his famous Prison Epistles.

QUESTIONS TO GUIDE YOUR STUDY

1. What did Paul accomplish in his three months on the island of Malta?
2. The Maltese people were lavish in their hospitality toward Paul and the others. Compare the reception from these pagan people with receptions he received from the many Jewish communities he visited.
3. What do we know about Paul's time in Rome? What do you think happened to Paul?

PAUL'S MISSIONARY JOURNEYS HARMONIZED WITH THE PAULINE EPISTLES

DATE	BOOK	EVENT
AD 29	Acts	Death and resurrection of Christ
AD 32	Acts	Conversion of Paul, followed by three-year period of preaching in Damascus and Arabia. Escaped a Jewish death plot in Damascus by being lowered over wall in city.
AD 32	Acts	Barnabas introduced Paul to Jerusalem church.
AD 32	Acts	Paul returned to Tarsus.
AD 32	Acts	Barnabas brought Paul to Syrian Antioch. Both took famine relief to Jerusalem.
AD 47		**I. FIRST MISSIONARY JOURNEY**
AD 47	Acts	Syrian Antioch Cyprus—Blinding of Elymas and conversion of proconsul Sergius Paulus
AD 47	Acts	Perga—Departure of John Mark Pisidian Antioch—Paul turned to Gentiles after preaching in synagogue.
AD 47	Acts	Iconium—Driven from the city after preaching in synagogue
AD 47	Acts	Lystra—After Paul healed a cripple, crowd tried to worship Barnabas and Paul as Zeus and Hermes. Paul was stoned.
AD 47	Acts	Derbe Lystra Iconium Pisidian Antioch Perga Attalia Syrian Antioch
AD 49	Galatians (under south Galatia theory)	Jerusalem council (Acts 15)
AD 50–52		**II. SECOND MISSIONARY JOURNEY**
AD 50–52	Galatians (under south Galatia theory)	Antioch in Syria Derbe Lystra—Paul took Timothy (Acts 16:1).
AD 50–52	Galatians (under south Galatia theory)	Iconium

PAUL'S MISSIONARY JOURNEYS HARMONIZED WITH THE PAULINE EPISTLES

DATE	BOOK	EVENT
AD 50–52		Pisidian Antioch Troas—Paul received Macedonian vision. Philippi—Conversion of Lydia and exorcism of demon-possessed girl.
AD 50–52	Galatians (under south Galatia theory)	Jailing of Paul and Silas. Earthquake at midnight. Conversion of jailer.
AD 50–52	Galatians (under south Galatia theory)	Thessalonica—Paul driven from city by mob attack on Jason's house.
AD 50–52	Galatians (under south Galatia theory)	Berea—Jews listened to Paul's message and searched Old Testament to verify it.
AD 50–52	Galatians (under south Galatia theory)	Athens—Paul preached sermon on Hill of Ares (Mar's Hill).
AD 50–52	1 and 2 Thessalonians	Corinth—Paul involved in tentmaking with Priscilla and Aquila.
AD 50–52	1 and 2 Thessalonians	Conversion of Crispus, the synagogue ruler
AD 50–52	1 and 2 Thessalonians	Paul remained one-and-a-half years in Corinth after the Roman governor Gallio refused to condemn his preaching.
AD 50–52	1 and 2 Thessalonians	Cenchrea—Paul took a Nazarite vow by shaving his head.
AD 50–52	1 and 2 Thessalonians	Ephesus—Left Priscilla and Aquila behind here.
AD 50–52	1 and 2 Thessalonians	Caesarea Jerusalem Syrian Antioch
AD 53–57		**III. THIRD MISSIONARY JOURNEY**
AD 53–57	1 and 2 Thessalonians	Syrian Antioch Galatia and Phrygia(Derbe, Lystra, Iconium, Pisidian Antioch)
AD 53–57	1 Corinthians	Ephesus—Preaching in school of Tyrannus. Converts renounced the occult by burning magical books. Demetrius led riot of silversmiths on behalf of goddess Artemis (Diana). Paul ministered for three years (20:31).
AD 53–57	2 Corinthians	Macedonia (Philippi,Thessalonica)
AD 53–57	Romans	Greece (Athens and Corinth)—Jews plotted to kill Paul on voyage to Palestine.

PAUL'S MISSIONARY JOURNEYS HARMONIZED WITH THE PAULINE EPISTLES

DATE	BOOK	EVENT
AD 53–57	Romans	Macedonia Troas—Healing of Eutychus after a fall from window during Paul's sermon
AD 53–57	Romans	Miletus—Farewell to Ephesian elders
AD 53–57	Romans	Tyre—Paul warned to avoid Jerusalem.
AD 53–57	Romans	Caesarea—Agabus warned Paul of suffering in Jerusalem.
AD 53–57	Romans	Jerusalem—Jews rioted against Paul in temple. He was rescued and arrested by Roman soldiers. Defended himself before Sanhedrin. Sent to Felix in Caesarea.
AD 53–57	Romans	Caesarea—Paul defended himself before Felix, Festus, and Agrippa. He appealed to trial in Rome.
AD 53–57		**IV. JOURNEY TO ROME**
AD 53–57	Romans	Crete—Paul advised sailors not to sail on to Mediterranean. Storm hit ship in which Paul was traveling.
AD 53–57	Romans	Malta—Paul's shipwrecked. Paul and companions remained here during winter.
AD 61	Philemon, Colossians, Ephesians, Philippians	Rome—Paul is housed in a rented home. Preached to Jews and Gentiles. Waited two years for trial before Nero.
AD 63	1 Timothy, Titus	Release from prison. Ministry in the east.
AD 67	2 Timothy	Reimprisonment
AD 67	2 Timothy	Martyrdom

* Taken from Thomas D. Lea, *The New Testament: Its Background and Message* (B&H), 304–8.

Romans

INTRODUCTION

By every measurement, Paul's letter to the church at Rome is one of the most important ever written. Indeed, from a Christian viewpoint, many would classify it as the greatest letter of all time.

Several considerations support this lofty estimate. For one, Romans has as author one of the most committed of all men, the apostle Paul. No one in the early churches or since has exceeded him in love for Jesus Christ, the Son of God. Furthermore, its message is the grandest of all themes—the grace of God. No New Testament writer experienced that grace more dramatically or proclaimed it more faithfully than Paul.

No wonder, then, that throughout Christian history Romans has played an important role in times of great spiritual renewal. Again and again, God has spoken to men and women at the level of their deepest need through its message.

"ROMANS IN A NUTSHELL"

Purpose:	To express the nature of the gospel, its relation to the Old Testament and Jewish law, and its transforming power
Major Doctrine:	Salvation
Key Passage:	Romans 3:21–26
Other Key Doctrines:	God, humanity, and the church
Influence of the Letter:	Martin Luther (1515), through preparing lectures on Romans, felt himself "to be reborn" after reading this letter

AUTHOR

As was the common practice in ancient letter writing, Romans opens with a statement identifying the author. The letter says it was written by "Paul, a servant of Christ Jesus, called as an apostle and set apart for the gospel of God" (1:1). It is rarely questioned today that the Paul who wrote the epistle to the Romans was the apostle of that name whose conversion to Christ is recorded in Acts 9 and whose missionary activities dominate the latter half of that book.

NEW TESTAMENT REFERENCE

The style and language of Romans is consistent with that of Galatians and 1 and 2 Corinthians, the other unquestioned letters of the apostle.

AUDIENCE

In the opening chapter, Paul indicated he was writing his letter to the believers "in Rome" (1:7). What was the makeup of the congregation at Rome? Were they primarily Jewish or Gentile believers? While some passages suggest that Paul's readers were primarily Jewish, other passages seem to require the conclusion that Paul's readers were primarily Gentile converts.

PURPOSE FOR WRITING

Paul wrote Romans with a threefold purpose:

1. He was seeking support for his projected visit to Spain (15:24, 28).
2. He wanted to explain his theology to the Romans and apply it to practical issues in daily life.
3. He wanted to urge the Romans to a greater unity (14:1–15:13).

DATE OF WRITING

Romans was apparently written between AD 54 and 58. Evidence indicates that Felix became procurator of Judea in AD 59, at which time Paul was in custody in Caesarea (Acts 23:33–27:2). Allowing time for the journey from Corinth to Jerusalem and Paul's subsequent activity before his appearance before Festus, a date somewhere around AD 56 is most likely for the composition of Romans.

MAJOR THEMES IN ROMANS

Natural Revelation. In Rom 1:20, Paul set forth two of God's "invisible attributes" that are clearly seen by all—his "eternal power and divine nature." By this Paul meant that the evidence of creation moves a person persuasively toward the conclusion that the Creator is a powerful being and that this power is not limited. Design calls for intelligence, and intelligence speaks of personality. It is God.

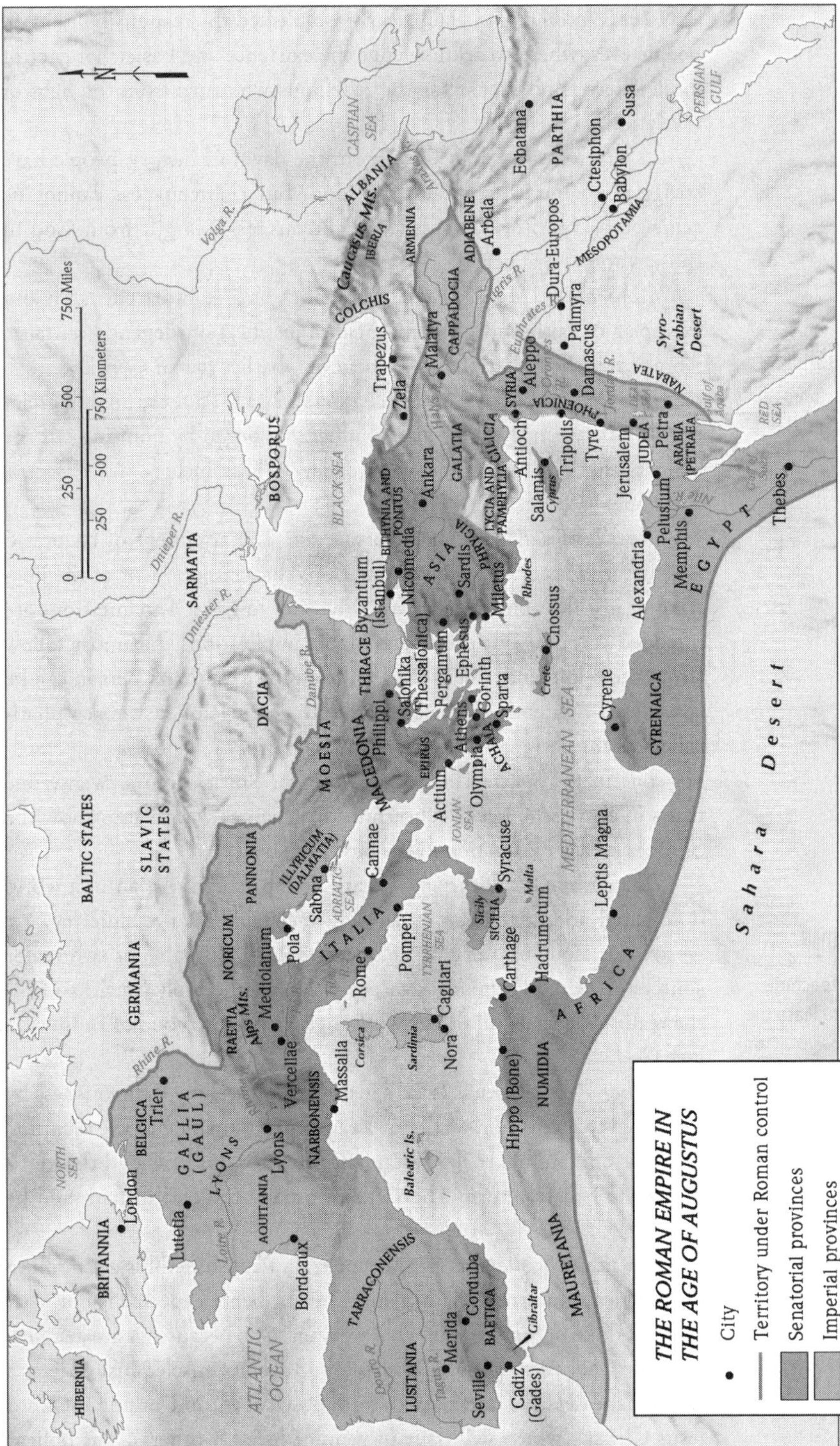

The Roman Empire

The Wrath of God. Paul clearly established the responsibility of all people everywhere to acknowledge the existence and basic character of God. There is no excuse for the rebellious who turn from the light of revelation.

A Righteousness from God. From the dawn of history, people have struggled to merit acceptance by God. But righteousness cannot be achieved by meritorious activity. Righteousness is a gift from God to those who live by faith

Abraham, a Man of Faith. Abraham was a stalwart patriarch and exemplar of faith and obedience. Since justification depends on faith, Abraham is the father of all who believe, whether Jew or Gentile.

OLD TESTAMENT REFERENCE

Genesis 15:6 declares that Abraham "believed the LORD, and it was credited to him as righteousness."

The Benefits of Believing. In chapters 12–15, Paul clarified the relationship between theology and conduct. He began by pointing out the benefits that accrue to those who believe. These include peace, access, and hope.

Does justification by faith promote sin? The argument of chapter 6 is structured around two basic questions that an opponent of the doctrine of justification by faith would be sure to raise. The questions are intended to point out the unacceptable implications that must follow (from the opponent's point of view) from the idea that a person can be considered righteous on the basis of faith alone. Paul answers emphatically, and the detractors' questions fall by the way.

Life in the Spirit. The Greek word for "spirit" occurs twenty-one times in chapter 8. Paul's concern in this chapter was to show how the Spirit is meant to function in the life of the believer.

The Triumph of Believing. Clearly, living as a Christian in a world dominated and controlled by sin will inevitably involve suffering. Yet we are not alone in our trials. Romans 8:26–30 points out two major sources of help: (1) the intercessory prayer of the Holy Spirit; and (2) the realization that " all things work together for the good of those who love God."

PERSONAL APPLICATION

To grasp Paul's teaching on the Spirit is to learn the secret of how to live victoriously while surrounded by sin and impaired by human frailty. It is the single most important lesson the Christian can learn.

What about the Jews? Israel's insistence on seeking righteousness by works led to a rejection of all but a remnant. In turning to the Gentiles, God not only fulfilled Old Testament promises but provided the motivation for Israel's return. They will eventually respond in faith and be saved.

Practical Christianity. With chapter 12, Paul shifted his attention to the practical concerns of daily living. The obedience expected is not what we must do to be justified but what we want to do because we are justified.

The Obligations of Love. In chapter 13 Paul counseled his readers to "discard the deeds of darkness" (a form of self-love) and "put on the Lord Jesus Christ" (which will issue in genuine love for others). The obligations of love will be fulfilled when we identify ourselves with him so that he who is pure love is allowed to express this love in practical ways.

THE LIFE AND MINISTRY OF PAUL

MAJOR EVENTS	BIBLICAL RECORDS		POSSIBLE DATES
	ACTS	GALATIANS	
Birth			AD 1
Conversion	9:1–25	1:11–17	33
First Jerusalem visit	9:26–30	1:18–20	36
Famine	11:25–30	2:1–10?	46
First missionary journey	13:1–14:28		47–48
Apostolic council in Jerusalem	15:1–29	2:1–10?	49
Second mission-ary journey	15:36– 18:21		
Letter to the Galatians			53–55
Third missionary journey	18:23–21:6		53–57
Letters to the Corinthians			55
Arrest and imprisonment in Jerusalem and Caesarea	21:8–26:32		57
Imprisonment in Rome	27:1–28:30		60–62
Letter to the Ephesians			60–62
Death			67

THEOLOGICAL SIGNIFICANCE OF ROMANS

Paul's message to the Romans means the church must proclaim that God is the Giver of salvation—the gift of righteousness—and this gift is for all who will receive it by faith. The church must not call for a faith that can be separated from faithfulness. Assurance must be grounded not in human decision but in the atoning and justifying work of Jesus Christ.

The believer's righteousness in Christ means our acceptance and worth before God cannot be earned but only received. When we feel depressed, discouraged, or defeated, we must remind ourselves that God has reconciled us, accepted us, and given us value and significance in his sight because of the atoning work of Jesus Christ.

When troubled from all sides, we are reminded that God is for us and that nothing can separate us from the love of Christ (8:31–39).

PERSONAL APPLICATION

When divisions occur in the church, we must turn to Paul's exhortation for mutual love, concern, and service for one another. No one has a superior place in Christ's body because of inherent worth, heritage, accomplishments, or background. There is no place for human boasting or claim of special privilege. All nations are invited to come to Christ, in whom there is no condemnation.

THE MESSAGE OF ROMANS FOR TODAY

Romans lays a solid foundation for an understanding of justification by faith. Faith as an absolute reliance on Jesus Christ and his work of redemption are clearly presented. Through his arguments and teaching, Paul reveals much about the character and heart of God. From chapter 12 on, Paul dealt with matters of practical Christianity and how life in the Spirit is to be lived out in our daily experience. Paul shows us where theology and conduct meet to produce the Spirit-filled life.

QUESTIONS TO GUIDE YOUR STUDY

1. What was Paul's purpose in writing his letter to the Roman believers?
2. Who were Paul's readers? What was the makeup of the congregation at Rome?
3. What key doctrines does Paul emphasize in his letter?
4. Given the various themes covered in Romans, what might we learn from a study of this letter?

ROMANS 1

SALUTATION (1:1–7)

When we write a letter, we put the name of the addressee at the beginning and our own at the end. In Paul's day, people did it differently. The writer placed his name first, the identity of his reader next, and attached a greeting. Furthermore, in our letters we are content to state the barest details about ourselves and our readers. The ancient letter writer often expanded the references to himself, his correspondents, and his greetings to enhance his purpose in writing.

Writer (v. 1)

Romans opens with a statement identifying its author. It is rarely questioned today that the Paul who wrote the epistle to the Romans was the apostle of that name whose conversion to Christ is told in Acts 9 and whose missionary activities dominate the latter half of that book.

Paul identified himself in three different ways:

1. *He was a "servant of Christ Jesus."* He belonged without reserve to the one who confronted him on the Damascus Road.

2. *He was "called as an apostle."* God initiated this process. Paul did not choose the role for himself.
3. *He had been "set apart."* He was set apart by God to serve in the interests of the gospel of God.

Paul's Purpose in Writing (vv. 2–6)

To establish his apostolic authority. In verse 1 Paul presented himself as "Paul, a servant of Christ Jesus, called as an apostle and set apart for the gospel of God." What a remarkable self-introduction! Formerly Paul's zeal for the ancestral tradition had brought him honor and advancement within the ranks of Judaism (Gal 1:1–14). But now he described himself as Christ's servant.

To Verify His Apostolic Message. Paul stated that God promised his gospel earlier "through his prophets in the Holy Scriptures." In keeping with other early Christians, Paul saw in the gospel the fulfillment of God's promise in the Old Testament. In verses 3–4 he centered the gospel in Jesus Christ, God's Son. Paul offered two affirmations regarding Jesus:

1. With respect to his fleshly existence or incarnation, he was descended from David.
2. With respect to his present status or exaltation, "Jesus Christ our Lord" was designated "Son of God according to the Spirit of holiness by the resurrection of the dead."

Readers (v. 7a)

Paul addressed his letter to the Christian believers in the city of Rome. Paul described them as "loved" by God and "called" to be saints.

"Grace . . . and Peace" (v. 7b)

The salutation "grace . . . and peace" combined a Christianized form of the Greek and Hebrew greetings. Real peace comes only as a result of the grace of God. *Grace* is what we receive; *peace* is what we experience as a result of the activities of God on our behalf.

HISTORICAL BACKGROUND

The Hellenistic Letter

Generally, Paul's epistles seemed to follow the normal pattern of the Hellenistic letter, the basic form of which consists of five major sections:

1. Opening (sender, addressee, greeting)
2. Thanksgiving or blessing (often with a prayer of intercession, well wishes, or personal greetings)
3. The burden of the letter (including citation of classical sources and arguments)
4. *Parenesis* (ethical instruction, exhortation)
5. Closing (mention of personal plans, mutual friends, benediction)

NEW TESTAMENT REFERENCE

Several New Testament passages bear witness to the Davidic descent of Jesus (Matt 1:1; Luke 1:31–33; Acts 2:29–30; Rev 5:5).

PAUL'S DESIRE TO VISIT ROME (1:8–15)

In keeping with the ancient letter form, Paul continued his opening remarks with expressions of thanksgiving and prayer on his readers' behalf.

The substance of his prayer is contained in verses 10–15. For a long time, Paul desired to visit Rome, but something always intervened to prevent a visit. His reasons for wanting to visit believers in the capital city were twofold: (1) he wanted to share some spiritual blessing that would strengthen them; and (2) he wanted to participate in the gospel harvest in Rome, even as elsewhere among the Gentiles.

Section Summary

Paul longed to see the believers at Rome. Commitment to a common Lord draws the people together. To be servants of the same Master is to be in harmony with one another. Paul's special concern was that he would be able to share with them some spiritual favor that would provide encouragement and strength.

RIGHTEOUSNESS FROM GOD (1:16–17)

These are pivotal verses in the New Testament. They state concisely and with unusual clarity a fundamental tenet of the Christian faith. The heart of verse 16 is that the gospel is the saving power of God.

In his opening remarks, Paul introduced two important features of the gospel and then added a third. We find these features of the gospel described in Romans 1:

1. It is the fulfillment of God's promises (v. 2).
2. It centers in the person of Jesus Christ (vv. 3–4).
3. It is the "power of God for salvation to everyone who believes" (v. 16).

What is the gospel able to accomplish? The gospel is not simply a display of power but the effective operation of God's power that leads to salvation. It has purpose and direction. The salvation Paul spoke of is more than forgiveness of sin. It included the full scope of deliverance from the results of Adam's sin.

OLD TESTAMENT REFERENCE

Paul found his basic concept of justification by faith in Hab 2:4, "The righteous one will live by his faith." The prophet used the term *faith* in the sense of faithfulness or steadfastness. The righteous will be preserved through times of difficulty by their steadfast loyalty to God.

THE POWER OF THE GOSPEL

ASPECT OF SALVATION	ITS WORK IN THE LIFE OF THE BELIEVER	SPHERE OF DELIVERANCE
Justification	Being set right with God	Deliverance from the penalty of sin
Sanctification	Growth in holiness	Deliverance from the power of sin
Glorification	Ultimate transformation into the likeness of Christ	Deliverance from the presence of sin

Section Summary

Verses 16–17 are pivotal verses in the New Testament. They state concisely and with unusual clarity a fundamental tenet of the Christian faith. The gospel is the saving power of God.

THE GENTILES (1:18–32)

God's Revelation Through Wrath (v. 18)

Paul next pointed to the revelation of God's wrath in his judgment on sin (v. 18). Romans 1:19–3:20 provides a commentary on this verse.

The revelation of God's righteousness in the gospel and the revelation of His wrath are parallel and continuous. That is, God's righteousness is always revealed through the preaching of the gospel of salvation. Also, God's wrath is always being revealed through his abandonment of humans to the consequences of their sinful choices (v. 18).

God's Revelation Through Nature (vv. 19–20)

The pagan world had an opportunity to know God through his revelation in nature (v. 20). Not only does this verse affirm God's disclosure of himself in nature, but it also indicates what may be learned about him—his eternal power and deity—and this knowledge was enough knowledge of God to place men under the responsibility of acknowledging him and rendering thanks to him.

We can make three observations about this passage (vv. 19–20):

1. God is the revealer, and nature is the medium of His revelation.
2. God's revelation in nature does not guarantee a positive response.
3. God's revelation of himself in nature establishes the minimal ground of every person's responsibility before him.

The age-old question about the salvation of the "heathen" is clearly answered in verse 20. God's revelation of himself through nature is clear enough to leave all people without excuse for their rebellion against him.

Section Summary

Paul pointed to the revelation of God's wrath in his judgment upon sin and God's disclosure of himself in nature. God's wrath is revealed through his abandonment of people to the consequences of their sinful choices. God's revelation of himself in nature establishes the minimal ground of every person's responsibility before him.

WORD PICTURE

Wrath of God

"Wrath" is from a word that means to "teem, to swell." (A. T. Robertson, *Word Pictures in the New Testament*, vol. 4, 328.) Millard Erickson says: "Anger is not something that God chooses to feel. His disapproval of sin is not an arbitrary matter, for his very nature is one of holiness; it automatically rejects sin. He is . . . 'allergic to sin,' as it were. The second comment is that we must avoid thinking of God's anger as being excessively emotional. It is not as if he is seething with anger, his temper virtually surging out of control. He is capable of exercising patience and long-suffering, and does so." (Millard Erickson, *Christian Theology* [Baker, 1985], 605.)

PAGAN RESPONSE (1:21–23,25)

Rebellion (vv. 21,25,28)

Individuals may respond to God's revelation in two ways: in faith or by rejection. They have the capacity to say yes or no to God. No is the answer of rebellion, whereas faith is the response of trust and commitment. Self-deification lies at the heart of all human rebellion.

PERSONAL APPLICATION

Homosexuality "cannot be understood as an alternative life-style, somehow acceptable to God" but rather is "a sign of one of the forms . . . God's wrath takes when he allows us free reign to continue in our abuse of creation and in our abuse of one another as creatures."

P. Achtemeier, *Romans* (John Knox, 1985), 41.

Arrogance (vv. 21–22)

In rejecting the knowledge of God available in creation, people claim to be wiser than God. When a person refuses to accept God as sovereign, that person is doomed to have less than God as his or her god.

Idolatry (vv. 23,25)

Just as rebellion is an improper attitude toward God, and arrogance is an improper attitude toward self, so idolatry reveals an improper attitude toward creation. A person's refusal to acknowledge God as sovereign Lord makes idolatry inevitable. It leads to a tragic reversal of the primeval order set forth in Gen 1:26.

GOD'S JUDGMENT (1:24–32)

WORD PICTURE

Corrupt

The word *corrupt* is a compound word that combines a negative particle (meaning "not") with the word "approved." It was often applied to metals. (W. E. Vine, "Paul," *Vine's Complete Expository Dictionary* [Thomas Nelson, 1996], 526–27). In this passage it carries the idea of "not standing the test" or "not passing the test." It is often translated "reprobate" or "depraved." A "depraved," "reprobate," or "corrupt" mind is one God cannot approve, and he must reject it.

For Impurity (vv. 24–25)

People are free to receive or reject God's revelation. However, they are not free to do so without consequences. Verse 24 speaks of "the desires of their hearts." Scripture is clear that the human heart is inclined toward evil. Those who rejected God were fools, and their hearts were darkened. Verse 24 tells us that God gave them over in their sinful desires, which is sexual impurity.

For Sexual Perversion (vv. 26–27)

Paul described this sexual impurity as "disgraceful passions . . . for one another." Romans 1:26–27 contains the clearest teaching in the New Testament on homosexuality. This passage makes the following observations about homosexuality.

1. Homosexuality is an abandonment to "disgraceful passions" (v. 26).
2. Homosexuality is "unnatural" (v. 26).
3. Homosexuality involves "shameless acts" (v. 27).
4. Homosexuality is sexual perversion, and it results in a serious breakdown for those involved (v. 27).

For Depraved Reason (vv. 28–32)

For the third time in five verses, Paul wrote that when people disregard God's revelation in nature, he gives them over to the normal consequences that follow. In verse 28 Paul declared that God gives them over to a "corrupt mind."

Turning from the light of revelation prevents a person from thinking correctly about the issues of life. God's will and his ways with humans are crucial factors in understanding the moral world in which we live. Secular education, which rules out the hand of God in history, is seriously flawed because it attempts to understand the whole world without acknowledging its source. This is an omission with enormous consequences.

Paul proceeded to characterize the lifestyle of the God-rejecting Gentiles by listing twenty-one negative qualities (vv. 29–32) of those abandoned to their own sinful natures.

Section Summary

The revelation of God's wrath is as authentic as his revelation of righteousness. People cannot reject God and build a society on a solid foundation. Every utopia ventured by God-rejecting men is doomed to crumble under the sheer weight of its moral corruption. Abandoned by God, every such undertaking is destined to self-destruct.

QUESTIONS TO GUIDE YOUR STUDY

1. In his salutation, how did Paul identify himself?
2. Describe the wrath of God. How does God's wrath differ from human wrath?
3. Describe the various pagan responses to God. What is God's judgment for each?
4. What is the Bible's position regarding homosexuality?
5. What does it mean for a person to have a "corrupt mind"?

ROMANS 2

Chapter 2 begins with "therefore," a term that normally introduces the result of that which immediately precedes. In this case, however, the connection with chapter 1 is not clear. The final section of that chapter established the need for righteousness among Gentiles, but by the time we reach 2:17, it is obvious that Paul is addressing his remarks to Jews.

GOD'S RIGHTEOUS JUDGMENT (2:1–16)

First, the Jews approved of God's judgment upon the pagan world. Unlike the Gentiles described in Rom 1:32, they did not applaud those who practiced pagan vices. Quite the contrary: They condemned them. In doing so, they revealed a knowledge of God, an awareness of sin, and an acknowledgment of his right to judge sin.

Did not the approval of God's judgment upon pagan wrong prove that the Jews were rightly related to God? It should have. But what if those who approved God's judgment upon others were themselves guilty of the same sins? Were they to suppose that they would escape the judgment of God?

Agreement Without Obedience (vv. 1–11)

No! Paul charged that by passing judgment on the Gentiles, the Jews condemned themselves, because they were doing the same things. To expect God to condone in themselves the sins he punishes in others is to invite God's judgment. It is to treat with contempt the great "kindness, restraint, and patience" of God.

Those three terms describe a revelation of God that went beyond the disclosure to the Gentiles through nature of his eternal power and deity (v. 4). They suggest the divine qualities shown through centuries of God's gracious dealings with the Jews.

NEW TESTAMENT REFERENCE

"But be doers of the word and not hearers only, deceiving yourselves. Because if anyone is a hearer of the word and not a doer, he is like someone looking at his own face in a mirror. For he looks at himself, goes away, and immediately forgets what kind of person he was." (Jas 1:22–24)

Judgment with or Without the Law (vv. 12–16)

Could the Jews expect preferential treatment for having the law? Or could the Gentiles plead special consideration for not having it? To be sure, God's revelation through the law provided a great advantage. It made known the will of God more completely, making possible a fuller knowledge of him.

But the greater opportunity for knowing the will of God included a greater responsibility for keeping it. "All who sin without the law will also perish without the law, and all who sin under the law will be judged by the law" (v. 12).

There was a real sense in which the Gentiles had access to the law of God—the inner law of conscience. Through the medium of conscience, God inscribed what the law required on the hearts of the Gentiles. Thus conscience, as well as nature, constituted a medium through which God sought to reveal himself to the pagan world. In this way, God brought all people, Gentiles and Jews, under the law of God.

Section Summary

Through the law of Moses, God revealed himself to the Jews, and through his law written on the heart, he revealed himself to the Gentiles. According to the gospel Paul preached, God would judge the secrets of both Jews and Gentiles by Christ Jesus on the last day (v. 16).

AUTHENTIC JEWISHNESS IS INWARD (2:17–29)

The Advantages of the Jews (vv. 17–20)

Observe the details Paul mentions in his elaboration of the advantages of the Jews and their pride regarding these advantages.

1. *"You call yourself a Jew"* (v. 17). We find the earliest use of the term *Jew* in the Old Testament in 2 Kings 16:6. The Jew was proud to be known as a Jew.
2. *You "rely on the law"* (v. 17). The verb translated "rely on" is used in the sense of finding rest or support in something. Thus, the Jew leaned on or found support in the law.
3. *You "boast in [brag about] God"* (v. 17). No man has a higher privilege than this: to have his or her glory in God. This is the heart of worship.
4. *You "know his will"* (v. 18). The law was regarded as the full revelation of the will of God.
5. *You "approve the things that are superior"* (v. 18). They were able to distinguish between right and wrong because they were instructed in the law.
6. *"You are convinced that you are a guide for the blind, a light to those in darkness" (vv. 19–20).* These terms express a low opinion of the Gentiles. They reveal both the high esteem in which the Jew held himself and the low regard he had for the Gentiles.

The Inconsistencies of the Jews (vv. 21–24)

The charge takes the form of five rhetorical questions and a pronouncement. Observe that in each of the questions Paul charged the Jews with a shocking gap between their profession and their practice. Thus, these verses serve to detail the charge made against the Jews in Rom 2:3:

1. *"You, then, who teach another, don't you teach yourself?* (v. 21). One has to know the truth to teach it. Will one venture to teach to others what he does not apply to himself?
2. *"You who preach, 'You must not steal'—do you steal?"* (v. 21). This is a reference to the eighth commandment.
3. *"You who say, 'You must not commit adultery'—do you commit adultery?"* (v. 22). This refers to the seventh commandment. One

calls to mind here the incident of the woman taken in adultery and brought before Jesus, as recorded in John 7:53–8:11.

4. *"You who detest idols, do you rob temples?"* (v. 22). This refers to those who rob temples, or more generally, to those who commit some irreverent act against a holy place.
5. *"You who boast in the law, do you dishonor God by breaking the law?"* (v. 23). Breaking the law made the Jews' bragging about it an empty gesture. God wanted no praise of his revelation in the law if his people refused to obey the law.

OLD TESTAMENT REFERENCE

There are many forms of robbery. The prophet Amos denounced the greedy merchants who were eager for religious holidays to pass so they could resume their sale of wheat with dishonest balances (Amos 8:5).

Section Summary

The Jews had no better standing in God's sight, even though they received God's special revelation through the law of Moses. Although they knew the will of God expressed in the law, they had not kept the law.

Obedience to the Requirement of Circumcision (vv. 25–29)

A third feature of Jewish lostness that obscured their alienation from God was their faithful observance of the law requiring circumcision.

A real circumcision was not merely external and physical. A person was a Jew only if he was one inwardly. The circumcision that counted was a circumcision of the heart (see Deut 30:6). Real circumcision was the work of the Spirit. It did not come through the mechanical observance of the written code. Authentic circumcision was the cutting away of the old sinful nature.

OLD TESTAMENT REFERENCE

Although this rite was practiced by others in the ancient world, it had special meaning for the Jews. God had commanded Abraham to circumcise every male as a sign of the covenant between Abraham and God (Gen 17:10–17).

Section Summary

One's heritage and adherence to the rituals of the law did not give a Jew a right standing before God. Rather, true Jews were those who had received the regenerating work of the Spirit in their lives.

QUESTIONS TO GUIDE YOUR STUDY

1. What makes God's judgments righteous? What do his judgments tell us about him?
2. What advantages did the Jews enjoy? Why did Paul list them?
3. What were the inconsistencies of the Jews? Why did Paul present these?
4. What is significant about a circumcision of the heart? What does it accomplish that observance of the law cannot?

ROMANS 3

At this point in his letter, Paul stopped to defend his indictment of Jewish lostness against the objections of an imaginary opponent. No doubt he encountered such questions from Jewish hearers during his missionary preaching.

THE FAITHFULNESS OF GOD (3:1–8)

Question 1: What Advantage Does the Jew Have? (vv. 1–12)

What Paul wrote previously about true Jewish identity and real circumcision was shocking to his fellow Jews (2:25–29). No wonder then that Jewish hearers likely asked him many questions. Paul's answer to this question is "considerable in every way." To begin with, Jews were entrusted with "the very words of God." Most likely this was a reference to the whole Old Testament. (Later Paul cited other reasons in Rom 9:1–5.)

Question 2: Does Jewish Unfaithfulness Nullify God's Faithfulness? (vv. 3–4)

In the previous chapter, Paul spoke of those hardened and impenitent Jews who were storing up wrath for themselves (2:5). He described those who were proclaiming the law fervently to the Gentiles but were practicing it in a shoddy manner before them (2:21–24). Obviously, they were being faithless regarding the covenant. Did the unfaithfulness of some Jews nullify or cancel the faithfulness of God?

Paul's response was emphatic: "Absolutely not! Let God be true, even though everyone is a liar." He supported his words with a quote from the last part of Ps 51:4. He referenced this psalm to emphasize God's vindication in judgment.

Question 3: Is God Unrighteous to Inflict His Wrath upon Us? (vv. 5–6)

The imaginary Jewish objector now began to question God's justice. He argued that his wickedness serves God by providing a contrasting background for God's righteousness. What a twisted concept of divine service this represented! Paul again replied emphatically, "Absolutely not!" If that were so, how could God judge the world? The moral governorship of the universe was at stake in such an absurd charge.

Question 4: Does Not My Lie Cause God's Truth to Abound? (vv. 7–8)

Here we see a contrast between the lie of the Jew and the truth of God. The Jew suggested that his lie caused the truth of God to abound to his

WORD PICTURE

Absolutely Not!

This is an emphatic statement, which we find frequently in the New Testament. It expresses a strong negation to a stated proposition or question. Paul used it here in verses 4 and 6. It is comprised of two Greek words, "not" and "to be." To convey their force, these two words have been variously translated as "Let it not happen!" "By no means!" "God forbid!" "Far from it!" "May it never be!"

"Fitzmyer calls this an 'indignant negative' (*Romans*, 327). Murray says that *me genoita* ["not at all!"] indicates 'the recoil of abhorrence' *(Romans*, 1:94, n.1.)"

Robert H. Mounce, *Romans*, New American Commentary 27, 104.

glory. This caused him to wonder why he was still being condemned as a sinner. This question and the previous one amounted to an evangelistic appeal that said, "Let us do what is evil that good may come" (v. 8). Paul retorted, "Their condemnation is deserved!"

God does not need our evil as a *contrast* to his goodness. Rather, he wants our goodness as a *reflection* of his likeness. It praises His glory when God is permitted to create his righteousness in us.

Section Summary

To suggest that God is unfair, as the questions of verses 3,5, and 7 appear to do, is to blaspheme God. Those who question God's judgment are condemned themselves.

PAUL'S CONCLUSION: ALL ARE GUILTY BEFORE GOD (3:9–20)

No Fear of God Before Their Eyes (vv. 9–18)

"Are we any better off?" Paul was once again emphatic: "Not at all!" The Jew was neither better off nor at a disadvantage since it was already established that both Jew and Gentile are under the condemnation of sin (see 1 Kgs 8:46; Gal 3:22).

To support his charge, Paul strung together several Old Testament passages (vv. 10–18): Ps 14:1–3 (vv. 10–12); Pss 5:9; 140:3 (v. 13); 10:7 (v. 14); Isa 59:7–8 (vv. 15–17); and Ps 36:1 (v. 18). Together they lead up to the ultimate condemnation of verse 18: "There is no fear of God before their eyes." This verse stated the disastrous effects listed in verses 10–17, which were so visible in Paul's day and in our own.

This entire section (3:9–20) reflects a courtroom scene, which the following chart attempts to capture.

PAUL'S "COURTROOM SCENE"

PHASE	VERSE	CONTENT
The Accusation	v. 9	"Jews and Greeks are all under sin."
The Evidence	vv. 10–18	"There is no one righteous, not even one. . . . There is no fear of God before their eyes."
The Courtroom Setting	v. 19	"Every mouth may be shut and the whole world may become subject to God's judgment."

PHASE	VERSE	CONTENT
The Verdict	v. 20	"For no one will be justified in his sight by the works of the law, because the knowledge of sin comes through the law."

The Whole World Is Accountable Before God (vv. 19–20)

In bringing his indictment of all men to a close, Paul wrote, "Now we know that whatever the law says, it speaks to those who are subject to the law, so that every mouth may be shut and the whole world may become subject to God's judgment." Those under the law were Jews. Paul focused attention on them that they might understand that they, as well as the Gentiles, were answerable to God. Both are without excuse before him (Rom 1:20; 2:1).

HISTORICAL BACKGROUND

Quoting rather freely from Ps 143:2, Paul added, "No one will be justified in his sight by the works of the law, because the knowledge of sin comes through the law." No human being can be brought into a right standing with God based on doing what the law requires. Why? Because the law makes a person conscious of sin. It reveals that we are unable to live up to the righteous requirements of a holy God.

Section Summary

Once again Paul reiterated the theme that was so difficult for his Jewish audience to understand and accept. No one can be brought into a right standing with God based on doing what the law requires. The purpose of the law is to guide conduct, not to provide a method to stand before God because of one's own righteousness.

GOD'S WAY OF MAKING US RIGHT WITH HIMSELF (3:21–31)

Apart from the Law (v. 21)

As a devout Pharisee, Paul believed he could achieve a right standing with God through keeping the law. Thus, he was zealous for the traditions of the fathers (Gal 1:14). He claimed he was blameless regarding righteousness under the law (Phil 3:6). However, his encounter with the risen Christ on the road to Damascus radically changed all that. No longer would Paul depend on his obedience to the law as the basis for his acceptance with God.

When God confronts us in the gospel of Jesus Christ, he does not lay down a new law for us to keep. We are not invited to attain a right standing with him through obedience to any religious code. Paul wrote, "But now, apart from the law, the righteousness of God has been revealed." The gospel is not legalistic. It is God's good news to a sinful race.

Attested by the Law and Prophets (v. 21)

In Rom 1:2, Paul indicated that God promised the gospel beforehand through his prophets in the holy Scriptures. Here he expanded the statement to include the law as well as the prophets. Through both, God bore witness to his saving acts in Jesus Christ. The gospel was no innovation. Thus, Paul shared with other early Christians the conviction that the Old Testament pointed forward to the coming of Jesus Christ. The great promises of the Old Testament have their fulfillment in the New.

WORD PICTURE

Propitiation

Many have objected to the concept of propitiation (CSB: "mercy seat") which says that God's wrath must be averted if humans are to be justified. John Murray says, "It is one thing to say that the wrathful God is made loving. That would be entirely false. It is another thing to say that the wrathful God is loving. That is profoundly true."

After quoting Murray, Millard Erickson elaborates, "The love which prompted God to send his Son was always there. While the Father's holiness and righteousness and justice required that their be a payment for sin, his love provided it. The propitiation is the fruit of the Father's divine love."

Millard Erickson, *Christian Theology*, 817–18.

Experienced Through Faith in Jesus Christ (vv. 22–25)

Paul affirmed that God made available to men and women a right relationship to himself through faith in Jesus Christ. All need to believe in him, "for all have sinned and fall short of the glory of God." This is the verdict Paul reached regarding the Gentiles, and he repeated it here.

Verses 24–25 are crucial for our understanding of Paul's teaching regarding the death of Jesus Christ on the cross. Here Paul uses three metaphors to describe what God has done for sinful men through Jesus Christ, his Son.

Courtroom. Through the legal metaphor, we see a condemned man in a courtroom as he hears the verdict of acquittal.

Slave. Through the slave metaphor, we see an enslaved man who is redeemed from his bondage and set free.

Ritual Sacrifice. Through the sacrificial metaphor, we see a guilty man from whom the wrath of God has been removed.

All of this is of grace. What God has accomplished through the death of his Son on the cross may be experienced by men through faith.

Shows the Justice of God (vv. 25–26)

God passed over sins previously committed. Does that mean he is indifferent to sin and justice? Paul argued that is not the case. Jesus, God's beloved Son, took on himself the consequences of sin. Through Jesus's death, God demonstrated at least two truths: (1) that he is a God of justice, and (2) that he justifies—or makes right with himself—those who have faith in Jesus.

PERSONAL APPLICATION

The redemptive work of God through his Son Christ Jesus is the most amazing event in the history of the universe. God brought a just sentence of death upon all, for all have sinned. He then provided a sinless sacrifice, his only Son, to atone for the unrighteousness of the wayward human race. What a tragedy when people misinterpret God's forbearance and mercy as indifference toward their sins! (see Eccl 8:11).

Excludes Pride (vv. 27–28)

What implications does justification by faith have for us at the point of our basic attitude toward God and ourselves? It should make a difference in our lives. Those who imagine they have attained a right standing with God by keeping the law tend to be proud. But when God's grace is rightly understood, pride becomes an early casualty. Paul declared, "It is excluded." Paul warned the Corinthians, "Let the one who boasts, boast in the Lord" (1 Cor 1:31).

Affirms God as the God of All Men (vv. 29–30)

Another important implication of justification by faith is that since God is one, he is the God of all men—Gentiles as well as Jews. This belief was stated by devout Jews every time they recited their traditional confession of faith (the *Shema*), "Listen, Israel: The LORD our God, the LORD is one. Love the LORD your God with all your heart, with all your soul, and with all your strength" (Deut 6:4–5).

Upholds the Law (v. 31)

Finally, Paul asked if the principle of faith robs the law of its rightful role. Does it "nullify" the law? His answer was, "Not for a moment!" (Moffat Bible). On the contrary, faith puts the law in its proper place. It plays an essential role in the divine plan, but it was never intended to make it possible for a person to earn righteousness. Faith upholds the law in the sense that it fulfills all the obligations of the law.

Section Summary

God's justification of those who believe is provided "freely by his grace." Grace points to God's free and unmerited favor by which God has declared believers to have a right standing in his sight.

QUESTIONS TO GUIDE YOUR STUDY

1. Why did the Jews think that keeping the law gave them a right standing before God? What was Paul's response to this belief?
2. Paul declared that all are guilty before God. How was the Jew guilty before God? How was the Gentile guilty before God?
3. How does a person become righteous before God? What does *atonement* mean?
4. What are two implications of justification by faith that Paul discusses?

ROMANS 4

Chapter 4 serves as clear proof that the principle of justification by faith apart from works was in fact the principal operative in the Old Testament. It was not some new doctrine created by Paul.

THE BASIS OF ABRAHAM'S RIGHTEOUSNESS (4:1–8)

What was the ground of Abraham's righteousness before God: faith or works? The answer given in Jewish tradition was works. One might wonder how Abraham managed to keep the law since it was not given until the time of Moses. According to some Jewish tradition, Abraham kept the law by anticipation.

It follows then that if Abraham were justified by works (or faith regarded as a work of merit), he had ground for boasting. However, Paul appealed to Gen 15:6 to show that this was not so: "Abraham believed

WORD PICTURE

The Doctrine of Justification by Faith

Basically, justification is a process by which an individual is brought into an unmerited, right relationship with God. Justification does not encompass the whole salvation process; it does, however, mark that instantaneous point of entry or transformation that makes a person "right with God." Christians are justified in the same way Abraham was—by faith (Rom 4:16; 5:1). Human works do not achieve or earn acceptance by God. The exercise of faith alone ushers us into an unmerited, right relationship with God (Gal 2:16; Titus 3:7).

the Lord, and it was credited to him as righteousness." This was a basic biblical teaching about Abraham. God revealed himself to Abraham, and Abraham responded in faith. This faith was reckoned to the patriarch as righteousness. He was justified by faith.

HISTORICAL BACKGROUND

Circumcision and Christianity

Controversy arose in the early church (Acts 10–15) about whether male Gentile converts needed to be circumcised. First-century AD Jews disdained the uncircumcised. The leadership of the apostle Paul in the Jerusalem Council was crucial in the settlement of the dispute: Circumcision of the heart by way of repentance and faith were the only requirements (Rom 4:9–12; Gal 2:15–21).

Section Summary

Paul offered proof that the principle of justification by faith apart from works was in fact the principle operative in the Old Testament. Abraham himself was the foremost Old Testament example (or prototype) of justification by faith.

THE MEANING OF CIRCUMCISION (4:9–12)

What about this blessing of a righteousness that is reckoned through faith? Is it for the circumcised only, or does it also include the uncircumcised? Once again, Paul appealed to what the Scriptures taught about Abraham's righteousness. The account of his justification by faith is recorded in Gen 15:6, and his circumcision is not described until Gen 17:22–27. This was several years later, when Ishmael was thirteen years old. Thus, at the time Abraham's faith was reckoned to him for righteousness, he was uncircumcised.

Then what was the meaning of circumcision for Abraham? Paul explained that circumcision was not the work by means of which Abraham attained a right relationship with God. Rather, it was a sign of the justifying faith he already had. Circumcision was a sign of faith, not a substitute for it.

HISTORICAL BACKGROUND

God's Promise to Abraham

Abraham's name means "father of a multitude." The first Hebrew patriarch, he became known as the prime example of faith. His name in the beginning was Abram, but this was changed subsequently to Abraham. It was to Abram that God made his covenantal promise in Gen 17:4–5.

"As for me, here is my covenant with you: You will become the father of many nations. Your name will no longer be Abram; your name will be Abraham, for I will make you the father of many nations. I will make you extremely fruitful and will make nations and kings come from you. I will confirm my covenant that is between me and you and your future offspring throughout their generations. It is a permanent covenant to be your God and the God of your offspring after you" (Gen 17:4–7).

Section Summary

Paul showed that God declared Abraham righteous by faith, not by any works or rituals of the law.

THE PROMISE OF MANY DESCENDANTS (4:13–25)

God's promises to Abraham and his descendants were not tied to their keeping a law. The promise was of grace—to be believed and received by faith. Putting the relationship between God and humans on a legalistic basis invites the wrath of God. Relationships with a legalistic basis require both parties to carry out perfectly both the spirit and the letter of the law. Failure to keep the spirit and letter of the law results in penalties (wrath) to the offending party. Knowing the weakness of human nature as he does, God knows right relationship must be founded on something other than a legal basis.

Paul climaxed his account of Abraham's justification by faith by reminding his readers that this had meaning for them, too—for "us who believe in him who raised Jesus our Lord from the dead" (v. 24) is also reckoned righteousness. Moreover, Jesus "was delivered up for our trespasses and raised for our justification" (v. 25).

Section Summary

Jesus Christ, crucified and raised to life, is God the Father's gracious provision for the sins of a fallen race. The simplicity of the message makes it clear for all who will hear. The power of the message is experienced by those who reach out in faith.

QUESTIONS TO GUIDE YOUR STUDY

1. What was the basis of Abraham's righteousness?
2. What does it mean to be justified by faith?
3. What was the meaning of circumcision for the Jew? Why did Paul declare this ritual unnecessary?
4. What did God promise to Abraham and his descendants?

ROMANS 5

The "therefore" with which chapter 5 begins connects it to what Paul had written in the previous verses. In fact, "since we have been justified by faith" (v. 1) summarizes the entire argument of chapters 1–4.

Those who have placed their trust in Christ can rest assured that their faith has been credited to them as righteousness. Their confidence is based on the fact that Christ was put to death for their sins and raised again that they might be declared just.

PERSONAL APPLICATION

Peace with God

"Peace" is a word rich in meaning. It speaks of the new relationship between God and those who turn to him in faith. As Paul uses the term here, it does not primarily depict a state of inner tranquility. It is external and objective. To have "peace with God" means to be in a relationship with God in which all hostility caused by sin has been removed.

THE BENEFITS OF JUSTIFICATION (5:1–11)

A New Relationship with God (vv. 1–2)

Our new relationship with God—based on our being justified by faith—is characterized by peace, access to God, and hope of glory.

Access to God. Through Christ, we have been ushered into the presence of God the Father. By faith we have gained access into this gracious relationship in which we now find ourselves (Eph 2:18).

Hope of Sharing the Glory of God. We rejoice in our hope of sharing "the glory of God." Thus, we can face the future with joy. In fact, God's plan that we should reflect his glory is now realized in the lives of obedient believers.

Section Summary

Those justified by faith enjoy a new relationship with God. This new standing with God is characterized by peace with God, access to God, and a joyous hope in sharing in God's glory.

A New Understanding in Suffering (vv. 3–5)

The joy of believers is not something they hope to experience in the future but a present reality even in times of trials and distress. Christian suffering is a source of joy because its purpose is to build character in the believer. Observe the sequence Paul describes:

WORD PICTURE

Produces

Each of the three steps in the process of Christian suffering (see table) are "produced." The word Paul used is an emphatic form of the word meaning "to work out." It is a word filled with meaning. Because the preposition *down* is often used with a perfective force in composition, a paraphrase might be, "work down to the finish," or "completely produce." A. T. Robertson, *A Grammar of the Greek New Testament in the Light of Historical Research*, 606.

THE LINKED-CHAIN PROCESS OF CHRISTIAN SUFFERING

LINK	PRODUCES	RESULT IN THE BELIEVER
Affliction		Endurance
Endurance		Character
Character		Hope

"Affliction produces endurance" (v. 3). The word translated "affliction" literally means "pressure." It describes distress that is brought upon us by outward circumstances.

"Endurance produces proven character" (v. 4). The word translated "character" describes the quality of being approved, what has been proved by trial.

"Character produces hope" (v. 4). Observe that "hope" is the final level in these three steps toward spiritual maturity. It always burns brightly in those whose character has been developed through overcoming many trials.

Paul maintained that the Christian hope "will not disappoint us." It will never prove to be illusory because "God's love has been poured out in our hearts through the Holy Spirit who was given to us."

PERSONAL APPLICATION

Hope is not the tuition we pay as we enroll in the school of adversity. Rather, it is the diploma awarded to those who by the grace of God do well on the tests.

Section Summary

Believers have a new understanding of suffering. Christian suffering is a source of joy because its purpose is to build character in the believer.

A New Assurance in Judgment (vv. 6–11)

Another benefit of justification is the assurance it brings about the final judgment. Christian hope is neither wishful thinking nor guesswork. Rather, it is based on the solid foundation of what God has done for us in the death of his Son.

God took this action on our behalf not because we were good. On the contrary, we were his enemies. We were at our worst.

Paul's argument is a *how-much-more* argument. If God did this for us when we were at our worst, how much more will he do for us, now that we have been made right with him by the death of his Son. Looking at the kind and degree of love God showed us, we have hope and confidence.

The Christian's assurance regarding the final judgment is based on what God has already done (v. 9). Because of it, believers will be saved from the wrath of the last day. God's gracious and decisive action on the believer's part places a solid historical basis under the assurance of final deliverance. That is why Christians "boast in God through our Lord Jesus Christ, through whom we have now received this reconciliation."

THE GIFT OF RIGHTEOUSNESS (5:12–21)

From Adam to Moses (vv. 12–14)

Beginning at verse 12, we enter Paul's extended contrast between Adam (the first man) and the results of his sin and Jesus Christ (the "second man") and the gracious provisions of his atoning life and death.

But what about those who lived between Adam and Moses? What about the presence of sin before the law was given? Paul asserted, "In fact, sin was in the world before the law, but sin is not charged to a person's account when there is no law." Adam's sin was expressed as a deliberate transgression of God's commandment. It was not possible for those who lived between Adam and Moses to sin in this way.

Paul explains in verse 14, "Nevertheless, death reigned from Adam to Moses, even over those who did not sin in the likeness of Adam's transgression. He is a type of the Coming One." This verse affirms that humanity headed by Adam was characterized by sin and death even during the time preceding the law. Also, with reference to Adam as a type of Christ, verse 14 provides a transition to the analogy in the following verses.

Adam and Christ: An Analogy (vv. 15–19)

There are five parallels between Adam and Christ in these verses. The first three are contrasts (vv. 15–17), and the last two are comparisons (vv. 18–19):

1. A contrast between Adam's *trespass*, through which many died, and the *free gift* of God's grace in Christ, which has abounded for many (v. 15).
2. A contrast between the *condemnation* that followed Adam's trespass and the *justification* that follows the free gift of God's grace (v. 16).

3. A contrast between the *death* that reigned through Adam's trespass and the much greater reign in *the life* of those who receive the free gift of God's grace (v. 17).
4. A comparison between the *condemnation* that came to all people through Adam's trespass and the *justification* that comes to all people through Christ's act of righteousness (v. 18).
5. A comparison between the *disobedience* of Adam, through which the many were made sinners, and the *obedience* of Christ, through which the many will be made righteous (v. 19).

WORD PICTURE

Grace Multiplied

Where sin increased, grace "superabounded," "surpassed by far," "exceeded immeasurably," "overflowed beyond."

Robert Mounce, *Romans,* New American Commentary 27, 145.

The Triumph of Grace (vv. 20–21)

If righteousness is by faith, it is reasonable to ask where the law fits into the picture. After all, God gave the Israelites an extended code of legislation with the expectation that it would guide their life and conduct. The answer is that the law was brought in so the offense might increase. The law makes wrongdoing all the worse. The law was never intended to provide salvation but to convince people of their need for it.

God lavished his grace upon us beyond all measure. His grace exceeded immeasurably the extent of human sin. God's ultimate purpose in grace is to triumph over the reign of sin and death. What a magnificent portrayal of the achievement of God's justifying work in Christ!

Section Summary

Paul, by way of typology, demonstrated that sin and death came to men and women through Adam; righteousness and life came through Jesus Christ. Sin had been intensified by the law. Thus, greater grace was needed. But where sin abounded, grace abounded all the more.

QUESTIONS TO GUIDE YOUR STUDY

1. What characterizes a believer's new relationship with God?
2. What does it mean to have "peace with God"?
3. Describe the three-step process of spiritual maturity through suffering in Rom 5:3–5. What should be the believer's attitude toward suffering?
4. In what ways does Paul contrast Adam and Christ?

ROMANS 6

Beginning with this chapter, Paul moved ahead to discuss what was to happen in believers' lives after their sins have been forgiven and they are declared righteous in God's sight. This process of growth in spiritual maturity is the subject of chapters 6–8. This process is called "sanctification," the lifelong process of transformation into the likeness of Christ.

DEAD TO SIN, ALIVE IN CHRIST (6:1–14)

In Rom 5:20 Paul stated that where sin abounds, God's grace superabounds. What wonderful news! It means that no matter how deep the stain of man's sin, the grace of God is greater. Thus, there is hope for all, and men should praise God for his amazing grace.

Yet this great truth about the gospel was liable to grievous distortion by sinful men: "Should we continue in sin so that grace may multiply?" Paul's answer to this rhetorical question is a resounding: "Absolutely not!" How could it be possible for those who have died to sin to continue to live in sin?

Paul describes the Christian's death to sin by reference to baptism. Baptism proclaims with eloquent simplicity what has happened in a person's life.

First, baptism is an identification with Jesus Christ's death, burial, and resurrection. The believer says to the world, "I am with him. I am his."

Second, baptism is a proclamation that we have died to sin. Our sin and its consequence were borne by Jesus, and our sins were what put him to death. Realizing the hideous nature of sin, the believer has an aversion to sin.

Third, baptism tells the world that just as God raised Jesus from death—never to die again—so we are being raised from the waters of baptism to "walk in newness of life" (v. 4).

Obviously, the believer doesn't die at baptism in the way Christ died. And he doesn't rise from death in a resurrected body the way Christ did and the way he will in the future. But baptism conveys to the world a change within the believer that is as radical as Jesus's death and resurrection.

Paul described this radical change in the following way. Prior to conversion, all persons are slaves to sin. In conversion, the old self is crucified with Christ so the body of sin might be done away with. The result is that our slavery to sin is broken.

The believer not only hates sin but has the power to say *no* to it. This is a posture that must be assumed every day from the time of conversion until the day the believer dies and is fully separated from the presence of sin.

When the believer dies and is in the presence of Christ, he will be incapable of sin. But until then, Paul admonished, "Consider yourselves dead to sin and alive to God in Christ Jesus" (Rom 6:11). Considering

PERSONAL APPLICATION

William Barclay said, "How despicable it would be for a son to consider himself free to sin, because he knew that his father would forgive."

Quoted in Robert Mounce, *Romans, New American Commentary* 27, 148.

HISTORICAL BACKGROUND

In many evangelical churches today, people are invited to confess publicly their faith in Christ by walking an aisle and shaking hands with a pastor. But in Paul's day there were no Christian buildings with aisles for people to walk. Instead, they made public their confession of faith in Christ by submitting to baptism. It is unlikely that Paul ever faced a situation in which one professed Christian faith and refused to be baptized. Baptism was both the time and the mode of confession whereby one made known his commitment in faith to Jesus Christ as Lord.

HISTORICAL BACKGROUND

"Most commentaries just assume immersion to be the original mode (of baptism) as all Christianity did until after the Reformation. Thomas Aquinas and John Calvin conceded this even when they argued for an alternate mode. Luther and Wesley were almost unbending in defense of immersion."

Dale Moody, *Broadman Bible Commentary*, vol. 10 (Broadman, 1970), 198.

PAUL'S COMMANDS IN ROMANS 6:11–13*

COMMAND	VERSE	KIND OF COMMAND	EXTENDED MEANING*
"Consider yourselves dead to sin."	v. 11	Imperative (do)	"A plea to live up to the ideal of the baptized life."
"Do not let sin reign in your mortal body."	v. 12	Prohibition (don't do)	Do not let sin "continue to reign as it once did."
"Do not offer any parts of [your body] to sin."	v. 13	Prohibition (don't do)	"Stop presenting your members or do not have the habit of doing so."
"Offer yourselves to God."	v. 13	Imperative (do)	"Do it now and completely."
Offer "all the parts of yourselves to God as weapons for righteousness."	v. 13	Imperative (do)	"Do not go on putting your members to sin."

* From A. T. Robertson, "Romans," *WPNT,* vol. 4, 363.

oneself dead to sin doesn't just happen. It's something the believer can and must do daily.

In verse 13 Paul pointed out that believers have a continuing choice of whether to present the members of their bodies as servants of sin or servants of God. He urged believers to present their bodies to God to serve his good purposes.

Section Summary

Salvation as exemplified in baptism so changes individuals that they receive a new nature which delights in serving God. In conversion, Christians pass from an experience of slavery to sin to the service of God.

HISTORICAL BACKGROUND

"The walk of grace is the day-by-day issue of the life of grace. Christian ethics are the expression of a relationship with Christ. If a Christian fails morally, it is not because the needed power was not *available*. It is because it was not *appropriated*."

J. W. MacGorman, *Romans*, Layman's Bible Book Commentary, 58.

SLAVES TO RIGHTEOUSNESS (6:15–23)

In Rom 6:14 Paul declared that Christians are no longer under law but grace. This verse provides the transition to a restatement of the same problem mentioned in Rom 6:1: "What should we say then? Should we continue in sin so that grace may multiply?" Paul's answer is, "Absolutely not!"

Evidently Paul encountered Jewish opponents who maintained the law was essential to keep believers from lapsing into pagan sins. Another possibility is that some believers felt that since they were under grace instead of law, they could sin without dire consequence. Paul used the analogy of slavery to combat a casual attitude toward sin.

He reminded his readers that, regardless of the religious claims they made, their real master was identified by the commands they obeyed. If they obeyed the commands of sin, then sin was their master and death was their destiny. If they obeyed the commands of righteousness, then righteousness was their master and life was their end.

Verses 20–23 summarize Paul's teaching on the moral consequences of justification by faith. He described two masters, two freedoms, two fruits, and two destinies.

CONTRASTED LIVES (ROM 6:20–23)

	BELIEVER	NONBELIEVER
Master	Righteousness	Sin
Freedom	Free from sin	Free from righteousness
Fruit	Sanctification	Shameful behavior
Destiny	Eternal life	Death

Section Summary

Slavery to sin results in death. Slavery to righteousness leads to eternal fellowship with God. It all comes down to this: The wages paid by sin are death, but the gift God gives is eternal life.

QUESTIONS TO GUIDE YOUR STUDY

1. What does it mean to be "baptized into Christ Jesus"?
2. What is the point of Paul's ethical commands in 6:11–13?
3. Contrast the life of a person who is a slave to sin and a person who is a slave to righteousness. What are the major differences?
4. Describe the doctrine of sanctification. How does it happen? What is its result?

ROMANS 7

In this chapter Paul pictured himself as one wanting to live righteously and fulfill the demands of the law but still within frustrated by sin. Nowhere else in Paul's letters, and nowhere else in ancient literature, is there such a penetrating description of the human plight as in Rom 7:1–25.

DEAD TO THE LAW (7:1–6)

Paul taught that Christians have died not only to sin but also to the law. Thus, the law no longer wields authority over them. Paul laid down the principle that the law exercises lordship over a person only as long as that person "lives." Death cancels the law's claim upon that individual.

HISTORICAL BACKGROUND

Sanctification

Sanctification is the process of being made holy, which results in a changed lifestyle for the believer. Christ's crucifixion makes possible the moving of the sinner from the profane to the holy (that is, "sanctifies," "makes holy") so that the believer can become a part of the temple where God dwells and is worshiped. Both Paul and Peter affirmed the work of the Holy Spirit in conversion as a sanctification, a making of the believer holy so he or she can come before God in acceptance. Especially in Paul, *justification* and *sanctification* are closely related concepts.

To illustrate this principle, Paul drew on the covenant of marriage. A married woman is legally bound to her husband as long as he lives. If she lives with another man while her husband is living, she violates the law and is an adulteress. However, if her husband dies, she is free to marry another man.

Having established the principle that death rendered the law inoperative, Paul then applied this analogy to the issue at hand—the relation of the Christian to the law in verse 4. Admittedly, the analogy is not exact.

The important point is that the marriage relationship was broken by the death of one of its participants. The death of the believer took place when by faith that person became identified with the crucified Christ. Christ's death to and for sin becomes our death to sin (Gal 2:19–20). The purpose of this death is that we might belong to another husband—to the one who was raised from the dead. Our Savior becomes our new "husband."

And this, in turn, is in order that we may bear fruit to God. If Paul intended us to carry on the analogy of marriage, "bear[ing] fruit" would refer to offspring. He probably had a more general idea in mind, such as "the new life characterized by the good works God prepared beforehand and in which we are to walk." F. F. Bruce, *The Letter of Paul to the Romans*, rev. ed., Tyndale New Testament Commentary (Eerdmans, 1985), 138.

Section Summary

Formerly we were in bondage to written regulations. law was our old master. But now we are set free to serve our new master in a new way, in the Spirit. Dead to sin and freed to live for righteousness, we now live lives that bear fruit for God.

THE LAW AND SIN (7:7–25)

NEW TESTAMENT REFERENCE

"I have been crucified with Christ, and I no longer live, but Christ lives in me. The life I now live in the body, I live by faith in the Son of God, who loved me and gave himself for me. I do not set aside the grace of God, for if righteousness comes through the law, then Christ died for nothing." (Gal 2:20–21)

"Is the law sin?" is Paul's self-imposed question. His emphatic answer is "Absolutely not!" Any equation of the law with sin was a shocking distortion to him. However, Paul saw a relationship between the law and sin, and in verses 7–11, he sought to explain it.

Paul casts his answer in the form of a personal testimony: "I would not have known sin if it were not for the law. For example, I would not have known what it is to covet if the law had not said, Do not covet. And sin, seizing an opportunity through the commandment, produced in me coveting of every kind" (vv. 7–8).

The law brought home to Paul the reality of sin. Law defines sin and makes us aware of it. Apart from the law sin exists but cannot be designated as "sin." There may be dangerous microbes in the air, but unless some instrument detects them, they will go unnoticed. The law does more than show sin for what it is. It provokes sin. Sin seizes the opportunity and arouses within a person a desire to do evil.

Paul raised a second question, "Therefore, did what is good become death to me?" (v. 13). Sin, not the law, was the culprit. And Paul affirmed that it was through the law that he came to realize how exceedingly sinful sin was. Suppose sin could accomplish its work through sinful means only. That would be bad enough, but a particularly treacherous feature of sin is that it can achieve its evil end through that which is good. It can take something as good as the law of God and accomplish death through it.

At this point Paul made a dramatic switch from past to present tense as he continued to explain the relation between the law and sin: "We know that the law is spiritual, but I am of the flesh, sold as a slave under sin."

A slave cannot act upon his own will. He is bound to obey his master. His noble desires will be overruled and crushed by the one who owns him. Through this analogy of slavery, Paul explained why he was unable to obey the law. As sin's slave, bought and paid for, he had to do his master's bidding. No matter how much he delighted in God's law, he was powerless to fulfill it.

In verses 21–25 Paul climaxed the account of the struggle in his life between the law of God and the law of sin. Both laws contended for mastery in him. Paul did not offer a neutral battleground. Instead, he was deeply biased in favor of the law of God, in which he delighted. It appealed to him, and he aspired to fulfill it (v. 22).

But the law of sin would not permit it. This dreadful alien law waged war against the law of God in Paul and took him captive (v. 23). As a prisoner, he cried out for deliverance, "What a wretched man I am! Who will rescue me from this body of death?" (v. 24). And in the same breath he provided the triumphant answer: "Thanks be to God through Jesus Christ our Lord!"

Romans 7 does not provide a complete picture of Paul's spiritual experience. In fact, it serves to prepare the reader for what follows. It sets the stage for the triumph of chapter 8. It probably is true that in the lives of most earnest Christians the two conditions Paul described exist in a sort of cycle. Recognition of our inability to live up to our deepest spiritual longings (chap. 7) leads us to cast ourselves upon God's Spirit for power and victory (chap. 8). Failure to continue in reliance on the power of the Spirit places us once again in a position inviting defeat.

Sanctification is a gradual process that repeatedly takes the believer through this recurring sequence of failure through dependency on self to triumph through the indwelling Spirit.

WORD PICTURE

Seizing an Opportunity

The word translated "opportunity" here and in verse 11 was used in a military context to designate a base of operations or a starting point from which an attack is launched. "A starting place from which to rush into acts of sin, excuses for doing what they [those who sin] want to do."

A. T. Robertson, *WPNT*, vol. 4, 367.

We find this same word in 2 Cor 5:12; 11:12, and in Gal 5:13, where Paul taught that Christian liberty can so easily turn to license. In such a case, a person uses his or her liberty as a springboard for sin. *Robertson, WPNT*, vol. 4, 311.

WORD PICTURE

Sold as a Slave Under Sin

This phrase means bought and delivered to sin, as a slave to a master. This same verb is used in Matt 18:25 to describe a debtor being sold into slavery.

PERSONAL APPLICATION

John Calvin observed, "This work of God is not completed on the day when it is begun in us, but gradually increases, and by daily advancement is brought by degrees to its completion." Quoted in Robert Mounce, *Romans*, New American Commentary 27, 151.

Section Summary

Paul pictured himself and all believers as those who long to live on a higher plane. But they are constantly dragged to the abyss of disobedience by the power of sin. Struggle and conflict are typical of Christian experience, but defeat and despair are not. Through the death and resurrection of Christ, God has provided the power for us to live in the freedom of the Spirit.

QUESTIONS TO GUIDE YOUR STUDY

1. How does one become dead to the law? Comment on Paul's marriage metaphor.
2. What is the relationship between law and sin?
3. What is the new way of the Spirit? What is its result?
4. In 7:21–25 Paul described a struggle. What was this struggle? How do you deal with this struggle in your own life?

ROMANS 8

With chapter 8 we arrive at what may be called the inspirational highlight of the book of Romans. The theme of this chapter is living by the Spirit.

Romans 8 is not mere theology. As Paul wrote, his pen gave evidence that he was caught up in an experience of profound worship and spiritual adoration.

DELIVERANCE FROM THE BONDAGE OF SIN (8:1–11)

The new life of the Spirit, made possible through faith in Jesus Christ as Lord, brings deliverance from the old bondage to sin and death. Paul launched this portion of his letter with a mighty declaration of freedom: "Therefore, there is now no condemnation for those in Christ Jesus, because the law of the Spirit of life in Christ Jesus has set you free from the law of sin and death."

Note the two laws mentioned in this passage: (1) the law of the Spirit of life in Christ Jesus, and (2) the law of sin and death (vv. 1–2).

The Law of Sin and Death. Paul described its work in Rom 7:14–25. It always lies close at hand, ready to challenge our every desire to do right. It wages a relentless warfare until it has made a captive out of the person who tries to fulfill God's law.

The Law of the Spirit. This law breaks the dominion of the old law of sin and death. Through Jesus Christ men are set free. Verse 3 tells us how this happens. The heart of the gospel of the grace of God is found in this verse. The doctrines of the incarnation and the atonement come into play here.

WORD PICTURE

Spirit

Twenty-one times in Rom 8 the Greek word for *Spirit* or *spirit* occurs. At least eighteen and perhaps twenty of these are references to the Holy Spirit. This means there are more references to the Holy Spirit in Rom 8 than in any other chapter of Paul's letters (1 Cor 12 ranks second with twelve). We have in Rom 8 Paul's fullest discussion of the new life of the Spirit.

The Incarnation. God is not an angry Father waiting to have his wrath against us appeased by the sacrificial intervention of a loving Son. Instead, God the Father acts on behalf of sinful man by sending his Son. Paul described the manner of Christ's coming as "in the likeness of sinful flesh." This is the incarnation. Jesus Christ, the Son of God, became one of us in our humanity.

The Atonement. Through the sacrificial death of Jesus on the cross, God achieved our deliverance by condemning sin in the flesh. In his death on the cross, Christ bore the full fury of sin's devastating power.

Paul reminded his readers in verse 9 that they were not under the control of their sinful nature. To the contrary, their lives were under the direction of the indwelling Spirit of God. Furthermore, the indwelling Spirit is the believer's guarantee of future resurrection (v. 11).

Section Summary

The new life of the Spirit, made possible through faith in Jesus Christ as Lord, brings deliverance from our old bondage to sin and death. Christians, controlled by the Spirit of God, can experience life and strength in their struggles against sin.

SONSHIP: AN INTIMATE PERSONAL RELATIONSHIP (8:12–17)

Paul next moved to the theme of sonship. He discussed the *test* of sonship, the *privilege* of sonship, and the *assurance* of sonship.

The Test of Sonship (v. 14)

"All those led by God's Spirit are God's sons" (v. 14). A day-by-day response to the leading of the Spirit indicates the one to whom we belong because we follow the one to whom we belong. This is a more dependable criterion than our emotional highs and lows. Elation without obedience is a fraud.

The Privilege of Sonship (v. 15)

Paul contrasted the ideas of slavery and adoption as children. He reminded his readers that in turning to Christ they were not enslaved once again to fear. On the contrary, the spirit they received was the consciousness that they had become adopted sons of God. Because of this, they have the privilege to address God as "*Abba,* Father!"

Privilege also involves responsibility. Paul reminded his fellow Christians that the assurance of resurrection by the indwelling Spirit placed them under obligation to be led by the Spirit of God and not by their sinful nature.

WORD PICTURE

Abba, Father!

Abba is the Aramaic word for *father.* It is the intimate and endearing term by which the child in a Jewish home addressed his father. This term is found only three times in the New Testament: Gal 4:6; Mark 14:36; and this passage. In Mark 14:36 Jesus used it as he called on God in Gethsemane. No term serves better than *Abba* or *Father* to qualify the warm, personal relationship to God that his grace has made possible.

The Assurance of Sonship (v. 17)

As God's children, we are "coheirs with Christ—if indeed we suffer with him so that we may also be glorified with him." Observe Paul's emphasis here on sharing Christ's sufferings (see also Phil 1:29; 3:10; Col 1:24). These are not the adversities that come because of our common humanity, such as illness, bereavement, or the loss of employment during a recession. Rather, they are the sufferings that come from following Christ.

Section Summary

In contrast to the control of sin, believers have received the Spirit of adoption and can approach God in an intimate way. The Christian's current suffering is only a prelude to being glorified together with him.

Having mentioned in verse 17 that suffering accompanies membership in the family of God, Paul next laid out three grounds of encouragement: (1) the glory that will be revealed (vv. 18–25), (2) the help of the Holy Spirit (vv. 26–27), and (3) the fact that all things work together for good (vv. 28–30).

HOPE OF GOD'S ULTIMATE TRIUMPH (8:18–25)

Paul contrasted the suffering of believers which is characteristic of this present age with the glory that will be theirs in the future. In verses 19–22 Paul described creation's involvement both in man's bondage to sin and in his hope of redemption. Genesis 3:17–19 provides background for this discussion. Paul made three statements about the creation:

1. It eagerly awaits the revelation of the sons of God.
2. It was subjected to futility, not willingly but by the will of God.
3. It is destined to be set free from enslavement to decay and to share in the glorious liberty of God's children.

In vv. 23–25 Paul resumed his discussion of the believers' present trials. Like creation, we also groan inwardly as we await the final day. Believers yearn for the full adoption as sons that will take place in the resurrection. And we do so as those who already "have the Spirit as the firstfruits." This is God's pledge of our complete triumph with Christ at the end. At present, this is a hope that we wait for with patience (vv. 24–25).

Section Summary

Hope transforms suffering. Paul pointed to creation's longing for its redemption and believers' eagerly awaiting their ultimate adoption and redemption. Here we see God's plan of redemptive suffering moving to its fulfillment at the end of the age.

HELP IN PRAYER THROUGH THE SPIRIT'S INTERCESSION (8:26–27)

Another benefit of the new life of the Spirit is that it is available at a point where we need it most—in our prayers.

Hope carries us through our times of suffering (vv. 24–25). The Spirit also comes to our aid when we find ourselves unable to pray as we ought. Prayer has always been one of the great mysteries of the spiritual life. We understand God is listening, but we sense our inadequacy when we are uncertain about how to pray or for what to pray. For example, how many times have we wondered how to pray for a friend suffering a serious illness?

When our lack of faith undermines certainty in prayer, the Spirit himself intercedes on our behalf. So intense is the Spirit's prayer that Paul described it as "inexpressible groanings." We may be assured that God understands what the Spirit desires, even though it is inexpressible in human terms. No passage in Scripture provides greater encouragement for prayer.

Section Summary

The Spirit comes to the aid of believers baffled by the perplexity of prayer and takes their concerns to God with an intensity far greater than we could ever imagine. Our groans become his as he intercedes on our behalf in accordance with God's will.

GOD'S OVERRULING CARE (8:28–30)

We come to one of the favorite verses in Romans. How often in times of trial have believers turned to Paul's reassuring words that God has not deserted us, but he is at work in every circumstance of life: "We know that all things work together for the good of those who love God, who are called according to his purpose" (v. 28). This is one of the greatest promises in all the Bible.

Notice the phrase that Paul attached to this promise: "Those who love God, who are called according to his purpose." Not only is God continually at work, but those for whom he works are steadfast in their love for him.

WORD PICTURE

The Spirit as Firstfruits

Paul used the term *firstfruits* in reference to the gift of the Spirit as a pledge (see 2 Cor 5:5, where the Spirit is given "as a down payment" for what is to come). The Spirit is evidence that at the present time we are the sons of God (Rom 8:14,16). He is the "down payment" on the inheritance that will be ours as members of the family of God.

"The Holy Spirit came on the great Pentecost and his blessings continue as seen in the 'gifts' in 1 Cor 12–14, in the moral and spiritual gifts of Gal 5:22f. And greater ones are to come, 1 Cor 15:44ff." A. T. Robertson, *WPNT*, vol. 4, 376.

WORD PICTURE

Helps

"The little English verb *helps* [Rom 8:26] translates a big verb in Greek. It is used elsewhere in the New Testament only when Martha called for Mary to help her prepare a meal (Luke 10:40)." Dale Moody, *Broadman Bible Commentary,* vol. 10, 220.

GOD'S REDEMPTIVE PURPOSE IN ROMANS 8:30

WORK OF GOD IN REDEMPTION	MEANING
Predestination	God's grace at work before the foundation of the world
Calling	God's grace confronting us
Justification	God's grace making us right with Himself in the midst of history
Glorification	God's grace in the consummation of this age

The good toward which God is working all things together is that every believer be conformed to the image of Christ. In verse 30 Paul bridged eternity past and future with his majestic summary of God's redemptive purpose.

Section Summary

Believers may gain assurance knowing that God is for them. All that happens to them rests in the sovereign hand of God, because "all things work together for the good of those who love God, who are called according to his purpose."

ASSURANCE OF SALVATION (8:31–39)

Predestination, Calling, Justification, and Glorification. These great terms encompass the scope of God's redemptive purpose. Having set forth God's redemptive purpose in verse 30, Paul asked, "What, then, are we to say about these things?" His answer provides the grandest passage on Christian assurance in the Bible. The following assurances form the solid foundation of our confidence:

1. Our assurance is based on the heavy investment that God has already made in our redemption (vv. 31–32).
2. Our assurance is based on God's acquittal and Christ's continuing intercession for us (vv. 33–34).
3. Our assurance is based on God's love for us in Christ, which guarantees that nothing will be able to separate us from Him (vv. 35–39).

PERSONAL APPLICATION

"For Paul, it is not fate, the stars, angelic powers, nor heaven or hell that determines the lives of believers; rather, the faithfulness of Jesus does." Craig S. Keener, *The IVP Bible Background Commentary* (InterVarsity Press, 1993), 432.

After enumerating the various calamities that have assailed God's people (vv. 35–36), Paul claimed, "We are more than conquerors through him who loved us." This statement provides the background for one of the greatest affirmations of faith in God: "For I am persuaded that neither death nor life, nor angels nor rulers, nor things present nor things to come, nor powers, nor height nor depth, nor any other created thing will be able to separate us from the love of God that is in Christ Jesus our Lord" (vv. 38–39).

Section Summary

Believers can expect difficulties in this age; yet they can be certain that nothing will be able to separate them from the love of God. This recognition of present victory and future hope because of God's gracious actions in Jesus inspired Paul to ecstatic praise and worship of God.

QUESTIONS TO GUIDE YOUR STUDY

1. What great encouragements is the believer promised in chapter 8? How does each encourage you?
2. What does being "God's sons" mean for the believer? What does it include? What does it require of us?
3. What does Paul mean by the "firstfruits" of the Spirit?
4. What is the basis for our own assurance of salvation?

ROMANS 9

The triumphant conclusion of Romans 8 turned to a minor key as Paul thought about Israel and its rejection of God's Messiah.

Romans 9–11 is best read and reread as a unit. These three chapters begin with a lament but end with a doxology.

WORD PICTURE

Grief

A. T. Robertson said the grief Paul felt at the thought of his brethren was consuming. A. T. Robertson, *WPNT*, vol. 4, 380.

PAUL'S LAMENT (9:1–5)

Ultimate Compassion (vv. 1–3)

When Paul thought of his people and their alienation from God, he felt an overwhelming grief. Placing himself under a solemn oath, he disclosed his anguish in their behalf (vv. 1–2).

How deep was Paul's compassion for his people? He stood ready to forfeit his own hope in Christ if only it could benefit them. This is compassion in its ultimate form. Love knows no greater expression than this. Being an apostle to the Gentiles meant no lessening of Paul's concern for the salvation of his fellow Jews.

The Advantages of the Jews (vv. 4–5)

In verses 4–5 Paul listed several advantages of the Jews that made their rejection even more tragic:

- They were Israelites.
- They were adopted as sons.

- They experienced the glory of God.
- They were covenant partners with God.
- They had God's law.
- They had the temple worship service.
- They had God's promises.
- They were descendants of the patriarchs.
- They were the people through whom the Messiah was given.

Yet with all these advantages of God's special blessings throughout their history, the Jews did not acknowledge Jesus as the Messiah. As a people, they rejected him.

OLD TESTAMENT REFERENCE

Paul's stance regarding Israel was similar to that of Moses when Israel sinned by creating the golden calf. "Now if you would only forgive their sin. But if not, please erase me from the book you have written!" (Exod 32:32).

Section Summary

Paul's heart was heavy with grief because his own people disdained God's deliverance through faith in Jesus Christ.

GOD'S SOVEREIGNTY (9:6–29)

The "Israel" Within Israel (vv. 6–13)

Paul insisted that the Word of God had not failed, although most of Israel did not believe in Jesus Christ. This was true because God's promises were not intended for all who could boast of racial descent from Abraham. They constituted the "Israel" within Israel.

Ishmael was as much a son of Abraham as was Isaac. Yet no Jew considered the Ishmaelites to be the children of God's promise to Abraham. Instead, the covenant relationship continued through Isaac.

WORD PICTURE

Sovereignty

Sovereignty is the biblical teaching that God is the source of all creation and that all things come from and depend on him (Ps 24:1). *Sovereignty* means that God is in all and over all.

In verses 10–13 Paul described God's choice of Jacob over Esau. Both sons had the same father and mother. Rebekah conceived both by Isaac (v. 10). Furthermore, God chose Jacob, the younger twin, rather than Esau before they were born (v. 11). Thus, the selection could not have been based on their doing right or wrong.

The Absolute Freedom of God (vv. 14–18)

God's action with respect to Jacob may have seemed unfair. Paul anticipated a possible charge of injustice against God, but he quickly dismissed it (v. 14). He cited God's message to Moses, "I will show mercy to whom I will show mercy, and I will have compassion on whom I will have compassion" (v. 15). It is not the exercise of man's will or his striving that compels God to withhold his judgment; it is his mercy (v. 16).

The opposite of showing mercy to the sinner is hardening the heart of the sinner. As God's word to Moses was an instance of the former (showing mercy), so his dealings with Pharaoh provided an example of the latter (v. 17). Paul attributed both the bestowal of mercy and the hardening of the sinner's heart to God's sovereign will (v. 18). Grace does not come as something owed: It is a gift. It has to be, or it's not grace.

The "Israel" Beyond Israel (vv. 19–29)

This is an exceedingly difficult teaching, and Paul felt the necessity of permitting his imaginary opponent to press his argument still further: "Why then does he still find fault? For who resists his will?" (v. 19). To this pertinent question, Paul gave a sharp rebuke (v. 20). He affirmed the right of the potter to fashion vessels of his choosing out of the same lump of clay. This was true whether the vessels were made for exalted or menial use (v. 21).

Against this background, Paul asked the lengthy hypothetical question in vv. 22–24. What if God executes judgment on objects of wrath to show His glory to those whom He had prepared to be objects of mercy? Paul did not stop at this point to answer this question. But from the tone of the question and from the context, we would expect Paul to say something like: "God is God. Who is qualified to evaluate His decisions and actions?"

In verses 25–26 Paul turned to several Old Testament passages to show that (1) some Gentiles are included in God's redemptive plans, and (2) only a remnant of believing Jews will be preserved.

OLD TESTAMENT REFERENCE

"So I went down to the potter's house, and there he was, working away at the wheel. But the jar that he was making from the clay became flawed in the potter's hand, so he made it into another jar, as it seemed right for him to do. The word of the LORD came to me: 'House of Israel, can I not treat you as this potter treats his clay?'—this is the LORD's declaration. 'Just like clay in the potter's hand, so are you in my hand, house of Israel.'" (Jer 18:3–6)

OLD TESTAMENT CONFIRMATION OF GOD'S REDEMPTIVE PLAN

PASSAGE	ACTION	OLD TESTAMENT CONFIRMATION
Romans 9:25–26	Redemption includes Gentiles.	Hosea 2:23; 1:10
Romans 9:27–29	Remnant of Israel will be saved.	Isaiah 10:22–23; 1:9

HISTORICAL BACKGROUND

This contrasts with the Greek understanding of God expressed in Plato's *Euthyphro*. On this view of right and wrong, justice and injustice were ideas separate from God. For that reason, God's actions could be evaluated by reference to these ideas.

Section Summary

Paul described God's sovereign choice of his people. Everything that had taken place in redemptive history had been due to God's faithfulness to the promise he gave Abraham and his descendants. He had chosen Israel to serve his purposes as Lord over all.

Note: Romans 9:30–33 is part of Paul's discussion of chapter 10 and should be studied as a unit with chapter 10. These verses are covered in the following chapter.

WORD PICTURE

Stone . . . to Stumble Over

A stumbling block, or a "stone . . . to stumble over," is anything that causes a person to stumble or fall. Although this term is sometimes used literally in the Bible, it is most often used as a metaphor. It is used of idols, of God's work with faithless people, and of God himself in relation to his people. The disobedient are warned that Jesus himself could be a stumbling block (Rom 9:32–33). The Greek word *skandalon* was used for the "bait stick" in a trap, the part of the trap to which the bait was attached. It was also used symbolically for the trap itself. In Rom 9:33 it is "a rock to trip over." The word came to refer to "temptation to sin" or "to have false faith."

QUESTIONS TO GUIDE YOUR STUDY

1. How did the alienation of his people, the Jews, affect Paul? What was his attitude toward them?
2. What added to the tragedy of the Jews' rejection of Jesus Christ?
3. What did Paul mean when he declared that God is sovereign?
4. In support of his argument, Paul provided Old Testament confirmation of God's redemptive plan. Why did he do so? How might this confirmation have impacted his Jewish audience?

ROMANS 10

We come now to the second part of Paul's discussion on the relationship of the Jews to the gospel of justification by faith. The last three verses of chapter 9 are part of Paul's discussion of chapter 10 and should be studied as a unit with chapter 10.

In the earlier verses of chapter 9, Paul reminded his readers that the Jews could not establish a legitimate claim on God's favor based on their national heritage. Their history demonstrated that God carries out his purposes with a freedom not limited by human notions of what ought to be. Here Paul showed that the Jews themselves were responsible for their rejection.

THE STONE OF STUMBLING (9:30–33)

Paul pointed to another apparent unfairness regarding Israel and then offered an explanation. The Gentiles, who did not pursue righteousness, attained it by faith, whereas Israel, having pursued righteousness based on the law, fell short of it (vv. 30–31). Israel did not understand God's way of making people right with him. They believed they could make themselves right with God by keeping God's law. This belief kept them from seeing the numerous ways they fell short of keeping the law.

A good example of the attitude of righteousness by keeping the law is seen in a parable Jesus told about a Pharisee who prayed, "God, I thank you that I'm not like other people—greedy, unrighteous, adulterers, or even like this tax collector." Jesus said that the man's prayer was to himself. Luke pointed out that Jesus told this parable to "some who trusted in themselves that they were righteous and looked down on everyone else" (Luke 18:9–14).

PERSONAL APPLICATION

Paul knew firsthand this zeal that was not informed by knowledge. Here he described it to the Galatians: "For you have heard about my former way of life in Judaism: I intensely persecuted God's church and tried to destroy it. I advanced in Judaism beyond many contemporaries among my people, because I was extremely zealous for the traditions of my ancestors" (Gal 1:13–14).

Section Summary

Israel's refusal to believe in Jesus Christ was the reason for their rejection. He was the stumbling block over whom they had tripped and fallen. Righteousness comes by faith and faith alone.

THE TWO WAYS OF SEEKING A RIGHT STANDING WITH GOD (10:1–17)

As he had done in Rom 9:1–5, Paul expressed again his concern for the salvation of his people. He bore witness to the Jews' zeal for God but lamented that it was not enlightened. Ignorant of the right standing with God made possible through faith, they sought to establish their own right standing with God by keeping the law. They failed to recognize that Christ put an end to the law as a way of achieving righteousness for everyone who believes (Rom 10:4; 3:21; Gal 3:19–4:7).

The law, instead of providing a way to arrive at a right standing with God, came to an end in Christ. "For Christ is the end of the law for righteousness to everyone who believes."

There was no question that Paul's Jewish brethren were zealous for God, but unfortunately their zeal was not guided by knowledge. They had no valid insight into God's plan for providing righteousness. They failed to recognize God's way of righteousness—that Christ is the end of the law.

Paul next contrasted the way of righteousness by law versus righteousness by faith. He quoted Moses as saying that if a person wants to be righteous based on the law, he will need to live in accord with that law (Lev 18:5). Earlier in Romans he had shown this to be an impossibility. The way of righteousness by faith simply recognized and trusted what God had done.

As there is no distinction between Jew and Greek in sinfulness (Rom 3:22–23), so there is none between them in salvation (Rom 10:12; 3:29–30). Belief is the key. Belief depends on hearing. If people hear, someone must proclaim the good news. Paul ended this section with a quotation from Joel 2:32, declaring the good news that "everyone who calls on the name of the Lord will be saved."

Section Summary

Nowhere in Scripture is the universal scope of salvation presented with greater clarity. Although God's redemptive plan was worked out in history through one particular race, it was meant from the beginning for the benefit of all people.

A DISOBEDIENT AND CONTRARY PEOPLE (10:18–21)

In this passage Paul set up a dialogue between someone who was an advocate for Israel. This advocate asked three questions designed to show that Israel was not at fault in their broken relationship with God. To each of these three questions, Paul cited answers from the Old Testament that showed that Israel was without excuse. Israel was responsible for her rejection. She herself had rejected the word of God.

WORD PICTURE

End

An alternate view of Rom 10:4 claims that Christ is the "end" of the law in the sense of its *aim* rather than its *termination*. Thus, the law has meaning and fulfillment in Christ.

HISTORICAL BACKGROUND

The Way of Salvation

Romans 10:9–10 has long served as one of the most helpful portions of Scripture for pointing out the way of salvation: confession that Jesus is Lord and belief in one's heart that God has raised him from death. This belief is not merely verbal assent but staking one's entire being on this truth.

OLD TESTAMENT REFERENCE

The final answer from Isa 65:2 is poignant, "I spread out my hands all day long to a rebellious people."

Section Summary

Israel's rejection had nothing to do with lack of opportunity or inability to understand. It rested solely on the nation's willful disobedience. They insisted on personal merit based on works as the way to gain God's approval. They had been equipped to understand that God's requirement for righteousness is faith.

QUESTIONS TO GUIDE YOUR STUDY

1. Why was Jesus Christ a stumbling block to Israel?
2. Paul described two ways of seeking a right standing before God. What is the way of salvation? Why does the way of the law fail?
3. What were the three objections of Paul's imaginary opponent who defends Israel? How did Paul respond to these objections? What is the point of his response to all three?
4. Paul used Isa 65:2 to illustrate the real explanation for Israel's rejection of the gospel. Who was responsible for Israel's rejection?

ROMANS 11

WORD PICTURE

The Remnant

"The remnant" consists of the righteous people of God who remained after divine judgment. Old Testament accounts of the remnant abound. For example, Noah and his family may be understood as survivors, or a remnant, of a divine judgment in the flood (Gen 6:5–8; 7:1–23). In the New Testament, Paul quoted (Rom 9:25–33) from the prophets Hosea and Isaiah to demonstrate that the saving of a remnant from among the Jewish people was still part of the Lord's method of redeeming his people. There would always be a future for anyone among the covenant people who would turn to the Lord for salvation.

Paul began this passage with the rhetorical question, "Has God rejected his people?" and his emphatic response, "Absolutely not!" He followed his answer with a discussion of the remnant of Israel, the evangelization of the Gentiles and Israel's jealousy because of the success of the Gentile mission, and the eventual turning of Israel to Christ.

THE REMNANT (11:1–10)

Paul followed up his emphatic denial that God had rejected his people by pointing to himself as a Jew who was brought to right relationship with God. After all, Paul was an Israelite. He was a descendant of the great patriarch Abraham and a member of the tribe of Benjamin. Thus, the rejection of Israel was partial rather than total. There was a remnant of Jewish believers, and Paul was one of them. Although Israel had been disobedient and obstinate, she was not repudiated as a nation.

If God rejected the entire nation of Israel, then Paul would not have been able to claim a right standing before God. The truth is that God had not rejected those whom he chose as his special people.

Paul found evidence for his teaching about the remnant in the experience of Elijah. At a time of national crisis, the prophet complained to God that he was the only one who remained faithful. God then told Elijah there were seven thousand men who had not bowed the knee to Baal (see 1 Kgs 19:18).

Making his application, Paul affirmed, "In the same way, then, there is also at the present time a remnant chosen by grace. Now if by grace, then it is not by works; otherwise grace ceases to be grace" (Rom 11:5–6).

Section Summary

Paul taught that since a remnant of Israel had believed the gospel, it was a clear indication that Israel as a whole would yet believe.

THE SALVATION OF THE GENTILES (11:11–24)

The description of the hardening of unbelieving Israel in the preceding verses drew from Paul a further question: "Have they stumbled so as to fall?" His inquiry was whether Israel's failure to believe had led to their ruin. Had they stumbled irretrievably? Once again, the answer was, "Absolutely not!"

Verses 11–12 reveal the main points of Paul's discussion for the remainder of the chapter:

1. Through the trespass of Israel, salvation has come to the Gentiles.
2. Through the salvation of the Gentiles, Israel will be provoked to jealousy.
3. Through the inclusion of Israel, great blessings will come to all. Not only was the rejection of Israel *partial;* it was also *temporary.*

OLD TESTAMENT REFERENCE

"The LORD named you a flourishing olive tree, beautiful with well-formed fruit. He has set fire to it, and its branches are consumed with the sound of a mighty tumult." (Jer 11:16)

In verses17–24 Paul used the allegory of an olive tree to warn the Gentiles against boasting. The olive tree represented true Israel. Unbelieving Jews were the natural branches that had been broken off. Gentiles were the wild olive branches that have been grafted in. Notice the reasons Paul gave to the Gentiles for not boasting over the Jews:

1. They should remember that they are wild olive shoots who have been engrafted (vv. 17–18).
2. They should understand that the natural branches were broken off because of their unbelief, taking heed not to presume on God (vv. 19–22).
3. They should realize that God has the power to graft the natural branches back into the olive tree, provided they do not persist in their unbelief (vv. 23–24).

Section Summary

Although God may have temporarily rejected Israel, he has not finally or irrevocably rejected them. When Israel rejected God's message, the opportunity was given to the Gentiles, who were grafted into the tree. Gentiles, however, were warned not to be proud of their acceptance but humbly to rely on God's grace.

THE SALVATION OF ISRAEL (11:25–36)

Verses 25–26 need to be understood in the larger context of what Paul has been saying about Israel as a nation. Here Paul boldly announced that all Israel would be saved. This is an amazing declaration regarding Israel's destiny.

What was the basis for such a claim? Paul described it as a "mystery," a special insight into God's saving plan given him by revelation. The content of the disclosure was that a hardening had come upon a part of Israel "until the fullness of the Gentiles" come to Christ.

Israel's salvation will be on the same basis as all other people—by responding in faith to the forgiveness made possible by the death and resurrection of Jesus Christ.

Much has been written about this "mystery." Interpreters differ widely in their understanding of this difficult passage. The most probable interpretation of the phrase "all Israel" is that it indicates a great turning of Israel to Christ, without specifying the conversion of every individual Jew, just as the "fullness of the Gentiles" does not mean every Gentile will be saved. Paul envisioned a great turning to Christ on the part of the Jewish people. Furthermore, he probably expected this to take place during his lifetime.

With this summation of God's gracious ways with men, Paul burst into praise. This doxology, thought by many to have been written by Paul himself, provides an appropriate finale of the doctrinal portion of Romans and an effective transition to Paul's instruction concerning the practical implications of the gospel.

He magnified the depth of God's riches, wisdom, and knowledge. Who but God could have conceived a plan that would turn disobedience into an occasion for mercy, reaching out universally to all who would believe?

God has set everything in motion by his creative Word. He is the source, the agent, and the goal of all that is. All things find their origin in him. Through him, everything that exists is sustained and directed. All things exist for his glory. Therefore, to him be praise and glory forever! Amen.

WORD PICTURE

Mystery

The New Testament uses the word *mystery* about twenty-five times, twenty-one of which occur in Paul's writings. The "mystery" of the New Testament has been described as an "open secret." Matters previously kept secret in God's eternal purposes have now been or are being revealed (Eph 3:3–5; 1 Cor 2:7–8). The mystery of the New Testament appears in the historical activity of the person of Jesus Christ (Col 2:2; Eph 1:9); the indwelling Christ is the hope of glory (Col 1:26–27). The mystery is received spiritually (Eph 3:4–5) and manifested in the proclamation of the gospel (Eph 6:19). Part of the mystery involves the disclosure that Gentiles share in the blessings of the gospel (Eph 2:11–13).

Section Summary

Paul boldly announced that all Israel would be saved. He described this as a "mystery." This mystery meant that a hardening would come upon a part of Israel "until the fullness of the Gentiles" had come to Christ. Upon this affirmation, Paul burst into praise for God's wisdom and knowledge.

QUESTIONS TO GUIDE YOUR STUDY

1. What was the result of God's rejection of Israel?
2. Describe the concept of "the remnant." How did it relate to Israel's rejection?
3. What is the "mystery" Paul spoke of?
4. Paul's doxology praised God for his plan to transform disobedience into an occasion for his mercy. What does this doxology reveal about the mind and attributes of God?

ROMANS 12

Through the first eleven chapters of Romans, we have followed Paul's presentation of the gospel. Now we come to the last major division of the letter (12:1–15:13), where Paul applies the gospel to everyday living. These four chapters provide the pattern of discipleship for believers.

In this chapter, Paul dealt with the call to commitment, spiritual gifts, and personal relationships.

CALL TO COMMITMENT (12:1–2)

The Greatest Sacrifice: Ourselves (v. 1)

Paul used the language of the altar to urge his readers to costly commitment. He encountered them to offer their bodies as a sacrifice to God. This sacrifice was to be "your true worship." These three qualities describe the believer's sacrifice:

1. *It is living.* This concept may provide a contrast with the dead bodies of animal sacrifices, or it could denote the new life the believer possesses in Christ.
2. *It is holy.* The Christian is set apart for and belongs to God.
3. *It is pleasing.* Sacrifices offered to God are not enough in themselves. The offerings must be acceptable to him.

WORD PICTURE

Therefore

When we encounter "therefore," we are directed to look at what has gone before and what is coming after and to discern the connection between them. You should always ask, "What is it there for?"

The Greatest Motivation: The Mercies of God (v. 1)

No greater demand can be made of any Christian than to climb upon God's altar as a living sacrifice. The motivation, therefore, must be equal to the demand. Paul appealed to the correct motivation in the words, "in view of the mercies of God." If gratitude to God for his mercies does not compel our devotion to him, nothing will. Paul never degraded the gospel by diluting its call to commitment.

Section Summary

Paul called on his readers to commit themselves as living sacrifices to God. This sacrifice is a spiritual act of worship.

The Greatest Threat: The Pressure to Conform to This World (v. 2)

Verse 2 tells of two ongoing activities that carry out the intention of the living sacrifice. The first is negative; the second, positive:

1. *"Do not be conformed to this age."* Believers are no longer to conform themselves to the present age. This present age is opposed to the world to come.
2. *"Be transformed." Transformation* is the outward expression of what springs from within. Rather than allowing the world to squeeze us into its own mold, Paul told his readers to be "transformed by the renewing of your mind." There is a continuing pressure to adopt the customs and behavior of the world in which we live. Although that influence must be rejected, this alone will never create the kind of change God has in mind for his followers. Genuine change comes from within. We must let ourselves be transformed.

NEW TESTAMENT REFERENCE

As citizens of heaven (Phil 3:20), we are to "set [our] mind on things above, not on earthly things" (Col 3:2). Paul reminded the Galatians that the present age is evil (Gal 1:4). This age cannot and must not serve as a model for Christian living. Its values and goals do not support growth in holiness.

The Greatest Discovery: The Will of God (v. 2)

The purpose of transformation by the renewing of our minds is that we may be able to "discern what is the good, pleasing, and perfect will of God."

The greatest discovery of all is the will of God. God's will is good, well pleasing, and complete:

1. It is *good* because it brings about moral and spiritual growth.
2. It is *pleasing to God* because it is an expression of his nature.
3. It is *perfect* (complete) in that no one could possibly improve on what God wants to happen.

Section Summary

Believers live as men and women of two ages: witnessing to the one that is dying and walking toward the one that is dawning. But the world does not like this, and it imposes relentless pressure on Christians to conform to its dying ways and values. Thus, Paul urged the Roman Christians to resist the efforts of a sinful age to press them into its mold. Instead, believers are to be transformed by the renewing of their minds so they may know what God has in mind for them.

SPIRITUAL GIFTS (12:3–8)

The Nature of the Church: One Body in Christ (vv. 3–5)

Paul was aware of the consequences of pride in believers. So he cautioned the Christians at Rome not to think of themselves more highly than they ought (v. 3), reminded them that they were all members of one body (vv. 4–5), and encouraged them to use their individual gifts for the benefit of the entire church (vv. 6–8).

They were to think of themselves "sensibly."

To each member of the church at Rome, God had given a measure of faith (see 1 Cor 12:11; Eph 4:7). Paul reminded them that as the physical body is made up of many members performing various functions, so also in Christ the many members form one body (see 1 Cor 12:12–31; Eph 4:25). Unity in diversity is the theme that runs through this section. Thus unity, however, which is spiritual, was possible only because the members were "in Christ," that is, joined by faith as part of the body of Christ.

The Christian faith is essentially a corporate experience. Although each member of the body comes to faith by an individual act of faith, the believing community lives out its Christian experience in fellowship with one another.

The Variety and Use of Spiritual Gifts (vv. 6–8)

Spiritual gifts are abilities or powers the Spirit of God bestows on all believers to equip them for service. These gifts are an important part of the gospel of grace. We are *saved* by grace; we *grow* by grace; and we are *endowed* by grace. Salvation, growth, and service—an experience of God's grace from beginning to end.

Paul mentioned seven different gifts and showed how they were to be exercised (see 1 Pet 4:10).

WORD PICTURE

Discern

The word *discern* describes gold tested by refining fires (1 Pet 1:7).

WORD PICTURE

Sensibly

Robert Mounce pointed out that the use of this term suggests how out of touch with reality the Roman Christians were in their opinions of themselves. Since the metaphor suggests intoxication, we might say they were in danger of becoming "egoholics!"

WORD PICTURE

Renewing of Your Mind

The word *renew* in the Greek text is a compound of two words: "back" or "again," and "new." This compound is translated "to make new" or "renew." To renew the mind is to adjust one's spiritual vision and thinking to the mind of God, which has a transforming effect on one's life.

A renewed mind is concerned with those issues of life that have lasting importance. By nature, our thoughts tend to dwell on the fleeting present. But that which passes quickly is normally inconsequential. As Paul explained in 2 Cor 4:18, "What is seen is temporary, but what is unseen is eternal." The renewed mind enables us to discern the will of God. Released from the control of the world around us, we can come to know what God has in mind for us.

PAUL'S LISTS OF SPIRITUAL GIFTS*

SPIRITUAL GIFT	ROM 12:6–8	1 COR 12:8–10	1 COR 12:28	1 COR 12:29–30	EPH 4:11
Apostle			1	1	1
Prophet	1	5	2	2	2
Teacher	3		3	3	5
Pastor					4
Miracles		4	4	4	
Discernment of Spirits		6			
Word of Wisdom, Knowledge		1			
Evangelists					3
Encouragers	4				
Faith		2			
Healings		3	5	5	
Tongues		7	8	6	
Interpretation		8		7	
Ministry/Serving	2				
Administration			7		
Leaders	6				
Helpers			6		
Mercy	7				
Giving	5				

* *Chart presents the order in which the gifts listed appear in the passage.*

Section Summary

Paul reminded his readers that as the physical body is made up of many members performing various functions, so also in Christ the many members form one body. The gift each believer has received is the result of the gracious outpouring of God's blessing on the church.

PERSONAL RELATIONSHIPS (12:9–21)

General Instructions (vv. 9–13,15–16)

Nowhere in Paul's writings do we find a more concise collection of ethical injunctions. In these verses are several exhortations ranging from love of Christians to hospitality for strangers.

Paul called his readers' attention to the absolute primacy of genuine love. Love must be genuine, not a form of role-playing.

SPIRITUAL GIFTS IN THE BODY OF CHRIST

GIFT	HOW TO BE EXERCISED
Prophecy	Communication of revealed truth that builds up believers
Service	Practical service to help others
Teaching	To provide guidance and moral instruction
Exhorting	Encouraging, comforting, and exhorting others
Giving	Cheerfully contributing to the needs of others
Leading	Service carried out for the benefit of others
Showing mercy	Helpful activities such as feeding the hungry, caring of the sick and aging

We are to "detest evil; cling to what is good." One cannot do the second without doing the first. This insight is one that permissiveness never grasps. Brotherly love is to prevail, and we are to honor others above ourselves.

Love has a capacity to identify with others in their joys or sorrows. To identify with persons in sorrow is sometimes easier than to identify with them in their joys, since we never envy the griefs of others. Love seeks harmony in all personal relationships. It associates readily with the lowly. Freedom from conceit helps make this possible.

Paul exhorted his readers to several actions:

"Do not lack diligence in zeal" (v. 11). In whatever believers do, they are to put their whole heart and soul into it.

"Be fervent in the Spirit" (v. 11). Believers are to be aglow with the Spirit. The life-giving presence of the Holy Spirit radically alters the way a person lives.

"Serve the Lord" (v. 11). Christians are to serve the Lord. This service is by no means drudgery.

"Rejoice in hope" (v. 12). Servants of God continually rejoice in their hope. The word Paul used here speaks of confident trust rather than uncertain expectation.

"Be patient in affliction" (v. 12). This world will present its share of difficulties, but the believer is to be steadfast in times of trouble.

"Be persistent in prayer" (v. 12). Most Christians confess the difficulty of maintaining a regular and effective prayer life. The reason is not difficult to discern. If Satan can keep us out of touch with God, he knows we won't cause any problems for his evil kingdom.

"Share with the saints in their needs" (v. 13). The level of poverty and the need for help were relatively high in the early church. It was critical for believers who had plenty to share their abundance with those in need.

"Pursue hospitality" (v. 13). In a day when inns were scarce and not always desirable, it was critical for believers to extend hospitality to Christians (and others) who were traveling.

When Wronged by Others (vv. 14,17–21)

Paul provided several exhortations for responding to those who have wronged us.

"Bless those who persecute you; bless and do not curse" (v. 14). Paul urged his readers to invoke God's blessing on behalf of those who persecuted them. This expressed the same attitude Jesus had in his Sermon on the Mount.

"Do not repay anyone evil for evil" (v. 17). We are not to repay evil for evil. This reflected Paul's concern about the impressions Christians make on unbelievers (see 1 Thess 4:12; 1 Cor 6:1; 2 Cor 8:20–21).

"Live at peace with everyone" (v. 18). As far as is possible, we are called to live at peace with everyone. Jesus pronounced a blessing upon the peacemaker (see Matt 5:9). The author of Hebrews wrote that we are to "pursue peace with everyone" (Heb 12:14).

"Do not avenge yourselves" (v. 19). We are not to take vengeance into our own hands. Instead, we are to do good to our enemy. By doing that, we "will be heaping fiery coals on his head."

WORD PICTURE

Heaping Fiery Coals

"The idea of heaping coals on an enemy's head has led to different interpretations. Some have proposed the remote "Egyptian ritual in which a penitent showed his repentance by carrying on his head a dish containing burning charcoals on a layer of ashes (Manson). This may be in the background of Proverbs 24:21–22, but it is more likely that Paul is advocating nonretaliation in the light of the future retribution of God." Dale Moody, *Broadman Bible Commentary*, vol. 10, 254–55.

Section Summary

The believer's most powerful weapon against evil is good. To respond to evil is not to overcome it but to add to it. Believers are called upon to live victoriously in a hostile world by following the example of Jesus. God will avenge the wicked and reward the righteous.

QUESTIONS TO GUIDE YOUR STUDY

1. Describe the kind of sacrifice Paul urged his readers to make. What characteristics describe it? What actions does true sacrifice involve on the part of the believer?
2. Contrast the world's pressures on the believer to conform with the inward transformation of the believer. How has God's love changed your attitude toward life and toward other people?
3. The gift each believer receives is the result of the gracious outpouring of God's blessing on the church. What is your gift?
4. What exhortations did Paul give regarding personal relationships? What are some ways these can be applied?

ROMANS 13

In this chapter Paul discussed the divinely sanctioned role of government and the believer's responsibility to those in power. Christians, like everyone else, are to submit to the governing authorities. Allegiance to God does not take away our responsibility to secular authority.

DUTIES TO THE STATE (13:1–7)

In verses 1–7 Paul provided his readers with instructions regarding governing authorities.

Christians Must Submit to Governing Authorities (vv. 1–2)

The authority of the state is grounded in the will of God (v. 1). To resist rulers is to resist what God has appointed and to incur judgment (v. 2). It is important to remember that government is God's way of maintaining the public good and directing the affairs of state.

Christians Must Recognize the Function of Governing Authorities (vv. 3–5)

Rulers maintain order in society by rewarding good conduct and punishing wrongdoing (v. 3). In wielding the sword (the power of life and death), rulers are God's servants who execute his wrath upon wrongdoers (v. 4). We are to submit to their authority because of the fear of punishment as well as the demands of conscience (v. 5). Here we have the biblical basis of the use of force by government for the maintenance of law and order.

Christians Must Support Governing Authorities (vv. 6–7)

Christians are obligated to pay taxes to support the governing authorities. They also are to respect and honor governing authorities (v. 7). Paul did not qualify his statements, and this troubles many modern readers. For example, he did not discuss the limits of Christian obedience, the possibility of the moral justification of revolution, or the duties of rulers to their subjects.

Section Summary

The social benefits that come from a properly managed state place the Christian under obligation to abide by the accepted regulations. Undergirding all secular law and order is the authority of God delegated to those who rule.

NEW TESTAMENT REFERENCE

"Give to Caesar the things that are Caesar's, and to God the things that are God's." (Mark 12:17)

WORD PICTURE

Submit

The word *submit* in the Greek text of the New Testament is a compound of two words, "under" and "to arrange." It means "to put to subjection." In Rom 13:1, the word means "to be in subjection" to governing authorities. "This word occurs thirty-eight times in the New Testament, most often in the middle voice, meaning 'to subordinate oneself.' It is used of submission to political authorities (Titus 3:1); wives to husbands (Col 3:18), the younger toward elders (1 Pet 5:5). Cranfield argues that the predominant thought is not obedience but the conduct that flows naturally from the recognition that the other person as Christ's representative has an infinitely greater claim on one than one has on oneself." *Romans,* 2:660–62, quoted in Robert H. Mounce, Romans, New American Commentary 27, 243, n. 62.

THE PRIMACY OF LOVE (13:8–10)

The previous paragraph dealt with the God-invested authority of the state, submission to rulers, the payment of taxes, and respect for those in public office. These three verses describe the Christian's obligation to all people—the obligation to love (v. 8). All the commandments are summed up in the one sentence, "Love your neighbor as yourself." The need to love is supremely important in view of the critical age in which we live. This obligation to love has no limit. Since love does no wrong to a neighbor, it is the fulfilling of the law (v. 10).

THE END OF THE AGE (13:11–14)

Here Paul wrote from the perspective of the closing period of the present age.

The world lives as though human history is destined to continue forever. The Christian knows that God is in control of people and nations and is directing history to a predetermined end. Since the end is near, we are to rouse ourselves from sleep. Every day brings us closer to that final day when all we have anticipated in Christ will become a reality.

Because the night is nearly over and the day is about to dawn, it is critical that believers rid themselves of the works of darkness (see Eph 5:11). It is time to clothe ourselves with the weapons of light. Our conduct is to be decent and honorable.

HISTORICAL BACKGROUND

God used these verses in the conversion of young Augustine in a garden in Milan. He heard some children playing and saying repeatedly, "Take and read; take and read." Augustine responded by opening the Scripture to this passage (Rom 13:11–14). Upon reading these words, Augustine said, "I had no wish to read more and no need to do so. For in an instant, as I came to the end of the sentence, it was as though the light of confidence flooded into my heart and all the darkness of doubt was dispelled." *Confessions, Book 8, xii.*

Section Summary

Christian conduct is vitally related to the hope of Christ's return and the believer's ultimate transformation.

QUESTIONS TO GUIDE YOUR STUDY

1. What was Paul's view of governing authorities?
2. What did Paul teach about the believer's role in submitting to governing authorities?
3. Why did Paul emphasize the primacy of love in Rom 13:8–9?
4. What truth prompted Paul's exhortation to the believer to "walk with decency"?

ROMANS 14

GUIDELINES FOR ISSUES CONFRONTING THE CHURCH (ROM 14:1–15:13)

THE PROBLEM (14:2,5,21)

Throughout this passage, Paul spoke of two groups of believers, whom he designated as the "weak" and the "strong." He mentioned three points at which the two groups held a sharp difference of opinion: (1) the eating of meat (v. 2); (2) the observance of special days (v. 5); and (3) the drinking of wine (v. 21).

It is interesting to observe how Paul approached a resolution to the problem at Rome. Paul's letters were not intended as abstract treatises on matters ethical and theological. Rather, they were pastoral notes addressed to real-life situations in first-century churches. He offered some Christian guidelines designed to achieve unity in an atmosphere of difference. To help the believers at Rome deal with their problem, he laid down three principles that he discussed in Rom 14:1–15:13.

PRINCIPLE 1: JUDGMENT IS GOD'S RIGHT, NOT MAN'S (14:1–12)

God has welcomed both the "weak" and the "strong." By grace, both are his servants. As servants, neither has the right to pass judgment on the other. That right belongs to God alone (v. 4). Each should act in the light of his own convictions regarding the religious scruples in question. Both the observer and the nonobserver of the food laws and special days may have an equal desire to honor the Lord (v. 6).

"None of us lives for himself" (v. 7) often has been understood in the sense of John Donne's statement, "No man is an island." Paul's statement, however, was not a sociological observation regarding the oneness of humanity. What he said is that all believers live out their lives accountable to God. Decisions about such matters as special days and eating meat are not made in isolation but in accordance with the will of God as understood by the individual.

But the "weak" (immature Christian) must stop passing judgment on his brother who does not share his convictions at such points. And the "strong" must stop scorning his brother who clings to them (v. 10). Both need to realize that they will stand before the judgment seat of God to give an account of themselves to him (vv. 10–12; see 2 Cor 5:10).

Paul characterized the "weak" by their lingering legalism. They tended to be harsh in their criticism of those in the church who did not share their opinions. The "strong" were convinced that Jesus Christ put an end to all religious legalisms. They rejoiced in their liberty in

WORD PICTURE

Weak Faith

Paul used the term *weak* in a figurative sense here. At Rome there were Jewish Christians who were reluctant to give up certain ceremonial aspects of their religious heritage. Therefore, they maintained a literal obedience to the ceremonial part of the Old Testament law. They were "weak" in the sense that they were uncertain about how faith in Christ affected the status of Old Testament regulations.

Christ. But the "strong" may have been tempted to look down on their less mature brothers. One *flouted;* the other *flaunted*—both were wrong!

Section Summary

The believers at Rome were experiencing disagreements about the eating of meat, the observance of special days, and the drinking of wine. Paul taught that harmonious relationships are important. Believers should live without judging others.

PRINCIPLE 2: LOVE REQUIRES SELF-LIMITATIONS FOR THE SAKE OF OTHERS (14:13–22)

Here Paul directed his counsel primarily to the mature. They were able to bear the greater responsibility for healing the breach in fellowship. Thus, he urged them never to place a stumbling block or an occasion to sin in the path of a weaker brother in Christ.

The old taboos on certain ceremonial foods were no longer in force. Jesus taught that it is not what goes into the mouth that makes a person unclean but what comes out (Matt 15:10–11,16–20). Nevertheless, Paul was concerned with the effect of this new freedom on those Christians who still felt the regulations of Judaism were not obsolete. Although no food was unclean in itself, if someone regarded it as unclean, then for that person it was.

If the mature ignored the influence of their conduct on the immature, Paul declared, they no longer walked in love (v. 15). Love willingly gives up all liberties that might cause a brother or sister to stumble.

God's reign is not fulfilled in food and drink laws, but in "righteousness, peace, and joy in the Holy Spirit" (v. 17). Therefore, we are to "pursue what promotes peace and what builds up one another" (v. 19). The peace Paul spoke of here is the peace within the family of believers (see Ps 34:15).

PERSONAL APPLICATION

God has called us to a life of faith. Trust is the willingness to put all of life before God for his approval. Any doubt about the rightness of an action removes it from the category of what is acceptable. This principle is of special help to the Christian in what is sometimes called the "gray area." If it is gray to you, it is wrong—not in itself but in the eyes of the one who considers it inappropriate.

Section Summary

Believers should not influence others to violate their consciences. The mature should not hinder the weak with their freedom. The weak should avoid restricting those who have discovered genuine Christian freedom. Mutual love and respect are the marks of true disciples.

QUESTIONS TO GUIDE YOUR STUDY

1. Paul taught that judgment is a right that belongs to God alone. Considering this, what should be our attitude toward other believers who share different convictions?

2. "None of us lives for himself" (v. 7). How do we apply this principle to our congregations and fellowships? To the larger body of Christ?
3. What is the obligation of the stronger believer toward the weaker believer? What is the obligation of the weaker believer toward the stronger believer?
4. All believers are to "pursue what promotes peace and what builds up one another." When differences arise, what steps can believers take to ensure peaceful and edifying results within the body of Christ?

ROMANS 15

The first thirteen verses of chapter 15 continue Paul's discussion of chapter 14. In dealing with the problem among the believers at Rome, Romans 15:1–13 concludes Paul's message to the Roman Christians. Rounding out chapter 15 is a discussion of Paul's future travel plans, and chapter 16 is the conclusion to his letter.

OLD TESTAMENT REFERENCE

Psalm 69:9 reflects the selfless life of Christ: "The insults of those who insult you have fallen on me." As Paul applied this verse, Christ became the speaker.

PRINCIPLE 3: FOLLOW CHRIST'S EXAMPLE OF FORBEARANCE (15:1–13)

Christ's Example of Self-Denial (vv. 1–3)

Paul's concern that weak and strong Christians live in harmony carries into chapter 15. He linked himself with the "strong" in his appeal that they "bear the weaknesses of those without strength." Rather than pleasing themselves, strong believers are to please their neighbors. By seeking our neighbor's good instead of pleasing ourselves, we follow Christ's example of forbearance. The goal is to help them develop into more mature Christians.

The great example of self-denial for the sake of others is, of course, Jesus Christ. If Christ, the Son of God, did not order his life to please himself, how much more should we give up all personal advantage and follow the path of the Suffering Servant.

The Relevance of Scripture (v. 4)

Verse 4 contains a principle of great significance for the believer. Everything that was written in Scripture in days gone by was written for us (see 1 Cor 10:11; Rom 4:23–24). Not only did it serve the needs of its own day, but it is still relevant in the modern world. Scripture is relevant because it meets our deepest needs.

Through the endurance taught in Scripture and the encouragement it brings, we are enabled to live in hope. The difficulties of today are bearable because God in his Word tells us of a better time to come. He mediates his comfort and encouragement by speaking through his Word to the hearts of receptive believers. To separate ourselves from the Scripture is to turn a deaf ear to the voice of a heavenly Father eager to console.

First Benediction (vv. 5–6)

Paul's wish was that God would grant the church at Rome a spirit of unity. In the benediction of verses 5–6, Paul prayed that his readers would live in harmony with one another and in such accord with Christ that they would be able to glorify God with one voice.

Paul's perspective was that of Jesus Christ, our model for Christian conduct. We are to think as he does and take on his values and priorities. As members of the church draw closer to Christ, they draw closer to other members of the body. The experience of Christian unity produces a symphony of praise to God in which each voice blends with all others to the glory of God.

Welcoming One Another (v. 7)

Both the weak and the strong are to accept one another. The word *welcome* carries the idea of a genuine and heartfelt acceptance. That is what it means to follow Christ.

Second Benediction (vv. 8–13)

This second benediction brings the main body of Paul's letter to the Romans to a close.

Christ became a servant of the Jews to demonstrate the truthfulness of God (v. 8). He confirmed the promises made to the patriarchs by fulfilling them. Now the Gentiles can glorify God for the mercy he has shown them.

God's redemptive plan was that through his Son, born a Jew as to his human nature, he might reach out in reconciling love to those of every nation. In support of the universal scope of God's redemptive work through Christ his Son, Paul cited four Old Testament Scriptures.

Section Summary

Believers are to follow Christ's example of self-denial. Such conduct will result in unity and the acceptance of one another. Christ's acceptance of both Jewish and Gentile believers, played out in the universal scope of his redemptive work, is to be the measure of their acceptance of one another.

OLD TESTAMENT SUPPORT FOR GOD'S REDEMPTIVE WORK THROUGH HIS SON

PASSAGE	EXPLANATION
1. 2 Samuel 22:50 and Psalm 18:49	David vows to praise God among the Gentiles. Israel was to be the instrument through whom God's redemptive work would extend to the Gentiles.
2. Deuteronomy 32:43	From Moses's great hymn celebrating God's victory over Pharaoh and his army: "Rejoice, you nations concerning his people."
3. Psalm 117:1	The salvation of the Gentiles was in God's mind from the very first.
4. Isaiah 11	The Messiah will come as a shoot springing up from the stump of David's family line. He will rule the nations, and the Gentiles will "hope in him."

PAUL'S TRAVEL PLANS (15:14–33)

The Goal of Paul's Ministry (vv. 14–21)

In bringing his letter to a close, Paul expressed his confidence in the character and competence of his readers. He admitted boldness in the way he has written to remind them "on some points" (v. 15). But as a minister of Christ to the Gentiles, he was eager that the offering of the Gentiles as a sacrifice to God would be acceptable.

In seeking to win obedience from the Gentiles, Paul preached the gospel from Jerusalem to Illyricum, a province bordering the Adriatic Sea. It was his ambition to preach the gospel in pioneer areas that had never heard it.

Plans to Visit Rome (vv. 22–29)

At the beginning of his letter, Paul mentioned his oft-delayed plans to visit Rome (1:10–15). Now at the end he repeated them. Only here he disclosed a further plan not mentioned earlier—the evangelization of Spain. Feeling that his work in the east was at a close, he wanted to visit Rome briefly and then press on to Spain (Rom 15:22–25). Obviously, he wrote this letter to gain the support of the Roman church for his mission to the west.

For the present, however, his visit to Rome and points beyond had to be postponed. First, he had to accompany the delegates from the Gentile churches to Jerusalem with the relief offering (vv. 25–28; see also Acts 20:3–6; 24:17). As soon as this mission was completed, Paul would visit Rome while enroute to Spain.

Requests for Prayer (vv. 30–33)

Concerned about the trip to Jerusalem, Paul asked his readers to pray: (1) that he would be delivered from unbelievers in Judea (v. 31), (2) that his ministry on behalf of the poor believers in Jerusalem would be acceptable to them (v. 31), and (3) that God would permit him his anticipated visit to Rome (v. 32).

NEW TESTAMENT REFERENCE

A study of Acts 21:15–28:31 provides insights regarding God's answer to these prayer requests.

Section Summary

This concluding section contains Paul's travel plans and role as a minister to the Gentiles. He wanted to go to Rome in order to extend the Christian mission westward to Spain. He requested prayer from the church for his upcoming mission to Jerusalem.

QUESTIONS TO GUIDE YOUR STUDY

1. Drawing from Paul's words here and in Gospel accounts, in what ways did Jesus demonstrate self-denial? As we follow his example, what principles might we draw on?
2. How is Scripture relevant to believers today? What does 1 Cor 10:11 teach?
3. What were Paul's travel plans for spreading the gospel? What was his driving force?
4. What support does the Old Testament provide about the universal scope of God's redemptive plan? Why was this plan such "news" to the Jewish leaders of Paul's day?

ROMANS 16

This chapter, made up of five separate segments, contains Paul's final words to the believers at Rome. First, the apostle commended Phoebe to the church at Rome. He followed this commendation with a long list of greetings to his friends and helpers living in the capital city, warnings against false teachers, a section of greetings from Paul's companions, and a closing doxology.

HISTORICAL BACKGROUND

Letters of Commendation

The letter of commendation or recommendation was the most common form of letter of mediation in secular letters.

Commendations of the following people are embedded in several of Paul's letters: Phoebe (Rom 16:1); Timothy (1 Cor 4:17; 16:10–11; Phil 2:19–24); and Epaphroditus (Phil 2:25–30).

COMMENDATION FOR PHOEBE (16:1–2)

Letters of commendation were well known in the ancient world. Phoebe, a servant of the church at Cenchreae, may well have been the bearer of this letter to Rome (v. 1). She was a faithful helper of many in the work of the gospel. Paul wanted the Roman Christians to receive and help her in any way she needed (v. 2).

PERSONAL GREETINGS (16:3–16, 21–23)

Paul named twenty-six people in verses 3–16. Nowhere else in Paul's writings do we find such a lengthy list of personal greetings. Furthermore,

Paul revealed an intimate knowledge of their family relationships and Christian service.

Some have argued that Paul could not have known so many in a church he had never visited. However, the many who are named here may have been Paul's friends and converts in other places who had moved to Rome. Since he had never been to Rome, he would have been eager to greet the ones he knew.

In verses 21–23, Paul sent greetings to the Roman believers from his companions. Those named were with Paul when he was writing the letter, likely from Corinth. One of his companions, Timothy, occupied a special place in Paul's heart and ministry.

Section Summary

Paul closed his letter typically with greetings and commendations from various individuals. Included was a commendation for Phoebe, a servant of the church at Cenchreae, who may have been the bearer of his letter to the Roman believers.

WARNING AGAINST THOSE WHO CREATE DISSENSIONS (16:17–20)

It is impossible to identify these creators of dissension with any particular group. They have been variously identified as Judaizers, antinomians, or charismatic enthusiasts. They opposed the doctrines that had been taught to the Roman believers. They were self-serving and smooth talking (v. 18).

Those who cause divisions are not serving the Lord but are "slaves of their own base desires" (Moffat, v. 18).

These kinds of people were to be noted and avoided by the church. And the alerted believers could rest assured that the God of peace would soon crush Satan under their feet (v. 20; see Gen 3:15). This would take place at the end of the age, which Paul expected soon. Verse 20 is a benediction.

OLD TESTAMENT REFERENCE

Among the "seven [things that] are detestable to [the Lord]," the writer of Proverbs listed in the most emphatic position "one who stirs up trouble among brothers" (Prov 6:16,19).

Section Summary

In every group there seem to be those intent on causing trouble. False teachers are identified by their teaching. The church must accept or reject that which claims to be true based on its consistency with revealed truth. God's Word stands as the only absolute.

DOXOLOGY (16:25–27)

Paul closed his letter with a magnificent doxology. In the original Greek text, these verses are one long, involved sentence that reads differently from the usual Pauline doxology. In it we find many of the major themes of the letter to the Romans:

- God is the one who is able to establish and strengthen the believer.
- The gospel is not taught by men but was received by direct revelation from Jesus Christ.
- The gospel centers in the life, death, and resurrection of Jesus Christ.
- The gospel is universal in its purpose.

In the coming ages the songs of the redeemed will ring throughout the courts of heaven. Redemption will be complete. The eternal purpose of God will reach its fulfillment. God will be forever praised.

Section Summary

The objective in preaching the gospel to all nations is "the obedience of faith among all the Gentiles." Therefore, "to the only wise God, through Jesus Christ—to him be the glory forever!"

QUESTIONS TO GUIDE YOUR STUDY

1. Who was Phoebe? What does her position and importance to Paul's mission say about the role of women in the early church?
2. Paul had never been to Rome. How did he know so many believers in the church at Rome?
3. Paul warned against false teachers. What is our basis for putting into check false teaching in the church?
4. Paul's doxology described several characteristics of God. What are they?

1 Corinthians

INTRODUCTION

For Paul's most complete statement of the gospel of God's grace, we must turn to Romans. But for his most extensive correspondence with a single church, we must turn to the Corinthian letters.

Here, several of his converts struggled with the responsibility of being the people of God in the midst of a pagan city. Some of them were saved out of lifestyles marked by gross sin (1 Cor 6:9–11), and the temptation to lapse into old vices remained strong. They all lived under the relentless pressures of a pagan society which sought to conform them to its corrupt ways. Thus, 1 Corinthians provides the most intimate disclosure of the inner life and workings of an early congregation to be found in the New Testament.

1 CORINTHIANS IN A "NUTSHELL"

Purpose:	To answer the Corinthians' questions and to restore their areas of weakness
Major Themes:	Christian wisdom, sexual immorality, marriage and divorce, spiritual gifts, women in the church, the Lord's Supper, and the resurrection

AUTHOR

The letter (1:1,2,16–21) as well as church tradition acknowledge Paul as the author of 1 Corinthians. This affirmation generally has gone unchallenged.

HISTORICAL BACKGROUND

The Apostle Paul

Paul is the official name of this outstanding missionary apostle. Paul's Jewish name was Saul. He was born on Turkey's southern shore in Tarsus. Well trained in Jewish Scriptures and tradition, he also learned the trade of tentmaking. He is the author of many New Testament epistles. Paul's third missionary journey centered in Ephesus, from which the gospel probably spread into the surrounding cities. From Ephesus he carried on a correspondence with the Corinthian church. While in Corinth at the end of this journey, he wrote his epistle to the Romans.

PURPOSE FOR WRITING

Paul dealt with several problems in this letter. He learned of these matters through the report from Chloe's people (1:11), common rumors (5:1), and from information received from the church (7:1; 8:1; 12:1; 16:1). Paul wrote to answer the questions the Corinthians put to him but had other concerns as well. Although the church was gifted (1:4–7), it was equally immature and unspiritual (3:1–4). Paul wanted to restore the church in its areas of weakness. Through the inspiration of the Holy Spirit, he articulated the New Testament's clearest exposition of the Lord's Supper, the resurrection, and spiritual gifts.

PROBLEMS REFLECTED IN 1 CORINTHIANS

PROBLEM	PASSAGE
Factions	1:10–17; 3:5–15
Worldly Wisdom	1:18–31; 2:6–3:4
Unethical Conduct	5:1–6:20
Marriage and Celibacy	7:1–40
Idols	8:1–11:2
Actions of Women Leaders	11:3–16
Lord's Supper	11:17–34
Spiritual Gifts	12:1–14:40
Unbelief in the Resurrection	15:1–58

Chart taken from Joe Blair, *Introducing the New Testament,* 155.

DATE OF WRITING

According to 1 Cor 16:8, 9, Paul was in Ephesus when he wrote this letter. Although we are not able to date this letter with great precision, we can be reasonably accurate if we date it AD 54 or 55.

A CHRONOLOGY OF PAUL'S RELATIONSHIP WITH THE CORINTHIAN CHURCH*

1. Paul evangelized Corinth during his second journey (Acts 18:1–11).
2. Paul wrote a letter to Corinth, now lost, in which he urged Christians to avoid association with professing believers who were immoral (1 Cor 5:9–11).
3. Paul wrote 1 Corinthians from Ephesus during his third missionary journey to advise the Corinthians on handling problems in the church.

A CHRONOLOGY OF PAUL'S RELATIONSHIP WITH THE CORINTHIAN CHURCH*

4. Paul made a "painful" visit to Corinth from Ephesus to correct problems in the church. His visit failed to achieve its aim (2 Cor 2:1).
5. Paul sent another letter, also lost, calling the Corinthians to repentance and urging discipline for an opponent in the church (2 Cor 2:4–11). Titus carried the letter to Corinth. Scholars have named this the "severe" letter.
6. Paul left Ephesus for Troas, and then to Macedonia, to await word on the success of Titus's visit (2 Cor 2:12–13).
7. Titus met Paul in Macedonia with the report of the Corinthian church's warm acceptance of Paul's letter and eagerness to see him (2 Cor 7:5–16).
8. Paul wrote 2 Corinthians from Macedonia and sent it to Corinth by Titus.
9. Paul went to Corinth for his third visit (2 Cor 12:14; 13:1; Acts 20:2).

*List taken from Thomas D. Lea, *The New Testament: Its Background and Message*, 412.

AUDIENCE

The church at Corinth was a picture of converts who came out of the environment and culture of the city of Corinth. The church had several problems, among them a leadership problem producing divisions in the church (1:10–17). Immoral practices were not being dealt with (5:1–6:20). An enthusiastic group in the church flaunted their spiritual gifts (12:1–14:40). A legalistic group was concerned about dietary laws (8:1–10:32). Some were abusing the Lord's Supper (11:17–34), and others were offering false teachings regarding the resurrection (15:1–58). These matters—in addition to its multiethnic makeup of Greeks, Romans, and Jews and a mixture of social classes including rich, poor, and slave—made for a unique and troubled congregation.

THE DOCTRINES OF 1 CORINTHIANS

The focus of 1 Corinthians is not on doctrinal theology but pastoral theology. This letter deals with:

- The problem of those who bring division to the body of Christ (1:11–3:4)
- The treatment of fellow Christians who sin (5:1–13)
- Matters of sexuality in marriage and divorce (7:1–40)
- Propriety in church worship (11:2–34)
- Disputes about food (8:1–11:1)

THE THEOLOGICAL SIGNIFICANCE AND RELEVANCE OF 1 CORINTHIANS

If Paul were to write a letter to the average church today, he probably would rewrite much of 1 Corinthians. The Corinthians' world was much like our modern world. The people had the same thirst for intellectualism, the same moral permissiveness, and certainly the same fascination for the spectacular. The church resembled our churches—extremely proud, affluent, and fiercely eager for acceptance by the world.

In doctrine, there existed a mixture of truth and error. In ethics, the church manifested widespread immorality and worldliness. Two valuable contributions come from this letter. First, we have the doctrinal and pastoral expositions of the topics discussed. Second, we have Paul's practical counsel for living as Christians in a pagan society. Paul carefully defined each issue and then offered helpful principles to deal with them. What we learn from the apostle's method is as important for the contemporary church as the solutions he articulated.

HISTORICAL BACKGROUND

The City of Corinth

The city of Corinth was located on a narrow strip of land that connected the Peloponnesian Peninsula with northern Greece. It had two seaports, Cenchrea on the Aegean side in the east and Lechaeum at the edge of the gulf of Corinth in the west. The city's location made it a crossroads for travel and commerce and contributed to its prosperity. Ship captains, eager to avoid the stormy dangers of sailing around the Peloponnesian Straits on the south, would dock at one port of Corinth. Their cargo was unloaded, hauled overland, and then loaded in another vessel in port on the opposite side. They avoided the risk of losing ships and lives in the dangerous voyage along the southern route. Corinth was also known for hosting athletic events known as the Isthmian games. These events took place every two years. Huge crowds thronged to the city for the festivities.

BASIC OUTLINE FOR 1 CORINTHIANS

I. Introduction (1:1–9)
II. Concerning Divisions (1:10–3:4)
III. Concerning Leadership (3:5–4:21)
IV. Concerning Immorality (5:1–6:20)
V. Concerning Marriage (7:1–40)
VI. Concerning Food Offered to Idols (8:1–11:1)
VII. Concerning Orderly Worship (11:2–34)
VIII. Concerning Spiritual Gifts (12:1–14:40)
IX. Concerning the Resurrection (15:1–58)
X. Concerning the Collection and Closing Remarks (16:1–24)

QUESTIONS TO GUIDE YOUR STUDY

1. Who were Paul's readers? Why did he write to them?
2. What problems did Paul address at Corinth?
3. What are the key doctrines Paul addressed in this letter?
4. What makes his message relevant to today's readers?

1 CORINTHIANS 1

Paul visited Corinth on his second missionary journey and began teaching immediately in the synagogue there. Some of the Jews believed, but

PAUL'S LISTS OF SPIRITUAL GIFTS*

SPIRITUAL GIFT	ROM 12:6–8	1 COR 12:8–10	1 COR 12:28	1 COR 12:29–30	EPH 4:11
Apostle			1	1	1
Prophet	1	4	2	2	2
Teacher	3		3	3	5
Pastor					4
Miracles		3	4	4	
Discernment of Spirits		5			
Word of Wisdom, Knowledge		1			
Evangelists					3
Encouragers	4				
Faith		2			
Tongues		6	8	6	
Interpretation		7		7	
Ministry/ Serving	2				
Administration			7		
Leaders	6				
Helpers			6		
Mercy	7				
Giving	5				

* Chart presents the order in which the gifts listed appear in the passage.

leaders and others rejected his witness. He continued his ministry in the home of a believer, Titius Justus, a Gentile who lived next door to the synagogue (Acts 18:7). Although Paul met resistance, his work went well, and a struggling church began with even the synagogue ruler and his family becoming Christians (Acts 18:7–8).

The Corinthian church, plagued with problems, needed Paul's firm guidance. The problems with which they were struggling presented challenges to the nature and unity of the church. In this first part of his letter, chapter 1, Paul addresses two of their problems:

- The challenge of factions within their church
- Believers' fascination with worldly wisdom

GREETINGS (1:1–3)

Writer (v. 1). The writer of 1 Corinthians identifies himself as the apostle Paul. This affirmation generally has gone unchallenged. The letter

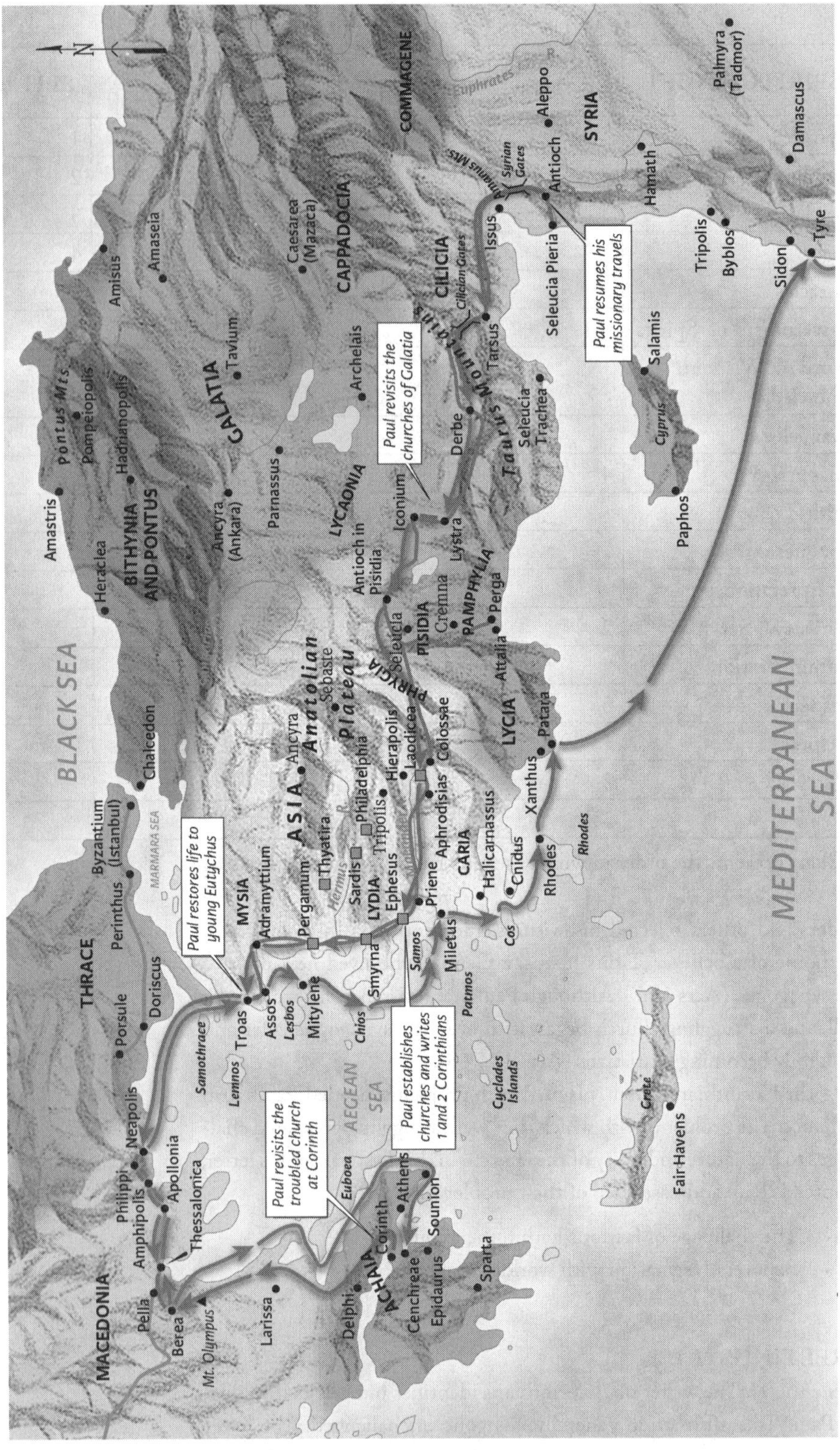
BLACK SEA
MEDITERRANEAN SEA
AEGEAN SEA
MARMARA SEA
MACEDONIA
THRACE
ACHAIA
MYSIA
LYDIA
CARIA
LYCIA
ASIA
Anatolian Plateau
PHRYGIA
PISIDIA
PAMPHYLIA
LYCAONIA
GALATIA
BITHYNIA AND PONTUS
Pontus Mts.
CAPPADOCIA
CILICIA
COMMAGENE
SYRIA
Taurus Mountains
Amanus Mts.
Euphrates R.
Paul revisits the troubled church at Corinth
Paul establishes churches and writes 1 and 2 Corinthians
Paul restores life to young Eutychus
Paul revisits the churches of Galatia
Paul resumes his missionary travels
Pella
Berea
Mt. Olympus
Amphipolis
Thessalonica
Philippi
Apollonia
Neapolis
Larissa
Delphi
Corinth
Cenchreae
Epidaurus
Sparta
Athens
Sounion
Euboea
Samothrace
Lemnos
Porsule
Doriscus
Perinthus
Byzantium (Istanbul)
Chalcedon
Troas
Assos
Lesbos
Mitylene
Adramyttium
Pergamum
Thyatira
Sardis
Smyrna
Chios
Ephesus
Samos
Patmos
Miletus
Priene
Cos
Halicarnassus
Cnidus
Rhodes
Cyclades Islands
Crete
Fair Havens
Philadelphia
Tripolis
Hierapolis
Laodicea
Colossae
Aphrodisias
Xanthus
Patara
Ancyra
Sebaste
Seleucia
Antioch in Pisidia
Cremna
Perga
Attalia
Iconium
Lystra
Derbe
Parnassus
Ancyra (Ankara)
Archelais
Tavium
Heraclea
Amastris
Hadrianopolis
Pompeiopolis
Amisus
Amaseia
Caesarea (Mazaca)
Tarsus
Cilician Gates
Seleucia Trachea
Issus
Syrian Gates
Antioch
Seleucia Pieria
Aleppo
Hamath
Cyprus
Salamis
Paphos
Tripolis
Byblos
Sidon
Tyre
Damascus
Palmyra (Tadmor)

was written sometime around AD 54 or 55, near the end of Paul's three-year ministry in Ephesus (1 Cor 16:5–9; Acts 20:31).

Recipients (v. 2). Paul addresses his letter "to the church of God at Corinth" (v. 2). The city of Corinth, an important city of trade, had a reputation for wickedness. The church at Corinth was Gentile, and its converts came from a wide variety of backgrounds and religious experiences. These members had little, if any, preparation for living the Christian life, unlike other churches that were made up of God-fearers, proselytes, and Jewish converts. In addressing the believers at Corinth, Paul had to deal with basic moral, church, and doctrinal matters.

We see a few notable expansions on the standard salutation:

Paul identified himself as one whom God called "as an apostle of Christ Jesus" (v. 1). Paul did not choose the vocation to which he was called of God. Rather, it was a divine summons that he obeyed.

Paul designated his readers as "the church of God at Corinth" (v. 2). The word *church* comes from a word made up of two words: "out of" and "a calling." It refers to a body of people who have been "called out" and gathered for God's purposes. They are those who, through faith in Jesus Christ, have been separated unto God. They belong to God and are at his disposal.

Paul magnified the grace and peace of God in his prayer for the Corinthian believers (v. 3). The two qualities—peace and grace—sum up the essence of the Christian gospel. *Grace* is the unmerited favor of God and the expression of his love that we could never deserve. *Peace* is the consequence of God's grace in the lives of those who confess Jesus Christ as Lord.

THANKSGIVING (1:4–9)

A customary feature of the Hellenistic letter was thanksgiving. As with the address and prayer, it preceded the main body of the letter.

Thanking God for the Corinthians (v. 4)

Paul knew he must address some tough problems at Corinth. He began with a word of affirmation—expressing what was right in the church. Paul thanked God for the evidence of his work among the Corinthians.

Paul's Readers Enriched in Every Way (vv. 5–6)

The effect of God's grace in the Corinthian church was seen in their gifts of speaking and knowledge. Both endowments from God were given so the Corinthian believers would not be lacking (see 1 Cor 12:8; 13:1–2). But both gifts were subject to abuse in the church.

HISTORICAL BACKGROUND

The Hellenistic Letter

Generally, Paul's epistles follow the normal pattern of the Hellenistic letter, the basic form of which consists of five major sections:

1. Opening (sender, addressee, greeting)
2. Thanksgiving or blessing (often with prayer of intercession, well wishes, or personal greetings)
3. The burden of the letter (including citation of classical sources and arguments)
4. Parenesis (ethical instruction, exhortation)
5. Closing (mention of personal plans, mutual friends, benediction)

HISTORICAL BACKGROUND

Paul's opening greeting to his readers contains some expansions on the standard salutation. He refers to his vocation as an apostle—a divine summons that he obeyed. He describes his readers as a "church," those who have been sanctified and called to be separated unto God.

NEW TESTAMENT REFERENCE

It seems that Paul anticipated that this event would occur in his own lifetime (1 Cor 15:51–52; 1 Thess 4:16–17). This would explain his statement that the Corinthians were eagerly awaiting "the revelation of our Lord Jesus Christ" (1 Cor 1:7).

FACTS ABOUT THE CHURCH

TERM	EXPANDED MEANING
A called-out group of people	The church is a group of people gathered for a specific reason.
"Sanctified"	The church is separated unto God for his purposes.

THE GIFTS BESTOWED ON THE CORINTHIAN BELIEVERS

GIFT OF GRACE	PURPOSE
"In all speech"	for telling the truth
"All knowledge"	for one's grasp of the truth

Anticipating the Lord's Return (vv. 7–8)

Early Christians believed not only that Jesus Christ had died for their sins and rose from the dead but that he would soon return triumphantly in glory.

Paul assured (v. 8) this gifted, expectant congregation that Christ would provide what they needed to strengthen and sustain them to the end. When they appear before him, they will be blameless. This theme appears elsewhere in Paul's New Testament writings (see Rom 5:9–11; 8:31–39).

WORD PICTURE

Eagerly wait

"This phrase is only one word in the Greek text and is an interesting compound consisting of three words. It is made up of two prefixed prepositions 'from' and 'out of' and the verb 'to wait for.' It means 'to await or expect eagerly,' 'to anxiously await,' and 'to wait eagerly but patiently for something. . . . The double preposition in compound implies a degree of earnestness and intensity of expectation. . . . The present tense emphasizes the continuous action and the participle expresses an attendant circumstance." Fritz Rienecker, *Linguistic Key to the Greek New Testament* (Zondervan, 1980), 386.

The Fellowship of Christ (v. 9)

The remarkable hope Paul expressed in verse 8 rests on a sure foundation, namely, the faithfulness of God. He is its unfailing guarantee. The word *fellowship* describes sharing with Christ. It refers to participation and communion. The call of God is a call to relationship and participation in the life of his Son.

Paul's salutation, in these first nine verses of chapter 1, reveals many aspects of God's call to us in Jesus Christ, as the following chart shows.

REVELATION ABOUT GOD'S CALL	VERSE
1. It sets us apart for God, making us saints.	v. 2
2. It relates us to the vibrant community of those in every place who call upon the name of Christ.	v. 2
3. It is an expression of God's grace and brings peace.	v. 3
4. It always enriches and endows us.	vv. 5,7
5. It is mediated through testimony borne to Christ.	v. 6
6. It plants a sustaining hope and assures an ultimate deliverance.	vv. 7–8

REVELATION ABOUT GOD'S CALL	VERSE
7. It rests on the faithfulness of God and invites us to share in the life of Christ.	v. 9

THE REPORT FROM CORINTH (1:10–17)

Following his affirmation of the Corinthians, Paul directed his attention (1:1–4:21) to the problem of divisions in the church. Not only did he address these divisions at the outset; he dealt with them at greater length than any other issue except the charismatic error in chapters 12–14.

Quarreling Among the Corinthians (vv. 10–12)

How did Paul know about the conflict among the Corinthians? Members of Chloe's household had told Paul about what was taking place. The New Testament reveals little about Chloe, but she was well-enough known to give validity to Paul's source of information.

In verse 12 Paul specified the division or factions within the Corinthian church: "I belong to Paul"; "I belong to Apollos"; "I belong to Cephas"; "I belong to Christ."

HISTORICAL BACKGROUND

Paul began his letter in the customary fashion, using the normal pattern of the Hellenistic letter: a greeting, a salutation, and a lengthy expression of his thanksgiving for the Corinthian believers. In his thanksgiving prayer, he offered thanks for their reception of the gospel, their giftedness, and particularly for God's faithfulness.

Three Probing Questions (v. 13)

Paul responded to this rivalry by asking three rhetorical questions. Paul's purpose for these questions was not to receive information from his readers but rather to make strong affirmations.

PAUL'S PROBING QUESTIONS

QUESTION	AFFIRMATION
1. "Is Christ divided?"	Christ is not one among many.
2. "Was Paul crucified for you?"	*Only* Christ can atone for sin.
3. "Were you baptized in Paul's name?"	A believer's allegiance can only be to Christ.

These three questions together form a collective affirmation: The person who responds in faith to Christ must give himself or herself totally to Christ.

PRACTICAL APPLICATION

Split churches today cannot improve upon this strategy. Healing and unity are found in Jesus Christ—in realizing both who he is and what he has done for us and will do for us if we will allow Him.

The Priority of Preaching (vv. 14–17)

Paul next emphasized the fact that he baptized few of his converts. This ministry he entrusted to others while he devoted his primary energies to preaching the gospel. Paul expressed this concern lest converts exaggerate the importance of the role of the baptizer (v. 15). He was equally concerned that no one exaggerate the skills one uses to proclaim the gospel. Actions that draw attention to the one proclaiming the message shift the focus from the message to the messenger. When this happens, the cross of Christ is "emptied of its effect" (v. 17).

Section Summary

Paul's first major topic was the problem of factions in the Corinthian church. Some were claiming to belong to Paul, some Apollos, others Cephas, and yet others Christ. Paul showed the sinfulness and folly of such division. God does not act in the way human wisdom might expect. God redeems men and women by the foolishness of the cross, not by anything that would enhance human pride. Paul taught that the gospel message did not originate in profound human thought but in the Holy Spirit himself.

THE MESSAGE OF THE CROSS (1:18–31)

The emphasis on the priority of preaching in verse 17 now advances to a focus on the message of the cross. It is certainly one of the greatest passages in the New Testament. At this point in his letter, Paul shifted to the message of the cross because the Corinthian church showed a great misunderstanding of the essential truth of the gospel:

- They had a wrong concept of wisdom (1:18–2:5).
- They had a wrong concept of the gospel (2:6–13).
- They had a wrong concept of spirituality (2:14–3:4).

In verses 18–31, Paul addressed the Corinthians' wrong concept of wisdom and set forth three distinct truths about the cross of Christ:

1. The cross of Christ is necessary to the knowledge of God (vv. 18–21).
2. The cross of Christ requires the response of faith (vv. 22–25).
3. The cross of Christ allows for no boasting in God's presence (vv. 26–31).

WORD PICTURE

Perishing

This word is a compound made up of the preposition "out of" and the verb "to destroy." It means "to ruin," "to be lost," "to lose utterly." "The preposition in the compound is perfective and the present tense indicates that the goal is ideally reached. A complete transformation of the subjects is required to bring them out of the ruin implicit in their state." Fritz Rienecker, *Linguistic Key to the Greek New Testament* (Zondervan, 1980), 387.

Necessary to the Knowledge of God (vv. 18–21)

God seeks to make himself known to us, and he uses many media to confront us. These include nature, conscience, the Scriptures, and his self-disclosure in the cross of Jesus Christ.

However, the world neither appreciates nor understands God's confrontations. The message of the cross is "foolishness to those who are perishing" (v. 18). The world has its own spokespersons: the wise man, the professional scholar, and the subtle debater (v. 20). It has its own criteria for acceptance or rejection, which is visible evidence or rational proofs. And it has its own prevailing attitude: self-sufficiency and confidence in the power of its own reasoning and technology.

GOD'S REVELATION TO US

MEDIA	PASSAGE
Nature	Romans 1:20
Conscience	Romans 2:14–16
Scriptures	Romans 3:1–2
Cross of Jesus Christ	1 Corinthians 1:18–21

In verse 21 Paul rendered the startling indictment of human wisdom: "The world did not know God through wisdom." The fatal flaw in man's wisdom and ingenuity is that it leaves him without the knowledge of God.

Paul went on to write that "God was pleased to save those who believe through the foolishness of what is preached" (v. 21). "What is preached" refers not to the act of preaching but to the content of the proclamation.

Requires the Response of Faith (vv. 22–25)

In verses 22–25 Paul mentioned two groups for whom the call to faith in a crucified Lord was especially offensive. These groups were:

The Jews. The Jews looked for signs that identify the Messiah, who would be their deliverer from Roman oppression. Because there was no place for a Messiah who would die on the cross, faith in Christ was a stumbling block to the Jew.

The Greeks. The Greeks embraced human wisdom and demanded rational, empirical proofs. That an itinerant Jewish teacher sentenced to die on the cross was the Son of God and Savior of the world seemed foolish.

Verse 25 affirmed to Paul's readers that all who respond in faith to God's call in Jesus Christ experience him as God's power and wisdom, whether Jews or Greeks.

Allows No Boasting in God's Presence (vv. 26–31)

Paul reminded the Corinthians of who they were and where they came from. Not many were rich, famous, and powerful. He then said something startling. God delights in taking those whom the world despises and raising them up. In this way, it becomes clear to all that what has been done is God's work.

Paul closed this chapter with the exclamation, "Let the one who boasts, boast in the Lord" (v. 31).

Section Summary

Paul shifted to the message of the cross because the Corinthian church showed a great misunderstanding of the essential truth of the gospel. He addressed the Corinthians' wrong concept of wisdom and set forth three distinct truths about the cross of Christ: (1) the cross of Christ is necessary to the knowledge of God; (2) the cross of Christ requires the response of faith; and (3) the cross of Christ allows for no boasting in God's presence.

QUESTIONS TO GUIDE YOUR STUDY

1. Paul opened this letter with an expanded salutation. From this salutation, what do we learn about the church?
2. Why was Paul thankful for the Corinthian believers? What was his prayer for them?
3. What kind of report had Paul received about the Corinthian church? What was Paul's response to the troubles at Corinth?
4. Describe the message of the cross. What are its essential truths?

1 CORINTHIANS 2

This chapter continues Paul's theme of the gospel and the wisdom of the world. Some of the Corinthian believers were enamored with the wisdom of certain men. They thought the church could benefit more from the world's wisdom and philosophy to win converts to Christ rather than relying on the message of the cross.

HISTORICAL BACKGROUND

Paul was one of the best-educated men of his day. He was thoroughly trained as a Jewish rabbi. But his learning likely went beyond his own religious tradition. His early years were spent in Tarsus, home of a major Jewish school. We don't know whether he studied at that school, but growing up in Tarsus prepared Paul to be at home in a variety of worlds. It's evident that he was skilled in numerous languages. Paul was a Roman citizen—an indication that he was born into a family cosmopolitan in outlook.

PAUL'S MINISTRY IN CORINTH (2:1–5)

Paul reminded the Corinthians about the message he brought, the way he brought it, and the motivation that impelled him when he came to Corinth. Recall that Paul affirmed both the speech and wisdom of the Corinthians as he opened his letter. Now he told them that in his communicating the gospel to them, he relied neither on impressive speech nor wisdom.

His Message (vv. 1–2)

Paul was single-minded. He intentionally focused on one truth: "Jesus Christ and him crucified." With his rich background, he could have imparted many things to the Corinthians. But he chose to focus on the most important.

His Manner (vv. 1,3–4)

Evidently Paul was not in his top form when he came to Corinth. He was suffering emotionally and physically, and he came across as weak.

Consequently, Paul relied not on his own power but the power of the Holy Spirit as he presented Christ.

His Motivation (v. 5).

Paul's compelling desire was for other people to place their faith in the power of God rather than in the wisdom of men.

Section Summary

Paul preached the gospel to Corinth, a great urban center of his day. His basic message was simple and clear: "Jesus Christ and him crucified." Throughout his ministry Paul understood his responsibility as a messenger of God and depended on God's power, not his own strength, to carry out his mission.

PERSONAL APPLICATION

Believers and churches today are seeking to meet the challenges of an increasingly urbanized society that depends on advancing, new technologies. But they cannot improve on the essential strategy Paul reveals here. Today's churches often fail to gain New Testament results because they do not rely on the power of the Holy Spirit to take the message and make it effective in the lives of hearers.

CHRISTIAN WISDOM (2:6–16)

To guard against his repudiation of worldly wisdom being interpreted as hostility toward all wisdom, Paul gave his readers a concept of wisdom that is distinctly Christian.

The Gospel Is Distinct from Human Wisdom (vv. 6–9)

The word *however* introduces a contrast between the world's wisdom and the Christian wisdom of which Paul spoke. Throughout this section of the chapter (vv. 6–16), Paul built his view of Christian wisdom, as the chart on page 382 shows.

OLD TESTAMENT REFERENCE

Borrowing from Isa 64:4, Paul quoted, "What no eye has seen, no ear has heard, and no human heart has conceived—God has prepared these things for those who love him" (1 Cor 2:9). He appears to be making two points here: (1) God's ways are not conceivable by the human mind. (2) The human mind is ignorant of the salvation God has prepared for those who love him. Therefore, our human methods of comprehension—eyes, ears, and understanding—cannot give us any idea of the wonderful things God has already prepared for "those who love him."

The Role of the Spirit (vv. 10–13)

The divine origin of the message is the Holy Spirit. Paul revealed at least two of the Spirit's activities regarding his role of revealing the wisdom of God.

"The Spirit searches everything" (v. 10). The phrase "searches everything" means that the Spirit penetrates all things, even the "depths of God." The word *deep* often refers to the unfathomable depths of the sea.

The Spirit knows the thoughts of God (v. 11). Paul presented the argument that nobody really knows what goes on inside a person's mind—the memories, reflections, motives—except for that person's spirit. In a similar way, no one can know what goes on in God's mind except the Spirit of God.

In verse 12 we come to the central issue of verses 6–16: When we come to Christ, we receive God's Spirit, who searches and knows the mind of God. He can impart the things of God to us. Worldly wisdom, however impressive, cannot begin to do for us what God's Spirit can.

PAUL'S VIEW ON CHRISTIAN WISDOM

KEY POINT	PASSAGE
1. Christian wisdom exists among mature believers.	v. 6
2. Christian wisdom is not to be confused with the world's wisdom.	vv. 6,8
3. Christian wisdom centers on God's redemptive plan through the ages.	vv. 7,9
4. Christian wisdom is revealed to us by the Spirit.	vv. 10–12
5. Christian wisdom is imparted to others by us who have been taught by the Spirit.	v. 13
6. Christian wisdom is folly to the unspiritual person.	vv. 14–16

Spiritual Discernment (vv. *14–16*). Paul contrasted the unspiritual person's inability to make right judgments with that of the spiritual person.

CHARACTERISTICS OF THE UNSPIRITUAL PERSON

CHARACTERISTIC	REASON
Does not accept the things that come from the Spirit	They are foolishness.
Cannot understand the things that come from the Spirit	They are spiritually discerned.

Section Summary

To guard against his repudiation of worldly wisdom being interpreted as discrediting all wisdom, Paul gave his readers a distinctly Christian concept of wisdom. Christian wisdom exists among mature believers, and the Holy Spirit reveals the wisdom of God to believers, for only the Spirit knows the mind of God.

QUESTIONS TO GUIDE YOUR STUDY

1. What characterized Paul's ministry at Corinth? What can we learn from his strategy that can be applied today?
2. What is the difference between worldly wisdom and Christian wisdom?
3. What is the role of the Spirit in revealing the wisdom of God?
4. What is spiritual discernment? How does it work in the believer?

1 CORINTHIANS 3

In this chapter Paul took a more direct approach with his indictment of the divisions in the church at Corinth. Using metaphors from agriculture, architecture, and Judaism, Paul delivered insight and warnings that define the proper roles of faithful servants. Key points of this chapter include:

- Although many laborers contribute to the planting and watering of the seed of the gospel, only God gives that seed growth.
- As Christians labor in doing the work of God's kingdom, only genuine building materials will stand the test of judgment.
- Believers are God's temple because God's Spirit dwells within them. They are not to destroy God's temple, or God will destroy them.
- Believers are to draw a distinction between worldly wisdom and God's wisdom and not be deceived by the world's way of thinking.

"WORLDLY" CHURCH MEMBERS (3:1–4)

Paul lamented that he could not address his readers as spiritual people (v. 1). Instead, he must address them as "worldly" because of the jealousy and strife in their midst (v. 3). As "babies in Christ," they still required a milk diet. Therefore, Paul could not set before them "solid food" to digest.

These first four verses set the stage for the rest of the chapter in which Paul dealt with the division within the church. What follows is vintage Paul—a powerful mixture of insight, warning, and appeal. He delivered three powerful metaphors regarding the work of the servant.

METAPHORS OF THE LABORER

METAPHOR	OBJECT	REASON FOR USE	KEY POINT
Agriculture (vv. 5–9)	Field	Insight	Only God gives growth.
Architecture (vv. 10–15)	Building	Warning	Only genuine building materials withstand the test.
Judaism (vv. 16–17)	Temple	Strong warning	Believers are God's temple, and God's temple is sacred.

Section Summary

Paul viewed the Corinthian believers as mere infants in Christ. Because of their jealousy and strife, they were not mature enough for the "solid food" he hoped to give them.

PERSONAL APPLICATION

This metaphor provides an encouraging truth for all Christians of all ages. It teaches that every believer has equal access to God's favor. Arduous labor is possible for all God's servants, whereas a large harvest is not always.

GOD GIVES THE GROWTH (3:5–9)

Paul used two key terms that require special attention from the reader: "servants" and "Lord." God's servants are many, but God alone is Lord. The roles of the two must never be confused. However, the Corinthians obviously were giving to certain servants of God their devotion that rightly belonged only to God.

To clarify the roles of the servant and the Lord, Paul used an agricultural metaphor to portray the important but subordinate role of man in the work of the gospel. Paul "planted" the gospel at Corinth, while Apollos, who came later, "watered" it. As a result of the faithfulness of both of these men, many were saved. But what was the proper explanation of this harvest? Did Paul or Apollos accomplish their salvation? The answer is no! It is *God* who gives the growth. Only he has the power to cause the seed of the gospel message to grow.

HISTORICAL BACKGROUND

Apollos

Apollos was an Alexandrian Jew who came to Ephesus following Paul's first visit and was taught Christian doctrine by Priscilla and Aquila. Apollos was skilled in interpreting Scripture, and there is evidence that he was a more polished speaker than Paul or Peter. Although one of the splinter groups in Corinth seemed to pit Apollos against Paul, there is no indication that Apollos encouraged this. In 1 Cor 16:12 Paul referred to Apollos as "our brother." In one of Paul's latest letters, Titus, Paul urged Titus to help Apollos on his way.

AN AGRICULTURAL LESSON

ANALOGY	EXPLANATION	AGENT	RESULTS
Field (v. 9)	The church at Corinth		A harvest
Planting (v. 6)	Spreading the seed of the gospel message	Christian laborers	Laborer rewarded for labor
Watering (v. 6)	Nurturing and cultivating the implanted seed	Christian laborers	Laborer rewarded for labor
Growth (v. 7)	Development and fruitfulness of the seed	God	God's blessings on the work of his laborers

Section Summary

To clarify the roles of the servant and the Lord, Paul used an agricultural metaphor to portray the important but subordinate role of humankind in the work of the gospel. Both "planting" and "watering" by the servants are required for an abundant harvest of the gospel message. But growth comes from God. Only he has the power to cause the seed of the gospel message to grow.

TEST OF FIRE (3:10–15)

Paul now employed an architectural metaphor. In this metaphor, Christ is the only foundation that could be laid. Paul already laid this foundation through his ministry of spreading the gospel message in Corinth. Now others were building on that foundation, and they needed to take care how they were doing it.

The adequacy or integrity of any building material is shown when it is subjected to a test. The Christian's work will be tested by fire on the day of judgment, showing it for what it is (v. 13).

The believer whose building materials are combustible, including wood, hay, or straw, will find his or her work consumed with fire—"burned up." This word refers to something that is burned up *completely*. Those who use noncombustible building materials such as gold, silver, or costly stones (granite and marble) will find their labor will stand the test. Such a laborer will "receive a reward." Those who have built poorly will suffer loss, but they themselves will be saved as a person who is rescued from a fire.

Paul intended that his reminder of God's impending judgment upon the work of all his servants should give pause to those in Corinth who were responsible for divisions in the church.

Section Summary

Paul used an architectural metaphor to drive home a point about the importance of the genuineness of one's building materials for the work of the kingdom. The adequacy or integrity of any building material depends on the test it will have to meet. That test for the Christian's building is fire on the day of judgment.

DESTROYING GOD'S TEMPLE (3:16–17)

Paul used yet another metaphor—a temple. This metaphor applies to all believers, anytime and anywhere. The temple does not refer to the structure in which believers meet to worship. Rather, Christians themselves *are* the temple of God. They are his temple because God's Spirit dwells within them. Paul's original readers, those responsible for the divisions in the church at Corinth, lost sight of this basic truth and needed correction. Nothing destroys a church more completely than dissension and strife.

Because of this, Paul issued this strong warning that God will destroy those who destroy his temple (vv. 16–17).

WORD PICTURE

Gold, Silver, Costly Stones

"The durable materials are three (gold, silver, marble or precious stone), perishable materials (pieces of wood, hay, stubble), of a palace on one hand, of a mud hut on the other (Lightfoot). Gold was freely used by the ancients in their palaces. Their marble and granite pillars are still the wonder and despair of modern man. The wooden huts had hay and stubble which were used to hold the wood pieces together and to thatch the roof. It is not clear whether Paul's metaphor refers to the persons as in God's building in verse 9 or to the character of the teaching as in verse 13. Probably both ideas are involved, considering the penalty for shoddy work (v. 15) and shoddy men (v. 17). The teaching may not always be vicious and harmful. It may only be indifferent and worthless. A co-worker with God in this great temple should put in his very best effort." A. T. Robertson, "Epistles of Paul," *Word Pictures in the New Testament*, vol. 4, 97.

Section Summary

Paul used the metaphor of a temple to illustrate the destructive nature of dissension and strife that existed in the Corinthian church. Because the Holy Spirit indwells believers, they are the temple of God and must not allow such destructive forces to control them. Paul issued his strongest warning yet: "If anyone destroys God's temple, God will destroy him."

FOLLY OF WORLDLY WISDOM (3:18–23)

The Believer Is to Avoid Self-Deception (v. 18)

In this final portion of chapter 3, Paul drew a sharp distinction between worldly wisdom and God's wisdom. Paul exhorted his readers, "Let no one deceive himself" (v. 18).

The Craftiness of the Worldly Wise (vv. 19–20)

God sees through the pretensions of human wisdom. Paul quoted two passages from the Old Testament to illustrate this truth.

OLD TESTAMENT REFERENCE

Paul supported his indictment of worldly wisdom by citing two passages from the Old Testament: (1) "He traps the wise in their craftiness" (Job 5:13); and (2) "The LORD knows the thoughts of mankind; they are futile" (Ps 94:11).

No More Boasting (vv. 21–23)

In these verses Paul sought to reverse the partisan cries of the Corinthian believers. They were boasting of their loyalties to their favorite leaders (Paul, Apollos, Cephas). These loyalties divided the church into rival factions. Paul reminded them that they all belonged to Christ.

Section Summary

Paul drew a sharp distinction between worldly wisdom and God's wisdom, and he exhorted his readers, "Let no one deceive himself." God views the wisdom of this world as foolishness. Believers are not to embrace such wisdom but rather to embrace the inheritance that is theirs in Jesus Christ.

QUESTIONS TO GUIDE YOUR STUDY

1. Paul used an agricultural metaphor to illustrate the work of the gospel. What is Paul teaching with this metaphor?
2. What is the point of Paul's architectural metaphor?
3. What is the point of Paul's metaphor of the temple?
4. In his teaching on the folly of wisdom, Paul instructed believers not to deceive themselves. What does it mean to deceive oneself? Are there consequences for doing so?

PAUL'S CONTRAST BETWEEN THE CORINTHIANS AND THE APOSTLES

THE CORINTHIANS	THE APOSTLES	CROSS-REFERENCE
1. "You are already full! You are already rich! You have begun to reign as kings without us." (v. 8)	1. "God has displayed us, the apostles, in last place, like men condemned to die." (v. 9)	1:18–25; 3:18–19
2. "You are wise in Christ!" (v. 10)	2. "We are fools for Christ." (v. 10)	1:18–25; 2:3–5
3. "You are strong!" (v. 10)	3. "We are weak." (v. 10.	
4. "You are distinguished." (v. 10)	4. "We are dishonored!" (v. 10)	

1 CORINTHIANS 4

Paul's warnings in the previous chapter do not imply that human leaders are unimportant. He was clear that people are saved only by Jesus Christ, and there is no other basis for salvation. Church leaders build on this foundation. From this thought, Paul appealed to the Corinthians to act on what he had written them. Paul's key points in this chapter include:

- The responsibility of church leaders and the importance of their example to other believers.
- The "mysteries of God" granted to leaders are things that human wisdom cannot discover but can only be revealed by God.

THE SERVANT'S ROLE (4:1–7)

Paul addressed a church that was divided into partisan groups who were boasting about their identity with one leader as over against another. Paul countered this misplaced devotion by instructing the Corinthians to consider their leaders as "managers of the mysteries of God" (v. 1). "Managers" are *stewards.*

The primary qualification of stewards is trustworthiness. Because they deal with what belongs to another, they must have their master's interests at heart and avoid any kind of self-serving.

Paul, apparently, was evaluated by some of the Corinthians. Perhaps he was even compared to Peter and Apollos. Paul didn't put a lot of weight on this evaluation or any other human evaluation—including his evaluation of himself. What mattered was God's appraisal of him.

He urged the Corinthians to be patient and await the judgment that would take place at Christ's second coming. At that time, the hearts of all people would be laid bare before the One who even now reads the thoughts, desires, and motives of each person. At that time, God would give appropriate praise to his servant.

HISTORICAL BACKGROUND

A steward was the "manager of a household, which often was a trusted slave put in charge of the whole household. The word emphasizes that one is entrusted with great responsibility and accountability." Fritz Rienecker, *Linguistic Key to the Greek New Testament* (Zondervan, 1980), 395.) In this passage, Paul referred to leaders who are stewards and what has been entrusted, or what they are to administer.

The purpose of Paul's referring to Apollos and himself in verses 6–7 was to keep the Corinthians from being "arrogant, favoring one person over another" (v. 6). Both Paul and Apollos were servants of Christ, not rival leaders.

Section Summary

Paul addressed a group of believers who were divided into partisan groups that were boasting about their identity with one leader as over against another. Paul countered this misplaced devotion by instructing the Corinthians to consider their leaders as stewards who are "managers of the mysteries of God." The primary qualification of stewards is that they be persons who are worthy of trust. Both Paul and Apollos were faithful servants of Christ, not rivals.

DEFLATION BY SATIRE (4:8–13)

Contrasts (vv. 8–11)

By favoring one leader over another, the Corinthians were judging the merits of the apostles. There was an implied claim of superiority in what they were doing. Paul sought to deflate their pride. In a series of exclamations, some of which echo themes he touched on earlier in his letter, Paul contrasted their imagined estate with the actual lot of the apostles, whom the Corinthians were presuming to judge.

Three Antitheses (vv. 12–13a)

In verses 12–13a, Paul delivered three antitheses that do more than state the apostles' hardships and their responses to improper treatment. They are clear reflections of the teachings of Jesus and are the responses of one who imitates Christ:

- "When we are reviled, we bless."
- "When we are persecuted, we endure it."
- "When we are slandered, we respond graciously."

A Final Metaphor of Humiliation (v. 13)

To accent the world's feeling toward the apostles, Paul used a graphic and unflattering description of him and his fellow apostles: "We are like the scum of the earth, like everyone's garbage" (v. 13).

Section Summary

By favoring one leader over another, the Corinthians were judging the merits of the apostles. Seeking to deflate their pride, Paul provided a series of exclamations that contrasted the Corinthians' imagined estate with the actual lot of the apostles, whom the Corinthians were presuming to judge. Paul closed this portion of his letter by embracing responses that are indicative of a person who is imitating Christ.

PAUL'S PERSONAL APPEAL (4:14–21)

In verses 14 and 15 Paul assumed the role of a father counseling his children: "I became your father in Christ Jesus through the gospel" (v. 15). He was clear that his hard words were not to shame them but to warn them so that they might do what is right. He encouraged the Corinthians to become imitators of him and announced that he was sending Timothy to minister to them for that reason. He also mentioned that he himself would be visiting them soon (v. 19).

Paul then pointed out that some of the Corinthian believers had become "arrogant." He urged the Corinthians to undergo a behavioral change, or they would be subject to Paul's discipline: "Should I come to you with a rod, or in love and a spirit of gentleness?" (v. 21). He placed the issue before them and left the choice to them.

Section Summary

Paul assumed the role of a father counseling his children and encouraged the Corinthians to become imitators of him. He also urged the Corinthians to undergo a behavior change or be subject to his discipline.

QUESTIONS TO GUIDE YOUR STUDY

1. Paul explained the responsibility of church leaders and said that they are really "managers." What is a manager, and what does a manager do?
2. In verses 8–13, what is the point of Paul's several exclamations?
3. How did the world perceive the apostles and their work, according to Paul?
4. How did Paul couch his personal appeal to the Corinthians? What was the content of his appeal?

1 CORINTHIANS 5

As in any day, the pressures to conform to an immoral society were strong in the church at Corinth. In chapter 5 Paul responded to reports that reached him about an incident of incest involving a member of the

HISTORICAL BACKGROUND

Garbage

This word is a compound made up of the preposition "around" and the verb "to wipe." It refers to that which is removed by the process of cleaning dirt off, scouring, scum. Whereas the word *scum* indicates a rinsing, this word indicates a "scrapping" of a dirty vessel. It was used in the papyri in a letter greeting conveying the idea of "your humble and devoted servant." Vine's Complete Expository Dictionary of Old and New Testament Words *(Thomas Nelson, 1996).*

WORD PICTURE

Sexual Immorality

"Sexual immorality" translates the Greek word *porneia.* It is used of illicit sexual intercourse and "refers to general sexual acts outside of legal marriage." (Fritz Rienecker, *Linguistic Key to the Greek New Testament* [Zondervan, 1980], 399.) The Greeks used a different word for the act of adultery: *"moicheia* is technically adultery on the part of the married (Mark 7:21)." A. T. Robertson, *WPNT*, "Epistles of Paul," vol.4, 111.

congregation. In this chapter, he rebuked the church for tolerating such flagrant immorality in its midst and demanded that they exclude the member from the congregation.

SHOCKING PERMISSIVENESS IN THE CORINTHIAN CHURCH (5:1–2)

Paul heard reports of sexual immorality among the Corinthians. The problem involved a man in the church who was living in an illicit sexual relationship with his stepmother (the probable meaning of the phrase "his father's wife"). She was probably a pagan, for Paul did not include her in his instructions.

The incident was especially shameful because the father and son engaged in sexual relationships with the same woman. The Old Testament Scriptures strictly forbade such behavior (Lev 18:7–8; 20:11). Even the Romans prohibited such unions. But the church's attitude toward the evil taking place within their congregation was one of pride and arrogance.

The Corinthians were so busy priding themselves on their spirituality that they were ignoring the immoral behavior of the member. At stake was the integrity of the Christian witness to an immoral society, but the proud Corinthian believers were too unspiritual to recognize the severity of the problem. Paul rebuked them for their failure to respond properly to the offending member (v. 2). "You are arrogant!" (v. 2), Paul declared.

Section Summary

Paul drew his readers' attention to a case of incest at Corinth. Although the Christian witness to an immoral society was at stake, the proud Corinthian believers were too unspiritual to recognize the severity and deal with the problem.

HISTORICAL BACKGROUND

Leaven in the Bible

Leaven was a small portion of fermented dough used to ferment other dough. It often symbolized corruptive influence. *Unleavened* bread was required for the Feast of Unleavened Bread, which was celebrated in conjunction with the Passover Festival (Lev 23:4–8). It reminded the Israelites of their hasty departure from Egypt and warned them against corruptive influences.

EXCLUSION OF THE OFFENDER DEMANDED (5:3–5)

Although he was not present with the Corinthian believers, Paul took responsibility for correcting the situation that existed in the congregation. He passed judgment on the member who was guilty of immoral conduct and instructed the entire fellowship to deal with the problem.

The congregation was to meet on the issue. After they gathered in the name of Jesus Christ and with his power, Paul ordered that they "hand that one over to Satan for the destruction of the flesh, so that his spirit may be saved in the day of the Lord" (v. 5). We can make at least three observations from Paul's handling of this incident of immorality in the Corinthian church:

1. The form of discipline applied here was exclusion from the church, which was suggested in verse 2.
2. Apparently, the world outside the church was regarded as Satan's domain.
3. The purpose of the actions was redemptive, not merely punitive.

Section Summary

Paul took responsibility for correcting the problem that existed in the congregation. He passed judgment on a member who was guilty of immoral conduct and instructed the entire fellowship to deal with the problem by excluding the offending member from the church.

EVIL AS LEAVEN (5:6–8)

Paul criticized the Corinthians for boasting. They prided themselves on being an exemplary congregation but condoned sin in their midst. He used the illustration of leaven to show them how dangerous their attitude was.

Several Old Testament passages shed light on the observance of Passover and the Feast of Unleavened Bread. These passages include Exod 12:1–51; Lev 23:4–6; and Deut 16:1–8. An understanding of those Old Testament Scriptures provides an appreciation for Paul's messages in verses 6–8.

Paul rebuked the Corinthians for their complacency regarding the immoral member. He likened the presence of this person in the church to old leaven that would contaminate the whole batch (v. 6). Paul called for a cleansing of the old leaven. Christ, our "Passover lamb," has been sacrificed, and the call given to celebrate the festival with "bread of sincerity and truth" (v. 8).

PERSONAL APPLICATION

Paul presented his readers with a principle of New Testament church discipline. When a congregation, or the church at large, condones immorality, the moral fiber of the church is weakened. None escape its contamination. The *whole* lump is affected. No church or fellowship may celebrate deliverance from sin while sheltering sin among its members.

Section Summary

The Corinthians prided themselves on being an exemplary congregation but condoned sin in their midst. Paul used the illustration of leaven to show them how dangerous their attitude was. When believers condone immorality among themselves, the moral fiber of the entire church is weakened.

PREVIOUS LETTER CLARIFIED (5:9–13)

At this point in his letter, Paul found it necessary to clear up a misunderstanding that occurred because of a letter he sent earlier to Corinth. He urged his readers not to continue in fellowship with immoral church members. The Corinthians, however, understood Paul to mean that they must withdraw from associations with all immoral persons in the world

(v. 10). Paul corrected this misunderstanding, indicating that it is God's responsibility to judge those outside the church (v. 13).

The problem with the church at Corinth was not that they were living amid an immoral society. Rather, it was their low estimate of what it means be the people of God in such a setting. They permitted the immoral society around them to invade their midst. For the fourth time in this chapter, Paul demanded that the congregation exclude the immoral church member from the fellowship.

Section Summary

Paul found it necessary to clear up a misunderstanding that occurred because of a letter he had sent earlier to Corinth. He had urged his readers not to continue in fellowship with immoral church members, reminding them that God will judge those outside their church.

QUESTIONS TO GUIDE YOUR STUDY

1. What prompted Paul's rebuke of the Corinthian believers in verses 1–2?
2. In Paul's instructions for dealing with members guilty of immoral conduct, what do we learn about church discipline?
3. What is the lesson *of leaven* Paul is teaching here?
4. Paul cleared up a misunderstanding from a previous letter to the Corinthians. What was this misunderstanding, and what was Paul's counsel to them?

1 CORINTHIANS 6

In this chapter Paul chastised the Corinthians for their factious spirit. Their active part in lawsuits before heathen judges was evidence of their unspiritual attitudes. Paul provided instructions on dealing with disputes within the Christian community. He then went on to discuss the kind of conduct that excludes people from the kingdom of God.

PERSONAL APPLICATION

Paul was not depreciating courts or implying that all pagan judges are corrupt and incapable of administering justice. His concern, instead, was that the Corinthians were depreciating the gospel by their readiness to sue one another.

THE PROBLEM (6:1–4)

Paul turned his attention to personal disputes among the church members. Evidently, some members of the congregation were contending about personal rights or business matters. Unable to resolve these differences, they were appealing to courts of law.

In these opening verses of the chapter, Paul presented two main points for his readers:

1. He considered it ludicrous for those destined to participate in the final judgment to show themselves "unworthy to judge trivial cases" (v. 2). Those who are to deal with the issues of the ages ought to be able to deal with the problems of the moment.

He considered it tragic for believers to carry their disputes before pagan judges. To do so was to discredit the gospel in the eyes of the pagan society to which they were to bear witness.

Section Summary

Members of the congregation were contending about personal rights or business matters. Unable to resolve these differences, they were appealing to courts of law. Paul provides instructions for keeping the resolution of disputes among believers rather than taking them before pagan judges, where the witness of the gospel could be discredited.

HISTORICAL BACKGROUND

Under Roman rule, the Jews enjoyed a large measure of autonomy. Disputes among those in the Jewish community were settled among themselves. Indeed, the rabbis taught that it was unlawful for a Jew to seek a judge's decision in pagan courts. Even within the pagan world, there were religious brotherhoods and mutual-benefit societies that pledged not to sue one another in the courts. Disputes among these groups were settled through arbitration among themselves.

ALTERNATIVES TO LITIGATION (6:5–8)

Arbitration within the Church (vv. 5–6)

The Corinthian believers boasted of their wisdom. Paul asked them why it was necessary for them to go outside their congregation to find a person competent to render a judgment in their disputes.

With arbitration within the Corinthian congregation an option, Paul was distressed that "brother goes to court against brother, and that before unbelievers" (v. 6).

Enduring the Wrong (vv. 7–8)

That serious disputes and breakdowns in relationships existed among the Corinthians was an indication that they have been defeated already (v. 7).

Rather than discrediting the gospel by dragging disputes into the pagan courts, Paul advised the Corinthians to endure the wrong done to them: "Why not rather be wronged?" Apparently, some of the Corinthians were suing others in the courts attempting to defraud one another (v. 8).

Section Summary

Because the Corinthians boasted of their wisdom, Paul asked them why it was necessary for them to go outside their congregation to settle their disputes. They were to settle their disputes by arbitration within the Corinthian congregation rather than discredit the gospel by dragging disputes into the pagan courts.

RELATION TO THE KINGDOM OF GOD (6:9–11)

In verses 1–8 Paul focused on a particular form of unrighteous conduct—the readiness to sue or defraud one another in court. He now broadened his discussion to include other forms of unrighteousness.

Warning to the Wicked (vv. 9–10)

Paul warned the Corinthians not to be deceived. Literally, he was telling his readers, "Do not continue to be deceived."

Twice he affirmed that the unrighteous have no inheritance in God's kingdom (v. 9). He repeated this warning in verse 10, where he listed several acts of unrighteousness that were characteristic of the wicked. Six of these repeat what Paul listed in 5:10–11, with four additions. The following chart lists these and their meanings.

SINS OF THE WICKED

SIN	MEANING
Sexual immorality	Unlawful sexual activity with the spouse of another person
Idolatry	Worshiping and serving idols
Adultery	Indulgence in fornication
Male prostitution	Technical term for a passive partner in homosexual relations
Homosexuality	Homosexual activities between males
Thievery	Use of force or violence in stealing
Greediness	Desire to have more and seek fulfillment by any means
Drunkenness	State of intoxication
Verbally abusive	Use of abusive language
Swindling	Act of extortion

The Basis of the Believer's Righteousness (v. 11)

Paul told the Corinthians that, as believers in Christ, they were no longer to be among those who commit such acts of unrighteousness. He now provided three metaphors that form the basis of his premise: "You were washed, you were sanctified, you were justified in the name of the Lord Jesus Christ and by the Spirit of our God" (v. 11).

THE BELIEVER'S BASIS FOR RIGHTEOUS LIVING

WORK OF SALVATION	SIGNIFICANCE TO BELIEVERS
"Washed"	They are washed from the filth of their former lifestyles.
"Sanctified"	They are set apart for holy, godly living that contrasts their former wickedness.
"Justified"	Because of their justification, they may inherit the kingdom of God.

Section Summary

Paul broadened his discussion to include other forms of unrighteousness. After commanding readers, "Do not be deceived," he listed several acts of unrighteousness that paint the character of the wicked. The Corinthians, however, were not to be among those who commit such acts of unrighteousness, for they had been washed, sanctified, and justified "in the name of the Lord Jesus Christ and by the Spirit of our God."

SEXUAL IMMORALITY (6:12–20)

Paul's discussion of sexual immorality is the most extensive on this subject in all his letters. He challenged the Corinthians' casual attitude toward sexual immorality and made a case for sexual purity.

Refuting Popular Slogans (vv. 12–14)

As today, the Corinthians used popular slogans, or catchphrases. Paul quoted two of these that some of the church members may have been using to rationalize their attitude regarding sexual indulgence. He used these quotes as points of departure for setting forth a Christian view of sexual behavior.

Sexual Immorality (6:12–20)

"Everything is permissible for me" (v. 12). Paul added a qualifier to this slogan that related it to Christian freedom: "But not everything is beneficial." Paul insisted that the Christian exercise freedom in a thoroughly responsible way. Otherwise, the believer's freedom becomes license. And license leads to slavery.

"Food for the stomach and the stomach for food" (v. 13). Here Paul confronted those who excused their sexual sins by declaring that the body had no significance. He tied the importance of the body to the coming resurrection (v. 14).

WORD PICTURE

Washed

This word is a compound in the Greek language and is made up of the preposition "away, off" and the verb "to wash." It means "to wash off something." The preposition has a "perfective" force, which means that it emphasizes the completeness of the action of the verb "to wash." With this word Paul told his readers at Corinth that they had been completely washed of their former filthy and wicked lifestyles.

The significance of Paul's refuting these slogans is that in both cases the Corinthians were rationalizing sexual immorality as allowable or irrelevant.

Intercourse with Prostitutes (vv. 15–17)

For the citizens of Corinth, sexual relations with cult prostitutes carried a religious significance. It signified consecration to the cult goddess. For visitors to the city, such as sailors, this prostitution was nothing less than debauchery.

Paul stated that intercourse with a prostitute was a desecration of the body. He considered the believer's identification with Christ so complete that when a believer committed fornication with a prostitute, he involved Christ in the act.

PERSONAL APPLICATION

Paul commanded the Corinthians to "flee" sexual immorality (v. 18). In its grammatical context, this word meant that the fleeing was to be a continual and habitual fleeing. Because some people insist on spending time where temptation abounds, they find it difficult to resist, and then fail morally. In resisting sexual temptation, the believer does well never to underestimate its power or overestimate one's strength to refuse.

Flee Sexual Immorality (vv. 18–20)

Paul followed this command to flee sexual immorality with four reasons:

1. *It has a tragic uniqueness as a sin against the body* (v. 18). No sin involves so complete a giving of the total person in a way that opposes God.
2. *It desecrates the body, which is the temple of the Holy Spirit* (v. 19). At conversion the Holy Spirit comes to dwell in the life of the believer, which makes the body of the believer a temple of the Holy Spirit. Sexual immorality profanes the Spirit's temple.
3. *It ignores the costliness of redemption* (vv. 19–20). The Christian is not his or her own but rather has been bought with a price—the sacrifice of Jesus Christ on the cross.
4. *It fails to glorify God in the body* (v. 20). The believer is to use his or her body to glorify God. Therefore, the body requires the highest level of Christian integrity in sexual relationships.

Section Summary

Here Paul wrote his most extensive section on sexual immorality. He challenged the Corinthians' casual attitude toward the sexual immorality that existed in their fellowship. He closed the section with a command to "flee" sexual immorality.

QUESTIONS TO GUIDE YOUR STUDY

1. What problem did Paul address in 6:1–4? What was distressing him about it?
2. What was Paul's counsel for believers who had disputes with others in the congregation?

3. In 6:9–10 Paul gave his readers a list of the sins of the wicked. Why? What is the believer's basis for righteous living?
4. Paul refuted two popular slogans of his day. What was his point?
5. What was Paul's practical counsel for avoiding sexual immorality? What reasons did he give for his counsel?

1 CORINTHIANS 7

The Corinthians raised a series of questions for Paul. In this chapter he responded to their concerns by addressing the issue of marriage and divorce. In this chapter Paul provided principles for marriage and gave advice to the married and the unmarried.

He moved on to offer further advice about contentment and then concluded this topic with counsel for virgins and widows.

WHERE BOTH HUSBAND AND WIFE ARE CHRISTIANS (7:1–7,10–11)

As the gospel was preached in Corinth, sometimes both a husband and a wife became Christians. Sometimes only one spouse became a believer, leaving a mixed marriage. Still others who responded to the gospel were unmarried or widows. The Corinthians wanted to know how becoming a Christian would affect these various relationships:

- Should a Christian continue to share life's most intimate union with a pagan partner?
- Should an unmarried Christian marry?
- Should a widowed believer remarry?
- How do these situations apply to various cultural and religious settings?

Paul answered these important questions, often deferring to the recorded teachings of Jesus. Where no recorded teachings of the Lord were available, Paul gave his own opinion "as one who by the Lord's mercy is faithful" (v. 25).

Paul's Preference for Celibacy (vv. 1–2,7)

In verse 1 Paul stated his preference for celibacy. In verse 7 he implied that his celibacy was a gift. In this sense, his gift fit his calling. Paul did acknowledge that not all have the gift of celibacy.

A Sexual Partnership (vv. 3–6)

For marriage to provide security against sexual temptation, both spouses must be generous with each other in the conjugal relationship. In such a relationship, "a wife does not have the right over her own body, but

HISTORICAL BACKGROUND

Some persons in Corinth may have been practicing celibacy within marriage without the consent of their spouse. This could have led to immorality on the part of the nonconsenting partner.

- Any abstinence is to be by common consent since the decision involves both spouses.
- It is to be for a limited time, not indefinitely.
- It is to be for a special season of prayer. The husband and wife are to resume their normal pattern of conjugal relations. "Otherwise, Satan may tempt" them because of a lack of control.

In these opening verses of chapter 7, Paul taught some important features of the Christian concept of marriage, as the chart.

her husband does. In the same way, a husband does not have the right over his own body, but his wife does" (v. 4). Neither are to refuse sexual relations to the other "except when you agree for a time" (v. 5). For such exceptional cases, Paul spelled out the details for this kind of arrangement:

THE CHRISTIAN MARRIAGE
1. It is a monogamous relationship: one husband and one wife for life.
2. No premarital or extramarital sex is permitted.
3. Sex contributes to the fulfillment of the marriage relationship and is not just limited to having children.
4. The principle of mutuality prevails. The husband is to fulfill his duty to his wife and the wife to her husband.

The Sanctity of Marriage (vv. 10–11)

A husband and wife are not to separate. Here Paul appealed to the teachings of Jesus but didn't deal with the issue of grounds for divorce. If a wife did separate from her husband, both were to remain single or be reconciled to each other.

Section Summary

Paul stated his preference for celibacy. For married Christians, marriage is a monogamous relationship: one husband and one wife for life. For those who are married, to provide security against sexual temptation, both spouses must be generous with each other. Neither is to refuse sexual relations to the other "except when you agree for a time."

WHERE ONLY ONE SPOUSE IS A CHRISTIAN (7:12–24)

One question posed to Paul by the Corinthians was whether a believer ought to continue in marriage with a pagan. To this Paul gave his own opinion by emphasizing two principles: (1) the initiative belongs to the unbeliever; and (2) God calls us to live in peace.

Initiative Belongs to the Unbeliever (vv. 12–16)

Paul taught that if the unbelieving spouse desires to continue in the marriage, then the Christian partner is to comply (vv. 12–13). If the unbelieving spouse desires to separate, the Christian partner should allow a peaceful dissolution of the marriage.

Section Summary

Where only one spouse is a believer, a question arises whether the two should continue in the marriage relationship. Paul's first principle is that the initiative belongs to the unbeliever. If it is the desire of the unbelieving spouse to continue in the marriage, then the Christian partner is to comply (vv. 12–13). If the unbelieving spouse desires to separate, the Christian partner should allow a peaceful dissolution of the marriage.

God Calls Us to Live in Peace (vv. 17–24)

Paul's second principle for dealing with a marriage where only one spouse is a believer is that "God has called you to live in peace" (v. 15). Paul's statement in verse 15 supports his instruction for Christians not to oppose an unbelieving spouse's determination to end the marriage. Verses 17–24 are an elaboration of his emphasis of verse 15. Paul then applied this principle to circumcision and slavery.

A religious application: circumcision (vv. 17–19). Whether circumcised or uncircumcised, a person should not seek to change his or her state.

A social application: slavery (vv. 20–24). Many slaves responded to the gospel and became believers. Whether a slave or a free person, one's status is not what matters. It is one's relationship to God that matters most.

Section Summary

Paul exhorted the Corinthians to continue in the state they were in when they were called to Christ. Conditions of life are secondary. Obedience to God is of primary importance.

COUNSEL FOR THE UNMARRIED AND WIDOWS (7:8–9, 25–40)

In verse 8 Paul repeated his statement that singleness is preferable to marriage. In this passage Paul identified several tensions associated with this issue.

The Moral Tension (vv. 8–9)

Paul began by advising unmarried and widows to remain single. He stated, however, that "it is better to marry than to burn with desire." Being married does not eliminate one's struggle with sexual temptation, but a good marriage is a strong defense against sexual immorality.

The "End Time" Tension (vv. 25–31)

It is clear from his writings that Paul believed he was living in the time that would precede the end of the world. In this passage alone he made

HISTORICAL BACKGROUND

The meaning of verse 14 is not entirely clear. J. W. MacGorman comments, "Certainly Paul was not teaching the salvation of a pagan by marriage to a Christian as an alternative to faith in Christ. Nevertheless the marriage of a Christian and a pagan had a quality not to be found in the marriage of two pagans. Somehow and in some sense, through the intimate association of marriage to a believer, the unbeliever was consecrated. And thus their children were holy. A benefit is described, though its precise nature and extent are not defined." (*Romans, 1 Corinthians,* Layman's Bible Book Commentary [Nashville: B&H, 1980], 121.) The New English Bible uniquely renders this passage: "Think of it: as a wife you may be your husband's salvation; as a husband you may be your wife's salvation."

three allusions (vv. 26,29,31). In view of the "present distress," Paul advised single believers not to seek a mate but to remain as he or she was.

The Domestic Tension (vv. 32–35)

In verses 32 and 34, Paul presented a rather idealistic view of an unmarried man and woman. Both are devoting their full energies to the Lord's work. On the other hand, he portrayed the married as having divided interests. Paul sees a married woman as "concerned about the things of the world—how she may please her husband" (v. 34).

Obviously, Paul's point is relative. The Christian man or woman who has no family responsibilities is free to devote more time and energy to ministry. But certainly not all Christian couples fit the pattern of distraction Paul describes here (see Priscilla and Aquila, Rom 16:3–5).

Individual Cases (vv. 36–38)

Paul now addressed individual cases involving virgins. There is some debate over the proper translation and interpretation of these verses, which makes this a difficult passage in some respects.

Remarriage for Widows (vv. 39–40)

According to Paul, a wife is bound to her husband for as long as he lives. However, if he dies, she is free to marry another man, but he must be a Christian (v. 39). Paul, however, believed that she is happier if she remains a widow.

WORD PICTURE

Virgin

This word refers to either a father and his daughter or to a man and woman who have entered upon a spiritual marriage and now live together without physical relations, or a case of levirate marriage and the word means "young widow," or it refers to a man and woman who are an engaged couple. Fritz Rienecker, *Linguistic Key to the Greek New Testament* (Zondervan, 1980), 410.

Section Summary

After repeating his statement that singleness is preferable to marriage, Paul identified several tensions associated with the issue of marrying or remarrying. His conclusion was that "keeping God's commands is what matters. Let each of you remain in the situation in which he was called." Paul also provided instruction for virgins and widows.

QUESTIONS TO GUIDE YOUR STUDY

1. What was Paul's concept of Christian marriage?
2. How should a believer handle a marriage where his or her spouse is not a believer?
3. What two principles govern the believer's decisions and actions?
4. What was Paul's counsel for unmarried Christians? For widows who are believers?

1 CORINTHIANS 8

First Corinthians 8:1–11:1 is the unit of Paul's letter that deals with the issue of food sacrificed to idols. Chapter 8 reveals how Paul dealt with this problem in the church at Corinth in relation to varying levels of maturity among believers in the congregation.

THE ISSUE OF EATING FOOD OFFERED TO IDOLS (8:1–3)

In the pagan temples at Corinth, animal sacrifices were offered to gods. Only certain portions of the animal were used for this purpose, leaving the greater portion of the animal to be consumed by the priests and worshipers in a cultic meal. Following the sacrifices, the magistrates sold whatever remained to the local butcher shops. Because this was often the best meat available, those having dinner parties would be sure to purchase this meat and serve it to guests.

Paul addressed several questions here: What is the Christian's responsibility in such a setting? If invited to participate in a cultic meal at a pagan temple, should a believer attend? Was a believer permitted to buy meat that had been consecrated in pagan worship? If invited to the home of a pagan friend, was the believer free to accept the invitation? To refuse to attend such gatherings was to cut oneself off from social activity with friends. Differences of opinion among the Corinthian believers caused division within the church.

In verse 3 Paul explained that *love*, not *knowledge*, is the basis for Christian conduct. In verse 1 he contrasted the two: "Knowledge puffs up, but love builds up." Knowledge, untempered by other qualities, fosters pride and arrogance. It can never be the only criterion as the guide to right conduct. But love never fosters pride and arrogance. Instead, it edifies or builds up the church.

LOVE, NOT KNOWLEDGE, IS THE GUIDE

	KNOWLEDGE	LOVE
What it does	"Puffs up"	"Builds up"
What it causes	Pride and arrogance	Character development
Its effects	Temporary	Permanent

WORD PICTURE

Knowledge Puffs UP

"Knowledge puffs up." Paul's use of knowledge is not something purely intellectual. It is the knowledge that has results and leads to action, especially religious action. "Puff up" means "to blow up like a billows." Applied to an individual, this word means "to be inflated with self-complacency," "to make conceited." Because it is in the present tense, this verb emphasizes that what Paul said here is a general truth.

Love Builds Up

The Greek word used here is a compound made up of the noun "house" and the verb "to build." Its basic meaning is applied to the building of something. It is the word used for describing the erection of buildings. Paul used it here as a metaphor for the development of Christian character.

Section Summary

Paul dealt with the issue of eating food offered to pagan idols. This issue raised several questions, including: Was a believer permitted to buy meat that had been consecrated in pagan worship? In such complex issues, Paul taught that love, not knowledge, is the basis for Christian conduct.

THE KNOWLEDGE OF THE MATURE BELIEVERS (8:4–6)

Paul addressed the mature members of the Corinthian congregation. In verse 4 he acknowledged their understanding about idols:

"*We know that 'an idol* is *nothing in the world*.'" There was no shortage of pagan gods in the ancient world. Their images and shrines were abundant. However, some Corinthian believers felt more mature because they knew these idols didn't exist.

"'*There is no God but one*.'" This statement reinforces a fundamental teaching of the Jewish religion. In the Shema, the Jewish confession of faith, Deuteronomy 6:4 teaches that "the LORD our God, the Lord is one." This expression of faith may have been an early Christian confession. (Later worship practice combined Deut 6:4–9; 11:13–21; Num 15:37–41 into the larger Shema as the summary of Jewish confession.) Because an idol represents something that does not exist, meat consecrated to it could not profane anyone. It remained simply meat, neither more nor less. This meant that the mature Christian could buy it and eat it with no defilement whatever. Christian liberty renders meaningless all such superstitions.

Section Summary

Paul addressed the mature members of the Corinthian congregation and acknowledged their understanding about idols. Because an idol represents something that did not exist, the consecrated meat could not profane anyone. Therefore, the mature Christian could buy it and eat it with no defilement whatever.

THE LIMITATIONS OF THE IMMATURE BELIEVERS (8:7–12)

Paul reminded his readers that not all members of the congregation were at the same level of understanding. As is often said today, "Perception is reality." There were Christians who came out of a pagan background whose consciences were weak and believed in pagan gods. When they turned to the living God, they turned away from the gods they worshiped, but they could not yet think of them as not existing.

PAUL'S THREE LIMITATIONS TO PERSONAL FREEDOM IN 1 CORINTHIANS

LIMITATION	FOCUS	PASSAGE
1. Paul indicated that one Christian should never eat meat if the eating offends a weaker Christian	A weaker Christian	8:13
2. Paul suggested that a believer should limit the right to eat meat if that freedom hindered the spread of the gospel.	The spread of the gospel	9:19–23
3. Paul warned that a Christian should never indulge the freedom to eat meat if that action threatens the personal spiritual life of the individual.	One's own spiritual life	9:24–27

So, when they thought of eating meat offered to these idols, they felt guilty. When they saw other Christians eating this meat, they were offended.

In verse 8 there is a hint that some of the mature believers may have been flaunting their freedom to eat such food, supposing that God esteemed them more highly for doing so. Paul refuted such thinking—"Food will not bring us close to God."

In 1 Corinthians Paul addressed the issue of personal freedom concerning the eating of meat sacrificed to pagan idols. In chapter 8 he addressed the first limitation.

Section Summary

Paul reminded his readers that not all members of the congregation are at the same level of understanding. And some of the mature believers may have been flaunting their freedom to eat such food, supposing that God esteemed them more highly for doing so. Paul taught that one Christian should never eat meat if the eating offends a weaker Christian.

LOVE'S REQUIREMENT (8:13)

Paul summed up his principle of self-limitation for the sake of others with the statement, "Therefore, if food causes my brother or sister to fall, I will never again eat meat, so that I won't cause my brother or sister to fall." The strong believer must adapt to the conscience of the weaker believer.

QUESTIONS TO GUIDE YOUR STUDY

1. The issue of eating food offered to pagan idols raised several questions for the Corinthians. What were some of those?

2. What did the mature believers at Corinth understand about idols that Paul agreed with? How had some of them crossed the line and erred with newer believers?
3. According to Paul, what is the basis for Christian conduct? Contrast love and knowledge.
4. What is love's requirement? Can you think of ways mature believers today might apply this principle in your church?

1 CORINTHIANS 9

In the preceding chapter Paul urged his mature readers to exercise their Christian freedom in a responsible way. In life, Paul practiced the principles he described.

He next devoted an entire chapter to a personal account of his own efforts to live on the level he recommended to his readers. Paul emphasized that one should subordinate one's own interests to those of others, especially those of Christ and his gospel. He identified four areas in which concerns for others led him to renounce or limit his rights:

WORD PICTURE

Rights

The Greek word translated *rights* can also be translated *freedom.*

- Marriage (v. 5)
- Financial support (vv. 4,6–18)
- Cultural bias (vv. 19–23)
- Self-discipline (vv. 24–27)

PAUL'S RIGHTS (9:1–3)

Paul began this chapter by defending his apostleship. Apparently, some Corinthian believers were criticizing Paul. Although he could have claimed privileges such as financial support from the church for his work and ministry, he did not. Rather, he was a tentmaker and worked to provide his own support.

MARRIAGE (9:5)

Paul presented a rhetorical question: "Don't we have the right to be accompanied by a believing wife like the other apostles, the Lord's brothers, and Cephas?" Paul was not expecting an answer or special information. It was his way of emphatically claiming that he did have a right to marry a Christian woman but that he yielded that right out of consideration for his ministry to others.

FINANCIAL SUPPORT (9:4,6–18)

Paul was sensitive about the issue of financial support in his relations with the Corinthians. Apparently, some in the congregation were ready to question his motives if he should accept financial support as a minister of the gospel. Paul gave his readers several evidences that established his right to receive such support:

- *He gave examples from everyday life (v. 7).* The soldier does not serve at his own expense. A person who plants a vineyard eats some of the fruit himself, and one who tends a flock is entitled to some of the milk.
- *He appealed to Scripture (vv. 8–12).* Paul cited Deut 25:4 as an illustration of the principle that the person doing the work requires material support.
- *He pointed to the prevailing custom in the temple service (v. 13).* Those who served at the altar shared in the sacrificial offerings (Num 18:8–32; Deut 18:1–8).
- *He appealed to the teachings of Jesus (v. 14).* "In the same way, the Lord has commanded that those who preach the gospel should earn their living by the gospel." But Paul did not ask for a contribution from the Corinthians.

NEW TESTAMENT REFERENCE

"Do not muzzle an ox while it treads out grain" (Deut 25:4).

Section Summary

Paul defended his rights to marriage and financial support. Although he could claim the privilege of financial support from the church for his work and ministry, he did not. He cited several evidences to prove his right. Rather than take compensation from the Corinthians, he worked as a tentmaker to raise his own support.

WORD PICTURE

I Have Become All Things

Paul used an interesting play on words in verse 22: I have become *all* things to *all* people, so that I may by every possible means save *some* (emphasis added). There is a pointed play on the word *all,* that I might save some. This was his goal and worth all the cost of adaptation. A. T. Robertson, "Epistles of Paul," *WPNT*, vol. 4, 148.

CULTURAL BIAS (9:19–23)

Paul had a remarkable history of spreading the gospel throughout many lands and in the midst of various cultures. His success was due partly to his flexibility and his willingness to take risks in moving beyond his own culture. For example, Paul wrote, "To the Jews I became like a Jew, to win Jews" (v. 20).

He had unusual skills in distinguishing between the nonessential and the essential as he proclaimed the gospel. He willingly adapted to the cultural bias of his listeners, and he did so without compromising the gospel. Indeed, Paul declared in verse 22, "I have become all things to all people, so that I may by every possible means save some."

Section Summary

Paul effectively spread the gospel in the midst of various cultures. His success was due partly to his flexibility and his willingness to take risks in moving beyond his own culture. Paul summed up his goal in this statement: "I have become all things to all people, so that I may by every possible means save some."

SELF-DISCIPLINE (9:24–27)

Paul turned his attention to one's struggle with bodily appetites. To illustrate the Christian's need for self-discipline, he drew upon the athletic arena. Because the Isthmian games were held in Corinth every two years, these kinds of illustrations were likely popular and communicated well to his readers.

The Runner (vv. 24–25)

A runner subjected himself to strict and rigid training to prepare for the games. To the runner who wanted the victor's wreath, no amount of self-control for peak performance was too great a price a pay. Paul's argument was that the Christian should train even harder for "an imperishable crown."

WORD PICTURE

Competes

This is the Greek verb *agōnizomai,* from which we get our English words *agony* and *agonize.* It means "to engage in an athletic contest, to strive, to contend." Paul was talking about an all-out effort, not a halfhearted attempt. Christians are always to give their best.

The Boxer (vv. 26–27)

Here Paul pictured the Greek boxer. The trained boxer does not win by "beating the air." Paul insisted that he deals decisive blows to his body to bring it under control. The boxer keeps his appetites under submission lest he disqualify himself.

Section Summary

Paul addressed a person's struggle with bodily appetites. The believer needs to bring his or her appetites under control. Paul used the illustrations of the runner and the boxer to make his point.

QUESTIONS TO GUIDE YOUR STUDY

1. Why did Paul "waive his rights" in the areas of marriage and financial support?
2. Paul gave his readers several evidences that established his right to receive such support. What were they?
3. Why was Paul so successful in spreading the gospel into so many different cultures?
4. What was the point of Paul's two illustration from the athletic games?

1 CORINTHIANS 10

Paul showed how the Israelites, despite their rights and privileges, suffered in the wilderness. Using typological interpretation of Old Testament events, Paul warned the Corinthians not to grumble or dabble with idolatry. Thus, Paul pointed to the disastrous experiences of Israel following the Exodus from Egypt to jolt them out of their complacency and arrogance (vv. 1–13).

Spiritual fellowship at the Lord's Supper served as a stern reminder that the Corinthians should have nothing to do with idols. One cannot share simultaneously in the Lord's Table and in the table of demons (vv. 14–22).

ISRAEL'S FOLLY (10:1–5)

Having experienced baptism and the Lord's Supper, the Corinthians felt that their standing with God was secure. They believed they could also harmlessly choose to participate in cultic meals in pagan temples. They were enjoying a false security, and Paul refuted them by recalling the experiences in the life of ancient Israel: (1) the Israelites "were baptized into Moses" (v. 2), and (2) they participated in their equivalent of the Lord's Supper (vv. 3–4). Despite these assurances, God was not pleased "with most of them," and "they were struck down in the wilderness" (v. 5).

Section Summary

Having experienced baptism and the Lord's Supper, the Corinthians believed their standing with God was secure. But the security they felt was false. Paul warned them by recalling the experiences in the life of ancient Israel, in which similar attitudes resulted in God's displeasure.

PAUL'S ADMONITION (10:6–13)

Paul pointed out that the Israelites' assurances did not guarantee them entrance into the promised land, and then he made the connection between the Israelites and the believers at Corinth: "Now these things took place as examples for us, so that we will not desire evil things as they did" (v. 6). A. T. Robertson comments, "More exactly, an example for us" (A. T. Robertson, "Epistles of Paul," *WPNT*, vol. 4, 152.)

THE SINS OF THE ISRAELITES AND THE SINS OF THE CORINTHIANS

SIN	1 COR 10	OLD TESTAMENT PASSAGE
Desiring evil	v. 6	Num 11:4–34
Worshiping idols	v. 7	Exod 32:1–6
Sexual immorality	v. 8	Num 25:1–9
Putting the Lord to the test	v. 9	Num 21:4–9

HISTORICAL BACKGROUND

Typology in the Bible

Typology is the method of interpreting some parts of Scripture by seeing a pattern that an earlier statement sets up and by which a later statement is explained. Typology involves a correspondence, usually in one particular matter, between a person, event, or thing in the Old Testament with a person, event, or thing in the New Testament.

1. *Old Testament warnings.* Paul rehearsed the experiences of the people of Israel in the Exodus in their forty years in the desert. All the people participated in these experiences, but God was not pleased with most of them who died in the desert (1 Cor 10). The majority were types or warning patterns (examples) for Christians (v. 6).
2. *Adam as a type of Christ.* Paul compared Adam and Christ (Rom 5:12–21). He argued that Christ's deed was much more powerful than Adam's transgression. The one point of correspondence in the passage is the effect of the influence upon humankind.

WORD PICTURE

Grumble

The meaning of the word *grumble* is "to murmur, grumble, say anything in a low tone." The word in Greek is spelled *gonguzō* and is an onomatopoetic word, representing the significance by the sound of the word. We get our English word *gong* from this word.

Vine's Complete Expository Dictionary of Old and New Testament Words (Thomas Nelson, 1996), p. 422.

PERSONAL APPLICATION

Paul then summed up the examples of the Israelites as warnings for Christians. The Corinthians were to take care not to be self-confident: "So, whoever thinks he stands must be careful not to fall" (v. 12). The Corinthians were experiencing what is "common to humanity" (v. 13). Whatever temptation they might face, they need not fall but could count on God's help. He is faithful and will provide them a way out so they can stand up under the temptation. "The 'way out' is always right there along with the temptation" (A. T. Robertson, "Epistles of Paul,"*WPNT,* vol. 4, 154.) These truths are a comfort and source of strength to all Christians in all ages.

THE SINS OF THE ISRAELITES AND THE SINS OF THE CORINTHIANS

SIN	1 COR 10	OLD TESTAMENT PASSAGE
Grumbling	v. 10	Num 16:1–50

If self-trust and self-will led to the results they did for the children of Israel, that should keep the Corinthians from setting their hearts on "evil things as they did" (v. 6). The following verses show four examples of what caused Israel's demise in the desert. In presenting these examples, Paul provided several directives for the Corinthians.

"Don't become idolaters" (v. *7*). The Corinthian believers were not to emulate the actions of the children of Israel in the desert. Idolatry among God's people exposes them to God's judgment.

"Let us not commit sexual immorality" (v. *8*). Paul instructed some of the members of the congregation to "cease practicing fornication as some were already doing (1 Cor 6:11). The connection between idolatry and fornication was very close. . . . It was very true of Corinth where prostitution was part of the worship of Aphrodite" (A. T. Robertson, "Epistles of Paul," *WPNT* vol. 4, 153.)

"Let us not test Christ" (v. *9*). The Corinthians were putting Christ to the test by eating at both the Lord's Supper and the table of demons.

"Don't grumble" (v. *10*). In Num 14 we find that each time the Israelites "grumbled," God sent a punishment. The point is that grumbling about God brings his judgment.

Section Summary

Paul pointed out that the Israelites' assurances did not guarantee them entrance into the promised land, and then he made the connection between the Israelites and the believers at Corinth: "These things took place as examples for us, so that we will not desire evil things as they did." Paul instructed the Corinthians to refrain from those sins that brought judgment to the Israelites.

WARNING TO FLEE IDOLATRY(10:14–22)

The phrase "So then" is important, as it signals that Paul was bringing his preceding argument to a logical conclusion. Paul had urgent counsel regarding sins of immorality and idolatry. His warning was abrupt but absolute. Christians are to "flee from idolatry" (v. 14). He supported his command by describing the believer's experience in the observance of the Lord's Supper.

By partaking of the elements of the Lord's Supper, the bread and the cup, believers participate in the blood and body of Christ. Paul appealed to the meaning of Jewish sacrifices— "consider the people of Israel" (v. 18). Those who ate sacrifices were partners in the altar.

What pagans sacrifice, they offer to demons—not to God. Although pagan idols represent gods that do not exist, the worship of those gods involves the worship of demons. Paul's question was, How can a believer participate with Christ in the Lord's Supper and also commune with demons in a pagan cultic meal? (v. 21). Attempting such a thing is "provoking the Lord to jealousy" (v. 22) and inviting the kind of judgment that fell on idolatrous Israel in the wilderness.

Section Summary

Paul issued a direct and abrupt warning to the Corinthians. They were to "flee from idolatry" (v. 14) and seek safety in flight. He supported his command by describing the believer's experience in the observance of the Lord's Supper. A believer cannot participate with Christ in the Lord's Supper and also commune with demons in a pagan cultic meal.

SPECIFIC INSTRUCTIONS (10:23–11:1)

Note: Because it is obviously part of Paul's discussion in chapter 10, 1 Corinthians 11:1 is included here.

Paul began this section by repeating a catchphrase he used in 6:12: "Everything is permissible." And, as in chapter 6, he added a qualifier, "But not everything is beneficial." Christian liberty is important, but actions that do not build up or help others should be avoided.

Paul closed his discussion with specific instructions about Christian liberty and eating meat offered to pagan idols.

At the Meat Market (vv. 25–26)

Believers were to go ahead and buy any meat sold in the meat market. It was impossible to know for certain whether any piece of meat was offered to idols. Ultimately, it does not matter, for idols represent gods that do not exist. Paul's reasoning was that "the earth is the Lord's, and all that is in it" (v. 26). All meat is a provision from God, and because of its origin, Christians may eat whatever meat they purchase at the meat market.

At an Unbeliever's Home (vv. 27–28)

Christians were often dinner guests in the homes of unbelievers. Paul's instruction for this contingency was to eat what was served, "without raising questions for the sake of conscience" (v. 25). If, however, a fellow believer present took offense at eating meat that was offered in sacrifice to idols, the other believer was not to eat the meat, in deference to the fellow believer's conscience.

GOD'S GLORY, THE PRIORITY (10:31–11:1)

Paul left this issue by providing the following instructions to his readers.

Whatever you do, do it for the glory of God (v. 31). Paul delivered this all-encompassing principle to his readers: "So whether you eat or drink, or whatever you do, do everything for the glory of God" (v. 31).

Don't be a stumbling block to others (v. 32). Paul specifically mentions Jews, Greeks, and those who are part of the church.

"Imitate me" (11:1). As he often did, Paul appealed to himself as his readers' example. Because his example imitated Christ, they were to imitate Paul.

PERSONAL APPLICATION

"This is the ruling motive in the Christian's life, not just having his own way about whims and preferences." A. T. Robertson, "Epistles of Paul," *WPNT*, vol. 4, 158.

Section Summary

Paul closed his discussion with specific instructions about Christian liberty and the eating of meat offered to pagan idols. Believers should go ahead and buy any meat sold in the meat market. But if a fellow believer present took offense at eating meat that was offered in sacrifice to idols, the other believer was not to eat the meat, in deference to the fellow believer's conscience. In all matters, the all-encompassing principle is to do everything for the glory of God.

QUESTIONS TO GUIDE YOUR STUDY

1. What was Israel's folly? Why did Paul remind the Corinthians of it?
2. What is a Bible type? What is its purpose? What did Paul intend to teach by using typology?
3. What does it mean to "grumble"? Why does this behavior bring God's judgment?
4. Some of the Corinthians struggled with idolatry. What was Paul's instruction to them? What modern-day applications might we find for his instruction?
5. Regarding the eating of meat offered to pagan idols, what principle did Paul give the Corinthians? Can you think of ways this principle is to be applied in today's church?

1 CORINTHIANS 11

Paul turned his attention to matters of public worship. Every church bears witness to its faith through public services of worship. For this reason, Christian congregations need to be sensitive to the impressions they make on the communities in which they serve.

In this chapter Paul brought to the attention of the Corinthians an area in which they needed his guidance. Some of the activities of the church were causing disturbances and discrediting the testimony of the church:

- Women were flouting prevailing customs by participating in public worship with uncovered heads (vv. 2–16).
- Some members were profaning the observance of the Lord's Supper by shameful conduct (vv. 17–34).
- Those who spoke in tongues were dividing the church by their exaggerated and erroneous claims regarding their gift (12:1–14:40).

Note: Because 11:1 is part of the discussion of chapter 10, we begin the discussion of chapter 11 with verse 2.

THE VEILING OF WOMEN (11:2–16)

Certain women in the church at Corinth were creating a disturbance by failing to wear veils. Some of the Corinthian Christian women perhaps understood Paul's emphasis on Christian freedom to mean that they no longer had to observe any of the old Jewish customs—including wearing a veil. The effect of a such change was disruptive to the worship services and the church's Christian witness in Corinth. This led Paul to state that a woman should cover her head during the worship service. At the same time, he encouraged the men to follow the Jewish custom of worshiping with uncovered heads. Paul cited several reasons for this teaching:

The order of creation (v. 3). Woman comes below man in the divine order and should wear the head covering as a sign of subjection.

The social customs of the time (vv. 4–6). An unveiled woman, like a woman with a shaved head, was looked down upon in disgrace.

The presence of angels (v. 10). It is not certain what Paul meant here. Possibly he meant that if people are shocked by the presence of veiled women in services of worship, how much *more* the angels.

Nature itself (vv. 13–15). Nature teaches that long hair is degrading to a man but commendable in a woman. That is, nature gives women longer hair than it does men. Paul did not specify precise length, as it was not important. He simply stated that it is longer, and this is accepted as "her glory" (v. 15).

The prevailing practice in churches (v. 16). Paul indicated that this practice was also observed elsewhere— "the churches of God."

HISTORICAL BACKGROUND

Covering the Head

The Jewish custom for all women was to show modesty and virtue by covering their heads with a veil when they went outside their homes. The veiling of a woman's head was not a new concept for the Corinthians. In Jewish synagogues it was required, and in Greek sanctuaries women were also to be veiled. It is likely that the women in the Corinthian congregation were simply reflecting the more daring styles of the day. The principle here is that Christians must be sensitive to the cultures in which they live and not needlessly flout local customs unless there is some moral reason to do so.

Section Summary

Some women in the church at Corinth were creating a disturbance by failing to wear a veil. Paul stated that a woman should cover her head during the worship service. At the same time, he encouraged the men to follow the Jewish custom of worshiping with uncovered heads.

OBSERVANCE OF THE LORD'S SUPPER (11:17–34)

Some members were profaning the observance of the Lord's Supper by their shameful conduct. The following verses describe this problem.

Abuses Associated with Its Observance (vv. 17–22)

A fractured fellowship (vv. 18–20). Paul repeated a similar concern that he expressed in 1 Cor 1:10–12. In that previous passage, divisions arose from conflicting loyalties to different leaders. Here the divisions were issuing from differences in economic and social status.

Disorder (v. 21). In addition to general disorder ("Each one eats his own supper"), Paul also cited instances of gluttony and drunkenness. Members were gorging themselves with food and getting drunk at the Lord's Supper.

Paul responded to these abuses with a series of rhetorical questions, which he used to hammer at the evils of their practice. Paul made clear that he could not commend their actions: "What should I say to you? Should I praise you? I do not praise you in this matter!"

Original Meaning of the Lord's Supper (vv. 23–26)

Because of the degree to which things had gotten out of hand at Corinth, Paul saw a need to remind his readers about the original meaning and purpose of the Lord's Supper. He began by describing the first Supper, as it was reported by the earliest Christians.

"In remembrance of me" (vv. 23–25). Paul associated the Supper with the meal Jesus ate with his disciples "on the night when he was betrayed" (v. 23).

On this solemn occasion, Jesus gave thanks and then broke the bread, saying, "This is my body, which is for you. Do this in remembrance of me" (v. 24).

Proclaiming "the Lord's death until he comes" (v. 26). When a congregation observes the Lord's Supper, it proclaims the gospel by its actions, and this proclamation of the Lord's death through the enactments of the Supper is to continue "until he comes." Even in the first century, the early Christians lived in the expectancy of the Lord's return. The observance of the Lord's Supper: (1) calls Christians to remember and proclaim Christ's sacrificial death on their behalf, (2) invites believers to celebrate his living presence, and (3) fixes the believers' hope on the victory that his coming will bring.

The Need for Self-Examination (vv. 27–34)

Having provided background about the original meaning and purpose of the Lord's Supper, Paul returned to the situation that existed in the Corinthian church and their observance of this ordinance.

HISTORICAL BACKGROUND

The Lord's Supper

The Lord's Supper was a memorial celebrated by the early church to signify Jesus's sacrificial death for humanity's sin. The form of the observance was established by the Lord at the Last Supper—the Passover meal Jesus shared with his disciples on the day before he was crucified. His actual death the following day fulfilled his words about his broken body and his shed blood. Only Paul uses the phrase "Lord's Supper" (1 Cor 11:20), although this phrase is implied in Rev 19:9 ("marriage feast of the Lamb"). Church fathers began to call the occasion the "Eucharist" (that is, "Thanksgiving") from the blessing pronounced over the bread and wine after about AD 100. Church groups celebrate the Lord's Supper regularly as a sign of the new covenant sealed by Christ's death and resurrection.

HISTORICAL BACKGROUND

Written about AD 54 or 55, this letter brings us within three decades of the first Lord's Supper.

The phrase "So, then" (v. 27) is one Paul used to draw a conclusion. In this case, it introduced the consequence for the inappropriate behavior of the Corinthians. Whoever observes the Lord's Supper "in an unworthy manner will be guilty of sin against the body and blood of the Lord."

Paul instructed the Corinthians to "examine" themselves before eating the bread and drinking the cup for the purpose of avoiding communicating unworthily (v. 27). Anyone who is unworthy while partaking of the Lord's Supper brings judgment. Paul stated that for this reason "many are sick and ill among you, and many have fallen asleep" (v. 30). Here Paul noted that the ill health and even deaths of some of the Corinthians had spiritual causes.

Paul closed this part of his instruction by telling the Corinthians to wait for one another in the common meal and to satisfy their hunger at home.

WORD PICTURE

Lord's Supper

Participating in the Lord's Supper requires that we recall the extent to which Christ was willing to go to forgive us and make us what God intended from the beginning. What would happen if every believer was acutely aware of God's love for him or her?

Section Summary

The Lord's Supper should be a celebration of unity; instead, divisions among the church members were magnified. Because they were participating in Christ's body and blood, to participate in an unworthy manner profaned the Supper and invited judgment. Paul exhorted the Corinthians to examine their motives, methods, and manners when they gathered to worship the Lord at his Supper.

QUESTIONS TO GUIDE YOUR STUDY

1. Why did women veil their heads? Why was the veiling of a woman's head such an issue? How does Paul's teaching on this issue impact today's church?
2. What is the Lord's Supper? What is meant by the "bread" and the "cup"? What is the significance of this ordinance for the believer?
3. Why did Paul take issue with the Corinthians over their observance of the Lord's Supper?
4. How does one partake of the Lord's Supper worthily? What is the consequence for observing the Supper unworthily?

1 CORINTHIANS 12

The exercise of spiritual (or charismatic) gifts in the church was a subject about which the Corinthians asked for advice. Many of them were attracted by the more spectacular gifts. Chapters 12–14 provide the most extensive passage in the New Testament on charismatic gifts.

These gifts were a divisive issue in the church at Corinth. Some members regarded their own spiritual gifts with pride and exclusiveness.

The Corinthians tended to place an extreme value on one the most dramatic of these gifts—speaking in tongues. The overemphasis of those who used this gift prompted the overreaction of those who did not speak in tongues. The result of the confusion over these gifts was further division.

Paul countered this crisis by raising questions about the problem of *glossolalia* with the following response pattern:

- He *taught* about the nature of the church as the body of Christ.
- He *appealed* to love as the more excellent way.
- He *confronted* those who spoke in tongues, who wrongly valued ecstatic utterance above prophetic utterance.

WORD PICTURE

Speaking in Tongues

The Greek word refers to the gift of speaking in tongues. It involved the ability to speak in a foreign language (or languages) not previously studied or to respond to and experience the Holy Spirit by uttering sounds that believers without the gift of interpreting tongues could not understand. At Corinth, some members of the church uttered sounds which the rest of the congregation did not understand (1 Cor 12–14). This led to controversy and division. Paul tried to reunite the church, assuring the church that there are different gifts but only one Spirit (1 Cor 12:4–11).

THE NATURE AND FUNCTION OF CHARISMATIC GIFTS (12:1–11)

"Jesus Is Lord" (vv. 1–3)

Paul established the ultimate test of the presence and power of the Spirit in the believer's life; it is the confession that "Jesus is Lord" (v. 3). The Holy Spirit alone can plant this confession in a person's heart. Therefore, a church is the body of Christ, consisting of members who experience him as Lord.

Enabling Graces (vv. 4–7)

As believers are saved by grace, so also are they equipped by grace to serve. Spiritual gifts are bestowed by the Holy Spirit upon every believer. In these verses Paul mentioned the varieties of spiritual gifts, emphasizing that each has the same divine source and operation. His statement in verse 7, "A manifestation of the Spirit is given to each person for the common good," provides two key points for the reader:

1. Every Christian receives some gift or enabling grace. No believer is overlooked when it comes to receiving a spiritual gift.
2. Gifts are given by the Holy Spirit to individual members for the good of the entire congregation. They equip members of the church to function as the body of Christ in a community.

Paul is clear that to regard a spiritual gift as a merit badge to designate God's elite or as evidence of total commitment is to misunderstand the purpose of the giving of these enabling gifts.

Section Summary

As believers are saved by grace, so also are they equipped by grace to serve. The enabling grace, or spiritual gifts, is bestowed by the Holy Spirit upon every believer. Paul emphasizes that each gift has the same divine source and operation.

The Charismatic Gifts (vv. 8–11)

The gifts listed (vv. *8–10*). Paul named a representative list of nine charismatic gifts:

LISTING OF GIFTS IN 1 CORINTHIANS 12:8–11

1. Wisdom	6. Prophecy
2. Knowledge	7. The ability to distinguish between spirits
3. Faith	8. Tongues
4. Gifts of healing	9. Interpretation of tongues
5. Performing of miracles	

Other New Testament passages that include some spiritual gifts or offices not mentioned here are 1 Cor 7:7; 12:28; Rom 12:6–8; Eph 4:11. (For an exhaustive list of gifts, see the chart, "Paul's Lists of Spiritual Gifts," in the introduction.)

The Sovereignty of the Spirit (v. *11*). The giving of spiritual gifts is not a do-it-yourself operation. Only the Holy Spirit can give these gifts. "One and the same Spirit is active in all these, distributing to each person as he wills." As a result, no Christian can boast that he or she has accomplished or attained his or her gift.

Section Summary

In this passage Paul listed some of the charismatic gifts. He emphasized that the source of each gift is the Holy Spirit: "One and the same Spirit is active in all these."

THE INTERDEPENDENCE OF CHARISMATIC GIFTS (12:12–31)

Baptized into One Body (vv. 12–13)

Paul used the analogy of the body to describe the church. The body has many different members and organs, yet these unique parts all work together to form the body. Paul applied this analogy to the body of believers: "So also is Christ. For we were all baptized by one Spirit into one body—whether Jews or Greeks, whether slaves or free—and we were all given one Spirit to drink."

WORD PICTURE

Baptism in the Spirit

With his phrase, "We were all baptized by one Spirit into one body," Paul did not use this word to refer to water baptism but rather spiritual transformation that puts the believer "in Christ." It is the effect of receiving the gift of the Spirit that takes place at the time of the believer's conversion.

As the body of Christ, the church is a unit of solidarity that transcends all ethnic and social distinctions (Gal 3:27–28; Col 3:11).

The Folly of Discord Within the Body (vv. 14–26)

Paul now turned to a method of argument that showed the Corinthians how ridiculous their discord was. He made two points.

1. *Paul imagined a dissatisfied foot and a proud ear* (vv. 15–20). The foot wants to be a hand, and the ear wants to be an eye. Because they are both unable to arrange such trades, they declare their intentions to secede from the body. Paul responded: "But as it is, God has arranged each one of the parts in the body just as he wanted" (v. 18).
2. *Paul imagined a proud eye and a proud head* (vv. 21–26). The proud eye scorns the hand, and the head scorns the feet. Paul maintained that this is folly, as all parts of the body unite in a remarkable interdependence. Each part is unique and essential. Paul explained, "Those parts of the body that are weaker are indispensable" (v. 22).

In this passage Paul taught these important truths about the body of Christ:

1. There should be no division within the body (v. 25).
2. If one part of the body suffers, the whole body suffers with it (v. 26).
3. If one part of the body is honored, the whole body rejoices with it (v. 26).

The God-Appointed Ministries of the Church (vv. 27–31)

Paul took his analogy of the body and applied it directly to the church at Corinth: "Now you are the body of Christ" (v. 27). Some of the members of the congregation were building a fellowship around the gift of tongues, and in doing so they were denying the nature of the church as the body of Christ.

Paul presented seven rhetorical questions to make a point that no Christian has all these charismatic gifts and that no one gift is bestowed upon all. He then cited God's appointments in the church to various ministries:

MINISTRIES OF THE CHURCH

1. Apostles	5. Healers
2. Prophets	6. Helpers
3. Teachers	7. Administrators
4. Workers of miracles	8. Speakers in tongues

Verse 31, "But desire the greater gifts," serves as a transition that points to chapter 13.

Section Summary

Paul took his analogy of the body and applied it directly to the church at Corinth. He cited God's appointments in the church to various ministries, emphasizing that no Christian has all these charismatic gifts and that no one gift is bestowed upon all.

QUESTIONS TO GUIDE YOUR STUDY

1. What is the gift of speaking in "tongues"?
2. Why did Paul take issue with some believers at Corinth who spoke in tongues?
3. From this portion of Paul's letter, what do we learn about the nature of spiritual gifts? About the proper exercise of these gifts?
4. In 12:12–21, what important truths does Paul teach about the body of Christ?

1 CORINTHIANS 13

Paul explained the proper way to exercise all spiritual gifts. He now showed the supreme fruit of the Spirit—a more excellent way.

LOVE: THE MORE EXCELLENT WAY (13:1–13)

The Necessity of Love (vv. 1–3)

How important is love? Christians may be talented, gifted, devoted, generous in their giving, or endowed with mountain-moving faith; but those are of no value if love is not present. Without love, none of the gifts can honor God and build up the church.

Paul presented four conditions that embrace important concepts of Christianity to show the meaninglessness of using the gifts without love.

The Gift of Tongues (v. 1). No earthly or heavenly language compares with the exercise of love. The use of tongues without interpretation has no meaning. If it is exercised without love, it results in nothing more than noise— "a noisy gong" or "a clanging cymbal."

"The Gift of Prophecy" (v. 2). "All knowledge" means the sum of all wisdom, both human and divine. The word "mysteries" has to do with those things we cannot know without revelation from God. Even if a person were able to fathom all this—without the expression of love—it would amount to nothing.

WORD PICTURE

If

In verses 1–3 the word *if* introduces what is known as a *condition.* Conditional constructions in the New Testament have four functions, one of which is to show the possibility of something occurring. That was Paul's intent here. Four times he used this grammatical construction to drive home the point that the proper use of the gifts of the Spirit is conditional. Indeed, it is possible for believers to use the gifts of the Spirit without bringing honor to God and building the church. Unless they are exercised as expressions of love, the gifts become meaningless and gain nothing.

The Gift of Faith (v. 2b). If a person were to exercise the kind of faith that works miracles and use it to its fullest extent but lacked love, the use of this gift would have no value.

The Gift of Giving (v. 3). Acts of giving and self-sacrifice, if not done in love, accomplish nothing. Even if one were to "give over [one's] body," if it is not done within the context of love, it is worthless.

In this passage Paul used the phrase "but do not have love." He did not refer to a possession of love but to the idea of acting lovingly.

WITHOUT LOVE . . .

"IF . . ."	APPARENT WORTH	RESULT
"If I speak . . . tongues"	"human or angelic"	I am . . . a clanging cymbal."
"If I have the gift of prophecy"	"understand all mysteries and all knowledge"	I am nothing."
"If I have all faith"	"that can move mountains"	I am nothing."
"If I give away all my possessions"	"give my body over"	I gain nothing."

Section Summary

Paul discussed the necessity of love in the exercise of the charismatic gifts. Christians may be talented, gifted, devoted, generous in their giving, or endowed with mountain-moving faith, but those are of no value if love is not present. Without love, none of the gifts can honor God and build up the church.

The Characteristic Actions of Love (vv. 4–7)

PERSONAL APPLICATION

In this passage Paul used fifteen words to describe the characteristic actions of love. Seven of these have to do with the positive actions of love, and eight have to do with what love does not do. We need to keep in mind that Paul was dealing with a congregation that needed to be reminded about many things that love does not do.

Paul made clear that genuine love is active, not static. Love is something people *do*.

Seven Positive Actions of Love

1. *It "is patient" (v. 4)*. One who is patient waits a long time before giving room to action or passion. It is the opposite of one who is short-tempered.
2. *It "is kind" (v. 4)*. Kindness is being gracious and useful to others.
3. *It "rejoices in the truth" (v. 6)*. Love rejoices in the truth of God and the gospel. The loving person rejoices with that which reflects the gospel, such as the forgiveness of sins and acts of kindness toward others.
4. *It "bears all things" (v. 7)*. Love covers. It conceals what is unbecoming or displeasing in another rather than bringing that person's "dirty laundry" out into full view of others.

5. *It always "believes" (v. 7).* Although love is not to be gullible or deceived by pretense, it does allow for circumstances and actions in others, and it tries to see the best in them.
6. *It always "hopes" (v. 7).* Love always has the forward look, no matter the circumstances. It never loses hope because it never ceases to have faith.
7. *It always "endures" (v. 7).* Love is not overwhelmed by circumstances, but it continues despite difficulty.

Eight Negative Actions of Love

1. *It "does not envy" (v. 4).* Love avoids acts of jealousy and envy toward others. It is not upset or displeased when others succeed.
2. *It "is not boastful" (v. 4).* One who loves does not assert oneself. A loving person is not arrogant or boastful. The Greek word Paul used here means to behave as a braggart or "windbag."
3. *It "is not arrogant" (v. 4).* Love does not cause one to be puffed up; it is not addicted to the sin of pride.
4. *It "is not rude" (v. 5).* A loving person is tactful and refrains from behaving indecently or in a shameful manner.
5. *It "is not self-seeking" (v. 5).* Love is not self-centered. It does not seek to have its own way.
6. *It is not easily angered* (v. 5). A loving person is not "touchy" or easily irritated. Such a person is not provoked to anger by others.
7. *It "does not keep a record of wrongs" (v. 5).* A loving person does not keep accounts of wrongdoing. Neither does a loving person take notice of every evil thing another does and then hold it against that person.
8. *It "finds no joy in unrighteousness" (v. 6).* Love does not take pleasure or satisfaction in evil of any kind.

HISTORICAL BACKGROUND

Patient

The church at Corinth had at least two kinds of people who were wronged: those involved in lawsuits and the poor who were made to feel their poverty at church meals. Love, on their part, would show itself as patience—not retaliating when wronged.

Section Summary

In this passage Paul used fifteen words to describe the characteristic actions of love. Seven of these have to do with the positive actions of love, and eight have to do with what love does not do.

THE SUPREMACY OF LOVE (13:8–13)

Love Never Fails (v. 8)

Paul makes a bold statement: "Love never ends" (v. 8). This means that love is never defeated. Nothing can cause it to collapse. He then contrasts love with the spiritual gifts. Love is greater than the gifts because it is *eternal* and the gifts are *temporal.*

Whereas love never ends, the temporal gifts will eventually disappear:

- Prophecies will cease.
- Tongues will be stilled.
- Knowledge will pass away.

The Complete Versus the Partial (vv. 9–12)

These verses explain what Paul asserted in verse 8 and illustrate the temporality of the gifts and the eternality of love.

Paul stated that when "the perfect comes, the partial will come to an end" (v. 10). In verses 11–12 Paul continued with two analogies that contrast the *partial* with the *complete*.

Human Growth (v. 11). Paul likened the imperfection of this present age with the perfection of the future by his analogy of human growth. As children grow up, their actions, speech, and thoughts mature. They put "childish things" behind them.

A *Mirror* (v. 12). The Christian's knowledge of God at present may be compared to the imperfect reflection of an ancient metal mirror. However, in eternity the believer's knowledge of God will be "face to face." The believer's partial understanding will yield to a full understanding of God.

HISTORICAL BACKGROUND

Mirrors

"A city like Corinth, famous for its bronze mirrors, would have particularly appreciated Paul's final illustration. The perfection and imperfection mentioned in verse 10 were deftly likened to the contrasting images obtained by the indirect reflection of one's face viewed in a bronze mirror and the same face when viewed directly." *The Bible Knowledge Commentary, New Testament* (Zondervan), 536.

The Three Great Realities (v. 13)

Paul closed this chapter with a brief discussion of the three great realities that will endure forever. These enduring realities are faith, hope, and love. Of the three, Paul said, "the greatest of these is love."

THE THREE GREAT REALITIES

REALITY	WHY THEY ENDURE
Faith	Because the believer's relationship to God will always be one of trust and commitment
Hope	Because the believer will participate with God in an eternal order that is dynamic
Love	Because where God is, love is

Section Summary

Paul stated that "love never ends." As he contrasted genuine love with spiritual gifts, he showed that love is greater that the gifts because it is eternal, whereas the gifts are temporal. Paul closed this chapter with a brief discussion of the three great realities that will endure forever: faith, hope, and love.

QUESTIONS TO GUIDE YOUR STUDY

1. Why is love necessary in the exercise of spiritual gifts?
2. Paul mentioned seven positive characteristics of love. What are they, and what does each contribute to the building up of the body of Christ?
3. Paul mentioned eight negative characteristics of love. What are they, and what does each contribute to the building up of the body of Christ?
4. What are the three realities that endure forever?

1 CORINTHIANS 14

In this chapter Paul confronted the erroneous claims of those who spoke in tongues. He sought to point out their error by comparing the relative values of the two gifts: prophecy and speaking in tongues.

PROPHECY IS MORE IMPORTANT THAN TONGUES (14:1–25)

Definitions

- *The Gift of Prophecy.* This gift has to do with Spirit-inspired utterance that is intelligible. It has a recognizable vocabulary through which God's message is communicated.
- *The Gift of Speaking in Tongues.* This gift is Spirit-inspired utterance that is *not* intelligible. It is a form of ecstatic utterance. It is *not* the ability to speak in foreign languages.

Paul informed the Corinthians that both the gifts of prophecy and speaking in tongues are valid spiritual gifts. However, they are not of equal importance in the ministries of the church. Whereas those speaking in tongues regarded their gift more highly than the other gifts, Paul taught that prophecy is more important. He gave the Corinthians three reasons:

1. Prophecy edifies the whole church.
2. Prophecy is understood by all.
3. Prophecy inspires conviction, confession, and worship.

Prophecy Edifies the Whole Church (vv. 1–12)

Speaking in tongues has a value, as does any gift bestowed by the Spirit. The Spirit alone determines the who, when, and where of all his gifts (v. 4). However, in Corinth, and often since, *tongues* was magnified out of proportion to its value. Self-edification is its primary contribution.

WORD PICTURE

Prophecy

Paul declared that one reason the gift of prophecy is more important than speaking in tongues is that it edifies the entire congregation. He used three words to describe how prophecy ministers to believers in the church. *Strengthening.* This word is a compound made up of the noun "a home" and the verb "to build" and denotes the act of building. Here it refers to the body of Christ and depicts the edification, the building up of others that is a result of the exercise of the gift of prophecy. *Encouragement.* This is a compound made up of the words "by the side" and "to call" and means "a calling to one's aid." Here it refers to exhortation of one another in the body of Christ through the exercise of the gift of prophecy. *Consolation.* This is yet another compound made up of the words *near* and *speech.* Literally, it means "a speaking closely to anyone." Here it refers to consolation and comfort that result from the exercise of the gift of prophecy within the body of Christ.

Unless accompanied by the gift of interpretation, it cannot build up the congregation (v. 5).

But prophecy is different. As speaking in tongues is ecstatic speech addressed to God by people, so prophecy is intelligible speech addressed by God through people to others. Paul claimed, "The person who speaks in a tongue builds himself up, but the one who prophesies builds up the church" (v. 4).

Section Summary

Although the gifts of prophecy and speaking in tongues were valid, they were not of equal importance in the ministries of the church. Whereas those speaking in tongues regarded their gift more highly than the other gifts, Paul taught that prophecy is more important. He provided three reasons to support his argument: (1) prophecy edifies the whole church; (2) prophecy is understood by all; and (3) prophecy inspires conviction, confession, and worship.

Prophecy Is Understood by All (vv. 13–19)

"Therefore" refers to the goal of strengthening the church. Paul instructed the one who speaks in tongues to "pray that he can interpret" what he says (v. 13). The problem was that although a person who is praising God in tongues may be expressing genuine thanks, others may not know when to respond with an "Amen" (v. 16).

Paul claimed that he spoke in tongues, but he placed greater value upon "five words with my understanding, in order to teach others also, than ten thousand words in a tongue" (v. 19). This statement should remind believers not to exaggerate the value of the gift of speaking in tongues.

THE RELATIVE VALUE OF TONGUES AND PROPHECY

AREA OF CONTRAST	SPEAKING IN TONGUES	PROPHECY
Edification	Self-edifying	Edifies the entire congregation
Understanding	Needs to be interpreted to be understood	Understood by all who are listening
How message is communicated	From people to God	From God through people to others

Section Summary

Whereas speaking in tongues cannot be understood by others, the gift of prophecy can be understood by the entire congregation. This elevates the gift of prophecy to a higher level of importance.

Prophecy Inspires Conviction, Confession, and Worship (vv. 20–25)

Paul was concerned about the impact the exercise of these charismatic gifts had on unbelievers. Here he contrasted the impressions prophecy and tongues had on those who were not Christians. He offered two kinds of responses from unbelievers:

1. *Speaking in tongues invites scorn (v. 23).* Paul imagined a situation in which visitors are present at worship and everyone is speaking in tongues. What will they think? What value will they take away from this?
2. *Prophecy inspires worship (vv. 24–25).* Clear communication, on the other hand, could bring conviction and could be used by the Spirit to bring the visitor to say, "God is really among you."

The point of Paul's contrast here was that the gift of prophecy that prompted them to worship God was superior to the gift of tongues that led unbelievers to respond with, "You are out of your minds."

Section Summary

Paul was concerned about the impact the exercise of these charismatic gifts had on unbelievers. Here he contrasted the impressions prophecy and tongues have on those who are not Christians: speaking in tongues invites scorn, whereas prophecy inspires worship.

PRACTICAL GUIDANCE IN WORSHIP (14:26–40)

Broad Principles (vv. 26,33,40)

Paul advocated orderly worship. Some of the Corinthians prized the more spectacular gifts, such as speaking in tongues, above all others. If the exercise of such gifts were not done in an orderly fashion, Christian worship and service could easily degenerate into an experience of frenzy and flamboyance with little moral substance. Paul's instructions in this section were designed to correct the abuses the Corinthians were allowing.

PERSONAL APPLICATION

Paul equipped his readers with three basic principles that he applied to their worship and service:

1. "Everything is to be done for building up." (v. 26.
2. "God is not a God of disorder but of peace." (v. 33.
3. "Everything is to be done decently and in order." (v. 40)

Specific Items (vv. 26–36)

The Proper Exercise of Charismatic Gifts (v. 26). Paul mentioned several activities of worship that take place when believers come together:

- A hymn
- A teaching
- A revelation
- A tongue
- An interpretation

Controlling principle: All of these activities were to be exercised according to the principle in verse 26: "Everything is to be done for building up."

The Number of Prophets or Speakers in Tongues Who May Take Part in a Service (vv. 27–32). At times, several members of the congregation at Corinth exercised the gift of tongues *simultaneously,* making for confusion. Paul taught that prophecy also needs to be regulated; that no more than "two or three prophets" should speak in a service. The purpose was that all might be instructed and encouraged.

Controlling principle: "God is not a God of disorder but of peace" (v. 33).

Restrictions on the Participation of Women (vv. 33–36). Paul instructed women to "be silent in the churches" (v. 34). The context of this passage does not discuss whether women were qualified to minister but rather was concerned with how they should learn (v. 35). Paul instructed his readers, "If they want to learn something, let them ask their own husbands at home" (v. 35).

In verses 37–40 Paul closed this section by appealing to those who considered themselves prophets. All are to "be eager to prophesy" and "not forbid speaking in tongues" (v. 39).

Controlling principle: Whether the participation of women in the church or the exercise of spiritual gifts, Paul reminded his readers that "everything is to be done decently and in order" (v. 40).

HISTORICAL BACKGROUND

It should be noted that Paul asked the Corinthians to conform to what was the accepted Christian practice of his day. In the eyes of most people, women assuming the role of instructor or teacher would have been a discredit to Christianity. Among the Greeks, for example, women were discouraged from saying anything in public. The Jews even regarded it a sin to teach a woman.

Section Summary

Paul advocated orderly worship, and his instructions in this section were designed to correct the abuses the Corinthians were allowing. He centered his teaching on three basic principles: (1) all must be done for the purpose of strengthening of the church; (2) the God they worship is not a God of disorder but of peace; and (3) everything must be done in an orderly way.

QUESTIONS TO GUIDE YOUR STUDY

1. What are the gifts of prophecy and speaking in tongues?
2. Why is prophecy the more important of the two gifts?
3. Paul presented three controlling principles for worship and service. Describe them. How well are these applied in our churches today?
4. What were Paul's instructions regarding the role of women in the church? How are we to apply these to today's church?

1 CORINTHIANS 15

In this chapter we have the earliest existing account of the resurrection of Jesus Christ. Some believers in Corinth were saying that there was no resurrection of the dead. We do not know the details of this denial. Earlier in his letter, Paul rebuked the arrogant Corinthians for acting as though the consummation had already occurred and they were basking in its glories (4:8–13). Paul sought to refute the denial of the resurrection by affirming the certainty of the resurrection (vv. 1–34) and describing the nature of the resurrected body (vv. 35–38).

TESTIMONY OF THE EYEWITNESSES (15:1–11)

The gospel message Paul understated has three vital emphases:

1. "Christ died for our sins according to the Scriptures." (v. 3).
2. "He was buried." (v. 4.
3. "He was raised on the third day according to the Scriptures." (v. 4)

Following his resurrection, Jesus appeared to several of his followers. Paul mentioned Jesus's post-resurrection appearances, capping his list with Paul's Damascus Road encounter.

Section Summary

Some believers in Corinth were saying that there was no resurrection of the dead. Paul refuted their denial of the resurrection, citing Jesus's post-resurrection appearances, capping his list with his own Damascus Road encounter with the resurrected Lord.

PAUL'S ACCOUNT OF JESUS'S POST-RESURRECTION APPEARANCES

APPEARANCE	PASSAGE
1. Peter	Luke 24:34; Mark 16:7; John 21:1–14
2. The Twelve	Matthew 28:16–20; Luke 24:36–49; John 20:19–25
3. Five hundred believers	1 Corinthians 15:6
4. James	1 Corinthians 15:7
5. The apostles	1 Corinthians 15:7
6. Paul	1 Corinthians 15:8

DENIAL OF THE RESURRECTION (15:12–19)

Now Paul more directly challenged the denial of the resurrection. Whether the Corinthians' denial of the resurrection included Jesus's resurrection is not known. However, Paul's argument against the denial of resurrection constituted a denial of Jesus's resurrection: "If there is no resurrection of the dead, then not even Christ has been raised" (v. 13).

Now for the sake of argument, Paul assumed that Jesus was not raised from the dead, and proceeded to draw conclusions based on this false premise:

- *Preaching the truth: "Our proclamation is in vain" (v. 14).* An unresurrected Christ would make Paul's preaching false witness.
- *Faith without forgiveness: "Your faith is worthless; you are still in your sins" (v. 17).* If Jesus remained a victim of sin and death following his resurrection, he would have been unable to deliver us from the power of sin and death.
- *Death without hope: "Those, then, who have fallen asleep in Christ have also perished" (v. 18).* The death of those who believed on Christ have the same end as those who denied him.
- *Sacrifice without meaning: "If we have put our hope in Christ for this life only, we should be pitied more than anyone" (v. 19).* Christ's sacrifice was wasted on an illusion.

HISTORICAL BACKGROUND

Christ's death, burial, and resurrection served as the foundation of all Paul preached and wrote.

Section Summary

Paul challenged the Corinthians' denial of the resurrection. For the sake of argument, Paul assumed that Jesus has not been raised from the dead and drew four conclusions based on this false premise. Christ's death, burial, and resurrection were the foundation of all Paul preached and wrote.

HISTORICAL BACKGROUND

Firstfruits

This word means the first installment of the crop which foreshadows and pledges the ultimate offering of the whole. The word was used in various ways in the papyri: a birth certificate, a certificate of authorization, a yearly offering for a god, or an inheritance tax. Fritz Rienecker, *Linguistic Key to the Greek New Testament* (Zondervan, 1980), 441.

CONSEQUENCES OF CHRIST'S RESURRECTION (15:20–28)

Paul now turned from drawing conclusions based on the premise of an unresurrected Christ to an affirmation of faith. Christ indeed was raised from the dead (v. 20) and is the "firstfruits of those who have fallen asleep."

Leviticus 23:4–11 is the background for the metaphor of the firstfruits. The waving of the sheaf of the firstfruits of the grain harvest before God consecrated the whole harvest to follow.

Drawing from that Old Testament concept, Paul taught that the resurrection of Christ as the firstfruits of those who have died is the assurance that those who trust Christ shall have a resurrection like his.

In verses 23–26 Paul showed order in the resurrection: Christ was the firstfruits; "afterward, at his coming, those who belong to Christ"

(v. 23). The resurrection of believers is related to the second coming of Christ. "Then comes the end, when he hands over the kingdom to God the Father, when he abolishes all rule and all authority and power" (v. 24). And death, described as the last enemy, will be destroyed (v. 26).

Paul now turned from drawing conclusions based on the premise of an unresurrected Christ to an affirmation of faith. Christ indeed has been raised from the dead (v. 20) and is the "firstfruits of those who have fallen asleep."

OTHER ARGUMENTS FOR THE RESURRECTION (15:29–34)

For the sake of argument, Paul draws two more negative conclusions:

1. *Baptism on behalf of the dead is futile (v. 29).* "Otherwise what will they do who are being baptized for the dead?" Although this is a puzzling verse, it probably refers to Paul's teaching that Christ was raised from the dead. If he wasn't, then any baptism would be for "the dead."
2. *Risking one's life for the sake of the gospel is folly (v. 30).* "Why are we in danger every hour?" The apostles were in constant danger. Why should anyone endure the risks associated with Christianity if death is final?

THE NATURE OF THE RESURRECTED BODY (15:35–58)

The discussion of the nature of the resurrected body begins in verse 35 with two questions: "How are the dead raised?" and "What kind of body will they have when they come?"

Paul's response to those questions was, "You fool! What you sow does not come to life unless it dies" (v. 36). He followed by presenting an analogy from nature and an appeal to Scripture.

Paul's Analogy from Nature (vv. 36–44)

Paul insisted that believers would experience resurrection with an imperishable body suited for life in the world beyond. His analogy from nature made the point that death is a transition to a higher life.

Grains and Plants (vv. 36–38). Paul used the metaphor of a *seed.* A seed goes through stages:

- It is planted in the ground.
- It dies (germinates).
- It yields a new body.

Men and animals (v. 39). Humans, animals, birds, and fish have different kinds of flesh. Through the idea that there are different kinds of

NEW TESTAMENT REFERENCE

Biblical examples of the use of the word *firstfruits* include:

- Christ in his resurrection is the "firstfruits" of those who sleep (1 Cor 15:20, 23).
- The Holy Spirit is spoken of as "firstfruits" (Rom 8:23).
- Believers are also spoken of as "a kind of firstfruits" (Jas 1:18).
- The saved remnant within Israel is described as "firstfruits" (Rom 11:16).
- The 144,000 of the tribulation period are described as "firstfruits" (Rev 14:4).
- The converts of an area were designated "firstfruits" (Rom 16:5; 1 Cor 16:15).

flesh, Paul prepared the way in his readers' minds that there can indeed be a difference in the kind of body one has *before* the resurrection and the body one has *after* the resurrection.

The Heavenly Bodies (vv. 40–41). In a smaller way, there is a difference between the heavenly bodies and earthly bodies. With the variety and adequacy with which God has clothed all kinds of celestial and terrestrial life, he should be able to provide suitable bodies for those who will share in the eternal order.

Application of the Analogy (vv. 42–44). The phrase "so it is" signaled to Paul's readers that Paul was now applying his analogy to the issue of the resurrection of the dead. "Paul now applies his illustrations to his argument to prove the kind of body we shall have after the resurrection. He does it by a series of marvelous contrasts that gather all his points. The earthly and the risen beings differ in duration, value, and power." A. T. Robertson, "Epistles of Paul," *WPNT*, vol. 4, 196.

THE RESURRECTION BODY

	BEFORE—"SOWN"	AFTER—"RAISED"
Its duration	Perishable	Imperishable
Its value	Dishonor	Glory
Its power	Weakness	Power
Its nature	Natural body	Spiritual body

Section Summary

Paul discussed the nature of the resurrected body by using an analogy from nature. His observations of seeds, flesh, and the variety and splendor of heavenly bodies proves there can be a difference in the kind of body one has before the resurrection and the body one has after the resurrection. With the variety and adequacy with which God has clothed all kinds of celestial and terrestrial life, he should be able to provide suitable bodies for those who will share in the eternal order.

Paul's Appeal to Scripture (vv. 45–50)

Paul now sought to support and expand his conclusion. He quoted Gen 2:7 with some modifications and then commented on it. "The first man Adam became a living being; the last Adam became a life-giving spirit." The first Adam was a man of dust, and because of our relationship to him, we all have a physical body. But the last Adam (Christ) is from heaven, not dust. Because of the believer's relationship to him, the believer will have a spiritual body.

Therefore, the spiritual body of the resurrected believer will be similar to the body of the risen Christ. Such a changed body will be necessary, for "flesh and blood cannot inherit the kingdom of God, nor can corruption inherit incorruption" (v. 50).

Section Summary

Paul expanded his conclusion by quoting Gen 2:7, where he made a comparison between the first Adam and the last Adam. He further concluded that because of the believer's relationship to Jesus, the believer will have a spiritual body.

Triumph over Death (15:51–58)

This is one of the most exalted New Testament passages describing the glorious consummation of God's kingdom. Because the eternal order is not one of flesh and blood, all believers must undergo a transformation when the Lord returns. Those whose death has preceded his coming will be resurrected, while those who survive until he returns will be transformed from the perishable to the imperishable, from the mortal to the immortal.

Paul expressed profound thanks to God for what he has done in Christ and what he is yet to do. Since Christ's resurrection provides victory over death, Christians have an incentive for unceasing labor to the glory of God (v. 58).

Section Summary

Because the eternal order is not one of flesh and blood, believers must be transformed when the Lord returns. Those whose death has preceded his coming will be resurrected, while those who survive until he returns will be transformed. When this happens, death will truly and finally be "swallowed up in victory"!

QUESTIONS TO GUIDE YOUR STUDY

1. How did Paul refute the Corinthians' denial of the resurrection of the dead? What do we learn from his argument?
2. What did Paul mean by describing Christ as the "firstfruits" of the resurrection?
3. Paul answered two hypothetical but valid questions regarding the bodily resurrection of the dead (v. 35). How did Paul answer these questions? What lessons did he teach about the resurrection?
4. In this chapter, what do we learn about the nature of the believer's resurrection body?

1 CORINTHIANS 16

Paul concluded his first letter to the Corinthians with several instructions and greetings. His chief concerns were (1) providing instructions for the offering for the poor in Jerusalem, and (2) exhorting the believers at Corinth regarding their church life.

RELIEF OFFERING FOR JERUSALEM (16:1–4)

These verses in 1 Corinthians show that Paul was true to his word. Evidently, the Corinthians wrote to Paul about their participation in the offering for the believers in Jerusalem. Paul responded with some specific guidance. We can see at least five principles of Christian giving in this passage:

1. *It is inclusive (v. 2).* Each member of the congregation was to have a part in the offering.
2. *It is systematic (v. 2).* They were to set aside a portion of money "on the first day of the week."
3. *It is proportionate (v. 2).* Members were to give as they had prospered.
4. *It is voluntary (v. 2).* In the Jewish system, a temple tax was levied annually on every male twenty years of age and older. Paul apparently made no attempt to adapt that practice here.
5. *It is administered wisely (v. 3).* Appointed delegates from the Corinthian church would take the gift to Jerusalem. That delegation would include Paul, if necessary.

NEW TESTAMENT REFERENCE

In Gal 2:10 we find the earliest reference to the proposed offering for the poor Christians in Jerusalem. The church leaders in Jerusalem had urged Paul and Barnabas to remember the poor, and Paul expressed an eagerness to help.

Section Summary

In response to the need for helping poor believers in Jerusalem, Paul instructed the Corinthians to set aside some money, week by week, so that it would be ready to be taken to Jerusalem.

PAUL'S TRAVEL PLANS (16:5–9)

Paul stated his intention to visit Corinth by taking a route through Macedonia rather than sailing directly from Ephesus (v. 5). Rather than making a brief visit, Paul desired to spend some extended time with the Corinthians, perhaps even a winter. Three times in this passage Paul used the word *you* emphatically. Its emphasis is even more pronounced in the language of Paul's Greek text of 1 Corinthians:

1. "I will remain with you." (v. 6.
2. "So that *you* may send me on my way." (v. 6.
3. "I hope to spend some time with you." (v. 7)

HISTORICAL BACKGROUND

Province of Macedonia

Macedonia was a crossroads for travel and commerce going north, south, east, and west. The Christian message came to Macedonia through the preaching of Paul, who followed God's vision there (Acts 16:9–10). The church founded at Thessalonica (Acts 17:2–12) was the recipient of the oldest Christian writing, 1 Thessalonians, which Paul wrote from Corinth after he had preached in Berea and Athens (vv. 13–15). In his travel plans for visiting the Corinthians in 1 Cor 16, Paul chose the overland route that would take him through Macedonia.

Section Summary

These emphases contrasted the Corinthians with the Macedonians and emphasized Paul's deep desire to be with the Christians at Corinth.

Paul also mentioned that he would stay in Ephesus until Pentecost, the Jewish feast that followed seven weeks after Passover. By doing this, he was hoping to take advantage of the opportunity he had to preach the gospel at Ephesus. "A wide door for effective ministry has opened for me—yet many oppose me" (v. 9).

Section Summary

Paul stated his intention to visit Corinth by taking a route through Macedonia rather than sailing directly from Ephesus. His desire was to spend some extended time with the Corinthians, perhaps even a winter.

PAUL'S FINAL APPEAL AND FAREWELL (16:10–24)

The Coming Visits of Timothy and Apollos (vv. 10–12)

Paul mentioned Timothy's forthcoming visit to Corinth and urged the church to receive him as one committed to the Lord's work (vv. 10–11). Another missionary, Apollos, would also arrive "when he has an opportunity" (v. 12).

Concluding Exhortations (vv. 13–14)

"*Be alert.*" This means to "stay awake." This word is used for being watchful of the Lord's return, but it can also be a call to watchfulness with regard to the enemy (1 Pet 5:8) or to destructive influences (Acts 20:31). Here it needs to be understood in view of the following exhortation to "stand firm in the faith."

"*Stand firm in the faith.*" Believers were to *stand* firm in Christ as opposed to *falling*.

"*Be courageous, be strong.*" Both of these exhortations recall Ps 31:24, "Be strong, and let your heart be courageous, all you who put your hope in the Lord." It means to conduct oneself in a courageous way. The Corinthians were to be courageous and strong in the face of the problems that plagued their fellowship.

"*Do everything in love.*" Echoing his theme of chapter 13, Paul's last exhortation to the Corinthians focuses on their relationships. "Everything" would include all Paul had discussed in his letter.

Recognition of Others (vv. 15–18)

In verses 13–14 Paul provided several concluding exhortations regarding the church life of the Corinthians. Although originally written to the

HISTORICAL BACKGROUND

Timothy

Timothy, whose name means "honoring God," was a friend and trusted coworker of Paul. When Timothy was a child, his mother Eunice and his grandmother Lois taught him the Scriptures (2 Tim 1:5; 3:15). A native of Lystra, he may have been converted on Paul's first missionary journey (Acts 14:6–23). Paul referred to Timothy as his child in the faith (1 Cor 4:17; 1 Tim 1:2; 2 Tim 1:2). This probably means that Paul was instrumental in Timothy's conversion. When Paul came to Lystra on his second journey, Timothy was a disciple who was well respected by the believers (Acts 16:1–2). Paul asked Timothy to accompany him. Timothy's father was a Greek, and Timothy had not been circumcised. Because they would be ministering to many Jews and because Timothy's mother was Jewish, Paul had Timothy circumcised (Acts 16:3). Timothy not only accompanied Paul but also was sent on many crucial missions by Paul.

believers at Corinth, these exhortations have application to believers in any age.

Final Greetings (vv. 19–24)

In closing his letter, Paul sent greetings from the Asian churches, with special mention of Aquila and Priscilla, both of whom were beloved by the Corinthians. Paul concluded his letter with a series of his standard greetings and his grace benediction. It ended with a heartwarming benediction to this troubled church: "The grace of the Lord Jesus be with you. My love be with all of you in Christ Jesus" (vv. 23–24).

WORD PICTURE

Tribute

Paul paid a tribute to the household of Stephanas for their faithful service and expressed joy over the arrival of two men, Fortunatus and Achaicus. We know nothing more about these men. Fortunatus, whose Latin name means "lucky" or "blessed," was probably one of the Roman citizens of Corinth. Achaicus means "one who is from Achaia." Paul related that the arrival of these men "refreshed my spirit and yours." Whether or not these men were leaders, Paul saw them as worthy of proper recognition.

Section Summary

In his final appeal and farewell, Paul mentioned Timothy's forthcoming visit to Corinth. He concluded by offering several exhortations and gave recognition to several others for their faithful service in the work of the gospel.

QUESTIONS TO GUIDE YOUR STUDY

1. What do we learn about Christian giving from Paul's instructions for the offering to the poor in Jerusalem?
2. What might have been Paul's reason for wanting to take the overland route to visit Corinth?
3. From his farewell, how do we know Paul desired to spend time with the Corinthians?
4. What encouragements for the life of faith might we claim from Paul's concluding exhortations?

2 Corinthians

INTRODUCTION

Second Corinthians is Paul's most personal and pastoral letter. While it is a different kind of letter from Romans or even 1 Corinthians, it is characterized by his style. It contains some of Paul's most profound theology. In this letter he reveals more about himself and his feelings than in any of his other writings. Yet this book is probably less read and understood than any of his other letters. This second letter to the Corinthians is third in length among his New Testament letters, second only to Romans and 1 Corinthians.

SECOND CORINTHIANS IN A NUTSHELL

Purpose: To prepare readers for Paul's third visit and to defend Paul and the gospel he taught against false teachers.

Key Passage: 2 Corinthians 5:11–12

Major Doctrines: The church, Jesus Christ, and salvation

Letter's Influence: C. K. Barrett called 2 Corinthians "the fullest and most passionate account of what Paul meant by apostleship."

AUTHOR

The apostle Paul is the author of 2 Corinthians (1:1; 10:1). An internal comparison of 1 and 2 Corinthians strongly supports this claim. The Pauline authorship of 2 Corinthians is accepted by both the early and the present church.

HISTORICAL BACKGROUND

The Apostle Paul

Paul is the official name of this outstanding missionary apostle, and his Jewish name was Saul. He was born on Turkey's southern shore in Tarsus. Well trained in Jewish Scriptures and tradition, he also learned the trade of tentmaking. He was the author of thirteen New Testament epistles.

Paul's third missionary journey centered in Ephesus, from which the gospel probably spread into the surrounding cities. From Ephesus he carried on correspondence with the Corinthian church. While in Corinth at the end of this journey, he wrote his epistle to the Romans.

PURPOSE FOR WRITING

Paul's primary purpose for writing 2 Corinthians was to prepare the Corinthian believers for his coming visit. Paul wrote this letter at a time when relations between him and the church at Corinth were strained. In this letter, Paul expressed relief that the crisis at Corinth showed signs of subsiding.

DATE OF WRITING

This letter is difficult to date, for we do not know the amount of time that separated 1 and 2 Corinthians. The content of the letter suggests that Paul wrote it soon after writing 1 Corinthians. The letter has been variously dated between AD 55 and 57.

THE UNITY OF THE LETTER

Some have suggested that chapters 10–13 were the severe (or painful) letter, written prior to chapters 1–9, but strong evidence for this claim is lacking. Most likely the severe letter has not survived. The letter, as we now have it, forms a coherent whole, as the structure and outline indicate. The history of the church has been nearly unanimous in affirming the letter's unity. No existing Greek manuscripts present the letter in any other form.

HISTORICAL BACKGROUND

Audience

Paul wrote to the church at Corinth, a body of believers who came out of an exceptionally pagan environment and culture. The church had several problems, among them a leadership problem producing divisions in the church (1 Cor 1:10–17). Immoral practices were not being dealt with (1 Cor 5:1–6:20). An enthusiastic group in the church flaunted their spiritual gifts (1 Cor 12:1–14:40). A legalistic group was concerned about dietary laws (1 Cor 8:1–10:32). Some were abusing the Lord's Supper (1 Cor 11:17–34), and others were offering false teachings regarding the resurrection (1 Cor 15:1–58). These matters—in addition to its multiethnic makeup of Greeks, Romans, and Jews and a mixture of social classes including rich, poor, and slave—made for a unique and troubled congregation.

THE DOCTRINES OF 2 CORINTHIANS

Dominant themes include Paul's gratitude to God and Christ (1:3; 5:14) and his ministry as a continuing triumph in Christ (2:14). Paul shared the risen life of Christ (4:10–11). Simultaneously he gloried in infirmities and was content with weaknesses, persecutions, and calamities for the sake of Christ (12:9). His ministry was characterized by integrity and suffering (1:8–12; 6:3–10; 11:23–29), marks of a true apostle. His message as an ambassador of Christ focused on the message of reconciliation (5:11–21) and Jesus Christ as Lord (4:5).

Paul's collection for the church at Jerusalem had an important role in his missionary efforts. He devoted two chapters to this matter (2 Cor 8–9). They provide some of the most helpful teaching on Christian stewardship found in the New Testament.

THE THEOLOGICAL SIGNIFICANCE OF 2 CORINTHIANS

In this letter we learn of the importance of restoring relationships in ministry. An important lesson on dealing with opponents and appealing to God for confirmation of one's ministry is contained herein. The most important aspect of this letter is Paul's inspired insights regarding the nature of ministry. Ministry involves suffering, joy, comfort, and hard work. Primarily, ministry is the power of God working in and through his people to accomplish his purposes.

We learn of the importance of sacrificial and spontaneous giving. These important principles regarding Christian stewardship need to be expounded in every congregation. Believers are to follow Christ in giving freely with joy and love.

Finally, we learn of the significance of Christ's reconciling work in restoring our broken relationship with God. Because of what he has done for us, we are a new creation, participants in the new covenant, and his ambassadors to proclaim the message of reconciliation. Because believers have been reconciled to God, they should be reconciled to other believers.

THE RELEVANCE OF 2 CORINTHIANS FOR CHRISTIANS TODAY

Second Corinthians was written from the heart of a great church leader. Because it was addressed to specific situations in the life of the church, it speaks as directly to the church today as it did to its original readers. Several relevant topics surface in Paul's second letter to the Corinthians, as shown below.

Suffering. Everyone experiences pain and distress in life. Suffering is one of Paul's major themes in 2 Corinthians. His inspired understanding of suffering speaks to every Christian. God gives the comfort and strength necessary to turn misery into ministry. As we see in Paul's life, suffering equips the Christian for ministry.

Ministry. What is the ministry of the church? is a question raised by each generation of believers. Paul's answer is that the church is a ministry of reconciliation that urges persons to be reconciled to God. Such a ministry requires that the church model Jesus Christ.

Leadership and Authority. Paul offers the pattern of Christlike leadership. This kind of leadership is centered in the example of Christ. The authority to lead comes only by sharing in the suffering of Christ.

The Nature of the Gospel. Human nature resists the implications of the gospel. There is a strong tendency to substitute schemes of human effort. Believers are newly created in Christ and have a new nature. This new nature is to determine the way believers live in the world.

Christian Giving. Today's culture, as was Paul's, is characterized by luxury, materialism, and inequality. Paul placed a strong emphasis on giving. Christian stewardship is based on the fact that God is a generous giver. He can continue to supply our needs as we give to others.

HISTORICAL BACKGROUND

The City of Corinth

The city of Corinth was located on a narrow strip of land that connected the Peloponnesian Peninsula with northern Greece. It had two seaports, Cenchrea on the Aegean side in the east and Lechaeum at the edge of the gulf of Corinth in the west. The city's location made it a crossroads for travel and commerce and contributed to its prosperity. Ship captains, eager to avoid the stormy dangers of sailing around the Peloponnesian Straits on the south, would dock at one port of Corinth. Their cargo was unloaded, hauled overland, and then loaded in another vessel on the opposite side. They avoided the risk of losing ships and lives in the dangerous voyage along the southern route.

Corinth was also known for hosting athletic events known as the Isthmian games. These events took place every two years and provided great financial rewards to the victors. Huge crowds thronged to the city for the festivities.

A CHRONOLOGY OF PAUL'S RELATIONSHIP WITH THE CORINTHIAN CHURCH

1. Paul evangelized Corinth during his second journey (Acts 18:1–11).
2. Paul wrote a letter to Corinth, now lost, in which he urged Christians to avoid association with professing believers who were immoral (1 Cor 5:9–11).
3. Paul wrote 1 Corinthians from Ephesus during his third missionary journey to advise the Corinthians on handling problems in the church.
4. Paul made a "painful" visit to Corinth from Ephesus to correct problems in the church. His visit failed to achieve its aim (2 Cor 2:1).
5. Paul sent another letter, also lost, calling the Corinthians to repentance and urging discipline for an opponent in the church (2 Cor 2:4–11). Titus carried the letter to Corinth. Scholars have named this letter the "severe" letter.
6. Paul left Ephesus, for Troas and then to Macedonia, to await word on the success of Titus's visit (2 Cor 2:12–13).
7. Titus met Paul in Macedonia with the report of the Corinthian church's warm acceptance of Paul's letter and eagerness to see him (2 Cor 7:5–16).
8. Paul wrote 2 Corinthians from Macedonia and sent it to Corinth by Titus.
9. Paul went to Corinth for his third visit (2 Cor 12:14; 13:1; Acts 20:2).

(List taken from Thomas D. Lea, *The* New *Testament: Its Background and Message*, 412.)

BASIC OUTLINE FOR 2 CORINTHIANS

I. Introduction (1:1–2)
II. Apostolic Experience (1:3–11)
III. Apostolic Explanation (1:12–2:11)
IV. Apostolic Ministry (2:12–7:16)
V. Apostolic Fellowship (8:1–9:15)
VI. Apostolic Defense (10:1–13:14)

QUESTIONS TO GUIDE YOUR STUDY

1. Who were Paul's readers? Why did he write a follow-up letter to 1 Corinthians?
2. What problems did Paul address at Corinth in this letter?

3. What key doctrines does Paul address in this letter?
4. What is unique about 2 Corinthians?
5. What makes Paul's message in this letter relevant to today's readers?

2 CORINTHIANS 1

In this first chapter Paul defended himself against his former detractors at Corinth and answered some of the attacks directed against him. Identifying himself as an apostle, one specially commissioned by Christ, was significant for Paul's defense of his calling and ministry.

In this opening chapter Paul introduced one of his major themes in this letter—suffering. Drawing from his own experience, Paul described the value of suffering for the believer.

GREETING (1:1–2)

Paul followed the pattern of the Hellenistic letter, a standard letter form in the ancient world. In his greeting, Paul identified himself as the writer, named his readers, and then gave them a blessing.

Writer (v. 1)

Paul is the author of this letter (1:1; 10:1). It is the apostle's most personal and pastoral letter, and it contains more biographical material than any of his other writings.

In his opening greeting, Paul told us some about himself and his calling.

Paul, an Apostle. The designation *apostle* refers to a messenger or delegate—one sent for a particular purpose. It means "one commissioned." An apostle is a person "holding the highest office in the Christian communities" (F. Wilbur Gingrich, *Shorter Lexicon of the Greek* New *Testament* [University of Chicago Press, 1957], 25). Paul is an apostle of "Christ Jesus by God's will." Here he emphasized the authority of his commission, which paralleled that of the twelve original apostles.

Timothy, Our Brother. While on his second missionary journey, Paul met Timothy. Paul recruited him as a member of his missionary team. Timothy is now with Paul, having been sent on to Macedonia from Ephesus (Acts 19:22).

Recipients (v. 1)

To the Church of God at Corinth. The audience is the same church to which he addressed 1 Corinthians: "To the church of God at Corinth" (v. 2). In the ancient world, Corinth was an important city of trade but had a reputation for wickedness. The church at Corinth was Gentile, and its

HISTORICAL BACKGROUND

The Hellenistic Letter

Generally, Paul's epistles seem to follow the normal pattern of the Hellenistic letter, the basic form of which consists of five major sections:

1. Opening (sender, addressee, greeting)
2. Thanksgiving or blessing (often with prayer of intercession, well wishes, or personal greetings)
3. Burden of the letter (including citation of classical sources and arguments)
4. Parenesis (ethical instruction, exhortation)
5. Closing (mention of personal plans, mutual friends, benediction)

converts came from a wide variety of backgrounds and religious experiences. These members had little preparation for living the Christian life, unlike other churches that were composed of God-fearers, proselytes, and Jewish converts. In addressing the believers at Corinth, Paul had to deal with basic moral, church, and doctrinal matters.

With All the saints. "Saints" means "holy ones." They are holy people set apart as God's possession. *Saints* is the title given to all believers because they are dedicated to God.

NEW TESTAMENT REFERENCE

In Matt 10:40 Jesus commissioned the Twelve. He told them, "The one who welcomes you welcomes me, and the one who welcomes me welcomes him who sent me."

Extended Greeting (v. 2)

Paul's opening greeting to the Corinthians is "grace to you and peace."

Grace. This is God's unmerited favor. Despite our sin, God loves us. Despite our unrighteousness, God clothes us with his righteousness. No person can earn this grace; it may only be received through faith.

Peace. This word was a common Jewish greeting. In the New Testament, however, it carries a deeper meaning. To the Jew, this word signified freedom from internal and external conflict. To the Christian, it describes all the blessings of salvation.

"These words, common in Paul's epistles, bear 'the stamp of Paul's experience' . . . no one word carries more meaning for Paul's messages than this word" (A. T. Robertson, "Epistles of Paul," *Word Pictures in the New Testament*, vol. 4, p. 7).

Section Summary

Paul's opening greeting followed the Hellenistic letter format but with an extension. He referred to his divine commission as an apostle. His readers were the members of the church at Corinth. He called them "saints," those who have been sanctified and called to be separated unto God.

WORD PICTURE

Comfort

This noun is a compound word made up of the preposition "alongside" and the verb "to call." It indicates a calling to one's side. Depending on its context, it is translated "exhortation," "consolation," "comfort," or "encouragement." "It is the standing beside a person to encourage him when he is undergoing severe testing" (Fritz Rienecker, *Linguistic Key to the Greek New Testament* [Zondervan, 1980], 450).

THANKSGIVING TO GOD (1:3)

This verse is an outpouring of praise to God that describes both comfort and suffering. Verse 3 focuses on God and reveals several truths about him.

- *The Father of Jesus Christ (v. 3).* God the Father shares the same nature, or essence, but is distinct from Jesus, his Son.
- *The Father of Mercies (v. 3).* This signifies that God is a merciful Father whose character is to show compassion.
- *The God of All Comfort (v. 3).* God is the encourager. He is the God of all comfort, which means that His comfort meets every need. Those with troubled hearts may find strength in him.

Section Summary

This verse is rich in meaning and truth. It focuses on God and reveals several truths about him. He is the Father of Jesus Christ, the Father of mercies, and the God of all comfort (v. 3).

THE MINISTRY OF SUFFERING (1:4–11)

The Jews expected the time of the Messiah would be preceded by the suffering of his people. It was Jesus, however, who suffered for his people. Those whom he called to follow him also suffered. Those who choose to engage in Christian service will experience many difficulties, but Paul teaches that this suffering is not purposeless.

Our sufferings are related to Christ's sufferings. Much of the comfort Paul received during his suffering came from knowing that his suffering was related to "the sufferings of Christ" (v. 5).

Suffering is a part of ministry. Paul used his own suffering as an example for the Corinthians and to witness to God's deliverance. Something terrible happened to him in Asia (the Roman province around Ephesus). Paul provided no details about the problem, but the best theory is that Paul referred to some serious threat. It might have been the attack on his ministry in Ephesus.

Suffering provides opportunity for partnership in prayer. Although the Corinthians were not mature believers, Paul confessed that he needed their help. The prayers of the Corinthians helped Paul, and God's blessings yielded joy and gratitude in their lives. In this way, intercessory prayer is an investment that pays dividends for those who pray as well as for those prayed for. The more prayer is offered, the more thanksgiving there will be when the prayer is answered.

PERSONAL APPLICATION

For those who suffer, God provides strength, and this strength becomes a rich resource for ministering to others. From this passage we see that Paul viewed his suffering as *ministry,* not misery. He provided three purposes of the suffering of God's people.

Section Summary

Jesus suffered for his people, and those whom he calls to follow him will also suffer. But Paul taught that there is purpose to the Christian's suffering. For those who suffer, God provides strength, and this strength becomes a rich resource for ministering to others.

SOMETHING TO BE PROUD OF (1:12–14)

Verse 12 looks back to verse 11. Paul had a right to ask for the prayers of the Corinthians because his conscience was clear about his behavior toward them. He spoke of a "boast." This word and its related forms occur twenty-nine times in 2 Corinthians, more than in the rest of the New Testament. It is a theme that runs throughout the letter.

Because others were boasting, Paul felt that he must engage in this foolish approach to set the record straight. He emphasized the propriety of his conduct toward the Corinthians because it was brought into question by his critics. His enemies were saying that Paul did not really mean what he said, so he affirmed that his present writing was clear and understandable. The Corinthians already knew enough to know his sincerity. They had better opportunity than most to know his character. He was with them many months. He expressed confidence that when they all stood before their Lord, they would be proud of each other.

PERSONAL APPLICATION

Through his own experience, Paul taught that through prayer even the weakest believer can help the greatest Christian.

Section Summary

Because others were boasting, Paul felt that he must engage in this foolish approach to set the record straight. Because it was brought into question, Paul emphasized the propriety of his conduct toward the Corinthians.

DEPENDABLE PROMISES (1:15–22)

Paul's Consistency (vv. *15–20*). At the end of 1 Corinthians (16:5–7), Paul announced a visit to Corinth after he passed through Macedonia. Later he changed his mind and planned two visits, one going to and one coming from Macedonia. When he learned of the Corinthians' hostility toward him, he again changed his plans. He believed a second visit would only bring added pain. The Corinthians thought, or were likely to think, that Paul was wishy-washy. If he were inconsistent, then this flaw would extend to his preaching as well. Such an inference was unthinkable to Paul.

WORD PICTURE

Boast

The Greek word translated *boast* and *pride* occurs twice in this passage (vv. 12 and 14). Its basic meaning is "that in which one glories, a matter or ground of glorying." The ending of the noun in the original language Paul used to write his letter (Greek) means "the act of glorying" in verse 12, but in verse 14 the word means "the thing boasted of."

Fritz Rienecker, *Linguistic Key to the Greek New Testament* [Zondervan, 1980], 452.

Not only was Paul's preaching consistent and positive, but it was also concerned with these characteristics in Christ himself. God has promised salvation to his people, and Christ fulfilled that promise.

God's Works in the Believer (vv. *21–22*). Paul introduced this section (1) to affirm his integrity as a messenger of the gospel, and (2) to show that the trustworthiness of his gospel message rested on the work of God. Paul made clear to his readers that his faithfulness was not the result of his own accomplishment. Here he revealed four works of God in the life of the believer.

God strengthens us (v. 21). The word *strengthen* means "steadfast" and "secure."

God anoints us (v. 21). This anointing refers to the anointing of the Holy Spirit that takes place at the time of a believer's conversion.

God has sealed us (v. 22). Paul said that "God put his seal on us."

God has given us his Spirit as a down payment (v. 22). The presence of God's Spirit in the believer's life witnesses to his inheritance in the kingdom of God and enables the believer to serve God. In this way the Spirit is a "down payment" or *earnest*, a guarantee of what is to come.

Section Summary

Despite accusations of inconsistency, Paul showed that the trustworthiness of his gospel message rests upon the work of God. He revealed four works of God at work in his life and ministry that confirmed Paul's own faithfulness was not the result of his own accomplishment.

DETERMINED TO DO NO HARM (1:23–2:4)

"God as a Witness" (1:23)

After his defense of his gospel, Paul returned to the immediate question about his change in plans. This change was to benefit the Corinthians. Paul felt it important to emphasize this fact that he was willing to call God as a witness against him if he were not telling the truth. Because he spoke so strongly, he did not want the Corinthians to think he was claiming too much authority. He did not see himself as their lord; rather, he was their fellow worker, and his aim was joy in their lives. He also did not think they needed an authoritarian leader, for they were firm in the faith.

WORD PICTURE

Firm

"The word was used in the papyri of making a legal guarantee and appears often in the guarantee clause of a bill of sale."

Fritz Rienecker, *Linguistic Key to the Greek New Testament* [Zondervan, 1980], 454.

A Change in Plans (2:1–4)

His decision not to make another visit, then, was to avoid causing pain to the church. His last visit did so, and Paul saw no reason to repeat the pain. For him, to hurt the believers at Corinth would be to hurt himself. They were his source of joy. If he caused them sorrow, they could not make him glad.

Instead of making a second, painful visit, Paul wrote a painful letter (which some believe is the material included in 2 Cor 10–13). Even this was difficult for him, and he wanted them to know he did it out of love to restore the joy that should exist in relationship.

HISTORICAL BACKGROUND

"A seal on a document in New Testament times identified it and indicated its owner, who would protect it. So too, in salvation the Holy Spirit, like a seal, confirms that Christians are identified with Christ and are God's property, protected by Him."

The Bible Knowledge Commentary, Victor Books, 556.

Section Summary

Paul changed his travel plans to benefit the Corinthian congregation. He decided not to make another visit to avoid causing further pain to the church.

QUESTIONS TO GUIDE YOUR STUDY

1. How did Paul's opening greeting differ from that found in the typical Hellenistic letter of his day?
2. For what was Paul thankful to God?
3. For the Christian, what is the purpose of suffering? What should be the Christian's attitude toward suffering?

4. Paul revealed four works of God that enable the believer to serve him. What are they, and what does each do for the believer?

WORD PICTURE

Down Payment

This is a word of Semitic origin (possibly Phoenician). It has a common use in the papyri as earnest money in a purchase for a cow or for a wife (a dowry). In the New Testament, the word appears only in 2 Cor 1:22 and Eph 1:4. "It is a part payment on the total obligation and we use the very expression today, 'earnest money.' It is God, says Paul, who has done all this for us and the Spirit is God's pledge that He is sincere. This earnest of the Spirit in our hearts is the witness of the Spirit that we are God's."

A. T. Robertson, "Epistles of Paul," *WPNT*,vol. 4, 214.

2 CORINTHIANS 2

Note: The first four verses of chapter 2 are part of the discussion of chapter 1 and are treated there.

A wrongdoer in the Corinthian congregation was punished by the majority of the members. Paul was concerned that Satan might gain a foothold in the Corinthian congregation if the offending member was overwhelmed with grief. To prevent this act, Paul urged the congregation to reaffirm their love for this person.

HOW TO TREAT A TROUBLEMAKER (2:5–11)

Here Paul began to address the specific problem between himself and the believers at Corinth. He wrote with such tact and restraint that he did not give enough details to provide an adequate explanation of the problem for the modern reader. What we know for certain is that one man did something to hurt the entire congregation and Paul as well. The most likely explanation is that it was Paul himself who was wronged by a member who questioned Paul's authority as an apostle, his integrity, and perhaps even his motives regarding money (2 Cor 12:14–18).

Paul mentioned this offense in 7:12. In that passage he indicated he did not want to focus on the wrongdoer or the one hurt. He wanted, instead, to influence the attitude of the congregation. At this point, we may assume that the wrongdoer was brought to repentance. Paul now urged the congregation to engage in the restoration of this person and, in verse 7, offered his twofold instruction to the Corinthians for doing so.

NEW TESTAMENT REFERENCE

"So even though I wrote to you, it was not because of the one who did wrong, or because of the one who was wronged, but in order that your devotion to us might be made plain to you in the sight of God." (2 Cor 7:12)

1. *They were to forgive and comfort the wrongdoer.* The Corinthians were to be gracious toward the wrongdoer and take steps in comforting him.
2. *They were to reaffirm their love for the wrongdoer.* Paul called on the members of the congregation to reaffirm their love for the wrongdoer. Most of the church members already disciplined the offender in some way, and Paul felt that was enough. The next step was for the congregation to forgive this person, lest he be overcome by sorrow.

Paul wanted the Corinthians to know that he joined them in forgiving this person. His purpose in writing the letter of rebuke was accomplished. He simply wanted to be sure that the Corinthian believers would be obedient to Christ and the integrity of his ministry was recognized. In forgiving the offender, Paul recognized that Christ was present in the situation and that he himself was seeking the welfare of the church. Not to forgive the offenders was to let Satan win the war after the church was already victorious.

Section Summary

Paul spoke of the specific problem between him and the believers at Corinth. Apparently, Paul himself was wronged by a member who questioned his authority as an apostle, his integrity, and perhaps his motives regarding money. Paul's response was to call for redemption, not retaliation.

WORD PICTURE

Comfort means "to encourage, to exhort, to urge on." "It is used of the speeches of leaders and of soldiers who urge each other on. It is the word used to send hesitant soldiers and sailors courageously into battle." Fritz Rienecker, *Linguistic Key to the Greek New Testament* [Zondervan, 1980], 456.

PAUL AWAITS TITUS (2:12–13)

Paul's pattern in this letter was to state a fact about his personal history and then launch a discussion of some larger idea. Here he prepared to plunge into an extended discussion of his ministry as an apostle, but his starting point was once again his personal experience.

Paul came to Troas to preach the gospel and found great opportunity. While in Troas, he awaited the return of Titus. When he did not find Titus, his anxiety about the situation moved him to go on to Macedonia.

Section Summary

Paul recounted his anxiety while awaiting the reply to his "severe" letter to the Corinthians. He journeyed to Troas and ultimately Macedonia to learn the results of Titus's visit.

WORD PICTURE

Overwhelmed by Excessive Grief

The word *overwhelm* is a compound word made up of the preposition "down" and the verb "to swallow." They combine to form a word that means "to swallow down," or "to swallow up completely." This word was used of waves that engulf things and people. Paul was concerned that if the congregation failed to forgive this repentant member, he might drown in his excessive grief. A lesson here is that God's people need to be sensitive about when enough punishment is sufficient for an offense.

GOD'S VICTORY MARCH (2:14–17)

Instead of describing his reunion with Titus, Paul broke into an exclamation of praise for the way God worked in their ministry. Not until 7:5 did he return to the subject of his trip to Macedonia. There he told how Titus met him in Macedonia with joyful news from Corinth. The thought of that joy seemed to be in Paul's mind as he began his discourse on ministry in verse 14.

The news that the Corinthians repented of their hard feelings (7:9) and were positive toward Paul (7:7) moved him to rejoice. He portrayed God as a Roman general "who always leads us in Christ's triumphal procession" (v. 14). Paul regarded himself as one taken captive by God, a trophy of his saving power. His missionary journeys were occasions when God led him. Just as burning incense filled the air for the Roman victory parades, Paul's ministry was the aroma of Christ to the people he encountered.

PERSONAL APPLICATION

"Some Satan destroyed through sin, others through the unmeasured sorrow following on repentance for it . . . conquering us with our own weapons" —Chrysostom.

Paul then contrasted this profound view of ministry with the approach taken by some of his critics at Corinth. He described these people as those who "market the word of God for profit" (v. 17).

Section Summary

The news that the Corinthians repented of their hard feelings and were positive toward Paul moved him to rejoice at the way God worked in his ministry. Paul shared the gospel with the Corinthians, not like a huckster peddling his wares but with the sincerity of a God-sent spokesman.

QUESTIONS TO GUIDE YOUR STUDY

1. What instruction did Paul give the Corinthians for dealing with the wrongdoer in their midst? What does this advice teach us about dealing with troublemakers in today's churches?
2. Why did Paul consider the punishment already dealt to the wrongdoer sufficient? What was his concern about this person? What might we as a church today learn from Paul's concern here?
3. What fueled Paul's anxiety as he awaited the report from Titus?
4. Why was Paul so joyful in verses 14–17?

WORD PICTURE

Marketing the Word of God

The word for "market" suggests a wine merchant who watered down his product; it could be translated "huckster." They sought their own advantage, neglecting the people and altering the message to make their sales on any terms that would profit them. Adapted from David C. George, 2 *Corinthians, Galatians, Ephesians,* Layman's Bible Book Commentary (B&H, 1979), 22.

"It is curious how hucksters were suspected of corrupting by putting the best fruit on top of the basket." A. T. Robertson, "Epistles of Paul," WPNT, vol. 4, *WPNT*, 219.

Paul, in contrast to peddlers and hucksters, was a sincere representative of Christ accredited by God himself.

2 CORINTHIANS 3

Paul discussed letters of recommendation (common in Paul's day) and explained that no letters of recommendation were necessary to authenticate his ministry to the Corinthians and his apostleship to the church in Corinth. Also in this chapter, Paul contrasted the ministries of the old and new covenants, proving the superiority of the new.

LIVING LETTER (3:1–3)

Paul just poured out his heart for what God did in his ministry. He also contrasted his ministry with others who were not sincere. But he did not want anyone to think he was writing a letter of recommendation for himself. Letters of introduction were common in the early church as Christians traveled about. The troublemakers who came to Corinth apparently had such letters, and they may have objected that Paul did not have them. Paul, however, had something better. His ministry to the people of Corinth made a direct impression on their lives. They, of all people, did not need anyone to vouch for Paul. They were living proof for all to see that Paul was a true minister.

Some apparently attacked the legitimacy of Paul's apostleship toward the Corinthian church. Paul insisted that he needed no special recommendation for his work with the Corinthian believers. The planting of the church and the transformation of their lives were Paul's recommendations for ministry and apostleship.

COMPETENT MINISTRY (3:4–6)

Paul was confident, but his confidence rested with God, not himself. He could not claim authority on his own. He had a sense of competence that came from being a minister of the new covenant, which was the new relationship between God and man created by Christ. A minister who offers such a covenant has a distinct advantage over those who present the old covenant or those who preach a legalistic faith. Such forms of legalism all rest on words and rules with a deadening effect. The new covenant is the work of the Spirit, and he provides the life needed for a new creation.

Paul introduced the contrasts between the covenants here because his critics at Corinth took pride in their Jewish background and because the contrast was a basic feature of his own experience. In Romans 7–8 Paul described how the law only served to expose his helplessness, while Christ delivered him and gave him new life.

Section Summary

Paul continued to defend his ministry before some of his detractors. He insisted that his competency in ministry came from God.

THE FADING GLORY OF THE LAW (3:7–11)

Paul continued to discuss the superiority of the new covenant to the old covenant. Moses was minister of the old covenant. Paul called it a ministry of death (v. 7) and condemnation (v. 9), but it did not mean the law was evil. To the contrary, God gave the law, and Paul was devoted to it. But he knew it did not bring life. It was provisional and needed to be replaced by something permanent. It was carved on stone (v. 7) and had only external authority. What was needed was a living, spiritual covenant that had inner force in people's lives. The old covenant was given with great splendor and glory. The face of Moses shone with the radiance of his encounter with God, but the glow was only temporary.

Paul argued that the new covenant is superior, and he provided several reasons for his readers.

1. *It involves the ministry of the Holy Spirit (v. 8).* The Spirit enables people to walk and live in the commandments of God. Paul called the old covenant the "ministry that brought death" (v. 7).

HISTORICAL BACKGROUND

Letters of Recommendation

"Jewish travelers often carried letters of recommendation indicating that Jewish householders could trust them and give them lodging on their journey. In Greco-Roman society, higher-class patrons would write letters recommending their subordinates."

The Bible Background Commentary: New Testament, InterVarsity Press, 496.

WORD PICTURE

Minister

The word *minister* is an important word for Paul. Either the noun, verb, or broader term "ministry" are found in all of Paul's letters except those to the Thessalonians. It means "servant," and it is the same word Jesus used of himself as one who came to minister (Mark 10:45). In its various forms it occurs often in 2 Corinthians. In 5:18 we see the "ministry of reconciliation." The word does not describe a special office, either *minister* in the modern professional sense or *deacon* in the sense of a lay officer of the church. Rather, it describes the function of service and the role of a servant.

2. *It brings righteousness (v. 9).* The new covenant is a glorious ministry that brings righteousness. The old covenant condemned people by exposing their sin.
3. *It is permanent (v. 11).* The new covenant is "what endures." The old covenant was temporary and had faded.

CONTRAST BETWEEN THE OLD AND NEW COVENANTS

OLD COVENANT	NEW COVENANT
Ministry of death	Ministry of the Spirit (life)
Brings condemnation	Brings righteousness
Temporary in nature	Permanent in nature

Section Summary

Paul proclaimed that the ministry of the new covenant is superior to that of Moses because the new covenant features the ministry of the Spirit, produces righteousness, and provides permanence.

THE LIFE-CHANGING GLORY OF CHRIST (3:12–18)

The minister of the new covenant is in a much better position than was Moses. Moses put a veil over his face because it shone (Exod 34:33–35). The Exodus account does not specify why he did so, but Paul explained that he did not want the Corinthians to see the fading of the glow of God's glory.

Paul went on to apply the idea of the veil to what happened when the people of Israel read the law in his own day. The lack of God's living presence in their hearts made them unable to see what God wanted to reveal. This "veil" or obstacle is removed when people turn to the Lord. "The Lord"—that is, Christ—"is the Spirit" (v. 17). It does not mean there is no difference between Christ and the Holy Spirit. Rather, it means Christ is present and acts in believers through the Spirit.

Paul then contrasted the old covenant with the Spirit's involvement with the new covenant. The Spirit liberates persons so they can receive God's revelation. Paul stated that "where the Spirit of the Lord is, there is freedom." This is what the law lacked. Moses had only the written law and a brief, fading glimpse of glory.

Christ has the life-changing Spirit and an ever-increasing glory. Paul wrote that believers "are being transformed into the same image from glory to glory" (v. 18). The word *transformed* is the Greek word *metamorphoō*, from which we get our English word *metamorphosis*.

Section Summary

Paul contrasted the old covenant with the Spirit's involvement with the new covenant. Where the life-changing Spirit of the Lord is, there is freedom. This is what the law lacked. Paul added that believers "are being transformed into the same image from glory to glory."

QUESTIONS TO GUIDE YOUR STUDY

1. What was the purpose of a letter of recommendation in Paul's day? Why did he insist on not needing one? Upon what did he base the competency of his ministry?
2. Paul contrasted the new and old covenants. Why is the new covenant superior?
3. What happens when a person "turns to" the Lord and removes the "veil" covering his or her heart?
4. How is the believer transformed into the likeness of God?

2 CORINTHIANS 4

Considering the ministry God entrusted to Paul, he described how he conducted himself to accomplish his mission. Paul closed the chapter by explaining the content of the gospel.

THE MINISTRY OF LIGHT (4:1–6)

Paul's Appeal to the Conscience (vv. 1–2)

Paul begins with the conjunction "therefore," which points to Paul's preceding words about the glory of ministry in the new covenant. Because he had such confidence in his gospel and in the mercy of God, Paul could not be discouraged despite the many problems he had endured as a minister of the gospel.

Neither did Paul allow his difficulties to pressure him into taking shortcuts in his ministerial duties. Other teachers at Corinth may have seemed to present a more popular approach to the faith. Unfortunately, ministers, like other people, were sometimes tempted to use questionable methods or to water down their message to make it more acceptable to the masses. Paul was determined not to do so. His Lord and the gospel demanded that he be open and truthful at all times and in all things. Paul's appeal was to the conscience, not to lower instincts.

"The God of This Age" (vv. 3–6)

Paul recognized that not everyone would understand and accept the gospel. Some were perishing in unbelief and could not see the light of

WORD PICTURE

Transformed into His Likeness

Christians are not deified but are transformed when they see the image of God in Jesus. The verb "being transformed" is in the present tense, indicating an extended process and emphasizing its progressive nature. The words "ever-increasing glory" are literally "from glory to glory." Christians are transformed into the image of God, as expressed in the life of Jesus, from one stage of glory to a higher stage . . .

Portions taken from Fritz Rienecker, *Linguistic Key to the Greek New Testament* (Zondervan, 1980, 461.

Christ because they were spiritually blind. Satan is the god of this age, not a true god but one whom people have mistaken for their god. He is a deceiver and works to keep people from seeing the truth of the person of Jesus Christ and of God's Word.

This passage is the only place in Scripture where Satan is called "the god of this age." This statement does not mean God has surrendered control of his world to Satan but rather that people give Satan a measure of power in their lives. Satan's corrupt rule is limited to this age only, whereas God's rule is for all ages to come.

SATAN'S REALM OF CONTROL

HIS TITLE	PASSAGE
"The god of this age"	2 Cor 4:4
"The ruler of the power of the air"	Eph 2:2
"The ruler of this world"	John 12:31

Whereas Satan is a false god, Jesus is the likeness of God. Paul pointed out that Jesus Christ was the subject of his preaching, not Paul himself. He made a point to describe himself as a servant of Christ whose concern was the welfare of the Corinthians.

Christ the Light (v. 6)

God has given his people a light in their hearts that comes from his self-revelation through the person of Christ. "Christ shares in God's real being and is a perfect manifestation of that being" (Fritz Rienecker, *Linguistic Key to the Greek* New *Testament* [Zondervan, 1980], 463). Here Paul agreed with the apostle John that those who have encountered Christ have beheld the glory of God (John 1:14,18; 14:9).

WORD PICTURE

Age

Although sometimes translated "world" in some English versions, this word is literally "age." Here it refers to all that floating mass of thoughts, opinions, maxims, speculations, hopes, impulses, aims, aspirations at any time current in the world.

Fritz Rienecker, *Linguistic Key to the Greek New Testament* [Zondervan, 1980], 463.

Section Summary

Paul did not allow his difficulties to pressure him into taking shortcuts in his ministerial duties. He realized that many unbelievers were spiritually blinded by Satan, the god of this age. However, God causes the light of the knowledge of his glory through Christ to shine "out of darkness" (v. 6).

A TREASURE IN JARS OF CLAY (4:7–12)

Despite Paul's best efforts, some Corinthians were not impressed. The difference lay in the fact that Paul's experience with the gospel was different from theirs. He suffered intense persecution, including imprisonment and stoning. The Corinthian believers had not faced this kind of opposition, nor had they faced strong Jewish opposition to the gospel or been pressured to worship Caesar. The church may have been on too good of terms with its culture and environment. Because they understood only internal strife rather than enduring external attacks, it may have been too easy for them to look down on Paul.

Paul devoted this portion of his letter to dealing with their differences in experience.

Believers Are a Treasure (v. 7)

A messenger of the gospel is like a clay jar carrying precious contents. The jar holds the treasure of the gospel. A key point here is that the treasure of the gospel does not receive its value from its container; rather, it derives its power from God. Paul made clear that this treasure is something that "we have" (v. 7), that is, all Christians possess it. The contents consist of "the knowledge of God's glory in the face of Jesus Christ" (v. 6).

Clay Jars Are Frail (vv. 8–12)

To show how the power of God works despite human frailty and weakness, Paul mentioned five crisis situations that can endanger the frail clay jar. Were it not for the strength from a higher power, these clay jars would have failed or broken.

Crisis 1: External Pressure (v. 8). An example is the persecution Paul endured for the sake of the gospel. In such situations, clay jars are "not abandoned" (v. 9). Christians are never without a way to endure or escape (1 Cor 10:13).

Crisis 2: Inner Perplexity (v. 8). "Perplexed" was used in Paul's day of a person who was ruined by creditors and at wit's end.

Crisis 3: Interpersonal Conflict (v. 8). This describes a person retreating from enemies who are pursuing him. Even in such dire straits, God gives support.

Crisis 4: Acute Danger (v. 9). The idea here is of one knocked or thrown down with force. This refers to the throwing down of an opponent in wrestling or striking down another with a sword. A warrior may be wounded and down, but he is not finished. God is still at work even amid defeat and mortal danger.

Crisis 5: Impending Death (v. 10). This refers to the process of dying or putting to death. In his missionary journeys, Paul was constantly exposed to death.

HISTORICAL BACKGROUND

Clay Jars

In the ancient world almost everything was stored in clay jars, including treasure. Corinthian pottery was well-known in the ancient world, and Paul may have been referring to the small pottery lamps that were cheap and fragile, or he may have been referring to earthenware vases or urns. The point seems to be that the valuable treasure is contained in weak, fragile, valueless containers.

Section Summary

A messenger of the gospel is like a clay jar carrying precious contents. The content of the jar is the treasure of the gospel. The frail clay jar is vulnerable, potentially placing its contents at risk. To show how the power of God works despite human frailty and weakness, Paul mentioned five crises that require God's strength to ensure that the jars are not broken.

THE SPIRIT OF FAITH (4:13–15)

Paul quoted the Greek version (the Septuagint) of Ps 116:10, "I believed, even when I said, 'I am severely oppressed.'" Like the psalmist, Paul bore witness to a faith that endures suffering. He also had something in common with the Corinthians. He and they would experience resurrection with Christ into the presence of God. Paul's suffering was for their sake, and the grace that flowed through his ministry would bring glory to God. Thus, the frail clay jars through his ministry would bring glory to God. They would prove to be carriers of heavenly treasure.

Section Summary

Paul quoted from Ps 116 to show that he bore witness to a faith that endures suffering. He informed the Corinthians that both he and they would experience resurrection with Christ. All of this would bring glory to God.

PREPARATION FOR GLORY (4:16–18)

Paul introduced a series of contrasts to drive home his points.

The outer nature is wasting away and the inner nature is being renewed. Although the body perishes, the believer's inner nature is daily renewed by God's power. Paul looked forward to the day when he would be in the presence of God in a resurrected body.

Temporary affliction and eternal glory. In a fallen world, Christians will suffer afflictions. These temporary afflictions are "producing" an eternal glory that far outweighs any afflictions that we may experience in this life. The word "producing" implies a prolonged process that is worked out completely.

What is seen is temporary, and what is not seen is eternal. Paul was not merely contrasting the visible with the invisible. He was contrasting what we see *now* in this life and *what will be revealed* in the future (e.g., Christ and his kingdom at the second coming).

Paul based his hope in unseen reality. While visible evidence can only be temporary, the unseen work of God is eternal.

PERSONAL APPLICATION

Paul's hope in Christ prevented him from becoming discouraged: "We do not give up" (v. 16). In fact, his inner life was gaining him new strength from God as Paul explained, "Our inner person is being renewed day by day." What God had in store for him was beyond description. It was vast and never-ending. "For our momentary light affliction is producing for us an absolutely incomparable eternal weight of glory" (v. 17).

Section Summary

The afflictions Paul faced were light in contrast with the glory God was storing up for him. God also gave Paul an ability to view events from an eternal rather than a temporal viewpoint.

QUESTIONS TO GUIDE YOUR STUDY

1. What did Paul mean when he called Satan the "god of this age"?
2. What was Paul conveying by his analogy of a treasure in clay jars?
3. What was Paul's point in his discussion of the five crisis situations that endanger frail clay jars?
4. Paul made a series of contrasts relating to the believer's future glory. What are these contrasts, and what truths do they convey?

2 CORINTHIANS 5

In this chapter Paul continued his topic of ministry. For him, ministry radiated with the hope of the resurrection. His discussion here revealed Paul's view about life after death. Also in this chapter, Paul defined his motive and message for ministry, both of which are rooted in the work of Christ on the cross.

A highlight is one of the apostle's major themes of his letter—reconciliation. God gave Paul a ministry of reconciliation to proclaim the gospel to all people, and Christ's love compelled him to endure unbelievable hardships in carrying out his mission.

AN EARTHLY TENT AND A HEAVENLY HOME (5:1–5)

As Paul compared his present, human frailty with the coming glory of resurrection, he returned his readers to a prominent theme from his first letter to the Corinthians (1 Cor 15)—the change that will take place in the believer's body. For all human beings, the present, physical life will someday end. Paul likened our bodies to a "tent" that will be taken down so that we can go home to our permanent houses. The Christian need not fear dismantling the tent because those in Christ have another, more permanent abode.

This heavenly dwelling, created by God, can also be compared to a garment. By striking the body-tent, death threatens to leave a person unprotected and vulnerable. But moving into the heavenly dwelling wraps the believer in a new covering of life. Although we naturally experience anxiety as we face death, we may find strength in the promise of new life. God prepares us for this event by giving us the Holy Spirit as an advance assurance of resurrection and heavenly life.

WORD PICTURE

Tent

Paul likened the believer's body to a tent. The verb used here that is translated as "destroyed" is the same word used for "striking down" a tent. Those on a journey strike their tents in order to move to the next destination.

Section Summary

Paul's ministry radiated with the hope of receiving the resurrection body at Christ's return. He considered his present possession of the Holy Spirit to be a deposit assuring him of future victory.

AT HOME OR AWAY (5:6–11)

Because Paul's security was in God, he could be confident even in the face of death. For the believer in Christ, earthly life in this present body is like a trip away from home. Death becomes a return home. Paul realized that being at home with God would be best, but he gave himself totally to life and to his ministry in the present by exercising faith and by doing what pleased God.

Whether on earth or in heaven, Paul knew that he was responsible to God for what he did in this life. He shifted his mind from the visions of death as a homecoming to the concept of death as judgment.

Paul saw Christ as the Judge of *all*. Everyone, including Paul himself, must stand before the judgment seat. Paul clearly taught that Christians are saved by grace, through faith, not by their own accomplishments (Eph 2:8–9). But he also knew that believers are saved to do God's work (v. 10). When they appear before the Lord, some of their works will be seen as unworthy. Others will receive his approval. This did not shake Paul's confidence in his relationship with Christ but made him aware of the need to live responsibly.

Section Summary

Paul's knowledge that he ultimately would be "at home with the Lord" filled him with a desire to please God through his present actions. It is important to live responsibly, for all will be made accountable at the judgment seat.

THE MOTIVE AND THE MESSAGE (5:12–15)

Paul's Motive (v. 12)

Paul may have been speaking of his evangelistic ministry when he said, "We try to persuade people" (v. 11). But because he was criticized by his opponents as being insincere, he was more likely referring to his efforts to persuade the Corinthians of his sincerity. In response to this criticism, Paul revealed that he was constantly aware of God's purpose and judgment. It was characteristic of Paul always to be mindful of God's seeing and knowing his every act.

Paul was not bragging; rather, he was trying to meet a need in the lives of his friends. The critics raised questions in their minds. While they put the emphasis on their outward standing in the church, Paul placed it on inner standing in relation to God. Motive is what counts, and God knew Paul's motives. The Corinthians needed to be reassured, and they needed to have ammunition to counter the critics. Any doubt at this point would injure the effectiveness of Paul's message. This he wanted to avoid at all costs. Chapters 10–12 provide extensive details about Paul's concern at this point.

Paul's Message (vv. 13–15)

There is some question about the interpretation of verse 13. Was Paul being accused of indulging in excessive ecstatic experience? Many interpreters take it that way. However, a closer study of the Corinthian situation makes it more likely that Paul refrained from public displays of such experiences (1 Cor 14:19). His critics, on the other hand, joined in this popular activity at Corinth and thought Paul unspiritual because of his restraint. He answered that he did know what it meant to be "out of [his] mind" with ecstasy, but this was only between him and God. In his relationship with the Corinthian believers, he found it more helpful to be in his right mind. This twofold concern with the glory of God and the good of the people is a constant theme of his ministry.

Verses 14–21 provide us with one of the most important statements of the gospel message in the New Testament. In these verses Paul emphasized that the controlling factor of his ministry was the love of Christ as seen in his death on the cross. Paul was deeply influenced by Christ's love. It was from his Lord that he learned such dedication. Paul wrote that "the love of Christ compels us." Paul did not have in mind the impulse that sent him on his mission but rather the restraint that kept him focused on the cross and from seeking his own advantage.

The word for "compel" has the sense of pressure that confines and restricts. Such a total commitment to the good of others prevented Paul from doing something that might falsify the gospel or hinder his Christian growth or those to whom he was ministering.

In verse 15 the *motive* of Paul's ministry and his *message* are viewed as the same, for both flowed from Christ's work on the cross. The death of Christ was the most important fact in Paul's thinking. It affected all people by making possible the most radical change in their lives. Paul saw Christ as the second Adam (Rom 5:14–17), God's new beginning in the creation of humanity. As such, Christ is the representative of humanity. What happened to him happens to all humanity in some sense. Those who accept their unity with Christ by faith take part in the death he died for them.

Death to sin and resurrection become a pattern for the Christian life. They no longer live to serve themselves. Instead, they live for Christ and others. This is more than mere acceptance of an idea; it is participation in a new reality. Paul saw his task as making all persons aware of

HISTORICAL BACKGROUND

Judgment Seat

In Bible times, a *judgment seat* was a raised platform or bench. Pontius Pilate occupied a judgment seat while deliberating the accusations made against Jesus (Matt 27:19; cp. Acts 18:12). In Rom 14:10 and 2 Cor 5:10, the judgment seat of Christ is a theological concept, emphasizing that individuals are accountable to the Lord for their lives and must one day face him in judgment.

WORD PICTURE

Compel

Writing of the usage of this word in the New Testament, Greek scholar A. T. Robertson tells us this word means "to hold together, to press the ears together (Acts 7:57), to press on every side (Luke 8:45), to hold oneself to (Acts 18:5), to be pressed (Luke 12:50; Phil 1:23). So here Paul's conception of Christ's love for him holds him together to his task whatever men think or say."

"Epistles of Paul," *WPNT*, vol. 4, 230.

this new possibility and enlisting them to experience it. Paul used the word *all* prominently in verses 14 and 15, which indicates the scope of his missionary goal.

CHRIST'S DEATH AND THE BELIEVER*

PURPOSE	PASSAGE
That we might live *through* Him	1 John 4:9
That we might live *with* Him	1 Thess. 5:10
That we might live *for* Him	2 Cor 5:15

*Developed from material in Warren Wiersbe, *Wiersbe's Expository Outlines in the New Testament* (Victor Books, 1992), 489.

Section Summary

God had given Paul a ministry of reconciliation to proclaim the gospel to all people. Christ's love compelled him to carry out that ministry.

WORD PICTURE

Reconcile

Paul uses a Greek word here that is used only six times in the New Testament. And Paul is the only New Testament writer to use this word. In five of the six uses, Paul dealt with the relationship between God and human beings. In 1 Corinthians Paul used this verb when describing the reconciliation between a husband and wife. Even though it is used so infrequently, it carries a lot of theological weight. It communicates the action God has taken which makes possible a peaceful relation between God and man.

THE NEW HAS COME (5:16–21)

Paul's critics valued persons based on outward appearances and superficial signs. They judged Paul and themselves "from a worldly perspective" (literally "according to the flesh"). Paul told the Corinthians that such evaluations are sub-Christian. To take a strictly human point of view is to miss what God is doing.

From the point of his conversion on, Paul did not evaluate others merely in terms of their human characteristics. He was most concerned with their hearts and the work of the Spirit in their lives. As a new person, he saw with new eyes. This led to his overwhelming concern for others.

In verse 17 "therefore" points back to Paul's words about Christ's death for all and all dying with him (vv. 4–15). With his resurrection from the dead, humanity gained a new beginning with God. All who unite with Christ by faith become part of this new creation. They are "in Christ," a phrase Paul used constantly throughout his letters to describe his relationship with Christ. It implies that those who exercise faith in Christ enter a real, personal union with him. In verse 17 Paul told his readers that two life-changing things take place:

1. "*The old has passed away.*" A new outlook takes hold of the believer. Although the old persists throughout this life, the *new* will be culminated at the resurrection.

2. "*The new has come!*" Believers have already begun their participation in the new creation. The new creation is God's doing and will not be fully revealed until the new heaven and the new earth appear and

Christians receive their resurrection bodies. But for those who are in Christ, the new order has already begun.

Such a new creation requires that the hostility and separation between man and God be ended. The need for reconciliation implies that a state of enmity has existed due to sin. In his discussion of reconciliation, Paul emphasized what God does for humanity to overcome their hostility toward him. He indicated that "in Christ, God was reconciling the world to himself" (v. 19).

Paul went on to make a forceful appeal in verse 20. The reconciliation of man to God has been accomplished in Christ, but it must be known and accepted to become effective. This has become Paul's ministry.

God's general appeal comes to persons through messengers like Paul, who are here called "ambassadors." Paul saw himself as the direct representative of God in foreign, hostile territory, inviting former enemies to come into God's family.

To reinforce his appeal, Paul restated the means and results of reconciliation (v. 21). Reconciliation between God and man is made possible by Christ's remedy for sin. "Made . . . [Christ] to be sin" (v. 21) means at least that God the Son bore the consequences of sin. But it is a daring phrase that may mean much more. In some mysterious sense, the sinless Christ became identified with our sin so we could become identified with his righteousness. As a result of this, those who are in Christ by faith "become the righteousness of God" (v. 21)—that is, they receive the benefits of God's righteousness. They take on the characteristics of Christ as he takes on their former characteristics as sinners. This is not simply a label of righteousness. They become righteous as they are transformed into the image of Christ.

THE DOCTRINE OF RECONCILIATION

CHRIST'S WORK	ASPECT OF RECONCILIATION
His death and resurrection	The *means* of reconciliation
His atonement	The *basis* of reconciliation
His incarnation	The *channel* of reconciliation

Section Summary

With Christ's resurrection from the dead, humans gained a new beginning with God. All who unite with Christ by faith become part of this new creation. For this to be possible, God reconciled the world to himself through Christ by having his Son bear the consequences of the sin of all mankind. Those who are in Christ receive the benefits of God's righteousness.

QUESTIONS TO GUIDE YOUR STUDY

1. What did Paul tell us about his view of the afterlife in this chapter?
2. What was Paul's motive for ministry? What was his message?
3. What is the "new creation"? Who participates in it?
4. What does it mean to be reconciled to God? What does this involve? How is it possible?

2 CORINTHIANS 6

Chapter 6 continues the thought of 5:20. From his side of the relationship, Paul was reconciled to the Corinthians. He had nothing against them. If there was any blockage in the relationship, it rested with the Corinthians.

HISTORICAL BACKGROUND

Ambassador

The Greeks used this word to describe an important official in the Roman Empire. Roman provinces that were peaceful were under the direct control of the emperor and his representative on the scene, called an *ambassador.* This person was the direct, personal representative of the emperor. When a country was in the process of becoming a Roman province, the senate would send ten ambassadors to arrange the terms of peace. Thus, an ambassador was one who brought former enemies into the family of Rome.

David C. George, *2 Corinthians, Galatians, Ephesians,* Layman's Bible Book Commentary (B&H, 1979), 32.

SERVANTS OF GOD IN EVERY WAY (6:1–10)

Paul's Appeal for Reconciliation (vv. 1–3)

In this section of his letter Paul made an appeal for reconciliation with the Corinthian congregation. Paul was cooperating with God in a partnership of preaching. Reconciliation requires both divine action and communication by a human witness. The plea to the Corinthians was that they not receive the grace of God in vain. Some of them might not have responded in faith to the message. More likely, Paul was telling the Corinthians to make use of the grace they had received. Don't let it go to waste.

Instead of this, he reminded them of the promise in Isa 49:8: "I will answer you in a time of favor, and I will help you in the day of salvation." Paul used this verse to emphasize the urgency of his appeal. The day of salvation had already come. The blessings of the kingdom were theirs. The present moment was the time to trust fully in God's redemption.

Paul again emphasized the positive nature of his ministry. Aware that some found fault with his work, he did not yield to their criticism. He was confident he had done nothing to hinder their faith. To the contrary, he did everything as a servant of God. Therefore, all his experiences worked to commend the gospel.

Section Summary

In this section of his letter, Paul made an appeal for reconciliation with the Corinthians. He used Isa 49:8 to emphasize the urgency of his appeal. Now is the time to trust fully in God's redemption.

Paul's Sufferings (vv. 4–5)

Paul then listed his sufferings as he did earlier in 4:8–9. He cited the things that made him unimpressive to his critics as ways of commending the gospel. His endurance throughout these hardships bore witness to the patient suffering of Christ. "By great endurance" seems to be the umbrella heading under which he listed nine kinds of suffering in three groups.

The first set of difficulties was the conditions under which Paul worked. They describe increasing degrees of difficulty.

- *Afflictions.* This is a much-used word in the New Testament. It describes the pressures or crushing burdens of life.
- *Hardships.* Literally, this means "necessities" or "things that cannot be avoided."
- *Difficulties.* This word means "a place that is too narrow." It describes those situations in life when there seems to be no way of escape.

The second triplet of troubles described the attacks Paul suffered from his opponents.

- *Beatings.* This refers to stripes from whips and rods with which Paul's persecutors beat him.
- *Imprisonments.* "Imprisonments" refers to the times Paul was put in jail.
- *Riots.* This refers to disorders and probably referred to the mob violence Paul often encountered.

This third set includes the hardships Paul accepted in doing the work of a missionary.

- *Labors.* This describes work to the point of exhaustion. It was a term Paul often used to describe his work, and it is almost synonymous with the Christian life in the New Testament.
- *Sleepless Nights.* Because of duty, discomfort, or danger, Paul spent some nights sleepless. These were times of prayer, witness, and even singing (Acts 16:25, and the entire chapter, where Paul's experience in prison at Philippi illustrates this whole list of difficulties).
- *Hunger.* Going without food because either time or money is lacking. It probably does not mean fasting for religious purposes. Like Jesus and his disciples, Paul sometimes had no "time to eat" (Mark 6:31). Paul's response to these sufferings turned defeat into triumph.

WORD PICTURE

Endurance

"Endurance" is one of the key words of the New Testament. It is a compound word made up of the preposition "under" and the verb "to remain." It means "a remaining under."

Vine's Complete Expository Dictionary of Old and New Testament Words (Nashville: Thomas Nelson, 1996), p. 200.

Paul had already used the verb form in 1:6 as he described the endurance of suffering which he and the Corinthians had in common. The word *endurance* occurs throughout Paul's writings, especially Romans and 2 Corinthians. It refers to constant strength under difficulty. Jesus gave it great emphasis (Luke 21:19; Mark 13:13; Matt 10:22; 24:13). Early Christian writers often described it as the chief Christian virtue. It does not mean passive acceptance of difficulty but the transformation of trouble into victory. In modern terms it could be described as coping successfully with life.

See David C. George, 2 *Corinthians, Galatians, Ephesians,* Layman's Bible Book Commentary (B&H, 1979, p. 33.

HISTORICAL BACKGROUND

Paul knew the inside of prisons in Philippi, Jerusalem, Caesarea, Rome, and probably many other places before his life was over.

PAUL'S SUFFERINGS FOR THE GOSPEL

WORK CONDITIONS	Troubles Hardships Distresses
ATTACKS FROM OPPONENTS	Beatings Imprisonments Riots
HARDSHIPS OF A MISSIONARY	Hard work Sleepless nights Hunger

Paul's Commendable Features (vv. 6–7)

Paul next listed features of his ministry by which he commended himself as a minister of the gospel. He referred to these as his "weapons of righteousness" (v. 7).

- *Purity.* Describes the clean heart and clean hands necessary to carry the message of the gospel. It describes moral purity and integrity.
- *Knowledge.* Includes not only understanding of the faith but also insight into people and common sense about what to do.
- *Patience.* Patience with people and control of one's temper.
- *Kindness.* A feature that refers to a sweet and gracious spirit that avoids harming others.
- *The Holy Spirit.* Although not a quality, the Holy Spirit is the source of all these qualities and the One who gives needed wisdom and skill for ministry. The phrase here might better be translated "a spirit that is holy" or "holiness of spirit."
- *Sincere Love.* Love without any pretense. It is the kind of love God shows.
- *The Word of Truth.* This phrase literally means "the declaration of the truth" and may refer to the preaching of the gospel or to truthfulness in general.
- *The Power of God.* The ability and authority of the one who sent him to do his work. This is a basic theme of the entire letter as Paul contrasted God's strength with his own weakness. To conclude his list, Paul testified that his equipment for ministry was complete. He had "weapons of righteousness," which were both offensive (the sword was held in the right hand) and defensive (the left hand held the shield).

The Two-Sided Nature of Ministry (vv. 8–10)

In these three verses Paul gave his readers nine contrasting pairs of characteristics that describe the two-sided nature of the ministry. There are many negative factors, but each is outweighed by the positive. Just as the experience of Christ includes both cross and resurrection, the Christian life is full of shadows that witness to the light all around.

MINISTRY'S CONTRASTING NATURES

NEGATIVE SIDE	POSITIVE SIDE
Dishonor	Glory
Slander	Good report
Deceivers	True
Unknown	Recognized
Dying	Living
Disciplined	Not yet killed
Grieving	Always rejoicing
Poor	Enriching many
Having nothing	Possessing everything

Dishonor . . . Glory. Describes the loss of rights as a citizen. But as a citizen of the kingdom, Paul had a higher honor than this world bestows.

Slander . . . Good Report. This is the way many thought of Paul, but with God and God's people his reputation was entirely different.

Deceivers . . . True. Paul and his fellow missionaries were looked upon as deceivers, a word meaning a wandering deceiver or seducer. To those who could recognize it, though, their message was truth itself.

Unknown . . . Recognized. Paul's enemies considered him an unknown, but he was well-known by those who received the gospel from him.

Dying . . . living. Paul and his associates were constantly in danger of dying, but they were more fully alive than most. Although they were punished or disciplined, it was never such as to bring death.

Grieving . . . Always Rejoicing. Paul had ample reason to be sorrowful, but nothing could take away his joy.

Poor . . . Enriching Many. Although poor in terms of earthly wealth, Paul could share the true wealth of the Spirit with all who would receive it.

Having Nothing . . . Possessing Everything. Paul committed himself to a life of having nothing, but in Christ everything belonged to him.

Section Summary

Paul presented a section rich with lists and paradoxes. His endurance throughout hardships bore witness to the patient suffering of Christ. While he waged the battle of the ministry, using the "weapons of righteousness," he remained Christlike in his conduct and character.

AN APPEAL TO THE HEART (6:11–13)

Now that Paul spoke to his friends in such bold terms, he paused to ask for their response. He was completely open with them. He opened his

OLD TESTAMENT REFERENCE

"Do not plow with an ox and a donkey together." (Deut 22:10)

WORD PICTURE

We Have Spoken Openly to You

This phrase is literally "Our mouth is open to you." It means "I am speaking to you frankly, with an open heart, hiding nothing."

Fritz Rienecker, *Linguistic Key to the Greek New Testament* (Zondervan, 1980), 473.

"The similar expression, 'He opened his mouth [and taught them]' is often used of Jesus in the Gospels (e.g., Matt 5:2; 13:35) and reflects a common Hebraic idiom meaning simply 'he spoke.' However, Paul's expression, our mouth is open to you, is a Greek idiom denoting candour, or straightforward speech. By adding, our heart is wide, Paul affirms that there is plenty of room for the Corinthians in his affections." Colin Kruse, *The Second Epistle of Paul to the Corinthians*, Tyndale New Testament Commentaries (Eerdmans, 1987), 135).

PERSONAL APPLICATION

Christians in today's society need this reminder to keep their lives clean and to live in dedication to God just as they did in pagan Corinth of Paul's day.

heart and offered love to all who would respond. They, however, were not so open. The problem was their attitude, not any unwillingness on his part. Now he asked them as he would have asked his own children, "We have spoken openly to you, Corinthians; our heart has been opened wide. . . . Open your heart to us" (vv. 11, 13).

Section Summary

Paul opened his heart to all who would respond. The Corinthians, however, were not so open to Paul. Now he asked them as he would have asked his own children, "Open your heart to us."

PAUL CAUTIONS AGAINST COMPROMISE (6:14–7:1)

In the middle of his appeal for open hearts, Paul switched gears to discuss the dangers of Christians getting too involved with pagan idol worshipers. Some think this passage was originally part of another letter to Corinth, perhaps the one mentioned in 1 Cor 5:9–13. But that letter clearly dealt with immoral Christians. This passage obviously refers to unbelievers. The unequal yoking may refer to Deut 22:10.

Turning to the Old Testament Scriptures to make his point, Paul cited Isa 52:11, where the prophet called the Israelites to leave Babylon with its spiritual uncleanness and return to the land of divine promise. Paul also pointed to other Old Testament passages (2 Sam 7:8,14; Isa 43:6; Jer 31:9) that show God's people are in a special relationship with the world.

Section Summary

Paul suspected that the block in their relationship was brought about by the Corinthians' love of the world. He pointed out that the light cannot be a part of the darkness. Christians must not be bound to unbelievers in a way that will affect their moral purity.

QUESTIONS TO GUIDE YOUR STUDY

1. As Paul appealed to the Corinthians to reconcile with him, he quoted Isa 49:8. Why did he select this verse from the Old Testament?
2. What is the point of Paul's recounting his sufferings in the ministry of the gospel?
3. Was Paul ready for reconciliation from the Corinthians? What step had he taken? What step did the Corinthians have to take?
4. Paul suspected that the Corinthians had a love for the world. What key point did he make?

2 CORINTHIANS 7

In this chapter Paul brought his conversation with the Corinthians to a climax. He renewed his appeal to the Corinthians to open their hearts to him. Paul's concern turned to joy when Titus brought the good news that the Corinthians wanted to be reconciled with Paul.

PAUL CONTINUES HIS APPEAL (7:2–4)

The mood is one of affirmation and joy. Like an evangelist pressing his invitation, Paul said, "Make room for us in your hearts" (v. 2). The issues had been dealt with. There was no longer reason to harbor hard feelings. But Paul knew that broken relationships take time to mend. So he spoke tenderly to his flock. Reminding them that he had done nothing to hurt them, he also let them know that he was not criticizing them for the strain in their relationship.

Paul's own heart was open to the Corinthians, and he asked them to do the same. Any restrictions in the relationship with Paul from here on would rest with the Corinthians. In verse 2 Paul made three statements that asserted his integrity and built a bridge to the Corinthians.

"We have wronged no one." To wrong someone has to do with treating someone unjustly or injuriously.

"We have . . . corrupted no one." To corrupt another is to ruin that person in the areas of money, morals, or doctrine.

"We have . . . taken advantage of no one." To exploit someone is to take advantage of that person for personal gain or to defraud for the purpose of gain.

Paul insisted to the Corinthians that he was not guilty of any of the above offenses.

The important point is in verse 3. Paul wanted to be in their hearts because they were in his. He was willing to die for them and did not want to live without them. In verse 4 Paul affirmed his friends by making statements of confidence and pride in them:

- "I am very frank with you."
- "I have great pride in you."

In spite of the suffering he experienced for them, he felt only joy and comfort.

WORD PICTURE

Make Room in Your Hearts

The Greek word used here means "to provide a place for, make room for." It is an imperative form of the verb, indicating that Paul was making a strong appeal to the wills of the Corinthian believers. Paul "wishes no further tightness of heart in them. He makes this plea to all, even the stubborn minority."

A. T. Robertson, "Epistles of Paul," *WPNT*, vol. 4, 238.

Section Summary

Paul asked the Corinthians to "make room for us in your hearts." Knowing that broken relationships must be mended slowly with love, Paul spoke tenderly to his flock. He reminded them that he had done nothing to hurt them and let them know that he was not criticizing them for the strain in their relationship.

COMFORTING NEWS FROM CORINTH (7:5–16)

The Crisis Is Resolved (vv. 5–7)

At the height of his expression of joy, Paul began to explain how the change came. He already mentioned his anxious waiting for Titus to return from Corinth (2:12–13). Now he finished the story. He suffered acute distress. On the outside, opponents of the gospel resisted him. On the inside, he was concerned about the problems at Corinth. What saved him from this crisis was the comfort he received from God. It came, as spiritual help so often does, through human means. Titus returned at last, and he brought good news.

No Regrets (vv. 8–11)

One of Paul's concerns was the harsh letter ("severe" letter) he sent them. Was it too strong? Would they be crushed? For a while he was sorry he wrote it, but no longer. Now he knew it provoked only a temporary grief, one that led them to repent. Because this godly grief led to a change for the better, neither he nor they had any cause to regret it. This process was the opposite of the world's grief over evil, which was despair with no hope of change. Because of their strong desire for change, the Corinthians proved that things were right again. His letter and its results helped the Corinthians realize how much Paul meant to them.

HISTORICAL BACKGROUND

Titus

Titus was a Gentile companion of Paul, and he may have been converted through Paul's ministry. He was the recipient of the New Testament letter bearing his name. He was overseer or bishop of the church at Crete. Paul entrusted him with the delicate task of delivering Paul's severe letter (2 Cor 2:1–4) to Corinth and correcting problems with the church there. Titus's genuine concern and evenhanded dealing with the Corinthians contributed to his success, which he reported in person to Paul. The apostle responded by writing 2 Corinthians, which Titus probably delivered.

Paul's Confidence in the Corinthians (vv. 12–16)

Titus, as well as Paul, was relieved at the way things turned out. He heard from Paul that the Corinthians were all right, but he was gratified to find that the Corinthians lived up to Paul's high estimation of them. Paul was glad they had justified his optimism. Titus then shared Paul's love for them, and Paul was filled with all joy and confidence.

Section Summary

Paul rejoiced when Titus told him that God had used his strong words to bring about repentance and a desire for reconciliation from the believers at Corinth. Paul affirmed his unchanged devotion toward the Corinthians and expressed confidence in them.

QUESTIONS TO GUIDE YOUR STUDY

1. What was Paul's appeal in verse 2? Why did he make it?
2. Paul made three statements to defend his integrity. What did these statements accomplish for Paul and the Corinthians?
3. What news did Titus bring from Corinth? What was Paul's response?
4. Why did Paul not regret that he had sent the Corinthians such a harsh letter?

2 CORINTHIANS 8

Chapters 8 and 9 provide the most extensive teaching on stewardship found in the New Testament. They also show Paul's brilliant leadership as a missionary statesman.

A GRACIOUS WORK (8:1–7)

The Example of the Macedonian Churches (vv. 1–5)

Because Jerusalem was a major city and a religious center, it attracted many poor people. Many of these impoverished people had become Christians. To compound this problem, Jewish persecution of Christians had increased the poverty of the churches in Palestine. Then, to make matters worse, famine struck the region.

In response to this emergency, Paul urged his missionary churches to give an offering to be sent to their Jewish brothers. This gracious work would reveal to the Jews the depth of Christian concern among the Gentiles and remind the Gentiles of their spiritual debt to the Jews who shared God's revelation with them.

HISTORICAL BACKGROUND

The Macedonian churches included those in Philippi, Thessalonica, and Berea.

Paul began his appeal to the Corinthians by sharing the example set by the churches of Macedonia. These churches suffered persecution for their faith which affected them financially, yet they contributed even beyond what they were able to the offering for the Christians in Jerusalem and greater Palestine. Paul wrote, "They gave themselves first to the Lord and then to us by God's will" (v. 5).

NEW TESTAMENT REFERENCE

Paul explained this concept in Phil 2:7, where he wrote that Jesus "emptied himself" for the sake of mankind.

Paul Urges the Corinthians to Respond (vv. 6–7)

In light of this example, Paul urged the Corinthians to respond because they had not suffered persecution as had the Macedonians. As a result, they should be able to do even more: "Excel also in this act of grace" (v. 7).

Section Summary

As incentive for completing the collection of funds, Paul commended to the Corinthians the unselfish example of the Macedonian churches. These churches sacrificed for the purpose of meeting the needs of their fellow believers in Palestine.

HISTORICAL BACKGROUND

The event described in Phil 2:5–8 is known as the *kenosis,* derived from the Greek word for "empty" (*kenoō*). In this passage we read that Christ "emptied himself, divested himself of his privileges" (William F. Arndt and F. Wilbur Gingrich, *A Greek–English Lexicon of the New Testament* [University of Chicago Press, 1957], 429). Christ gave up the appearance of divinity and took on the form of a slave.

"Of what did Christ empty Himself? Not of His divine nature. That was impossible. He continued to be the Son of God. There has arisen a great controversy on this word, a *kenosis* doctrine. Undoubtedly Christ gave up His environment of glory. He took upon Himself limitation of place and knowledge and of power, though still on earth retaining more of these than any mere man. It is here that men should show restraint and modesty, though it is hard to believe that Jesus limited Himself by error of knowledge and certainly not by error of conduct. He was without sin, though tempted as we are."

A. T. Robertson, "Epistles of Paul," *WPNT*, vol. 4, 444.

THE WHY AND HOW OF GIVING (8:8–15)

The Example of Jesus (vv. 8–9)

Paul did not want the Corinthians to think he was ordering them to give. He wanted them to be motivated by the examples of others because they already had a genuine Christian love. This led him to the heart of the stewardship motive—the gift of God in Christ.

Paul wrote, "For you know the grace of our Lord Jesus Christ, Though he was rich, for your sake he became poor, so that by his poverty you might become rich" (v. 9). Jesus willingly gave himself, emptying himself of his divine wealth.

Guideline for Giving (vv. 10–15)

The guideline for giving is "according to what you have" (v. 11). A person with much should give much; a person with little should give what is possible. The goal Paul had in mind was equality of needs being met among the Christian churches.

Section Summary

Paul referred to the example of Jesus's self-giving. His intent in urging the Corinthians to take part in the offering was to allow their "surplus" to offset the "poverty" of the Jewish Christians in Jerusalem.

THE CORINTHIANS AS HELPERS IN GIVING (8:16–24)

Paul also let the Corinthians know that Titus shared his pastoral concern for them. He was not carrying out Paul's instructions; he was leading them in the fundraising effort because he wanted to do it. This effort was not only to help the Jewish Christians at Jerusalem; Titus was doing it out of concern for the Corinthians.

Paul mentioned two others who were coming to Corinth with Titus. There are at least three reasons for this.

It was social. Christ's ministers enjoy companionship in service, and the Corinthians would enjoy fellowship with these men.

It was strategic. These men were designated by the churches to share in the work of fundraising.

It was precautionary. Paul did not want anyone to suspect him or Titus of wrongdoing in handling money.

Paul did not name the two helpers. It may be that they were not yet known by those at Corinth. Both were Christians with some reputation. One was known for his preaching, and the other was recognized for his earnestness.

Paul closed this chapter by challenging the Corinthians to prove their love to him and to the two trusted helpers and their churches.

OLD TESTAMENT REFERENCE

In verse 15 Paul quoted Exod 16:18: "The person who gathered a lot had no surplus, and the person who gathered a little had no shortage." The Israelites were not permitted to hoard excess manna, but neither was anyone left without enough.

Section Summary

Paul made wise, honest plans for receiving and transporting the collection to Jerusalem so no one could accuse him of dishonesty.

QUESTIONS TO GUIDE YOUR STUDY

1. According to Paul, in addition to helping meet the financial needs of believers in Jerusalem, what would this gracious act of giving accomplish within the Christian community?
2. Why were the Macedonian believers an example for the Corinthians? How did Paul expect them to respond?
3. What were Paul's guidelines for giving?
4. Why did Paul enlist helpers to aid Titus?

2 CORINTHIANS 9

In this chapter Paul continued to deal with the collection for needy believers in Jerusalem. In this discussion Paul explained his theology of giving, including guidelines and features of Christian giving.

PLANNING FOR A WILLING GIFT (9:1–5)

Paul knew the Corinthians were willing and ready to give an offering. He did not need to inform or persuade them. But he did see the need to encourage them.

Because recent problems at Corinth slowed the offering effort to a virtual standstill, Paul renewed the effort to ensure that the task was accomplished. The urgency for moving ahead was dictated, in part, by the time schedule, the need to coordinate the collection effort with other churches, and with Paul's travel plans.

Previously Paul used the example of the Corinthians to inspire the Macedonians, just as he now used the Macedonians' generosity to inspire the Corinthians. He stated this to remind them that they had a responsibility to live up to. He also wanted to give them enough time to act freely and avoid the pressure of a last-minute drive.

Section Summary

Paul explained features about the proper manner of giving to the needy believers at Jerusalem. Paul asked the Corinthians for a generous offering rather than a grudging donation.

PERSONAL APPLICATION

Christians often need help to move from the point of good intentions to action.

PAUL'S THEOLOGY OF GIVING (9:6–15)

Guidelines for Giving (vv. 6–7)

Paul challenged the Corinthians about the spirit in which they needed to make the gift. They should give it bountifully. Paul set forth the principle of planting and harvest and applied it to the entire Christian faith, making several points about the proper manner of giving:

1. Generous giving yields generous results.
2. Each person should give as his or her heart determines.
3. Each person should contribute cheerfully to the gift.

Giving and the Grace of God (vv. 8–11)

In the act of giving, the believer's inner attitude is as important to God as the outward gift. Paul based Christian giving on the biblical understanding of God. If God is a miser, then we need to hang on to and even hoard what we have. But the Bible teaches that God is a generous provider. Everything has its source in him, and he will continue to supply our needs.

The Christian's Ministry of Giving (vv. 12–15)

Paul described a balance of grace somewhat like the balance of nature. He identified these results of the ministry of giving.

Giving supplies the needs of God's people (v. 12). As long as each member of the system is functioning properly, the needs of everyone are met. People give to God by giving to one another. The giver is strengthened, the recipient is helped, and God is glorified.

Giving causes God's people to overflow with thanksgiving to God (v. 12). When Christians give generously to meet the needs of others, gratitude flows to both God and others. When Paul thought of this marvelous economy of grace, he shouted, "Thanks be to God for his indescribable gift!" (v. 16).

OLD TESTAMENT REFERENCE

In verse 9 Paul quoted Ps 112:9: "He distributes freely to the poor." Because he "distributes freely" and gives gifts "to the poor," God's people can both trust him to be generous and follow his example.

Giving unifies all believers (*vv.* 13–14). Through Christians who give generously from their hearts, God supplies the needs of all people. The reality of the matter is that true Christian giving affects "everyone." In Paul's day, such giving served to unify Jewish and Gentile believers.

Section Summary

In this section Paul presented his theology of giving. He offered guidelines for giving and informed his readers that Christian giving is based on the biblical understanding of God. He went on to identify several results of the ministry of giving: (1) giving supplies the needs of God's people; (2) giving causes God's people to overflow with thanksgiving to God; and (3) giving serves to unify all believers.

QUESTIONS TO GUIDE YOUR STUDY

1. What guidelines did Paul offer for Christian giving?
2. Paul told his readers that Christian giving is based on the biblical understanding of God. What do we know about God that shapes our view of giving?
3. What results of Christian giving did Paul mention?
4. What is God's indescribable gift?

2 CORINTHIANS 10

We see a noticeable change in the tone of Paul's letter as we move into chapters 10–13. Chapters 1–9 are characterized by comfort and confidence in both God and the Corinthians. From this point on in the letter, Paul engages in personal defense, replete with satire and sarcasm, and levels an attack against those who are negatively influencing the Corinthian believers. Clearly, he is dealing with those who have opposed him or are determined to do so.

PAUL'S POTENTIAL FOR BOLDNESS (10:1–6)

Paul's words in these verses imply that he was being criticized as a coward. His critics claimed that he was bold when he wrote from afar but humble when present before the Corinthians. Paul responded by appealing to the *meekness* and *gentleness* of Christ. That is the way Jesus chose to deal with people, and Paul would follow the example of his Lord. So he pleaded with the Corinthians not to force him to use strong tactics when he came, but rather he let them know he was fully prepared to use his strength if necessary.

Paul went on to show that difference between his kind of strength and that of his critics. They were accusing him of "living according to the flesh" (v. 2). Like the Gnostic heretics who came later, these critics prided themselves on being spiritual. Paul acknowledged that all live "according to the flesh," the realm of human weakness, but he insisted that his ministry was being carried out on spiritual resources.

WORD PICTURE

Meekness and Gentleness

Jesus described himself as meek and declared that all with this character trait are blessed. Jesus exemplified meekness when he prayed that his enemies be forgiven (Luke 23:34). In translating Plato, Aristotle, and Plutarch, Matthew Arnold suggests "sweet reasonableness" for the Greek word translated in this verse as *gentleness*. A. T. Robertson says this kind of person "does not press for the last farthing of his rights."

Paul knew he was fighting a spiritual war but indicated that he had the necessary weapons to win. Although Paul did not specifically identify his weapon in this passage, he was confident that these weapons "are powerful through God for the demolition of strongholds" (v. 4). So equipped, Paul was ready to deal with the argument, pride, and rebellious thoughts of the enemy. He wanted all to understand that he would discipline those who had not been obedient to Christ.

Section Summary

Paul dealt with the charges of his critics, who claimed that he was showing timidity in face-to-face contacts but operated with excessive boldness in the remote safety of a letter. In a meek and gentle approach, Paul insisted that his attitude and behavior were consistent, whether with the Corinthians or absent from them.

HISTORICAL BACKGROUND

Strongholds

This word is found only here in the New Testament. It is a military metaphor and refers to a stronghold or fortress. "It is used in a literal sense in Proverbs 21:22 (the Septuagint, the Greek translation of the Old Testament) while Philo uses it figuratively of a stronghold prepared by persuasive words against the honor of God (*Confusion of Tongues*, 129). But more important is the fact that the military practice of building strongholds (there was a large one on Acrocorinth) provided the imagery used in Cynic and Stoic philosophers, and in particular by Seneca, a contemporary of Paul, to describe the fortification of the soul by reasonable arguments to render it impregnable under attack of adverse fortune."

Colin Kruse, *Second Epistle of Paul to the Corinthians*, Tyndale New Testament Commentaries (Eerdmans, 1987), 174.

PAUL ASSERTS HIS AUTHORITY (10:7–11)

Paul challenged the Corinthians to examine the facts, not what others were saying about him. The false teachers were claiming to belong to Christ in a unique way. There was even a "Christ party" in Corinth (1 Cor 1:12). But if they were only to reflect on their experience with Paul, they would know that Paul belonged to Christ if anyone did. He had no fear that he would claim too much in his letters and then fail to live up to it in person. His letters may have seemed strong at times, but they were not simply an empty show of force. In effect, the false teachers were claiming, "Oh, his letters are fierce, but when you hear him in person, he is unimpressive." Such accusations did not intimidate Paul. He knew that his conduct in person matched his words and that the Corinthians needed to understand this.

Section Summary

In view of the charges from his critics, Paul challenged the Corinthians to examine the facts rather than listen to hearsay. The Corinthians' history with Paul was evidence that he belonged to Christ.

THE MEASURE OF A PERSON (10:12–18)

Paul did not intend to engage in comparing himself with the false apostles. They were comparing themselves with one another and their own standards. Paul knew this was an unwise course for a servant of Christ. Taking his cue from the word *measure* (v. 12), Paul went on to speak of limits ("beyond measure," vv. 13, 15). His critics questioned Paul's right to minister in Corinth. They wanted to declare the area "off limits" to him. Paul recognized that God set limits to his ministry. His assignment was to go to the Gentiles and preach in new mission fields. Corinth was well within those guidelines. He was the first to open the work in Corinth. He was certainly not overreaching himself to minister there. His goal was to enlarge the work in Corinth and then go on to other new fields. He would not, like the false apostles, work in someone else's field.

Lest he seem to be engaged in some sort of self-glorification contest with his critics, Paul reminded them that the only proper glorying for the believer is in God. After all, it is God's commendation, not one's own or any other person's, that matters.

OLD TESTAMENT REFERENCE

"A wise person went up against a city of warriors and brought down its secure fortress." (Prov 21:22)

WORD PICTURE

Measure

This word is often translated "rule." It is also used to indicate *sphere of influence* and, in these cases, is translated "province, limits." (See William F. Arndt and F. Wilbur Gingrich, *A Greek-English Lexicon of the New Testament* [University of Chicago Press, 1957], 403.) According to Fritz Rienecker (*Linguistic Key to the Greek New Testament* [Zondervan, 1980], 487), it has to do with "rule, measuring rod, the fixed bounds of a territory. It may be that Paul has in mind the marked out lanes as used by runners in athletic contests."

Section Summary

Paul's critics boasted of their ministry in Corinth and tried to claim credit for what Paul had accomplished there. Paul insisted that he would not boast of the work of another but would boast only of what the Lord had done through him.

QUESTIONS TO GUIDE YOUR STUDY

1. Paul's approach to dealing with the Corinthians was one of meekness and gentleness. What do these terms mean? Why is it important for all Christians to take this same approach?
2. What is the "stronghold" Paul referred to in verse 4?
3. How did Paul assert his authority with the Corinthians? What point did he drive home?
4. What did Paul consider to be the limits of his ministry?

2 CORINTHIANS 11

The Corinthian rebellion was serious enough to force Paul into the corner of self-defense. In this chapter, he turned his opponents' method of boasting on themselves.

THE THREAT OF "SUPER-APOSTLES" (11:1–6)

Paul asked his readers to indulge him in some momentary foolishness for the sake of argument. In effect he was saying, "I'll play their little game." He did not want to boast or compare, but if that is what they wanted, he would show them he could do it better than they. He boasted of his jealousy over the Corinthian church, his generosity to the church, and his sufferings for the sake of the church. However, rather than engage in self-glory as his opponents did, he gave the glory to God.

Although he feigned foolishness, Paul was serious. With deep feeling he told them that their relationship to Christ was a sacred marriage. This relationship was now threatened by the false teachers who undermined their devotion to Christ, just as the serpent seduced Eve in the garden of Eden.

The false teachers spoke of Christ, but their presentation of him was as though they were talking about a different Jesus. Their spirit and their gospel were different from Paul's, and he was disappointed that the Corinthian believers were so easily misled.

Paul boldly rejected the idea that he was inferior to the false teachers. He called them "super-apostles." They accused Paul of being unskilled—that is, a layman in speaking. The Greeks valued gifts of speech, and these teachers were likely well trained in oratory. But Paul knew, and the Corinthians had reason to know, that he was highly skilled in knowledge, even if a poor speaker by their standards. "Even if I am untrained in public speaking, I am certainly not untrained in knowledge" (v. 6).

WORD PICTURE

Deceived

The word Paul used here (v. 3) means to be completely deceived, as was Eve. Paul feared that the Corinthians would buy the false apostles' teachings and fall from their commitment to Christ.

Section Summary

Cunning, deceitful teachers were going to the Corinthians and enticing Paul's friends away from their pure commitment to Christ. Their methods included attacking Paul's speaking abilities and claiming a greater knowledge of God's plans and workings than Paul. Paul was concerned that the Corinthian believers might accept the claims of the false apostles.

PAUL REFUSES TO ACCEPT MONEY (11:7–11)

When Paul came to Corinth, he worked as a tentmaker with Aquila and Priscilla (Acts 18:1–3). It was customary for Jewish teachers to support themselves by a trade, but the Greeks considered manual labor beneath the dignity of a teacher.

The right of missionaries to be supported by the churches was clear to Paul, but he took special care at Corinth not to depend on the church financially (1 Cor 9:6–15). He also accepted support from the churches of Macedonia rather than burden the Corinthians. His critics seem to have contended that these practices were not dignified enough for a true apostle, and perhaps they viewed this as a disgrace to the church. However, it was not from lack of love for the Corinthians that Paul refused their money. He dearly loved the believers there.

HISTORICAL BACKGROUND

Support Ministry in the Early Church

In Old Testament life, the temple tithe and offerings primarily supported the Levites and priests (Num 18:20–24; Ezek 44:28–30). Both Christ and Paul affirmed that supporting God-called ministers is the duty of the Christian church. Paul was anxious to assure the Corinthians that he was not after their money but desired that they know Christ. Paul apologized for permitting them to be "inferior" to other churches by not supporting his ministry. His self-support as a tentmaker was for their good and was not an example to be followed in all churches *Disciple's Study Bible* (B&H, 1988), 1484).

Section Summary

Paul had not accepted financial support from the Corinthians and insisted that he had never been a financial burden to them. His opponents wrongly interpreted this independence as evidence of Paul's lack of love for the Corinthians.

FALSE APOSTLES (11:12–15)

Paul's reason for consistently refusing financial support from the Corinthians was to show the contrast between himself and the false teachers. They claimed to be equal to Paul or even superior to him, yet they encouraged the Corinthians to support them financially. Paul realized that this put the false teachers at a disadvantage. His strongest attack on them came in verse 13. They were "false apostles, deceitful workers, disguising themselves as apostles of Christ." Worse still, their behavior proved that they were servants of Satan, not apostles of Christ. Like Satan, they disguised themselves with the appearance of righteousness. Their future fate, Paul warned, would be appropriate. In 5:10 Paul reminded his readers that all must appear before the judgment seat someday. At that time, false teachers would face God's judgment.

Section Summary

Paul insisted that he would never change his practice of refusing financial support because his refusal to accept funds from the Corinthians prevented his enemies from boasting that they worked on the same basis.

WORD PICTURE

"Angel of Light"

"The prince of darkness puts on the garb of light and sets the fashion for his followers in the masquerade to deceive the saints."

–A. T. Robertson

PAUL'S TACTICS AND THEIRS (11:16–21A)

This section begins Paul's celebrated "fool's speech." Paul did not want to be considered foolish, but since he was so accused, he intended to act the part to make his point. This boastful role had no divine authority in Paul's view. But as long as that was the game his opponents were playing, he would show that he could beat them by their own rules. There was, however, one important difference. They boasted of worldly things, whereas Paul boasted of his sufferings.

The Corinthians, Paul noted, showed a willingness to be led by such aggressive, authoritarian tactics. He sarcastically called them "wise" because his approach had been termed "foolish." The false teachers made servants of the Corinthians, taken their money, and humiliated them (literally, "slap in the face"). If refusing to use such high-handed leadership was weakness, then Paul pleaded guilty to this weakness.

PAUL'S BOASTS

BOAST	PASSAGE
His jealousy over the Corinthian church	vv. 1–6
His generosity to the Corinthians	vv. 7–21
His sufferings for the church at large	vv. 22–23

Section Summary

The Corinthians had shown a willingness to be led by the aggressive, authoritarian tactics of his opponents. As a result, they were humiliated and taken advantage of. Paul admitted his "weakness" in not stooping to such tactics.

THE CREDENTIALS OF A SERVANT OF CHRIST (11:21B–29)

Jewish Ancestry (vv. 21b–22)

Paul then showed that he could match the "super-apostles" in a bragging match.

- They boasted of being Hebrews, those who spoke the language of their ancestors and read the sacred writings.
- They were Israelites, members of the chosen nation.
- They were heirs of Abraham and, therefore, to the promises made to him. But Paul was all of these, too.

Beyond Jewish Ancestry (vv. 23–27)

The false apostles passed the test of Jewish ancestry, but Paul asked, "Are they servants of Christ?" (v. 23). They called themselves servants of Christ. Paul not only matched them, but he also went far beyond them. The evidence he listed was not a string of victories; it was a list of hardships suffered. He, not they, showed the true marks of a servant of Christ: his sufferings. Most of the occasions listed do not appear in the book of Acts, which gives only a partial history of Paul's career.

Verses 23–37 list the many forms of persecution Paul suffered, most of which came from his own people, the Jewish religious leaders.

PAUL'S PERSECUTIONS

STRENUOUS EXERTION	• Severe beatings
	• Exposure to death
	• Five times received thirty-nine lashes
	• Three times beaten with rods
TRIALS OF TRAVEL	• Three times shipwrecked
	• Robbers
	• Dangerous river
	• Dangers from false brothers

HARDSHIPS	• Sleeplessness
	• Hunger
	• Thirst
	• Cold and nakedness

Verses 28–29 tell of another kind of suffering, the pressures of a pastor-evangelist as he cared for his churches. Paul agonized daily with his converts as they encountered difficulties.

This, Paul wrote, is the kind of boasting an apostle should do. He must tell of his weakness because that is where the strength of God touches the needs of people. Paul gave one more example, one that must have been well known to his friends (Acts 9:19–21). The picture of Paul being hidden in a basket and smuggled out of Damascus was not heroic. But it showed the courage and humility of the apostle and the providence of God in his life.

Section Summary

Paul encountered opponents who boasted of their apostolic credentials and questioned Paul's. Paul had no option but to resort to the foolish practice of boasting of his own credentials as an apostle in ministry.

QUESTIONS TO GUIDE YOUR STUDY

1. What was the "foolishness" Paul took part in? Why did he ask the Corinthians to indulge him?
2. Paul refused to accept financial support from the Corinthian congregation. Why did he do this? Why did his decision not to take money create a problem for the false teachers?
3. What is a false teacher? What makes them dangerous to the church? How prevalent are false teachers in today's church?
4. What are the credentials of a true servant of Christ?

2 CORINTHIANS 12

Criticism from Paul's opponents forced him to say what he did in this chapter. In the first part of the chapter, he shifted from his apostolic trials to issues of visions and revelation. In the second part he assured the Corinthians that he had no interest in their money or material possessions. He gladly poured out his own possessions and personality for their benefit.

PAUL'S VISION (12:1–10)

Paul's opponents claimed that true apostles had special revelations. Therefore, the Corinthians may have thought that a spiritual leader should be able to point to visions and mystical experiences as qualification. It is probable that false prophets of Paul's day may have claimed such experiences themselves. In this passage Paul let the Corinthians know that he experienced a vision, but he made it clear it was not the key to his effectiveness as a minister.

The "Third Heaven" (vv. 1–6)

Paul told his readers that he was caught up to the "third heaven" (v. 2). Jewish thought speculated that there were levels of heaven, as many as seven. The third level probably refers to the highest. So unusual was his experience that Paul twice remarked that he was not certain whether he was "in the body or out of the body" (v. 3). The term *paradise* (v. 4), one Paul borrows from the Persians, means a park or garden.

In his account, Paul was reserved about the details of this experience and spoke as if it had happened to someone else. Paul's account did not relay what he saw—only what he heard. While caught up in paradise, Paul told his readers, he "heard inexpressible words, which a human being is not allowed to speak" (v. 4). "The word was often used of divine secrets which were not intended for human beings" (Fritz Rienecker, *Linguistic Key to the Greek New Testament* [Zondervan, 1980], 494).

In speaking of himself, he spoke only of his "weaknesses," for in these he found the real point of his ministry. His emphasis here makes clear that he understood his mission was to preach the gospel of Christ, not visions.

HISTORICAL BACKGROUND

The Third Heaven and Paradise

"The identification of *the third heaven* and the *Paradise* which is made by Paul . . . has a parallel in the *Apocalypse of Moses* 37:5, where God hands Adam over to the archangel Michael and says: 'Lift him up into Paradise unto the third heaven, and leave him there until that fearful day of my reckoning, which I will make in the world.' In the literature of both the Jewish (e.g., 1 Enoch 39:3f) and Gentile (e.g., Plato, *Republic*, 10:614–621) worlds there are parallels to the apostle's experience of rapture. And in the Babylonian Talmud (*Hagigah* 14b) there is the story of four rabbis who were temporarily taken up to Paradise, but so awesome was the experience that only one, Rabbi Akiba, returned unharmed."

Colin Kruse, *The Second Epistle of Paul to the Corinthians*, Tyndale New Testament Commentaries (Eerdmans, 1987), 202.

Paul's Thorn in the Flesh (vv. 7–10)

It was possible that such an experience could have gone to Paul's head. But God was at work in Paul's life to prevent this from happening. God gave Paul a "thorn in the flesh" to ensure that he remained humble. Paul described this thorn as a "messenger of Satan" (v. 7). We do not know the exact nature of this thorn. Some have speculated that it may have been mental and spiritual anguish arising from the hardships he endured or his own grief over having persecuted the church. Most conclude that Paul is referring to a physical ailment of some sort. (For more information, see the article, "Paul's Thorn in the Flesh.")

Whatever the thorn was, the lesson Paul learned from it is clear. Three times he asked God to remove the thorn, but God did not. It was God's design that Paul depend on his grace, not on Paul's own strength: "My grace is sufficient for you, for my power is perfected in weakness"

(v. 9). Because they were channels of God's power, Paul could affirm his disabilities.

Section Summary

Paul related a time when he experienced the inside of heaven. Although he disliked sharing this account, he knew that God's strength is more easily seen in the apostle's weakness. In fact, God allowed Satan to afflict Paul to keep him humble and to demonstrate the power of God in his life. If his own vulnerability revealed God's power, Paul gladly accepted the weakness.

FOOLISH TALK (12:11–13)

Having had to boast and draw so much attention to himself, Paul exclaimed, "I have been a fool" (v. 11). Rather than take this approach to make his point, Paul should have been commended by the Corinthians. He was clearly grieved, for the believers at Corinth were aware of Paul's ministry and sacrifices on their behalf. His sacrifices and the changes in the lives of the Corinthians were the "signs of an apostle" (v. 12). Paul mentioned three marks of an apostle: signs, wonders, and miracles.

MARKS OF AN APOSTLE

MARK	MEANING	EMPHASIS
Signs	Miracles that convey a significance such as Jesus's seven signs in the Gospel of John	Appeal to one's understanding
Wonders	Unusual events that evoke awe on the part of those who witness them	Appeal to one's imagination
Miracles	Showed Paul's works to have a supernatural origin rather than a natural or human agent	Indicate a supernatural source

Section Summary

Paul was grieved that he had to boast of himself to make the point of his genuine apostleship. He added that the marks of an apostle are signs, wonders, and miracles—all of which were part of his divinely powered ministry to them.

PAUL REFUSES TO BE A BURDEN (12:14–18)

Paul refused in the past to accept monetary support from the Corinthian church. Even though he was criticized for doing so, he did not intend to

HISTORICAL BACKGROUND

Paul's Thorn in the Flesh

One good explanation relates to the context of 2 Cor 12:1–10 where "thorn in the flesh" parallels both "messenger of Satan" in verse 7 and the "weaknesses," "insults," "hardships," "persecutions," and "difficulties" of verse 10. The Old Testament use of the term *thorn* also offers some help. In Num 33:55 and Ezek 28:24 we read of enemies who are "thorns" in Israel's side, a constant harassment to Israel as the agent of the Lord's redemptive judgments (cp. Josh 23:13; Hos 2:6).

Therefore, in 2 Cor 12:7, "thorn in the flesh" refers more to the enemy, the "messenger of Satan," than to any specific physical ailment. The "messenger of Satan" was a redemptive judgment (as Israel's enemies were also used) of God upon Paul "so that I would not exalt myself." Thus, Paul's entire apostolic experience of suffering, abetted by Satan and operative through the evils of this world, was the "messenger of Satan," a "thorn in the flesh," which God gave and used to keep the great apostle humbly obedient. Paul could truly say that he was an earthen vessel (4:7), one who shared the sufferings of Christ (1:5), so that the life of Jesus might be manifested through his very mortality (4:11); "for when I am weak, then I am strong" (12:10).

change this position when he made his next visit. Paul's motivation for ministry was not gain but grace.

Ironically, his pure motive was interpreted as trickery by some in the congregation. Those helpers whom Paul previously sent to Corinth to minister also did not take advantage of the people. Paul questioned the Corinthians to confirm that there was no evidence for this charge of trickery. "Did I take advantage of you by any of those I sent you?" (v. 17). Clearly, Paul's policy in ministering to the believers in Corinth had been consistent.

Section Summary

Paul planned to visit the Corinthians again. As previously, he would again refuse their money. Paul's ministry was characterized by constant concern for people and a consistency in both his actions and motives.

SIGNS

A sign is something which points to something else; an object, occurrence, or person through which one recognizes, remembers, or validates something; military signal (Josh 2:12); or military standard (Num 2:2; Ps 74:4). Signs may be classed according to seven somewhat overlapping functions:

1. *Signs can impart knowledge or give identity.* These signs typically characterize God as Lord of history and champion of oppressed Israel (e.g., Exod 7:5; 8:22; 10:2).
2. *Signs protect.* The mark of Cain (Gen 4:15), blood on the doorposts at Passover (Exod 12:13), and the seal of God upon the foreheads protected those under the sign (Rev. 9:4).
3. *Signs motivated faith and worship.* Israel's unbelief in spite of signs is often condemned (Num 14:11,22; Deut 1:29–33). The signs fulfill their goal when they inspire obedience (Deut 11:3, 8), worship (Deut 26:8, 10), and loyalty to the Lord (Josh 24:16–17).
4. *Signs serve as reminders of significant events.* Eating unleavened bread at Passover (Exod 13:9) and redeeming the firstborn (Exod 13:16) are reminders of God's liberation of Israel.
5. *Other signs serve as reminders of a covenant or established relationship.* Rainbow, covenant with Noah (Gen 9:12–17); circumcision, covenant with Abraham (Gen 17:11; Rom 4:11); Sabbath, covenant with Moses (Exod 31:13,17; Ezek 20:12). The Lord's Supper points to Jesus's new covenant.
6. *Signs serve as confirmation.* Signs often authenticated God's special call of Moses (Exod 3:12,48); of Gideon (Judg 6:17); of

Saul (1 Sam 10:2–9), and confirmed God's word of judgment (1 Sam 2:34; Jer 44:29–30) or promise of healing (2 Kgs 20:8).

7. *Signs take the form of prophetic acts.* The names of Isaiah ("Yahweh is salvation") and his sons Shear-jashub ("A remnant shall return") and Maher-shalal-hash-baz ("The spoil speeds, the prey hastens") illustrate Israel's fate (Isa 7:3; 8:3).

The New Testament often rebukes the demand for a sign to confirm God's work (Matt 16:1; John 2:18; 5:48; 1 Cor 1:22). A sign may evoke faith in a receptive heart, but no sign will convince the hard–hearted.

From the *Holman Concise Bible Dictionary*, 605.

A PASTOR'S CONCERN (12:19–21)

Paul now turned to the motives for his discussion in this chapter. The church at Corinth was an angry, divided church. A fear of Paul's was that his next arrival would find the believers there gripped by negative attitudes and actions. Here he attempted to build them up spiritually.

Paul listed eight kinds of sins, or vices, that he feared might exist at Corinth. His list here is similar to the one we find in his letter to the Galatians (5:19–21). The following chart shows these vices and provides a brief description for each.

PAUL'S LIST OF VICES AT CORINTH

VICE	EXTENDED MEANING
Quarreling	Strife or rivalry among people
Jealousy	A mean spirit that begrudges the good of others
Angry outbursts	A sudden flare-up of burning anger
Selfish ambitions	Those who are selfish
Slander	Those who speak against others, backbiters
Gossip	Those who "whisper" behind the backs of others
Arrogance	Those who have an inflated opinion of themselves
Disorder	Out-of-control situations because people act without the thought of the common good

Paul closed this section of this letter by grieving over those who may have not repented of their former ways. He mentioned three sins that were formerly practiced by some of the Corinthian believers:

Moral Impurity. This refers to uncleanness of any kind and here, more specifically, to sexual sins of impurity.

Sexual Immorality. This refers to fornication or improper sexual relations.

Sensuality. This is a deliberate defiance of public decency. It is unrestrained and lawless insolence.

Section Summary

Fearing what he might find at Corinth, Paul alerted the Corinthian believers to several vices they must avoid. His goal was to strengthen the congregation and build them spiritually.

QUESTIONS TO GUIDE YOUR STUDY

1. What kind of vision did Paul have? What was his purpose for relating it to the Corinthians?
2. What did Paul mean by a "thorn in the flesh" (v. 7)? Why did God allow Satan to so inflict Paul?
3. What are the marks of an apostle? What does each convey about Paul's ministry?
4. Why did Paul list the eight sins in verses 19–21? What was he hoping to accomplish by discussing them?

2 CORINTHIANS 13

This concluding chapter includes words of warning from Paul as he anticipated a visit to Corinth. The discipline of wrongdoers within the congregation was on his mind. Paul concluded his letter without the usual greetings, but he provided a unique trinitarian benediction.

WORDS OF WARNING FROM PAUL (13:1–4)

Before his "third" visit (v. 1) to the Corinthians, Paul issued a stern warning. In this warning he cited Old Testament law to show that two or three witnesses served to establish charges. This implied that Paul intended to conduct a thorough investigation and discipline any wrongdoers in the Corinthian church.

To address any doubters, Paul spoke of his authority. He was as weak as Christ was weak on the cross. But he could also show the strength of one who lives by the power of God.

Section Summary

Paul claimed that he would not fail to make another trip to visit the Corinthian believers. He warned them that during this visit he would deal with their sin firmly and in the power of God.

MEETING THE TEST (13:5–10)

Some were judging Paul. To him, the real issue for them was not his authority but rather his opponents' own relationship with Jesus Christ. Rather than proving himself right, Paul was more concerned that his doubters succeed in their relationship to Christ. To them he issued two commands: "examine yourselves" and "test yourselves."

"Examine yourselves" (*v.* 5). The Corinthian believers needed to search their hearts to see that their attitudes were in keeping with the faith they professed.

"Test yourselves" (*v.* 5). This self-examination was to approve that they were indeed in Christ Jesus. "Such a testing of themselves will give them full knowledge that Paul is not reprobate. The best way for vacillating Christians to stop it is to draw close to Christ" (A. T. Robertson, "Epistles of Paul," *WPNT*, vol. 4, 270).

MEETING THE TEST

COMMAND	PURPOSE
"Examine yourselves"	To see whether one is "in the faith"
"Test yourselves"	To approve one's relationship with Christ after the examination

If Christ were not in these doubters, then they would have failed the only test that matters.

Section Summary

Paul was concerned that his doubters succeed in their relationship to Christ. In anticipation of his approaching visit, he issued two commands to them: "examine yourselves" and "test yourselves."

PAUL'S PARTING PLEA (13:11–13)

Paul's parting plea was a series of exhortations to his brothers and sisters in Christ at Corinth. In verse 11 he delivered the following exhortations.

"Become mature." It is the same word he used in verse 9. The NRSV translates this phrase "put things in order." Mark, in his Gospel, used this word of James and John mending their nets. After the Corinthians made things right on the human level, they would enjoy fellowship with God on the divine level.

"Be of the same mind." Paul encouraged the believers at Corinth to agree with one another, to think alike, and to be of the same mind.

"Be at peace." Each believer of the congregation was to be peaceable so each might live and work together in harmony. Those who did so would receive the promise that "the God of love and peace will be with you" (v. 11).

OLD TESTAMENT REFERENCE

"One witness cannot establish any iniquity or sin against a person, whatever that person has done. A fact must be established by the testimony of two or three witnesses." (Deut 19:15)

PAUL'S CLOSING EXHORTATIONS

EXHORTATION	GOAL
Be restored to one another	Reconciliation
Be encouraged to agree with one another	Common purpose
Be at peace with one another	Harmony

Section Summary

Paul's parting plea was a series of exhortations to his brothers and sisters in Christ at Corinth. He exhorted them to be restored to one another, to be encouraged to agree with one another, and to be at peace with one another.

HISTORICAL BACKGROUND

Holy Kiss

"In the Jewish synagogues where the sexes were separated, men kissed men, the women, women. This apparently was the Christian custom also. This custom is still observed in the Coptic and the Russian churches. It was dropped because of the charges made against the Christians by the pagans. In England in 1250 Archbishop Walter of York introduced a pax-board which was first kissed by the clergy and then passed around. Think of the germ theory of disease and that kissing tablet!"

A. T. Robertson, "Epistles of Paul," *WPNT*, vol. 4.

PAUL'S THREEFOLD BLESSING FOR THE CORINTHIANS (13:14)

For a congregation desperately in need of God's love and the fellowship of the Holy Spirit, Paul sent them a longer-than-normal final blessing. His last sentence has become a familiar benediction in public worship. "This benediction is the most complete of them all. It presents the persons of the Trinity in full form" (A. T. Robertson, "Epistles of Paul," *WPNT*, vol. 4, 271)."The grace of the Lord Jesus Christ, and the love of God, and the fellowship of the Holy Spirit be with you all" (v. 13).

PAUL'S TRINITARIAN BENEDICTION

PERSON OF THE TRINITY	BLESSING
Jesus Christ	Grace
God the Father	Love
Holy Spirit	Fellowship

Section Summary

Paul concluded his letter with a beautiful benediction. The benediction was trinitarian in form and has played an important role in the worship of God's people through the centuries.

QUESTIONS TO GUIDE YOUR STUDY

1. Why did Paul issue a stern warning to the Corinthians in verse 2?
2. In view of his approaching visit to meet with the Corinthians, Paul commanded them to "examine themselves" and "test themselves." What did Paul mean by these? What was his goal?
3. Paul left his readers with a series of closing exhortations. What were they, and how applicable are they for today's congregations?
4. Describe Paul's benediction in verse 14. What makes it unique?

Galatians

INTRODUCTION

Galatians ranks as one of the most important books in the New Testament. It is crucial for understanding the apostle Paul. Written in the heat of one of his most important battles, it gives us vital insights into the mind and heart of the apostle. Galatians is basic for understanding the Christian faith. It probes the question, How does a person come into a right relationship with God?

This letter is pivotal in the unfolding of Christian history. Fifteen hundred years after Paul wrote this letter, a German monk named Martin Luther found it to be his guide out of bondage into Christian freedom. Luther loved this letter so much he called it his *Katie von Bora*—his wife!

Galatians is pertinent for today, for Christianity is still threatened from one side by legalistic cults and self-righteous pride and from the other by those who would turn Christian liberty into license.

A close look at the letter in its original setting will help us understand its message and apply its truth to our lives.

AUTHOR

Except for one or two extreme critics of an earlier period, no one questions that Paul the apostle was the author of Galatians. Not only did he give us his name at the beginning (1:1) and near the end (5:2), but he also devoted the first two chapters to describing his experience as apostle to the Gentiles. Only Paul fits the description given there.

Some important characteristics of the apostle shine through the letter. He was a preacher who stated his theology against a background of intense personal experience. He received his message by revelation of Jesus Christ (1:12). He faithfully communicated this revelation with passion and power. Deeply spiritual, he was also thoroughly human. He expressed surprise (1:6), disappointment, and fear (4:11). He was perplexed (4:20). He showed anger and impatience (1:9; 2:14; 5:12; 6:17).

AUDIENCE

Paul addressed his letter "to the churches of Galatia" (1:2) and called the readers "Galatians" (3:1). Where is Galatia, and who are the Galatians? There are two possible answers to this question and much disagreement as to which is correct.

First, Galatia was a mountainous territory in central Asia Minor (modern-day Turkey). It included the cities of Pessinus, Ancyra (Ankara, capital of Turkey today), and Tavium.

The Romans expanded the province of Galatia southward to include parts of Lycaonia, Phrygia, and Pisidia. Thus, the name Galatia could mean the old kingdom in the northern highlands or the Roman province that included other territory in the south.

Throughout much of Christian history it was thought that Paul addressed his letter to territorial or ethnic Galatia, the area of the old Gallic kingdom. This view is called the North Galatia Theory. It assumes that Paul did missionary work in North Galatia (Acts 16:6) on his second missionary journey and at the beginning of the third journey (Acts 18:23). Some commentators, mostly European scholars, continue to hold to this view today.

HISTORICAL BACKGROUND

In the third century BC, wandering tribes of Gauls from Europe entered the area. They fought with the inhabitants until they were overcome and confined to the region that came to be known as the kingdom of Galatia, after the name "Gaul." Galatia continued to be an independent kingdom until the death of King Amyntas in 25 BC. At this time the area came under Roman control.

Other commentators, including most British and American scholars, prefer the South Galatia Theory, although they admit there are some good arguments on both sides. In this view, Galatia refers to the Roman province, particularly the southern part where Paul on his first missionary journey founded churches at Antioch of Pisidia, Iconium, Lystra, and Derbe.

Advocates of the North Galatia Theory point out that in the book of Acts, Luke did not speak of Antioch, Lystra, Derbe, and Iconium as towns of Galatia, so Paul would not likely do so. They assert that Galatia must be a geographical term because Luke used geographical designations such as Pisidia, Phrygia, and Lycaonia in Acts. Furthermore, they say, the people of the southern area would not be called Galatians, even when their province was called Galatia.

Proponents of the South Galatia Theory say that in his other writings Paul spoke in terms of Roman provinces, not geographical territories. They also think the isolated, mountainous area of north Galatia would not likely be the scene of activity by the Judaizers who worked against Paul. Paul spoke of Barnabas as one well known to the Galatians, and we know Barnabas accompanied Paul on his campaign in the southern territory. Finally, they contend, there is no clear evidence that Paul was ever in the territory of North Galatia. It is more reasonable, they say, to think in terms of the area where we have abundant records of Paul's activity.

The evidence for the South Galatia Theory seems more convincing, although not irrefutable. In either case, the interpretation of the letter is not changed. The major point of difference would be in the dating.

DATE OF WRITING

The North Galatia Theory would require a later date for the writing since the supposed work in that area began later than in the south. Those who hold that view date the writing during the third missionary journey, possibly from Ephesus around AD 55.

The South Galatia Theory permits, but does not require, an earlier date. Some scholars believe it was written before the Jerusalem Council, described in Acts 15, because it does not mention that momentous decision regarding ministry to the Gentiles. If it were written before that council, it would be dated around AD 49 and would be the earliest of Paul's letters. This early date would make it easier to understand Peter's inconsistent attitude toward fellowship with Gentiles (Gal 2:11–14).

Others believe the theology expressed in Galatians is closer to that found in Romans and 1 and 2 Corinthians, which were written later. They maintain that an earlier writing would reflect more of the doctrinal concerns seen in 1 and 2 Thessalonians, which were written earlier. They, whether North or South Galatianists, date the letter around AD 55. The following chart contrasts the two views.

NORTH GALATIA THEORY	SOUTH GALATIA THEORY
1. Paul's first missionary journey	1. Paul's first missionary journey
2. Jerusalem Council	2. Writing of Galatians
3. Paul's second missionary journey	3. Jerusalem Council
4. Writing of Galatians	4. Paul's second missionary journey

OCCASION AND PURPOSE

Occasion. Paul had been as devoted to the law and the traditions of Judaism as anyone, but he was the first to see fully and clearly that these things were not necessary. God led him to preach salvation to the Gentiles, and he quickly saw that faith in Christ, not works of the law, made a person righteous.

There were other Christians besides Paul who had been Pharisees. When Paul and Barnabas returned from the first missionary journey, they found some of these at Antioch telling the believers that circumcision was essential for salvation (Acts 15:1). This discovery led to a conference at Jerusalem where, again, converted Pharisees urged obedience to the law of Moses (Acts 15:5). The council, under the leadership of James and Peter, decreed that Gentile believers were not to be burdened with the Jewish law. Their letter to this effect indicated that the Judaizers had already been active not only at Antioch but throughout Syria and in Cilicia (Acts 15:23–24).

Purpose. With that background in mind, it is easy to understand what must have happened in the Galatian churches. Paul had come to Galatia with the good news of salvation in Christ. Paul had three closely related purposes in mind when he wrote Galatians:

- He was defending his authority as an apostle against those who claimed otherwise.
- He was stating, explaining, and proving the gospel message.
- He was applying the gospel message to daily living by the power of the Holy Spirit.

Historical Background

Christians today sometimes forget that the first believers were Jews. They continued to be Jews after they became Christians. At first it did not dawn on them that one could be a Christian and not be a Jew. Only gradually did they come to appreciate that the gospel provided a radically new and different basis for right relationship with God. It was hard for them to conceive of a person who was in right standing with God but was not circumcised and did not keep the requirements of the Jewish law.

Most of those Galatians who believed were Gentiles. They had no background in Judaism. They found salvation and freedom in Christ. But when Paul left the area, his opponents, the Judaizers, were not far behind. Soon the Galatian believers were led astray (Gal 1:6). Like most new converts, they were eager to do right and to prove their faithfulness. When these new teachers came, claiming the authority of the Jerusalem apostles, their appeal was irresistible. The new Christians were ready to add circumcision and the law to their faith in Christ.

To Paul this was a serious crisis. If this were allowed to go unchecked, Christianity would lapse into being a cult of Judaism. Freedom in Christ would be exchanged for a new kind of slavery. The gospel would be hopelessly distorted. Strong, decisive action was called for. The apostle sat down and, under the leadership of the Holy Spirit, wrote an impassioned restatement of the gospel of grace.

STRUCTURE OF THE LETTER

In recent years, New Testament scholars have devoted much attention to the structure and form of the Pauline letters, analyzing their literary features and comparing them with other letters that have survived from the Hellenistic world. By the time of Paul, letter writing in the Roman Empire had developed into a fine art among the professional clientele of the educated elite.

Generally, Paul's epistles do seem to follow the normal pattern of the Hellenistic letter, the basic form of which consists of five major sections.

OUTLINE

A quick look at the text of Galatians will show that it fits this pattern rather neatly with one exception: There is no thanksgiving or blessing. Otherwise, using this structure, we could lay out this structural outline for Galatians:

I. Opening (1:1–5)
II. Body (1:6–4:31)
III. Ethical instruction/exhortation (5:1–6:10)
IV. Closing (6:11–18)

HISTORICAL BACKGROUND

1. Opening (sender, addressee, greeting)
2. Thanksgiving or blessing (often with prayer of intercession, well wishes, or personal greetings)
3. The burden of the letter (including citation of classical sources and arguments)
4. Parenesis (ethical instruction, exhortation)
5. Closing (mention of personal plans, mutual friends, benediction)

CONTENTS AND LITERARY STYLE

Contorts. The message of Galatians can be summed up in one key verse: "For freedom, Christ set us free. Stand firm, then, and don't submit again to a yoke of slavery" (5:1).

The book is composed of three sections of two chapters each. Chapters 1–2 give Paul's personal history as the basis for his appeal to the Galatians. Chapters 3–4 give his theological, or doctrinal, appeal. Chapters 5–6 give his challenge to spiritual living.

The argument is strong and thorough. Paul detailed the history of his apostleship to counter the false claims of the Judaizers (1:1–2:14). He developed his doctrine of salvation by grace from many angles, beginning with his own personal testimony (2:15–21). He then appealed to the Galatians' own experience (3:1–5).

Next, he turned to the Old Testament, showing Abraham as the prototype of justification by faith (3:6–18). He went on to discuss law and promise, showing that the role of the law is temporary, while faith in God's Word is permanent (3:19–29). He warned against returning to bondage and reminded the Galatians of his experience with them (4:8–20). He climaxed this doctrinal section with an allegory drawn from the life of Abraham, illustrating spiritual truth with historical events—an approach much used in the ancient world (4:21–31). On this basis, Paul made his practical appeal.

Literary Style. The style of the letter is interesting and impressive. Paul used many colorful figures of speech. There are numerous rhetorical questions. Personal references give the letter warmth. By using the first-person plural *we*, Paul identified with his readers. Although we do not know the effect the letter had in Galatia, the fact that it was preserved and treasured in the churches would indicate that it was effective in its mission. Paul's skill as a communicator is evident throughout.

THE MEANING OF GALATIANS FOR TODAY

At first glance, the book of Galatians seems to be an argument against circumcision and other requirements of Jewish legalism. If that is all we see, it will not seem meaningful for contemporary life. Those issues were settled long ago. The key to reading Galatians in the present tense is to see the larger, basic issues.

It is significant that almost every cult and distorted form of religion involves some kind of legalism. And even within the major Christian churches, there is always the danger that we will substitute our own requirements for God's way of redemption. Why is legalism such a persistent danger?

PERSONAL APPLICATION

Galatians is a book about the relationship between persons and God. How can a man or woman find peace with God and live in harmony with him? The answer is, through faith in Jesus Christ The problem comes when we try to add other requirements. There is a strong tendency for people to add other requirements or to substitute them for faith in Christ altogether. Although circumcision may not be an issue today, other things are.

For one thing, legalism appeals to pride, while faith in Christ requires repentance and humility. As long as religion can be reduced to regulations, those who try hard can feel good about their accomplishments. To say, "My only hope is the grace of God in Christ" is hard on the ego.

Legalism is also more natural to human experience. It puts religion on the same basis as most of the rest of our experiences, which are transactions involving effort and competition.

Legalism is also easier to manage than grace. If righteousness can be reduced to certain well-defined duties, a person can do these more easily than he can exercise a life-changing faith. Christian freedom requires the inner motivation of the Holy Spirit, but legalism provides the external force of laws and punishments. Those who administer the regulations can control other people, as many cult leaders do, by defining the rules their way.

Finally, legalism seems safer than grace. Freedom is dangerous. If matters are left up to the conscience of the individual, there is more danger of confusion and mistakes. Insecure people fear that life will get out of control, and they feel better if someone with authority will tell them what to do.

Galatians speaks not only to the endless danger of legalism; it also speaks to another trend in modern life—the abuse of freedom and the absence of moral order. Legalists are right in that control is needed. They are wrong about where the control must come from. Outward restrictions of the law are mostly ineffective in creating moral living. Such morality can only come from within as persons are energized by the Spirit of God.

QUESTIONS TO GUIDE YOUR STUDY

1. How do we know Paul is the author of Galatians?
2. What is the debate over north or south Galatia?

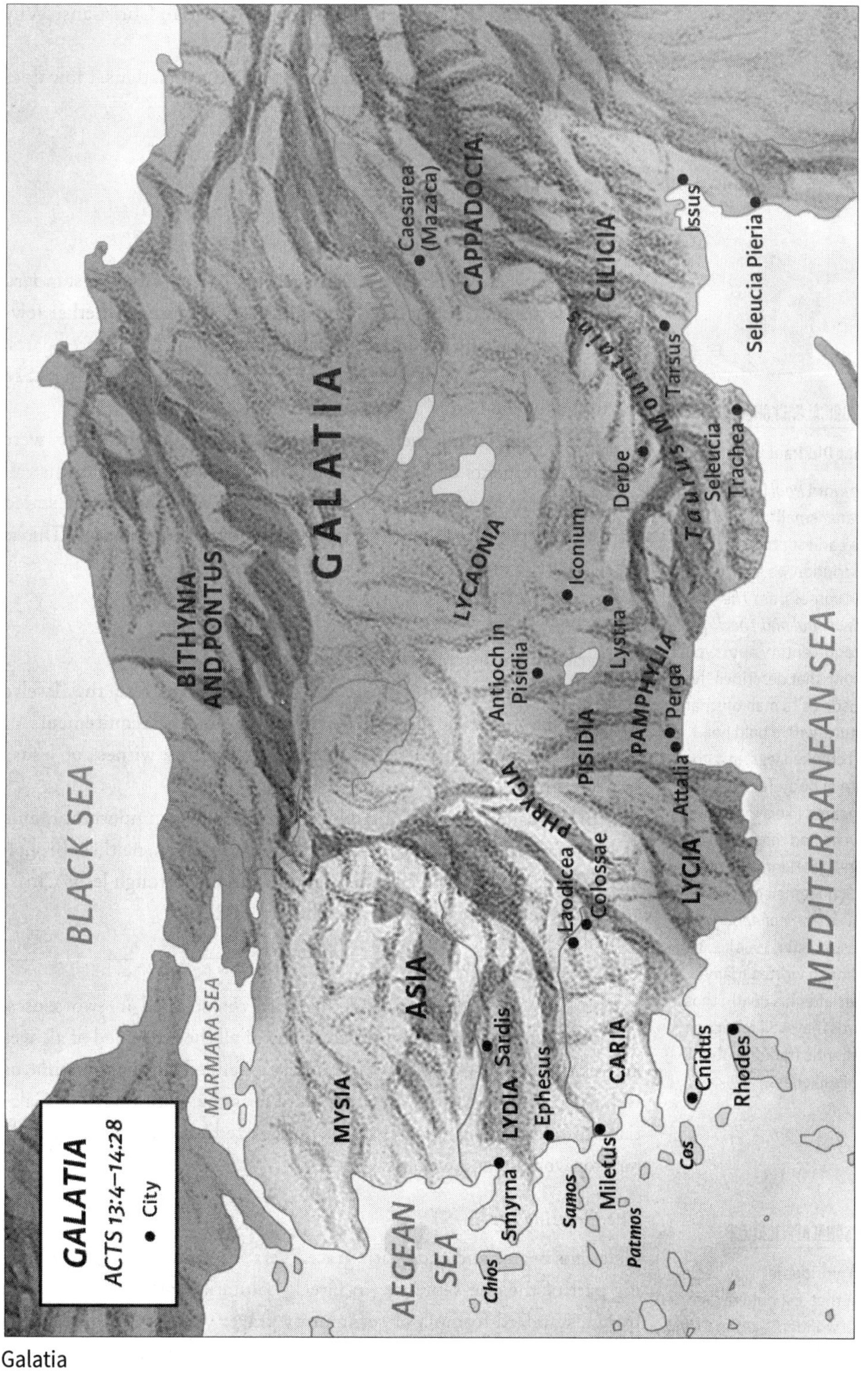
GALATIA
ACTS 13:4–14:28
● City
BLACK SEA
MARMARA SEA
AEGEAN SEA
MEDITERRANEAN SEA
BITHYNIA AND PONTUS
GALATIA
CAPPADOCIA
LYCAONIA
CILICIA
MYSIA
ASIA
LYDIA
CARIA
PHRYGIA
PISIDIA
PAMPHYLIA
LYCIA
Taurus Mountains
Caesarea (Mazaca)
Antioch in Pisidia
Iconium
Lystra
Derbe
Tarsus
Issus
Seleucia Pieria
Seleucia Trachea
Perga
Attalia
Laodicea
Colossae
Sardis
Ephesus
Smyrna
Miletus
Cnidus
Rhodes
Cos
Samos
Patmos
Chios
Galatia

3. Why did Paul write this letter to the Galatian Christians? Why is its message relevant to us today?
4. Describe the structure of the letter to the Galatians. How does Paul present his argument.

GALATIANS 1

THE APOSTOLIC SALUTATION (1:1–5)

When Paul wrote to believers, he began his letters with the standard form for letters of the that day. Letters in the first century, whether Jewish or Greek, usually began with a salutation that included three parts: name of sender, name of the recipient, and a formula of greeting. (See "Structure of the Letter" in Introduction.)

But Paul's letters were more than ordinary letters. They were inspired statements of the gospel and impassioned defenses of his call and mission as an apostle. Even in the greeting of each letter he stated his deepest convictions and outlined key points in his message. This is especially true in these first verses of Galatians.

HISTORICAL BACKGROUND

What Did Paul Look Like?

The word *Paul* literally means "small" or "little." The earliest physical description we have of Paul comes from *The Acts of Paul and Thecla*, a second-century apocryphal writing that describes the apostle as "a man of small stature, with a bald head and crooked legs, in a good state of body; for now he appeared like a man, and now he had the face of an angel" (E. Hennecke and W. Schneemelcher, eds., *New Testament Apocrypha* [Westminster, 1964], 2:354). Although written many years after his death, those words may well reflect an authentic tradition about Paul's likeness.

The Sender (vv. 1–2a)

The writer identifies himself as "Paul, an apostle."

In the New Testament, *apostle* applies primarily to the Twelve whom Jesus called as his first disciples. One of the requirements of being an apostle in this sense is that the person be a witness of Jesus's resurrection.

In this salutation Paul introduces what will be an important theme of Galatians. He is an apostle—literally "not from men, neither through man." Rather, his call and commission were directly through Jesus Christ and God the Father who had raised him from death.

The Recipient (v. 2b)

In the New Testament we find the word *church* used in two senses. Sometimes it refers to the whole company of all the redeemed of all ages and places, the place, the body of Christ extended throughout time as well as space. More often, however, Paul uses the word *church* in Galatians to refer to local congregations of baptized believers who regularly met for worship and witness.

PERSONAL APPLICATION

"So glorious is his redemption that it should ravage us with wonder." —John Calvin (Taken from Calvin, *CNT* 11)

The Greeting (vv. 3–5)

Galatians begins and ends with "grace." Verses 3–5, which form the closing part of the one-sentence (in Greek) salutation, are no doubt taken from a standard formula of community prayer with its liturgical opening, "Grace . . . and peace," and its concluding affirmation, "Amen." In fact, each of Paul's letters in the New Testament begins with a reference to "grace and peace." But for Paul this is more than a liturgical formula. "Grace . . . and peace" summarize God's way with human beings. Grace is God's undeserved kind intention carried out on behalf of sinful human beings. Peace is the result of grace received.

Paul attributes this double blessing to a single source—the one God who knows himself and reveals himself as Father, Son, and Holy Spirit. Grace is seen (v. 4) in Christ's giving himself over to death for our sins. Peace results as he delivers us out of this present evil world.

"This present evil age" Paul speaks of is the context in which God's purpose of salvation is now unfolding. Christ has rescued us from this evil present age through justifying us by faith and pouring out his Spirit in our lives. But while Christ has rescued us from this evil age, he has not taken us out of it.

Paul concludes his greeting with an expression of praise and worship—a doxology: "To him be the glory forever and ever. Amen." Its inclusion is no mere formality. Paul's point here is that to contemplate who God is and what he has done in Christ Jesus is to fall on our knees in worship, thanksgiving, and praise.

NO OTHER GOSPEL (1:6–10)

The Crisis in Galatia (vv. 6–7)

Paul usually began his letters with words of appreciation for his readers. Even for the Corinthians (1 Cor 1:4–9), whose carelessness had created numerous problems, Paul had words of praise and commendation. Not so for the churches in Galatia.

The transition from his greeting to the body of the letter is so abrupt as to be almost jarring. Paul marveled at what the Galatians were doing. Olaf M. Norlie translates this phrase as, "I am dumfounded." The verb tense implies that Paul is in a continual state of being dumfounded at what the Galatians had done (Herschel H. Hobbs, *Galatians* [Word, 1978], 23). He wanted them to know how shocked he was at the new turn they had taken, as if astonishment would startle them into awareness. He also let them know in no uncertain terms that the course they had taken was wrong.

They were "turning away from him" who called them to the grace of Christ and instead turning to a "different gospel." Paul contrasted the message of the Judaizers with the gospel. It seemed to be another gospel, but it was so different that it was not a gospel at all. In turning to legalism, the Galatians deserted the one who called them, God himself. The grace of Christ was their rightful allegiance, and they had abandoned this.

WORD PICTURE

Turning Away

In verse 6 Paul told the Galatians that they were "turning away from" God, or as some translations say, "deserting" God. The word *desert* is striking. Literally, it means "to bring to another place." Historically, the word was used of desertion or revolt in a military or political defection. It often expressed the idea of a change in one's religion, philosophy, or morals. By using this word, Paul was calling the Galatians spiritual turncoats!

What the Galatians failed to realize was the decisive character of who Jesus was and what he accomplished in his atoning death on the cross. To Christ's completed work, they wanted to add something that, from their own perspective, seemed so right, so reasonable, and so religious. They were not aware that adding *anything* to grace changes grace to something other than grace and undermines the way God has provided for sinful human beings to be made right with him.

The Counterfeit Gospel: Anathema! (vv. 8–9)

WORD PICTURE

Anathema is a Greek word that has been carried over into English. It was used to translate a Hebrew word meaning "devoted to God for destruction." It denotes something that is totally rejected by God, such as idols and valuable goods that Israelites captured in battle with their enemies, and which they were commanded to destroy.

In these verses Paul paints two future scenarios to drive home his point. He says, let's suppose I, Paul, came to you at some future date and preached a new and different gospel to you. If I did that, let me be eternally condemned. Or suppose an angel from heaven came to you and preached a different gospel. Let him, too, be eternally condemned. The fact that Paul issued this condemnation in the strongest words possible and then repeated it for emphasis makes this one of the harshest statements in the entire New Testament. The word translated "a curse be on" is the word *anathema!*

Herschel Hobbs observes that Paul's words sound overly harsh to modern ears. In an age of relativism, Paul's stance here is far from being politically correct. But Hobbs says, "No sane person wants a banker who says that two plus two equals three. . . . We do not want a pharmacist who just throws together any drugs which may suit his fancy. We want him to follow exactly the doctor's prescription. This is true narrow-mindedness. We commend this quality in matters of lesser importance—finances and health. But many condemn it in matters of religion" (Hobbs, *Galatians,* 27).

Paul's Motive for Ministry (v. 10)

Paul says that his strong reaction to the direction the Galatians are taking is not motivated by his desire to win their approval. He may have at one time been motivated by human approval but no longer. One who becomes a servant of Jesus Christ sets his heart on pleasing Christ first and lets the chips fall where they may.

Section Summary

In the first ten verses of Galatians, Paul moves from formal greeting to an impassioned warning that the Galatian Christians were on the brink of a course of action that would be destructive to them and to other churches.

GOD'S REVELATION TO PAUL (1:11–17)

Having stated the problem, Paul now begins to develop his argument. His first line of argument is personal history, contained in the first two chapters of Galatians.

Paul's Call from Above (vv. 11–12)

These two verses introduce the theme Paul alluded to in the introduction and will more fully develop in the following narrative—that the gospel he preached to the Galatians was not devised by any human source but came directly from God himself—a "revelation of Jesus Christ." To impress the truth of this upon his readers, Paul introduced it with a solemn disclosure formula: "I want you to know."

The phrase translated "of human origin" relates back to and encompasses the twin negatives found in 1:1, "*not* from men *or* by man." Paul's apostleship and his gospel was neither *from* nor by any human source.

Paul then elaborated this denial by adding two additional negative qualifications concerning his gospel's nonhuman character: He neither received it through tradition nor was taught it through the ordinary means of instruction. These two additional denials both point to the same reality and are nearly identical in meaning.

Having asserted that the gospel was not of human origin and that it came through a direct revelation to him by Christ, Paul offers five pieces of evidence in support of his claim.

EVIDENCE	PASSAGE
1. Nothing in Paul's religious background could account for his acceptance of the gospel.	1:13–17
2. Paul was not commissioned by the Jerusalem church.	1:18–20
3. Those Paul formerly persecuted glorified God because of the change wrought in him.	1:21–24
4. Paul's apostolic work was recognized by church leaders at Jerusalem.	2:1–10
5. Paul defended the gospel against Peter's vacillation at Antioch.	2:11–14

Following this extensive historical section, Paul summarizes the central theme of his letter (2:15–21) and then reminds the Galatians of how God worked among them at his first preaching of the gospel in their midst (3:1–5). Thus, the entire historical section of the letter moves from Paul the persecutor to Paul the preacher. It is the record of the gospel's movement from Damascus to Galatia.

WORD PICTURE

Revelation

Revelation is an unveiling or a disclosure. It "refers to God's actions of making Himself known to humans. This action is necessary because humans, being limited, are unable to know God by their own ability of discovery. Just as dogs or cats cannot investigate their master, and if they could, would not really understand him, so humans do not have the capability of finding God by their own effort. Because God loves His human creatures and wants to have fellowship with them, He has therefore made Himself known."

Millard J. Erickson, *Foundations for Biblical Interpretation)*

Paul's Life before Christ (vv. 13–14)

Paul's main point in these verses is to show that nothing in his religious background and his life before his conversion could have prepared him for a positive response to the gospel. Quite the contrary. His early career and lifestyle were shaped by a confident attachment to the strictest traditions of Judaism, which in turn led him to take up arms against believers in Jesus.

Paul's use of the term *church* stands in marked contrast to his earlier address to the "churches in Galatia." Clearly, here he has in mind the church universal, the body of Christ, which is the company of all the redeemed throughout the world.

Section Summary

Paul's background did not explain his conversion. For such a Jewish leader to change would require divine intervention. Paul's changed life was proof of the validity of his experience, "a revelation of Jesus Christ."

WORD PICTURE

Paul used the word we translate as "set . . . apart" also in Rom 1:1, where he describes himself as being "set apart for the gospel of God." Literally, the word means "to determine beforehand." Paul had in mind something that was even prior to the occasion of his birth—God's eternal predestination and good pleasure by which he chose us in Christ before the creation of the world (Eph 1:4).

Paul's Conversion and Calling (vv. 15–17)

Paul described the sovereign initiative of God in terms of three distinct acts, all of which were according to God's good pleasure:

- *Paul was set apart.*
- *Paul was called.* Not only was Paul chosen from eternity and set apart from his mother's womb; he was also called by God at a specific point in his life.
- *God revealed his Son through Paul.* Many commentators believe Paul was here referring to his encounter with the risen Christ on the road to Damascus. Thus, "to reveal his Son in me" is another way of describing the call Paul received at this decisive juncture of his life.

HISTORICAL BACKGROUND

Arabia

The Arabia of Paul's day was not identical with the boundaries of contemporary Saudi Arabia. This was a vast territory lying between the Red Sea on the southwest and the Persian Gulf and Euphrates River on the northeast.

PAUL'S FIRST VISIT TO JERUSALEM (1:18–24)

Paul now begins a second line of defense, a tightly woven alibi designed to show that his contacts with the Jerusalem church were such that he could not possibly have been dependent on the Jerusalem church or its leaders for his authority or for that portion of revelation imparted directly to him by Christ.

Following his conversion, Paul didn't go to Jerusalem. Rather, he went to Arabia.

Some have suggested that Paul went to Arabia to preach the gospel. Luke tells us that he began preaching in Damascus immediately following his conversion. Others believe he went to Arabia for a retreat—for time to study the Scriptures, to meditate on them, and to pray. Such a time was needed for Paul to assimilate his encounter with Christ on the road to Damascus.

These reasons for going to Arabia are not mutually exclusive. Both may be true.

Paul Meets with Peter (vv. 18–19)

Paul says he went to Jerusalem "to get to know Cephas."

The reference to "three years" is not precise. It doesn't necessarily mean that Paul spent three years in Arabia. It does imply that there were at least three years between his conversion and his journey to Jerusalem. By this time, the gospel imparted to him by the Lord would have been well assimilated.

Upon arriving in Jerusalem, Paul was a house guest of Peter. We wish we could have been a fly on the wall during their dinner conversations!

A. T. Robertson paints a possible scenario:

> It is pleasant to think of them here together for two weeks in Jerusalem. Paul would naturally be the learner and let Peter tell the history of Jesus in particular as it was connected with Jerusalem. There was Bethany; here was the road of the Triumphant Entry; down there was Gethsemane, where Peter went to sleep; here Jesus was arrested; at this place the trial took place and just here Peter had denied him; and on yonder hill they crucified him; and in that tomb they buried him; lo! here was the spot where Jesus had appeared to Peter after his resurrection; in this upper room he had appeared to the disciples twice; up here on Olivet was the place where they had caught the last glimpse of him as he went up on the cloud. (A. T. Robertson, *Epochs in the Life of Paul* [Broadman Press, 1974], 81–82.)

Paul learned historical details of Jesus's life. Peter learned from Paul what the risen Lord imparted to Paul concerning the gospel and how it related to God's revelation prior to Christ.

An important point here is that Paul did not seek authorization of his message or validation of his ministry from Peter. He did seek a close fellowship in the things of the Lord as well as a strategic partnership in their common apostolic mission.

The only other apostle Paul met was James, the Lord's brother. Paul includes James among the other apostles, even though he was not one of the Twelve. Apparently, the term *apostle* extended to other leaders beyond the original circle.

So Help Me God! (v. 20)

Paul then asserted a solemn warning that what he was saying was the truth. The issue was so important that Paul felt he must set the record straight in the clearest possible terms: "I declare in the sight of God: I am

HISTORICAL BACKGROUND

James, the Brother of Jesus

Here are seven fairly well-established facts about James.

James is one of the most important and fascinating characters in the history of the early church, although there is much about him we do not know. However, the following facts are firmly established.

1. James was not a follower of Jesus during his earthly life.
2. Jesus made a special resurrection appearance to James (1 Cor 15:7).
3. James became a member of the church at Jerusalem.
4. James quickly rose to a position of leadership within the Jerusalem church.
5. James is known as the "Just," obviously because of his personal piety and strict observance of Jewish customs.
6. In all likelihood James wrote the epistle that bears his name.
7. In AD 62 James was put to death through the conniving of the Sadducees who administered the temple.

not lying in what I write to you." He was not a secondary apostle, dependent on others for his message and, therefore, subject to their correction. His faith and calling came by revelation from Christ himself.

A Mission to Syria and Cilicia (v. 21)

Paul left Jerusalem, according to Acts 9:26–30, because his preaching aroused the anger of the Greek-speaking Jews there. His life was in danger, so he went to Tarsus. He referred to the regions of Syria and Cilicia, neighboring territories that were part of the same Roman province. What was the result of Paul's ministry in these places? We cannot say for sure, but it is clear from later references in Acts that Paul's witness bore fruit in the conversion of new believers and the planting of several churches.

Reaction to Paul in Judea (vv. 22–24)

In these closing verses, Paul shifted the perspective away from his missionary activities back to the local environment around Jerusalem. Paul registered the reaction of the Jerusalem churches to his early ministry. He did this by referring to three facts: (1) his lack of personal acquaintance with the Judean churches, (2) the impression of his work that was conveyed to them, and (3) their jubilant reaction at the report of the persecutor turned proclaimer.

The doxology in verse 24, "And they glorified God because of me," echoes the earlier doxology at the conclusion of the introduction (1:5). The first doxology is a hymn of praise for what God has done through the atoning death and triumphant resurrection of Jesus Christ. This second doxology celebrates that same victory as seen in the calling and apostolic ministry of Paul.

Section Summary

Paul was well thought of by the Christians in Jerusalem, but he was in no way dependent on them. He was an apostle in his own right.

NEW TESTAMENT REFERENCE

"All who heard him were astounded and said, 'Isn't this the man in Jerusalem who was causing havoc for those who called on this name and came here for the purpose of taking them as prisoners to the chief priests?'" (Acts 9:21)

QUESTIONS TO GUIDE YOUR STUDY

1. Describe the crisis taking place in Galatia. What was Paul's point about the gospel the Galatians were preaching?
2. What reasons did Paul give to support his claim that his calling was independent of the other apostles?
3. What are the implications of the doctrines of election and predestination for us?
4. What was Paul's purpose for visiting Peter during his first visit to Jerusalem? What do you suppose they discussed?

GALATIANS 2

THE APOSTOLIC MESSAGE—CONFIRMATION AND CHALLENGE (2:1–21)

Chapter 2 continues Paul's defense of his commission as an apostle and of the integrity of the gospel he received directly from Jesus Christ.

The chapter divides naturally into two major sections.

In the first (2:1–10), Paul recounts an important meeting he had with the Jerusalem church—the issue of circumcision, which now dominates the appeal being made to his Galatian converts by the false teachers.

The second section (2:11–21) centers on another meeting between Peter and Paul, this time at Antioch, where again the issue of legalism threatened to disrupt the unity of the church.

HISTORICAL BACKGROUND

Fourteen years passed. It is not clear whether Paul was counting these years from his conversion or from his first visit to Jerusalem. The latter seems a more natural interpretation of the word *then,* immediately following the account of the first visit.

PAUL'S SECOND VISIT TO JERUSALEM (2:1–10)

In these opening verses the stage is set for the drama that is about to unfold. Let us notice the event itself, the parties involved, and the motive behind Paul's action.

The Event (vv. 1–2)

Paul established the fact that he was independent of the leaders of the church at Jerusalem. Now he proceeded to show that the leaders of the Jerusalem church approved his gospel and his mission to the Gentiles without asking him to require circumcision.

The Parties Involved (v. 2)

In the narrative that follows, there are three groups of principal actors, each of which plays a distinct role in the decision of the conference and its aftermath.

First, we have the Pauline party consisting of Barnabas, Titus, and Paul.

Second, we have the "false brothers" who agitated for Titus to become circumcised and later imported their teachings to Antioch itself.

The third party that plays a prominent role in the narrative is comprised of the leaders of the Jerusalem church—James, Peter, and John—whose prominence had given them the name "pillars."

Paul's main negotiations were with these church leaders, not with his Judaizing detractors, although the close relationship between the "pillars" and some of their more zealous disciples must have created a situation of great tension for everyone involved.

Paul's Motive (v. 2)

Paul made three important points about his motivation for his second visit to Jerusalem:

1. He insisted that he was prompted to call this meeting "according to a revelation."

This is the same word Paul used in 1:12 which describes the revelation of the risen Christ on the road to Damascus as well as other revelations Paul had.

2. In such a setting the leaders in Jerusalem could hear with their own ears what Paul was proclaiming to the Gentiles. He wanted to reach agreement with the Jerusalem leaders on the message God had given to him.

If this message were from God, why did Paul need consensus with the Jerusalem church?

In one sense, he didn't need their approval or consensus. What God has commissioned and communicated doesn't require human approval. On the other hand, for the health and well-being of the church, what God has revealed needs to be recognized and acted on by the church. Otherwise, it will remain hidden at least for a time.

3. Thus, Paul sought to resolve a crisis that could have led to a major division within the body of Christ. Paul would later say, "So then, let us pursue what promotes peace and what builds up one another" (Rom 14:19).

WORD PICTURE

In this case, Paul was speaking most likely about a specific word from the Lord related to the growing rift and controversy concerning Paul's message and its reception throughout the church at large.

The Judaizers probably painted caricatures of Paul as one who was departing from God's revelation to Israel. God's Spirit made clear to Paul, directly or through the church at Antioch, the need to sit down face-to-face with the leaders of the Jerusalem church.

Titus and the False Brothers (vv. 3–5)

Verse 3 is the first mention of circumcision in the epistle. It is easy to see why the question of circumcision arose regarding Titus. Here, in Jerusalem itself, Paul introduced a Gentile as a brother in Christ. For the ancient Hebrews, circumcision was a sign of the covenant relationship with God dating back to Abraham (Gen 17:11–14). It was commanded of God's chosen people. Under Moses it became a requirement of the law (Exod 12:43–48). No wonder the Jews who were Christians had doubts about Christians who were not circumcised. Judaizers had already advanced the claim, "Unless you are circumcised . . . , you cannot be saved" (Acts 15:1).

Paul emphasized that Titus was not compelled to be circumcised. The Jerusalem apostles did not require it, even though there were agitators present who tried to force the issue. Their aim, Paul said, was to undermine the freedom we have in Christ—a step that would result in bondage. Paul stood his ground to preserve the gospel for the sake of Gentile believers. Those who demanded circumcision of the Galatians

PERSONAL APPLICATION

Meeting face-to-face over differences is a healthy first step toward handling church conflict constructively. Hearing directly what a brother or sister is saying is far better than relying on secondhand sources of information.

were asking for something that had not been required by the apostles at Jerusalem.

Paul used two unusual words to characterize the activity of the false brothers. These words are from the world of political and military espionage, but they are applied to the conflict raging in the early church.

Perhaps Paul is making a deliberate contrast between the proper oversight of a godly pastor and the arrogant usurping of church power the false brothers had assumed for themselves.

WORD PICTURE

Infiltrated

The idea is that of a conspiracy of error, a secret plot concocted by enemies of the faith, informants, and double agents deliberately planted to ferret out confidential information. This word can also express the idea of activity carried out for sinister purposes. Here in Galatians, it points unmistakably to the unworthy motives of the false brother

Spy

This word means "to spy on, to destroy in a sneaky manner." This word is related to another word, oversight, which Paul used in a positive sense to describe pastoral authority in the governing of a New Testament congregation.

Section Summary

We can summarize what we have learned about the false brothers with these four propositions:

1. ***They were not what they seemed to be.***
2. ***They were secretive in their work of disruption.***
3. ***They carried out their destructive mission step-by-step.***
4. ***They demonstrated the connection between false teaching and unworthy behavior.***

Paul and the Pillars (vv. 6–9)

Having interrupted his narration of the Jerusalem meeting to describe the intrusion of the false brothers and the Titus test case, Paul resumed the flow of his account he left off with at the end of verse 2. He drew a sharp distinction between the false brothers and the church leaders with whom he had come to Jerusalem to confer. The former were pseudo-Christians; the latter were respected leaders and dialogue partners with Paul in his strategic missionary summit.

In verse 9 we learn the identity of the "pillars." They were James, Peter, and John. Paul described them as "those recognized as pillars." Some scholars have argued that Paul's repeated use of this expression indicates a disparagement or slighting of the authority of these church leaders. On this view, Paul would have been saying that they were reputed to be pillars, they appeared to be something, they seemed to be real leaders; but in reality, their appearances were deceiving. In other words, the reality did not match the reputation.

The basic drift of this passage (vv. 6–9), however, points not to opposition or confrontation between Paul and these leaders, but to their fundamental unity and shared task of fulfilling the Great Commission. Here, Paul rejected the idea that there is any rank or authority that determines spiritual truth. God shows no partiality toward men of reputation, and neither did Paul.

It was, however, significant to Paul that those recognized leaders did not add anything to the gospel he had received from the Lord. Therefore, the Judaizers in Galatia had no grounds for doing so.

Positive Affirmations (vv. 7–9)

Much of what Paul states in this chapter is negative in nature. However, the climax of the meeting was the mutual recognition symbolized by the right hand of fellowship and the agreed-upon division of labor in the worldwide missionary enterprise.

WORD PICTURE

Recognized As

The expression "those recognized as" need not carry such a derogatory meaning. Here Paul may have been using a common term of respect to refer to those leaders who were men of high reputation and considered to be authorities among the believers in Jerusalem.

Section Summary

We have three affirmations in this passage. One gospel. Paul focused on the one gospel shared by all the participants. Two apostles. The two apostles represented the two spheres of missionary outreach. Three pillars. The three pillars—James, Peter, and John—whose affirmation of Paul and Barnabas was crucial to the positive outcome of the conference.

Concern for the Poor (v. 10)

This verse is a kind of postscript to the agreement Paul and Barnabas had concluded in verse 9. Paul and Barnabas were asked to remember the poor. The "poor" were the Christians in Jerusalem who were suffering persecution and loss of property. Paul was already doing so, having brought an offering for the poor from Antioch, either on this visit or an earlier one. He was eager to continue this practice to meet a pressing need—cementing the bond of friendship between Jewish and Gentile Christians. Throughout his ministry Paul gave much attention to such relief work (1 Cor 16:1–4; 2 Cor 8–9; Rom 15:25–29).

Section Summary

The two key themes of the first ten verses of Gal 2 are widespread recognition of the truth of the gospel Paul received and the unity of the church. This passage shows a pattern of cooperation around the truth of the gospel. Paul was eager to work closely with other Christian leaders who shared with him a common commitment to the good news of salvation through Jesus Christ. As a result of their conference, the apostles found it desirable to do the work of evangelization by a practical division of labor.

PAUL'S CONFRONTATION WITH PETER AT ANTIOCH (2:11–14)

The Problem (vv. 11–13)

Following the consensus in Jerusalem, a problem arose that centered on the issue of table fellowship. In the fast-food culture of modern Western civilization, it is difficult to appreciate the religious significance ancient peoples attached to the simple act of eating.

The problem became clear when Peter paid a visit to Antioch. There he found Jews and Gentiles enjoying unbroken fellowship, including a common meal.

This was revolutionary, for Jews simply did not eat with Gentiles. The law did not specifically forbid it, but it did impose restrictions on diet that would exclude Jews from a Gentile table. Developments in Jewish history caused them to take extreme measures to avoid contaminating their way of life with Gentile contacts. There were traditional Jewish restrictions against eating unclean food, including the consumption of pork, eating food offered to idols, and partaking of meat from which the blood had not been properly drained in accordance with the law of Moses (Lev 3:17; 7:26–27; 17:10–14).

OLD TESTAMENT REFERENCE

"This is a permanent statute throughout your generations, wherever you live: you must not eat any fat or any blood." (Lev 3:17).

The agreement worked out earlier at Jerusalem said that Gentiles did not have to assume the burden of the Jewish law. It did not say that Jews could be free from it. It approved sending missionaries to the Gentiles, but it said nothing about close fellowship with them. Peter accepted the open fellowship of the congregation at Antioch and joined in.

But the other Jewish believers were also interested in what was going on at Antioch. James himself did not come, but some of his associates did. Their presence, and perhaps their reaction, caused Peter to fear the circumcision party. He withdrew from the group meals. Worse, the other Jews joined him in his hypocrisy. Even Barnabas was swept along by their hypocritical behavior.

WORD PICTURE

Hypocrisy

The word translated "hypocrisy" comes from the world of the theater, where it refers to the act of wearing a mask or playing a part in a drama. Negatively, it came to mean "pretense, insincerity, acting in a fashion that belies one's true convictions."

The Protest (v. 14)

What happened at Antioch must have been a severe blow to Christian fellowship. Paul acted quickly and decisively. He opposed Peter to his face because Peter was clearly in the wrong. He confronted Peter in the presence of the whole congregation since the whole congregation was involved in what he was doing, and the principle was vital for all concerned. He pointed out Peter's inconsistency.

Peter was formally holding to Jewish law but was living much like the Gentiles. It was wrong for him, then, to expect Gentiles to live up to a way of life that he did not support by his own behavior. Or, as Paul put it, Peter was "deviating from the truth of the gospel."

There are three practical truths we can apply from this passage to the life of the church today.

1. *Great leaders can be in error.* There was every reason for Peter to resist the pressure to compromise his convictions in the face of pressure. He had been in the intimate circle of Jesus's closest disciples. He was a primary witness to the resurrection. Yet, in a moment of crisis, he failed, and the force of his example led many others astray as well. May God help us to test every message we hear by the touchstone of his Word and save us from exalting any human leader above the clear voice of God.

WORD PICTURE

Acting in Line With

This phrase is only one word *(orthopodeō)* in the Greek text. Literally, it means "to walk with straight feet." Paul was saying that Peter was not "walking a straight course." Elsewhere in his letters Paul had much to say about the importance of the Christian's "walk" (Eph 4:1,17; Col 1:10; 2:6; Rom 13:13). And later in Galatians Paul also admonished his readers to "keep in step with the Spirit" (Gal 5:25).

2. *God's grace means no second-class Christians.* The withdrawal of Jewish believers from table fellowship with their Gentile brothers and sisters precipitated a serious breach within the church at Antioch. Racism of any brand within any culture is incompatible with the truth of the gospel. Later in Galatians (3:26–29) Paul spelled out the implications of Christian unity in terms of the promise of grace fulfilled in Jesus Christ. Any religious system or theology that denies this truth stands in opposition to the "new creation" God is bringing into being. The body of Christ is based not on caste, color, or social condition but on grace alone.
3. *Standing for the gospel can be a lonely business.* When the crisis became more intense, Barnabas sided with Peter in the confrontation with Paul. The apostle to the Gentiles stood alone on behalf of the gospel. Throughout church history others have done the same. Thank God for those brave warriors of the faith who did not flinch in the hour of temptation—who refused to flirt with the false gods of their age and thus have passed on to us a goodly heritage of courage and faith.

Section Summary

This section centers on the issue of table fellowship. Paul publicly confronted and rebuked Peter, pointing out Peter's inconsistency and hypocrisy regarding the issue. Peter was formally holding to Jewish law, but he was living much like the Gentiles who did not hold to the law. It was wrong for him, then, to expect Gentiles to live up to a way of life that he did not support by his own behavior.

THE PRINCIPLE: JUSTIFICATION BY FAITH (2:15–21)

In this concluding section of chapter 2, Paul concludes the historical argument he has been pursuing and launches into the doctrinal exposition that will cover the next two chapters.

These seven verses contain some of the most compressed language found anywhere in Paul's epistles. Here Paul sets forth his main point—his big idea—that he wants to impress upon the Galatians: *Acceptance with God is effected through a simple act of trust in Jesus Christ and not through anything else.*

The Doctrine Declared (vv. 15–16)

In these verses Paul introduces three expressions that encompass the idea of the believer's justification by faith: *justification, the works of the law,* and *faith in Christ.* Paul uses each of these for the first time in his letter.

Justification. In its most basic meaning, justification is the declaration that somebody is right. Justification should not be confused with forgiveness, which is the fruit of justification. Neither should it be confused with atonement, which is the basis of justification. Rather, it is the favorite verdict of God, the righteous Judge, that one who formerly stood condemned has now been granted a new status at the bar of divine justice.

The Works of the Law. The law Paul usually refers to is the specific requirements God gave to Israel through Moses. Paul's argument here is that the nature of the law is such that it cannot produce a right relationship with God. As Paul will show in Gal 3, the law was given by God to play a special role in leading persons to Christ, who is the "end of the law" (Rom 10:4).

Faith in Christ. Paul speaks of faith as essential for justification. Faith is the necessary human response to what God has objectively accomplished on the cross of Christ. At the same time, we must recognize the instrumental character of such faith. Paul always tells us that we are saved "by" faith, not "on account of" faith. We must guard against the temptation to turn faith itself into one of the "works of the law." Saving faith is a gift from God, never a mere human possibility (Eph 2:8–9). Faith is not an achievement that earns salvation any more than circumcision is. Rather, faith is the evidence of saving grace manifested in the renewal of the heart by the Holy Spirit.

Section Summary

Here Paul sets forth his big idea that he wants to impress upon the Galatians: Acceptance with God is effected through a simple act of trust in Jesus Christ and not through anything else.

Objections Answered (vv. 17–20)

These verses take us back to the troubles in the fractured church at Antioch. We may have in Paul's coded language an actual piece of the debate that raged in Antioch.

The First Objection. "If we ourselves are also found to be 'sinners' while seeking to be justified by Christ, is Christ then a promoter of sin?" Paul's response is, "Absolutely not!" It is one of the strongest exclamations in his vocabulary. It is not Christ who causes people to be sinners.

The fact that Jewish Christians now shared table fellowship with Gentile believers did not make them sinners. Rather, this was an expression of the Christian freedom that was theirs through the righteousness of faith.

HISTORICAL BACKGROUND

Martin Luther on the Doctrine of Justification by Faith

For the issue before us is grave and vital; it involves the death of the Son of God, who, by the will and command of the Father, became flesh, was crucified, and died for the sins of the world. If faith yields on this point, the death of the Son of God will be in vain. Then it is only a fable that Christ is the Savior of the world. Then God is a liar, for he has not lived up to his promises. Therefore our stubbornness on this issue is pious and holy; for by it we are striving to preserve the freedom we have in Christ Jesus and to keep the truth of the gospel. If we lose this, we lose God, Christ, all the promises, faith, righteousness, and eternal life.

Martin Luther (Taken from *Luther's Works* 26, 90–91).

NEW TESTAMENT REFERENCE

"For you are saved by grace through faith, and this is not from yourselves; it is God's gift." (Eph 2:8)

In verse 18 Paul points his finger of blame at those who try to establish their legal righteousness, as Peter did, by going back to the law after they already recognized the futility of the law.

The Second Objection. By displacing the law as the proper channel for a right standing before God, had not Paul undermined the basis for living a righteous life? Had he left no place for the practical outworking of faith in the life of the believer?

Paul uses four theses to refute the second objection to his doctrine of justification by faith:

1. "Through the law I died to the law, so that I might live for God." When Paul says he died to the law, he was referring to nothing less than the God-given commandments and decrees contained in Old Testament Scriptures. However, he is not saying that the law of God lost all meaning or relevance for the Christian believer. Rather, he is saying that his relationship to self, sin, the world, and the law had been so altered by his union with Christ that they no longer controlled, dominated, or defined his existence.

The law is the instrument of a sinner's death. But the sinner's death is not sufficient to create a right relationship with a holy God. Only God himself, as man, can accomplish that.

By faith, the believing sinner sees Christ's dying and recognizes that he, too, is there. His orientation to God has heretofore been either ignoring God or trying to establish right relationship with God through keeping God's law. But because of his sinful nature, he couldn't possibly do that.

Christ's death puts to death the self which tries to please God by keeping the law and opens a new way—the way of faith. Faith recognizes that right relationship with God is not a human achievement but a gift from God to be received.

2. "I have been crucified with Christ." When Jewish believers witnessed the death of a sacrificial animal, such as a lamb, they recognized that this animal was dying as a consequence of their sin.

When Christian believers see the death of Christ, they see Jesus receiving the consequences of their sin. They identify with him in his death.

3. "I no longer live, but Christ lives in me." Paul set forth in this expression his doctrine of the indwelling Christ. The indwelling of Christ does not mean that persons are delivered from their current realm of suffering, sin, and death. Christ takes up residence in the believers, sanctifying our bodies as temples of the

Holy Spirit and enabling us to approach the throne of God in prayer.

Christ's death, which happened in space and time, is appropriated by the believer so it is no longer an external event but one that transforms and gives life. John Calvin says, "As long as Christ remains outside of us, and we are separated from him, all that he has suffered and done for the salvation of the human race remains useless and of no value for us" (John Calvin, *Institutes* 3.1.1, quoted in Timothy George, *Galatians*, New American Commentary 30 [B&H, 1994]).

4. "The life I now live in the body, I live by faith in the Son of God, who loved me and gave himself for me." While the Christian life takes place in the flesh, it is nonetheless lived by faith Not only are we justified by faith; we also live by faith. This means that saving faith cannot be reduced to a one-time decision or event in the past; it is a living, dynamic reality permeating every aspect of the believer's life. The object of this faith is Jesus Christ, the Son of God, "who loved me and gave himself for me." It was the love of God—unmerited, immeasurable, infinite—that sent Jesus to the cross.

HISTORICAL BACKGROUND

Martin Luther on Being Crucified with Christ

For we are called Christians because we may look at the Christ and say: "Dear Lord, You took all my sins upon Yourself. You became Martin, Peter, and Paul, and thus you crushed and destroyed my sin. There (on the cross) I must and will seek my sin. You have directed me to find it there. On Good Friday I clearly see my sin, but on the Day of Easter no sin is any longer to be seen" (Easter Sermon, Coburg, April 7, 530, WLS I, 182; WA 32, 47, as quoted in Thomas C. Oden, *The Word of Life* [Harper & Row 1989], 382).

Section Summary

Paul responded to two major objections to his doctrine of justification by faith. His four theses present the truths taught in verse 20. The believer has died to the law, shares in Christ's suffering, is the temple of the Holy Spirit, and lives by faith.

The Terrible Alternative (v. 21)

As we have seen, grace is the operative word in Galatians. In this concluding verse of chapter 2, Paul defends himself against the charge that by displacing the law as a means of salvation he has thwarted God's grace. The opposite is true. If it were possible to obtain a right standing before God through the works of the law, then Christ had no business dying! Was Christ a false messiah, a common criminal whose death was merely a footnote in history? Any true Christian must tremble in horror at such a prospect.

Paul says that as believers we must not persist in building again the wall that Christ has torn down. If we add works of the law to the sacrifice of the cross, then indeed we make a mockery of Jesus's death.

OLD TESTAMENT REFERENCE

"For no one alive is righteous in your sight." (Ps. 143:2b)

Galatians 2:15–21 summarizes the themes developed thus far and introduces the theological exposition of justification by faith that Paul will pursue in chapters 3 and 4. The key verse in this section is 2:16. It contains both an appeal to Christian experience ("Even we ourselves have believed in Christ Jesus") and an argument from Scripture, the quotation from Psalm 143:2 about no human being justified by observing the law. Paul anticipated objections to his doctrine of justification and emphasized the life of faith to which he will return in greater detail in Gal 5–6.

We are now ready to look at the centerpiece of Paul's doctrine of justification which he unfolds in the next two chapters.

QUESTIONS TO GUIDE YOUR STUDY

1. What was Paul's motive for returning to Jerusalem?
2. Describe the "false brothers." What was their error?
3. What was unique about Paul's status as an apostle in contrast to the Jerusalem apostles? What did he have in common with them?
4. Why did Paul rebuke Peter? Describe the issue that forced this confrontation.

GALATIANS 3

SECTION INTRODUCTION: THE THEOLOGICAL ARGUMENT (3:1–5:1)

Paul's argument in this section fulfills these three purposes:

1. He wanted to show the Galatians that their contemplated return to right standing with God by keeping the law as a method of relating to God was a contradiction of their experience (3:1–5).
2. He wanted to convince his readers that their experience had been identified with that of their forefather Abraham (3:6–9).
3. He wanted to explain the purpose and intent of the law (3:19–25).

In chapters 3 and 4 Paul turns from the evidence of his personal experience to evidence based on theology as revealed in several doctrines he will teach. But the transition in verses 1–5 is based on an appeal to the experience of the Galatian Christians.

WORD PICTURE

Cast a Spell

Paul is asking the Galatians who has led them astray by the evil eye or through evil arts. This is the only occurrence of this concept in the New Testament, although this is an old and persistent concept (Deut 28:54).

PROBING QUESTIONS (3:1–5)

Paul asked the Galatians a question that showed his astonishment at their deviation and directed their attention to its unreasonableness. "You foolish Galatians! Who has cast a spell on you?"

Paul follows this dramatic question with four rhetorical questions.

***Rhetorical Question 1: "Did you receive the Spirit by the works of the law or by believing what you heard?"* (v. 2)**

Restated, the question is, Why should the Galatians go back to the law when it was hearing and faith that brought the life of God into their lives? Paul's point was that the Galatians did not come to experience life in the Spirit by doing works of the law but by hearing the gospel and receiving it by faith. Here Paul describes the Christian life in terms of receiving the Spirit instead of being justified. Justification is God's activity in salvation; receiving the Spirit is man's experience. Paul is focusing on the experience of his Galatian friends. (He later contrasts the law and the Spirit in chapter 5.)

WORD PICTURE

Receive the Spirit

The word *receive* (in v. 2 and in 3:14) refers not to a self-prompted taking but to a grateful reception of that which is offered. Therefore, the Galatians received the Holy Spirit as an unfettered gift from the sovereign God apart from any contribution of good works or human merit on their part.

QUESTION	VERSE
1. "Did you receive the Spirit by the works of the law or by believing what you heard?"	v. 2
2. "After beginning by the Spirit, are you now finishing by the flesh?"	v. 3
3. "Did you experience so much for nothing—if in fact it was for nothing?"	v. 4
4. "Does God give you the Spirit and work miracles among you by your doing the works of the law?"	v. 5

***Rhetorical Question 2: "After beginning by the Spirit, are you now finishing by the flesh?"* (v. 3)**

Paul next raised the contrast between the Spirit and the flesh, a basic concept in the latter part of the book. How foolish and tragic to start out with the Spirit, the presence of God in a person's life, and to go from there to the flesh/human nature as it was apart from God.

***Rhetorical Question 3: "Did you experience so much for nothing—if in fact it was for nothing?"* (v. 4)**

Paul went on to question whether the Galatians learned anything from their experience. Paul's point was, Did you learn anything from what you experienced, or has it been wasted? Paul was not sure that it was in vain, so he added a statement to that effect after the question.

***Rhetorical Question 4: "Does God give you the Spirit and work miracles among you by your doing the works of the law?"* (v. 5)**

The fourth and final rhetorical question concerned the wonderful things God had done in the lives of the Galatians. He had given his Spirit. God worked miracles. Those things happened in their lives not because of their law-keeping but because they responded in faith to the gospel they heard.

Section Summary

Paul asked the Galatians a question that showed his astonishment at their deviation and directed their attention to its unreasonableness. "You foolish Galatians! Who has cast a spell on you?" Paul followed this dramatic question with four rhetorical questions to help the Galatians understand how they had gone wrong by accepting a false gospel in place of the true gospel of Jesus Christ.

WORD PICTURE

Hearing by Faith

The phrase translated "believing what you heard" in 3:2 and 3:5 is literally "hearing by faith." Much has been written about this expression, which could mean variously "the faculty or organ of hearing," or "the act of hearing." However, while the content of what is heard is crucial, Paul was thinking of the process by which one comes within the orbit of God's saving grace. As Paul said elsewhere, faith comes by hearing and hearing by the Word of God (Rom 10:17). The term *hearing* refers to the passive posture of the recipient. Thus, Martin Luther could write that the only organs of a Christian are his ears. The focus is not merely on the physical faculty of hearing but on the awakening of faith that comes through the preaching of the gospel. Thus, the contrast Paul was drawing between doing works and believing in Christ.

THE EXAMPLE OF ABRAHAM (3:6–9)

A Text from Genesis (v. 6)

Paul now turned from experience to Scripture as the basis of his argument. The point he had been making, that salvation comes through faith and not through law, was proved by Abraham. The patriarch Abraham, who is mentioned nineteen times in Paul's letters, is the pivotal figure in all of Paul's arguments from Scripture in Galatians.

Abraham was the father of the Jewish people, and circumcision began with him (Gen 17:10–14). But Paul pointed to Gen 15:6 to show that Abraham's righteousness came as he accepted God's promise by faith. Before Abraham was circumcised, and long before the law was given to Moses, Abraham was righteous in the sight of God simply by faith in God's promise.

True Children of Abraham (vv. 7–9)

In verse 7 Paul extended his argument from Abraham to Abraham's posterity and raised for the first time the question that would dominate the remainder of Galatians 3 and 4: Who are the true children of Abraham? This train of thought later will find a conclusion in the allegory of the two mothers, Sarah and Hagar, and their sons, Isaac and Ishmael (4:21–31).

Abraham was justified not on account of his outstanding virtues and holy works but solely because he believed God. And his faith was reckoned as righteousness long before he knew anything about circumcision or had taken the first step in his long journey toward the promised land. Although he became the father of the Jews, he was justified and received the Holy Spirit through the hearing of faith, not through works of the law.

Paul's rebuttal was a stinging rebuke to the theology of the Judaizers. Descent by blood or physical procreation does not create sons of Abraham in the sight of God any more than circumcision does. The true children of Abraham are those who believe—literally, those who ground their existence on faith in what God has said and done.

In these verses Paul makes two critical points:

1. He redefines the Abrahamic family in such a way as to undercut the appeal of his opponents to this biblical model.
2. Paul interprets the blessing promised through Abraham to "all the nations" as a prophecy of his own law-free mission to the Gentiles.

Paul's entire argument in this passage (vv. 6–9) hinges on one assumption: the continuity of the covenant of grace. From the creation of Adam and Eve until the second coming of Christ, God has provided one and only one way of salvation for all peoples everywhere: The atoning death of his Son on the cross applied to all the elect through the regenerating ministry of the Holy Spirit.

Section Summary

In verses 6–9, Paul turns from his own experience to Scripture as the basis of his argument. The point he had been making, that salvation comes through faith and not through law, was proved by Abraham. Abraham was justified not on account of his outstanding virtues and holy works but solely because he believed God.

In verses 6–9 Paul set forth a positive argument for justification by faith. In verses 10–14 he turned the tables and argued negatively against the possibility of justification by works.

CHRIST AND THE CURSE OF THE LAW (3:10–14)

The Curse of the Law (vv. 10–12)

Not only does the law not bring blessing; it imposes a curse. Paul cited Deut 27:26, which says that anyone who does not keep the law is cursed. Paul knew that no person could keep all the law. Therefore, all were under this curse. Furthermore, Paul maintained that keeping the law was never intended to be the way to be right with God. Quoting Hab 2:4, he said, "The righteous will live *by faith*" (emphasis added). The original statement in Habakkuk uses *faith* in the sense of faithfulness, but the idea of trusting God is still present.

The way of the law is different from the way of faith. Quoting Lev 18:5, Paul pointed out that the law requires doing, not trusting. The law dealt with actions. Only if one could do what the law required could he hope to gain life that way. Thus, the law and the hopeless burden of trying to keep the law were seen to be a curse.

NEW TESTAMENT REFERENCE

Justification by Faith

Basically, justification is a process by which an individual is brought into an unmerited, right relationship with God. Justification does not encompass the whole salvation process; it does, however, mark that instantaneous point of entry or transformation that makes one right with God. Christians are justified in the same way Abraham was, by faith (Rom 4:16; 5:1). Human works do not achieve or earn acceptance by God. The exercise of faith alone ushers us into an unmerited, right relationship with God (Gal 2:16; Titus 3:7).

OLD TESTAMENT REFERENCE

God Speaking to Abram

"All the peoples of the earth will be blessed through you." (Gen 12:3)

Redemption Through the Cross (vv. 13–14)

Verses 10–12 paint a grim picture of the human situation. The law requires a life of perfect obedience in order to be right with God. Yet no person can meet such a high standard. Consequently, everyone in the world has been "imprisoned" (3:22), suffering the just condemnation of the curse of the law. Given this situation, we are prompted to ask with the disciples, "Then who can be saved?" (Luke 18:26).

OLD TESTAMENT REFERENCE

"If anyone is found guilty of an offense deserving the death penalty and is executed, and you hang his body on a tree, you are not to leave his corpse on the tree overnight but are to bury him that day, for anyone hung on a tree is under God's curse. You must not defile the land the LORD your God is giving you as an inheritance." (Deut 21:22–23)

Paul's answer to this dilemma comes in the form of a confessional statement that may well have circulated in early Jewish Christian communities as a kind of shorthand summary of the gospel itself: Christ "redeemed us from the curse of the law by becoming a curse for us." Everything is different for those who trust in Christ. By becoming a curse for us, he has redeemed believers from the curse of the law.

Paul then quoted Deut 21:23, which prohibited hanging a body of an executed person from a tree. The condemned man was thought to be under a curse, and to leave the body publicly displayed would bring a curse on the land. Therefore, the executed person was to be buried and not left in the open. Christ, then, became our substitute and representative, taking upon himself the curse of the law.

As an aside, this verse from Deuteronomy may have been a stumbling block to Paul before his encounter with the risen Christ. Knowing this verse and the crucifixion of Jesus, Paul assumed that Jesus was under a curse. For that reason, he couldn't be the Messiah.

HISTORICAL BACKGROUND

Redeemed

The word *redeemed* means "to buy off" or "set free by the payment of a price." It was used to describe the purchase of slaves. The root word for *redemption* is Greek is *agora*, "marketplace," the site of the slave auction where, every day in ancient Rome, human beings were put up for sale to the highest bidder. Paul's use of the word *redemption* declares that we have been bought with a price. The ransom for our sins was nothing less than the lifeblood of the Son of God.

Following his conversion, Paul saw that, indeed, Jesus bore a curse but not for himself. Moreover, the resurrection vindicated him as God's anointed.

In his death, Jesus broke the curse on humankind and provided the needed alternative. Now in Christ, the blessing God spoke to Abraham can come to the Gentiles. Anyone who will put his or her faith in Christ can receive the Spirit, the experience of God in his life that comes by being in right relationship with God.

Section Summary

One way to summarize this passage is in terms of two major propositions, each of which is confirmed and clarified by a citation from the Old Testament.

PROPOSITION	OT QUOTE
1. Those who rely on observing the law are under a curse.	Deut 27:26
2. No one can be justified by means of the law.	Hab 2:4

THE LAW AND THE PROMISED INHERITANCE (3:15–25)

Paul now moves to a second level of argument, where he speaks about the nature of salvation. He shows the validity of the law as God's free and gracious favor promised to Abraham. This is a favor secured by Christ and sealed in the hearts of believers by the Holy Spirit. Paul argues exclusively from the Scriptures, quoting the Pentateuch five times and from the Prophets once. He shows how God's promise to Abraham—that all peoples would be blessed through him—has been fulfilled by Christ, whose death on the cross wrought redemption and justification by faith for Jews and Gentiles alike.

Paul now moves to a second level of argument, showing first how God's covenant with Abraham stands in stark contrast to the law of Moses and yet how, in the providence of God, even the law played a crucial role in the unfolding drama of redemption.

The Priority of the Promise (vv. 15–18)

Paul illustrated his argument by giving an example from common experience. He spoke of making a "covenant," likely any kind of contract or formal agreement, such as an exchange of property. His point was that such a contract was binding and was not changed except by the party who made it.

Paul then interrupted his thought to indicate that he was thinking of the covenant God made with Abraham in Genesis 13:15 and 17:7–8.

This covenant was not only promised to Abraham; it was also promised to his offspring ("seed"). Paul finds profound significance in the fact that a singular word was used of this offspring. Abraham's seed is Jesus the Messiah, who is head of the new humanity.

Christ was head of the new humanity which God was creating. As such, he included in himself all who are Abraham's spiritual descendants. Paul is not proving this truth from the Old Testament, simply illustrating from it.

In mentioning the coming of the law 430 years after Abraham, Paul's point was simply that it was a long time and that the covenant of promise had lasted that long without the addition of the law. The giving of the law did not annul God's promise, especially since it was later fulfilled by Christ. If the giving of the law was intended to provide a new way of receiving God's blessings, then the way of promise would have been annulled.

HISTORICAL BACKGROUND

Covenant

The basic definition of *covenant* is a "pact, treaty, alliance, or agreement between two parties of equal or unequal authority." The covenant or testament is a central, unifying theme in Scripture. God made covenants with individuals, and the nation Israel found final fulfillment in the new covenant in Christ Jesus. God's covenants can be understood by humans because they are modeled on human covenants or treaties.

Section Summary

The law was never intended to replace faith in God's promise as the way of salvation. There has always been only one way to be saved, and it is not by keeping the law.

The Purpose of the law (vv. 19–25)

Structurally, these verses divide neatly into three parts, with the first two sections introduced by leading questions. Paul seems to be speaking in a kind of theological shorthand that is not easy to unpack. For this reason, and not ignoring the context of Paul's argument here, we will find that the best commentary on Galatians is the book of Romans.

Paul's first question is, "Why, then, was the law given?" This question arises from the logic of Paul's argument that he has pursued relentlessly since 2:16. Paul flings out his answer in four terse statements (vv. 19–20): (1) it was added because of transgressions (cf. Rom 5:20); (2) until the seed had come, it was put into effect; (3) through angels; (4) by a mediator.

His second question is, "Is the law therefore contrary to God's promises?" This elicits Paul's immediate and indignant response, "Absolutely not!"

At this point we might think the law opposed or contradicted the promise of God. Paul is saying that the law would be bad if it were given to bring spiritual life and then failed to do so. But no law can bring life. The law was not given for that purpose, so it cannot be judged a failure on that basis. The law, like everything else in human experience, was limited by sin.

Paul now moves on to the three functions of the law.

The law enters that it might fail (v. 21). The failure of the law to save has been turned into a blessing. The "side road" of the law, which can only lead to the gallows, has by the great mercy of God directed us back toward the road of salvation.

The law condemns that it might save (vv. 22–23). By exposing human wickedness, the law eliminates every area of self-justification from which the conscience-driven sinner might draw.

The law disciplines that it might set free (vv. 24–25). The law is a stern disciplinarian and a harsh taskmaster. Yet in its harshness there is a note of grace, for the function of discipline, as opposed to mere torture, is always remedial. "With its whippings, the law . . . draws us to Christ" (Martin Luther, *Luther's Works* 26, 346).

WORD PICTURE

Absolutely Not!

The Greek expression Paul uses here conveys horror and shock at the concept under consideration—"absolutely not!" Literally, it can be translated "may it never be!" Or, as A. T. Robertson puts it, "Far from it!" Of its fifteen occurrences in the New Testament, thirteen are in Paul's writings. Other occurrences of this expression are in Rom 3:6,31; 6:1–2; 9:14; and Gal 2:17.

Section Summary

Because all have sinned, the law cannot bring life. Recognizing this fact leads persons to see that only faith in Christ can enable them to receive God's promise.

A Shift in Paul's Argument

The note: copy on copyright page correctly notes a major break in Paul's argument at this point (3:26), a new turn in his continuing scriptural demonstration of the doctrine of justification by faith. To this point Paul has presented the grand sweep of redemptive history from Abraham to Christ. Now he shifts his focus from the historical to the personal, from the institutional to the individual.

The following diagram taken from Timothy George, *Galatians*, New American Commentary 30 (Nashville,B&H, 1994), 271.

3:6–14 Promise (Abraham)
▼
3:15–22 Law (Moses)
▼
3:23–25 Faith (Christ)
▼
3:26 "Through faith you are all sons of God in Christ Jesus."
▲
3:27–4:7 Faith (Spirit)
▲
4:8–11 Law ("the elements of the world")
▲
4:21–31 Promise (Sarah)

BAPTISM AND THE NEW COMMUNITY (3:26–29)

The New Status of Believers (v. 26)

In this section Paul makes three astounding statements about the new status of"all"of"all" true believers.

"You are all sons of God." Jesus is uniquely and exclusively *the* Son of God, equal with the Father from all eternity, unrivaled by any creatures in his essential deity. Even more remarkable, then, is Paul's description of the redeemed as "sons of God." He developed this theme in the verses that follow by showing how the sonship of Christians derives from the sonship of Christ.

NEW TESTAMENT REFERENCE

"To all who did receive him, he gave them the right to be children of God, to those who believe in his name." (John 1:12; cp. Hos 1:10)

- "Through faith you are all sons of God." Not by natural descent or human contrivance but through faith alone have we entered this new relationship with the heavenly Father.
- "Through faith you are all sons of God in Christ Jesus." The expression "in Christ" is found 172 times in Paul's writings. Most often it is used to describe that participation in and union with Jesus Christ that is effected for every believer by the indwelling of the Holy Spirit.

HISTORICAL BACKGROUND

Guardianship

The picture in this passage is one of a boy in a home of wealth and standing who is legally the heir. This owner or "young master" of the family estate is still a minor and so lives under rules much like a slave.

The guardians Paul refers to may have been the overseers set up by Roman law, a guardian or tutor until age fourteen, and a trustee or curator until age twenty-five. Or the terms may have described a personal guardian and a trustee of property who acted at the same time. These officers acted until the time set by the father. Under Roman law, the father did not set the time for the son to cease being a minor. It is not certain which legal system Paul was thinking about, but there were some parallels in Syrian history.

Paul's point here was that the son, until he became of age, was no better off than a slave. He was under the direction of others.

The Significance of Baptism (vv. 27–29)

For Paul, baptism, with its symbolic association with the death, burial, and resurrection of Christ, models justification, although it can never effect it. For New Testament believers, baptism with the Holy Spirit is antecedent to baptism with water, the latter being a confession and public witness to the former.

Paul described all that baptism was given to represent in one of the most striking metaphors found anywhere in the New Testament—being "clothed with" Christ. This comparison could have recalled several parallel practices that would have been familiar to Paul's Gentile converts in Galatia.

Section Summary

Paul focuses on the new status the believer enjoys through justification by faith. Paul then uses the baptismal rite as a symbolic model of justification.

QUESTIONS TO GUIDE YOUR STUDY

1. What is a rhetorical question? How did Paul use this device, and how effective do you think he was in using it to make his point?
2. What is the significance of the example of Abraham to Paul's argument on justification by faith?
3. Why is the law a curse? How is it limiting?
4. According to Paul, what was the purpose of the law?

GALATIANS 4

THE RADICAL CHANGE: FROM SLAVERY TO SONSHIP (4:1–7)

Our Past Condition (vv. 1–3)

Paul continued to contrast law-keeping and living by faith, presenting another illustration drawn from common experience. He shifts his emphasis from the inheritance to the heir. He describes a child who has been left his father's estate but is too young to take possession of it and so is placed under guardians and trustees.

We, Paul explained (apparently referring to himself and his readers), were like that. Before the coming of Christ, all were slaves to "the elements of the world."

Two basic interpretations of the phrase "the elements of the world" are favored:

1. The "elements" may be elementary principles, religious and moral "ABCs," such as the Jewish law.
2. The "elements" may be spirits, or spiritual powers, that were thought to move the heavenly bodies.

No matter which interpretation one favors, Paul was speaking of people who lived under the yoke of some force other than the Spirit of God as experienced in Christ.

The Coming of Christ (vv. 4–5)

Verses 4–5 contain one of the most compressed and highly charged passages in the entire letter because they present the objective basis for the doctrine of justification by faith.

Paul and his fellow believers moved out of their immature bondage when Christ came. As in the illustration where the date was set by the father, Christ came "when the time came to completion."

From the human point of view, Jesus was born at a favorable time. Roman law, the wonderful system of Roman highways, the political stability maintained by the Romans, the Greek language, and Jewish religious teaching all combined to create a situation in which the gospel could spread.

But the emphasis is on God's sovereign choice. God sent his Son into the world. This was a gift of grace. He was born of a woman and shared our human nature. He was born under the law—that is, he was a Jew and submitted to the curse that the law imposed. He did this to redeem those who were under the law.

An examination of the grammatical structure of these verses reveals the four central ideas of the passage brought together within a single literary unit:

- The *temporal* introduction: "When the time came to completion."
- A *parallel participle* describing the condition of the incarnate Son: "Born of a woman."
- *A parallel participle* describing the status of the incarnate Son: "Born under law."
- Two purpose clauses that describe the reason for Christ's coming and the great benefit believers receive through faith in him: *In order* that he might "redeem those under law" and *in order* that we might "receive adoption as sons."

In verse 5 Paul focuses on the divine person and eternal deity of Jesus Christ as it relates to his saving work in redemption and regeneration. The Son of God became a human being and was put under the law in order to redeem those who were under the law, and so we might become God's sons.

As redemption implies a basically negative concept—we are redeemed *from* the curse and *from* the slave market of sin—Paul goes on to show the positive purpose for Christ's sacrificial suffering and death. The Son of God was born of woman and put under the law to redeem us from the law so that we might receive "adoption as sons."

The Spirit Within (vv. 6–7)

Paul now moves to the Spirit's role as the foundation of our justification by faith. Just as God sent his Son into the world, so he has sent the Spirit of his Son into our hearts.

The best commentary on this text is Paul's parallel statement in Rom 8:15–16: "For you did not receive a spirit of slavery to fall back into fear. Instead, you received the Spirit of adoption, by whom we cry out, '*Abba,* Father!' The Spirit himself testifies together with our spirit that we are God's children." The most basic indication of our adoption is that we have a new form of address for God. The Spirit invites us to join in his invocation, crying, "Abba, Father."

Section Summary

No longer is a person's relationship to God determined by race, rank, or role. No longer are we under the curse of the law. The promise given to Abraham and fulfilled in his prophetic Seed, Jesus Christ, has now been extended to all of those who through faith in him have become sons, crying "Abba!" and heirs of the living God.

WORD PICTURE

Abba

Abba is the Aramaic word for "father." It is the term a child would have used much as children today use "Daddy." It is still heard throughout the Middle East as a word of address used by young children to greet their father. However, Abba, used here in Galatians, is more associated with intimacy than infancy. Jesus introduced its use in reference to God. Before that, it would have been considered much too familiar and personal. Those who are in Christ enter into this intimate relation with God and inherit the promises of God.

AREA OF THEOLOGY	KEY DOCTRINE	GALATIANS PASSAGE
Study of Christ	Our adoption as sons	4:4
Study of Salvation	Our redemption through the cross	4:5
Study of the Spirit	Our regeneration through the Spirit	4:6–7

From 3:6 through 4:7, Paul develops a tightly woven and carefully crafted argument for the doctrine of justification by faith. He offers an analysis of redemptive history centered on the true identity of the children of Abraham. The remainder of chapter 4 can be divided into three literary units:

Verses 8–11 are an exhortation in which Paul reminds his Galatian converts of their former way of life, the great transformation that has happened to them through their adoption into God's family, and his deep concern that they are about to exchange their spiritual heritage for a mess of pottage.

Verses 12–20 extend the theme of Paul's fear by his recalling the endearing bonds of friendship and love he and the Galatians had enjoyed in days past. He pleads with them to remain faithful to the one and only gospel he had first preached among them.

Verses 21–31 contain the allegory of Hagar and Sarah whose sons, Ishmael and Isaac, are taken as representative types of spiritual slavery and spiritual sonship.

THE DANGER OF TURNING BACK (4:8–11)

Before the Galatians became Christians, they worshiped the pagan deities. Paul acknowledged their existence as some kind of spirits, but he denied that they were gods. Those who worshiped them were in bondage to them. Then the Galatians came to know God, or as Paul put it, "have become known by God." This emphasizes that God takes the initiative. Our relationship with him does not depend on our initiative.

To turn to the works of the law would be to give up this relationship and return to a state of bondage. Paul implies that bondage to the law is the same as their bondage to pagan gods. Both systems demanded that their followers observe special days and seasons. Both systems were heavily motivated by fear and kept their adherents uncertain and intimidated.

This would have been one of the appeals that Jewish legalism made to former pagans. Both the works of the law and the pagan gods were "weak and worthless elements [spirits]." Both lacked the power to save and bring abundant life.

The thought of the Galatians accepting such a condition made Paul feel that he failed. We can understand Paul's feeling here, as it is possible that some may have "tasted God's good word and the powers of the coming age" (Heb 6:5) without being converted. This helps us make sense of his closing lamentation, "I am fearful for you, that perhaps my labor for you has been wasted."

Section Summary

To turn to the works of the law would be to give up a relationship with God and knowing him to return to a state of bondage. Paul rebuked the Galatian believers to keep them from being drawn into a legalistic religious system.

WORD PICTURE

Turn Back

Some have implied that by using the phrase "turn back," Paul was implying that the Galatians could lose their salvation. It is significant that the word Paul uses for "turn back" is a technical term used for both religious conversion (1 Thess 1:9; Acts 9:35; 15:19) and religious apostasy (2 Pet 2:21–22). However, real apostasy, as opposed to a temporary backsliding, is possible only for those who have never been genuinely converted.

HISTORICAL BACKGROUND

Paul's Affliction

Verse 13 has fascinated scholars primarily because of its reference to the undisclosed illness that afflicted Paul during his first visit to Galatia. In the early church, Jerome interpreted Paul's affliction as the temptation of sexual desire that he identified with the "thorn in the flesh" of 2 Cor 12:7. During the Reformation, Martin Luther dismissed a reference to the suffering and affliction Paul bore as the result of the persecutions he endured.

In recent years, however, most commentators have discarded both of those traditional interpretations in favor of the idea that Paul was referring here in Galatians to some actual bodily illness that affected his missionary labors.

PAUL'S PERSONAL APPEAL (4:12–20)

This section forms a personal parenthesis in Paul's overall argument for justification by faith, which he resumes and concludes in verses 21–31 with an additional proof from Scripture.

Paul's Labors Among the Galatians (vv. 12–16)

The mention of his work previously among the Galatians led Paul to speak personally of his ministry in Galatia. He began with a strong appeal for the Galatians to "become as I me"—that is, free from the law. This he urged "for I also have become as you are." Becoming like them may mean that Paul had virtually become a Gentile. Or perhaps it referred to the fact that he had once been in bondage to the law and had been set free. In either case, Paul was telling his readers that he had a lot in common with them. He knew what they were going through and urged them to follow his example.

Paul's Love for Them (vv. 17–20)

Before declaring again (vv. 19–20) his enduring love and anguished concern for the Galatians, Paul took a long sidewards glance at his opponents, whose evil activities had precipitated the present crisis in Paul's relationship with the Galatians. Neither here nor anywhere else in Galatians did Paul name these troublesome agitators. The problem with the agitators was not the interest they had shown in the Galatians but their evil intentions and selfish motivation ("it is for their own ends," Phillips; "but for a dishonorable purpose," Knox).

Section Summary

During his argument for justification by faith, Paul made a personal appeal to the Galatians. He appealed to them to "become as I am"—that is, free from the law. Paul told his readers that he had a lot in common with them, he knew what they were going through, and he urged them to follow his example.

PERSONAL APPLICATION

Paul was a pioneer in what we call today *contextualization*, the communication of the gospel in such a way that it speaks to the total context of the people to whom it is addressed. Insofar as we can separate the heart of the gospel from its cultural cocoon—to contextualize the message of Christ without compromising its content—we too should become imitators of Paul.

THE ANALOGY OF HAGAR AND SARAH (4:21–31)

The Analogy (vv. 21–23)

Paul now brings his doctrinal argument to a climax. He calls for the attention of those who were considering putting themselves under the law and asks whether they really heard what the law said. After all, Paul was a lifelong student of the law and trained in the schools of the rabbis. He proceeds to pick up again the theme of Abraham and his descendants by pointing to the story of Abraham, Sarah, and Hagar.

Hagar, the slave woman, symbolized Mount Sinai, the system of obedience to the Mosaic law. Her son Ishmael represented those enslaved to legalism. Sarah corresponded to the freedom in Christ. Her son Isaac represented spiritual children of Abraham, who were freed from the law by faith in Christ. The Galatians were the children born in freedom, but they acted as if they were the descendants of the slave-wife. Paul urged them to take their stand in freedom to avoid the harness of slavery (5:1).

The Figurative Meaning (vv. 24–27)

In verse 24 we come to one the most difficult and controversial words in the entire epistle. Referring to the historical summary he had just given in verses 22–23, Paul declared, "These things are being taken figuratively." Allegorical interpretation seeks to discern a hidden meaning in each story or text—a meaning that may be divorced from the historical events and facts alluded to in the text itself.

Clearly, however, Paul was not advocating a departure from the basic meaning of Scripture as found in its natural and literal sense. What he called an allegory might be better termed *typology:* a narrative from Old Testament history interpreted in terms of new covenant realities.

The entire analogy involves five sets of twos: two mothers, two sons, two covenants, two mountains (Mount Sinai and Mount Zion, the latter being understood but not expressed), and two cities. The following chart contrasts the two women and what they represent.

WORD PICTURE

Typology

A method of interpretation whereby Christian truths are symbolized in Old Testament events.

HAGAR	SARAH
Ishmael, the son of slavery	Isaac, the son of freedom
Birth "as a result of the flesh"	Birth "through promise"
Old covenant	New covenant
Mount Sinai	Mount Zion
Present Jerusalem	Heavenly Jerusalem

The two women stood for two covenants—law and promise. The law covenant, represented by Hagar, came from Mount Sinai. This was where Moses received the law. It was not located in the promised land but in Arabia, the area settled by the descendants of Ishmael. Paul links Hagar and Jerusalem, the center of Judaism and the law. She and her children were slaves. It must have come as a shock to the Judaizers to read this, for the Jews would have said they descended from Isaac, not Ishmael. They thought they were free, not slaves, as they said to Jesus on one occasion (John 8:33).

However, Paul was speaking not of biological relationships but spiritual realities. The Judaizers insisted on the slavery of the law, and the Isaac family was characterized by freedom and promise.

Sarah represented the Jerusalem above, a New Testament designation of the church and the heavenly home of God's people (Heb 12:22; Rev 3:12; 21:2,9ff). This Jerusalem is free and is the mother of all who are in Christ.

Paul breaks into a joyful quotation from Isa 54:1, in which the fruitfulness of restored Jerusalem is contrasted with the barrenness of Jerusalem destroyed by the conquerors. Sarah had been barren, and the church might seem barren at times. But according to God's promise, the children of freedom would be many. Paul reminded the Galatians that they, along with him, belonged in the Isaac family, the family of promise.

OLD TESTAMENT REFERENCE

"'Rejoice, childless one,
who did not give birth;
burst into song and shout,
you who have not been in labor!
For the children of the desolate one will be more than the children of the married woman,'
says the LORD" (Isa 54:1).

Section Summary

Paul brings his doctrinal argument to a climax by pointing to the story of Abraham, Sarah, and Hagar. He uses typology, a narrative from Old Testament history that he interprets in terms of new covenant realities. With this analogy, Paul makes his point that the Galatians, along with him, belonged to the family of promise.

THE PERSONAL APPLICATION (4:28–31)

Quoting from Gen 21:8–14, Paul adapts the words of Sarah concerning Ishmael to the situation in Galatia: "Drive out the slave and her son." This passage from Genesis speaks of Sarah's displeasure at the continued presence of Ishmael alongside Isaac. Later Jewish tradition spoke of the persecution of Isaac by Ishmael.

Paul sees a reenactment of this in the trouble being given the Galatians by the Judaizers. Sarah had demanded that Hagar and Ishmael be sent away. The inheritance could not go to both the slave's son and the free woman's son. Paul is calling for a strong solution to the problem in Galatia. The legalists would have to be cast out. He again reminds the Galatians in verse 31 that they were the children of freedom.

QUESTIONS TO GUIDE YOUR STUDY

1. Describe the doctrine of adoption. What does it include?
2. Why was the concept of sonship such good news for those who were in bondage to the law?
3. What danger did Paul warn the Galatians about? What stake did he have in their growth as believers?
4. What is the significance of Paul's analogy of Hagar and Sarah?

GALATIANS 5

SECTION INTRODUCTION: THE PRACTICAL ARGUMENT (5:2–6:10)

Chapter 5 begins Paul's practical, concluding section. In this final section Paul warned against the cavalier attitude that freedom from the law created in some people who lived in disobedience. He reminded the Galatians that they must respond to the urgings of the Holy Spirit and not be captured by the cravings of the flesh. He also entreated them to show concern for one another and to demonstrate persistence in their commitment to Christ.

A PASSIONATE CALL TO FREEDOM IN CHRIST (5:1–12)

Stand Firm in Freedom (v. 1)

Verse 1 is a transitional sentence and could easily relate to chapter 4. It is a stirring challenge to embrace freedom, not slavery. If Galatians is the Magna Carta of Christian liberty, then Gal 5:1 has reason to be considered one of the key verses of the epistle.

Falling from Grace (vv. 2–6)

Verses 2–3 state two terrible consequences of a lapse into legalism for the Galatians: (1) it would cancel the benefits of Christ for them, and (2) it would put them under the necessity of keeping all of the law. Perhaps the Galatians had not thought of it, but they could not submit to circumcision and stop there. Once they admitted that this was necessary, they would be admitting that all the rest of the law was necessary. As James noted, to break one point of the law was to be guilty of all the law (Jas 2:10).

Paul spoke further on the first danger, the result of turning to the law, which cancels the benefits of Christ in a person's life. Paul explained that for those who turn to the law, "Christ will not benefit" them. That is because the way of Christ is a totally different approach to righteousness. If Christ and the law were simply two items in a category of ways to please God, then by all means they should have used both. But the way of the law is the way of human effort, and the way of Christ is denial of human effort. The two are mutually exclusive.

Paul carries the idea further in verse 4 where he says, "You who are trying to be justified by the law are alienated from Christ; you have fallen from grace." Such a person removes himself or herself from the relationship in which Christ can be of benefit. Such a person has "fallen from grace."

NEW TESTAMENT REFERENCE

"For whoever keeps the entire law, and yet stumbles at one point, is guilty of breaking it all." (Jas 2:10)

WORD PICTURE

"Whoever wants to have a half-Christ loses the whole."

John Calvin, *CNTC* 11.93.]

Because that phrase has come to mean to some that a person may be saved through faith in Christ and later lose his or her salvation through some sin they commit, it requires careful study. We need to note first that Paul is speaking of the catastrophic loss of the benefits of Christ. This clear statement should not be explained away. (It has been suggested, for example, that they would have been fallen from sanctifying grace but not from justifying grace.) But it is equally clear that Paul is not speaking of losing salvation by committing sin. He is speaking of substituting law for grace as the basis of salvation.

Second, we must remember that Paul is talking about a hypothetical situation. For emphasis he is speaking as if the Galatians had already fallen from grace. He is simply carrying his argument to its logical conclusion to show the Galatians how great is their danger. His concern here is practical guidance, not theoretical argument.

The promise of righteousness through the law is appealing because it is definite and tangible. The righteousness that comes through faith, Paul argues, is no less real. Although this righteousness may not be fully experienced until God's final judgment, it is already present in the form of hope as the Spirit works in the believer now.

Verse 6 is a key as it cuts through all the debate about circumcision to show what really matters. Circumcision accomplished nothing, but neither did uncircumcision. It was an equally serious error if the Galatians refused circumcision and then prided themselves on that, thinking they had earned some merit in the sight of God. There can be a legalism of doing and a legalism of not doing. The only thing that really matters is "faith working through love."

Circumcision or the Cross (vv. 7–12)

"Who prevented you from obeying the truth?" is a rhetorical question like "Who has bewitched you?" in 3:1. The result in this sinister interference in the life race of the Galatians is that they had not continued to obey the truth. Earlier in his letter, Paul summarized his entire message under the rubric the "truth of the gospel" (2:5,14). This was precisely what the Galatians were on the verge of deserting through their alliance with the unbelieving theology of false teachers. Here Paul is calling them back from the brink of disaster.

WORD PICTURE

Running a Race

Paul compares the Christian life to running a race, an athletic image found in many of his writings (1 Cor 9:24–26; Phil 3:14; 2 Tim 4:7). The image is of an Olympic athlete who dashes from the starting line with great vigor, perhaps accelerating past his competitors, only to have someone from the stands suddenly enter the race and trip him at an unexpected turn in the road.

As Paul continues his letter, he speaks of the methods of the false teachers and considers the end result of their meddlesome interference. He does this by quoting a proverbial saying from the world of bread-making: "A little leaven leavens the whole batch of dough." This is a commonsense saying similar to our own English maxim, "Just one rotten apple spoils the whole barrel."

Paul's point is clear: His opponents had not overturned the whole system of Christian teaching but were only making a seemingly minor adjustment to it—the imposition of the harmless rite of circumcision. But even a seemingly slight deviation on such a fundamental matter of the faith can bring total ruin to the Christian community. Just a little poison, if it is toxic enough, will destroy the entire body.

Verse 9 ended on a note of sourdough, a batch of bread thoroughly infested from a little morsel of yeast. The churches in Galatia were in turmoil. They were wavering and perhaps even tilting toward Paul's opponents, but they had not yet completely succumbed to the false teachers' persuasive appeals. Paul's primary purpose in writing his letter probably was to provide a counterweight to the false teachers.

Evidently a part of the confusion in verse 10 stemmed from a false accusation, a slanderous lie, that Paul's opponents circulated about him when they first met the Galatians. In urging circumcision upon the Gentile believers there, they apparently whispered, "Haven't you heard that Paul himself is an advocate of circumcision?" To us this seems like a preposterous charge, and Paul certainly thought it to be maliciously intended.

Verse 12 is the strongest statement in the epistle, and it showed how deeply disturbed Paul was over this crisis. It has been considered by some as the most startling of all Paul's recorded statements in the New Testament. In referring to the act of circumcision, Paul expresses his wish that those preaching circumcision would "let themselves be mutilated." The Jerusalem Bible translates verse 12, "Tell those who are disturbing you I would like to see the knife slip." However we choose to translate verse 12, we must not imagine that Paul meant any literal, physical harm to his opponents. He did not fight with carnal weapons but rather with "the sword of the Spirit—which is the word of God" (Eph 6:17).

WORD PICTURE

Persuasion

It is obvious that the circumcision-preaching agitators had exerted a powerful influence over Paul's converts. They had bewitched them and tripped them up in their race toward the finish line. What was the secret of their success? Paul answered this question by using (v. 8) a unique word, "the persuasion" (Gr. *peismonē*), a term found nowhere else in earlier Greek literature.

Section Summary

In this section Paul describes the dangers of giving in to the Judaizers' demand for circumcision. We feel the clash of turbulent and conflicting emotions as Paul vacillates between consolation and anger, exasperation and hope. Paul registered many strong words against the Judaizers whose false teachings were poisoning the Galatian churches.

FLESH AND THE SPIRIT (5:13–26)

The Law of Love (vv. 13–15)

Paul once again repeats his challenge. As in verse 1, he points to freedom. As in verse 8, he reminds them of his calling. As he had done several times before (3:15; 4:12,31), he calls them brothers. Then, having made his point about freedom, he clarifies what that Christian freedom means.

There is always the danger that freedom will be mistaken for license. It could become, Paul said, "an opportunity for the flesh." By "flesh," Paul meant human nature without the motivation of the Holy Spirit.

If the Christian is not under the law, then what is to prevent him from giving in to the desires of the flesh? Paul's answer to this question is the commitment to be servants of one another through love. This is what the law is all about. If you love your neighbor as yourself (Lev 19:18; Luke 10:27), then you have fulfilled the intent of the law (Rom 13:8–10). Thus, Paul showed that he did not deny what the law aimed at, which was righteousness. He simply said that the law cannot bring it about, but Christ can.

Life without love would be chaos and destruction. This is true of legalism as well as license. Without love, persons would "bite and devour one another" like wild animals tearing at each other's throats.

PERSONAL APPLICATION

"The only bondage in God's Creation that is tolerable and desirable is the law of love. No man knows true happiness till he has learned how to love—how to love not a little, but a great deal."

Henry Ward Beecher, "The Fruits of the Spirit," from *20 Centuries of Great Preaching*, vol. IV (Waco: Word Books, 1971), p. 316.

Conflict and Victory (vv. 16–18)

Paul has just described the kind of life that lapses into uncontrolled indulgences of the flesh. He now presents the Christian alternative, which is not law but the Spirit. Paul uses several distinct verbs to illustrate the Spirit-controlled life of the believer, all of which are roughly equivalent in meaning. He urges believers to:

- Be led by the Spirit (v. 18).
- Live by the Spirit (v. 25a).
- Keep in step with the Spirit (v. 25b). Each of these verbs suggests a relationship of dynamic interaction, direction, and purpose. The Spirit in the life of the believer means the presence and power of God in the believer's life.

PICTURES OF FLESH IN THE NEW TESTAMENT (5:19–21)

The fifteen items Paul lists in his "catalog of evil" are by no means intended to be exhaustive. And so as he concludes his list, he adds "and anything similar."

Sins of Immorality (v. 19)

Sexual Immorality. The first three acts in Paul's list of sins have to do with loose sexual relations. This typically Pauline feature characterizes his listing of evil offenses in other writings as well (1 Cor 6:9; 6:18; Eph 5:5; 1 Thess 4:3).

The Greek word for "sexual immorality" originally meant "prostitution." By Paul's time it was used to denote a whole range of immoral sexual relationships, including incest (1 Cor 5:1). For believers to be caught up in sexual misconduct deeply grieves the Holy Spirit, whose presence within their lives has made their bodies temples unto the Lord.

Acts of sexual immorality, although often done in the name of love, are really the antithesis of love, which is the foremost fruit of the Spirit.

Moral Impurity. This word literally means "uncleanness" and has both a medical and a ceremonial connotation. Even today doctors speak of cleaning a wound before they apply medication to it.

Under the Mosaic law, ceremonial impurity barred one from participation in the worship rituals of the temple until the impediment was removed. Uncleanness, then, speaks of the defilement of sexual sin and the separation from God that it brings. The remedy for such sins is confession and repentance. If we confess and repent, the promise of God's Word is that Christ is faithful and just to forgive and purify us from all unrighteousness (1 John 1:9).

Promiscuity. William Barclay defines this particular vice as "a love of sin so reckless and so audacious that a man has ceased to care what God or man thinks of his actions" (*Flesh and Spirit: An Examination of Galatians 5:19–23* [SCM, 1962], 31). Promiscuity speaks of the total loss of limits, the lack of restraint, decency, and self-respect.

Sins of Idolatry (v. 20)

Idolatry. From the ancient fertility cult of Baal to the sacral prostitution at the temple of Aphrodite in Corinth, the homage paid to false gods was often accompanied by shameful displays of sensuality. The word *idolatry* is not found in the texts of the classical writers but belongs to the unique Christian vocabulary of the New Testament.

Sorcery. At the root of this word is *pharmakon*, literally "drug." In classical Greek, the word *pharmakeia* referred to the use of drugs, whether for medicinal or more sinister purposes (e.g., poisoning). In the New Testament, however, it is invariably associated with the occult, both here in Galatians and in Revelation, where it occurs twice (Rev 9:21; 18:23).

Sins of Animosity (vv. 20–21)

Hatreds. This is the first of eight nouns Paul mentions, all of which refer to the breakdown of interpersonal relationships. Hatred, or enmity, is the opposite of love. In Rom 8:7 Paul used the same word to describe the hostility of the sinful mind to God. Here in Galatians, however, its destructive force is played out on the plane of human relationships. The specific forms this hatred can take in tearing down community life are "strife, jealousy, outbursts of anger, selfish ambitions, dissensions, factions, envy."

Strife. In the New Testament this word is unique to Paul, who used it nine times to characterize the discord that beset so many of his congregations. Paul was aware of some who even preached Christ "out of envy and rivalry" (Phil 1:15). This shows that it is possible for the servants of the Lord to use even unworthy motives and selfish means to

WORD PICTURE

Flesh

The word translated *flesh* is a complex term with various meanings, depending on the context in which it is used. Elsewhere in Galatians Paul uses the word *flesh* to refer to human life in its material dimension, our physical body, or to that which is merely human as opposed to spiritual or divine (2:20; 4:29). However, throughout Gal 5–6, *flesh* is used as an ethical term with a decidedly negative connotation. *Flesh* refers to fallen human nature, the center of human pride. Flesh is the arena of indulgence and self-assertion. We cannot restrict the use of the term *flesh* to the human body, although the "works of the flesh" Paul will shortly describe (5:19–21) are manifested in connection with bodily life. Paul warns the Galatians that they must not turn their freedom into license or use it as an occasion to gratify their fleshly desires.

accomplish the greatest good. But the damage is done to the body of Christ when ministers of the gospel do not walk in the Spirit but are pulled aside by petty bickering and pride!

Jealousy. Jealousy can be used in the Bible in a good sense to describe even God Himself. But here Paul uses the word with a negative connotation. A jealous person is someone who wants what other people have. A jealous pastor looks with envious eyes on the more prosperous church field of a neighboring minister.

Outbursts of Anger. Here is another word (one word in the Greek New Testament) with various shades of meaning, depending on the context in which it is used. For example, this same word is used in Revelation to refer both to God's wrath (14:10; 19:15) and to Satan's rage (12:12). Here in Galatians, it means a passionate outburst of anger or hostile feeling.

Such displays of uncontrollable verbal violence should not be excused as a natural propensity to "fly off the handle." Such fits of rage are a form of conduct unbecoming to a Christian. They drag us away from God and the promptings of his Spirit and further enmesh us in the works of the flesh.

Selfish Ambitions. This is a term that derives from the political culture of ancient Greece, where it meant "office seeking" or "canvassing for office." Although many godly men and women have been called to live out their Christian vocation in political life, it is also true that politics attracts those persons given to self-promotion and self-service rather than the service of others. For such "political animals," climbing the ladder of success or manipulating the process for personal gain is all a part of a self-seeking lifestyle.

While the characteristics are bad enough in secular politics, they are especially corrupting to the community of faith whose Lord and Savior modeled the opposite of this vice. He came not to be served but to serve—to give his life as a ransom for many.

Dissensions. Paul used this word on only one other occasion (Rom 16:17). "Dissensions" carries political overtones suggesting the cultivation of a party spirit or exclusive elite within the church. Whenever this happens, the unity and fellowship of the body of Christ fractures. Soon the backbiting, badmouthing, and mutual destruction Paul warned the Galatians of (5:15) manifest themselves to the detriment of the life and witness of God's people.

Factions. This word also occurs only one other time in Paul's writings. In 1 Cor 11:19 Paul speaks of the various factions in the church at Corinth. The basic meaning of the word *factions* comes from the verb "to choose" (from which we also get our English word *heresy*). This verse from 1 Corinthians reminds us that the divisive tendency so evident in many congregations is the result of intentional choices to walk in the

HISTORICAL BACKGROUND

In New Testament times, drugs were used for occult purposes including, and especially, abortion. In the early church both infanticide, often effected through the exposure of newborn babies to the harsh elements, and abortion, commonly brought about by the use of drugs, were regarded as murderous acts. Both are flagrant violations of Jesus's command to "love your neighbor as yourself."

HISTORICAL BACKGROUND

Jealousy often leads to bitterness and sometimes erupts into violence, as when Joseph's brothers seized him in anger and sold him into slavery (Gen 37:12–26). At the root of all sentiments of jealousy is the basic posture of ingratitude to God, a failure to accept one's life as a gift from God. To envy what someone else has is to fling one's own gifts before God in rebellion and spite.

way of selfish pride, envy, and bickering rather than the royal road of love, forgiveness, and magnanimity.

Envy. This is another word similar in meaning to the trait of jealousy listed earlier, except that this word is plural, suggesting the multitudinous expressions of envious desire. Here in Gal 5:21 it refers to the unacceptable rivalry that had sprung up from the malice and ill will of the Galatians toward one another.

WORD PICTURE

Heresy

The English word *heresy* is a derivative of the Greek word translated here as "factions."

Sins of Intemperance (v. 21)

Drunkenness. We come now to the fourth group of sinful deeds Paul included in his catalog of the works of the flesh. There is no place for drunkenness in a Spirit-directed life. Alcohol abuse was a common feature of urban life in the Roman Empire, but Paul expected a higher standard of conduct among those who belonged to Christ.

He later wrote to the Ephesians: "Don't get drunk with wine, which leads to reckless living, but be filled by the Spirit" (Eph 5:18). In addition to the common abuse of alcohol, Paul may also have had in mind the cultic inebriation practiced by the mystery religion of Dionysus, the wine god. Some of those who were in the habit of getting drunk before participating in the Lord's Supper at Corinth may have been influenced by this pagan ritual (1 Cor 11:21). Paul portrayed excessive drinking as incompatible with real Christian commitment.

Carousing. This word is variously translated "revelings" (KJV) and "wild parties" (TLB). It occurs three times in the New Testament (here and in Rom 13:13 and 1 Pet 4:3). In each case it is linked to the sin of drunkenness. In New Testament times, as in our day, the abuse of alcohol contributed to marital infidelity, child and spouse abuse, the erosion of family life, and the moral chaos in society.

PERSONAL APPLICATION

It is supremely important that Christians learn to live together in love. When Christians forget this, two horrible consequences follow. First, the worship of the church is disrupted as the gifts of the Spirit are placed in competition with the fruit of the Spirit, as happened in Corinth. Second, the witness of the church is damaged as unbelievers stumble and fall over the obvious lack of love within the body of Christ.

A CATALOG OF EVIL

SINS OF IMMORALITY	SINS OF IDOLATRY	SINS OF ANIMOSITY	SINS OF INTEMPERANCE
Sexual immorality	Idolatry	Hatreds	Drunkenness
Moral impurity	Sorcery	Strife	Carousing
Promiscuity		Jealousy	Outbursts of anger
		Selfish ambitions	
		Dissensions	
		Factions	
		Envy	

Section Summary

Throughout Gal 5:19–21, Paul leads us down fifteen steps into the pit of depravity. He shows us the ugly reality of the flesh. He could have gone on and on as he indicates by his closing tag "and anything similar." Only divine grace, through the transforming power of the Spirit, can rescue us from the snare of such a loveless life.

NEW TESTAMENT REFERENCE

For Paul, love was foundational to everything he had and would yet say in Galatians— "I live by faith in the Son of God, who loved me and gave himself for me" (Gal 2:20). The result of the transforming, sanctifying ministry of the Holy Spirit in our lives is just this: We are enabled to love one another with the same kind of love that God loves us. Paul profiled this kind of love in 1 Cor 13.

The Fruit of the Spirit (vv. 22–26)

After listing fifteen specific misdeeds—fifteen one-word illustrations of the works of the flesh—Paul turns to consider the contrasting graces of the Spirit-controlled life.

Paul groups these nine graces into three triads that give a sense of order and completion, although there is no attempt to provide an exhaustive list of the Christian virtues.

Love. The word is used frequently by Paul. It is significant that love heads the list of these nine graces of the Christian life. Paul might well have placed a period after love and moved on to the conclusion of his letter.

Love is not merely "first among equals" in this listing but rather the source and fountain from which all of the other graces flow. Love as a characteristic of the Christian life issues from God's unfathomable love and infinite mercy toward us.

The triad love-joy-peace was a familiar watchword among the early Christians, and comparable to faith, hope, and love. Clearly these three graces cover the whole range of Christian existence.

PERSONAL APPLICATION

Gentleness

This word connotes a submissive and teachable spirit toward God that manifests itself in genuine humility and consideration toward others. It is regrettable that the English word *gentleness* has come to have the popular connotation of a wimpish weakness and nonassertive lack of vigor.

Gentleness is not incompatible with decisive action and firm convictions. It was, after all, Jesus who expelled the mercenaries from the temple because of their defilement of His Father's house. This same Jesus is meek and humble (Matt 11:29).

Section Summary

After cataloging fifteen sins that are the works of the flesh, Paul contrasts them with the fruit of the Spirit. These three triads of the Christian graces are the evidence of a Spirit-filled life.

QUESTIONS TO GUIDE YOUR STUDY

1. What are the critical contrasts between the works of the flesh and the fruit of the Spirit?
2. What did Paul mean when he said that the Galatians had "fallen from grace"?
3. Paul labels the nine Christian virtues that he describes as the "fruit of the Spirit." What are the implications of the term *fruit*?

4. How might we go about cultivating the fruit of the Spirit in our lives?

GALATIANS 6

FREEDOM IN SERVICE TO OTHERS (6:1–10)

Thus far in his exhortation, Paul has presented the case for Christian ethics—not in terms of a general theory of human behavior but as the unfolding of the principle of freedom in the life of the individual believer and that of the community to which the believer belongs.

Bearing One Another's Burdens (vv. 1–3)

Verse 1 is important in understanding the character of congregational discipline in the life of the early church. Paul returns to his favorite word of address for the Galatians: "Brothers and sisters." When Paul does this, he not only indicates a new topic to be discussed, but he also reminds his readers of his affectionate regard for them.

Much speculation surrounds the exact meaning of Paul's comment, "If someone is overtaken in any wrongdoing."

What particular transgression Paul is referring to here, we do not know. Neither can we be sure whether Paul is referring to an actual "case study" that had come to his attention or providing a general guideline for dealing with serious moral lapses among the Galatians.

Clearly, Paul is responding to a real-life situation in which concrete acts of wrongdoing, such as those he just listed among the works of the flesh (5:19–21), are involved. Paul addressed his advice to those "who are spiritual," or the "spirituals." These are Christians who walk in the Spirit, are led by the Spirit, and keep in step with the Spirit.

It is best to understand the "spirituals" in the same kind of positive sense Paul uses it in 1 Cor 2:15–3:4. There he contrasts the spiritual believers at Corinth with those who were "of the flesh," or worldly-minded. These were "baby" Christians more concerned with status and self-gratification than with the mind of Christ or service toward others.

Paul acknowledges that believers can and do sin and fall. While all sin is detestable before God and should be resisted, certain transgressors are especially hurtful to the fellowship of the church. These must be dealt with according to the canons of Christian discipline. Those who are spiritually minded and whose lives give evidence of the fruit of the Spirit have a responsibility to take the initiative in seeking restoration and reconciliation with those who have been caught in such an error.

How is this done? The lapsed brother or sister should be restored "with a gentle spirit." Here in Galatians Paul did not outline a specific

WORD PICTURE

Overtaken

The word for "overtaken" means literally to be "detected, overtaken, surprised."

WORD PICTURE

Restore

This word means "to put in order, to restore to its former condition." Elsewhere in the New Testament (Matt 4:21; Mark 1:19), this same word is used for the mending or overhauling of fishing nets. It was also part of the medical vocabulary of ancient Greece, where it meant "to set a fractured or dislocated bone."

procedure of church discipline, but he likely knew and presupposed the one given by Jesus in Matt 18:15–17.

NEW TESTAMENT REFERENCE

Mocked

This word is found nowhere else in the New Testament, although it is well attested in other Greek literature. It means literally "turn up the nose in mockery or contempt." The Old Testament references are mostly to the mocking of God's prophets. Only once is this graphic word applied to a blasphemous mocking of God Himself.

Carrying One's Own Load (vv. 4–5)

Paul tells us bluntly, "Examine [your] own work." God will not hold us accountable for the gifts he gives others. The word for *examine* is the word used for the fiery testing of gold to determine its purity. We are not to compare ourselves with "Pastor Jim," "Deacon Smith," or "Sister Jones." God wants us to bring our lives before the pages of his Holy Word.

There are two aspects of scrutiny and examination before God: (1) serious self-examination, and (2) evaluation that will be disclosed by Christ when every believer appears before his judgment seat to give an account of the stewardship of his life. This verse has important implications for Christian spirituality, and we do well to heed its message.

During many parts of his letter to the Galatians, Paul presupposes a strong orientation to the doctrine of the last days. He places the verb for the carrying of one's own load in the future tense. This placement indicates that he was thinking not merely of an individual's bearing his own responsibility here in this life but more particularly the future reckoning of every Christian before the judgment seat of Christ.

Sharing with Teachers (v. 6)

Paul introduces another practical matter of behavior as an example of spiritual responsibility.

Christians who are taught by a teacher are to contribute to that teacher's support. Paul may have feared that the mention of each person carrying his own load in verse 5 would lead the Galatians to abandon the support of those who ministered to him.

There seems to have been developing in the early church a group of teachers who gave enough time to this important task that they required some support from the congregation. Paul himself believed he had a right to support from those whom he served. He accepted help from the Philippians because they wanted to share in his ministry, but he refused support from the Corinthians because he was being accused of taking advantage of them (Phil 4:14–18; 1 Cor 9:6–18; 2 Cor 11:7–11).

WORD PICTURE

Burdens and Loads

Verses 2 and 5 seem to contradict each other. Thomas Lea points out that the two Greek words translated "burden" and "load" clarify the apparent difficulty. The term *burden* used in verse 2 describes a crushing weight or load in life. The term *load* (v. 5) was frequently used to refer to the pack of a soldier and described one of life's responsibilities which cannot be shared with another. Some burdens are so heavy, we need help with them. Other burdens we must carry ourselves.

Sowing and Reaping (vv. 7–8)

"Don't be deceived: God is not mocked. For whatever a person sows he will also reap" is a familiar and often-quoted verse. Its three statements are presented in staccato-like fashion.

Earlier Paul referred to the Galatians as "foolish" Christians upon whom some evil deceiver had "cast a spell" (3:1). Now he instructs them not to be misled in such a dangerous way. This is a strong statement that Paul uses twice in 1 Corinthians, in both cases as an introductory formula to a severe warning about immoral behavior.

Here in Galatians, the deception into which the Galatians were in danger of falling was even worse. Paul pleaded with them. God will not be mocked.

Paul moves on to apply these truths to the Galatian situation in terms of his earlier contrast of the flesh and Spirit.

If we continue to indulge in the works of the flesh, moving deeper and deeper into the pit of depravity, we can be certain of the harvest we will receive—destruction.

WORD PICTURE

Destruction

The word *destruction* conveys the idea of a corpse in the process of decomposition. The consequences of sins are nowhere more vividly seen than in the ravaging of the human body through disease, decay, and death.

Section Summary

A person who invests in the concerns of the flesh reaps destruction. A person who invests in the things of the Spirit reaps a harvest of eternal life.

Don't Quit! (vv. 9–10)

Still using the agricultural imagery of planting time and harvest, Paul admonishes his readers to persevere in the faith, knowing that at the proper time God will fulfill his promise and bring to completion all things in accordance with the good pleasure of his own divine will.

Throughout Gal 5–6 Paul instructs the Christians of Galatia to do a number of specific things: expel the agitators, love your neighbor as yourself, keep in step with the Spirit by manifesting the fruit of the Spirit in your lives, practice church discipline by restoring those who have fallen, bear one another's burdens, examine yourself in the light of the judgment seat of Christ, and provide material support for those who instruct you in the faith. In verse 9 Paul summarizes all these duties under the rubric of "doing good."

Section Summary

Paul's message to the Galatians is simply, "Don't quit!" Faced with the temptation of legalism on one hand and libertinism on the other, many of Paul's converts in Galatia were beginning to lose heart. Having begun well in the life of the Spirit, they were in danger of losing their first love—being diverted from witness and service into petty bickering and greedy self-concern. To these fatigued and spiritually exhausted Christians, Paul made his appeal: "Let us not get tired of doing good."

THE APOSTOLIC SEAL (6:11–16)

Verse 11 begins the final paragraph of Paul's letter to the Galatians. Despite its lack of personal greetings and intimate disclosures, Paul did not lose sight of his primary reason for writing his letter to the Galatians.

Paul's Autograph (v. 11)

Most scholars and commentators believe that here Paul took the stylus from the hand of his secretary and finished the letter in his own handwriting, using unusually large letters to which he drew their attention.

HISTORICAL BACKGROUND

Why did Paul write in such large letters?

Much speculation revolves around this question. Was it Paul's poor eyesight (cf. 4:15) that required him to write in this unusual manner? Or was his writing hand twisted or defective as a result of some harsh persecution he had received? Was it that he was not a professional scribe but a workman more accustomed to shaping leather and making tents than using precise penmanship? All of these are intriguing possibilities, but none can be set forth with certainty. It is likely that in addition to authenticating the letter as genuine and attesting that he had meant what he said Paul wanted to underscore and reemphasize both the central message of the letter and his own personal investment in its message.

Boasting in the Cross (vv. 12–16)

A Parting Blow (vv. 12–13). Throughout Galatians Paul waged a steady campaign against a group of false teachers, commonly known as Judaizers. These false teachers sowed great confusion among the apostle's recent converts by teaching that becoming Jewish was necessary for salvation. Paul's opponents evidently were Jewish Christian missionaries who were waging an aggressive evangelistic campaign of their own. It is not far-fetched to imagine that they had strong ties to the "mother church" at Jerusalem, especially to its ultra-legalistic wing.

In these two verses, Paul levels a dual charge against his opponents. He accuses them not only of dangerous doctrinal deviation but also of unscrupulous and unworthy motives.

Paul did not deny that there was an element of sincere and self-serving motivation among his opponents, but he did claim that there was a more sinister and self-serving motivation at work as well. These Judaizers wanted to boast and brag about how many Gentile Christians they converted into Jewish proselytes.

The Cross and the New Creation (vv. 14–16). In contrast to the false teachers, who boasted about their accomplishments and who were especially proud of their success in winning Gentile believers to the requirement of circumcision, Paul declared in the strongest possible terms that the only possible ground of his own boasting was the cross of the Lord Jesus Christ.

Paul developed the theme of boasting more than any other New Testament writer, for the kind of self-confident assertion it conveyed stood in marked contrast to the attitudes of humility called forth by divine grace. Thus, in Rom 3:21–27, immediately following his exposition of the righteousness of God that is apart from the law, Paul posed the question, "Where, then, is boasting?" His answer is dogmatic: "It is excluded."

When confronted with the amazing grace of God, the thought of self-glorification or spiritual ego-stroking vanishes.

Verse 16 is a conditional benediction: "May peace come to all those who follow this standard, and mercy even to the Israel of God!" This is no large-hearted conclusion like the one at the close of Paul's letter to the Philippians. Paul knew well that he was writing to churches caught up in intense conflict over a serious doctrinal matter.

Rather than smoothing over the difficulty in the interest of a superficial harmony, Paul did the opposite: He emphasized the sharp differences between him and his opponents and forced the Galatians to make a choice. On one side of that choice was the apostolic curse; on the other, the apostolic blessing.

Brand Marks of Jesus (v. 17)

When Paul said that he carried around in his body the death of Jesus (cf. 2 Cor 4:10), that he constantly bore the Lord's brand marks, he was referring to the actual scars of persecution and marks of physical suffering which he had received through his apostolic ministry because of his unflinching witness for the gospel.

Why did Paul mention the brand marks here at the end of his letter?

1. Paul's readers would have identified the branding of the flesh with slavery.
2. Paul's reference to the brand marks also recalls his bitter opposition to the false teachers and their penchant for "boasting" in the flesh. Paul had already said that he would boast only in the cross of the Lord Jesus Christ (v. 14). Regarding Paul's ministry, the brand marks are a seal and sure evidence of true doctrine and faith.
3. The brand marks recall the fact of Christian baptism to which Paul refers in the heart of his letter (3:26–28). We cannot and should not try to duplicate Paul's sufferings, for they were unique to his own apostolic mission. But every believer who has been baptized "into Christ" has become identified with Jesus in his sufferings no less than in the triumph of his resurrection. Baptism signals a separation from the world and a passage from the realm of Satan into the ownership of Christ.

HISTORICAL BACKGROUND

Slaves in the ancient world frequently were marked with the insignia of their master as a badge of identification. Paul was saying, "Look, I too have been branded! I am a slave of my faithful Savior Jesus Christ."

Section Summary

In this final paragraph of his letter, Paul summarizes the main themes which he has pursued throughout his letter. He did not lose sight of his primary reason—to win the Galatians back from the brink of apostasy to a full-orbed faith in the one and only gospel of Jesus Christ.

BENEDICTION (6:18)

Paul had already provided a benediction of peace in verse 16. Here he concludes his letter with a second benediction. This one was a prayer for the grace of the Lord Jesus Christ to be with the Galatians, whom he again called his brothers. Paul began his letter with a customary salutation of grace (1:3), and he closed it with this same formula, pointing to the central theme that had been his primary concern throughout the epistle. This is a fitting conclusion to such a tumultuous letter. It is as though Paul is saying to the Galatians:

Dear brothers, in writing to you in this way, I have put it all on the line. Now you know exactly the burden of my heart. I will end the letter as I began it, commending to you the awesome and marvelous grace of our Lord Jesus Christ. The only thing left for me to do is to pray from my heart that Christ will confirm my labors among you, restoring you to the truth of the gospel and granting you the gift of perseverance unto life eternal. So may it be. Amen!

QUESTIONS TO GUIDE YOUR STUDY

1. Paul contrasted those who were "fleshly" with those who were "spiritual." What did Paul mean by "spiritual"?
2. What does it mean to "restore" a brother who has lapsed into sin?
3. Describe Paul's principle of reaping and sowing. How does he specifically apply it to the situation at Galatia?
4. What did Paul mean by boasting in the cross? How did he contrast his boasting to that of the false teachers?

Ephesians

INTRODUCTION

Ephesians is a special New Testament book. Here the teachings of Paul find their highest expression in a sweeping summary of his faith. This letter to the Christians at Ephesus is the one that best sets out the basic concepts of the Christian faith. An insightful and powerful book, Ephesians is both devotional and theological, holding a place all its own among Paul's New Testament letters.

EPHESIANS IN A NUTSHELL

Purpose:	To emphasize the unity of the church in Christ through the power of the Spirit
Major Doctrine:	Re-creation of the human family as God originally intended it
Key Passage:	Ephesians 1:10: "To bring everything together in Christ, both things in heaven and things on earth in him."
Other Key Doctrines:	Predestination, reconciliation, and union with Christ

AUTHOR

Paul the apostle referred to himself as the author in two places in the letter: 1:1 and 3:1. Some scholars think Ephesians contains a writing style, vocabulary, and even some teachings that are not typical of the apostle Paul. Yet others regard the book of Ephesians as the crown of all of Paul's writings. In line with the undisputed acceptance of Pauline authorship in the early church, we can conclude that there is no reason to dispute Paul as author of Ephesians.

Paul was the outstanding missionary and writer of the early church. Both he and his theology are important in the New Testament not only because thirteen epistles bear his name but also because of the extended biographical information given in the book of Acts. From the information in these two sources, we can piece together a picture of one of the major personalities of early Christianity. The letters of Paul, as listed in the New Testament, include Romans through Philemon. His experience of radical change and call to proclaim the gospel to the Gentiles provided his motivation to travel throughout the Roman world, preaching the way of Christ.

PURPOSE FOR WRITING

Paul wrote most of his letters to meet specific needs in the churches, but it is difficult to determine the specific occasion for which Ephesians was written.

The letter itself, however, hints at several purposes. The apostle taught that Jewish and Gentile believers are one in Christ. This oneness is to be demonstrated by their love for one another. Paul used the noun form of the verb "to love" (*agapē*) nineteen times (about one-sixth of the total uses in all of Paul's letters). Ephesians begins with love (1:4–6) and ends with love (6:23–24).

Ephesians is a general statement of Christian truth concerning the church, Christian unity, and the Christian walk. The understanding of this truth is as necessary for the church today as it was in Paul's day.

DATE AND PLACE OF WRITING

Interpreters are divided on the question of the time and place of the writing of Ephesians. Paul's imprisonments in Acts 21:15–26:32 and 27:1–28:31 are the only ones that might bear on the question of where and when the Prison Epistles (Ephesians, Colossians, Philemon, Philippians) were written. In all four of these letters, Paul mentioned his imprisonment.

Date. The traditional view is that Ephesians was written during the early sixties (60–62). References in Eph 6:21–22 suggest that Tychicus carried the letter to its destination.

Place. Careful review of this extensive and complex issue leaves the subjective opinion that all four Prison Epistles were written from Rome while Paul was imprisoned there about AD 60–62.

AUDIENCE

Despite the traditional heading (1:1), relatively little is known about the recipients of the letter who are called "Ephesians." Several important and early manuscripts do not contain the words "at Ephesus" (v. 1).

Some interpreters have suggested that Ephesians was originally a circular letter, sent perhaps to churches throughout Asia. The church at Ephesus kept a copy of this letter without an address. As time passed, readers outside Ephesus might have assumed that Ephesus received the letter initially. The hypothesis of a circular letter, though not without problems, provides the most logical explanation of the omission of "at Ephesus" from the greetings of the letter.

HISTORICAL BACKGROUND

Tychicus

Tychicus, whose name means "fortunate," was one of Paul's fellow workers in the ministry. Tychicus and Onesimus carried the Colossian letter from Paul; they were also the bearers of this letter to Ephesus. Tradition holds that Tychicus died a martyr.

PAUL'S MINISTRY AT EPHESUS

At the close of his second missionary journey (ca. AD 49–52), Paul left Achaia (Greece), taking Aquila and Priscilla with him. They stopped at Ephesus and surveyed the situation in that city where religions flourished. The Ephesians urged Paul to stay, but he declined. Leaving Aquila and Priscilla and perhaps Timothy there to carry on the Christian witness (Acts 18:18–21), Paul sailed to Antioch. He returned to Ephesus during a third missionary journey and experienced triumph over the challenge of Jewish religious leaders as well as that of the Greco-Roman religions represented in the worship of the Greek goddess Artemis (Roman name, Diana; Acts 19:24).

Paul's ministry in Ephesus lasted three years (Acts 20:31). From there he journeyed to Jerusalem, where he was arrested by the Jews and turned over to the Romans.

STRUCTURE OF THE LETTER

Ephesians follows the pattern common to Paul's letters—discussing doctrine in the first half, followed by practice in the second half. The content of Ephesians falls naturally into two divisions:

1. Chapters 1–3 discuss the spiritual privileges of the church, spelling out the great Christian truths of experience and belief.
2. Chapters 4–6 present the responsibilities of believers in their Christian walk in light of the truths of the first three chapters.

Unique Features of Ephesians. Although Ephesians and Colossians contain many similarities, it is important to observe the distinctives of Ephesians. When the content of Ephesians that is common to Colossians is removed, units of material that are unique to Ephesians remain, (See the chart "Comparing Ephesians and Colossians" on p. 607.)

DISTINCTIVES IN EPHESIANS

PASSAGE	TOPIC
1:3–14	An expanded benediction
2:1–10	A confessional statement on the new life
3:14–21	A prayer to understand the mystery of Christ
4:1–16	An extended exhortation to Christian unity
5:8–14	A section on walking in the light
5:23–32	A theological expansion on the household roles
6:10–17	A unique picture of the Christian's spiritual warfare

LITERARY FEATURES IN EPHESIANS

A Comparison of Ephesians and Colossians. The salutation and structure of Ephesians are similar to Colossians. Many of the same topics are treated in both letters, and the message is strikingly similar. Of the 155 verses in Ephesians, more than half contain expressions identical with those in Colossians. While Colossians is abrupt, argumentative, and seemingly compressed, Ephesians presents a bigger, finished picture that is meditative, instructive, and expansive.

THE THEOLOGY OF EPHESIANS

Doctrinal Emphasis

Central to the message of Ephesians is the re-creation of the human family according to God's original intention. The new creation destroys the misguided view of some people that God accepts the Jew and rejects the Gentile. Paul claimed that this distinction was abolished at Christ's sacrificial death. Thus, a hindrance no longer remains to reuniting all humanity as the people of God, with Christ as the head (1:22–23). The new body—the church—has been endowed by the power of the Holy Spirit to enable them to live out their new life (1:3–2:10) and put into practice the new standards (4:1–6:9).

Theological Significance of Paul's Letter to the Ephesians

This letter lifts its readers to a new vantage point from which they are united with the risen and ascended Christ. Believers are not to have a limited or merely earthly perspective. When we view life from the heavenly realms (1:3), we can understand that the church's strength is not in human resources but in the grace and strength of God.

The church, God's people, does not function just to carry out routine activities. It reveals the wisdom of God and proclaims the rich redemption provided by Jesus Christ (1:3–11; 3:2–13). This grand letter gives us a purpose for living in line with God's history (1:10). This is accomplished as we live in submission to Christ, the head of the church, and indeed the supreme authority over all things (1:22).

THE RELEVANCE OF EPHESIANS FOR BELIEVERS TODAY

Ephesians has been called the most modern of all the New Testament writings. The breadth and depth of its doctrinal teachings make it a lively source of ideas for every situation. Its emphasis on the inclusive nature of the church makes it a rich source of inspiration and challenge for churches of any age.

Christ for the Whole Universe

Ephesians is one of the major sources for our vision of Christ as the Lord of all creation. Although New Testament writers could not have envisioned our modern technology, they had no doubt that Christ was big enough to be Lord of the entire creation. He was "far above every ruler and authority, power and dominion, and every title given, not only in this age but also in the one to come. And he subjected everything under his feet and appointed him as head over everything for the church" (Eph 1:21–22).

Ephesians rekindles our vision of the church as the body of Christ in which gifts are recognized and leaders equip people for the work of the ministry.

The Nature and Purpose of the Church

No biblical book provides a higher view of the church than Ephesians, and none has had a greater impact on modern church life and theory.

Bringing Together a Divided World

From Ephesians we learn that God's plan is "to bring everything together in Christ" (Eph 1:10). Paul's letter sets forth a church in which both Jews and Gentiles join in one faith, serving one Lord. Paul's message of peace and unified purpose in Christ is both relevant and pertinent to the modern world.

A Sense of Calling

Ephesians challenges its readers to their best with Paul's exhortation to "walk worthy of the calling you have received" (4:1). Institutions, organizations, and individuals often lack a sense of purpose. Even churches sometimes languish because they lack a compelling goal. The view of life offered by Ephesians is a powerful motivation for believers to get involved in what God is doing in the world.

Worthy Living

In today's pluralistic culture where moral values are widely questioned and abandoned, Ephesians describes Christian living as walking in the light amid a world of darkness. It presents a radically different lifestyle for Christians and describes appropriate patterns of behavior in detail.

QUESTIONS TO GUIDE YOUR STUDY

1. What prompted Paul to write his letter to the Ephesians?
2. What was Paul's goal for this letter?
3. What is the major doctrine of this letter? What are some of its other themes?
4. What is the relevance of Ephesians to the believer today?

BASIC OUTLINE FOR EPHESIANS

I. Introduction (1:1–2)
II. God's Purposes in Christ (1:3–3:21)
III. God's Purposes in the Church (4:1–6:20)
IV. Conclusion (6:21–24)

EPHESIANS 1

In this first chapter, Paul focused on the spiritual blessings Christians have because they are in Christ. The chapter breaks down into two major sections: (1) the blessings of the believer in Christ, and (2) Paul's prayer that believers might understand these blessings and the power they can bring to one's life.

The opening words of the letter to the Ephesians are in the standard form for letters in New Testament times. This form is known as the *Hellenistic letter.*

SALUTATION (1:1–2)

Paul introduced himself by name and calling. In his salutation, he offered greetings in the manner common to all his letters.

Name. The author declared himself to be Paul, which scholars take as a reference to the apostle Paul. Tradition supports Paul as author, and many scholars see 6:20 as internal evidence pointing to Paul. A unique feature of this salutation is the absence of any mention of Paul's companions. Usually, Paul included the names of those who were accompanying him at the time of writing.

Calling. Paul referred to himself as an "apostle." This term describes "one who is sent." It is what we would call a missionary. His reference

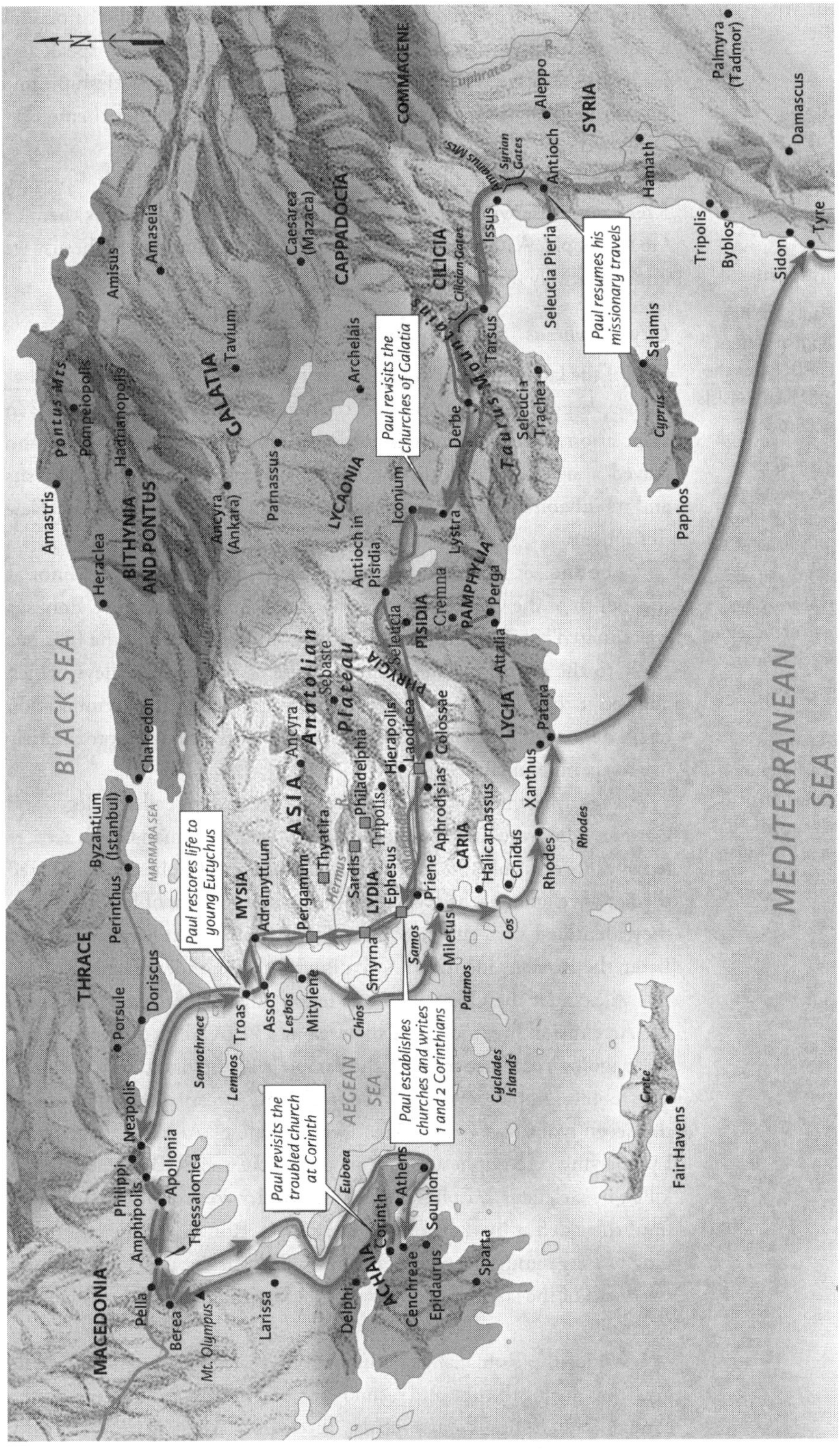
BLACK SEA
MEDITERRANEAN SEA
AEGEAN SEA
MARMARA SEA
MACEDONIA
THRACE
ACHAIA
MYSIA
ASIA
LYDIA
CARIA
LYCIA
PHRYGIA
PISIDIA
PAMPHYLIA
LYCAONIA
GALATIA
BITHYNIA AND PONTUS
CAPPADOCIA
CILICIA
COMMAGENE
SYRIA
Anatolian Plateau
Pontus Mts.
Taurus Mountains
Amanus Mts.
Cilician Gates
Syrian Gates
Euphrates R.
Hermus
Mt. Olympus
Paul revisits the troubled church at Corinth
Paul establishes churches and writes 1 and 2 Corinthians
Paul restores life to young Eutychus
Paul revisits the churches of Galatia
Paul resumes his missionary travels
Pella
Berea
Larissa
Amphipolis
Thessalonica
Philippi
Apollonia
Neapolis
Porsule
Doriscus
Perinthus
Byzantium (Istanbul)
Chalcedon
Heraclea
Amastris
Amisus
Amaseia
Pompeiopolis
Hadrianopolis
Tavium
Ancyra (Ankara)
Parnassus
Archelais
Caesarea (Mazaca)
Delphi
Corinth
Cenchreae
Epidaurus
Sparta
Athens
Sounion
Euboea
Samothrace
Lemnos
Lesbos
Chios
Samos
Patmos
Cyclades Islands
Crete
Fair Havens
Troas
Assos
Mitylene
Adramyttium
Pergamum
Thyatira
Sardis
Smyrna
Ephesus
Philadelphia
Tripolis
Hierapolis
Laodicea
Colossae
Aphrodisias
Priene
Miletus
Halicarnassus
Cnidus
Cos
Rhodes
Xanthus
Patara
Attalia
Perga
Cremna
Seleucia
Sebaste
Ancyra
Antioch in Pisidia
Iconium
Lystra
Derbe
Seleucia Trachea
Tarsus
Issus
Antioch
Seleucia Pieria
Aleppo
Hamath
Cyprus
Paphos
Salamis
Tripolis
Byblos
Sidon
Tyre
Damascus
Palmyra (Tadmor)
N

to his apostleship served two purposes: (1) it identified him as one on a mission from Christ, and (2) it pointed to his authority to speak as a leader. Because he was an apostle "by God's will," his apostleship came not through any human agent. The will of God is a major theme that Paul expands upon in his letter.

Paul's Readers. Paul addressed his letter to the "saints" in Ephesus. *Saints are* those who are "set apart for God," which designates them as God's people. As for the demographics of the church at Ephesus, we know relatively little.

WORD PICTURE

The Hellenistic Letter

Generally, Paul's epistles follow the normal pattern of the Hellenistic letter, the basic form of which consists of five major sections:

1. Opening (sender, addressee, greeting)
2. Thanksgiving or blessing (often with prayer of intercession, well wishes, or personal greetings)
3. The burden of the letter (including citation of classical sources and arguments)
4. Parenesis (ethical instruction, and exhortation)
5. Closing (mention of personal plans, mutual friends, and benediction)

City of Ephesus

One of the largest and most impressive cities in the ancient world, Ephesus was a political, religious, and commercial center in Asia Minor. In association with the ministries of Paul, Timothy and the apostle John played a significant role in the spread of early Christianity. Ephesus and its inhabitants are mentioned more than twenty times in the New Testament.

The ancient city of Ephesus was located in western Asia Minor at the mouth of the Cayster River and was an important seaport. Ephesus was situated between the Maeander River to the south and the Hermus River to the north; it had excellent access to both river valleys, which allowed it to flourish as a commercial center. Due to the accumulation of silt deposited by the river, the present site of the city is approximately five to six miles inland.

The earliest inhabitants of Ephesus were groups called Leleges and Carians, who were driven out around 1000 BC by Ionian Greek settlers led by Androclus of Athens. The new inhabitants of Ephesus assimilated the native religion of the area, the worship of a goddess of fertility whom they identified with the Greek goddess Artemis—the virgin huntress. Later, the Romans identified Artemis with their goddess Diana.

Alexander the Great, who was reportedly born on the same day as the Artemision fire, took over the area in 334 BC. His offer to finance the ongoing reconstruction of the temple was diplomatically declined. The rebuilt temple, completed about 250 BC, became known as one of the seven wonders of the ancient world. One of Alexander's generals, Lysimachus, ruled Ephesus from about 301 BC to 281 BC, when he was killed by Seleucus I. Ephesus remained under control of the Seleucids until their defeat by the Romans in 189 BC. Rome gave the city to the king of Pergamum as a reward for his military assistance. In 133 BC, at the death of the last Pergamum ruler, the city came under direct Roman control.

Under the Romans, Ephesus thrived, reaching the pinnacle of its greatness during the first and second centuries of the Christian era. At the time of Paul, Ephesus was probably the fourth largest city in the world, with a population of about 250,000. During the reign of the emperor Hadrian, Ephesus was designated the capital of the Roman province of Asia. The grandeur of the ancient city is evident in the remains uncovered by archaeologists, including the ruins of the Artemision, the civic agora, the temple of Domitian, gymnasiums, public baths, a theater with seating for twenty-four thousand people, a library, and the commercial agora, as well as several streets and private residences. Also discovered were the head and forearm of a huge statue of the emperor Domitian. Today, the Turkish town of Seljuk occupies the site of ancient Ephesus.

WORD PICTURE

"*Blessed* is the God . . . who has *blessed* us with every spiritual *blessing*" (v. 3).

The word translated "bless" is a compound of two words: "well" and "a word." Its literal, root meaning is "to speak well of." Paul uses a form of this word three times in verse 3, as noted by A. T. Robertson. "Paul lovingly plays with the idea. The believer is a citizen of heaven and the spiritual blessings count the most for *him*" "Epistles of Paul," *(Word Pictures in the New Testament,* vol. 4, 517). When we address this word toward God, it is an acknowledgment of his attribute of goodness.

Section Summary

Paul identified himself by name and calling. He offered greetings in the manner common to his letters. Absent is the usual mention of Paul's companions. Also absent in the earlier manuscript copies of Ephesians is the address "at Ephesus."

BLESSINGS IN CHRIST (1:3–14)

God the Father's Purpose (vv. 3–6)

Paul began his letter with a great statement of praise to God for his blessings in Christ. This section is one long sentence in the original text, made up of carefully balanced clauses. This extended benediction surveys the redemptive activity of the triune God. The grand theme of this section is God's eternal purpose in history (v. 9). Some have seen here a hymn of three stanzas: vv. 3–6, vv. 7–12, and vv. 13–14, with each stanza concluding with a reference to the praise of God's glorious grace.

We are blessed with spiritual blessings "in Christ" (v. 3).

The expression "in Christ" occurs some thirty-five times in Ephesians. The motive behind God's plan is love. His loving purpose aims at personal relationship.

God has chosen us (vv. 3–4).

To "choose" means to "call out, select." God has claimed those in Christ for himself and his own purpose. Commenting on this passage, A. T. Robertson says that it is a "definitive statement of God's elective grace concerning believers in Christ" ("Epistles of Paul," *WPNT,* vol. 4, 517). Although this is difficult to comprehend, God has chosen us to be his own.

WORD PICTURE

Chose

The word Paul uses here—"chose"—is a compound word in the original text. It is made up of the preposition "out of" prefixed to the verb "to call, say, or tell." It is translated "to pick out, select."

Given the grammatical elements of the word in this context, it means that God *himself* chose us.

God has adopted us (v. 5).

Here the use of *adoption* is a family concept. It involves the placing of a family member into the privileges and blessings of adulthood.

God has graciously favored us (v. 6).

Although unacceptable to God by our own merits, God has accepted us through Christ. Paul declared, "To the praise of his glorious grace that he lavished on us in the Beloved One." God has generously favored us by giving many provisions of his grace.

Section Summary

Paul began by discussing the blessings of Christ as they relate to God the Father's purposes. He chose us before the creation of the world to be adopted and accepted through his Son Jesus Christ.

HISTORICAL BACKGROUND

Adoption

Regarding the New Testament concept of adoption, William Barclay said, "The person who had been adopted had all the rights of a legitimate son in his new family and completely lost all rights in his old family. In the eyes of the law, he was a new person. So new was he that even all debts and obligations connected with his previous family were abolished as if they had never existed. That is what Paul says that God has done for us." *The Letter to the Galatians and Ephesians* (Westminster, 1976), 80.

God the Son's Accomplishments (vv. 7–10)

In this section we see three of the greatest concepts of the Christian faith:

- Deliverance from the penalty of sin
- Forgiveness of sins
- Understanding of the will of God

Christ has redeemed us (v. 7a).

Redemption is a term that occurs throughout the Old Testament. The idea of redemption is vitally related to the themes of liberation, deliverance, and ransom. Within this model we see a struggle between the kingdom of God and the hostile powers enslaving humankind. Redemption is the idea of bringing sinners out of hostile bondage into authentic freedom (Col 2:15). As Redeemer, Jesus breaks the power of sin and creates a new and obedient heart by delivering us from the powers of sin, guilt, death, and Satan. He brings about a people who have been bought with a price (1 Pet 1:18–19).

Christ has forgiven us (7b).

The word for *forgiveness* means "to send forth, send away." It refers to the removal of a person's sins. This word for "trespasses" is the term for false steps or a deviation from the right.

Christ has revealed God's will to us (vv. 8–10).

This passage reaches its high point as Paul reveals what God has made known in Christ. It is the "mystery of his will." *Mystery* was a word common to Paul's readers. In the first century, cults known as mystery religions were built around secret spiritual lore known only to a few people. Some of these religions advanced the idea that salvation was offered to a select few who shared in their special knowledge. Paul countered this teaching in this letter and in his letter to the Colossians.

The mystery Paul spoke of is not something hidden but something "made known." It was a mystery in the sense that it was previously unknown. It could only be known by a revelation from God. In Christ, such a revelation is available. The content of the mystery was the will and purpose of God. This purpose was set forth in Christ. Apart from Christ, the contents of the mystery could not be known. Only as people receive Christ and begin to see life in the light of his revelation do they realize what God is working to accomplish in human lives.

In describing the believer's understanding of the mystery of God's will, Paul used two synonymous terms. Although similar in meaning, these terms were distinguished by Paul's Greek readers:

- *Wisdom* is the ability to see into the heart of things and understand them. It is the knowledge that satisfies the intellect.
- *Understanding* is insight that leads to wise action. It enables a person to handle the day-to-day problems of practical life and living.

Paul explained that God's making known the mystery of his will is part of his pursuing a plan for "the right time" (v. 10). God will accomplish his strategy when the time is right.

God plans to unite all things in Christ. When the time is right, God will "bring everything together in Christ, both things in heaven and things on earth in him" (v. 10). Paul declared that all of reality—physical and spiritual—will be included in the unity of Christ.

WORD PICTURE

The Right Time

The word Paul used for "time" *(kairos)* speaks of a particular time of opportunity, not simply the passing of days and years.

Christ has made us an inheritance (vv. 11–12).

Verse 11 reads, "In him we have also received an inheritance." The word Paul used here literally means "we were *made* an inheritance" (emphasis added). Not only has God given us an inheritance in Christ (1 Pet 1:3–4); he has also given us as an inheritance for Christ! The church is his body and bride and will share in his glory.

WORD PICTURE

To Bring Everything Together

The phrase "to bring together" is only one word in the original text, but it is loaded with meaning. It refers to the process of gathering something together to present as a whole. In the New Testament, it is used only here and in Rom 13:9, where Paul summed up the Commandments into one rule: "Love your neighbor as yourself."

Section Summary

The believer's blessings in Christ include the Son's redemptive work. The believer has been redeemed and forgiven by Christ. Through him, God's will is revealed. As his body, temple, and bride, Christ also has made us an inheritance that he will someday claim for himself.

God the Spirit's Ministry (vv. 13–14)

The sealing of the Spirit occurs at the time of believing: "When you heard the word of truth" (v. 13). Those "also . . . sealed" (v. 13) were the Gentiles. Paul's change of pronouns from "we" to "you" indicates that he was referring to second-generation converts of the Christian message—Gentiles.

WORD PICTURE

Down Payment

This is a word of Semitic origin (possibly Phoenician). It has a common use in the papyri as earnest money in a purchase for a cow or for a wife (a dowry). In the New Testament, the word appears only in 2 Cor 1:22 and Eph 1:14. "It is a part payment on the total obligation, and we use the very expression today, 'earnest money.' It is God, says Paul, who has done all this for us and the Spirit is God's pledge that He is sincere. This earnest deposit of the Spirit in our hearts is the witness of the Spirit that we are God's." A. T. Robertson, "Epistles of Paul," *WPNT,* vol. 4, 214.

The Spirit has given us a down payment (v. 14).

Down payment is a business term used for money given as a deposit for a purchase. Because we as believers have not entered our final salvation, God has given us the Holy Spirit as a deposit, a down payment, to assure us that the "goods" will be delivered. Through the Spirit we have an advance experience of what we will have fully in heaven.

Section Summary

The blessings in Christ involve the ministry of God the Spirit. The Spirit has sealed us, ensuring God's ownership of us. The Spirit is also our earnest, our down payment on the fulfillment of salvation that is yet to come.

THE BELIEVER'S BLESSINGS IN CHRIST

BLESSING	EXPLANATION
Chosen (v. 4)	God claims those in Christ for himself and his own purpose.
Adopted (v. 5)	The placing of a family member into the privileges and blessings of adulthood.
Lavished on (v. 6)	The grace of God freely given to those in Christ.
Redeemed (v. 7)	The purchase of our deliverance was made at a great cost: "through his blood."
Forgiven (v. 7)	The removal of one's sins.
Made known God's will to us (v. 9)	What God has made known in Christ.
Received an inheritance (v. 11)	God has given those in Christ as an inheritance for Christ, and they will share in his glory.
Sealed (v. 13)	God owns those in Christ and will keep them.
Gave the Holy Spirit as a down payment (v. 14)	God has given the Holy Spirit as a guarantee of the future glory to come.

HISTORICAL BACKGROUND

The Spirit Has Sealed Us (v. 13)

A seal was a mark, perhaps on wax, which showed that a letter or a delivery was authentic and had been delivered intact. "Seals were used as a guarantee indicating not only ownership but also to guarantee the correctness of the contents (see 2 Cor 1:22)." (Fritz Rienecker, *Linguistic Key to the Greek New Testament* [Zondervan, 1980], 523). Sealing means that God owns us and will keep us.

PAUL'S PRAYER FOR HIS READERS (1:15–23)

Paul's entire letter to the Ephesians was written within the framework of prayer. This section functions as an extended prayer.

Paul's Reason for Praying (vv. 15–16)

Although Paul may not have known his readers personally, he heard of their faith and love, perhaps through Epaphras, as in Col 1:4–8. Whatever Paul's relationship with these Christians, he prayed for them in this passage. His prayers were continuous and intense, characterized by thanksgiving.

PAUL'S PRAYER REQUESTS

REQUEST	STATEMENT
1. That his readers might know that God had called them to a great hope (v. 18)	"What is the hope of his calling"
2. That his readers might know the quality and extent of their blessings in Christ (v. 18)	"What is the wealth of his glorious inheritance"
3. That his readers might understand and experience the power of God (v. 19)	"What is the immeasurable greatness of his power"

Paul's Prayer for His Readers' Understanding (vv. 17–19)

Paul's prayer was addressed to God in his relation to Jesus Christ as in 1:3. He further described him as "the glorious Father." This is in line with Paul's emphasis in this chapter on the fullness and richness of God's nature and blessings.

In his prayer, we see three objects of the knowledge Paul desired for his readers. Paul introduced the content of each request with the words "what is." As A. T. Robertson commented, "Note three indirect questions after 'to know' (what is the hope, riches, and surpassing greatness). When the Holy Spirit opens the eyes of the heart, one will be able to see all these great truths." "Epistles of Paul," *WPNT*, vol. 4, 521.

Paul made three requests for the Ephesian believers:

1. *He wanted them to know that God called them to a great hope (v. 18).* Paul emphasized the origin of their calling and urged them to take part in it.
2. *He wanted them to realize the quality and the extent of the blessings they had in Christ (v. 18).* Paul has already described these blessings as an inheritance (v. 14). That they are an inheritance emphasizes the fact that they are received as a gift and already guaranteed, even though they are not yet fully bestowed upon believers.
3. *He wanted them to understand and experience the power of God (v. 19).* God's power is unlimited—a concept we cannot fully understand. What Paul wanted to convey to his readers is that God is at work in the life of a Christian in a powerful way. By piling up four synonyms for strength, Paul strained the limits of language to suggest something that cannot be put into words.

PERSONAL APPLICATION

Being aware of our calling, our blessing, and our empowerment will impact the way we live every day.

SYNONYMS FOR POWER IN EPHESIANS 1:19

ENGLISH TERM	GREEK WORD	EXPANDED MEANING
Power	*dunameōs*	Inherent ability; ability to perform anything
Working	*energeian*	The effectual working of ability
Mighty	*kratous*	Strength in relation to an end to be gained or dominion to be exercised
Strength	*ischuos*	Strength that a person has; power in possession, ability, or latent power

What God Has Done for Us in Christ (vv. 20–23)

The mention of God's great power in verse 19 led Paul to expound upon the greatest demonstration of that power—the *resurrection.* When Old Testament writers spoke of God's power, they referred to the Exodus from Egypt and the creation of the world. New Testament writers, however, pointed to the resurrection. Paul referred to this in Phil 3:10 as "the power of his resurrection."

As a result of his resurrection, Jesus is now enthroned at the right hand of God, a position of greatest honor and authority. God has put all powers in existence at his feet. Christ is now the head of all things.

PERSONAL APPLICATION

Think about the tremendous power and creativity that transformed Jesus's lifeless body into a body that transcends space as we know it and can never be again subject to death. What difference does it make to realize that this same power is with you?

In verse 22 we have the first use of the word *church* in Ephesians. Paul declared that Christ is the head of the church. Not only is Christ the church's guide and authority, but Paul explained that Christ and his church exist in an organic unity. Paul closed this chapter by describing the church as "his body, the fullness of the one who fills all things in every way." Although interpreted variously, this statement seems to mean that Christ fills everything and that God wants the church to be the full expression of Christ.

Section Summary

Paul prayed for his readers and made three requests on their behalf: (1) he wanted them to know that God had called them to a great hope; (2) he wanted them to realize the quality and the extent of the blessings they had in Christ; and (3) he wanted them to have an understanding and experience of the power of God.

QUESTIONS TO GUIDE YOUR STUDY

1. In what sense does God choose Christians? What does this tell us about God's true character?
2. The grand theme of verses 3–14 is God's eternal purpose in history (v. 9). How does each of God's spiritual blessings help accomplish that purpose?
3. Paul prayed for his readers. What is the content of his requests on their behalf?
4. In verse 19 Paul used four synonyms to describe God's strength. What does each contribute to our understanding? What idea or ideas do these collectively convey to the reader?
5. What is the greatest demonstration of God's power? Why is it the greatest?

EPHESIANS 2

Paul will return to his theme of the church in 2:11, but in the first section of this chapter he describes the work of Christ in the lives of God's people. Verses 1–10 are one long sentence in the original Greek text, bringing together all of Paul's teachings about grace, faith, and the Christian life.

FROM DEATH TO LIFE (2:1–10)

Dead in Sin (vv. 1–3)

Paul explained that those who are now alive in Christ were not always alive. A look at their former lives would show that they did not have life at all. The tense of the Greek verb for "previously walked" summarizes one's total past life as a point. The sum of their past spiritual experience was death.

Paul outlined several characteristics of the past walk of believers:

They were dead in their "trespasses and sins" (v. 1).

"Trespasses" and "sins" are close synonyms but with different backgrounds. *Trespasses* indicates wrong steps taken or a deliberate breaking of the law. To *sin* means "to miss the mark." Paul used these two words together for emphasis by repetition. The sins he speaks of here are not mere isolated acts; they speak of a way of life or a pattern of conduct in which these people walked.

WORD PICTURE

Previously Walked

"Walked" is a compound word made up of the preposition "around" and the verb "to walk." "Figuratively, it signifies the whole round of activities of the individual life, whether of the unregenerate (Eph 4:17), or of the believer, 1 Cor 7:17; Col 2:6." (*Vine's Complete Expository Dictionary of Old and New Testament Words* [Thomas Nelson, 1996], 664). Life is a walk, an active process that moves along step-by-step.

DEAD IN SIN, ALIVE IN CHRIST

DEAD IN SIN	ALIVE IN CHRIST
"You were dead in your trespasses and sins." (Eph 2:1)	"God . . . made us alive with Christ even though we were dead in trespasses." (Eph 2:4–5)
"You previously walked according to the ways of this world." (Eph 2:2)	"We are [God's] workmanship, created in Christ Jesus for good works, which God prepared ahead of time for us to [walk in]." (Eph 2:10)
"You previously walked . . . according to the ruler of the power of the air, the spirit now working in the disobedient." (Eph 2:2)	"In the coming ages [God] might display the immeasurable riches of his grace through his kindness to us in Christ Jesus." (Eph 2:7)
"We were by nature children under wrath." (Eph 2:3)	"You are saved by grace! . . . This is not from yourselves; it is God's gift—not from works, so that no one can boast." (Eph 2:5,8b–9)
"We too all previously lived among them in our fleshly desires, carrying out the inclinations of our flesh and thoughts." (Eph 2:3a)	"He also raised us up with him and seated us with him in the heavens in Christ Jesus." (Eph 2:6)

They followed the ways of this world (v. 2).

Powerful factors influenced their deadly walk. First, the "ways of this world" describes the present world order and its present course. The pressures of society and culture led them away from God.

They were disobedient (v. 2).

There is a superhuman, spiritual power of evil that generates a spirit of disobedience in people. He is Satan, called here the "ruler of the power of the air" (v. 2). *Air* refers to the spiritual realm. It is important to note that the disobedience Paul mentioned here is our own choice and not simply the effect of Satan on the ways of the world.

They gratified the desires of their sinful nature (v. 3).

An important part of our disobedience is rooted in our own sinful desires. These desires originate in our lower, sinful nature. Paul emphasized that this sinful nature involves both the physical body *and* the mind: "inclinations . . . and thoughts."

Throughout this passage, Paul emphasized that we all once lived in the way described above: "We were by nature children under wrath" (v. 3). What he described here is true of every person, Jew or Gentile.

Section Summary

Paul described the human condition and how all people were dead in their trespasses and sins. They were controlled by their own selfish desires and cut off from the life of God. As a result, men and women apart from Christ were without life, without freedom, and without hope.

The Riches of God's Grace (vv. 4–7)

Against the dark and hopeless background which he described in verses 1–3, Paul changed the entire landscape with the words "but God"! These words signal God's intervention into our hopeless, sinful condition. If it were left up to humankind, there would only be death. But God is not a God of wrath only; he is also a God of mercy. He is "rich in mercy," and his mercy is rooted in his "great love . . . for us."

God shows us his mercy by what he has done in Christ. Believers are brought to life from a state of death. Then they are raised to the presence of God and seated "in the heavens"—or the spiritual realm. In verses 5–7, Paul considered the riches of God's grace.

"Made us alive with Christ" (v. 5).

Christ gives us new life through his resurrection. The word translated "made us alive" is a synonym for "raised," but it also can mean "to keep alive" or "to preserve life." Through Christ, believers are quickened and granted a new spiritual life. (For more on this subject, see Rom 6:1–10.)

"Raised us up with him" (v. 6).

Believers have been raised together with Christ; that is, they have been united with him in his resurrected life.

"Seated us with him" (v. 6).

Believers sit together with Christ in the heavenly realms. Although believers have yet to be physically resurrected and seated in the heavenlies, spiritually speaking, it has already been accomplished.

Section Summary

By his grace God grants new life to believers. The basis for the new life is God's great love and mercy. Believers have been reunited with Christ in his resurrected life. Formerly, people apart from Christ were dead, enslaved, and objects of wrath. In Christ, believers are now alive, enthroned, and objects of God's grace.

"Saved . . . Through Faith" (vv. 8–9)

This passage is one of the best summaries of the gospel in the New Testament. It contains many key themes Paul developed elsewhere in his

WORD PICTURE

With

Each of the verbs for "made us alive," "raised us," and "seated us" is a compound word. All three have the prepositional prefix "with." God has raised us up with Christ. What happened to Christ will happen to us as we enter into union with him in Christ. The believer's resurrection, ascension, and enthronement must await complete fulfillment in the resurrection of the body at the end of time, but spiritually this has already happened. Those who are in Christ by faith already share in his fellowship with God.

writings, but here he expressed them in a new way to communicate to a wide audience in the Gentile world.

In verses 8–10, Paul focused on three themes:

Grace. The word "grace" occurs twelve times in Ephesians. To the people of Paul's day, it carried the meaning of pleasantness, favor, or gratitude. Early Christians, however, gave this word new significance. They used it to describe the utter generosity that God gives to sinners even though they do not deserve it. This grace is not only forgiveness of sins but the gift of God's power in their lives which brings about a new kind of life.

Salvation. Paul used the term "saved" in these verses to refer to the various aspects of redemption. The grammatical tense he used indicates something accomplished in the past that continues to have results in the present. Paul usually spoke of salvation in more technical terms, such as justification, reconciliation, or adoption. *Saved* is a general term that includes all those various concepts, and it was probably more understandable to Gentiles.

Faith. This is one of Paul's favorite words. It means far more than simply agreeing with an idea. It refers to a total openness to letting God give the benefits of salvation and to obeying the will of God. It is important to note, however, that this does not mean faith is something we do by our own ability. Rather, faith is our willingness to let God into our lives. It includes both trust and commitment.

Paul emphasized that salvation is not something given because of good works. It is not an accomplishment; it is a gift.

The words "and this" (v. 8) are grammatically significant. A. T. Robertson pointed out that the gender of these words is "neuter, not feminine, and so refers not to *faith* (feminine) or to *grace* (feminine also), but to the act of being saved by grace appropriated through faith. Paul shows that salvation does not have its source in men, but in God. Besides, it is God's gift and not the result of our work." "Epistles of Paul," WPNT, vol. 4, 525.

THE BELIEVER'S WALK

POSITIVELY	NEGATIVELY
"In newness of life" (Rom 6:4)	"Not . . . according to the flesh" (Rom 8:4)
"According to the Spirit" (Rom 8:4)	"Not . . . like mere humans" (1 Cor 3:3)
"With decency" (Rom 13:13)	"Not . . . deceitfully" (2 Cor 4:2)
"By faith" (2 Cor 5:7)	"Not by sigh"t (2 Cor 5:7)
"For good works" (Eph 2:10)	Not "in the futility of . . . thoughts"(Eph 4:17

THE BELIEVER'S WALK

POSITIVELY	NEGATIVELY
"In love" (Eph 5:2)	Not disorderly (2 Cor 12:20)
"Wisely" (Col 4:5)	
"In truth" (2 John 4)	
"According to [God's] commandments" (2 John 6)	

For What Purpose (v. 10)

God saves us for a purpose. We are his workmanship. This term "workmanship" can also be translated "handiwork." We are a work of art God is in the process of designing.

This creative process God is carrying out takes place in Christ. We are being made anew for good works.

We are saved from a lot that is negative and destructive, but there is more. We are being saved to do good works. This has been God's plan for us from the beginning, and it's something that begins now. Paul uses one of his phrases here—"for us to do."

Another way of saying it is that God's transforming grace will increasingly result in our doing works that are pleasing to him as a part of our lives every day.

NEW TESTAMENT REFERENCE

Philippians 2:13 tells us that "it is God who is working in you both to will and to work according to his good purpose."

Section Summary

God spells out his purpose for believers in this section. He has restored them. He provides salvation as his gift to men and women. He then creates a dispensation of faith within them so they may receive his gracious gift. Salvation is completely God's achievement, a pure gift of God.

UNITY IN CHRIST (2:11–22)

Gentiles Without Hope (vv. 11–12)

The phrase "so, then" signals a transition is Paul's writing. Paul had been discussing the blessings God gives to the Christian with its emphasis on what Christians as individuals received in Christ. Beginning here he pointed to Christians as a group. He reminded his Gentile readers that they formerly were not part of the people of God, but in Christ they had been included.

Paul explained Christ's peace mission in this section. Those who had been separated from the covenant were united, those who had been alienated were reconciled, and those who had been far off were brought near. Paul said they had been "without God" (Greek word *atheos,* v. 12). This is a term from which the word *atheist* is taken. He described them as such even though the pagans had many gods.

WORD PICTURE

Reconciliation

Reconciliation involves bringing fallen humanity out of alienation into a state of peace and harmony with God. Jesus, as Reconciler, heals the separation and brokenness created by sin and restores communion between God and humankind. Reconciliation is not a process by which men and women become more acceptable to God. Rather, it is an act by which we are delivered from estrangement to fellowship with God. Because of Christ's work on the cross, God has chosen to treat men and women in sin as children rather than transgressors (2 Cor 5:18–20; Eph 2:12–16; Col 1:20–22).

PERSONAL APPLICATION

Some modern theologians assert that God has acted in Christ to reconcile all the world to himself. Consequently, the church's primary concern is not to seek to effect the reconciliation of all people to Christ but merely to proclaim that all have already been reconciled. This kind of universalism is not what Paul teaches in this chapter and is not consistent with his teaching in other letters.

Christ Reconciles All (vv. 13–18)

Apart from Christ, the Gentiles were hopeless. "But now in Christ Jesus" (v. 13), Gentiles and Jews are reconciled to God and to one another. The enmity, the barrier, that existed for hundreds of years has been removed. This is the meaning of reconciliation—to *bring together again*. In Jesus Christ, Jew and Gentile are one because of his work on the cross. Not only has Christ made peace; "he is our peace" (v. 14). Jews and Gentiles are no longer strangers; they are called in one hope as one people of God.

A Holy Temple (vv. 19–22)

Only in response to the cross of Christ (called "faith" in 2:8) does peace exists vertically between humans and God and horizontally among humans. Paul called this new society the church.

Paul pictured the church as a nation ("fellow citizens"), a family ("household"), and a "building." This new building is "built on the foundation of the apostles and prophets, with Christ Jesus himself as the cornerstone" (v. 20). The purpose of the church is to become "God's dwelling in the Spirit" (v. 22).

PICTURES OF THE CHURCH IN EPHESIANS 2

PICTURE	REFERENCE	EXPLANATION
As a nation	v. 19a	All believers are God's people—fellow citizens of "Israel."
As a family	v. 21b	Both Jews and Gentiles now belong to the household or family of God.
As a building	vv. 20–22	God's people are a structure—a temple—where God dwells.

Section Summary

Those who were separated from the covenant have been united, those who were alienated have been reconciled, and those who were far off have been brought near. Jews and Gentiles are no longer strangers; they are called in one hope as one people of God.

QUESTIONS TO GUIDE YOUR STUDY

1. Describe the believer's past life of sin and new life in Christ. Why has God saved us from the consequences of our past sins?
2. What riches in Christ does the believer have? Describe them.
3. What was the Gentiles' relationship to God and his promises before Christ?

4. What is the new relationship between the Jews and the Gentiles? How was it established?
5. Paul used three pictures of the church. How does each of these pictures contribute to our understanding of what the church is?

EPHESIANS 3

After discussing the union of Jewish and Gentile believers in the church (2:11–22), Paul began to offer a prayer on their behalf. However, he stopped unexpectedly in the middle of his sentence and digressed about the divine mystery. He did not return to his prayer until verse 14.

THE DIVINE MYSTERY (3:1–13)

The Stewardship of the Mystery (vv. 1–6)

The phrase "for this reason" refers to the unity of the church in the previous chapter. The point here is that Paul had been given a stewardship. The concept of the Christian as a steward was common in New Testament time. The steward was a household manager entrusted by the master of the house with the responsibility of taking care of things for him. The grace of God that Paul described at such length had been given to him for this specific purpose.

As Paul indicated in 1:9, the inclusion of the Gentiles was a mystery—something no one could have foreseen. But now the secret was open because God had revealed it to Paul in his conversion and call to missions. In verse 6 Paul summed up the mystery for his readers: "The Gentiles are coheirs, members of the same body, and partners in the promise in Christ Jesus through the gospel."

The content of the mystery is Christ—Christ for us in giving his life on our behalf and now Christ in us—accomplishing his purpose by working in each member of his body.

This mystery is received spiritually (Eph 3:4–5) and demonstrated in the proclamation of the gospel. Part of the mystery involves the disclosure that Gentiles share in the blessings of the gospel (2:11–13).

WORD PICTURE

Mystery

The ordinary English sense of this word implies knowledge withheld. The biblical sense is *truth revealed.* The word "mystery" refers to what is known by the "initiated." The mystery was made known only by divine revelation and to those illuminated by the Spirit.

Paul Made a Minister (vv. 7–13)

Paul's Ministry

In verse 6 Paul mentioned the focus of his ministry. This was not something he chose for himself; he *was made* a servant of the gospel by God. He considered himself the "least of all the saints" (v. 8). This was not likely a false modesty on his part.

Before his conversion, Paul was one of the leading persecutors of the church. For him to become a minister of the gospel was a complete reversal of his life's course and not his own accomplishment. This happened through the working of God's power. Paul referred to his appointment as a "gift of God's grace." The purpose of his appointment was "to proclaim to the Gentiles the incalculable riches of Christ, and to shed light for all about the administration of the mystery hidden for ages in God who created all things" (vv. 8–9). Paul traced this mystery all the way back to creation.

God's Plan

God chose to unfold His wise and wonderful plan in the arena of the church. Here we see God's work of redeeming and unifying taking place. One result of this revealing process taking place is the church, God's plan was made known to the "rulers and authorities in the heavens" (v. 10). Angels, both good and bad, were learning about God's grace as it was being revealed in the church. God's plan to undo the work of evil power was successful.

The Believer's Access to God

God's plan, however, was more than a successful operation. It became a personal experience. In Christ we have a free approach to God. "Rather than being overwhelmed by the greatness and power of God's magnificent plan, the believer in Christ finds himself in a close personal relationship with God. Christ gives him the boldness and confidence to come to God in faith." David C. George, *2 Corinthians, Galatians, Ephesians,* Layman's Bible Book Commentary, vol. 21 (B&H, 1979), 113.

Section Summary

The purpose of Paul's appointment to the ministry is "to proclaim to the Gentiles the incalculable riches of Christ, and to shed light for all about the administration of the mystery hidden for ages in God who created all things" (vv. 8–9). God chose to unfold his wise and wonderful plan and reveal the divine mystery in the arena of the church. It is here that we see God's work of redeeming and unifying taking place.

PRAYER AND PRAISE (3:14–21)

Paul's Prayer of Intercession for His Readers (vv. 14–19)

Paul now returned to the prayer he began in verse 1 and prayed that his readers would experience strength through the Holy Spirit and grasp the depth of God's love for them. Obviously, his vision of God's grand

NEW TESTAMENT REFERENCE

The unsearchable riches of Christ are matters that far surpass our human ability to understand. In a doxology in his letter to the Romans, Paul described God's riches. Using this same word in Rom 11:33, Paul exclaimed, "Oh, the depth of the riches and the wisdom and the knowledge of God! How unsearchable his judgments and untraceable his ways!" God's riches are so vast that no one can plumb their depths.

WORD PICTURE

Multifaceted Wisdom

Paul used an interesting word to describe God's wisdom. The word translated *multifaceted* is a compound word made up of the prefix *much or many* and the word *many-sided.* It conveys an idea that is difficult to express in English. It describes something as being "(very) many-sided," "many-faceted," or "many-colored." Paul wanted his readers to understand that this wisdom was richly diversified:

"The idea in this word is that the grace of God will match any situation which life may bring us. There is nothing of light or of dark, of sunshine or of shadow, for which it is not triumphantly adequate." William Barclay, *The Letters to the Galatians and Ephesians* (Westminster, 1976), 127.

grace and the blessings of Christ moved Paul to an attitude of humility and prayer.

Paul again referred to "riches of his glory." From such vast resources God can supply all the needs of his people. These are resources which his people may draw upon in prayer. Having defined this resource, Paul went on to ask for several blessings from these riches to be given to his readers. Paul made five requests for his readers:

PAUL'S FIVE PETITIONS FOR HIS READERS IN 3:16–19

PETITION	PURPOSE
1. Inner strength	That God may work in them and through them
2. Faith	That Christ may dwell in their hearts
3. Love	That they may exercise a new orientation toward others
4. Spiritual understanding	That they may grasp the dimensions of God's love
5. The fullness of God	That they may personally and fully experience God's power

1. Inner strength (v. 16)

The "inner being" is the center of a person's life. Herein lies a person's real strength. The believer's strength comes from God, who is present and active in a believer's life. His power works in and through the believer.

2. "That Christ may dwell in your hearts through faith" (v. 17)

The strength God gives is himself, which Paul explains with his request "that Christ may dwell in your hearts through faith."

3. A new orientation toward others (v. 17)

With a new inner strength and the presence of Christ dwelling within, the believer has a new orientation toward others. Love is the foundation of the believer's life, and so Paul requested in this prayer that his readers be "rooted and firmly established in love."

4. Spiritual understanding (v. 18)

Paul wanted his readers to comprehend the dimensions of Christ's love. His request was that they "may be able to comprehend with all the saints what is the length and width, height and depth of God's love."

5. To be filled with the fullness of God (v. 19)

This is God's ultimate purpose for the lives of his people. God's Spirit dwells in believers, and the Christian life is a process of growth to this end.

In verse 19, Paul further explained that this love of Christ "surpasses knowledge."

Christ's love excels beyond and surpasses what one might gain through knowledge. Paul wanted his readers to have more than an intellectual knowledge of God; he wanted them to experience the fullness of God.

WORD PICTURE

Surpass

The word "surpass" is a compound word made of the preposition "beyond" and the verb "to throw." It means "to throw over and beyond," and it is translated "surpass" or "excel."

Paul's Doxology of Praise (vv. 20–21)

Paul's letter to the Ephesians reached a climax at this point. He delivered a stirring benediction, assuring his readers that God's power at work within them was able to carry out His work more abundantly than they could imagine. The wonderful news to Paul's readers is that this power was *working in them!* This power is active in all believers, and it is a means of glorifying God.

Section Summary

Referring to God's glorious riches, Paul informed his readers that God can supply all the needs of his people. Paul went on to ask for several blessings from these riches to be given to his readers. A stirring benediction emphasizing God's infinite power working in his people closes this section.

HISTORICAL BACKGROUND

Above and Beyond

Paul used an extraordinary word to describe God's power to work on behalf of Christians. It is a compound word constructed of three words to show the highest form of comparison imaginable. Paul connected the words *above, out of,* and *exceedingly* to form this word. It means "exceedingly abundantly, superabundantly, quite beyond all measure, infinitely more." The idea the apostle conveyed here is that God's power is a concept that goes beyond the expression of language. It exceeds what we can "ask or think" (v. 20).

QUESTIONS TO GUIDE YOUR STUDY

1. What did Paul mean by "mystery"? What is the content of this mystery?
2. What was Paul's attitude toward ministry? What might we learn from his attitude and teaching about service to God?
3. What did Paul mean when he said that God's riches are "incalculable"? That His wisdom is "multi-faceted"? In what ways do these truths affect the Christian? How should the believer respond to these truths?
4. In desiring that his readers understand the dimensions of Christ's love for them, Paul prayed for his readers and made several requests on their behalf. What do we learn from Paul's prayer about the dimensions of Christ's love?

EPHESIANS 4

Chapter 4 began the second half of Paul's letter. Chapters 1–3 discussed the spiritual privileges of the church, spelling out the great Christian truths. In the last three chapters, 4–6, Paul drew out the practical implications and responsibilities that follow from the truths of the gospel.

THE UNITY OF THE CHURCH (4:1–6)

A Worthy Life (vv. 1–3)

Paul strengthened his appeal to his readers by referring to himself as a "prisoner in the Lord" (v. 1). His response to God's grace resulted in his being in prison chains. What Paul urged his readers to do summarized all that he would write in chapters 4–6. He compared the Christian life to a walk, then asked them to "walk worthy of the calling you have received."

Paul informed his readers that they had a calling. He placed the Christian life in a category beyond that of a gift or privilege; a calling comes from someone who has the right to claim loyalty. Here it implies that Christian living is goal oriented and dynamic.

This calling, however, is more than simply a vocation or mission. To Paul, it was to a way of life—the Christian walk. He went on to define this walk in terms of attitudes and actions, listing four virtues. These same four virtues also appear in Paul's letter to the Colossians (3:12). These virtues are not to be static qualities; they are to be dynamic actions. Christians are to exercise:

- Humility of mind
- A gentleness with patience
- A bearing with one another in love

Paul emphasized these virtues of the Christian walk:

Humility

Because the ancients did not have a word for humility that was not degrading, Christians gave new meaning to this word. People who are humble consider themselves "small," but at the same time they recognize God's power and ability working in them.

Gentleness

This was another word for "meekness." However, it is not a synonym for weakness. It was used to speak of a wild animal that had been tamed, suggesting controlled strength or power under control.

HISTORICAL BACKGROUND

Urge

The word "urge" is translated in other versions as "beg" or "exhort." In the original Greek text, this word is a compound made up of the preposition "alongside" and the verb "to call." It means "to appeal to, exhort, encourage." "The word signifies a will of the writer that is at the same time warm, personal, and urgent." Fritz Rienecker, *Linguistic Key to the Greek New Testament* (Zondervan, 1980), 530.

NEW TESTAMENT REFERENCE

The New Testament writers regularly took the best words available to express new realties and put meaning into those words by the way they lived. In this way, they had a transforming influence on their society and its language.

Patience

This involves endurance and the attitude Christians are to show toward others as well as suffering. "Bearing with one another" is the practical expression of patience. *Patience* stays with someone until the problem or provocation is past.

Love

The background quality to the three preceding virtues is *love* (see 3:17). In bearing with others, love accepts and overlooks another's weakness and loves others despite their faults.

All these virtues relate to and support the unity of the church. The unity Paul spoke of here is not organizational unity. Rather, it is a dynamic, living union of believers energized and united by the Holy Spirit who already indwells them. Those who are part of the body of Christ are to make "every effort to keep the unity of the Spirit through the bond of peace" (v. 3).

Section Summary

Paul compared the Christian life to a walk, asking his readers to walk worthy of the calling to which they have been called. He went on to define this walk in terms of attitudes and actions, listing four dynamic virtues that ought to characterize every believer in Christ.

All in One—Unity (vv. 4–6)

Paul now turned his attention to the great spiritual realities that unite all Christians.

One Body (v. 4)

The church is the body of Christ. With Christ as its head, the body cannot be divided. Christ's body includes the redeemed of all time as well as local assemblies of believers. Believers everywhere should strive to achieve unity with one another regarding primary truths and values.

One Spirit (v. 4)

There is one Holy Spirit who unites a group of believers. In each believer, the same power and person is at work. Paul already made clear (1:13) that anyone who has received Christ has received the Holy Spirit.

One Hope (v. 4)

Paul's mention of the Spirit led him to an affirmation of hope. Christians everywhere share in the call of God to his great purpose. All look ahead to the same future; all pursue the same goal.

One Lord (v. 5)

At the heart of Christian experience and faith is Christ, who is the "one Lord." Just as the spokes of a wheel are held together and arranged around a common hub, so all Christians come together around the one Lord.

One Faith (v. 5)

The original meaning of "faith" was the common commitment believers have to one Lord. The idea of faith as personal trust and commitment gradually extended to faith as a body of truths to which Christians adhere.

One Baptism (v. 5)

Baptism signals the beginning of the Christian life. Although there is much disagreement about the form and meaning of baptism, all believers share in this act.

One God (v. 6)

This is the central item in the list—the foundation piece. The ultimate basis for all unity is the oneness of God.

THE ONENESS OF BELIEVERS IN CHRIST

UNIFYING FACTOR	KEY IDEA
One body	All believers are part of a body of which Christ is the head.
One Spirit	The same power and person is at work in all believers.
One hope	All believers have the same future and pursue the same goal.
One Lord	At the heart of every believer's Christian experience and faith is Christ.
One faith	The common commitment believers have to one Lord.
One baptism	Signals the beginning of the Christian life and an act which all believers share.
One God	The foundation piece, the ultimate basis for all unity.

Section Summary

In this section Paul focused on the great spiritual realities that unite all Christians and provided a sort of checklist of unifying factors that bind all believers together. The central item in the list is the oneness of God, the ultimate basis for all unity.

PAUL'S LISTS OF SPIRITUAL GIFTS

SPIRITUAL GIFTS	ROM 12:6–8	1 COR 12:8–10	1 COR 12:28	1 COR 12:29–30	EPH 4:11
Apostle			v. 28	v. 29	v. 11
Prophet	v. 6	v. 10	v. 28	v. 29	v. 11
Teacher	v. 7		v. 28	v. 29	v. 11
Pastor					v. 11
Miracles		v. 10	v. 28	v. 29	
Discernment of spirits		v. 10			
Word of wisdom, Knowledge		v. 8			
Evangelists					v. 11
Encouragers	v. 8				
Faith		v. 9			
Healings		v. 9	v. 28	v. 30	
Tongues		v. 10	v. 28	v. 30	
Interpretation		v. 10		v. 30	
Ministry/Serving	v. 7				
Administration			v. 28		
Leaders	v. 8				
Helpers			v. 28		
Mercy	v. 8				
Giving	v. 8				

BUILDING UP THE BODY OF CHRIST (4:7–16)

Each Member of the Body Given a Gift (vv. 7–10)

Having spent the first part of this chapter on the theme of unity in the body, Paul next turned to the idea of *diversity* within the body. "Grace was given to each one of us according to the measure of Christ's gift" (v. 7). This idea of measure suggests that the gift is individually tailored to each Christian.

To further develop this idea, Paul cited Ps 68:18. The phrase "for it says" is a literary device, a formula that "introduces a citation from the Old Testament and is characterized by the absence of a legalistic and polemic undertone. It is an urgent invitation to listen attentively." Fritz Rienecker, *Linguistic Key to the Greek* New *Testament* (Zondervan, 1980), 531.

Christ's Ascending and Descending

Paul further explained that his reference to Christ's ascending implies that he had first descended. This descent seems to correspond to his emptying himself and coming in the flesh to dwell among people and to die (Phil 2:5:11; John 1:1–18). Two other interpretations of the verse are sometimes proposed. Some interpreters think the descent was what was described in 1 Pet 3:19 and that it refers to a visit to the realm of the dead between Christ's death and resurrection. Others suggest this descent was the coming of the Holy Spirit at Pentecost. Paul emphasized the fact that the one who ascended was the same as the one who descended. This seems to have been aimed at the early false teachers who said the glorified Christ could not have experienced real human life and death.

The impact of Eph 4:8–10 is that Christ—by his incarnation, death, resurrection, and ascension—had become available to "fill all things" (v. 10). He is able to give his people all that is needed to fulfill their calling. David C. George, 2 *Corinthians, Galatians, Ephesians,* Layman's Bible Book Commentary 21, 119.

OLD TESTAMENT REFERENCE

Psalm 68:18 describes God returning in triumph after the defeat of the enemies of his people. As was the custom of returning conquerors, he led a parade of captives as he returned. The original Hebrew text reads, "received gifts from men." Paul rendered that phrase here in Ephesians as "he gave gifts to people" (v. 8). There is some evidence that Jewish writers quoted Ps. 68:18 with this same variation. The point of Paul's quoting this passage from the Old Testament is to show that Christ has ascended as conqueror of sin and death, and from his wealth he has given gifts to his people.

Spiritual Gifts Given to the Church (vv. 11–12)

In verse 11 Paul named the gifts Christ has given to his church. Of course, in general terms, Christ's gift to the church is the Holy Spirit (Acts 1:8). But the Spirit himself is said to give a variety of gifts. Paul categorized these gifts in terms of functions that they perform in the church and those who perform those functions.

Apostles

In its most basic meaning, an *apostle* is a delegate, envoy, or messenger—a "sent one." The apostles were the original witnesses of Christ's life, death, and resurrection. Their function was to give a true representation of the gospel and to launch the missionary movement.

Prophets

These were persons who were recognized as speaking with authority. Their words were especially important before the New Testament writers became available to the churches to interpret the will of God. Prophets were able to speak the word of God in special situations to foretell (Acts 11:28; 21:9,11), to convict (1 Cor 14:24–25), and to encourage (Acts 15:32).

Evangelists

These were persons who proclaimed the gospel to those outside the church or to new regions. Philip is called an evangelist in Acts 21:8, and

Paul encouraged Timothy to do the work of an evangelist in 2 Tim 4:5. Today we would call such a person a missionary.

Pastors and Teachers

The word *pastor* means "shepherd." Paul's "image of a shepherd with his flock pictures the relation of a spiritual leader to those committed to his charge." (Fritz Rienecker, *Linguistic Key to the Greek* New *Testament* [Zondervan, 1980], 531.) A *teacher* is one who instructs others in the way of truth. Paul linked *pastor* and *teacher* and, therefore, may have viewed them as a common group—that is, as *teaching shepherds.* Certainly, the church needs both functions within the body.

All of these persons and functions aim at the purpose Paul described in verses 12–13: "To equip the saints for the work of ministry, to build up the body of Christ, until we all reach unity in the faith and in the knowledge of God's Son, growing into maturity with a stature measured by Christ's fullness."

The verb form of this word is used in Matt 4:21 to describe the mending or preparing of nets and in Gal. 6:1 to refer to restoring Christians to spiritual health. It designates a "fitting or fully preparing." *Vine's Complete Expository Dictionary of Old and* New *Testament Words* (Thomas Nelson, 1996), 467.

Section Summary

All members of the church have received spiritual gifts for use in the fellowship. Leaders of the church are to prepare all people for the works of service so that the entire body might experience growth and unity.

The Church's Goal: Spiritual Growth (vv. 13–16)

Unity in the Faith

Paul emphasized this part is verses 3–6. Unity grows out of the common faith believers share.

Unity in Knowledge of the Son

This kind of knowledge speaks about that which is directed toward a particular object. In this case, it involves knowing the Son of God. By knowing Christ intimately, believers experience him as the one who knows God's character and brings God's presence as no one else does. In addition, this knowledge serves to bind Christians together in unity.

Maturity

The word "maturity" carries the idea of being complete or reaching the goal. For the church to reach its goal of Christlikeness, it must have members who are attaining God's will for their lives. This kind of maturity is necessary if there is to be unity in the church. Paul contrasted this maturity with instability in verse 14 by comparing those who are "tossed by the waves and blown around by every wind of teaching, by human cunning with cleverness in the techniques of deceit."

A Stature Measured by Christ's Fullness

A complete person is one who measures up to the pattern of personhood displayed by Jesus Christ. This involves far more than our human standards or definitions of maturity. The fullness of Christ means all that Christ wants in the lives of his people.

Believers are not to be like those Paul warned about in verse 14. Those who use "cunning" and "cleverness" are deceivers and manipulators of the immature.

Paul closed this section by shifting his focus from the church and its members to the subject of Christ as the head and the parts of the body working together. All the members with their various gifts depend on Christ, the head. The body's growth and effectiveness depend on all members of the body working together. Again, Paul emphasized love as the means and manner for building up the church.

WORD PICTURE

Cunning

The word "cunning" means "wicked dice playing" and refers to someone involved with intentional fraud. In contrast, those who follow Christ are to speak "the truth in love" (v. 15). By holding both truth and love in balance, Christians grow to be like Christ in their practical living.

Section Summary

The church's gifts are to be used "to build up the body of Christ" (v. 12). Paul taught a process that moves toward the goal of Christlikeness, and he described four parts of the process: unity in the faith, unity in knowledge of the Son, maturity, and a stature measured by Christ's fullness. The body's growth and effectiveness depend on all members of the body working together, holding truth and love in balance.

PUTTING ON THE NEW NATURE (4:17–24)

Paul's opening phrase, "Therefore, I say this," was an urgent signal to his readers that what he was about to say was important. He used this attention-getter to give a warning: "You should no longer walk as the Gentiles do" (v. 17).

The minds of the Gentiles were completely out of touch with the reality of God, so they were going nowhere. Not only did they lack understanding; they were hard-hearted, blind, shameless, and greedy. Paul pointed to the Gentiles and said, "You're not to be like this. This is the exact opposite of what Christ is."

Rather, believers need to do the following:

1. *Take off the old self (v. 22).* The way the believer puts off the old self is likened to the way one might take off clothes. The tense of the verb signifies a once-for-all, concluding action. The putting off is done once, permanently.

WORD PICTURE

The Commands of 4:25–5:2

Most of the commands in this passage are in the present tense. The present tense with the command indicates that the actions of the verbs used are to be habitual. This applies to both negative and positive commands. This formula in use with positive commands means the reader is to continually act in a certain way. In the case of the command, "Be imitators of God," the believer is to continually imitate God. It is to be a habit. This formula used with negative commands, such as, "Don't grieve God's Holy Spirit," is considered a *prohibition.* This particular prohibition means that the person grieving the Spirit is to *stop* doing so and is to *continue* not grieving the Spirit.

2. *Be made new in the attitude of the mind (v. 23).* This change is not only outward, but it also involves the inner person. The present tense of the infinitive "to renew" emphasizes that spiritual renewal taking place is a continuing process.
3. *"Put on the new self" (v. 24).* The word for "put on" is also used in the sense of putting on a garment. Indeed, the NRSVUE translates this passage, "Clothe yourselves with the new self." This new self is "created according to God's likeness" (v. 24). This verse might possibly mean that a new self is created in God's image.

Section Summary

Becoming a Christian involves far more than learning truths with the mind. It requires a complete break with the past life of sin. The person who believes in Christ takes off the old, corrupted self and then puts on the new self, which is created to be like God.

EXAMPLES OF THE NEW WAY OF LIFE (4:25–5:2)

In this practical and challenging section, Paul focused on holy living. Believers are to walk in purity as well as unity. The apostle first showed negatively how believers should not walk and issued several commands to his readers.

Paul suggested several positive aspects of Christian conduct.

Speaking the Truth (v. 25)

Falsehood is not a characteristic of the believer's new nature. Not only are we to put away lies, but our lives are also to be characterized by speaking the truth. Because Christians depend on one another, they must be able to trust others' words and deeds.

Dealing with Anger (vv. 26–27)

Paul quoted Ps 4:4, "Be angry and do not sin." It is a Hebrew way of saying, "When you are angry, do not sin." This command is not a license to anger. Paul recognized that anger is a part of life and must be handled realistically and constructively. Paul urged believers to settle negative feelings before sundown. A failure to do so keeps one's anger alive and provides the devil with an "opportunity"—room to work his evil in a person's life.

PERSONAL APPLICATION

"Paul's antidote for a habit of taking is to develop a habit of giving." David C. George, 2 *Corinthians, Galatians, Ephesians,* Layman's Bible Book Commentary, vol. 21, 125.

Honest Work (v. 28)

Hands that were previously involved in stealing must now engage in honest work. Paul advocated a change in behavior. Those who were inclined to dishonest gain by stealing should stop that kind of behavior immediately, replacing it with hard work and giving to others in need.

WALKING IN THE NEW WAY

ASPECT	COMMAND, PROHIBITION, OR ENTREATY	REASON
"Putting away lying, speak the truth." (v. 25)	Commands	For "we are members of one another."
"Be angry and do not sin." (vv. 26–27)	Prohibition	So the devil will not gain an opportunity.
"No longer steal." (v. 28)	Entreaty	To work honestly and help those in need.
"No foul language should come from your mouth." (v. 29)	Prohibition	So that we may exhibit God's grace to others and build them up.
"Don't grieve God's Holy Spirit." (v. 30)	Prohibition	We are God's vessel and the temple of the Holy Spirit.
Get rid of "all bitterness, anger and wrath." (v. 31)	Entreaty	So we may maintain and cultivate good relationships.
"Be kind and compassionate." (v. 32)	Command	So we may be considerate and meet the needs of others.
"Be imitators of God." (5:1–2)	Command	So we may exhibit the nature of God in word and deed to our world.

Gracious Speech (v. 29)

Becoming a Christian changes the way a person speaks. Speech controlled by the new nature will exhibit three characteristics:

1. It edifies or builds up.
2. It is appropriate.
3. It has a redemptive effect on those who hear it.

Harmony with the Spirit (v. 30)

The new nature at work within the believer is the work of the Spirit. God is saddened and disappointed when his people fail to live up to their new nature. The Spirit is grieved. The Spirit is the seal and guarantee of the believer's future complete redemption (for a review of the Spirit's ministry of sealing, see 1:13).

Christlike Relationships (v. 31)

Immediately following his warning against grieving the Spirit, Paul listed six forms of sin that must be put away. These sins are normally expressed within the context of speech, and all six involve relationships with others. The following chart lists these sins and their specific meanings.

OLD TESTAMENT REFERENCE

"'These are the things you must do: Speak truth to one another; make true and sound decisions within your city gates. Do not plot evil in your hearts against your neighbor, and do not love perjury, for I hate all this'—this is the LORD's declaration." (Zech 8:16–17)

SIX SINS OF SPEECH

SIN	EXPANDED MEANING
Bitterness	A spirit of resentment that refuses to be reconciled
Wrath	A subtle, deep-flowing, persistent antagonism against someone
Anger	A temporary outburst of temper
Shouting	Loud expressions of grievance, shouting
Slander	Speaking evil of others and God
All malice	A general term that includes any evil word or act against another; the root of the above vices

Being Imitators of God (5:1–2)

Paul challenged his readers to the highest standard possible: "Be imitators of God." He taught that what Christians became when they believed on Christ, they must diligently continue in their daily behavior. He challenged his readers with two commands: "Be imitators of God," and, "Walk in love."

"Be imitators of God" (v. 1).

If we are to be like God, we must imitate him. This command is in the present tense, indicating that this should be a continuous, ongoing action by the Christian.

"Walk in love" (v. 2).

Paul highlighted two areas in which believers are to imitate: by exercising love and forgiveness toward others.

NEW TESTAMENT REFERENCE

"Dear friend, do not imitate what is evil, but what is good. The one who does good is of God; the one who does evil has not seen God" (3 John 11).

Section Summary

In this practical and challenging section, Paul focused on holy living. Believers are to walk in purity as well as unity. The apostle first showed negatively how believers should not walk and then issued several commands to his readers.

QUESTIONS TO GUIDE YOUR STUDY

1. Paul listed several character qualities in verse 2. How do these equip the believer to fulfill Paul's command in verse 3?
2. What was Paul's point in verses 4–6? What is the foundation or key unifying factor of this oneness?
3. Paul mentioned several spiritual gifts. How does each contribute to the growth of the body of Christ? What does the word *equip* mean? What is the goal of spiritual growth?

4. Contrast the believer's old and new natures. How does a person "put on" the new nature?
5. What changes take place when a person puts on the new nature?
6. What did Paul mean by urging Christians to imitate God?

EPHESIANS 5

This chapter continues Paul's instruction on the Christian walk. His main topics are warnings against immorality, instruction on walking in wisdom, and submission within the marital relationship. Because 5:1–2 logically is part of the closing section of chapter 4, it is treated there.

FURTHER WARNINGS AGAINST SIN (5:3–14)

Immoral Behavior and Talk (vv. 3–7)

After his summary statement in 5:1–2, Paul appeared to double back and attack the sins of the pagan world. This served to emphasize the urgency of the problem Paul saw. Here he listed several sins, the first of which are concerned with sexual immorality:

- *"Sexual immorality."* This refers to illicit sexual activity or sexual activity outside of marriage. From the Greek word for *fornication* we get the English word *pornography*.
- *Impurity*. This is a broad term for immorality or uncleanness.
- *Greed*. This word was often used to describe uncontrolled sexual desire.

Paul next shifted to sins of conversation:

- *"Obscene . . . talking."* This refers to shameful, filthy, or obscene speech.
- *"Foolish talking."* Known as the "talk of fools," it is the conversation of the drunkard.
- *"Crude joking."* This is the language that makes light of human weakness or human goodness and ultimately tears down the quality of life.

Paul declared that his readers should not make these topics a matter of conversation and should not associate with people who practice and talk about these things: "Do not become their partners" (v. 7). To underscore the seriousness of this kind of immoral behavior, Paul stated that those who practice these evils will not share in the inheritance of the kingdom of God.

WORD PICTURE

Imitator

The term *imitator* was understood by Paul's readers. "Imitation was the main part of the training of an orator. The teachers of rhetoric declared that the learning of oratory depended on three things—theory, imitation and practice. The main part of their training was the study and the imitation of the masters who had gone before. It is as if Paul said: 'If you were to train to be an orator, you would be told to imitate the masters of speech. Since you are training in life, you must imitate the Lord of all good life.'" William Barclay, *The Letters to the Galatians and Ephesians* (Westminster, 1976), 160–61.

Light and Darkness (vv. 8–14)

Light, because it is the nature of Christ, is powerful. Paul provided some specific details about the light that Jesus Christ brings to humankind.

Light produces good fruit (v. 9).

Paul listed goodness, righteousness, and truth as the products of light. Those who walk in the light exhibit a spirit of generosity.

Light exposes motives (v. 10).

Light enables the Christian to discriminate between what is pleasing and what is not pleasing to God. It is in this light that all motives, attitudes, and actions must be tested. Believers are to test "what is pleasing to the Lord."

PERSONAL APPLICATION

Believers walk in the light, and evildoers live in darkness. Believers themselves once "were once darkness, but now you are light in the Lord" (v. 8). Because of their standing in Christ, Paul urged his readers to "walk as children of light." Another way of saying this is, "Try to learn what is pleasing to the Lord." The guiding rule in this walk is whether an attitude or action is pleasing to God.

Light exposes evil (v. 12).

Light exposes the unfruitful works of darkness. Evil activity, when dragged into the light of Christ, is seen for what it is and dies a natural death.

Light cleanses (v. 13–14).

Although this (v. 13) is a difficult verse to interpret, it seems that Paul declared that light has a cleansing effect. What is exposed by the light becomes influenced by the light. In addition to the light's function of condemning evil, light heals. Certainly, light is a witness to people in darkness. The effect of light on a sinful heart can result in the healing of the soul.

CONTRAST BETWEEN DARKNESS AND LIGHT

DARKNESS	LIGHT
Produces lies (v. 6)	Embraces truth (v. 9)
Produces sin (v. 6)	Produces righteousness (v. 9)
Unfruitful (v. 11)	Produces fruit (v. 9) (goodness, truth, righteousness)
Shameful (v. 12)	Pleasing to God (v. 10)

To conclude this section. Paul introduced an indirect quotation from Isa 60:1: "Get up, sleeper, and rise up from the dead, and Christ will shine on you." This quotation includes the name of Christ, leading most scholars to believe that it is from an early Christian hymn.

This passage from Isaiah describes the beginning of the Christian life as waking from sleep, as rising from the dead, and as receiving light. Certainly, those who have experienced Christ cannot take part in the ways of sleep, death, and darkness.

Section Summary

Paul attacked the sins of the pagan world and listed sins of sexual immorality and sins of conversation that Christians are to avoid. Not only are believers to avoid evil deeds; they are also to avoid associating with those who practice such deeds.

WALKING IN WISDOM (5:15–20)

The way believers conduct their Christian walk is critical. They are to exercise wisdom. Considering their redemption from darkness into light, they must take decisive steps. Paul addressed his readers with several exhortations. He did this to appeal to the will, the volitional side of a person. Paul intended that these exhortations guide believers into patterns of wise living. It was his desire that they develop the following qualities in their Christian lives.

THE CHRISTIAN WALK OF WISDOM

AREA	PAUL'S EXHORTATION
	Walk carefully.
Opportunities for doing good	Seize opportunities.
God's guidance	Understand God's will.
Control and stability	Be filled with the Spirit.
Encouraging one another	Speak praises to one another.

Walk Carefully (v. 15)

The idea Paul conveyed here is that of looking around carefully to avoid stumbling and falling. Christians are to be aware and alert, taking advantage of the light they have in a dark world.

Make the Most of the Time (vv. 15–16)

"Redeeming the time" is how some other versions have translated this phrase. Paul is teaching here that wise living involves making the most of our time. The kind of time Paul spoke of here is not the passing of hours, days, and years but strategic time in the form of windows of opportunity. Timely action is especially important because "the days are evil."

Understand God's Will (v. 17)

Understanding God's will is directly related to understanding God's Word. God's will as revealed in his Word is always the criterion and the motivation for Christian living.

Be Filled with the Spirit (v. 18)

The key idea of the word *filled* is control. The indwelling Spirit of God ought to be the dominant and controlling factor in a believer's life. Those

WORD PICTURE

Making the Most of the Time

The King James Version translates Paul's phrase in verse 16 as "redeeming the time." The word for "redeeming" ("making the most") is a compound word made up of the preposition "out" prefixed to the verb "to buy." This compound means "to buy out." The "time" Paul refers to is "a season" of time. Opportunities that cannot be recalled are missed. Believers are to grab each opportunity for doing good, turning it into the best advantage for the cause of Christ.

not controlled by the Spirit are vulnerable to evil influences and will ultimately give way to control by their own lusts and desires.

Sing Praises to God (v. 19)

The early church was a singing church. Paul described the gathering of believers as they were filled with the Spirit. "Psalms" refers to the songs of Israel in the Old Testament, and "hymns" may have been new songs of the Christian faith. While these spiritual songs were shared among believers, their purpose was to praise God. This praise was to be accompanied with thanksgiving, a quality possible only to those whom God had redeemed through Jesus Christ his Son. From Scripture we find that the early church was indeed a thankful church.

Section Summary

The way believers conduct their Christian walk is critical. This involves taking decisive steps. Paul addressed his readers with several exhortations to guide them into patterns of wise living.

WIVES AND HUSBANDS (5:21–33)

PAUL'S WRITINGS ON THE MARRIAGE RELATIONSHIP

Ephesians 5:22–6:4
Colossians3:18–21
1 Corinthians 7:1–17
1 Timothy 2:8–15

Mutual Submission (v. 21)

Paul exhorted believers to be submissive to one another: "Submitting to one another in the fear of Christ" (v. 21). Although in the following verse Paul applied this exhortation to husbands and wives, he did not limit his emphasis to the husband-wife relationship. His emphasis on unity and harmony applies to the entire body of Christ.

WORD PICTURE

Fear of Christ

This is not the kind of fear that arouses alarm or terror. Rather, it is the biblical meaning of the word to indicate profound respect. A reverential fear of Christ will inspire a constant care and consideration in one's dealings with others. This is important because the submission of both husband and wife to Christ's authority will ensure proper attitudes within the relationship.

Counsel to Wives (vv. 22–24)

Wives are to submit to their husbands in everything: "Submit to your husbands" (v. 22). The term "submit" means "to be subject to."

This word is common to specific New Testament instruction regarding the relationship between husband and wife (see Col 3:18; 1 Pet 3:1, 5). It is "used in a military sense of soldiers submitting to their superior or slaves to their masters. The word has primarily the idea of giving up one's own rights and will, i.e., 'to subordinate one's self.'" Fritz

Rienecker, *Linguistic Key to the Greek* New *Testament* (Zondervan, 1980), 538.

The term for "submit" is also used in a variety of other contexts, including the subjection of all things to Christ, the subjection of persons to civil authorities, and the subjection of one Christian to another. In his *The Epistle to the Romans*, C. E. B. Cranfield, speaking of this subjection, stated, "It is the responsible acceptance of a relationship in which God has placed one and the resulting honest attempt to fulfill the duties which it imposes on one" (p. 662).

Submission has nothing to do with worth before God or before one another. Submission does not imply inferiority. Rather, it is an expression of a God-ordained role. Verse 23 is critical. The wife is to be subject to her husband because the husband is head of his wife in the same way that Christ is head of the church. The husband is the God-appointed leader of the home, and he is held accountable for that role.

Counsel to Husbands (vv. 25–33)

Paul's command to husbands was to "love your wives" (v. 25), and he immediately told husbands what it meant to do so. Paul pointed to Christ and said in effect, "You see how much Christ loved the church? You see how he demonstrated that love to the church? In that way—to that degree—you husbands are to love your wives."

Section Summary

Paul exhorted believers to be submissive to one another, and then he made a special application to the husband-wife relationship. Wise believers, filled with the Spirit, who mutually submit to one another contribute to the unity and harmony of the entire body of Christ.

PERSONAL APPLICATION

What difference would it make in your home if the wife were subject to the husband in all things and the husband put the good of his wife ahead of his needs and wants in every decision and action?

QUESTIONS TO GUIDE YOUR STUDY

1. Paul listed several sins of immorality and conversation. What was his point?
2. Paul exhorted believers to walk in the light. Contrast this spiritual light with spiritual darkness. What does the light that Christ brings accomplish in the life of the believer? How does it affect the unbeliever?
3. What are some of the steps of walking in wisdom?
4. Paul urged his readers to make "the most of the time." What are some ways Christians can do this?
5. Regarding Paul's teaching on submission, what was his counsel to wives? To husbands? What does *submit* mean for the wife in the context of the marital relationship?

EPHESIANS 6

Continuing the theme from the previous chapter, Paul began this final chapter by providing counsel for children and parents, slaves (or workers) and masters. He then shifted to the subject of spiritual warfare and God's provisions for the believer's battle against evil.

Counsel to Children (vv. 1–3)

Paul's counsel for children came in the form of two commands: obey and honor. Both should be exercised continuously.

"Obey your parents" (v. 1).

Children are to obey the instruction of their parents. Paul added a reason: "Because this is right." This phrase could have more than one meaning. It could mean that a child's obedience is recognized as right by all people. Or it could mean that a child cannot always understand the reasons for a parent's instructions and must obey because it is the right thing to do.

PERSONAL APPLICATION

Children and Parents

Paul first focused on the relationship between children and their parents. He emphasized that there is to be harmony in the home, and he provided counsel for both children and parents.

"Honor your father and mother" (v. 2).

To honor something is to value it or revere it. Here Paul cited the fifth commandment: "Honor your father and your mother" (Exod 20:12). "Honor" is a broader word than "obey." In the case of younger children, it calls for obedience. In the case of older children, it calls for respect and care for the parents.

Counsel to Parents (v. 4)

Paul included a word to parents. He probably used the word "fathers" in a general sense that would include both parents. He delivered his counsel in the form of one negative command and one positive command.

WORD PICTURE

Obey

The Greek word translated "obey" is a compound word made up of the prepositional prefix "under" and the verb "to listen, attend." This word is also translated "to submit." It describes the proper response in certain kinds of relationships, such as children to parents and servants to masters.

BIBLICAL INSTRUCTION FROM PAUL FOR CHILDREN

PASSAGE	FORM OF INSTRUCTION	COUNSEL
Ephesians 6:1–3	Command	"Children, obey your parents in the Lord."
Colossians 3:20	Command	"Children, obey your parents in everything."
Exodus 20:12 (the fifth commandment)	Command (Old Testament quote)	"Honor your father and your mother."

"Don't stir up anger in your children" (v. 4).

Parents are not to provoke their children to anger. Their exercise of authority is not to be harsh. Rather, parental authority is to be exercised with due regard for the child, recognizing the child's rights and feelings.

"Bring them up in the training and instruction of the Lord" (v. 4).

To "bring up" a child is to nourish and care for that child. Parents are to raise their children in the training and instruction of the Lord.

WORD PICTURE

Training and Instruction

The word *training* speaks of discipline used to correct transgressions of laws. The word *instruction* literally means "a putting in mind." It is often translated "admonition" and refers to verbal instruction. *Instruction* is "the training by word," whether of encouragement, or, if necessary, by reproof. *Vine's Complete Expository Dictionary of Old and New Testament Words* (Thomas Nelson, 1996), 13.

Section Summary

Paul addressed the relationship between children and parents. Children are to obey their parents. Parents are to exercise their authority with due regard for their children and bring them up in the training and instruction of the Lord.

SLAVES AND MASTERS (6:5–9)

Counsel to Slaves (vv. 6–8)

The Roman world lived with slavery. From the earliest times, the government accepted and promoted the practice. In the Roman world, treatment of slaves varied considerably. By the first century, however, the institution of slavery was changing. Public sentiment was against harsh treatment of slaves, and many leading orators spoke against the institution. This caused many masters to free their slaves.

Christianity arose in a real-life, tension-filled setting. The slaves' insurrections had already failed, causing significant injury, sorrow, and loss of life. Working within these tensions, however, the seeds of abolition were sown.

In the Roman Empire of Paul's day, nearly all work was done by slaves. A large portion of the population consisted of those in forced servitude either as captives of the Romans or as debtors unable to pay their obligations. It is likely that many early Christians were slaves. Therefore, Paul included Christian instruction for those in slave-master relationships. His approach to the slavery problem of his day was to urge both slaves and masters to acknowledge Christ as their Lord.

Paul's words, "slave or free," remind us today that Paul's instruction is just as applicable to the modern-day employee as to the first-century slave. He urged workers to:

Obey with respect and sincerity (v. 5).

Servants are to obey their masters in the same way they obey Christ. Paul mentioned qualities of this obedience:

- *Fear and trembling.* This phrase elsewhere is translated "with respect and trembling" (NRSVUE).
- *Sincerity.* This word conveys the ideas of simplicity, uprightness, and "singleness of heart" (NRSVUE).

Serve from the heart (v. 7).

Paul instructed that service to masters should be done wholeheartedly, as if the servants were serving the Lord directly. Christians are serving Christ, even in their daily duties. This word suggests a good will that does not wait to be compelled to action.

NEW TESTAMENT REFERENCE

When Paul Wrote to Philemon

Encouraging him to take back his runaway slave, Onesimus, the apostle said, " For perhaps this is why he was separated from you for a brief time, so that you might get him back permanently, no longer as a slave, but more than a slave—as a dearly loved brother. He is especially so to me, but how much more to you, both in the flesh and in the Lord" (Phlm 15–16).

Counsel to Masters (v. 9)

There was much cruelty and abuse of slaves in the Roman Empire, but Christian masters were to be different. They were to do good to their slaves. Their relationship with their slaves was to be governed by the awareness of their accountability to God for what they did. In situations where both slave and master were Christians, they were in a master-slave relationship at one level, but at a more important level, they were equals as brothers in Christ.

Section Summary

In this passage Paul addressed the relationship between servants and masters. Servants are to obey their masters and serve them wholeheartedly. Masters are to treat their servants with goodness. Both are to conduct themselves as if they were serving Christ himself.

THE WHOLE ARMOR OF GOD (6:10–20)

Paul concluded his letter to the Ephesians by preparing his readers for the spiritual conflict of life. He made them aware of the enemy, Satan, and exhorted them to put on the "armor" that God supplies so they may be equipped for the battle.

WORD PICTURE

Stand

The word *stand* "could be used in a military sense indicating either 'to take over,' 'to hold a watch post,' or it could also mean 'to stand and hold out in a critical position in a battlefield' (Barth)." Fritz Rienecker, *Linguistic Key to the Greek New Testament* (Zondervan, 1980), 541.

The Believer's Fight Against Evil (vv. 10–13)

Paul's use of the word "finally" indicated to his readers that he was beginning to draw his letter to a conclusion. It drew together several themes from throughout the letter but particularly pointed to 5:3–18, where Paul described evil deeds and evil days as enemies of God's people. Paul began his instruction with three commands: "Be strengthened by the Lord," "Put on the full armor of God," and "Stand against the schemes of the devil."

"Be strengthened by the Lord" (v. 10).

Paul exhorted believers to be strengthened or empowered for the battle. Human effort is not enough; the strength and power for the fight must come from God, his "vast strength." The Christian draws strength from:

- Realizing that believers are seated with Christ "in the heavens" (1:19–23), a much higher position than Satan and his principalities.
- The fact that the power of God is available to every believer through the power of the indwelling Spirit (3:14–21).

"Put on the full armor of God" (v. 11).

To put on the armor of God is to clothe oneself with the necessary equipment for battle. It is important to include all the parts of the armor to protect oneself completely from the attacks of the enemy.

"Stand against the schemes of the devil" (v. 11).

Just as an enemy will come up with a variety of schemes to try to gain victory in combat, so it is with Satan against God's people.

SATAN, THE ENEMY

HIS WEAPON	PASSAGE	OUR DEFENSE
Crafty schemes	Eph 6:11	Putting on the full armor of God and standing against the enemy
Strategy and devices	2 Cor 2:5–11	Confessing our sins, forgiving others, and claiming God's forgiveness for ourselves
Snares	1 Tim 3:7	Maintaining a good testimony among the unsaved
Ignorance and lies	2 Cor 4:1; Luke 22:53	Not succumbing to Satan's power and authority

The Believer's Equipment for Battle (vv. 14–17a)

In this graphic passage, Paul pictured the Christian soldier being outfitted for a battle. To wage this battle with human effort is foolish. The believer must put on God's full armor in order to be strengthened "by his vast strength" (v. 10). Human effort is inadequate in spiritual warfare, but God's power is invincible.

Armor is essentially a shield worn directly on the body. Since the body is most vulnerable in the head and chest regions, it was especially there where armor was worn. Saul and Goliath wore helmets (1 Sam 17:5,38), as did the entire army of Judah, at least in the time of Uzziah (2 Chr 26:14). The helmet was usually made of leather or metal. It was designed in various shapes depending on the army and even on the unit within the army so the commander could distinguish one unit from another while viewing from a higher vantage point. The different helmets helped the soldier tell whether he was near an enemy or comrade in the confusion of tight hand-to-hand combat.

With the rise in popularity of the arrow with its speed and quickness, the mail came to be more and more necessary to cover the torso. Fish-scale-like construction of small metal plates sewn to cloth or leather was the breastplate for the ancient soldier. These scales could number as high as seven hundred to one thousand per "coat." Each coat obviously could be heavy and expensive to produce in volume. The distant enemy units of archers who might find themselves firing on each other would wear mail, along with archers riding in chariots. While in a chariot, Ahab was hit and killed by an arrow exactly where the mail was least protective—at the seam where the sleeve and breast of the coat met (1 Kgs 22:34). Leg armor, like the bronze leglets of Goliath (1 Sam 17:6), was not regularly used in Old Testament times.

Arms and armor surfaced on only a few occasions in the New Testament. In New Testament times, Roman imperial soldiers were equipped with metal helmets, protective leather and metal vests, leg armor, shields, swords and spears.

The armor of God is both the armor he supplies and the armor he himself uses in the battle. Paul listed the items in the order in which they would be put on. He identified each one by the spiritual quality each represents. Because Paul emphasized the "full armor of God," the details of the individual pieces should not be pressed too far.

Truth

The first step in preparing for battle was to gird the loins. Because men in ancient times wore long robes, their movement in battle or work could be hindered. To eliminate this hindrance, they would pull up the robe and tie it about the waist and hips with a girdle or belt. Paul says this belt is *truth,* which means sincerity of character.

Righteousness

In battle, the breastplate was vital, for it protected the heart and lungs. This is what *righteousness* does for the believer.

PERSONAL APPLICATION

Christians who go to war against the lies of Satan, the father of lies, must not be tripped up by their own untruth.

Peace

Shoes are important to the foot soldier. For the Christian, the gospel of peace makes his feet spring lightly across the field or makes it possible for him to stand firmly in position when such a stance is required. Just as shoes provide foundation to our standing or moving, so the gospel is the foundation on which we stand.

Faith

A shield was indispensable for battle. The kind of shield Paul spoke of was large enough to cover the body, about two-and-one-half feet by four feet in size. These shields were made of leather and were often soaked in water to ensure protection from flaming arrows. The Christian's shield is faith, which is a complete confidence in God's power. It is important to note that to "take up" the shield (v. 16) does not mean to grab with one's own strength; rather, it is *receiving* what is given by God.

Salvation

The helmet protects the most vital and vulnerable part of the body—the head.

"The Roman soldier wore a bronze helmet equipped with cheek pieces. The helmet was a heavy decorative and expensive item that had an inside lining of felt or sponge which made the weight bearable. Nothing short of an axe or hammer could pierce a heavy helmet." Fritz Rienecker, *Linguistic Key to the Greek* New *Testament* (Zondervan, 1980), 542.

Therefore, the helmet of salvation is the Christian's most basic protection. Armed with God's grace and the guarantee of eternal life, the Christian soldier can remain fearless. Nothing the enemy will do can break the bond that holds the believer to God. Although believers may experience setbacks during the battle, they will be able to hold their heads up when the battle is over.

PERSONAL APPLICATION

This willingness to let God work in the believer's life can effectively protect one from all the enemy can deliver.

The Believer's Preparation Through Prayer (vv. 17b–20)

Two offensive weapons are included with the armor of God: (1) the "sword of the Spirit," which is the Word of God, and (2) prayer.

PERSONAL APPLICATION

A Christian's basic defense against evil is obedience to God's Word and will and an uprightness in his or her conduct. Improper attitudes and actions become "kinks" in the armor—weak areas through which the enemy may thrust his weapons.

"The Sword of the Spirit" (v. 17)

The kind of sword Paul described is the short, straight sword the Roman soldier used. It was used as a close-range weapon. The sword given by the Spirit to be wielded as an offensive weapon is the Word of God. God's sword has life and power, and we learn from Heb 4:12 that it never grows dull. Indeed, it is an effective weapon, "penetrating as far as the separation of soul and spirit, joints and marrow. It is able to judge the thoughts and intentions of the heart." Christians learn to conquer the enemy on the spiritual battlefield when they understand Scripture, apply its life-changing truths to themselves, and obey its commands and precepts.

THE ARMOR OF GOD

ARMOR PIECE	SYMBOL	MEANING
Belt	Truth	Sincerity of character
Breastplate	Righteousness	Uprightness in conduct
Shoes	Peace	Gospel of peace
Shield	Faith	Complete confidence in God's power
Helmet	Salvation	God's grace and the guarantee of eternal life

NEW TESTAMENT REFERENCE

On many occasions Jesus urged his disciples to watch and pray. In Luke 18 Jesus told a parable to his disciples "on the need for them to pray always and not give up" (Luke 18:1).

Prayer (v. 18)

Prayer is what energizes the Christian. Paul set forth several guidelines for this prayer. The Christian is to pray:

- In the Spirit
- On all occasions
- With all kinds of prayers and requests

The attitude of the prayer warrior should be one of alertness and persistence. It is to be constant and intense. Like a guard keeping watch over the camp, the Christian is to be vigilant without a letdown.

Paul concluded this section by describing himself as "an ambassador in chains" (v. 20). He was in prison, wearing iron prison chains. In Paul's time, Rome housed many ambassadors in fine embassies. Paul, an ambassador of Christ, found himself imprisoned. Because ambassadors normally would not be arrested, Paul indicated the wrong he was suffering.

HISTORICAL BACKGROUND

Stay Alert

The word Paul used in verse 18 for "stay alert" means "to stay awake, to lie sleepless, to be watchful, vigilant." The grammatical elements of this verb speak of continuous, unbroken action. This command is coupled with the word "perseverance," intensifying the action. From our study of papyrus documents of New Testament times, we know that the verb form of *persevere* was used to describe "waiting until one's trial came before the court or diligently remaining at one's work." Fritz Rienecker, *Linguistic Key to the Greek New Testament* (Zondervan, 1980), 543.

Section Summary

Paul concluded his letter to the Ephesians by preparing his readers for the spiritual conflict of life. He used the Roman soldier's weapons and armor as images to express the virtues necessary to defend the believer against Satan. To ensure victory, the Christian warrior is to put on the full armor of God and to use the sword of the Spirit and prayer on the spiritual battlefield.

PAUL'S FINAL WORDS TO HIS READERS (6:21–24)

Acknowledgments (vv. 21–22)

At the end of his letter, Paul acknowledged the personal ties between himself and some of his readers. He would send a special messenger, Tychicus, to hand deliver the letter. Verses 21–22 are nearly identical to Col 4:7–9, indicating that Tychicus carried both letters.

Benediction (vv. 23–24)

The book closed with a rich benediction. Familiar themes of peace, brotherhood, love, faith, and grace are the blessings Paul pronounced on God's people. He spoke eloquently of Christ's love for his church. At the end he graced them with the title, "all who have undying love for our Lord Jesus Christ." By "undying" Paul meant a love that is incorruptible not only in its endurance but also in its character.

Section Summary

Paul's final words to his readers were an acknowledgment of his personal ties with his readers and a benediction.

QUESTIONS TO GUIDE YOUR STUDY

1. Regarding harmony in the family, what is Paul's counsel to children? To parents? Explain his commands to both.
2. How should Paul's instruction in verse 4 affect a parent's attitude and behavior toward his or her child or children? How does a parent bring up a child "in the training and instruction of the Lord"?
3. Paul included counsel for the slave-master relationship. What was his counsel to both, and what of his counsel is applicable to our modern work environment?
4. Describe the believer's fight against evil. What commands did Paul give his readers to prepare them for the battle?
5. Describe God's armor for fighting the battle. What does each part of the armor represent? What offensive weapons does God provide the Christian warrior?

Philippians

INTRODUCTION

Philippians, more than most other epistles of the apostle Paul, reveals Paul's situation, his personal history, and his deep and abiding affection for a church that loved him.

In addition to revealing Paul's heart, the epistle contains a fresh presentation of Jesus Christ. In a lofty hymn about Jesus Christ, Paul called his readers to an examination and interpretation of the mind of Christ. Paul's life had been transformed radically by his encounter with Christ and by the obedience Christ's love brought from him.

This letter reads easily. Apart from Philemon, Philippians is the most personal of all Paul's letters.

THE CITY OF PHILIPPI

Philippi is one of the better-known New Testament cities. It was in the eastern part of the Roman province of Macedonia, on the Egnatian Way, the principal highway from Asia to the west. About eight hundred miles from Rome and approximately ten miles from the seaport of Neapolis, it was a strategic city in ancient times. Abundant resources such as water supplies, timber, and metals made the city important commercially.

Its most imposing geographical feature was a 750-foot-high rock cliff that overlooked Philippi. Many reliefs, depicting the religious cults popular at Philippi, were sculpted on it. Everyone who entered the city was immediately confronted with the religious symbolism of the area.

AUTHOR

The book of Philippians claims the apostle Paul as its author and reflects his personality. Early acceptance of Pauline authorship by such leaders as Clement of Rome and Ignatius provides additional support for this position.

HISTORICAL BACKGROUND

In the first century, Philippi contained a diverse population. Three primary ethnic groups lived there, but many others came to Philippi for various reasons. The three groups were the native Thracians, the Greeks, and the Romans, who occupied the territory. From appearances, the Roman element was the strongest. Philippi was no doubt the most Roman of all the cities Paul visited.

HISTORICAL BACKGROUND

Epaphroditus

The name *Epaphroditus* was common in the first-century Greek-speaking world. His personal name means "favored by Aphrodite or Venus." He was a friend and fellow worker of Paul the apostle. He delivered to Paul a gift from the church at Philippi while the apostle was in prison. While he was with Paul, Epaphroditus became seriously ill. After his recovery, Paul sent him back to Philippi, urging the church to receive him with gladness.

ORIGIN AND DATE OF WRITING

Origin. The traditional view is that Paul wrote the letter from Rome during his first Roman imprisonment.

Date of Writing. The date of the epistle depends on the origin. Those who affirm the traditional view, from Rome, generally date the epistle at about AD 60–62.

OCCASION AND PURPOSE

Occasion. Why did Paul write the epistle when he did? The Philippian church sent Epaphroditus to Paul with a gift (2:25–30). Paul likely wanted to thank the Philippians for this gift which had been sent for his support.

Purpose. Some members of the Philippian church showed a tendency toward disunity and contentiousness. Paul encouraged them to consider the mind of Christ (2:1–11) and urged them to practice the humility evident in Christ as they related to one another. The church faced a challenge from false teachers who diluted or added to God's way for salvation (3:1–6). Paul made his readers aware of the dangers of legalism, on the one hand, and the dangers of sensuality and materialistic greed, on the other. Each of these teachings required strong resistance, and Paul intended to help the church deal with them.

Paul's letter also prepared the way for a forthcoming visit to the church by both Timothy and Paul (2:19–24). His expression of hope to see his Christian friends soon (2:24) indicated that Paul's long imprisonment in Rome was nearing its end.

AUDIENCE

The Philippian church became a model. From its beginning, it was healthy, even though at the time of Paul's writing it was experiencing a minor problem of disunity (4:2–7). We find several characteristics about this congregation:

- It was primarily a Gentile congregation.
- Women played an important role in the life of the church.
- The Philippians were a model of generosity.
- The church was loyal, as evidenced by its gifts of support to Paul and its desire to know Paul's state during his imprisonment in Rome.

BASIC OUTLINE OF PHILIPPIANS

I. Greetings (1:1–2)
II. Paul's Joyful Concern for the Church (1:3–11)

III. Paul's Joyful Response in the Midst of Difficult Circumstances (1:12–26)
IV. Paul's Personal Plea for Christian Unity and Humility (1:27–2:18)
V. Paul's Pastoral Commendation for His Coworkers and Their Examples of Humility (2:19–30)
VI. Paul's Warning Against the Error of Self-righteousness (3:1–11)
VII. Paul's Single-Minded Exhortation to Christian Maturity (3:12–4:1)
VIII. Paul's Gentle Advice for Joy and Peace Among the Saints (4:2–9)
IX. Paul's Genuine Thanksgiving for the Church's Generosity (4:10–20)
X. Conclusion (4:21–23)

QUESTIONS TO GUIDE YOUR STUDY

1. Describe the city of Philippi, including its political and social environment.
2. What was Paul's purpose in writing to the believers at Philippi?
3. Describe the church at Philippi. What were its characteristics?
4. What is the basic value of the book of Philippians to the present-day believer?

PHILIPPIANS 1

THE SALUTATION (1:1–2)

The greeting Paul sent the church at Philippi resembled the greetings of other first-century letters. Commonly, letters contained three elements: (1) identification of the writers, (2) identification of the readers, and (3) the greeting. Some differences occur, however, which reinforce the Christian nature of Paul's letters.

The Writers (v. 1a)

This letter names two writers: Paul and Timothy. Timothy, along with Silas, participated in the original mission to Philippi (Acts 16:1ff.).

Readers (v. 1b)

Paul identified two groups of readers. They were the church at large and special persons within the congregation at the Philippian church. The special group consisted of overseers and deacons. Their precise functions are not clear.

HISTORICAL BACKGROUND

The Hellenistic Letter

Generally, Paul's letters do seem to follow the normal pattern of the Hellenistic letter, the basic form of which consists of five major sections:

1. Opening (sender, addressee, greeting)
2. Thanksgiving or Blessing (often with prayer of intercession, well wishes, or personal greetings)
3. The burden of the letter (including citation of classical sources and arguments)
4. Parenesis (ethical instruction, exhortation)
5. Closing (mention of personal plans, mutual friends, benediction)

Section Summary

The characteristic greeting in Paul's letters brings together two great words. "Grace" is God's undeserved favor toward us, manifested in the giving of his Son. The usual Jewish greeting was shalom or "peace." For Paul, that word describes the new relationship between God and believers and among believers themselves.

PAUL'S THANKSGIVING AND PRAYER FOR THE PHILIPPIANS (1:3–11)

Philippians 1:3–11 forms a unit of thought in two movements: verses 3–8 express praise and affection for the Philippians, whereas verses 9–11 express Paul's prayer for them.

Paul's Thanksgiving (vv. 3–8)

Paul expresses his thanksgiving for the church at Philippi and tells them he does so every time they came to mind.

Characteristics of Paul's Thankfulness (vv. 3–7a)

We can see at least three characteristics of Paul's thankfulness for them:

1. *It is joyful.* Here is the first mention of joy, which will become a major theme in the letter.
2. *It is prayed with confidence.* Paul's confidence was based on the working of God in their midst, not in his own ability or persuasiveness.
3. *It is proper.* Paul maintains a sense of propriety. He balanced the two actions of "always praying" and being "sure."

Paul's Reasons for His Thankfulness (vv. 7b–8)

Paul provides three reasons for his attitude of thankfulness:

1. *Paul had the Philippians "in [his] heart."* Although the church at Philippi started under difficult circumstances, the difficulties forged a bond of affection between Paul and those in the Philippian church.
2. *The Philippians' fellow service in the apostolic ministry.* The love and respect were mutual. The Philippians carried Paul in their hearts and proved it by their support of him as he bore witness to Christ as a prisoner in Rome.
3. *The deep Christian tie between Paul and the Philippian believers.* The mutual affection between Paul and the Philippian believers was so strong that he longed for them with a love much like the love Christ had for both Paul and the Philippians.

HISTORICAL BACKGROUND

Timothy

Timothy, whose name means "honoring God," was h friend and trusted coworker of Paul. He is listed as coauthor of this letter. Paul tells the Philippians (2:19–23) he hopes to send Timothy to them soon.

HISTORICAL BACKGROUND

Philippi

Philippi was a city in the Roman province of Macedonia. Paul did missionary work in Philippi (Acts 16:12) and later wrote a letter to the church there (Phil 1:1). Paul first visited Philippi on his second missionary journey in response to his Macedonian vision (Acts 16:9). The Roman character of the city is apparent from Paul's other experiences in Philippi. (See also "The City of Philippi" in the Introduction.)

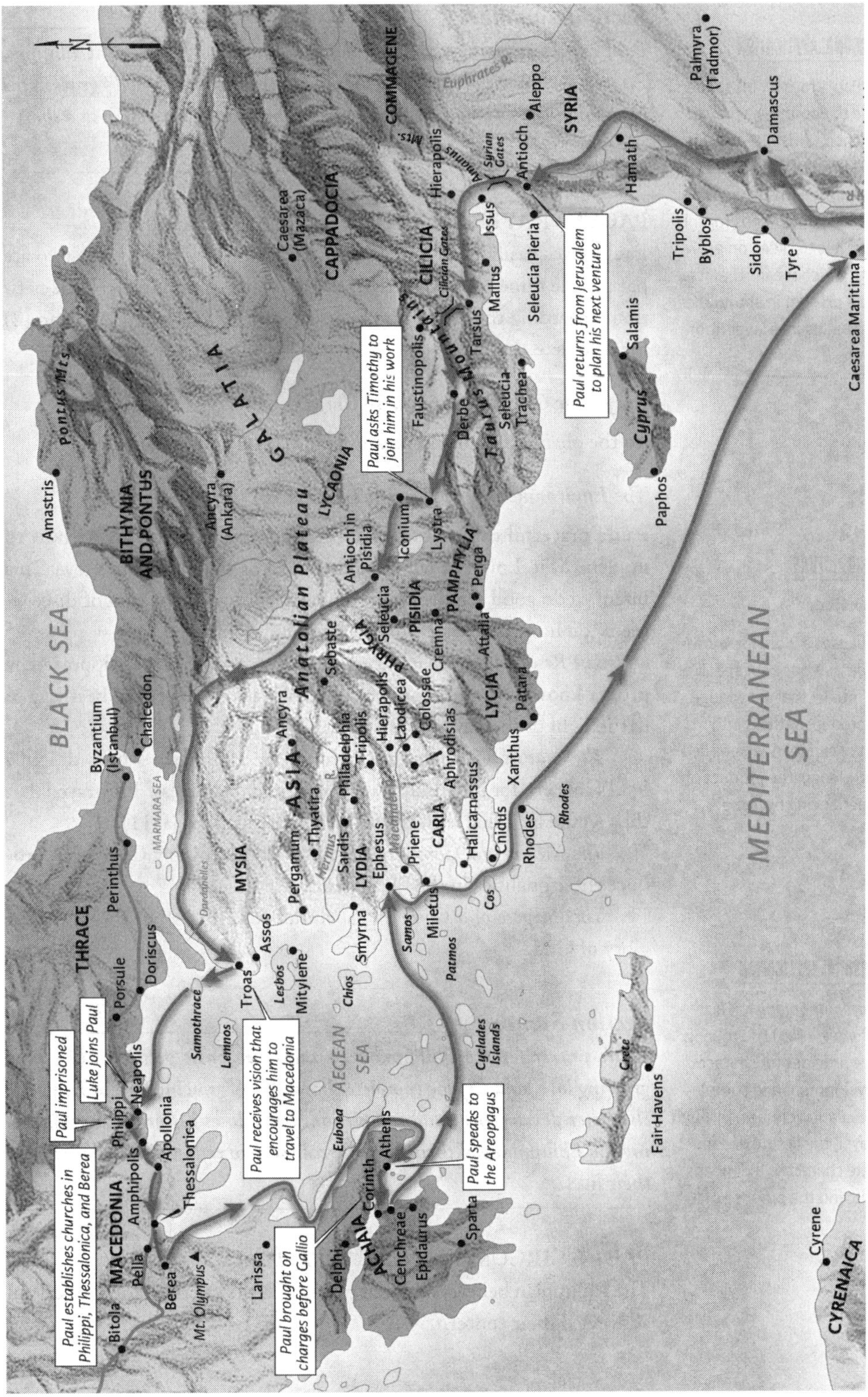
BLACK SEA
MEDITERRANEAN SEA
AEGEAN SEA
MARMARA SEA
MACEDONIA
THRACE
MYSIA
ASIA
LYDIA
CARIA
PHRYGIA
PISIDIA
LYCIA
PAMPHYLIA
LYCAONIA
GALATIA
CAPPADOCIA
CILICIA
COMMAGENE
SYRIA
BITHYNIA AND PONTUS
ACHAIA
CYRENAICA
Anatolian Plateau
Taurus Mountains
Pontus Mts.
Amanus Mts.
Euphrates R.
Paul establishes churches in Philippi, Thessalonica, and Berea
Paul imprisoned
Luke joins Paul
Paul receives vision that encourages him to travel to Macedonia
Paul brought on charges before Gallio
Paul speaks to the Areopagus
Paul asks Timothy to join him in his work
Paul returns from Jerusalem to plan his next venture
Bitola
Pella
Berea
Mt. Olympus
Amphipolis
Thessalonica
Apollonia
Philippi
Neapolis
Porsule
Doriscus
Perinthus
Byzantium (Istanbul)
Chalcedon
Amastris
Larissa
Delphi
Corinth
Cenchreae
Epidaurus
Sparta
Athens
Samothrace
Lemnos
Troas
Assos
Lesbos
Mitylene
Pergamum
Thyatira
Sardis
Smyrna
Chios
Ephesus
Samos
Patmos
Priene
Miletus
Cos
Halicarnassus
Cnidus
Rhodes
Philadelphia
Tripolis
Hierapolis
Laodicea
Colossae
Aphrodisias
Xanthus
Patara
Ancyra
Sebaste
Seleucia
Cremna
Attalia
Perga
Antioch in Pisidia
Iconium
Lystra
Derbe
Ancyra (Ankara)
Faustinopolis
Seleucia Trachea
Tarsus
Cilician Gates
Mallus
Issus
Hierapolis
Syrian Gates
Antioch
Seleucia Pieria
Aleppo
Caesarea (Mazaca)
Salamis
Cyprus
Paphos
Hamath
Tripolis
Byblos
Sidon
Tyre
Damascus
Palmyra (Tadmor)
Caesarea Maritima
Cyclades Islands
Crete
Fair Havens
Cyrene
Euboea

Section Summary

Paul expresses genuine thankfulness for his fellow believers at Philippi. As partners in the gospel, they shared in the blessings of God's grace. This resulted in strong emotional ties between them and partnership in a shared mission.

PERSONAL APPLICATION

As Paul prays for his readers' love to abound, he prayed for their Christlike attitude of self-sacrifice to continue. We can see the dynamic growth Paul intends for this love. It is to "keep on growing," which means that it is to be present in abundance and builds love layer upon layer.

PAUL'S PRAYER FOR THE PHILIPPIANS (1:9–11)

Paul moves easily from thanksgiving to petitioning prayer. The two are part of the same spiritual activity. Paul's prayer contains two basic petitions regarding the Philippian believers: (1) for a growing love, and (2) for complete character.

Prayer for Growing Love (v. 9–10a)

To the obvious command regarding love, Paul adds his own insights.

The Environment of a Growing Love (v. 9b)

Paul's prayerful exhortation to love came with instructions on how to implement it. Love is a will to do good to the objects of one's love. This intent to do good requires both "knowledge" and "every kind of discernment" on how to do that which is good for another person.

The Result of a Growing Love (v. 10a). A growing love, supported by proper knowledge and moral insight, enables one to see the best way to live in light of the day of Christ.

The Nature of Complete Character (v. 10b). Two words describe Paul's concern for the Philippians: "pure" and "blameless." He prayed that they would be "filled with the fruit of righteousness" (v. 11).

The Means to a Complete Character (v. 11a). Only Christ can produce these qualities in the Philippians.

The Purpose of a Complete Character (v. 11b). All of this is for the glory of God.

WORD PICTURE

Knowledge

Paul uses a word for *knowledge* that does not speak of an intellectual knowledge (a product of the mind) but of experiential, applied knowledge (the product of experiencing by living).

PERSONAL APPLICATION

Prayer for Complete Character (vv. 10b–11). Growing love provides for character development and completion. Paul identifies, through prayer, the nature of complete character, the means to it, and the purpose of it.

Section Summary

Paul's prayer for the Philippians contains two basic petitions: (1) for a growing love, and (2) for complete character. A growing love provides for character development and completion. Paul closes his prayer by reminding the Philippians of their ultimate calling—to reflect God's character in their lives.

PAUL'S CIRCUMSTANCES (1:12–17)

The Philippian believers desired to know Paul's circumstances, and Paul addressed their concern.

His Imprisonment (v. 12)

Rather than detail the hardships he faced, Paul takes a higher road. His primary concern was that the gospel advances.

Reactions of Others to Paul's Imprisonment (vv. 13–17)

In explaining the situation at Rome, Paul discloses two important results of the events that happened to him. Neither of these was expected, and thus Paul's word was news to them. At the same time, both reactions advanced the gospel.

The first reaction was that the gospel spread through the ranks of the soldiers. Paul says they knew he was a prisoner of Christ.

The second result of Paul's circumstances involved the church at Rome. A new evangelistic effort sprang up, touching the entire community. Some members were encouraged by Paul and preached out of sympathy. Others, who were antagonistic toward Paul, preached in hope that they would create further trouble for Paul while he was in prison.

Section Summary

Paul made known to the Philippians the real purpose of his imprisonment. He had been placed there "in the defense . . . of the gospel"—that is, to present its claims. Indeed, the gospel spread among the Roman soldiers, and a new evangelistic effort sprang up in Rome from these difficult circumstances.

PAUL'S ATTITUDE (1:19–26)

Paul's situation caused him to reflect deeply. He has two concerns: the outcome of his imprisonment and the trial and the possibility of his death. These verses reveal the tensions in Paul's life, and the carefully composed following section expresses Paul's emotions.

Paul's Joy in Salvation (vv. 18–24a)

Paul is obviously optimistic, and this section provides a description of Paul's joy.

Paul's Salvation and Hope (vv. 18b–20). Paul fully expected deliverance.

Paul then expresses hope in two ways, which are really two sides of the same coin. First, he expresses the hope that he will not be ashamed but rather, second, that he will honor Christ.

Paul is not so much concerned that he will be ashamed of Christ. Rather, his desire is that he would never bring dishonor to Christ. He wanted to act and speak boldly in even the most difficult of circumstances in such a way that Christ will be highly esteemed by those who are observing his behavior.

WORD PICTURE

Salvation

Also translated "deliverance," this word has been interpreted in two ways. First, it can mean deliverance from prison. Second, it can mean deliverance from this life to the full presence of Christ. Or, third, Paul could well have had both these ideas in mind.

To Live Is Christ (vv. 21). For Paul, life *was* Christ. Before he encountered Christ on the Damascus Road, Paul [called Saul at that time in Acts] had been the center of his own world. It was a world of which God was a part. But the focus of Paul's pre-Christian life was his own righteousness before God—how well he was performing.

Paul's conversion was a revolution. Paul was no longer the center of his universe. Christ was. What Paul thought about himself and how he perceived himself mattered far less than what Christ thought of him. And Christ held Paul in such esteem that he "loved me and gave himself for me" (Gal 2:20). For Paul, death was simply much more of Christ—it was gain.

Paul's Commitment to the Philippians (vv. 21–26). Paul's words reveal a deep inner struggle. He came down on the side of expressing his confidence that he would remain with the Philippians to advance the gospel and further their progress and joy in the faith.

Section Summary

Paul's attitude was one of sober optimism. His joy was anchored in the certainty of his salvation, the hope that he will not be ashamed on the day of judgment, and his commitment to the Philippians. His love for them dictated that he place their needs above his own desires.

THREE EXHORTATIONS (1:27–2:18)

This verse begins a new section of the epistle: 1:27–2:18. A change of tone signals a change of direction. Paul moved from information to exhortation. Three exhortations occur: 1:27–30; 2:1–4; 2:12–18.

A UNIFIED STAND (1:27–30)

The Philippians had the opportunity to witness to the world by their unified stand for the gospel. This would be particularly impressive if they stood strong through the sufferings they were called to endure. To address this issue, Paul discusses two matters: the nature of the stand (vv. 27–28) and Christian suffering (vv. 29–30).

The Nature of the Philippians' Stand (vv. 27–28)

The command "live your life worthy of the gospel" calls the church to appropriate conduct. Paul is reminding the Philippians of the obligations of people who participate in a society. In this case, the society was one of Christians whose strongest ties were in heaven. Paul explains this stand in two w1ys:

1. *In One Spirit.* This refers to the attitude that should be a mark of the church. To describe the function of the body, Paul draws on the imagery of persons—"contending together."

2. *"Not Being Frightened."* The church was to have unflinching steadfastness, even in the midst of persecution. Whoever the opponents were, they were not to intimidate the Philippians.

Christian Suffering (vv. 29–30)

The Pauline Model of Suffering (v. 30). Paul's life provided the model of suffering he identified in this verse by reminding the Philippians that they witnessed him suffer.

Section Summary

The Philippians had the opportunity to witness to the world by their unified stand for the gospel. This would be particularly impressive if they stood strong through the sufferings they were called to endure. Suffering confirms the believer's faith, bringing him or her in closer contact with the Lord and providing a vehicle for making commitment real and tangible.

QUESTIONS TO GUIDE YOUR STUDY

1. What are the characteristics of thankfulness?
2. What prompted Paul's attitude of thankfulness toward the Philippians?
3. Describe the nature of Paul's prayer for the Philippians. What aspects of that prayer might we appropriately apply to our present-day churches?
4. How would you describe Paul's attitude while being imprisoned? Why did he have this outlook?

HISTORICAL BACKGROUND

Paul's Suffering

Paul may be referring to the imprisonment and beating he and Silas experienced in Philippi after they prayed for an evil spirit to come out of a slave girl who was being used to tell fortunes. The beatings resulted in wounds which the Philippian jailer washed following his conversion. It's likely that the early members of the church at Philippi saw these wounds.

Paul reminds them that he continues to be involved in the same conflict which caused suffering in Philippi. He calls on the Philippians to step up and not to shrink back from the suffering which results from following Christ.

PHILIPPIANS 2

A UNIFIED MIND (2:1–4)

Paul's thoughts turn from the need to withstand pressure from the outside to the attitudes that were to characterize Christians. In 1:27 he exhorted the Philippians to unity, and here he continues that thought. This passage unfolds in three parts:

The basis of Paul's appeal (2:1)
The essence of Paul's appeal (2:2a)
The expression of unity (2:3–4)

These become the resources for Christian unity.

PERSONAL APPLICATION

Paul spoke straightforwardly about Christian suffering. He states clearly that God has given them the privilege of believing in Christ and suffering for him. God is honored by both.

WORD PICTURE

Emptied Himself

A. T. Robertson asks, "Of what did Christ empty himself? Not his divine nature. That was impossible. He continued to be the Son of God. . . . Undoubtedly Christ gave up his environment of glory. He took upon himself limitations of place (space) and of knowledge and of power, though still on earth retaining more of these than any mere man. It is here that men should show restraint and modesty, though it is hard to believe that Jesus limited himself by error of knowledge and certainly not by error of conduct. He was without sin, though tempted as we are. 'He stripped himself of the insignia of majesty" (Lightfoot)."

A. T. Robertson, *WPNT*, vol. 4, 444.

HISTORICAL BACKGROUND

Many New Testament interpreters believe this passage is an earl' Christian hymn. Its structure has two parts. Philippians 2:6–8 speaks of Jesus's servanthood, and 2:9–11 speaks of his exaltation. If these verses do constitute a hymn, which seems reasonable, they reveal something of the worship of the early church and how Jesus Christ was viewed by the churches.

Basis of Paul's Appeal to Unity (v. 1)

Four statements form the basis of Paul's appeal. Introduced by the word "if," they recall the blessings of being in a Christian community:

- *If you have any consolation or encouragement in Christ*
- *If you draw comfort from his love*
- *If you have any fellowship with the Spirit*
- *If you have any tenderness and compassion*

The Essence of Unity (v. 2)

Paul assumes that each of the four conditions set forth in the above "if" clauses exists among the Philippians. Based on these realities experienced by the Philippians, Paul urges them to fill his cup with joy by (1) thinking and feeling the same, (2) loving one another with the same love, and (3) having their souls in harmony with one another and with Jesus Christ.

Nothing would make Paul happier than for this unity of thought and feeling to pervade the church.

The Expression of Unity (vv. 3–4)

The unity of mind and heart will be strengthened and will express itself in actions that take the pattern—

DON'T DO THIS	DO THIS
The first "don't" is: don't act from motives where you are trying to outdo or outshine a brother or sister and build up your own ego.	The way to avoid this is to consider others better than yourself.
The second "don't" is: don't focus just on your own interest. To be sure, you must be concerned about your own interest. Not to be so concerned could result in irresponsibility.	But balance the concern with your own affairs by being concerned about the interests of others. Step outside yourself and look at things through the perspective of others.

Section Summary

Paul exhorts the Philippian believers to strive for unity and then provides the resources for Christian unity. To function as a community of believers, the church needs to be of one mind.

THE EXAMPLE OF CHRIST (2:5–11)

In 2:5 Paul repeats the exhortation he made in 2:1–4. This repetition emphasizes its importance. Even more, it introduces the strongest possible model of humility and servanthood: the Lord Jesus Christ himself.

Philippians 2:6–11 recalls the attitude and actions of Christ as he left the glories of his eternal state to become a man and die for our sins. The Philippians were to imitate him because, in doing so, any problems of disunity that were beginning to appear could be solved.

The Introduction to the Hymn (v. 5)

Paul introduces this hymn to Christ by urging the Philippians to have the same mind as Christ.

The Hymn to Christ (vv. 6–11)

If this passage indeed was a hymn, it may well have been used in worship in Philippi. And so, Paul may have been reminding them of a text that was familiar to them.

The hymn reminded Paul's readers of the glory of Christ prior to the incarnation. He was God by nature—just as God the Father was. But he didn't cling to what was his by nature; rather, he emptied himself.

In verse 9 the passage changes both tone and structure. The hymn continues, but the Father, rather than Christ, becomes the subject:

God "highly exalted him." The word actually means "superexalted." This action occurred because of Jesus's voluntary humility and his servant-like attitude and actions.

God "gave him the name that is above every name." Jesus, by virtue of his humility, has become the object of highest adoration. The one who was humiliated by men was "exalted" by God. Because of his matchless obedience, God gave him a matchless name. "Every knee" will bow, and "every tongue" will acknowledge him to be Lord. The end result of the universal dominion of Christ will be that God will receive the "glory" due him.

OBEDIENCE: THE BELIEVERS' APPROPRIATE RESPONSE (2:12–18)

Following his extended hymn to Christ, Paul returned to his primary concern of 1:27—working together with one mind.

Practical Christianity (vv. 12–13)

Paul observed that the Philippians practiced obedience while he was among them. He told them that while he was away from them, it was even more important that they be obedient to the teaching they received from him.

He urges the believers to work out their salvation (v. 12) and provides a reason for doing so (v. 13).

The Command to Work Out Their Salvation (vv. 12–13). The Philippians were to make salvation work in their lives.

WORD PICTURE

Obedient

Obedient and *obey* come from an old word that means "to give ear to, to listen to." *Obedience* listens to and follows the wishes of another. The thought of death on a cross and the spiritual implications were overwhelming to Jesus as he prayed in Gethsemane. In his prayer to the Father, he asked if there were any way around drinking the cup he was about to drink. Three times after asking the question, he listened to his Father. There was no other way.

HISTORICAL BACKGROUND

Cicero, the Roman philosopher, characterized crucifixion as "the most cruel and abominable form of punishment" (*Verrine Orations* 5.64). In another context Cicero said, "The very word 'cross' should be foreign not only to the body of a Roman citizen, but to his thoughts, his eyes, his ears" (*Oration in Defense of C. Rabirius*, 16) (Both of these quotes are found in F. F. Bruce, *Philippians*, Harper & Row, 54.)

NEW TESTAMENT REFERENCE

Salvation was central to Paul's theology. In his other letters, Paul describes salvation as a past event (Eph 2:8–9) and as a future consummation (Rom 13:11). Here, he spoke of working out salvation in the present.

They were to work out their salvation with an attitude of "fear and trembling."

Positive Steadfastness (vv. 14–16)

Here Paul warns his readers of the dangers of murmuring and arguing. Paul knew that selfishness and vainglory led to complaints. He may have been attempting to head off even more problems in the community.

The Command to Stop Complaining (v. 14). "Do everything without grumbling or arguing." Those activities are unworthy of Christ's servants, and they have a negatively contagious effect among a body of Christians.

The Purpose of the Command (vv. 15–16). When individuals and churches have the mind of Christ and refrain from grumbling and arguing, they will be innocent and pure. There will be a marked difference between believers and the surrounding world.

Personal Joy in Ministry (vv. 17–18)

Paul's concern for the Philippians' steadfastness did not replace his joy for them and their service to the Lord. Paul uses three words that recall the sacrificial system: "poured out," "sacrifice," and "service." Paul indicated he was being "poured out" like a drink offering along with those he loved so much. Rather than being discouraged about his circumstances, Paul had great joy.

WORD PICTURE

Fear and Trembling

This phrase doesn't indicate a cowardly sort of fear. It was intended as an encouragement for believers to have an awe that is appropriate in the presence of God. Wuest translates this phrase like this: "carry to its ultimate conclusion your own salvation with a wholesome, serious caution and trembling, for God is the One who is constantly putting forth his energy in you both in the form your being desirous of and your doing his good pleasure."

Section Summary

Paul commands the Philippians to "work out" their salvation by being faithful in living the Christian life. He also urges them to have the mind of Christ and to grow toward the goal of blamelessness. Above all, they were called to be like Christ.

The following verses form a break in the letter. Here Paul provides information about his situation and his intent to visit the Philippian church when he could.

PAUL'S PLANS FOR TIMOTHY (2:19–24)

The Sending of Timothy (vv. 19–22)

Knowing that he could not visit Philippi, Paul hopes to send Timothy in whom he had complete confidence because he was "like-souled" ("I have no one else like-minded"). Paul provided the evidence to support his commendation of Timothy:

- Timothy had a genuine interest in the affairs of the church at Philippi.
- Timothy sought the things of Christ rather than his own interests.

The Importance of Timothy (vv. 23–24)

Obviously, Timothy had a significant role in Paul's work. Paul makes two statements that reveal Timothy's importance to Paul and the work of the gospel. First, Paul needed Timothy a while longer. Second, Timothy replaced Paul, who desired to come when he could. In sending Timothy, Paul sent the best he had—an extension of himself—a costly gift to them.

PAUL'S PLANS FOR EPAPHRODITUS (2:25–30)

The Commendation of Epaphroditus (v. 25)

Paul wanted to send Timothy, but he also found it necessary to send Epaphroditus. That raises many questions. Why should Paul have felt that way? Would Epaphroditus not be of service to Paul as the church originally intended? Did something happen to sour him or Paul? Paul provides us with no answers to these questions.

The Reason Paul Sent Epaphroditus (vv. 26–28)

Paul mentions Epaphroditus's sickness. On the way to Rome, Epaphroditus apparently fell sick and nearly died. It was better for Epaphroditus to return home than to die in service to Paul. Further, Paul expected that the church would be eager to see him.

The Command to Honor Epaphroditus (vv. 29–30)

Paul urges the church members at Philippi to welcome Epaphroditus appropriately, with the honor due him. If the church had any doubts about whether Epaphroditus failed, Paul relieves those concerns. Epaphroditus risked his life for Paul, but he had also done it in demonstration of his love for them. He endured sickness near to death for their sakes.

Section Summary

Paul commends the service of two Christlike men. Both thought of others before their own concerns, and both served the Lord and his church. They would journey to the church in Paul's place, in the hope that he would follow soon.

QUESTIONS TO GUIDE YOUR STUDY

1. Paul exhorted the Philippians to think "the same way." What did he mean by that?

2. What does it mean that Christ "emptied" himself? What should be our response to this?
3. What does it mean for us to "work out" our salvation?
4. What can we learn through the examples of Timothy and Epaphroditus?

PHILIPPIANS 3

At this point in the epistle, Paul turns his thoughts more directly to the false teachers and to Christian living. Paul provides an interchange of instruction and exhortation. Commands predominate again until 4:10.

Two concerns occupy Paul's mind. First, certain persons attempted to undermine his ministry, and he had to counter them. Second, the problem of disunity demanded one final appeal, and Paul provided it with more direct language. These two concerns form the logical divisions of 3:1–4:19.

PAUL'S EXHORTATION TO AVOID FALSE TEACHERS (3:1–21)

Be Joyful in the Lord (v. 1a)

Halfway through the letter Paul says, "In addition."

As he is approaching the close of his letter, he echoes a key theme: rejoice in the Lord.

Be on Guard Against False Teachers (vv. 1b–3)

There is humor in the way Paul begins this section of warning. He is admitting repetition in what he is about to say. But like the skilled educator he was, he felt it was for the good and safety of his beloved Philippians.

Paul speaks from experience. He traveled the road the false teachers were traveling. He knew the weaknesses of a legalistic approach to salvation, and he knew the joys of coming to God through Christ. A subtle danger, however, was the threat that some would become legalistic Christians. In their enthusiasm, they might not be able to distinguish legalistic Christianity from the real thing and might not be able to see the dangers of legalism.

With three rapid statements, Paul warns the Philippians about false teachers. Three times he uses the verb "watch our for" in connection with false teachers whom he characterizes as dogs, those who do evil, and mutilators.

HISTORICAL BACKGROUND

Dogs

Eastern people generally hated dogs. The Jews often described Gentiles that way, but here Paul applies that term to false teachers. Perhaps he was envisioning the packs of ravenous dogs that roamed the countryside eating whatever they could.

Section Summary

Paul warns the Philippian believers about the threat posed to them by false teachers. These teachers were legalists who exalted the physical rite of circumcision. Genuine believers do not trust in any physical distinctions or in their own achievements. Their trust is in a God of power and glory who redeems them through Jesus Christ.

Paul's Testimony (vv. 4–6)

Paul gives a firsthand testimony of the bankruptcy of the flesh. He says if anyone could boast of fleshly status and achievement, he could. His background naturally divides into two logical categories: heritage and achievement.

His Heritage. Paul was circumcised on the eighth day. This mean he was an Israelite by birth and not a proselyte.

He was of the tribe of Benjamin—the youngest of Jacob's sons and the only one born in Canaan. Although a small tribe, Benjamin produced Israel's first king—Saul—for whom Paul may have been named.

He was a Hebrew of Hebrews. Although Paul was born in Tarsus, both of his parents were Hebrews. It's likely his lineage was well known to him and solidly Hebrew.

His Achievements. Paul gives his readers three items that provide the standard to measure his achievements: the law, zeal for the nation, and righteousness.

Paul had chosen to be a Pharisee. Pharisees were known for their love of the law, their strict interpretation of it, and their ethical consistency. Paul's zeal was at the core of his persecution of the church. Finally, as a staunch observer of the law, Paul sought to attain the righteousness of the law.

These characteristics of heritage and achievement reveal that Paul's acceptance of Christ did not occur because he was marginally Jewish. He had not failed at his own religion. The point of his testimony is that he had seen a better way and chosen to follow it.

OLD TESTAMENT REFERENCE

Circumcision

"This is my covenant between me and you and your offspring after you, which you are to keep: Every one of your males must be circumcised. . . . Throughout your generations, every male among you is to be circumcised at eight days old" (Gen 17:10, 12).

Section Summary

Paul's heritage and achievement revealed that his acceptance of Christ did not occur because he was marginally Jewish. He had seen a better way (the gospel of Jesus Christ) than the law and chosen to follow it instead.

The Righteousness of Faith (vv. 7–11)

When Paul was confronted by Christ (Acts 9:1–19), he made a radical decision. He could hold on to his advantages of birth and moral achievement that he possessed, or he could trust Christ for salvation. But he could not do both. He had to make a choice.

WORD PICTURE

Knowing Christ Jesus

The word *knowing* means "to have personal acquaintance or experience with." To "know" Christ is to be in an intimate relationship with him through faith. The person who knows Christ experiences the power of his resurrection.

HISTORICAL BACKGROUND

To explain what he means, Paul uses the illustration of athletic games. He was like a runner in a race. In races the winner's prize, the laurel wreath of the victor, was often placed at the finish line as an added incentive to the contestants. Since the Greek athletic games captured the imagination of all people in this area, Macedonia included, this illustration spoke vividly to Paul's readers.

The content of Paul's goal revolved around his repetitive use of the verb "take hold" (vv. 12,13). Paul attaches two activities for attaining his goal.

"Forgetting what is behind" expresses Paul's future orientation. For him, every day was a new adventure.

"Reached forward to what is ahead" captures the athletic metaphor of the Greek games. It is graphic, bringing to mind the straining muscles, clear focus, and complete dedication of the runner to his race to the prize. Both mental and physical discipline were necessary.

This section of Paul's warning explains Paul's real values. The real value Paul found was in knowing Christ personally. That brought zeal for perfect character not found through the law.

Paul considered his previous gains as loss (v. 7). He continued to affirm that decision and expressed that conviction even more firmly by saying he counted all things as trash compared to knowing Christ (v. 8).

Three times in verses 7–8 Paul expresses that his goal is Christ. For him, knowing Christ was better than the combined value of his former life. Christ exceeded everything else.

The Power of Christ's Resurrection. Christ was crucified. He was dead and buried, but God raised him from death.

Those in Christ, believers, participate in his resurrection. Paul experienced that resurrection life first on the road to Damascus, but from that point on he wanted to have greater personal knowledge of the risen Christ.

There is another mark of the person who knows Christ. He shares in the sufferings of his Lord.

The Fellowship of Sharing in His Sufferings. Knowing Christ also means identifying with his death. Being united with Christ in his death was a spiritual reality, but being conformed to his death was the daily process of living. Paul realized that conformity to Jesus's death made him a candidate for resurrection power. This helps explain the spiritual discipline Paul mentions in 3:12–16.

Section Summary

Paul tried the way of right relationship with God by heritage and achievement. Although he doesn't say so explicitly in this letter, he found this approach to right relationship with God to be a dead end because of the sinfulness of human beings. But God provided a way of right standing through the death and resurrection of Jesus Christ. Paul found in Christ what he had been seeking all his life. And once he found what he had been looking for, he left all for the knowledge of Christ.

PRESSING TOWARD THE GOAL (3:12–16)

Paul's Desire to Fulfill His Call (vv. 12–14)

Paul wanted to guard against any misunderstanding of his previous comments. He wanted his readers to know that he had not crossed the finish line in the Christian race yet. He also wanted them to know that he had not achieved perfection.

Paul's Encouragement to Other Believers (vv. 15–16)

Paul's experience set a pattern for all believers. If they would understand it and join with him, then they would avoid the influence of false teachers. Three movements occur in this command:

1. A call to unity
2. A warning of misconduct
3. An exhortation to continue

He calls the Philippians to unity (v. 15). He calls on those who are perfect or spiritually mature to "think this way." It includes thoughts, values, and intentions. Paul knew everyone would not see things as he did, so he urged them to be open to God's view of the matter.

He gives them an exhortation (v. 16). The believers were to remain steadfast. They were to remain true to what they had and with a collective discipline that was to characterize the entire church. This meant they were not to follow the false teachings of Paul's opponents.

Section Summary

Paul's experience correctly set a pattern for all believers. If they would understand it and join with him, they would avoid the influence of false teachers.

THE FALSE TEACHERS' CHARACTER EXPOSED (3:17–21)

Paul continues to warn the church about false teachers. In this passage he moves to plural rather than singular subjects so that the entire church is included.

Encouragement to Imitate Paul (v. 17)

Earlier Paul urged the church to imitate Christ (2:5–11). Here he urged the Philippians to imitate him. There is no egotism involved, however, as Paul realized they would follow ("pay careful attention to") other Christian models as well. In Paul's absence, they were to find other models who were true to his commitments.

Characteristics of Paul's Opponents (vv. 18–19)

Then Paul delivers his final blow against the false teachers. Emotion fills his words here, and he confesses his tears as he writes. These teachers followed Paul about, seeking to entice people away from the truth. They opposed the message of the cross, hindering those who would take advantage of its work. Paul cherished the cross. The fact that the false teachers did not honor the cross reveals who they were. Theirs was organized, active opposition to the gospel.

HISTORICAL BACKGROUND

Citizenship

A. T. Robertson points out that Paul was proud of his Roman citizenship—just as the Philippians were proud of theirs. With this citizenship came protection and many other privileges. But Paul was prouder of the fact that he and his fellow Christians at Philippi were citizens of heaven. A. T. Robertson, *WPNT*, "Epistles of Paul," vol. 4, 457.

Paul exposed these teachers by revealing their character, providing four statements about their doctrine and practice:

1. They followed their appetites—"their God is their stomach."
2. They are proud of what they should be ashamed of.
3. Their focus is exclusively on this world.
4. Their end is destruction.

Paul ends this section by presenting a Christian perspective in which he contrasts the earthly and the heavenly. This metaphor had rich meaning to the Philippians, as they were proud of their Roman citizenship. Although the term *citizenship* may imply a place, Paul uses it of a people. Genuine believers are not citizens of this world but belong to a heavenly commonwealth. Their "citizenship is in heaven."

Paul also makes a point in verse 21 to focus on the physical body, which would be transformed to become like Christ's body. This body is destined for eternity. Paul's hope involved a physical transformation. The power of the resurrection would be complete when Jesus exerted his power in the bodies of believers. This hope should have caused the believers to press on toward that great day.

Section Summary

Paul delivers his final blow against the false teachers by revealing their character and outcome. They opposed the message of the cross and hindered those who would take advantage of its work. He contrasts them by discussing the characteristics of the true believer, who has the hope of being transformed into a new resurrection body.

QUESTIONS TO GUIDE YOUR STUDY

1. How did Paul describe the false teachers who were trying to entice the Philippians with their doctrines?
2. What was the point of Paul's personal testimony?
3. What does it mean for the believer to "know" Jesus?
4. How did Paul view his calling? What lessons on calling might we apply from Paul?

PHILIPPIANS 4

Throughout Paul's letter to the Philippians are hints of disunity among the members of the congregation. Paul confronted the disunity with strong doctrinal and practical instruction. Paul gave several exhortations: to steadfastness, to unity, to joy and peace, and to the proper outlook.

AN EXHORTATION TO STEADFASTNESS (4:1)

The previous passage contains the emotion of argumentation. In this passage, Paul speaks with the warmth of a friend.

The Address to the Readers

In his address, Paul makes three statements about his readers at the Philippian church:

1. *They were brothers and sisters.* Through the Holy Spirit, they had oneness with one another and with Paul.
2. *They were "my dearly loved and longed for."* This speaks of Paul's desire to fellowship with them.
3. *They were Paul's "joy and crown."* For Paul, life was better because he knew these believers. They brought him joy even while he was awaiting trial.

Clearly, a strong tie existed between Paul and the church.

The Exhortation

Out of this friendship grew exhortation. Paul urged the Philippians to steadfastness. Roman armies were well known for standing unmoved against the enemy. The church was to stand in the same way. How was the church to stand? It was not to be weakened by disunity, turmoil, or wrong values. It was to stand together to accomplish God's will. This exhortation recalls Paul's instruction in 1:27.

WORD PICTURE

Euodia and Syntyche

Euodia means literally "good or prosperous journey." Syntyche means "pleasant acquaintance" or "good luck."

In writing to solve the problem, Paul identified a process and reasons for helping these women.

The Process. The process began with the women themselves. Naturally, the best solution was for the women to solve their own problem. The word "agree" means that the women were to have the same attitudes and values that Christ had and which Paul expressed earlier in the letter (2:5–11).

The Reasons. Paul provides us with two reasons for helping the women. First, they were Christian sisters. Second, they fought with Paul for the gospel.

AN EXHORTATION TO UNITY (4:2–3)

At this point, Paul addresses the problem of unity. The problem that erupted was a dispute between two women, Euodia and Syntyche. This problem was more than a passing disagreement. It had the potential of splitting the church. But Paul had faith in the women themselves and the church's ability to correct the problem.

Section Summary

Paul exhorts the Philippian congregation to unity. A dispute between two women within the church threatened to divide the fellowship. Paul appeals to the women and offers a solution to their problem.

AN EXHORTATION TO JOY AND PEACE (4:4–9)

The Exhortation (vv. 4–7)

These six verses divide naturally into two major sections (vv. 4–7 and vv. 8–9), but they unite around the theme of peace. In 4:7 Paul writes of the peace of God that sustains Christians during times of hardship. In 4:9 he writes of the result of a proper thought life (4:8).

Philippians 4:4–7 speaks primarily to those occasions when peace is lacking. There are those times when troublesome circumstances interrupt the normal flow of events. Paul gives his readers three commands to help them solve these kinds of problems:

1. *He commanded them to rejoice.* Their joy was to be in the Lord, and it was to be unchanging. Paul's own circumstances reminded him of the joy available in the Lord, and he wished that joy for them as well. Paul knows that no situation is beyond the Lord's help. Christians can rejoice in that, if nothing else. "The Lord is near" expresses the confident expectation of early Christians.
2. *He exhorts them to graciousness.* The word for "graciousness" has a variety of meanings. Gentleness or kindness in relation to others is a central idea. The gentle person does not insist on his or her rights.
3. *"Don't worry about anything."* This is a negative command that has a positive thrust. Anxiety is a contradiction of the life of faith. It is the destructive, self-defeating worry about whether our needs are going to be met. It expresses itself in the idolatry of things. Jesus in the Sermon on the Mount spoke of anxiety (Matt 6:25–34), where he stated the most common causes of anxiety. They are clothing, food and drink, and the future. Even in our contemporary life, with its complexities, the same simple concerns cause anxiety. Prayer cures anxiety, and Paul uses three words to describe prayer: "prayer," "petition," and "thanksgiving." Each contributes to a proper understanding of the comprehensive nature of the prayer life.

Paul's answer to anxiety is the peace of God. He makes three statements about this peace:

1. *It is divine.* Paul did not envision a situation where circumstances changed or external needs were met. This peace was a characteristic of God that invaded the Christian.
2. *It "surpasses all understanding."* The word *transcends* means "excellent." Peace excels over knowledge. Paul probably had in mind situations where knowledge is insufficient. Sometimes knowledge cannot explain, and sometimes explanations do not help. Peace, however, is a reality Christians experience even when they don't understand the *whys*.
3. *It will "guard your hearts and minds in Christ Jesus."*

For these three reasons, prayerful people are peaceful people.

WORD PICTURE

Guard

"Guard" is a military term, implying that peace stands on duty to keep out anything that brings care and anxiety.

The Environment of Peace (vv. 8–9)

In verses 8–9 Paul turns his thoughts to providing an environment of peace by unity of thought. The church is to make these matters its collective goal, with God ruling in them. This section contains two lists. The first list is completed by the exhortation to "dwell on these things." The second list concludes with "do."

Paul addresses the thought life first, identifying eight qualities that should characterize Christians. The following chart lists these qualities and provides their extended meanings. These characteristics would unite the church and present a good testimony to the world.

"DWELL ON THESE THINGS" QUALITIES LIST

VIRTUE	EXTENDED MEANING
Whatever is true	truthfulness, dependability
Whatever is honorable	worthy of respect, honor
Whatever is just	giving to God and people a justness that is worthy of them
Whatever is pure	holy in relation to God
Whatever is lovely	that which calls forth love; persons should be attractive, lovable
Whatever is commendable	praiseworthy, attractive
Whatever is excellent	morally excellent
Whatever is praiseworthy	worthy of praising God

"Do" instructions list. After presenting the standard for the thought life, Paul turns to Christian practice. Paul urges the Philippians to use him as a model of effective Christian living. The church is to model and cultivate these things it saw in Paul:

- Whatever you have learned
- Whatever you received
- Whatever you heard

The result of this kind of living would be the God of peace abiding with them.

The above two sets of instructions on peace complement each other. When anxiety appears, the cure is prayer. When the life is disorderly, the cure is mental and practical discipline.

Section Summary

Paul's exhortation addresses the anxieties of life and presents an environment of peace. When anxiety appears, the cure is prayer. When life is disorderly, the cure is mental and practical discipline.

PAUL'S EXPRESSION OF THANKS FOR THE PHILIPPIAN SUPPORT (4:10–20)

The final section of the epistle addresses finances. Paul thanks the Philippians for remembering him and his needs, as they had before. Because of their pattern of giving, they were a double blessing to him. Paul identifies some of the benefits for those who gave.

Paul's Situation (vv. 10–14)

Appreciation (v. 10). It may have been years between the gifts mentioned in 2 Cor 8 and the one delivered by Epaphroditus. In the meantime, Paul learned to be content with whatever God supplied to him. He states three reasons he fared well even during the time before he received their gift.

Contentment (v. 11). The first reason Paul did not need the gift was his own contentment. Twice Paul mentions that he learned contentment. Paul came to grips with his circumstances and fared well in and through them because of his relationship to Christ.

PERSONAL APPLICATION

"God's work, done God's way, will never lack God's blessing." —Hudson Taylor

Adaptability (v. 12). Circumstances are the arena of spiritual growth, and through them Paul developed adaptability.

In these varied experiences Paul displayed spiritual equilibrium. He was equally unaffected by poverty and riches. One learns this kind of knowledge by walking with Christ—who is the sufficient one—and by developing a biblical perspective of material things. By doing so, Paul learned to rise above any circumstances.

Dependency (v. 13). Paul depends on Christ for strength. The expression "through him who strengthens me" clearly refers to the indwelling Christ. Paul could accomplish all that God wanted through the strength he provided.

Blessing (v. 14). Paul reminded his readers that their share in his work was good: "You did well by partnering with me in my hardship." First, they participated with him.

Second, Paul identified their partnership specifically with his troubles. The term *hardship* implies hardships of any kind, but it had a deeper meaning for Paul. In Col 1:24 Paul speaks of suffering "Christ's afflictions" so that his difficulties in spreading the gospel related to the Messiah.

The gift of the Philippians was good because it demonstrated that they understood God's working in the world and that they willingly supported it through God's servants.

Section Summary

Paul thanks the Philippians for remembering him and his needs. Because of their pattern of giving, they were a blessing to him. Paul identifies some of the benefits in store for those who gave.

Paul's Attitude Toward Those Who Gave (vv. 15–20)

Paul's thankfulness turns to commendation and promise of reward. Both the nature of their giving and its motivation pleased the Lord.

Commendation (vv. 15–17). Paul commended the Philippian church for the way it supported him. Its support was unique, for it was the only Macedonian church to support him. He also commends them because their support was immediate and consistent. Finally, Paul commends them because their gifts were an investment in the work of God and in their future.

Blessings (vv. 18–19). Paul's commendation leads him to speak of how the Philippians benefited from supporting him. He indicates two benefits to the giver. First, God was pleased. Paul pointed out that their gift was an acceptable Christian sacrifice (see Rom 12:1–2). The second benefit was that the believers would experience God's provision. Just as God had met his needs, he would also meet theirs.

Doxology (v. 20). Fittingly, Paul ends this passage with a doxology. God is the source of all good things. The love of God was expressed in the Philippians' gift. Paul remembers the ultimate purpose of life—to bring glory to God now and forever. The last word, therefore, is one of praise.

Section Summary

Paul promises the Philippians they would be rewarded for their support. Both the nature of their giving and its motivation pleased the Lord.

CONCLUSION (4:21–23)

The final greeting is typical. "Every saint in Christ Jesus" is everyone who trusts in Christ. Paul uses the word where we often employ the term *Christian*. The reference to "Caesar's household" shows the opportunities Paul's imprisonment opened for witness at the highest levels of Roman government.

HISTORICAL BACKGROUND

Caesar's Household

"Not members of the imperial family connected with the imperial establishment. . . . Christianity has begun to undermine the theme of the Caesars."

A. T. Robertson, *WPNT*, vol. 4, 463.

QUESTIONS TO GUIDE YOUR STUDY

1. What problem at the church in Philippi prompted Paul's exhortations in this chapter?
2. List Paul's several exhortations in this chapter. What are the main thrusts of each? What is their common denominator?

3. What steps must a follower of Christ take to create an environment of peace?
4. Explain Paul's view of contentment. What practical and spiritual lessons might we learn from Paul as a model of contentment?

Colossians

INTRODUCTION

Christianity faced one of its most severe challenges in the complex and confusing intellectual climate of ancient Colossae. False teachers were urging the people to move away from their Christian roots and to accept other religious ideas. Although Paul did not found the church at Colossae, it bore his imprint, and Paul felt the responsibility to address its problems.

This epistle contains distinctive teachings about the person and work of Christ, Christian living and relationships, and Paul's conception of his ministry.

Studying the epistle is an adventure. Its pages are alive with relevance and challenge to those of us who live in an age of relativism and religious syncretism.

One theme predominates in Colossians: the centrality of Christ. No other epistle is as Christ centered as this one. Whether the reader spends countless hours with Colossians or reads it only casually, every encounter with the text brings one face-to-face with the Lord whom the text introduces so well.

AUTHOR

Tradition supports the letter's claim that Paul was the author (Col 1:1). Paul had never been to Colossae, but he wrote to them to address matters raised by Epaphras (1:7) who was with Paul at the time the letter was written (4:12). Some people doubt Pauline authorship on the grounds of the book's theology and style. But some obvious differences in the theological perspective do not automatically force the conclusion that someone other than Paul wrote Colossians.

HISTORICAL BACKGROUND

Colossae

The city of Colossae had a mixed population. The natives were Phrygian. Because of the military and commercial heritage of the area, however, Greeks may have settled there during the Greek period of dominance. To this were added Jews of the Diaspora, Romans involved in politics, and various ethnic groups drawn by commercial interests. From the epistle we know that both Jews and Gentiles lived at Colossae and became part of the church.

DATE OF WRITING

From the earliest times, most scholars have dated the letter to the Colossians to the time of Paul's first Roman imprisonment. The letter would have been written about the same time as Philippians and Philemon, around AD 60–61.

PURPOSE

Paul's purpose for writing the letter was to address false teachings in the church. Apparently these false teachings attempted to supplement the gospel and in the process of doing so were undermining it. We don't have a direct description of these false teachings, but on the basis of what Paul says in the letter, we can make some inferences about these teachings. They:

- Undermined the centrality of Christ
- Focused on speculative philosophical traditions
- Observed dietary prescriptions and prohibitions
- Observed certain religious rites of a Jewish nature
- Venerated angels
- Tended toward asceticism

AUDIENCE

Paul addressed his letter to "the saints in Christ at Colossae."

THE MESSAGE OF COLOSSIANS

The theme of this letter centers on the supremacy of Christ. In his letter, Paul emphasizes that Christ was sufficient for the total Christian life from beginning to end. Only he is worthy of worship and obedience, for the fullness of God is in him and in him alone (1:15–20). Believers needed no other source of understanding and knowledge (2:2).

NEW TESTAMENT REFERENCE

Although the problem addressed in Galatians was entirely different, Paul feared the same consequences. Adding to the gospel of Christ is, in effect, to subtract from it.

The worship of the principalities and powers—if intermediaries—is both evil and foolish, for Christ is supreme in his authority over all of them (1:16). The unity and growth of the church depended on its faithful relationship to Christ, who is its head (2:19).

We know from Paul's letters that he was able to tolerate a great diversity of opinion and beliefs in the Christian body. But he resisted fiercely any teaching that denied to Christ his unique place as the only Savior and Lord of the church.

The church at Colossae had indeed held firm to its initial faith in Christ (2:15). But Paul must have feared that the Colossians could yet be seduced by false teachings which were subtly undermining the gospel.

Paul wrote his letter to the Colossians, therefore, to encourage them to remain true to Christ and to assure them that they had in him all they needed to live and grow in faith.

NEW TESTAMENT REFERENCE

"God . . . has spoken to us by his Son. God has appointed him heir of all things and made the universe through him." (Heb 1:1–2)

THE THEOLOGY OF COLOSSIANS

Paul's major teaching centered on the question, Who is Jesus Christ? The apostle insisted that no chasm existed between the transcendent God and his material creation. Christ is both the Creator and Reconciler (1:15–23). He is the exact expression of God and brings together heaven and earth. A hierarchy of angelic powers or ruling spirits to mediate between God and humans is unnecessary. Christ is fully divine and fully human. Indeed, "the entire fullness of God's nature dwells bodily in Christ, and you have been filled by him, who is the head over every ruler and authority" (2:9–10).

Second, he dealt with the issue of genuine spirituality. Paul developed the basis for genuine worship and spirituality by refuting the false spirituality that encouraged an unspiritual pride (2:6–23). He exhorted the Colossians to abandon sins of the old life and cultivate the virtues of the new life (3:5–4:6).

COMPARING EPHESIANS AND COLOSSIANS

EPHESIANS	COLOSSIANS	THEME
1:7	1:14–20	The Son's redemptive work
1:10	1:20	Everything comes together in Christ
1:15–17	1:3–4,9	Prayers for Paul's readers
1:18	1:27	Inheritance and hope for those in Christ's glory
1:21–22	1:16–18	Christ's authority over all
2:5	1:16–18	Believers are alive in Christ
2:12–13	1:21–22	Citizenship/redemption through Christ's blood
2:15	2:14	Abolished the law
3:1	4:3	Paul as a prisoner

COMPARING EPHESIANS AND COLOSSIANS

EPHESIANS	COLOSSIANS	THEME
3:2–3	1:25–26	Hidden mystery is made known
3:6–7	1:23–25	Paul, servant of the gospel
4:1	1:10	Live worthy of your calling
4:2	3:12–13	Humility, gentleness, patience, bearing with one another in love
4:15–16	2:19	Christ is the head of the body
4:22–23	3:5–12	Put off the old nature and put on the new
5:3–6	3:5–9	No immorality, impurity, or greed
5:15	4:5	Live wisely
5:19–20	3:16–17	Sing and give thanks to God
5:21–6:9	3:18–4:1	Specific instructions for wives, husbands, children, parents, slaves, and masters
6:18–20	4:2–3	Perseverance in prayer
6:21–22	4:7–8	Tychicus sent to give updates on Paul and encourage the churches

UNIQUENESS OF COLOSSIANS

Most of Paul's letters are addressed to churches made up of Jews and Gentiles. There may well have been no Jews in the congregation at Colossae.

Conspicuously absent from the letter are any Old Testament quotations or allusions. Paul's teaching on Christ in this letter does not refer to him as Messiah of Israel. The letter does mention the Sabbath (2:16) and circumcision (2:11).

BASIC OUTLINE OF COLOSSIANS

I. Introduction (1:1–14)
II. Explanation of the Supremacy of Christ (1:15–23)
III. Ministry for the Church (1:24–2:5)
IV. Warnings Against False Spirituality (2:6–3:4)
V. Exhortations for Ethical Living (3:5–4:6)
VI. Conclusion (4:7–18)

To see the geographical location of Colossae, refer to the map in Philippians 1, p. 585.

QUESTIONS TO GUIDE YOUR STUDY

1. What was Paul's purpose in writing Colossians?
2. Describe the nature of the heresy that threatened the believers at Colossae. How serious was this threat?
3. What theme rings throughout Paul's letter to the Colossian Christians?
4. What is the relevance of Colossians to present-day believers?

COLOSSIANS 1

SALUTATION (1:1–2)

Paul addressed this epistle to a congregation previously unknown to him (1:4; 2:1). While Paul knew many of the churches in the area by "face," he did not know them all. It is inconceivable, however, that these churches did not know of him. Paul's lack of personal knowledge does not significantly change his introduction, which contains the three elements normally included in first-century correspondence: the writer(s), the readers, and a greeting.

The Writers (v. 1)

This letter has two writers, Paul and Timothy, although later the epistle clarifies the fact that Paul is primary writer. Paul included Timothy because of his share in the ministry.

The Readers (v. 2a)

The readers are Colossian Christians. They were located in Colossae, and Paul addressed them as "saints in Christ . . ., who are faithful brothers and sisters."

The Greeting (v. 2b)

This greeting was typical for Christian and non-Christian epistles. "Grace" points the readers to the basis of their new life in Christ, as well

HISTORICAL BACKGROUND

Colossae

Shortly after Paul wrote this letter to the Colossians, the entire Lycus Valley was devastated by an earthquake (about AD 61), which probably ended occupation of the city.

The city was located in the southwest corner of Asia Minor in what was then the Roman province of Asia. Hierapolis and Laodicea were situated only a few miles away. All three were in the Lycus Valley. A main road from Ephesus to the east ran through the region.

Colossae was prominent during the Greek period. By Paul's day, it lost much of its importance, perhaps due to the growth of the neighboring cities. Extremely detrimental to all the cities of the region were earthquakes that occasionally did severe damage.

WORD PICTURE

Christian Love

Paul's understanding and discussion of love make it a central theme, and his use of the noun *agape* makes the term almost a technical term. Prior to Paul, in fact, the Greek term *agape* was little used. Instead of using a word for *love* already filled with meaning, Paul took the seldom-used term and filled it with Christian meaning. Christian love is not simply an emotion that arises because of the character of the one loved. It is not due to the loving quality of the lover. It is a relationship of self-giving that results from God's activity in Christ. The source of Christian love is God (Rom 5:8), and the believer's response of faith makes love a human possibility (Rom 5:5).

as the state of grace in which they were to conduct their lives. "Peace" is a consequence of grace received.

PAUL'S THANKSGIVING AND PRAYER FOR THE COLOSSIANS (1:3–23)

Paul's Thanksgiving for the Colossians (vv. 3–8)

Paul typically opens his epistles with an expression of thanksgiving for the church and his assurance that he was praying for them.

Paul's thanksgiving embraces three growing aspects of the Colossian church—their faith, love, and hope. Although Paul never visited the church, he knew well their Christian experience and accepted it as genuine.

Nature of the Growth. The presence of faith, love, and hope showed the Christian character of the Colossian church. The phrase "faith in Christ Jesus" is not the same as faith directed toward Jesus Christ. Paul assumes that the object of their faith was Christ.

The original Greek focuses on the Colossians, existence "in Christ" and the faith they exercised in that new context.

Another evidence of their growth was the presence of *love*. Paul used the term *agape* for Christian love. Paul advanced two truths about this love. First, it is sacrificial. The term *agape* reminded them of the sacrificial love of Christ for them. Second, within the Christian community, love is indiscriminate. The love was directed to all the saints. Love, however, has little value if it is held only among the saints. It must be expressed to others. *Agape* love fulfills two objectives: (1) it represents Jesus to the world, especially in his bodily absence, and (2) it perfects the body of Christ.

Basis of the Growth. After expressing thanksgiving for the Colossian Christians' maturity in Christ, Paul presents the reason for their growth. It is their hope. Hope provides the basis for Christian growth since the most basic elements of faith toward God and love toward others grow out of hope.

Without hope, faith and love are greatly diminished.

This hope is both objective and subjective. The first is the object of hope—complete redemption already secure in heaven. The second is the activity of hope in their hearts as they anticipate future blessing. This hope is both object and activity of the heart.

Section Summary

The church at Colossae was healthy in many respects. It had a living love for all Christians and a solid hope of life eternal through the gospel. These virtues are solid ground for genuine thanksgiving.

Paul's Prayer for the Colossians (vv. 9–14)

The Character of Paul's Prayer. Three statements describe the character of Paul's prayer on behalf of the Colossians:

The Occasion for Its Prompting. The condition of the church at Colossae and the danger of heresy to the church prompted Paul's prayer.

The Specific Nature of the Prayer. "Praying" covers the entirety of the prayer life. "Asking" expresses a particular request that God intervene in the lives of the people for whom Paul prayed.

Its Consistency. Paul prayed regularly and consistently for the Colossians.

The Content of Paul's Prayer. Paul prayed specifically for a knowledge of the will of God for the Colossians. The prayer is informed and motivated by Paul's awareness of developments in the church at Colossae.

The Purpose of Paul's Prayer. Paul prayed with a goal in mind. His stated purpose to the Colossians is "that you may walk worthy of the Lord." He is speaking of wisdom applied to living, not simply wisdom applied to knowledge. His prayer is directed toward the transformation of the Colossians' character and witness. He speaks in terms of the characteristics of those who walk in God's will. And he highlights three characteristics:

They have continued growth in the spiritual life. This involves effective service and growth in knowledge. "Bearing fruit in every good work" refers to the reproductive aspect of the Christian's calling. This can take the form of evangelism or the fruit of the Spirit in a Christian's life (Gal 5:22–23) which, at times, is called fruit bearing. This first characteristic has two focal points. First, it clearly demonstrates that God's will is related to growth in Christian experience. Second, Christian service is a natural response to the will of God, but so is gaining spiritual understanding. A close relationship exists between these two.

They have the power to persevere. People need to know what God wants them to do. They also need the strength to live by the will of God. Paul believed the possibilities of spiritual power were unlimited for the believer. God strengthens us "according to his glorious might." Paul emphasizes the nature and application of the power available to the Christian.

They exhibit joyful thanksgiving to the Father. This is heartfelt, genuine thankfulness that grows out of the experience of salvation. Christians should never forget what God has done for them. They should allow this life-changing experience to bring them daily joy.

God is to be thanked because he qualified believers for an inheritance (v. 12); he rescued believers from darkness (v. 13a); and he brought believers into the Son's kingdom (v. 13b).

WORD PICTURE

Knowledge

The Greek word Paul used for *knowledge* had many applications, both religious and nonreligious. It is a compound word form that includes the word *knowledge (gnōsis)* and a preposition (*epi*, "on, upon, over"), which at times slightly changes its meaning. A secular use of the term occurs in the New Testament in 1 Pet 3:7, where Peter urges husbands to love their wives according to knowledge. He meant they should have a personal understanding of their wives' specific needs. Generally, in the New Testament, however, the word has a religious use. It was likely a favorite word of the teachers in Colossae who sought to add to the gospel.

WORD PICTURE

Being Strengthened

Paul uses two different words for *power* in verse 11. The power he describes as strengthening may be defined as "the potential to exert a force to perform some function." The word *power* refers to "the power to rule or control."

Believers need God's power to endure the circumstances of life and to relate positively to other people. Paul uses two terms to explain the empowering of the believer in the will of God: endurance and patience.

WORD PICTURE

The word translated *image* does not mean just a replica or a likeness. The reality itself is present in the image. God himself, the invisible one, had become visible and accessible to humans through Jesus Christ. To see Jesus is to see God (John 14:9).

Section Summary

A personal knowledge of God's will is accompanied by three characteristics. First, continued growth in the knowledge of God comes in the arena of service. Second, power is given to endure both difficult circumstances and people who seem to counter the work of God. Finally, joyful thanksgiving is offered to God the Father for what he has done in planning and effecting salvation.

THE PERSON OF CHRIST (1:15–20)

From Paul's perspective, to add to the gospel is to fail to understand who Christ is. When a person rightly understands who Christ is, he will see that it's impossible to add to who he is and what He has done.

Evidently these false teachers in Colossae valued knowledge and wisdom. They were seeking to enlighten the believers in Colossae to enable them to grow in wisdom and knowledge.

Paul says, in effect, they're pointing in the wrong direction. Christ himself is the source of knowledge, wisdom, and life-transforming power. What the Colossians needed was an adequate understanding of Christ.

Many believe Paul's presentation of Christ in this context is a hymn that was sung or spoken in worship, much like Phil 2:5–10.

The first section presents Christ's relation to the created world. Paul answers basic questions about the origin and purposes of creation.

The other section presents Jesus's relationship to the redemption of what he created. Paul reminds his readers of the redemptive purposes of God in and through Christ.

Jesus: Lord of Creation (vv. 15–17). Paul makes two assertions about this theme. First, "He is the image of the invisible God."

Second, Jesus is "the firstborn over all creation." Some have wrongly interpreted this to mean that Christ—prior to his incarnation—was a creature, the first creature born. This claim is an ancient heresy called Arianism. But in the context of what follows, this can't be the meaning of that phrase.

Christ is the agent of creation. Name anything in the visible world (physical objects) or in unseen worlds (whether invisible particles or spirits). Christ created it, and it exists for Christ.

Moreover, Paul says that Christ is the one who holds all reality together. Not only that, as Redeemer, he is creating a new order amid the old order. This new order is the church, of which he is the head. Just as in the human body the head exercises control over the body, so Christ is head of the church.

Paul's first claim about Jesus is that God's fullness indwelled him (v. 19).

WORD PICTURE

Fullness

This is a technical theological term meaning "the totality of the Divine powers and attributes" (Lightfoot). The fact that all the fullness of the Godhead dwelt in Christ was shocking. The false teachers were right. The distance between God and sinful human beings was great. How could such a gap be bridged? Their proposal was likely that a chain of spiritual beings bridged this gap. And so sinful human beings had to recognize these intermediaries, including Christ, in relating to God. The truth of the gospel is far simpler: that the fullness of God dwells in Christ.

The second claim has to do with God's purpose in Christ (v. 20). The universe was fragmented and in disharmony. Paul understood this in cosmic terms. Not only were there hostile people; there were also rebellious spiritual powers that were against God. God's purpose in Christ is to bring the universe, fragmented by rebellion and sin, back together to restore the harmony that existed at creation when God looked at everything and declared it to be good.

Peace is achieved through the blood of Christ. One of the deepest human perceptions is that wrong must be punished. Our sin against God was such that only God could pay the cost. And that he did in his Son, Jesus Christ.

Section Summary

To understand Christ is to know him as supreme over all created beings and to know him as our Redeemer.

THE SALVATION OF THE COLOSSIANS (1:21–23)

Having spoken of the universal and cosmic nature of the work of Christ, Paul now applies it specifically to the church at Colossae.

The Colossians' Former Condition (v. 21)

Paul reminded the Colossians of the blessings of reconciliation. When Paul uses the term *alienated,* it obviously meant that at one time the Colossians had been outside the sphere of God's blessing. These Gentiles were far removed from the promises of God's blessings. Furthermore, their minds were opposed to God; their actions were evil rather than good. In such a condition, the possibility of reconciliation seemed remote.

The Colossians' Present Condition (vv. 22–23)

The present condition is one of reconciliation—reconciliation achieved in the fleshly body of Christ. It was not just an apparent body. Christ was fully human. The Colossians owed their salvation to the initiative of God in their lives. They voluntarily responded to God's offer of reconciliation. Being reconciled to God, they had new values, motivations, and outlooks.

But the purpose of God in Christ had not been exhausted in the conversion of the Colossian Christians. It looked toward the future when the Colossian believers would be presented to God as the people God intended them to be, pure, without blame.

Since these believers had not seen Paul personally, he included an extended section on the nature of his ministry.

WORD PICTURE

What Is Lacking

This is a startling expression. Bratcher and Nida observe, "In no sense does Paul mean that Christ's sufferings and death for the redemption of mankind was not sufficient; what is meant is that in the service of Christ his servants are called upon to suffer as he did; suffering is an integral part of the ministry of Christ's servants, as it was of Christ himself. Barclay translates 'the uncompleted sufferings which the work of Christ still entails.'" (Bratcher and Nida, p. 37).

.WORD PICTURE

Mystery

"The word *mystery* is used in the New Testament in a rather special sense, of those secret things, which man could have never discovered for himself, but have now become known because God has been pleased to reveal them. The New Testament 'secret' is a secret proclaimed to all men and revealed to faith; the 'mystery' of the pagan world was a secret, the knowledge of which is made available only to the initiated, and received through the rites of initiation." Stephen Neill, *Paul to the Colossians*, 36.

PAUL'S MINISTRY TO THE CHURCHES (1:24–29)

In this summary statement of Paul's ministry, two focal points emerge. Paul sees two dimensions to his mission: suffering and completion of the work God gave him.

To Complete the Afflictions of Christ (v. 24)

The first aspect of Paul's ministry involved suffering. Paul knew from the time of his conversion that unique suffering would be his lot. Paul addresses two areas of his suffering.

Suffering for the Colossians. Paul's mission to the Gentiles brought suffering at the hands of Jews and Gentiles alike.

Suffering for Christ. Paul stated that his call involved "I am completing in my flesh what is lacking in Christ's afflictions for his body" (1:24).

To Complete the Word of God (vv. 25–27)

The second aspect of Paul's ministry involved the Word of God.

Paul's Role (v. 25). Paul saw his role as a servant of the church. His stewardship fulfilled a part of the divine plan that God foresaw long ago but which he clarified through the events in Paul's life.

The Revelation to Paul (vv. 26–27). Paul's role in the administration of God's plan related to the "the mystery hidden for ages and generations but now revealed to his saints" (v. 26).

Paul may have used the concept of mystery because the false teachers were seeking to pull the Colossians away from the gospel by using the concept of mystery. We humans are attracted to mysteries and even more to the idea that we may be among the few who understand such mysteries.

The content of the mystery is: "Christ in you, the hope of glory." Believers could expect to share in the inheritance of the saints because Christ lived in them and Christ in them now constitutes the hope of glory in the future.

Paul's Message, Method, and Purpose (vv. 28–29)

His Message. Paul's message was Christ. The gospel is not a system, a hierarchy, or a set of regulations. It is the person and work of Jesus Christ. He is the beginning, center, and end of it. It is only as life is lived in him, subject to his will and direction, that Christians become "mature."

His Method. Paul states his method with two verbs: *warning* and *teaching.* Teaching complements admonishing.

His Purpose. Paul's purpose is to "present everyone mature in Christ." This purpose has three emphases:

Two times Paul referred to "everyone." Clearly, he could not rest until all Christians lived up to what God expected.

Paul had a perspective of the last days. When he stated to "present" every person, he thought in terms of the return of Jesus and the desire to see each Christian mature in Christ.

Paul willingly exerted himself toward the end. The term *striving* was used of athletes who painfully pursued athletic glory.

WORD PICTURE

Striving with His Strength

A. T. Robertson translates this phrase literally as "how great a contest I am having," a metaphor from the athletic arena.

Section Summary

In this passage, Paul shows us how he viewed his ministry. Suffering had been an inescapable part of it. His attitude was, "I rejoice in my sufferings." His task as an apostle was to make the gospel fully known. Paul took no credit for all he had accomplished, as it had been due to the energy and power of Christ at work in him.

QUESTIONS TO GUIDE YOUR STUDY

1. Describe Paul's prayer for the Colossians. What were the elements of his prayer? What was its purpose?
2. Why was Paul thankful for the Colossian believers?
3. What is the theme of verses 15–20?
4. Describe Paul's ministry to the churches. What were the goals of his mission?

COLOSSIANS 2

PAUL'S MINISTRY TO THE COLOSSIANS (2:1–7)

As Paul applied his ministry to the Colossians, he began the struggle. His struggle was emotional rather than physical. In verse 1 we learn for the first time that Paul was not personally acquainted with the Christians in Colossians or Laodicea, a neighboring city to Colossae.

The Object of Paul's Concerns (v. 1)

Paul desired to be faithful to his calling. This could best be accomplished by a face-to-face meeting with the Colossians and with their fellow Christians in Laodicea.

The Purpose of Paul's Concerns (vv. 2–3)

Paul's Main Purpose. Paul's main purpose was that the Colossians might be encouraged in heart. Their encouragement grew out of a genuine love that formed a tie stronger than a mere physical tie and from the riches of an understanding that contains assurance and certainty. Moreover, such understanding yields a true knowledge of God's mystery—Christ Jesus.

The Reason for Paul's Concern (vv. 4–5)

Paul expresses his reasons for concern in a twofold way. He uses doctrinal and personal perspectives.

Doctrinally. Paul is concerned that the Colossians are not deceived by "arguments that sound reasonable." Their heretical arguments came with the appearance of "deeper theology." In reality, they were subtle inroads of heresy. The church needed to see past these arguments the false teachers were presenting. The best antidote to this false teaching was the true knowledge that is in God's disclosure of himself in Christ.

Personally. Paul also had a personal reason for his concern. He had not seen the Colossians in person, but he felt a strong tie to them. He was with them in spirit. Paul was delighted to hear of their steady faith in Christ.

WORD PICTURE

Rooted and Built Up

The first metaphor pictures sinking the roots of faith into the soil of Christian truth. The other calls to mind building on the foundation of faith. These point to the continued growth of the church, but with a distinct emphasis. The strength is related to its faith. The attack of the false teachers was against "the faith," the system of Christian truth and its ramifications in life.

The Application to the Colossians (vv. 6–7)

In making specific application of these things to the Colossians, Paul's primary concern was that they continue to grow in Christ.

They already received Christ. Paul wanted them to reflect on *how* they received him, and that was to be a model for their present lives. The word "as" (v. 6) draws attention to the relationship between receiving and continuing. Paul is calling them to a focused faith in the all-sufficiency of Jesus not only for the first step of salvation but as they live out the day-to-day reality of that salvation.

They were "rooted and built up in him and established in the faith." Notice the two metaphors "rooted" (from the agricultural world) and "built up" (from the construction world) in the faith.

They were "overflowing with gratitude." Paul frequently used thankfulness as one of the litmus tests of Christian health. Thankfulness is an antidote to the poison of false teaching.

HISTORICAL BACKGROUND

Elements of the World

"A general belief in Paul's time was that spiritual beings—frequently associated with planets and stars—controlled every man's future. This ancient astrology, coupled with the ideas that secret knowledge enable man to control the power of these things, seems to have formed a basic element in the false teaching in Colossae. Astrology, secret knowledge, and strange regulations all promised a super-Christian life. But Paul wrote that this was deceptive." Harold S. Songer, *Colossians: Christ Above All*, Convention Press, p. 67.

Section Summary

This section ties Paul to the Colossians, identifies his tribulation with their faith, and encourages them to continue the same path on which they have begun so well.

PAUL'S DEFENSE AGAINST DOCTRINAL THREAT (2:8–19)

The threat concerned two major tenets of the Christian faith.

1. The doctrine of salvation, the person and work of Christ specifically related to the cross
2. Sanctification, the application of the cross to the development of personal purity

The Doctrine of Salvation (vv. 8–15)

The attack of the heretics struck at the heart of the Christian faith. It was a direct attack on the doctrine of salvation. In this section Paul addresses two concerns: (1) the worship of angels, and (2) the practice of the law.

The Nature of the Threat (v. 8). Paul saw the heresy as a planned, organized attack against what God has revealed through his prophets and apostles. This false teaching made inroads at Colossae through what Paul calls "philosophy and empty deceit." Paul states three characteristics about this philosophy. Together, these provide a standard of measurement not only for the Colossians but for us as well.

The philosophy was human. Basically, the false teaching represented man's attempt to arrive at the truth apart from God's help. Paul explains that it is "based on human tradition."

The philosophy was viewed as coming from the elements of the world. Paul may have been referring to angelic powers, which the Colossians incorrectly perceived as being in authority over the world. Whatever the specific interpretation, Paul's point is that the elements were inferior.

The philosophy was non-Christian. This characteristic perhaps points to the heart of the danger. The philosophy was not according to Christ.

Section Summary

The Colossian Christians were being confronted with a heresy that threatened two major tenets of the Christian faith: the first is the doctrine of salvation, and the person and work of Christ. In his letter to the Colossians, Paul offers a defense against this false teaching.

The Answer to the Threat (vv. 9–15)

To answer the teaching of the heretics, Paul now focuses on the person and work of Christ. He relates the work of Christ to both the supernatural powers and the law.

Jesus is the sufficient Savior. Paul emphasizes Jesus's work in relation to the law and his dominion over other spiritual beings.

Jesus is completely God. Paul argues for the deity of Christ by stating that "for the entire fullness of God's nature dwells bodily in Christ." This is Paul's way of saying that Jesus is fully God—just as the Father and Spirit are fully God.

Paul informs the Colossians that they "have been filled by him." He means that they are complete in him. Although the blessings of salvation may increase, in Christ they have the "fullness" of God. There is no need to be concerned about other spiritual beings or powers.

To describe the absolute adequacy of what Christ brings to the Colossian Christians, Paul uses the figures of circumcision and baptism.

WORD PICTURE

The Entire Fullness of God's Nature

Stephen Neill paraphrases this expression in the following way: "When God entered into the world in the incarnation of Christ, it was the whole of Himself that he was pleased to give to us. Your new teachers imagine that the fullness of the divine essence is distributed among a whole crowd of beings, divine and semi-divine. This is a fundamental error. Everything of God that can be known by man was seen and understood in the human bodily life of Jesus Christ. Whenever we touch Him, we touch the reality of God, the whole reality of God." Stephen Neill, *Paul to the Colossians*, pp. 41–42.

Circumcision. Presumably the Colossians were Gentiles. They had not been circumcised physically. But Paul describes their experience of conversion as circumcision. In this experience they had put off "the body of flesh." That stood for the old life of rebellion against God. When they became Christians, the Colossians were freed from the power of rebellion that enslaved their lives.

Baptism. The Colossians, of course, had been baptized. Paul equates Christian baptism with dying and being buried. Christ died and was buried in a tomb. We die and are buried with him in a watery grave. This means there is a radical dividing line between what the Christian now is and what he used to be. He not only died but is also raised with Christ.

The decisive phrase in verse 12 is "through faith." Paul did not believe the physical act of being put under the water changed a person any more than physical circumcision did. What is important is our trust in God. What is even more important is what God does for the believer. God makes him or her "alive" with him.

Paul uses two metaphors to express the heart of what Christ did for believers: the handwriting of ordinances being removed ("the certificate of debt") and nailing the accusations to the cross ("nailing it to the cross").

These two metaphors present Paul's doctrinal conclusions regarding the law and the work of Christ. God forgave, canceled the condemnatory aspects of the law, and paid the accusations in full.

WORD PICTURE

The Certificate of Debt

This handwriting represents the certificate of indebtedness written in one's own hand. This means that the personal note that testifies against us is canceled.

WORD PICTURE

Nailing It to the Cross

Most likely this refers to the indictment hung over the prisoner's head when he was crucified. By such action, the criminal's debt to society was canceled since he paid for the crime.

Section Summary

The central error of the false teachers was their failure to recognize the sufficiency of Christ to meet the needs of believers. Paul's argument countered his opponents at every point. No one should follow these false teachers. They were defeated, disgraced, and powerless because of the work of Christ. Jesus is the sufficient and sovereign Savior.

The Doctrine of Sanctification (vv. 16–19)

In these three verses Paul focuses his attention on the implications of his teaching for Christian living. He discusses the Colossians' relationship to the law (vv. 16–17) and to the supernatural powers (vv. 18–19). The commands of verses 16 and 18 predominate this section.

Concerning Asceticism (vv. 16–17). "Don't let anyone judge you." The nature of asceticism was related to matters of the law. However, Paul also sees a need to address the attitude of some of the members of the Colossian congregation, as they were critical and demanding. The problem was that the heresy gave great importance to dietary laws. Certain foods and drink were forbidden. The heresy also placed great emphasis on holy days.

WORD PICTURE

Sanctification

Sanctification is vitally linked to the salvation experience. It is concerned with the moral and spiritual obligations assumed in that experience. We are set apart to God in conversion, and we live out that dedication to God in holiness.

However, Paul maintains that the reality of the Christian life is not determined by holding to dietary laws or observing holy days. The person who has Christ does not need to worry about keeping those laws.

Concerning Angel Worship (vv. 18–19). "Let no one condemn you by delighting in ascetic practices and the worship of angels, claiming access to a visionary realm." False humility may have expressed itself as severe ascetical practices and self-mortification and the worshiping of angels. Such practices have the paradoxical effect of increasing a person's pride, which is the core of human sinfulness.

Section Summary

Paul discusses doctrines of Christian growth with two specific reference points that were the foundations of the false teaching: asceticism and angel worship. Christians should realize that they need only Christ. Whatever one experiences, the objective tests of truth must prevail. Christ, not experiences, determines spiritual reality.

PAUL'S DEFENSE AGAINST THE PRACTICAL THREAT (2:20–3:4)

The Doctrine of Salvation (vv. 20–23)

Paul looks back to the time of the Colossians' conversion, which he calls their death with Christ which freed them from the ruling principles of the universe. Christian growth and freedom consist in understanding and living out the consequences of this truth.

The Nature of the Attacks (vv. 20–21). The false teachers brought with them definite ideas about religious life. They had an organized system that forbade certain practices. Paul defines these practices and reveals their character as enslaving and legalistic.

Reasons Not to Submit (vv. 22–23). Paul provides two reasons not to submit to false teachers. The first reason is the nature of the believer's conversion. Christ's death already delivered believers from the "elements" of the world (v. 20).

The second reason is that such practices are superficial and fail to address the sinful self which Christ desires to transform into his own likeness. Only he can accomplish that. Therefore, trust in him is not only the first step in salvation but the basis of every other step.

Section Summary

Paul defends the faith against the practical threats of the false teachers. The false teachers held to an organized system that forbade certain practices. Paul explains that such systems have no value in the sanctification of the believer and that they will perish.

QUESTIONS TO GUIDE YOUR STUDY

1. What was Paul's concern for the Colossians? Why was he concerned for them?
2. What false teaching had invaded the Colossian church? What was the nature of the heresy? What was wrong with it?
3. What specific points and truths did Paul use to counter the false teaching? What are the implications of Paul's teaching in Colossians for the church's contemporary response to such philosophies as the New Age movement?
4. Describe the doctrines of salvation and sanctification. How are they related?

COLOSSIANS 3

In this section Paul maintains his defense against the practical threats of the teaching of the false teachers.

THE NEW LIFE IN CHRIST (3:1–4)

The Nature of the Christian's Higher Calling (vv. 1–2)

PERSONAL APPLICATION

Robert Murray M'Cheyne used to counsel: "For every look you take at your sinful self, take ten looks at Christ."

People are not changed by imposing legalistic restrictions on what they eat or drink. They are changed by the power of Christ.

Paul urges the Colossians to take their eyes off earthly concerns and look to Christ.

The higher things, those above, Paul defines in 3:1 as "where Christ is, seated at the right hand of God." This imagery called to mind the enthronement of Christ.

Reasons to Seek the Higher Calling (vv. 3–4)

Paul presents three reasons Christians should seek things above:

The Resurrection of Christ (v. 1). The believer lives in resurrection as a new creation of God.

The New Life Source (vv. 3–4). The new life is Christ. His life energizes Christians, enabling them to be and do what they should.

The Future Manifestation of Glory (v. 4). The believer's life, which is hidden in Christ, will be revealed. The second coming of Christ will be a time of glory.

Section Summary

The life of Christ is a profound reality. It is a life that draws its existence from the center of all reality, Jesus Christ himself. The Christian has a higher calling, which is to set one's mind and heart on things above. Paul's admonitions that follow are controlled by the thought of the full life that belongs to all who are in Christ.

WORD PICTURE

Right Hand

Perhaps Mark 14:62 provides the insight to understand this metaphor. There Jesus told the high priest, "You will see the Son of Man seated at the right hand of Power and coming with the clouds of heaven." The right hand was the place of power. The term may also refer to a position of privilege.

With the doctrinal foundations in place, Paul addresses the false teachers and exposes their errant positions. The apostle turns his thoughts more directly to the specifics of Christian living. This second part of the epistle falls into three logical groupings, and each contributes to Paul's thought uniquely. They are: (1) individual and corporate responsibilities (3:5–4:1); (2) exhortation to the Colossians to be careful witnesses (4:2–9); and (3) miscellaneous greetings (4:10–18).

In this first section (3:5–4:1), Paul's theme is the preeminence of Christ in Christian living. In it, he addresses order in the Christian life and church. Paul's primary ethical concern surfaces. If the Colossians were not to live like those around them, how were they to live? In response to God's grace, they had specific duties. To spell out those duties, Paul issues a series of commands, all of which seem to have equal weight.

THE NEW PERSON (3:5–17)

UNION WITH CHRIST: PAST, PRESENT, AND FUTURE

RAISED WITH CHRIST (PAST)	HIDDEN WITH CHRIST (PRESENT)	GLORIFIED WITH CHRIST (FUTURE)
"If you have been raised with Christ, seek the things above, where Christ is, seated at the right hand of God." *(Col 3:1)*	"For you died, and your life is hidden with Christ in God." *(Col 3:3)*	"When Christ, who is your life, appears, then you also will appear with him in glory." *(Col 3:4)*

The Old Nature and the New (vv. 5–11)

Paul commands the Colossians to "put to death" the old self or nature. The old self is to be crucified in order that sin might be rendered ineffective in the believer's life (Rom 6:6).

This old self is characterized by attitudes and actions which Paul lists. The first of these are in verses 5–6. Paul identifies these vices and then gives a reason to leave them.

Sexual Immorality. This refers to illicit sexual intercourse. More specifically, "adultery" identifies sexual intercourse as the breaking of a

HISTORICAL BACKGROUND

God's Wrath

"Wrath (*orgē*) differs from passionate anger, which is immediate and strong; wrath is more settled in the long term. The wrath of God suggests the continuing revulsion of the holiness of God against sin. The holy God cannot abide injustice, pride, deception, and willful diminution of the good. God's righteous wrath is directed against sin."

Thomas C. Oden, *The Word of Life*, p. 394.

PERSONAL APPLICATION

We notice that the emphasis is on attitudes and actions that determine the believer's relationship to the community of the redeemed. Furthermore, the relationship is one of love. All the elements in the list speak about different ways of expressing the love of God that has become the central fact of the believer's life. The unbeliever makes himself the center of his life. His thoughts and efforts are directed toward himself. The Christian makes others the center of his life, subordinating his own desires and ambitions to the welfare of his brother.

covenant of marriage. "Fornication" generally refers to the act itself outside of a covenant relationship.

Impurity. Failure to have the proper attitude to God's gift of sexuality.

Lust and Evil Desire. These two words belong together. They generally refer to strong desires gone bad.

Greed. This word can also be translated "covetousness." It is the longing for something that belongs to someone else, placing supreme value on something that belongs to someone else, or placing supreme value on something not (yet) possessed.

These five are sins of personal aggression. The individual who commits them thinks more of himself than he does of others. Paul gives two reasons Christians should never practice these sins. They bring the wrath of God (v. 6), and they characterize the former life of sin and rebellion (v. 7).

The Character of the New Nature (vv. 12–17)

Paul gives three commands that form the backbone of this section:

- He commands believers to clothe themselves with Christian characteristics.
- He commands the church to let the peace of Christ rule it.
- He urges the church to let the Word of Christ dwell in its midst.

Social Relationships in the Church. Every social group has its set of problems, and the church is no exception. Paul, therefore, calls the Colossians individually and collectively to be characterized by Christian graces that enhance their relationships.

Believers are God's "chosen" people. They belong to God as his redeemed community because of his saving initiative. As such, they are to be clothed with a new kind of life. Paul earlier spoke of the old that had to be put off; now he speaks of the new that must be "put on." He listed five virtues that characterize the people of God.

The new clothing of the Christian begins with personal attributes. Because Christians sometimes are difficult to live with, we need the grace of forbearance. People are prone to offend, so we need the grace of forgiveness. Everything on the list so far is an aspect or expansion of Christian love. *Love* is more important than anything else in the Christian life. It is the love of God expressed in his redemption for the Christian.

This love must be put on "above all," for it is the identifying mark of the genuine believer.

Harmony in the Church (v. 15). The second command of Paul calls the church to harmony. The peace of Christ is to rule in the believers' hearts. It stresses harmony in the group rather than personal peace.

Freedom of the Word of God (vv. 16–17). Paul's third command to the church at Colossae is to allow the word of Christ to dwell richly in their midst. This passage parallels Eph 5:18–21, as the two passages speak to the same concern. Colossians says, "Let the word of Christ dwell richly among you." Ephesians declares, "Be filled by the Spirit." When the word of Christ dwells in the church, three activities result:

Teach. Instruction in the word of the Lord was evidently central from the beginning of Christian history.

Admonish. Christians have a responsibility for the moral and spiritual lives of one another.

Sing as an Expression of Gratitude and Worship. This is characteristic of the church's response to the word of her Lord. That word is the message of God's love and redemption in Jesus Christ.

PERSONAL APPLICATION

Rule

This peace is to "rule" in the congregation. This word is often translated "umpire." The reason for such peace is that believers have been called into one body. The spiritual environment of the believer is the one body they must share.

Section Summary

Issuing three commands that form the backbone of this section, Paul addresses social relationships in the church. He called the Colossians individually and then collectively to be characterized by Christian graces that enhance their relationships.

FAMILY RELATIONSHIPS (3:18–4:1)

Now Paul turns to some concrete advice about Christian living. Christian commitment affects every area of life, including the family. It was natural, therefore, for Paul to address Christian responsibilities in this area.

Wives and Husbands (vv. 18–19)

Paul believed there was an order for the family. It seems that he believed the order was God given. In this order the husband functions as the head of the family.

Wives (v. 18). Wives are to submit to their husbands. Paul's term "submit" means "to subject or subordinate." The wife's submission is different from the submission of children or slaves. Children and slaves are told to obey; the wife is not. The wife has a different relationship to her husband than children to parents or slaves to masters. The motivation for voluntary submission is that it is a proper Christian attitude. Such submission is an outworking of the lordship of Christ.

Husbands (v. 19). The counterpart of the wife's responsibility is that of the husband. The simple command is to love.

WORD PICTURE

The term *agape*, used here, never occurred in secular households. The command, therefore, appears to be a distinctively Christian element of the marriage commitment. Paul follows this positive command with a negative one: "Don't be bitter toward them." Paul probably meant that the marriage relationship could become an irritant to the one who does not love properly. The husband was to take care to see that bitterness did not develop.

Children and Parents (vv. 20–21)

Moving from the innermost family circle, Paul addressed the parent-child relationship.

Children (v. 20). Paul commands children to obey their parents. The word *obey* is stronger than the word *submit* used of wives. Paul reinforces this by using the phrase "in everything." Obedience is expected. Children have a responsibility in the Christian family order. To be pleasing to the Lord as Christians, they should obey their parents.

Parents (v. 21). In the Lord, parents have a mutual responsibility to children. Paul issues a command and a practical reason. "Fathers, do not exasperate your children." The reason for this command is to avoid discouragement. Constant nagging produces a situation where children are discouraged either because they cannot please those they love or because they feel they are of no worth to anybody. In God's sight, children and parents have equal worth. Parents are to treat their children with respect as persons.

Servants and Masters (vv. 22–4:1)

The guidelines for slavery were more complex than any of the other relationships.

Servants. Paul's guidelines about slaves' responsibilities were twofold: obey and serve genuinely. Paul uses the word "obey" rather than "submit." Slaves, like children, were to obey in everything. Paul commands the servants to genuine service by urging them to work "wholeheartedly." Paul mentions three motivations for such service:

- Reward: "You will receive . . . an inheritance from the Lord."
- The sovereignty of the Lord
- "The wrongdoer will be paid back for whatever wrong he has done."

Surely Christian masters came under God's judgment. God's righteousness demands that any injustice be punished.

Masters (4:1). There was much cruelty and abuse of slaves in the Roman Empire. Christian masters were to be different. Justice and equality were to be the guiding principles of their conduct. The motivation Paul gave to masters reminded them that they, too, were slaves. Their heavenly Master rules over all things. If masters were to avoid judgment, they had to have a concern for fairness. Although slaves did not receive salaries, their basic needs were to be met in keeping with the value of human effort, time, and life. Paul gives masters a motivation by reminding them that they, too, were slaves. The heavenly Master rules over all.

Section Summary

Paul provides practical advice about family relationships, including husband-wife, parents-children, and master-slave. Ultimately, individuals are judged by their personal responses to the Lord in each situation.

QUESTIONS TO GUIDE YOUR STUDY

1. What are the aspects of the Christian's higher calling? Why should believers seek it?
2. Paul speaks of the old and new natures. Why is there a struggle between the two?
3. Describe the new nature of the believer. What should characterize this new nature?
4. How does Christian commitment affect family relationships?

COLOSSIANS 4

Note: Colossians 4:1 belongs to the context of the last section of chapter 3, so it is covered in the previous chapter.

PRAYERFUL COOPERATION IN MINISTRY (4:2–6)

Paul concludes his epistle by reminding the church of some basic concerns: prayer (vv. 2–4), wisdom (v. 5), and using careful communication (v. 6).

Prayer (vv. 2–4)

Prayer is a basic expression of the Christian faith. Because God is personal, a heavenly Father who cares for us, we should pray. In this passage Paul gives us three characteristics and the content of Christian prayer:

1. *Devotedness.* In other epistles, Paul said, "Pray constantly" (1 Thess 5:17) or its equivalent. The same general tone occurs here.
2. *Staying Alert.* "Staying alert" implies mental alertness. Presumably this meant the Colossian Christians were to know the circumstances of life, particularly those that affected the spread of the gospel. Informed prayer is likely to be more purposeful, personal, and powerful.
3. *Thanksgiving.* Thankfulness is the environment of good praying, and it provides a safeguard for informed praying. All believers may be thankful for what God has done, is doing, and is going to do for us through his Son.

Paul provides two specific petitions regarding the content of Christian prayer. Paul requested that the Colossians pray for an open door for the gospel. He was always seeking ways to communicate the gospel to others. Here he discloses the secret of his success in witness. He was successful because he looked to the Lord to supply the wisdom for the opportunity.

Wisdom (v. 5)

Having discussed a door of opportunity in ministry, Paul turned his thoughts to wise conduct. In the Bible, wisdom is God-given insight into God's will and purpose.

Careful Communication (v. 6)

In the give-and-take of life, both the content of words spoken and the method of speaking matter. Paul continued his exhortations to the believers by addressing their speech. He makes two statements that illustrate the nature of the Christian's talk: in grace and with salt.

Gracious. This may be used in its full Christian sense, in a generic sense of charming, or with a combination of both. The third option seems most likely. However, Paul could hardly think of a Christian word so grand as *grace* and not fill it with Christian meaning. We could express Paul's words here as, "Let speech be always with the graciousness appropriate to Christians, that is, those who love in a state of grace."

With Salt. Salt had three uses in Paul's day: it could (1) preserve a food, (2) "sterilize" a food, or (3) season a food. In this passage, Paul takes the last meaning. Conversation is to be seasoned, that is, acceptable and inoffensive.

Finally, Paul teaches in this passage that conversation is to be suited to each person: "That you may know how you should answer each person." Sound answers offered with a positive spirit overcome many obstacles to the gospel. Paul's text emphasizes the method of answering more than the content. It calls for Christian graciousness and sensitivity to the specific person and situation.

Paul ends his letter to the Colossians with this call to Christian virtues. He prays for wisdom to walk worthy of the Lord. This wisdom involves growth, power for endurance and patience, and joyful thanksgiving. That the epistle should end on a note like its beginning is fitting. It is also fitting that Paul should think in terms of reaching non-Christians with the gospel.

PERSONAL APPLICATION

Wisdom was necessary because of their Christian testimony. "Outsiders" (nonbelievers) needed examples of their Christian testimony. "Making the most" is a translation of the Greek verb that means to buy back. It conveys the idea of "making the most of your time." Paul is calling for the Colossians to make the time count for Christian purposes. Perhaps he was reflecting on his own limited opportunities as he awaited trial. The church should realize all of its opportunities to be of service to God and the world.

CONCLUSION (4:7–18)

Those Who Journeyed to the Church (vv. 7–9)

In the first century, letters were often carried by personal messengers. The Roman government provided an adequate mail system, but personal couriers made the communication more meaningful. Often a particular situation required such letters. Paul identifies both the courier and the immediate situation that prompted the letter.

THOSE WHO JOURNEYED TO THE CHURCH

RECIPIENT	OCCASION	BACKGROUND PASSAGES
Tychicus	A loved brother, faithful minister, and fellow servant to whom Paul entrusted with considerable responsibility	Acts 20:4; 2 Tim 4:12; Titus 3:12
Onesimus	A "dear friend and coworker"	Philemon

Those Who Sent Greetings (vv. 10–14)

Paul continues his closing by sending greetings from six men who were with him in Rome. They obviously had a close relationship with both Paul and the church. In some cases, the connection with Paul is clear, but history is silent about their connection with the church.

THOSE WHO SENT GREETINGS

RECIPIENT	OCCASION	BACKGROUND PASSAGES
Aristarchus	A fellow prisoner and one of the three Jewish believers with Paul at the time	Acts 19:29; 20:4
Mark	A fellow worker with Paul	Acts 12:12; 13:5, 13; 15:39; 1 Pet 5:13; 15:39; 1 Pet 5:13; 2 Tim 4:11; 2 Tim 4:11
Jesus (Justus)	One of the three Jews with Paul at the time of the writing; he also comforted Paul in his trial.	Col 4:11 is the only mention of this man.
Epaphras	A fellow servant and faithful minister who originally brought the Colossians the gospel	Col l:7; Philem 23
Luke	Writer of Acts and the Gospel of Luke; he had a significant role in the early church.	Philem 24; 2 Tim 4:11
Demas	Accompanied Paul to Rome but later departed because he "loved this present world."	2 Tim 4:10

Those to Whom Greetings Were Being Sent (vv. 15–17)

Paul sent greetings to a final group of persons. The readers of the letter were instructed to greet them for Paul. Among other things, this reveals the closeness of the Christian communities in the area and the Gase of communication from one to another. He sent his greetings to the church at Laodicea, to Nympha, and also to Archippus.

THOSE TO WHOM GREETINGS WERE BEING SENT

RECIPIENT	OCCASION	BACKGROUND PASSAGES
Laodicea (church)	To encourage the believers at this church	Rev 3:14–22; Col 4:13
Nympha	The church at Laodicea met at her house	Acts 12:12;Rom 16:5
Archippus	To encourage him; to complete the work God had given him to do	Philem 2

Final Greeting from Paul (v. 18)

The letter ends with a personal touch. Paul signed the greeting in his hand. This means that someone else penned the epistle, which happened commonly in the first century and with Paul's letters. Paul's eyesight may have prohibited his present writing these letters. The authenticity, however, came from Paul's signature.

Here Paul gives two final reminders. They encapsulate the entire message of the letter:

Paul reminded the Colossians to "remember my chains." As Paul was with the Colossians in spirit and had a passion for their well-being, so he asked them to remember and intercede for him.

Paul reminded the Colossians of God's grace. He ends his letter where he began. In a sense, the entire epistle argues for the principle of grace, that God supplies salvation freely, that he requires nothing but a trust in the work of his Son, Jesus, and that grace sustains the Christian's life. If God's grace is with the Colossians, they need nothing else.

QUESTIONS TO GUIDE YOUR STUDY

1. Examine Paul's opening prayer for the Colossians. What does it teach us about Christian prayer?
2. What does Paul mean when he says to "act wisely" in our Christian walk?
3. From Paul's teaching here, what should characterize Christian communication?
4. What is the significance of Paul's closing reminders to the Colossians?

1–2 Thessalonians

INTRODUCTION

1 FIRST THESSALONIANS

Galatians probably was the first letter Paul wrote, and 1 Thessalonians was the second. Paul traveled to Thessalonica on his second missionary journey around AD 51. Luke reported this brief visit, Paul's preaching ministry there with Silas, and the subsequent persecution that drove him and his companions out of the city (Acts 17:1–9). Many people believed in Jesus Christ before they were compelled to leave.

From Thessalonica, Paul went to Berea and Athens and then to Corinth. Timothy and Silas, who had been with Paul at Thessalonica, rejoined him in Corinth. Paul wrote 1 Thessalonians in response to Timothy's report shortly after his arrival.

1 THESSALONIANS IN A "NUTSHELL"

Purpose:	To encourage new converts during persecution; to instruct them in Christian living and to assure them concerning the Second Coming.
Major Doctrine:	Last Things
Key Passage:	1 Thess 4:13–18
Other Key Doctrines:	Evangelism, prayer, and God
Influence of the Letter:	Every chapter of 1 Thessalonians ends with a reference to the second coming of Christ.

HISTORICAL BACKGROUND

Thessalonica, the capital of Macedonia, was larger than Philippi. It was a free city, having no Roman garrison within its walls. Like Corinth, it was a cosmopolitan city.

AUTHOR

Both 1 and 2 Thessalonians claim Paul as author. The vocabulary, style, and theology are Paul's. No decisive objections to Paul's authorship have swayed the convictions of centuries of Christian opinion.

PURPOSE FOR WRITING

Paul received the report that the Thessalonians were strong in faith and were making favorable progress. After receiving this information about the church, Paul wrote 1 Thessalonians to accomplish several purposes:

1. He wanted to encourage believers as they stood firm against intense persecution (1 Thess 2:14; 3:1–4).
2. He responded to criticism against his motives in Christian service by explaining how he had conducted his ministry in Thessalonica (1 Thess 2:1–12).
3. The presence of low moral standards in Thessalonica led Paul to explain Christian standards for sexual purity (1 Thess 4:1–8).
4. The death of some members in the congregation sparked questions about how deceased members would participate in the coming return of Christ, and Paul answered their questions (1 Thess 4:13–18).
5. The church needed instruction about the appropriate use of spiritual gifts (1 Thess 5:19–22).

HISTORICAL BACKGROUND

"His [Paul's] signature at the close was the proof of genuineness (2 Thess 3:17) against all spurious claimants (2 Thess 2:2). Unfortunately the brittle papyrus on which he wrote easily perished outside of the sand heaps and tombs of Egypt or the lava covered ruins of Herculaneum. What a treasure that autograph would be!"

A. T. Robertson, *Word Pictures in the New Testament*, vol. 4, 5–6.

PLACE AND DATE OF WRITING

First Thessalonians was probably written while Paul was in Corinth.

Some have suggested that 2 Thessalonians was written before 1 Thessalonians. Neither letter claims to come before the other, and it is also possible that this suggestion is correct.

AUDIENCE

Paul's readership was the congregation in the church at Thessalonica. Since Paul's ministry there, the church had grown, according to the report Timothy brought to Paul. But the church was experiencing persecution. The believers were new converts, and they needed encouragement to remain faithful under these pressures.

THEOLOGICAL SIGNIFICANCE OF 1 THESSALONIANS

The letter is more practical than theological. It is God centered throughout. God chose the Thessalonians unto salvation (1 Thess 1:4). His will is the guide for all believers (4:3). He calls his people to holy living (4:7) and enables them to live obediently. He raised Jesus from the dead (4:14) and will raise believers to be with him at the Lord's return (4:13–5:11).

This letter was written specifically to reassure those who were concerned about believers who had already died.

HISTORICAL BACKGROUND

The letter can be dated with the help of the Delphi Inscription, which provides information about the service of the proconsul Gallio. Gallio probably assumed office in the summer of AD 51 and served through the summer of AD 52. Paul was brought before Gallio shortly after the governor's arrival in Corinth, near the end of Paul's eighteen-month stay in the city (Acts 18:9–18). Paul's Corinthian ministry probably began in AD 50, and Paul wrote 1 Thessalonians either in this year or the following year.

BASIC OUTLINE OF 1 THESSALONIANS

I. Salutation (1:1)
II. Personal Relations (1:2–3:13)
III. Church Problems (4:1–5:11)
IV. Concluding Exhortations (5:12–28)

2 THESSALONIANS

Paul's second letter to the Thessalonians was apparently evoked by alarm on the part of believers who had been informed that the day of the Lord had arrived. The agitator who confused the Thessalonians apparently appealed for authority to the utterances of inspired prophets within the church, or to some phrases from Paul's writings, or possibly to a forged letter (2 Thess 2:1–2). Some who anticipated the Lord's imminent return stopped working and were depending on others to supply them with life's necessities (3:11).

Because of inexperience, the church members were uncertain of their position. They needed reassurance to cope with the opposition of pagan culture and with doubts raised by their misunderstandings (2:15), and discipline was needed to keep the lazy members from disrupting community life (3:13–15).

PERSONAL APPLICATION

Words of comfort and hope from Paul about the resurrection of believers provide good news for the church at all times in all places. This good news serves as a basis for practical and godly living.

2 THESSALONIANS IN A "NUTSHELL"

Purpose:	To encourage new converts in persecution and to correct their misunderstanding about the Lord's return.
Major Doctrine:	Last Things
Key Passage:	2 Thess 1:3–12
Other Key Doctrines:	Prayer, the church, evil, and suffering
Influence of the Letter:	With only three chapters, the letter is one of Paul's shortest. But because of 2:3–10, it is one the most extensively studied.

AUTHOR

In 2 Thessalonians 1:1 we read, "Paul, Silvanus, and Timothy." Some scholars have questioned Paul's authorship of 2 Thessalonians because of variations with the doctrine of Christ's return as presented in 1 Thessalonians. However, as with Paul's authorship of 1 Thessalonians, no decisive objections have changed centuries of Christian opinion about Paul's authorship.

PURPOSE FOR WRITING

Paul's purpose in writing 2 Thessalonians paralleled his first letter to these believers. Several reasons for this letter are prominent:

1. He wrote to encourage the persecuted church (1:4–10).
2. He attempted to correct their misunderstanding about the Lord's return.
3. He exhorted the church to be steadfast in all things (2:13–3:15).
4. Paul's emphasis was on the return of Christ when the church would be gathered to him (2:1), and the wicked would be judged (1:6–9; 2:8).
5. Paul also instructed the church concerning the man of lawlessness (2:1–12).

DATE OF WRITING

Assuming that Paul was the author along with the traditional sequence of the two letters, 2 Thessalonians would be dated several months after the writing of 1 Thessalonians. This would place the date of writing toward the end of Paul's Corinthian ministry—late AD 50 or early AD 51.

AUDIENCE

The audience was the same as 1 Thessalonians. (See "Audience" for 1 Thessalonians above.)

THEOLOGICAL SIGNIFICANCE OF 2 THESSALONIANS

The emphasis of this epistle on the second coming of Christ reminds us to be ready for Christ's coming at any time.

Likewise, we must be alert to the evil schemes of the man of lawlessness. The church gains strength from the instruction about the wicked activity of Satan with his power and pretended signs and wonders. Believers are empowered with the truth that the man of lawlessness will be finally destroyed by the Lord Jesus at his coming (2 Thess 2:12).

In the meantime, the church must remain faithful and steadfast to the goodwill and providential purposes of God.

BASIC OUTLINE OF 2 THESSALONIANS

I. Salutation (1:1–2)
II. Encouragement for the Church (1:3–12)
III. Instructions to Correct Misunderstandings (2:1–12)
IV. Injunctions to Steadfastness (2:13–3:18)

PERSONAL APPLICATION

We must be prepared, for he will come as suddenly as a thief in the night. Those who have died and those who are still alive will be united with Christ at his return. These words provide hope and encouragement for the church at all times.

MAJOR THEMES IN THE THESSALONIAN LETTERS

Persecution and Peace. Both Thessalonian letters deal with the problem of persecution of the church. Both begin and conclude with Paul's concern of peace for the Thessalonian believers.

The End Times and Endurance. Several sections of both letters address various aspects of the end time. In 1 Thessalonians, Paul comforted grieving believers in the church, whereas in 2 Thessalonians he assured the persecuted church that their persecutors would suffer punishment.

Election and Faith. The word for *church* refers to people who are "called out." These people are chosen by God (1 Thess 1:4). Along with the reality of God's sovereignty Paul recognized the reality of the human response—faith.

HISTORICAL BACKGROUND

City of Thessalonica

Cassander, a general of Alexander the Great, founded the city of Thessalonica in 315 BC, naming it after his wife. Located on the Thermaic Gulf (Gulf of Salonika) with an excellent harbor—and at the termination of a major trade route from the Danube—it became one of the most important commercial centers in Greece. In the Roman period, it retained its Greek cultural orientation and functioned as the capital of Macedonia after 146 BC.

QUESTIONS TO GUIDE YOUR STUDY

1. What prompted Paul to write 1 Thessalonians? 2 Thessalonians?
2. What was Paul's goal in writing 1 Thessalonians? 2 Thessalonians?
3. What were the Thessalonian believers like? What had been their history with Paul?
4. What major doctrines does Paul address in the Thessalonian letters?
5. When Paul visited the city, it was larger than Philippi, which reflected a predominantly Roman culture. Thessalonica was a free city, having no Roman garrison within its walls and maintaining the privilege of minting its own coins. Like Corinth, it had a cosmopolitan population due to the commercial prowess of the city.

THE LIFE AND MINISTRY OF PAUL

MAJOR EVENTS	BIBLICAL RECORDS		POSSIBLE DATES
	Acts	Galatians	
Birth			AD 1
Conversion	9:1–25	1:11–17	33
First Jerusalem Visit	9:26–30	1:18–20	36
Famine	11:25–30	2:1–10?	46
First Missionary Journey	13:1–14:28		47–48
Apostolic council in Jerusalem	15:1–29	2:1–10?	49
Second missionary journey	15:36–18:21		
Letter to the Galatians			53–55
Third missionary journey	18:23–21:6		53–57
Letters to the Corinthians			55
Arrest and prison in Jerusalem and Caesarea	21:8–26:32		57
Prison in Rome	27:1–28:30		60–62
Letter to the Ephesians			60–62
Death			67

HISTORICAL BACKGROUND

Paul began his letter with the name of the writer, the name of the recipient, a greeting, and a prayer of gratitude and intercession. This was the way letters generally began in the Hellenistic world of the first century.

See "The Hellenistic Letter" sidebar in this book's treatment of 2 Thessalonians 1.

1 THESSALONIANS 1

THE LIFE AND MINISTRY OF PAUL

The first several verses of this letter introduced the topics with which Paul's letter would deal (especially the first three chapters) and established rapport with the readers. Paul gave thanks for the Thessalonians and affirmed the church's success. Thanksgiving and affirmation together praised past actions of the Thessalonians with the intent of encouraging the continuing growth of their Christian behavior and character.

THE SALUTATION (1:1)

Authors and Addresses (v. 1a)

The three men involved in the writing of the letter were Paul, Silas, and Timothy. Timothy joined Paul and Silas on the missionary journey that took them to Thessalonica.

Greeting (v. 1b)

Paul's greeting was simply "grace to you and peace." "Grace" is God's unmerited favor that is given to us through the Lord Jesus Christ regardless of who we are or what we have done. It is the reason for our salvation and our relationship to God. "Peace" describes this new relationship that exists between a believer and God and among believers themselves. It is the total well-being that flows from the new life of grace. The combined effect of these two words transforms a routine "hello" into a theologically meaningful salutation.

HISTORICAL BACKGROUND

Paul—The renowned apostle and leading personality among the three writers.

Silvanus—A trusted leader of the church in Jerusalem and later Paul's companion on his second missionary journey.

Timothy—A prominent person both in Acts and in Paul's Letters. He was a resident of Lystra and a member of the church there.

THE THANKSGIVING (1:2–7)

Paul's expression of thanksgiving in this passage operated on several levels:

- It expressed a genuine appreciation for the faithfulness of the Thessalonian Christians.
- The thanksgiving was a way of establishing rapport with the readers.
- The thanksgiving praised several points of the Thessalonians' Christian character that Paul later encouraged and elaborated on in the body of his letter.

Paul's Prayer of Gratitude (vv. 2–3)

What caused Paul to be so thankful to God? It was the "faith," "love," and "hope" of the Thessalonian church. These words describe the total response of the believer to what God has done in the past, is doing now, and will do in the future.

Faith is not assent to a code of rules or a body of dogma. It is the position of complete trust in God. The life of faith is also the life of love. One cannot be a believer without loving God and the children of God. Hope describes the believer's eager expectation and confident waiting for the future that God has promised to his children.

Although Paul cited faith, love, and hope as prime Christian virtues (see 1 Thess 5:8; 1 Cor 13:13; Col 1:5), they were not the focal point of verses 2–3. These virtues serve to identify that which motivates and produces Christian actions. The actions themselves are what Paul emphasized.

The "work produced by faith" that Paul praised here is the Christian life, specifically the deeds that result from the indwelling Spirit (Gal 5:16–26; see also Eph 2:10).

These are not prerequisites of salvation but rather the results of salvation in the lives of those who are transformed by Christ (1 Cor 6:1–4; 12:1–2).

PERSONAL APPLICATION

"We are justified by faith, but faith produces works (Romans 6–8) as [John] the Baptist taught and as Jesus taught and as James does in James 2."

A. T. Robertson, *WPNT*, vol. 4, 8.

CHRISTIANITY IN ACTION AT THESSALONICA

VIRTUE	VIRTUE IN ACTION	EXPLANATION
Faith	"work produced by faith"	Action inspired by action or carried out by faith
Love	"labor motivated by love"	Strenuous work carried out in love
Hope	"endurance inspired by hope"	Patience involved in the practice of hope

Section Summary

After a brief greeting, Paul expressed gratitude for the Thessalonians' faith, love, and hope. These three virtues motivated and produced their Christian actions.

The Success of the Mission in Thessalonica (vv. 4–7)

Paul was convinced that his labors and that of his colleagues had been in keeping with God's initiative in reaching out to Thessalonian citizens—that they were chosen.

Paul had not just spoken words. God affirmed his preaching with demonstrations of "power, in the Holy Spirit, and with full assurance."

PERSONAL APPLICATION

"Election (Gk. *ekloge*) took place 'before the creation of the world' (Eph 1:4), but its effects are seen in the life of the elect. . . . Election is a way of saying that God takes the initiative in salvation. It underscores the fact that salvation is entirely of God's grace."

David Ewart, *Evangelical Commentary on the Bible*, ed. Walter Elwell (Baker, 1989), 1070.

Power. The word Paul used here for "power" was also one of the words used by the Gospel writers for Jesus's miracles. Paul's point here was that God's power, not his, had been demonstrated among the Thessalonians.

Holy Spirit. The inclusion of the Holy Spirit broadened Paul's statement to more than the miraculous. The Spirit's power to call, convict, enlighten, transform, assure, and comfort is far more effective than words alone can express. In a sense, the work of the Spirit is the guarantor of truth.

Full Assurance. This may refer either to the conviction demonstrated by the missionaries or the assurance that developed in the hearers of the gospel.

Section Summary

Paul described the exemplary response of the Thessalonians to the gospel. In spite of severe suffering, the Thessalonians had a joy that could be supplied only by the Spirit. They had become imitators of Paul and the Lord, thus providing a model for all believers in Macedonia and Achaia.

WORD PICTURE

Election or Choice

The Greek word *eloge*, translated as "election" or "choice" occurs only seven times in the New Testament and always denotes God's choice of human beings.

A. T. Robertson, *WPNT*, vol. 4, 10.

THE NEWS SPREADS (1:8–10)

The news about the response of the Thessalonian believers to the gospel spread rapidly. Indeed, this news preceded the arrival of the missionaries elsewhere. Instead of the missionaries themselves having to talk about what God had done in Thessalonica, they heard it from other people. "Every place" of course, is only hyperbole. Paul means "everywhere they traveled." Even more specifically, he was probably referring to Christian places of assembly (Acts 4:31; 1 Cor 2:1; 2 Cor 2:14), where news of churches, persecution, and perseverance would be shared by traveling Christian merchants and missionaries.

The Thessalonians became both models (v. 7) and messengers (v. 8) of the gospel. Through their words and lives, they helped spread "the word of the Lord" throughout their province, impacting the entire region of Macedonia and Achaia.

Paul revealed the extent of their response to the gospel:

- *How they received the missionaries* (v. 9). They received the missionaries into the Thessalonian community. The difficulty and persecution associated with Paul's work in the city made the reception given by those who became believers even more remarkable.
- *How they turned from idols to serve God* (v. 9). Conversion is pictured here as a willful act of turning from one path and moving in another direction. The Thessalonians turned "to God" and "from idols." This would indicate that they were pagans and not Jews.
- *How they persistently expected the return of the Lord* (v. 10). This was the result of their genuine conversion—perseverance to the end. They awaited Jesus, who would rescue them from "the coming wrath." Believers live in anticipation of a coronation (2 Tim 4:8) rather than a condemnation.

PERSONAL APPLICATION

Because of the way the Thessalonians had received the gospel amid affliction, they became an "example" for believers in Macedonia and Achaia. We do not become Christians or act like Christians by following the example of anyone. We can only be Christians by means of the presence and power of God through our personal faith. The example of the Thessalonians bore witness to the divinely given realities of a life of faith. This same course of conduct was possible to others who, inspired by the Thessalonians, also trusted God.

Section Summary

News of the response of the Thessalonian believers to the gospel had spread rapidly. They welcomed the missionaries Paul sent; they turned from idols to serve God; and they eagerly anticipated Jesus's return.

QUESTIONS TO GUIDE YOUR STUDY

1. What is the meaning of Paul's greeting of "grace . . . and peace"?
2. Why was Paul thankful for the Thessalonian Christians?
3. How were the Thessalonians an example for other believers? In what ways are they a model for believers today?
4. How had the Thessalonians responded to the gospel?

NEW TESTAMENT REFERENCE

In Acts 16:12–40, we read about the planting of the church at Philippi—a church that would be a joy to Paul over the years. In this same city, on this same trip, Paul and his colleagues experienced great suffering and humiliation. Assaulted by a mob, beaten, and imprisoned, they had suffered physical pain and emotional trauma.

1 THESSALONIANS 2

In this section Paul presented a summary of the motivations and actions of him and his companions during their ministry in Thessalonica. He placed several statements of thanksgiving in the narrative material of chapters 2–3.

Chapter 2 was new material, but it was closely related to chapter 1 as the following chart shows.

TIES BETWEEN CHAPTER 1 AND 2

PASSAGE IN CHAPTER 2	TREATMENT	CHAPTER 1 PASSAGE
2:1–6	expands	1:4–10
2:7–12	restates	1:5,9
2:13–16	echoes	1:6–8,10

THE DIFFICULTIES CONFRONTED (2:1–2)

In the preceding verses Paul wrote about the glowing reports that had gone out from Thessalonica. In chapter 2 he turned to more specific comments about the ministry of the missionaries in that city.

The missionaries' experience in Philippi prior to their arrival in Thessalonica was one of great blessing and great difficulty.

The result of their persecution was the opposite of what we might have expected. Despite strong "opposition" in Thessalonica, the missionaries had openly and courageously proclaimed the gospel.

WORD PICTURE

Great Opposition

The word translated "opposition" (Greek word, *agōn*) was used of the "struggle" of an athlete engaged in training or in a contest, and it was also used frequently as a metaphor for moral struggles. It speaks of the strenuous effort required to overcome an opponent. Paul did not identify the opponent in this passage. No doubt, the Thessalonians did not have to be reminded of the struggles they had encountered in the early days of their congregation.

Section Summary

Despite their previous persecution in Philippi, Paul and his missionary companions faithfully proclaimed the message God had entrusted to them. The success of their mission, despite sustained opposition, was due largely to their courage inspired by God.

THE PURITY OF PAUL'S MOTIVES (2:3–5)

For some reason Paul was anxious to defend the purity of the missionaries' motives during their stay in Thessalonica. People in the Mediterranean world were accustomed to traveling philosophers, teachers, and religionists who sometimes exploited gullible people for their own gain. Perhaps the character of Paul and his companions had also been degraded by their Jewish enemies in Thessalonica.

Paul and his companions faithfully proclaimed the message God entrusted to them. Faithfulness in adverse conditions is one proof of pure motives.

These witnesses, however, were responsible not only for witnessing to Paul's behavior but also for imitating it. Whether Paul was fending off an attack against the gospel, his narrative was intended to encourage the church to live as he had taught them to live.

In this passage Paul denied two specific impure motives behind the actions of many people: greed and flattery. Paul emphasized that the readers themselves must testify to the character of him and his missionary companions. "You know" is an emphatic phrase in the original Greek text. The missionaries spoke not from any wrong motives but because God approved them to be entrusted with the gospel.

WORD PICTURE

Approved by God

This phrase translates one word in the original Greek text. It refers to the approval of something as the result of careful examination. The verb tense refers to a past event of testing or examination, resulting in a current state of approval. The term *approval* does imply some standard of judgment.

Section Summary

The approval of God was more significant for Paul and his team than the success of the mission. Paul had sufficient reason to endure suffering and the questions surrounding his character. He denied flattery as his means of mission. His motivations were neither greed nor human praise.

GENTLE AS A NURSING MOTHER (2:6–8)

The Thessalonians might have expected Paul and his team to exert their rights and authority as "Christ's apostles." After all, they were commissioned and sent out by the Lord himself. Even though they "could have been a burden as Christ's apostles," the evangelists were "gentle . . . as a nurse nurtures her own children" (v. 7).

Paul was painting a word picture of his relationship to the Thessalonians. It was characterized not by his authoritarian assertion of his desires but of gentle kindness demonstrated by a mother who nurses a small baby.

The great love the missionaries grew to feel for their Thessalonian converts could be seen in their ministry in their city. Not only were they glad to share the gospel, but they were willing to share their "lives" as well.

THE MISSIONARIES' ASSERTIONS OF LOVE*

ASSERTION	PROOF
1. "We never used flattering speech, . . . or had greedy motives" (v. 5).	1. "You know." 2. "God is our witness."
2. "We didn't seek glory from people, either from you or from others" (v. 6).	"We could have been a burden as Christ's apostles."
3. "We were gentle among you, as a nurse nurtures her own children" (v. 7).	"We cared so much for you."
4. "We were pleased to share with you not only the gospel of God but also our own lives" (v. 8).	"Because you had become so dear to us."

*Chart adapted from D. Michael Martin, *1, 2 Thessalonians*, New American Commentary, 80.

Section Summary

Rather than exhibiting flattery, greed, and exploitation, Paul and his coworkers demonstrated pure motives and a parental gentleness born of love.

THE UNSELFISHNESS OF THEIR LABOR (2:9–12)

In verse 9 Paul elaborated on the way the missionaries shared their lives with the Thessalonians. They engaged in strenuous, difficult manual labor to support themselves so that they would not have to be a financial burden to any of the converts.

THE POSITIVE ACTIONS OF THE MISSIONARIES

ACTION	VERSE
Gentleness	v. 7
Love and a desire to share the good things of the gospel	v. 8
Hard work and financial independence	v. 9
Holiness, righteousness, and blamelessness	v. 10

Verses 9–10 paint a picture of a self-reliant, considerate, and righteous missionary. Paul's use of another family analogy—a father—added warmth and a personal touch to the depiction of his relationship with the Thessalonian church.

A good father encourages and provides guidance, and he is concerned about the moral development of his children. Moral problems were especially acute among believers newly won from pagan religions.

Such was the case in Thessalonica. They did not have the benefit of moral training as did the Jews. Ignorance of Christian ethics, the pull of the old life, and the pressures of heathen society combined to hinder some believers from leading lives worthy of the gospel.

That is why so much of Paul's letter was dedicated to basic moral exhortation. Paul believed that one of his basic responsibilities was to support new converts in their Christian life through exhortation and encouragement. High moral standards were in keeping with the high calling believers had received from God.

Section Summary

Paul's behavior resembled a father offering help to his struggling children. To the hesitant he offered exhortation; to the weary he offered encouragement; to the weak he offered strength and direction. His motivation was to help each convert see what it meant to "walk worthy of God, who calls you into his own kingdom and glory."

THE ACCEPTANCE OF THE MESSAGE (2:13–16)

The missionaries had been true, honorable, and loving in their ministry. Likewise, the Thessalonian believers had been responsive to the proclamation of the gospel. So many of their neighbors dismissed the missionaries' message as "a human message."

But when the message was preached to the Thessalonian believers, their subsequent experience confirmed that the message was indeed "the word of God," which "works effectively" in them.

Section Summary

After receiving the gospel, the Thessalonian believers endured intense persecution. Paul expressed his deep concern and exasperation with his countrymen. Their rejection of the gospel moved Paul to bitter denunciation similar to the Old Testament prophets.

PAUL'S DESIRE TO VISIT THE CHURCH (2:17–20)

From Paul's comments about his departure, we see how much he wanted to stay. Evidently, he feared that the Thessalonians were not strong enough to confront the hostility toward their new faith. Paul used emotionally charged language to describe his separation and absence from the church. Paul said that the missionaries were "forced to leave" the church. The word Paul used here means literally "orphaned." The strong bond between Paul and the church, comparable to the bond between loving parent and beloved child, made separation emotionally painful for

WORD PICTURE

Encouraged, Comforted, Implored

These verbs indicate the act of encouraging or cheering someone. "Encouraged" more frequently than "comforted" carries the idea of exhortation, yet both are also used in contexts of admonition. The combination of those two verbs in Paul's writings seems to indicate a positive encouragement to Christian living. "Implored" speaks of the delivery of truth and is likely intended to convey the more directive functions of a father.

Previously Paul had mentioned that his readers had experienced affliction when they received the word. He now revealed that the affliction was persecution from their own people. Paul saw his own persecution by fellow Jews as part of an age-old pattern of rebellion against God. They had "killed the Lord Jesus." Before that, they had murdered the "prophets." They had driven out Paul and his associates.

The result of the opposition of the Jews to the advance of the gospel was that "they are constantly filling up their sins to the limit." Commenting on this phrase, A. T. Robertson said, "It may be God's conceived plan to allow the Jews to go on and fill up (fill up full), or it may be the natural result from the continual sins of the Jews." (*WPNT*, vol. 4, 22.

the apostle. Paul's description of his separation was designed to express clearly that his absence did not result from indifference on his part.

Paul made repeated attempts to return to Thessalonica, but Satan thwarted his efforts. Sometimes Paul saw obstacles and problems as expressing the will of God (Rom 1:13). In this case, they expressed Satan's opposition to God.

How important were the Thessalonians to Paul? He made every effort to let them know that they were indispensable. They were his "glory and joy," both in the present and at the future coming of Christ.

WORD PICTURE

At His Coming

This phrase translates the New Testament word *parousia*. It denotes the manifestation of a deity or the visit of a king or emperor. Early Christians used this phrase to refer to the coming of Jesus in power and glory at the end of the age.

Section Summary

Paul longed to see the Thessalonians again with the joyful anticipation similar to that of parents eager to look upon their firstborn.

QUESTIONS TO GUIDE YOUR STUDY

1. What are some ways the missionaries asserted their love for the believers at Thessalonica?
2. In defending the motives of his ministry with the Thessalonians, on what basis did Paul do so?
3. In describing his relationship with the Thessalonians, Paul used the analogies of a nurse (vv. 6–8) and a father (vv. 9–10). In what ways did he function as both toward the Thessalonians?
4. Paul greatly desired to visit the Thessalonians. What was his motivation? Why had he been prevented from returning to the church?

1 THESSALONIANS 3

We get a view into Paul's heart in this chapter of 1 Thessalonians. He expressed his deepest concerns for the church. He needed to know how the Thessalonians were doing in the midst of persecution.

NEW TESTAMENT REFERENCE

The Acts account offers little insight at this point. There we are told that Jewish opposition drove Paul from Thessalonica to Berea and then to Athens (Acts 17:1–5). Acts 17:14–15 indicates that Timothy and Silas stayed in Berea when Paul fled to Athens, but they were expected to join Paul in Athens as soon as possible.

THE DECISION TO SEND TIMOTHY (3:1–5)

Unable to make the desired visit to Thessalonica personally, Paul's anxiety about the new converts there became unbearable. In this situation he decided to send Timothy back to visit them, even though it meant he had to remain in Athens without his trusted friend.

Paul's reason for sending Timothy to visit the Thessalonians is clear. The Thessalonians were under great pressure from their adversaries. Timothy was to perform the pastoral function of encouraging and exhorting the believers to remain true to Jesus Christ in spite of persecution. Paul knew that the lot of believers is persecution, such as the Thessalonians were experiencing.

Paul used three infinitives to explain Timothy's mission as highlighted in the following chart:

TIMOTHY'S MISSION TO THE THESSALONIANS

	MINISTRY DIRECTIVES	DESIRED RESULT
1.	To strengthen them in the faith	That the Thessalonians might remain true to Christ.
2.	To encourage them in the faith	Same as above.
3.	To prevent them from being "shaken" by affliction	That the Thessalonians might resist being discouraged by affliction.

Verse 5 reveals why Paul was anxious for the Thessalonians. He wants to find out about their faith—that is, if their trust in Jesus was of the quality that could stand up under persecution. Also, he wanted to feel that he had engaged in useful and lasting labor regarding the Thessalonian church.

"Tempter" is another name for Satan. The believers at Thessalonica faced both temptation (v. 3) and affliction (v. 5). What is the temptation in the time of opposition and suffering? It comes from the sense that we have been abandoned by God. Suffering can also lead us to believe that our trust is absurd. If the Thessalonians renounced their faith in the midst of their persecution, Paul would have considered his labor with the Thessalonians as fruitless.

HISTORICAL BACKGROUND

Timothy, whose name means "honoring God," was a friend and trusted coworker of Paul. When Timothy was a child, his mother Eunice and his grandmother Lois taught him the Scriptures (2 Tim 1:5; 3:15). A native of Lystra, he may have been converted on Paul's first missionary journey (Acts 14:6–23). Paul referred to Timothy as his child in the faith (1 Cor 4:17; 1 Tim 1:2; 2 Tim 1:2). This probably means that Paul was instrumental in Timothy's conversion.

Section Summary

Paul sent Timothy to visit the believers at Thessalonica. He was anxious about them and wanted to know that the church had persisted in its commitment to Jesus Christ. In addition, he wanted to feel that he had engaged in useful and lasting labor.

TIMOTHY RETURNS WITH GOOD NEWS (3:6–10)

Timothy returned from his mission to the Thessalonians with the kind of report Paul hoped to hear. Timothy's good news encouraged the missionaries. Overjoyed by the news from the little band of besieged Christians, Paul decides to communicate with them by letter. His enthusiasm was conveyed by the speed with which he responded to the news. "Timothy has come" implies that Paul was making his response a high priority.

The good news Timothy brought was twofold:

He told about the "faith and love" of the Christian community at Thessalonica. The Thessalonians trusted God and had not abandoned this trust under pressure.

Timothy also reported that the Thessalonians always remembered their missionaries with respect and love. They shared Paul's desire for a reunion.

"If you stand firm" is conditional, implying a future expectation rather than a statement about the past.

"What is lacking" (v. 10) may refer to a natural growth toward completion or, more negatively, a deficiency or inadequacy that needed to be corrected. In none of Paul's letters do we get the idea that Christians in the churches had arrived at the zenith of their development. No matter what their progress, there was always room for further development.

WORD PICTURE

Stand Firm

This verb means "to stand firm, to be steadfast." It is used repeatedly in the New Testament as a call for continued perseverance. The Thessalonian believers were persevering in godliness during affliction. Other New Testament uses of this word include "stand[ing] firm" in the faith (1 Cor 16:13); in the Spirit (Phil 1:27); in one's fellowship with the Lord (Phil 4:1); and in Christian freedom (Gal 5:1).

Section Summary

Timothy's encouraging report of the favorable feelings of the Thessalonians toward Paul—and the fact that they trusted God and had not abandoned that trust under pressure—were reasons for joy.

PAUL'S PRAYER (3:11–13)

Paul concluded this first major section of his letter with a prayer. The apostle addressed three requests to God: (1) he wanted God to "direct" their "way" for his visit to Thessalonica; (2) he wanted God to cause their love to overflow; and (3) he asked God to "make your hearts blameless."

WORD PICTURE

The word translated "direct our way" can mean "to straighten out, to make straight" or simply "to direct." The former would imply the need to remove obstacles, and it seems more likely to be Paul's intent in this context. Some spiritual hindrance had kept them from visiting the Thessalonians: "Satan hindered us" (2:18). Spiritual power is required to remove a spiritual hindrance. According to travels recorded in Acts, Paul's visit to Thessalonica did not happen for several years, not until after the Ephesian ministry (20:1–6).

"Direct Our Way" (v. 11)

Paul's first request was that God would "direct our way" for his personal visit to the church.

"May the Lord Cause You to Increase and Overflow with Love" (v. 12)

Paul's second prayer petition is that the Lord might cause the believers to "increase and overflow" in their love for others. Together those two words form an emphatic prayer-wish for the spiritual growth of the Thessalonians. This love was not exclusive; it is expressed to "one another" and "everyone" else.

"Make Your Hearts Blameless" (v. 13)

The heart is the center of the intellect and will. Paul, in this verse, referred to resolution and commitment. Paul's goal for requesting that God make blameless the hearts of the Thessalonians was that they be "blameless in holiness" in the presence of God. God's saints, or holy ones, are those dedicated to him and his service. He wants them to be strengthened in their dedication to a holy life—one completely devoted to God.

Section Summary

Paul's prayer reflected the transition in his life from anguish to exhilaration. He prayed that God would enable him to visit his friends. He then asked God to perfect and enlarge the love which the Thessalonians had already displayed toward one another.

QUESTIONS TO GUIDE YOUR STUDY

1. Why did Paul send Timothy to the Thessalonians? And what specifically was his mission?
2. What was the content of Timothy's report to Paul about the Thessalonians?
3. Timothy reported that the Thessalonians were "stand[ing] firm in the Lord." Given their circumstances, what did that mean?
4. Describe the petitions of Paul's prayer in verses 11–13. What was the occasion for the prayer? What was the goal of his prayer?

1 THESSALONIANS 4

Paul could have ended his letter with chapter 3, for he discussed the most important concern on his mind. Instead, he added to the letter a second section that contains ethical appeals and instructions. Some of these subjects probably were suggested by Timothy's good report from Thessalonica.

AN INTRODUCTORY CALL TO OBEDIENCE (4:1–2)

Paul began this section by appealing to the Thessalonians. "Ask" and "encourage" are synonyms. They come after "additionally, then, brothers and sisters" in the original Greek text, providing a sense of urgency to Paul's words and creating anticipation on the part of the readers.

"In the Lord Jesus" describes the context of his appeal. Jesus was Lord of Paul's life and theirs. The apostle had given the Thessalonians instructions about Christian behavior—how they were to live and to "please God." He diplomatically affirmed that the Thessalonians were indeed following those instructions. Yet there was room for development and growth, so Paul urged them to "do this even more." His challenges to continue in Christian growth, however, did not minimize the progress his readers had already made toward living out the implications of the gospel.

Paul used two comparative clauses (introduced by the phrase *as*) to express what the Thessalonians were to do. "We ask and encourage you in the Lord Jesus, that *as* you have received instruction from us on how

WORD PICTURE

How You Should Live and You are Doing

The words of this phrase translate the verb that means "walk." Forms of this word occur twice in 1 Thess 4:1, and they are translated "live" and "doing." Both refer to behavior or conduct. "Paul is fond of the metaphor 'walk' (*peripateō*)."

A. T. Robertson, *WPNT*, vol. 4, 410.

you should live and please God—*as* you are doing—do this even more" (emphasis added).

This instruction guided the new believers in how they were to "live" and to "please God." Paul used the present tense with both verbs to imply that consistent behavior was expected and not just the occasional acts of obedience.

Continuing to live in a way that pleased God did not require the return of the apostle or the revelation of new traditions. It required obedience to the commands the church had already received. It also required obedience to the commands of Jesus. The verses that followed provided some specific content in places where Paul apparently felt the Thessalonians needed clarification or encouragement.

WORD PICTURE

Sanctification

Sanctification is the gradual process of being made holy, of being set apart for God, resulting in a changed lifestyle for the believer. This process takes the believer through failure because of self-dependency to triumph through the indwelling Spirit. What does it mean to live a sanctified life? At its basic level, it means living in a manner consistent with the character and commands of God.

Paul made clear in his letters that high moral standards were important to the Christian life. If believers are to be holy, certain practices must be rejected. In this context, Paul highlighted three aspects of sanctification. One who is sanctified:

- Should avoid sexual immorality (v. 3).
- Should know how to control his or her own body (vv. 4–5).
- Should not "transgress against and take advantage of a brother or sister" (v. 6).

Section Summary

Continuing to live in a way that pleased God required obedience to the commands of Jesus. Paul instructed the Thessalonians to continue in their Christian growth.

EXHORTATIONS ABOUT SANCTIFICATION (4:3–8)

Holiness in the Sexual Life (vv. 3–6a)

This first of several exhortations began with the statement that what follows is "God's will." The theme of this section is a call to *sanctification*. The specific commands in verses 3b–6 are examples of sanctified living regarding sexual purity.

A Solemn Warning (vv. 6b–8)

These verses present a fourfold warning. They are not directed to the pagan but to those members of the church who choose to live in a manner that denies the God they claim to serve. Paul gave four reasons Christians should adhere to a life of moral purity.

1. *God will punish sinful behavior (v. 6b).* Salvation does not grant believers the right to sin without suffering the consequences.
2. *Sexual sins are inconsistent with the sanctified life (v. 7).* The "call" Paul referred to seems to look back at their initial commitment to follow Christ. The nature of the Thessalonians' call and the purpose to which he called them require not impurity but sanctification.
3. *He who rejects this instruction rejects God (v. 8a).* Because God calls believers to a sanctified life rather than immoral behavior, living immorally is a rejection of God. Rejection indicates a settled attitude, not a single incident of disobedience.

4. *Living an unsanctified life is inconsistent with the character of the Holy Spirit, who indwells the believer (v. 8b).* To live an immoral lifestyle is to reject God's gift of the Spirit. The work of the Holy Spirit must be evident in the sanctified living of believers (Gal 5:16–26). This is the will of God for his people. To live immorally is to deny the presence of the Spirit.

Section Summary

The prevailing sexual laxity Paul witnessed throughout the Roman Empire compelled him to remind his readers that sexual purity was the will of God. Anyone who violated God's standards at this point faced certain punishment from the Lord. Paul made clear that God had not called believers to a life of impurity but a life of holiness.

EXHORTATIONS ABOUT BROTHERLY LOVE (4:9–12)

In his exhortations to the churches to which he ministered, Paul usually put love and unity in the community ahead of his call for personal morality. In this section he reversed the order and turned to the matter of love after talking about the need for sexual purity.

Love Among Brothers and Sisters (vv. 9–10)

Paul's theme for these two verses was love for fellow Christians, whereas he dealt with the theme of relating to non-Christian society in verses 11–12.

Paul's only directive in this passage was "we encourage you." He expanded this directive with a series of suggested actions that would allow the Thessalonians to excel on a path that leads to the final, intended outcome.

The love of the Thessalonian congregation was to include "all the brothers and sisters in the entire region of Macedonia." We may assume their love was lived out in concrete ministry to the needs of other Christians. We get some notion of this spirit of the Macedonian believers when we read 2 Cor 8:1–5.

Paul urged the Thessalonians to love the brothers "even more." No Christian reaches the zenith of such love in his or her spiritual life in this world.

Conduct in the Community (vv. 11–12)

Paul moved naturally from relationships in the church to the Christian's conduct in society. The believer's manner of life should be the kind that would earn respect from unbelieving neighbors.

WORD PICTURE

Brotherly Love

The phrase "brotherly love" (the Greek word, *philadelphia*) is a translation of a word that is made up of two words: "love" and "brother." Outside of the New Testament, both Greek and Jewish writers used "brotherly love" primarily of love within actual families, not of love within religious groups. In the New Testament, however, it is always used as it is here—of love between members of the Christian family (Rom 12:10; Heb 13:1; 1 Pet 1:22; 2 Pet 1:7).

HISTORICAL BACKGROUND

Christians in the first century were often found in the center of trouble and disorder because of preaching the gospel. Paul himself had that experience. But he did not believe Christians should get into trouble because of disorderly conduct, interference in other people's business, or failure to earn a living.

PAUL'S EXHORTATIONS TO BROTHERLY LOVE

ACTION		VERSE
Love the brothers even more		v. 10b
Aspire to lead a quiet life		v. 11
Mind their own affairs		v. 11
Work with their own hands		v. 11
Goals:		
1.	To win the respect "of outsiders."	
2.	To "not be dependent on anyone"	v. 12

Section Summary

God's will for believers includes moral purity and love relationships with people, which demands openness and self-sacrifice.

EXHORTATIONS REGARDING THOSE WHO HAVE ALREADY DIED (4:13–18)

"Do Not . . . Be Uninformed" (vv. 13–14)

Apparently, early Christians expected the Lord would return before they died. In Thessalonica, some of the believers already died. The church evidently had some questions about this. What would happen to their brothers and sisters who were not alive when Jesus appeared? In this passage Paul answered that question.

For Paul the future of believers after death was tied to the resurrection of Jesus Christ. Christians believed that God raised Jesus from the dead. They needed to be confident also that the relationship of believers to God in Christ did not end with death. The physical death of Christians, however, presented no problem to the God who brought Jesus back from the dead.

Those Who Are Alive Will "Certainly Not Precede Those Who Have Fallen Asleep" (vv. 15–18)

Verses 15–17 describe the scenario of the end time. The main point in the passage was Paul's insistence that being alive at the return of the Lord would give no advantage to his readers. They would not "precede those who have fallen asleep."

Paul made two primary statements in verse 16 and one in verse 17; these provide the core sequence of events regarding Jesus's coming. Three key events constitute Paul's vision of Jesus's return:

1. The Lord will appear (16a).
2. The "dead in Christ" will be raised (16b).
3. All believers will be caught up to "meet the Lord in the air" (v. 17).

The following chart depicts the sequence and details of these events.

THE LORD'S RETURN (THE RAPTURE)*

	EVENT	VERSE	DETAILS OF THE EVENT
1.	Appearing of the Lord	v. 16a	• The Lord will come down from heaven → with a loud command → with the voice of the archangel → with the trumpet call of God
2.	Raising of the "dead in Christ"	v. 16b	• The dead will rise first
3.	Believers "caught up"	v. 17	• Together with the "dead in Christ" → in the clouds → to meet the Lord in the air

*For more information on the Lord's return, see the article, "The Return of Christ" at the end of this chapter.

Living believers are said to be "caught up" to meet the Lord at his coming. But this is not understood in the same way by all interpreters. Those of varying millennial views about end-time events all hold firmly to the biblical truth of such a rapture. However, within the premillennial view the teaching of the rapture finds major emphasis. This view sees a tribulation period immediately before the second coming of Christ. Postmillennial and amillennial perspectives generally understand the rapture as a part of the day of the Lord when Jesus will return to gather his people to himself.

The period of tribulation mentioned above is referred to as the great tribulation. It is a seven-year period of intense trouble on earth prior to the second coming of Christ. There are three basic views regarding the tribulation, as explained in the following chart.

WORD PICTURE

The Rapture

The event described in verses 16–17, commonly referred to as the "rapture," holds a prominent place in the study of the last days. It refers to the catching up of believers by Christ at the time of his return.

VIEWS OF THE TRIBULATION

VIEW	EXPLANATION
Pretribulational	Sees the rapture occurring prior to the tribulation.
Midtribulational	Places the rapture at the midpoint of a seven-year tribulation period.
Posttribulational	Holds that the church will remain on earth during the tribulation period.

PERSONAL APPLICATION

Paul wanted his readers to believe physical death was no problem for believers, so he closed this section with the command to "encourage one another" with these words. Just as the Thessalonians were called to comfort one another, so believers of every age are called to "rejoice with those who rejoice" and "weep with those who weep" (Rom 12:15). This is Paul's message of comfort.

Section Summary

The believing community should not grieve over those who have died in Jesus, for God will bring them with Jesus at the return of the Lord. At the Lord's appearing, the Christian dead will be raised to meet the Lord in the air together with those have been "caught up" (who are alive and remaining). Paul exhorted believers to comfort one another with these words.

QUESTIONS TO GUIDE YOUR STUDY

1. What was the point of Paul's introductory call to obedience at the beginning of this chapter?
2. What is the doctrine of sanctification? What did Paul teach about holiness in the sexual life?
3. Paul exhorted the Thessalonians to "brotherly love." How might we apply his exhortation to the modern-day church?
4. What does the term *rapture* mean? What events does Paul describe regarding the Lord's return? What should be the believer's attitude toward the Lord's return?

WORD PICTURE

Day of the Lord

The phrase "day of the Lord" is full of meaning to anyone familiar with the Jewish Scriptures. In the Old Testament, it is a day of judgment. Yahweh will punish the evil within Israel (Amos 5:18–20) on that day, and the wicked among the nations will face a day of terrible wrath (Isa 13:6–13; Obad 15). Those who have not repented will face "devastation from the Almighty" (Joel 1:13–15). Yet the punishment of the evil is at the same time the deliverance of the righteous (Joel 2:31–32; Zech 14:1–21; Mal 4:5). In the New Testament, Jesus is the Lord whom God has appointed to judge the world (Acts 17:31), so the Day of the Lord (2 Thess 2:2; 1 Cor 5:5; 2 Pet 3:10) is the Day of the Lord Jesus Christ (1 Cor 1:8; 2 Cor 1:14; Phil 1:6–10; 2:16).

1 THESSALONIANS 5

This chapter contains two major sections. In the first, Paul continued his discussion about the Lord's return with an emphasis on the Day of the Lord. The concluding section emphasized responsibilities to the different people in the Christian community.

THE DAY OF THE LORD (5:1–11)

This section continues Paul's discussion of the Lord's coming from chapter 4, but with this section he changed his emphasis. Whereas 4:13–18 addressed the concerns regarding believers who had already died, these verses addressed the responsibility of living believers as they await the Lord's return.

The Thessalonians' Question (v. 1)

When is the Lord going to return? is a question that has been on the minds of believers for centuries. Paul's response to a specific time was: "About the times and the seasons . . . you do not need anything to be written to you." He did, however, remind the Thessalonians that the Lord's return is inevitable and will surprise unbelievers. In contrast to unbelievers, believers need to remain alert and watchful for his return.

Descriptions of the Lord's Return (vv. 2–3)

Paul used two analogies to describe the manner of the Lord's return:

Its *unexpectedness*. The Lord will come "like a thief in the night." A thief does not announce his coming, so the specific time of his arrival is unknown. Only those who are unbelievers, however, will be taken by surprise.

Its *suddenness*. Its suddenness will be like the onslaught of labor pains which a pregnant woman experiences. In addition, when a pregnant woman begins labor, there is no "escape" (v. 3). Its conclusion is inevitable.

Anticipating the Return (vv. 4–11)

How should believers live in light of the Lord's return? Paul provided additional instruction to address this question. Believers should prepare for the Lord's return by disciplined, godly living supported by hope, love, and faith. Watching for Jesus's return involves consistent living in obedience to the Lord's commands. Paul gave his readers these exhortations:

5. *"Let us stay awake."* Believers need to be like a watchman that never falls asleep at his post.
6. *"Let us be self-controlled."* This is a word that means "to be calm, sober-minded" (see A. T. Robertson, *WPNT*, vol. 4, 35).

A person like this is aware of what is happening around him.

The believer is to be alert, similar to a soldier putting on armor. The Christian soldier's armor includes those qualities and attributes already in the believer's possession: (1) the "armor" of love and faith; and (2) the "helmet" of the "hope of salvation."

Paul closed this section by admonishing his readers to encourage one another with these truths about the Lord's return. Believers should encourage and build up one another in the faith, knowing that one day they will live with Christ.

Section Summary

Because the Day of the Lord will come suddenly and unexpectedly, bringing destruction on those who are spiritually insensitive, believers should maintain spiritual alertness.

CONCLUDING EXHORTATIONS (5:12–22)

This concluding section emphasized the church's responsibilities to different people within the Christian community.

Leaders and Followers (vv. 12–13)

Leaders are to respect those who follow their leadership. Paul identified three areas associated with this relationship between the leaders and followers:

WORD PICTURE

Idle or Unruly

The Greek word behind these translations is a military term that describes soldiers who don't keep in the ranks.

Leon Morris, *The Epistles of Paul to the Thessalonians* (Eerdmans, 1958), 100.

WORD PICTURE

"Modern discussions generally insist that a prophet's function was rather to 'forth-tell' than to 'fore-tell.' While there is truth in this it should not be forgotten that on occasion the prophet would foretell the future."

Leon Morris, *The First and Second Epistles to the Thessalonians* (Eerdmans, 1959), 176–77.

PERSONAL APPLICATION

"Henri Nouwen's image of the wounded healer is a model for the church's ministry to the weak. The man sits at the gate with the other sick and diseased. His wounds are just as deep; his suffering is just as severe as others who live the life of hurt. But he takes time out from dressing his own wounds to clean and bandage the wounds of others."

John D. Hendrix, *To Thessalonians with Love* (Broadman, 1982), 116.

Those Who Work Hard (v. 12). These were laborers who worked hard in the work of the ministry so as to earn the respect of the congregation.

Those Who Lead You (v. 12). These were individuals who directed or cared for others in the church.

Those Who Admonish You (v. 12). These were leaders or members of the congregation who admonished one another to proper behavior.

Paul exhorted the congregation at Thessalonica to acknowledge and respect those who were ministering in their midst. They were to "be at peace among yourselves" (v. 13).

The Weak and the Strong (vv. 14–15)

In verse 14 Paul provided four brief exhortations for the church that encouraged it to take protective measures to assist troublesome or weak Christians:

"Warn those who are idle." Those who were idle had entered an unacceptable lifestyle, and they needed to be confronted about their behavior.

"Comfort the discouraged." Those who were fainthearted or "discouraged" by their circumstances or a turn of events needed to be encouraged.

"Help the weak." This can refer to those who were physically weak or ill as well as those who were spiritually weak or immature. The church was to support these weak members and not desert them.

"Be patient with everyone." Patience is a characteristic of God. The believers at Thessalonica were to demonstrate godly patience in dealing with troublesome members, just as God had demonstrated his patience in their lives.

Optimists and Pessimists (vv. 16–18)

These three brief exhortations commend joyful worship directed toward God and should be evident in all assemblies where Christians gather for worship:

"Rejoice always" (v. 16). Joy is a work produced in the believer by the Spirit. The believer who is joyful rejoices in the good fortune of others and is obedient to the Lord.

"Pray constantly" (v. 17). "God is with us whatever befalls us. It is God's will that we find joy in prayer in Christ Jesus in every condition of life" (A. T. Robertson, *WPNT*, vol. 4, 37).

"Give thanks in everything" (v. 18). Believers should constantly give thanks to God for what he has done in their lives. Paul was particularly thankful for what God had done in the Thessalonian church.

The Cynical and the Gullible (vv. 19–22)

Paul wrote this group of five exhortations to help the Thessalonians hold their ground in the midst of conflicting claims about truth:

"Don't stifle the Spirit" (v. 19). This exhortation is a prohibition that forbids the Thessalonians from suppressing or stifling the work of the Spirit in their church. The following exhortation provided an example of stifling the Spirit.

"Don't despise prophecies" (v. 20). Those with the gift of prophecy proclaimed the word of God to the congregation. The congregation might "stifle the Spirit" by refusing to hear the word of the prophet.

"Test all things. Hold on to what is good" (v. 21). To "test" something is to examine it carefully. This included the church carefully examining the teaching of visiting teachers and prophets as well as its own members and leaders. What proved to be "good" they were to retain and allow it to shape their lives.

"Stay away from every kind of evil" (v. 22). "Kind of evil" is a translation of a word that means "look" or "appearance." Upon careful testing, whatever appeared evil Paul called on the church to avoid. "Evil had a way of showing itself even in the spiritual gifts including prophecy" (A. T. Robertson, *WPNT*, vol. 4, 38).

WORD PICTURE

Test, Prove

These terms are "often used in testing metals or checking out budgets. 'Prove all things' (KJV) refers to the process of sifting out the genuine from the counterfeit. Paul was not saying to try everything once. He was saying that we should test everything that represents itself as good. The good should be accepted. Every kind of evil should be avoided."

John D. Hendrix, *To Thessalonians with Love* (Broadman, 1982), 122–23.

Section Summary

In this section Paul reflected on the church's responsibilities to different people within the Christian community. With a series of brief exhortations, he urged the church members to embrace one another as well as the community in ways that honor and glorify God.

BENEDICTION AND CONCLUSION (5:23–28)

Benediction (vv. 23–24)

Paul concluded his letter with a prayer that highlights two of the key themes of the letter. His first prayer request was that God might sanctify the Thessalonians "completely." His second request was for the preservation of the church.

Paul concluded his prayer by assuring the Thessalonians that God is faithful and will do what he promises. Paul left his readers with the assurances that those who are in Christ will be sanctified and kept, making their future secure.

Concluding Remarks (vv. 25–27)

Following his prayer for the Thessalonian congregation, Paul presented them with three brief exhortations:

"Pray for us." Paul pleaded for the prayers of his converts at Thessalonica. Paul used the present tense, which indicated that he wanted them to "pray constantly."

"Greet all the brothers and sisters with a holy kiss." The holy kiss was widely practiced among the early Christians as a greeting, a sign of acceptance, and as an impartation of blessing. This custom may have been used to express the unity of Christian fellowship.

"I charge you . . . that this letter be read." According to A. T. Robertson, the word "charge" means "to put one to oath" (*WPNT*, vol. 4, 39). Paul was requiring a pledge from the Thessalonians that they would read his letter "to all the brothers and sisters."

Conclusion of the Letter (v. 28)

The typical closing to an ancient letter was a simple farewell Paul replaced the secular formula with a benediction. Paul's signature theme "—the grace of our Lord Jesus Christ"—concluded this letter. He reminded his readers that Jesus Christ is the source of God's grace then applied that grace to his readers.

HISTORICAL BACKGROUND

"Many people could not read, so reading his letter aloud was the only way everyone in the congregation could be acquainted with it."

Craig S. Keener, *The IVP Bible Background Commentary* (InterVarsity Press, 1993), 596.

Section Summary

Paul offered edifying words of assurance and blessing for the church. These comments underscore the importance of prayer in carrying out the purposes of God.

QUESTIONS TO GUIDE YOUR STUDY

1. How did Paul respond to questions about the time of the Lord's return? Is it really necessary that we know when his return will be?
2. What is the "day of the Lord"? What does it mean to believers? To unbelievers?
3. How should believers live in anticipation of the Lord's return?
4. Paul gave several concluding exhortations to the church at Thessalonica regarding its responsibilities to different people within the Christian community. Do any of these apply to your church?

2 THESSALONIANS 1

Paul wrote this letter to the Thessalonians to deal with three major issues. First, there was the matter of continued persecution to which the church was still subjected and which it apparently continued to meet with courage and faithfulness. Second, some person or persons proclaimed to the church that the Day of the Lord had already come. Third, some members of the church were guilty of idleness and disorderly conduct.

In this first chapter, Paul emphasized the dire consequences that awaited the persecutors of the Thessalonians through the judgment of God.

THE SALUTATION (1:1–2)

Authors (v. 1a)

As with 1 Thessalonians, the three men involved in the writing of the letter were Paul, Silvanus, and Timothy. (See 1 Thess 1:1 for information about these men.)

Recipients (v. 1b)

Here, as in all his letters, Paul followed the conventional Hellenistic form of address. Although he followed this form, he did so with a distinctly Christian flair.

Greeting (v. 2)

The greeting of 2 Thessalonians is identical to that in 1 Thessalonians except for the addition of the pronoun *our* in the first verse and the phrase "from God our Father and the Lord Jesus Christ" (v. 2). (See 1 Thess 1:1 for a discussion of the terms *grace* and *peace*.) God's gracious act in Christ and the well-being that can result form is the basic tenet of the Christian faith.

Paul used the term *Father* as his first designation of God. This title reminded his readers that a relationship exists not only between the father and his children but also between the siblings. Children who share the same Father are bound together in a single family and should demonstrate love and concern for one another.

HISTORICAL BACKGROUND

The Hellenistic Letter

Generally, Paul's epistles seem to follow the normal pattern of the Hellenistic letter, which consists of five major sections:

1. Opening (sender, addressee, greeting)
2. Thanksgiving or blessing (often with a prayer of intercession, well wishes, or personal greetings)
3. The burden of the letter (including citation of classical sources and arguments)
4. *Parenesis* (ethical instruction, exhortation)
5. Closing (mention of personal plans, mutual friends, benediction)

Section Summary

The second letter to the Thessalonians begins by identifying Paul, Silvanus, and Timothy as its senders. No doubt, Paul was the primary author. The letter's beginning follows the pattern of most of Paul's letters.

PAUL'S GRATITUDE FOR THE BELIEVERS (1:3–4)

Before turning to the problems in the churches to which he wrote, Paul usually expressed thanksgiving for the good things in their lives. He did the same here but with a different twist. His expressions of thanksgiving, here and in 2 Thess 2:13, are unusual in that they included a sense of obligation. "We ought" implies that the giving of thanks was not an option. He also expressed that thanksgiving was fitting, which emphasized further the Christian sense of moral obligation.

Why did Paul use these expressions? Some interpreters suggest that the Thessalonians protested their unworthiness of Paul's praise in the previous letter. Where "faith" and "love" existed in the church, however, it was wrong not to be grateful to God who was their source.

"Flourishing" faith and "increasing" love were cause for Paul's thanksgiving in this letter. Faith and love are not static; they are dynamic. We can never trust or love as much we ought, so we need to be concerned about increasing these as well as their presence.

WORD PICTURE

Boast

The word *boast* means "to make a boast of, take pride in." In all the New Testament, it is used only here. Its compounded form ("in" + "boast" = "to boast in") gives it more emphasis than the uncompounded form ("boast") that Paul frequently used.

"Paul was not above praising one church to other churches to provoke them to good works. Here he is boasting of Thessalonica in Macedonia to the Corinthians as he did later to the Corinthians about the collection (2 Cor 8:1–15) after first boasting to the Macedonians about the Corinthians (2 Cor 9:1–5)."

A. T. Robertson, *WPNT*, vol. 4, 42.

CHRISTIAN DYNAMICS AT WORK IN THESSALONICA

VIRTUE	DYNAMIC AT WORK	DIRECTED TOWARD
Faith	"flourishing"	God
Love	"increasing"	Other believers

Paul's emphasis on this boast before other congregations served two purposes: (1) it intensified the affirmation; and (2) it implied that the Thessalonians had a reputation to live up to, thus encouraging continued perseverance.

Section Summary

Paul commended the Thessalonians for their growing faith and their maturing love and patience. They became the object of his boasting to other congregations.

THE OUTCOME OF PERSEVERANCE (1:5–10)

These verses are an elaboration that addressed one of the great hopes the apostle had for the church—that they would persevere. Paul encouraged the Thessalonians' perseverance by pointing out its result as well as the end result of opposition to faith. Because God is just, he will ultimately reward the faithful and punish the wicked.

The Perseverance of the Thessalonians (v. 5)

It is difficult to determine what exactly Paul considered to be "evidence of God's righteous judgment." It could have been both the fact that they are suffering and that they are bearing up under their suffering. Today, this is evidence of God's presence in the church. The power of God in the life of the believers was proof that they would emerge victorious.

Evil had not prevailed. The enemy could not accomplish his purpose. This was evidence of the weakness of the forces opposed to God. Perseverance in persecution meant that God would count the Thessalonians "worthy of God's kingdom" (that is, His victorious rule).

God's Righteous Vindication (vv. 6–10)

Vindication of the persecuted is one aspect of the righteousness of God's judgment. The other aspect is the punishment that will be meted out to the persecutors. The just judgment of God will "repay" those who afflict with affliction and give rest to the afflicted (v. 7; see Dt 32:35). In the context of the unjust suffering of the righteous at the hands of the unrighteous, this promise is an assurance that evil persons ultimately will receive the punishment they deserve.

WORDS FOR SUFFERING

TERM	MEANING	EXAMPLES	CROSS-REFERENCES
"Persecutions"	Especially religious persecutions	Political opposition to the preaching of the gospel; physical violence, such as stoning	Rom. 8:35; 2 Tim. 3:11
"Affliction(s)"	Pressure; metaphorically, some burdensome or chafing oppression	Pressure of circumstances; antagonism of persons	1 Thess. 1:6; 3:3,7

The promise of balancing accounts in the future will not remove suffering from believers, but it does help them put suffering in perspective.

Just as persecutors will be punished for inflicting suffering on the righteous, faithful believers can anticipate God's rest ("relief," v. 7) in the glorious kingdom of the Lord Jesus.

Section Summary

In the coming judgment, God will reverse the present roles of the persecuted and the persecutors. God's people can be encouraged by knowing they will be vindicated at the Lord's coming and will realize they have neither believed nor suffered in vain.

WORD PICTURE

Relief

The word Paul used to indicate *relief* originally meant the release of the tension on a bowstring. According to A. T. Robertson, *rest* means "let up, release . . . from troubles here (2 Cor 2:13; 7:5; 8:13), and hereafter. Vivid word. They shared suffering with Paul (v. 5) and so will share the *rest*."

A. T. Robertson, *WPNT*, vol. 4, 43.

PAUL'S PRAYER FOR THE THESSALONIANS (1:11–12)

Paul was always conscious that the future of believers was dependent on God. Therefore, it was not at all contradictory for him to assure his readers that God would count them worthy and at the same time constantly pray to God that he would do so.

"Your work produced by faith" should be understood as the resolve and work of the believers. Both resolve and action are essential in the life of holiness. Good resolve needs to be carried out in work that expresses confidence in God. God is the one, however, who fulfills our resolve and gives us the energy for the work of faith. The result is that we cannot take credit for carrying them out in action.

We can rest assured that God will own us as his people in Jesus Christ—that is, because of our relationship of living for and belonging to him.

WORD PICTURE

Work Produced by Faith

Paul prays for rich fruition of what he had seen in the beginning. Work marked by faith, springs from faith, sustained by faith."

A. T. Robertson, *WPNT*, vol. 4, 45–46.

Section Summary

Paul prayed that God's purposes for the church would be fulfilled in them. He expressed his desire that glory would be ascribed to Christ for all he would do in the lives of believers.

QUESTIONS TO GUIDE YOUR STUDY

1. Paul identified two dynamics of Christian living evident in the believers at Thessalonica. What were they?
2. Paul "boasted" of the Thessalonians to other congregations. What does "boasting" mean in this context? Why did he do this?
3. How will God deal with those who persecute the righteous?
4. What promise does God make to believers who suffer persecution?

2 THESSALONIANS 2

This passage is one of the most difficult and problematic for the interpreter of Paul's letters. Its subject is what is known as the day of the Lord, when the Lord will return as Judge.

The coming of the Lord will be a day of judgment. The persecutors of the church will reap the harsh punishment of being banished from the presence of God.

THE PROBLEM (2:1–2)

Paul's teaching about the end time was directed at a problem in the Thessalonian congregation. Evidently someone told them that "the day of the Lord" had already come. Clearly the "coming of our Lord" and the gathering of the saints to meet him had not yet occurred. But the "day of the Lord" could refer to a whole series of events connected with and preceding the coming of the Lord.

We may guess that the Thessalonians had been told that certain events already transpired, which meant the second coming of the Lord was about to take place. As a result, the believers were "easily upset." In addition, the Thessalonians also were not to become alarmed by "a prophecy" they received.

How did this false teaching come to the Thessalonian church? Paul mentioned three possible sources:

5. *By a "Prophecy."* This literally means "by spirit." The word probably refers to a Spirit-inspired utterance of some sort with emphasis on the revelatory nature of the utterance. Prophecy, interpreted tongues (see 1 Cor 14:5,12), or any other exercise by which a speaker claimed to guide the church by Spirit-inspired insight could serve as the specific avenue of the teaching.
6. *By a "Message."* This means literally "by word." If it was intended by Paul as a contrast to "by spirit" (prophecy), it referred to speech, emphasizing its rational nature. Arguments derived by reasoning from the Old Testament or from the life of Jesus might fall into this category.
7. *By a "Letter."* The final possible source of the church's confusion and anxiety about the "day of the Lord" was a letter. Possibly a letter attributed to Paul also had appeared in Thessalonica, and this may have put the apostle's authority behind the erroneous teaching.

Section Summary

Some false teachers were claiming that the Day of the Lord had already occurred. Paul countered these false teachers.

THE EVENTS OF THE END TIME (2:3–12)

Paul immediately got to the point and told his readers that the Day of the Lord could not have come because the events associated with his return had not yet taken place. What Paul saw as the events of the end were easy to see. How they should be understood is the difficulty—one we cannot resolve with the knowledge we have.

The Main Events (vv. 3–8)

Paul identified three things that must take place before the day of the Lord will come:

1. *Apostasy must occur (v. 3).* Paul chose not to elaborate on the nature of this "rebellion" or "apostasy." Religiously, it means to desert one's faith. This was probably an already well-defined concept for the Thessalonians. "It is not clear whether Paul means revolt of the Jews from God, of Gentiles from God, of Christians from God, or of the apostasy that includes all classes within and without the body of Christians" (A. T. Robertson, *WPNT*, vol. 4, 49).
2. *The man of lawlessness must be revealed (v. 3).* Paul literally described this man as "the man doomed to destruction." This man of lawlessness would demand worship as God, display

WORD PICTURE

Upset and Troubled

"To become unsettled" used literally refers to something that has been shaken by a storm (Luke 6:48) or caused to totter in an earthquake (see Acts 16:26). The addition of the phrase "from the mind" (in the original Greek text but not translated in the CSB), meaning something like "in mind" (NRSV), implies that Paul was worried about the believers becoming disoriented or confused by false teaching. The combination implies a spiritual instability that ought not characterize believers grounded in the truth and maturing in Christ (see Eph 4:14).

To be "troubled" means to be inwardly disturbed, depicting a frightened or disturbed state. The same word occurs in Mark 13:7 as a caution against premature expectation of the end. Such alarm and confusion in the face of false teaching is the opposite of standing firm in the faith.

satanically inspired, counterfeit miracles, and inspire all kind of evil in his followers. "He seems to be the Antichrist of 1 John 2:18" (A. T. Robertson, *WPNT*, vol. 4, 50).

3. *The restrainer must be removed (vv. 6–8).* "Unfortunately we do not know what Paul means by *that which retrains* (holds back), neuter here and masculine in verse 7" (A. T. Robertson, *Word Pictures in the New Testament*, vol. 4, p. 51). After the restrainer's influence is removed, the lawless one "will be revealed" and his display of power will increase.

NT REFERENCE

"Children, it is the last hour. And as you have heard that antichrist is coming, even now many antichrists have come. By this we know that it is the last hour." (1 John 2:18)

The Deceptions of the Man of Lawlessness (vv. 9–10)

His grandest delusion will be his pretension to deity. This lawless one will demand worship as God. His coming will be in accordance with the work of Satan, and the powers he will display will be impressive, but they will have their source in Satan. These works of Satan will involve "every kind of miracle, both signs and wonders."

The "Lie" (vv. 11–12)

Because of their deliberate rejection of truth, God will send those unbelievers who follow the man of lawlessness "a strong delusion so that they will believe the lie" (v. 11). The "lie" will not be just any lie but the great lie that the man of lawlessness is God (v. 12). By refusing the truth, they choose to believe "the lie."

THE TRUTH VERSES THE "LIE"*

	THE TRUTH	THE LIE
SOURCE	GOD	SATAN
Those who believe	will be saved	will perish
Destiny of those who follow	will share in the glory of Christ	will share in the condemnation of the son of perdition

For more information on the Lord's return, see the article, "The Return of Christ" at the end of this chapter.

Section Summary

Paul's statements in this section make a direct contribution to the question of whether the return of Christ can happen at any moment. Paul taught that a falling way from God and the appearance of the man of lawlessness will precede the Lord's return.

CHOSEN FOR SALVATION (2:13–15)

Paul told the Thessalonians that God had "chosen" them to be saved. The relationship they had with God was possible only because God had taken the initiative. Apart from God's choosing and calling, salvation was impossible.

Paul went on to explain the means of their salvation:

"Through sanctification by the Spirit" (v. 13). Sanctification is the ongoing process of spiritual growth through the direction and power of the Spirit. Through this process believers become what God wants them to be.

"Through belief in the truth" (v. 13). Truth is not assent to a body of doctrine or a code of rules. The truth is personal: it is Christ. Christians believe in the truth by expressing trust in Jesus Christ.

Verse 15 is a summary exhortation. The church is to "stand firm" in the truth they already received from Paul's teaching.

Paul offered thanksgiving for the Spirit's work in the life of the Thessalonian church. He also encouraged them to remain faithful to what they had been taught.

A CONCLUDING PRAYER (2:16–17)

Paul concluded this section with a prayer for the church. Regarding the Thessalonians, Paul asked that God:

Encourage their hearts. In their present state of distress, the believers at Thessalonica were in need of divine encouragement and comfort.

Strengthen them in every good work and word. "Work and word" speaks of behavior. Paul wanted the church to maintain a consistent pattern of Christian behavior. His hope was that God's strengthening of the church would allow it to stand firm against opposition and error.

Section Summary

Paul concluded this section with a prayer requesting encouragement and assistance that the Thessalonians might remain firm in the faith.

QUESTIONS TO GUIDE YOUR STUDY

1. What problem was Paul addressing in the Thessalonian congregation in this chapter?
2. Why were the new converts at Thessalonica in a state of alarm? How did they get this way?
3. According to Paul, what three things had to take place before the day of the Lord?
4. What did Paul mean when he declared that the Thessalonians were "chosen for salvation"?

WORD PICTURE

Choose

Choose is one of a number of words used to convey the idea of election. This is the only place in the New Testament where it is used in this sense (though it is found with this meaning in the Greek Old Testament). No one word constantly expresses the idea of election, but the fundamental thought is clear. The salvation of believers rests on divine choice—not human effort. Nor was this some afterthought on God's part. He chose them "from the beginning."

Leon Morris, *The First and Second Epistles to the Thessalonians* (Eerdmans, 1959), 237.

2 THESSALONIANS 3

This chapter is the last major division of the letter. After requesting prayer for his own ministry and protection, Paul expressed confidence that his readers (1) would persevere in their obedience; (2) involve themselves in proper conduct; (3) and be obedient to his teaching.

PAUL'S REQUEST FOR PRAYER (3:1–5)

Two Requests (vv. 1–2)

The apostle Paul prayed for believers. He also felt a need for their prayers on his behalf. In his prayers, he expressed no concern for things like good health, material prosperity, or good fortune. His interest was focused on his role as a minister of the gospel. Paul made two prayer requests:

He asked the Thessalonians to pray that "the word of the Lord may spread rapidly and be honored" (v. 1). The idea Paul was conveying here was *unhindered* progress rather than the effort required to make progress. Because the rapid proclamation of the gospel does not guarantee its acceptance, Paul also urged prayer that the gospel would be accepted by those who heard it.

He requested deliverance from evil and wicked men (v. 2). The word *deliver* was used to indicate future deliverance (see Rom 11:26; Col. 1:13; 1 Thess 1:10) and deliverance from dangers in this present age (see Rom 15:31; 2 Cor 1:10). The latter is what Paul had in mind here.

WORD PICTURE

Spread Rapidly

This word can also be translated "run" and is a metaphor taken from the world of competition in the stadium. Psalm 147:15 pictures God's Word as running swiftly.

Section Summary

Paul requested that the Thessalonians pray for him and his associates. He wanted God to bless and prosper the proclaimed word. He also expressed his concern to be delivered from wicked and evil men.

Encouragement Offered (vv. 3–4)

Paul shifted from his concern regarding the persecutions missionaries would experience to the difficulties his readers would experience.

Persecution was a stark reality for the Thessalonians. Persevering in this environment required their constant realization that the Lord is faithful.

Paul then offered encouragement to those in the midst of persecution. This encouragement further described God's faithfulness: "He will strengthen you and guard you from the evil one." Satan was referred to in the early church as "the evil one" (Matt 6:13; Eph 6:16). Likewise, Paul referred in a personal manner to the activity of Satan in his letters to the Thessalonians, both in the future (2:9) and in the present. He described

Satan as a hinderer of his work (1 Thess 2:18) and as a tempter attempting to short-circuit the faith of the church.

God's faithfulness is seen not only in judgment but also in his care for his church. Paul sent Timothy to the church with this same goal, to "strengthen and encourage" them so that "no one will be shaken by these afflictions" (1 Thess 3:2–3).

Confidence in the Lord as the one who strengthens and protects his people leads to confidence and the perseverance of the faithful. Because of God's faithfulness, believers can look beyond their suffering and continue in the faith.

Thus, God's faithfulness guarantees:

That our suffering has meaning.

That our persecutors will reap their just reward.

That our future is secure in him.

Section Summary

Paul offered encouragement to those in the midst of persecution. It is the Lord who strengthens and protects his people. Because he is faithful, believers can persevere in the faith and look beyond their period of persecution, knowing their future is secure in him.

A Concluding Benediction (v. 5)

It was Paul's desire that the church live in a manner consistent with "God's love and Christ's endurance." Christian behavior results from a genuine, inner commitment. Thus, Paul prayed that the Lord would "direct" the church in love reflective of God's love and in perseverance like Christ exhibited in the face of his persecutors. Paul, in effect, prayed that the church's love for God would endure and grow.

WORD PICTURE

Direct

The word *direct* is a compound word in the Greek text (the preposition "down" + the verb "to make straight"). Prefixing the verb with the preposition *down* intensifies the idea of the verb. According to A. T. Robertson, this use of the word is a "bold figure for making smooth and direct road."

A. T. Robertson, *WPNT*, vol. 4, 57.

Section Summary

Paul's benediction was an expression of confidence that God would continue to direct the paths of the believers at Thessalonica.

THE PROBLEM OF IDLE CHURCH MEMBERS (3:6–15)

Paul's Exhortation and Example (vv. 6–10)

The problem Paul dealt with in this passage was that of certain members of the Thessalonian church who were living in an "idle" manner. He wanted them to "work quietly and provide for themselves" (v. 12). Rather than leading orderly lives, however, they had become troublemakers.

Paul's Commands to Idle Church Members (vv. 11–12)

Paul called these idlers "busybodies." Instead of being productive individuals, they were using their time and energy to stir up trouble.

Paul commanded these idlers to "work quietly" and earn their own living. This way they would not drain the church's resources and would regain respect from those in the community.

HISTORICAL BACKGROUND

Busybodies

The word for "busybody" is a compound comprised of two words: the preposition *around* and the participle *working*. It means to be "working around" or "working about" in nonproductive activities instead of tending to one's own business. "Literally, *doing nothing but doing around*."

A. T. Robertson, *WPNT*, vol. 4, 60.

The addition of the preposition *around* to the verb "implies activity that lies outside the sphere of constructive or productive labor. Such busybodies could disrupt the work of the church either with their passivity or with their activity."

D. Michael Martin, *1, 2 Thessalonians*, New American Commentary, 282.

Paul's Commands to the Church (vv. 13–15)

Paul balanced his command to the idle members of the Thessalonian church with a series of commands to the church.

"Do not grow weary in doing good." Literally, this command means "do not lose heart doing good." Paul urged the Thessalonians not to lose courage so they might continue to do good toward others. He wanted them to focus on doing good toward those who were idle members. Encouragement was part of his instruction for bringing idle members back into the fold.

"Take note" of those who do not obey instruction, and "don't associate" with idle members. For Paul's instruction to be effective, the entire congregation needed to participate in any disciplinary process. Offenders were to be "noted" so that a cooperative effort from the congregation could be made.

"Don't consider" idle members as enemies but "warn" them as brothers. The church was not to treat the problem members like enemies. Rather, they were to treat these idlers as brothers for whom Christ had died but as brothers who needed to change their ways. The church had a responsibility to "warn" any such member "as a brother" (that is, in a spirit of love and with a desire to help him).

The purpose of Paul's instruction in these verses was to bring problem members back into the fold, where they could again become productive by using their gifts and talents for the cause of Christ.

Section Summary

A concern of Paul's was the inappropriate conduct by some of the believers at Thessalonica. Paul urged them to avoid a habit of idleness, settle into productive labor, and earn their own living. He also urged the church to administer firm but sensitive discipline to those who rebelled against his teaching.

CONCLUSION (3:16–18)

A Prayer for Peace (v. 16)

The conclusion to the letter contains some typical remarks. Paul was always concerned about peace in the church as an expression of the members' relationship with their Lord. Because Jesus is the Lord of peace, peace in the church would serve as evidence that the Thessalonians were under his authority. Peace is a gift that must be accepted; it is not the product of human effort.

Authenticity Assured (v. 17)

This verse contains an unusual comment. Evidently, Paul's handwriting was distinctive and easily recognized. Normally, he wrote his closing greeting in his own hand. Paul told the church that this was the "authenticating mark" in every letter he had written. Perhaps the reason for this was to guard against forgery. Paul hinted even in this letter that the Thessalonians had received a forged letter (2:2).

Benediction (v. 18)

Paul concluded his letter to the Thessalonians with a benediction identical to the one in 1 Thess 5:28, except for the addition of the word "all."

Section Summary

Paul's closing remarks expressed concern about peace in the church as an expression of the members' relationship with the Lord. Because Jesus is the Lord of peace, peace in the church would show that the Thessalonians were under his authority.

QUESTIONS TO GUIDE YOUR STUDY

1. For what specifically did Paul request prayer? From this passage, what can we learn of his view of prayer?
2. What encouragements did Paul offer to those who were suffering persecution? How might we apply those encouragements to believers suffering persecution today?
3. According to Paul, what is a "busybody"? Why are such people disruptive to the work of God?
4. How is the church to deal with such people ("busybodies") in our churches? What should be the goal of such action?

EXCURSUS: THE RETURN OF CHRIST

The Lord Jesus, who was raised from the dead and ascended to the Father, will return. This conviction is expressed repeatedly in the New Testament.

The church used several terms to refer to the return of Christ. *Parousia*, meaning either "coming" or "presence," often described the Lord's return (see Matt 24:3; 1 Cor 15:23; 1 Thess 2:19). *Epiphaneia* in religious usage described the appearing of an unseen god (see Titus

2:13). The revelation (*apocalypsis*) of the power and glory of the Lord was eagerly anticipated by the church (for example, see Luke 17:30; Rom 8:18).

The phrase "the Day of the Lord" (an Old Testament theme) is also common in the New Testament. "That day," "the day of Christ," and similar phrases were used as synonyms.

Often the writer implied that he was living in the last days (Acts 2:17; 1 John 2:18). The reference to time in many passages listed above, however, is ambiguous (see 1 Cor 1:8; 5:5; Phil 1:6,10; 1 Thess 5:2; 2 Thess 1:10). The character of that "day" is clearer than its timing. It is the day of judgment.

The Gospels. Jesus taught his disciples to expect a catastrophic conclusion to history. At that time God would effect a general resurrection and a final judgment with appropriate rewards for the just and the unjust (Matt 7:21–27; 24:1–51; Mark 12:24–27; 13:1–37; Luke 11:31–32; 21:5–36).

Although the signs of the end receive considerable attention in the Gospels (Matt 24; Mark 13; Luke 21), the time of the end remains obscure. Some sayings imply the end is near (Matt 10:23; Mark 9:1; 13:30). Others imply a delay (Matt 25:5; Mark 13:7,10). The clearest statements indicate that the time cannot be known (Matt 24:36,42–44; Mark 13:32–37; Luke 12:35–40).

Acts 1:6–8 expresses the same conviction: The time cannot be known. According to Jesus, the disciples' task was to bear witness to the gospel. The time was left in the Father's hands.

The Epistles. As the church aged, questions arose. What happened to those who die before Jesus's return (1 Thess 4:13–18)? What will his return be like, and when will it occur (1 Thess 5:1–11; 2 Thess 2:1–12)? What will happen to us and our world (1 Cor 15:12–13,23–28)? Does his delay make his promised return a lie (2 Pet 3:3–10)?

The New Testament answers these questions with a strong affirmation concerning Christ's return. The New Testament is not clear regarding the time of his appearing. Yet the epistles clearly reveal a persistent faith in the return of Christ (Rom 8:19–39; 2 Tim 4:1). His lordship is real. His victory is assured. His people will share his glory at his return (Rev 19:6–22:17). Thus, the responsibility of the church is patience, faithfulness, and witness (see Acts 1:7–8; 1 Cor 15:58; 1 Thess 4:18). Taken from *Holman Bible Handbook*, 735.

1–2 Timothy, Titus

INTRODUCTION

This introduction covers the books of 1 and 2 Timothy and Titus. This group of letters is known as the Pastoral Epistles or the Pastoral Letters. These letters were written near the end of Paul's life to guide his two younger associates.

AUTHOR

The apostle Paul is credited with writing the Pastoral Epistles. Each of the Pastoral Letters includes Paul as its writer. Although some scholars have raised questions about stylistic contrasts between these letters and other Pauline Epistles, it is unnecessary to reject Paul as author on that basis. After all considerations, much weight of evidence exists to support direct or indirect authorship of Paul for these three letters.

PLACE AND DATE OF WRITING

First Timothy. The place of this epistle's origination is uncertain, but somewhere in Macedonia seems to be the most likely location, a conclusion drawn from 1:3. The time of writing is difficult to determine, but probably sometime between AD 63 and 67 is a good possibility.

Second Timothy. This letter supports Rome as the place of imprisonment (1:16–17). The most likely date for 2 Timothy is between AD 63 and 67.

Titus. The place of origin was somewhere in Macedonia. Paul wrote Titus before 2 Timothy and perhaps before 1 Timothy. For Paul to have written the letter, the date most likely would be the same as for 1 and 2 Timothy, AD 63–67.

OCCASION AND PURPOSE OF WRITING OF THE PASTORALS

Occasion. The Pastoral Letters were written to deal with the false teaching that was negatively impacting the young churches. The churches were apparently in more danger from internal threats than from external persecution. Paul urged his apostolic associates to counter the internal danger with sound teaching, by providing an example of godly living, and by organizing and training leaders for the congregations.

Purpose. These letters address the need for pastoral oversight in the churches. They focus on church organization, the importance of apostolic doctrine, and the refutation of false doctrine. First Timothy and Titus carefully describe the qualifications of Christian leaders.

AUDIENCE

First Timothy. Timothy was the primary reader of this epistle, but certainly he shared the contents with the church. He was a trusted friend and fellow laborer to Paul in the Gentile mission.

Second Timothy. The letter names Timothy as the recipient. Paul's worst fears, hinted at in 1 Timothy, have been realized, and he is once again in prison (4:8,16).

Titus. Titus is the recipient. He had leadership responsibilities for the church at Crete. A Gentile, Titus was an important fellow worker with Paul. The instructions are general enough in Titus so as to be read by or to the entire church.

MAJOR THEMES IN THE PASTORAL LETTERS

The Gospel. In all three of the Pastoral Epistles a concern for the truth of the gospel is a powerful influence. Paul uses both the courtroom image of justification and the social image of redemption to describe the results of responding to the gospel. Paul presents faith as the proper response to the gospel and emphasizes that godly living must be a result of this faith response.

Church Government. Paul pictures the church in the Pastoral Epistles as a united family ministering to its constituency and organized for service. The church is the family of God, and believers are brothers and sisters. Paul charged the church with a responsibility to the poor and to serve as a foundation of doctrinal and ethical truth. Leaders of the church were known as overseers or elders, and they were assisted by deacons. Women also filled a special position of service in the church.

Heresy. In the second century, Christianity became involved in a fierce struggle with a heretical movement known as Gnosticism. This false teaching denied the resurrection of Christ, vacillated between moral license and rigid asceticism, and insisted that sinful human beings could not enjoy fellowship and full contact with the transcendent God. The heresy Paul describes in the Pastoral Epistles was characterized by an interest in Jewish law (1 Tim 1:6–7) and showed the influence of "those of the circumcision party" (Titus 1:10).

Salvation. The Pastoral Epistles recognize the universal problem of sin and God's desire to redeem humanity from sin's power and penalty. Both God and Jesus Christ are referred to as "Savior" throughout the Pastorals. Paul boldly asserts that "Christ Jesus came into the world to save sinners" (1 Tim 1:15) Salvation is God's work alone, promised by God before the beginning of time and historically realized "in his own time" (Titus 1:3). Believers are referred to as Christ's elect, as redeemed through Christ's self-sacrifice, and can be described as "saved," "heirs," "renew[ed]," and "justified" (Titus 3:5–7).

The Trinity. Paul describes God the Father by reference to his attributes and his actions. He portrays God as living and as observing the moral actions of his creatures. Paul refers to God as eternal, immortal, invisible, and as the only God. He reflects monotheism by his reference to God as one. The majesty of God is such that he is unapproachable, deserving of blessing and thanksgiving from his creatures. God is also faithful and truthful to his promises, merciful in salvation, and generous in giving the Holy Spirit. Paul also describes God as Creator and the bestower of life. He is the sovereign Ruler who has condescended to reveal himself in Scripture. The course of all history is in his hands.

THEOLOGICAL SIGNIFICANCE OF THE PASTORAL LETTERS

First Timothy. The letter to Timothy develops a theology of the church. The church needs organization to do its work effectively. Church leaders give guidance and enablement for the Christian community to carry out its service. The church is to be a pillar and bulwark, a custodian of the truth. The church must always strive to avoid heresy and to teach the truths of the gospel to succeeding generations.

Second Timothy. This second letter to Timothy teaches us about the importance of our theological heritage (1:14). Paul had much to say about what God has done in Christ, our Savior. Jesus Christ has been revealed, has destroyed death, and has given us life and immortality (1:8–10). The foundation of the Christian life is what God has already done for us in Christ. We should live boldly, for we have received a "spirit of . . . power, love, and sound judgment" (1:7). These truths about the gospel and Christian living are available to us in God's inspired Scripture (3:15–17). Now we, like Timothy, should pass on these truths to faithful men and women who can also teach others (2:2).

Titus. Like the other Pastoral Letters, Paul's Letter to Titus focuses on keeping the faith and refuting heresy. Especially significant, considering the nature of the Cretan heresy, are the repeated emphases on doctrinal fidelity (2:11–14; 3:4–7) and faithful living (1:16; 2:7,14; 3:1,8, 14). The letter makes it plain that the Christian life is grounded in the grace of God (2:11–14). Believers must recognize this truth and rebuke heresy and avoid legalism (1:10–16). This can be done only by grace—grace that saves, grace that teaches, grace that strengthens, and grace that enables. In so doing, we can see the relationship between doctrine and practice.

THE VALUE OF THE PASTORAL LETTERS FOR TODAY

The Pastorals provide insight. They help us in dealing with contemporary problems of heresy, divisiveness, and leadership difficulties. They are not a collection of rigid rules for church organization but guidelines which provide direction for facing problems and church needs.

The Pastorals are realistic. They present the churches Paul founded with all their needs, weaknesses, and shortcomings (1 Tim 4:1–3). However, they also present the mighty power of God as a prescription for human failure (1 Tim 1:17) and show this divine power at work in the lives of people (1 Tim 1:12–17).

The Pastorals provide encouragement. In spite of the likelihood that Paul was facing death as he wrote 2 Timothy, he remained steadfastly optimistic (2 Tim 4:6–8). He was lonely, but he was vigilant, irrepressibly a preacher, and confident in the Lord. The Pastorals provide a picture of the early church as it faced error, greed, and moral corruption. In spite of these shortcomings, there is a clear sign of anticipated victory and hopeful moral restitution. Churches today need a heavy dose of such realism and encouragement.

One additional feature of significance in the Pastorals is their influence on hymnody. Some of the better-known hymns based on the Pastorals include "Immortal, Invisible, God Only Wise" (1 Tim 1:17), "Fight the Good Fight" (1 Tim 6:12), and "I Know Whom I Have Believed" (2 Tim 1:12).

OUTLINES OF THE PASTORAL LETTERS

Basic Outline of 1 Timothy

I. Introduction (1:1–2)
II. Warning Against False Teachers (1:3–20)
III. Guidelines for Church Worship (2:1–15)
IV. Instructions for Church Leaders (3:1–13)
V. Maintaining the Truth (3:14–4:16)

VI. Miscellaneous Instructions for the Church (5:1–6:10)
VII. Personal Charge to Timothy (6:11–21)

Basic Outline of Second Timothy

I. Introduction (1:1–7)
II. Suffering and the Gospel (1:8–18)
III. Encouragement to Faithfulness (2:1–13)
IV. Contrasts in the Church (2:14–26)
V. Godlessness in the Last Days (3:1–9)
VI. Final Advice to Timothy (3:10–4:18)
VII. Final Greetings (4:19–22)

Basic Outline of Titus

I. Introduction (1:1–4)
II. The Appointment of Elders (1:5–9)
III. The Rebuke of False Teachers (1:10–16)
IV. The Different Groups in the Church (2:1–15)
V. The Responsibility of Christian Living (3:1–11)
VI. Personal Concluding Requests (3:12–15)

GUIDING QUESTIONS

1. What issues prompted Paul's letters to Timothy and Titus?
2. What were Paul's circumstances at the time of his writing of the Pastoral Epistles?
3. Examine the major themes in the Pastorals. How are these relevant to the mission and work of the church today?
4. What is the value of the Pastoral Letters to the church today?

First Timothy

1 TIMOTHY 1

SALUTATION (1:1–2)

In the address of his letters, Paul follows the form of first-century letter writing. Three of the elements of that form give structure to the opening of 1 Timothy: the name of the writer, the name of the recipient, and a greeting.

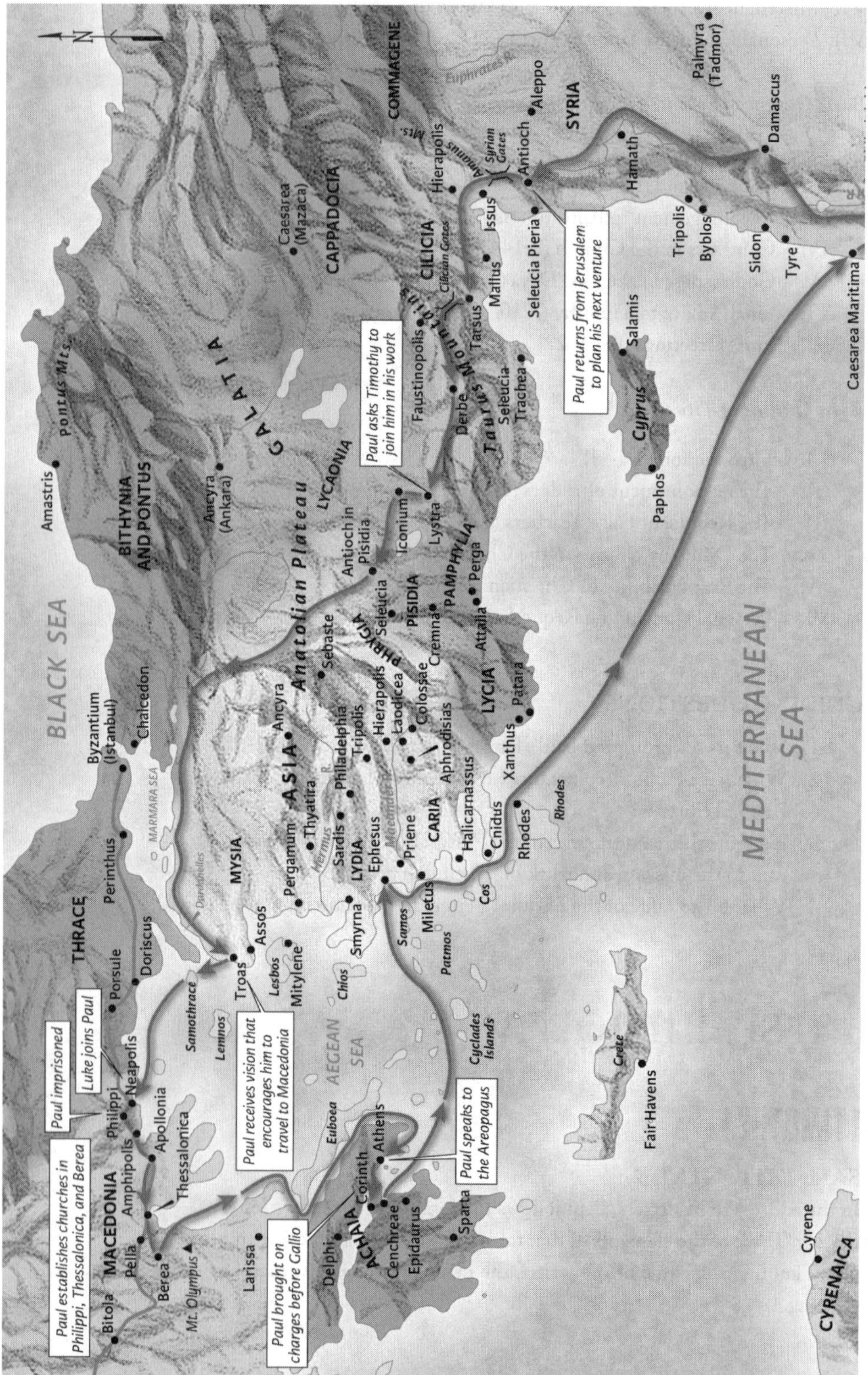
N
BLACK SEA
MEDITERRANEAN SEA
AEGEAN SEA
MARMARA SEA
Paul establishes churches in Philippi, Thessalonica, and Berea
Paul imprisoned
Luke joins Paul
Paul receives vision that encourages him to travel to Macedonia
Paul brought on charges before Gallio
Paul speaks to the Areopagus
Paul asks Timothy to join him in his work
Paul returns from Jerusalem to plan his next venture
MACEDONIA
THRACE
MYSIA
ASIA
LYDIA
CARIA
PHRYGIA
PISIDIA
PAMPHYLIA
LYCIA
LYCAONIA
GALATIA
BITHYNIA AND PONTUS
CAPPADOCIA
CILICIA
COMMAGENE
SYRIA
ACHAIA
CYRENAICA
Anatolian Plateau
Pontus Mts.
Taurus Mountains
Amanus Mts.
Cilician Gates
Syrian Gates
Euphrates R.
Hermus R.
Meander R.
Dardanelles
Mt. Olympus
Bitola
Pella
Berea
Amphipolis
Thessalonica
Philippi
Apollonia
Neapolis
Larissa
Delphi
Corinth
Cenchreae
Epidaurus
Sparta
Athens
Euboea
Samothrace
Lemnos
Lesbos
Chios
Samos
Patmos
Cos
Cyclades Islands
Crete
Fair Havens
Cyrene
Porsule
Doriscus
Perinthus
Byzantium (Istanbul)
Chalcedon
Troas
Assos
Mitylene
Pergamum
Thyatira
Smyrna
Sardis
Philadelphia
Ephesus
Priene
Miletus
Halicarnassus
Cnidus
Rhodes
Aphrodisias
Tripolis
Hierapolis
Laodicea
Colossae
Ancyra
Sebaste
Xanthus
Patara
Attalia
Perga
Cremna
Seleucia
Antioch in Pisidia
Iconium
Lystra
Derbe
Faustinopolis
Seleucia Trachea
Tarsus
Mallus
Issus
Hierapolis
Antioch
Seleucia Pieria
Aleppo
Amastris
Ancyra (Ankara)
Caesarea (Mazaca)
Cyprus
Paphos
Salamis
Hamath
Tripolis
Byblos
Sidon
Tyre
Caesarea Maritima
Damascus
Palmyra (Tadmor)

Author (v. 1)

The letter's author is Paul the apostle. "Paul" was the Gentile name of the great missionary statesman and was used to designate the writer in each of the thirteen Pauline Epistles.

Recipient (v. 2a)

Timothy is the recipient of this letter. He was one of the close associates of Paul in his missionary labors. In fact, Timothy accompanied Paul on his second and third missionary journeys. The biblical portrait of Timothy is that of a young man, somewhat retiring and perhaps shy. Paul urged his young disciple to stand firm for the gospel against menacing opponents and circumstances.

Greeting (v. 2b)

Outside of this letter among Paul's writings, only 2 Tim 1:2 employs a threefold greeting of "grace, mercy, and peace." As Paul's special representative in a difficult situation, Timothy had great need for an abundant supply of all three qualities. Detailed, these qualities mean:

- *Grace* describes the goodness God offers to undeserving sinners.
- *Mercy* is God's help offered to the discouraged and stumbling (Heb 4:16).
- *Peace* describes a state of salvation that results from the grace and mercy of God.

THE EXPLANATION OF THE TASK TO TIMOTHY (1:3–20)

Paul wasted no time in explaining the aim and purpose of the letter. He directed Timothy to remain in Ephesus so that he could warn church leaders not to involve themselves in the spread of false belief and practice.

Paul charged Timothy to maintain his commitment and obedience to the Lord to avoid the decline of commitment that had overtaken Hymenaeus and Alexander.

PREVENT THE SPREAD OF FALSE TEACHING (1:3–11)

Timothy was to order certain men in Ephesus to stop spreading speculative ideas that promoted controversy rather than the work of God.

Content of the Warning (vv. 3–4)

Paul warns against "myths and endless genealogies" (v. 4). Interpreters see these stories as either fictitious distortions of the Old Testament or Gnostic myths about creation. Paul opposes these myths because they get God's people sidetracked in speculation and argument rather than

HISTORICAL BACKGROUND

Timothy

Timothy's name means "honoring God." When Timothy was a child, his mother Eunice and his grandmother Lois taught him the Scriptures (2 Tim 1:5; 3:15). A native of Lystra, he may have been converted on Paul's first missionary journey (Acts 14:6–23). Paul referred to Timothy as his child in the faith (1 Cor 4:17; 1 Tim 1:2; 2 Tim 1:2). This probably means Paul was instrumental in Timothy's conversion.

When Paul came to Lystra on his second journey, Timothy was a disciple who was well respected by the believers (Acts 16:1–2). Paul asked Timothy to accompany him. Timothy's father was Greek, and Timothy had not been circumcised. Because they would be ministering to many Jews and because Timothy's mother was Jewish, Paul had Timothy circumcised (Acts 16:3).

HISTORICAL BACKGROUND

Timothy not only accompanied Paul but also was sent on many crucial missions by Paul. For example, when Paul was unable to go to Corinth, he sent Timothy to represent Paul and his teachings (1 Cor 4:17). Later, when Paul was in prison, he sent Timothy to Philippi (Phil 2:19). Paul felt that no one had more compassion and commitment than Timothy (vv. 20–22). So close were Paul and Timothy that both names are listed as the authors on six of Paul's letters.

WORD PICTURE

Christian Love

The special kind of love Paul speaks of here is known as *agape* love. Paul's understanding and discussion of love make it a central theme, and his use of the noun *agape* makes the term almost a technical word. Prior to Paul, in fact, the Greek term *agape* was little used. Instead of using a word for love already filled with meaning, Paul took the seldom-used term and filled it with Christian meaning.

Christian love is not simply an emotion that arises because of the character of the one loved. It is not due to the loving quality of the lover. It is a relationship of self-giving that results from God's activity in Christ. The source of Christian love is God (Rom 5:8), and the believer's response of faith makes love a human possibility (Rom 5:5).

focusing on the work of proclaiming the gospel and nurturing believers in the Christian life.

Goal of the Warning (vv. 5–7)

The purpose of Christian instruction or preaching is to lead people to grow in both their love of God and other human beings. Mature love flows from hearts that are being purified, consciences which are cleansed, and faith that is without pretense.

By describing the false teachers as "teachers of the law," Paul pictures them as aspiring to be like Jewish rabbis and spinning out sterile interpretations of Old Testament stories and regulations. These "teachers" pretended to be wise sages, but they were really talking about matters they didn't begin to understand.

Reason for the Warning (vv. 8–11)

Paul's reason for warning against the false teachers at Ephesus was that they misunderstood the intent and the use of God's law. They were using the law *unlawfully* and perverting its true function in God's plan.

What is the right use of the law? From Paul's other writings, we see that the primary function of the law is to make us aware of sin and of our need for Christ's forgiveness.

In his statement that the law "is not meant for a righteous person," Paul is saying that committed believers do not need the law to propel them to holy living. Their new heart takes pleasure in God's law, and they are open to the promptings of the Holy Spirit that lead them to act in ways that fulfill God's law (Gal 5:22–24).

Section Summary

Paul warns against the false doctrines permeating Ephesus. His statements are blunt and incisive. He accuses the heretics of not properly understanding and using the law.

TO PREACH THE GOSPEL (1:12–17)

In this passage, Paul explains the unlimited power of the gospel. These verses are a sort of parenthesis that is an outburst of praise for the grace of God.

Thanksgiving to God (vv. 12–14)

Paul expresses three attitudes that are characteristic of his view of ministry:

1. Christ himself is the source of Paul's strength. Paul doesn't take credit for any of his accomplishments.

2. Being a servant of Jesus Christ is a privilege beyond comprehension. He considers it a blessing he did not deserve.
3. When Christ calls a person into his service, this implies trust. Paul felt great responsibility for living up to that trust.

Statement of the Gospel (vv. 15–16)

In this verse, Paul succinctly summarizes the gospel. In contrast to the complex arguments and speculations of false teachers, Paul states the gospel in nine words: "Christ Jesus came into the world to save sinners."

He goes on to say that he himself was the worst case—as if to say, *He saved me; therefore, he can save anyone.*

THE "TRUSTWORTHY SAYINGS" FORMULA IN THE PASTORAL EPISTLES

"THIS SAYING IS TRUSTWORTHY"
1 Timothy 1:15
1 Timothy 3:1
1 Timothy 4:9
2 Timothy 2:11
Titus 3:8

Doxology (v. 17)

As Paul contemplates the incredible redeeming grace of God, what had begun as a thanksgiving now concludes with a doxology of divine praise. He ascribes these characteristics to God:

- "The King eternal." His rule is universal and eternal.
- "Immortal." He is immune from decay and corruption.
- "Invisible." But believers can view the splendid glory of God residing in the person of Jesus (2 Cor 4:6; John 1:14).

Section Summary

Paul summarizes the gospel in clear language, presenting himself as Exhibit A of what the gospel can do in the life of a sinner. The thought of this causes him to thank God for what he has done and to praise him for who he is.

AN ENCOURAGING REMINDER (1:18–20)

Paul is about to instruct Timothy regarding the situation in Ephesus. He prefaces his instruction with three reminders—two positive and one negative.

First, Timothy will find strength for fighting the good fight by remembering the prophecies made at the time he was set apart for Christian ministry.

Second, two characteristics that will contribute to Timothy's strength as God's man in Ephesus are faith and a good conscience.

Third, Paul reminds Timothy of what happens when Christians jettison faith and a good conscience. Hymenaeus and Alexander "shipwrecked the faith" in Ephesus. As a result, Paul delivered them to Satan to teach them not to blaspheme.

Section Summary

Paul takes a moment to encourage Timothy, reminding him of truths that would equip him for his leadership role in Ephesus.

NEW TESTAMENT REFERENCE

Delivered to Satan

Many scholars believe this means that the church withdrew fellowship from these men in order to enable them to realize the gravity of what they were doing. We see an instance of this at Corinth (1 Cor 5:1–5; 2 Cor 4:4–8).

GUIDING QUESTIONS

1. Describe Paul's warning to Timothy about false teachers. What was Paul's greatest concern?
2. What is *agape*, or Christian, love? Contrast it with the attitudes of those false teachers.
3. What was Paul's view of ministry? How applicable is his view for those in ministry today?
4. What is the point of the "trustworthy sayings" in the Pastoral Epistles? What do some scholars think about these?

1 TIMOTHY 2

Paul turns from warnings about false teachers to the subject of worship and how it should be conducted.

NEW TESTAMENT REFERENCE

Kings and all those who are in authority—all temporal authorities derived their role from God—whether they knew it or not. "Let every soul put himself habitually in subjection to authorities who hold position over them, for there is not an authority except that ordained by God." Rom 13:1, *The New Testament, An Expanded* Translation, Kenneth S. Wuest.

THE SCOPE OF PUBLIC PRAYER (2:1–7)

The Objects and Content of Prayer (vv. 1–2)

Objects of Prayer. The church has a role as intercessor not only for those in its fellowship but also for everybody outside its community. Paul specifically mentions kings—those who have authority over temporal matters.

Content of Prayer. Paul lists four words for prayer: "petitions, prayers, intercessions, and thanksgivings."

FOUR WORDS FOR PRAYER IN 1 TIMOTHY 2:1

WORD	ITS USE
Petitions	Used of petitions to God based on a sense of deep spiritual need
Prayers	For all kinds of prayers to God including the general requests or specific petitions
Intercessions	Used of Christ's prayers for believers
Thanksgivings	Adds gratitude as a motivation for asking

Paul probably did not intend any sharp distinction between these words. Perhaps he was collecting synonyms that effectively communicate the importance of prayer.

The Goal of Prayer (vv. 3–4)

The goal of the prayers Paul urges is that all people be saved. This is to include all human beings, without distinctions of race or social standing. That God desires ("wants") the salvation of all people does not guarantee that all will be saved.

The will of God does not function as a ruthless bulldozer, crushing and forcing into obedience any who resist it. God urges us to repentance with his goodness rather than coercing us toward the truth with his power. "To come to the knowledge of the truth" is a synonym for conversion.

The Goal of Prayer (vv. 5–7)

As he has done earlier in the letter, Paul simply states foundational truths which stand in sharp contrast to complicated speculations.

- There is one God.
- There is a single Mediator between God and humankind.
- Christ's death was a ransom.

Paul himself was an example of God's universal purpose. By divine appointment he was a "herald, an apostle." Through him, God was reaching out to the pagan world which his fellow Jews had excluded from the covenant community.

Section Summary

The goal of the prayers Paul urges is that all people be saved. Jesus's death is the price paid for the release of humankind from captivity to sin. Although Christ's death has the potential to save all people, it is effective only with those who come to Christ in faith and repentance.

INSTRUCTIONS FOR WORSHIP (2:8–15)

Paul turns to instructions regarding public worship.

An Appeal to the Men (v. 8)

WORD PICTURE

Ransom

This word is made up of two words, one of which has the primary meaning of freeing slaves and prisoners. The second word means "on behalf of" or "instead of." It suggests substitution.

In the early church, the place of worship was usually the home of some believer. By implication, the men were to do the public praying. A common Jewish posture in prayer was evidently widely adopted by early Christians. While they stood, they looked upward toward heaven, lifting their arms with their palms turned upward. This may have symbolized the expectation of receiving God's blessings in answer to their petitions. Of course, no specific posture in prayer is sacred. Various postures are found in Scripture.

Paul's primary point in this passage, however, is not the posture of prayer but the attitude which the men were to bring to prayer. They were to pray "without anger or argument."

An Appeal to Women (vv. 9–15)

The Moral Behavior of the Women (vv. 9–10). Paul's first point has to do with the way women were to dress when they attended the public worship of the church. Modesty is to be the governing principle. The worship service is not the place for a fashion show. He urges the women to produce good works instead of devoting attention to their physical appearance. There should be a relationship between behavior and belief, between deeds and profession.

The Church Activity of the Women (vv. 11–12). By modern standards, Paul is far from politically correct, but he is clear that women are to focus on being learners rather than teachers in the context of a congregation of believers.

An Explanation of Paul's Appeal (vv. 13–14). Drawing on the account of the creation in Gen 2, Paul argues that Adam was chronologically prior to Eve. This chronological priority becomes the support of Paul's command that the women were to show a spirit of attentiveness to learning and were to avoid an attempt at dominating men. Paul apparently feels that the spiritual equality of both men and women in Christ (Gal 3:28) does not negate differences in role that are part of God's creative design.

NEW TESTAMENT REFERENCE

"So if you are offering your gift on the altar, and there you remember that your brother or sister has something against you, leave your gift there in front of the altar. First go and be reconciled with your brother or sister, and then come and offer your gift." (Matt 5:23–24)

Moreover, Paul relates his prohibition to the history of the fall in Gen 3. Eve was deceived by the serpent and so fell into sin. In describing Adam, Paul denies that he was deceived. Adam listened to Eve and sinned with his eyes wide open. Paul's point is that men, including those in Ephesus, are more susceptible to mistake and error when they carelessly surrender their God-given responsibilities to women.

A *Promise of Obedient Women* (v. *15*). But Paul expresses a promise for those women who showed obedience: Women "will be saved through childbearing." C. A. Trentham says Paul saw this truth most profoundly: "Woman's true fulfillment is in her devotion to that for which she was created, the bearing and rearing of children. . . . [This] is a loftier work for her even than being a leader in the church." *Studies in Timothy* (Convention Press, 1959), 35.

Section Summary

Both men and women must assume their respective places of responsibility in the church.

1 TIMOTHY 3

CHURCH LEADERSHIP (3:1–13)

There seems to be no doubt that development took place in the organization of the church from the time of Paul's earlier epistles to the time when he wrote the letters to Timothy and Titus. In 1 Cor 12:4–10 and Rom 12:6–8, the situation in the church seems to have been much more fluid and less organized than that reflected in the Pastoral Epistles.

In this section Paul discusses the qualifications of three groups: (1) overseers or pastors, (2) deacons, and (3) wives, or women helpers.

Qualifications of Overseers (vv. 1–7)

A Commendation (v. 1). We have here the second of five "trustworthy sayings" in this letter: "If anyone aspires to be an overseer, he desires a noble work."

Desiring this noble task or good work is only one of many qualifications. Paul lists others.

An Appeal for Obedient Behavior (vv. 2–3). The qualifications mentioned in verse 2 are largely positive and are traits that can be observed in one's behavior. The demands of verse 3 are negative. For a listing of these qualifications, see the chart below, "Qualifications of Overseers (Bishops)."

Leadership of the Family (vv. 4–5). A church leader must "manage his own household competently."

One of Paul's key points here is that the experience the leader gained in the home would develop sensitive compassion for this role in the church. The development of proper leadership skills in the home was a prerequisite for using them in the church.

An Experienced Leader (v. 6). Only the first converts to Christianity could assume office immediately after their conversion. Eventually, it would be important to select leaders with enough maturity to avoid the pitfalls of pride. The danger of appointing a recent convert to a place of

WORD PICTURE

Manage

The verb *manage* carries the idea of governing, leading, and giving direction to the family. It demands an effective exercise of authority bolstered by a character of integrity and compassion.

leadership is that he may become a victim of the conceit that sometimes accompanies an important new position.

Respected by Unbelievers (v. 7). An effective church leader needs the respect of even the unsaved world. If the behavior of the leader does not present a credible witness, the devil can entrap the church by making outsiders wary of believing the gospel. "Outsiders" are those who have not believed the gospel. A "good reputation" is literally a "good witness." Christians must realize that unbelievers scrutinize their actions with a searchlight. Paul's implied appeal is that church leaders give no opportunity for unbelievers genuinely to find fault.

QUALIFICATIONS OF OVERSEERS (BISHOPS)

QUALIFICATION	EXPLANATION
Above reproach	A man of blameless character
Husband of one wife	Faithful to his one wife
Self-controlled	A sensible person, trustworthy, and balanced in judgment
Sensible	Free from rash actions
Respectable	Demands dignity and orderliness in behavior
Hospitable	Caring for Christians and others
Able to teach	Competent and skillful in communicating Christian truth
Not an excessive drinker	Controls his thirst for wine
Not a bully but gentle	Forbearing in relationships with troublemakers
Not quarrelsome	Not contentious, grasping, pugnacious
Not greedy	Not given to questionable money making
Manages his own household competently	Exemplary in controlling and directing his family unit; teaches his children obedience and respect

Second, who does the testing? Again, Paul provides no specific statement. Acts 6:5 implies that the Seven were chosen by the congregation, but Titus 1:5 highlights the role of Titus in selecting leaders for the church at Crete. Perhaps a more mature congregation would act as a body in selecting its leaders, but a fledgling flock might rely on the wise insight of its founding pastor. The examination may have been informal, but the deacon candidate needed to convince the church of his genuine Christian faith.

After the experience of testing, those who "prove blameless" could serve as deacons.

Excelling at Home (v. 12). Like overseers, deacons are to manage their children and their families well.

A *Promise for Performance* (v. 13). A Deacon who serves well has the following two rewards:

He will receive a "good standing" for his effective service.

He will receive "great boldness." His confidence in Christ will grow.

For a full list of qualifications, see page 681.

QUALIFICATIONS OF DEACONS (CHURCH HELPERS)

QUALIFICATION	EXPLANATION
Worthy of respect	Serious-minded person whose character merits respect
Not hypocritical	Controlling speech; not engaging in double talk
Not drinking a lot of wine	Does not love alcohol
Not greedy for money	Not given to questionable money making
Hold the mystery of the faith with a clear conscience	Has an inner guide to life that demonstrates obedience to God
Must be tested first	Convinces church of his genuine Christian faith
Husband of one wife	Faithful to his one wife
Manages children and household competently	Exemplary in controlling and directing his family unit; teaches his children obedience and respect

Qualifications of Wives (or Women Helpers) (v. 11)

The word "wives" is the same word translated "women" in 2:9–10 or "woman" in 2:11–12. The context will usually show whether the word refers to a married woman ("wife") or to the female gender ("women"). The question here is whether Paul was discussing the wives of the deacons, or was he presenting a special order of female helpers in Christian work?

New Testament Greek language did not have a special word for *deaconess*. Paul's failure to use a more specific title for these women was because there was not one in use at that time. His use of the term *wives* or *women* implies that these were women who helped the church in some manner. The early church did have women whose special responsibility was to work with women and children. They provided assistance with the sick and the poor and helped at baptism.

Paul outlines four requirements for a woman helper, which are detailed in the following chart.

QUALIFICATIONS OF WIVES (OR WOMEN HELPERS)

QUALIFICATION	EXPLANATION
Worthy of respect	Exhibits character that merits respect
Not slanderers	The literal meaning of "malicious talker" is "slanderer" or "accuser"
Self-controlled	Shows control or moderation in behavior
Faithful	Is reliable and faithful

Section Summary

Paul's appeals to the men and women leaders called for visible, mature, righteous living that commended Christianity to its observers. He wants them to show a maturity that has been proven by obedience and endurance under testing. God desires that the righteousness of spiritual leaders shine forth (Matt 5:16) so the transforming power of Christianity might be evident for all to see (1 Tim 3:7).

CORRECT APPLICATION OF CHRISTIAN TRUTH (3:14–16)

This passage serves as a bridge between the guidelines Paul gives in 2:1–3:13 and the warnings about false teaching that follow.

Paul's Plans for a Visit (v. 14)

Paul fully intends to make a visit "soon" to Timothy in Ephesus. However, his travel plans were always subject to the will of God. Did Paul make his anticipated visit to Ephesus? Nothing in any of the Pastorals confirms that he made the journey.

Paul's Purpose for Writing (v. 15)

Paul's concern is for correct behavior in the church. He is interested in the relationships of people in God's "household," and he sets forth principles to guide those relationships. It is also apparent that "church" here has a broader connotation than just the local church at Ephesus. It includes the people of the living God, wherever they may be found.

The church has a responsibility for the truth. Paul speaks of the "pillar and foundation of the truth." That truth was under attack by people who were involved in wild speculations.

A Hymn for Believers (v. 16)

Christian truth is expressed in the central event of our faith—the event of the incarnation. Several aspects of this truth are expressed in this hymn. Paul probably did not compose this hymn but found it in the life of the church. The hymn contains six distinct statements with Christ as the understood subject of each line.

Paul uses this hymn as an example of the mystery of godliness which the church proclaimed. This mystery relates to the incarnation and resurrection of Christ and the church's proclamation of the gospel.

What stands out is the simplicity of the mystery of godliness in comparison with complex speculations of false teachers.

WORD PICTURE

Soon

This adverb comes from the Greek word *tachos* which means "quickness" or "speed." We derive the word *tachometer*— a device that measures engine speed— from this *tachos.*

HYMN FOR BELIEVERS

STATEMENT ABOUT CHRIST	SIGNIFICANCE
1. "He was manifested in the flesh"	A reference to Jesus's incarnation
2. "Vindicated in the Spirit"	Recalls the statements about Christ's resurrection
3. "Seen by angels"	A reference to the worship given by angels to the ascended Christ
4. "Preached among the nations"	Refers to the proclamation of the gospel among the nations of the world
5. "Believed on in the world"	Described as the response to the proclamation
6. "Taken up in glory"	A reference to the brightness and majesty of God's presence in Jesus

Section Summary

Christians are to distinguish themselves by a lifestyle of holiness. Believers are those whose behavior designates them as God's children and demonstrates the reality of their faith. They are to build their lives on the strong foundation of the gospel.

GUIDING QUESTIONS

1. Compare the positions of overseer and deacons in the church. What is the function of each? What are the responsibilities of each?
2. What were the roles of women helpers in the early church?
3. What is the promise of reward to deacons for effective service?
4. What is the focus of Paul's "hymn for believers"? What might we learn from reflecting on it?

1 TIMOTHY 4

UNDERSTANDING FALSE PRACTICE (4:1–5)

The Christian faith was preached, accepted, and lived out in a world where many ideas threatened it. There is always a danger of the gospel being distorted either by adding to it or taking something from it. In this passage, Paul elaborates on the errors in Ephesus and calls on Timothy to oppose them.

A Warning Against Apostasy (vv. 1–3)

The Holy Spirit has expressly warned that some people will fall away from the faith. Rather than focusing on the profound simplicity of the gospel, they will turn aside and give attention to spirits who will deceive them and to doctrines promoted by demons. The spokespersons for these deceptions are people who are given to hypocrisy and lying. The result of this behavior is that their consciences no longer work as God intended, but they have been cauterized as if by a branding iron.

Paul calls his readers' attention to two features that characterize the teaching of the false teachers: (1) forbidding marriage, and (2) abstaining from certain foods.

An Argument Against Asceticism (v. 4)

Paul rejects any division of foods into two categories—good and evil. He presents two reasons this division should not occur. First, he affirms that God's creation is good. All that God has made is good. The facts of God's benevolent creation implies that we can eat all that God has made. Second, we must eat with thanksgiving what God has created.

HISTORICAL BACKGROUND

One perennial idea that came from certain schools of Greek philosophy was that the spirit was good while matter was evil. When these concepts intersected with Christian teaching, numerous distortions of the faith occurred.

An Argument for Blessing Food (v. 5)

Paul was probably suggesting that in responding to the gospel, the believers in Ephesus learned that there are no food laws. The gospel brought them into a proper understanding of food, and they acknowledged by prayer that it was a gift from God. This act of blessing the food made it special or consecrated before God.

Section Summary

Paul describes a destructive legalism in this section. This legalism prevented one's grasp of the freedom and power of the Holy Spirit, and it destroyed gratitude toward God. Legalism, however, cannot endure long in the presence of an attitude of gratitude to God.

WORD PICTURE

Apostasy

Apostasy is the act of rebelling against, forsaking, abandoning, or falling away from what one has believed. Our English word *apostasy* is derived from a Greek word that means "to stand away from." Paul taught that apostasy would precede the day of the Lord. The Holy Spirit has explicitly revealed this falling away from the faith (1 Tim 4:1). Such apostasy in the latter times will involve doctrinal deception, moral insensitivity, and ethical departures from God's truth.

TIMOTHY'S PERFORMANCE OF HIS TASK (4:6–16)

Facing Falsehood (vv. 6–10)

What should be our strategy when we live in a world inundated with false teaching? Paul teaches that we must (1) expose the errors we oppose and (2) develop personal holiness to assure continuation in integrity. The combination of exposing error and practicing truth is a powerful antidote to heresy.

Demonstrating Christian Behavior (vv. 11–16)

Timothy had begun well in obeying God's commands. Paul desired that Timothy continue in the path he had started to provide an example for others.

Timothy was possibly a timid young man. His timidity could hinder him from making a bold assertion of Christian truth. Paul wanted Timothy to speak with authority. He wanted Timothy to "teach these things." By issuing the directives and instruction of 4:6–10, Paul provided several emphases that should characterize Timothy's ministry:

- Timothy was to live as a spiritual example of what a believer can be.
- He was to apply himself to reading, preaching, and teaching.
- He was not to neglect the spiritual gift he received.
- He was to be consistent in his spiritual growth.

Section Summary

The best antidote for error is a positive presentation of the truth. As a teacher of the truth, Timothy was to demonstrate a personal godliness that he might be a living example to his congregation. Church members will follow someone whom they respect.

GUIDING QUESTIONS

1. What did the false teachers teach? What was Paul's response?
2. What are practical ways for the church to guard the gospel from heresy and false teachers?
3. What is *apostasy?* How is it evident in our churches today? What should be our course of action to address it?
4. What actions did Paul emphasize when instructing Timothy on how to perform his tasks?

1 TIMOTHY 5

RESPONSIBILITIES TOWARD CHURCH GROUPS (5:1–16)

The New Testament has many metaphors for the church. One of the most meaningful is the family of God. How is the younger minister to relate to the various age groups in his church? Paul takes his cue from relationships in the family. He requests treatment that recognizes these family relationships.

Paul gives Timothy directions for meeting the needs of three groups within the church at Ephesus.

Proper Treatment for All Ages (vv. 1–2)

Older Men. Paul urges Timothy not to rebuke an older man.

The youthful Timothy faced a delicate situation in appealing to older men, but the difference between their ages did not make admonition of these men any less necessary.

Younger Men. Timothy was not to talk down to younger men, but he was to treat them as equals. The term *exhort* demands a kindlier, more considerate approach than "rebuke." Those who err would need to receive some rebuke for their behavior, but Timothy is to avoid a pompous approach in relating to them.

Older Women. Paul directs Timothy to treat the older women respectfully as mothers (Rom 16:13). A church leader would find it virtually impossible to heap verbal abuse on an older woman if he shows respect for her.

Younger Women. Younger women posed a special problem for Timothy. He was to treat them as sisters and maintain a purity that would banish all evil in thought and deed. "Purity" calls for modesty and chastity in all relationships.

WORD PICTURE

Rebuke

The term *rebuke* used here occurs nowhere else in the New Testament; it describes a severe verbal pounding. Such treatment would show no appreciation for age.

The Care of True Widows (vv. 3–8)

Paul identifies two types of widows: those who had relatives to care for them and those who had no living family members. Those who had family were to receive support from their family. Caring for one's own family should have high priority in a Christian's life.

Those who fail to do so deny the faith and are worse than unbelievers (v. 8) who may have a better track record of caring for their families.

The True Widow. Paul describes the true widow—one who is really in need—with three phrases. His description outlines more precisely the kind of person Paul exhorted Timothy to honor. The true widow is one who:

- *Was "left all alone."* She had no relatives to support her and no source of income or encouragement.
- *"Put her hope in God."* She has developed a settled and continuous confidence in God.
- *Was a woman of prayer who prayed "night and day."* This phrase is a metaphor describing a person who prays continually.

NEW TESTAMENT REFERENCE

"Pure and undefiled religion before God the Father is this: to look after orphans and widows in their distress and to keep oneself unstained from the world." (James 1:27)

The opposite of this ministry of prayer is the life of self-indulgence or pleasure. The widow who abandons herself to pleasure and comfort is in complete contrast with the godly widow who prays and seeks God. A widow, supported by the church, could not use her idle time in seeking self-gratification. Paul was aware of this possibility and felt that steps should be taken to guard against it.

Section Summary

Three terms sum up this section: respect, compassion, and responsibility. Paul speaks to the church and individual families about the urgency for showing compassion to needy widows. At the center of what it means to be a Christian is the responsibility of providing material support for the helpless members of one's own family.

A Warning to Younger Widows (vv. 9–16)

Paul's chief concern in this section is to single out the younger widows who were apparently a source of great difficulty for the Ephesian church (2 Tim 5:15). Paul recommends the behavior of true widows as a desirable contrast to the actions of the frivolous younger widows.

Paul names three basic requirements for anyone on this list:

1. The widow could not be less than sixty years of age.
2. The widow must have been "the wife of one husband."
3. Specific works should characterize the life of the widow.

These "works" are actions the widow must already have performed and on which her reputation was based. The younger widows failed to meet these requirements.

Therefore, Paul states that the younger widows should not be counted among the true widows. The younger widows, therefore, are encouraged to remarry and fulfill the functions of wife and mother.

The point of verse 16 is that relatives should assume responsibility for the widows in their families. This would free the churches to use their meager resources for the widows who were left completely alone in the world.

Section Summary

The younger widows do not meet the requirements of a true widow. Therefore, Paul encourages the younger widows to remarry and urges them to assume the responsible behavior appropriate to a married woman rather than the idle, meddling actions of a tattletale.

THE PROPER HANDLING OF LEADERS (5:17–25)

Recognition and Discipline of Leaders (vv. 17–20)

Recognition (vv. 17–18). An elder who showed himself proficient in leadership was "worthy of double honor." *Honor* means "pay or financial remuneration." Simply stated, it means the best leader should get twice as much. Paul asks that special consideration be given to those who labored in "preaching and teaching." The ministry of the Word was the highest responsibility of all.

Discipline (vv. 19–20). Paul discusses the process of discipline for erring leaders. First, he warns against accepting an accusation against an elder unless two or three witnesses support it. Paul is not urging special treatment for the elder, but he is urging fair protection from any capricious accusations.

Those who continued to sin after being warned in private should be rebuked before the entire congregation. The open rebuke was designed to change the course of the erring pastor's life as well as to put the fear of God within the entire congregation.

OLD TESTAMENT REFERENCE

Paul quotes two biblical sources in support of this command: "Do not muzzle an ox while it treads out grain" (Deut 25:4), and "The worker is worthy of his wages" (Luke 10:7).

Section Summary

Today's churches resemble the church in Ephesus in that they have leaders who deserve recognition as well as those who merit correction. Paul provides advice for recognizing those leaders who do their job well and instructions for dealing with those elders who face accusation. Paul's goal is to avoid partiality toward important leaders and to provide fair treatment for all.

Special Directions to Timothy (vv. 21–25)

OLD TESTAMENT REFERENCE

Paul is here drawing on a time-honored principle of justice among God's people: "The one condemned to die is to be executed on the testimony of two or three witnesses. No one is to be executed on the testimony of a single witness" (Deut 17:6).

Paul now charges Timothy to assume initiative in handling the problems of church leadership. This charge involves several elements.

He warns Timothy of making hasty appointments to Christian offices. He hints that one who participates in such an appointment shares in the sinful results that can easily follow.

He appeals for personal purity in Timothy. "Purity" involves separation from immorality and single-mindedness of purpose.

He urges Timothy to "use a little wine" for his apparent stomach ailment. Contaminated water may have aggravated Timothy's problems. Wine was widely used for such medicinal purposes.

He warns Timothy against hasty acceptance and hasty rejection of the "sins" of the elders. Paul did not believe evil could remain hidden forever in God's order. Nor did he believe that goodness would be covered up ultimately.

Section Summary

The church has a responsibility for the moral quality of its leaders. That responsibility is limited, however, because our knowledge of the good and evil in others is limited. Eventually, all will be apparent. We may be sure of this, for God, the ultimate Judge, knows our hearts.

GUIDING QUESTIONS

1. What relationship did Paul see between the older and younger men?
2. What did relationship did Paul see between the older and younger women?
3. What is the church's responsibility for the care of widows?
4. What practical advice does Paul give Timothy for handling the problems of their church leadership?

1 TIMOTHY 6

A WARNING TO SLAVES AND SINNERS (6:1–10)

The Responsibility of Christian Slaves (vv. 1–2a)

The phrase "under the yoke" describes the galling, humiliating result of slavery. Paul insists, however, that Christian slaves are to have a genuine respect for their owners. This would produce an outward expression in word, manner, and performance. The great object of Paul's concern was the glory of God. Bad behavior by professing Christian slaves could only lead an owner to mock Christianity.

Slaves who have Christian masters are to honor them and not be disrespectful to them or presumptuous with them because they are brothers in Christ. Rather, they should show all the more respect to them.

HISTORICAL BACKGROUND

"Many members of the early church were slaves. The question arises, Why does Paul seem to countenance slavery? It must be remembered that a direct attack upon the practice would have caused misunderstanding in the church and would probably have led to an ineffectual, open rebellion against a deeply entrenched institution, which would, no doubt, have resulted in widespread suffering." C. A. Trentham, *Studies in Timothy*, (Convention Press, 1959), 68.

Section Summary

Regarding slaves, Paul did not emphasize individual rights but individual responsibilities. His chief concern was the glory of God, not the liberation of the slaves or an increase in the privilege for the owners. Equality before God does not guarantee that all human beings enjoy equal roles or life status. While Paul accepted a different status for master and slave, he demanded a changed attitude from both.

An Indictment of the False Teachers (vv. 2b–5)

After a brief diversion to deal with the servant-master relationship, Paul exposes further the shortcomings of the false teachers. "These things" that Paul urges Timothy to teach most likely refer to the teachings Paul has enunciated throughout this letter. The unhealthy teaching of the false teachers stands in contrast to the healthy instruction from Jesus's teaching. This is a rare reference in the epistles to the actual teachings of Jesus.

Paul mentions three unhealthy traits of the false teachers:

1. They were pompous or "conceited."
2. Despite their arrogance, they lacked genuine spiritual knowledge.
3. They were ailing with the disease of controversy and word battles.

Paul goes on to describe the products of their impaired instruction. These include an envy that shows annoyance at the success of others and feeds a spirit of dissension. Also included are "slander," wicked denunciations of others, "evil suspicions," faultfinding, and misgivings about the integrity of others. The vividness of Paul's description suggests he was facing a concrete situation that aroused his indignant protest. Paul saw that a sense of real community had been destroyed.

Paul's last criticism is a devastating one. He accuses the false teachers of being motivated by a desire for "material gain." From early on, the Christian religion was seized upon by people for personal exploitation. These were men "whose minds are depraved and deprived of the truth."

The Greed of the False Teachers (vv. 6–10)

Paul's accusation about the profiteering motive of the false teachers leads to his statements about the relation between the believer and money. Genuine Christian faith brings great gain when coupled with contentment.

In these verses Paul shows two reasons for which contentment should be a companion to godliness and then explains the desire for wealth as a trap that plunges the unwary into spiritual ruin.

Why do godliness and contentment represent great gain? Paul offers two reasons:

After a brief stay, we shall depart this life as we came in. It is sheer folly to concern ourselves with earthly matters. Material gain is irrelevant, and greed is irrational.

We must be content when we possess life's necessities. Paul is contrasting the believer's attitude with that of the greedy heretics. His words reflect the teaching of Jesus (Matt 6:25–34).

Paul also warns that the greedy person becomes entrapped by the snare of his own desires. The end of such people is "ruin and destruction." Paul paints three progressive pitfalls in which the willful wealth-seeker becomes entangled:

1. Wealth tempts like a lure and causes people to covet the wrong objects.
2. Individuals become entangled like animals dangling in a trap.
3. The trapped ones drown in an almost personified wealth that becomes a personal monster.

WORD PICTURE

Contentment

The word *contentment* means "to be sufficient in oneself, adequate, and needing no assistance." It expresses the essence of the Stoic ideal, which was to be independent of external circumstances. Paul Christianized this term, using it to refer to an attitude of mind independent of externals and dependent only on God. He was not advocating godless self-sufficiency as a source of contentment. Rather, Paul believed that true sufficiency is Christ-sufficiency (Phil 4:13).

Section Summary

Godliness is not a trait from which to make material profit. True godliness has contentment for its companion. Since we cannot take life's luxuries into God's presence, we should be content with basic necessities.

INSTRUCTIONS TO TIMOTHY AND THE WEALTHY (6:11–21)

A Program for Godliness (vv. 11–16)

Paul's statements in this section consist of a series of commands, a solemn charge, and an outpouring of praise to God

Commands for Timothy. Paul delivers several commands to Timothy to warn and challenge him regarding the task ahead:

- *Flee* the heresy of the false teachers. Timothy was to stand in contrast to the false teachers.
- *Pursue* the six virtues that Paul lists. The Williams New Testament translates "pursue" as "constantly strive for," expressing the grammatical force of the verb. The list of virtues includes righteousness, godliness, faith, love, endurance, and gentleness.
- *Fight the good fight of faith.* To fight for "the faith" includes at least a struggle for the truth of the gospel, but it may also refer to the whole of Timothy's Christian life as a great contest requiring discipline and purpose.
- *Take hold of eternal life.* Timothy was to continue in the contest until it ended in triumphant conclusion. Depending on the context, eternal life could be a blessing to be realized at the journey's end or a present experience.
- *Charge.* Paul's charge in the presence of God and of Jesus Christ to Timothy was to keep the "command" until Jesus returns. It may refer to directives given to Timothy at his baptism or during the laying on of hands. Or it may be a commandment to Timothy to persevere in his own faith and ministry. He reminded Timothy that Jesus's good confession before Pontius Pilate was his model
- *An Outpouring of Praise to God.* Paul expresses seven statements of majestic praise to God in a moving doxology. In verse 15 he uses three titles in a description of God. In verse 16 he focuses on God's divine essence. All these phrases are Jewish in style, uniquely expressing the sovereignty of God.

WORD PICTURE

For the love of Money

Paul supports his warning about wealth with a contemporary proverb: "For the love of money is a root of all kinds of evil" (v. 10). The Greek text does not say, "The love of money is the root of all evils." Literally, it says that it is a root of evil. It is one of the sources of evil. We can make three general observations about this proverb:

1. It does not condemn money but rather the love of money.
2. It does not state that all evil comes from the love of money, but such misplaced love can cause a great variety of evil.
3. The wandering elders from Ephesus who had sold out to greed were living proof of this maxim.

NEW TESTAMENT REFERENCE

"So Pilate asked him, 'Are you the king of the Jews?'

He answered him, "You say so."

And the chief priests accused him of many things. Pilate questioned him again, 'Aren't you going to answer? Look how many things they are accusing you of!' But Jesus still did not answer, and so Pilate was amazed." (Mark 15:2–5)

PAUL'S DOXOLOGY

STATEMENT OF PRAISE		MEANING
"Blessed and only Sovereign"	Title	God has the universal authority to decide the precise time of Christ's return.
"King of kings"	Title	God's sovereign authority over all powers, both human and divine.
"Lord of lords"	Title	Same as for "King of kings."
"Immortal"	Attribute	God is self-existent and so One who will not die.
Glory ("lives in unapproachable light")	Attribute	God is unapproachable physically by human beings.
"Honor"	Attribute	God's worthiness in receiving esteem and reverence.
"Power"	Attribute	The power of God expressed in sovereign acts.

Section Summary

Paul provides positive action for Timothy to undertake after warning him to flee the evil desire for wealth. Paul's practice was wise and sensible. He prohibits Timothy's pursuit of wealth but urges him to follow hard after the traits of righteousness and godliness and to continue the struggle for the truth of the gospel in the Christian life.

A Promise for the Prosperous (vv. 17–19)

From the available evidence, we conclude that the churches did not have many rich members. As time went on, however, their number probably grew as the churches grew. This passage shows that some believers, at least, had to deal with the temptation presented by wealth.

One problem of riches was its threat to Christian fellowship. So Paul contrasts the right and wrong responses to wealth. A rich person might be tempted to be "arrogant" toward the poor or to make wealth the hope of one's life.

In contrast, Paul mentions four ways to use wealth wisely:

1. *"To do what is good."* This involves using wealth in a positive way instead of letting it feed a life of personal luxury.
2. *"To be rich in good deeds."* This points the wealthy in the direction in which they are to be truly rich.
3. *"To be generous."* This demands a liberal sharing of wealth with others.
4. *"To be . . . willing to share."* This shows that the generous act of giving is to spring up from internal generosity.

The outcome of this kind of generosity is twofold: (1) the giver stores up treasure for the coming age; and (2) it allows the giver to lay hold of eternal life here and now.

Section Summary

Paul urges the wealthy to enrich their lives with all kinds of good deeds. He particularly urges them to share their wealth to help the needy.

A Concluding Caution (vv. 20–21)

This final exhortation to Timothy once again involves both the positive and negative aspects of Christian living.

Timothy is to "guard" the genuine teachings of the gospel. They have been given to him as a trust. In each generation, much depends on the faithfulness of the ministers to that trust.

Timothy is to avoid "irreverent and empty speech." He is to avoid the kinds of ideas that have threatened the sound teachings of the faith. The "knowledge" of the heretics included empty fables, genealogies, and asceticism. In this tension in which Timothy found himself, he needed "grace" above all. He needed the presence, help, and love of a gracious God. That's exactly what Paul wished for him in the closing words of the letter.

GUIDING QUESTIONS

1. The role of a slave during the days of the early church was often difficult. What warnings and exhortations did Paul give to Christian slaves?
2. Describe the unhealthy traits of the false teachers. What was the result of their teaching to others? How did it affect some of the Ephesian believers? What is the Christian view of contentment?
3. Describe God's "program for godliness" for Timothy. Might today's young pastors heed these same commands and Pauline exhortations?

NEW TESTAMENT REFERENCE

"Don't store up for yourselves treasures on earth, where moth and rust destroy and where thieves break in and steal. But store up for yourselves treasures in heaven, where neither moth nor rust destroys, and where thieves don't break in and steal. For where your treasure is, there your heart will be also." (Matt 6:19–21)

WORD PICTURE

Guard

Paul exhorts Timothy to guard what has been entrusted to him. Literally, this is "guard the deposit." The "deposit" is a banking term denoting a sum deposited to the responsibility of a bank. (Compare the same word used in 2 Tim 1:12,14.)

Second Timothy

2 TIMOTHY 1

SALUTATION (1:1–2)

Paul wrote his second letter to Timothy from the loneliness of a dungeon while awaiting death (4:6–8). Paul's salutation is brief and like 1 Timothy. The apostle gave a lengthy salutation to Titus; but in this, his final letter, he uses a standard form.

The Author (v. 1)

Paul speaks of himself as an "apostle." This is a term that refers to one selected by God to serve as an ambassador to herald the approach of the gospel. He uses the term to lend credibility to his directives for Timothy, which reinforces Paul's urgent appeals to Timothy to heed and follow Paul and his gospel.

The Recipient (v. 2a)

In 1 Timothy, Paul addresses Timothy as "my true son." That expression underscores the special relationship between the older apostle and the younger helper. It also gives a public legitimacy to Timothy before the Ephesian church.

The Greeting (v. 2b)

Paul uses the identical wording for expressing the greeting here and in 1 Timothy: "Grace, mercy, and peace." Each of these words has special meaning for Paul's readers:

Grace describes the goodness God offers to undeserving sinners.

Mercy is God's help offered to the discouraged and stumbling (Heb 4:16).

Peace describes a state of salvation that results from the grace and mercy of God.

NEW TESTAMENT REFERENCE

Timothy's Spiritual Lineage

Timothy's grandmother Lois and mother Eunice had been women of sincere faith. To know and be influenced by persons of this caliber is one of God's greatest gifts. Paul met these women and got to know them well on his first and second missionary journeys to Lystra.

PAUL'S GRATITUDE (1:3–5)

Paul's letters ordinarily include a thanksgiving at the beginning. His gratitude to God for Timothy is a consistent element in prayers for his younger associate. Paul served the God his "ancestors" served. Both he and his ancestors were loyal to the same God and were involved in the same redemptive purpose.

The last parting between Paul and Timothy had been painful and emotional. Paul vividly remembers Timothy's tears. He experienced constant longing to be reunited with his friend and fellow servant of Christ.

One of the character traits that attracted Paul to Timothy, and that gave Paul confidence in entrusting the work of the gospel to him, was Timothy's sincere faith. Although our faith doesn't come from our family, a godly family provides the environment in which a sincere faith can flourish.

QUALITIES NEEDED IN MINISTRY (1:6–18)

*A **Call for Courage** (vv. 6–7)*

Paul's conviction that Timothy had genuine faith leads him to urge Timothy to fan his gift into an open flame. The gift to which Paul refers is Timothy's gift for ministry. Timothy had to function in an environment of fear, heresy, and challenges to his leadership. His gift related to administration and organization rather than evangelization.

Throughout this epistle, Paul pictures Timothy as a younger and more hesitant colleague. He reminds Timothy of his spiritual gift for ministry to encourage a revitalized commitment. This is not so much a command as a reminder. Paul's approach to Timothy shows the gentleness of a seasoned pastor.

Paul's reference to the "spirit" does not refer to the Holy Spirit but to those traits of which the Spirit is the author. These traits represent gifts for performing special ministries. The Holy Spirit does not produce "fear" or cowardice. A spirit of cowardice would falter under the load of responsibility Paul was placing on Timothy. Instead, the Holy Spirit produces three special gifts:

Power—a reference to a forcefulness of character that can use authority boldly and fulfill difficult tasks.

Love—a love that endures even the most cantankerous opposition, conquering opposition by forgiveness and a refusal to seek revenge.

Sound Judgment—to correct and warn the wayward and careless.

Section Summary

Paul calls on Timothy to demonstrate courage. His conviction that Timothy had genuine faith leads him to urge Timothy to fan his gift of ministry into an open flame. The Holy Spirit would provide three gifts for performing special ministries—power, love, and sound judgment—that would enable Timothy to carry out his mission.

*A **Readiness to Suffer** (vv. 8–12)*

Now we come to the point of Paul's concern. He was aware that Timothy was being tested by those opposing the genuine gospel of Jesus Christ.

NEW TESTAMENT REFERENCE

The tears Paul remembers Timothy shedding may have been on the occasion when Paul met the Ephesian Christians at Miletus just before Paul traveled to Jerusalem for the last time.

Luke describes the parting as follows: "After [Paul] said this, he knelt down and prayed with all of them. There were many tears shed by everyone. They embraced Paul and kissed him, grieving most of all over his statement that they would never see his face again. And they accompanied him to the ship" (Acts 20:36–38).

WORD PICTURE

The Laying On of . . . Hands

This is a reference to a time when Timothy's gifts were officially recognized. Paul focused only on his role in the recognition of Timothy's gifts because he wanted to emphasize the close personal relationship between himself and Timothy. The act of laying on of hands was symbolic. It was not the cause of Timothy's receipt of a spiritual gift, but it was a visible representation and symbol of it.

Paul appeals to Timothy to join Paul in suffering for the gospel. First, the epistle mentions two truths of the gospel that would promote a readiness to endure hardship for Jesus. Second, he refers to features of his own life that would provide an example for Timothy to imitate:

- *The gospel provides access to divine power.* Paul outlines the process of salvation, the purpose of salvation, and the basis of salvation:
- *Process*—a call from God to share in his kingdom, outwardly by the preaching of the gospel; inwardly by the Spirit working through the Word.
- *Purpose*—that each believer might produce a life of obedience and holiness to God instead of self.
- *Basis*—the purpose and grace of God, not human merit.

The Powerful Effect of the Gospel. Paul now moves to a discussion of God's purposes in eternity to Christ's appearance in time. He makes three points:

1. *God's plan to save has been revealed by Jesus's appearance as Savior.* God's saving power through Christ has been at work before the world was founded. Christ is the Mediator through whom the divine grace comes to human beings.
2. *Jesus has destroyed death.* He put death out of action. Although Christians are not released from physical death, their approach to it means that it is no longer to be feared (Heb 2:14–15), and it has lost its sting (1 Cor 15:55).
3. *Jesus has "brought life and immortality to light through the gospel."* The resurrection of Christ brought eternal life and immortality out into the open for the first time where people could see it. What had been a hope was now a certainty.

It was for proclamation of this good news that Paul suffered, but he was not ashamed to do so. He knew the one whom he believed. Knowing Christ, Paul knew that the deposit he had made with him was secure—Christ would keep it until that day—the *day* of his appearing once again.

An Imitation of Paul's Example (vv. 13–14)

Knowing Christ's absolute dependability, Paul calls on Timothy to mirror that dependability by adhering to the pattern of sound words which Paul imparted to Timothy and by guarding that deposit with the help of the Holy Spirit.

The task of preserving the truth of the gospel is so demanding and difficult that human strength alone cannot assure it. Maintaining the purity of the gospel demands the might and wisdom of the Holy Spirit.

These sound and saving words are to be communicated to the churches not just as words but in the faith and love of Christ.

An Incentive for Faithfulness (vv. 15–18)

An Example of Disloyalty. A poignant, personal note intrudes at this point. The apostle in prison was saddened because he had been deserted by people who should have supported him. We do not know at what point the people in the province of Asia turned against him.

Paul grieves at this neglect, but the encouragement Onesiphorus gave him greatly cheers him. Paul wants Timothy to imitate the example of Onesiphorus and avoid the shame of those who had deserted him.

What was the nature of the desertion? These former friends of Paul turned against him personally, but they also seem to have rejected the gospel he preached. We know nothing more about either Phygelus or Hermogenes from Scripture.

An Example of Loyalty. In contrast to the behavior of the profane pair above was the commendable behavior of Onesiphorus. Paul speaks affectionately of his diligent, unselfish service. What is unclear is the situation Onesiphorus faced. Was he alive or deceased?

Paul prayed that Onesiphorus would "obtain mercy from [the Lord] on that day" (the day of judgment). This underlies the fact that he, like all others, must depend solely on the mercy of God in the future judgment.

WORD PICTURE

I Know

"The word 'know' is not *ginosko,* 'experiential knowledge,' but *oida,* 'absolute, beyond a peradventure of a doubt knowledge,' the latter being the stronger word. The knowledge here is not personal knowledge gained by experience, such as fellowship with God, but a knowledge of what God is in Himself which makes Him absolutely dependable in any circumstances." Kenneth S. Wuest, *The Pastoral Epistles in the Greek New Testament* (Eerdmans), 123.

HISTORICAL BACKGROUND

Onesiphorus

His name means "profit bearing." Ephesian Christians praised his effort to seek out the place of Paul's arrest, his disregard of the shame connected with befriending one in chains, and his past service in Ephesus (2 Tim 1:16–18). The greeting of and prayer for the household of Onesiphorus has suggested to some that Onesiphorus was already dead. All that can be assumed is that Onesiphorus was not at Ephesus.

Section Summary

Paul also calls on Timothy to demonstrate a readiness to suffer for the cause of Christ. Paul was not ashamed to present himself as the initial example for Timothy. Ultimately, moral behavior cannot be taught by character-building courses. Christians must see moral commitment as a sterling example in others.

GUIDING QUESTIONS

1. What are Paul's circumstances as he writes this letter? What is the basis of his gratitude?
2. What gifts from the Holy Spirit did Timothy rely on for performing special ministry? Might today's minister expect the same kind of strength and resources from the Spirit?
3. What does a "laying on of hands" signify?
4. What truths about the gospel promote a readiness to suffer?

HISTORICAL BACKGROUND

In other literature (the apocryphal book Acts of Paul and Thecla), Phygelus and Hermogenes are described as "full of hypocrisy." They may have served as ringleaders of the trouble in Ephesus along with Hymenaeus and Philetus (2 Tim 2:17–18).

2 TIMOTHY 2

IMAGES OF EFFECTIVENESS IN MINISTRY (2:1–7)

After appealing for qualities such as courage, willingness to suffer, and faithfulness in the life of a minister, Paul borrows images from daily

WORD PICTURE

Be strong

This is a vigorous word that implies Timothy is to keep on being empowered by God. Paul's command demands Timothy's continuous active cooperation with God. "Keep in touch with the power." A. T. Robertson, *WPNT*, vol. 4 616.

WORD PICTURE

Share in Suffering

This phrase is a two-word compound ("with" + "suffer hardship") that means literally "to suffer together with someone" or "to take one's share of suffering hardship." The text mentions no specific person with whom Timothy was to share this suffering. Goodspeed's translation, "Join the ranks of those who bear suffering," catches the sense of the command.

WORD PICTURE

In the Grace

Paul shows the need for living by the means of God's grace and constantly within the sphere of strength given by God's grace. "Christ is the dynamo for power only when and while we keep in touch with Him." A. T. Robertson, *WPNT*, vol. 4, 616.

life to illustrate the traits necessary for effective service. He pictures a teacher, a soldier, an athlete, and a farmer.

The Teacher (vv. 1–2)

Paul charges Timothy to send on faithfully the message he received. Paul demanded Timothy's active involvement in the training of a future generation of Christian servants.

To be equal to this task, Paul challenges Timothy to be strong in the grace of Christ Jesus.

"What You Have Heard." These are the foundational truths of the gospel Timothy is to send to trustworthy believers. These men needed to be able to pass along these truths to others by their ability and willingness to teach.

The Soldier (vv. 3–4)

Because of the soldierlike hardship of life, Timothy desperately needed an abundant supply of grace, which Paul describes.

Paul uses the imagery of the soldier to make at least three points:

1. *Spiritual Growth.* To commend growth or accomplishment in some aspect of Christian behavior (1 Cor 9:7; Phil 2:25).
2. *Proper Ambition.* To show that the soldier's ambition must be that of pleasing the commander.
3. *Right Priorities.* To show the importance of developing an ability to distinguish between doing *good* things and doing the *best* things.

The Athlete (v. 5)

Paul uses the picture of an athlete to illustrate the importance of complete devotion and stamina in Christian living. Performing as an athlete demands a commitment to a regimen of training and to the rules for the game.

Paul implies to Timothy that the Christian athlete could expect suffering, but he also holds out the promise of a prize for the committed athlete. In the Pastoral Epistles, Paul uses athletic images in 1 Tim 4:7–8; 6:12 in order to emphasize that the Christian life demands the practice of self-discipline, affecting both personal behavior and inner attitude.

Christians must practice self-control. Each Christian must also have an inner preparedness to endure cheerfully the demands and hardships that spiritual commitment will bring (cf. 1 Cor 9:24–27).

The Farmer (v. 6)

Paul uses the analogy of a farmer to show that the one who works hard has first claim on the fruits of the work. Paul frequently uses the word "hardworking" to describe the work of ministry. The farmer who works hard will be the first to enjoy the fruits, and the diligent Christian servant can expect the same.

This passage emphasizes the anticipation of a final reward from the Lord for earnest, steady work in Christ's service. The time of enjoyment of these fruits is in the future, at the time of Christ's return (2 Cor 5:10).

PERSONAL APPLICATION

In verse 7 Paul asks Timothy to reflect on these images and emphasizes the traits that believers need to demonstrate their service for the Lord. These include:

- Faithful skills of a competent teacher
- The willingness to suffer and the priority choices of a soldier
- The self-discipline of an athlete
- The hard work of a farmer

As we also reflect on these images, God will provide the understanding for applying these truths.

Section Summary

Effective ministry requires such qualities as courage, willingness to suffer, and faithfulness in the life of a minister. The positive images Paul presents—teacher, soldier, athlete, and farmer—demand our consideration and reflection for their proper application in our lives.

TRUTHS THAT PROMOTE EFFECTIVENESS IN MINISTRY (2:8–13)

A Proper Understanding of Christ (v. 8)

Paul now urges Timothy to rivet his attention on Christ, mentioning two features of Christ's person and work:

He emphasizes Christ's resurrection. Jesus's resurrection from the dead is the prime example of victory over death. It provides an encouragement for any believer who faces suffering.

He points out that Christ "descended from David." This shows that Christ has messianic qualifications and is the heir to the glorious promises of God for David.

The memory of Christ cloaked with resurrection power and messianic dignity is an inspiration for Christian service.

The Goal of Paul's Suffering (vv. 9–10)

Paul explains the aim of his suffering. He suffered to enable God's chosen people (the "elect") to obtain their salvation. "The word of God is not bound" is Paul's way of saying that while people could silence him, they could not silence the power of God's Word (Phil 1:12–18). This is a reminder that, above all, the spread of the gospel is a work of divine power (2 Tim 1:7).

The knowledge that the gospel was not chained or bound provides Paul with an incentive to endure.

The Certainty of Reward (vv. 11–13)

These verses are another of Paul's "trustworthy sayings" (cf. 1 Tim 1:15; 3:1; 4:9). (For additional treatment of these, see commentary on 1 Tim 1:15 in this volume.)

This saying is structured by four conditional statements, each starting with the word "if." Each statement describes an action of a believer.

A TRUSTWORTHY SAYING

CONDITION	CONCLUSION
"If we died with him,"	"we will also live with him."
"If we endure,"	"we will also reign with him."
"If we deny him,"	"he will also deny us."
"If we are faithless,"	"he remains faithful."

Paul's main point with this section is the faithfulness of God. Paul wants to make clear that this is an area where no parallel exists. Human beings are often unfaithful. God is never unfaithful. Human faithlessness only serves to decorate God's faithfulness. We can always trust him to act according to his character and promises.

Paul's certainty of reward derives largely from the certainty that God was faithful to care for and love his people. God's faithfulness means future life and glory for believers.

WORD PICTURE

Correctly Teaching

This phrase translates a two-word compound from the Greek text ("straight" + "to cut"), with the emphasis on "straight." In reference to handling the word of truth, it means to be diligent in its study and to be accurate in its teaching.

"It [the word for "correctly teaching"] occurs in Prov 3:6; 11:5 for making straight paths, with which compare Heb 12:13 and 'the Way' in Acts 9:2. Theodoret explains it to mean ploughing a straight furrow. Parry argues that the metaphor is the stone mason cutting the stone straight. Since Paul was a tent-maker and knew how to cut straight the rough camel-hair cloth, why not let that be the metaphor? Certainly plenty of exegesis is crooked enough (crazy-quilt patterns) to call for careful cutting to set it straight." A. T. Robertson, *WPNT*, vol. 4, 619–20.

Section Summary

We find this section dominated by several certainties: Christ's resurrection, his messianic majesty, and the power of God's Word to provide stamina and motivation for endurance of hardship. Paul's certainty of future reward is based on God's faithfulness—his love continues, and he remains true to his promises.

THE CONFUSION OF FALSE TEACHING AND LIVING (2:14–26)

Resistance of the False Teachers (vv. 14–19)

Paul's opening appeal is for Timothy to do his duty for the people. He is to remind his audience continually to endure in their commitment while proclaiming the Christian message.

He then charges Timothy to warn the Ephesians not to "fight about words." The quarreling had a negative effect on the Ephesian believers: (1) it accomplished no good purpose, and (2) it worked to the ruin of those who participated in it.

Paul's solution for Timothy is to encourage good conduct. This conduct includes three features:

1. Timothy is to make it his supreme ambition to obtain God's approval.
2. Timothy is to be a workman with no reason to be ashamed.
3. Timothy is to be accurate in developing the truth.

The truth is the gospel. Paul shows concern that Timothy will present the gospel without perverting or distorting it. He is not to be turned aside by disputes about words or mere empty prattle.

Although saddened by the denial of Christian truths by the false teachers, whose teaching would "spread like gangrene," Paul recognizes the durability of the main structures of Christianity. God's solid foundation is unshakable.

Timothy's Response to Error (vv. 22–26)

The Content of Paul's Instructions. Paul delivers two imperatives to Timothy: (1) "flee" and (2) "pursue."

"Flee from youthful passions."

"Pursue righteousness, faith, love, and peace, along with those who call on the Lord from a pure heart."

The Purpose of Paul's Instructions. "Perhaps God will grant" signals Paul's two-pronged purpose for his gentle instructions for Timothy:

1. Paul wants the false teachers to experience repentance so they will acknowledge the truth.
2. Paul wants the false teachers to return to sober thinking and win release from Satan's stranglehold.

PERSONAL APPLICATION

In verses 20–21, Paul uses the "large house" as a metaphor for the church. The church contains both faithful and unfaithful believers. Some serve for desirable ends; others accomplish shameful ends. Paul urges his readers to avoid those who would hinder their good work, namely the false teachers. Paul has three encouraging words about the believer who is an instrument "for honorable" purposes:

1. Such a person is made holy, set apart for a special purpose before God.
2. Such a person is "useful to the Master." His level of consecration can affect his level of usefulness to God.
3. Such a person is "prepared for every good work." He will be ready to undertake whatever God calls him to do.

Those who are most useful to God will find they must avoid certain practices, attitudes, and ideas. He urges his readers to make such a separation.

Section Summary

Paul warns Timothy to resist the false teachers, appeals for Timothy to separate from them, and outlines Timothy's proper response to them. The best prescription for avoiding enticing errors is a proper presentation of the truth. Paul urges this on Timothy.

GUIDING QUESTIONS

1. Paul uses five images from the daily life of his culture. What lessons might we learn from each of these images?
2. What is the point of Paul's trustworthy saying? How might we embrace the truths it teaches?
3. What does Paul mean by "correctly teaching the word of truth"? Cite some examples of failing to correctly handle the word of truth.

4. Why did Paul appeal to his readers to separate from the false teachers? What is to be Timothy's response to the error of the heretics?

2 TIMOTHY 3

THE STUBBORN CHARACTER OF THE FALSE TEACHERS (3:1–9)

In this section Paul prepares Timothy for the kinds of people he can expect to deal with in his ministry.

What They Are (vv. 1–5)

Paul provides a long list of vices that resemble collections in Rom 1:29–31 and 1 Tim 1:9–10. Unbridled egotism, greed, disregard for authority, and cruel, callous attitudes toward others are the kinds of things Paul describes here. The presence of people with these vices demonstrates that these were hard times.

Paul applies the catalog of vices to the false teachers. He summarizes their behavior with a description that contains these two elements:

1. They maintain a form of godliness.
2. They deny the power of godliness.

For Paul, there was only one solution: stay away from these people.

What They Do (vv. 6–9)

Paul further describes the false teachers. Their methods were most effective among gullible, undisciplined women whose instability resulted from guilt. These woman were constantly learning but never came to know anything.

Paul indicates these teachers opposed the truth with the same level of intensity that the Egyptian magicians, Jannes and Jambres, opposed Moses and Aaron. The minds of the teachers were corrupted.

NEW TESTAMENT REFERENCE

In another letter Paul wrote to Ephesus, he describes what may have been this same phenomenon. "Growing into maturity with a stature measured by Christ's fullness. Then we will no longer be little children, tossed by the waves and blown around by every wind of teaching, by human cunning with cleverness in the techniques of deceit" (Eph 4:13–14).

Section Summary

Paul provides a description of the false teachers. Paul reminds Timothy that this wasn't the first time God's servants have been opposed by hypocrites and that such teacher's real motives will eventually be exposed.

SOURCES OF STRENGTH FOR ENDURANCE (3:10–17)

Paul uses a frightening picture to portray the opposition Timothy would face. Where could anyone find the strength and wisdom to resist and overcome such opposition? Two sources were Paul's sterling example and the instruction of Scripture.

The Example of Paul (vv. 10–13)

Paul provides a condensed autobiography to draw out lessons from his life for the benefit of his younger disciple. The older apostle's counsel did not come from an ivory-tower existence. He knew what it was to suffer hardship for the gospel.

Although the enemies of the faith might have seemed victorious for the moment, they would not gain ultimate victory because they were opposed to God. Timothy was not without guidance as he faced the challenge of the false teachers. His guidance consisted of three elements:

1. The truth of the gospel from Paul's teaching and example.
2. His commitment of faith to Jesus Christ, as opposed to new and deceptive teachings.
3. The help of "sacred Scriptures."

The Enrichment of Scripture (vv. 14–17)

Paul reminds Timothy that his inspired source of instruction is the "sacred Scriptures," or literally, the *sacred writings.*

The affirmation of Scripture's inspired nature leads Paul to a discussion of its usefulness. He describes four uses to which Scripture can be put:

Teaching. Scripture is a positive source of Christian doctrine. Out of the many times the term *teaching* appears in the New Testament, Paul uses it fifteen times in the Pastoral Epistles. Because of the prominence of heresy among his readers, Paul emphasizes sound doctrine.

Rebuking. This may refer to a rebuke that exposes the errors of false teachers. It may also refer to reproof in our personal lives. Scripture can show sinners their failures, clarify the point or doctrine, and lead them to a new sense of peace and wholeness.

Correcting. Scripture is helpful for convicting the misguided and disobedient of their errors and restoring them to the right paths.

Moral Training. This is training that leads to righteous living. In Eph 6:4 the term for "training" (the same term used in 2 Tim 3:16) denotes a system of discipline used by a parent to develop Christian character in a child. Here it describes a system of discipline in Scripture that leads to a holy lifestyle.

The reason for using Scripture in these ways is "so that the man of God may be complete, equipped for every good work." For Timothy, this meant that he was furnished completely to do whatever God called him to perform. What a tragedy for any Christian to be labeled spiritually unprepared for a task when the means of preparation are readily at hand!

WORD PICTURE

All Scripture Is Inspired by God

"In contrast with the teaching of imposters, the Christian faith rests securely on its inspired Scriptures, which have been carefully preserved from generation to generation. Therefore, Paul calls Timothy to remember that 'all scripture is given by inspiration of God,' or is 'God-breathed.' The Scriptures are the result of God's personal intervention on the plane of human history and of his personal encounter through the Spirit with his people and prophets. 'Revelation' means God's presence in the events of history. 'Inspiration' means his presence in the recording of those events." C. A. Trentham, *Studies in Timothy*, 128.

HISTORICAL BACKGROUND

"Reproof was especially important in Judaism, where it had to be done privately and gently first."

Craig S. Keener, *IVP Bible Background Commentary*, 630.

Section Summary

Paul teaches Timothy several lessons in these verses that are applicable to us today. Christians receive strength for their pilgrimage from two sources—the lives of other believers and the instruction of God's Word.

GUIDING QUESTIONS

1. Describe the character of the false teachers. What two principles for our consideration emerge from Paul's description of these heretics?
2. Who were the victims of these false teachers? Why were they able to subvert their victims?
3. What does "inspired by God" mean? Why is the inspiration of Scripture such an important Christian doctrine?

2 TIMOTHY 4

A CHARGE FOR CONSISTENT BEHAVIOR (4:1–5)

In this section Paul continues the appeal for doctrinal soundness, which he began in 2:14. He underscores Timothy's role in thwarting the advance of heresy in Ephesus. The intensity of Paul's feeling is evident from his use of nine imperatives in this part of his letter.

Context of the Charge (v. 1)

Paul makes this solemn charge to Timothy not just as man to man but in the presence of God the Father and Jesus Christ, who will serve as judge of both the living and the dead.

Charge to Ministry (v. 2)

Paul's charge to Timothy is to "preach the word." He then follows this charge with four commands that indicate how Timothy is to carry out his charge:

1. Timothy is to stand "ready in season and out of season." This means he must always be on duty and take advantage of every opportunity for service.
2. Timothy is to correct error using reasoned judgment.
3. Timothy is to give hope to the fainthearted by providing tender encouragement in the face of discouraging opposition.

Timothy is to encourage with "great patience and teaching."

Reason for the Charge (vv. 3–4)

Paul gives a stern charge to Timothy to declare the truth because he foresees Christendom increasing its appetite for error rather than truth.

Only sturdy pastors can endure such unstable congregations. Paul sees three developments that emphasize the need for countering error:

1. Listeners would no longer "tolerate sound doctrine." They would find the content and demands of the gospel unpalatable.
2. They would raise up teachers "according to their own desires."
3. They will do all this to satisfy the "itch[ing]" in their ears.

Paul is warning professing believers in this passage.

Timothy's Personal Charge (v. 5)

What should be the stance of the pastor who sees these developments? He is to remain poised ("exercise self-control") and suffer any hardship that results from his faithfulness to his charge. Timothy is to continue his work by spreading the gospel and discharging his ministerial duties.

WORD PICTURE

Be Ready

A. T. Robertson gives these translations of this Greek term: "Take a stand," "carry on," "stick to it."

Section Summary

Indifference from listeners must not be permitted to shut off the proclamation of the gospel by believers. Timothy is to remain alert and watchful of opposition while enduring all necessary afflictions in spreading the gospel. There is encouragement. Christians committed to declaring God's message to indifferent audiences can expect God's strength, power, and ultimate blessing.

THE REWARD FOR SELF-SACRIFICE (4:6–8)

Paul now speaks of the expectation of his approaching death. Here he outlines the sacrifice he has made, the service he has rendered, and the reward he anticipates.

The Sacrifice of Life (v. 6)

In these verses Paul shares his own attitude and faith in the face of his impending execution. His statements may have been dictated just days or hours before his death. Here we can see how one great Christian viewed the possibility of sacrificing his own life for the sake of the gospel.

He uses sacrificial imagery to portray his own death. First, he compares the pouring out of his energy in ministry to the pouring out of the wine of an Old Testament drink offering. Second, he describes his death as a "departure" of a ship by the lifting its anchor and the breaking up of a camp of soldiers. Both the ship and the soldiers were going home.

By faith Paul gives a marvelous appraisal of the grim prospects of his death. Timothy may have read the story of this buoyant faith through a covering of tears.

HISTORICAL BACKGROUND

"Paul had had his preliminary hearing before Nero, and was expecting the final one, and death. He knew it would not be crucifixion, for a citizen of the Roman Empire was not crucified. If the death penalty was demanded by the State, it would be decapitation, hence the figurative reference to a libation." Kenneth S. Wuest, *The Pastoral Epistles in the Greek New Testament*, 160.

The Service of Ministry (v. 7)

But Paul has no regrets as he nears the end. He uses three metaphors to reflect the struggle of his ministry:

1. *"I have fought the good fight."* Paul did his best in the contest.
2. *"I have finished the race."* He faithfully followed the course laid out by his Lord.
3. *"I have kept the faith."* This may have involved either maintaining the sound doctrine of Christianity intact or by keeping loyalty to the trust that the Father had given him.

With these words Paul is not boasting of his accomplishments but reflecting on the cause of his life with a statement of confidence. He is describing what the grace of God has produced in him.

The Reward of Obedience (v. 8)

When a runner in an athletic contest of the first century crossed the finish line as the victor, he was assured of receiving the emblem of victory. Paul is also sure he will receive a victor's crown: a "crown of righteousness." This may refer to a reward for righteous behavior or a gift consisting of righteousness awarded by the Judge when he returns.

WORD PICTURE

Bring the Cloak

"Paul also wanted his cloak, which probably was a heavy wool garment, to protect him from the winter. It was getting cold in Rome. The cold, wintry winds would pass through the subterranean corridors of the Mamertine Prison, chilling the bones of the aged apostle to the very marrow. This was the only cloak Paul had. Those who seem to feel that the Christian gospel promises an abundance of material comforts to all followers to Christ need to remember that Paul was so poor that he could not afford to lose an old cloak at Troas. We know nothing about Carpus save that he was the custodian of the cloak of Paul." C. A. Trentham, *Studies in Timothy*, 138–39.

Section Summary

The knowledge that God rewards and recognizes faithful Christian service is an incentive to godly living. God is faithful to believers; he will not ignore their works but will justly evaluate all of them.

A FEW REQUESTS AND WARNINGS (4:9–15)

As Paul wrote these verses, he seems to have been convinced of the nearness of his death. There may have been some possibility, however, of a further delay in the execution of the sentence imposed on him. He urges Timothy, therefore, to come to him soon.

The apostle asks Timothy to bring his cloak along with his scrolls and parchments. There has been much speculation about the nature of these scrolls and parchments. It's possible that nothing was written on them. Perhaps they were simply writing materials for Paul's use.

Paul makes special mention of a coppersmith named Alexander. He warned Timothy about this man as the fellow had vigorously resisted Paul. Timothy was to be on his guard for him.

A REMINDER OF GOD'S DELIVERING POWER (4:16–18)

Paul gives Timothy fresh information about his lack of support from Christian friends and the magnificent strength the Lord had supplied. The memory of divine protection leads Paul to an outburst of praise.

"The Lord stood with me and strengthened me." In contrast to the desertion of friends, the Lord stood beside Paul to provide strength. Two results developed from the help and strength God provided in the trial:

The gospel was fully proclaimed so the heathen heard it. God gave Paul the courage and opportunity to preach. By doing so, Paul fulfilled his plans of reaching Rome with the gospel.

Paul's Deliverance from the "Lion's Mouth." Interpreters have identified the lion as one of these three: the literal lions of the amphitheater, the emperor Nero, or Satan.

Section Summary

Paul had been deserted by friends and wronged by others. In the midst of difficult circumstances and approaching death, Paul gave testimony to God's faithfulness. He was totally confident that God was in control of his life. As Christians we, too, must learn to rejoice in divine victory and avoid succumbing to disappointments in a spirit of vindictiveness.

CONCLUSION (4:19–21)

As was customary in letters of the first century, Paul concludes his letter with personal greetings. These include Priscilla and Aquila, Onesiphorus, and Trophimus. Paul makes a final request to Timothy to visit him "before winter" so there would not be an additional delay.

BENEDICTION (4:22)

In the benediction, Paul expresses a personal word for Timothy. He wishes that God might strengthen Timothy personally so the younger leader might faithfully discharge his task. These are likely the last written words of Paul.

NEW TESTAMENT REFERENCE

Paul first met Aquila and Priscilla in Corinth (Acts 18:2). His relationship with them had remained strong and a source of comfort over many years of ministry.

GUIDING QUESTIONS

1. Upon what realities did Paul base his charge to Timothy? How do we relate today to these realities in our ministries?
2. Specifically, what was Paul's charge to Timothy? Why was it so important that Timothy follow through?
3. Describe Paul's attitude toward his approaching death. What are your thoughts about death?
4. Why is it so important to preach the Word?

Titus

TITUS 1

SALUTATION (1:1–4)

Author (vv. 1–3)

In his letters to churches or individuals, Paul uses the form of introductory greeting customary in first-century letter writing. In this epistle to Titus, Paul identifies himself as the source of the letter and Titus as the recipient, followed by his stated desire for God's blessing upon Titus.

Paul typically includes several self-descriptions to establish his authority and right to speak. He does this by identifying himself as "a servant of God and an apostle of Jesus Christ." The term *apostle* means "one who is sent." Paul classifies himself among those earlier apostles, such as Peter, James, and John, who had been called and commissioned directly by the risen Lord.

The goal of Paul's apostolic ministry was the "hope of eternal life." The "word" Paul preached is the message of God's redemptive deed in the death and resurrection of Jesus Christ. This was the message Paul proclaimed in obedience to the trust God had placed in him by calling him as an apostle.

HISTORICAL BACKGROUND

Crete

Crete is a long, narrow mountainous island (175 miles long, 35 miles at its widest point) south of mainland Greece. Crete was the center of the Minoan maritime empire named after the legendary King Minos. This brilliant civilization fell suddenly, perhaps by an earthquake followed by conquest, about 1400 BC, leaving written tablets in the oldest known scripts of Europe.

By the second century BC, Crete had a substantial Jewish population, powerful enough to obtain the protection of Rome. The large and influential Jewish population on Crete, as well as the initial exposure of Cretan Jews to the gospel at Pentecost, suggests that Crete was a fertile location for missionary work.

The character of the people is described in a quotation from a prophet of their own: "Cretans are always liars, evil beasts, lazy gluttons" (Titus 1:12), words attributed to the Cretan seer Epimenides, who was also credited with having advised the Athenians to set up altars to unknown gods (cf. Acts 17:23).

Recipient (v. 4a)

Titus is the recipient of the letter. He was one of Paul's closest missionary associates. Paul calls Titus his "true son." In common usage, this phrase means biological, as opposed to an adopted or foster child. This father-son relationship, however, is understood in the context of the community of faith. Perhaps Paul had won Titus to Christ.

Paul's greeting is standard. "Grace," God's unmerited love, is the basis of our relationship with him. "Peace" is the new relationship we enjoy with God and his people because of his grace. We have been reconciled to God and to one another.

THE CHARGE TO APPOINT ELDERS ON CRETE (1:5)

Paul now turns his attention to Titus's immediate task with the churches at Crete. There was work yet to be accomplished in Crete, and Paul instructs Titus to complete the work that had been started there. He gives Titus a primary directive, which is to "appoint elders in every town." This meant he was to appoint elders in every Cretan town where a Christian congregation was located.

THE QUALIFICATIONS FOR ELDERS ON CRETE (1:6–9)

The qualifications presented require acceptable conditions in three basic areas of the prospective elder's life, namely:

1. His marriage and family
2. His personality and character traits
3. His devotion to God's Word and his commitment to teaching and preaching the true gospel message

Marriage and Family Qualifications (v. 6)

Two aspects of the prospective elder's family life are noted: his marriage and the faith and conduct of his children.

"The Husband of One Wife." These simple words have proven difficult to understand, and the interpretations derived from them are many and varied. A basic question concerning this qualification is whether the elder is restricted to *one* marriage to *one* woman in his lifetime. Obviously, this phrase would eliminate a bigamist or polygamist from consideration. Since the Scriptures do not prohibit remarriage after the death of a spouse, and encourage it in some cases, it is unlikely that such a remarried man should be disqualified.

While it was not Paul's intention to prohibit unmarried men from becoming elders, it may be assumed that the majority of candidates would be married, and Paul may have preferred married men to hold these positions because of their experience in leading the family unit.

"Faithful Children." The second aspect of the prospective elder's family life concerns his children, specifically their faith and personal conduct. This passage and 1 Tim 3:4 are similar in that they both require that children be well-behaved and obedient. However, the addition of "faithful children" in Titus makes this condition even more stringent. This additional requirement that the elder is capable of influencing his own children to become Christians demonstrates Paul's conviction that effective spiritual leadership in the home suggests that same probability of effective leadership in the church.

Personality and Character Qualifications (vv. 7–8)

Paul provides a succinct list of five negative and six positive personality and character traits of the prospective elder. The following chart lists these and adds their extended meanings:

WORD PICTURE

Elder

The term *elder* simply means "an aged man." However, in the context of New Testament church organization, *elder* is a technical term signifying a church leader. It is likely that this term was carried over from the synagogue, which probably served as a limited model for early church organization.

PERSONALITY AND CHARACTER QUALIFICATIONS OF ELDERS

TRAIT		EXTENDED MEANING
	NEGATIVE ("NOT")	
Not arrogant		Flexible in his own opinions; considerate of other viewpoints
Not hot-tempered		Controls his emotions and exercises proper judgment
Not an excessive drinker		Is not given to much wine; considerate of weaker brothers in this area
Not a bully		Not given to physical (or verbal) violence
Not greedy for money		Absolutely honest in money matters; does not use his Christian service as an opportunity for financial profit
	POSITIVE	
Hospitable		Devoted to the welfare of others
Loving what is good		Includes good things as well as good men
Sensible		Mastery of his mind, emotions, words, and deeds
Righteous		Committed to doing what is right; to a life of devotion and service to God
Holy		Separated to devotion and service of God
Self-controlled		Exhibits the power of lordship over oneself

Devotion to Sound Doctrine (v. 9)

The elder must hold firmly to orthodox biblical teaching. Two basic functions of the elder's role in the church emanate from his own personal devotion to the truth of God's Word:

To Encourage Others. Here, within the context of the elder's function toward believers, "to encourage with sound teaching" indicates comfort and edification in "the faithful message."

To Refute Those Who Oppose Sound Teaching. The goal of the refutation of false teaching is not to destroy the opponent but rather to restore him to "sound teaching." Such a situation would also require that the elder be courageous in his willingness to confront a so-called Christian brother.

Section Summary

Paul presents qualifications for church leaders. Elder candidates must meet certain standards regarding home life, personality and character traits, and doctrinal integrity.

THE NEED FOR QUALIFIED CHURCH LEADERSHIP (1:10–16)

The problem confronting the churches in Crete was serious. They were being disrupted by false teachers. The impact of these false teachers was considerable; they were "ruining entire households." Paul feels that they are exploiting the churches "in order to get money dishonestly " and believes that "it is necessary to silence them." Paul's response to their rebelliousness and false teaching is to command Titus to "rebuke" them.

Paul provides two descriptions of their false teachings:

"Jewish Myths." The myths Paul refers to possibly were concerned with Jewish and Gnostic ideas combined in Hellenistic Judaism and transferred to Christianity by Jewish-Christian converts.

"The Commands of People Who Reject the Truth." This description recalls Isa 29:13: "These people approach me with their speeches to honor me with lip-service, yet their hearts are far from me, and human rules direct their worship of me." Jesus quoted this passage to the Pharisees when they disputed him concerning religious ceremony and the matter of being clean or unclean. Those persons who tenaciously hold to these human commandments or tradition (that is, religious rituals that have no real meaning) are "people who reject the truth," according to Paul (1:14), or who "abandon[ed] the commands of God," according to Jesus (Mark 7:8).

Titus 1:14–16 should be studied in light of Jesus's teaching in Mark 7:1–23 and its parallel passage in Matt 15:1–20.

Section Summary

Paul attempts to expose and rebuke the false teachers who were endangering the Cretan churches. He uses strong language as he exposes their error of adding external religious requirements to the gospel of God's grace. Because of the serious perversion of the doctrine of salvation, it is evident how much the churches of Crete needed strong, qualified leaders.

NEW TESTAMENT REFERENCE

"I know and am persuaded in the Lord Jesus that nothing is unclean in itself. Still, to someone who considers a thing to be unclean, to that one it is unclean." (Rom 14:14)

GUIDING QUESTIONS

1. Who was Titus? What was his mission?
2. What qualifications did Paul lay down for prospective elders?
3. What is proper interpretation of the requirement: "husband of one wife"? How does a church apply this requirement to a man who has remarried? To one who has divorced?
4. How can we avoid the trap of legalistic Christianity and other false teachings?

TITUS 2

EXHORTATIONS FOR THE RIGHT BEHAVIOR (2:1–10)

Having addressed Titus's duties regarding church organizational leadership and the confrontation of false teaching, Paul encourages Titus to exhort various groups within the church to meet certain standards of behavior. Five specific groups are to receive specific exhortations: the older men (v. 2), the older women (v. 3), the young women (vv. 4–5), the young men (vv. 6–8), and slaves (vv. 9–10). These groups, designated by age, sex, and social position, would certainly include each believer and church member on Crete.

Especially noteworthy is the occurrence of the phrase "so that" (four times, vv. 4, 5,8,10). Each occurrence begins a clause that expresses the goal or purpose of the behavior that is encouraged. Furthermore, these clauses indicate that proper Christian behavior has a significant impact on pagan attitudes toward Christianity (v. 5), silencing opponents by correct Christian teaching (v. 8), and attracting a lost world to Christianity (v. 10), thus affecting the entire missionary enterprise of the church.

In contrast to the opponents in 1:10–16, who taught error that resulted in their being "unfit for any good work" (v. 16), Paul emphasizes in 2:1–10 that good works are a necessary and natural result of believing "sound teaching." To be rescued from sin and death through faith in Jesus Christ must result in a changed life that displays self-control and reflects God's love and grace.

Behavior in Accord with Sound Doctrine (v. 1)

Paul begins with a sharp command for Titus. His message to Titus is "proclaim things consistent with sound teaching." He asserts Titus's personal responsibility for instructing the Cretan believers regarding their own appropriate Christian behavior and responsibilities.

Exhortation for Older Men (v. 2)

This group may have been men of an age sufficient to have raised a family and seen their children begin families of their own. Titus was to exhort or encourage these older men to be:

- *Self-controlled*—possessing complete clarity of mind and its resulting good judgment.
- *Worthy of Respect*—with dignity; not frivolous or silly.
- *Sensible*—behaving sensibly.
- *Sound*—doctrinally healthy.

Furthermore, the older men are to be sound in these three areas:

- *Faith*—trust in God, manifested in loyal Christian living.

HISTORICAL BACKGROUND

"Early Christian adaptation of Roman social relations was important for the church's witness to society and for diminishing preventable opposition to the gospel." Craig S. Keener, *IVP Bible Background Commentary*, 637.

WORD PICTURE

Self-Controlled

The way modern translators render this word indicates a sober, temperate, calm, and dispassionate approach to life, having mastered personal desires and passions. Biblical admonitions expect God's people to exercise self-control (Prov 25:28; 1 Cor 7:5; 1 Thess. 5:6; 1 Tim 3:2; 2 Tim 3:3; Gal 5:23; 2 Tim 1:7; 2 Pet 1:6).

Freedom in Christ does not give believers liberty to cast off all moral restraint as some members in Galatia and other churches apparently believed. Nor does it call for a withdrawal from life and its temptations. It calls for a self-disciplined life following Christ's example of being in the world but not of the world.

Paul repeatedly uses the term "self-control" throughout this passage in Titus and applies it to all the groups he addresses. This indicates the need for Christians to live sensibly and reasonably within a fragmented world characterized by chaos and confusion.

- *Love*—commitment to the welfare of others without regard for merit.
- *Endurance*—a triumphant stance in the face of persecution and difficulties.

The Older Women (v. 3)

As children grow up and leave home, the older woman's focus may become less defined as her familial responsibilities become less demanding. This may contribute to feelings of uselessness, loneliness, low self-esteem, and self-pity.

Paul suggests in this passage that older women should possess personal godliness, be worthy of respect, and play an essential role in the lives of the young women in the church. The concept of spiritual mentoring is evident in this passage.

Titus is to encourage the older women with the following exhortations.

"*Be Reverent*—a way of life appropriate to a priestess serving in God's temple. The phrase "in behavior" indicates the outward expression of an inner character.

"*Not Slanderers*"—avoiding lies, false accusations, and malicious gossip.

"*Not Slaves to Excessive Drinking*"—control over physical appetites.

"*Teach What Is Good*"—advising the young women.

The Younger Women (vv. 4–5)

The young women are to "love their husbands and . . . children." Because Paul expresses this first, it may suggest the high value Paul gave to the congenial and cohesive Christian family unit.

Communicating Paul's exhortations for the younger women was not Titus's direct responsibility. Rather, this was to be the duty of the older women. Of the desirable qualities for Christian young women, several presuppose a life involving marriage and family:

- "To love their husbands and . . . children"
- "Self-controlled, pure"
- "Workers at home"
- "Kind"
- "In submission to their husbands"

It must also be noted that "in submission to" does not imply a position of inferiority of being. As a general rule, all Christian doctrinal discussion concerning relationships between men and women should begin with Paul's statement in Gal 3:28 that "there is no . . . male and female . . . in Christ."

WORD PICTURE

Submission

This phrase is an instruction regarding the relationship between husband and wife (cf. Eph 5:24; Col 3:18; 1 Pet 3:1,5). The term is also used in a variety of other contexts, including, for example, the subjection of all things to Christ, the subjection of persons to civil authorities, the subjection of slaves to masters, and the subjection of one Christian to another. In his *The Epistle to the Romans*, C. E. B. Cranfield, speaking of this subjection, states, "It is the responsible acceptance of a relationship in which God has placed one and the resulting honest attempt to fulfill the duties which it imposes on one" (p. 662).

The Younger Men (vv. 7–8)

Paul's exhortation for the younger men is to be conveyed by Titus's words and personal example. Titus is to encourage them toward these qualities:

To achieve self-control—self-mastery and sensibleness

To "make yourself an example of good works"—to be a role model of good works, in contrast to the false teachers

To show integrity in their teaching—the art of effectively communicating the true gospel message

To demonstrate seriousness—characterized by dignity and what will inspire respect from hearers

To demonstrate soundness of speech—healthy, well-thought-out presentations of the Christian gospel.

Paul's stated goal for exhorting these qualities in younger men is "so that any opponent will be ashamed, because he doesn't have anything bad to say about us." Hostile critics will ultimately be ashamed in the sense of publicly suffering loss of respect as it becomes apparent that their criticisms are groundless.

Instructions for Slaves (vv. 9–10)

The institution of slavery is indefensible from the Christian point of view. Paul expresses his belief that the division between slave and free belonged to the old order that was under the judgment of God. In Christ's church, which belonged to the new order, there is "no . . . slave or free" (Gal 3:28).

Under the conditions of the ancient world, the only advice the apostle could give to believing slaves was to be Christian in their slavery. Their Christian character could be demonstrated through obedience, honesty, and faithfulness. Paul exhorts Titus to encourage these qualities in slaves:

- "To submit to their masters in everything."
- "To be well-pleasing" to their masters.
- "Not talking back" to their masters.
- "Not . . . stealing" from their masters.
- "Demonstrating utter faithfulness."
- Make attractive the teaching about God and Jesus in every way.

Section Summary

Paul's specific exhortations to the various groups within the Cretan church in 2:1–10 reveal two foundational aspects of Christian behavior. First, his repeated use of the term "self-control" throughout this passage is applicable to all groups. Second, the repeated use of the phrase "so that" (indicating purpose) demonstrates the missionary aspects of everyday Christian behavior within a hostile and lost world.

THE DOCTRINAL BASIS FOR CHRISTIAN BEHAVIOR (2:11–15)

The material in this section is highly compressed but incredibly rich.

The Truths of God's Grace (v. 11)

Paul uses the connecting word *for* to link what follows with what has gone before. What he says, in effect, is to take on this new lifestyle—whatever your station in life, *for* or *because* God's grace has appeared.

A person who sees, understands, and accepts this grace can't easily go back to his or her former lifestyle.

God's Grace as a Teacher (vv. 12–15)

God's grace educates us in Christian behavior. The force of the verb *instructing* is that of present tense, continuous action, which conveys ongoing results rather than a once-for-all action.

God's grace teaches us to "deny" godlessness. This refers to a conscious, willful repudiation of thoughts, words, and actions that are opposed to true godliness.

God's grace teaches us to "live in a sensible, righteous, and godly way." Self-control involves being sensible and sober minded. *Righteous* denotes conduct that cannot be condemned. *Godly* denotes lives that are pleasing to God.

Through Jesus's work of redemption, God brought into being a people who are his priceless possession. Immorality is inconsistent with this status conferred upon us by God. In view of this special relation with God, believers are to take their moral and ethical lives seriously. We are to be "eager to do good works."

WORD PICTURE

Grace

Kenneth Wuest points out that the Greeks used *charis* (grace) to refer to a favor that one does for another person, expecting no return. But these favors were always done for friends. Christ gave *grace* a far richer meaning because the favor he did at Calvary was done not for friends but for those who hated him. Paul reminds the Romans that while we were still his enemies, he provided a way of reconciliation to God through his death (Rom 5:10).

WORD PICTURE

Instructing Us

The Greek verb translated "instruct" means "to teach, educate." However, its biblical usage may contain the nuance of discipline or chastisement. Education in Christian behavior is seldom a painless process as it involves the correction of human behavior that by nature stands in opposition to God. Paul states the aspects of this education both negatively and positively.

Section Summary

The highest and purest motivation for Christian behavior is not based on what we can do for God but upon what God has done for us and will yet do. The false teachers on Crete assumed their religious works earned them God's favor. The apostle Paul teaches that only as we grasp the significance of God's grace can we eagerly do what is pleasing to him.

GUIDING QUESTIONS

1. Describe Paul's concept of "self-control." Why does he give it such high priority?
2. What instructions does Paul provide for the older men? The younger men?
3. What instructions does Paul provide for the older women? The younger women?

4. In the New Testament, what does it mean for a wife to be subject to her husband?
5. How does the grace of God "instruct" us? What does it teach us?

TITUS 3

THE NEED FOR CHRISTIAN BEHAVIORAL STANDARDS (3:1–2)

Paul takes up the matter of standards of Christian conduct with regard to pagan society in general. His exhortations in 2:1–10 appear to relate more directly to Christian behavior among believers and the impact such behavior has on the unbeliever. Here Paul addresses the direct relationship the Cretan Christians had with the pagan world.

Respect for Governmental Authorities (v. 1)

Paul takes a positive attitude toward the government, as is also true of Peter (1 Pet 2:13–14). When the Pastoral Epistles were written, the government was viewed as beneficent rather than a hindrance to the gospel. According to this passage, the duty of the believer in civic matters is threefold:

1. Be submissive.
2. Be obedient.
3. Be honest.

This exhortation extends the Christian's responsibilities from a passive posture (obeying laws) to an active, positive involvement in society.

Respect for All (v. 2)

The question of how Christians are to relate to their pagan neighbors was especially difficult in the early days of Christianity. Church members, a minority of the population, were often objects of pagan and Jewish hostility and slander.

According to Paul's instructions, the relation of believers to non-Christians is to be governed by the principles of love. Their conversation with their unbelieving contemporaries should be loving, gentle, and courteous.

NEW TESTAMENT REFERENCE

This idea is a practical outworking of Jesus's teaching about being "the salt of the earth . . . [and] the light of the world . . . that they may see your good works and give glory to your father in heaven" (Matt 5:13–16).

Section Summary

In this section Paul takes up the matter of standards of Christian conduct regarding pagan society in general. This conduct includes believers' respect for governmental authorities and maintaining civic responsibilities. It also requires that they be governed by the principles of love in their relationship to non-Christians in a pagan society.

THE THEOLOGICAL BASIS FOR PROPER BEHAVIOR (3:3–8)

In this section Paul describes the degenerate conditions of the pagan society in which Christians had to live. Interestingly, his comments focus on the human condition within society. Paul identifies himself and all Christians with sinful and degenerate humanity. Christians, though at one time degenerate and lost, are objects of God's kindness and love, which results in their salvation. Christians are to demonstrate this same kindness and love toward lost individuals and society, making Christianity attractive and resulting in the salvation of others.

Verses 4–7 eloquently summarize God's work in humanity's salvation. Paul presents several key doctrinal ideas.

"*The kindness of God . . . and his love . . . appeared.*" God's kindness includes his generosity and goodness, especially toward humanity and for humanity's benefit. God's love speaks of his love for humankind. The purpose of God's kindness and love is to bring salvation.

"*He saved us.*" Salvation is not through humankind's attempts to achieve salvation through its own efforts. It comes as a result of God's mercy.

"*According to his mercy.*" Salvation depends solely and completely on God's grace, displayed in "his mercy," revealed and achieved by his Son, Jesus Christ, and applied to humankind by the Holy Spirit.

Section Summary

Paul describes the degenerate condition of the pagan society in which Christians had to live. Christians are to demonstrate kindness and love to lost individuals and society, making Christianity attractive and resulting in the salvation of others.

WORD PICTURE

This Saying Is Trustworthy

This phrase is used in all three of the Pastoral Epistles (1 Tim 1:5; 3:1; 4:9; 2 Tim 2:11; Titus 3:8). It serves to emphasize either what is to be said or what has been said and may indicate Paul's intentional use of creeds, catechisms, hymns, or liturgical material. The "trustworthy saying" in this passage probably includes verses 4–7.

PAUL'S FINAL WARNING CONCERNING FALSE TEACHING AND DIVISION (3:9–11)

Having offered an eloquent doctrinal summary of the gospel and its motivation to profitable good works, Paul again warns Titus about the "unprofitable" works of the false teachers.

PAUL'S WARNINGS ABOUT FALSE TEACHINGS IN THE PASTORAL EPISTLES

PASSAGE	TOPIC
1 Timothy 1:4	Genealogies
1 Timothy 6:4	Disputes and arguments
2 Timothy 2:16	Irreverent and empty speech
2 Timothy 2:23	Foolish and ignorant disputes

These occurrences suggest that similar if not identical false doctrines were common during this period of church history.

Paul describes a false teacher as a "divisive person." Concerning those persons who promote false teaching, Paul commands that Titus "reject a divisive person after a first and second warning" (v. 10).

NEW TESTAMENT REFERENCE

This process is similar to what Jesus commands: "If your brother sins against you, go tell him his fault, between you and him alone. If he listens to you, you have won your brother. But if he won't listen, take one or two others with you, so that by the testimony of two or three witnesses every fact may be established. If he doesn't pay attention to them, tell the church. If he doesn't pay attention even to the church, let him be like a Gentile and a tax collector to you" (Matt 18:15–17).

Division can be destructive. Divisions within the church result in believers who are confused, frustrated, angry, and hurt. They become ineffective in ministering to one another and to a lost world in desperate need of the gospel of Jesus Christ.

Paul concludes by saying, "For you know that such a person has gone astray and is sinning; he is self-condemned." We can be sure about these three things about a divisive person.

He has "gone astray." The force of the verb Paul uses here means that this person has been and remains off track.

He is "sinning." This is a present-tense verb, meaning that he willfully *continues* to sin. He has been perverted and persists in his sinful way.

He is "self-condemned." He refuses to heed the counsel of those who are trying to win him from his erring ways. This refusal amounts to his own condemnation of himself.

Section Summary

Paul closes his instruction to Titus by reemphasizing the significance of refuting false teaching. The goal of false teachers is to deny a true knowledge of God and destroy the doctrinal unity of the church. When the church cannot agree on the essentials of Christianity and is characterized by conflict and divisions, it is ineffective in a lost world as well as displeasing to God.

CONCLUDING REMARKS (3:12–15)

Paul ends this letter with personal directions, comments, and greetings.

Personal Directions (vv. 12–14)

When either Artemas or Tychicus was sent to Crete, Titus is to make an effort to rejoin Paul. Artemas is not mentioned elsewhere. Tychicus was the bearer of the epistle to the Colossians. Paul plans to send one of them to take the place of Titus so he will be free to leave his responsibility in their hands.

HISTORICAL BACKGROUND

"Paul is going to replace Titus on Crete with someone and therefore urges him to join him in doing ministry in Nicopolis (v. 12)." George W. Knight III, *Evangelical Commentary on the Bible* (Baker), 118.

Titus is to do all he can to provide for Zenas and Apollos in their journey. Supplying the needs of traveling missionaries as they departed so they would not suffer from lack of food on their journey was an honored expectation among early Christians.

Closing Salutations (v. 15)

The close of this letter is in keeping with the practice of letter writing of the day. The final greeting is typically Pauline. From his point of view, the Christian life is a matter of grace from beginning to end. We are saved by grace and sustained by grace, and we enter into our inheritance by grace.

"Grace be with you all" is a prayer for God's grace to be realized in each believer's life. "You all" suggests that although this letter is designated for Titus, Paul expects it to be shared with the entire Cretan church. Paul could ask no higher blessing on Titus and his charges than that they continue to receive the grace of God.

Section Summary

Paul closes the letter by commending Titus and the Cretan believers to the grace of God.

GUIDING QUESTIONS

1. What is the believer's proper attitude toward civic responsibilities?
2. What should govern the relationship of believers to non-Christians?
3. Discuss the doctrinal basis for Christian behavior. What are the key concepts involved?
4. What are the three sure things about a divisive person?

Philemon

INTRODUCTION

This beautiful and touching letter was written by the apostle Paul on behalf of Onesimus, a runaway slave. Paul was a prisoner when he wrote the letter. Customarily, interpreters have assumed this was Paul's Roman imprisonment mentioned in Acts. Caesarea and Ephesus have been suggested, however, as other possibilities.

After escaping from his master, Onesimus came into contact with the imprisoned apostle. Subsequently, Paul decided that Onesimus should return to his master. He wrote this brief letter to be delivered to Philemon at the slave's arrival.

HISTORICAL BACKGROUND

In a letter written in the early second century, Ignatius of Antioch mentioned an Onesimus who was the bishop of the church at Ephesus. The supposition that Onesimus the slave and Onesimus the bishop were the same person is attractive. If this is true, Philemon may have decided to free his slave in response to Paul's letter. Onesimus then showed himself to be worthy of the love and trust of Paul and Philemon by rising to a place of leadership in the church.

AUTHOR

Few scholars seriously question the Pauline authorship of this epistle. From the early Christian centuries, it has enjoyed almost unanimous acceptance as a letter written by Paul. The earliest collections of the New Testament letters included Philemon without dispute. Today, virtually all scholars accept Pauline authorship.

DATE OF WRITING

As with the other prison epistles, questions of place and origin interrelate. Three options have been suggested for the place of origin: Rome, Caesarea, and Ephesus. Clearly Paul was in prison at the time of writing (vv. 1,9,13,23). The traditional view identifies Rome as the origin of the letter.

HISTORICAL BACKGROUND

Those who decide for an Ephesian imprisonment place it early, about AD 55. Those who accept a Caesarean hypothesis place the letter at about AD 58. The traditional dating at Rome places the epistle at about AD 61.

OCCASION AND PURPOSE

Occasion. The letter makes clear the occasion for writing. Onesimus, a slave of Philemon—a wealthy Christian convert in the Lycus Valley—ran away from his master. After leaving his master, Onesimus became a Christian through his contact with Paul while Paul was in prison.

Onesimus served Paul faithfully for a time (v. 13), but he determined to return to Philemon to put his past life in order. A strong friendship developed, and Paul reminded Philemon of their relationship and suggested that his Christian commitment required such loving actions.

Purpose. Paul wrote Philemon to implore him to forgive and receive his runaway slave, Onesimus (v. 10). No doubt when Onesimus determined to get matters straight at home, some fear entered his heart. Even though his master was a good man (vv. 4–7), as a runaway slave, Onesimus deserved punishment. Paul took the role of a mediator, imploring Philemon to have mercy on this new Christian.

AUDIENCE

The mention of Archippus both in Col 4:17 and in verse 2 of Philemon suggests that the recipients of this letter lived in Colossae. Philemon was the principal recipient. He apparently was a slave owner from whom Onesimus had fled. Probably Philemon had been converted during Paul's three-year ministry in Ephesus (Acts 20:31).

We cannot positively identify Apphia and Archippus. Some have supposed that Apphia is the wife of Philemon and Archippus is their son. Paul also addressed the letter to the house church meeting at Philemon's home.

WORD PICTURE

Slavery in the First Century

The Roman world lived with slavery. From the earliest times, the government accepted and promoted the practice. In the Roman world, treatment of slaves varied considerably. By the first century, however, the institution of slavery was changing. Public sentiment decried harsh treatment of slaves, and many leading orators spoke against the institution. This caused many masters to free their slaves. Many slaves took the opportunity to run from their masters. They normally fled to large cities, where they could hide from the authorities. Although officially the government recognized the value of human life, many masters treated their slaves harshly. No doubt that was a fear in Onesimus's heart.

THEMES IN PHILEMON

Paul and Slavery

The obvious concern to contemporary Christians is the social institution of slavery. Many questions arise about the way Paul handled it. Why did he not forbid the institution? Why did he not recommend that Philemon release Onesimus? Why were his instructions so vague? Many people believe Paul moved too slowly in not condemning an evil institution.

Paul, however, taught equality. Colossians 3:18–4:1 contains some basic principles. Slaves served Christ despite their economic situation. Their owners were also slaves, only they were slaves to the Master in heaven. This equality was to lead the way to sympathy for each other. Further, God called people to serve him in varied circumstances, and he judged impartially. The application of these principles would, in fact, bring an end to the institution.

Philemon does not forbid slavery overtly. Slavery was not even the issue it was written to solve: It was the occasion that provided the opportunity to address another matter. The issue was Christian relationships. Nevertheless, Christian relationships bring an end to such evils as slavery. (For a more detailed treatment of this topic, see the article "Paul and Slavery" at the back of this book.)

Christian Fellowship

The primary message of this epistle is Christian fellowship. The idea occurs at strategic locations throughout the epistle. Fellowship is participation in the lives of others. Partners' lives interrelate at the deepest levels, and partnership became the main avenue of appeal from Paul to Philemon.

Embodiment of the Christian Mind

A third powerful message from the epistle is the expression of Christian thought in action. Expressions of Christian thought permeate the letter:

- Two people needed reconciliation;
- Paul pleaded the case of Onesimus, taking the side of the guilty in calling for forgiveness;
- Paul offered to pay the debt Onesimus owed, even though it was not his responsibility; and
- The reconciliation was, in essence, effected in Paul.

This epistle provides insight into Paul that no other does. Paul pondered the meaning of grace, the cross, and the nature of salvation. Apart from personal salvation, nothing equals Christlikeness in attitudes and actions. The gospel demands it. In the epistle to Philemon, Paul demonstrated it.

THE VALUE OF PHILEMON

Two features of this letter make it of great value in New Testament study. First, the letter provides an example of a Christian approach to the social problem of slavery. Attacking the institution forthrightly would have been futile. Paul, both in Philemon and in Col 4:1, urged masters to treat their slaves with compassion. Paul sounded no call for slaves to rise in armed rebellion, but he melted the resistance of both groups with a lavish outpouring of Christian love. He urged Philemon to receive Onesimus as a "dearly loved brother."

When a slave owner could refer to his slave as a brother in Christ, emancipation should not be far away. Christianity thus established conditions that made it impossible for slavery to endure.

This letter also presents an intimate, personal account of Paul. He writes not so much as a theologian or apostle to the Gentiles. Rather, he writes as a Christian man applying the gospel he has preached. His words show his integrity (v. 19) and genuine compassion for both Philemon (v. 7) and Onesimus (v. 16).

BASIC OUTLINE OF PHILEMON

I. The Salutation (vv. 1–3)
II. Prayer of Thanksgiving for Philemon (vv. 4–7)
III. A Good Word on Behalf of Onesimus (vv. 8–21)
IV. Paul's Personal Request (v. 22)
V. Greetings and Benediction (vv. 23–25)

QUESTIONS TO GUIDE YOUR STUDY

1. Describe the setting for this epistle. Who are the key characters?
2. How did Christians in Paul's day view the institution of slavery?
3. From this short letter, what can we learn about Paul's view of Christian fellowship?
4. What is the value of Philemon for present-day believers?

PHILEMON

THE SALUTATION (1–3)

Paul began this letter like his other epistles. He identified two writers, the readers, and sent a greeting. At the same time, this salutation is unique. Its brevity is noteworthy. But more significantly, Paul did not use his usual title in describing himself.

HISTORICAL BACKGROUND

Philemon

Philemon, whose name means "affectionate," owed his conversion to the Christian faith to the apostle Paul. Paul and Philemon became devoted friends. Paul's only epistle of a personal and private nature included in the New Testament was written to Philemon. A slave of Philemon, Onesimus, robbed him and fled to Rome. Paul wrote to Philemon concerning Onesimus. Philemon had a judicial right to punish severely or even kill Onesimus. Paul's short letter challenged Philemon to apply Christian love in dealing with Onesimus.

The Writers (v. 1a)

The epistle identifies two writers in the opening verse: Paul and Timothy. Normally Paul uses a title appropriate to his position. He did, however, refer to his situation by stating that he was a "prisoner of Christ Jesus."

The Readers (vv. 1b–2)

The letter appears to address four readers: Philemon, Apphia (probably his wife), Archippus, and "the church that meets in your home." The letter makes clear, however, that Paul directed his comments to Philemon alone. Most likely Paul included the others because they were part of Philemon's family and courtesy demanded it.

The Greeting (v. 3)

Paul's greeting was a standard greeting for that day to which he added distinctively Christian elements. The logical order preserves the way God works: Grace precedes and produces peace. These qualities come jointly from God the Father and Jesus. For Paul, Jesus performed the same activities as God. Particularly, he can supply grace and peace for the hearts of people.

PRAYER OF THANKSGIVING FOR PHILEMON (4–7)

As is common in Paul's letters, a prayer for the recipient follows the greeting. The prayer follows his customary pattern of thanksgiving and intercession.

Paul's Prayer (vv. 4–6)

When Paul thought of Philemon, he did so with joy and thankfulness. From Paul's prayer, two outstanding qualities of Philemon appear: faith and love. These two primary aspects of the Christian life are the cause of Paul's gratitude to God.

Commendation of Philemon (v. 7)

After concluding his prayer for Philemon, Paul stated a reason he expected Philemon to respond. In commending Philemon, Paul built on the expectation expressed in his prayer. He expected Philemon to do the "good thing" regarding Onesimus because Philemon was a man accustomed to doing "good things" for Christian people.

Paul accomplished three important tasks through this thanksgiving. First, he established goodwill between Philemon and himself. Second, Paul anticipated his case by stressing some of Philemon's good qualities. Third, he alluded to some particular matters that would be helpful to him later in summarizing his letter.

Section Summary

Paul referred to Philemon's generous acts of love toward other believers because he was about to address an important appeal to his friend. He wanted Philemon to do yet another loving act that would inspire his brothers.

WORD PICTURE

"Useful" and "Useless"

In describing this change of character, Paul used a double play on words. Both "useful" and "useless" are compound words containing a word that sounded exactly like *Christos* (Christ). What made such a difference in Onesimus's life? Christ had brought about the transformation.

PAUL'S PLEA FOR ACCEPTANCE OF ONESIMUS (8–21)

An Appeal to Love (vv. 8–14)

Paul knew he had the authority "in Christ" to command Philemon. He probably also believed Philemon would obey an apostolic injunction because he also recognized that authority. But Paul spurned the way of command. He preferred to appeal to the love of which Philemon had given such clear evidence.

Three people were intensely and personally involved in the transaction Paul had in mind. Paul, Onesimus, and Philemon all had a stake in it. Paul wanted all three, not just Onesimus and himself, to benefit from any decision made. Thus, he had to give Philemon an opportunity to act according to his faith and love. He would not deprive his friend of the privilege of doing a genuinely Christian deed.

In verse 10 the motive for Paul's letter becomes apparent. He is making an appeal for a slave belonging to Philemon. This is a "father" pleading for his "son." Onesimus had trusted Christ through the witness of the imprisoned apostle.

Onesimus's New Life. Christ brought about a change in Onesimus. He had gone from being a "useless" to a "useful" person.

Paul desired to keep Onesimus with him. Indeed, he could have justified it as a service rendered to him by his friend in his imprisonment. But to do so would have been wrong, for it would have taken the decision out of Philemon's hand. But Paul emphasized how difficult the decision was. It was like sending his very "heart." It was as though Paul himself stood before Philemon in the person of the slave.

The Conclusion of the Appeal (vv. 15–22)

The Providence of God (vv. 15–16). We must assume Onesimus had run away from Philemon. There is a great deal about the whole episode we would like to know. Why had Philemon not won Onesimus to Christ? Perhaps his influence bore fruit later when his slave came to know Paul. At any rate, Paul suggests (v. 15) that the providence of God was at work in the whole affair. If Onesimus had not run away, he might not have become a believer. Because he was a Christian, however, the temporary relationship between the slave and his owner had become eternal. They would inherit the kingdom together.

Paul's Relationship to Philemon (vv. 17–21). "Partner" is one of Paul's favorite words for describing relationships among Christians. They share together the mutual life in Christ, in terms of both its benefits and its responsibilities. Paul and Philemon were partners in the greatest of all enterprises. Paul emphasized this partnership in the address when he called Philemon a "coworker."

The apostle went even further. If Philemon suffered any loss, he was not to look to Onesimus for repayment. Paul himself would stand good for any debt incurred because of the slave's escape. We have no way of knowing how Paul meant to repay such a debt.

Philemon refreshed the hearts of the saints (v. 7). Now Paul made the request that his friend might do the same for him.

PERSONAL APPLICATION

Love and confidence are much more effective than hostility and suspicion in calling forth the best in other people. We generally strive to fulfill the expectations of those we love.

Section Summary

By virtue of his new life in Christ, Onesimus had a new character. He had been transformed by the gospel.

PAUL'S FINAL REMARKS AND PERSONAL REQUEST (22–25)

Paul reinforced his appeal to Philemon by an affirmation of confidence in him. He expected his friend to go beyond what he asked him to do in his letter. If Philemon merited this confidence at all, Paul did not have to spell out clearly what he should do. Love always goes far beyond duty.

Paul was in prison, but he was evidently optimistic about the future. He believed he would be freed, and he apparently planned to return to the area of his former ministry to visit the churches. Believers normally provided food and lodging for traveling evangelists like Paul. The request for a "guest room" was normal under the circumstances.

Paul usually ended his letters with a prayer for the greatest blessing for all of his recipients. That blessing is "grace." Paul's request is that God's grace be given to the whole church.

QUESTIONS TO GUIDE YOUR STUDY

1. Why did Paul write his letter to Philemon?
2. What characteristics make this letter unique in the New Testament?
3. What lessons about Christian attitudes might we learn from the interaction we see in these verses? What can we learn from Paul about dealing with conflict situations?
4. We have no record of Philemon's answer to Paul. What do you suppose was Philemon's response?

Hebrews

INTRODUCTION

Since no author is readily identified, the author of the book of Hebrews is anonymous. Despite the difficulties in determining the author, the book's majestic picture of Christ commended its contents to the early church.

The writer of Hebrews presented Christ as superior to the Old Testament prophets, angels, Moses, Joshua, and Aaron. He laced magnificent discussions of Christ's person and work into frightening passages that warn against apostasy (1:1–2:4). The superiority of Christ led the writer to appeal for faith (chap. 2), stamina (12:3–11), and good works (13:16).

HEBREWS IN A NUTSHELL

Purpose:	To urge Christians to continue their profession of Christ.
Key Words:	*Better, Superior.* Christ is superior to the angels, Moses, and Aaron. Hebrews has a *better* priesthood, covenant, and sacrifice.
Theme:	Jesus Christ is the High Priest who offered himself as the perfect sacrifice for sins.
Major Doctrines:	The person of Christ—both his humanity and his deity; Christ's atonement for our sins.

AUTHOR

Hebrews is anonymous, and attempts to establish its authorship are conjecture. Nowhere in its thirteen chapters does Hebrews mention any possibilities. The readers obviously knew who the writer was, but the name has not been preserved.

The early church was uncertain about the author of this anonymous letter. Eastern Christendom usually regarded Paul as the author, while Western Christendom doubted Pauline authorship and initially excluded Hebrews from the canon because of this uncertainty.

The early church historian Eusebius quoted the biblical scholar Origen as saying, "Who it was that really wrote the epistle Hebrews, God only knows" *(Ecclesiastical History*, 6.25). Despite this verdict, many varied opinions about the authorship have arisen.

Christians in the Eastern Roman Empire regarded Paul as the author. Hebrews contains statements like Paul's view of the preexistence and creatorship of Christ (cp. Heb 1:1–4 with Col 1:15–17). Both Heb 8:6 and 2 Cor 3:4–11 discuss the new covenant. These factors inclined some observers to consider Paul as the author.

Christians in the Western Roman Empire originally questioned Pauline authorship of Hebrews. They observed that the statement of 2:3 suggests that the author was not an apostle. Also, the Old Testament quotations in Hebrews come from the Greek Septuagint, but Paul used both the Hebrew text and the Septuagint. Furthermore, none of Paul's other writings are anonymous, and the polished Greek style of Hebrews does not resemble the explosive, dynamic style of most of Paul's writings. Shortly before AD 400, Christian leaders in the West extended acceptance to the book of Hebrews. They absorbed it into the Pauline collection of writings without distinguishing it from the rest.

Tertullian advocated Barnabas as the author of Hebrews. Barnabas's background as a Levite would have qualified him to write the book, but support for his authorship is lacking in the early church. Martin Luther suggested Apollos as the author. In Apollos's favor is his reputation for eloquence (Acts 18:24), but against him is the absence of early church tradition accepting him as author. Some have suggested Luke since his knowledge of Greek would favor him, but Luke was a Gentile. The outlook of Hebrews is definitely Jewish. The nineteenth-century church historian Adolf von Harnack suggested Priscilla, the wife of Aquila, as the author. She and her husband would have known Pauline theology and Jewish practice, but the early church was silent about nominating her as author.

Modern Greek texts of Hebrews bear the title "To the Hebrews." It is best to accept this title and recognize that we cannot know for sure who wrote Hebrews. Despite our ignorance of the author, we can use and understand what he wrote.

AUDIENCE

The title "to the Hebrews" reflects the conviction that Jewish Christians were the original readers of the writing. Frequent appeals to the Old Testament, an extensive knowledge of Jewish ritual, and the warning not to return to Jewish ritual support this conviction.

One might believe that the Jewish Christians who read Hebrews lived in Palestine. According to 2:3, however, the readers may not have seen or heard Jesus during his earthly ministry. The verse suggests that the readers had been dependent on the first hearers of the Christian message to share it with them. Doubtless, most Palestinian Christians heard Jesus preach and teach.

According to 6:10, the readers of Hebrews had resources enough to assist other believers; Palestinian Christians were poor and needed aid (Acts 11:27–30; Rom 15:26). These facts indicate that the readers were not from Palestine.

The statement in 13:24, "Those who are from Italy send you greetings," sounds as if Italians away from their home were returning greetings to friends in Rome. If this is true, Rome is the probable destination of the writing. A second fact favoring this view is that a knowledge of Hebrews first appears in Clement's First Epistle, which was written in Rome.

PURPOSE FOR WRITING

The purpose of Hebrews is closely linked to the identity of its recipients. All agree that the letter is written for Christians who are being urged to continue their profession of faith in Christ.

Wherever the recipients lived, they were well known to the writer. He described them as generous (6:10) but immature (5:11–14). He is aware of their persecution (10:32–34; 12:4), and he plans to visit them soon (13:19,23).

The writer rebuked the readers for not meeting together often enough (10:24–25). They are in danger of lapsing into sin (3:12–14). Perhaps the readers were a Jewish-Christian group who had broken away from the chief body of Christians in the area. They were considering returning to Judaism to avoid persecution. The author wrote to warn them against such apostasy (6:4–9; 10:26–31) and to help them return to the mainstream of Christian fellowship.

DATE OF WRITING

The date of the writing of Hebrews is difficult to determine. We must date the book before AD 95, when Clement referred to it. The writer used a present-tense verb in 10:11 ("stands") to describe the ministry of the priests in the Jerusalem temple. This indicates that sacrifices were still being offered in the days of the writer.

The Roman army destroyed the temple in AD 70. Persecution intensified as that day drew near (see 10:32–34). Timothy was still alive (13:23). The best option for the date is the mid-to-late 60s before the Romans destroyed the temple.

LITERARY FORM

Opening. Letters in the New Testament period began with specific salutations and concluded with benedictions and farewells. They were written to meet needs in the life of the church. Hebrews has some, but not all, of these characteristics. The letter begins without a salutation and omits the naming of the author and addressees.

Language. The language of Hebrews is elegant and carefully constructed. Its excellent Greek, the language in which the letter was originally written, does not clearly show up in English translations that strive for readability.

Oratorical Style. Was the writer penning a letter to a specific group of Christians, or was the letter a summary of a sermon made available to several Christian congregations? "Time is too short for me to tell" (11:32) seems to indicate a sermon; however, the writer knew specific details about the congregation (5:11–12; 6:9–10; 10:32–34; 12:4; 13:7). This suggests a letter written to a specific location. The statement in 13:22 also requires that we view the writing as a letter penned in the style of an earnest warning to a specific congregation.

Closing. The book concludes with a benediction, some personal observations, and a farewell (13:20–25).

SPECIAL FEATURES OF LETTER TO THE HEBREWS

Original Greek Text. The Greek text of the letter to the Hebrews has high literary qualities and reflects an elegant vocabulary.

Use of Old Testament Quotations. It also makes frequent allusions to and quotes from the Old Testament. Some passages such as Ps 110:1, 4 appear repeatedly (1:13; 6:20; 7:17,21; 10:12–13). The quotations do not serve as mere confirmations of the author's opinions; they provide the foundation for the presentation itself.

Doctrines of Christ. The Christology of Hebrews is incredibly rich and varied. Over twenty titles or names are used for Christ. Both the humanity and the deity of Christ are emphasized in Hebrews.

Warnings. A group of five warnings appear in the argument of Hebrews. These warnings are found in 2:1–4; 3:7–4:13; 5:11–6:20; 10:26–39; and 12:15–29. The writer was anxious that his listeners pay special attention to the voice of the living God. Most of the warnings deal with the danger of neglecting the salvation in Christ or missing out on it because of unbelief, apostasy, or compromise.

THE DOCTRINES OF HEBREWS

The Letter to the Hebrews emphasizes the person of Christ. It presents a Jesus who is truly human (2:18), realistically tempted (4:15), and obedient to death (3:2; 13:12). The suffering of Jesus taught him the value of obedience (5:8).

Hebrews also emphasizes the finality of Christ's work. The sacrifices offered by Jewish priests in the temple reminded the worshipers of sin, but the sacrifice of Christ removed sin (10:1–4). The priests of Judaism repeatedly offered sacrifices that did not take away sin (10:11). Christ's single offering of himself forever removed the sin that hindered fellowship with God (10:12–14).

THE THEOLOGICAL SIGNIFICANCE OF HEBREWS

The author of Hebrews pointed his readers to the superiority of Jesus Christ. He is superior to the prophets (1:1–3), superior to the angels (1:4–2:18), and superior to Moses (3:1–13). He provides a superior priesthood on the basis of a superior covenant (4:14–10:31). Not only is Jesus superior to the foundational aspects of Judaism, but he also is superior to any aspect of contemporary religion. This means that Jesus is not just one good option among many ways of drawing near to God; he is the *only* way. Because of the superiority of Jesus, we must not neglect such a great salvation that he has provided with his sacrificial death (2:3; 10:1–18).

Jesus, the superior Savior, is also the superior Priest. We can come to him in times of trouble, suffering, and struggle. In him we will find a sympathetic Priest (4:14–16) who offers grace in time of need. Thus, we can and should draw near to him in worship (10:19–25), live by faith (11:1–40), persevere to the end (12:1–29), and live a life of love (13:1–25).

THE RELEVANCE OF HEBREWS FOR CHRISTIANS TODAY

Hebrews is among the least read, least studied, and least preached from books of the New Testament. Modern readers sometimes have problems with its descriptions of ancient religious practices. Readers in every century have been confused and disturbed by its harsh warnings. However, those who dig into Hebrews discover that it has much to say to us today.

Above all, Hebrews challenges us to be faithful to Christ, no matter what the cost. Fair-weather Christianity finds no comfort in the book of Hebrews. Our lukewarm complacency is shattered by its words of warning, and our faith is stirred by its words of challenge. We are warned against becoming too comfortable with this world and its values. We are reminded that we are pilgrims on the way to glory and that we are to live in light of the values of that eternal kingdom.

As we walk this pilgrim way, Christ is fully adequate to meet our needs. Through him, we have access to God in prayer and worship, and we have a fellowship of mutual encouragement with others who are marching to Zion. Christ has passed this way himself; therefore, he helps and encourages us as we encounter various trials and temptations.

BASIC OUTLINE FOR HEBREWS

1. The Superiority of Christ over the Old Testament Prophets (1:1–2)
2. The Superiority of Christ over Angels (1:4–2:18)
3. The Superiority of Christ over Moses (3:1–19)
4. The Superiority of Christ over Joshua (4:1–13)
5. The Superiority of Christ over Aaron (4:14–10:18)
6. The Practice of Spiritual Endurance (10:19–12:29)
7. Final Exhortations (13:1–25)

QUESTIONS TO GUIDE YOUR STUDY

1. Who were the readers of the book of Hebrews?
2. What was the writer's purpose for his letter?
3. What key doctrines does the author address in this letter?
4. What is unique about Hebrews?
5. What in this letter makes it relevant to today's readers?

HEBREWS 1

The revelation of God given through Christ is both superior and final. The writer's majestic descriptions of Jesus in these verses implies that in both *quality* and *quantity* God has no further revelation to give other than what he has already given in Jesus.

JESUS IS SUPERIOR TO THE PROPHETS (1:1–4)

God Spoke Through the Prophets (v. 1)

Without any salutation, the writer of Hebrews launched his letter. From the first sentence, he issued a powerful proclamation of the good news of God through Jesus Christ the Son. This introduction is concise. At the same time, it is astoundingly broad in its scope. "God spoke to our ancestors by the prophets" (v. 1), leaves the clear impression the original readers of this letter were Jewish. The Hebrew prophets were God's spokesmen who uniquely brought the word of the Lord's judgment and the word of the Lord's loving-kindness to his chosen people.

The Hebrew people built their theology on the conviction that God *exists*, that he is *one*, and that he *has spoken*. The prophetic tradition was forward-looking. In that tradition, men like Amos and Micah and women like Miriam (Exod 15:20) and Anna (Luke 2:36) were caught up by God's Spirit and compelled to proclaim his Word in a language clearly understood by the common people. As Amos said, "A lion has roared; who will not fear? The Lord God has spoken, who will not prophesy?" (Amos 3:8).

The prophets' saying, "The Lord God has spoken," was the standard that marked Israel's dynamic progression toward the Messiah. The prophets were both seers of the messianic hope and speakers for God concerning the coming revelation of redemption.

God Now Speaks Through His Son (vv. 2–4)

Now, however, "in these last days" God "has spoken to us by his Son. God has appointed him heir of all things and made the universe through him" (v. 2).

No longer must God's message be relayed through the prophets. It now comes directly through the Son, who is "the exact expression of his nature, sustaining all things by his powerful word." (v. 3). This verse reminds the reader of John's insight that "through him, and apart from him not one thing was created that has been created" (John 1:3), and of Paul's profound word that "by him all things hold together" (Col 1:17). In Christ all the galaxies of the universe and every last atomic particle in all creation hold together.

As the writer asserted that Christ is superior to the Old Testament prophets, he made seven descriptive statements about Christ:

- He is the Son of God.
- He is the Heir of the universe.
- He is the Creator.
- He is the Radiance of divine glory.
- He is the Sustainer of the universe.
- He is the Redeemer from sin.
- He is the Exalted One.

These statements effectively drive home the writer's point that Christ is God's final and most complete message to human beings.

When the Son finished his redemptive work on earth, he sat down "at the right hand of the Majesty on high" (v. 3). As a result, he "became

WORD PICTURE

Exact Expression

These words are the translation of the Greek word *charakter*. It means "impression, stamp." It refers to an engraved character or impress made by a die or a seal. It also indicates the characteristic trait or distinctive mark. It was used with special reference to any distinguishing peculiarity and, hence, indicated an exact reproduction. Fritz Rienecker, *Linguistic Key to the Greek New Testament* (Zondervan, 1980), 664.

superior to the angels, just as the name he inherited is more excellent than theirs" (v. 4). Christians are redeemed by a mighty Savior whose name is above every name. Seldom do we see so much "heavy" doctrine compressed into so few verses. These four verses have been called by some the most beautiful passage in the New Testament.

In the wake of these inspired words, the author of Hebrews has stirred the imagination of his readers. He has rooted them in their spiritual heritage, reminded them of their cleansing, and pointed them to their destiny.

Section Summary

The Hebrew prophets had been God's spokespeople who uniquely brought the word to his chosen people. No longer now must God's message be relayed through the prophets. It now comes directly through the Son, who is "the exact expression of his nature, sustaining all things by his powerful word" (1:3).

JESUS IS SUPERIOR TO THE ANGELS (1:5–14)

The writer first declared that Jesus is superior to the angels and that his name is more excellent than theirs (v. 4). Next, he focused on the witness of the Scriptures in support of that declaration. For the most part, the writer drew his quotes from the Septuagint.

Psalm 2:7 and 2 Samuel 7:14. Quoting from the Septuagint, the Greek translation of Ps 2:7 and 2 Sam 7:14, he stated that the superiority of Jesus Christ to angels is demonstrated by the fact that of none of the angels did God ever say, "You are my Son; today I have become your Father," or, "I will be his Father, and he will be my Son" (v. 5).

Deuteronomy 32:43 and Psalms 97:7; 104:4. Later, when God "brings his firstborn into the world" (v. 6), the Scriptures (Deut 32:43 and Ps 97:7) demand, "Let all God's angels worship him" (v. 6). Then, referring to the angels as messengers, note the witness of Psalm 104:4: "He makes his angels winds, and his servants a fiery flame" (v. 7).

Psalm 45:6–7. The writer of Hebrews quoted Ps 45:6–7 to magnify God's moral uprightness: "The scepter of your kingdom is a scepter of justice. You have loved righteousness and hated lawlessness" and to demonstrate how God anointed the Son "with the oil of joy" above his companions (vv. 8–9).

Psalms 102:25–27; 110:1. The writer of Hebrews quoted from Ps 102:25–27 and Ps 110:1 to illustrate God's permanence and the Son's exaltation at God's "right hand," together with his ultimate victory over all his spiritual and mortal enemies (vv. 10–13).

The angels, according to the Scriptures, are "ministering spirits sent out to serve those who are going to inherit salvation" (v. 14).

HISTORICAL BACKGROUND

The Septuagint

The Septuagint is the oldest Greek translation of the Hebrew Old Testament. It contains several apocryphal books. Most New Testament quotations of the Old Testament are from the Septuagint.

Section Summary

The writer of Hebrews brought to bear the witness of the Scriptures in support of the declaration that Jesus is superior to the angels. He used several Old Testament passages to demonstrate Christ's superiority.

QUESTIONS TO GUIDE YOUR STUDY

1. Before Christ came, what was the role of the prophets?
2. Why is Christ superior to the prophets?
3. The writer made seven statements regarding Christ. What point do these statements collectively make?
4. From the writer's use of the Old Testament, what do we learn about Christ's superiority to the angels?

HEBREWS 2

The writer of Hebrews presented his first exhortation to remain faithful to Christ (vv. 1–4). If the giving of the law in the Old Testament led its violators to be punished, how much greater will be the punishment for those who neglect the great salvation in Christ.

In the second part of this chapter, the writer discussed the incarnation, which resulted in two benefits for believers: (1) The death and resurrection of Jesus made it possible for all believers to overcome the fear of death (vv. 14–15). (2) Because the incarnate Christ suffered and overcame temptation, he is able to help believers when they are tempted (v. 18).

A WARNING AGAINST NEGLECTING CHRIST (2:1–3)

The writer warned his readers that in the light of all God's redemptive activity, his angelic messengers, and what he communicated through his Son, they need to pay close attention. God communicated a message that is a matter of life and death. If they really understand this, they won't drift away (v. 1).

At this point the writer used a how-much-more argument. He reminded his readers that when angels delivered God's message and it was not obeyed, those who failed to listen received the punishment they deserved. If this were true of a message delivered by angels, *how much more* would it be true of a message delivered by God's Son (v. 2).

This great salvation "had its beginning when it was spoken of by the Lord" (v. 3), Jesus Christ. He declared the good news by:

- His preaching
- His teaching
- His good works

WORD PICTURE

Drift Away

The Greek verb for *drift away* is used only this one time in the New Testament. Xenophon used it of a river flowing by. B. F. Westcott said it's a picture "of being swept along past the sure anchorage which is within reach." A. T. Robertson, *Word Pictures in the New Testament*, vol. 5, 342.

PERSONAL APPLICATION

Verse 3 contains one of the great texts of the Bible, "How will we escape if we neglect such a great salvation?" While this text, in recent times, has most often been used as an evangelistic call to commit one's life to Christ, it is actually a word directly addressed to Christians. Read in this light, it calls believers to moral alertness and spiritual watchfulness. It warns against laziness. It reminds believers not to ignore the salvation God has given, is giving, and will give to those who trust and obey him.

- His virgin birth
- His sinless life
- His personal example
- His sacrificial death
- His powerful resurrection

The readers of this letter were not personal witnesses of what Jesus did and taught. But they had been instructed by those who had been with Jesus. Moreover, the testimony concerning Jesus had been confirmed to these Christians by the Holy Spirit. This confirmation came through:

- Signs and wonders
- Variety of miracles
- Gifts of the Holy Spirit

SO GREAT SALVATION (2:4)

For the sake of convenience, salvation can be viewed from the two perspectives of Christ's saving work and the believer's experience of salvation. Christ's saving work involves already completed, ongoing, and future saving activity. The apex of Christ's completed work is his sacrificial death: Christ came to "give his life as a ransom for many" (Mark 10:45); Christ "entered the most holy place once for all time . . . by his own blood, having obtained eternal redemption" (Heb 9:12); "In Christ, God was reconciling the world to himself, not counting their trespasses against them, and he has committed the message of reconciliation to us" (2 Cor 5:19). Here *ransom, redemption,* and *reconciliation* are synonyms for salvation. With reference to Christ's atoning work, the believer can confess, "I was saved when Jesus died for me."

Christ's present saving work primarily concerns Christ's role as Mediator (Rom 8:34; Heb 7:25; 1 John 2:1). Christ's future saving work chiefly concerns Christ's coming again "to bring salvation to those who are waiting for him" (Heb 9:28) and salvation from the wrath of God's final judgment (Rom 5:9–10). Though Christ's sacrificial death is central, Christ's saving activity extends to the whole of his life, including his birth (Gal 4:4–5), resurrection (Rom 4:25; 1 Cor 15:17), and ascension (Rom 8:34).

The believer's experience also offers a perspective for viewing salvation. The experience again embraces the past, present, and future. God's initial work in the believer's life breaks down into various scenes: conviction of sin (John 16:8); repentance (turning) from sin to God (Luke 15:7,10; 2 Cor 7:10); faith which involves commitment of one's whole life to Christ (John 3:16,36); and confession of Christ as Lord (Acts 2:21; Rom 10:9–10). Scripture uses a wealth of images to describe this act: *new birth* (John 3:3; Titus 3:5); *new creation* (2 Cor 5:17); *adoption*

(Rom 8:15; Gal 4:4–5; Eph 1:5); *empowerment to be God's children* (John 1:12); *the status of "saints"* (1 Cor 1:2; 2 Cor 1:1). This initial work in the believer's life is often termed *justification*. Justification, however, also embraces God's final judgment (Rom 2:13; 3:20,30).

God's ongoing work in the believer's life concerns the process of maturing in Christ (Heb 2:3; 1 Pet 2:2), growing in Christ's service (Eph 4:15; 2 Pet 3:18), and experiencing victory over sin through the power of the Holy Spirit (Rom 7–8). Here sin remains a reality in the believer's life (Rom 7; 1 John 1:8–2:1). The believer is caught in between what God has begun and what God is yet to complete (Phil 1:6; 2:12).

God's yet-to-be-finished work in the lives of all believers is sometimes called *glorification* (Rom 8:17; Heb 2:10). Scripture, however, uses a wealth of terms for this future saving work: *adoption* (Rom 8:23); *redemption* (Luke 21:28; Rom 8:23; Eph 4:30); *salvation* (Rom 13:11; Heb 1:14; 9:28; 1 Pet 1:5; 2:2); and *sanctification* (1 Thess 5:23). God's future work involves more than the individual; God's future work extends to the renewal of heaven and earth.

Section Summary

The writer presented his first exhortation to his readers to remain faithful to Christ and warned them against ignoring him. The superiority of Christ makes the failure to believe on him a feared experience.

THE VALUE OF CHRIST'S INCARNATION (2:5–13)

The World Is Subjected to the Crucified Lord (vv. 5–9)

God hasn't put angels in charge of the world to come. God's intent is to give human beings dominion in the world to come. Here the writer quoted Ps 8.

The writer observed that the world is not yet subject to human beings. He interprets Ps 8 as applying to the world to come.

While we don't see the present world subject to man, we see Jesus who, for a time, was made lower than the angels. The Son became human so that he might suffer and taste death for everyone. God's love of and grace toward sinful human beings led the Son to be made lower than the angels for the purpose of fully tasting death for everyone.

Jesus Is the Author of Our Salvation (vv. 10–13)

As the "pioneer" of our salvation, the Son has been made "perfect through sufferings" (v. 10). The word *pioneer* here may be translated "leader," "originator," or "trailblazer." He didn't need to be made perfect or complete because he was sinful. He entered time and became subject to the processes of time so that he might bring with him many sons to glory.

HISTORICAL BACKGROUND

It has been claimed that the Dead Sea Scrolls show the sectarians of Qumran believed that the coming age would be marked by the dominion of Michael and his angelic subordinates.

OLD TESTAMENT REFERENCE

"What is a human being that you remember him,
a son of man that you look after him?
You made him little less than God
and crowned him with glory and honor.
You made him ruler over the works of your hands;
you put everything under his feet." (Ps 8:4–6)

WORD PICTURE

Taste Death

"The phrase to taste death occurs in the gospels (Matt 16:28; Mark 9:1; Luke 9:27; John 8:52), though not in ancient Greek. It means to see death (Heb 11:5), a bitter experience, not a rapid sip (Moffatt). The death of Christ (Andrew Fuller) was sufficient for all, efficient for some." A. T. Robertson, *WPNT*, vol. 5, 346.

The writer of Hebrews went on to explain that because of the incarnation, believers become part of God's spiritual family. As God is our Father, so Jesus is our elder Brother. He is not ashamed to identify with us as members of his own family. In God's gracious providence, we are his kin. Christ, who sets Christians apart in salvation and authentic holiness of life, and the ones who are so set apart have the same source.

WORD PICTURE

As Christians, our roots are established fully and firmly in God's Son, the pioneer of our great salvation and the source of our entire being. Our fruits are nurtured by God's indwelling Spirit, who is the source of the believer's productivity. If we are rightly rooted in the source, fruit bearing will appropriately come. If we are truly fruitful, it is because our life and work have him as our spiritual source.

Section Summary

The author concluded that Christ's incarnation and crucifixion enhance his superiority and qualify him to become a spiritual trailblazer for believers—that is, the pioneer of their salvation.

RESULTS OF THE INCARNATION (2:14–18)

Christians Are No Longer Enslaved to Death (vv. 14–15)

Jesus shared our human nature and became subject to death. His tasting death had the result of destroying the devil, the one who has the power of death. In doing so, he liberates human beings who have been enslaved by the fear of death all of their lives.

Adam and Eve disobeyed God and ate the forbidden fruit of which God had said, "For on the day you eat from it, you will certainly die" (Gen 2:17). The moment they willfully disobeyed him, they began to die; and the human race has been dying ever since. Because of man's fallen and sinful condition, he is enslaved to death—his last, great enemy. However, Jesus conquered this last great enemy in the resurrection. His resurrection took the sting out of death and the victory out of the grave, and now death is swallowed up in life (v. 15).

PERSONAL APPLICATION

Make an inventory of some of your fears. Notice how each of those fears is related to the fear of death. There is an inverse relationship between fear of death and enjoyment of life. The less fear of death, the greater the capacity to live—even in this world.

Jesus Helps Us Overcome Temptation (vv. 16–18)

The writer revealed a second great benefit of the incarnation for believers. Jesus identified not with angels (v. 16) but with us "so that he could become a merciful and faithful high priest in matters pertaining to God, to make atonement for the sins of the people" (v. 17).

In the Jewish system, the sins of the people were forgiven as the priests made prescribed sacrifices on behalf of sinners. Atonement of some kind is at the heart of every religion. That is, religion universally offers some way for sinners to get rid of their sin. In most religious systems, human acts are required to banish sin and bridge the chasm between humanity and deity. In Christianity, however, it is Jesus Christ himself, the "faithful high priest," whose divine act of self-sacrifice on the cross has banished our sin and bridged the gap.

WORD PICTURE

Because Jesus Christ knows human life personally, with its suffering and temptation, "he is able to help those who are tempted" (v. 18). In what ways have you been tempted recently? Being tempted is not a sin. Jesus was sinless, yet he knew temptation better than any human being. Next time you are tempted remember Jesus.

The pioneer of our salvation is our trailblazer to glory. The writer simply stated that "he is able" (v. 18). What an incomparable affirmation about our Lord and Savior!

Section Summary

Christ's incarnation gives believers two benefits. First, the death and resurrection of Jesus make it possible for all believers to overcome the fear of death. Second, because the incarnate Christ suffered and overcame temptation, he is able to help believers when they are tempted.

QUESTIONS TO GUIDE YOUR STUDY

1. What is the content of the writer's warning in Hebrews 2:1–4?
2. How would you define *salvation?* What does it entail? How is it made possible?
3. One of the believer's benefits of the incarnation is that Christians must no longer fear death. How did Jesus accomplish this?
4. A second benefit of the incarnation is that Christ is able to aid us in our temptation. What has qualified him to do so?

WORD PICTURE

He Himself Has Suffered

The tense of the verb suffer (the Greek *perfect* tense) is important in understanding the impact of this statement. "The perfect tense serves to emphasize that, though the temptation Christ suffered in the flesh is a thing of the past, yet its effect is permanent, the effect of compassion and understanding as He aids us in the hour of our temptation." (Fritz Rienecker, *Linguistic Key to the Greek New Testament* [Grand Rapids: Zondervan, 1980], p. 671)

HEBREWS 3

In this chapter the author contrasted Moses with Christ and clearly proved the superiority of Christ over Moses and his ministry. He also mentioned the unbelief shown by the Jewish generations in the time of Moses and warned his readers not to follow their evil example.

In comparing Jesus to Moses, the writer pointed out that Moses was a servant of God in God's house, that is, among the people of God. In contrast, however, Jesus was God's Son, serving *over* that house. The superiority of Jesus's position is obvious (vv. 5–6).

Joshua led the Jews of his generation to rest in Canaan. Jesus, however, brought the people of God into a resting place that provided eternal spiritual benefits (4:1–10). The superiority of the destination provided by Jesus is again obvious.

The writer was aware that a crisis faced his readers just as the Jews in the lifetime of Moses and Joshua confronted crises. He warned that unbelief could prevent them from entering a relationship of promise just as it had in an earlier generation. The problem earlier was unbelief (3:18; 4:11), and he wanted his readers to avoid the spiritual defeat caused by unbelief.

THE SUPERIORITY OF JESUS TO MOSES (3:1–6)

Because of Christ's superiority in providing salvation to those who are willing to receive it, Christians are to consider Jesus further (v. 1). The writer, for the first time, addressed and identified the first recipients of this letter. The writer called them "holy brothers and sisters." That is, they are brothers and sisters together with the writer in the family of God, and they are "holy" in the sense that they are separated to God in their life and conduct.

THE SUPERIORITY OF CHRIST'S WORK IN HEBREWS

WORK	PASSAGE	RESULT
1. Priesthood	4:14–7:28	He pointed to the superior priesthood of Christ.
2. Covenant	8:1–13	He explained the superior covenant Christ founded in relationship to human beings.
3. Sacrifice	9:1–10:18	He described the superior sacrifice Christ offered for our redemption.

This is a powerful reminder that the church must never draw its net of evangelism so loosely and so irresponsibly as to count its membership as anything other than a holy brotherhood closely related to our holy God. A Christian's relationship to him should show up in every relationship and circumstance.

Christians share in a "heavenly calling" (v. 1). All believers have a gift. Some are chosen for one office and some for another, but God has called from heaven to bring life and light through the gospel. The writer urged his readers to "consider Jesus, the apostle and high priest of our confession." This is a unique challenge. Nowhere else in the Bible do we find one that compares precisely to it. To consider Jesus is to observe him to understand his profound significance. It is an effort to perceive him in all his fullness, concentrating on the true meaning of his life and work.

Jesus the Apostle. As "the apostle," Jesus is God's special Messenger and authoritative Spokesman concerning his new covenant of grace made with his believing and behaving people.

Jesus the High Priest. As the "high priest," he is the One who enables and mediates our confession. As God's special Apostle, Jesus has come from God to us; and as High Priest, he has gone to God for us. He has done, once for all, the work of going between "the Judge of the whole earth" (Gen 18:25) and us. Our confession, as Christians, is that Jesus Christ, God's Apostle and our High Priest, is our Lord. No formula, no creed, no set of doctrines, no human document can ever be the proper object of the believer's confession. We confess Christ. With our minds and hearts we believe and are justified (Rom 10:10), and with our lives and mouths we confess and are saved.

CONSIDERING JESUS

HIS ROLE	HIS MINISTRY
Apostle	God's special Messenger and Spokesman concerning his new covenant of grace
High Priest	The One who enables and mediates our confession before God

We are to consider Jesus because of his faithfulness (v. 2). Jesus was "faithful" to the Father "who appointed him" or commissioned him as Moses had been "faithful . . . in all God's household" (v. 2). This reference to Moses picks up the statement attributed to the Lord in Num 12:7 and acknowledges the special respect or even veneration paid by the Jews to Moses, their great deliverer from Egyptian bondage. The house of God is God's entire household or family, and this term is meant to include all God's redeemed people delivered from the bondage of sin by his grace.

Jesus is more worthy of glory than Moses, just as the builder of a house is worthy of more honor than the house he has built (v. 3). "The one who built everything," it is observed parenthetically, is God (v. 4). Moses was faithful as a steward, "but Christ was faithful as a son" (vv. 5–6).

The writer sounded a word of caution to keep his readers from turning aside from their commitment to God: "We are that household if we hold on to our confidence and the hope in which we boast" (v. 6). Christians have always been prone to relax in their spiritual discipline, to drift, to grow lukewarm, and even to let go of their first love. This word is an antidote for the poison of such carelessness. Believers are the family in God's own household if they hold fast to him as he holds fast to them. If we proudly hold to our hope in Him, remaining steadfast to the end, he will surely provide his loving care and never-failing protection.

Section Summary

Jesus is God's Son who reigns over the household of God's people. He was superior to Moses, who was merely a servant within God's household. Moses was faithful as a steward, but Christ is faithful as a Son.

A WARNING AGAINST UNBELIEF (3:7–19)

Hebrews 3:7–11 is a quotation of Ps 95:7–11. The preacher of Hebrews loved the Bible. He quoted it freely and at length. He skillfully appropriated it to make some of his important points. Here he called it to mind with special attribution, "As the Holy Spirit says" (v. 7). It was God's Spirit who warned the Jews in the psalmist's time, and it is his Spirit who warns Christians in our own time not to harden their hearts in rebellion (vv. 7–11).

The author of Hebrews appropriately used this psalm to remind his readers to keep on hearing God's voice, to keep on walking in God's ways, and to keep on holding fast to the hope of entering God's eternal rest, which he is preparing for his faithful people. The psalmist here linked together two dramatic events from Israel's Exodus from Egypt: (1) their murmuring anxiety over the apparent lack of water in the wilderness, and (2) the pessimistic report of the apprehensive spies who caused the people to shrink back from the immediate conquest of the promised land that God intended. Both incidents illustrate their lack of faith. This passage in Hebrews deals with that same kind of complaining and fearful unbelief in the lives of Christians today.

"Watch out" (v. 12) is a solemn warning. Caution in the presence of aggressive evil is appropriate. Humility is in order. Those who think they are standing must be careful they don't fall (1 Cor 10:12). The writer issued this particularly forceful warning so that none of his readers has "an evil, unbelieving heart that turns away from the living God" (v. 12). He urged his Christian "brothers and sisters" to avoid the fate of those who wandered in the wilderness for forty years and died because they would not put their faith to work.

When the heart harbors unbelief, that unbelief leads to:

- Separation from God by giving way to "sin's deception" (vv. 12–13)
- Hardness of heart and rebellion (v. 15)
- Disobedience (v. 18)
- Inability to enter God's rest (v. 19)

THE CYCLE OF UNBELIEF

STEP	PROGRESSION	RESULT
Unbelief	leads to →	Disobedience
Disobedience	issues in →	Sin
Sin	brings on →	punishment

God's oath of exclusion (v. 11) is a solemn warning for us to bear in mind against the great judgment day.

The writer reminded his audience that "today" (v. 15) is the time when opportunity is still knocking, when hope is still beckoning, when God is still speaking, and when the Spirit is still calling. He will not be stopped short of calling believers to hold firmly to their original confidence in Christ and to maintain steadfast commitment to him (v. 14). His point is that we keep on enjoying Christ as we keep on enduring. We keep on being delivered from disobedience, rebellion, callousness of spirit, sin, and death as we keep on believing. Though the unbelieving

Hebrew children were "unable to enter" the promised land "because of unbelief" (v. 19), we who maintain our faith and endure to the end are assured of entering God's rest.

This chapter begins with a compelling presentation of Jesus's superiority and ends with a ringing challenge for Christians to endure.

Section Summary

The writer warns his readers not to harden their hearts in rebellion as did the Israelites in the wilderness wandering. Jesus's superiority to Moses makes it a more serious matter to reject Jesus than to reject Moses. Unbelieving people will not enter God's heavenly rest.

QUESTIONS TO GUIDE YOUR STUDY

1. Why is Christ superior to Moses?
2. How does Jesus function as both an *apostle* and our *High Priest?*
3. The writer warned his readers of unbelief. Why was he so concerned? What would be the result of their unbelief?
4. The writer advised his readers to "encourage each other daily." What are some ways Christians can do this?

PERSONAL APPLICATION

The writer advised his readers to "encourage each other daily" (v. 13). It is a part of our continuing responsibility as Christians to prop up one another. In the community of obedient and active faith, believers are to cultivate an ever-lastingly vigilant concern for one another. Such daily encouragement helps the family of believers avoid the deceitfulness of sin. The mutual admonishment of believers involves the sharing of the warnings and cautions, affirmations and encouragements, and the edification and nourishment that are required for Christians to grow in the grace and the knowledge of Christ. For this to take place effectively, it is imperative that God's people be steeped in God's Word.

HEBREWS 4

Joshua led the Jews of his generation to rest in Canaan. Jesus, however, brings the people of God into a resting place that provides eternal, spiritual benefits. The superiority of what Jesus provides is again obvious.

The writer was aware that his readers face a crisis just as the Jews in the lifetime of Moses and Joshua confronted crises. He warned that unbelief could prevent them from entering a relationship of promise just as it had in an earlier generation. As expressed in chapter 3, the writer of Hebrews wanted his readers to avoid the spiritual defeat caused by unbelief.

THE SUPERIORITY OF JESUS TO JOSHUA (4:1–8)

A Caution Against Missing God's Rest (vv. 1–2)

The writer called Christians to moral alertness. God's offer of rest is open. They need to press on and not fall short of the promised rest (v. 1).

He admonished his readers to "beware." One of the aids to pressing on is to cultivate a healthy fear of the awful consequences of failing to reach God's rest. Again, the pastoral concern of the author of Hebrews is coming through loud and clear. This is the concern of the church, God's caring community. The phrase "the promise . . . remains" reminds us of the attention the book of Hebrews gives to the promises of God.

WORD PICTURE

God's Rest

The word *rest* is a compound word made up of the preposition *down* and the word *cease*. It refers to a "causing to cease" or "putting to rest" (Acts 7:49; Heb 3:11; 4:8). It refers primarily to the rest in Canaan and then the heavenly rest in which God dwells. A. T. Robertson, "The Epistle to the Hebrews," *WPNT*, vol. 5, 357.

As good news came from Moses to the Israelites during their bondage in Egypt, so through Jesus Christ "we also have received the good news" (v. 2) while we were in bondage to sin. The message they heard from Moses did not benefit them because it was not met with personal faith on their part (v. 2). Recalling the Israelites' example, the writer urged Christians to hear with faith the good news that had been proclaimed to them.

The Scope of God's Rest (vv. 3–8)

In these verses the writer mentioned three kinds of rest:

- God's resting from his work on the seventh day of creation
- The rest of God's people in Canaan
- The eternal rest of God's people

Many, through unbelief, refused to enter the rest in Canaan when Joshua led the Israelites. Even those who entered the rest in Canaan found that this was not a permanent rest.

God has made provision for an eternal rest for his people. Jesus is the leader who opens the way for this rest. On the human side, faith is the condition that enables persons to enter this rest. This rest is both present and future. Believers begin to experience this rest now and will experience this eternal rest in its fullness in the world to come.

God's rest has been ready from the beginning. No works on the part of the Creator-Redeemer remain to be done, for "on the seventh day God rested from all his works" (v. 4). His rest was denied to the disobedient Hebrew children (v. 5); "it remains for some to enter it" who choose to turn to God through faith in Jesus Christ (v. 6). He has set today as the "certain day" of salvation (v. 7). Even Joshua was not able to deliver rest to God's people (v. 8).

Section Summary

The writer shows that Joshua failed to lead the people of God to rest because of their unbelief. However, those who have received the gospel of Christ may enter that rest. Salvation is an accomplished fact. Those who make the commitment to Christ enter God's rest without delay.

WORD PICTURE

Let Us Make Every Effort

This exhortation contains an interesting contrast: "make every effort" and "enter that rest." Diligent activity, effort, exertion, work precede the entry into the rest God has promised.

THE URGENCY OF SEEKING GOD'S REST (4:9–13)

A time will come when the blessed repose and perfect peace that God has promised Christians will be theirs: "Therefore, a Sabbath rest remains for God's people" (v. 9).

This passage is a thumbnail sketch of the interaction between God and humankind in history. The writer of this letter issued yet another strong challenge to his readers: "Let us, then, make every effort to enter that rest, so that no one will fall into the same pattern of disobedience." (v. 11).

God's people need not stumble in disobedience, drift in disbelief, or fall away in apostasy. Here the writer brought the strongest imaginable antidote to taking a destructive path: the Word of God.

God's Word is alive and active. It is exceedingly sharp and able to probe and discern the contents of the human heart. In fact, nothing in the human heart can escape the gaze of God.

Sinners love "darkness rather than light because their deeds [are] evil" (John 3:19). Like Adam and Eve, attempting to hide from God after their rebellious disobedience, sinful humans seek to avoid God's sight. The writer called his readers to realize that every day and every moment God sees every act, hears every word, knows every motive, numbers every heartbeat, and counts every hair. As we—open to the gaze of God—realize all we are and all God wants to be and do for us, we will stay on course to the rest God has for us.

Section Summary

The writer issued yet another strong challenge to his readers: "Let us, then, make every effort to enter that rest, so that no one will fall into the same pattern of disobedience." (v. 11). Jesus promised rest to his people if they believe and follow the promises of the gospel.

CHRISTIAN CONFESSION TO BE HELD LAST (4:14–16)

The writer further encouraged faithfulness on the part of believers by reminding them that they have a great high priest who has entered heaven on their behalf. As the high priest on earth entered the holy of holies, so Jesus has entered the heavens on our behalf. With that in view, the writer urged his readers to hold fast to their profession of faith.

Consider further the character of our great High Priest.

He is sympathetic with our weaknesses. Although he is God's Son, when he took on human flesh, he came to know firsthand what it was to live as a human being in a fallen world. He also came to know what it is like to be tempted. In every case he resisted the temptation and was completely without sin.

In light of these truths, God's people can "approach the throne of grace with boldness," so they may receive mercy and find grace to help in their time of need (v. 16). This text is another of those brilliant gems from the treasure box of Hebrews. The writer of Hebrews was tender and pastoral here. God opened his heart of grace and love to us. It is now possible for us to approach him.

In Jesus Christ, God has shown us his face. In Jesus Christ, God has borne to us his heart. In his loving presence, we "receive mercy and

NEW TESTAMENT REFERENCE

"This is the judgment: The light has come into the world, and people loved darkness rather than the light because their deeds were evil. For everyone who does evil hates the light and avoids it, so that his deeds may not be exposed. But anyone who lives by the truth comes to the light, so that his works may be shown to be accomplished by God." (John 3:19–21)

OLD TESTAMENT REFERENCE

High Priest

The high priest was the priest in charge of the temple worship. In the Levitical priesthood, the high priest went once each year, on the great Day of Atonement, through the curtain into the holy of holies, the innermost and holiest place, to make special sacrifice for his own sins and for the sins of all the people. Sprinkling the blood of the sin offering seven times before and on the mercy seat, he symbolically covered the sins of the people from the eyes of the Lord. Now Jesus, our great High Priest, has passed, once for all, not through the inner curtain of a tabernacle made with human hands, but "through the heavens" (v. 14) to God himself to make atonement for all our sins.

find grace to help us in time of need" (v. 16). Our "time of need" is always. Thank God for his grace, which supplies every need we have according to his riches in glory through Christ Jesus (Phil 4:19). He is ever eager to supply our need. Let us then approach him with confidence.

Section Summary

Christ is our great High Priest who represents us in God's presence. Because his sacrifice made atonement for all our sins, salvation may be appropriated by anyone who wants it. Therefore, God's people can "approach the throne of grace with boldness" to receive mercy and find grace to help in their time of need.

QUESTIONS TO GUIDE YOUR STUDY

1. Why is Jesus superior to Joshua?
2. What is God's rest? What did it mean to the Israelites wandering in the desert? What is its significance to believers in Christ?
3. Why is it urgent for believers to seek God's rest?
4. The writer explained that Christians have in Jesus a High Priest. What does that mean to the believer in Christ?

HISTORICAL BACKGROUND

The High Priest's Offering for Sin

Under special appointment from God "every high priest taken from among men is appointed in matters pertaining to God for the people, to offer both gifts and sacrifices for sins" (v. 1). Sins cannot be taken lightly. The high priest's offering was "for sins" of rebellion against God, of willful disobedience, of intentional mark missing, of perversity, of transgression, of trespasses, of evil, of violence, of injustice, of unrighteousness. A righteous God dealing with a morally responsible human race requires that sin be taken seriously and that it be dealt with seriously.

WORD PICTURE

Grace

The most frequent use of *grace* in Old Testament times had to do with finding favor in the sight of God or some human authority like an earthly ruler. Now, through Christ, all believers may approach God and find his unmerited favor. He is not willing that any should perish but that all should come to life. "'I take no pleasure in anyone's death.' This is the declaration of the Lord God. 'So repent and live!'" (Ezek 18:32). In Christ we come to the throne of grace, respond to this prophetic call to turn or to repent, and receive from God his great gift of life eternal and life abundant.

HEBREWS 5

In this chapter the writer outlined two similarities between Christ as High Priest and the priests after Aaron. Both showed the ability to understand sympathetically the needs of human beings before God, and both were called by God to carry out their work.

In this passage the writer issued his most serious warning against committing apostasy and turning away from Christ. He urged them to move beyond spiritual infancy into maturity, a theme he continued in the next chapter.

THE COMPARISON OF CHRIST AND AARON (5:1–4)

The statement in 4:15–16 declared that as believers hold on to their confession, they may confidently approach God's throne of grace. Through the special ministry of Jesus Christ, the great High Priest, they may receive mercy and find grace to help in time of need.

Called by God (vv. 1–3)

The writer informed us that "every high priest taken from among men is appointed in matters pertaining to God for the people, to offer both gifts and sacrifices for sins" (v. 1). The high priest does not take the office on his own initiative, nor is he elected by the people. God established the office, and the person occupying the office must be "called by God, just as Aaron was" (v. 4). Further, he "did not exalt himself to become a high priest" (v. 5).

The high priest under the Levitical system could "deal gently with those who are ignorant and are going astray, since he is also clothed with weakness. Because of this, he must make an offering for his own sins as well as for the people" (vv. 2–3).

Aaron's Priesthood (v. 4)

To be especially chosen, appointed, or ordained is to be entrusted with special responsibility by the one choosing, appointing, or ordaining. The writer mentioned Aaron because the priestly line began with him. Aaron served with prominence and distinction as the first one to be particularly consecrated or set apart for what God called his priesthood (Exod 28:1–3).

THE PRIESTHOOD OF CHRIST (5:5–10)

Jesus Christ, our great High Priest under God's new covenant, also was called by the Father. Nor did he exalt himself to do the high priestly work. The Father exalted him (v. 5). His special ordination from God was, "You are a priest forever according to the order of Melchizedek" (v. 6). This is the first reference in Hebrews to Melchizedek, but eight other references in the letter to the Hebrews follow (chaps. 5–7).

Who was Melchizedek? Genesis 14:18 identifies him as "king of Salem" and as the priest of "God Most High." To him Abraham, the father of the faithful, gave tithes (Gen 14:20).

Old Testament. When Abraham returned from the Valley of Siddim where he defeated Chedorlaomer, king of Elam, and the kings aligned with Chedorlaomer, Melchizedek greeted Abraham with bread and wine. He blessed Abraham in the name of "God Most High." In return, Abraham gave Melchizedek a tenth of everything. Melchizedek and Abraham both worshiped the one true God. Abraham also appeared to recognize the role of Melchizedek as a priest. Psalm 110:4 refers to one who would be forever a priest "according to the pattern of Melchizedek." This messianic psalm teaches that the leader or ruler of the Hebrew nation would be able to reflect in his person the role of priest as well as the role of king.

HISTORICAL BACKGROUND

Melchizedek

The name *Melchizedek* means "Zedek is my king" or "my king is righteousness." He was a priest and king of Salem, a city identified with Jerusalem.

New Testament. The writer of Hebrews made several references in chapters 5–7 to Jesus's priesthood being of the "order of Melchizedek" as opposed to Levitical in nature. The author of Hebrews cited Ps 110:4. For the writer of Hebrews, only Jesus, whose life could not be destroyed by death, fit the psalmist's description of a priest of the "order of Melchizedek."

Christ's Humanity. Combining the high priesthood of Aaron and the unique high priesthood of Melchizedek, Jesus prayed and made earnest supplication to God. In his complete identification with humanity, Jesus prayed as we pray. He petitioned God as we do. He cried aloud as we do in times of personal crisis. He wept as we sometimes do. As with all who truly trust God, Jesus "was heard because of his reverence" (v. 7).

Christ's Suffering. Although God's only begotten Son, Jesus "learned obedience from what he suffered" (v. 8).

Christ's Perfection. Jesus "was perfected, he became the source of eternal salvation for all who obey him" (v. 9). The treasure chest of Hebrews is open again, and another priceless jewel is flashing here in verses 8–9. The *perfection* Jesus achieved was accomplished through his death and resurrection.

Christ's Obedience. God appointed him, and he responded with absolute faith, complete obedience, and redemptive suffering. His obedience was not a conditioned response to external stimuli. It was rather a supremely moral, absolutely responsible response to the Father's leadership. Though Jesus was God's Son, his humanity was so total that he "learned obedience" through the things he suffered along life's way, such painful experiences as the great temptation, Lazarus's death, Jerusalem's refusal to know the things that make for peace, the disciples' petty jealousies, Peter's denial, Pilate's harsh sentence, and the agony of crucifixion.

PERSONAL APPLICATION

The eternal salvation which has Jesus as its source is given to "all who obey him" (v. 9). The divine imperative is for us to obey him. There is no other way out of the dark valley of sin and death except the high and narrow way of obedience to him.

Section Summary

God appointed Aaron as a high priest to represent people before God. Because Aaron was surrounded with weakness, he was able to have compassion on other weak, sinful people. Christ also faced hardship, and he learned the value of obedience by his commitment to God's will. He is the source of eternal salvation for all those who obey him.

COUNSEL TO KEEP MOVING TOWARD MATURITY (5:11–14)

The writer declared to his readers that they are "too lazy to understand" (v. 11). They once heard the word of the gospel with keenly attentive ears. Familiarity with the good news, however, seems gradually to have hardened their hearing. "By this time" they ought to have disciplined themselves in the faith and developed in their own Christian experience that they could "be teachers" (v. 12), bringing others to the knowledge of Christ and obedience to him in their daily lives.

Certainly, without qualified and able teachers and serious teaching, any church is in deep trouble. Discipleship is at the heart of all authentic church life. Where there is no real learning, there can be no committed disciples.

The writer continued his chastisement: "You need milk, not solid food" (v. 12). They ought to have been ashamed. They were behaving like babies, like immature children not acquainted with "the message about righteousness" (v. 13). He challenged his readers to realize that "solid food is for the mature—for those whose senses have been trained to distinguish between good and evil" (v. 14).

Formal teaching is valuable and has its place, but the real proof that the lesson has been learned is when it is put into practice. When we become disciplined to discern between good and evil, we then consistently choose the right and reject the wrong and move responsibly toward maturity in Christ.

Mature Christians "have been trained to distinguish between good and evil" (v. 14), have made the "message about righteousness" part of their lifestyle. Christians are not to abandon the basics but to build on them. A foundation is absolutely necessary, but it is no substitute for a superstructure.

PERSONAL APPLICATION

The writer of Hebrews delivered a powerful moral meaning in this passage. He distinguished the mature adult from the immature child by the commitment to be morally responsible, to be morally discriminating, and to make consistently moral judgments. Christian maturity is related to the development of skill in the use of "the message about righteousness" (v. 13). This phrase is a reference to moral truth. It has to do with the "glue" that holds civilization together. Without "the message about righteousness," both religious institutions and civil structures would crumble and fall apart.

Section Summary

The writer declared to his readers that they are "too lazy to understand." He challenged his readers to become disciplined to discern between good and evil, consistently to choose the right and reject the wrong and move responsibly toward maturity in Christ.

QUESTIONS TO GUIDE YOUR STUDY

1. Why does the writer mention Aaron's priesthood?
2. Describe Christ's priesthood. How does it differ from the Aaronic priesthood?
3. What is the result of Christ's priesthood?
4. What is the "message about righteousness" the writer mentioned in verse 13?

PERSONAL APPLICATION

Senses Have Been Trained to Distinguish

This word is also translated "practice" (v. 14, NRSVUE). It is the word for *habit*, referring to a habit of body or mind indicating not the process but the result. That is, the condition has been produced by past exercise and is then the habitual or normal condition, the disposition or character. Fritz Rienecker, *Linguistic Key to the Greek New Testament* (Zondervan, 1980), 680.

HEBREWS 6

In this chapter the writer described his readers as immature and urged them to move beyond spiritual infancy into maturity (vv. 1–2). He warned that if they finally renounce Christ, they will forfeit all hope of eternal salvation (vv. 3–6). He also reminded his readers that they have borne fruit that demonstrates salvation, but he wanted them to avoid becoming lazy and careless in their Christian profession (vv. 7–12).

ELEMENTARY TEACHINGS (6:1–3)

The writer now challenged his readers to move on to maturity. Apparently, they were stuck in laying the foundations of the Christian faith over and over again. The foundations are important, but they are designed to enable believers to grow in their faith.

THE ELEMENTARY TEACHINGS OF THE FAITH

- Repentance from dead works
- Faith in God
- Instruction about ritual washings
- Instruction about the laying on of hands
- The resurrection of the dead
- Eternal judgment

"Repentance from Dead Works" (v. 1)

Repentance is a keynote in the New Testament message. Its great prominence in the early church is reason enough for its being mentioned first in this passage. *Repentance* is godly sorrow for and an intentional turning away from sin.

For those who have trusted in works to make them right with God, repentance is necessary so that the work of the great High Priest, Jesus Christ, can take effect.

The phrase "dead works" does not refer to Hebrew ceremonialism but rather to those activities, interests, and pleasures that pertain to spiritual death. They are moral offenses from which a person must break away in order to become a Christian. Dead works are like a sheepskin over a wolf. One is still a wolf even though he or she may be in sheep's clothing. In conversion, Christians learn to trust Christ for new hearts while distrusting the former covering of dead works that once occupied their energies.

"Faith in God" (v. 1)

This is the saving faith that believers direct to the Lord when they first believe. It is closely connected to repentance. It is not merely the belief that there is a God or simply faith in his existence. It is a genuine trust in him as Redeemer, Savior, and Lord.

"Teaching About Ritual Washings" (v. 2)

This reference is not clear. Because it is part of a list of the elementary teachings of the Christian faith, it is better understood as singular (baptism) instead of plural (baptisms). Some believe the reference is to immersions such as those practiced by some of the Jewish cults for initiates, proselytes, and regular gatherings of the faithful. Many ancient religions used all kinds of purification rites connected with water. The distinctively Christian use of water for believer's baptism, therefore, had to be carefully taught to early Christians, who needed to distinguish between similar rites practiced by non-Christians.

Instruction About "Laying on of Hands" (v. 2)

This is the early church's recognition of special needs for the Holy Spirit's indwelling and empowering for Christian work. Ordination in any highly formal sense for a special class of ministers like preachers, teachers, deacons, or missionaries is apparently not intended here.

NEW TESTAMENT REFERENCE

"If Christ has not been raised, your faith is worthless; you are still in your sins" (1 Cor 15:17).

"The Resurrection of the Dead" (v. 2)

This is a crucial doctrine of Christian faith. It is vital that all believers understand this teaching and its significance early in the Christian life.

"Eternal Judgment" (v. 2)

This is another vital doctrine the readers of this letter needed to understand, as do modern readers. Human beings do not die as animals, with no hope for eternity. On the contrary, all people will experience God's righteous judgment following death. Then, for eternity, each person will live with the choices he or she made in life.

The writer apparently did not intend to mention every single elementary doctrine that Christians embrace. He drew out, under the Holy Spirit's leadership, these primary points with which his Christian converts would be familiar. Churches today would also do well to make sure every convert gains a working knowledge of these basic concepts.

Note that although the writer of Hebrews admonished believers to leave these elementary teachings, they are not to lose them. Instead, they are to build on, add to, and fulfill them. "And we will do this if God permits" (v. 3), is a way of saying that forward movement in the Christian life is our doing by his mercy.

Section Summary

The writer described his readers as immature and urged them to move beyond spiritual infancy into maturity. He did not intend that they abandon the basics but rather build on them and add to them.

PERSEVERANCE IN CHRIST (6:4–8)

Bringing One Back to Repentance (vv. 4–6)

These three verses are among the most solemn and most discussed in all the Scriptures. A key word in these verses is *impossible.*

WORD PICTURE

Fallen Away

John Calvin noted that a lot is at stake in our understanding what the writer meant here by *fallen away*: "Whoever then understands its meaning, can easily extricate himself from every difficulty. But it must be noticed, that there is a twofold falling away, one particular, and the other general. He who has in anything, or in anyway offended, has fallen away from his state as a Christian; therefore all sins are so many fallings. But the Apostle speaks not here of theft, or perjury, or murder, or drunkenness, or adultery; but he refers to a total defection or falling away from the Gospel, when a sinner offends not God in some one thing, but entirely renounces his grace."

What is impossible? It is impossible to bring some people back to repentance.

Who are these people?

- They have been enlightened.
- They have tasted the heavenly gift.
- They have shared in the Holy Spirit.
- They have known firsthand how good God's Word is.
- They have experienced the powers of the world to come.

Under what conditions is it impossible to bring such persons back to repentance? If they fall away. A person who falls away continues to crucify the Son of God and hold him in contempt.

A key question in interpreting this passage is whether the people described above have been saved. Some take the position that despite all they have experienced they haven't been saved. Salvation is from first to last a work of God that cannot be reversed by human beings.

Some interpret the falling away as a hypothetical possibility that can't happen.

However we interpret this passage, it is a grave warning—a wake-up call on the sufficiency and finality of Christ.

Illustration from Nature (vv. 7–8)

The reminder that land that produces good crops receives a "blessing from God" (v. 7) illustrates the teaching of this passage. But land that bears nothing but weeds and brush is worthless and "at the end will be burned" (v. 8).

Section Summary

The sin of falling away is the sin of deliberately, willfully, intentionally rejecting God. Hebrews 6:4–8 does not teach that Christians can fall from grace, but it does warn that if Christian salvation should ever be abandoned, it could never be recovered.

CHARACTER OF THE GENUINE BELIEVER (6:9–12)

After his stern warning about falling away from the faith, the author turned immediately to a pastoral expression of affection and encouragement. He focused specifically on those things that pertain to salvation.

NEW TESTAMENT REFERENCE

Paul wrote about the fruit of the Spirit in Gal 5:22–23: "love, joy, peace, patience, kindness, goodness, faithfulness, gentleness, and self-control."

Better Things That Accompany Salvation (vv. 9–10)

The writer addresses his readers as "dearly loved friends" (v. 9). They were people to whom the writer was apparently close and for whom he felt special warmth. He expressed confidence in those to whom he wrote.

He believed they were bearing fruit as a result of God's salvation in their lives. Fruit gives evidence of righteousness.

Salvation is not simply a theological transaction, a psychological phenomenon, or an emotional experience. Rather it is a reality that translates into Christian character and works of righteousness. Its marks are self-sacrifice, giving, discipline, obedience, and faithfulness. Christians may be assured their labors are not in vain. Their works and ministries are all known to the Lord.

Characteristics of True Believers (vv. 11–12)

"We desire each of you to demonstrate . . . diligence " (v. 11). Each one is to show spiritual earnestness and confident hope "until the end."

"So that you won't become lazy" (v. 12). Christians must avoid sluggishness, realizing that enthusiasm and excitement in the work of the Lord are winsomely contagious.

"Be imitators of those who inherit the promises through faith and perseverance" (v. 12). The counsel to "be imitators of" (v. 12) is advice to follow the example of those who worked faithfully and patiently and who always found God absolutely trustworthy.

Section Summary

After his stern warning about falling away from the faith, the author focused on the "things that are better" that accompany salvation and the characteristics of true believers.

SECURITY OF GOD'S PROMISE (6:13–20)

The letter now moves on with a fairly long and involved discussion of God's new covenant by which believers experience complete security in Christ. When God makes a covenant, he keeps it. His promises are sure. His dealings with Abraham (vv. 13–15) appropriately illustrate "his unchangeable purpose" (v. 17) and show how "it is impossible for God to lie" (v. 18). God's promise was that he would bless Abraham and multiply him (v. 14).

The continuing purpose of God was that "the heirs of the promise" (v. 17) maintain absolute confidence in him. The human part of the covenant, however, is not to be ignored, for it must be remembered that it was only after "waiting patiently" that faithful Abraham "obtained the promise" (v. 15).

Christians, as latter-day heirs of God's promise to Abraham, the father of the faithful, have taken refuge in Jesus that they may "have strong encouragement" (v. 18). Believers have a new covenant and a sure and steadfast anchor in Christ.

NEW TESTAMENT REFERENCE

Anchor for the Soul

In the ancient world, as ships were entering a harbor, some of the sailors got into a smaller craft and went ahead of the large vessel. Their job was to carry the anchor into the harbor and find a place where it could be securely fastened. In the same way, Jesus went into the inner sanctuary, into the holy of holies, the presence of God, taking with him the anchor of the soul. *The Bible Knowledge Commentary: New Testament* (Victor Books), 797.

Section Summary

When God makes a covenant, he keeps it. The writer discussed God's new covenant by which believers experience complete security in Christ. He illustrated the unchanging nature of God's purpose by recounting God's dealings with Abraham.

QUESTIONS TO GUIDE YOUR STUDY

1. What are the elementary teachings of the faith? What is the writer's point in discussing them?
2. What was the writer teaching in verses 4–6? What was he *not* teaching?
3. What characterizes the true believer?
4. What is the basis of the believer's security in Christ?

HEBREWS 7

In this section of his letter, the author pointed out two features that prove the superiority of the priesthood of Jesus over that of the Aaronic priests. Christ became a high priest by a divine oath which established him in a new priestly order, the order of Melchizedek.

MELCHIZEDEK THE PRIEST (7:1–10)

As both priest and king, Melchizedek was a type of Christ. The writer mentioned these similarities between the two.

He Was a King (vv. 1–2)

The name *Melchizedek* means "king of righteousness" (v. 2). As king of Salem, he was, by translation of the place name *Salem*, the "king of peace" (v. 2).

He Was a Priest (vv. 1–2)

As "priest of God Most High," he received Abraham's tithes (v. 4) and, symbolically through Abraham, the tithes of all the Levitical priesthood (vv. 5–10).

He Had No Record of Human Descendants (v. 3)

As a person "without father, mother, or genealogy," he was without any historical reference regarding his human descendants.

Like "the Son of God, he remains a priest forever" (v. 3). Of the eternal Christ, the writer noted that it is not that Jesus resembled Melchizedek but rather that Melchizedek resembled the Son of God. As God's peculiarly ordained priest, Melchizedek both received Abraham's tithes and "blessed the one who had the promises" (v. 6). Who is superior and has the power to bless the inferior (v. 7) except one who is especially set apart by "God Most High"?

Section Summary

As both priest and king, Melchizedek was a type of Christ. He was king of Salem. As priest of God Most High, he received Abraham's tithes and, symbolically through Abraham, the tithes of all the Levitical priesthood. The writer of Hebrews declared that he resembled the Son of God.

A HIGH PRIEST LIKE MELCHIZEDEK (7:11–19)

This impressive line of reasoning now moves forward. Perfection was not possible under the Levitical priesthood, so it was necessary for God to raise up the ultimate High Priest, not from the tribe of Levi at all but from the tribe of Judah (vv. 11–14).

"Now if perfection came through the Levitical priesthood (for on the basis of it the people received the law), what further need was there for another priest to appear, said to be according to the order of Melchizedek and not according to the order of Aaron?" (v. 11).

Jesus was God's great High Priest not "based on a legal regulation about physical descent but based on the power of an indestructible life" (v. 16). The centuries saw other high priests come and go, receiving their office by inheritance and relinquishing it at death. Jesus, however, knew no such limitation, for as God's Son he has life indestructible and eternal. In him Christians have life, abundant and everlasting.

The "previous command" concerning the Levitical priesthood is now set aside "because it was weak and unprofitable" (v. 18). In Jesus Christ, "a better hope is introduced, through which we draw near to God" (v. 19). No longer do we need a human mediator to approach God on our behalf. By this "better hope" every believer, through Christ, personally draws near to God. Nowhere in the Bible is the profoundly important Christian doctrine of the priesthood of the believer so beautifully stated and so clearly explained as in this passage in Hebrews.

Section Summary

Perfection was not possible under the Levitical priesthood, so it was necessary for God to raise up the truly ultimate High Priest. No longer do we need a human mediator to approach God on our behalf. By this "better hope" every believer, through Christ, personally draws near to God.

WORD PICTURE

Perfection

This word means "perfection, reaching the goal." "It denotes a fulfillment, completion, perfection, an end accomplished as the effect of a process." (*Vine's Complete Expository Dictionary of Old and New Testament Words* [Thomas Nelson, 1996], 467.) The Old Testament law and the Levitical system could not produce forgiveness or the holiness of heart demanded by God. It failed to provide an adequate relation to God. Fritz Rienecker, *Linguistic Key to the Greek New Testament* (Zondervan, 1980), 686.

OLD TESTAMENT REFERENCE

Of Abraham God said, "For I have chosen him, so that he will direct his children and his household after him to keep the way of the LORD by doing what is right and just" (Gen 18:19).

JESUS, THE SUPERIOR PRIEST (7:20–28)

God's Guarantee (vv. 20–22)

That Jesus is "the guarantee of a better covenant" (v. 22) means that God's Son is the certain guarantee of God's agreement to save and to bless. The covenant is still God's covenant with faithful people like Abraham.

A Trustworthy Priest (vv. 23–25)

The generations of earthly priests lived and died. Jesus lives forever, and his priesthood is permanent. He stands ready at all times to save those who come to God through him. His continuing purpose is to intercede for his people (v. 25).

A Perfect Sin Offering (vv. 26–28)

Jesus is unlike the priests of the Levitical priesthood in the fact that he has made a once-for-all offering for sin (v. 27). What he has done is sufficient to save those who call on him. Our great High Priest is "holy, innocent, undefiled, separated from sinners, and exalted above the heavens" (v. 26), a perfect High Priest and a perfect sin offering. This is God's "Son, who has been perfected forever" (v. 28).

Section Summary

Jesus is God's agreement to save and to bless. His priesthood is superior to the Levitical priesthood.

HISTORICAL BACKGROUND

Mediator

The term *mediator* in the New Testament conveys several ideas. Primarily it meant an umpire or peacemaker who came between two contestants, a negotiator who established a certain relationship, or some neutral person who could guarantee an agreement reached (of Moses in a negative sense in Gal 3:19–28). Christ is the only necessary Mediator (1 Tim 2:5). Full communion with God comes through faith in the Mediator who gave himself a ransom for others, mediating a new eternal covenant through his sacrificial death (Heb 7:22–25; 8:6; 9:15; 12:24).

QUESTIONS TO GUIDE YOUR STUDY

1. Why is Melchizedek significant to the writer's argument?
2. How is Christ's priesthood "perfect"?
3. What does the writer mean by declaring that Jesus is the "guarantee of a better covenant"? (v. 22).
4. God is committed to his covenant with us. What is the responsibility on the human side of the agreement?

HEBREWS 8

In this chapter the author of Hebrews indicated that, in addition to beginning a new order of priesthood, Christ inaugurated a new covenant.

THE NEW ORDER OF PRIESTHOOD (8:1–6)

The writer of Hebrews pointed out that Christians have in Jesus a Mediator "who sat down at the right hand of the throne of the Majesty in the heavens, a minister of the sanctuary and the true tabernacle that was set up by the Lord and not man" (vv. 1–2). Priests on earth, offering gifts according to the law, have always worked in a tent made with human hands according to the divine pattern given by God to Moses.

The earthly sanctuary is but "a copy and shadow of the heavenly things" (v. 5). The old covenant was incomplete and therefore flawed. The new covenant mediated by Jesus, the Son of God himself, is better because it "has been established on better promises" (v. 6). Likewise, his ministry is superior to the ministry of the priests under the old covenant. Christ's is a ministry of incarnation, self-denial, suffering, and final self-sacrifice.

Christ is the great Intercessor, praying for his disciples while on earth and continuing to do so in heaven (John 17; Rom 8:34). He is the supreme High Priest who enters once for all into the sanctuary to make a sacrifice of himself that brings eternal redemption (Heb 9:11–12).

OLD TESTAMENT REFERENCE

Jeremiah 31:31–34 is the longest passage directly quoted in Hebrews. The author calls on one of the major Old Testament prophets to illustrate his point that the old covenant was inadequate, requiring that God mandate a new covenant. With prophetic vision, Jeremiah had foreseen the day when God would establish a new covenant with his people (Heb 8:8), not like the one originally made when he first took them by the hand and led them out of bondage (v. 9). "I showed no concern for them . . . because they did not continue in my covenant," God said.

Section Summary

Christians have in Jesus a Mediator who is seated at the right hand of the throne of Majesty in heaven. Jesus is the great Intercessor, praying for his disciples on earth. He is the supreme High Priest whose self-sacrifice brings eternal redemption.

THE SUPERIOR COVENANT OF CHRIST (8:7–13)

In addition to beginning a new order of priesthood, Christ inaugurated a new covenant. It provided three benefits for those who lived under it. The covenant of Christ is superior in these three areas:

1. The new covenant offered an internalization of the law.
2. Christ's covenant provided a new, direct knowledge of God.
3. The new covenant promised complete forgiveness of sins.

In Jesus, the promised new covenant with God's people is realized: "I will put my laws into their minds and write them on their hearts. I will be their God, and they will be my people. And each person will not teach his fellow citizen, and each his brother or sister, saying, 'Know the Lord,' because they all know me, from the least to the greatest of them. For I will forgive their wrongdoing, and I will never again remember their sins" (vv. 10–12).

The author of Hebrews then commented that Jeremiah's reference to a new covenant treated the old covenant even then as already essentially obsolete. He concluded this lesson with the observation that "what is obsolete and growing old is about to pass away" (v. 13).

WORD PICTURE

Obsolete

This word means "to declare or treat as old or obsolete." The word was used in the papyri for a temple and a wall which had become old and obsolete and needed repairing. Fritz Rienecker, *Linguistic Key to the Greek New Testament* (Zondervan, 1980), 692.

Section Summary

Christ's covenant with God's people is superior in three ways: (1) it provided a new awareness of God's laws and a new nature by which to obey God; (2) it gave a personal knowledge of God that inspired a loyalty and commitment to him; and (3) it provided a complete forgiveness of sins (8:8–12). Christians today have inherited the benefits of this new covenant in their relationship with God.

QUESTIONS TO GUIDE YOUR STUDY

1. As our great High Priest, Jesus sacrificed himself. What did his sacrifice accomplish?
2. What does Christ accomplish as our Mediator?
3. In what ways is Christ's new covenant superior to the old covenant?
4. The writer declares the old covenant "obsolete." In what ways does Christ's new covenant render it obsolete?

HEBREWS 9

The author shared several effects of Christ's sacrifice to demonstrate its superiority. The death of Christ was more effective than the sacrifices offered by the Aaronic priests because Christ's sacrifice cleansed the conscience, brought forgiveness, and dealt with heavenly realities, not mere earthly symbols.

HISTORICAL BACKGROUND

The Holy Places

Holy place. The courts, the inner room, and the outer room of the tabernacle (Exod 26:33). Later the expression was used in reference to the temple and its environs. It was a holy place in the sense of being a place set apart for Yahweh.

Holy of holies. This was the innermost sanctuary of the tabernacle and later the temple. It was separated from the other parts of the temple by a thick curtain. The holy of holies was specially associated with the presence of Yahweh. In the early years of the existence of the temple, the holy of holies contained the ark of the covenant.

A SACRIFICE THAT CLEANSES THE CONSCIENCE (9:1–14)

The First Covenant (vv. 1–10)

The first covenant included regulations for formal worship (v. 1). The author gave a concise but adequate description of the outer tabernacle, called the "holy place," and the inner tabernacle, called "the most holy place."

The priests continually went into the outer tabernacle or tent for the performance of their ritual duties (v. 6). The high priest went into the inner tent once a year on the Day of Atonement to make a blood offering for his own sins and for the sins of the people (v. 7). While the outer tabernacle still stood, the way into the holy of holies was not disclosed (v. 8). This inability of the priests to go beyond the holy place and into the holy of holies was a symbol of that time (v. 9). According to the old arrangement, sacrifices were made for sins, but those sacrifices could not "perfect the worshiper's conscience" (v. 9). Instead, they dealt only with regulations imposed "until the time of the new order" (v. 10), washings for the body but not for the heart, gifts for time but not for eternity, sacrifices for sins but not a perfect sacrifice for all sin. In Jesus the time of reformation came, and God's great drama of redemption was perfected.

The Second Covenant (vv. 11–14)

The second covenant was brought into effect by a sacrifice of an entirely different order from the first covenant. Christ entered through an earthly tabernacle—one that is part of creation. He did not bring with him the blood of animals. Christ entered a more perfect tabernacle with his own blood. Christ's blood, offered through the Holy Spirit, brought about a radical change in the hearts of those who received his gift. This change cleanses the consciences of works that lead to death. The believer is prepared to serve the living God.

The author of Hebrews combined the concept of the high priest with that of the blood offering to explain how Jesus both did the high priestly work and made himself the offering. Jesus did not walk away from suffering. He walked through suffering and death to break sin's dominion over all who want salvation's glorious freedom. This brief passage (vv. 11–14) contains the doctrinal heart of the letter to the Hebrews.

Section Summary

The old covenant made provision for removing external pollution using animal sacrifices and familiar rituals. Under the new covenant Jesus surrendered his life to God in sacrifice for sin. The sacrifice of Christ is more effective for us today in three ways. First, it did not limit itself to the mere removal of ceremonial pollution. It cleansed the conscience from guilt and thus inspired holy living.

A SACRIFICE THAT REMOVES SIN (9:15–22)

The death of Christ redeems believers from the sins that would have left them dead under the old covenant (v. 15). In dying, Jesus became the "mediator of a new covenant, so that those who are called might receive the promise of the eternal inheritance" (v. 15). The author continued this careful line of reasoning. Where a will is involved, the death of the one who made it must be verified (v. 16). A will takes effect only at the death of the one making it (v. 17). The first covenant was not ratified except by the life blood that signified life given (v. 18).

Then, "when every command had been proclaimed by Moses to all the people according to the law," he took the blood of the sacrificial animals and sprinkled the book of the law, the people, the tent, and the vessels used in the formal ceremony of worship (vv. 19–21). Moses's words, "This is the blood of the covenant that God has ordained for" (v. 20),

PERSONAL APPLICATION

In the light of the great truth that Christians are cleansed by the blood of Christ to serve God, it is important to consider the service God expects. The matter will surface later in the letter, but at this point we should observe that the intention of service here is not formal worship. The recurring emphasis on obedience, growth, maturity, and the things that accompany salvation argue for assigning a meaning to service that would encompass the doing of truth, righteousness, justice, and peace. When questioned about what reasonable service to God might have as its absolute minimum, Jesus answered that we are to love God with our entire being and our neighbors as ourselves (Matt 22:34–40).

remind readers of Hebrews that "according to the law almost everything is purified with blood, and without the shedding of blood there is no forgiveness" (v. 22).

This profound theological insight is not one believers today may ignore. This is the heart of the gospel. Preaching or teaching that ignores this isn't the gospel of Jesus Christ.

WORD PICTURE

Blood

Hebrews 9 has twelve references to *blood,* more than in any other entire book of the New Testament with the exception of Revelation, which also has twelve references to blood. This emphasis on blood represents a major concern for the life of the people of God by the sacrifice of the life of God's Son.

The term *blood of Christ* in the New Testament designates the atoning death of Christ. *Atonement* refers to the basis and process by which estranged people become at one with God. At his last Passover, Jesus inaugurated the new covenant in his blood "poured out for many for the forgiveness of sins" (Matt 26:28; cp. Luke 22:20). Jesus died as a sin-bearer that we might live for righteousness and become healed (1 Pet 2:24).

Section Summary

Christ's sacrifice resulted in the removal of sin by the shedding of Christ's blood.

A SACRIFICE THAT AFFECTS HEAVENLY REALITIES (9:23–28)

The writer continued a vivid comparison between animal sacrifices under the old covenant with Jesus's sacrifice. Under the old covenant it was necessary for both the tabernacle and the things in it to be purified through prescribed rites (v. 21). "The heavenly things" (v. 23), the things of heaven itself, are somehow purified and given special glory and honor in the presence of the crucified and risen and ascended Lamb of God whose "better" sacrifice transforms not only earth but also heaven itself. He entered not into an earthly tent of sanctuary but "into heaven itself, so that he might now appear in the presence of God for us" (vv. 23–24). Christ does not offer himself repeatedly but "he has appeared one time, at the end of the ages, for the removal of sin by the sacrifice of himself" (v. 26).

The Greek word translated "judgment" (v. 27), when transliterated into English letters, makes our word *crisis*. The crisis of final determination of the everlasting fate of every person will come after death at the time of judgment.

In the normal course of human events people die, and they are not then allowed to come back to life in this world to start all over again (v. 27). As judgment follows death in the normal course of human events, so Christ's sinless life and sacrificial death will not be repeated. However, he "will appear a second time, not to bear sin" as he did on the cross, "but to bring salvation to those who are waiting for him" (v. 28).

Christians are not to fear the judgment of the Lord. Instead, we joyfully anticipate the second coming when there will be a final consummation in eternity of our salvation that began in time.

Section Summary

By entering God's presence, Christ showed that he has offered a perfect sacrifice. Because Christ has fully removed all sins, Christians have the hope that he will one day return to complete their salvation by taking them to be with the Father.

QUESTIONS TO GUIDE YOUR STUDY

1. What is the first covenant? The second covenant?
2. What acts lead to death?
3. What does the blood of Christ do in the believer's heart?
4. What should be the believer's response to being cleansed by the blood of Christ?

WORD PICTURE

Shadow

This word refers to the outline or shadow cast by the object, which is the reality. In the New Testament, it is used of ceremonies under the law and its sacrifices and offerings (Col 2:17).

HEBREWS 10

In the first part of this chapter, the author explained the permanence of Christ's sacrifice. Because his once-for-all death forever took away all sins, there remains no further need for sacrifice.

In the second half, the writer explained that because Christians now have complete access to God, they can draw near to him with an inward and outward cleansing. He expressed several concerns along these lines. Finally, as a body of believers, Christians need to consider how to stimulate one another to good works by meeting together.

CHRIST'S PERMANENT SACRIFICE (10:1–18)

OLD TESTAMENT REFERENCE

The writer quoted from a psalm of David, Ps 40:6–8:

"Therefore, as he was coming into the world, he said: You did not desire sacrifice and offering, but you prepared a body for me. You did not delight in whole burnt offerings and sin offerings. Then I said, 'See—it is written about me in the scroll—I have come to do your will, God.'" (Heb 10:5–7)

The Law Is "Only a Shadow" (vv. 1–9)

The writer is about to end his exhaustive statement about Abraham, Moses, Melchizedek, the tabernacle, the Levitical priesthood, the high priests, and the sin offerings. The law and the sacrifices are but shadows of the true redemption achieved through Christ's sacrifice.

These acts of sacrifice did not bring to perfection those for whom they were offered year after year. The writer asked a rhetorical question. Would these sacrifices have ceased if they cleansed the people? He followed this question with an assertion: It's impossible for the blood of bulls and goats to take away sin. Only Christ through his perfect obedience to death can accomplish the removal of sin and the perfection of sinners.

Christ's Sacrifice Is Superior (vv. 10–18)

Once for All. The death of Christ was more effective than the sacrifices offered by the Aaronic priests because Christ's sacrifice cleansed the conscience, brought forgiveness, and dealt with heavenly realities, not mere earthly symbols. Christ's sacrifice was also superior because he offered himself voluntarily in a once-for-all, never-to-be-repeated death.

All Christians are sanctified. Having come to earth to do the Father's will, he abolished the old order and established a new order (v. 10). According to the will of God, "we have been sanctified through the offering of the body of Jesus Christ once for all time" (v. 10). All Christians are sanctified by Christ who brings us pure, spotlessly cleansed by his own blood, before the Father.

OLD TESTAMENT REFERENCE

The author then quoted from Jeremiah 31:33: "This is the covenant I will make with them after those days, the Lord says. I will put my laws on their hearts and write them on their minds, and I will never again remember their sins and lawless acts." (Heb 10:16–17)

We have no further need for sacrifice. When Christ's great high priestly work was finished, he "sat down at the right hand of God. He is now waiting until his enemies are made his footstool" (vv. 12–13). By his single offering of himself, he "perfected forever those who are sanctified" (v. 14).

Where such forgiveness is fully given by God in Christ and fully received through personal repentance for sin and personal faith in the Lord Jesus, there need be "no longer an offering for sin" (v. 18).

The author of Hebrews carefully shared his mind and heart about these immensely important matters. No more about them needed to be said. The writer of Hebrews finished preaching his sermon; he turned next to the exhortation.

Section Summary

The once-for-all death of Christ forever took away all sins. When these sins are removed, no further need for sacrifice remains.

Note: Here the writer of Hebrews began his section on advice for practical Christian living. This part covers the remainder of the letter up to the conclusion (10:19–13:19).

STAMINA IN OBEDIENCE (10:19–39)

Counsel to Draw Near to God and Encourage One Another (vv. 19–25)

By God's grace, Christians can boldly approach him. Christians "have boldness to enter the sanctuary through the blood of Jesus" (v. 19). They are enabled to live a new life, to walk in "a new and living way" (v. 20). Since we have in Christ "a great high priest" (v. 21), we are called to draw near with a true heart "in full assurance of faith" (v. 22). The concept of drawing near to God is a prominent one in this letter, and its use again in this context is particularly important. Needy believers draw near to

WORD PICTURE

True

The word translated *true* conveys the idea of truth, loyalty, and dependability.

him for cleansing, for renewal, for strength, for comfort, for help, and for guidance.

The writer urged believers, himself included, to "draw near with a true heart" (v. 22).

Faith (v. 22). In drawing near to God, the believer's first concern is faith. As Christians draw near to God with a true heart, we are to do so "in full assurance of faith" (v. 22). A primary aim of the writer of Hebrews was to bring his readers to this full assurance of faith, to complete confidence in God, to positive certainty about him to whom we have committed everything for time and eternity. We must know whom we have believed (2 Tim 1:12) in order to have this full assurance of faith.

DRAWING NEAR TO GOD

CONCERN	VERSE(S)	ACTION INVOLVED
Faith	v. 22	Living with complete confidence in God.
Hope	vv. 22–23	Enduring trials, conquering temptations, and following righteousness.
Christian Love	v. 24	Acts of kindness and righteousness toward others in Christ's name for his glory.
Good Works	v. 24	To do good without ceasing. Faith, hope, and love all find both validation and fruition in good works.

Hope (vv. 22–23). The writer's second concern is hope. He urges his readers, "Let us hold on to the confession of our hope without wavering" (v. 23). In hope Christians endure trials, conquer temptations, bear witness, follow righteousness, do the things that make for peace, and await the return of their Lord.

Love (v. 24). The writer's third concern in drawing near to God was love. "Let us consider one another in order to provoke love and good works" (v. 24). Love is not something we think, say, or feel. Love is something we do. As important as it is, love cannot be taken for granted. It must be stirred up, aroused, fanned into flame, and encouraged.

"Good Works" (v. 24). A fourth concern in drawing near to God is "good works" (v. 24). The writer treated the subject of good deeds in the context of love. Christian love and good works belong together; in fact, they are inseparable.

The writer closed this section with an admonition for "not neglecting to gather together" (v. 25).

Section Summary

Because Christians have complete access to God, they can draw near to him with an inward and outward cleansing. They also need to consider how to encourage one another to good works by meeting together.

Warning of Judgment to Fall on the Disobedient (vv. 26–39)

Avoid acts of disobedience. Because Christians "see the day approaching" (v. 25), the writer of Hebrews listed several acts of disobedience he wanted his readers to avoid:

- They must be vigilant to avoid deliberate sin (v. 26).
- They must also be careful not to spurn the Son of God (v. 29).
- They must not profane the blood of the covenant (v. 29).
- They must not throw away their confidence (v. 35) or shrink back from our commitment (v. 39).

Avoid apostasy. He now returned to the topic of apostasy which he previously dealt with in 6:4–8. Perhaps an evil spirit of apostasy was actually working among the particular Christians to whom this letter was originally sent. Or perhaps here, as earlier, he meant to sound the note of grave warning that would keep them decisively turned away from lukewarmness, coldness, and subsequent apostasy.

The deliberate sin in 10:26 is willful, intentional abandonment of Christ after receiving "the knowledge of the truth" (v. 26). If such a thing should be, then "there no longer remains a sacrifice for sins" (v. 26). Instead, there would be "a terrifying expectation of judgment and the fury of a fire about to consume the adversaries" (v. 27).

PERSONAL APPLICATION

The vengeance and judgment of God (v. 30) were in mind when the writer issued this solemn warning: "It is a terrifying thing to fall into the hands of the living God" (v. 31). This theme inspired the preaching of Jonathan Edwards as he called multitudes to repentance in the First Great Awakening in America. Today, we would do well to respond to this warning by cultivating a continuing spirit of personal repentance and personal faith. God's promises of judgment are as certain as his promises of grace, and believers ought never to forget it.

Under the Mosaic law, the death penalty had been prescribed for the twenty-five offenses when guilt was confirmed by "the testimony of two or three witnesses" (v. 28). Such a death was awful, but "how much worse" will a person be punished who spurns the Son of God and profanes the blood of the covenant by which he was sanctified? (v. 29).

The writer reminded the original recipients of this letter of their struggles and sufferings in the time of persecution through which they had passed. They had been able to endure because they knew they "have a better and enduring possession" (v. 34). He urged them not to "throw away your confidence, which has a great reward" (v. 35).

Persevere in the will of God. Believers are to persevere, endure to do the will of God and receive what is promised (v. 36). The author then quoted the well-known Hab 2:3–4 to call attention to the fact that the just, or righteous, shall live by faith, but that God can have no pleasure in anyone who shrinks back (vv. 37–38). Christians, however, "are not those who draw back and are destroyed, but those who have faith and are saved" (v. 39).

Section Summary

The author warned his readers that turning away from Christ would expose them to divine judgment. He insisted that his readers show genuine faith by their continued commitment to Christ. They had already suffered for their faith, but they needed to demonstrate stamina by obeying God.

QUESTIONS TO GUIDE YOUR STUDY

1. Although the sacrifices of the Levitical system met the needs of the law, why was God not pleased with these sacrifices?
2. What reasons did the writer give to show the superiority of Christ's sacrifice over those of the Levitical priesthood?
3. What specifically did the author warn his readers in about verses 26–39?
4. How does a believer persevere in the will of God?

HEBREWS 11

Hebrews 11 is not only the best-known chapter in this letter, but it is also one of the best-loved chapters in the Bible. It is more than simply a chapter about faith; it is a chapter about *faith in action*. It is about faith at work, faith that does not shrink from battle, faith that does not flee from confrontation, faith that does not bend under pressure, faith that does not wither under the heat of persecution. With almost incomparable beauty and excellence, the author painted a masterpiece of the word picture of faith.

In verses 1–3 the author described the nature of faith as a conviction of certainty about what we do not see. This kind of faith motivated the godly men and women of the past to move toward the promises, even though they did not inherit them (vv. 4–40).

THE NATURE OF FAITH (11:1–3)

What is faith? Verse 1 describes the nature of faith. Notice how these three Bible versions translate the text:

- "Now faith is the reality of what is hoped for, the proof of what is not seen" (CSB).
- "Now faith is confidence in what we hope for and assurance about what we do not see" (NIV).
- "Now faith is the assurance of things hoped for, the conviction of things not seen" (ESV).

WORD PICTURE

Reality

The word translated "reality" is a compound made up of the preposition "under" and the verb "to stand." Literally, it means "a standing under, support." The word has several connotations and usages, such as *essence, substance, foundation, confident assurance, guarantee,* and *attestation,* that is, documents that attest or provide evidence of ownership. According to the Greek scholar A. T. Robertson, this word "is a very common word from Aristotle" and refers to "what stands under anything (a building, a contract, a promise). . . . It is common in the papyri in business documents as the basis or guarantee of transactions." A. T. Robertson, "The Epistle to the Hebrews," *WPNT,* vol. 5, 418.

Faith Is the Foundation for Hope (v. 1)

Faith is the foundation of hope, standing under hope, providing the ground on which hope is built.

Faith Is the Proof of What We Do Not See (v. 1)

What does faith do? It is the evidence, proof, or conviction that enables us to perceive unseen things just as if they were seen, to sense spiritual realities just as truly as we sense things by seeing and smelling, hearing and touching. Faith claims the future in the present. It gives things that are yet to come all the certainty of things that already are. Through faith, unseen things take on substance, and future things take on present reality.

Faith transcends the time-space framework in which we live this present life. It reaches to the high places where eternity can be seen beyond all present boundaries and barriers. By faith we hold clear title to the property of salvation. With faith in our possession, history becomes filled with meanings, life's present puzzle is no longer an insoluble mystery, and the unseen future comes into plain view and into clear focus.

Faith is not the gift of seeing something that is not there. Rather, it is the gift of seeing through all the haze of doubt and the pollution of sin to the distant city of God set on the mountain of eternity. Faith is not believing something despite the evidence; it is living life for the Lord God in scorn of all earthly consequences.

WORD PICTURE

Proof

The words *evidence* and *conviction* carry the concept of proof. The word was used in the papyri for legal proofs of an accusation. The word *conviction* implies an outward response of the inner assurance of faith. "When the Holy Spirit gives us faith through the Word, the very presence of that faith in our hearts is all the assurance and evidence we need!" Warren W. Wiersbe, *Wiersbe's Expository Outlines on the New Testament* (Victor Books), 706.

Faith Receives God's Approval (v. 2)

By faith, our spiritual forebears "were approved" (v. 2). As they demonstrated their trust in God, he affirmed and blessed them.

Faith in God's Creative Word (v. 3)

"By faith we understand that the universe was created by the word of God" (v. 3). Scientists continually come forward with new theories about the when of creation. Yet, the "how" of creation is a theological perception to which the author of Hebrews spoke with profound insight. By faith we understand that, whenever it was done, creation was done "by the word of God" that he made the material out of the immaterial, "so that what is seen was made from things that are not visible" (v. 3).

The writer's point here is that his readers believed that God created the universe even though they did not witness it. They accepted the fact of creation through the power of his word by faith, not sight. In a sense, they had a start in faith.

PERSONAL APPLICATION

"Faith is like a muscle. As we exercise it, it grows and develops. God asks us to do that today. He does not want us to take his Word for granted. He wants us to check it out. He wants us to commit ourselves to him and see if he will not do what he has promised. Faith is the substance, the title deed of the things we hope for and desire. Everything we dream for in life is ours by faith." James T. Draper

Section Summary

Faith is the support for the believer's hope. It gives reality to things that cannot be seen. It is evidence that God is absolutely trustworthy and that his promises are completely sure. By this faith Old Testament believers received a positive witness from God.

FAITH IN ACTION: THE ROLL CALL (11:4–40)

This chapter often has been called the Westminster Abbey of the Old Testament, for as the great London cathedral contains the graves and appropriate markers for most of the famous men and women of the British Empire, so this passage contains appropriate markers for many of the great men and women who are the spiritual giants of the Bible.

The writer's purpose for the illustrations that follow is to show how faith was put into action by men and women like us. These illustrations are windows. Like the parables of Jesus, when appropriately used, they provide earthly examples with heavenly meanings. It is heavenly meaning, not the details of history, with which the writer was primarily concerned.

Abel: Worshiping in Faith (v. 4)

By faith Abel offered a better sacrifice than Cain. Abel received God's approval as righteous but not because he used the right words. Instead, it was his right deed, his offering to God of the better or more acceptable sacrifice, that God approved. Although Abel died, his faith still speaks to us today about the importance of obedient and active faith.

Enoch: Walking in Faith (vv. 5–6)

We know from the Old Testament that Enoch "walked with God" (Gen 5:24) by faith and that he "was taken away, and so he did not experience death" (v. 5). Enoch's communion with God was so complete that his journey from time to eternity was not interrupted by the detour of death. In active faith, Enoch walked with the Lord and by so doing "pleased God" (v. 5).

Whoever comes to God in faith for salvation must use the mind so as to understand both God's existence and his justice in rewarding those who seek his face. Adapting what the great missionary William Carey once said, faith expects great things from God and attempts great things for him.

Noah: Obeying by Faith (v. 7)

Noah is the first specific example of faith given. God warned Noah that a flood was coming. He commanded Noah to build an ark that would save him and his family in the coming deluge. After being warned by God of

NEW TESTAMENT REFERENCE

John Calvin said this verse teaches the same truth as Romans 1:20, "where it is said, that the invisible things of God are made known to us by the creation of the world, they being seen in his works. God has given us, throughout the whole framework of this world, clear evidences of his eternal wisdom, goodness, and power; and though he is in himself invisible, he in a manner becomes visible to us in his works." *Commentary on Hebrews.*

WORD PICTURE

Taken Away

The Greek word used here is "one of the most beautiful words to be found in the Bible." It means "to replace." "We could put it like this, 'Enoch was transposed.' He exchanged earth for heaven. God loved him so much, and he was so true to God, that God just took him on to glory." James T. Draper, *Hebrews*, 307.

PERSONAL APPLICATION

Faith pleases God. In fact, without faith, pleasing God is impossible. Faith is manifest in two ways: (1) The person believes that God exists and (2) that God rewards those who seek him. The demons believe that God exists (James 2:19), but they do not respond to his righteous character, which demands that they cease to do evil and learn to do well (Isa 1:16–18).

the flood to come, by faith Noah constructed an ark to save his household (v. 7). Noah had no evidence of what was about to happen except what God told him. He believed God and built the ark.

Abraham: The Life of Faith (vv. 8–12,17–19)

Abraham, the father of the faithful, holds the place of greatest prominence in this list. The Genesis account tells us that Abraham believed God and that God reckoned it to him as righteousness (Gen 15:6). This passage in Hebrews highlights his life of faith.

- In response to God's call, Abraham obeyed and left his ancestral home. He didn't have anything like a complete picture of where he was going or the outcome of his journey, but he believed God and obeyed (v. 8).
- Abraham lived or sojourned as a stranger in the land God would later give his descendants. He lived in tents as did his son, Isaac, and his grandson, Jacob. He was content with these arrangements because he was looking for a substantial city—one God had built (v. 10).
- Abraham exhibited exceptional faith when he responded to God's command to sacrifice Isaac. He recognized God's ownership of Isaac and believed God could raise Isaac from death (v. 19).

WORD PICTURE

Stayed as a foreigner

"This verb is related to a noun which refers to a licensed sojourner. Such a person paid for the privilege of living in a land without becoming a citizen in order to do business in the land." Herschel H. Hobbs, *Hebrews*, 113.

Sarah: The Power of Faith (v. 11)

Because she is a heroine of the faith, Sarah received special attention. By faith Sarah received power to conceive, even when she was past the age of childbearing. Conception, birth, and child-rearing require concentration of strength, energy, and will. Sarah's faith was so active that it reckoned "the one who had promised was faithful" (v. 11) to enable her, even in old age, to receive such a blessing.

Because the writer of the letter did not want his readers to forget his main point with these illustrations, he paused a moment to remind them of his purpose before continuing (vv. 13–16). All of these—Abel, Enoch, Noah, Abraham, and Sarah—"died in faith" without receiving the complete realization of the promises of God. With eyes of faith, they saw "from a distance" the promise of God's redemption and greeted it, remaining essentially "foreigners and temporary residents on the earth" (v. 13).

The writer proceeded to mention briefly several other Old Testament heroes and heroines of the faith.

PERSONAL APPLICATION

This review reminds us also not to set our own minds to things on earth. We, too, are sojourners on our way to a better country. We are to maintain an orientation to God's unfolding future.

Others (vv. 20–40)

Isaac. Like his father Abraham, Isaac believed God and acted on his faith by passing on his blessing to Jacob and Esau and, through that blessing, to succeeding generations (v. 20). He showed faith that his own death would not cancel out the promises of God.

Jacob. Likewise Jacob, "when he was dying, blessed each of the sons of Joseph" (v. 21) as a sign that he was looking ahead to the future for the fulfillment of the promises of God. Although famine forced Jacob and his family to emigrate to Egypt, his ties to the land of promise were not severed, and his confidence in the promises of God was not shaken.

Joseph. By faith Joseph is said to have spoken at the end of his life of "the exodus of the Israelites" and to have given them instructions to take his bones back for burial in the land of promise, when they themselves returned (v. 22).

Moses. By faith Moses's parents hid him to save his life (v. 23). By faith Moses identified with the Israelites, refusing to be called the son of Pharaoh's daughter. He chose to suffer with God's people rather than indulge in the pleasures of sin (v. 25).

Rahab. By faith, the life of Rahab the harlot was spared. She did not perish with the disobedient because she "welcomed the spies" (v. 31), thus proving herself to be believing.

As the writer of Hebrews drew to the end of his roll call, he also mentioned Gideon, Barak, Samson, Jephthah, David, Samuel, and the prophets (vv. 33–34).

This great chapter concludes with this summary: "These were approved through their faith, but they did not receive what was promised, since God had provided something better for us, so that they would not be made perfect without us" (vv. 39–40).

These people lived in faith, worked in faith, and died in faith. God was the object of their faith. He did great things for them under the old covenant promise, and he has done and is doing something far better for us under the new covenant through Christ.

Section Summary

As an incentive to his readers' endurance before God, the writer presented a gallery of Old Testament heroes of faith. We, too, are sojourners on our way to a better country. We are to maintain an orientation to God's unfolding future. By faith, like those in the writer's roll call, we too, are to cling to righteousness and unchanging values.

QUESTIONS TO GUIDE YOUR STUDY

1. According to the writer of Hebrews, what is faith?

2. What does faith do?
3. What are we to learn from the author's list of Old Testament illustrations of faith? Why is each example included?
4. Because Rahab was a harlot, some people might be reluctant to include her in a hall of fame of faith. Why did the writer of Hebrews include her here?

WORD PICTURE

Cloud

We find the word *cloud* used only here in the New Testament. It is the Greek word for a vast mass of clouds *(nephos)*. The metaphor refers to the great amphitheater with the arena for the runners and the tiers upon tiers of seats rising like a cloud. The "witnesses" here are not mere spectators but those who testify from their own experience to God's fulfilling his promises (11:2,4,5,33,39). A. T. Robertson, "The Epistle to the Hebrews," *WPNT,* vol. 5, 432.

HEBREWS 12

In this chapter the writer of Hebrews provided incentives to the believer for enduring hardships. He mentioned the example of Jesus (vv. 1–3) and the benevolent discipline of God (vv. 4–11). Describing the dramatic circumstances under which the old covenant began, he presented Jesus as the Mediator of a new and better covenant (vv. 18–29).

To promote holiness and fear in the readers, the writer noted that the character of God resembles a consuming fire.

AN ADMONITION TO PUT FAITH TO WORK (12:1–13)

The Example of Christ (vv. 1–3)

The author of Hebrews wrote that we are surrounded by "a large cloud of witnesses" (v. 1).

Because Christians are surrounded by a great "cloud of witnesses," they are called to action (v 1). They are to "lay aside every hindrance" so that their working faith will not be frustrated. Our God-given freedom guarantees that we may choose to run with handicaps, that we may pet the sin that dogs our feet, but we will do well to lay aside every hindering weight and shun every distraction and sin.

The purpose of this personal initiative to reject sin is that Christians may "run with endurance" (v. 1) the race marked out for them. The example of Christ should motivate and encourage the believer so that he or she "won't grow weary and give up" (v. 3).

WORD PICTURE

Lay Aside

Throw off ["lay aside" in the CSB] is a compound word made up of the preposition *off* and the verb *to throw.* A. T. Robertson wrote that "the runners ran in the stadium nearly naked." For the believer, *everything* is "every encumbrance that handicaps like doubt, pride, sloth, anything. No trailing garment to hinder or trip one." "The Epistle to the Hebrews," *WPNT* vol. 5, 432.

Section Summary

Believers are to lay aside every hindering weight and shun every distracting and hobbling sin so they may "run with endurance" the race marked out for them. They are to look to the example of Christ as an encouragement.

God's Purpose (vv. 4–13)

Christians are to demonstrate subjection to God by their obedience in suffering and through trials, by patient endurance of hostility, and even through open persecution (v. 9). The result of this endurance is "the peaceful fruit of righteousness to those who have been trained by it" (v.

11). The writer of Hebrews issued three exhortations to his readers as a track for discipline:

1. *"Strengthen your tired hands"* (*v. 12*). The writer's reference to tired hands and weakened knees is from Isa 35:3, where the prophet was encouraging the people to endure with the assurance that God would come and save them.
2. *Strengthen your "weakened knees"* (*v. 12*). Believers need strength for the heavy loads they will lift and the hard tasks they will undertake.
3. *"Make straight paths for your feet"* (*v. 13*). The path is to be level "so that what is lame may not be dislocated but healed instead." Runners leave tracks behind them that either lead or mislead others who follow. The path of the believer is not to be "turned out of the way." A. T. Robertson, "The Epistle to the Hebrews," *WPNT*, vol. 5, 437.

It is God's intention that Christians should march into spiritual battle in full spiritual health and vibrant faith. The door to God was opened through Jesus Christ, and we are to walk confidently through that door and in his way.

PERSONAL APPLICATION

"We may wonder why God wants us to follow after peace before holiness, as our text suggests. We need to remind ourselves that Christians are being reminded that they cannot be right with God if they are not right with their fellowmen. A lost man must get right with God first, and then with his fellowman. But a Christian cannot be right with God if he is not right with his fellowman." James T. Draper, *Hebrews*, 347.

Section Summary

The writer also found encouragement for endurance from Jesus's example (12:1–11). Jesus had already run the race of faith, and God had placed him on the throne. When Christians consider the hardships he faced, they can find strength and fresh courage. God allows all Christians to experience hardship so that they might develop holiness. Even though God's chastisement seems hard for the time, it will eventually produce righteousness in those who follow him.

A WARNING AGAINST REJECTING GOD (12:14–29)

The Beauty of Holiness (vv. 14–17)

A Call for Holiness (v. 14). Hebrews 12:14 is one of the great ethical texts in the Bible. It is a clarion call for holiness. After reminding his readers of how discipline from the Lord comes so "that we can share his holiness" (v. 10), they are to "pursue peace with everyone."

The "peace with everyone" for which we are to strive is a natural result of one's peace with God. Such peace, however, is not a routine result. The believer must determine to work out a right relationship with God and right relationships with others. The believer achieves true peace with others by working faithfully for the things that make for

WORD PICTURE

Holiness

Holiness is a drawing near to God with a cleansed conscience. The Bible provides several reasons we as believers need holiness:

1. We need holiness because God commands it: "Be holy, for I am the LORD your God" (Lev 20:7; 1 Pet 1:16).

2. We need holiness because our nature is such that we can never be at rest until we are at rest in God who is holy.

3. We need holiness because holiness in the lives of believers is the only thing to which the lost world has ever paid attention. It is the only thing in the world that authenticates our faith to the lost multitudes.

WORD PICTURE

Make Sure

The writer of Hebrews used this phrase repeatedly throughout this passage. It is one word in the Greek text. It is made up of the words *over* and *to watch*. It means "to watch over, to watch out for." This verb is a present-tense participle, indicating that this action is to be continuous. "The word expresses that careful regard of those who occupy a position of responsibility (as a physician, or a superintendent)." Fritz Rienecker, *Linguistic Key to the Greek New Testament* (Zondervan, 1980), 716.

peace: justice and righteousness, honesty and fairness, selflessness and kindness, mercy and love.

Holiness is available to those in Christ (v. *14*). Holiness is available to those who come to Christ in faith and then strive for it with all their hearts. It is sobering to realize that without holiness, "no one will see the Lord" (v. 14).

The Root of Bitterness (vv. *15–16*). The author next issued a three-dimensioned admonition. Believers are to "make sure":

- "That no one falls short of the grace of God."
- "That no root of bitterness springs up, causing trouble and defiling many."
- That no one be immoral or irreligious like Esau, "who sold his birthright in exchange for a single meal."

The "root of bitterness" is a reference from Deut 29:18 that warns against turning away from the Lord. As tares could choke out the wheat in Bible times, and as Johnson grass can ruin a crop in our times, so the Christian is to ensure that no bitter root of evil doctrine or evil doing is allowed to grow in the garden of faith, lest trouble and defilement prevail.

Sexual Immorality and Godlessness (vv. *15–16*). Christians also are to "make sure . . . that there isn't any immoral or irreverent person." The first reference seems to be to sexual immorality. The word used is the one from which our word *pornography* is derived. The word is generally taken to mean sexual vice. The second warning against being irreligious or profane is bolstered by a stern reminder of the awful fate of Esau who so despised the heritage which should have been his in line with the promises of God that he sold it all "for a single meal" (v. 16). Christians are to be everlastingly vigilant to "make sure" that none be sexually immoral or profanely irreligious. Those qualities are outward signs of inner chaos.

Section Summary

God provides the Christian with another incentive for endurance. God desires that all persons seek after holiness.

Requirement for Grateful Service (vv. 18–29)

Christians have not come to Mount Sinai with its terrifying manifestations of the awful presence of the Almighty (vv. 18–21) but "to Mount Zion, to the city of the living God (the heavenly Jerusalem)." If the former was awesome, how much more awesome is the city of God.

God shook the earth at Sinai. Many who saw the display of power and holiness at Sinai still refused to listen and obey. As a result, they died in the desert, outside the land God had promised them.

God is going to shake the earth again and not only the earth but heaven as well. The result of this shaking will be that only those things which are unshakable will remain. Everything else will be consumed.

Christians are called to be grateful for "receiving a kingdom that cannot be shaken" (v. 28). Therefore, and never forgetting that "our God is a consuming fire" (v. 29), we are to "serve God acceptably, with reverence and awe" (v. 28).

PERSONAL APPLICATION

"Many years ago President Pat Neff of Baylor University commented on laying up treasures in heaven. He said that preachers had been telling him to do this, but that no one had told him how to get his treasures into heaven. He concluded that to do this one must invest his earthly treasure in things that are going to heaven. Not cattle, land, stocks, bonds, oil, or other earthy things—but in men, women, boys, and girls." Hershel H. Hobbs, *Hebrews,* 131.

Section Summary

God will not tolerate a disobedient, self-serving lifestyle. The presence of God at Sinai caused thunder, lightning, and fright among the people who saw him. If God's speaking on earth at Sinai produced fear, how much more would his words from heaven through Jesus produce fear. God's kingdom is unmovable. This gives Christians the grace to serve him with stamina and reverence.

QUESTIONS TO GUIDE YOUR STUDY

1. The author of Hebrews wrote that Christians are surrounded by "a large cloud of witnesses." What does this phrase mean?
2. What is the content of the author's warning against rejecting God?
3. What is the main point of the author's relating Old Testament experiences in verses 18–29?
4. What is the relationship between a Christian's salvation and grateful service?

HEBREWS 13

This chapter contains the writer's final exhortations and conclusion. The letter of Hebrews is profoundly theological, and its emphasis on the great high priestly work of Christ is unsurpassed in the Bible. It is deeply ethical, however, from its beginning to its ending. In the last chapter of the book, ethical issues of great importance are raised and dealt with by the writer in the knowledge that Christians need help in knowing how to live while seeking the city of God. The writer did not conclude his letter with chapter 12. Instead, he climaxed it with chapter 13 and its immensely important moral teachings.

EXHORTATIONS FOR CHRISTIAN BEHAVIOR TOWARD OTHERS (13:1–3)

The writer delivered these exhortations regarding the believer's behavior toward others.

"Let Brotherly Love Continue" (v. 1)

Where the Spirit of Christ is, there is brotherly love. Christians are not to let their brotherly love fade. Instead, they are to cultivate it diligently.

"Don't Neglect to Show Hospitality" (v. 2)

This exhortation shows the importance of hospitality as an expression of brotherly love among the early Christians. By showing such hospitality, many have entertained "angels," the messengers of God, "without knowing it." Some risks are taken when strangers are entertained, but living the Christian life was never meant to be a risk-free adventure. The moral ministry of hospitality, therefore, is not to be neglected.

"Remember Those in Prison . . . and the Mistreated" (v. 3)

This exhortation reminds us that Christians are to maintain a deeply genuine concern for common, poor, powerless, and downtrodden people of the world. The writer was not claiming the innocence of most prisoners but rather that they are all needy, lonely, and frustrated by their self-made shackles inside their society-made walls. We are to remember them as if we were there with them, in the knowledge that, as we render moral ministries to them and to needy people like them in Jesus's name, we actually serve our Lord (Matt 25:31–46).

HISTORICAL BACKGROUND

When John Calvin wrote his commentary on Hebrews in the sixteenth century, he observed that hospitality had, at that time, ceased to be practiced by most people. "For the ancient hospitality, celebrated in histories, is unknown to us, and inns now supply the place of accommodations for strangers."

Section Summary

Christians have practical duties with one another. They must show sympathy to others, including those in prison.

EXHORTATIONS FOR CHRISTIAN BEHAVIOR TOWARD OURSELVES (13:4–6)

The writer delivered these exhortations regarding believers' behavior toward ourselves.

PERSONAL APPLICATION

"Nothing is to break the bond of marriage. God is deeply concerned about it, because a broken home will give an occasion for the enemies of God to delight in the tragic life of a Christian." James T. Draper, *Hebrews*, 366.

"Marriage Is to Be Honored by All and the Marriage Bed Kept Undefiled" (v. 4)

This is the clearest statement related to marriage and sexual ethics in the book of Hebrews. "God will judge the sexually immoral and adulterers" (v. 4), but Christians are assured of escaping that judgment because God has called us not to sexual immorality but to purity. "The marriage bed," or sexual union, is extremely important to individuals, families, churches, nations, and society at large. Only as its sacredness is preserved can the institution of marriage be "honored" and kept pure.

"Keep Your Life Free from the Love of Money" (v. 5)

Greed is a sickness of the soul, a malignancy in the spirit, a bottomless pit that Christians are to steer away from at all costs. The love of money is the root of all kinds of evil because it is a kind of addictive idolatry (1 Tim 6:10). The more the greedy person gets, the more he or she wants.

Such a person is like the rich farmer in Jesus's parable who so lusted for increased possessions that he determined to tear down adequate barns in order to build even bigger ones.

Christians need not be anxious about money because the Lord is their helper.

OLD TESTAMENT REFERENCE

To encourage his readers along these lines, the author quoted an Old Testament promise (Deut 31:6 and Josh 1:5). The reason Christians should be content with what they have is that God has promised, "I will never leave you or abandon you."

Section Summary

Christians are to (1) keep the marriage union pure and to avoid sexual immorality; and (2) keep their lives free from the love of money. God offers the promise that he will never leave Christians, and that promise helps them to banish greed (v. 6).

EXHORTATIONS FOR CHRISTIAN BEHAVIOR TOWARD GOD (13:7–9)

The writer delivered these exhortations regarding the believer's behavior toward God.

"Remember Your Leaders" (v. 7)

This is an admonition to honor and imitate those "who have spoken God's word" by which faith came. They are gone, but by their precept and example, they have left us firmly anchored to "Jesus Christ" who "is the same yesterday, today, and forever" (v. 8).

"Don't Be Led Astray by Various Kinds of Strange Teachings . . . Be Established by Grace" (v. 9)

This exhortation has to do with "food regulations" (v. 9). It is a warning against any new religious fad that foolishly focuses on foods while turning away from faith in God whose grace is uniquely mediated through Christ. Bread can sustain the body, but only grace can sustain the heart.

HISTORICAL BACKGROUND

Christ's Sacrifice

The book of Hebrews portrays Christ as the sinless High Priest who offered up himself as a sacrifice for sinners (Heb 7:27). The superiority of Christ's sacrifice over the Levitical sacrificial system is seen in that his sacrifice had to be offered only once. First Peter 2 calls believers a holy and royal priesthood who offer up spiritual sacrifices. Jesus's death was an offering and sacrifice to God and, as such, a fragrant aroma (Eph 5:2). Jesus was associated with the Passover sacrifice (1 Cor 5:7).

Section Summary

In these verses, the writer exhorted his readers to "remember your leaders" and "don't be led astray by various kinds of strange teachings." Instead, they are to be strengthened by grace, not by regulations about food.

SACRIFICES PLEASING TO GOD (13:10–16)

A spiritual sacrifice is an act done or given in the name of Christ for his glory. In the verses that follow, the writer mentioned several such sacrifices that are pleasing to God.

Christ's Supreme Sacrifice on the Cross (vv. 10–12)

Christ's sacrifice which he made outside the city gate (v. 12) does not require or involve or even allow any special meal. It is faith in him alone on which the Christian's right relationship to God depends.

Our Sacrifice of Bearing Disgrace for Christ's Sake (vv. 13–14)

Here the writer called on Christians not to be at home where Jesus was homeless, not to get all settled down when Jesus had no place to lay his head, not to seek the world's praise when it has heaped abuse on our Lord, and not to cling so selfishly to life inside the camp that we will not risk life outside the camp for Him who loved us and gave himself for us.

Christians are to live always with the realization that "we do not have an enduring city here" (v. 14). Rather, they are a people who seek "the one to come."

Our Sacrifice of Praise to God (v. 15)

"Through him let us continually offer up to God a sacrifice of praise, that is, the fruit of lips that confess his name" (v. 15). Such an acceptable sacrifice of praise to God might also include, however, mouths that preach his gospel and lives that demonstrate his love. The "fruit of lips that confess his name" has always been the fruit of more believers, inasmuch as God's Word never returns to him void.

Our Sacrifice of Self for the Sake of Others (v. 16)

"Don't neglect to do what is good and to share" (v. 16) is a powerful reminder that those who rail out against do-gooders are not on God's side. The alternatives to doing good are to do evil or to do nothing. Christians of every age do well to heed this call "to do what is good" and "to share" what we have. Such self-sacrifice is the authentication of the genuineness of the words of profession and confession which we have uttered with our mouths.

Section Summary

The writer mentioned several sacrifices that are pleasing to God. These include Christ's supreme sacrifice on the cross, the believer's sacrifices of bearing abuse for Christ's sake, sacrifice of praise to God, and sacrifice of self for the sake of others.

A COMMAND TO OBEY TO LEADERS (13:17)

The readers of Hebrews now receive advice on submitting to their leaders: "Obey your leaders and submit to them" (v. 17). This advice provides unqualified endorsement of Christian leaders in the particular fellowship to whom this letter was originally sent. The advice also intends to provide encouragement for the members to obey the teachings and to submit to the spiritual leadership of those who were called to keep watch over their souls "as those who will give an account" to God.

The special responsibility of church leaders is to be carried out joyfully: "So that they can do this with joy and not with grief" (v. 17). When a spirit of joy prevails, those in their spiritual charge are helped, comforted, reproved, and strengthened.

PERSONAL APPLICATION

There is a timelessness about this advice. God-called leaders are universally concerned for the highest interests of all the Christians to whom they are related. As a group and individually, they provide spiritual direction for the community of faith. They rightly divide the word of truth and preach God's Word in season and out of season. They press the claims of Christ on both unbelievers who need to come to him and on believers who need to come closer to him. As the shepherd sleeplessly keeps watch over his flocks by night or as the soldier remains wakefully vigilant through the long watches of the night, so the spiritual leader is spiritually alert to discharge his pastoral responsibilities.

Section Summary

Christians must follow the faith of their leaders by obeying them and submitting to their authority. When Christians submit to those who care for their spiritual needs, their leaders are free to do their jobs with joy, not with hardship or frustration.

BENEDICTION AND CONCLUSION (13:18–25)

Benediction (vv. 18–20)

The writer of Hebrews exhorted his readers to "pray for us" (v. 18). He could make this request because he had a clear conscience in knowing that he desired to live honorably in every way toward his readers. Using the first person for the first time in his letter, he wrote, "I urge you all the more to pray that I may be restored to you very soon" (v. 19); that is, that he might quickly be with them again.

Conclusion (vv. 20–25)

The writer made a final appeal at the end of his letter. He asked his readers to "receive this message of exhortation, for I have written to you briefly" (v. 22). He shared the good news that Timothy had been released.

The readers were to greet all their leaders on behalf of the writer. He added that those from Italy send their greetings. Then with this beautifully simple word the letter is concluded, "Grace be with you all" (v. 25).

Because the most majestic and memorable benediction in the whole Bible is recorded in Hebrews 13:20–21, it is fitting to use it as the benediction for this look at the book of Hebrews: "Now may the God of peace, who brought up from the dead our Lord Jesus—the great Shepherd of the sheep—through the blood of the everlasting covenant, equip you with everything good to do his will, working in us what is pleasing in his sight, through Jesus Christ, to whom be glory forever and ever. Amen."

Section Summary

The writer made a final appeal at the end of his letter. He included, as part of his conclusion, one of the most majestic and memorable benedictions in the whole Bible (vv. 20–21).

QUESTIONS TO GUIDE YOUR STUDY

1. The writer provided several final exhortations for his readers. What are his exhortations for Christian behavior toward others? Why is each so important?
2. What are the writer's exhortations for Christian behavior toward ourselves? Why is each so important?
3. What are the writer's exhortations for Christian behavior toward God? Why is each so important?
4. What spiritual sacrifices are pleasing to God?
5. Why does the writer issue a command for Christians to obey their spiritual leaders?

James

INTRODUCTION

The letter of James belongs to the section of the New Testament usually described as the General Epistles. The letter is one of exhortation for practical Christianity. The author states principles of conduct and then frequently provides poignant illustrations. The author's concerns are clearly more practical and less abstract than those of any other New Testament writer. No other New Testament book has received the level of criticism encountered by this epistle.

JAMES IN A "NUTSHELL"

Purpose:	To call individuals and the church to full commitment to God and to concern for one another
Major Doctrine:	Genuine faith that is evidenced by good works
Key Passage:	James 1:22
Other Key Doctrines:	Prayer, judgment, grace, intercession

THE MAIN THEME OF JAMES

James's letter makes a unique contribution in the New Testament with its strong ethical emphasis. Its ethical teaching is scattered throughout his writing. James clearly taught that a faith that lacks works is empty, vain, and useless. James's frequent use of the imperative mood (in the Greek language which he used to write the letter) indicates his passionate feeling about the issues he faced. His fiery words resemble those of an Old Testament prophet. He shared ethical commands that touched upon both personal morality and social justice.

AUTHOR

The book of James came slowly into widespread circulation in the early church. Many factors contributed to this. Its brevity and practical nature made it seem of small significance in comparison to a book like Romans. Christians in the early church also disagreed concerning the identity of James, the author of the letter. Those who identified the name with the Lord's brother tended to view the letter as genuine Scripture. Those who rejected the link between James and Jesus tended to ignore the letter.

Bible students debate the precise meaning of "the Lord's brother" (Gal 1:19). Possibilities are the literal brother or stepbrother, a cousin, or intimate friend or associate. The literal meaning is preferred.

Paul, seeking out Peter in Jerusalem after his conversion, reported "I didn't see any of the other apostles except James, the Lord's brother" (Gal 1:19). In time, James assumed the leadership of the Jerusalem church, originally held by Peter. Evidently, such was achieved not through a power struggle but by James's constancy with the church while Peter and other apostles traveled.

HISTORICAL BACKGROUND

Church councils meeting at Rome (AD 382) and Carthage (AD 397) accepted the book of James as Scripture. This acceptance gave support to the view that James, the Lord's brother, was the author.

In a Jerusalem conference called regarding Paul's Gentile mission, James presided as spokesman for the Jerusalem church (Acts 15). James perceived his calling as to the "circumcised," that is, the Jews (Gal 2:9), and is portrayed as loyal to Jewish tradition. He was, however, unwilling to make the law normative for all people who responded to God's new action in Christ.

The death of James reportedly was at the order of priestly authorities in Jerusalem and was either by stoning (according to Flavius Josephus, first-century historian of the Jews) or by being cast down from the temple tower (after Hegesippus, early Christian writer, quoted by the third-century historian Eusebius). These accounts of James's death (ca. AD 66) are not confirmed in the New Testament.

The text of James provides little information about the author other than his name, but its mention provides an important clue to his identity. Few persons with the name of James could succeed in identifying themselves merely by their first name. The writer must have been an important James.

Other features of the letter also confirm the likelihood of identifying the author with Jesus's brother. James 1:22 and 5:12 contain echoes of Jesus's teaching in Matt 7:20–24 and 5:34–37, respectively. The brother of the Lord could have heard this teaching. While it is not possible to prove beyond a shadow of a doubt that the Lord's brother is the author of this letter, he is the most likely candidate from among the men named James mentioned in the New Testament.

PURPOSE FOR WRITING

The letter is pastoral in purpose, and we see several purposes that James targets within its pages:

- It encourages those besieged by trials.
- It rebukes the prejudiced.
- It condemns an idle faith that will not work.
- It instructs regarding the tongue.
- It explains the nature of pure religion.
- It counsels concerning the ministries to the sick.
- It shows concern for evangelism.

"In a book written in 1915, the great Greek scholar A. T. Robertson chose for his title *Practical and Social Aspects of Christianity*. That title appropriately picks up the theme of this particularly powerful epistle" (taken from Foy Valentine, *Hebrews, James, 1 & 2 Peter*, Layman's Bible Book Commentary [B&H, 1981], 67).

DATE OF WRITING

Many scholars think the book of James is one of the earlier New Testament writings. Three features suggest an early date:

1. James describes a large gap between the rich and the poor (5:1–6). When the war against Rome broke out in AD 66, the rich suffered great losses, and conflict between the rich and poor ceased. The impact of this observation pushes the writing to an earlier time rather than later.
2. The church organization mentioned in James seems undeveloped as seen in the mention only of elders as church leaders (5:14).
3. Christians were fervently expecting the return of Christ (5:7–9). Such fervor would be truer of the initial generations of Christians.

All of these features support the acceptance of an earlier date for the writing of James.

HISTORICAL BACKGROUND

James, the Lord's brother, was martyred in AD 62. If he was the author of the letter, the letter was written before AD 62.

AUDIENCE

The letter lacks an address to a specific church. The address of the letter is to "the twelve tribes dispersed abroad" (1:1). The twelve tribes were social and political groups in Israel claiming descent from one of the twelve sons of Jacob. These tribes were Reuben, Simeon, Levi, Judah, Issachar, Zebulun, Joseph, Ephraim, Manasseh, Benjamin, Dan, and Naphtali. Each tribe had its own history within its allotment of land.

The tribes became scattered across many nations. The dispersion, or *diaspora*, refers to this scattering of the tribes. The dispersion of the tribes most likely began at the time of the Assyrian captivity and took place over a span of several centuries. The result of the *diaspora* was that by New Testament times, as many Jews lived outside of Palestine as lived within the land. In almost every city Paul visited in his missionary journeys, he found a Jewish synagogue. The *diaspora* helped pave the way for the gospel.

This suggests that the readers were Jewish Christians who lived outside of Palestine. Several features confirm the truth of this suggestion:

- The term for "meeting" (2:2) is the Greek word for "synagogue." The word does not suggest that the readers met in a Jewish synagogue, but it indicates that Jewish Christians used this name to describe their place of meeting.
- The phrase "dispersed abroad" (1:1) reflects a single Greek word that referred to Jews who lived out of their homeland.

These facts suggest that the Lord's brother directed a message to Jewish believers who left their native country of Palestine.

LITERARY FEATURES IN JAMES

Literary Form

James's writing is similar to Old Testament wisdom literature in Proverbs and Psalms. Both James and Old Testament wisdom literature treat such subjects as the tongue, the dangers of wealth, and the need for self-control. The content of the letter moves quickly from one subject to another. Some scholars have also pointed out a similarity with synagogue homilies or sermons.

James's writing reflects a vivid imagination. We can see his use of various figures of speech in his comparison of the wavering person to "the surging sea, driven and tossed by the wind" (1:6). He was also a close observer of nature. We can see this from his description of the effects of the sun's heat (1:11), horticulture (3:12), and rainfall (5:7,18).

James used several basic literary forms to deliver his letter:

- The entire book is framed in the *epistolary*, or letter, form.
- He uses the *diatribe*, a teaching device for exhorting moral reform in his readers.
- He also uses *parenesis*, traditional moral instruction in the form of loose sets of proverbs.

Key Words

Throughout James we see recurring connecting or "chain" words that form threads of the key themes in the letter. These words include *temptation, patience, perfection, lacking, asking, wavering, lust, sin, slowness, wrath, word, hearer, beholding,* and *doer.*

WORD PICTURE

"These connecting words are designed for didactic purposes, to render the teaching easy to memorize." Nigel Turner, *Grammar of the Greek New Testament*, vol. IV (T &T Clark, 1976), 116.

Literary Devices

James employed several literary devices throughout his writing that are effective tools for providing emphasis, gaining the reader's attention, and communicating spiritual truth. The following are a few of his most-used devices.

Short Questions and Answers. Regularly throughout these chapters James poses short, staccato-like questions that he then follows with an answer. For example:

- "Who among you is wise and understanding?" (3:13)
- " Is anyone among you suffering? (5:13)

Rhetorical Questions. James is fond of this kind of question, for which he does not provide a direct answer. For example:

- "Didn't God choose the poor in this world to be rich in faith and heirs of the kingdom that he has promised to those who love him?" (2:5)
- "What good is it . . . ?" (2:14)
- "Can a fig tree produce olives . . . ?" (3:12)

Irony. Irony is expression of a thought that naturally conveys its opposite. Irony is often connected with serious words and concepts. For example:

- "What good is it . . . if someone claims to have faith but does not have works?" (2:14)
- "You rich people, weep and wail." (5:1)

JAMES AND THE GOSPELS

James echoes many of the themes found in the four Gospels. In his letter are many parallels to the teachings of Jesus, including several striking passages from the Sermon on the Mount (Matt 5–7). The themes he did not include are somewhat surprising, such as the person and work of Jesus Christ, the work of the Holy Spirit, the practice of baptism and the Lord's Supper, and the gifts of the church and its nature as a spiritual body.

JAMES AND THE WRITINGS OF PAUL

The contradiction between James and Paul regarding faith and works is apparent. James was not struggling against Judaizing Christianity, which sought to require circumcision in addition to faith in Christ. He was not trying to "correct" Paul at key points (e.g., Rom 3:20; Gal 2:16). He was concerned with the consistency of genuine faith as evidenced by its results, that faith should be active, not a mere profession covering a life of sin.

JAMES AND THEOLOGY

Doctrines in the Book of James

Some students of James suggest that the book lacks doctrinal emphases. It is true that James assumed some doctrinal similarity between himself and his readers and did not elaborate on all his beliefs. He does affirm the unity of God (2:19; 4:12) together with an emphasis on divine goodness (1:17), graciousness (4:6–8), and judgment (2:13). He emphasizes strongly the return of Christ (5:7–11). In 1:12–15 he presents an analysis of temptation and sin, suggesting that human desire was the source of sin. Much of the content of James represents an effort to call individuals and the church back to full commitment to God and to concern for one another.

NEW TESTAMENT REFERENCE

"Every good and perfect gift is from above, coming down from the Father of lights, who does not change like shifting shadows." (Jas 1:17)

End Time. Trials and testings are presented in view of the revelation of the end-time rule of God. It is this prospect over which believers are called to rejoice and persevere. Judgment is certain, especially upon the rich who have oppressed others.

Faith and Deeds. Deeds demonstrate the genuineness of one's faith. The way believers live must correspond to the claims they make for their faith. James harshly attacks contradictions between faith and life. Faith is primary in his letter but only faith that is true, active, consistent, and genuine.

Ethical Teachings. James showed a concern for reforming Christian behavior. He effectively developed several ethical topics: speech, trials, wealth, and mercy. His contrast between the rich and poor is obvious. Like the Old Testament prophets, James attacked wealthy believers who contradicted the truth of their faith by withholding the acts of love and mercy required of them.

OLD TESTAMENT REFERENCE

"Do not take revenge or bear a grudge against members of your community, but love your neighbor as yourself; I am the LORD." (Lev 19:18)

Law. James's concept of the law draws upon Lev 19:18, which sums up the whole law in the command to love God and neighbor. This law is integral to faith, leading to the mercy and love God requires of those who trust him.

Wisdom. Wisdom is the gift of God. By wisdom, believers translated their present trials into opportunities to trust in and do the will of God. The necessity of wisdom deepens as James comes closer to the description of true faith that contrasts with the foolishness of those who imagine that living faith does not express itself in obedience.

Human Nature. James pointed out that conflicts between faith and the temptation to sin find their source within fallen human nature. Human beings are created in and possess the qualities of the image of God, but they are also their own sources of evil desire.

Church. James does not supply direct teaching on the nature of the church but presupposes it. The local church possessed a plurality of elders upon whom the sick were to call for prayer, but James gave no indication of the nature of their authority.

God. God the Creator receives praise throughout the body of James's letter. That he created the universe and sustains it is summed up by the title "Father of lights." God is generous and merciful, but he is also the Judge and Lawgiver. The doctrine of God is presupposed in James rather than extensively developed.

Christ. James made clear that Jesus Christ is the Lord whom he served. Christ shares this title with God (the Father). He is also called "glorious," fully sharing the glory that belongs to God alone. With these titles, Christ is identified with God.

WORD PICTURE

In 2:1 James refers to Christ as "our glorious Lord."

Theological Significance of the Book of James

James reminds us in a forthright way that faith involves doing. It is not enough to be hearers of the word; we must be doers as well. We cannot just say we are believers; we must show it in our lives. This must be evident in the way we control our tongues and the way we relate to others. The rich must share with the poor. The Christian community must live out its faith by demonstrating love and a working faith to those inside and outside the body of Christ.

THE RELEVANCE OF JAMES FOR BELIEVERS TODAY

James encouraged his readers in the trials and tribulations of life and challenged them to engage in right living. His letter remains of lasting value and consequence to the Christian confronted by an increasingly secular world. The theme and mandate of James is that Christ ought to make a difference in a believer's life. That mandate is just as relevant today as it was when James addressed his original readers.

BASIC OUTLINE FOR JAMES

I. Greeting (1:1)
II. How to Face Trials (1:2–18)
III. A Correct Response to God's Word (1:19–27)
IV. The Avoidance of Partiality (2:1–13)
V. The Production of Works of Mercy (2:14–26)
VI. The Practice of Personal Discipline (3:1–18)
VII. The Avoidance of Worldliness (4:1–17)

VIII. The Demonstration of Justice (5:1–6)
IX. The Practice of Endurance (5:7–12)
X. The Proper Use of Prayer (5:13–18)
XI. The Reclamation of Straying Christians (5:19–20)

QUESTIONS TO GUIDE YOUR STUDY

1. What is the main theme of James's letter?
2. Who were James's readers? What makes his message relevant to today's readers?
3. What do we know about the author of this letter?
4. What is the apparent contradiction some see between what James taught and the writings of the apostle Paul?

JAMES 1

In this first chapter, James began by showing the attitude of a compassionate pastor shepherding his flock through trials. Then he wrote with the fire of an Old Testament prophet as he warned against sinful activities and attitudes and called for changed behavior. In the midst of times of trial, believers may take comfort in the certainty of God's goodness and draw strength from God's Word.

HISTORICAL BACKGROUND

The Diaspora

The diaspora was the scattering of the Jews from the land of Palestine into other parts of the world. The term *dispersion* is often used to describe this process.

GREETINGS (1:1)

From the Author. The writer of this letter identified himself only as "James, a servant of God and of the Lord Jesus Christ." It is significant that James chose not to mention his relationship to Jesus. His statement that he is a servant of Jesus indicates his humility. He did not allow his special relationship to Jesus to imply a unique authority for his teaching (See "Introduction" for a discussion of the authorship of the book of James.)

To His Readers. James's readers were the "twelve tribes dispersed abroad." The "twelve tribes" was a term commonly used to describe the nation Israel, God's chosen people. Comparing this passage with the apostle Paul's view of the church (Eph 2; Rom 11), we see that the church does not displace Israel as God's beloved people but that it does participate in a new covenant that will ultimately be the fulfillment of God's original covenant with Abraham and Moses.

HOW TO FACE TRIALS (1:2–8)

This first section of James presents trials in both their positive and negative aspects. Trials are to be viewed as a reason for rejoicing since vital faith is required by God. Trials serve as faith's stimulus. The guiding principle of this entire first chapter is the right understanding of wisdom. A right understanding refers to a life that puts faith and action together.

Trials Lead to Maturity (vv. 2–4)

The first readers of this letter, scattered and living outside Palestine, are likely experiencing serious adversity. This adversity could have taken many forms, such as loneliness, grief, suffering, hardship, rejection, frustration, homesickness, social isolation, language barriers, and culture shock. Actual persecution might have already begun.

James began with encouragement. He exhorted his readers to "consider it a great joy . . . whenever you experience various trials" (v. 2). James's reference to trials had in mind specific sufferings his readers were enduring. Because all things, including one's trials, work together for good for those who love God and are called according to his purpose, Christians are not to thrash about in frustration as troubles come.

Believers face many kinds of trials. These trials come from different sources—opponents, doubts, fears, and tribulation.

The Greek word behind the English word for "face" is an interesting compound word made up of the preposition "around" and the verb "to fall." It can be rendered "to fall in with or among," or "to come across, encounter." One who "falls into" a trial normally does not have the option of taking or leaving it. These are unwanted and unwelcome experiences. In a sense, one is "surrounded" without avenues for escape. When encountered, trials are to be endured and worked through. For the believer, this is a necessary process for maturing in the faith.

For the believer, trials are not accidents or purposeless. In verses 3–4 James provides his readers with the purpose for trials:

- The testing of the believer's faith produces perseverance.
- Perseverance produces spiritual maturity.

James tells us that the testing of the believer's faith "produces" perseverance and that this perseverance has "its full effect" in maturity.

PURPOSE IN THE TESTING OF THE BELIEVER'S FAITH

PROCESS	PROCESS	FINAL RESULT
Testing	Perseverance	Maturity
Develops	Develops	

In verse 4 James revealed the grand goal of the testing of the believer's faith: "that you may be mature and complete, lacking nothing."

WORD PICTURE

Various

The Greek word for this phrase can also mean multi-faceted or multicolored.

WORD PICTURE

Testing of Faith

The word for "testing" is the word meaning "tested and approved." The purpose of the testing is not to find a person lacking but to approve the genuineness of one's faith, or the genuine element of one's faith. The result of the trial is that true faith is proven to be authentic. The Greeks used this word to describe the testing of metals. "Your faith like gold stands the test of fire and is approved as standard." A. T. Robertson, "General Epistles and Revelation of John," *WPNT*, vol. 6, 12.

"So that you may be mature and complete, lacking nothing" (v. 4) is not James's advice for Christians to achieve an obviously impossible sinless perfection. It is, rather, a powerful reminder that God's people must not surrender to trouble. On the contrary, believers must endure trials faithfully and stand steady through the storms of life. When such steadfastness has "its full effect," then God's faithful people will be "mature and complete, lacking nothing." Foy Valentine, *Hebrews, James, 1 & 2 Peter,* Layman's Bible Book Commentary 23 (B&H, 1981), 70.

Section Summary

James urged his readers to look at trials from God's point of view. The trial itself is not an occasion of joy, but it could promote joy by becoming an occasion for producing stamina in the life of a believer.

Seeking Wisdom Through Prayer (vv. 5–8)

James's letter might appropriately be titled "The Wisdom of James." A quick reading of the entire letter reveals the author's deep concern for wisdom. At an early point in the letter, he introduces this topic of special importance.

Wisdom is attainment of worthy ends using worthy means. As used by James, wisdom is right understanding, moral discernment, spiritual insight, responsible words, and worthy deeds. *Wisdom* is not a word that occurs often in our modern-day newspapers, TV, radio, at the cafeteria, or on the internet.

Praying for Wisdom (v. 5). James encouraged his readers, "If any of you lacks wisdom, he should ask God—who gives to all generously and ungrudgingly—and it will be given to him" (v. 5). Facts may be gathered by inquiring minds, and scientific data can be accumulated and processed by experts in their fields, but wisdom is the special provision of God. To pray to God for wisdom is to recognize the fact that he knows all and to acknowledge his providence. God delights in freely giving his great gift of wisdom, without finding fault with those who ask him.

The wisdom that Christians are to pray for has deep roots in the soil of faith. James taught that there is a close connection between faith, prayer, and wisdom. The Christian who asks for wisdom asks in faith; asking in faith requires divine wisdom. To ask for this wisdom is wise in itself. Growth in wisdom is to understand that everything of faith is from God. Such wisdom sought through prayer is a fundamental characteristic of the believer's life in Christ.

Asking with Doubting (vv. 6–7). In verse 6, however, James warned his readers that those who ask must believe and not doubt that they will receive wisdom from God. James then used simile, a picture from nature, to illustrate the kind of person who doubts. That person is "like the surging sea, driven and tossed by the wind." It is the picture of a rudderless ship on the restless, swaying surface of the sea that is being whipped into whitecaps by the buffeting winds. It is a picture of an unstable vessel going nowhere fast. The believer who doubts his or her relationship with God exposes the instability of faith and will not receive wisdom from God.

"Being Double-Minded" (v. 8). To pursue good and evil at the same time is to divide oneself. The result is hypocrisy and a superficial faith. A person's entire relationship with God is affected, especially in the prayer life.

Double-minded is a word made up of the words "two" and "soul." It refers to a person who is double-minded about something—one whose soul is divided between faith and the world. Such a person "is a walking civil war in which trust and distrust of God wage a continual battle within each other." William Barclay, *The Letters of James and Peter* (Westminster, 1976), 46.

WORD PICTURE

The word James used for "surging sea" is one that refers to a dashing or surging wave in contrast to successive waves. A. T. Robertson, "General Epistles and Revelation of John," *WPNT,* vol. 6, 14.

CONTRAST BETWEEN FAITH AND DOUBT *

PERSON OF FAITH	PERSON OF DOUBT
Has "faith"	Has "doubt"
Asks for "wisdom"	Does not ask for "wisdom from God" or asks with "doubt"
Receives "wisdom" from God	Receives nothing from God

*Kurt A. Richardson, *James,* NAC, vol. 36 (B&H, 1997), 68.

Section Summary

In the midst of trial, the believer must ask for an understanding of the purpose behind the divine permission of the difficulty. An incentive to do this is that God will give generously to those who ask and will not humiliate them for asking. But the believer must not ask in doubt, for such an unstable person will not receive wisdom from God.

POVERTY AND WEALTH (1:9–11)

In these three verses James introduced one of the cardinal teachings of the gospel—the theme of reversal.

The Boast of the Poor (v. 9)

Those in the humblest condition should boast in the high position that will be theirs in the future with God. They are to rejoice that God has lifted them up to make his strength perfect in their weakness. The rich, the beautiful, and the strong are to rejoice that God helped them down

NEW TESTAMENT REFERENCE

"Many who are first will be last, and the last first" (Matt 19:30; cp. Luke 1:46–55).

PERSONAL APPLICATION

The church has always been reluctant to hear God's Word about wealth. The words of Jesus on this point are often glossed over. Many people consider James's teaching on the subject offensive. But the context for this hard truth about the wealthy is the instruction James gave to the Christian community. Riches may hold a special status in the world's way of thinking, but in the church, bought by the blood of Jesus Christ, everybody is somebody. Therefore, the wealth and position of the rich are to be carried under an umbrella of humility.

from their rickety ladders of self-love. The ground at the foot of the cross is level.

The Reduction of the Rich (vv. 10–11)

The rich are to take pride in their "humiliation" (v. 10); that is, they should humble themselves now. James was telling the rich that they need to humble themselves against the temptation of trusting in their wealth rather than placing trust in God.

James began to express the full force of his indignation against the injustice perpetrated by the rich against the poor. Again, drawing a picture from nature, he said that the rich are like a wildflower, which is an Old Testament image of fragility (Isa 40:6; Pss 89:6; 103:15). Under oppressive, scorching heat, its blossom falls, its beauty fades, and the flower withers and dies. Winds coming off the deserts of the south and east were balmy at times, but more often they would sear the land and dry up the vegetation. Like a blast of heat from an oven, this scorching, blistering wind, known as the *sirocco,* had the power to wither flowers in a matter of minutes. Such is the existence of the rich. "The rich person will wither away while pursuing his activities" (v. 11). He will perish along with all his undertakings. His wealth will prove to be an illusion.

Section Summary

Jesus said that "many who are first will be last, and the last first." James told his readers that such would be the case with the rich. James told the rich that they needed to resist the temptation of trusting in their wealth rather than placing trust in God. They were like vulnerable wildflowers that faded in the scorching heat of the desert winds of summer.

ENDURE TRIALS AND RESIST TEMPTATION (1:12–15)

Trials as Life-Giving (v. 12)

Turning again to the subject of trials, James used the only beatitude of his letter: "Blessed is the one who endures trials, because when he has stood the test he will receive the crown of life that God has promised to those who love him."

OLD TESTAMENT REFERENCE

"The wealth of the rich is his fortified city; in his imagination it is like a high wall." (Prov 18:11)

Beatitudes are generally introduced with the term *blessed.* They reflect a person's right relationship to God. We see them in the Old Testament (Deut 33:29; Pss 1:1; 2:12; 144:15; Prov 3:13), and Jesus used them in the Gospel accounts (Matt 5; 13:16). Because the believer's faithfulness is under trial, James declared such a person "blessed."

For the promised reward, James used the phrase "crown of life." This crown was a head wreath, the victor's prize in the Greek games. It might also be given to the person whom the public wished to honor, and it was worn in religious and secular feasts. The grammar of the text allows for two different renderings of this phrase. It could mean (1) "the crown of life," or (2) "a living crown," in contrast to a perishable crown. Most translators prefer the former.

Temptations as Life Taking (vv. 13–15)

Temptations are different from trials. Trials beset us from without. They are an inevitable part of living in a fallen, sin-cursed world. Temptations, however, spring from within when a person is tempted by his or her "own evil desire" (v. 14). James clearly stated that God is not the origin of our temptations. Temptation to sin is the operation of evil forces and the devil.

"Evil desires" originate from within the believer. These may be sexual appetites, the most manipulative, self-gratifying form. Or evil desires may be material goods, money, fame, position, influence, prestige, power, or even comfort. No matter how destructive a sin may be, the believer can find a source of sin outside himself. Our evil desires harbor a reproductive life of their own. Desire conceives an offspring—sin.

The believer must make every effort to resist temptation. For "after desire has conceived, it gives birth to sin, and when sin is fully grown, it gives birth to death."

PROGRESSION OF AN UNCONTROLLED EVIL DESIRE

STAGE	
1. Conception	Temptation—the believer is enticed by own evil desires.
2. Birth	Sin—the believer gives way to the evil desire, and sin lives in the believer.
3. Maturity	Death—sin become fully grown and eventually slays the host.

Section Summary

James warned believers not to blame God for temptation in their lives. God does not dangle evil before people to entice them to sin. Their own evil desires lure them to disobedience. Believers must resist giving in to temptation because it will conceive sin and lead to death.

The Father and the Firstfruits (vv. 16–18)

Because of the complexity of temptation and sin in a believer's life, James was concerned that his readers may have adopted some false ideas about the life of faith. He commanded them, "Don't be deceived, my dear brothers and sisters" (v. 16). If they were being deceived, they were to stop. If they had not yet been deceived, they were to beware.

To emphasize that God is not the source of temptation, James proclaimed that God is the source of "every good and perfect gift" (v. 17).

Therefore, the believer is to understand that God is never involved in the evil when we are tempted or enticed by our own desires. Instead, he is the source of good in the believer's life. James described God's gifts as "good and perfect." Such gifts include wisdom (1:5). The Old Testament has much to say about God's good gifts (e.g., Ps 94:12; Deut 26:11).

James described God as "the Father of lights, who does not change like shifting shadows" (v. 17). James was making the point that the Father of lights, who made them all and directs their course, does not change. He is constant, steady, and unchanging. Although the sun, moon, and stars are constantly moving and periodically are concealed, no shadow comes from God.

WORD PICTURE

Shadows

"Shadows from the sun shift, but not the One who made the sun!" J. Ronald Blue, *The Bible Knowledge Commentary* (Victor Books), 822.

James concluded this section by contemplating God's "good and perfect" gift of salvation. Certainly, God's supreme good and perfect gift is salvation, the new birth through God's good news in Jesus Christ. James made clear that believers have faith because God gives them spiritual birth (John 1:13; Phil 1:29). He clearly contrasted God's action of engendering life with the death that results from allowing sin to conceive in one's life and bring death. This spiritual life is given birth through the "word of truth" that is like a seed that produces a fruit-bearing plant. The word of truth from God, which brought forth the first creation, now brings about the regeneration of human beings.

Section Summary

James taught that God gives only "good and perfect" gifts to believers and he will not vary from that principle. God's supreme good and perfect gift is salvation—the new birth through God's good news in Jesus Christ.

A CORRECT RESPONSE TO GOD'S WORD (1:19–27)

Developing Character (vv. 19–21)

As the life of faith begins with the good gifts of God, so it continues with the development of Christian character. James asked his readers to "understand" the three exhortations he was about to give them. His first two were references to speech and the tongue.

"Be quick to listen." James emphasized listening rather than reacting quickly by speaking.

Wherever wisdom is honored, listening becomes a virtue. Christians are to cultivate the grace of sympathetic listening.

Be *"slow to speak."* In tandem with listening, the believer is to practice the wisdom of careful and deliberate speaking.

Be "slow to anger." One's anger may not be completely controllable, but it can be kept in check by avoiding impetuous remarks.

Certainly, believers are not to indulge in temper tantrums. Anger in a believer's life "does not accomplish God's righteousness" (v. 20). In other words, God's righteousness cannot be accomplished through human anger.

James strongly exhorted his readers to get rid of "all moral filth and . . . evil" (v. 21). All believers need to exercise the spiritual discipline of ferreting out any moral decay in their hearts. Doing so makes room for the "word" that has been implanted in believers. The word James referred to is God's Word that brings salvation in a believer's life. This word continues to grow and mature as believers continue to live committed to the lordship of Jesus. God intends that his children live victorious and abundant lives.

Section Summary

Developing character involves the wisdom of listening and keeping one's anger in check. Believers are to be rid of all "moral filth and . . . evil" so they can receive the implanted word and allow it to take root.

Putting Faith to Work (vv. 22–27)

Do the word. Because the implanted word is dynamic, working salvation in the believers' lives, it is imperative that they are "doers of the word" (v. 22). Those who only hear the word but do not do it are deceiving themselves, James declared.

James went on to use figures of speech to describe the function of the word in the believer's life.

The Word is a mirror (vv. 23–24). James used the illustration of a person looking intently into the mirror. This "mirror" concept is the reader's key for understanding this section of James's letter.

James implied two mistakes that occur when the believer fails to act upon the word: (1) the believer doesn't treat the truth of the word as reality, and (2) the believer ignores the message of the word.

The Word is the perfect law (v. 25). The law is "perfect" in the sense that it participates in God's goodness and is essential to his gifts bestowed in wisdom upon believers. James told his readers that it is "the perfect law of freedom." This combination of law and freedom recalls the apostle Paul's theology of the believer's freedom in Christ (see Rom 6:18–22; 2 Cor 3:17; Gal 2:4; 5:1,13–14; 6:2).

NEW TESTAMENT REFERENCE

What James means is well illustrated in Jesus's parable of the sower (Mark 4:1–9): the believer has to provide the right climate for the growth of God's Word in his life—he has to be "good ground."" Thus there is need to clear out the weeds of moral filth and evil. James's reference to the word as being planted in us may allude to Jesus's parable but probably also hints at the fulfillment of Jeremiah's famous prophecy about the new covenant, in which God promised to "put [his] teaching within them and write it on their hearts" (Jer 31:33). Douglas Moo, *Evangelical Commentary on the Bible*, vol. 1 (Baker Book House, 1989), 155.

HISTORICAL BACKGROUND

Mirrors in Ancient Literature

In the ancient world, the *mirror,* a specially shaped piece of polished metal, was used to inspect or decorate a person's body. The ancient literature is replete with references to the mirror and its use as a metaphor for moral development. Kurt A. Richardson, *James,* New American Commentary 36 (B&H, 1997), 95–96.

HOW GOD'S WORD HELPS BELIEVERS

FIGURE OF SPEECH	PASSAGE	LESSON
Seed	v. 21	The implanted word works out salvation in the believer.
Mirror	vv. 23–24	The word reflects the believer's spiritual condition.
Law	v. 25	The perfect law of God sets the believer free.

James closed this section of his letter by writing that those who do the will of God according to his Word will be blessed.

Section Summary

It is imperative that believers not only hear the Word implanted in them but that they do what it says. James presented three figures of speech that explain how God's Word helps the believer: (1) a seed that could be planted with a Christian to grow into salvation, (2) a mirror that clearly reflects the condition of the one looking into it, and (3) a law that provides freedom.

WORTHLESS RELIGION AND GENUINE RELIGION (1:26–27)

Worthless Religion (v. 26)

A person who imagines himself to be religious while avoiding discipline that is required for "controlling his tongue" has fallen prey to self-deception. One characteristic of self-deception in the believer's life is an empty show of religious devotion. James taught that such religion is "useless."

Genuine Religion (v. 27)

WORD PICTURE

A true response to God's Word is both outward activity and inward control. Ministry to orphans and widows is the outward activity. Separation from the world is evidence of inner control.

Genuine religion is "pure and undefiled," thrusting the believer into the real world of struggles, tears, broken relationships, and raging animosities. This kind of religion involves itself in practical care for "orphans and widows in their distress."

The Christian must always be cautious to avoid compromise with the world. James used the graphic term "unstained" to make this point. This word refers to the ongoing practice of staying free of contamination from the ungodly attitudes and actions of the world.

Section Summary

James contrasted what is worthless religion with what is genuine. Those who practice worthless religion have fallen prey to self-deception. Those who practice genuine religion are careful to avoid being polluted by the world.

QUESTIONS TO GUIDE YOUR STUDY

1. According to James, what is the purpose of trials in the life of the believer?
2. James exhorted his readers to ask God for wisdom. How were they to go about doing so? What does it mean to be "double-minded"?
3. What were James's commands to the poor? To the rich? How were they to respond to his teaching?
4. James said much about temptation in the life of the believer. What is the source of temptation? What happens when a believer gives in to temptation?

JAMES 2

James opens this chapter with a warning. It serves as an intentional break and signals the beginning of four exhortations on authentic faith.

In this chapter James shows how believers should live out their faith in relation to others within the body of believers. For James, faith and works are inseparable. He sets forth three arguments in support of his position.

JAMES'S THREE ARGUMENTS IN CHAPTER 2

PASSAGE	ARGUMENT
2:1–7	Authentic faith does not play favorites.
2:8–13	The "royal law" is "love your neighbor as yourself."
2:14–25	Faith must have deeds.

DO NOT SHOW FAVORITISM (2:1–7)

The Glorious Christ (v. 1)

People play favorites but God doesn't. In the opening verse of chapter 2, James told his readers, "Do not show favoritism." Playing favorites or showing partiality is incompatible with the ways of Christ.

The word translated "favoritism" is a compound word and a distinctive Christian word. It is made up of the words *face* or *person* and *to lay hold of*. Having its roots in the Old Testament, it is a Hebrew idiom meaning "to lift up the face on a person," or "to be favorable and so partial."

OLD TESTAMENT REFERENCE

There is a strong affinity between what James wrote in this passage and Lev 19:15: "Do not act unjustly when deciding a case. Do not be partial to the poor or give preference to the rich; judge your neighbor fairly."

PERSONAL APPLICATION

Taking this parable to heart is painful for many believers and congregations. Although the gospel requires a change in social relations within the church, in contemporary Western middle-class churches, the poor rarely would visit. The church needs to refrain from favoritism based on economic, educational, and social status and practice the redemptive role given God's people by Christ. Moving from favoritism to fairness will please Christ and will raise the credibility of the church in the community in which it is planted.

PERSONAL APPLICATION

The church of Jesus Christ must live by the principles of Christ rather than those of the world.

Favoritism becomes a fault when a person responsible to give judgment gives respect to a person's position, popularity, or circumstances instead of that person's intrinsic conditions. In the Old Testament, evil judges often showed favoritism toward rich and powerful people at the expense of those who were not (see Ps 82:2; Prov 18:5; Mal 2:9). This behavior or attitude is *not* characteristic of God. See this word used in this sense of partiality (respect of persons) in Rom 2:11; Col 3:25; and Eph 6:9. A. T. Robertson, "General Epistles and Revelation of John," *WPNT,* vol. 6, 27; and *Vine's Complete Expository Dictionary of Old and* New *Testament Words* (Thomas Nelson, 1996), 469.

When a Christian shows favoritism, he is being double-minded. A Christian has identified with Jesus and his interests and concerns. Jesus, God's unique Son, chose to identify with the poor and helpless during his ministry on earth. His attitude is the model for every believer. So, when a Christian plays favorites, he's at odds with his Lord.

An Illustration of Favoritism (vv. 2–4)

To drive home his point, James gave a case study of favoritism (v. 1). It may well be not just a hypothetical case but something he observed in the churches.

The illustration presents two church visitors and an usher. The usher favors the high-class visitor and provides him with a "good place" but relegates the low-class visitor to a position of inferiority and humiliation: "Sit here on the floor by my footstool." For the members of this congregation, the visit of the rich man became a test of their Christian faith. Sadly, they didn't pass this test.

CONTRASTS BETWEEN THE RICH MAN AND THE POOR MAN

RICH MAN	POINT OF CONTRAST	POOR MAN
Well-dressed ("fine clothes")	Attire	Unsightly ("filthy clothes")
Required preferential treatment	Attitude	Expected fair treatment
Favored	Treatment	Discriminated against

GOD'S DISCRIMINATION (2:5–7)

James followed his illustration with the emphatic words, "Listen, my dear brothers and sisters." He wanted his readers' attention, for he was ready to give them a statement of truth about God's discrimination. He framed this section with a series of rhetorical questions:

- "Didn't God choose the poor in this world to be rich in faith and heirs of the kingdom that he has promised to those who love him?" (v. 5).
- "Don't the rich oppress you and drag you into court?" (v. 6).
- "Don't they blaspheme the good name that was invoked over you?" (v. 7).

The expected, though unexpressed, answer to these questions is yes. James told his readers that they insulted the poor and honored the rich. They disregarded the honor God bestows on the poor. In addition, they failed to confront the rich for depriving others of what was due them.

James made two important statements about the poor:

1. *The poor believers are made wealthy in faith.* God chooses to make the poor heirs of the treasures of the kingdom that cannot perish. Bestowing these eternal treasures is beyond human ability. Only God can do this.
2. *The poor are heirs of the kingdom of God.* God especially delights in raising the poor from where they are to be his sons and daughters.

To be heirs of God's kingdom is to become his children and to share in his nature through resurrection. Jesus is saying that the poor are God's prime subjects of this inheritance in Christ. The church of Christ is to make every effort to ennoble the poor and to rejoice in salvation together with them.

WORD PICTURE

Rhetorical Question

A question asked primarily for effect and not expecting an answer.

PERSONAL APPLICATION

Most of us know how it feels to be on the wrong end of favoritism. It doesn't feel good.

Remembering how it feels, and practicing the royal law, we will avoid showing partiality when dealing with others—regardless of their station in life.

NEW TESTAMENT REFERENCE

We are reminded of the words of our Lord in Luke 6:20: "Blessed are you who are poor, because the kingdom of God is yours."

Section Summary

Favoritism is a complex sin—an evil—that leads to division within the fellowship of believers. James commanded his readers to refrain from demonstrating favoritism to the rich who attended their services while ignoring the poor, for God has chosen the poor to be wealthy in faith and heirs of his kingdom. The church of Jesus Christ must unite around the principles of Christ rather than follow the practices of the world.

THE ROYAL LAW (2:8–13)

The Excellent Deed (v. 8)

James argued that rather than showing favoritism, Christians are to follow the royal law. Echoing the words of Jesus, James defined this law as "Love your neighbor as yourself" (v. 8).

TEACHINGS ON THE ROYAL LAW

JESUS	JAMES	PAUL
"Love your neighbor as yourself." (Matt 22:39)	"Love your neighbor as yourself." (Jas 2:8)	"What matters is faith working through love." (Gal 5:6)

Offensive at Every Point (vv. 9–11)

At this point, James forestalled our responding to him by saying something like, "Favoritism isn't all that bad. It's so common, it couldn't be too bad."

James then made a strong claim. If a person fails to keep even the small points of the law, they break God's entire law.

He illustrated this claim with an example. If a person doesn't commit adultery but murders someone, he breaks the entire law.

A key point to gain from this section is that God's law exposes sin and its true nature. Sin in a person's life is never a question of breaking a single command but rather of violating the integrity of the whole law.

The Freedom-Giving Law (vv. 12–13)

James stirred his readers into action by commanding them to "speak and act" (v. 12) as those who are going to be judged by the law. Both of those words speak of ongoing actions or habits. (See A. T. Robertson, "General Epistles and Revelation of John," *WPNT,* vol. 6, 33.) James closed this section on the royal law with two main points.

The Christian lives under the law of freedom. What does it mean to live under the law of freedom? This is the second time (1:25) this phrase, "the law of freedom," occurs in James. From the perspective of sinful human beings, any kind of law seems like a burden—especially at those points where the law opposes what we want to do at the moment.

NEW TESTAMENT REFERENCE

Jesus was clear in his teaching on this truth:

"For if you forgive others their offenses, your heavenly Father will forgive you as well. But if you don't forgive others, your Father will not forgive your offenses." (Matt 6:14–15)

"Do not judge, so that you won't be judged. For you will be judged by the same standard with which you judge others, and you will be measured by the same measure you use." (Matt 7:1–2)

From the Christian's point of view, the law looks different. We now see that living our life in harmony with God's law is the way of joy and fulfillment. It's like a train running on the tracks for which it was designed rather than running off in fields and forests. Conversion gives us the power and the desire to live as God made us. This is the law of liberty.

Coming back to the problem of favoritism, we might say that it's in our interest not to hurt other people by showing favoritism. We're following the law of freedom when we treat others as we want to be treated.

He who shows mercy will find mercy. James's statement about impending judgment is harsh: "For judgment is without mercy to the one who has not shown mercy" (v. 13).

Mercy is an important ingredient in human relationships because it is a direct indicator of how much we're aware of God's forgiveness of us.

In verse 13 James offered one of the highest principles in all of Scripture: "Mercy triumphs over judgment." On judgment day, God will reserve his judgment where merciful faith is evident. His will to condemn will be emptied by his will to show mercy, and judgment will be swallowed up in mercy.

PERSONAL APPLICATION

"Mercy should be the mark of a regenerated person. If it is present in a believer's life, he will have nothing to fear at the judgment." Donald W. Burdick, *Expositor's Bible Commentary*, vol. 12 (Zondervan, 1981), 180.

Section Summary

James supplied the antidote to wrong thinking and false judgments of the rich: "Love your neighbor as yourself." To play favorites is to commit sin, and breaking the law on this point is serious business. Instead, believers are to "speak and act" as those who will be judged by the law. Those who show no mercy will be judged harshly. James assured the Christian that in the grace of God "mercy triumphs over judgment."

FAITH MUST HAVE DEEDS (2:14–26)

This passage is the third argument of this chapter, delivering the true content of faith according to James. Demonstrating the authenticity of faith is its primary focus.

The relationship between faith and works has been the cause of debate and division among Christians since the first century. Verses 14–26 have been a battlefield for this controversy. The great reformer Martin Luther found this portion of James's letter especially objectionable to his understanding of salvation and faith.

Although James's and Paul's teachings seem to be in conflict at this point, it can be shown that they are consistent with each other.

James and Paul approached faith and works from different points of view. James had a viewpoint that was essentially pastoral. Paul's viewpoint was essentially mission focused. James saw faith and works in light of what God requires of those who have already become Christians, while Paul saw faith and works in the light of what God requires for a person to become a Christian.

This portion of God's truth (2:14–26) can deliver Christians from the false dichotomy that mistakenly assumes a conflict between faith and works in the lives of God's people.

An Open Question (v. 14)

James presented an example and then asked a rhetorical question. Let's suppose a person says that he has faith but has no works. James asked, "Can such faith save him?"

The answer he expected is no.

USAGE OF THE TERMS *FAITH, WORKS,* AND *JUSTIFICATION* BY JAMES AND PAUL

TERM	JAMES	PAUL
Faith	The giving of intellectual assent to the facts of Christianity, an assent that was barren of good works, inactive, and therefore, useless.	Saving faith in Jesus Christ, which faith issues normally and naturally in works of righteousness.
Works	Acts of ministry, mercy, love, and justice done in obedience to the demands of God's indwelling Spirit.	Acts performed legalistically in obedience to the letter of the law in order to earn salvation.
Justification	The believer's final acceptance by God at the last judgment.	God's immediate acceptance of any sinner who repented and believed in obedience to the call of the gospel.

Need Without Deed (vv. 15–16)

At this point, James brought a strong illustration to bear. Suppose a brother or sister in Christ lacks food or clothing. Suppose further that a person thought to be a Christian tells this needy person, "Go in peace, stay warm, and be well fed," without raising a finger to help the person find warmth and food.

A Pronouncement of Faith's Death (v. 17)

James concluded that this is dead faith. It's dead because it shows no signs of life. The kind of faith James is criticizing is mere words. Apparently, this was a problem in James's day. Some people were equating faith with the simple verbal claim that they had faith. These claims apart from works were not the real thing.

PERSONAL APPLICATION

This illustration from James is like a Christian meeting a needy person in his or her fellowship but responding with "Have a nice day!" or "Good luck!" and moving on. Such "faith" lacks Christian action. We see a similar issue in 1 John 3:17–18: "If anyone has this world's goods and sees a fellow believer in need but withholds compassion from him—how does God's love reside in him? Little children, let us not love in word or speech, but in action and in truth."

A Question of Proof (vv. 18–19)

Perhaps Christians had come to see some believers in the church as having faith and others as people of works. James didn't allow this as a valid dichotomy. For James, faith is shown in and by works.

Let's suppose a person believes God exists, James declared. This belief isn't faith. After all, the demons not only believe, but they know that God exists, and they shudder at the thought of God. But they don't have faith. They are against God. Authentic faith is something more than belief. What could it be?

Faith and Deeds (v. 20)

James began this section of his argument by saying once again to his imagined opponent, "Are you willing to learn that faith without works is useless?"

He then proceeded to deliver the answer. In these next few verses James provided two examples of a faith evidenced by works. He used two Old Testament characters: Abraham and Rahab.

The Example of Abraham (vv. 20–24)

God commanded Abraham (Gen 22) to take his only son Isaac to the land of Moriah. On one of the mountains there, he was to offer his son as a burnt offering. Abraham proceeded to act according to God's command. James saw Abraham's belief in God and his action as working together. Abraham's action made his faith in God complete.

James asked rhetorically, "Wasn't Abraham our father justified by works in offering Isaac his son on the altar?" He assumed we will answer yes.

What's the relationship of this claim with Paul's teaching that we are justified by faith alone apart from the deeds of the law (Rom 3:27–28)? Both James and Paul used the same Greek word for *justify*. Both James and Paul appealed to Abraham's action to support their different claims.

The supposed conflict between James and Paul involves the use of some of the same key words: *justify*, *faith*, and *works*. Let's look more closely.

James (2:23) quotes Gen 15:6: "Abraham believed God, and it was credited to him as righteousness." James then declared (v. 24), "You see that a person is justified by works and not by faith alone."

Compare what Paul said: "For we conclude that a person is justified by faith apart from the works of the law" (Rom 3:28).

Paul and James were dealing with two different situations. Apparently, the kind of faith James encountered was *belief that* rather than *belief in*. There's a vast difference between the two. The demons *believe that* God exists, but they don't *believe in* or trust in God.

For Paul, faith included *belief that*, but he added to it *belief in* to the point of obedience. Paul saw faith resulting in good works. It's likely Paul would agree with James that good works give evidence of faith. But Paul maintained that works of the law—merely human effort—do not make a person right before God. God justifies. Humans receive what God has done by faith. Good deeds follow from saving faith.

WORD PICTURE

Made Complete

This is one word in the Greek text, and it means "to bring to completion, to bring to maturity, to perfect, to consummate." "As the tree is perfected by its fruits, so faith by its works. Works do not animate faith; but faith produces works, and works perfect faith. Faith itself 'is perfected,' that is, shown to be true, by works." Fritz Rienecker, *Linguistic Key to the Greek New Testament* (Zondervan, 1980), 731.

The Example of Rahab (v. 25)

James turned to the example of "Rahab the prostitute." In James's day, prostitutes were ranked with tax collectors among the lowest class of people. James used such a person to underscore his emphasis on vital, useful faith. We find Rahab's story in Josh 2:1–21. She mercifully hid the Israelite spies from her own countrymen and cared for their needs before the destruction of Jericho. She exemplified faith in that she recognized the truth of God in his works of delivering Israel, and she demonstrated that faith. It is for her faith that she is remembered (see Heb 11:31).

There Is No Faith Without Deeds (v. 26)

James closed this chapter by reemphasizing verse 17, which is the beginning of the current portion of his letter begun at verse 17, stating that "just as the body without the spirit is dead, so also faith without works is dead." He used the image of a corpse to emphasize a lifeless faith.

PERSONAL APPLICATION

All believers need to nurture a living faith that issues in works of righteousness to the glory of God and the advancement of Christ's kingdom. This means that believers demonstrate their faith by doing what God requires.

Section Summary

Demonstrating the authenticity of faith was James's focus in this section. For him, a living faith cannot be disjoined from deeds that are evidence of that faith. James used the illustration of Abraham, whose faith was made complete by his obedient actions. Because of his faith, God "credited" it to him as righteousness. Justification from God comes to those who put faith to work and who perceive that faith and works are the two sides of the coin of God's saving grace.

QUESTIONS TO GUIDE YOUR STUDY

1. Why is it sin to show favoritism?
2. James wrote about the royal law. What is it? What is its application to modern-day believers?
3. What is the nature of the faith James described? What is the relationship between faith and works?
4. What was the main point of James's illustrations of Abraham and Rahab?

JAMES 3

We all know what damage can be done by falsehoods, gossip, and degrading, abusive language. James insisted that Christians obey God by controlling their tongues and all their desires. The tongue has power for both good and evil. Characteristics of the tongue include stubbornness and inconsistency. In this chapter James urged his readers to demonstrate heavenly wisdom rather than earthly folly.

THE RESPONSIBILITY OF TEACHERS (3:1)

In the early church, teachers were important people. Wherever genuine teachers are mentioned, it is with honor. Teachers who failed in their responsibilities were considered false teachers (Acts 15:24; Rom 2:17–29).

A teacher was one who held something of an office within the church (Acts 13:1; 1 Cor 12:28; Eph 4:11; 2 Tim 1:11). He was a person who mastered the Scriptures and how they were to be applied to faith and life. The teacher's primary tool was speech, and its instrument was the tongue.

The church's teaching ministry has several dimensions.

- *The church teaches about Jesus.* The church presents the basic details of Jesus's life and ministry: His death, burial, and resurrection. It helps members understand the meaning of these events for all time.
- *The church teaches spirituality.* New Christians are not to remain infants in Christ but to increase in "grace and knowledge" of the Lord Jesus Christ (2 Pet 3:18). Christian spirituality is the process of growing in faith. In its teaching ministry, the church guides Christians in the life of faith through prayer, Bible study, and spiritual reflection.
- *The church teaches Christian ethics.* Those who follow Christ must be conformed to his image. The church instructs its members in faithfulness, morality, honesty, and integrity. Ethical instruction is not focused on legalism but on a way of life according to Christ's new commandment to love one another (John 13:34–35). Jesus is the ultimate moral teacher and example for the people of God.
- *The church instructs in Christian doctrine.* The church teaches the basic truths of the Christian faith. It guides Christians in understanding significant beliefs. It opens the Scriptures to determine those doctrinal ideals upon which the church is founded.

As the church teaches, it also evangelizes. The teaching ministry of the church is another way in which the people of God declare their faith in order that others may know Christ and grow up in him. It is no wonder that James warned teachers to control the primary instrument of their vocation—the tongue.

James was not trying to recruit as many teachers as possible. He said plainly that not many people should become teachers because teachers are judged more strictly than others.

Teaching has great potential to build up individual believers and the church. At the same time, wrongful teaching can be destructive.

HISTORICAL BACKGROUND

Teachers in the New Testament

Instruction, or the gift of teaching, is one of the abilities God gives certain Christians to equip them to serve in the Christian community. Teachers were those who provided instruction and exhortation on aspects of Christian life and thought and directed to persons who had already made a faith commitment. Instruction is frequently distinguished from evangelistic preaching.

PERSONAL APPLICATION

We want workers who build airplanes to be well taught. We want physicians to be taught by those who know what they're talking about. How much more should we expect competency from those who teach concerning issues with eternal consequences?

Section Summary

In New Testament times, a teacher was a person who had mastered the Scriptures and how they were to be applied to faith and life. The teacher's primary tool was speech, and its instrument was the tongue. James warned teachers to control the tongue, for they would be judged more strictly for its use.

THE UNCONTROLLABLE TONGUE (3:2–12)

The tongue receives major attention in the Bible. The tongue was thought of as expressing a person's true nature since speech was viewed as more than just a verbal phenomenon (Pss 64:2–3; 45:1; Prov 10:20; 17:20). The wisdom writings of the Old Testament emphasized the practical results of the use of the tongue (Prov 12:18; 18:21; 21:6; 21:23; 25:23; 26:28). Like a bit in a horse's mouth or the rudder of a ship, the tongue could control the direction of a person's life (Jas 3:3–8). Since the tongue reveals what is in a person's heart, its use has ethical consequences, whether good or bad (Pss 34:13; 37:30; 109:2; 120:2; 140:2–3; Isa 59:3).

The tongue was considered an organ of the body that played a central role in the expression of a person's religious commitment. The tongue could be used to praise God (Pss 35:28; 51:14; 71:24; Rom 14:11; Phil 2:11). On the other hand, the tongue could cause separation from God (Job 15:4–5; Pss 39:1; 78:35–37). The potential for good or bad, which is a part of human nature, is actualized through the tongue (Jas 3:9–10).

The tongue is influential in all human relationships. Its strength is out of proportion to its size, and it has an almost limitless potential for good or bad. In verses 2–12 James presented several analogies regarding the tongue to describe its nature and potential.

Analogies of Size (vv. 2–5)

James commented that "though the tongue is a small part of the body, it boasts great things" (v. 5). Here he delivered for his readers three analogies that illustrate how small things can have control over large things, relating those to the nature of the tongue.

1. *A Horse's Bit (v. 3).* Bits are placed in the mouths of big horses to direct them. With this small bit, the rider controls the entire horse. James's analogy provides a clear connection between the turning, or controlling, of the "whole bodies" with a bit, and the controlling of the "whole body" with the tongue (v. 2).
2. *A Ship's Rudder* (v. 4). Small rudders are used by pilots to guide large ships. A ship is an excellent illustration of bringing under control a large object with a small but effective instrument. The analogy is heightened by the fact that on the open sea, and

PERSONAL APPLICATION

Just as a rider can control a horse, so a person can control his or her willfulness and appetites.

against the wind, a vessel without a rudder is uncontrollable. Such a ship is driven and tossed about by the waves that move it along (Jas 1:6).

3. *A Small Fire in the Forest (v. 5).* Although deceptively small and seemingly insignificant, a small spark has potential for massive destruction. One small, unattended spark in the forest can kindle a fire of great force. Many forest fires have been caused by careless campers who failed to douse that last single spark, which then grew into an uncontrollable inferno after being fanned by the wind.

PERSONAL APPLICATION

Just as a rudder in the hands of the trained pilot can steer a vessel through the harshest of winds, the Christian who wisely controls the tongue can direct the potential and impact of his or her speech.

Section Summary

James wrote that "though the tongue is a small part of the body, it boasts great things" (v. 5). In this section he delivered three analogies that illustrate how small things can have control over large things, and he related those to the nature of the tongue.

PERSONAL APPLICATION

Just as a small spark can lead to a great fire of destruction, a word or words of boasting from the tongue can reap much destruction.

Analogies of Force (vv. 6–8)

James turned next to two analogies of force regarding the tongue: a fire and an uncontrollable animal. These become forces of corruption and destruction. James was clear that the tongue cannot be tamed; it must be kept in check.

Fire (v. 6). James wrote that the tongue is a "fire" that corrupts the whole person. The tongue is set on fire by hell itself. "In a most powerful image, the fire that is the little tongue, a little spark causing great fires, has another fire that causes it. Hell has outcroppings in the world, and one of them is evil speaking." Kurt A. Richardson, *James*, New American Commentary 36 (B&H, 1997), p. 154.

PERSONAL APPLICATION

The tongue is "a fire," "a world of unrighteousness," with far-reaching consequences. The person who fails with speech certainly will fail in actions.

To show the extent of its potential, James set forth three cause-and-effect relationships of the tongue as a fire:

1. Corrupt speech corrupts the whole body.
2. The corrupted body sets in motion the evil course of an entire life.
3. The destructiveness of evil speech is derived from the destructiveness of hell.

PERSONAL APPLICATION

In contrast to man's ability to control and tame animals, he has failed to tame the tongue. As a result, the tongue constantly must be kept under the lordship of Jesus Christ.

An Uncontrollable Animal (vv. 7–8). We have tamed all kinds of creatures from the animal world, but humans generally fail to tame the tongue. "It is a restless evil, full of deadly poison," James declared. "This does not mean that for Christians our talk is uncontrollable. It means that the tongue needs everlasting supervision, that it can never be trusted completely, that it can never be left alone without careful direction from the morally responsible and socially sensitive people of God."

Foy Valentine, *Hebrews, James, 1 & 2 Peter*, Layman's Bible Book Commentary 23 (B&H, 1981), 83.

WORD PICTURE

Full of Deadly Poison

The word *deadly* is a compound term made up of two words: the noun "death" and the verb "to bring." The word describes something that is *death bringing*. In this case, the death-bringing agent is poison. It is used only here in the New Testament. "Like the restless death-bringing tongue of the asp before it strikes." A. T. Robertson, "General Epistles and Revelation of John," *WPNT*, vol. 6, 44.

Section Summary

James offered two analogies of force regarding the tongue: It is a fire and an uncontrollable animal. These become forces of corruption and destruction. James was clear that the tongue cannot be tamed; it must be kept in check.

Analogies of Incompatibility (vv. 9–12)

At the outset of these verses, James referred to the fact that men and women have been made in the image of God, "God's likeness" (v. 9). Every human has the stamp of God's likeness. James's point here was that God's image in others is to be respected and not made the object of malediction. To dishonor others is to dishonor God.

James continued his pattern of analogies with three analogies of incompatibility.

Praise and Cursing (v. 10). The tongue has the capacity both to give praise and to curse. The obvious question that arises is, How can speech that builds up and speech that tears down come from the same mouth?

Fresh Water and Salt Water (v. 11). Fresh water corresponds to water that is good or desirable, such as for bathing, drinking, or irrigating crops. Salt water corresponds to water that is bad or undesirable. Salt water is unfit for drinking, irrigating, or bathing.

Fruit Trees and Their Fruit (v. 12). James closed his series of analogies with two illustrations about the fig tree and the grapevine. Rather than presenting a contrast here, he focused on the natural order of living things: Fig trees produce figs, not olives, and grapevines produce grapes, not figs. The believer's speech is a revelation of his or her character. A person's speech comes from the heart.

PERSONAL APPLICATION

Just as a spring that produces fresh water will not produce salty water, the source of the believer's speech should produce "fresh" or wholesome speech.

More friendships are broken, more families are divided, and more churches are split by what is said than by what is done. Foy Valentine observed, "A fist can only reach three feet, but the tongue is an intercontinental ballistic missile." Foy Valentine, *Hebrews, James, 1 & 2 Peter*, Layman's Bible Book Commentary 23 (B&H, 1981), 83.

PERSONAL APPLICATION

Believers are to avoid the temptation to speak evil against others.

Section Summary

James provided two more analogies that were based on incompatibilities. The lessons for his readers were that believers are to be careful in their speech in order to avoid evil speaking. Speech should be wholesome and from the heart.

THE TWO "WISDOMS" (3:13–15)

The Nature of Heavenly Wisdom (v. 13)

In the passage that covers 3:13–4:10, James focused on two main ideas: those who are friends of *God* and those who are friends of the *world*. Those who are friends of God embrace heavenly wisdom; those who are friends of the world embrace "earthly, unspiritual, demonic" (v. 15)wisdom. His opening rhetorical question asked his readers to take inventory of themselves and determine which wisdom was guiding them.

James coupled the terms "wise and understanding" to describe people who embrace heavenly wisdom. Such people measure up to God's standards with both attitudes and proper behavior. In addition, the coupling of these two words views not only the objective truth but also the application of the truth.

THE COOPERATION OF WISDOM AND UNDERSTANDING

WISDOM	UNDERSTANDING
Knows how to do good	Knows why wisdom is good
Concerned with the conduct of one's life	Involves the demonstration of a good life

Wisdom that comes from God leads a person in a life that grows in understanding. The "word of truth" (Jas 1:18), which is implanted in the believer's heart, becomes a primary source of God's wisdom. Kurt Richardson explains the process:

> Wisdom in the life of the believer advances in cycles. Wisdom entails understanding, which entails the demonstration of a good life, which entails humble deeds, which entail wisdom. True wisdom constantly engenders a cycle of increasing virtue that continues throughout a lifetime. The seed of the Word of God grows within and grows up in a believer according to the standard of well-being and well-doing established for us by God. *James*, New American Commentary 36 (B&H, 1997), 163.

HISTORICAL BACKGROUND

"Wisdom does not show itself so much in precept as in life." Seneca

The word "wise" comes from the term that describes "the wisdom of ultimate things" and "knowledge of the most exalted subjects." It speaks of wisdom that is divine in nature and origin. In Matt 23:34, we see Jesus sending out wise men who were experienced and knowledgeable in the things of God. This word *wise* is the technical term for "teacher." The Jewish use of this word spoke of a person who has a knowledge of practical, moral wisdom, resting on the knowledge of God. It is in contrast to the Greek philosophical term that meant "theoretical wisdom." Fritz Rienecker, *Linguistic Key to the Greek* New *Testament* (Zondervan,

1980), 734; and William Barclay, *New Testament Words* (Westminster, 1974), 258–59.

Section Summary

Heavenly wisdom involves both wisdom and understanding—knowing the truth and acting on it. Those who embrace heavenly wisdom measure up to God's standards with both their attitudes and their conduct.

The Nature of Earthly Wisdom (vv. 14–15)

James sharply contrasted heavenly wisdom with earthly wisdom. The word "but" indicates a contrast of values and definition with heavenly wisdom. He describes earthly wisdom as "demoic." Signs of this wisdom in the life of a person are "bitter envy" and "selfish ambition." James made a contrast between the Word of God growing in the heart of the believer who embraces heavenly wisdom and the envy and selfish ambition that grows within the person who embraces earthly wisdom.

James provided his readers with more information about this earthy wisdom.

- *It is unspiritual.* Rather than taking hold of the gifts of God and anticipating the joy that is to come, this wisdom is self-centered and oriented to personal gain. It is concerned only with physical needs and urges and is driven by the dictates of the selfish mind and heart.
- *It is demonic.* "The demonic is an umbrella description for both the directly satanic and all human opposition to God and his Spirit. Thus, the faith that merely assents to gospel truths is on par with demonic faith (2:19b). As soon as believers act out of wrath, they are no longer serving God and so are opposed to God (1:20)." Kurt A. Richardson, *James*, New American Commentary 36 (B&H, 1997), 167.

WORD PICTURE

Bitter Envy

The phrase "bitter envy" translates one Greek word that is sometimes rendered "zeal" or "bitter jealousy." The idea here is of a fierce desire to promote one's own opinion to the exclusion of others.

The believer needs to be alert and careful not to allow a foothold for earthly wisdom. The tongue is influenced strongly by such unspiritual and demonic wisdom.

Section Summary

James sharply contrasted heavenly wisdom with earthly wisdom. The signs of earthly wisdom in the life of a person are bitter envy and selfish ambition. Believers are not to allow a place for such wisdom in their life.

THE TWO WISDOMS AND THEIR HARVESTS (3:16–18)

In the last three verses of this chapter, James categorized the characteristics of the two wisdoms, focusing primarily on the virtues of true, heavenly wisdom.

The Harvest of Earthly Wisdom (v. 16)

"Disorder." This word is also translated "confusion." It carries with it the ideas of trouble, disturbance, and instability. In political contexts it means "anarchy."

"Every Evil Practice." James did not teach that believers who return to earthly wisdom become experts in all kinds of evil. What was likely in his mind here is that when believers return to earthly wisdom, which is demonic and unspiritual, anything can happen. People fueled by ambition and this kind of wisdom will do whatever it takes.

OLD TESTAMENT REFERENCE

"There is a way that seems right to a person, but its end is the way to death" (Prov 14:12).

The Harvest of Heavenly Wisdom (vv. 17–18)

- *'Pure.'* This term speaks of sincere, moral, and spiritual integrity.
- *'Peace-Loving.'* A person governed by true wisdom is one who promotes peace.
- *'Gentle.'* The believer's example is the gentleness exhibited by the Lord Jesus Christ. The process of spreading the good news is not to be mixed with harshness or anger.
- *'Compliant.'* This kind of person is compliant, approachable, and willing to yield—one who willingly receives instruction about the truth.
- *'Full of Mercy.'* This can involve forgiving others or acting generously toward others in need.
- *'Full of . . . Good Fruits.'* To James, being merciful and bearing good fruit were nearly synonymous. Good deeds are the fruit of righteousness.
- *'Unwavering.'* An unwavering person is one who does not deviate in the way he or she relates to others. For James, this word was the opposite of double-mindedness, a condition he wrote about frequently.
- *'Without Pretense.'* This refers to a person of integrity who exhibits a singleness of heart. His speech and actions are consistent, and they do not betray each other. This kind of person is without hypocrisy and pretense.

WORD PICTURE

Selfish Ambition

This phrase is one word in the Greek text, meaning the vice of a leader of a party created for his own pride. It is "pushing forward for one's personal ends, partisanship." (A. T. Robertson, "General Epistles and Revelation of John," *WPNT,* vol. 6, 46). It is partly ambition; partly rivalry. (Fritz Rienecker, *Linguistic Key to the Greek New Testament* [Zondervan, 1980], 734–35.)

JAMES'S CONTRAST BETWEEN EARTHLY WISDOM AND HEAVENLY WISDOM

	ELEMENTS	RESULT
EARTHLY WISDOM	Envy Selfish ambition	Disorder and every evil practice
HEAVENLY WISDOM	Pure, peace-loving, gentle, compliant, full of mercy and good fruits, unwavering, without pretense	Fruit of righteousness

Section Summary

James focused on the differing harvests of the two wisdoms. Earthly wisdom yields disorder and all kind of evil, whereas heavenly wisdom produces fruit of righteousness.

PERSONAL APPLICATION

"A church that is rich in reconciling activities, that is, evangelism, the defense of the poor, counseling the troubled, offering hospitality to the stranger, providing shelter for the battered, sending gospel missionaries throughout the world, and many more, certainly reaps a rich harvest of righteousness. Whenever the church of Christ is doing these things, the kingdom of God is evidence. This harvest precisely is what Jesus meant by the admonition to 'seek first the kingdom of God and its righteousness' (Matt 6:33)." Kurt A. Richardson, *James*, New American Commentary 36 (B&H, 1997), 172.

QUESTIONS TO GUIDE YOUR STUDY

1. What responsibility did James assign to teachers of God's Word? Describe the church's ministry of teaching.
2. Why did James place such an emphasis on the use of the tongue?
3. What do James's analogies about the tongue and speech teach us? What truths especially stand out for you?
4. Contrast the two wisdoms. What is the product of each?

JAMES 4

The break between chapters 3 and 4 falls in the midst of the first part of James's letter (3:13–4:10). The first part of this chapter (vv. 1–10), therefore, is a continuation of his theme about the two kinds of wisdom and how they play out in a person's life.

In this chapter James depicted the issues of right and wrong in a context outside the church. In addition to urging ethical action, James warned about conflicts that result in quarrels and fights. His answer to such divisiveness is the believer's submission to God.

THE TRUTH ABOUT CONFLICTS (4:1–5)

Their Source (v. 1)

James's readers apparently were plagued by conflicts and disputes. He addressed these conflicts directly. In effect, his opening in verse 1 was a question to ask his readers whether they wanted to submit to the will of

God or satisfy their own desires for the pleasures of this world. The two choices before them were (1) friendship with the world, or (2) friendship with God.

James identified the source of their conflicts as "passions." The point of verse 1 is that evil desires are within every human being, and they must be confronted.

Their Outcome (vv. 2–3)

James moved on to describe the outcome of unchecked evil desire in a person's life. He returned to his theme of 1:14–15, where he wrote of the deadly effects of evil desire in a person's life: "Each person is tempted when he is drawn away and enticed by his own evil desire. Then after desire has conceived, it gives birth to sin, and when sin is fully grown, it gives birth to death."

James identified their "passions" in two different ways: "You desire and do not have" and "You murder and covet and cannot obtain." These two cravings likely parallel the twin evils of chapter 3—bitter envy and selfish ambition.

Desiring What They Do Not Have. At the root of the conflict James wrote about *desire*. Throughout the New Testament, its writers warn that the desires for the things of this world are always a threat to the spiritual life of the believer.

Coveting What They Cannot Obtain. Coveting is the willingness to steal what belongs to someone else. Such desire becomes idolatry.

The result of the ruthlessness in the hearts of these believers is quarreling and fighting, which has the potential to lead to murder. (See the words of Jesus in Matt 15:19.) Although some interpreters take James's reference to murder as a metaphor, the connection between the frustration of not having and envying with the act of murder is certainly a reality in today's world.

James closed this section with a reference to prayer that is consistent with true faith. These quarrelers did not rely on God for provision but rather were driven to fight for what they wanted. When they did ask of God, they did so with the wrong motives.

"You do not have because you do not ask" (v. 2). Rather than asking God for wisdom (Jas 1:5), they relied on wisdom that comes from the world. Had they asked God, they would have found wisdom and peace as the outcome.

"You ask and don't receive because you ask with wrong motives" *(v. 3).* These believers failed to receive because they asked wrongly. Their motives were shaped not by God's wisdom but by their own evil desires. Those motives were rooted in their own "pleasures." James wrote that they intended to "spend" what God gives them on their pleasures. The word *spend* refers to the act of securing enjoyment. It is the same word

WORD PICTURE

Desire

This word is a compound word in the Greek text. It is made up of the preposition "upon" and the verb "to desire." It means "to desire something earnestly," emphasizing the inward impulse rather than the object desired. *Vine's Complete Expository Dictionary of Old and New Testament Words* (Thomas Nelson, 1996), 162.

Jesus used in his parable of the prodigal son in describing the lost son's squandering of his wealth in "foolish living" (Luke 15:13–15). Their goal was to exchange, or cash in, for whatever gain they could make from God's gifts.

James's observation on the prayer life of these individuals revealed that they were impatient people bent on exercising their own will over God's. They were not interested in being guided by God's Word or his will. True prayer is not self-centered but an act of humility before God.

OLD TESTAMENT REFERENCE

Psalm 34:14–17 reinforces James's teaching in this passage: "Turn away from evil and do what is good; seek peace and purse it. The eyes of the LORD are on the righteous, and his ears are open to their cry for help; the face of the LORD is set against those who do what is evil. . . . The righteous cry out, and the LORD hears."

The Enmity of Friendship with the World (vv. 4–5)

James addressed his readers harshly as "adulterous people!" This term is an Old Testament metaphor for unfaithfulness. His mention of it likely brought to his readers' minds the standard Old Testament image of the covenant relationship between God and his people (Isa 54:4–8). In that image, Israel is the wife of the Lord (Jer 31:21; Hos 3:1; Ezek 23:45). By making this correlation, James implied that his readers were "committing adultery" with the world.

WARNINGS AGAINST BELIEVERS FLIRTING WITH THE WORLD		
PASSAGE	**WRITER**	**WARNING**
Matt 6:24	Matthew, quoting Jesus	"No one can serve two masters, since either he will hate one and love the other, or he will be devoted to one and despise the other. You cannot serve both God and money."
2 Tim 3:2, 4	Paul, writing to Timothy	"People will be lovers . . . of pleasure rather than lovers of God."
1 John 2:15	John, writing to believers	"Do not love the world or the things in the world. If anyone loves the world, the love of the Father is not in him."

WORD PICTURE

Hostility

The word translated "hostility" is literally the word *enmity.* It is a word that indicates active hostility toward God. In this passage, it is intended to be the opposite of friendship.

James labeled this condition as "friendship with the world" (v. 4). This indicates their hatred toward God. A person cannot be friends with the world and love God at the same time. In this way, spiritual adultery is synonymous with being an enemy of God.

Scholars have found verse 5 difficult to translate, as there are a variety of ways the verse can be punctuated, leading to different translations. Here are some of the possible interpretations:

- James is asking if the spirit which God has put in us longs to the point of envying (ASV).
- God's Spirit which he placed in us yearns with jealousy over us (Weymouth).
- God yearns jealously over the Spirit which he has placed within us.

Because James's readers were plagued by conflicts and disputes, he asked them whether they wanted to submit to the will of God or to satisfy their own desires for the pleasures of this world. The two choices before them were friendship with the world or friendship with God. Friendship with the world is spiritual adultery, making them enemies of God.

BEING A FRIEND OF GOD (4:6–10)

Grace for the Humble (v. 6)

James provided the antidote to spiritual adultery by quoting from the Old Testament book of Proverbs: "God resists the proud but gives grace to the humble" (Prov 3:34). In addition to this Old Testament quotation, James reminded his readers that God gives "greater" grace and that by appropriating that grace, they could overcome their spiritual sins. Paul's words, "where sin multiplied, grace multiplied even more" (Rom 5:20), would certainly support James's text. A key point to be gained from this verse is that unlike some of James's readers, whose envy was directed toward all, God maintains a favorable disposition toward believing sinners.

Exercising for Humility (vv. 7–10)

Building on the foundation he laid in verse 6, James began a series of imperatives that span the next four verses. These commands, in effect, are his recipe for humility or a how-to on repentance. James provided his readers with these progressive steps of spiritual self-discipline, each being a means of entering into an intimate relationship with God.

"Submit to God" (v. 7). To "submit" was a military term, meaning literally to be "arranged or ordered under." To submit is to align oneself under the authority of another. All conflict resolution needs to start with a renewed submission to God by the internal act of submission to his authority.

"Resist the devil" (v. 7). James next instructed his readers to put up an active resistance to the devil and the influence he wields in their lives. James did not advocate an offensive approach toward the devil but rather a defensive posture.

Resistance is an effective attack for the believer. The result is that the devil will flee. This picture brings to mind Luke 4:13: "After the devil had finished every temptation, he departed from him for a time." When met with Jesus's resistance toward his temptation, Satan's course of action was to leave. Note that Jesus used Scripture in his resistance to the devil's wiles. The believer will do well to take the Lord's example to heart.

"Draw near to God" (v. 8). This step begins with a positive exhortation and concludes with a promise. Nearness to God is a basic call of

WORD PICTURE

Proud

Our English translation of the word *proud* is an interesting word in James's Greek text. It is a compound word made up of the preposition "above" or "beyond" and the basic word "proud." The prefixed preposition heightens the word's basic meaning. This word refers to a person who is *haughty* or *arrogant*, a person who thinks above and beyond that which is proper. "Like our vernacular 'stuck-up folks.'" A. T. Robertson, "General Epistles and Revelation of John," *WPNT*, vol. 6, 52.

WORD PICTURE

Resist

The word *resist* is a compound word in the Greek text, made up of the prefixed preposition "against" and the verb "to cause to stand." It carries the ideas of withstanding and opposing and is rendered "resist." A modern-day application of this Greek word *(anthistēmi)* relates to medicine. A person suffering from an allergy might take an *antihistamine* to block histamines and reduce, or resist, the effects of allergens.

the Christian faith. It is an act of contrition, and it involves letting go of and rejecting all evil practices and false teachings. The promise to James's readers was that if they took this step, God would draw near to them.

"Cleanse your hands . . . and purify your hearts" (v. 8). These are reconciling actions that recall the ritual purity required of worshipers and priests at the temple. The second prophetic call is to the purification of the heart. Drawing near to God involves a commitment of the will to cleanse one's hands to assume a submissive spirit so that one may purify the heart. By washing the hands and purifying the heart, the believer is turning from sin and double-mindedness.

James intentionally combined the hand and the heart, as they both must move in harmony in action and commitment before God. A morality rooted in sincere faith requires an inner life that is purified and that corresponds with the character of God (cp. Matt 5:8; 1 Tim 1:5). As the believer draws near to God, God and the heart of the believer come together, and one should mirror the other. Noted Bible teacher Warren Wiersbe states that the concept of drawing near to God is more a case of "nearness is likeness" (Prayer, Praise & Promise, 29). It is an observation that James's teaching here would seem to validate.

"Be miserable and mourn and weep"; change your laughter to mourning and "your joy to gloom" (v. 9). These four commands call for a deep transformation of a person's attitude toward God. James presented a progression that the believer is to use for attacking his or her own heart and bringing it into submission to God.

"Be miserable." This word means to undergo hardship. It refers to dealing with one's inner attitude of repentance.

"Mourn." This action is self-contained and is the expression of one's grief.

"Weep." The grief James described here is more than a heartache; it's a heavy grief that brings tears to the eyes. Certainly, the removal of deeply rooted sin would result in such a release.

Change laughter to mourning. This refers to the act of turning from the laughter of an arrogant, autonomous fool to true humility before God.

"Humble yourselves before the Lord" (v. 10). This is a command to the believer to humble himself or herself before God. This humility is a matter of the believer's relating wholeheartedly to God in recognition of God's total claim upon the believer's life. To this command James attached the promise that "he will exalt you."

PERSONAL APPLICATION

Matthew 23:12 provides insight into the meaning of this promise: "Whoever exalts himself will be humbled, and whoever humbles himself will be exalted."

Section Summary

James provided the antidote to spiritual adultery by quoting from the Old Testament book of Proverbs: "God resists the proud but gives grace to the humble" (Prov 3:34). Then he provided his recipe for humility—a progression of steps, each being a means of entering into a more intimate relationship with God.

Warning Against Criticism (4:11)

James opened this section by addressing his readers as "brothers and sisters" rather than "adulterous people." He began his teaching by issuing the command to "not criticize [slander] one another." (He used the verb for "criticize" three times.) "Slander was considered a vice in the ancient world, and by interjecting it here, James pronounced a judgment on their behavior that perhaps they were not expecting." Kurt A. Richardson, *James*, New American Commentary 36 (B&H, 1997), 194.

WORD PICTURE

Criticize

The word for "criticize" is a compound word made up of two words: a prefixed preposition meaning "against" and the verb "to speak." Literally, the word means "to speak against," "to defame," "to speak evil of." The word is applied to scenarios where harsh words are spoken about a person who is not present.

JAMES'S RECIPE FOR HUMILITY

COMMAND	VERSE	THE BELIEVER'S PROPER RESPONSE
Submit yourselves.	v. 7	The believer is to submit to the authority of God.
"Resist the devil."	v. 7	The believer is to put up an active resistance to the devil and the influence he wields.
"Draw near to God."	v. 8	The believer must reject all evil practices and false teachings and approach God with a submissive spirit.
"Cleanse your hands . . . and purify your hearts."	v. 8	The believer needs to make a commitment to purify the heart and turn from sin and double-mindedness.
"Be miserable and mourn and weep."	v. 9	The believer is to attack his or her own heart and bring it into submission to God.
Change your laughter "to mourning and your joy to gloom."	v. 9	The believer needs to turn from an attitude of arrogance to true humility before God.
"Humble yourselves before the Lord."	v. 10	The believer needs to relate wholeheartedly to God in recognition of God's total claim upon his or her life.

James went on to reveal more about the realities of slander.

- *Slander is an act of condemnation.* Those who slander are really condemning the one they speak against because they are passing judgment on that person. Only God can judge because only he knows the secrets of the heart and can judge them. Believers certainly have the right to preach the gospel, announce God's forgiveness of sins, and forgive the sins of others committed against them personally. But no person has the right to judge another person who has sinned, thereby claiming to know God's final judgment about a person.

- *Slander judges God's law.* When believers engage in judging others, they slander the law of God. Believers are to accept the law. They are not to place themselves in a position of rival judgment with God's. This law requires them to exercise mercy toward others since they themselves have received God's mercy.

GOD ALONE IS THE LAWGIVER (4:12)

His Authority (v. 12a)

The Greek text does not use the word *only* but says "there is one lawgiver." This implies that God is the only lawgiver.

His Abilities (v. 12b)

God—the only lawgiver—can save and destroy. Judgment is his alone.

He is able to save. God is the great deliverer, and only he has the ability eternally to save or rescue a person.

He is able to destroy. Likewise, only God can condemn a person.

The combination of the terms *save* and *destroy* is a picture of God's power (see Matt 10:28). It is also a common idea in the Old Testament (Deut 32:39; 2 Kgs 5:7).

HISTORICAL BACKGROUND

Mists in the Bible

"In the Bible, a mist often appears as a symbol for something that quickly passes away. It can refer to water, fog, or clouds. The metaphor of the mist in James 4:14 is quantitative rather than qualitative. Mists do not last long in Palestine. Their form is transitory. This evaporation is a fitting way to refer to the ephemeral attribute of human life." Taken from the *Holman Bible Dictionary* and Kurt A. Richardson, *James*, New American Commentary 36 (B&H, 1997), 199.

Section Summary

James emphatically issued the command: "Don't criticize one another." Criticism is an act of condemnation, and it judges God's law. Believers need to be careful not to judge others but rather exercise mercy toward others. Only God can judge.

WHEN BUSINESS IS A SPIRITUAL LIABILITY (4:13–17)

The Irony of Boasting (vv. 13–14)

As an example of boasting, James used the hypothetical, overconfident business dealer. He made the point that this businessman is confidently predicting the future but without involving or considering God.

James focused on the irony of boasting about tomorrow, reminding his readers that they know nothing about their future. He then presented a metaphor to illustrate the shortness of life: "You are like vapor." Vapor is transitory; it is here now and then gone! Our lives are like a morning mist that the sun soon burns away. The lesson is that human life is transitory; therefore, the believer must place his or her trust in God. Our lives are in his hands.

The Norm of Human Activities (v. 15)

James informed his readers that there is one norm by which the life of faith is to be lived out in the temporal environment of the world—"the Lord wills." Life is lived but only if God wills.

The Sinfulness of Presumption (vv. 16–17)

The only rightful place boasting has in the Christian life is if it is done in reference to the work of God. But this is not the kind of boasting to which James referred in these verses. His readers were, instead, boasting arrogantly. To boast means to glory in something. Those who were boasting were doing so without any reference to God. Not only were these people boasting; they boasted about the fact that they boasted! They took pride in being this kind of people.

This chapter concludes with the Bible's best statement, negatively expressed, of the Christian ethic: "So it is sin to know the good and yet not do it."

Section Summary

Human life is transitory; it is but a morning mist that the sun quickly burns away. Because we know nothing about what tomorrow holds, it is imperative that we place our trust in God. Our lives are in his hands.

QUESTIONS TO GUIDE YOUR STUDY

1. What is the source of conflict in the believer's life? What can be the outcome of such conflict? What is the believer's responsibility regarding conflict?
2. What did James mean by the phrase "friendship with the world"?
3. James presented a sort of "recipe" for humility. What are the steps to humility, and what must the Christian do to maintain progress toward humility?
4. What is slander? Why is it so destructive? What can a believer do to avoid slander?

JAMES 5

In this final chapter, James began by returning to the theme of the rich. He delivered strong words about the dependence on and the abuse of wealth. Other themes include patience in the face of suffering and prayer as a central activity of the church.

JUDGMENTS AGAINST THE RICH (5:1–6)

James returned to his theme of the sins of the rich and the dangers of their wealth. His previous treatments are 1:10–11 and 2:3–6. Of all the New Testament passages about sins of the rich, these six verses stand out. The tremendous importance of this topic seems to have compelled James to return to it in the closing portion of his letter.

The Misery of Hoarding (vv. 1–3)

Here James expressed anger against the rich because of the way they treated the poor and less fortunate. Immediately he addressed the future condemnation of the wicked rich: "miseries . . . are coming on you." In verse 2 he presented the truth about the greed and selfish hoarding that had consumed some of the rich among his readers. He used several graphic statements to portray the degrading influence of wealth.

"Your wealth has rotted" (v. 2). In the ancient world, land and its produce were considered wealth. The picture is of the produce or crop having rotted. The verb tense James used indicates the state or condition of the wealth. This statement and the following two are prophetic in their anticipation.

"Your clothes are moth-eaten" (v. 2). The clothing of the rich had been moth-eaten. James might have intended a connection between the "fine clothes" of 2:2 and the moth-eaten garments here.

"Your gold and silver are corroded" (v. 3). The precious metals of the rich were corroded and rusted. (Although gold and silver do not rust, James used his prophetic license here to make a point.) Rusted metals are no longer useful. James prophesied that the gold and silver of the rich would lose their value as investments when God's judgment comes.

With these three illustrations, James made a statement that trusting in wealth is a mistake because the idea that it retains its value is a myth. Amassing and trusting in wealth is a damaging and degrading attitude (see Matt 13:22; Mark 4:19; Luke 8:14; 12:21; 1 Tim 6:9). The ill-gotten wealth of these rich people was evidence of their moral depravity. James wrote: "Their corrosion will be a witness against you and will eat your flesh like fire." In the end, corrosion destroys both the wealth and its holder.

NEW TESTAMENT REFERENCE

These strong words echo the insights of our Lord, who warned, "Don't store up for yourselves treasures on earth, where moth and rust destroy and where thieves break in and steal. But store up for yourselves treasures in heaven, where neither moth nor rust destroys, and where thieves don't break in and steal. For where your treasure is, there your heart will be also." (Matt 6:19–21)

GOD'S FUTURE JUDGMENT OF THE WICKED RICH

RICHES	IN JUDGMENT	TRUTH ABOUT ILL-GOTTEN WEALTH
Wealth	Will be "rotted"	Hoarded wealth will be gone.
Clothing	Will be "moth-eaten"	Clothing will be destroyed.

GOD'S FUTURE JUDGMENT OF THE WICKED RICH		
RICHES	IN JUDGMENT	TRUTH ABOUT ILL-GOTTEN WEALTH
Gold and silver	Will be "corroded"	Investment values will be lost.

The Misery of the Innocent (vv. 4–6)

James condemned the ill-gotten wealth of the rich because it had been accumulated through fraud and at the expense of others. He issued several indictments against the rich.

Failure to Pay the Workmen (v. 4). Because of their greed, the rich landowners failed to pay their workers for services rendered.

The Defrauded Cry Out in Accusation (v. 4). The anguished cries of the defrauded "has reached the ears of the Lord of Armies." In ancient times, fraud was perpetrated by rich landowners against the poor day laborers. In today's complex, industrialized nations, however, fraud by the rich is perpetrated not just against manual laborers but against consumers, taxpayers, underprivileged nations, and disorganized masses of common people without an earthly advocate. The fraud is perpetrated through fixed prices, fixed taxes, fixed tariffs, and fixed programs designed to protect the vested interests of the rich at the expense of the poor.

HISTORICAL BACKGROUND

Such economic oppression was an urgent matter, as many of the laborers of the ancient world were transients or foreigners. Sadly, the wages due them never left the vaults of the rich.

James told his readers that God is patient, but he is not asleep. At the right time he will deliver his judgment.

The Luxury and Self-indulgence of the Rich (v. 5). The callousness of the rich was rooted in their self-indulgence. They lived in luxury and self-centered pleasure at the expense of their laborers. In the ancient world, luxurious living was regarded as moral laxity. James told these wealthy ones that they were fattening themselves for the "slaughter."

The Murder of Innocent Men (v. 6). James declared that the rich "condemned [and] . . . murdered the righteous." He added that these men were not opposing the rich. James used a present tense of the verb "resist" to bring the action to the attention of his readers. The treatment of the laborers was senseless, emphasizing the depraved nature of the rich.

Section Summary

James expressed anger toward the rich because of their mistreatment of the poor and less fortunate. Immediately he addressed the future condemnation of the wicked rich. God will eventually judge the wicked rich.

THE PRACTICE OF ENDURANCE (5:7–12)

This concluding section of James is united by the theme of the believers' exercise of faith and submission to James's teaching. The goal of his exhortations was to encourage and unite his readers as a community of Christ. It is to be a patience that endures "until the Lord's coming" (v. 7).

Patience Among Friends (vv. 7–11)

James began by encouraging his "brothers and sisters" to be patient during their suffering. He referred to trials brought about by injustices done to them.

WORD PICTURE

Patient

The Greek word behind our English translation "patient" is an interesting compound word. It is made up of the words "long" and "temper," and means "to be long-tempered." "The word describes the attitude which can endure delay and bear suffering and never give in." Fritz Rienecker, *Linguistic Key to the Greek New Testament* (Zondervan, 1980]), 740.

James used three illustrations to encourage a lifestyle of persistent devotion in serving God.

1. *The Farmer (v. 7).* James used the illustration of a farmer who plants and then waits for the rains to produce a crop. Because many of his readers were agrarian laborers, "farm hands," this was likely an appropriate illustration for James's original audience. Eventually, the farmer's patient endurance pays off, and the land yields its valuable crop. The wise farmer learns to wait patiently for the harvest. James exhorted his readers to do the same regarding the Lord's coming. In addition to patiently waiting, his readers are also to "strengthen your hearts" and not "complain about one another." All three actions are involved in waiting for the Lord's coming.

WAITING FOR THE HARVEST

EXHORTATION	EXTENDED MEANING
Be patient.	Patiently wait.
Strengthen yourselves.	Strengthen your heart.
Don't complain.	Don't cultivate a spirit of complaining.

OLD TESTAMENT REFERENCE

"Then the LORD said to Satan, 'Have you considered my servant Job? No one else on earth is like him, a man of perfect integrity, who fears God and turns away from evil. He still retains his integrity, even though you incited me against him, to destroy him for no good reason.'" (Job 2:3)

2. *Old Testament Prophets (v. 10).* The prophets suffered greatly because of their faithfulness and obedience to God. They displayed the proper attitude of faith during trials. They are worthy of imitation. James, in fact, invited his readers to do just that, as believers (then and now) share with the prophets the experience of suffering in patience.

3. *Job (v. 11).* Job is an example of patient endurance in suffering. The words of the Lord as he addressed Satan in Job 2:3 provide us with an important insight about Job.

What James showed with the illustration of Job is this great truth about trials: God allows the righteous to be tested so he may prove their faith.

OUR EXAMPLES OF PATIENCE

EXAMPLE	LESSON TO BE LEARNED
The farmer	We must patiently wait for God.
The prophets	We must maintain attitudes of faithfulness and obedience.
Job	We must suffer trials to prove our faith.

James closed this section with mention that "the Lord is compassionate and merciful" (v. 11). The significance in his focus on these attributes of God is that they are the primary attributes of God in his covenant with Israel. These character traits identify the God who blessed Job and the prophets and who will bless James's readers.

Section Summary

The goal of this section of James's letter was to encourage and unite his readers as a community of Christ. Their patience is to be one that endures "until the Lord's coming" (v. 7). Using illustrations of the farmer, the prophets, and Job, James showed the character of the kind of patience that endures life's circumstances and experiences.

Rejection of Oaths (v. 12)

Returning to the grave concern about speech and the tongue, which he has frequently addressed in his letter, James sounded his final note on the subject. To his readers he commanded, "Do not swear." This command referred to the taking of oaths.

In times of distress, Christians could easily use God's name in a careless, irreverent way. James warned against invoking God's name to guarantee truth, calling for truthfulness so consistent that no oath was needed. "Let your 'yes' mean 'yes,' and your 'no' mean 'no,' so that you won't fall under judgment."

HISTORICAL BACKGROUND

Oaths

In the Bible, symbolic acts often accompanied an oath. Invoking the name of the reigning monarch was another symbolic act joined with oath-taking. Using the Lord's name in an oath appeals directly to his involvement regarding testimony and establishes him as the supreme enforcer and judge. To violate the Lord's name is to violate the Lord; therefore, oaths that use God's name carelessly are condemned (Exod 20:7; Lev 19:12).

EFFECTIVE PRAYER (5:13–18)

James urged his readers to pray in all circumstances, including blessing, trouble, sickness, and sin. Using the illustration of Elijah, James showed that the prayer of the righteous person is powerful and effective.

Prayer for Times of Trouble (v. 13a)

"Is anyone among you suffering?" was James's opening question to his readers regarding prayer. The kind of "suffering" he referred to is when believers suffer evil or hardship. When believers are tempted to grumble against one another, prayer serves as the antidote to grumbling. James's previous instructions on prayer tell us that this prayer should be:

- For wisdom (1:5)
- Wholehearted (1:6)

NEW TESTAMENT REFERENCE

Paul wrote in Col 3:16: "Let the word of Christ dwell richly among you, in all wisdom teaching and admonishing one another through psalms, hymns, and spiritual songs, singing to God with gratitude in your hearts."

Prayer for Times of Blessing (v. 13b)

James posed a second question, "Is anyone cheerful?" Times of happiness are a blessing from God. The believer's proper response for these times is praise and gratitude toward God. James's implication seems to be that this praise is to be shared with the rest of the local Christian community or church.

Prayer for Times of Sickness (vv. 14–15)

NT REFERENCE

"Brothers and sisters, if someone is overtaken in any wrongdoing, you who are spiritual, restore such a person with a gentle spirit, watching out for yourselves so that you also won't be tempted. Carry one another's burdens; in this way you will fulfill the law of Christ." (Gal 6:1–2)

In these two verses, James's teaching emphasized the community of Christian faith. Problems of sin and sickness challenge unity within a church or fellowship of believers. As with happiness, times of sickness are to be shared with other believers. In verse 14 James set forth a threefold pattern for prayer on behalf of the sick:

- The sick person is to call the elders.
- The elders are to anoint the sick person with oil.
- The elders are to pray over the sick person for healing.

James told his readers that "the prayer of faith," not prayer based on the wrong motives (Jas 4:3), will heal the sick person. In describing God's response to their praying, James wrote that the Lord will "raise . . . up" the sick person. It is a word used for resurrection—a restoration of life.

HISTORICAL BACKGROUND

"While Calvin, Luther and other expositors think that the practice of anointing, along with the power to heal, was meant to be confined to the apostolic age, it is doubtful that such a restriction can be maintained." Douglas J. Moo, *James*, Tyndale New Testament Commentaries (Eerdmans, 1985), p. 179.

In Bible times, oil or ointment was used as a medicine in the treatment of wounds (Luke 10:34). James 5:14 may refer either to a symbolic use of oil or to its medicinal use. The anointing with oil is not merely a kind of home remedy. As it is applied, the name of the Lord Jesus is to be invoked. Olive oil, according to Old Testament and Jewish understanding, was prized for its nurturing of human well-being and for its healing properties. In the ministries of Jesus and his disciples, olive oil was used in their healings of the sick when combined with the preaching of repentance. "So they went out and preached that people should repent. They drove out many demons, anointed many sick people with oil and healed them" (Mark 6:12–14). Taken from the *Holman Bible Dictionary* and Kurt A. Richardson, *James*, New American Commentary 36 (B&H, 1997), 233.

James's next statement (v. 15b) raised the question about the connection between sin and sickness. Although sickness can be a consequence of sin, this is not always the case.

In John's Gospel, Jesus encountered a man who had been blind all his life. His disciples asked whether the man sinned or his parents. Jesus answered that it was neither the man nor his parents, but "this came about so that God's works might be displayed in him" (John 9:3).

Earlier in John's Gospel (5:1–18), Jesus healed a man who had been crippled for thirty-eight years. Not long after Jesus healed the man, he saw him in the temple and said, "See, you are well. Do not sin anymore, so that something worse doesn't happen to you."

Prayer for Times of Sin (v. 16)

James continued his instruction on prayer by telling his readers that their entire church or community should be characterized by mutual confession of sin. Paul's instruction for correcting a believer who has fallen into sin surely included mutual confession.

A key point here is that mutual confession leads to prayer for each other. Under the covenant with Israel, specific men were designated as priests. Under the new covenant, all believers are priests and have the privilege of interceding for their brothers and sisters in Christ—bringing them to Jesus Christ, our great High Priest.

James described the prayer of the true believer as "powerful in its effect." This phrase provides unique insight into the kind of prayer that accomplishes God's purposes.

Four friends brought a paralyzed man to Jesus. Jesus surprised and angered some of the crowd by telling the paralytic that his sins were forgiven. This was surprising because the most obvious need of the man was for physical healing. But Jesus went to the primary need first. Some of the religious leaders were angry, thinking to themselves that only God could forgive sin. Jesus perceived their thoughts and responded: "'Why are you thinking these things in your hearts? Which is easier: to say to the paralytic, 'Your sins are forgiven,' or to say, 'Get up, take your mat, and walk'? But so that you may know that the Son of Man has authority on earth to forgive sins'—he told the paralytic—'I tell you: get up, take your mat, and go home.' Immediately he got up, took the mat, and went out in front of everyone" (Mark 2:8–12).

WORD PICTURE

Powerful in Its Effect

J. B. Phillips's paraphrase illuminates these characteristics of a righteous person's prayer: "Tremendous power is made available through a good man's earnest prayer." *The Amplified Bible* Classic Edition says that such a prayer "makes tremendous power available[dynamic in its working]."

The Example of Elijah (v. 17)

James used an Old Testament example to illustrate effective prayer. Elijah prayed, and God withheld rain from the earth for three and one-half years. Then God sent rain again at Elijah's request. First Kings 17:1 records his first prayer: "Now Elijah the Tishbite . . . said to Ahab, 'As the LORD God of Israel lives, in whose presence I stand, there will be no dew or rain during these years except by my command!'" His prayer to restore the rain is found in 1 Kgs 18:41–42.

"Elijah was a human being as we are" means that he had the same kinds of feelings we have, endured the same kind of circumstances we face, and had the same life experiences as we do. The idea that he had our same nature "indicates that the power of Elijah's prayer did not lie in his supernatural greatness, but rather in his humanity." Fritz Rienecker, *Linguistic Key to the Greek* New *Testament* (Zondervan, 1980), 742.

Elijah's example illustrates everything James wrote about a faith that rejects worldly standards of judgment in favor of divine standards. An important point of this illustration is that Elijah knew the will of God concerning the signs of drought and rain. This knowledge was why he prayed so fervently. By applying the Word of God, all believers can know God's will and then do his will through their own fervent praying. James's statement, "If the Lord wills" (4:15), comes to mind. This fervent praying is appropriate for all seasons and circumstances of life.

PRAYER FOR EVERY SEASON

SEASON OF LIFE	NATURE OF THE BELIEVER'S PRAYER
In times of suffering	For strength to endure
In times of blessing	A song of praise
In times of sickness	A request for healing
In times of sin	Intercession

Section Summary

James urged his readers to pray in all circumstances, including times of blessing, suffering, sickness, and sin. Using the illustration of Elijah, James showed that the prayer of the righteous person is powerful and effective.

THE MINISTRY OF RESTORATION (5:19–20)

The disciplined Christian life involves not only patience and purity of speech and prayer but also persistence in rescuing the perishing. At the heart of the life and work of the church is restoration of the fallen, the finding of the lost, and the saving of sinners. Again, in this passage James used the only word for sin that he employed in his writing, and that is the word that means "to miss the mark." It is the nature of human beings to stray from God's way, to miss the moral targets he has established, and to turn from the ideals God has ordained.

Restoration takes place in view of:

- God's mercy, which James tells us triumphs over judgment (2:13)
- God's requirement that believers humble themselves (4:6–10)

To anyone willing, the way "back" to God and to life is to turn "from the error of his way" to save one's soul from "death and cover over a multitude of sins" (v. 20). Morally stumbling men and women who are missing God's mark of their lives, who are sick unto death, can find grace and the good life when they trust and obey him.

WORD PICTURE

Turns

This word is a compound word made up of the prefixed preposition "toward" and the verb "to turn." It literally means "to turn about" or "to turn toward" something. It is often translated "convert" because it describes a person's turning around or about. Associated with this turning around is repentance and faith.

Section Summary

At the heart of the life and work of the church is restoration of the fallen, the finding of the lost, and the saving of sinners. To anyone willing, the way "back" to God and to life is the way of turning "from the error of his way" to save one's soul from "death and cover over a multitude of sins" (v. 20).

CONCLUSION

The call of James to do the gospel has been debated, criticized, and even ignored. His call needs to be heard. There may be several keys to the lost radiance of the modern church, but one of those keys is in plain view in the gospel according to James. It is the key that unlocks the door between faith and works and once again joins that which God never meant to be separated. The joys, victories, and triumphs of pure religion are for those who live under the conviction that Jesus Christ is Lord and who are doers of the Word.

QUESTIONS TO GUIDE YOUR STUDY

1. According to James, what judgment awaits the rich who oppress the poor and hoard wealth?
2. What can we learn from James's illustrations about patience in 5:7–12?
3. What is effective prayer? What makes it so powerful in the life of the believer?
4. What is the significance of the ministry of restoration? Why is it necessary? What does it involve?

1 Peter

INTRODUCTION

First Peter provides a message of encouragement for Christians in northern Asia Minor who were facing unbelievable opposition and persecution. Martin Luther named 1 Peter, along with the Gospel of John, 1 John, Romans, Galatians, and Ephesians, as one of the New Testament books that shows us Christ and teaches how Christians ought to live in the world.

1 PETER IN A "NUTSHELL"

Purpose:	To provide encouragement in Christian living
Major Doctrine:	The sufficiency of God's grace
Other Key Doctrines:	The return of Christ; the sufferings and sacrifice of Christ on the cross; godly living

AUTHOR

First Peter begins with an affirmation of Simon Peter's authorship of the letter. Other claims made in the letter support that affirmation. In addition, leaders of the church made frequent references to 1 Peter, and there is no evidence of any dispute about authorship at that time. Only in the twentieth century have some students of 1 Peter questioned whether the apostle wrote the letter.

PURPOSE FOR WRITING

Peter urged his readers to live in accordance with the hope they had received in Christ (1:3). He gave guidance for them to use in their relationships with one another (3:1–12), and he urged them to endure suffering joyfully for Jesus's sake (4:19). His chief aim in writing was to provide them encouragement in Christian living.

DATE AND PLACE OF WRITING

Date. The theme of suffering appears in every chapter of 1 Peter. During Nero's reign there was great persecution of believers. Therefore, the most likely time for the writing of 1 Peter is around AD 62–64.

Place. Peter identified Babylon as the place from which he wrote his letter (5:13). Old Testament Babylon in Mesopotamia was deserted during this period. Most likely, he was using the name symbolically to refer to the arrogant idolatry and lust for power that characterized biblical Babylon. He probably used the term as a cryptic designation for Rome.

AUDIENCE

The readers of the letter are identified in 1:1. They lived in Asia Minor north of the Taurus mountains. This was far off the beaten path of travel and commerce. The Bible does not record how the gospel reached this area. Although the area contained colonies of Jews, Gentiles were numerically predominant.

Although *exiles* is the Jewish term for those dispersed from the homeland of Palestine (1:1), Peter probably used it to refer to the church. Peter saw believers as a pilgrim people on earth who had been set apart by God to do his will.

HISTORICAL CONTEXT

The order in which the provinces are mentioned might suggest the route followed by the letter carrier. He could have landed in Pontus, followed a circuit through the provinces, and left the area at Bithynia.

LITERARY FORM

Students of 1 Peter have discussed widely the literary forms within the book. Many find extensive evidence of the presence of hymns, creeds, or fragments of sermons in such passages as 2:4–8 and 2:21–25.

Although these discussions are enlightening and enriching, they are often inconclusive and unconvincing. Peter may have used material from different sources in writing the letter, but it is best to see that he made it his own material under the leadership of the Holy Spirit.

Peter made frequent references to the Old Testament, sometimes by quotation (2:6–8) and sometimes by allusion (3:6,20). This frequent use suggests that Jewish readers were at least among the recipients of the letter. Some of Peter's emphases resemble those of Paul. For example, there is similarity between Peter's words about relationships between wives and husbands in 3:1–7 and Paul's discussion in Eph 5:22–33.

1 PETER AND THE BOOK OF ACTS

Several themes in 1 Peter also appear in the speeches attributed to Peter in Acts, as shown in the following chart.

COMMON THEMES IN 1 PETER AND ACTS*

THEME	ACTS	1 PETER
God is no respecter of persons.	10:34	1:17
Christ is identified as a stone rejected by the builders.	4:10–11	2:7–8
The "name" of Christ has a prominent place.	3:6,16; 4:10, 12; 5:41	4:14,16

* Information taken from Thomas D. Lea, *The New Testament: Its Background and Message*, 534.

1 PETER AND THE GOSPELS

First Peter also contains information we can link to the Gospels. We would expect this to be the case with a letter written by one of the three disciples of the "inner circle."

COMMON THEMES IN 1 PETER AND THE GOSPEL OF JOHN *

THEME	JOHN	1 PETER
Jesus's conversation with Peter	21:1–25	5:2–4
Jesus as the "chief Shepherd"	10:14	5:4
Being clothed with humility	13:2–17	5:5

*Information taken from Thomas D. Lea, *The New Testament: Its Background and Message*, 534.

THE THEOLOGY OF 1 PETER

Peter often used theological ideas to drive home his ethical demands. He presented the death of Christ as a stimulus for Christians to endure suffering (2:21–25). He also affirmed the resurrection as a chief source of Christian hope and confidence (1:3). He presented the return of Christ as an incentive for holy living (1:13). He portrayed the nature of the Christian call (2:9–10) as a basis for individual Christians to obey Christ at home (3:1–7), to obey him as servants (2:18–20), and to follow him as citizens (2:13–17).

HISTORICAL CONTEXT

Some view the entire writing as a sermon preached at the baptism of a group of Christians, viewing the opening section through 4:11 as a message spoken to candidates for baptism. They locate the actual baptism at 1:21–22 and feel that the "Amen" at 4:11 concludes the address to the candidates. The concluding section beginning with 4:12 is viewed as an address to the entire church gathered for the rite of baptism.

BASIC OUTLINE FOR 1 PETER

I. Greetings (1:1–2)
II. The Method and Nature of Salvation (1:3–12)
III. A Demand for Holiness (1:2–2:3)
IV. A Description of the People of God (2:4–10)
V. The Christian Witness in the World (2:11–3:12)
VI. Appeals and Promises to the Persecuted (3:13–4:19)
VII. Praises to God and Greetings to the Church (5:10–14)

QUESTIONS TO GUIDE YOUR STUDY

1. What was Peter's purpose for writing this letter?
2. Who was his audience? Where were they located?
3. When was 1 Peter written? Why is this dating of the letter significant?
4. How does 1 Peter relate to other portions of the New Testament?

WORD PICTURE

Peter

Peter's personal name means "Rock." *Simon* is often found in combination with Peter, reminding the reader that Simon was the earlier name and that Peter was a name given later by Jesus.

1 PETER 1

SALUTATION (1:1–2)

Author (v. 1)

The author of this book identified himself as "Peter, an apostle of Jesus Christ" (v. 1). *Apostles* were the disciples of Jesus called of God and responsible for carrying out God's work in the world.

Peter is credited with being the leader of the original twelve disciples whom Jesus called. As a member of the inner circle, Peter was present with Jesus at the raising of the synagogue ruler's daughter (Mark 5:35–41), at the transfiguration (Mark 9:2–8), and at the arrest of Jesus in Gethsemane (Mark 14:43–50). As a representative disciple, Peter frequently typified the disciple of *little faith*. His inconsistent behavior reached a climax with his infamous denial scene (Mark 14:66–72). Peter was, however, rehabilitated in the scene where the resurrected Jesus restored Peter to his position of prominence (John 21:15–19).

Readers (vv. 2–3)

Peter addressed his readers as "chosen" and "exiles" who were "dispersed." His letter was addressed to Christian exiles who were displaced throughout much of Asia Minor. In his letter, we see Peter clearly addressing the needs of his readers. He urged them to live in accordance with the hope they received in Christ, gave them guidance for their relationships with one another, and urged them to endure suffering joyfully for Jesus's sake.

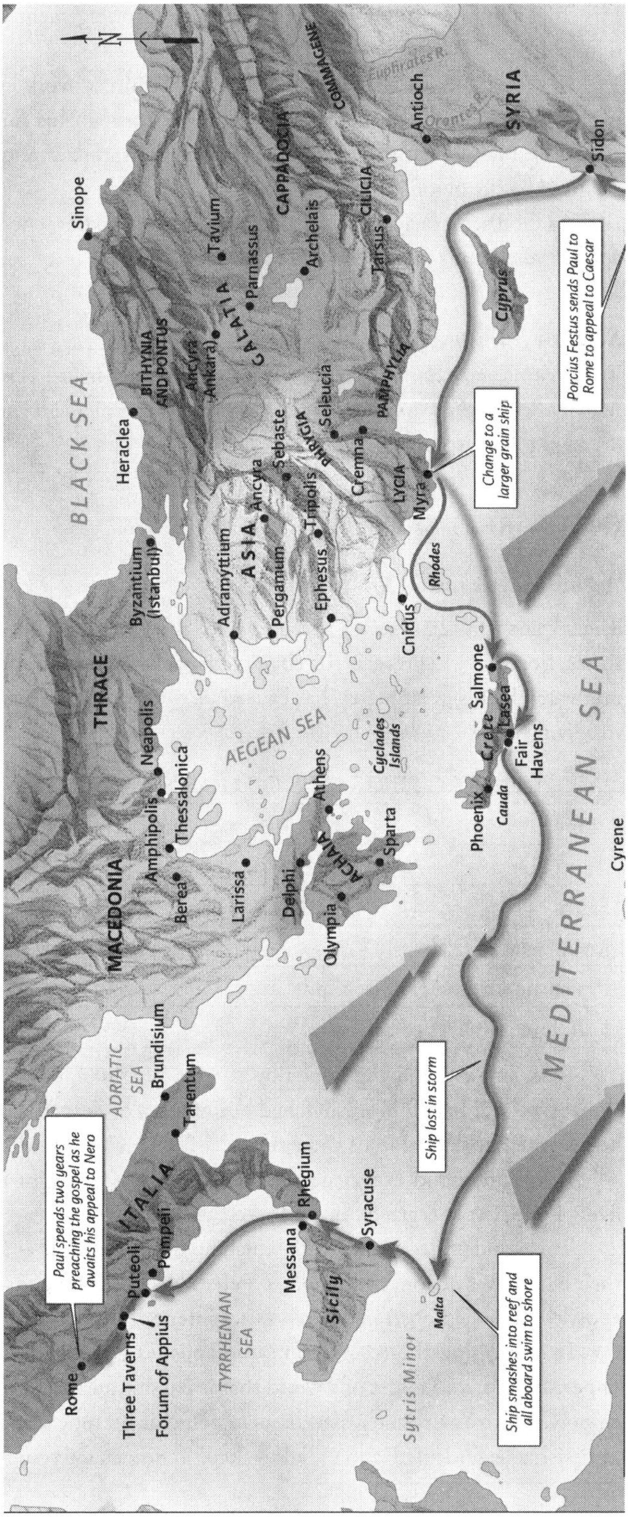
BLACK SEA
Sinope
Heraclea
BITHYNIA AND PONTUS
Byzantium (Istanbul)
THRACE
Neapolis
Amphipolis
Thessalonica
MACEDONIA
Berea
Larissa
AEGEAN SEA
Cyclades Islands
Athens
Delphi
ACHAIA
Olympia
Sparta
Adramyttium
Pergamum
ASIA
Ancyra
Ephesus
Tripolis
Sebaste
PHRYGIA
Seleucia
Cnidus
Rhodes
Myra
LYCIA
Cremna
PAMPHYLIA
Ancyra (Ankara)
GALATIA
Tavium
Parnassus
Archelais
CAPPADOCIA
CILICIA
Tarsus
COMMAGENE
Euphrates R.
Antioch
Orontes R.
SYRIA
Sidon
Cyprus
Porcius Festus sends Paul to Rome to appeal to Caesar
Change to a larger grain ship
Salmone
Crete
Lasea
Fair Havens
Phoenix
Cauda
Cyrene
MEDITERRANEAN SEA
Ship lost in storm
Ship smashes into reef and all aboard swim to shore
Malta
Sytris Minor
Syracuse
Sicily
Messana
Rhegium
TYRRHENIAN SEA
ADRIATIC SEA
Brundisium
Tarentum
ITALIA
Pompeii
Puteoli
Paul spends two years preaching the gospel as he awaits his appeal to Nero
Rome
Three Taverns
Forum of Appius
N

His chief aim in writing was to provide them encouragement in Christian living.

In verses 1–2, we see each person in the Trinity at work in the salvation of God's people. God the Father *chose* through his foreknowledge. The Holy Spirit *sanctifies* believers who are *sprinkled* and thereby cleansed by the blood of Jesus.

As God set Israel apart as his own possession, he now chooses, sets apart, and cleanses those who will receive his Son.

HISTORICAL BACKGROUND

Tradition holds that Peter died as a martyr in Rome in the 60s. His legacy, however, lived on long after his death. To a great extent, subsequent generations of the church rely on the confession, witness, and ministry of Peter, the devoted but fallible follower of Christ.

Section Summary

The opening verse claims Peter as author of this letter to believers in Asia Minor. Peter's chief aim in writing this letter is to provide them encouragement in Christian living.

GOD'S GREAT SALVATION (1:3–12)

An Inheritance (vv. 3–5)

The section 1:3–2:10 serves as a survey of the Christian life. This initial section (1:3–12) reveals the characteristics of God's salvation. God, motivated by his great mercy, has caused us to be brought from despair to a living hope.

CHARACTERISTICS OF GOD'S SALVATION

Hope	v. 3
Assurance	v. 4
Faith	vv. 5,9
Joy in spite of trials	vv. 6,8
Praise, honor, and glory to God	v. 7
Fulfillment in lives of believers	vv. 10–12

Peter knew this living hope not as a teaching handed down from someone else. He had been snatched out of a sea of despair into which he fell when he denied Jesus three times.

Peter's firsthand experience of the risen Christ brought him to a living hope that energized him and re-created his world.

The world of decay and death which holds most people as slaves for their entire lives no longer dominated Peter's life. For Peter and the other apostles, Jesus demonstrated just how impotent death really is.

In witnessing the resurrection, the apostles got a glimpse of the imperishable in the midst of a world that is passing away, and they were empowered to assure the generations to come of "an inheritance that is imperishable, undefiled, and unfading, kept in heaven for you" (v. 4).

The believers to whom Peter wrote did not have the firsthand experience of Jesus's resurrection that Peter had, but they might as well have.

Here is the secret of the resilience of Christian faith. The Holy Spirit, who raised Jesus from death, is the key agent in the communication of the gospel. He took the apostles's word—God's Word—and made it real in the hearts of those who heard it.

They were suffering (v. 6) and on the verge of suffering more. But they felt God's present protection and had an inward assurance of God's saving action that would appear in the future.

This assurance made them joyful—even in the midst of sufferings. Moreover, Peter reminds them that their sufferings were strengthening their faith and purifying it (v. 7).

The Spirit's work was such that even though they had not seen Jesus in the flesh, they believed in him and they loved him. This invisible union with their Lord caused them to "rejoice with inexpressible and glorious joy" (v. 8).

A Deliverance Foreseen by the Prophets (vv. 10–12)

Peter reminded his readers that the prophets foretold the salvation that came in Jesus Christ. God's Spirit was at work in these prophets, causing them to search out the time and place when Messiah would come. God's Spirit showed them that Messiah must suffer and enter glory. What they did not anticipate was the present church age that would separate the events of the crucifixion and resurrection from God's bringing history to a conclusion with the second coming of Christ.

The risen Christ, walking incognito with the disciples on the road from Jerusalem to Emmaus, said to them: "'How foolish you are, and how slow to believe all that the prophets have spoken! Wasn't it necessary for the Messiah to suffer these things and enter into his glory?' Then beginning with Moses and all the Prophets, he interpreted for them the things concerning himself in all the Scriptures" (Luke 24:25–27).

All aspects of God's salvation are encompassed by his grace. The salvation that God began by his grace will continue by his grace and will finally be consummated in heaven by his grace.

Through Christ, Christians can be heirs of God and "coheirs with Christ" (Rom 8:17; cp. Eph 3:6). Only the book of Hebrews makes explicit use of the idea of "inheritance" as requiring the death of the testator, Christ. A "will" requires a death to come into effect, so the death of Christ keeps the new "covenant"/"will" in effect (Heb 9:16–17).

In this passage (1 Pet 1), the believer's inheritance is kept not on earth but in heaven. Here, "inheritance" is another name for the *salvation* "that is ready to be revealed" (v. 5).

WORD PICTURE

Inheritance

In the New Testament, *inheritance* can refer to property (Luke 12:13), but most often it refers to the rewards of discipleship: (1) eternal life (e.g., Matt 5:5; 19:29); and (2) the kingdom (e.g., Matt 25:34).

Section Summary

Salvation begins with the living hope established by the resurrection of Christ from the dead. Although believers must endure the suffering of this present age, they have the promise of God's protection.

A CHALLENGE TO HOLINESS (1:13–21)

Exhortations for Holy Living (vv. 13–16)

After dealing with the fundamental matters of salvation, Peter shifted his focus to a more pastoral approach. His words in verse 13 are equivalent to saying, "Roll up your sleeves and go to work." The return of Jesus is to give Christians hope and stability in the face of persecution. They are to show their response to God's holiness by leaving the "desires" of their past ignorance (v. 14) and adopting God's own behavior as their pattern.

The conjunction "therefore" signals the change from statements to conclusions. Peter now exhorted his readers with several commands to guide them to a pattern of holy living.

"Your minds ready for action" (v. 13). Believers are forbidden to lapse into intellectual slothfulness. Dullness of the mind is inexcusable and shameful. The word *mind* refers not merely to the intellect but rather to that which guides and directs one's conduct.

WORD PICTURE

Your Minds Ready for Action

The literal expression here is "gird up your minds." Persons living in the Mediterranean world often wore robes. When they began to move quickly, they would gather their robe up so that it wouldn't impede their progress. Peter was saying to do that to your minds.

"Be sober-minded" (v. 13). The root meaning for the word *sober-minded* is "to be free from the influence of intoxicants." It is important to maintain a sharp mind and collected thoughts.

"Set your hope" (v. 13). Peter's readers are to set their hope on Christ's return. This hope will give them stability and strength in the midst of persecution.

"Do not be conformed" (v. 14). Each believer has a responsibility to avoid being fashioned by his or her evil desires. Instead, each must adopt God's own behavior as a pattern.

"Be holy" (v. 15). To be holy is to be set apart to God. Peter quoted Lev 11:44–45: "Be holy, because I am holy." Believers, who are separated to God, are to behave in a manner that shows them to be "like" God.

God's Judgment (v. 17)

Another motivation to holiness is God's judgment. God does not judge arbitrarily or with prejudice; he judges every person's work impartially. Christians, therefore, should conduct themselves in such a way as to give evidence of God's presence.

The Price of the Cross (vv. 18–21)

Peter indicated that the proper reverence for God and an appreciation of the high cost of redemption demands holy living.

The payment that releases believers from an "empty way of life" is the "blood of Christ."

Peter noted that God determined the performance of this work of Christ before the beginning of time. He has only recently made his plan evident in the incarnation, passion, and resurrection of Jesus (v. 20).

WORD PICTURE

Redemption

Peter's readers would have understood redemption as the freeing of a slave by paying a price.

Section Summary

Offering several commands and motivations, Peter challenged his readers to a pattern of holiness. Peter explained that the character of God and the high cost of redemption are incentives to produce holiness in his readers.

A CALL TO HARMONY (1:22–25)

Peter again emphasized the importance of obedience. He now urged his readers to express their holiness by a deep love, from the heart, for one another. Peter's quotation from Isa 40:6–8 shows that the experience of this love comes from the creative activity of God.

WORD PICTURE

Sincere Brotherly Love . . . Love One Another Constantly

"Peter uses two words for 'love' in v. 22: one means brotherly love and the other divine love *(agape)*. The Christian possesses brotherly love; but he needs to exert spiritual energy and love others the way God loves him. Even unsaved people can show brotherly love; it takes a Christian, controlled by the Spirit, to show *agape* love." Taken from Warren Wiersbe, *Wiersbe's Expository Outlines on the New Testament* (Victor, 1992), 743.

Section Summary

Peter urged his readers to express their holiness by a deep love for one another. Quoting from the Old Testament, Peter showed that the experience of this love comes from the creative activity of God.

QUESTIONS TO GUIDE YOUR STUDY

1. What is the believer's inheritance?
2. What is to be the believer's posture in the face of persecution and trial?
3. What does it mean for a Christian to be *holy?*
4. Peter provides his readers with several exhortations to be holy. What should be the believer's pattern for holy living?

1 PETER 2

The opening word of this chapter, "therefore," logically ties the reader back to the theme of being "born again" in 1:23. Because of the new birth and the new life that must follow, Peter offered his readers good advice on living the Christian life.

ADVICE FOR LIVING THE CHRISTIAN LIFE (2:1–3)

Avoiding Sin (v. 1)

Living the Christian life involves making choices, discharging responsibilities, and doing the work of the gospel. It is imperative that believers expressly avoid those things that can undermine progress in their personal and spiritual growth. Therefore, Peter charged his readers to take the responsibility of ridding from their own lives any stumbling blocks that might prevent that growth: "Rid yourselves of all malice, all deceit, hypocrisy, envy, and all slander" (v. 1).

SINS THAT EASILY BESET US

SPECIFIC SIN	EXPANDED MEANING
All malice	Every form of wickedness
All deceit	Not being straightforward
Hypocrisy	Forms of pretense
Envy	Desiring something another possesses
All slander	Disparaging or discrediting someone by evil speaking or backbiting

Note that not one of the sins on this list is physical. Rather, all issue from one's *mind, spirit,* and *heart.* Believers of all ages are vulnerable to each of these sins. Once this kind of sin takes hold in a believer's life, the result can be spiritually degrading and personally ruinous. Believers must absolutely and completely discard such sins. The word "rid" carries the idea of rejecting *any* connection with such sins.

Growing in the Lord (vv. 2–3)

Peter used the picture of an infant figuratively, using a word that refers to a baby that is nursing at its mother's breast. In like manner, Christians are to cultivate an appetite for nourishment—pure spiritual milk—that they may grow in their salvation.

In the New Testament, we find the word for *spiritual* "only here and in Rom 12:1, used here with an allusion to *logos* (12:3) and *rēma* (1:25), 'the sincere milk of the word' ('the milk belonging to the word,' either the milk which is the word or the milk contained in the word, that is Christ)." A. T. Robertson, "The General Epistles," vol. 6, *Word Pictures in the New Testament,* 95.

PERSONAL APPLICATION

"One of the most dangerous symptoms is the loss of appetite. It is the danger-signal warning that evil lurks unseen within. And there is no surer indication of religious declension and ill-health than the cessation of desire for the Word of God." F. B. Meyer, *Tried by Fire* (Marshall, Morgan, and Scott, 1950), 66–67.

CHRIST: THE LIVING STONE (2:4–10)

Peter used three images to describe the church in this section: living stones, a spiritual house, and a select nation.

Living Stones (vv. 4–5)

Peter portrayed the church as living stones that give sacrificial service to God. These "living stones" are believers who are built on the living Stone, Jesus Christ. He enables his followers to produce "spiritual sacrifices acceptable to God through Jesus Christ" (v. 5). Such sacrifices are those inspired by the Holy Spirit.

OUR SPIRITUAL SACRIFICES TO GOD

SACRIFICE	REFERENCE
Obedience	Rom 12:1
Praise	Heb 13:15–16
Practical ministry	Heb 13:15–16

A Building (vv. 6–8)

Peter also described the church as a building or spiritual house founded on Christ as the Cornerstone. He quoted Old Testament passages from Isa 8:14; 28:16 and Ps 118:22 to show that Christ is the foundation Stone for believers and a rock that causes unbelievers to trip and fall.

A Nation (vv. 9–10)

Finally, Peter used the language of Exod 19:5–6 and Hos 2:23 to portray believers as a select nation reflecting the glories of God (2:9–10). God fashioned special recipients of his mercy from those who previously never belonged to anyone.

DEFINITION OF THE "CHURCH" IN 1 PETER 2:9

PICTURE	EXPLANATION
"A chosen race"	Believers are the "spiritual Israel" through the new birth.
"A royal priesthood"	Because Christ is their King and Priest, believers are a royal priesthood.
"A holy nation"	The "spiritual Israel" of believers, who are God's own possession.

Section Summary

Peter used three images to describe the church: a living body, a building, and a nation. The church built on the living Stone, Jesus Christ, produces spiritual sacrifices and reflects the glories of God.

THE PRACTICE OF GOOD WORKS (2:11–25)

Peter was eager for God's people to demonstrate distinctive, obedient behavior in order to convince critics of their faith. Over a section

PERSONAL APPLICATION

"A stone can look most unimpressive—but it can perform a vital function if made the cornerstone of a large building; or it can bring a person tumbling to the ground if he or she stumbles over it. Jesus has become the cornerstone of God's spiritual temple, and there are two possible responses. We can either take our own angle and position from the Cornerstone, and line ourselves up on him; or we can refuse to live by reference to him, and stumble over him instead. It is a vivid picture." Stephen Motyer, *Evangelical Commentary on the Bible* (Baker Book House, 1989), 1166.

spanning 2:11–3:12, he urged them to apply this behavior in relation to their rulers—their earthly masters, in their families, and toward one another.

A Call to Personal Discipline (vv. 11–12)

Peter exhorted his readers to "conduct yourselves honorably among the Gentiles" (v. 12). He suggested three reasons Christians must discipline their lives:

1. Christians are foreigners to their pagan environment and not adjusted to it.
2. If Christians yield to the flesh, they will wage battle against their best selves.
3. Self-discipline and obedience have a wholesome influence on unbelievers.

Submission to Government Authorities (vv. 13–17)

Believers are to practice responsible citizenship by submitting to "every human authority" (v. 13). Peter urged voluntary submission on the part of believers for the purpose of commending Jesus's lordship. At this point he picked up on the theme of freedom. Christians are responsibly free to "love the brothers and sisters. Fear God. Honor the emperor [that is, their political leaders]."

WORD PICTURE

Slavery

"In today's world where slavery has been almost universally abolished and where the actual terms 'servants' and 'master' have been dropped from most vocabularies, what does this passage mean? Christians, no matter whom we are accountable to, are obligated to do our work responsibly. We are obligated to maintain the kind of relationship to those to whom we are accountable and to those who may be accountable to us that will conform to the example set by Christ. Paul states this same point, 'Whatever your task, work heartily, as serving the Lord (Col 3:23).'" Foy Valentine, *1 & 2 Peter*, vol. 23, *Layman's Bible Book Commentary*, 105.

Submission of Servants to Masters (vv. 18–25)

Peter's era was one in which slavery was an accepted part of the social system. From the earliest times, the Roman government accepted and promoted the practice. In the Roman world, treatment of slaves varied considerably. By the first century, however, the institution of slavery was changing. Public sentiment decried harsh treatment of slaves, and many leading orators spoke against the institution. Christianity arose in a real-life, tension-filled setting. The slaves' insurrections already failed, causing significant injury, sorrow, and loss of life. Working within these tensions, however, the seeds of abolition were sown.

As servants responded to the gospel of Jesus Christ, it became imperative for church leaders to address the issues of servant-master relationships. In the New Testament, we find both Peter and the apostle Paul providing guidance on this subject.

Peter provided special counsel to those who are servants of slave owners. Slaves are to be subject to their masters and submit to them with all respect. The incentive for showing this kind of subjection, even in the presence of provocation, is the moving example of Christ's obedience. As Christ suffered for all, also as his followers, Christians may be called to suffer wrongfully for doing right.

CHRIST AS THE EXAMPLE OF RIGHTEOUSNESS (2:21–25)

Although directed primarily to slaves, Peter's counsel about submission to masters in this section has rich contemporary application.

Righteous living in daily existence is made possible because of Christ's sacrifice. He is now the believer's Shepherd who cares for his sheep in every area and relationship of life (v. 25). Jesus is the believer's example of righteousness lived out in daily life. Through his power believers may follow "in his steps" (v. 21).

QUESTIONS TO GUIDE YOUR STUDY

1. Peter presented a list of certain sins that can easily beset us. What is unique about these sins?
2. Peter described three images that picture the church. What do we learn from these?
3. What is the believer's incentive for submitting to authority?
4. In verse 25, Peter stated that Jesus is the Shepherd and Overseer of our souls. What are the implications of his statement? What other biblical truths can you think of that support that statement?

1 PETER 3

Peter continued his theme of submission from chapter 2 and emphasized the need for submission in three areas of the believer's life: in the home, in the midst of suffering, and toward Christ.

SUBMISSION IN THE HOME (3:1–7)

This section is one of the most intensely practical parts of Peter's letter. It is helpful to read and compare what other portions of the New Testament have to say on the subject. The apostle Paul had a good deal to say about the subject of marital relationships in his writings.

PAUL'S WRITINGS ON THE MARITAL RELATIONSHIP

Eph 5:22–6:4
1 Cor 7:1–17
Col 3:18–21
1 Tim 2:8–15

Although it in no way diminishes the authority of God's Word, often it has been pointed out that Paul himself was not married. Peter, however, was married. In his Gospel, Matthew referred to Peter's wife's mother, who had a fever and was healed by Jesus (8:14–15).

Counsel to Wives (vv. 1–6)

PERSONAL APPLICATION

"Submission is voluntarily cooperating with someone, first out of love and respect for God and then out of love and respect for that person. Submitting to nonbelievers is difficult, but it is a vital part of leading them to Jesus Christ. We are not called to submit to nonbelievers to the point that we compromise our relationship with God, but we must look for every opportunity to humbly serve in the power of God's Spirit." *Life Application Study Bible* (Tyndale House, 1996), 2001.

As Peter counseled servants to be submissive to their masters, so he counseled wives to "submit yourselves" to their husbands. The term *submit* means "to subject or subordinate." A matter to note is that in the biblical passages dealing with the submission of the wife, the nature of the wife's submission is different from the submission of children or slaves. Children and slaves are told to obey; the wife is not. The wife has a different relationship to her husband from children to parents or slaves to masters. The motivation for voluntary submission is that it is a proper Christian attitude.

In these verses Peter had in mind here a situation where the husband is not a believer. Wives are to be submissive so that if her husband does "disobey the word," he may be "won over without a word by the way their wives live."

The submission Peter counseled wives to observe in relationship to their husbands reflects the acceptance of the husband-wife relationship, which, like the acceptance of human slavery, prevailed throughout the world of Peter's day. The power of the Christian gospel was just beginning to work on behalf of slaves, government, and women. At the time of Peter's writing of his letter to Asia Minor, there had been insufficient time for the gospel to change significantly the established and structured institutions of society.

Counsel to Husbands (v. 7)

WORD PICTURE

Weaker Partner

The phrase "weaker partner" is a reference to the physical body. According to A. T. Robertson, "She is termed 'the weaker,' not for intellectual or moral weakness, but purely for physical reasons, which the husband must recognize with due consideration for marital happiness." "The General Epistles," vol. 6, *WPNT*, 111.

The apostle also had a word for husbands. Christian husbands are to recognize their wives as "coheirs" of the gracious gift of life. Peter was affirming here that marriage is indeed a partnership. Husbands are to live in understanding of their wives, maintaining a considerate spirit, kindness, and honor to them. To fail in this area will result in an ineffective prayer life.

Section Summary

Peter continues his theme of submission, focusing on submission within the marital relationship. Marriage is a partnership that demands submission from the wife and loving understanding and consideration from the husband.

SUBMISSION IN THE MIDST OF SUFFERING (3:8–17)

Living in Harmony with One Another (vv. 8–13)

Here Peter discussed the mutual love between his readers and the harmony that should prevail: "be like-minded" (v. 8). He urged them to practice vital qualities of the Christian life that will lead to this harmony. Peter summed up this section by quoting Ps 34:12–16, one of the great passages of Scripture that encourages us to be "devoted to what is good" (v. 13).

Suffering Persecution (v. 14)

Believers who are faithful to Christ and his teachings may expect suffering. It should not come as a surprise to those who follow Christ, who is our example in suffering. When suffering does come, Peter said, "If you should suffer for righteousness, you are blessed" (v. 14). Eventually, those who persecute will "be put to shame" (v. 16).

The New Testament speaks clearly about the certainty of believers suffering persecution for their faith. Several writers deal with the subject. The following chart highlights a few of those passages.

THE CHURCH IN HARMONY

COMMAND	EXPANDED MEANING
"Be like-minded" (v. 8).	Having a unity of spirit and an attitude in spiritual matters.
"Be . . . sympathetic" (v. 8).	Sharing in the feelings of others, whether in sorrow or in joy.
"Love one another" (v. 8).	Expressing brotherly and sisterly love among God's people.
"Be compassionate and humble" (v. 8).	Being tenderhearted or goodhearted toward others with a humble spirit.
"Not paying back evil for evil" (v. 9).	Repaying acts of evil with acts of blessing.

PERSONAL APPLICATION

We are to prepare ourselves for trials and tribulations that come from a hostile world, not simply by hardening our minds or steeling our wills but by immersing ourselves in righteousness. That unqualified and uncompromised righteousness before God and others is the Christian's finest armor against the attack of persecution.

Dealing with Persecution (vv. 15–17)

Believers are not to fear those who persecute them. Rather, they are to "regard Christ the Lord as holy." In verse 15 Peter provided two steps a believer may take to respond righteously to those who persecute them:

1. Be prepared to give an answer.
2. Maintain a spirit of gentleness and respect.

By practicing these steps, the Christian will keep a clear conscience because of his or her behavior, and the accuser or accusers will be put to shame for their slander.

PERSONAL APPLICATION

"There is a sense, of course, in which our Saviour suffered for our sins *once*.... But we must not suppose that Jesus has passed into an unsuffering heaven. He still suffers in each of his members. He is crucified afresh when we yield to willful sins. He travails in birth until his kingdom come. He is touched with the feeling of our infirmities. How can He be at rest, whilst his beloved are tossing in the storm, and the members of his bride are not complete? And through his sufferings blessing is accruing; they cannot be in vain: we shall all see soon; meanwhile let us bear fellowship with Him in his anguish, drinking of his cup, that we may share his glory." F. B. Meyer, *Tried by Fire*, 123–24.

WORD PICTURE

Made Proclamation

The word Peter uses for "made proclamation" *(kerussō)* to the spirits in prison is not the same word the New Testament used for "preaching the gospel" (*euangelizō*). Peter opted for a word that means "to proclaim" or "to announce." Jesus's act of "proclamation" following his resurrection was a proclamation of his *victory* to the fallen angels in Hades rather than a proclamation of the gospel.

THE PERSECUTION OF THE SAINTS

REFERENCE	SPEAKER OR WRITER	KEY TRUTH
Jas 4:4	James	"Don't you know that friendship with the world is hostility toward God?"
2 Tim 3:12	Paul	"All who want to live a godly life in Christ Jesus will be persecuted."
John 16:33	Jesus	"You will have suffering in this world. Be courageous! I have conquered the world."

Section Summary

Believers who are faithful to Christ and his teachings may expect suffering. They may prepare themselves for times of suffering by immersing themselves in the righteousness of Christ.

SUBMISSION TO CHRIST (3:18–22)

Jesus: The Believer's Example in Suffering (v. 18)

Christ is the believer's best example of how to bear suffering for the sake of righteousness. His example should encourage us to endure our own suffering patiently.

"The Spirits in Prison" (vv. 19–20)

Some have interpreted the spirits in prison to mean departed human spirits. But the word for "spirits," *pneumata,* is never used in the Bible to refer to human spirits. More likely is that these are the spirits of fallen angels to whom Jesus announced his victory over evil and their own judgment.

Christian Baptism (vv. 21–22)

Peter ties the account of Noah's ark to Christian baptism. The flood is a picture of judgment. The ark is salvation, deliverance of Noah and his family from God's judgment. Baptism is a picture that tells forth the death, burial, and resurrection of Christ. These events, pictured by baptism, are the ark through which believers are saved from the judgment of God that fell on Christ.

Section Summary

As believers we show our submission to Christ by following his example in our suffering as well as in the act of Christian baptism. Even the fallen angels in Hades must recognize and submit to the authority of the resurrected Christ.

QUESTIONS TO GUIDE YOUR STUDY

1. Peter spoke of marital relationships. What is the responsibility of the wife? of the husband? What do other New Testament writers have to say about the subject?
2. What should be the view of Christians regarding suffering? What steps can believers take to remain submissive to Christ during times of persecution and suffering?
3. One of most difficult passages for interpreters over the years has been 1 Peter 3:19–20. What do you think Peter meant by his statement that Jesus "made proclamation to the spirits in prison"?
4. Why did Peter tie in Christian baptism with Noah and the flood? What was he teaching here?

1 PETER 4

This chapter opens with the word *therefore,* which introduces the reader to the main lesson to be drawn from the previous section, 3:18–22. Both this chapter and chapter 5 treat the general theme of God's grace in the midst of suffering. Indeed, in 4:12 Peter spoke of a "fiery ordeal," persecution that some were already suffering and which others would soon suffer.

LIVING IN THE WILL OF GOD (4:1–6)

Suffering with Christ (v. 1)

One of the Christian's great challenges is to "arm" oneself with the same attitude as that of Christ toward suffering. Jesus said, "Anyone who finds his life will lose it, and anyone who loses his life because of me will find it" (Matt 10:39). In the Gospels, we have a representative record of how Jesus dealt with life's challenges and responsibilities. His attitudes and approaches are the believer's ideal.

Redeeming the Time (vv. 2–3)

As believers live for the will of God, their values change; and they align their lives with God's desires, the stated principles and commands in his Word. For the Christian, life's deepest concern is not what human

HISTORICAL BACKGROUND

Arm

The word *arm* means "to equip" or "to arm" oneself. It is part of the New Testament motif of the Christian soldier (see Eph 6:10–18). Although this word is used only here in the New Testament, it was used in classical Greek, where its usage provides insight into what Peter had in mind and his readers understood.

For example, to arm oneself was to prepare by acquiring the necessary provisions for the way, such as a meal, lamps, horses, and ships. One usage even speaks of arming oneself with the attribute of *boldness.* Here, Peter was urging believers to arm themselves with the same attitude Christ had toward suffering. That includes aligning with his stated thoughts and convictions about the topic. See G. Kittel and G. Friedrich, *Theological Dictionary of the New Testament* (Eerdmans, 1967), vol. 5, 294–95.

appetites desire but what God's will dictates. Life becomes a precious resource that cannot be wasted by "doing what the Gentiles choose to do" (v. 3).

Relating to God's Judgment (vv. 4–6)

Because Christians do not join in practicing sin with the world, the world abuses them. Believers may take comfort in knowing that God will someday judge such people.

Some have misinterpreted the words of verse 6, "The gospel was also preached to those who are now dead," to suggest that unbelievers who die will have an opportunity to hear and respond to the gospel message after death. There is no hint in the Bible of a second chance after death. Rather, Peter was speaking of believers who died and were enjoying spiritual life with God in heaven. Warren Wiersbe offered a paraphrase that provides insight for this complex passage:

> There are people now dead physically, but alive with God in the spirit, who were judged by the world. But they heard the Gospel before they died and believed. They suffered and died because of their faith—but they are living with God! It is better to suffer for Christ and to be with God than to follow the world and be lost. Warren W. Wiersbe, *Wiersbe's Expository Outlines on the* New *Testament* (Victor, 1992), 751.

Section Summary

Peter urged a full commitment by believers to the will of God. Arming themselves with the same attitude that Christ had toward suffering is a starting point. They are then to live out the rest of life controlled not by their "human desires" but by the will of God.

LIVING THAT GLORIFIES GOD (4:7–11)

"The end of all things is near" is a reference to the end of history, or this present age. This emphasis on the expected end of the age is shared by the apostle Paul in his writings. It is also found in the books of Matthew, Hebrews, James, Mark, and Revelation.

Early Christians and the New Testament writers viewed the early return of Christ as a challenge to maintain a moral lifestyle. This ought to be the case for believers today. In view of the expected return of Christ ("therefore"), Peter set forth several exhortations that serve as guidelines for living a life that brings glory to God.

"Be alert and sober-minded." A clear mind and self-control are essential to effective, focused praying. An active and effective prayer life should characterize all believers anticipating Jesus's return.

"Maintain constant love for one another." The love Peter spoke about here is a strenuous, intense love. It is an unselfish love that stretches to reach to the other without breaking.

Use your gift. The nearness of the Lord's coming should lead believers to make vigorous use of their spiritual gifts.

LIVING THAT GLORIFIES GOD

EXHORTATION	REASON
"Be alert and sober-minded."	For effective prayer
"Maintain constant love for one another."	Love restores and reconciles
"Be hospitable."	To serve others
Use your gift.	To glorify God

Section Summary

Early Christians viewed the return of Christ as a challenge to maintain a moral lifestyle. This ought also to be the case for believers today. In view of the expected return of Christ, Peter set forth several exhortations that serve as guidelines for living a life that brings glory to God.

LIVING UNDER SUFFERING (4:12–19)

Peter presented a threefold perspective to encourage his readers not to be surprised at the prospect of the painful trial that lay ahead.

Sharing in Christ's Suffering (vv. 12–13)

Peter reminded his readers that their suffering could lead them to share in Christ's own experiences, a development that would link them more closely with their Savior. The "fiery ordeal" is a test, which by purifying and refining them, will make them more like Jesus.

Suffering and Special Blessing (vv. 14–16)

Peter suggests to his readers that their bearing insults for the name of Christ could lead to a richer supply of the Holy Spirit in their lives: "If you are ridiculed for the name of Christ, you are blessed, because the Spirit of glory and of God rests on you" (v. 14). The "glow" of God's glory on the believer will certainly be a witness to those who persecute God's people.

Suffering as a Witness to Unbelievers (vv. 17–18)

"For the time has come for judgment to begin with God's household" (v. 17). Although the time had come for persecution to fall on the church, the outcome for God's people will be victory. The final judgment of unbelievers, however, is left fearfully hanging: "What will the outcome

PERSONAL APPLICATION

Be Hospitable

Hospitality was a ministry during the time of the early church. But this practice was by no means limited to the church. And Eastern hospitality was not merely a custom; it was a sacred duty that everyone was expected to observe. Believers would entertain or receive strangers as well as traveling missionaries. In doing so, they would provide their guests with food, shelter, and protection. Christians ought to be ready always to extend hospitality and minister to the needs of others.

WORD PICTURE

Fiery Ordeal

This word is often used in a purifying or refining sense, which is the case here as Peter referred to the "fiery ordeal" as a "test." Used metaphorically, such an ordeal is truly a "trial by fire."

be for those who disobey the gospel of God?" In other words, what will happen when the time comes for unbelievers to be judged?

Suffering and God's Faithfulness (v. 19)

Peter closed this chapter by providing his readers the motivation for their obedient, trusting service. Peter reminded them that God is their faithful Creator. Based on His proven faithfulness, when Christians "suffer according to God's will," they are to commit themselves to Him and continue to do good.

HISTORICAL BACKGROUND

Entrust Themselves

The phrase "entrust themselves" is a compound word made up of the preposition "over" and the verb "to place or lay." The word is a banking term meaning "to deposit" (as in 1 Tim 1:18; 2 Tim 2:2). In the context of this passage, 1 Pet 4:19, it means "to give over oneself" or "to commit to one's charge." It is the word Jesus used as he died on the cross (Luke 23:46): "Father, into your hands I commit my spirit." A. T. Robertson, "The General Epistles," vol. 6, *WPNT,* 129.

Section Summary

Peter presented a threefold perspective to encourage his readers not to be surprised at the prospect of the painful trial that lay ahead: (1) they would share in Christ's sufferings; (2) they could have a richer supply of the Holy Spirit in their lives; and (3) their motivation for obedience is the faithfulness of God.

QUESTIONS TO GUIDE YOUR STUDY

1. What does it mean for Christians to "arm" themselves with Christ's attitude toward suffering? How does one do this?
2. What guidelines did Peter set forth for living a life that brings glory to God?
3. Why does God allow "fiery ordeals" in our lives? What good comes from them?
4. When Christians suffer according to God's will, what does it mean to "entrust" oneself to God?

1 PETER 5

In this final chapter, Peter focused on directives to church leaders and general exhortations and warnings to all Christians. After a short preaching section, he closed his letter with a final greeting.

ASSURANCES FOR FAITHFUL SERVANTS (5:1–11)

To Elders (vv. 1–4)

This first exhortation is to elders in the churches. Peter himself was a fellow elder. The purpose of this part of the letter, however, was not to discuss the duties of elders. Rather, he was addressing the elders as *older* church leaders and urged them to be faithful shepherds from a willing heart with a desire to serve as an example to the flock.

To Younger Christians (v. 5)

As elders have responsibilities, so do younger members of the church. Peter charged them to "be subject to the elders." The submission Peter spoke of here is most likely a reference to the recognition that the younger people have much to learn from the older believers in the church. Inexperienced young people in the church should profit from older members' experiences. In addition, exuberance and enthusiasm can be properly directed and channeled by older believers' experience and wisdom.

Peter especially exhorted younger believers to "clothe" themselves with humility toward one another. He then quoted Prov 3:34: "God resists the proud but gives grace to the humble."

To the Faithful Who Persevere (vv. 6–11)

Now directing his words to all believers, Peter encouraged them to persevere by cultivating the following special qualities of the Christian life.

"Humble yourselves" (v. 6). Peter urged his readers to practice humility. Those who humble themselves under "the mighty hand of God" may do so with the assurance that God will "exalt" them when the time is just right.

"Casting all your cares on him" (v. 7). Rather than wait for God to take the initiative and remove those anxieties troubling their hearts, believers are to take the responsibility of casting their anxieties upon him.

"Be sober-minded, be alert" (v. 8). These two imperatives are strong exhortations not to be slack in remaining watchful. Although we may be confident in God's care for us, we must ever be vigilant. Christians are in the midst of constant spiritual warfare and are the targets of Satan's attacks. Peter depicted the enemy as prowling around "like a roaring lion, looking for anyone he can devour" (v. 8).

"Resist him, firm in the faith" (v. 9). Christians who are tempted or threatened by the devil's evil presence are to "resist" him. Believers may stand against the devil and firm in the faith, taking comfort that other believers throughout the world are experiencing the same kind of suffering.

WORD PICTURE

Casting All Your Cares on Him

The word translated "casting . . . on" is a compound word in Greek. It is a construction of the preposition "upon" and the verb "to hurl, to throw off." The basic meaning of this word in 1 Pet 5:7 is "to throw onto." "Subjection to God's lordship is demonstrated in the fact that the community casts all its care on the Lord and is thus relieved of its burden." G. Kittel and G. Friedrich, *Theological Dictionary of the New Testament* (Eerdmans, 1968), vol. 6, 994.

Section Summary

Peter encouraged persevering believers to cultivate special qualities of the Christian life. They are to exercise humility, give their anxieties to God, and to be alert for the attacks of the enemy. It is important that believers not be slack in their vigilance and that they stand against the wiles of the devil.

CONCLUSION (5:12–14)

Final Greetings (vv. 12–14a)

Peter's summary of his purpose is: "I have written to you briefly in order to encourage you and to testify that this is the true grace of God" (v. 12). Even in his closing words, he continued to admonish his readers to "stand firm" in their Christian lives. He then sent greetings from those at his location, referring to it as "Babylon."

Benediction (v. 14b)

With a simple but powerful statement, Peter concluded his letter: "Peace to all of you who are in Christ." It is a statement of unity that underscores the message of his letter.

WORD PICTURE

Babylon

It is generally believed that the "Babylon" mentioned here is Rome. "The use of the code name for Rome was widespread among early Christians, particularly after the waves of persecution began to emanate from the city of the Caesars." Foy Valentine, *1, 2 Peter,* vol. 23, *Layman's Bible Book Commentary,* 119–20.

Section Summary

Peter concluded his letter by exhorting his readers to stand fast in their Christian lives. This is especially significant as waves of persecution from Rome against the church had already begun.

QUESTIONS TO GUIDE YOUR STUDY

1. What exhortations did Peter give to the elders of the churches. To the younger believers?
2. What special qualities of the Christian life did Peter encourage the persevering faithful to cultivate?
3. What does it mean for Christians to cast their anxiety onto God? What does it involve?
4. What can a Christian do to prepare against the attacks of the devil?

2 Peter

INTRODUCTION 2 PETER

Peter wrote his second letter to counter the influence of heresy within the church (2 Pet 2:1). He appealed for spiritual growth as an antidote to defeat the heretics who infiltrated the community and urged his readers to live holy lives in anticipation of Jesus's return (2 Pet 3:11–12). It is a message of pastoral encouragement, support for living the Christian life, prophetic warning against false doctrine, and concern for the proper preparation for a day of judgment.

Second Peter is brief, more like a short sermon or an essay than an actual letter. The brevity of this letter resulted in its being ignored for centuries by the church. Few Christians made use of it until the time of Origen (AD 250).

2 PETER IN A "NUTSHELL"

PURPOSE:	Encouragement for persecuted and suffering Christians
Major Doctrine:	Knowledge; the influence of Scripture
Key Passage:	2 Peter 1:16–21
Other Key Doctrines:	Judgment; practical Christian living; spiritual growth

AUTHOR

The author claimed to be Peter in 1:1 and asserted that he was an eyewitness to the transfiguration (1:16–18). His claim to be an apostle and his admission of friendship to Paul (3:15) clearly indicat that the writer intended to be seen as Peter.

PURPOSE FOR WRITING

Peter felt strongly that his death was near (2 Pet 1:14–15). He wanted to leave a spiritual testament to provide helpful instruction after his departure. He warned against the character and false teachings of heretics who would infiltrate the church (2:1–19; 3:1–4). To provide protection against errors, he urged a development of Christian virtues (1:3–11) and constant growth in God's grace (3:17–18).

HISTORICAL BACKGROUND

Eusebius places Peter's death in the fourteenth year of Nero that is variously dated from AD 64 to 68.

DATE AND PLACE OF WRITING

Date. Peter anticipated that his death would be soon (1:14–15). Assuming Peter wrote both 1 and 2 Peter, we can observe that Peter called this his second writing to the same readers (3:1). There is little specific information by which to arrive at an exact date, but it seems likely that 2 Peter was written shortly after 1 Peter. A time in the mid-to-late 60s, shortly before Peter's death, seems likely.

Place. Peter's letter contains little indication of his location. We may leave this as an open question, for a decision on this issue does not affect one's interpretation of the letter.

AUDIENCE

The letter lacks a specific address, something that 1 Peter does contain. So other data must be considered. If we assume Peter wrote the letter, "the second letter" (3:1) would indicate that he was writing to the same group who had received the first letter. The statement of 1:16 suggests that Peter spoke or preached to this group, but we have no knowledge of when or how this occurred. It seems best to suggest that Peter wrote to churches located in the northern part of Asia Minor.

LITERARY FORM

Several passages in 2 Peter indicate that Peter wrote to a specific congregation (1:16; 2:1; 3:1). The entire letter is an earnest warning against false teachers and an appeal for growth in maturity. Peter made little use of the Old Testament in quotations (but see 2:22), yet there are frequent allusions to Old Testament characters and events (2:4–8).

THE THEOLOGY OF 2 PETER

Peter held to a high view of Scripture (1:19–21), and he viewed Paul's writings as "Scripture" (3:16). He designated Jesus Christ as "Savior" and "Lord" (1:1–2), and he outlined his observation of Jesus's transfiguration (1:6–8). He affirmed the return of Christ (3:1–4) and asserted God's sovereign control of the events of history (3:13). He used the certainty of Christ's return as an incentive to appeal for godly living (3:14).

BASIC OUTLINE FOR 2 PETER

I. Greetings (1:1–2)
II. Provisions for Spiritual Growth (1:3–21)
III. The Danger of False Teaching (2:1–22)
IV. A Reminder of God's Hope (3:1–3)
V. Closing Commands (3:14–18)

QUESTIONS TO GUIDE YOUR STUDY

1. What was Peter's purpose for writing this letter?
2. Who was his audience? We don't know where Peter was when he wrote this letter. Is this a problem for our understanding its message?
3. What is Peter's main theme of this letter?
4. In his letter, Peter sought to protect his readers from the errors of false teachers. From what can be seen in the introductory material here, what tact did Peter follow to prepare his readers?

2 PETER 1

The theme of this chapter is Christ's return. Peter gave final warning against the false teachers and provided his readers assurance and encouragement. In the last chapter of this letter, he closed with advice to the faithful in view of the coming judgment.

SALUTATION (1:1–2)

Peter identified himself as a servant and an apostle of Jesus Christ. His salutation here and the one in 1 Peter differ in two ways: (1) here Peter used his full name, Simon Peter; and (2) although he did not address his letter to a specific geographic location, his references in 1:16; 2:1; and 3:1 suggest that he had a specific congregation in mind.

Peter addressed his letter to those who had "received a faith" in Christ. This faith is a precious gift shared by Peter and those to whom he wrote. Such faith is imparted by "the righteousness of our God and Savior Jesus Christ."

It is evident that Peter wanted his readers to experience God's loving favor and spiritual wholeness because of their clear, personal knowledge of Jesus.

HISTORICAL BACKGROUND

Righteousness

Righteousness is an attribute of God. God is righteous. God also works to make things right, and in this latter sense, God's righteousness imparts the gift of faith to sinful human beings.

PROVISIONS FOR SPIRITUAL GROWTH (1:3–4)

Peter reminded his readers that God not only provides faith but also provides everything they need for spiritual life and godly living. These gifts come through knowledge of God.

In this chapter he provided four sources of power, or incentives, for spiritual development in his readers: (1) God's calling and election, (2) Peter's witness to his readers, (3) God's majestic glory, and (4) the prophetic message of Scripture.

God's intended result of these provisions is that "you may share in the divine nature, escaping the corruption that is in the world because of evil desire" (v. 4).

HISTORICAL BACKGROUND

Peter may have been writing to combat a gnostic-like teaching that said that, in addition to knowledge of Christ, believers needed to learn a hidden knowledge which contains the key to spiritual growth.

Section Summary

Living the Christian life does not depend on one's own strength and resources. Here Peter reminded his readers that God provides everything believers need for spiritual life and godly living.

A CALL TO MORAL AND SPIRITUAL DEVELOPMENT (1:5–11)

Many refer to this section as the "ladder of faith." It teaches a progressive growth from the foundation of faith to the greatest of the ethical qualities for which Christians are to strive—love. Peter taught that believers need to strive to "supplement" or add to their saving faith. The most debilitating sin of modern believers is the failure to go on to maturity in Christ.

In verses 5–7, Peter showed that each quality builds on the previous one. Believers are never to pause in their upward climb until they have supplemented:

- Faith with goodness
- Goodness with knowledge
- Knowledge with self-control
- Self-control with endurance
- Endurance with godliness
- Godliness with brotherly affection
- Brotherly affection with love

Love is faith's finished product. "God is love" (1 John 4:16); therefore, Christians are to "be like him" (1 John 3:2).

WORD PICTURE

Supplement

The word translated "add" is a compound word in the Greek New Testament. It is made up of the preposition "upon" attached to the verb "to place." The preposition in compound words like this often makes the verb to which it is attached emphatic, thereby creating a new word with a unique meaning. Here the word seems to have taken on an accumulative force, which carries the idea of increasing and adding to the supplies. This word is often translated "put upon," "supplement," or "add."

WORD PICTURE

Given

The word translated "given" uses a tense in the Greek New Testament that emphasizes the continuing nature of what is given. Therefore, the spiritual resources God gives to believers are continually available to them as reliable sources of strength and growth.

THE LADDER OF MORAL DEVELOPMENT

RUNG OF THE LADDER	EXTENDED MEANING
Love	Self-giving for the good of others
Brotherly affection	Love for brothers and sisters in Christ
Godliness	Quality of being like God in daily life
Endurance	Endurance, perseverance, and courageous patience
Self-control	Mastery of self and control of one's appetites and drives
Knowledge	Practical understanding of the truth
Faith	Moral excellence
Goodness	Saving faith in God

Section Summary

Peter taught a progressive growth from the foundation of faith to the greatest of the ethical qualities for which Christians are to strive—love. Peter taught that believers need to strive to supplement or add these qualities to their saving faith.

COUNSEL FOR CONTINUED SPIRITUAL GROWTH (1:12–21)

More Incentives to Spiritual Growth (vv. 12–19)

Peter began this section by refreshing the memory of his readers. Although they are "established in the truth," Peter saw value in bringing to remembrance those things that would cause them to develop the qualities he had just mentioned and to grow spiritually. At this point, Peter was convinced that his death was approaching (he spoke of his "departure"). From his remarks in verse 15, it appears that he intended for his letter to continue to be circulated generally.

Peter now elaborated on two more incentives for the spiritual growth of his readers: God's glory and the prophetic message of Scripture.

God's Glory. The recipients of 2 Peter likely encountered those who mocked the idea of a powerful, heavenly Christ who could strengthen them for godly living. Peter had been an eyewitness of Christ's majesty in the transfiguration. He could testify that the glory of Jesus was a reality they could experience.

The Prophetic Message of Scripture. The final incentive Peter provided in this passage is the prophetic message of Scripture. Peter thought the transfiguration and other events in Jesus's life made the scriptural picture

HISTORICAL BACKGROUND

The Transfiguration

The transfiguration was an open display for the disciples of the glory Jesus had before the incarnation. It was also a foreshadowing of his resurrection and return. This event occurred most likely on Mount Hermon (elevation, 9,100 ft.). It is full of meaning, as much that took place there was highly symbolic. A mountain was often a place of revelation. Also present at the transfiguration were Moses and Elijah. They represented the Law and the Prophets respectively, which testify to but must give way to Jesus. The transfiguration experience provided needed reassurance for the disciples as they contemplated Jesus's death and their own future suffering.

of Jesus more sure and certain. Christians can find guidance from this word until Christ returns in person. Peter stated that Scripture is reliable because it has a divine rather than a human origin.

NEWTESTAMENEW TESTAMENT REFERENCE

Paul wrote to Timothy: "All Scripture is inspired by God and is profitable for teaching, for rebuking, for correcting, for training in righteousness" (2 Tim 3:16).

INCENTIVES FOR SPIRITUAL GROWTH IN CHAPTER 1

PROVISION	PASSAGE
1. God's calling and election	1:3–11
2. Peter's witness	1:12–15
3. The glory of God	1:16–18
4. The prophetic message of Scripture	1:19–21

The "Prophecy of Scripture" (vv. 20–21)

This passage has been understood variously. Among the views that have been advanced are:

1. Scripture should not be interpreted according to one's own bias.
2. Scripture cannot be interpreted properly without the Holy Spirit.
3. Scripture cannot be interpreted apart from the rest of Scripture.
4. The prophecies did not originate from the prophets but from God.

While all those views may have a measure of validity, the grammar of the underlying Greek text of our English translation seems to favor the last view. It suggests that Peter was speaking more about the source of Scripture than its proper interpretation. As believers, we can be certain the Scriptures are of divine origin, not human.

Section Summary

Convinced that his death was approaching, Peter reminded his readers about the qualities they should be developing in the course of their spiritual growth. Bringing to remembrance God's glory and the prophetic message of Scripture are powerful incentives.

QUESTIONS TO GUIDE YOUR STUDY

1. Describe the "ladder of faith" Peter provided in this chapter. Where does it start? Where does it lead?
2. What did Peter mean by "adding to to" or "supplementingone's faith?
3. Peter mentioned his ttransfiguration experience with Jesus. Why did this event mean so much to Peter?
4. What was Peter saying to his readers in 1:20–21?

2 PETER 2

Christianity has always been plagued by false teachers and false teachings. During the occasion of this letter, Peter's readers currently were under threat by false teachers "among" them. In this chapter Peter instructed his readers about the infiltrators and issued warnings against deceivers and false teachers.

THE AGENDA OF FALSE TEACHERS (2:1–3)

They Deny Christ (v. 1)

False teachers introduce "destructive heresies." These heresies are clever arguments against the true deity of Jesus Christ or persuasive contention against the true humanity of Christ. Both kinds of heresies sprang up among the early Christians. Heresies have reared their ugly heads many times over the centuries, and even today their modern counterparts are alive and active among Christians.

They Falsely Lead Others (v. 2)

The denial of Christ leads to immorality. False teachers are characterized by immorality and greed. Both of those sins have a common source in the rejection of God's will. "Many will follow their depraved ways."

As a result of the influence of false teachers, many people are enticed into blatant immoralities. In opposition to the teachings and activities of those heretics, the Bible teaches that Jesus is "the way, the truth, and the life" (John 14:6). A denial of Jesus leads to a denial of his way of truth and his moral uprightness.

"The way of truth will be maligned because of" (v. 2) those leaders who deny Christ and practice sexual corruption and depravity bring. Those believers who follow false leaders and their teachings shamefully compromise their Christian witness and become ineffective witnesses for Christ.

They Exploit the Weak (v. 3)

False teachers are deceivers and seducers, not disciples. They invent stories, which they use to exploit the weak. Their motivation is greed. When their deception works, they lure unwary believers away from Christ and into lust. Words have enormous power; they can be used to bless or curse. It is paramount that Christians speak God's truth in love and avoid using false words or "made-up stories."

HISTORICAL BACKGROUND

Heresy

A *heresy* is an opinion or doctrine not in line with the accepted teaching of a church, the opposite of orthodoxy. In the New Testament, the concept of heresy had to do both with right doctrine and right ethics. The New Testament writers were certainly concerned about false teachings; they apparently were just as disturbed by improper attitudes.

In the writings of Ignatius, a leader of the church in the early second century, the word *heresy* takes on a technical meaning. Most frequently in the writings of the early church fathers, the heresy about which they were most concerned was Gnosticism, a teaching that denied that Jesus was fully human.

Section Summary

Peter explained the agenda of false teachers. Their activity is destructive. They deny Christ, falsely lead others, and exploit the weak.

THE DESTINY OF THOSE WHO DENY CHRIST (2:4–10A)

In this section Peter used Old Testament examples of judgment on sin to show the certainty of punishment for followers of false teachers. This group of verses (4–10a) is a long, complete sentence that needs to be studied as a unit. Peter illustrated the destiny of the disobedient with illustrations from three historical events: (1) the casting out of fallen angels, (2) the flood, and (3) Sodom and Gomorrah.

WORD PICTURE

Cast Them into Hell

The particular word used here for "hell" appears only in 2 Pet 2:4. In classical Greek, this word refers to a subterranean region, doleful and dark, regarded by the ancient Greeks as the abode for the wicked dead. It was thought of as a place of punishment. In this sole New Testament use of the word, it refers to the place of punishment for rebellious angels.

The Fallen Angels (v. 4)

This illustration involves God's condemnation of the fallen angels who sinned and were cast out of heaven. Some believe this event refers to "the sons of God" in Gen 6:2. Revelation 12:7–12 indicates that rebellious angels long ago were cast out of their special places of service to God. Even though these beings were angels, God did not overlook their disobedience; he "didn't spare" them. He punished them by sending them into hell until the time of judgment.

The Flood (v. 5)

Because of the ungodliness of people of the ancient world, God brought a flood that destroyed them. It was a great and awful judgment. Whereas the judgment of the angels is being partly reserved until the end time, the flood was judgment that came at the time of provocation. To the false teachers Peter was addressing, it is a powerful illustration of the certainty of God's wrath against evil.

Sodom and Gomorrah (v. 6)

God burned the cities of Sodom and Gomorrah to ashes because of their rebellion and immoral behavior. We can see from the account of these cities that it is a terrible thing for rebellious and unrepentant sinners to fall into the hands of a righteous God. Whenever Christians become comfortable in the presence of sin, they are in grave danger of accepting it in others and of embracing it for themselves.

PERSONAL APPLICATION

Within these illustrations, we see a lesson. God delivered both Noah and Lot from the judgment that befell their evil worlds.

Section Summary

Peter used three Old Testament examples of judgment on sin to show the certainty of punishment for followers of false teachers: (1) the casting out of fallen angels; (2) the flood; and (3) Sodom and Gomorrah.

THE CHARACTERISTICS OF FALSE TEACHERS (2:10–22)

THE DESTINY OF THE DISOBEDIENT

ILLUSTRATION	OFFENDING SIN	GOD'S ACTION	DESTINY
Fallen Angels	Rebellion against God	"Didn't spare the angels"	Angels sent into hell; will be judged at the end time
People of the Ancient World	Rebellion against God	"Didn't spare the ancient world"	Unbelievers destroyed
Cites of Sodom and Gomorrah	Rebellion against God	Made "them an example"	Cities condemned to extinction

They Are Arrogant (vv. 10b–11)

These false teachers are so bold as to "slander the glorious ones." They recklessly dare to defy God, not hesitating to scoff or scorn the Almighty. Even the more powerful angels do not commit such slander.

They Are Brutes in Their Understanding (v. 12)

False teachers speak evil of matters they do not understand. Peter said they are like "irrational animals—creatures of instinct born to be caught and destroyed" (v. 12). Their end is destruction.

They Are Dominated by Lust and Greed (vv. 13–16)

These deceivers live constantly for luxury and sensuality. Peter called them "spots and blemishes" (v. 13). In verse 14 he listed several telltale activities of their lust and greed:

- Their eyes are "full of adultery."
- They "never stop looking for sin."
- They "seduce unstable people."
- They "have hearts trained in greed."

Not only are these deceivers unbelieving and immoral, but they are also clearly slaves of their unbelief and victims of their immorality.

They Falsely Claim to Know Jesus (vv. 17–22)

Here Peter warned that that those who make a superficial commitment to Jesus Christ and turn back are in a more culpable state than before their initial response to Christ. The false teachers experienced some knowledge of Christian truth that had given them a short victory over worldly corruption. A true knowledge of Jesus would have affected them permanently. However, having turned from the truth about Christ, which they had once believed, they are now in a worse condition. As a result, their willful rejection makes their disobedience a more blameworthy experience.

A real danger here to the Christian community is that the influence of false teachers can tempt Christians to fail in their commitment to Jesus and to "backslide."

In verse 22, Peter used two proverbs to hammer home his point:

1. "A dog returns to its own vomit."
2. "A washed sow returns to wallowing in the mud."

Those who use their freedom to become again entangled and overpowered by the defilements of sin are like the dog and sow. They never genuinely change.

PERSONAL APPLICATION

To reform one's life without regenerating one's life is futile.

Section Summary

False teachers are characterized by arrogance, lust, and greed. Although they make a pretense of faith, their faith is not genuine.

WORD PICTURE

Return of Christ

The New Testament clearly teaches that Jesus will return. His second coming will be physical and personal, as were hhis resurrection and ascension (Acts 1:10–11). His coming will be immediately preceded by cosmic and terrestrial distress (Luke 21:25–27). Christ's return will bring upon the world judgment that is sudden, unexpected, and inescapable (Matt 24:42–44). The aantichrist figure is to arise prior to the second coming. He will be decisively overthrown (2 Thess 2:1–8). The kingdom of God, God's rule and reign, will be fully established at Christ's return.

QUESTIONS TO GUIDE YOUR STUDY

1. What are false teachers? According to Peter, what is their agenda?
2. What is a "heresy?" Why are heresies so potentially destructive?
3. Peter provided three illustrations of the destiny of those who rebel against God. What lessons do we learn from them?
4. What are the characteristics of false teachers? What can believers do to guard against these "irrational animals" (2 Pet 2:12)?

2 PETER 3

The theme of this chapter is Christ's return. Here Peter gave his final warnings to the false teachers while providing his readers with encouragement and assurance by reminding them of the certainty of Christ's return.

The fact of Jesus's promised return should spark a new attitude of holiness and commitment in the minds of Jesus's followers. In fact, Peter hinted that Christians can "hasten" Jesus's return by renewed vigor in evangelism and devout living.

THE UNRIGHTEOUS AND THE FAITHFUL (3:1–13)

God's Judgment on the Unrighteous (vv. 1–7)

Peter began this section by reminding his readers that this letter to them is his second. He desires that they recall the words of the prophets and "command of our Lord and Savior given through your apostles."

Raising questions about Jesus's return was one of the ways false teachers were seeking to undermine the faith of Peter's readers. Understanding that the second coming was imminent, many early Christians were making the mistake of setting the date of his return during their lifetime.

Peter discouraged date setting, explaining that God's schedule is from a different perspective than ours and much more patiently worked out. In addition, scoffers will come and question Jesus's coming: "Where is his 'coming' that he promised?" (v. 4).

Once again, using a triad formula, Peter offers three examples of God's scheduling:

1. Creation (Gen 1)
2. The Flood (Gen 6)
3. The final judgment

These three examples refute the scoffer's argument that "all things continue as they have been since the beginning of creation." They show that God indeed has broken into history and, as in the case of the flood, he did so when men were convinced nothing would befall them.

God's Deliverance for the Faithful (vv. 8–13)

God's plan shows patience (vv. 8–9). Although God accomplishes his purposes by his own timetable, he "does not delay his promise" (v. 9). Time, although considered a crucial commodity among human beings, is not a great issue with God. Indeed, "with the Lord one day is like a thousand years, and a thousand years like one day." God will act at precisely the right time to fulfill his promises.

There is a greater plan at work here. Peter emphasized that God's patience leads to salvation for many. He is "not wanting any to perish but all to come to repentance" (v. 9).

Christ's return will be sudden (vv. 10–12). Peter believed that Christ's promise to return will be fulfilled with destructive power at a time when sinners will least expect it. It will "come like a thief." Peter described the accompanying destruction with three phases:

1. "The heavens will pass away with a loud noise."
2. "The elements will burn and be dissolved."
3. "The earth and the works on it will be disclosed."

WORD PICTURE

Heavens Will Pass Away with a Loud Noise

The word *loud noise* is from a Greek word, an adverb that means "with great suddenness," "with a loud noise," or "with a loud roar." Fritz Reinecker's *Linguistic Key to the Greek New Testament* provides this insight: "This word means 'with a hissing or crackling sound.' The word is onomatopoeic, expressing the whizzing sound produced by rapid motion through the air and was used of shrill rushing sounds, the hissing of a snake, the whir of a bird's wings, the hurtling of an arrow and is then used for the rushing movement itself or the accompanying crash or roar. Here probably the roaring of flame is meant" (p. 781).

God will keep his promise (v. 13). But God will deliver the faithful. When he finishes clearing out the old order, he will bring in his new order characterized by righteousness: "But based on his promise, we wait for new heavens and a new earth, where righteousness dwells." While waiting for the Lord's return, Christians are to cultivate holiness and godliness in their lives.

THE OLD ORDER VERSUS THE NEW ORDER

POINT OF CONTRAST	OLD ORDER	NEW ORDER
Dwelling plac	Fallen world	New heaven and new earth
Characterized b	Sin	Righteousness

Section Summary

According to his own timetable, God will surely send sudden and destructive judgment upon the unrighteous. God will keep his promise and deliver his faithful to "new heavens and a new earth, where righteousness dwells" (v. 13).

CLOSING COMMANDS (3:14–18a)

Referring to his readers as "dear friends," Peter reminded them that an anticipation of Christ's return carries with it the incentive to maintain and produce a holy life. He referred to Paul's writings as a support for Peter's belief that divine patience was a factor in the delay of Jesus's return. Many see here a reference by Peter to Romans, but Peter leaves his Pauline source unstated.

Be blameless and at peace with God. While awaiting the Lord's return, Christians are to make an effort to maintain the purity of their lives and remain at peace with God. In Romans, we also find that the apostle Paul admonishes believers to "present your bodies as a living sacrifice, holy and pleasing to God" (12:1).

Bear in mind God's patience. Because God is patiently waiting for all people to come to repentance, he has delayed his judgment. Christians need to understand this current period, known as the church age, as a time of continued opportunity for winning others to Christ.

Be on guard. Believers are to keep watch and guard themselves against lawless people and prevent losing their stability. God establishes believers in the faith, but they must constantly be on their guard against false teachers, false doctrines, and false ethics to avoid stumbling.

Grow in grace and knowledge. Peter boldly stated that believers may protect themselves spiritually by mature spiritual growth. This "knowledge" they need is a development in personal acquaintance with Christ.

WORD PICTURE

Grow in Grace

The word grow means "to advance," or "to increase." It is used of both physical and spiritual growth. Grammatically, the preposition *in* can express two meanings. It can mean: (1) grace as the sphere of one's growth, or (2) grace as the means of one's growth.

Section Summary

Peter reminded his readers that an anticipation of Christ's return carries with it the incentive to produce a holy life. He then set forth a series of commands intended to encourage his readers to godly living in anticipation of the Lord's return.

CONCLUSION (3:18b)

Peter now drew his letter to a close. He covered several key themes:

- Living the Christian life
- Rejecting the influence of false teachers
- Preparing for the Lord's retur

In closing, Peter pronounced a simple but beautiful benediction. It is a powerful affirmation of faith and focuses on the person and work of Jesus Christ. "To him be the glory both now and to the day of eternity" is the shout of triumphant faith of all Christians in all ages.

QUESTIONS TO GUIDE YOUR STUDY

1. Why has God delayed Jesus's return?
2. From Peter's words in this chapter, what do we learn about the nature of Christ's return?
3. As Christians anticipate Christ's return, what kind of attitude should it instill in them?
4. As Christians await Christ's return, in what sort of activities should they engage?

1 John

INTRODUCTION

First John is important and practical for the modern reader. It is a strong letter written from a pastor to his flock and addresses a first-century situation. However, its message resonates with significant application for the church and the world today. The study of 1 John will assist believers in finding security, increasing joy, and moving forward in their faith while serving as a reliable and poignant warning for the unbelievers.

Reading 1 John casually, one is struck by its simplicity. Reading and rereading it, one comes to discover its depth and complexity and to derive even greater benefit from it. First John is one book of the Bible that can assist even the simplest of readers, yet prompt the most skilled of scholars to scratch their heads while remaining uncertain as to the complete depth of the meaning within the text.

This letter is listed among the General Epistles, but it is uniquely different from others included in this category. The message of 1 John and the means in which that message is communicated provide for exciting and rewarding study. In order to appreciate the details of the text itself, it will help to discuss a few introductory matters first.

WORD PICTURE

The terms *General* or *Catholic* Epistles are traditional ways of designating the New Testament letters not attributed to Paul and written to a more general or unidentifiable audience: James; 1 and 2 Peter; 1, 2, and 3 John; Jude. The two shorter letters of John are included with 1 John even though they are seemingly addressed to specific readers.

AUTHORSHIP OF 1 JOHN

This letter has no signature and no obviously intentional clues to identify the author. Traditionally, the apostle John, the son of Zebedee, the author of the Gospel known by his name, is credited with the authorship of this letter. Both internal and external evidence supports this view, though admittedly some students disagree with the traditional view.

The external evidence supports the conclusion that the apostle John wrote this letter. Allusions and veiled references to John's letters are found in many early patristic writings such as *Clement of Rome* and in the *Didache,* although they do not identify John as the author. Irenaeus (ca AD 130–200) is noted as the first to clearly attribute 1 and 2 John to John, the apostle and author of the Fourth Gospel (*Against Heresies*

HISTORICAL BACKGROUND

External/Internal Evidence

External evidence is information gained from a source outside the given text. *Internal evidence* is information gained from the study of the given text.

3.16.8). The Muratorian Canon testifies to the authority of John's letters and to John as the author. Origen (d. ca AD 255) relied on 1 John, often naming John the apostle as its author. He was the first to include all three epistles as a part of John's work.

The internal evidence also points to John as the author in two ways. First, the internal evidence supports the conclusion that the author of the letter is the same as the author of the Fourth Gospel. If the author of that Gospel is John (as I believe him to be), there is good reason to believe he is also the writer of this letter. The discussion of authorship of the Gospel is much too complicated to be discussed in this book. For a concise argument for Johannine authorship of the Gospel, see Thomas D. Lea, *The* New *Testament*, 153–256.

The Gospel of John and 1 John are clearly similar in both substance and syntax, providing further internal evidence for their having the same author. The author of each uses the same set of opposite phrases: "light and darkness," "life and death," "love and hate," and "truth and falsehood." People are placed in only one of two groups: "children of God" or "children of the devil"; they belong to the world or do not belong to the world; they have life and know God, or they do not have life and do not know God. Both books use a similar Greek syntax involving the simplest of constructions filled with parallelisms. The Gospel and the letter have similar vocabulary and an overwhelmingly identical phraseology of ideas, such as believers being called God's "children," the Holy Spirit being the "Spirit of truth," and the "remaining/abiding" union of believer and Christ, as well as many others. Therefore, there appears to be one author for both works. With this conclusion, whatever can be learned about the author of the Fourth Gospel can be said of the author of 1 John and vice versa.

The second way the internal evidence points toward John as the author is that the author claims to be an eyewitness to Jesus's life. In 1 John 1–4, he describes himself as one having had a close personal relationship with Christ. Throughout his letter he also writes as one having authority. His use of an authoritative tone (i.e., "my little children," 2:1) and his authoritative commands reveal his authoritative position. His authority and eyewitness testimony lead to the conclusion that the author of 1 John was an apostle.

Therefore, although he did not identify himself by name, the combination of all these elements suggests it is best to accept the apostle John, the son of Zebedee, the "disciple Jesus loved," as the author of 1 John.

HISTORICAL BACKGROUND

The *Didache* is an early church manual of instruction regarding Christian life and church government that was composed no later than the early second century. Its longer title helps explain its nature: "The Teaching of the Lord, Through the Twelve Apostles, to the Gentiles." The Muratorian Canon includes those New Testament books recognized as Scripture by the church at Rome around AD 200. This list was first printed in 1740 by L. A. Muratori from an eighth-century manuscript.

NEW TESTAMENT REFERENCE

The author of the Gospel of John refers to himself as the "disciple Jesus loved." In this way John revealed his personal and close relationship to Jesus and his presence with him at some important moments. You can see John's relationship with Jesus as the "disciple Jesus loved" at the prediction of Judas's betrayal (John 13:23), when Jesus asked him from the cross to care for his mother (John 19:26–27), where John outran Peter to the empty tomb (John 20:2), when he followed the resurrected Jesus and Peter along the beach and became the subject of Peter's misdirected question (John 21:20), and when he identified himself as the one who wrote the Gospel (John 21:24).

LITERARY FORM OF 1 JOHN

First John is a letter that on the surface does not look like one. Interestingly, 1 John has none of the formal elements most letters of the period had except the body. Yet it was clearly a written document, not a sermon or homily (2:1,12–14). Furthermore, it was written to a specific group of people with whom John had a relationship (see 2:7,12–14,19,26). It appears to be a letter with the introductory and concluding elements cut off. Therefore, although it may read more like a homily or a theological treatise, it should be interpreted as a letter to a specific group of people for a specific occasion in a specific context.

RECIPIENTS AND ORIGINATION OF 1 JOHN

John does not directly tell who the recipients of his letter were, although it does appear that he had a specific audience in mind. This omission could be because he hoped it would be sent around to various churches in the area beyond the one specific church to whom he was writing. The designations "my little children" (2:1) and "dear friends" (2:7) reveal his relationship with the recipients and his intention of sending it to these specific people. His knowledge of the situation and challenges facing the recipients (2:19; 5:13–14,21) further support an intended audience. Even a superficial reading of the letter reveals the intimate care John had for the readers and the personal relationship they had together, even though he does not mention a single name.

Early church tradition claims that John spent the last part of his life living in and ministering around the city of Ephesus. Following the death of Mary, the mother of Jesus, tradition has it that John moved to this area in the middle of the first century. Although it cannot be determined for certain, it appears that John wrote from Ephesus and sent his letter to the churches he had been ministering to in and around the city of Ephesus located in the Roman province of Asia.

DATE OF THE WRITING OF 1 JOHN

When did John write this letter? That is not an easy question. Evidence within the letter is slight. The dating of the letter is generally tied to two issues: (1) the relationship of the date for 1 John as compared to that of the Gospel, and (2) the understanding of what type of false teaching John was writing to combat.

First John appears to have been written after the composition of the Gospel of John (AD 80–90). The Gospel was written for the purpose of evangelism (John 20:31) and the letter for the purpose of strengthening the faith of the believer (1 John 5:13). The letter appears to be answering follow-up questions generated from the Gospel and the misuse of the Gospel by the false teachers.

NEW TESTAMENT REFERENCE

Here is a snapshot of the author: Name: John. Nickname: Son of Thunder. Father: Zebedee. Mother: Salome, possibly a sister of Jesus's mother Mary. Brother: James. Hometown: Capernaum or Bethsaida in Galilee. Midlife residence: Jerusalem. Later life residence: Ephesus. Family business: Fishing. Family class: Well-to-do enough to have servants. Political connections: Known by the high priest with access to his court. Calling: Apostle of Jesus. Closest ministry partners: James, his brother, and Simon Peter. Biblical writings: Gospel of John; 1, 2, 3 John; Revelation.

HISTORICAL BACKGROUND

Elements of a Letter

Letters of this period had the following six elements: (1) the sender's name, (2) the recipient's name, (3) a greeting, (4) a prayer wish and/or thanksgiving, (5) the body of the letter, and (6) a final greeting and farewell.

WORD PICTURE

Some scholars distinguish between a "letter" and an "epistle." A letter is thought to be more personal and not written for public reading. An epistle was more of an artistic literary form intended to be read to the public. In this sense, 1 John would more formally be called an epistle while 2 and 3 John would be letters.

The letter seems to be combating a false teaching found in the latter part of the first century. John is concerned to strengthen his readers against the false claims of the Gnostic or proto-Gnostic teachers. This late first-century movement helps place John's letter in that time period.

Furthermore, John treated his readers as younger and of a different generation than he. All of this evidence supports a date later than the same author's Gospel and perhaps closer to the end of his life. Although it is difficult to date the letter precisely, it seems best to place it in the final decades if not the final decade of the first century (AD 85–95).

HISTORICAL BACKGROUND

Ephesus was one of the largest and most impressive cities in the ancient world. It was a political, religious, and commercial center in Asia Minor with a population of more than 250,000 people, making it the fourth largest city in the world during the end of the first century. Paul, Timothy, and John all played a significant role in the spread of Christianity in and around Ephesus. The grandeur of the city was created by the temple of Artemis, the civic agora, the temple of Domitian, gymnasiums, public baths, a 24,000-seat theater, a library, public streets, a commercial agora, and many private homes.

THE PURPOSES OF 1 JOHN

Prior to delving into the text of any letter, it is helpful to know the purpose for which it was written. John's first letter has several specific and stated purposes. His purposes cover two general categories: pastoral and polemical.

John's pastoral purposes reveal his care for his flock and identify ways he desires them to be established in the Christian life. He listed four pastoral purposes: (1) to increase their fellowship with him (1:3), (2) to complete his and their joy (1:4), (3) to help keep them from sinning (2:1), and (4) to provide a foundation for the assurance of their salvation (5:13).

His polemical purpose reveals his understanding of the false teaching they were encountering and his desire to protect them from it (2:26; 3:7; 4:1–3). This purpose is seen in nearly every verse of his letter as he fights both the theological and ethical errors of the false teachers invading the area around Ephesus. His pastoral care drives his theological battle.

NEW TESTAMENT REFERENCE

John also included a clearly stated purpose in his Gospel. He writes, "Jesus performed many other signs in the presence of his disciples that are not written in this book. But these are written so that you may believe that Jesus is the Messiah, the Son of God, and that by believing you may have life in his name" (John 20:30–31).

THE HERESY CONTESTED IN 1 JOHN

Since John's first letter is so driven by the false teaching from which he was trying to protect his flock, it is important for the student of this letter to gain a grasp of what the heretical teaching entailed. It is generally agreed that John directed much of his letter against a variety of Gnostic teachings. Gnosticism was one of the most dangerous heresies of the first two centuries of the church. It was a combination of oriental mysticism and Greek philosophy. It blended in just enough of the Christian perspective to make it an effective counterfeit Christianity. The Gnosticism in the first century was an early form of the more intricately developed system found in the second and third centuries.

Although the many Gnostic sects had variations in their systems, Gnosticism had two basic beliefs. First, knowledge was the one condition for salvation and the one test of fellowship with God. Faith was inferior to knowledge, and salvation was attained through enlightenment.

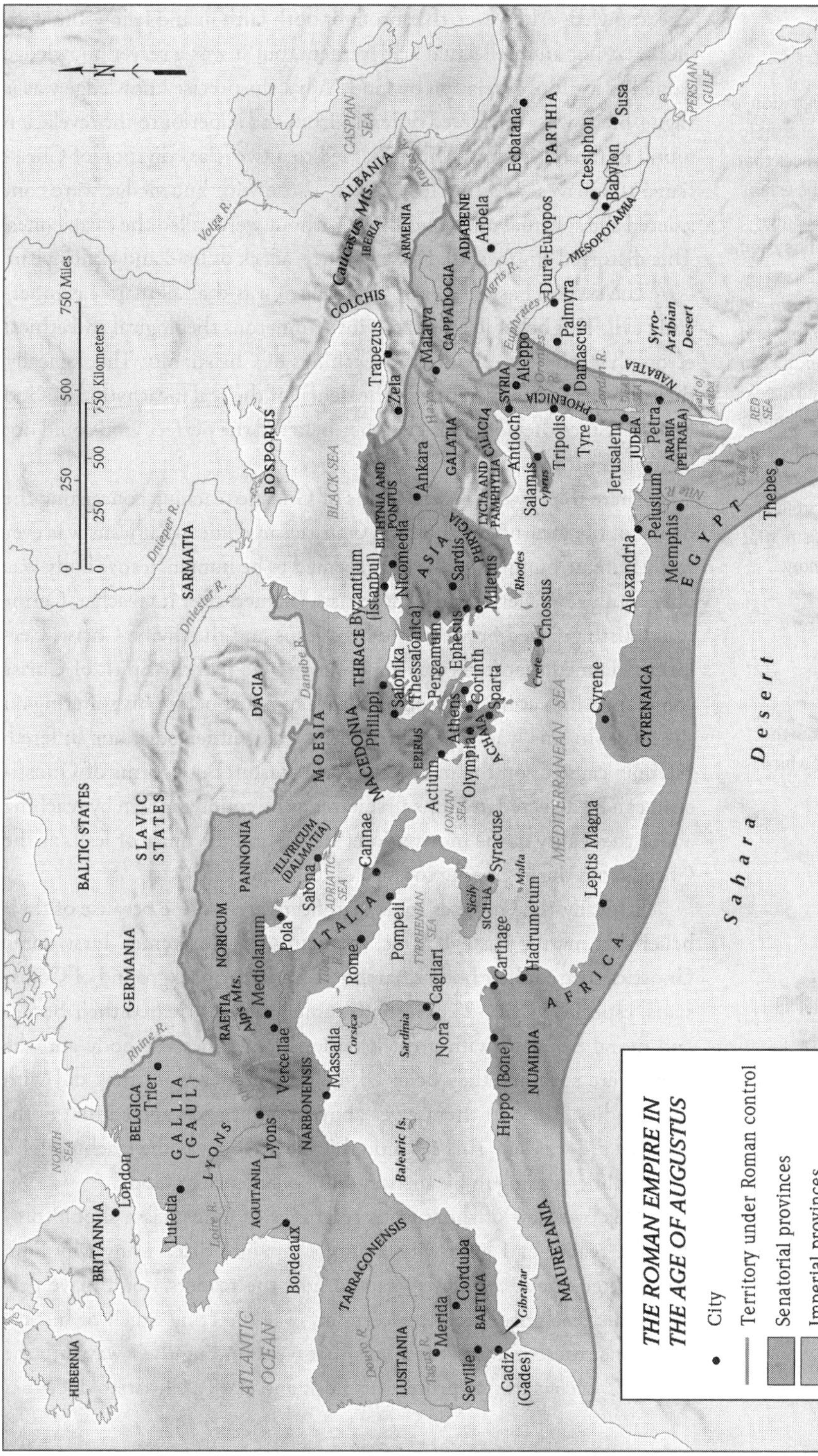

The Roman Empire

WORD PICTURE

Gnosticism

The modern designation for certain religious and philosophical perspectives that existed prior to the establishment of Christianity and for the specific systems of belief, characterized by these ideas, which emerged in the second century and later. The term *Gnosticism* is derived from the Greek word *gnosis* (knowledge) because secret knowledge was so crucial a doctrine in Gnosticism. Harold S. Songer, "Gnosticism," *Holman Bible Dictionary*.

WORD PICTURE

Docetic

Docetic comes from the Greek word *doke* which means "to seem."

HISTORICAL BACKGROUND

Eusebius recorded the story of how the apostle John once scurried out of a public bath house when he learned that Cerinthus had come inside. While running away, he beckoned others to join him by yelling, "Let us flee, lest the bath fall; for Cerinthus, the enemy of the truth, is within." See Eusebius, *Church History*, 3.28.6.

The knowledge, however, that brought both faith in and fellowship with God was not an intellectual achievement, but it was a secret knowledge gained as a gift of revelation by God. What the precise knowledge was is vague, but it was considered different from and superior to the revelation found in the Scriptures. This belief led to a two-class division of Christians: the "haves" and the "have nots." Those with knowledge were considered the spiritual ones, and those without were called the carnal ones. This distorted emphasis led to arrogance, a lack of love, and exclusivism.

The second basic belief in Gnosticism was that all matter is inherently evil. This belief led Gnostics into numerous theological and ethical errors that ran head-on into the teachings of Christianity. Theologically, their most significant error was the denial of the real incarnation of God in Jesus. Since the body was evil, they believed the perfect God could not be united with it.

There were two different forms of Gnostic teaching concerning the denial of the incarnation. Docetic Gnosticism denied that Jesus was ever really human, but insisted he only seemed to be human. Jesus's body was only an illusion. Cerinthian Gnosticism (named after its teacher, Cerinthus) distinguished between the man Jesus and the divine Christ. Cerinthus claimed that Jesus was a mere man who had the Spirit of Christ come upon him at his baptism and leave him just before his suffering on the cross. In this way, the divine Christ was neither born nor suffered. He only came upon the man Jesus for a season. Both forms of Gnosticism can be detected in John's first letter as he counters them by teaching about the reality of the incarnation (4:1–3) and the unity of Jesus as the Christ from the beginning to the end of his life (5:6).

Ethically, the Gnostics' most significant error came because of their belief that matter was evil. This led them to two extremes. First, some Gnostics treated their bodies harshly (seen in the background of Colossians, especially 2:21–23). Second, some Gnostics treated their bodies and moral behavior with great licentiousness. Since the body and the spirit were separate, they believed it didn't matter what they did with their bodies. They set themselves above morality and agreed that nothing they did was sin. This second ethical extreme was the teaching John was battling, leading to his insistence on obedience to God.

This overview of the various teachings of Gnosticism should provide the reader of 1 John with a jump-start into discovering why John was written about certain issues and how the readers would have perceived his teachings. He most certainly was directing much of his letter against these Gnostic teachings that were finding their way into the churches. He wanted to protect his flock and clarify Christian doctrine.

THE STRUCTURE OF 1 JOHN

Setting forth the structure of 1 John has proven difficult since the time the letter was written. Some ancient interpreters saw no form at all to this letter and thought of the writer as simply presenting his informal disconnected thoughts. A superficial reading of the text can reinforce this initial impression. Many today still hold to this view, seeing the sections of the letter to be connected by association of ideas rather than a logical flow of thought. Other commentators have interpreted the letter to have an exceptionally high degree of structure, while still others view the letter as having some structure. Since there does appear to be some logical structure, an understanding of the general framework of the letter should aid in proper interpretation.

This letter was written to people whose convictions and security were under attack. It was written to help provide assurance of who Christ is and of who really belongs to Christ. In order to bring about this assurance, John provided and repeated three tests by which a person can judge if he or she truly possesses eternal life. The three tests are moral, social, and theological, and they test a person's behavior, love, and beliefs, respectively. The repetitions of these three tests provide the skeletal structure of 1 John.

THE PRACTICAL VALUE OF 1 JOHN

As you engage in the study of this letter, you should not expect to find only an ancient message for those in the first century who were battling the burdens of Gnosticism. You can be assured that you will find a message for today that is powerful and applicable.

God has left for today's Christian a deposit of guidance and hope in this letter of John. There is guidance into the right way to live the Christian life and the right beliefs that are the basis of that life. There is hope in the assurance that can be gained through understanding the beliefs which are necessary for a person to receive eternal life and what characteristics that life will naturally produce. In an uncertain world, this book provides certainty. This benefit alone makes 1 John valuable for today.

WORD PICTURE

Before you begin the study of this letter, it may be helpful to pause and consider modern teachings or ideas that are similar to Gnosticism. First John will help you counter those teachings from a Christian perspective and ground you in the correct doctrine that will sensitize you to counterfeits of the Christian faith.

Section Summary

First John is a letter written by the apostle John at the end of the first century to Christians in the area of Ephesus. John's desire was to gird them up in their faith so they would find assurance in their salvation and be equipped to refute the false teachers of the Gnostic movement. He did this in his letter with the repetition of three tests of life: moral, social, and doctrinal.

QUESTIONS TO GUIDE YOUR STUDY

1. Who do you think wrote 1 John? What evidence can you give to prove your opinion?
2. What type of false teaching is encountered today that would be similar to Gnosticism?
3. What is the likely place and time when 1 John was written?

NEW TESTAMENT REFERENCE

This preface has many similarities to the prologue of John's Gospel (John 1:1–18). He used similar words in each (e.g., "word," "life," "testify") and parallel phrases (e.g., "In the beginning was the Word," and "What was from the beginning"). Furthermore, both focus on the person of Jesus. The prologue, however, dwells on his deity where the letter's preface turns the focus on his real humanity while acknowledging his deity. As in the Gospel, the initial verses of this letter dive headlong into the essential topics to be elaborated in the rest of the letter. After one paragraph, John challenged the false teaching and began to help his flock find security.

1 JOHN 1

PREFACE: THE BASIS OF FELLOWSHIP AND JOY (1:1–4)

The first four verses of John's letter are unlike the beginning of most letters in the New Testament. There are no preliminaries. John quickly jumps to his point. The absence of such expected elements draws attention to the urgency of the situation and leads the reader right into the heart of the letter. Although John did not use the traditional opening, he prefaced his letter with four verses of foundational matters concerning the apostolic proclamation (vv. 1,3a), the source of the proclamation (v. 2), and its purposes (vv. 3b–4).

The Proclamation (vv.1,3a)

John began his letter by proclaiming to his readers what the apostles ("we testify and declare") proclaimed, namely, "the word of life." But what is "the word of life"? Since it is the subject of the proclamation, it becomes an important question. There are two possibilities. The first takes the phrase to be impersonal and means the life-giving message. The second possibility takes the phrase "the word of life" to be personal and means the living Word of God. In this sense, it is a personal name for Jesus Christ. The earliest Greek manuscripts we have today are written with all capital letters (uncials) and provide no help in determining if the author wanted "word" *(logos)* capitalized or not. The best support for this view comes from John's similar uses of the term *logos* in the prologue to his Gospel (John 1:1,14) and in Revelation (19:13).

NEW TESTAMENT REFERENCE

"In the beginning was the Word, and the Word was with God, and the Word was God. He was with God in the beginning. . . . The Word became flesh and dwelt among us. We observed his glory, the glory as the one and only Son from the Father, full of grace and truth" (John 1:1–2,14).

If John wrote his letters shortly after the Gospel and as a companion piece, then it seems he would be using the terms in the same way. Therefore, the second interpretation seems correct. The "word of life" is Jesus Christ himself. "Word" is a special, almost technical term that John borrowed from either Jewish or Greek use and redefined it to represent Jesus. Christ is the subject of the proclamation.

The substance of this proclamation is filled out with four relative clauses. These apparently were placed at the beginning of the sentence and the letter for emphasis. The first deals with Christ's eternal preexistence, and the last three deal with his humanity. Each example serves both to strengthen the readers' understanding of who Jesus is and to confront the false teaching that challenged these understandings.

Jesus's eternal preexistence is confirmed in the first clause of the letter. "From the beginning" is equivalent to "from eternity." The phrase is used of the eternal God in 1 John 2:13–14 and of the sinning activity of Satan in 1 John 3:8. Although it is not stated with exactly the same words as in the Gospel, the meaning appears to be the same. The Gospel claims that "in the beginning was the Word, and the Word was with God" (John 1:1). The letter claims, "What was from the beginning," and he "was with the Father" (1 John 1:2). In every instance the verb ("was") is an imperfect tense, suggesting a continual existence that always has been. John's claim is that Jesus is preexistent, or that he has always been.

Moreover, John claimed that Jesus was really human. He succinctly unites the divine with the human, the timeless with the historical, the preexistent Word with the visible and tangible Jesus. By tying the doctrine he is about to teach to the authority that he had to teach, John testified to his eyewitness account of the reality of Jesus's humanity.

The phrases "we have heard," and "we have seen with our eyes" begin to prove the humanity of Jesus. Although Jesus existed from the beginning, John heard him and saw him. Both statements are in the perfect tense, which denotes a past action with present implications. They point to the many audible and visual experiences of the apostles. John adds "with our eyes" to emphasize that the experiences were actual.

When John stated, "We have observed and have touched with our hands," he developed his case even more. The tense changes from perfect to the aorist. This may indicate a single act in the past. If so, it probably referred to a time when John and the other apostles saw and touched Jesus's resurrected body. John talked about such a time in his Gospel (John 20:24–29; cp. Luke 24:39). John emphasized his historical experience of seeing and touching Jesus, thereby testifying of his humanity.

Section Summary

John began this preface with the subject of his whole letter: Jesus Christ. Calling him "the word of life," John proclaimed his deity and his humanity and gave his eyewitness account to support such claims.

The Source of the Proclamation (v. 2)

Verse 2 serves as an aside or as a parenthesis in thought. John stopped in mid-sentence and explained how that which was from the beginning could have been experienced by the three main human senses. He did this by explaining that the life "was revealed" before he elaborated on what the "life" in the "word of life" is.

WORD PICTURE

Word (Logos)

Why would John use the term *word (logos)* for Jesus? The term *logos* was used in many different religious and philosophical contexts in the first century, and scholars suggest each of these as possible backgrounds for John's use. Whatever the background of the original readers, they would have had a familiarity with the term *logos* that we do not have today.

OLD TESTAMENT REFERENCE

The Bible begins with the claim, "In the beginning God created the heavens and the earth" (Gen 1:1). The first verse of the Bible assumes the existence of God and makes a reference to his activity at the beginning of time. John, in the Gospel and in this letter, indicated that when the beginning started, Jesus already was.

WORD PICTURE

We Have Touched

The Greek root word for "we have touched" *(psēlaphaō)* is a picturesque word. It means "to grope after," "to handle," or "to feel for something like a blind man in the dark." In this context it means to examine something closely. This examination of John and the apostles is one of the bases for our faith.

How was it possible for people to see, hear, and handle the eternal Word? John explained this in verse 2. Although "life" may be a reference to the life offered in Christ, it seems to be another distinct reference to Jesus himself. This life is both "eternal"—a reference to a quality of life that transcends time—and "was with the Father," implying a face-to-face relationship.

NEW TESTAMENT REFERENCE

Jesus is referred to as "life" in other places by John. "We are in the true one—that is, in his Son, Jesus Christ. He is the true God and eternal life" (1 John 5:20). "In him was life, and that life was the light of men" (John 1:4). "Jesus told him, 'I am the way, the truth, and the life'" (John 14:6).

John maintained that this "life was revealed." The word "was revealed" can be translated "to manifest" and more literally means "to bring to light that which already exists." The life was manifested in a human body. John's testimony reveals the progressive experience of the human senses from the most unreliable to the most reliable, from the most abstract to the most tangible. He heard, saw, and felt the human body of Christ, proving it was real.

After the first sentence (vv. 1–3a), John took aim at the two primary tenets of the false teachers. To those who were claiming that Christ simply appeared to be human, John said he had heard, seen, and felt him. To those who said the man Jesus was not the Christ, John said he was the one who was from the beginning. While declaring the foundation of his doctrine, John refuted the foundation of his opponents.

PERSONAL APPLICATION

What does faith in Jesus mean to you? If someone should ask you to explain why you believe in Jesus, could you give them a compelling reason? John helps us here. He gives an eyewitness testimony and passes it on to us so that our faith is more than "blind."

Section Summary

John made such bold claims about who Jesus is because Jesus appeared on the earth and the apostles had physically encountered Him. John's was a personal testimony of God in the flesh.

The Purposes Of The Proclamation (vv. 3b–4)

With the two aspects of the apostolic proclamation out on the table (the preexistent [eternal] and human aspects of the Word of life), John gave the purposes of that proclamation in verses 3b and 4. John revealed two purposes for telling these readers about this apostolic proclamation.

WORD PICTURE

Fellowship

"Fellowship" *(koinōnia)* is a wonderful New Testament word. Its basic meaning is "to share something in common with another." Here it describes the unique Christian relationship that occurs when people share their experiences with Christ and their daily lives. True koinonia is a distinctly Christian experience.

The first purpose was for John's readers to have fellowship with him and with God (v. 3b). It is a natural result of the proclamation and acceptance of the Word of life. Salvation is understood to be the foundation for this fellowship, and fellowship is the visible social consequence of converted hearts. Community is created. The shared life is begun. Church happens when Christ is proclaimed and apprehended. Fellowship grows when life in Christ is the common thread and the central focus.

The second purpose is found in verse 4. John wanted their joy to be complete. He may echo the words of Jesus here as recorded in John's Gospel (15:11; 16:24). John reminded his readers of that teaching, clarifying that true joy is a result of true fellowship, which is a result of understanding and personally accepting the truth about Christ. In the churches that were about to be torn asunder by false doctrine, John gave a clarion call, proclaiming that the right doctrine doesn't pull people apart; it brings believers together.

In this preface, John took his readers from one extreme of eternity to the other while grounding them in the basics of true fellowship and true joy. With his final words being "so that our joy may be complete," he described a perfect and permanent situation that will occur only in heaven (the Greek uses a perfect tense for "may be complete"). In this way, he led his readers back to before time existed ("from the beginning," v. 1) and forward to when time as we know it will no longer exist. In order for them to experience this fellowship and joy, they must hold to the right basis, which is the reality of the apostolic proclamation about Jesus Christ.

PERSONAL APPLICATION

Have you come to the place in your Christian walk where you understand that the Christian life is not a life lived in isolation? The New Testament writers, and especially John, would not recognize a "Lone Ranger" Christian. Fellowship is not only a luxury; it is a necessity for the Christian to grow to his or her fullest potential and to find true joy. Our twenty-first-century culture pushes us away from honest, vulnerable relationships with others. What could you do today to increase your fellowship with other believers? Authentic church fellowship should always be in vogue.

Section Summary

To a church under attack, John proclaimed who Jesus really is because he knew that an acceptance of this teaching would result in supernatural fellowship and joy. He introduced his letter with high expectations and solid confidence in their realization.

QUESTIONS TO GUIDE YOUR STUDY

1. Why do you think John referred to Jesus as the "word of life"?
2. If you were a Gnostic-type false teacher, what about this preface would bother you the most?
3. Write a clear, concise, and comprehensive statement about who Jesus Christ is and how you know that.
4. Does your church have authentic koinonia and joy? If so, what can you do to preserve it? If not, what steps can you take to help your church find it?

PERSONAL APPLICATION

John teaches that there is no real fellowship resulting in real joy outside of Christ. This should prompt us to understand that all meaningful relationships will be those in which each person has been initiated into saving fellowship with Christ. Are there relationships you could naturally deepen by introducing your spouse, friend, or family member to Christ? Are there relationships in which you realize your level of expected intimacy is too high since Christ is not a part of them?

THE CHRISTIAN MESSAGE AND MORALITY (1:5–2:2)

Following the preface, John launched into a description of who God is and the moral implication of his character on the character of true believers. Verse 5 contains John's understanding of the basic Christian message. Based on that message, John then countered three different claims the false teachers were making.

The Basic Christian Message (v. 5)

The apostle John had a basic but profound message about the character of God that he "heard" and now was declaring. He could have heard this specific saying from Jesus, although it is nowhere recorded that Jesus made such a statement. Or John could have meant that the substance of the revelation of God in the life of Christ was contained in this statement.

NEW TESTAMENT REFERENCE

John appears to attempt to define God in his writings. He said, "God is Spirit" (John 4:24); "God is love" (1 John 4:8); he is "the true one" (1 John 5:20); and "God is light" (1 John 1:5, cp. John 1:4). The writer of Hebrews added that God is a "consuming fire" (Heb 12:29).

The statement of the message is simple and straightforward, but its meaning is evasive. The use of opposites and emphatic structures heighten the impact of the message. "Light" is placed first in the Greek sentence, highlighting its emphasis; while its opposite, "darkness," is used with a double-negative to underscore its emphasis.

Some people think the statement "God is light" was a way of showing God's self-revealing character while others see it describing his moral purity. It probably means both. As it is natural for light to shine, so God is a revealing God. In opposition to the arrogant and elitist Gnostics who believed in a privately enlightened group, John declared, "God is light." He shines forth on everyone and is capable of being apprehended by all.

Light is not mixed with impurities. It is perfect and cannot exist with darkness. As John wrote, "There is absolutely no darkness in him." If "light" is moral purity, then "darkness" is moral evil. God and sin are mutually exclusive.

WORD PICTURE

We

John used the pronoun "we" throughout this section. The use of "we" positioned John with his readers (not with the apostles as in the preface). In the first "if" statement of each new false claim, he used "if we" to hypothesize what would happen if they adopted this false teaching. He then used "we" in the true statements to reveal universal principles applicable to all people—even the apostles.

Section Summary

All things are declared true or false based on a standard. John preempted his discussion of the false claims with a presentation of a standard. The standard is God, and he is self-revealing and morally pure "light."

CHRISTIAN MORALITY (1:6–2:2)

If God is light, then fellowship with him is dependent on moral purity. False teachers were apparently teaching the opposite. To them, fellowship with God was not related to moral character.

In the next seven verses, the false claims can be read between the lines as John countered three false statements of this heresy. Each of John's statements follows a pattern.

1. He introduced the false claim with an "if" statement and quickly refuted it in the same sentence.
2. He altered the false claim to make it true in a second "if" statement.
3. He gave the encouraging results that come when someone holds to that truth.

OLD TESTAMENT REFERENCE

The life of sin and the life for God are often referred to as "darkness" and "light," respectively, in the Bible. "The people walking in darkness have seen a great light; a light has dawned on those living in the land of darkness" (Isa 9:2).

In this way John brought to light the false claims and went on to reveal a believer's true moral character. In each of the three teachings, John demonstrated how Christians must take sin seriously and how they must look to Christ for the solution to help sinners live in relationship with the light.

The First Claim and Its Refutation (vv. 6–7)

The first false assertion must have gone something like this: "It is possible to live in sin and still have fellowship with God." But John said, "If we say, 'We have fellowship with him,' and yet we walk in darkness, we are lying and are not practicing the truth" (v. 6). "Walk" is a present-tense verb. The word commonly refers to a person's moral activity. In this tense it draws attention not to a few dark acts but to the habitual lifestyle of walking in the darkness. John described a life lived in sin either void of adherence to God's self-revelation or filled with moral impurity.

The Gnostics believed that knowledge was the key to life and that righteous living was not important. To them, sin did not matter because righteousness and right moral conduct were of no value. Their claim was that an enlightened person could have fellowship with God and walk in sin at the same time.

John responded to this false claim boldly, declaring that the person is "lying" and is not "practicing the truth" (v. 6). A person's words and his actions do not mesh with the truth. "Truth" relates to either right doctrine or correct conduct. Such a person speaks and lives a lie. Living in darkness makes fellowship with God impossible.

In verse 7 John showed what a true believer's lifestyle is like. It is to "walk in the light." Again, "walk" is in the present tense and reflects a habitual lifestyle of walking in the light of God's revelation in conformity with his moral standards.

Two benefits emerge from such a lifestyle (v. 7b). First, such people have fellowship "with one another." Who is "one another"? Some think this refers to Christians and God. Others think it refers to Christians and other believers. Each is possible, and each works hand in hand with the other. Since the life in darkness breaks fellowship, the life in the light naturally bonds fellowship. John included himself in the circle of fellowship by saying, "We have fellowship."

The second benefit arises naturally from the first: The believer is cleansed from all sin. "Blood" is a word in the New Testament that represents all that Christ did for us through his perfect life and sacrificial death. The blood of Christ does more than forgive; it erases the stain and "cleanses us from all sin." How this happens is not clear, but God said it does happen, and for that we are deeply glad.

PERSONAL APPLICATION

Gnosticism is not a formal religion today, but many people claim to have fellowship with the holy God even though they live a life of sin. John taught that religion without morality is an illusion. Can a person really be in the light while living a life in the darkness of sin? John said no to his first-century readers, and he says the same to us today.

NEW TESTAMENT REFERENCE

"In him we have redemption through his blood, the forgiveness of our trespasses, according to the riches of his grace that he richly poured out on us with all wisdom and understanding" (Eph 1:7–8). "To him who loves us and has set us free from our sins by his blood, and made us a kingdom, priests to his God and Father—to him be glory and dominion forever and ever. Amen" (Rev 1:5b–6).

Section Summary

An authentic Christian cannot live a lifestyle of habitual sin. The Christian's life is one of moral purity that produces fellowship with God because of the purification from sin that he gives us.

The Second Claim and Its Refutation (vv. 8–9)

Verse 8 contains the second false claim. This one moves a step farther from the truth. To claim that you live in sin but sin doesn't affect your fellowship with God is one thing. To claim that you have no sin is another.

The denial of these people must have been bold. "Sin" is again in the singular and more than likely refers to the principle of sin, or specifically, the sinful nature. The heretical teachers may have maintained that those who had been enlightened with their *gnosis* were also cured of their sinful natures. Or they may have been claiming that though they sinned in their bodies, the flesh had nothing to do with their spirits.

In either case, they were boldly declaring themselves to be without sin.

John quickly contradicted their teaching. "If we say, 'We have no sin,'" he declared, "we are deceiving ourselves." People who make this claim are out of touch with reality. Their lives are built on a shaky foundation.

The positive claim is given in verse 9. Confession, not denial, is the beginning answer to our sin problem. What are we to confess? John declared, "Our sins." This word is now plural ("sins"). John taught that confession is specific and not general. It involves consciously calling to mind each sinful deed, one by one, admitting with God that it was wrong, and then forsaking the sin. Christians don't deny their sinful bent. They acknowledge it and then confess to God specific sins as they are brought to awareness.

The results of confession are both forgiveness and purification. Sins are forgiven because they are seen as debts that are released. The sinner is purified because sin is like a stain that needs to be removed.

God has promised to forgive sin upon our repentance. To this promise he is both faithful and just. It's clear what God's faithfulness means in this context. What does it mean to say God is just to forgive us our sins? It is not just for a holy God to allow sin to be removed and the sinner to be released. Justice implies that deeds receive what they deserve. Here is the marvel of grace. Jesus took the consequences of our sins. The nail scars on Christ portray the Father's justice. Forgiveness is "righteous" because Jesus shed his blood for the sinner. He received our punishment for us. God is "faithful" because he does what he promised and this because His Son died in our place.

Section Summary

No matter what a person claims, an authentic Christian cannot deny his or her sinful nature. The Christian's life is one of regular and specific confession that finds real forgiveness and purification from a faithful and just God.

PERSONAL APPLICATION

It is important to notice how meticulously John chose his words. He highlighted exactly whose blood it is that does the work of purification. It is Jesus's blood. More specifically, Jesus is God's son ("Jesus his Son"). John probably chose these words carefully. He revealed that Christ was genuinely human and, therefore, qualified to offer the sacrifice for humanity. Also, he revealed that Jesus was God's Son and, therefore, able to be the perfect sacrifice.

WORD PICTURE

Confess Your Sins

To "confess our sins" means more than simply admitting them. The verb literally means "to speak the same thing," or "to agree with." It provides a word picture of confession as a nodding of the head in agreement with God's judgment on our act. We admit to God our guilt.

NEW TESTAMENT REFERENCE

John's readers who were especially familiar with the Old Testament would understand the importance of "blood." The Old Testament Jews regarded the blood of a person or animal as representing its physical life. To give up the blood was to give up the life.

The Third Claim And Its Refutation (1:10–2:2)

The third false claim is found in verse 10. It goes even one step deeper into heresy, and it is the most blatant denial of all. Whereas the first false claim was that a person could sin and still be in fellowship with God, and the second was that sin is not a part of one's personal nature, the third false claim dares to state that the enlightened have never sinned. To disagree that fellowship with God is broken by sin or that sin is still a part of your nature is totally wrong, but to go on and claim that one has never sinned is to call God a liar. The climatic ascension of error is also seen in the corresponding counters offered by John: "We are lying" (v. 6); "We are deceiving ourselves" (v. 8); and "We make him a liar" (v. 10).

The false claim was that they had never committed an act of sin. "We have not sinned" translates a verb in the perfect tense. John used this to describe a person claiming to be in a condition of never having committed a sinful deed.

God has spoken. He has declared that all people have sinned. Moreover, God has provided a solution to our sinful condition. To deny what God has said—to deny what one is and has been—is to put oneself beyond the solution God offers for sin.

John broke his parallel pattern in 2:1–2. He did not begin with an "if" clause; instead, he began with a direct statement, addressing his readers in an affectionate way.

John countered the false claim of verse 10 with two important and integrated thoughts. First, his purpose in writing this to them is so they will not sin. Second, if they do sin, he wanted them to know of God's plan for their sinfulness. Both ideas must be maintained; both thoughts must be balanced.

John declared that the reason he is writing to them is so they will not commit a single act of sin. The tense of the verb (aorist) speaks of acts of sin, not a habitual lifestyle. John did not want them to be generally godly people. He desired for them to be people who "may not sin." This is the ideal.

John understood that this ideal will not often be met, so he quickly acknowledged that by saying, "But if anyone does sin." Again, the tense is aorist ("does sin") and reveals that John did believe that specific acts of sin are possible in a believer's life, although later he spoke in more detail about the incongruity of a sinful lifestyle with the believer.

If this sinless ideal is not met, John reminded his readers that God has made provision. The provision is found in Jesus Christ, who is presented in three roles. First, he is our "advocate with the Father." When a believer sins, Christ pleads his or her case to God. What is the case he pleads? It is not a plea of innocence or even a plea for mercy. Christ is the

NEW TESTAMENT REFERENCE

Speaking of Jesus, Paul said, "God presented him as the mercy seat by his blood, through faith, to demonstrate his righteousness, because in his restraint God passed over the sins previously committed. God presented him to demonstrate his righteousness at the present time, so that he would be just and justify the one who has faith in Jesus" (Rom 3:25–26).

OLD TESTAMENT REFERENCE

"'This is the covenant I will make with the house of Israel after those days'—the LORD's declaration. 'I will put my teaching within them and write it on their hearts. I will be their God, and they will be my people. No longer will one teach his neighbor or his brother, saying, "Know the LORD," for they will all know me, from the least to the greatest of them'—this is the LORD's declaration. 'For I will forgive their iniquity and never again remember their sin'" (Jer 31:33–34).

WORD PICTURE

Little Children

For the first time, John referred to his readers as "little children." He did this eight other times in this letter (2:12,13,18,28; 3:7,18; 4:4; 5:21). The designation reveals John's older age, his authoritative position, and his tender care of the readers. This (2:2) is the only time he called them his children ("my"), portraying an especially tender touch.

perfect advocate for the believer because his case is built on his applying his death to our misdeeds.

Second, Jesus is able to take care of our sin because he is "the righteous one." The name *Jesus* highlights his humanity and, therefore, his understanding. The name *Christ* highlights his messianic office and, therefore, his qualification to help. The title "righteous one" emphasizes his ability to approach God on our behalf. The sinless One can approach the holy and plead the case of the sinful ones.

Third, Jesus is able to forgive our sinful acts because his is the "atoning sacrifice" for all sins. This "atoning sacrifice" is currently available. He "is" (present tense) still the "propitiation" for the believer and for the whole world. His death is not effective for the whole world; it is only available to the whole world. It must be accepted by faith to gain its benefit. John clearly stated this teaching in his writings (1 John 4:9,14; John 1:29; 3:16; 5:24).

WORD PICTURE

Advocate

"Advocate" translates the Greek word (*paraklētos*). It is found in the New Testament only here and in the teachings of Jesus during his farewell discourse (John 14:16,26; 15:26; 16:7). Jesus used it of the Holy Spirit and indirectly about himself (calling the Holy Spirit "another" *paraklētos,* John 14:16). John used it here as a reference to Jesus. The word literally means "one called alongside to help another," and it is often used of a counsel for the defense in a legal setting. The Holy Spirit as *paraklētos* pleads Christ's causes against a hostile world; Christ pleads the believer's case against Satan (Rev 12:10) and to the Father.

Section Summary

No matter what a person claims, all people have committed acts of sin. The Christian tries not to sin but recognizes sin when it is committed. A believer's hope is not for strength not to sin, but it rests on Jesus Christ, the righteous One, the atoning sacrifice for our sins. All three false claims have been refuted, and the picture of a real Christian has been composed, revealing the right attitude toward sin.

QUESTIONS TO GUIDE YOUR STUDY

1. How would a first-century person living around Ephesus have understood John's statement: "God is light"? Would it be understood differently today?
2. What were the three false claims John refuted in this section of his letter?
3. How does the regular and specific confession of sins for forgiveness relate to the forgiveness that comes once and for all at salvation?
4. Are there any warnings that churches should be giving nominal Christians as a result of John's teachings in this section of his letter? Are there any different practices in which churches should be involved?

WORD PICTURE

Atoning Sacrifice

The main idea behind the word translated "atoning sacrifice" *(hilasmos)* is "to appease an offended person," and it is translated in the KJV as "the propitiation." John presented Jesus Christ not as the one who offers the appeasement but as the offering itself. He is "the propitiation," "the atoning sacrifice" that appeased the wrath of God. God is just. Wrong must be paid for. But God himself in the person of his Son takes the punishment for our sins.

1 JOHN 2

THE FIRST APPLICATION OF THE TESTS OF LIFE (2:3–27)

With the third verse of chapter 2, we begin to study the third major section of John's first letter. In this section John presented the first round of his three tests by which the readers can judge if they possess eternal life. Between the lines of each test, you can read the arguments of the false teachers which prompted John to discuss these issues. You can also see the solid application of the biblical doctrine of salvation that holds true for every generation.

The tests are moral, social, and doctrinal in nature, and they test, respectively, a person's behavior, beliefs, and attitude. While each test serves as a measure for assurance of salvation (or a prompt to the validity of the lack of it), each test also presents a challenge to the believer to become truer to the characteristic measured in the test.

WORD PICTURE

This is How

Twice in this section John used his common word "this" (at the beginning of v. 3, and in v. 5b, "This is how"). Throughout this letter it is difficult to know if the phrase points forward or refers to what has already been said. In most cases, as in both of these occurrences, it appears to point forward to what is about to be said.

THE MORAL TEST: A CALL TO OBEDIENT BEHAVIOR (2:3–6)

The structure of this paragraph is simple and somewhat repetitive. John began in verse 3 by stating the test. Verse 4 states the negative side of the same test. In verse 5 the test is elaborated, and in verse 6 it is made more specific with a call to action. The paragraph is an encouragement for assurance and an exhortation to action.

An Encouragement for Assurance (vv. 3–5a)

As the initial test is presented in verse 3, two foundational truths are also revealed. John indicated that we can both know Jesus and know that we know him. In the face of a heresy which claimed that only certain special people were chosen to receive knowledge (*gnosis*), John declared we can know God and know that we do. He used the word "know" in two different ways: (1) We can know intellectually and experientially, and (2) we can have intimate and saving fellowship with Jesus Christ.

The question now becomes, How can we know that we know him? The answer to that question provides the substance of the first test of life. John made it clear, "This is how we know that we know him: if we keep his commands" (2:3). The test is the test of behavior. In order to pass the test and gain assurance of salvation, a person must be obedient to God's commands. It is that simple. Obedient behavior is the sign of a life that is saved and in relationship with Jesus.

WORD PICTURE

Know

There are two Greek words translated by the English word *know (ginoskō* and *oida*), but generally they are similar in meaning. One meaning is "intellectual knowledge" that is often gained by experience. It is the second meaning that John uses characteristically. This is the kind of knowledge that comes from intimate fellowship with God.

John reiterated this test in three different ways. In verse 3 he used the idea of obedience to God's "commands"—referring to the specific commands in Scripture or to Jesus's explicit commands. In verse 5 he stated it as obedience to God's "word"—referring to the total revelation of his will in the Scriptures. In verse 6 he described it as walking as Jesus walked—referring to the perfect portrayal of God's moral will in the life of Jesus. In each case, John used a present-tense verb as a way of describing a lifestyle of obedience.

It doesn't matter if a person claims to know God; the test is found in the lifestyle one lives. If a person is an authentic Christian, he or she will have a lifestyle of obedience. If there is not a lifestyle of obedience, then the person claiming to know God is in reality "a liar, and the truth is not in him" (v. 4).

While repeating the test, verse 5 also presents a result of obedience to God's Word. John wrote, "Truly in him the love of God is made complete." In obedience, love is "made complete"—not perfect but brought to its proper end. True love is voiced best not in language but in action.

NEW TESTAMENT REFERENCE

"Remain in me, and I in you. Just as a branch is unable to produce fruit by itself unless it remains on the vine, neither can you unless you remain in me. I am the vine; you are the branches. The one who remains in me and I in him produces much fruit, because you can do nothing without me" (John 15:4–5). Each word translated "remain" in this passage is the same Greek word translated "remains." in 1 John 2:6.

An Exhortation for Action (vv. 5b–6)

The climactic description of the test comes in verse 6 as well as the natural call to action that should follow. John set up the test of verse 6 with his familiar "This is how we know" in verse 5. While verse 3 talks about knowing God, and verse 5 refers to being "in him," verse 6 underscores the intimacy of the relationship by using the term "remaining/abiding" in him. This word brings the test to a descriptive crescendo with an echo of John's earlier presentation of Jesus's vine and branches metaphor. It relates the continual aspect of the relationship between God and the person who truly knows him.

The test is made even more specific. Obedience to God's "commands" or "word" is now illustrated with Jesus's life. An authentic Christian is one who walks as Jesus walked. "Walk" is a figurative word for how you conduct your life, how you live, what you do. To be in him is to live like him.

Not only does this become an illustration of the test; it also serves as an exhortation to action. "Should" is a business term that means we are "obligated" or "in debt" or "bound." The person who is in relationship with Jesus must not only follow his commands but must act like him as well. Our actions are not only a test of our relationship, but our Christlike actions are an obligation of our relationship.

In this brief clause, John simplified all the ethical commands and teachings of the Scriptures into a perfect picture of someone who exemplifies them all. A real Christian is one who is true to his or her name—a Christlike one. A truly authentic Christian must walk as Jesus walked.

HISTORICAL BACKGROUND

Upon reflection of Jesus's initial call found in Matt 4:19, "Follow me," and his closing exhortation found in John 20:21, "As the Father has sent me, I also send you," T. B. Maston wrote, "One test of whether we have heard and responded to His invitation, 'Come, follow me,' is whether we have heard and heeded His exhortation or command to go." T. B. Maston, *To Walk as He Walked* (1985), 27.

Section Summary

The first and most obvious test to see if a person knows Christ is the test of obedient moral behavior. The encouragement for assurance and the exhortation for action are found in obeying God's commands, his Scripture, and walking like Jesus walked. These actions are the evidence for assurance of salvation.

QUESTIONS TO GUIDE YOUR STUDY

1. Based on this test, what counsel would you give a person who doubts his or her salvation?
2. What are some things Jesus did that would *not* apply to our lives? What would apply?

THE SOCIAL TEST: A CALL TO A LOVING ATTITUDE (2:7–11)

After showing that moral obedience is a test of relationship with God, John then drew out one specific aspect of that obedience. Though specific, it may also be said that this new command envelops all the other commands. This is the social test—the test of love.

Once again, John did not deal with a hypothetical situation. He did not set up a straw man to knock down. He dealt with a real situation. If we are correct in our understanding of the background of this letter, the Gnostic teachers created the need for this test. These people were arrogant, exclusive, and unloving. John called his readers to a test and to a lifestyle of love.

An Old-New Command (vv. 7–8)

John transitioned into his second test with a discussion of a command that is both old and new. He began in verse 7 with an affectionate term of address that is literally "beloved." He used the same word in 3:2,21; 4:1,7,11—an appropriate address in light of the coming topic. What this command is, we are never clearly told, but it seems to be the command to love others that is discussed in verses 9–11.

John first declared that it is not "a new command but an old command" (v. 7). By new *(keinen)* he meant novel, or new in kind or quality. It was not a novel idea; it was an "old" command. They should have been familiar with it because John said they have had it "from the beginning." John referred to the beginning of their experience as Christians as he did in 2:24; 3:11; and 2 John 6 with this identical expression (the same phrase is also used of the beginning of creation in 1 John 1:1 and John 1:1). The command to love has been around since Old Testament times (Lev 19:18; Deut 6:5). The point is that this teaching is not novel like

PERSONAL APPLICATION

There are two things you should do after hearing John's exhortation for action. First, you should study the Gospels to learn about Jesus's life. To attempt to walk like Jesus walked without knowing how he walked will lead to further false teaching and living. John presupposed that these people had knowledge or factual information about what Jesus's life was like, probably because they had his Gospel. Second, you should commit to apply all you learn about Jesus to your lifestyle.

WORD PICTURE

New

There were two basic words for "new" in the Greek New Testament. *Neos* signifies new in respect of time. It is used to say something is recent or young. *Kainos* signifies new in respect of quality or character. It is used to say something is different or novel. You may buy the most recent, brand-new *(neos)* computer, but if you buy one that is revolutionary in its technology, it would be a new *(kainos)* type of computer. In both verses 7 and 8, John used *kainos* to signify that this command is not a novel one, but then again it is. When Jesus referred to the command to love as a "new" command in John 13:34, he also used the word *kainos*.

OLD TESTAMENT REFERENCE

The Old Testament clearly mandated love toward other people and God. "Do not take revenge or bear a grudge against members of your community, but love your neighbor as yourself; I am the LORD" (Lev 19:18). "Love the LORD your God with all your heart, with all your soul, and with all your strength" (Deut 6:5).

WORD PICTURE

Darkness

"Darkness" is a term John uses with double meaning. Although it can mean "to be absent of physical light," its most prominent meaning is "the realm of spiritual decay, evil, and hopelessness." When Judas left the disciples to betray Jesus, John succinctly added, "And it was night." In this letter, John continued to use the physical picture of "darkness" to draw out the spiritual reality of the nonbeliever's world—a dark, evil world.

NEW TESTAMENT REFERENCE

John used this word for "true" *(alēthinos)* more than twenty-three times in his writings, including four times in 1 John (it is used only five other times in the New Testament). He used it in several ways to describe Jesus. John said he is the "true light" (John 1:9; 1 John 2:8), the "true bread from heaven" (John 6:32), the "true vine" (John 15:1), and even the "true God" (1 John 5:20).

the Gnostic's "new" teaching. It has been in effect for a long time, and they heard it (v. 7b) through the teaching of Jesus presented in John's Gospel.

Verse 8 appears to be a contradiction, but it is not. It is a further teaching about this old-new command. In other words, John declared, "Though this is old, in another sense this command is radically a new kind of command." The command is to love one another as Jesus did. John went on and said, "which is true," meaning the reality of its newness, "in him and in you." The idea of love was not new, but Jesus filled the old command with new meaning. Its newness can be seen in several ways:

- In its authority: Jesus took the old command and put his sanction on it (John 13:34).
- In its standard: Jesus filled the command with new meaning by presenting his own love as the model for ours (John 13:34). We are not to love others so much as we would love ourselves but as Christ himself loved us. This is an incredibly high standard.
- In its emphasis: Jesus tied all the teachings of the Law and the Prophets together with the command to love (Matt 22:37–40). It is new in that its emphasis is central to obedience and is to be primary in our behavior.
- In its experience: As the truth of its newness is seen "in you" (1 John 2:8), the experience of the newness of the command is realized every moment a believer practices it. It creates a new way of life in us.

The reason the reality of the newness could be seen was "because the darkness is passing away and the true light is already shining" (1 John 2:8). The "darkness" is the present age of the world. In John it represents the arena of sin, ignorance, and absence from God. It is the old order. The "true light" is Jesus himself. He is "true" not in the sense that a statement is true as opposed to false, but he is the genuine or real thing as opposed to unreal. We experience the reality of this new command because it is a part of the new age that is coming as the darkness passes away and the light continues to shine.

The Test of Love (vv. 9–11)

Having set the test up with the explanation of the command (vv. 7–8), John now moved directly into his second test of life. In the first test (vv. 3–6) he gave the principle followed by an example. Here he gave the example (v. 9) followed by the general principle (vv. 10–11). This is the moral test, and it calls the reader to investigate his or her loving attitude.

The false claim is revealed in verse 9. Anyone who claims to be in the light but lives a life of hate is making a false claim. The falsity of their claim is uncovered now, not by their disobedience but by their hatred.

The word "hates" in verses 9 and 11 relates a fixed and settled way of living (present tense). A person cannot simultaneously walk in hate and in the light. Darkness is the realm for hate. If a person lives a lifestyle of hatred, he or she fails the test and is "in the darkness until now."

Next, John gave the general principle. It is first stated positively (v. 10), then negatively (v. 11). A person either lives a life of hatred or love and finds himself either in the light or in the dark. There is no middle ground.

If a person "loves his brother or sister," two things are true. First, he "remains in the light." The test is a lifestyle of love. If that is the lifestyle, John said that person "remains in the light"—the person is a true believer.

Second, if a person "loves his brother or sister," then "there is no cause for stumbling in him." That phrase can be translated, "There is nothing to cause himself to stumble" or "There is nothing to cause others to stumble." Literally it says, "A stumbling block is not in him." Not only do those who love walk in the light, but they also have nothing to stumble over or anything to cause others to stumble.

The person who hates his brother experiences three negative effects (v. 11). First, he exists in the darkness ("is in the darkness"). In verse 9 John made the statement emphatic by saying he is in the darkness "until now." He is a person who has not experienced a life-changing relationship with the "true light," Jesus Christ. Second, he also "walks" in the darkness. He lives his life as a person in the darkness with no firm stance, no confident character, no ability to live like someone in the light. Finally, he has no direction: "He doesn't know where he's going."

John explained why it is so. He cannot find direction "because the darkness has blinded his eyes." Hatred has distorted his perspective; it has stolen his ability to see. A. T. Robertson wrote about the blinding power of darkness: "In the Mammoth Cave of Kentucky the fish in Echo River have eye sockets, but no eyes" (A. T. Robertson, *Word Pictures in the* New *Testament,* vol. 6, 212). Furthermore, it may suggest that persons of hate cannot really see where they are headed. They are walking headlong into eternal moral and spiritual darkness.

Section Summary

The command to love is as old as God's relating to his people. It is familiar to these believers because it was a part of the original instructions they received. Yet, this old command has received new meaning as "love" was fleshed out before us in Jesus's life. Whether a person has this "new" kind of love in his or her life is the test of salvation.

WORD PICTURE

Love

The word for *love* in this passage is a form of the Greek word *agape.* Many people are familiar with the various Greek words for *love.* There are three: *agapaō* (and the noun *agapē*), *phileō,* and *eros. Agapē* carries the general meaning of "God's kind of love." It is a perfect, sacrificing, and caring love. *Phileō* means a tender affection and is often thought of as "friendship love" (seen in the name *Philadelphia*). *Eros* is a passionate type of love from which we get our word *erotic. Eros* is not used in the New Testament. Although the words *agape* and *phileō* often carry these unique meanings, at times they share a similar meaning. Here, however, in 1 John, the test of love is clearly a call to "God's kind of love" to be activated in the believer's life. It is more than an emotion (as it is popularly defined); it is about an attitude that prompts action.

NEW TESTAMENT REFERENCE

If love is the key that keeps us from causing others to stumble, then love we must. The words of Jesus provide even more powerful motivation. "Offenses will certainly come, but woe to the one through whom they come! It would be better for him if a millstone were hung around his neck and he were thrown into the sea than for him to cause one of these little ones to stumble. Be on your guard" (Luke 17:1–3).

QUESTIONS TO GUIDE YOUR STUDY

1. How would you define the concept of love to a child?
2. In what ways did Jesus make new the old command to love?
3. Do you think it is possible to examine a person's attitude and action of love and determine if he or she is a believer? Why?

AN ASIDE ABOUT THE CHURCH (2:12–14)

As you read through this letter, the paragraph that begins in verse 12 appears to be an intrusion into the thought of John. The address becomes more personal, the structure turns more poetic, and the content seems out of context. For these reasons some scholars argue that the text is not authentic or a later addition. However, this is an unnecessary conclusion.

PERSONAL APPLICATION

This is a good point to reflect on your spiritual maturity. Do not judge yourself based on your physical age but on your spiritual maturity. Our spiritual maturity should increase in proportion to the number of years we have known Jesus. How sad it would be to have walked with him for a long time but to still be considered a spiritual "child."

Although the landscape of the text changes for a few verses, these words are an appropriate aside about the believers to whom John is writing. After giving some critical remarks and some decisive claims about what an authentic believer is—and preparing to make a few even more exacting and searching claims—John paused to assure his readers of what he believed to be true about their faith. He wanted to take away the false assurance of the heretical teachers, but he did not want to put undue doubt in the Christians. He wanted to assure the true believers.

In these three verses John used six statements, each revealing why he was writing: he knew of their authentic Christian faith. Each of the statements made that point in a slightly different way. The six statements break down into two sets of three statements (vv. 12–13a; 13b–14).

WORD PICTURE

Little Children

John used two different words for "little children." In verse 12 he called them *teknia*, and in verse 13c he called them *paidia*. Generally, *teknia* carries the idea of relationship or affection (and so, "little children"), and *paidia* relates the idea of inferiority or age subordination (and so, "children"). John probably used the words interchangeably without any distinction in meaning since he used both to refer to all the believers together in 2:1 (*teknia*) and 2:18 *(paidia)*.

John used three different terms of address: "little children," "fathers," and "young men." To whom do these terms refer? The best solution sees these three groups as representing three different levels of spiritual maturity: newborns in Christ (little children), more developed believers (young men), and strong and mature Christians (fathers).

John wrote to each group for a different reason and one that was appropriate for their spiritual maturity level. In all six statements the verb used to describe that maturity level is a perfect tense. It relates the present consequence of a past action.

The children have assurance because their "sins have been forgiven" (v. 12). This is the beginning of the Christian life and is the foundation for new life. The perfect aspect means their sins were forgiven in the past (when they put their faith in Christ), and the results remain. The phrase "on account of his name" means their faith was based on Jesus's revealed character. A person's "name" represented his or her character. Forgiveness is based on who Christ is and what he has done.

The second address to the "children" (v. 14) highlights the same idea of forgiveness as in the first. "You have come to know the Father" means to be in relationship with him, which is only accomplished through forgiveness. Also, John's use of the word "Father" points out who Christ is again. As in verse 12, he is God's Son.

The "fathers" have assurance because they "have come to know the one who is from the beginning" (identical in verses 13 and 14). The same verb ("have come to know") is used here as with the "children" in verse 14. It signifies not head knowledge as much as relational experience. The emphasis for the "fathers" is, however, in the degree of knowledge. "The one" may refer to God or to Jesus. John left it vague. All believers know God and Jesus, even spiritual babes or "children," but mature believers know him in a deeper sense. If "the one" refers to God, the "fathers" know him as the one who "is from the beginning," the one who is consistent and never changing. If "the one" refers to Jesus, the "fathers" know him as the preexistent Christ (as in 1 John 1:1).

The "young men" have assurance because they are victorious over evil. They "have conquered the evil one" (vv. 13,14c). Those people who are not new to their faith and who have not grown old with their beliefs are the people who are engaged in the battle of Christian living. Theirs is not so much a fresh experience with forgiveness or a peaceful touch of fellowship as it is a war with the enemy. So John encouraged these "adolescent" Christians by reminding them that they have already overcome and remain victorious (the perfect tense again). The victory may have been over the heretical teachers, or it may have been over a variety of evils.

Two further qualities of these "young men" are mentioned in verse 14. First, they "are strong." This strength surely has more to do with spiritual might than physical fortitude. Second, they are intimately tied to the Word of God: "God's word remains in you." The "word" here is the same as is used for Jesus (*logos*), but here it means the gospel message. They have made the truth behind that message and its ethical teachings a part of their lives. Both statements use present-tense verbs, demonstrating that these are permanent and dynamic forces in their lives.

Section Summary

John stopped for a moment to give his readers assurance. Based on his relationship with them, he encouraged each person according to his or her own level of maturity. A person can find assurance at whatever stage of Christian maturity they have achieved.

OLD TESTAMENT REFERENCE

The psalmist had the same type of understanding about God as these "fathers." "Lord, you have been our refuge in every generation. Before the mountains were born, before you gave birth to the earth and the world, from eternity to eternity, you are God" (Ps 90:1–2). Malachi revealed God declaring about himself, his consistent character: "I, the Lord, have not changed" (Mal 3:6).

NEW TESTAMENT REFERENCE

Jesus gave assurance to believers in the same way as John did here with the young men. "Then Jesus said to the Jews who had believed him, 'If you continue in my word, you really are my disciples'" (John 8:31). "Continue" translates the same verb as in 1 John 2:14. Again, the same word is used by Jesus but is translated "remain" in John 15:7: "If you remain in me and my words remain in you, ask whatever you want and it will be done for you."

PERSONAL APPLICATION

By describing the assurance of these "young men" who are in the process of growth, John gave three steps to Christian growth: Be strong, by being studious, so you can be striving for real growth and effective Christian living. We have no chance of growing into maturity outside of the study of God's Word.

AN ASIDE ABOUT THE WORLD (2:15–17)

The topic now changes and so does the mood. The theme is not assurance but warning. The tense is not the perfect but the present imperative—the mood of command. In the midst of assurance, the believers needed to be aware of the reality of temptation. So John commanded them, "Do not love the world or the things in the world" (1 John 2:15). That is the central thought of this aside about the world. The rest of the paragraph gives support to this command by explaining two reasons it should be heeded.

The "World" in John

It is important to have a good grasp on how John used the word *world* in his writings. He used the term more than all the New Testament writers together. Of the 185 times it appears in the New Testament, 105 occur in the writings of John (seventy-eight times in his Gospel, twenty-four times in his letters, three times in Revelation). John did not use "world" in only one way with only one clear definition. He appears to use it with a variety of meanings. Determining which meaning is used at any given time is an important matter for correct interpretation.

WORD PICTURE

make bold sidebar subhead: World Morris gives a helpful hint about interpreting this word *kosmos* in John's Gospel that applies to all of John's writings. He writes, "The word thus has many shades of meaning. This diversity must be kept in mind in studying this Gospel, because the boundaries between the classifications are not hard-and-fast. John moves freely from one to another, or even uses the term in ways that may evoke more than one of its possible meanings." Leon Morris, *The Gospel According to John*, 113.

The Greek Word: *kosmos*

How John uses the word:

- In reference to the universe at large (e.g., John 1:10; 8:12; 9:5).
- In reference to the earth, the world in which we live (e.g., John 16:33; 1 John 4:17).
- In reference to a large group or majority of people, somewhat as hyperbole (e.g., John 12:19).
- In reference to the whole race of sinful people who are in opposition to God (e.g., John 3:16; 1 John 2:2; 4:9).
- In reference to the whole moral order of society organized under the powers of evil and in rebellion against God (John 14:30; 1 John 2:15–17; 5:19). There are no believers who are a part of the "world" in this sense. They have been rescued from the world (John 15:19). This usage is how John normally uses *kosmos.*

The Command Not to Love (2:15a)

On the heels of the second test of life, the test of love, John commanded his readers not to love the world. The imperative "love" is from the same verb (agape) as in verses 9–11. How do we reconcile this prohibition with both the second test and Jesus's command to love our brothers, our neighbors, and even our enemies? The key is to understand what John referred to when he used the word *world* six times in this paragraph. The "world" is the whole moral order of society organized under the powers of evil against God. We are to love the people in the world as God does

(John 3:16), but we are commanded not to love the world's system or its ways. This becomes clear in verse 16 when the "world" is described.

Two Reasons for the Command (vv. 15a–17)

In verses 15a–17 John gave two reasons his command should be heeded. The first reason is that love for the world and love for God are mutually exclusive. A person cannot do both. As John stated it, "If anyone loves the world, the love of the Father is not in him" (v. 15). You cannot be involved in the ways of the world, which are in constant rebellion against God, and still love God.

John used three concise statements in verse 16 to explain the major characteristics of "everything in the world." First, "the lust of the flesh" describes the wrongful desires of our sinful nature. John described how the world's temptations begin from within us. Second, "the lust of the eyes" describes the wrongful desires that are inspired through our vision. The world tempts us by its physical attraction. Its ways appear good, but its beauty has no substance. Third, "the pride in one's possessions" describes arrogance due to material possessions. Literally, this phrase is "the boasting of life," where "life" (*bios*) means life in its human or material form. In context, it refers to material possessions. The world's system encourages us to outshine others in wealth and possessions.

Believers should not love the world because the world is temporal and believers are eternal. John explained that the "world with its lust is passing away" (17). "Passing away" is the same verb in the same tense (present) as was used in verse 8 to describe the present downfall of the darkness. Here the "darkness" is described as the "world," and again John described it as in the process passing away. The assumption is when the world passes, those who are a part of it will pass too.

However, the opposite is also true. Whoever "does the will of God," or loves God, "remains forever" (17). "Remains" translates a word that also means "lives/abides." This serves as a motivation to overcome the temptations of the world and not to love it. There can be no permanent satisfaction from anything in the world; it is all temporal. The only thing of permanent value is that associated with God and his will. As Williams translates, "He who perseveres in doing God's will lives on forever." Charles B. Williams, *The* New *Testament in the Language of the People.*

NEW TESTAMENT REFERENCE

"No one can serve two masters, since either he will hate one and love the other, or he will be devoted to one and despise the other. You cannot serve both God and money" (Matt 6:24). James also emphasized Jesus's point: "You adulterous people! Don't you know that friendship with the world is hostility toward God? So whoever wants to be the friend of the world becomes the enemy of God" (James 4:4).

WORD PICTURE

Flesh

The Greek word for "flesh" in verse 16 is *sarx*, which literally means "flesh." It can mean "the body," but it is the typical way of describing the sinful nature and is often contrasted with the Spirit-led life.

Section Summary

Christians are characterized by their love. However, a true believer is selective in the object of his or her love. You cannot love both God and the world because they are mutually exclusive realities and because the world is temporal, and believers are eternal. John declared, "Be in the world, but don't love it."

QUESTIONS TO GUIDE YOUR STUDY

1. What are the primary differences between the church and the "world"?
2. What did John mean when he said, "God's word remains in you"?
3. Why can't a Christian love both God and the world? Does this ring true to you? Why?

HISTORICAL BACKGROUND

John and the other New Testament writers viewed Christ's incarnation as the beginning of the beginning of the end, the inauguration of the "last days" or the "new age." Here John claimed that the "last hour" has come. Though there are numerous opinions about what this means, it appears that he spoke of the period before Christ's return that is marked by a last surge of the evil forces against his kingdom.

THE DOCTRINAL TEST: A CALL TO RIGHT BELIEF (2:18–27)

John now returned to his major purpose—to show the difference between false and true believers. He moved to his third test—the doctrinal test, the test of belief. He presented this by distinguishing between the heretics and the true believers (vv. 18–21), by describing their wrong teaching (vv. 22–23), and by giving safeguards to prevent wrong belief (vv. 24–27).

HISTORICAL BACKGROUND

The New Testament church believed that the coming of the antichrist, the personal embodiment of evil, would be a hallmark of the resurgence of evil that would precede the second coming of Christ. These "antichrists" around John's churches were not "the antichrist," but they manifested his spirit.

The Difference Between the Heretics and the True Believers (vv. 18–21)

John began by stating with confidence that they were living in the "last hour," which in essence means the final days before the second coming of Christ. He then gave evidence that this is the last hour by describing the events which signify it. Finally, he described the life of the true believers.

The evidence ("By this we know," v. 18) that the "last hour" is here was the appearance of "antichrists." The appearance of the antichrist was long thought to be a sign of the approaching end. The believers around Ephesus knew of this teaching because it was a part of the apostolic teaching they received (2 Thess 2:5). For John, the "many antichrists" (v. 18) are forerunners of the antichrist still to come. In 1 John 4:3 he spoke of the "spirit of the antichrist" that is now in the world.

These antichrists were not evil spiritual creatures but false teachers. John unmasked their identity in verse 19, and they were probably the same as the "false prophets" of 4:1. These "antichrists" revealed their true colors when they left the believers ("went out"). This is the same verb that described Judas's departure from the disciples on the night of his betrayal (John 13:30; "he . . . left").

John drew a sharp distinction between the heretics and the true believers. Their going proved they never really belonged to the community of faith, although they had a superficial connection. John was so convinced of this that he could write, "For if they had belonged to us, they would have remained with us" (v. 19).

In verses 20 and 21, John gave assurance to the true believers in the church, the ones who remained after the antichrists left. Their assurance comes from two things.

First, they "have an anointing from the Holy One" (v. 20). The "Holy One" could be a title designating either God or Christ. The "anointing" probably refers to the giving of the Holy Spirit to believers as Christ himself was anointed not with oil but by the Holy Spirit at his baptism (Luke 4:18; Acts 4:27; 10:38). The antichrists were against Christ and were falsely claiming to be like him, while the true believers were like him and were striving to be for him. The personal pronoun "you" is emphatic, emphasizing John's confidence in their salvation.

Second, John's readers could have assurance because they "know the truth" (v. 20). This thought is elaborated in verse 27. Here we should make the connection between the Holy Spirit and truth. John taught that the Holy Spirit, the "Spirit of truth" (John 14:17), would become their teacher (John 14:26). John claimed that all the readers have knowledge because they all received the "anointing," the Holy Spirit. In verse 21 he stated that he was writing them to give them this assurance.

PERSONAL APPLICATION

John demonstrated two important doctrines of the church. The first is the perseverance of the saints, which teaches that those who are truly saved will remain true to Christ until the end. It is not endurance that saves, but endurance is the characteristic of the truly saved. The second is the doctrine of the true church, which teaches that only those who are true to Christ are members of the church, and only Christ knows who that is. Remember, a time is coming when who we are will be revealed by the honest and clear vision of Christ. Are you a member of the true church, or do you just give the appearance of membership? Time will tell.

Section Summary

The "last hour" is here, but John didn't want his readers to panic. They could see that they were different from the heretics and, therefore, could find assurance. Their reception of the Holy Spirit and his teaching them of truth firmly established them as different from the antichrists.

The Explanation and Effects of the Heresy (vv. 22–23)

The false teaching of those who left the church is revealed in these verses. They denied that Jesus is the Christ. These teachers must have taught a false doctrine similar to full-blown Gnosticism of the second century. Some of the Gnostics said that Jesus, the man, was not the same as Christ, the divine being. To them, Christ was only united with Jesus the man during a portion of his earthly ministry. Therefore, Jesus was not the Christ. He was just a man. The incarnation wasn't real.

John made the standard for this test of belief clear. He already declared that one who disobeys God's commands or hates his brother but claims to know God is a "liar" (1:6; 2:4). The same is true in this third test for the person who believes this heresy and denies that Jesus is the Christ. The basic doctrinal test for salvation is one's belief about who Jesus is. To deny his deity and his humanity is not just a wrong belief; it is a belief that eliminates one from the family of God. John was direct: "This one is the antichrist" (v. 22)—one of those who exemplify the spirit of the Antichrist to come.

NEW TESTAMENT REFERENCE

Paul gave similar assurance to the church in Corinth. He wrote, "Now it is God who strengthens us together with you in Christ, and who has anointed us. He has also put his seal on us and given us the Spirit in our hearts as a down payment" (2 Cor 1:21–22).

PERSONAL APPLICATION

Many "religions" and cults can be singled out as carrying the spirit of the antichrist and as being wrong in their belief system simply by checking their doctrine about the character of Jesus. Do not be deceived. Any group which does not believe that Jesus is the Christ, the Son of God, is not in right relationship with the Father.

The effects of belief are described clearly in verses 22c–23. The one who "confesses" Jesus is in relationship with both the Father and the Son. John must have had in mind a public denial and acknowledgment since he used the same two verbs that Jesus used on the same subject (Matt 10:32–33). Of course, inward belief precedes public acknowledgment.

NEW TESTAMENT REFERENCE

"For the time will come when people will not tolerate sound doctrine, but according to their own desires, will multiply teachers for themselves because they have an itch to hear what they want to hear. They will turn away from hearing the truth and will turn aside to myths" (2 Tim 4:3–4).

Section Summary

To buy into the belief that Jesus is not the Christ is to reject a saving relationship with the Father and his Son.

Protection Against the Heresy (vv. 24–27)

John next exhorted his readers to protect themselves from falling prey to the false teaching. They could do so by remaining true to the apostolic teaching and the heavenly teacher.

He first commanded them to let the original gospel message, the apostolic teaching, "remain in" them. This is described as "what you have heard from the beginning" (v. 24a). The Greek begins with an emphatic "you" (as does v. 27). This was John's way of setting the readers over against the heretics. John assumes they must work to keep the apostolic teaching part of their lives. They must not allow themselves to be caught up in false ideas and incorrect doctrines. If they kept apostolic teaching a part of their lives, then they would "remain in the Son and in the Father" (v. 24), which is simply another description of "eternal life" (v. 25).

WORD PICTURE

Eternal Life

Remember, "eternal life" in John's writings is not so much about time as it is about a quality of life. It begins with salvation and crosses through death into all eternity. It is seen as union with God and Christ (1 John 2:24–25) and knowing God and Christ (John 17:3).

Next John commanded believers to let the Holy Spirit, "his anointing," remain in them (v. 27).

They "heard" (v. 24) the apostolic teaching from the apostles, and they had "received" the Holy Spirit "from him" (v. 27). This referred to the Holy One, Jesus Christ. Both were means of staying true to the Lord.

John provided his readers with two forms of protection: the truth of the Word and the Spirit of truth. John claimed they needed to remain in both. He reminded all of his readers of this important balance. A person should not focus on the Scripture over against the Spirit or vice versa. What John claimed is that the best safeguard against false teaching is a real knowledge of the truth as gained through study and Spirit-guided illumination.

WORD PICTURE

Emphatically stating that true believers had the Holy Spirit (the personal pronoun "you" is placed at the front of the sentence in Greek), John commanded them to remain in him.

This ends the first set of three tests that John offered. There are two more sets coming. He gave his readers assurance and stole the assurance of the false teachers by guiding his readers to the revealing tests of obedience, love, and belief.

Section Summary

The Word of God and the Holy Spirit's illumination of that word will keep a person true to the heavenly Father. The proper understanding and application of Scriptures is the key to a person's security in the Lord.

QUESTIONS TO GUIDE YOUR STUDY

1. Who is "the antichrist" and how do "antichrists" differ from him?
2. Is the "anointing" only for certain believers? Does John teach that the Holy Spirit is received more than once?
3. What are the two forms of protection against heretical teachings that John gave? How do they work together?

HISTORICAL BACKGROUND

John Calvin on Scripture and the Holy Spirit

"Therefore Scripture will ultimately suffice for a saving knowledge of God only when its certainty is founded upon the inward persuasion of the Holy Spirit." *Institutes,* I, vii, 5.

1 JOHN 2-4

THE SECOND APPLICATION OF THE TESTS OF LIFE (2:28–4:6)

John now circled back for a second look at each of his three tests. With each new look came a more solid affirmation of the test's validity as well as a further development of the idea behind it. John looked again at the test of obedience (2:28–3:10), the test of love (3:11–18), and the test of belief (4:1–6). In between the second and third test, he inserted an aside about assurance and the condemning heart (3:19–24).

A new topic should be noticed at this point. John introduced an idea in verse 29 that permeates the rest of this letter. It is the idea of believers being "born" of God and, therefore, being children of God. While "fellowship" has dominated the letter up to this point, "family relationship" carries the thought from here on out. Paul used similar language, but he emphasized sonship and, therefore, adoption. John focused on believers as children (he never used *sons*) and, therefore, regeneration.

HISTORICAL BACKGROUND

The two Greek words translated "appear" and "coming" have some interesting meanings that help describe Christ's second coming. The word for "appear" suggests an unveiling, an uncovering, a revealing, or manifestation. Christ and his glory are now hidden in some degree as he resides at the Father's right hand. At his future appearance, he and his glory will be revealed. The word for "coming" (used only here by John but often by Paul) is a technical term for a royal visit. It describes Christ's second coming into the presence of his people.

A SECOND LOOK AT THE TEST OF OBEDIENCE (2:28–3:10)

John took a second look at the moral test of obedience. He now framed the test with the standard of righteousness and the call to do "what is right." A form of the word *appearing* occurs six times in these verses, signifying John's method. He motivated the believers to obey Christ because of Christ's two appearances: his future appearance (2:28–3:3) and his past appearance (3:4–10).

Motivation to Obedience from Christ's Future Appearance (2:28–3:3)

John mentioned the second coming of Christ as a motivation to "remain in him" (v. 28) before he discussed the test of obedience (vv. 29–3:3).

The phrases in verse 28 translated "when he appears" and "coming" are clear references to Christ's future appearance. John encouraged believers to stay in relationship with Christ for two reasons related to this second coming.

The first reason we should continue in Christ is so "we may have confidence" (v. 28) when he returns. This word means "freedom of speech" or "outspokenness." Used in this context, it means "boldness, courage, unreserved confidence." It portrays dramatically the freedom from inhibitions that Christ desires us to have as we approach him now (see Heb 4:16; 10:19) and in his future coming.

The second reason we should continue in Jesus is so we may "not be ashamed" (v. 28) when he returns. This phrase may more literally be translated "and not be shamed away from him." Those who have not remained in him will instinctively shrink away from him at his second coming with feelings of guilt and disgrace. Both of these motivations should spur the reader on to obedience.

NEW TESTAMENT REFERENCE

Jesus vividly portrayed the judgment of his second coming in the parable of the wedding banquet. Here we see a person who lacks confidence. "When the king came in to see the guests, he saw a man there who was not dressed for a wedding. So he said to him, 'Friend, how did you get in here without wedding clothes?' The man was speechless. Then the king told the attendants, 'Tie him up hand and foot, and throw him into the outer darkness, where there will be weeping and gnashing of teeth'" (Matt 22:11–13).

John now held out the test of obedience for a second time (2:29–3:3). Doing "what is right" (v. 29) is the mark of a true believer. This standard is based on the character of Christ and God. John used two different words for "know" to explain the test. The first "know" is a word for intuition (knowing as a matter of fact). The second "know" refers to experiential knowledge or perception. If you know for a fact that he is righteous, then you can perceive that those who do right are "born of him." The character of the Father is revealed in the child. Knowledge is not the best indicator of the regenerated. A righteous life of obedience is the true test.

The mention of this new birth caused John to cry out in wonder at God's gift. In the first three verses of chapter 3, he described what it means to be a child of God.

Five ideas summarize John's thoughts on what it means to be a child of God: (1) We are recipients of God's love (v. 1a). (2) We are true children, not just title bearers (v. 1b). (3) We do not know for sure the full glory of our future destiny (v. 2a). (4) We will ultimately be conformed to Christ's image (v. 2b). (5) We will someday be face-to-face with God (v. 2c).

From these incredible truths related to Christ's second coming, John again saw motivation to obey him. The proposition that we will see and be like Christ some day is a powerful incentive to grow in conformity to him now. John said, "Everyone who has this hope in him purifies himself just as he is pure" (v. 3). The person who has the confident expectation of seeing Christ at his second coming naturally gets ready. To *purify* means "to put away all that defiles," and in context it specifically relates to moral sins. Although Christ's work is the only thing that can purify us completely (1 John 1:7), we have a responsibility to seek to purify ourselves daily (see 2 Cor 7:1; 1 Tim 5:22; Jas 4:8).

Section Summary

The test is the moral one. The standard is the righteous and pure Christ himself. The motivation is the fact that we will see him and he will see us. The natural correlation is that true believers should live a righteous and pure life.

Motivation to Obedience from Christ's Past Appearance (vv. 4–10)

The motivation to live a life of obedience is now linked to the past appearance of Christ. In the previous verses, the motivation was from the expected return of Christ. Now it is from the first coming of Christ. Since he came to remove sins, a righteous life is required from those who are united with him. The argument is presented twice in these seven verses with a slightly different angle in each. The first discusses the nature of sin and the second the origin of it. Both call the believer to moral obedience. Notice the similarities (adapted from Stott, 125):

	VERSES 4–7	VERSES 8–10
The Introductory Phrase	"Everyone who commits sin." (v. 4)	"The one who commits sin." (v. 8)
The Theme	The nature of sin is lawlessness.	The origin of sin is the devil.
The Purpose of Christ's Appearing	"He might take away sins." (v. 5)	"To destroy the devil's works." (v. 8)
The Logical Conclusion	"Everyone who remains in him does not sin." (v. 6)	"Everyone who has been born of God does not sin." (v. 9)

The Nature of Sin vv. 4–7)

John first defined the nature of sin by stating a universal principle: "Everyone who commits sin practices lawlessness" (v. 4). The present tense behind "sins" (v. 3) suggests the doing of sin as a practice, not the committing of an individual act of sin.

John then defined sin: "Sin is lawlessness" (v. 4). He indicated the two are equal. Sin does not *result* in rebellion against God; sin is rebellion against God and his will.

John next showed how sin is contrary to Christ and his work. His appearing and his incarnation had a purpose: "So that he might take away sins" (v. 5). "Take away" has the meaning of "to lift" or "to carry" and may mean to take away by bearing. It is our "sins" (plural) that Christ

PERSONAL APPLICATION

Have you ever lacked confidence or felt too ashamed to pray to God because of your lack of obedience? If we feel that way now in our prayers, imagine what it will be like when we stand face- to-face with Almighty God. Maybe we, too, should be motivated by His second coming to obey him now.

PERSONAL APPLICATION

The phrase translated "what great" (3:1) comes from one Greek word *(potapēn)*. Originally the word meant "of what country" and came to mean "of what sort." John recognized that the Father's love is so "unearthly," so "out of this world," that he wondered from where it came. God's love is unlike anything else in this world.

NEW TESTAMENT REFERENCE

"He made the one who did not know sin to be sin for us, so that in him we might become the righteousness of God" (2 Cor 5:21; see also Heb 7:26; 1 Pet 1:19; 2:22).

WORD PICTURE

Sin

The root meaning of sin (*hamartia*) is "missing the mark." "Lawlessness" *(anomia)* suggests defiance or rebellion against God's moral law. It denotes the attitude or spirit of a person that prompts sinful actions.

came to take away, where in John 1:29 it is our "sin" (singular). The plural may suggest the fruit of the singular root. Probably in both places, expiation and sanctification are meant. Christ was able to do this because "there is no sin in him" (v. 5).

The logical conclusion is that the person living in sin cannot be associated with Christ, and the person associated with Christ will not be living a life of sin (v. 6). With a broad brush, John declared that true believers do not have sin as the ruling principle of their lives. If it is, then they are not true believers. John did not contradict himself. He knew that believers commit sinful acts (1:8), but they do not live sinful lifestyles.

John concluded this thought with a strong warning: Righteousness is important. "Let no one deceive you" (v. 7), he warned. You cannot be righteous without practicing righteousness. Our nature is shown in our actions.

HISTORICAL BACKGROUND

A fully defined doctrine of Satan does not appear in the Old Testament, though when he does appear he is always the adversary of God and his people. The New Testament authors gave a more clear-cut doctrine of Satan. The origin of evil is within Satan, and he has fallen angels or demons assisting him in his work. Jesus was tempted by Satan, and Paul referred to him as the god of this age. Satan is a creature, so he is always in subordination to God. He was defeated by Christ at the cross, but God has allowed him to work until Christ returns. Although he poses a great threat to all people, Jesus promised we would never be tempted by him in such a way that we couldn't resist.

The Origin of Sin (vv. 8–10)

Where does sin come from? The person habitually practicing sin is "of the devil." The one who sins has the devil as his father. Sin is characteristic of the devil. He has been sinning since the beginning of his rebellious state and is still sinning. The person who sins shows who his father is.

Jesus came in his incarnation "to destroy the devil's work" (v. 8). The Greek word for "to destroy" *(luō)* means "to loose," "to release," " to break." Christ is pictured as having come in his first appearance to break the bondage of sin and sin's effects in our lives.

The logical conclusion is found in verse 9 in the form of a universal principle. The true believer, the one "born of God," does not "sin" or go on sinning. Again, as in verse 6, these are both present-tense verbs denoting a continual and habitual lifestyle of sin.

PERSONAL APPLICATION

John did not deny that true believers may sin occasionally. He denied that people with a sinful lifestyle can be true believers. Sinful acts are often a part of a true believer's life, but sinful lifestyles are never a part of a believer's life. The true believer hates sin and diligently resists it settling into his or her life.

Why is this true? John answered with two causal statements in verse 9: "because his seed remains in him" and because he "has been born of God." These two phrases are parallel. "His seed" is John's way of saying God's nature. The person born of God has received God's divine nature as a mark of his or her new birth. This new nature works from within believers to transform them—conforming them to Christ. If a person lives a lifestyle of sin, then it is obvious that the new nature is not a part of his or her life. He or she is not a true believer. Verse 10 is a transition summarizing and concluding the above discussion while paving the way for the social test of love.

Section Summary

John restated the moral test as "doing right" and gave the motivation based on Christ's past appearance. How a person measures up in that test lands him in one of two camps. There is no middle ground. You are either a child of the devil or a child of God. Whose you are is evident in how you live.

NEW TESTAMENT REFERENCE

"His divine power has given us everything required for life and godliness through the knowledge of him who called us by his own glory and goodness. By these he has given us very great and precious promises, so that through them you may share in the divine nature, escaping the corruption that is in the world because of evil desire" (2 Pet 1:3–4).

QUESTIONS TO GUIDE YOUR STUDY

1. In what way is the second coming of Christ a motivation for obedience in the present?
2. What did John mean when he said someone has been "born of him" (2:29)?
3. What is the nature of sin and the origin of sin? How can they motivate you to obedience?

A SECOND LOOK AT THE TEST OF LOVE (3:11–18)

John is now ready to lead his readers into a second look at the second test. Having shown them a preliminary outline of the test of love in 2:7–11, he distinguished between the hatred of the world exemplified in Cain (3:12–13) and the love of believers exemplified in Christ (3:14–18).

OLD TESTAMENT REFERENCE

"In the course of time Cain presented some of the land's produce as an offering to the LORD. And Abel also presented an offering—some of the firstborn of his flock and their fat portions. The LORD had regard for Abel and his offering, but he did not have regard for Cain and his offering. Cain was furious, and he looked despondent. Then the LORD said to Cain, 'Why are you furious? And why do you look despondent? If you do what is right, won't you be accepted? But if you do not do what is right, sin is crouching at the door. Its desire is for you, but you must rule over it.' Cain said to his brother Abel, 'Let's go out to the field.' And while they were in the field, Cain attacked his brother Abel and killed him" (Gen 4:3–8).

The Message of Love v. 11)

The old-new command of chapter 2 was the command to love. Here what "you have heard from the beginning" is made emphatically clear. The love commanded is both mutual and reciprocal. No target is mentioned. It is a love for all people.

The Hatred of the World (vv.12–13)

To contrast love with hate, John drew an illustration from the world's second generation. In the conflict between Cain and Abel, we see the awful consequences of anger, hate, and making wrong choices. Cain's murderous act revealed his family of origin. He "was of the evil one" (v. 12). His jealousy turned into hatred. Hatred resulted in murder. In this deed, his identity was revealed.

Based on the truth behind this real-life illustration, a command is given (v. 13). Believers are not to be surprised if the world hates them. Why? Because hatred is all the world knows. Cain's life is simply a picture of how the world works. Children of the devil act like the devil, and the people of the world hate like their "father."

The Love of Believers (vv. 14–18)

The contrast between true believers and people of the world is now presented. What do loving attitudes prove about a person (vv. 14–15)? What does love look like (vv. 16–18)?

A life of love is an indication that a person is saved. "We know" means that John and the true believers *know* for a fact. What they know is that they are saved from death. The classic picture of salvation is painted here by John when he refers to the passing "from death to life" (v. 14). The perfect tense of the verb *passed* signifies an act accomplished in the past with the results remaining in the present. "Life," meaning eternal life, is the permanent state of the believer that came about as an act of faith.

WORD PICTURE

"We have passed" translates a picturesque Greek word *(metabainō)*. It is normally used of a topographical change of place. For example, it is translated "leave" in John 7:3: "Leave here and go to Judea." In John 13:1, Jesus used it to describe his departure from this world to go to the Father. When used of "passing" from death to life, a literal spiritual change of address is meant. Jesus taught this reality when he said, "Truly I tell you, anyone who hears my word and believes him who sent me has eternal life and will not come under judgment but has passed from death to life" (John 5:24).

The opposite is also true. The person without love is still in death. The present tense of the verb *remains* (v. 14) signifies the current and abiding position of the person who does not love. The reason for this condition is stated in verse 15. The person who lives a lifestyle of hatred is essentially a murderer and does not possess eternal life.

John is finally ready to give some substance to his teaching on love. Here in verses 16–18, he defined love by way of example. No longer is this a vague command but a specific duty.

John began by writing literally: "In this we know love" (v. 16). "We know" translates the word for *know* that means to "know by experience." How do we come to understand the nature of love? It was not possible to grasp this until Christ had "laid down his life for us" (v. 16). He sacrificed his physical life for us. This is love. As Cain was the supreme example of hate, Christ is the perfect picture of love. To rob a person of his or her life (murder) is the worst of sins. To give up one's life for another is the supreme example of love.

NEW TESTAMENT REFERENCE

"Adopt the same attitude as that of Christ Jesus, who, existing in the form of God,- did not consider equality with God as something to be exploited. Instead he emptied himself by assuming the form of a servant, taking on the likeness of humanity. And when he had come as a man, he humbled himself by becoming obedient to the point of death—even to death on a cross" (Phil 2:5–8).

John quickly turned from the definition to the response. He focused on the example and then pointed the way toward action. If love is the mark of a true believer, and if love is defined by Christ's laying down his life for us, then "we should also lay down our lives for our brothers and sisters" (v. 16). The effects of Christ's loving self-sacrifice are unique, but the pattern for our social behavior is set by him. We must sacrifice for others.

If John's readers thought death is the only way to love others, he reminded them in verses 17–18 that love is eminently practical. John switched the target of love from plural ("our brothers and sisters," v. 16) to singular ("fellow believer," v. 17). By doing so, he brought the command from the world of theory to the world of practical and attainable action. True believers love by sharing what they have with those who are in need. If they don't, "how does God's love reside in him?"

Section Summary

The world is characterized by hatred that comes from the devil. Such hatred produces murder, proving their existence in spiritual death. The true believer is characterized by love that comes from the Father. This produces self-sacrifice and proves their existence in eternal life.

QUESTIONS TO GUIDE YOUR STUDY

1. What does it mean to *hate* someone? Can hate be a part of a Christian's life?
2. What does it mean to "lay down our lives for our brothers and sisters?"
3. How did John enhance his teaching on love in this test as compared to the first one?

AN ASIDE ABOUT ASSURANCE AND THE CONDEMNING HEART (3:19–24)

This passage is an "aside," but it is important. Verses 19–20 relate how assurance is gained, and verses 21–24 describe some benefits of this assurance.

How Assurance Is Gained (vv. 19–20)

Two types of assurance are described here: (1) the assurance that comes in normal times and (2) the assurance that is needed in times of crisis when our own hearts condemn us. In both cases the assurance comes from the same source. "This is how" points backward toward the truth that love toward others carried through in actions is proof of a person's true relationship with Christ. This genuine love provides the assurance that "we belong to the truth."

The crisis John brought up is the crisis of a condemning heart. The phrase "whenever our hearts condemn us" in verse 20 reveals that this may not be such an abnormal or infrequent crisis. When it does occur, it is a continual, persistent work of our conscience. At times the true believer may experience thoughts which encourage doubt.

When this happens, John says there is a way in which assurance can be gained, a way in which our hearts can be "reassure[d]." In those moments when doubt enters a believer's heart, it is not the feelings that are to be trusted; it is knowledge. What we know about the truth and our compliance with it can bring assurance. If there is evidence of a sacrificial, loving lifestyle, then assurance is gained. This kind of love is not natural; it is bred into those who have become God's children. So the visible evidence of Christlike love produces the assurance of a Christ-saved life.

WORD PICTURE

Reassure

The word *reassure* translates a unique word in the New Testament *(peisomen)*. It only occurs here and in Matt 28:14. The basic meaning of the word is "to convince" or "to persuade." In context it takes on the meaning of "pacify," "soothe," or "reassure."

NEW TESTAMENT REFERENCE

Paul spoke about the reverse effect of his conscience. He said that even though his conscience did not condemn him, he didn't trust it. He felt that we could be led astray by our hearts' silence into a false assurance. He wrote, "I am not conscious of anything against myself, but I am not justified by this. It is the Lord who judges me" (1 Cor 4:4).

Our hearts or our consciences cannot always be trusted. John declared, "God is greater than our hearts, and he knows all things." God is greater in that he is more knowledgeable and more true. Sometimes our hearts will condemn us, but if a true believer is condemned, then the accusations are unjust, and we are to rely on the justice and mercy of God.

The Benefits of Assurance (vv. 21–24)

PERSONAL APPLICATION

The process of salvation is an objective event. When people trust in the Christ who died for their sins, then they "will be saved" (Rom 10:9). Whether a person feels saved is never the issue. Assurance is never based on subjective standards; it rests on objective facts. Our feelings or conscience can prompt us to investigate the facts. Never ask yourself or anyone else if they feel saved. Ask if you have done what the Scriptures teach in order to be saved. Look for the evidence that John speaks about in this letter. Feelings are not one of the tests of salvation.

John moved into the wonderful benefits of assurance with a term of endearment. With the title "dear friends" (literally "beloved"), the heaviness of his discussion lightens somewhat, and the freshness of relief is felt. John listed two benefits of assurance (vv. 21–22) and gave a summary of God's commands (v. 23) before he gave his final thought on assurance (v. 24).

Two primary benefits of assurance are mentioned in verses 21–22. First, there is "confidence before God." John mentioned this confidence in 2:28 in the context of the believer before Christ at the second coming of Christ. Here he said this can be a present experience. The principle is that the true believer obeys the love command and has confidence to speak boldly before God.

The second benefit is the assurance of answered prayer: "And receive whatever we ask from him" (v. 22). "Ask" and "receive" are both in the present tense, suggesting an ongoing activity and experience of immediate response by God to our prayers. There is a condition for such a benefit (not a cause). This condition is that the believers "keep his commands and do what is pleasing in his sight" (v. 22). This obedience and pleasing action (namely to love others) are evidence that our will is in harmony with God's. God doesn't just grant whatever a believer asks. He gives when the prayer is asked according to his will (1 John 5:14).

NEW TESTAMENT REFERENCE

John reflected his earlier writing where Jesus taught, "If you remain in me and my words remain in you, ask whatever you want and it will be done for you" (John 15:7).

What are the commands that we are to obey? John gave them in verse 23, but he listed them only as one command (note the singular, "command") with two parts. First, we are to "believe in the name of his Son, Jesus Christ." To believe in the name means "to accept the character of." We are commanded to believe that the man Jesus is the Messiah, the Christ who is the Son of God. The verb *believe* is in the aorist tense and signifies a single, once-for-all act. Second, we are to "love one another as he commanded us." To "love" translates a present-tense verb that signifies ongoing, continual action. Faith and love are combined into a single command. Obedience of this command keeps the believer in the heart of God's will.

In verse 24, John added that the Spirit aids in our assurance. John's mention of the Spirit does not introduce a new inward or subjective test. John is saying that the Spirit in us is the one who can lead us to obey, love, and believe. Therefore, assurance comes as we look for and find evidence of the Holy Spirit in our lives.

Section Summary

An unsettled heart in a believer can be soothed by understanding what the Scriptures teach about a believer's lifestyle and comparing that standard to his or her own life. True assurance is a wonderful thing that gives confidence to pray and receive answers.

QUESTIONS TO GUIDE YOUR STUDY

1. How do you think our hearts become unsettled in the first place?
2. What is the key to receiving answered prayers?
3. How can a person pray in God's will?

1 JOHN 4

A SECOND LOOK AT THE TEST OF BELIEF (4:1–6)

The readers of this letter were members of a church in controversy. The opponents whom John was engaging were not professed pagans but people who claimed to be Christians. They had the intellectual ammunition to be persuasive. Their effect on the church was to lead other people astray and to plant doubt in authentic believers.

In this type of setting, John needed to teach his readers how to discern between true and false teachers. He explained to them that the content of their teaching is the test of the teachers' authenticity (vv. 1–3). He then explained that the character of the listeners is a test of their authenticity (vv. 4–6).

The Content of the Teaching (vv. 1–3)

After explaining what we should believe (3:23), John focused on what we should not believe. There is no such thing as "blind faith" for a true believer. The object of our faith is to be carefully chosen. We have the Holy Spirit in us, but there are other spirits in this world. We are commanded: "Do not believe every spirit, but test the spirits" (4:1).

The testing of the spirits was necessary because many "false prophets have gone out into the world" (v. 1). A prophet was someone who spoke a message more than someone who foretold the future. Many who appeared as prophets were actually "false prophets" (*pseudoprophētai*). These are equated with the "many antichrists" of 2:18–19.

HISTORICAL BACKGROUND

With the words "do not believe every spirit" (1 John 4:1), John brought his readers into a world with which they were familiar. Perhaps many people today are not aware of this world. The church services of the apostolic period were much more free and "spiritual" than is true of many churches today. The structure was less formal and less rigid. Many different people participated in the service. Anyone was free to address the congregation. In such an atmosphere, false teaching could easily be established.

WORD PICTURE

Spirit

Spirit comes from a word that can mean "wind" or "spirit." It is the same word used for the Holy Spirit. What did John mean by "spirit" in this passage? He spoke about a superhuman spirit that lies behind the human teacher. Behind every human is some spirit (either the Holy Spirit or an evil spirit), and behind every spirit is his head (either God or the devil). John indicated that we should test the spirit behind the teacher "to see if they are from God" (v. 1).

How do you test the spirits? Verses 2–3 answer that question. It is a test of belief. The authenticity of the spirit can be discerned from the words of the teacher.

The content of correct doctrine is narrowed to one simple truth, found in what a person "confesses" (v. 2). To *confess* means "to confess openly and publicly." The Spirit from God leads a person to acknowledge that "Jesus Christ has come in the flesh" (v. 2). This simple phrase carries the essential elements of Christian faith. It is the test of what one believes about Jesus. The correct belief involves acceptance of Jesus as the preexistent, incarnate Christ.

HISTORICAL BACKGROUND

The confession of verse 2 countered Cerinthus's teaching that the Spirit of Christ only came on Jesus for a time. John declared he "has come" (a perfect tense) in the flesh. This means the incarnation is an abiding reality. God did come in the form of a man. His name is Jesus, and he is the Christ.

This is the crucial doctrinal test. In order to be a God-given, Spirit-led confession, the substance of the confession must have the right perspective on Jesus Christ. To make sure he was understood, John states the opposite in verse 3: "Every spirit that does not confess Jesus is not from God." He shortened the phrase, but the substance of the confession is meant to be the same. These are not just false teachers. John called them the "spirit of the antichrist," and they are already in the world.

Section Summary

To test the spirit of a teacher, you should examine his or her teaching about Christ. The true teacher will teach the truth about him: he is Jesus, the Christ, the Son of God.

PERSONAL APPLICATION

This is not a history lesson. The denial of the Jesus of history, who is also the eternal God, is a modern-day teaching as well. In the twenty-first century, it is making its way into popular "Christian" books and interesting "Christian" sermons. It is doing so under the guise of scholarly credentials. You should be aware of this phenomenon. No matter how educated the teacher or how smooth the talker, if his or her doctrine teaches that Jesus Christ is someone other than God who entered history as a real person to save sinners, then he or she is a false teacher who serves an evil spirit.

The Character of the Listeners (vv. 4–6)

John now turned from the content of the message to the character of the listeners. Each verse in this section begins with a different personal pronoun: "you" (plural, v. 4), "they" (v. 5), and "we" (v. 6), referring respectively to John's readers (i.e., true believers), the false prophets, and John as a representative of the apostles. He encouraged the readers in verse 4 and then applied the doctrinal test by way of the character of the listeners in verses 5–6.

John gave his readers assurance of their status with God: "You are from God, little children, and you have conquered them" (v. 4). Earlier in verses 2–3 he maintained that the Spirit that passes the doctrinal test is "from God." Now he assured his readers that they, too, have passed this test and have overcome the false teachers. They have tested the spirits, found them to be false, and held to the proper doctrine. The perfect tense of "have conquered" is assuring, reflecting that the victory has come and the results will abide. This, no doubt, is why the false teachers "went out from" them (2:19).

The reason for their victory has nothing to do with their own abilities, but John credited "the one who is in" them (v. 4). This must be a reference to the Holy Spirit (2:20,27), whom John identified later as the

"Spirit of truth" (4:6). No matter how great "the one who is in the world" may be, the victory of the true believers is secure because the Holy Spirit is greater than the devil. The Spirit continues to illumine the apostolic teaching and help true believers discern false doctrine.

John turned from this strong word of encouragement to a strong contrast. In verses 5–6, he explained that the difference between true prophets and false prophets is not just the doctrine they teach but the character of those who listen to them. Verse 5 describes the false prophets ("they"), and verse 6 describes the apostolic teachers ("we") before John made a concluding remark.

The false prophets and the true teachers differ in origin and content of their teaching, but one key to recognizing who they are is to identify the character of their audience. The people of the world—those not born of God—listen to the false prophets. They like what they hear from them. However, those who know God, the true believers, listen to the apostolic message.

Originally, the doctrinal test was about content. Do you accept that "Jesus Christ has come in the flesh" (v. 2)? Now the doctrine is tested by whether it is accepted by Christians and rejected by non-Christians. The people of God will listen to the Word of God while the people of the world will not. True believers have the Holy Spirit to encourage and help them listen, while those in the world do not. "This is how we know the Spirit of truth and the spirit of deception" (v. 6).

Section Summary

Not only is a true "spirit" recognized by the content of the teaching, but they are also recognized by the character of their audience. True believers listen to true doctrine, and false believers listen to false doctrine.

QUESTIONS TO GUIDE YOUR STUDY

1. What did John mean by "spirits" and the call to "test the spirits"?
2. What test would you give to see if a teacher is of God or of the devil?
3. How would you go about using the test concerning the character of the listeners?

NEW TESTAMENT REFERENCE

John echoed the teaching of Jesus that he recorded in his Gospel. "The one who is from God listens to God's words. This is why you don't listen, because you are not from God" (John 8:47). "When he has brought all his own outside, he goes ahead of them. The sheep follow him because they know his voice. They will never follow a stranger; instead they will run away from him, because they don't know the voice of strangers" (John 10:4–5).

1 JOHN 4-5

THE THIRD APPLICATION OF THE TESTS OF LIFE (4:7–5:5)

So far John has presented two rounds of tests that help establish the authenticity of a believer. He has twice presented the three tests in order:

the test of obedience (2:3–6; 2:28–3:10), the test of love (2:7–11; 3:11–18), and the test of belief (2:18–27; 4:1–6). With each new presentation, he has both elaborated and deepened the requirements of the test. Along with the tests themselves, he has put forward a call for each true believer to find assurance and to move forward in the application of these truths to their lives.

John is now ready to present the third round of the tests. This time the order is different, and the strategy is altered. Following the command within the "aside" at 3:23 ("believe . . . and love"), John presented the second test of belief in 4:1–6. Now, with a new round of tests, instead of beginning again with the test of obedience, he quickly turned to the test of love (4:7–11) as commanded in 3:23. John then presented a combination of the tests of love and belief (4:12–21) before combining all three tests at the beginning of chapter 5. The switch in order underscores the greatest commandment: to love.

A CONCLUDING CALL TO LOVE (4:7–12)

This is perhaps the most loved and best-known portion of John's letter. It is a glorious statement about agape love, but its order is somewhat difficult to follow. However, the phrase "love one another" in its various forms holds the passage together. It is used as an appeal (vv. 7–10), as an obligation (v. 11), and finally as the substance of the test of true relationship with God (v. 12).

The Appeal to Love (vv. 7–10)

John began his concluding call to love with a tender but urgent appeal. He abruptly ended his former discussion and stated, "Dear friends" (literally, "beloved"), "let us love one another" (v. 7). The present tense of this appeal reflects the call to a continual mutual love.

The difference between this and John's original calls to mutual love (3:11,23) is the basis he gave for such an appeal. Here he listed two reasons for carrying out this call. First, God is the source and origin of love. John said it this way: "Because love is from God" (v. 7). If God is the source of real love, then all who exemplify love in their lives must have gotten it from God. Thus, love becomes a test of a person's relationship with God: "Everyone who loves has been born of God and knows God" (v. 7).

NEW TESTAMENT REFERENCE

The heresy invading the churches in and around Ephesus claimed much authority due to their special *gnosis* or knowledge. The statement that they "do not know God" would not only be true but also would be offensive to such an arrogant group of false teachers.

The opposite is also true. The person who does not have a lifestyle of love proves he or she does not know God. The change of tense in the verb *know* is important. In verse 7c it is present, signifying a relationship that is both intimate and continuing. The tense in verse 8a is not present, but aorist (past). It underscores the reality that the unloving person has never known God. Regardless of what a person says, if love is not the controlling principle of his or her life, he or she has have never known the source of love: God himself.

John gave his second reason or basis for his appeal to love one another in the brief phrase at the end of verse 8: "God is love." This is one of the most profound sentences in the entire Bible. Perhaps its fullest meaning could never be completely explained. It reveals a part of the character of God. The construction of the Greek does not completely equate love with God. In other words, you couldn't say, "Love is God." Love does not completely describe God, but God completely defines love. He is love. His nature is loving, and love can never be absent from his being or any of his actions.

In verses 9–10 John told how we know what God's love is and how great that love is. We know what it is because it was shown or revealed to us in the sending of Jesus (v. 9a). Love was first seen in Jesus's self-sacrifice (3:16); now it is seen in God's sending of his Son.

The greatness of this love is described by John in four ways. First, it is seen in the value of God's gift (v. 9b). Not only was the gift in the person of Jesus, God's Son, but he was his "one and only" *(monogenēs)* Son. His uniqueness made the gift valuable. Second, the greatness of the gift is seen in the purpose of the Son's mission: "That we might live through him" (v. 9). Third, it is seen in the condition of the recipients of his love. We were not worthy and were completely undeserving ("not that we loved God," v. 10); yet, his love was great enough that he still sent his Son for us. Fourth, it is seen in the manner in which the gift ultimately had to be given: "To be the atoning sacrifice for our sins" (v. 10). In order for us to "live through him," he not only had to come, but he had to die (see commentary at 2:2 for explanation of "atoning"). This truly is a great love.

Section Summary

John appealed to his readers to love one another because authentic Christians are people who love others in the way that God loves them.

The Obligation to Love (v. 11)

After giving the appeal to love and reflecting on the love of God, John now returned to the appeal by way of our obligation. The call to love one another is now mentioned as a factual obligation. The key word is "must" (Greek *opheilomen*, used in 2:6; 3:16). It is a strong word describing a moral obligation. After seeing the love of God in the gift of Christ, it is not that we "ought" to love others in the sense that we "should" do it. It is that we are bound and obligated to love others in the same self-sacrificing way.

PERSONAL APPLICATION

How can a loving God allow this to happen? or, If God is love, how can he send people to hell? These questions are often asked. Job asked similar questions. God is big enough to handle these questions. As with Job, God will bring to clarity what initially was puzzling. We will come to acknowledge that all of God's actions are loving. When our understanding of love seems to conflict with what we see God doing, we should bring our concerns to God and wait before him for light.

NEW TESTAMENT REFERENCE

"For God loved the world in this way: He gave his one and only Son, so that everyone who believes in him will not perish but have eternal life. For God did not send his Son into the world to condemn the world, but to save the world through him" (John 3:16–17).

PERSONAL APPLICATION

It is good for Christians to remind themselves of God's gift by way of prayer, reading, telling, and listening to the story of Christ's incarnation and death. The story of the "old rugged cross" should never be allowed to grow cold in our lives. We should rekindle our humility and appreciation often so that we will feel the obligation to love others and to share his love with them. But whether we feel it or not, we are obligated to do so.

The Substance of the Test of Love (v. 12)

John abruptly made a big statement: "No one has ever seen God." The truth of this statement is revealed throughout the Bible.

OLD TESTAMENT REFERENCE

Even in Moses's close encounter with God, he could not see God visibly. "He said, 'I will cause all my goodness to pass in front of you, and I will proclaim the name 'the LORD' before you. I will be gracious to whom I will be gracious, and I will have compassion on whom I will have compassion.' But he added, 'You cannot see my face, for humans cannot see me and live'" (Exod 33:19–20).

John went on to make an even more incredible statement. He said that the invisible God "remains in us" if we love one another. Love is not the condition for which God is waiting to come to us. If God lives in you, the natural outcome is love for others. Visible love is the test for the presence of the invisible God. Our loving attitude and action are evidence that we pass the test.

John went one step further before he ended this magnificent paragraph. Reciprocal Christian love is not only evidence of God's abiding presence, but John says it is evidence that God's love is being completed in us. "In us" can mean in each individual believer or in mutual Christian relationships. Both are probably true. In some indescribable manner, God is making his love perfect in us as we reflect his love to others. His love is brought to its proper end in us when we are busy loving others.

Section Summary

Love is the test of real relationship; as believers, we are obligated to love others. We should be motivated by the fact that God is love, his love was demonstrated in Jesus, and his love is now being made complete in us.

NEW TESTAMENT REFERENCE

John indicated that the invisible God was revealed in Christ. "No one has ever seen God. The one and only Son, who is himself God and is at the Father's side—he has revealed him" (John 1:18).

QUESTIONS TO GUIDE YOUR STUDY

1. What does the phrase "God is love" (v. 8) mean?
2. How would you explain to a new Christian that we have a social obligation to love everyone?
3. What do you think John meant when he said God's love is made "complete in us" (v. 12)?

A COMBINING OF THE TESTS OF BELIEF AND LOVE (4:13–21)

The two concluding statements in verse 12 are now picked up and elaborated in the following section. While combining the tests of belief and love, John discussed further the indwelling of God (vv. 13–16) and the perfecting of God's love within the true believer (vv. 17–21).

The Indwelling of God (vv. 13–16)

Three different times in this paragraph John mentioned the mutual indwelling of the true believer and God (vv. 13,15,16). Each time he gave the evidence of this mutual indwelling. We can check on ourselves by looking for these three kinds of evidence.

The first statement of God's indwelling occurs in verse 13, and the evidence is, "He has given us of his Spirit." How is this evidence? We can't see his Spirit, but we can see the evidence or fruit of his Spirit. In fact, the following two evidences (in vv. 15–16) are built on this one. We cannot believe in Christ or love one another unless the Spirit empowers us to do so (see 1 Cor 12:3; Gal 5:22; 1 John 3:23–24; 4:1–3). If a person has confessed Christ and loves other people, then the Spirit is in him. And if the Spirit is in him, then God also is indwelling him. Furthermore, the Spirit himself will bear witness to us that we belong to him (Rom 8:16).

In verse 14 John gave the apostolic testimony to the Son's saving mission. The "we" refers to John and the other apostles, demonstrating how faith in Christ is based on the testimony of firsthand witnesses of Christ. Their testimony is that the world needs salvation, the Son came as the Savior, and the Father sent him.

The grounds for John's three tests are found in this concise statement of the gospel. He has not arbitrarily chosen the tests. As John Stott writes, "Within this statement of the gospel all three of the apostle's tests are implicitly contained, the doctrinal (it was his Son himself whom the Father sent), the social (God's love seen in the sending of his Son, 9–10, 16, obligates us to love each other), and the ethical (if Christ came to be our Saviour, we must forsake the sins from which he came to save us)." John Stott, *The Letters of John*.

The test for assurance is now given. It is the doctrinal test. The statement, "Whoever confesses that Jesus is the Son of God," is the condition. To "confess" means a public confession (as in 4:2). This, however, does not simply mean to recite the phrase. It is to say what a person believes and has accepted as true. The aorist tense refers to a single and decisive act. The only way a person can understand and have the courage to make the confession is if the Spirit prompts him to do so (4:2). Therefore, this is a valid and necessary test for the assurance that "God remains in him and he in God."

John again gave his testimony in verse 16 before he brought the test of true life. John testified that he knew and relied on God's love. But, since "God is love," the evidence that a person is in God and God in him is the character of God being lived out in his or her life. Loving attitudes and actions as well as right beliefs prove that God is living in a person.

NEW TESTAMENT REFERENCE

The word *trinity* is never mentioned in the New Testament. There is much debate as to when the doctrine of the three-in-oneness of God developed, and some believe it is not a biblical concept. However, it seems clear that John accepted this doctrine and understood it well enough to feel he didn't need to explain it. For example, here we have all three members of the Godhead interrelated. The Father sends both the Spirit and Jesus. They are distinct, but they are all God.

Section Summary

There is evidence which demonstrates the mutual indwelling of God and the true believer. If this evidence is seen, assurance is real.

The Perfecting of Love (vv. 17–21)

John ended verse 12 with the affirmation that if we love one another, God dwells in us and his love is perfected in us. The idea of God's indwelling was expanded in verses 13–16. Now John elaborated on the idea of the perfecting of love. Previously God's love was the topic, here it is our love that is perfected (v. 17). John described the results of our perfected love: confidence in the day of judgment (vv. 17b–18) and love for other Christians (vv. 19–21).

First, perfected love results in confidence when Christ returns in judgment. The word *confidence (parrēsia)* was previously used to describe the unshakable confidence we should have at Christ's second coming (2:28) and during our prayers (3:21). Here it is used to explain the inner assurance of the true believer to face the judgment. There can be confidence because the true believer is in the same position as Christ ("as he is," v. 17), both a child of God and the object of his love. This confidence is a sign that our love is perfected

John stated this same truth negatively in verse 18. Whereas true love toward God (due to a true relationship with God) produces confidence, a lack of love (due to a lack of relationship) produces fear. Fear or terror is the opposite of confidence. They are mutually exclusive. As John stated, "Perfect love drives out fear." Fear is present when there is no saving relationship because the judgment will result in punishment. Love is perfected when there is no trace of fear at all.

Second, perfected love results in love for others (vv. 19–21). God "first loved us" (v. 19). Because of that, we love as well. God takes the initiative. We respond to his love not only in our heads but in our hearts and with our hands.

Genuine Christian love is not only expressed toward God, but it goes out to our brothers as well. While perfect love casts out fear, it also dispels hatred. As John stated earlier, a person cannot be in the light and hate his brother (2:9); neither can he claim to love God and hate his brother (4:20). That person "is a liar."

John concluded by giving two reasons love for God results in love for others. First, it is a logical conclusion. If we can't love the people we see, then it is illogical to think we could love God whom we can't see. If we have God's love in us, then we will naturally give it to those closest to us. Second, it is a matter of obedience. If God's love is in us, then we will obey his commands (2:5). Jesus made the command clear—that we are to love God and our neighbors. We cannot separate the duties or be exclusive with our love.

PERSONAL APPLICATION

John has now listed three types of people who are "liars." They are persons who claim to be true believers but either walk in the darkness of disobedience (1:6; 2:4), deny the deity of Jesus (2:22–23), and/or hate their brother or sister (4:20). All liars, when faced with the truth, lose their confidence. A day is coming when all masks will be dropped, and all tests will be final. Shouldn't we make decisions that will lead to confidence in the end and not the revelation of our lies?

Section Summary

Authentic Christian love is a perfecting love that results in confidence to face the judgment and loving action toward others.

QUESTIONS TO GUIDE YOUR STUDY

1. Why did John choose these three specific tests?
2. What is the evidence of the believer and God's mutual indwelling?
3. What are the results of perfected love? How are these played out in a person's life?

THE RELATIONSHIP BETWEEN THE THREE TESTS (5:1–5)

John concluded his discussion of the three tests (moral, social, and doctrinal) by affirming that it is important for the true believer to demonstrate all three signs of the presence of authentic Christianity (right actions, love, and belief). He showed how the three tests are closely related and intricately interwoven into an essential unity. All three are present in a true believer, and none can be missing in an authentic Christian.

John began with a universal principle relating to the doctrinal test of belief: "Everyone who believes that Jesus is the Christ has been born of God" (5:1). The substance of the belief is acceptance that Jesus the man is Christ the divine Son who became incarnate. The tenses of the verbs are important as well. "Believes" is present tense, signifying a present and ongoing belief. "Has been born" is perfect tense, meaning "has been born in the past and the results remain." Ongoing belief is the result of the new birth—not the cause of it.

Section Summary

First John 5:1–5 is difficult to outline, like most of this letter. The relationship between the three tests is described in such a way that it is difficult to unravel. Perhaps the three tests are so closely related that it is impossible to place them together in a specific order and to unpack these verses cleanly. The complexity of the argument reveals the inherent unity of the tests.

This new birth that brings about our believing also involves our loving. To be given birth by God naturally leads to loving God. "Everyone who loves the Father also loves the one born of him" (v. 1). John applied a social proverb to the Christian family. Love for a parent carries with it love for the parent's children as well. Anyone who loves God must also love God's children.

Verse 2 shows the relationship between love for others and love for God as well as obedience to God. Authentic love for others is grounded in love for and obedience to God. Love and obedience are so related that obedience defines love. John wrote, "This is what love for God is: to keep his commands" (v. 3). John also added that "his commands are not a burden" (v. 3). Love is practical and leads to obedient actions—actions which are not difficult to fulfill.

Right belief, right actions, right love—all of these evidences sound burdensome. How can John claim they are not? He quickly gives the answer: "Because everyone who has been born of God conquers the world" (v. 4). The new birth provides the power continually to win victory over the world and its evil powers. The burden of obedience is lifted because the power of victory is inherent within the new birth.

NEW TESTAMENT REFERENCE

Jesus stated, "Come to me, all of you who are weary and burdened, and I will give you rest. Take my yoke upon you and learn from me, because I am lowly and humble in heart, and you will find rest for your souls. For my yoke is easy and my burden is light" (Matt 11:28–30).

John referred to victory over the world two more times. In verse 4b the verb points to a definite act. It is probably referring to their past victory over the false teachers. What was it that helped bring the victory over the heretics? It was not their new birth specifically but their belief, "our faith" (v. 4). The last occurrence is with a present tense (v. 5), as was the first one (v. 4a), signaling the present and ongoing victory. The person who has such a daily victory is the one who believes correctly that "Jesus is the Son of God."

Section Summary

The argument has gone full circle, and all three tests have been related to one another. Authentic Christians are those who believe correctly who Jesus is and are born of God. They love both the Father and his children and keep his commands. They can keep his commands because they overcome the world. They overcome the world because they believe correctly and are, therefore, born of God. Remove any of these evidences and one fails the test. Fail one test and enough proof is gathered to pronounce the verdict that the one being tested is not authentic. The true believer will see all the evidence in some degree in his or her life, while perfection will not occur until the end of time.

QUESTIONS TO GUIDE YOUR STUDY

1. Will all believers pass all three of the tests John presented?
2. How are John's three tests interrelated?

1 JOHN 5

THE TESTIMONIES FOR OUR ASSURANCE (5:6–17)

After John began and ended his last paragraph with the aspect of faith in Jesus, the natural question arises: How can a person come to faith in Jesus as the Son of God? John answered the question by claiming that faith is dependent on having the right kind of witnesses. In this section of John's letter, he explained that idea by first presenting the three witnesses (vv. 6–9), the results due to their testimonies (vv. 10–12), and finally our resulting assurances (vv. 13–17).

The Three Testimonies (vv. 6–9)

In verses 6–9 John presented three different witnesses who testified that Jesus is in fact the Christ. The first witness is the "water." The second witness is the "blood." The third witness is the "Spirit."

Various interpretations have been given as to the identity of the first two witnesses: "water and blood." They generally break down into three different lines of thought: (1) they refer to baptism and the Lord's Supper; (2) they are symbolic references to the water and blood that flowed from Jesus's side at his death as a result of the spear thrust (John 19:34–35); and (3) "water" refers to his baptism, and "blood" refers to his death.

The third interpretation seems to be the best, although John could be using these as terms with one primary meaning along with other shades of meaning. Blood would be an unprecedented symbol for the Lord's Supper as well as the object that it is pointing to as a sign. Furthermore, it is difficult to see how John could say Jesus "came" (aorist) through the ordinances. In the same way it is difficult to see how Jesus "came" through the water and blood at his death when they actually flowed out of him.

Baptism and death offer the best interpretation for the meaning of "water and blood." God voiced his approval of Jesus at his baptism (Matt 3:16–17). He also voiced it again before Jesus's death (John 12:27–30). Water and blood seem to be unique and strange words to represent these events, but they must have been understood by John's readers because he didn't explain them. If they do represent baptism and death, then John presented an objective witness to both the beginning and ending of Jesus's earthly mission.

By referring to the water and the blood (Jesus's baptism and death) as witnesses, John gave a valid testimony for establishing faith as well as refuting the false teachers. Gnosticism taught that Jesus was born a man and died a man, that the Christ came upon him at his baptism and left him before his death. John refuted this teaching when he claimed, "He is the one who came by water and blood, not by water only, but by

NEW TESTAMENT REFERENCE

"When Jesus was baptized, he went up immediately from the water. The heavens suddenly opened for him, and he saw the Spirit of God descending like a dove and coming down on him. And a voice from heaven said, 'This is my beloved Son, with whom I am well-pleased'" (Matt 3:16–17). "'Now my soul is troubled. What should I say—Father, save me from this hour? But that is why I came to this hour. Father, glorify your name.' Then a voice came from heaven: 'I have glorified it, and I will glorify it again.' The crowd standing there heard it and said it was thunder. Others said, 'An angel has spoken to him.' Jesus responded, 'This voice came, not for me, but for you'" (John 12:27–30).

water and by blood" (v. 6). In other words, he is Jesus Christ—the man who was simultaneously the Christ at both his baptism and in his death, as he always was and will be just one person.

The third witness is the Spirit. The content of John's testimony is not mentioned, but the context of the letter as well as John's Gospel indicate that it must have been a testimony about Christ (4:2; John 15:26). John indicated the Spirit testifies because he "is the truth" (v. 6) and, therefore, is trustworthy. John must have referred to the inner testimony of the Holy Spirit (2:20,27; 4:1–6; 1 Cor 12:3), and he may have included the total witness of the Spirit as well (including that at Jesus's baptism and Pentecost).

John went on to establish the validity of these three witnesses. First, he claimed the witnesses agree in their testimonies (vv. 7–8). The law required the collaboration of two or three witnesses before a testimony was considered admissible (Deut 19:15; cp. John 8:17–18). John showed that the testimonies describing who Jesus is meet even these requirements. Second, John gave both objective (baptism and death) and subjective (the Spirit's inner testimony) witnesses. Finally, the testimonies are valid because they are the testimonies that God himself, through these three vessels, "has given about his Son" (v. 9, perfect tense indicating continuing validity).

PERSONAL APPLICATION

This is not a technical or insignificant detail. Anyone who does not accept that Jesus was and is always the Christ will have a confused doctrine of salvation. If the divine Son of God did not take both our nature and our sins upon him, then he has no effect in our reconciliation to God. Any church, person, or religious organization that teaches such false doctrine should be refuted and avoided.

HISTORICAL BACKGROUND

If you compare the texts of the CSB and the KJV, you will see that there is a difference in verses 7–8. The CSB reveals the original text, and the KJV "addition" is not found in any Greek manuscript prior to the fourth century. The added text provides an explicit reference to the Trinity and holds emotional value to some people. Through pressure, Erasmus included the text in his 1522 Greek New Testament (though he was sure it was not original). From there it found its way into the King James Bible. Most current textual critics are in agreement that the variant is not original. Bruce Metzger writes, "That these words are spurious and have no right to stand in the New Testament is certain." Bruce Metzger, *A Textual Commentary on the Greek New Testament*, 3rd ed. (United Bible Societies, 1975), 715.

Section Summary

The three witnesses that testify about Jesus are the water, the blood, and the Spirit. Each assists the believer toward salvation.

The Results from the Testimonies (vv. 10–12)

There are two different types of responses to the testimonies about Christ. One response is to believe in the Son of God (v. 10a). This is described by John as being synonymous with accepting the testimony of God about Christ (v. 9). The other is not to "believe God" (v. 10), which is the same as not believing in the Son and not accepting the testimony of God. To *believe* means "to rely upon, to trust in, or to commit to the Son of God." Not to believe is to not make such commitments.

The result from not believing is simply stated by John: "The one who does not believe God has made him a liar" (v. 10). As in 1:10, this does not mean it shows God to be a liar; rather, it means that the unbeliever is accusing God of a lie. Therefore, unbelief is not simply a lack of faith, but it is a deplorable sin. The unbeliever hears the true testimonies of God and tags them false, thereby rejecting Christ, accusing God of lying, and forsaking salvation ("does not have life," v. 12).

John continued to discuss the results that come to the believer. The first result is that "this testimony" is "within himself" (v. 10). In other words, he is given a deeper and inner assurance of his salvation by the testimony of the Spirit. It is the historical testimony of "water and blood" and the objective/subjective testimony of the Holy Spirit that leads to belief, but, also, it is the deeper subjective testimony of the Spirit that results from belief.

The second result for the believer is the assurance of eternal life. The "testimony" of verse 11 is now the deeper testimony of the Spirit that comes because of belief. The Spirit assures the believer of his "eternal life." This is John's special term that encompasses salvation, the kingdom of God, and relationship with Christ. It includes eternity in time, but it is much more than that. Before John restated the two different resulting conditions of the believers and the unbelievers, he claimed that the Spirit assures the believer of this grand result of faith—eternal life.

Section Summary

The three testimonies produce in a person either salvation or rejection of God. If a person is a believer, then these testimonies result in a deeper assurance and understanding of eternal life.

Our Resulting Assurance (vv. 13–17)

John quickly headed toward his conclusion by adding some final words of assurance to end this section of his letter. He spoke again about the assurance of eternal life (v. 13) and confidence in prayer (vv. 14–17). These two main thoughts concluded his section about the three witnesses and our assurance.

Verse 13 contains another of John's purpose statements for the writing of this letter. Perhaps this one serves as the primary purpose. He wanted the true believers he was writing to "know" they had eternal life. He delivered to them some accurate but strong criteria to test their relationship with Christ, but his purpose was to instill assurance into those who knew Christ.

John discussed another assurance of believers in verses 14–17. They can be assured that God will answer their prayers: "We know that we have what we asked of him" (v. 15). He began by claiming that they have "confidence" (*parrēsia,* same as in 2:28; 3:21; 4:17) that God hears our prayers: "If we ask anything according to his will" (v. 14). The idea of "hearing" probably means that God listens to and answers our prayers. It is not an unqualified promise of answered prayer. The condition of answered prayer in 3:22 was living in God's will—here it is praying in God's will. This is the inclusive statement on the conditions of effectual prayer in the New Testament. The promise is a present granting of the request.

NEW TESTAMENT REFERENCE

In 5:6–12 John spoke in detail about what he said briefly in his Gospel. John clearly stated his purpose for writing the Fourth Gospel. In speaking of all he wrote, he stated, "But these are written so that you may believe that Jesus is the Messiah, the Son of God,and that by believing you may have life in his name" (John 20:31). Life comes by believing, and believing comes from a testimony about Christ. In John 21:24, John spoke about himself and called what he was doing in the Gospel a testimony: "This is the disciple who testifies to these things and who wrote them down. We know that his testimony is true."

Before John closed his thoughts on prayer, he gave a specific example of the efficacy of intercessory prayer (vv. 16–17). The example John chose was, "If anyone sees a fellow believer committing a sin that doesn't lead to death" (v. 16). These verses have a few interpretative knots that are seen in this statement. First, who is the "fellow believer"? Although some interpreters think this refers to people or neighbors in general, it is probably another instance of John's technical use of the term referring to fellow Christians in their community (2:9–11; 3:10,13–17; 4:20–21).

Second, what is the "sin that leads to death"? Volumes have been written on this subject, and opinions are varied. The main options are: (1) a specific act of sin, such as murder, adultery, intentional sins, and so on; (2) a lifestyle of sin; (3) apostasy, or total renunciation of Christ and faith; or (4) blasphemy against the Holy Spirit.

PERSONAL APPLICATION

Some people think that holding some degree of doubt about your salvation and future life in heaven is a sign of righteous humility. This is not so. God's desire, according to his revealed will (5:13), is that his children will know without doubt that they have eternal life.

John's readers must have known exactly what he was talking about, or at least he seems to have assumed they did. This thought is simply a parenthetical idea. John's main point is that prayer asked in accordance with God's will, will be answered. The "sin that leads to death" is an example that his readers would have understood.

The best solution is perhaps found in the historical context. The Gnostic opponents willfully and vigorously rejected the Spirit's witness to the work and person of Christ. The "sin that leads to death" must have been a reference to their denial of the truth. This seems to be the best solution. The "fellow believer" (discussed above) may be a reference to someone who appears to be a brother but whose sin will reveal otherwise. Whatever the solution, the idea John communicated is that it is a type of sinning that leads to spiritual death.

NEW TESTAMENT REFERENCE

The "unpardonable sin" was considered blaspheming the Holy Spirit. In the context of the Gospels, this sin was attributing to Satan the work done by Christ. Jesus said, "Anyone who is not with me is against me, and anyone who does not gather with me scatters. Therefore, I tell you, people will be forgiven every sin and blasphemy, but the blasphemy against the Spirit will not be forgiven" (Matt 12:30–31). "'But whoever blasphemes against the Holy Spirit never has forgiveness, but is guilty of an eternal sin'—because they were saying, 'He has an unclean spirit'" (Mark 3:29–30).

In John's example, he pointed out that if you see a brother sinning in a way other than in a sin that leads to death, you should pray for him (v. 16). Through these kinds of prayer the sinning person will gain eternal life. This illustrates John's earlier point. Prayer in accordance with God's will results in God's answers.

Verse 17 serves as a clarification. Just in case people get the wrong idea about sinful deeds since John mentioned two different "classes" of sins, he reminds the readers that all sin is wrong and no sin is trivial. Earlier he said, "Sin is lawlessness" (3:4). Now he indicated it is "unrighteousness." All activities against the law or justice are sin, and all sin is serious.

Section Summary

John concluded this section and readied his readers for the conclusion by reminding them of the assurance and confidence that comes when a person accepts the validity of the three witnesses and believes in Jesus.

QUESTIONS TO GUIDE YOUR STUDY

1. What are the three witnesses, and how do they bear witness to Jesus?
2. How can a lack of belief be considered sin?
3. What did John mean by the "sin that leads to death"?

THREE CERTAINTIES AND A CHARGE (5:18–21)

John concluded his first letter by reminding and challenging his readers. He concisely stated three certainties a believer can have (vv. 18–20) before he concluded with one quick but solemn charge (v. 21).

The Three Certainties (vv. 18–20)

John used three rapid-fire "we know" statements (vv. 18,19,20) to rally his final thoughts.

First, John states that we know the true believer does not live a lifestyle of sin (v. 18a). There may be acts of sin in the true believer's life, but the old life of sin will not be present. This is a general statement about all believers.

Two reasons are given for this (v. 18b). One, because Christ ("the one who was born of God") "keeps him." Christ watches over and protects the Christian. It is not the believer who is able to overcome Satan and his ways; it is up to Christ to do the protecting. Two, the believer doesn't continue to sin because the "evil one does not touch him." To "touch" doesn't mean to engage or feel, but "to grasp." Satan may assault or attack, but he cannot lay hold of us enough to defeat us because Christ is on guard.

Second, John stated that we know something about John and his readers and something about the world (v. 19). John included himself when he wrote, "We know that we are of God." They had assurance of their salvation in the family of God. They had truly been born of him. The world, on the other hand, "is under the sway of the evil one." The evil one, Satan himself, has the people of the world and the evil powers in the world under his control.

Third, John stated that we know Jesus has both come and given us understanding (v. 20). This is his last and most foundational statement of the three. It includes the acknowledgment of Jesus being the "Son of God" (v. 19) as well as God's "Son, Jesus Christ" (v. 20). The statement reconfirms both the historical ("has come") and experiential ("has given") knowledge which he has brought. The purpose of his coming is so that we may know (relationally) the true One, which in fact the readers do ("we are in the true one," v. 20). The true One is God, and the experiential understanding of our relationship with him is mediated through "his Son, Jesus Christ."

PERSONAL APPLICATION

John's definitions of sin go against the standards of right and wrong held by pop culture today. John clearly declared there is a standard of right and wrong, although the culture maintains that right and wrong are individual matters. To be a Christian is to be in the world but not to live by the world's standards. Jesus said, "If you continue in my word, you really are my disciples. You will know the truth, and the truth will set you free" (John 8:31–32).

WORD PICTURE

Under the Sway

The Greek word translated "is under the sway" in verse 19 is *keitai*. It literally means "to lie." It paints a sad but true picture of the state of the world. Satan has it, and it lies helplessly in his power. The word portrays the world as a calm and almost sleeping victim that does not even struggle to get loose.

OLD TESTAMENT REFERENCE

The psalmist recorded God's desires of protection for his people. The statement in 1 John 5:18 may be an allusion to Ps 105:15: "Do not touch my anointed ones, or harm my prophets."

The final statement ("He is the true God and eternal life") is probably a reference to God. It could refer to Jesus. If so, it would be the clearest statement to the deity of Jesus in the New Testament. However, it is best to see it as another reference to the "true one." As such, God is defined as both the only "true" God and "eternal life."

Section Summary

John moved toward the conclusion of his letter by claiming three certainties: (1) true believers do not live sinful lifestyles, (2) the readers are true believers, and (3) Jesus is the incarnated Christ. If all this is truly and factually known, salvation is sure.

THE CHARGE (5:21)

John closed his letter not with a formal closing but with a gentle address of affection and a concise charge. Identifying his readers again as his "little children," he tenderly charged them to "guard yourselves from idols."

This entire letter is a detailed delineation of what a true believer is and does. Moral obedience, genuine love, and right beliefs are the marks of a Christian. Anything else is incongruent with our Father's character and our new nature. Now, with the image of the true God and his divine Son in the foreground and the false teachers and their heresy in the background, John summarized the true believer's important responsibility by charging them to worship nothing other than God.

QUESTIONS TO GUIDE YOUR STUDY

1. What are the three certainties listed by John in this section?
2. How do you think God keeps his children safe from Satan?
3. Why do you think John ended his letter with a command and not a normal salutation?

2–3 John

INTRODUCTION TO 2 AND 3 JOHN

The short length of both 2 and 3 John, as well as the relative neglect of these books by the early church, adds to their interest. These are the two shortest books in the New Testament, each containing fewer than 250 Greek words. Many of the themes discussed in detail in 1 John appear in these letters. A look at the issues of authorship, recipients, date, purpose, and structure will assist in understanding these letters. These issues will be discussed for both letters before the commentary is given on 2 and 3 John separately.

AUTHORSHIP OF 2 AND 3 JOHN

The external evidence for authorship of both letters is much less than for 1 John. Their canonicity was questioned in the early period of church history, as they were listed among the "disputed letters." However, no early Christian writer attributed the authorship of 2 and 3 John to anyone other than the apostle John.

The internal evidence lends support to Johannine authorship. Both the vocabulary and general themes of the letters are similar to 1 John. For example, the reality of Christ having come "in the flesh" (1 John 4:2; 2 John 7) and the importance of obedience to verify that one is a child of God (1 John 3:10; 3 John 11) are also important in these letters.

The author identified himself in both of these letters with the phrase "the elder" (*presbuteros*, 2 John 1; 3 John 1). Although this can lend support to John as the author, it has also been the point of much debate against Johannine authorship. Yet this would not be the first time an apostle referred to himself as an elder (1 Pet 5:1). It was probably John's way of referring to his advanced age as well as his authoritative position among the churches of Ephesus.

NEW TESTAMENT REFERENCE

Peter the apostle wrote, "I exhort the elders among you as a fellow elder and witness to the sufferings of Christ, as well as one who shares in the glory about to be revealed" (1 Pet 5:1).

RECIPIENTS AND ORIGINATION OF 2 AND 3 JOHN

In both letters a recipient is named. In 2 John the letter is written to "the elect lady and her children" (v. 1). Again, who this refers to specifically is uncertain. Some scholars view this as a title of a personal friend of John's. Others see it as a personification designating a local congregation of believers. The latter seems the best interpretation for several reasons: the language of love and the command given to love in verse 5 seem inappropriate for an individual; there are no explicit personal references such as those found in 3 John; the writer switches between "you" singular and "you" plural often in the letter (unobservable in most modern translations) while being consistent with the singular in 3 John; and it was normal to personify towns or institutions in the first century much as we do today.

The third letter of John was written to "Gaius" (v. 1). He appears to have been a leading member of a local church. Exactly where Gaius lived is unknown, but it was probably around Ephesus, where John continued to live and write these two letters.

NEW TESTAMENT REFERENCE

Thanks to the expansion and economic developments of the Roman Empire during the first century, travel had become much easier than ever before. The Romans had established a fine network of roads that connected most of the empire. The *Pax Romana* (peace of Rome) made traveling safer, and the spread of Greek and Latin as universal languages made it more inviting. All of these changes helped the spread of Christianity during the first century.

DATE OF THE WRITING OF 2 AND 3 JOHN

The data for a solid conviction on the date of the writing of either of these letters is vague. Again, as with 1 John, it appears best to place them after John's Gospel because of content. How they related to 1 John is difficult to determine. It appears best to see them as written after 1 John, possibly even sent together with it in a bundle. The referral to "the antichrist" in 2 John 7 without a more detailed discussion (see 1 John 2:18–23) seems to suggest this followed that letter in time. These were probably written shortly after 1 John or at the same time as 1 John (ca AD 85–95).

NEW TESTAMENT REFERENCE

As both Christian people and itinerant Christian teachers traveled, they would need a place to stay. Inns and hotels as we know them today were nonexistent in the first century. The ancient inns were not as comfortable as a private home. They usually housed as many fleas and as much dust as they did guests. They were also generally known for their dishonorable atmosphere, which was prompted by the poor character of most innkeepers. So it became a common practice for local Christians to open their homes to traveling Christians. Such hospitality is seen throughout the New Testament (Acts 16:15; 17:7; 21:8,16; Rom 16:23). This genuine hospitality was also abused by people who were simply looking for free lodging.

THE PURPOSES OF 2 AND 3 JOHN

John did not explicitly state a purpose in either of these two letters as he did in his Gospel and in his first letter. However, it appears that 2 John was written to warn against showing hospitality to false teachers (v. 10). This would have assisted the spread of errant doctrine. Intertwined in this discussion is John's teaching of the correct doctrines and actions of true believers.

Third John appears to be John's effort to confront a church problem by encouraging Gaius (vv. 2–8) and Demetrius (v. 12), discussing the problems caused by Diotrephes (vv. 9–11), and setting up an upcoming personal visit (vv. 13–14). Diotrephes had not welcomed the itinerant Christian teachers with the proper hospitality and had discouraged others from doing so. Therefore, 2 John and 3 John have the same background and similar purposes. Second John is more negative while 3 John is more positive on the issue of Christian hospitality.

THE STRUCTURE OF 2 AND 3 JOHN

The structure of both letters is simple. They both contain the elements of a traditional first-century letter (except 3 John omits a formal greeting). Each letter would probably fit on a single sheet of papyrus as a normal letter. Each has a simple outline as follows.

Section Summary

Second and 3 John were both written by the apostle John to a local church and a church leader, respectively, shortly after 1 John was written (ca AD 85–95). Second John was written to warn against showing hospitality to false teachers, and 3 John was written to encourage proper hospitality to Christian teachers.

2 JOHN

INTRODUCTION TO 2 JOHN (1–3)

John's introduction to this letter is in the typical pattern of ancient letters. He mentioned the sender and the recipients and gave a greeting. John identified himself as "the elder" (v. 1). This could be an official title or simply a designation of his age. The "elect lady and her children" are the addressees of the letter. This was John's way of addressing a specific church and its members.

After mentioning the recipients, John gave a long qualification about the church ("whom" of v. 1, masculine in Greek, refers to the lady and the children). First, he said he loved them in "the truth," which means in sincerity. Second, he declared that all the believers loved this church as well. "Truth" at the end of verse 1 is the revelation of Christ in the gospel or Christ himself. Therefore, to know this truth is to be a true believer. The love for this church was as broad as the community of faith. Finally, the reason for this love was because the truth was in them. This was not some fanciful or fickle type of love.

In John's description of the truth within them (v. 2), he struck a wonderful note of security. The truth is said to be a present, indwelling reality ("that remains in us") that will continue forever ("and will be with us forever"). The "with us" is emphatic and drawing a strong contrast between the heretics who will leave eventually (v. 7; 1 John 2:19) and the enduring truth within the individual that sustains the fellowship of the true community of Christ.

The greeting of this letter (v. 3) has some unique features which shed light on John's point. Any adjustments to the normal pattern of

WORD PICTURE

Elder

The term *elder* could have been an official title of John. While some see a distinction between elder *(presbuteros)*, bishop/overseer *(episkopos)*, and pastor/shepherd *(poimēn)*, the New Testament uses these titles interchangeably for the leaders of a local church. For example, Paul referred to the same people by all three names: "Now from Miletus, he sent to Ephesus and summoned the elders of the church. . . . Be on guard for yourselves and for all the flock of which the Holy Spirit has appointed you as overseers, to shepherd the church of God, which he purchased with his own blood" (Acts 20:17,28). The same thing occurs in 1 Pet 5:1–2.

PERSONAL APPLICATION

Church leaders should find good counsel from John's reaction. Joy is a natural part of ministry. Can there be any better joy than seeing people's lives changed and being conformed to the image of Christ? But his joy was the result of "some" of the church members' lives. His ministry was not 100 percent effective. The whole flock was not obediently following Christ. He couldn't say that all the church's members were "walking in truth." He could just say "some." Maybe we should not be surprised when we discover that every church member is not living in obedience to Christ.

PERSONAL APPLICATION

It is helpful to note how John encouraged and led this church. The use of the proper personal pronouns in our discussions with other church members is crucial. John included himself in the commands by using "we." Although he was the elder, it is as if he stepped from behind the pulpit, sat in the pew with his people, and said, "Now here is what we must do." A leader should follow his or her own teaching.

a greeting are intentional and reveal something the writer was trying to emphasize. John added "mercy" to the normal "grace and peace" formula, emphasizing salvation as well as our need of it. John also added the phrase "the Son of the Father" to the customary greeting as a way of relating his familiar theme of sonship. Finally, he added the phrase "in truth and love" as a way of reiterating the characteristics of the Christian life.

Section Summary

John opened his letter to this church with words of encouragement. He shared with them his love and built them up in the security of their faith.

PURPOSE OF 2 JOHN (4–11)

The purpose of this letter is now unfolded. John was concerned for both the fellowship of the congregation and a coming threat to the local church. He encouraged them and challenged them in their love and obedience (vv. 4–6) before he warned them and instructed them about the antichrist (vv. 7–11).

Encouragement for Fellowship Within the Congregation (vv. 4–6)

John was "very glad" because he found some of the members "walking in truth." Either he himself met them or he received word about them. He rejoiced because they believed the truth and obeyed its teaching, which is what they had been commanded to do.

John next encouraged the church to heed the commands of love and obedience. The command to love was not new *(kainos)* to them; it was one they had known since the beginning of their Christian life and had been around since the Old Testament (see discussion on 1 John 2:7–11). Love and obedience are reciprocal duties. Love was defined by John as walking "according to his commands," and his command was to walk in love (v. 6). In this brief encouragement to the church, John again alluded to the three tests in his first letter (truth/belief, love, and obedience). Here he celebrated their faithfulness to these tests and encouraged them to press on toward further application of these truths in their lives.

Section Summary

Having found members of the church living their lives faithfully, John rejoiced and pushed them forward in their duties of love and obedience.

Warning About a Threat from Outside the Congregation (vv. 7–11)

After rejoicing over and encouraging the true believers, John turned to the topic of how believers are to be related to those who are persistent in wrong behavior and on believing sound doctrine. Though "some" (v. 4) were walking in the truth, he warned about the "many" (v. 7) who were opposed to the truth. In verse 7 he described these "deceivers" before issuing two warnings to the church (vv. 8–9 and 10–11).

John warned about the "deceivers" of the church as opposed to the children of the church. The deceivers were out to lead others astray, to cause them to drift away from the truth. They should be seen as identical with the "false prophets" and "antichrists" of 1 John 2:18–19; 4:1. Their having "gone out into the world" (v. 7) is a reference probably to their leaving the church as well as their mission to teach lies.

These false teachers' most recognizable characteristic was their rejection of the incarnation of Christ. John did not say that they taught against the truth of the incarnation of Jesus but that they "do not confess the coming of Jesus Christ in the flesh" (v. 7). They were deceivers, and they may not have revealed their true beliefs, but their true position was to reject the incarnation. This was a double offense. They rejected Christ, and they deceived people, and, therefore, each one was "the deceiver and the antichrist" (v. 7).

With the deceivers presented for who they really were, John warned the church to watch out for this false teaching lest they fall prey to it. This is the same warning given by Jesus in Mark 13:23. The false teachers were deceivers, and so they were subtle and clever, mischievous and deceptive. A sharp eye was the true believers' best method of defense.

One reason was given for the need to watch out. John presented it negatively and then positively: "So that you don't lose what we have worked for, but that you may receive a full reward" (v. 8). John was surely not talking about their salvation. They did not work for that; it was a gift (see John 4:10). He referred to their reward to be given at Christ's return. John didn't want their reward to be stolen away by these false teachers. He wanted them to "receive a full reward," so he warned them to "watch yourselves."

John added support to this first warning by contradicting a claim of the false teachers (v. 9). These Gnostic-type teachers claimed a superior knowledge that moved them ahead of the normal Christians. John sarcastically claimed that these false teachers had run too far. In their leaving of the true teachings about Christ, they also left behind God. It is only the one who "remains in that teaching" who has "both the Father and the Son" (v. 9). John taught this in his first letter (1 John 2:22–23) and reminded them here so it would help them "watch yourselves."

John's second warning was not about buying into the false teaching but about assisting its distribution. The person who "comes to you" (v. 10) is one who approaches with the purpose of teaching you his ways. He is not just a person with different views who is coming for a casual visit. He is a false teacher. In fact, it may be that this is a visit to the

HISTORICAL BACKGROUND

The Christians were not the only traveling teachers in the first-century world. Many devoted followers of various religions hit the roads to extol their beliefs and win a material profit at the same time. Such schemes were not always easily detectable. The question of whom to host was a practical concern for these believers.

NEW TESTAMENT REFERENCE

Jesus taught about false, deceiving teachers also: "For false messiahs and false prophets will arise and will perform signs and wonders to lead astray, if possible, the elect. And you must watch! I have told you everything in advance" (Mark 13:22–23).

WORD PICTURE

Reward

Reward (*misthos*) has as its basic meaning "a workman's wages." In this passage John picked up on its common New Testament usage—a payment or honor to be received in heaven. The heavenly "reward" is never described precisely in the New Testament, although it is often held up as a motivation for doing right while we live on this earth. Paul painted the clearest picture of the reward ceremony. Both motivational and convicting, his description is found in 1 Cor 3:8–15.

church (since "you" is plural) which generally met in a home. However, the warning applies to both a church and a personal home.

John gives a clear command to the Christian about how to respond when a false teacher comes: "Do not receive him into your home, and do not greet him" (v. 10). In other words, do not encourage his ways or assist him. To do so would be to further the effectiveness of the false teaching and move the teacher deeper into its errant system. John's descriptive words for this person's efforts is "evil works" (v. 11). In order not to become an accomplice in such an evil adventure, John warned us not to encourage or assist its teacher.

PERSONAL APPLICATION

Here we have some helpful hints on how to deal with members of false religions who come knocking on our doors selling their "stuff." Recognize first that the false teaching concerns the doctrine of Christ. These are not guidelines from John on how to deal with fellow Christians who have different opinions on "minor" doctrines. First, the Christian response to the person must always be given in love. Rudeness and unkindness are not the marks of a Christian. Second, the Christian response must be assertive and direct. No compromise of one's doctrinal position should be made, and no assistance or encouragement should be given in the spread of such false teachings. It is not more loving to be tolerant of such teachings. Love points people to Christ, not away from him.

Section Summary

John warned the believers to keep an eye out for the false teachers so they wouldn't get caught in their false doctrine or lose their heavenly rewards. He also instructed them not to welcome them into their homes to assist their errant mission.

Conclusion of 2 John (12–13)

John closed his second letter, but he was not finished with the conversation. He wanted to hold his remaining comments for a personal visit. "Paper and ink" seemed to be the inappropriate medium in which to continue. The reason he wanted to visit them and talk with them was "so that our joy may be complete" (v. 12). He hoped the joy that was embarked upon when he found some of their members living in the truth would be brought to completion when he united with the whole church in personal Christian fellowship.

The final sentence of the letter was John's way of sending a greeting from a fellow congregation. "Your elect sister" (v. 13) corresponds with "the elect lady" (v. 1). So as John came to the end of his papyrus sheet, he signed the letter and got ready to pack his bags for a visit.

WORD PICTURE

Although books and papers have their place, such statements as these concluding ones by John reassure us of the value of preaching and teaching. While the communication age rushes forward with its new technologies, perhaps nothing will ever replace human-to-human, face-to-face communication for the encouragement and growth of Christians. Preaching, teaching, talking, and listening are still the best tools for encouraging spiritual growth.

QUESTIONS TO GUIDE YOUR STUDY

1. Why did John identify himself as "the elder"?
2. How do John's teachings about traveling teachers relate to our modern situation?
3. How does the concept of rewards mesh with selfless motives?
4. Is there ever a reason to show hospitality to a false teacher?

3 JOHN

SALUTATION OF 3 JOHN (1)

This letter begins the same as John's second letter but immediately reveals its more personal nature. John identified himself again as "the elder" (see commentary on 2 John 1). He addressed the letter this time not to a church but to a man named "Gaius." More information about this man is not given in this letter.

Two things about Gaius are apparent from the content of the letter. First, he must have held some position in the local church. If he was not its pastor, then he was a layman with some authority. Second, he held a fond place in John's heart. John explicitly declared his love (agape type) for him in verse 1 and later referred to him as "dear friend" (literally "beloved") (vv. 2,5,11). His love is "in the truth," an identical phrase to 2 John 1 and 3 John 4. This seems to indicate that Gaius was a person whom John had personally helped to come to know Jesus ("my children," v. 4).

PRAYER AND COMMENDATION OF GAIUS (2–8)

John moved into the body of his letter with a prayer for Gaius (v. 2) before he commended him for his faithfulness. He used an ancient, customary statement to pray for his good health and general success. Although these were common words found in most letters of the time, John meant them sincerely. In the midst of this polite prayer is a word of encouragement: "Your whole life is going well." John did not pray for this specifically; he used Gaius's spiritual growth as a standard to pray for his physical condition. John was confident in Gaius's spiritual condition.

After the brief prayer, John commended his walk (vv. 3–4) and encouraged his Christian hospitality (vv. 5–8). Just as some of the members of the church whom John had written in 2 John had brought joy to him, Gaius's personal spiritual walk had done the same (v. 3). A few fellow Christians ("fellow believers") visited Gaius's church and brought back a good report to John.

They reported two things: Gaius's continuing faithfulness to the truth in his lifestyle (v. 3b) and his love (v. 6a). These two reports combine to give a picture of a person who accepted the teachings of Christ and put them into practice through his daily behavior. For John, the "Son of Thunder" turned gentle elder, there could be "no greater joy" than "to hear that my children are walking in truth" (v. 4).

In verse 5 John commended Gaius for his past love, and specifically for his past Christian hospitality. John described him as faithful in what he was doing. His work matched his belief. He was true to his conviction, and this was seen in his treatment of the "brothers and sisters" who were

WORD PICTURE

Gaius

"Gaius" is considered by many to be the most common name in the Roman Empire. Several men with this name appear in the New Testament: Gaius of Ephesus, a traveling companion of Paul (Acts 19:29); Gaius of Derbe, who traveled with Paul on his last journey (Acts 20:4); and Gaius of Corinth, who was baptized by Paul (1 Cor 1:14) and who hosted him and the church of Corinth (Rom 16:23). There is no evidence that any of these men are the Gaius of 3 John 1.

NEW TESTAMENT REFERENCE

Truth and love are key elements in spiritual maturity. As Paul wrote, "Then we will no longer be little children, tossed by the waves and blown around by every wind of teaching, by human cunning with cleverness in the techniques of deceit. But speaking the truth in love, let us grow in every way into him who is the head—Christ. From him the whole body, fitted and knit together by every supporting ligament, promotes the growth of the body for building itself up in love by the proper working of each individual part" (Eph 4:14–16).

PERSONAL APPLICATION

We can learn a lesson in leadership from both of John's shorter letters. Although there may be times for tough, confrontational leadership, most members of a church need encouragement in what they are doing well before their ears are attentive to what they could do better. John built up people before he broke down the problems. Perhaps most importantly, when he encouraged his people, he did not flatter them with general or unbelievable fluff. Instead, he cast light on the specific areas in which they were excelling. We need more leaders like John—well trained and equipped, excelling in character and commitment, and caring enough about the spiritual success of others that they are not afraid to be vulnerable and transparent in their conversation.

WORD PICTURE

Hospitality

The Greek words translated "hospitality" *(philoxenia)* or "hospitable" *(philoxenos)* are made up of two separate Greek words. *Philos* means loving, and *xenos* refers to a stranger. Therefore, the literal meaning of *hospitality* is "love of strangers." Neither of these words appears in this passage, but they are fleshed out in what John said about Gaius having a love for strangers and brothers (vv. 5–6a).

"strangers" to him. From verse 6 we learn that these fellow Christians had come to Gaius and he had welcomed them and allowed them to stay with him. They reported back to John and the church about Gaius's love.

John gave instructions to Gaius for his future hospitality, and then he included a general guideline for all Christian hospitality. When Gaius sends these "brothers and sisters" on their way, he should do it "in a manner worthy of God" (v. 6). These are God's servants, traveling teachers, and they should be treated as such. John meant that they should be treated with kindness in attitude and probably in the giving of supplies.

John listed three reasons proper hospitality should be given to these traveling Christian teachers. First, they were on a mission for Christ ("They set out for the sake of the Name," v. 7). This was an authentic Christian mission, and the missionaries' motives were pure. The second reason was more practical. They would need help, but they had received no help from the non-Christian community. Because of this, John said, "We ought" ("we" is emphatic, v. 8) to support them. We are obligated to help our fellow Christians who are on mission for Christ. The last reason for supporting these people is "so that we can be coworkers with the truth" (v. 8). By showing them hospitality, we cooperate in the effort of spreading the truth and doing the truth. For all these reasons, Gaius as well as the readers of this letter must "support such people" (v. 8).

Section Summary

John encouraged his friend Gaius in his Christian lifestyle. Gaius represented all John wrote about true believers in 1 John. John also instructed Gaius on the proper type of Christian hospitality that should be shown to Christian teachers.

WARNING ABOUT DIOTREPHES (9–11)

Diotrephes was some type of leader in the local church to which John wrote. He may have been the pastor. Or perhaps he was a prominent layperson. He was the counterpart to Gaius in his character and conduct and was causing trouble in the church.

Diotrephes rejected one of John's earlier letters to the church (v. 9a). What this letter was is not certain. It could not have been the current letter of 3 John since Diotrephes had already responded poorly to it. It could not have been 1 or 2 John because nothing is mentioned in those letters about hosting authentic missionaries. So it must have been a letter that is now lost.

Diotrephes was causing trouble by doing at least four wrong things. First, he was rejecting the authority of John (he "does not receive our authority," v. 9). Second, he was spreading slanderous gossip about John ("slandering us with malicious words," v. 10). The Greek word for "slandering" means "talking nonsense," or "spreading inaccurate tales." Third, he opposed John's teaching by refusing "to welcome fellow believers" (v. 10). Fourth, he didn't show hospitality himself, and he stopped those "who want to do so and expels them from the church" (v. 10).

Why was Diotrephes such a troublemaker? John told us what Diotrephes's problem was. It was the sin of selfish ambition. John said Diotrephes "loves to have first place" (v. 9). He had a problem with anyone being ahead of him, whether Christ, Gaius, or John. His selfish ambition apparently led to his bullying for position in the church.

John concluded his warning about Diotrephes by instructing Gaius ("dear friend") in verse 11. With the powerful and negative activity of Diotrephes being felt in the church, perhaps John was fearful that Gaius would slip into his ways. So he told him, "Do not imitate what is evil, but what is good." His reason for making this statement reflects back on his moral test of his first letter. The moral activity of people reveals their spiritual condition. The person who does good is a true believer ("of God"). The one who does evil is not a believer ("has not seen God"). If John had Diotrephes in mind, he not only encouraged Gaius in his activity, but he questioned Diotrephes's spiritual condition.

WORD PICTURE

Notice in verses 9–10 that John switched pronouns when referring to himself. Sometimes he said "I" and sometimes he said "us." It is doubtful that he was revealing a change in who was writing the letter or in who was representing what was being said. The plural "us" is probably the plural of authority. It was John's way of referring to himself with the authority of the church.

PERSONAL APPLICATION

We should be careful not to judge but to reflect. Diotrephes had fallen into a familiar trap for leaders. With the first taste of authority and recognition, a person's appetite can easily be whetted for more of each. Humility must be sought when responsibility is given.

Section Summary

Diotrephes's selfish ambition was causing trouble in the local church because he was defying John's authority and teaching. Diotrephes was slandering John's character and trying to expel from the congregation those who were showing the proper Christian hospitality. John explained his errors and warned Gaius away from them.

COMMENDATION OF DEMETRIUS (12)

As John wrote about doing good, his thoughts naturally turned away from Diotrephes and toward Demetrius. The exact identity of Demetrius and his relationship to John and the church of Gaius are not known. He may have been the person chosen to deliver the letter to its destination.

John commended Demetrius for three things. First, he had a strong reputation ("Everyone speaks well of Demetrius"). Second, Demetrius's reputation was justified. He was "for real." Third, John gave his stamp of approval on his life. This was probably the strongest commendation that John could give because John could say confidently to Gaius, "You know that our testimony is true."

WORD PICTURE

When John called Gaius to a life of imitation, he helped us see the necessity of role models. Everyone imitates someone. The key issue is how good the original is. Just as a photocopy can be no better than the original, so a person's life will be no better than whom they are trying to emulate. That is why the best "original" for the Christian is God as revealed in his Son Jesus.

WORD PICTURE

Friends

In the closing words of John's letters, he used an interesting word: "friends" *(philoi)*. The normal designation in the New Testament of fellow Christians was "brothers." As John closed his last personal letter to the churches of which he was "the elder," he used a striking word that Jesus used to describe his relationship with his disciples. Jesus said, "No one has greater love than this: to lay down his life for his friends. You are my friends if you do what I command you. I do not call you servants anymore, because a servant doesn't know what his master is doing. I have called you friends, because I have made known to you everything I have heard from my Father" (John 15:13–15).

CONCLUSION (13–14)

The conclusion of this letter is different from that in his second letter, but there are some similarities. John had more to say, but he wanted to speak it to Gaius rather than write it. So he concluded with his hope to come and visit soon.

Before ending his letter, John added a closing word of greeting. "Peace to you" was a common wish in many letters, but it was especially appropriate for Gaius with Diotrephes in his church. After sending the greetings from the members of his church to Gaius, John asked Gaius to greet the members of his church by name as a personal gesture of care.

QUESTIONS TO GUIDE YOUR STUDY

1. What do you know about the person to whom this letter was written? How do you know it?
2. What can you learn about dealing with rebellious people from John's treatment of Diotrephes?
3. Are there any other people named Demetrius in the Bible?
4. What did John teach about proper hospitality?

Jude

INTRODUCTION TO JUDE

Although a brief letter, Jude makes a significant contribution to early Christian literature that calls on believers to defend the faith God has entrusted to the church.

Jude says that his intention was to write about the salvation believers share. However, a situation arose which caused him to address false teaching in the church.

These teachers erred both in their theology and, as a consequence, in their ethics. These teachings had some of the features that appeared in a second-century phenomenon called Gnosticism.

One of the key errors of these teachers was that they believed God's grace implied that there were no moral guidelines.

AUTHOR

The author identified himself as "a servant of Jesus Christ and a brother of James" (v. 1). In presenting himself as a brother of the Lord's half brother (Jas 1:1), he modestly neglected to mention his own relationship to Jesus (Matt 13:55; Mark 6:3). Some have identified Jude as "Judas the son of James" (Luke 6:16), but the author does not claim apostleship.

DATE OF WRITING

Date. Suggestions for dating this letter vary widely. Little evidence is available for making a conclusive decision. We cannot be certain whether Jude was younger or older than Jesus, but it is likely that he was younger. If Jude were born during the early part of the first century, the letter could have been written aroundd AD 65–80. Because of the uncertainty of the time of its writing, scholars have assigned dates ranging from AD 60 to AD 140.

AUDIENCE

No address for a reader appears within the letter. The readers might have been Jews or Gentiles who lived anywhere. Jude had a concrete situation in mind, but it is impossible to locate it precisely. The statements of verses 17–18 have led some to suggest that the readers knew apostles within the region of Palestine. This is a possible but unproven hypothesis.

PURPOSE FOR WRITING

Jude intended to produce a message about the common salvation he shared with his readers (v. 3). His awareness of the appearance of heresy led him to change his emphasis to a denunciation of the heresy surrounding him. Jude gave direction for halting the advance of heresy among his readers in verses 17–23.

THEME

Jude began with the intention of discussing the theme of "salvation." Awareness of the infiltration of false teachers led Jude to emphasize two features:

1. He warned against and condemned false teachers who were heavily influencing his area.
2. He urged his readers to greater firmness and commitment.

RELATIONSHIP OF JUDE'S LETTER TO 2 PETER

Most of Jude is included in 2 Peter, but it is an agreement in thought and vocabulary rather than a verbatim reproduction. It is difficult to determine which writer borrowed from the other or whether both used a third, common source. Conclusions reached about this relationship do influence views of authorship and date.

LITERARY FORM

Despite the lack of a specific address, Jude's letter is directed to a specific situation. It is more impersonal than John's epistles. Jude was fond of mentioned items in triads (v. 2: "mercy, peace, and love";; v. 11: Cain, Balaam, and Korah). The majestic doxology provides a moving conclusion to Jude's words (vv. 24–25).

THE THEOLOGY OF JUDE

The epistle contains little theological content because the purpose was largely practical. One controversial feature of the book is the references to the apocryphal books of *1 Enoch* (v. 14) and the *Assumption of Moses*

(v. 9). Some have seen these references as a liability to accepting the authority of Jude, but Paul quoted a heathen poet in Acts 17:28. He also referred to a noncanonical writing in 2 Tim 3:8.

Jude appears to have viewed his references to the Apocrypha as authoritative, and he apparently accepted the historicity of the incident in the *Assumption of Moses*. He used his reference more as an illustration to substantiate his points.

BASIC OUTLINE FOR JUDE

I. Greetings (vv. 1–2)
II. Occasion for Writing (vv. 3–4)
III. Description of the False Teachers (vv. 5–16)
IV. Resisting the False Teachers (vv. 17–23)
V. Doxology (vv. 24–25)

QUESTIONS TO GUIDE YOUR STUDY

1. What was Jude's purpose for writing this letter?
2. Who was his audience? Where were they located?
3. What is the relationship of Jude's letter to 2 Peter?
4. What is Gnosticism? Why did Jude react so strongly to its presence in the Christian community?

JUDE

SALUTATION (1–2)

Jude identified himself as a follower of Christ and "a brother of James" (v. 1). Jude is listed among the brothers of Jesus (Mark 6:3). His brother James gave no geographical designation to his readers, but he presented them as those who were "called," "loved by God," and "kept for Jesus Christ." This threefold wish is an example of Jude's affinity for triads, groupings of threes.

CHARACTERISTICS OF JUDE'S READERS IN VERSE 2

READER CHARACTERISTIC	EXPLANATION
"Called"	Those who accepted the invitation to become disciples of Jesus..
"Loved by God"	Divine love that always includes positive goodwill towar its object..
"Kept for Jesus Christ"	Jesus keeps a watchful care over them and protects them from harm..

HISTORICAL BACKGROUND

Apocrypha

The Apocrypha is a collective term referring to a large body of religious writings dating back to the early Christian centuries. These writings are similar in form to the New Testament but were never included as a part of the canon of Scripture. In the formation of the Christian canon of Scripture, *apocrypha* came to mean works that were not divinely inspired and authoritative.

The Apocrypha is significant for those who study church history. Even though these writings are not included in the Christian canon, they still have value. They give a sample of the ideas, convictions, and imaginations of a portion of Christian history. While the New Testament Apocrypha is often interesting and informative, it is usually unreliable historically and always unauthoritative for matters of faith and practice.

PERSONAL APPLICATION

The force (tense) of the verbs "loved" and "kept" emphasize God's continuing love and protection. Believers of Jesus today may also take comfort in Jude's greeting to his brothers and sisters in Christ, knowing that God exercises the same love and protection for us.

Jude wished his readers an experience of mercy that would allow them to know the benefits of love and peace. By using the word "multiplied," Jude was wishing they might see mercy, love, and peace increase in their Christian experience.

Section Summary

Jude's greeting is a wish of God's love and protection upon his readers as well as a desire to see God's love and peace multiply in their lives.

A PLEA FOR SOUND DOCTRINE (3–4)

A Shared Salvation (v. 3)

Most scholars agree that Jude originally prepared to write a letter about the mutual body of Christian teachings ("the salvation we share") but diverted his attention toward a growing heresy because of its imminent threat to the faith of hhis readers.

A Defense for the Faith (v. 3)

When Jude learned of the presence of heretics among them who denied Christ, he urged his friends into a continuous, vigorous defense of the faith: "contend for the faith" (v. 3). The word translated *contend* is used only here in the New Testament. This verb expresses the kind of intensity seen in wrestlers. This contention for the faith is not a one-time action but is continuous.

The faith is that body of truth that came to be recognized as the essentials of Christianity.

Contending for the faith involves (1) defending the faith against threat or attack, and (2) living godly, obedient lives to resist heresy.

WORD PICTURE

Faith

Although the term *faith* usually means a personal commitment in the Bible, here it has the definite article ("the") and clearly seems to refer to a body of Christian teachings or doctrines. That this faith "delivered to the saints once for all" further underscores that Jude was referring to an established body of teachings.

The Problem Group (v. 4)

Apparently, a group has "come in by stealth" to the Christian community. Jude described this group as "ungodly" who stood condemned before God because of their denial of Jesus's lordship. These men crept in secretly, were teaching false doctrines, and were were living in sin. There are two likely ways these men were denying Christ:

1. By rejecting his deity
2. By living sinful lives contrary to Jesus's teaching (see 2 Pet 2:1

Section Summary

The salvation the believers possessed was a common salvatio—that is, one they shared. Jude urged his readers to defend the faith vigorously, the body of teachings that had been entrusted to them.

A WARNING AGAINST FALSE DOCTRINE (5–16)

A Lesson from History (vv. 5–7)

The teaching about God's grace and forgiveness has been distorted repeatedly from tbeginning to imply that we can do anything we want and still be God's people.

The tendency to sentimentalize God's love in the last two centuries has come from a neglect of the Old Testament and a reading of the New Testament selectively.

Here Jude cites three cases of God's judgment in history. These cases show God's eternal opposition to evil:

1. The judgment of God in the wilderness (Num 32:10–13

God graciously delivered his people from slavery in Egypt. He provided food and water for them daily on their journey from Egypt to Canaan. He protected them from their enemies in miraculous ways. His intention was to give them and their children a rich inheritance in the land he promised to Abraham.

And ye almost all of Israel rebelled against God. As a consequence, his anger burned against them, and he determined that only Joshua and Caleb would enter the promised land. He allowed the rest to wander in the wilderness for forty years and die.

2. The angels who lost their positions of authority because they disobeyed Go
3. As a result, they have been imprisoned until the day of judgment. The likely reference here is Gen 6:4 as interpreted in the book of Enoch.
4. The destruction of Sodom and Gomorrah (Gen 19:24–29

The sins of these cities were so great that God destroyed them—sparing only Lot and his family.

These three instances show God's strong aversion to sin. Jude implies that God hasn't changed—that he is still opposed to sin.

HISTORICAL BACKGROUND

Contend

The word for *contend* is a compound word made up of two words: (1) a preposition that means "upon" or "about," attached to (2) a verb that means "to contest." The attached preposition serves to intensify the verb. In some translations, the word *earnestly* is added to convey the intensive force of the preposition.

Therefore, *contend* means "to struggle for, to contend for, to exercise great effort and exertion for something." It was often used of those who participated in athletic contests, describing their struggles and efforts to win the prize.See *Vine's Complete Expository Dictionary of Old and New Testament Words* (Thomas Nelson, 1996) 125.

A Description of the False Teachers (vv. 8–13)

Jude characterizes the false teachers as dreamers, which could refer to their relying on dreams as a source of their teaching, or they could be so out of touch with reality that they were characterized as dreamers.

He charges them with defiling their bodies, rebelling against authority, and making fun of angels. Apparently, they were so focused on the flesh that they talked glibly about spiritual realities, the existence of which they may have doubted.

Examples from the Old Testament. Here Jude used historical examples from the Old Testament to characterize the false teachers as materialistic and immoral. These characteristics include:

- Unreasoning animal
- Shepherds who feed only themselve
- Clouds without rai
- Barren tree without fruit and uproote
- Wild waves of the sea that wash up refuse
- Wandering stars for whom blackest darkness has been reserve

Jude charged the false teachers with leading others astray. He then referred to some well-known examples of Old Testament deceivers who led many astray: Cain, Balaam, and Korah.

HISTORICAL BACKGROUND

"'Wandering stars' referred to the erratic orbits of planets, sometimes attributed to disobedient angels, who were to be imprisoned under God's judgement and are called 'stars' in 1 Enoch."*The IVP Bible Background Commentary, New Testament* (InterVarsity Press, 1993) 755.

OLD TESTAMENT DECEIVERS'"HALL OF SHAME"

CHARACTER	SIN
Cain	"The way of Cain"; rejected God's revelation and refused to make a blood sacrifice; worshiped God his own way
Balaam	Greed; led others into sins for personal gain
Korah	Rebelliousness; rejected the authority of Moses and tried to assume power for himself

A Picture from 1 Enoch. Jude cited a statement, a picture of judgment, from 1 Enoch 1:9 to prove the reality of divine judgment upon the ungodly. It speaks of the eventual judgment of wicked people like false teachers. Jesus made a similar statement when he said, "When the Son of Man comes in his glory, and all the angels with him" (Matt 25:31). Jude is not necessarily viewing *1 Enoch* as inspired Scripture, but he is referring to a book his readers would know and respect.

Concluding Remarks. Jude closed this section by making a final characterization of the false teachers. The characteristics he chose to describe them include:

- Grumbler
- Faultfinder
- Lustfu
- Boastful
- Flatterer

Section Summary

Jude issued warnings to the false teachers. He drew examples from history, the Old Testament, and extrabiblical literature to expose the evil characteristics of these heretics. God will hold these evil men accountable for their actions.

ENCOURAGEMENT TO FAITHFULNESS (17–23)

Contending for the Faith Through Argument (vv. 17–19)

Jude reminded his readers "what was predicted by the apostles of our Lord Jesus Christ" (v. 17). This body of apostolic writings included predictions that "in the end time there will be scoffers living according to their own ungodly desires" (v. 18). The scoffers would come, bringing their divisiveness and spiritual emptiness. Likely, Jude was referring to such general warnings as Acts 20:29–30 and 1 Tim 4:1–3 to show that the apostles foretold the coming of these men.

Contending for the Faith Through Spiritual Growth (vv. 20–23)

Jude wanted his readers to build up themselves with prayer and obedience. He urged his readers to practice five disciplines that would prepare them to resist the false teachers who had infiltrated their community:

1. To build up themselves in their knowledge of God's trut
2. To pray ferventl.
3. To live in the sphere of God's love by obeying his command
4. To fan the flames of Christian hop.
5. To practice evangelism and pastoral care with those who might be enticed into following false teaching

Section Summary

Jude wanted his readers to remain faithful to God. They were to contend for the faith by remembering what the apostles foretold and by growing spiritually, practicing several disciplines Jude set forth.

DOXOLOGY (24–25)

Jude closed his letter with an unusually beautiful and meaningful doxology. His mind focused on the power of almighty God, who alone provides the strength for full obedience.

In verse 24 he praised God for his sustaining power toward believers. "To him who is able to protect you from stumbling" refers to God who can keep believers from yielding to temptation, whether or not it relates to false teaching.

In verse 25 he ascribed "glory, majesty, power, and authority" to God because of the work of Jesus Christ. Although Jude devoted a good deal of his letter to false teachers and the works of darkness, he concluded by focusing his letter on the attributes of God.

PERSONAL APPLICATION

"This conclusion of the epistle of Jude is grand and soul-stirring. It lifts the thoughts from earthly conflicts with which the author has been compelled to busy himself, up to the heavenly realms, where God is enthroned amidst eternal might and honor. The fight against evil forces in this narrow and dark world should always be viewed in such a luminous cosmic perspective."Bo Reike from *The Epistles of James, Peter, and Jude*, Anchor Bible (Doubleday , 1964), 217.

QUESTIONS TO GUIDE YOUR STUDY

1. What is the best way to "contend" for Christian truth? (See also John 13:34–35; 14:21.)
2. What are some of the characteristics of false teachers Jude mentioned in verses 5–16? How common are these traits today?
3. Drawing from the content of his letter, what did Jude's readers have in common with believers today?
4. What are some of the truths about God that we see in Jude's doxology in verses 24–25?

Revelation

INTRODUCTION

WHAT KIND OF BOOK IS THIS?

The book of Revelation is unique. There is nothing like it in the rest of the New Testament or in the Old Testament. It is a letter (like Paul's Letters) sent to seven historical churches. It identifies itself as a prophecy (1:3; 19:10; 22:7). It has numerous symbols and features like Jewish apocalyptic writings. So it is an apocalyptic-prophetic letter or an apocalyptic prophecy in the form of a circular letter.

Revelation is a book that is full of allusions and references to the Old Testament, but it has hardly any full quotations like many New Testament books. The title for this book in the first line is *The Revelation of Jesus Christ.* The revelation is *of* Jesus Christ in two ways. First, he is the revealer (cp. Matt 11:27; John 1:18), and second, he is the content or object of the revelation. We learn about the nature and activities of Jesus of Nazareth as he is today and his future victory or reign in this world. Revelation is a fitting conclusion to the whole Bible. So as the Bible is read, themes in early books like Genesis and Exodus come to completion. The biblical narrative comes to its goals. The kingdom of God is established, sinful rebellion in the world and in heaven is punished, and humanity is redeemed and restored to personal fellowship with God.

HISTORICAL BACKGROUND

Apocalyptic describes writings that employ symbolic language to tell of a divine intervention which will take place in the future.

WORD PICTURE

Revelation

Revelation means "unveiling" or making known what was previously hidden.

WHAT IS REVELATION ABOUT?

Revelation describes a great conflict which began with a rebellion among the angels in heaven itself (cp. 12:7–8). This war between the forces of light and the forces of darkness spread to earth and has continued from the time of Gen 3 until today. Revelation describes the intensification and the culmination of the struggle in the climax of the ages. This warfare is between two kingdoms and two cities: God's kingdom versus Satan's kingdom (including rebellious humans); Babylon the great versus the new Jerusalem. Elements of this conflict include martyrs, persecutions,

PERSONAL APPLICATION

Revelation promises to bless the person who reads it and applies it to his or her life (1:3; 22:7).

battles, and great judgments (cp. 1:9; 2:10; 2:13; 3:10; 6:9–11; 7:14; 11:7; 12:4,6–7,13; 17:14; 19:19; 20:7–8).

At face value, a good part of the book (chaps. 4–19) describes what it calls "the great tribulation" (7:14) or "the hour of testing" (3:10). This is a unique period in the history of the world that Jesus himself predicted would be "days of tribulation" unequaled in the long time from creation (cp. Mark 13:14–19). This is a period of the reign of the antichrist and also a time of great judgments on the earth. The following passages of Scripture are related to this "great tribulation" (Dan 12:1; Joel 2:31; Jer 30:7–8; Matt 24:15–24; 2 Thess 2:3–12; Rev 13:8).

The major themes of this book are related to two symbols: "the lamb," used twenty-nine times, and "the throne," which occurs forty times. The *Lamb* is a title of Jesus, and the *throne* is a symbol of God's rule and authority. The book describes the triumph of Jesus as God's Messiah and unique Son and how the sovereignty of God is manifested in redemption, judgment, rule, and the new creation.

WHO WROTE REVELATION?

The writer identifies himself as "John" (1:1,4,9; 22:8) and his writing as a prophecy (22:19). The book was accepted as Scripture, and the author was understood to be John the apostle, who wrote 1–3 John and the Gospel of John.

However, beginning with Dionysius of Alexandria (died around 264), many have been opposed to the millennial (Rev 20:1–7) teaching of the book, and arguments have developed against the authorship by John, son of Zebedee. Many modern scholars reject Johannine authorship, and there has been a neglect of this writing among the theologians. For example, Luther and Zwingli, early reformers, had little respect for the book. Calvin wrote commentaries on each New Testament book except for Revelation and on a large part of the Old Testament. Part of the problem has been the use of the book by unorthodox teachers or by fanatics. Part of the neglect is due to its symbolism. Another part is its Jewishness or its millennial teaching which is contrary to the European church tradition since Augustine (died AD 430).

A good defense of Johannine authorship can be made. The early witness of the six church fathers named above could hardly be better. The following list shows some of the links between John's Gospel, his epistles, and Revelation.

HISTORICAL BACKGROUND

The testimony of Justin Martyr, Irenaeus, Hippolytus, Tertullian, Clement of Alexandria, and Origen is strong support for John the apostle as the writer of the book.

All books use simple, common Greek vocabulary.

- In the Gospel and Revelation, there is a similar use of *logos.*
- In the Gospel and Revelation, there is a similar use of sign and *signify*.

- In the Gospel and Revelation, common key terms are *witness* and *testify*.
- Common use of the verb (*nikaō*) to *conquer*, or *overcome*.
- Both the Gospel (6:31) and Revelation (2:17) use a *manna* theme.
- Both the Gospel (4:21) and Revelation (21:22) say that a temple is not needed for worship.
- Both the Gospel (10:1) and Revelation (7:17) say Jesus is the Shepherd.
- Both the Gospel (4:10,14; 7:38) and Revelation (7:17; 21:6; 22:17) use the terms *water* and *springs* to describe salvation or eternal life.
- Both the Gospel (19:37) and Revelation (1:7) have a unique citation from Zech 12:10. Neither book cites Scripture often.
- The structures of both the Gospel and Revelation are built on *sevens:* seven signs, seven churches, and so forth.
- Common usage in John's Gospel, his epistles, and Revelation of the charge to keep God's commandments.
- Common dualism in all John's writings: God/Satan; world/church; good/evil; light/darkness.

While it cannot be absolutely proven that John son of Zebedee wrote Revelation, the weight of evidence is heavy in favor of this conclusion.

WHEN WAS IT WRITTEN?

From Irenaeus in AD 180 (John saw the revelation at the close of Domitian's reign), the majority view has been that the date is AD 95. This fits with internal and external evidence.

WORD PICTURE

True, Truth

The Greek word *alēthinos* (true, truth) occurs twenty-eight times in the New Testament. Of these, it occurs in John's Gospel nine times, John's epistles four times, and Revelation ten times—or twenty-three of the twenty-eight usages in the New Testament. Other similarities can be found with the use of a concordance to compare the usage of words and phrases.

AUTHOR AND AUDIENCE

According to Revelation, John was exiled to the prison island of Patmos during the reign of the Roman emperor Domitian because of his commitment to Jesus Christ and his word (1:9). John, who was a member of the "inner circle" of Jesus's disciples (Peter, James, and John), ministered first in the Jerusalem church but later moved to Ephesus. John's later ministry during the reign of Domitian (AD 81–96) ran into conflict with the Roman government. Since the time of Nero (AD 64), Christians were viewed as "enemies of mankind" who practiced an illegal religion.

The audience for Revelation was seven literal churches in Roman Asia. But the whole letter was sent to each one and applied to all Christians (1:4,11; 2:1,8,18, etc.). For the universal application, see 1:3; 2:7, 11,17,29; 22:6–7,9,16,18–19. As a book of the Bible, it is God's Word not only to the churches of the first century but also to the churches of all ages.

HISTORICAL BACKGROUND

Ephesus was a leading church in the Roman province of Asia. Under Paul, Ephesus became a center for evangelism and teaching (Acts 19:9–10).

STRUCTURE AND OUTLINE	
Prologue	1:1–8
John's Commission and Vision of Jesus	1:9–20
The Letters to the Seven Churches	Chapters 2–3
The Vision of the Heavenly Throne Room	Chapters 4–5
The Seven Seal Judgments	6:1–8:5
The Sealing of the 144,000	7:1–17
The Great Multitude in White Robes	8:1–5
The Seven Trumpet Judgments	8:6–11:19
The Angel with the Little Scroll	10:1–11:13
The Two Witnesses	11:14–19
The Cosmic and Earthly Struggles	Chapters 12–14
The Beast out of the Sea	13:1–10
The Beast out of the Land	13:11–18
The Seven Bowl Judgments	Chapters 15–16
Babylon the Great Doomed	17:1–19:10
The Return of the Lord	19:11–21
The Thousand-Year Reign of Christ	20:1–6
The Final Judgments	20:7–15
The New Heaven and New Earth	21:1–22:5
The New Jerusalem	
Epilogue	22:6–21

HOW SHOULD REVELATION BE INTERPRETED?

Because this book is unique, it has been interpreted in many ways down through the centuries. The following synopsis will outline the major options which are not entirely in opposition to one another:

- *Poetic-Symbolic View*. The book is understood as a dramatic poem of the triumph of God. The poem is more like an abstract or expressionist painting than a blueprint for the ages. Others do not call it a poem but emphasize spiritual interpretation.
- *Historical-Critical View*. This view does not usually hold to prophecy as a genuine gift which is able to "see" the future. The events of the book are understood in terms of the first-century Roman Empire and the fall of Jerusalem (AD 70).

- *Historicist View.* This approach sees the course of church history revealed in the visions.
- *The Futurist, or Eschatological View.* This view holds that the main thrust of the book concerns the future. The events from chapter 4 to the end are mainly but not exclusively about events of the great tribulation, the return of Jesus Christ, the thousand-year reign, the last judgment, and the eternal state.

This *Shepherd's Notes'* interpretation will be futurist while using insights from the other points of view. As indicated in the section entitled *What Is This Book About?*, a normal reading of the text puts a large part (chaps. 4–19) into the future tribulation. While using many symbols, John did intend that his readers would be able to grasp the meaning and understand what was coming in the future.

REVELATION 1

PROLOGUE (1:1–8)

Introduction to the Book (1:1–3)

John explains what this writing is about. It is an *apokalupsis* or "unveiling" of Jesus Christ that God gave to him. The Father and the Son are united in revealing the nature and future of Jesus (cp. Matt 11:25–27; John 5:19; 8:26). Jesus sends an angel to help John in the understanding of the visions. John is given this revelation so he can transmit it for the church's profit.

Revelation 1:3 indicates that the oral reading of this book would be done in the Christian congregations (cp. Col 4:16; 1 Thess 5:27). A blessing is pronounced upon everyone who responds positively to the message. This blessing is the first of seven in the book (1:3; 14:13; 16:15; 19:9; 20:6; 22:7; 22:14), and all seven point out what is of special importance.

THE SEVEN BLESSINGS

BLESSED ARE THOSE	REF.
Who hear and obey	1:3
Who die in the Lord	14:13
Who look for Christ's return	16:15
Who are invited to the messianic banquet	19:9
Who have part in the first resurrection	20:6
Who keep the words of the prophecy of this book	22:7
Who wash their robes (cp. 7:14)	22:14

John says that "the time is near" (v. 3). From John the Baptist, from Jesus, and from the apostles, there is a constant emphasis on the time of crisis or decision. In Revelation, the following passages announce the nearness of the end: 1:1,3; 2:16,25; 3:11,20; 6:11; 10:6; 11:2–3; 12:6, 12; 17:10; 22:6–7,10,12,20.

The Address, Greeting, and Ascription (1:4–6)

John addresses his prophecy to the seven churches in Roman proconsular Asia (this today is western Turkey). These churches were chosen because of John's knowledge of them and ministry among them. These churches are representative of all churches at that time and of churches today. So the message has individual and local significance as well as universal application.

The message comes from both the Father and the Son. The "seven spirits" cannot be exactly identified (cp. Isa 11:2; Rev 4:5; 5:6). The Son is depicted in a number of titles that show his nature and work. Christians are a kingdom of priests (cp. Exod 19:6) who have direct access to God and minister to him in worship and minister to a world in darkness.

OLD TESTAMENT REFERENCE

The use of an interpreting angel is common in what is called apocalyptic literature, and this sometimes is found in the Old Testament prophetic books, especially in Zechariah (1:9,12,14; 2:3; 3:6; 4:1,11).

The Theme (1:7–8)

The theme of the book is the return of Jesus the Messiah in the second coming. He is the same person who came to Bethlehem as a baby and went to the cross as the Suffering Servant of Isa 53. But in his return, he comes as the victorious Son of Man who will judge the earth in righteousness and inaugurate God's rule as the kingdom of God on earth. Verse 7 combines elements from two key Old Testament prophecies: Daniel 7:13, which describes the coming reign of the Son of Man, and Zech 12:10, which predicts the piercing of the Messiah (John 19:37). All the "tribes of the earth" (not just of Israel) will have regret and remorse when the regal nature of Jesus is revealed in its divine splendor.

HISTORICAL BACKGROUND

In the ancient world, not everyone could read (some estimate only 20–30 percent were able), and not many could afford books.

PERSONAL APPLICATION

Christians today should remember that Jesus told his disciples to watch and wait and that no one knows the exact time of his return except the Father in heaven (Mark 13:32–33).

THE CIRCUMSTANCES OF THE COMMISSION (1:9–11)

John was in exile on a prison island called Patmos. Most likely, around AD 95, the Roman government began some scattered persecution of Christians. Nero had already done this in Rome in AD 64, and soon after both Peter and Paul were killed. John's ministry focused on Jesus and his word. Rome was beginning to exalt the emperor as a semidivine being, and the Christian faith was illegal.

John's commission came in a dramatic way while he was worshiping on a Sunday. A trumpet voice summoned him to write a scroll and send it to the seven churches.

THE REVELATION OF THE GLORIFIED JESUS (1:12–16)

John first saw seven golden lampstands and someone like "the Son of Man." The lampstand (cp. Exod 25:31–37) is a symbol of the church (according to 1:20), and its function is to bring light to a darkened world (cp. Matt 5:14–16). "Son of Man" was a favorite self-designation of Jesus. It had several Old Testament connections. Jesus on earth was the suffering Son of Man, but now he is seen as a heavenly high priest with holiness and power. Just as we cannot look directly at the midday sun, so John could not look directly at his glory (cp. the similar experience John had at the transfiguration—Matt 17:5–8).

JOHN'S RESPONSE AND JESUS'S REASSURANCE (1:17–20)

Paul says that God dwells in unapproachable light (1 Tim 6:15–16), and the ancient Israelites trembled before Mount Sinai as it blazed with divine fire. But Jesus touched John and reassured him that he had come to commission John to a special prophetic task. Verse 19 is often understood as an inspired three-point outline of the contents of the book: "what you have seen" (glorified Christ), "what is" (the churches), and "what will take place after this" (the tribulation, millennium, judgment, and consummation). Others see a commission to write what he has seen—both what is and what is to follow (a two-point division). The three-point view seems better since John had only seen the risen Lord and not the churches or coming events at this time.

A major interpretive problem revolves around the "stars," which are interpreted as the "angels" of the churches. Four views are common: (1) A guardian angel for each church. Pro: "star" is interpreted by Christ as "angel." The normal meaning of "angel" in Revelation is a spirit being. Con: How do you write to an angel? (2) "Angel" = pastor, elder, or bishop. This is possible but unusual language. (3) "Angel" = messenger. The Greek word is sometimes used for this (Mal 2:7; 3:1; Luke 9:52) and fits historical context. Roman postal service was for imperial use. Businesses and congregations had to develop their own mail system. (4) "Angel" = the church personified. This view seems best.

Section Summary

Jesus, the resurrected Lord, appeared to John in a vision and commissioned him to write to seven churches in the Roman province of Asia. The content of his writing is to be a series of visions of the future and of the present.

HISTORICAL BACKGROUND

Patmos was a small island (ten miles by six miles) in the Aegean Sea located about thirty-seven miles southwest of Miletus. The Romans used such places for political exiles. John's mention of the island in Rev 1:9 probably means that he was such a prisoner, having been sent there for preaching the gospel. Eusebius (an early church father) wrote that John was sent to Patmos by Emperor Domitian in AD 95 and released after one and one-half years.

OLD TESTAMENT REFERENCE

The vision that preceded John's writing is similar to Isaiah's (6:1) and Ezekiel's (chap. 1).

OLD TESTAMENT REFERENCE

When only a little of God's glory shows, it is common to fall on one's face. "The appearance of the brilliant light all around was like that of a rainbow in a cloud on a rainy day. This was the appearance of the likeness of the LORD's glory. When I saw it, I fell facedown and heard a voice speaking" (Ezek 1:28). "So he approached where I was standing; when he came near, I was terrified and fell facedown. 'Son of man,' he said to me, 'understand that the vision refers to the time of the end'" (Dan 8:17; see also Isa 6 and Josh 5:14).

PERSONAL APPLICATION

The purpose of Christians and churches is to show God and Jesus to the world.

QUESTIONS TO GUIDE YOUR STUDY

1. What are the seven blessings promised in Revelation?
2. Where was John when he saw the vision recorded in Revelation?
3. What was John's response to Jesus's appearance?

REVELATION 2

THE LETTER TO EPHESUS: THE LOVELESS CHURCH (2:1–6)

Each letter follows a similar pattern, but not all elements occur in each:

- Command to write
- Description of the glorified Lord
- Positive evaluation
- Encouragement, warning
- Exhortation to the spiritually alert
- Promise to the overcomer

OLD TESTAMENT REFERENCE

"The LORD God said, 'Since the man has become like one of us, knowing good and evil, he must not reach out, take from the tree of life, eat, and live forever.' So the LORD God sent him away from the garden of Eden to work the ground from which he was taken. He drove the man out and stationed the cherubim and the flaming, whirling sword east of the garden of Eden to guard the way to the tree of life" (Gen 3:22–24).

Jesus is in the midst of the churches, and he knows what is going on. The church in Ephesus was battle-tested and orthodox, but somehow it lost its love. Love is primary. Without it the church has no reason to exist. The exhortation is to all the churches and so is the promise. The tree of life (Gen 2:9; 3:22–24) lost in Eden is regained in paradise (Rev 22:2). The dying thief on the cross was promised this by Jesus (Luke 23:43).

THE LETTER TO SMYRNA: THE PERSECUTED CHURCH (2:7–11)

The word *Smyrna* is connected to myrrh and to suffering in the Bible. Some people and some churches are called to suffer. Today in ninety countries in the world (of 193 in the United Nations), there is persecution of Christians. Jesus reveals himself as sovereign over death. He calls his people to be faithful to him despite economic or political persecution which may lead to death. The Christian is the winner in the race of life and receives a wreath or garland which is a picture of eternal life (cp. 1 Cor 9:25; 2 Tim 4:8; James 1:2; 1 Pet 5:4).

NEW TESTAMENT REFERENCE

"The tree of life was on each side of the river, bearing twelve kinds of fruit, producing its fruit every month. The leaves of the tree are for healing the nations" (Rev 22:2).

THE LETTER TO PERGAMUM: THE COMPROMISING CHURCH (2:12–17)

This church was located in the first city in Asia Minor that was the official center for emperor worship. The city was also a center for the worship of Askepios Soter and Zeus Soter. Both were connected to the serpent image. The expression "where Satan's throne is" may refer to a large throne altar on top of a high granite citadel. One of the major

The Seven Churches of Revelation

issues of first-century Christianity was separation or accommodation to paganism. Much of the business life was connected to trade guilds or organizations which met for meals that were held in temple halls. The meat sacrificed to these idols was served at their banquets. Often sexual immorality was part of these banquets. From Balaam (about 1400 BC; cp. Num 22:1–24 and 25:1–3), who corrupted Israel, to the Nicolaitans of John's days, God's people have been tempted to make accommodations to pagan culture and its destructive practices. Paul wrote often of this issue (1 Cor 8:1–12; 10:14–33).

To those who compromise, Jesus warned of his coming judgment. To those who resist, he promised "hidden manna" and a "white stone." Manna was the food God's people lived on in the wilderness wanderings (Exod 16:32–34). Jesus is the real manna for Christians to live on (John 6:48–51). The "white stone" means acceptance by God (compare our idiom "blackballed"). On the stone is a new name. Jesus changed the name of Simon to *Peter,* and often in the Old Testament God changed the names of his people as he gave them spiritual blessings (cp. *Jacob* = *Heel-Grabber* to *Israel* = *Prince of God* or *He Who Struggles with God;* Gen 32:28).

PERSONAL APPLICATION

Today, Christians in business must be wary of compromise at trade conventions, drinking parties, and other similar occasions. Often in the business world, people are corrupted by gambling, immorality, alcohol, and drugs. In some cultures, these are tools for business advantage over the weak.

THE LETTER TO THYATIRA: THE CORRUPT CHURCH (2:18–29)

This letter addresses a church which compromised with paganism. However, this church seems more corrupt. The city was prominent for its trade guilds. Christian workers were at the mercy of organized pagan society. A woman claiming to be a prophetess arose. She encouraged accommodation to pagan culture. Her promotion of paganism was like that of Jezebel in the Old Testament (1 Kgs 16:29; 2 Kgs 9:30).

Jesus reveals himself to this church as One who disciplines his people. Physical death was the penalty for some sins in the early church as God taught about his holiness (cp. Acts 5:1–11; 1 Cor 11:27–30).

Jesus rewards the overcomer with a gift of himself in a new and special way—"the morning star" (cp. 22:16; Num 24:17). The believer will share in the messianic rule of Jesus over the pagan nations of the world (Ps 2:8–9). But a compromise now will lead to judgment. Resist the world now and rule with Christ in the millennium.

NEW TESTAMENT REFERENCE

The decision of the first major church meeting (recorded in Acts 15) spoke to sexual immorality and meats offered to idols.

REVELATION 3

THE LETTER TO SARDIS: THE DEAD CHURCH (3:1–6)

"Pride goes before a fall." This proud city had been the capital of an empire and the home of the famous king Croesus. Twice in its history, secure in a high acropolis, the city failed to watch its defenses. An enemy army came and by stealth took the city. Jesus warns the sleeping church of his coming. "Christians—wake up!" "Be spiritually alert!" "Are you prepared for his coming?"

The faithful Christian will participate in the victory triumph of Jesus. The white garment was worn in Roman triumphs. We receive a white garment from Jesus symbolizing our righteousness. Our names are enrolled—not in a state citizen-register or a synagogue roll or even a royal archive but in God's book of life (cp. Exod 32:32–33). Jesus will bring our names before God the Father. He owns us as his friends and his brothers and calls each of us by name (John 15:13–14; Heb 2:11–13; 1 John 3:1).

THE LETTER TO PHILADELPHIA: THE FAITHFUL CHURCH (3:7–13)

Jesus is in control of our lives. He is the Holy One (Isa 40:25; John 6:69) who has the key of David (Isa 22:22). This "key" is to the messianic kingdom. He rules over it and has brought us into it (Col 1:13) to reign with him (Rev 20:4, 6). Christ gives spiritual opportunities to his people (cp. 1 Cor 16:9) and to churches. When God opens a door, no power can resist. As Jesus promised Peter, not even Hades can resist (Matt 16:18–19).

Jesus warns of a time of trial for the whole pagan world. It is called the "great tribulation" or "the hour of testing" (Rev 3:10; cp. Mark 13:19; Jesus calls it a uniquely horrible period of human history). This "testing" is upon the unbelieving inhabitants of the earth (3:10; 6:10; 8:13; 11:10; 13:8,12,14; 17:2,8). Although many people will be saved during these years—7:9 says a "vast multitude"—the day is a day of great wrath and judgment on human sin and rebellion (Rev 6:17).

The faithful church is preserved and protected, and the individual is inscribed with God's name. This denotes permanent ownership. We are also promised to be a "pillar" in God's temple—an essential part with permanence.

PERSONAL APPLICATION

We live in a day of great spiritual opportunity. The churches in America and in many other countries have a "door flung wide open" by God. Missions, radio, TV, the Internet, movies, podcasts, CDs, books, magazines, the Bible in English as a global language, little government interference—all combine to offer amazing outreach for the church.

THE LETTER TO LAODICEA: THE LUKEWARM CHURCH (3:14–22)

The descriptions of Jesus in verse 14—"the Amen," "the faithful and true witness"—have strong connections to the Gospel of John as major themes in that book. The phrase "the originator of God's creation" means Jesus Christ is the Source of all creation (cp. John 1:1–3)—not that he is a part of the creation.

The city of Laodicea had problems with its water supply. Unlike the nearby cities of Colossae with good cold water or Hierapolis with hot

CHURCHES OF REVELATION

CHURCH	STRENGTHS	WEAKNESSES	CHALLENGE	TO THE ONE WHO CONQUERS
Ephesus 2:1–7	Right theology, defense of the faith, and moral behavior	Abandoned the love they had at first	Remember how far they had fallen, repent, and do the works they did at first.	Jesus will give the right to eat from the tree of life, which is in the paradise of God.
Smyrna 2:8–11	Rich in faith despite affliction and poverty	–	Don't fear suffering but remain faithful, even to the point of death.	Jesus will give the crown of life, never harmed by the second death.
Pergamum 2:12–17	Holding on to Jesus's name without denying their faith in him despite persecution	Some hold to false teachings, living lives of immorality	Repent.	Jesus will give some of the hidden manna; he will also give a white stone with a new name.
Thyatira 2:18–29	Love faithfulness, service, endurance; last works greater than the first	Tolerating a false prophetess and teacher who encouraged immorality	Those who commit adultery with her must repent; those who don't hold this teaching must hold on to what they have until he comes.	Jesus will give authority over the nations, just as Jesus received from his Father; he will also give the morning star.
Sardis 3:1–6	A few people have not defiled their clothes (v. 4)	Had a reputation for being alive, but they were dead	Be alert and strengthen what remains, which is about to die; remember what they have received and heard: keep it and repent.	Will be dressed in white clothes and name will never be erased from the book of life; will be acknowledged by Jesus before his Father and the angels.

CHURCHES OF REVELATION

CHURCH	STRENGTHS	WEAKNESSES	CHALLENGE	TO THE ONE WHO CONQUERS
Philadelphia 3:7–13	Kept Jesus's word and did not deny his name; kept his command to endure	–	Hold on to what they have so that no one takes their crown.	Jesus will make them pillars in the temple of God, never to go out again; Jesus will write on them the name of the city of God and his new name.
Laodicea 3:14–22	–	Neither cold nor hot (useful) but lukewarm; self-focused and deceived	Focus on Jesus; be zealous and repent.	Jesus will give the right to sit with him on his throne, just as he conquered and sat down with his Father on the throne.

water for thermal baths, Laodicea had only lukewarm water that made a person vomit!

Unfortunately, a church is often like its environment. This city was rich, and this apparently led to complacency. How many "rich" Americans today are thankful enough to say "thanks" at their beautiful and bountiful meals? After a great earthquake in AD 60, the city of Laodicea declared, "I don't need any help from the government to rebuild—I'm rich." The church can become complacent and lukewarm and fail to recognize its need of the Lord and his grace. This church was spiritually blind to its true condition.

Paul reminded the Corinthian church: "What do you have that you didn't receive?" (1 Cor 4:7). All comes from God; therefore, we must constantly go to him. Jesus reveals himself to this church as One who stands at the door and knocks. Perhaps this alludes to a monumental triple gate at the entrance to the city. But in the spiritual realm, Jesus is before each individual and graciously inviting each one to personal fellowship with him (3:20).

PERSONAL APPLICATION

Although each letter is addressed to a specific local church with its own unique problems, each letter has individual and universal applications to every Christian in every age. Jesus, the Lord, is in the center of our local churches, and he knows what each one is doing. For the church to prosper, it needs to follow the orders of the Lord.

QUESTIONS TO GUIDE YOUR STUDY

1. Which of these seven churches is most like your local church?
2. Summarize briefly Jesus's appraisal of each church.
3. What is the greatest danger to your church today?

REVELATION 4

THE THRONE ROOM IN HEAVEN (4:1–6)

Just as "mission control" is the place that directs space exploration, the throne room in heaven controls the universe and, specifically, the action about to take place on earth. John was taken to heaven to see a vision of the future (4:1). What does God look like? John did not say other than his appearance of jasper and carnelian stone (cp. 1 Tim 6:16).

WORD PICTURE

Angel

The Hebrew and Greek words (*malak* and *angelos*) are not as specific as our EngKgsh word. They mean "messenger" and describe the function of angels.

THE WORSHIP OF HEAVEN (4:6b-11)

Because we do not see God as he is in his glory and power, we do not worship him as we should. Other created beings—the living creatures and the twenty-four elders—have a clearer vision so they can teach us. Both groups are most likely heavenly creatures of different classes of angels. We are not alone in the universe (cp. 2 Kgs 6:16–17; Matt 26:53; Heb 12:22), but we share it with many other intelligent beings. Paul says other intelligent heavenly creatures are learning about God's wisdom through God's plan of salvation in the church (Eph 3:10).

Since the worship of God is the center of the spiritual universe, should it not be the center of our lives? John saw the throne of God where the control of the universe takes place.

PERSONAL APPLICATION

How many other biblical people have been taken to heaven? (See Gen 5:24; Heb 11:5; 2 Kgs 2:11; Ps 73:24; 2 Cor 12:2; Phil 1:23; 1 Thess 4:17). What is your future destiny?

QUESTIONS TO GUIDE YOUR STUDY

1. How do biblical angels differ from the popular image of angels in today's culture?
2. Why should people worship the Lord?
3. What makes a person into a true worshiper (John 4:23)?

WORD PICTURE

Worship

The most common Greek word is *proskuneō* which means to "fall down before" or to prostrate oneself. In addition to the physical posture, the inner attitude of true worship is reverence, humility, and adoration.

REVELATION 5

THE LAMB TAKES THE SCROLL OF DESTINY (5:1–5)

Only the Lamb of God who is also the Lion from Judah's tribe (Gen 49:9–10) has the moral right to open the scroll which will reveal and bring about history's completion. The lion and the lamb represent two aspects of Jesus's nature: the royal and the sacrificial.

THE WORSHIP OF THE LAMB AND OF GOD THE FATHER (5:6–14)

A possible background for this chapter is in Deut 17:18–20 and 2 Kgs 11:12, where a king took his position to rule. At the enthronement ceremony a covenant book was in his hand to guide him in his rule.

The fact that Jesus is to be worshiped shows that he is God. Yet he is not identical with the Father. But this doesn't mean Christians have two or three Gods (Father, Son, and Spirit). The solution to this problem is the doctrine of the Trinity—three eternal persons within one Godhead or divine essence. The Athanasian Creed states: "We worship one God in Trinity, and Trinity in Unity; neither confounding the Persons, nor dividing the Substance."

When God delivered Israel out of Egypt, his people sang a song (Exod 15). Because Jesus has won the victory over Satan, sin, and death, the whole heaven explodes into praise of the Lamb. The four living creatures, the twenty-four elders, the prayers of God's people, and myriads of angels combine in universal adoration: "You made them a kingdom and priests to our God, and they will reign on the earth" (5:10).

Christians are now serving as Israel did (Exod 19:6) with the tasks of worshiping God and making him known to the world. The future is to share Christ's rule on earth (cp. Matt 5:5; Rom 8:17; Rev 20:4). Jesus, as the One who died and is now victorious, holds the book of destiny for the world. By our union with him, we have confidence as we face our future.

HISTORICAL BACKGROUND

The Old Testament background of this scene is Dan 7:10. Ten thousand times ten thousand ministered to God, and the "Son of Man" was invested with the kingdom.

OLD TESTAMENT REFERENCE

The background for this vision is Ezekiel's book of woe (Ezek 2; see also Ps 139:16; Deut 17:18–20; 2 Kgs 11:12). This book is in the form of a scroll with seals. As each seal is opened, more of the scroll can be unfolded (cp. Dan 12:4).

QUESTIONS TO GUIDE YOUR STUDY

1. What do angels do?
2. What does it mean for evangelism that the Lamb has purchased people from every tribe, language, people, and nation?
3. What does the word *worthy* (5:2,9) mean?

REVELATION 6

THE LAMB BREAKS THE SEALS (6:1–17)

In the breaking of each seal, a divine messenger of judgment is summoned to go out into the world. The rider on the white horse symbolizes military power. This rider is not the same as the "Word of God" who also rides a white horse in chapter 19:11–16. This rider starts a series of the tribulation horrors, while the rider in 19:11 represents the victorious return of Jesus to defeat his enemies.

The second rider is on a blood-red horse and pictures a plunging of the world into a great war. The twentieth century brought the deaths

PERSONAL APPLICATION

Singing to the Lord is a vital part of our Christian life. Redemption will lead to worship. Paul told Christians to speak "to one another in psalms, hymns, and spiritual songs, singing and making music with your heart to the Lord" (Eph 5:19). How much do you sing?

of over one hundred million people in wars (fifty million occurred in WWII alone!). Although mankind is advancing in technology, mass destruction has also advanced.

The third horse is black with a scale in the rider's hand. The image is of the famine and scarcity which comes through warfare. The cost of food has multiplied twelve times! Yet this famine is limited by God's mercy.

The fourth rider is on a pale horse. The color is most likely "cadaverous," and the rider is death personified. Hades is closely associated with death as the place where the dead go. This first series of judgments results in a global war over one-fourth of the earth which produces economic hardship, famine, and death.

The fifth seal gives a glimpse of Christian martyrs in heaven. These died for God's Word and his witness. To die in the Lord is to go to be with him (Phil 1:21–23). There is no "soul-sleep" but an immediate translation into his presence. The martyrs are aware of what is transpiring on earth and long for God's justice to be manifested. Each martyr is comforted and clothed by God in white, which symbolizes victory, honor, and righteousness (cp. 3:4; 7:9,13; 19:8). But others will die and join them as they anticipate God's consummation.

The breaking of the sixth seal brings great cosmic disturbances which herald the coming of the day of the Lord or the day of Christ. This "day" is a time to which both the Old Testament and New Testament continually look forward (Joel 2:31; Mal 4:5; Isa 2:12; Jer 25:15; Dan 2:28,44). This is the time of the final establishment of justice and righteousness on earth. Sin will be punished, and the nations will know God's sovereignty and his Messiah.

WORD PICTURE

Hades

Hades equals the Old Testament Sheol and is sometimes translated as "the grave," but it is not the final destiny for humans (cp. Rev 20:13–14).

HISTORICAL BACKGROUND

The vision of judgments poured out on the earth is modeled on the vision of Zech 6:1–8, where colored horses represent God's agents who execute his judgments on the rebellious nations.

WORD PICTURE

Star

Star in the original language does not mean a star in the scientific sense. It is a general term which covers meteorites, planets, as well as stars in the scientific sense. Most likely the usage here is like our "shooting stars" or meteor showers.

QUESTIONS TO GUIDE YOUR STUDY

1. What parallels are there between the events in this chapter and what Jesus predicted in Matthew 24?
2. What comfort can come to believers from the content of the fifth seal?
3. Why does humankind fear God's day? How can this fear be taken away?

OLD TESTAMENT REFERENCE

Many Old Testament passages refer to cosmic events that mark the end-time revelation of God (cp. Isa 50:3; Jer 10:10; Isa 2:2, 10,12–21; 13:10–13; Ezek 32:7–8; Joel 2:31; 3:15; Zech 14:1–6; Zeph 1:14–18).

REVELATION 7

THE 144,000 SEALED (7:1–8)

Chapter 7 is an interlude in the action, and it describes two significant groups. The first is the 144,000 who are sealed. Many different opinions are held on the identity of this group: Jehovah's Witnesses claim it is their group; some say it is the church; others say it is converted Jewish people. Romans 11 predicts a future conversion of Israel, and the term *Israel* occurs sixty-eight times in the New Testament. All the usages are of Jewish people. (Galatians 6:16 is no exception.) So the literal sense makes good sense. Doubtless in the last days the identification of God's people and God's enemies (the beast's people) will be evident (cp. Rev 13:16–17). Economic and physical persecution will come to God's people, but divine wrath will be on those who receive Satan's mark. Just what these marks will be is not known.

OLD TESTAMENT REFERENCE

The background for this vision is Ezek 9:4,6, where God's judgment does not fall on those with a mark on their foreheads.

THE GREAT MULTITUDE IN WHITE ROBES (7:9–17)

The second group in this chapter is a great multitude of people who come out of the great tribulation. These people are in heaven and so have died during this terrible period. How they die is not revealed here (cp. 17:6; 18:24; 19:2; 20:4), but they are killed for the faith. The great tribulation will be a period of great evangelization as well as of judgments. The ministry of the witnesses (described in chap. 11) is a 1,260-day-long event of signs and wonders with the Word that brings God's truth to the world. In addition, the nation of Israel may have a supernatural ministry to the Gentile world during this time (cp. Rom 11:12,25–26; possibly the 144,000; and Rev 12:13–17). In Rev 14:6–7, an angel warns the world of the need to know and worship God. The signs and cosmic disturbances (6:12–14) may also wake a sleepy world from its spiritual slumber. Many people will come to faith, and many will die for their faith.

QUESTIONS TO GUIDE YOUR STUDY

1. What does the white robe mean in this vision?
2. What picture is given of heaven in this scene?
3. In what way are Christians sealed today and for what purpose (2 Cor 1:22; Eph 1:13; 4:30)?

REVELATION 8

THE SEVENTH SEAL AND THE TRUMPET JUDGMENTS (8:1–6)

The relationship of the seals, trumpets, and bowls judgments can be charted as follows:

In the recapitulation view, the same judgments are described over and over again in increasing detail. In the linear view, each series of judgments is distinct and issues into the next series of more intense judgments. If the tribulation is taken as a seven-year period or as a three-and-one-half-year period, the difference is not too great. A linear view seems to be the simple reading of the text.

The trumpet judgments are introduced with solemnity. First there is a dramatic pause. Then seven angels prepare to execute God's will. Then another angel takes fire from the heavenly altar and casts it to earth. The judgment which comes is in response to the prayers of God's people, who long for his victory and his righteousness to be manifested.

OLD TESTAMENT REFERENCE

Trumpets were used in Israel to summon the people to attention. They were often used to announce a battle or a solemn emergency. Joel 2:1 is typical: "Blow the ram's horn in Zion; sound the alarm on my holy mountain! Let all the residents of the land tremble, for the day of the LORD is coming; in fact, it is near" (cp. Judg. 3:27; 7:8; Neh. 4:18; Ezek 33:1).

THE FIRST TRUMPET (8:7)

The trumpet judgments have similarities to the plagues and judgments which God poured out on Egypt at the time of Israel's exodus (Exod 7–11). However, the trumpets signal much greater and universal disasters which are not confined to one nation. The purpose is similar: to warn, to punish, and to bring people to repentance and faith. Hail, fire, and blood come to the earth. Many understand the fire to be lightning. Blood-red rain does occur in places of volcanic activity or near the red sands from the Sahara Desert. The result of this first trumpet judgment is the destruction of a third of the earth's vegetation. This will greatly affect humanity's food supply.

OLD TESTAMENT REFERENCE

Joel predicts similar signs before the final day of the Lord: "I will display wonders in the heavens and on the earth: blood, fire, and columns of smoke" (Joel 2:30).

THE SECOND TRUMPET (8:8–9)

As the second trumpet sounds, something like a gigantic meteor crashes into the sea, causing a third of the sea to turn bloody (cp. Exod 7:20). A third of sea life dies, and a third of the world's shipping is destroyed. Much of the world today depends on food supplies from other parts of the world, transported on the seas. Terrible economic disasters and suffering will take place.

WORD PICTURE

Altar

In contrast to *bomos* which is used to describe pagan altars, the Septuagint (Greek Old Testament) is the first hlace where the *thusiastērion*, "sacrificial table," or altar occurs. It occurs in the Septuagint 419 times. In Revelation it occurs eight times.

THE THIRD TRUMPET (8:10–11)

Another heavenly body comes crashing down. This star (meteorite) is named "Wormwood" for its effect on the inland waters—the great rivers. All the water is polluted, and many people die (cp. Jer 9:14–15; 23:15).

THE FOURTH TRUMPET (8:12)

With the blowing of this trumpet, the Egyptian plague of darkness is recalled (Exod 10:21–23). Sun, moon, and stars lose a third of their luminosity, so both day and night are darker.

The judgment of darkness is to warn the world to flee to Christ, who has come as light into the world (John 8:12). The great tragedy is that people often stay in the dark because their practices are evil (John 3:19–21). The final destiny of the rebellious is a place of outer darkness (Matt 8:12; 22:13).

THE VISION OF THE FLYING EAGLE (8:13)

The word translated "eagle" may also be a "vulture" (some manuscripts have the word *angel* instead). The warning of the heavenly messenger is a threefold "woe" which corresponds to the next three trumpet judgments. The first four were upon the elements or nature. The last will be upon humanity. Jesus himself warned, "Wherever the carcass is, there the vultures [or eagles] will gather" (Matt 24:28). Death is coming!

REVELATION 9

THE FIFTH TRUMPET—FIRST WOE (9:1–12)

The plague of locusts in this vision is different from normal locusts. These seem demonic as they come up out of the "abyss" or bottomless pit. In Luke 8:31, the abyss is the place of demons. These locusts do not feed on vegetation like normal locusts, but they torture people for five months. Not everyone is under this plague. Like the later plagues of Egypt, the Lord makes a distinction between his people and those under judgment (Exod 3:22–23). The believers are not appointed for wrath, and they have a seal from God (7:1–8). The limitation of this plague to five months is a warning and an opportunity to repent. As terrible as this demonic plague is, people will not die from it, but they will wish they could.

The leader of the locusts is named Apollyon, or "Destroyer." He is a fallen angel or demon and may be referred to in 2 Pet 2:4. The physical descriptions of these horrors are appalling—part human, part animal. It must be remembered that John was seeing a vision filled with symbols.

THE SIXTH TRUMPET (9:13–21)

At the border of the Roman Empire to the east was the River Euphrates. Beyond lived the Parthians, an Iranian people, who were a grave threat to the world of Rome. Several times their mounted troops constituted a terror from the east. The plague of the sixth trumpet shows a similar imagery: (1) origin near the Euphrates River; (2) the bright-plated armor of the horses and riders; (3) the Parthian tactic of shooting a volley of arrows while charging and retreating (cp. 9:19).

In a number of end-time prophecies in the Bible, there are predictions of invasions from the east or the north. (Because of Israel's location, most invasions from the east circled the desert and came in from the north.) In the history of the Jewish people, they suffered attacks from the Assyrians, Babylonians, and Persians who invaded from the east and north. Ezekiel prophesied of an end-time invasion of Gog and Magog (38:1–39:16). In the pseudepigraphal book of 1 Enoch (56:5–7), a vision similar to Revelation 9:13–21 occurs:

HISTORICAL BACKGROUND

When Krakatoa, a volcano in Indonesia, exploded on August 27, 1883, nearly five cubic miles of rock and dust were thrown into the air. The surrounding region was dark for two and one-half days, and dust drifted around the earth several times, causing bright red sunsets for a year. Something similar may happen with this series of judgments.

HISTORICAL BACKGROUND

The plant in the ancient world called "wormwood" was not poisonous, but it was proverbial for its bitterness and so was used as a symbol for the bitter result of sin. Sin often is pleasurable at first—with the outcome of bitterness and death. Thus, Deut 29:18 warns in the Hebrew language that the fruit of idolatry is "gall and wormwood" (KJV).

HISTORICAL BACKGROUND

The fifth and sixth trumpet judgments use some common Old Testament and contemporary symbolism. In the fifth, there is a plague of locusts—a calamity which came all too often in the Middle East. In the sixth, there is a plague of horsemen similar to the Parthian warriors who threatened Rome from the East. The eighth plague of Egypt (Exod 10:12–20) was the locusts, while Joel describes an army invasion in terms of locusts which is the clear background for this vision (Joel 1–2).

> In those days, the angels will assemble and throw themselves down to the east at the Parthians and Medes. They will shake up the kings (so that) a spirit of unrest shall come upon them, and stir them up from their thrones; and they will break forth . . . like lions . . . like hyenas. And they will go up and trample upon the land of My elect ones, and the land of My elect ones will be before them like a threshing floor or a highway.

PERSONAL APPLICATION

The visual description should not be pushed into excessive literalism. For example, Jesus is seen in chapter 1 with a long priestly garment. In chapter 6, he is the slain and victorious lamb or ram, while in chapter 19 he rides a white horse into battle with a sword coming out of his mouth. Each vision presents truth about Jesus's person and office, but we should not try to paint a picture of his pysical nature.

In the sixth plague, four angels (demonic) who were bound at the Euphrates are unleashed. The coming judgment is ordained to come at a precise time (9:15) marked out by God. The events set loose will bring the death of one-third of mankind. Previous disasters such as the flood on Noah or the black death of the Middle Ages are the only comparisons in history. The destructive forces consist of a cavalry of 200 million horsemen. Some interpreters argue for literal armies from the east. Others emphasize that these are demonic forces from hell and that literal human armies are not intended. The horses and their riders have elements like animals, like humans, and with fire, smoke, and sulfur (brimstone) that are hellish. As in the previous plague, the historical background is the Parthian cavalry. But these horrible hordes are demon inspired and demon led, resulting in unparalleled death and destruction.

As the plague comes upon the world, the two-thirds of humanity not killed might be expected to turn to the Lord in faith and repentance. But they are so enmeshed in their false religions that they do not see the truth. While it's true that "an idol is nothing in the world" (1 Cor 8:4), demon forces are involved in false religions, and they deceive people. In later visions of this book, satanic deceptions and false worship are described in more detail.

PERSONAL APPLICATION

Paul warned us that the god of this age (Satan) has "blinded the minds of the unbelievers to keep them from seeing the light of the gospel of the glory of Christ, who is the image of God" (2 Cor 4:4). Not only do people hang on to their false worship, but they also continue in their wicked lifestyles. If the first part of the Ten Commandments is broken, then violations of the second tablet are sure to come. Love of God and love of humanity are linked. True biblical love for God is a response to his love for us (1 John 4:19). True biblical love for God has ethical results (1 John 4:7–8,11, 20–21; Rom 13:8–10).

QUESTIONS TO GUIDE YOUR STUDY

1. How does God use angels (good) to work out his purposes?
2. How do Satan and the fallen angels (demons) fit into the plan of God?
3. What role do humans have in relation to angels (1 Cor 4:9; 6:3; Heb 2:5; Eph 3:10)?
4. Why is it so hard for unbelievers to see God's grace?
5. What is the connection between faith and works?
6. What are some modern forms of idolatry?

REVELATION 10

THE MIGHTY ANGEL AND THE LITTLE SCROLL (10:1–7)

As the seventh trumpet is anticipated, another interlude takes place (cp. 7:1–8). The sounding of the trumpet is delayed until 11:14–19. In this interlude, another series of seven thunders is announced, but they are mysteriously sealed up and not revealed (cp. 2 Cor 12:2–4). In this interlude, John tells of a great angel from heaven who gives him a little book to eat. He also records the measuring of the temple and the ministry of the two witnesses.

The mighty angel of Revelation is so glorious that some have thought him to be Jesus himself. While the term *angel* is not decisive (for it can be used of men, spirit beings, or even of God), he is one of a series of messengers (cp. 6:4; 5:2; 10:3). The angel takes a stance on land and sea with an uplifted arm. He announces that "there will no longer be a delay." (Not the end of "time" in a metaphysical sense.)

The great question is always "how long?" Now, heaven swears, the end of Satan's kingdom has come; God's kingdom will be established on earth. The restrainer of 2 Thess 2:3 is removed, and the prayers of the martyrs answered (Rev 6:11). Since the time of Moses, a long series of prophets have given predictions of the purpose of God in his Messiah without understanding the exact time sequences of suffering and glory (1 Pet 1:10–12). The "mystery" is now to be fully made known because God is not only giving revelation, but he is working out the actual events.

OLD TESTAMENT REFERENCE

John's vision is full of Old Testament images and themes. On the angel, compare Dan 8:16; 12:7. On the cloud, compare Ps 104:3; Dan 7:13; Acts 1:9. But the strongest similarities to this vision come from Ezek 1:26–28; 2:8–3:3. The angel has the glory of the Lord upon him. Ezekiel was shown a scroll which was unrolled and full of lament, mourning, and woe.He was told to eat the scroll, and it was sweet in his mouth.

JOHN CONSUMES THE SCROLL AND IS COMPELLED TO PROPHESY (10:8–11)

John is now commanded to take and eat a scroll. The content of this little scroll is about the completion of God's mystery which the prophets of the Old Testament proclaimed. This is a "mystery" because unless God discloses to humans what he is going to do, they will never be able to figure out his plan.

Several Old Testament prophets had an experience similar to John's. Ezekiel heard a voice and saw a hand outstretched to him with a written scroll. He was told to eat this scroll, which was sweet in his mouth (Ezek 2:8–3:3). Jeremiah in a poetic passage declared: "Your words were found, and I ate them. Your words became a delight to me and the joy of my heart" (Jer 15:16).

Both Ezekiel and Jeremiah found that the messages of judgment they had to deliver to the people caused a lot of pain for them. So John found the scroll "was as sweet as honey in my mouth, but when I ate it, my stomach became bitter" (v. 10). Why would the message be first

NEW TESTAMENT REFERENCE

Paul, after explaining part of God's plan in Jew, Gentile, and church interactions (see Rom 9–11), wrote: "Oh, the depth of the riches and the wisdom and the knowledge of God! How unsearchable his judgments and untraceable his ways! For who has known the mind of the Lord? Or who has been his counselor? And who has ever given to God, that he should be repaid. For from him and through him and to him are all things. To him be the glory forever. Amen" (Rom 11:33–36).

sweet, then cause bitterness? Probably the answer is that all of God's revelation is, as Ps 119:103 says: "How sweet your word is to my taste—sweeter than honey in my mouth."

Yet John's message contains elements of judgment, martyrdom, persecution, and eternal punishment. God himself says that he takes no pleasure in the death of the ungodly or of anyone (Ezek 18:32) but wants them to turn and live. He wants them to get a new heart and a new spirit! It is a bitter thing to contemplate the second death (Rev 20:11–15).

John's commission is to prophesy again. The content is not certain, but it most likely contains the material of the later part of his book (Rev 11–22).

Section Summary

God, in his kindness, reveals his purposes to people today in a written book. In the past the revelation came in many ways, including dreams, visions, and trances. To have a written record of God's prophecy is a great privilege.

QUESTIONS TO GUIDE YOUR STUDY

1. What features make the angel in 10:1–4 impressive?
2. Why are the seven thunders sealed?
3. How certain is this prophecy?

HISTORICAL BACKGROUND

Measuring the Temple

Ezekiel 40–42 describes the prophet watching a man measuring various parts of the temple and its courts. The glory of the Lord returns to the temple with the promise that this temple will never be defiled, again as the previous temples had been by foreign invaders. Zechariah (2:1–13) also describes a measuring of the city of Jerusalem as a prelude to God's working for hs people.

REVELATION 11

JOHN MEASURES THE TEMPLE (11:1–2)

John is given a bamboo-like cane and is told to measure the temple. When we see people surveying, we normally think that a new building or a renovation will soon take place. Interpreters differ on the significance of this vision. The symbolic interpretations see the preservation of the church in this passage. The more literal interpretations see a fulfillment in the city of Jerusalem on the ancient temple site of Mount Moriah. They look forward to a rebuilding of the Jewish temple and point to 2 Thess 2:4. In this passage, Paul reminds Christians of a future desecration of the temple. Jesus also warns of a sign in the future of an abomination that causes desolation (Matt 24:15; Mark 13:14) in the holy place. John is writing down his prophecy after the destruction of the second temple (Herod's) in AD 70. Most likely, his vision concerns the end-time temple.

THE TWO WITNESSES (11:3–14)

In 11:2 the Gentiles are to trample the Holy City for forty-two months. This time notation is a reference to the prophecy of Dan 9, which concerns "seventy weeks" of years. The last seven years are divided into two segments and referred to in a number of passages. Sometimes the days are numbered as 1,260 (three years of thirty-day months). Sometimes a period of tribulation is said to be "a time, times, and half a time" (Dan 7:25; 12:7). This same period is found in Rev 12:6,14; 13:5. The two witnesses are two end-time prophets whom God will raise up. They remind us of Moses (the miracles) and Elijah (the miracles and three-year judgment). They prophesy in sackcloth or mourning garments. These garments were of a coarse material and were often black, to distinguish them from normal clothing. They had supernatural power and protection. They minister most likely during the first three years of the period, known as Daniel's seventieth week. Many interpreters take a symbolic interpretation and see this prophecy fulfilled in the church. A more literal interpretation sees the fulfillment in the land of Israel during the last days. The city where Christ was crucified is Jerusalem (11:8), and it is a bit of a stretch to see this city as Babylon or Rome or Egypt. The mention of "Sodom and Egypt" refers to both as the enemies of God with their immorality, slavery, and idolatry.

At the completion of their witness to God, they become martyrs. They are killed by the beast (or the antichrist as he is known). This end-time person is a main character in the book of Revelation and is the same as the "man of lawlessness" mentioned by Paul in 2 Thess 2. To let a body lie in the streets of a city was a terrible dishonor during biblical times. A devil's Christmas celebration takes place as people rejoice in their opposition to God's message and messengers. But their joy turns to terror as the witnesses are resurrected and taken before their eyes to heaven. A judgment of an earthquake occurs which kills many people but also causes repentance toward God. This event may be significant in the conversion of the Jews during the tribulation.

WORD PICTURE

Martyrs, Witness

A witness in legal terms testifies concerning what he has seen and heard. In biblical terms the witness proclaims what he knows. Jesus is called "the faithful and true witness" (Rev 1:5; 3:14). By the end of the first century, the name *martyr* was given to the persons who sealed their testimony with their blood. So, in Rev 2:13, "Antipas, my faithful witness who was put to death."

OLD TESTAMENT REFERENCE

Olive Trees and Lampstands

In Zech 4, a vision of a lampstand and olive trees representing the testimony and power of God is seen. The olive trees are two men selected to do the work of rebuilding the temple.

Section Summary

Even as the Gentiles trampled the city of Jerusalem, God did not forget his ancient people (Rom 11:28–29). He raised up two prophets to witness to the nation.

THE SEVENTH TRUMPET (11:15–19)

The seventh angel blew his trumpet. With this trumpet blast, the earthly establishment of God's kingdom is announced. This concludes the series which began in chapter 8 (cp. vv. 6,10,12,13). The content of chapters 10:1–11:13 is parenthetical. No immediate content of the seventh trumpet is revealed, but the seven bowl judgments are the content. Before John describes the events that will bring in the King with his kingdom, more parenthetical revelation is given about the actors in this great drama of history (chaps. 12–14).

The response of heaven is first given. Later, both humankind's and nature's responses are revealed (vv. 18–19). Heaven solemnly proclaims that "the kingdom of the world" has become the kingdom of God and of his Messiah. The theme of the kingdom is a major theme of the Bible. The kingdom was the message of John the Baptist and of Jesus (Matt 3:2; 4:23).

A kingdom is the sphere or realm over which a ruler exercises his authority. The realm can be physical, spiritual, or both. In the political realm, the Jewish people achieved a significant kingdom under David and his son Solomon (2 Sam 5:1–1 Kgs 11). But because of disobedience, the Jewish political state was reduced and placed in servitude to various pagan nations—Assyrians, Babylonians, Persians, Greeks, and Romans. The people of Jesus's day longed for freedom from the Gentile or pagan domination (cp. Luke 1:68–75; John 6:14; and Acts 1:6).

The great mistake for Israel was its tendency to forget the spiritual realm and to think that political deliverance was all-important. As early as the foundation of the Hebrew monarchy, the people rejected God's rule and demanded an earthly solution to their troubles (1 Sam 8:1–22). The spiritual realm is more important than the human or political kingdom. The Bible opens our minds to spiritual forces and realms of which we would be totally ignorant if God didn't reveal them to us. Behind earthly kingdoms are spiritual powers headed by one who is called the *archōn* or ruler of this world.

Jesus faced this individual in his temptation (Matt 4:1–11). This *archōn* offered Jesus "all the kingdoms of the world." Jesus, in obedience, conquered Satan (the *archōn*) (John 12:31; 14:30; 16:11). Today, while the decisive battle has been won on the cross, there is still the "mopping-up operation." The world system lies under the control of the wicked one (1 John 5:19).

PERSONAL APPLICATION

While the Bible reveals spiritual forces opposed to God, the believer is not to fear (cp. 2 Kgs 6:16). "Those who are with us outnumber" the enemies of God. John encouraged his people by reminding us that "the one who his in you [God in the person of the Holy Spirit] is greater than the one who is in the world" (1 John 4:4). The major message of the book of Revelation is the triumph of God over evil in this world.

Jesus came into the world of darkness to destroy the works of the devil (1 John 3:8). Satan has a spiritual kingdom of darkness (1 John 3:14; Col 1:13), as well as control over the physical kingdoms of this world. Paul wrote that the "god of this age" blinds the minds of people so they do not see "the light of the gospel of the glory of Christ, who is the image of God" (2 Cor 4:4).

Revelation 11:15 states that the Messiah will reign forever when he takes over the kingdom of the world. When Jesus was born, the angel Gabriel told Mary that her Son would have David's throne and that he would rule forever and his kingdom would never end (Luke 1:32–33). The angelic promise embraces a number of Old Testament predictions.

In 2 Sam 7:15 David is promised that his lineage will be established forever. In Dan 2:44 God predicts a kingdom which will destroy the Gentile world empires, and in Dan 7:14,28 the prediction is of a messianic eternal kingdom. The one-thousand-year reign of Christ in Rev 20:4–6 and in 1 Cor 15:24–28 is best understood as the initial phase of God's eternal kingdom.

In 11:16 the heavenly beings—the twenty-four elders—prostrate themselves in worship before God at the wonder of his coming rule. The angels in heaven must be puzzled over the whole drama of redemption. Two references in the epistles seem to teach this. Peter said that "angels long to catch a glimpse of these things" (1 Pet 1:12). And Paul revealed that the church is an object lesson of God's grace to heavenly beings (Eph 3:10). The incarnation of our Lord was an act of grace in which he took on humanity, "for it is clear that he does not reach out to help angels, but to help Abraham's offspring" (Heb 2:16). Although there is angelic sin (see Rev 12:7), yet there is no revelation of salvation for angels.

The coming of the King with his kingdom means that he will rule in righteousness. Rebellion will be put down and punished, and rewards will be given for those who have been loyal to the King. The Old Testament day of the Lord is the time when God will come and visit his people in judgment (Isa 2:1–4; Joel 1:15; Amos 5:18–24; Mal 4:1–6). The rewards given to God's faithful are in this world (Rev 3:10) but mainly in the resurrection or in heaven (cp. Jesus's beatitudes, Matt 5:2–10 and Rev 2:7,10,17,28; 3:5,21; Rev 21:13). In Rev 11:18–19, the nations are angry at the kingdom of God while nature displays its awe before the Lord in lightning, thunder, hail, and earthquake.

OLD TESTAMENT REFERENCE

Psalm 2 describes the long conflict between God's rule and pagan insurrection. The psalm first reveals the revolt against the anointed of Israel. But God laughs at the insolence and firmly establishes his kingdom. Jesus as David's Son faced the same opposition and rejection. The New Testament quotes this psalm in reference to Jesus as God's Messiah (cp. Acts 4:25; 13:33; Heb 1:5; 5:5).

Section Summary

The final series of judgments is announced. The long-awaited kingdom is coming to earth with Jesus the King.

QUESTIONS TO GUIDE YOUR STUDY

1. Why is Jerusalem the city of importance?
2. How could the whole world see the dead bodies of the martyrs?
3. Why would people follow the antichrist and refuse to respond to God's prophets?
4. Why do the angels fall on their faces before God? Review Old Testament visitations of God to humans.
5. Why has the kingdom taken so much time to be established on earth?
6. Why should we pray for the coming of the kingdom (cp. Matt 6:10)?

HISTORICAL BACKGROUND

The vision seems like a myth rather than a historical account. Although many pagan myths have similar motifs, the birth of Jesus and the opposition of Satan really occur in our world and datable history. C. S. Lewis has written helpful material on the "true myth" or the mythical becoming historical ("on myth" in *An Experiment in Criticism*, 1961; cp. *C. S. Lewis: Defender of the Faith* by Richard Cunningham, 1967, 141–200; "The Myth of Deep Heaven" in *The Christian World of C. S. Lewis* by Clyde S. Kilby, 1964, 79–116; especially "Myth, Fact, and Truth," pp. 93–99 in *C. S. Lewis: Apostle to the Skeptics* by Chad Walsh, 1949). Thus, a myth can be a literary form like an allegory and used to depict historical truth.

REVELATION 12

THE WOMAN, THE CHILD, AND THE DRAGON (12:1–6)

This next section is most unusual. John usually introduces new visions with expressions like "I turned to see" (1:12), "After this I looked" (4:1), "Then I saw" (5:1; 6:1,12). Here he sees the appearance of a "sign" in heaven.

Here the word *sign* seems to have the sense of a striking phenomenon or a portent. The sign is a brilliant woman, and the reader of the Bible would naturally connect the image to the dream of Joseph in Gen 37:9. If this is correct, the woman has something to do with Israel. The identity of the great red dragon is clearly revealed in verse 9 as Satan or the devil. The identity of the man-child (v. 5) is clearly the Messiah since the text uses the language of the Second Psalm, where it indicated that God's Messiah "will break [all nations] with an iron scepter" (Ps 2:9). This expression occurs in Revelation at 2:27 and 19:15. In the first passage, Jesus is sharing his rule with his people. In the second, Jesus is returning as the conquering Messiah.

The section (12:1–6) may be understood in this way. Israel, the woman, after a long pregnancy, finally gives birth to the Messiah who will rule. The great cosmic struggle between good and evil, God and Satan, which is described in brief in the next section, is seen here on earth.

Satan (v. 9) is pictured in this vision as a great red dragon with seven heads and ten horns. In 17:9, the last world empire is described in similar language. The terminology of beasts, heads, and horns is based on Dan 7:1–28 and Zech 1:18–21. The dragon is similar to the pictures in the Old Testament of monsters who are enemies of God and his people (Isa 27:1; Pss 74:12–14; 89:9–10). The biblical picture of Satan is of a fallen angel who has great but limited power. He is an opponent of God and his people, seeking to destroy God's work (cp. Matt 4:1–11; 1 Pet 5:8–9). He is called the "ruler of the world" (or ruler, Gk. *archōn*) by Jesus (John 14:30), and John declared that the whole world is under his control.

WORD PICTURE

The word sign (*sēmeion*) is an organizing theme of the Gospel of John (cp. John 2:11; 4:54; 6:2; 7:31; 11:47; 12:18,37; 20:30).

Satan's opposition to God is manifested in hatred of his servants, and he attempts to destroy the child at his birth (v. 4). It is easy to see why many interpreters see Satan at work in Herod's attempt to kill the infant Jesus (Matt 22:1–18). Since the devil was foiled in his efforts to destroy the Redeemer who is taken to heaven, he turns to attack the woman who gave birth. She flees into the wilderness where God preserves her. The reference is to God's protection of his people (most likely converted Jews in the tribulation) during Daniel's three and one-half years (9:27). This period is the same as in 7:1–8; 11:3–10; 13:5–8.

Section Summary

The great battle between God and Satan is revealed in picture form with God's miraculous protection of his people.

WAR IN HEAVEN, SATAN CAST OUT, WRATH ON EARTH (12:7–12)

The Bible is clear about the outcome of the great cosmic struggle. The devil and his angels are doomed. Jesus says they will go into eternal fire which has been prepared for them (Matt 25:41). John sees the devil, the beast, and the false prophet all thrown into the lake of fire and sulfur, where they will remain forever. But in the revelation to John, he is shown part of a great mystery: war in heaven!

Two great archangels with their hosts go into battle. Michael is an archangel mentioned in Daniel as a guardian of the Jewish people (12:1; 10:13,21), and in the book of Jude (v. 9) he "was disputing with the devil in an argument about Moses's body." How angels could sin and how there could be a battle in heaven are unknown. Satan is pictured as defeated—but not by Michael's great power. As in the letter of Jude where the Lord rebukes Satan, so here victory is the Lord's. By his death and resurrection, Jesus has defeated Satan and his hosts.

The overthrow of Satan's kingdom and the coming to earth of the messianic kingdom is announced again by a heavenly voice. In the Bible, Satan has many titles and descriptions. His two principle names are "Satan" (Hebrew, "accuser" or "adversary") and "devil" (Greek, "slanderer"). Peter warns Christians about "your adversary the devil" (1 Pet 5:8). Somehow Satan has a perverted sense which points out the flaws and sins—real or possible—in God's people (cp. Job 1–2; Zech 3:1–5). In the Rev 12:10 passage, heaven is rejoicing at the overthrow of the "accuser of our brothers and sisters." God's people in heaven are ecstatic over the victory won by the blood of the Lamb.

What does this mean? By Jesus's death on the cross, human sin is now atoned for. God's rightness is vindicated, and his righteousness is granted as a gift to those who trust the finished work of Jesus.

Section Summary

The victory of Jesus on the cross and his resurrection ensure the defeat of Satan. God's people rejoice in heaven, but Satan is about to turn earth into a living hell.

NEW TESTAMENT REFERENCE

As Paul writes, "Who can bring an accusation against God's elect? God is the one who justifies. Who is the one who condemns? Christ Jesus is the one who died, but even more, has been raised" (Rom 8:33–34; see Rom 8:31; 3:21–31; 2 Cor 5:19–21; 1 John 2:1–2). Our sins are imputed to Jesus on the cross and his righteousness is imputed (or "credited to our account") to us. The accuser now has nothing to accuse against us. Jesus has put it all to his account and settled it once for all with his mighty shout from the cross: *Tetelestai*—"It is finished" (John 19:30).

WORD PICTURE

Satan's Titles

In the Bible, Satan is called the great red dragon, the deceiver of the world, the wicked one, the archon of the world, Lucifer, the tempter, the old serpent, the prince of darkness, the adversary, the accuser of the brothers, the father of lies, Beelzebub, the prince of the power of the air, the father of the children of evil.

THE DRAGON PERSECUTES THE WOMAN AND HER CHILDREN (12:13–17)

When Satan is confined to the earth, his activities are intensified against humanity, and his fury is unleashed because he knows he has only a limited time (12:12). Jesus has come to destroy the works of the devil (1 John 3:8) and to deliver people from Satan, who keeps people in bondage through fear of death (Heb 2:14). Jesus has come as the stronger one and raided Satan's house and kingdom (Matt 12:29; Col 1:13).

The woman represents converted Israel (Rom 11:26–27), or perhaps as Barnhouse held, "The woman represents all the saved of God from the time of Eve who received the promise that her seed would bruise the serpent's head" (*Revelation*, 229). She is now the object of Satan's wrath. Today God's people come out from mainly Gentile origins, but in the tribulation a great number will be from Jewish origins, for that time is called Jacob's trouble (Jer 30:7). The 144,000 Israelites of 7:4–8 is another indication of a large scale turning to Jesus during the tribulation.

Right from the beginning of the Hebrew nation, as God was freeing Israel from Egypt, Pharaoh and his host sought to destroy the infant nation. God reminded his people of his salvation in Exodus 19:4: "You have seen what I did to the Egyptians and how I carried you on eagles' wings and brought you to myself."

So in the tribulation God will protect his people in their wilderness experience for the period of forty-two months or "a time, times, and half a time" (Dan 7:25). Satan's failure will result in his turning to attack God's faithful throughout the whole world. The reference to the floodwater and the earth helping the woman (12:15–16) recalls the sea parting for Israel so they could cross on dry ground and escape their enemies.

Section Summary

Persecution of God's people will be rampant, but God knows how to protect and deliver his own in the midst of their troubles.

QUESTIONS TO GUIDE YOUR STUDY

1. Why does John use this picture language?
2. How has Satan been at work in modern times?
3. Why is Satan opposed to Christians?
4. How does Satan deceive the whole world (12:9)?
5. What will the devil's wrath produce on earth (12:12)?
6. Where and why are Christians being persecuted today?
7. What do Christians learn in persecution?
8. In what ways has Satan attacked the Jewish people?

REVELATION 13

THE BEAST OUT OF THE SEA (13:1–4)

Following the frustration of Satan in chapter 12, the dragon takes his stand on the sand of the sea (12:18). He almost seems to be pondering his next strategy. The sea is often a symbol for the people (Isa 57:20–21; Rev 17:15). But perhaps here John sees this beast come out of the Mediterranean Sea. The beasts of Daniel's book are world empires: Babylon, Medo-Persia, Greece, and Rome. The last two were distinctively Mediterranean-based world powers. As John sees his visions and writes his Revelation, the ruling world empire is Rome. Almost all interpreters see the Roman Empire reflected in some way in this book. But since Rome is no longer a world power, how is this to be understood?

Explanations include a revival of the Roman Empire with the European Union or the Common Market developing into something sinister. Others see Rome as the Roman Catholic Church developing into the beast. Still others see the rise of Islam around the Mediterranean Sea and its developing into a major world power as it was in its early days. At least ten Islamic powers ring the sea with hatred for the state of Israel.

The beast is like the leopard, the bear, and the lion of Daniel's three world empires, and it is energized and characterized by the dragon (13:1–4; 12:3). In the tribulation period, a final world power hostile to God will arise and demand to be worshiped. Deification of a human leader and an anti-Christian state have occurred throughout history. The "beast" in John's vision has a remarkable power of recuperation as it is "fatally wounded" but survives. John will receive more information on this beast from an angel in chapter 17 (vv. 7–18).

This satanic kingdom will have worldwide power: "The whole earth was amazed and followed the beast" (Rev 13:3).

Prediction is perilous. But the Bible does warn us of one called the antichrist (1 John 2:18). Paul calls him the "man of lawlessness" (2 Thess 2:3), and the "lawless one" (2 Thess 2:8). He is probably the "little horn" of Dan 7:8–12,21–22,24–28, and perhaps the "coming ruler" of Dan 9:26.

The beast out of the sea will be given great power and authority by Satan. The leader of this beastly kingdom will be a human but will be empowered by Satan himself. Paul said of him: "He opposes and exalts himself above every so-called god or object of worship, so that he sits in God's temple, proclaiming that he himself is God" (2 Thess 2:4).

OLD TESTAMENT REFERENCE

Beasts in the Old Testament

In the book of Daniel, visions of world empires hostile to God's people are seen as "beasts" or animals (Dan 7:1–12; 17–18; 19–28; 8:1–27). "Horns" on the "beasts" are often symbols of other kings or kingdoms that develop (Dan 8:22–23; 7:24–25). The "horns" are symbols of their power (Zech 1:18–21; Rev 17:12).

Section Summary

At the end of this age, the beast or the antichrist will arise with great satanic power. He is foreshadowed in the Roman Empire and other tyrannical dictator states.

PERSONAL APPLICATION

As this booklet is being written, neither Russia, nor Islam, nor a European federation seems as likely a candidate for the beast as they perhaps once did. The anti-Catholics point to the past when Rome under Innocent III (1160–1216) dominated the European rulers and claimed the right of investiture of the emperor. Islam once ruled a unified kingdom from Tours, France, all around the Mediterranean Sea to Vienna. Hitler would have been a great candidate for the satanic beast in 1941–1942 when he ruled Europe and a good part of North Africa. He also deified himself and placed an earthly authority over the church. Mass rallies exalted the leader, and even university professors had to begin their classes with a "Heil Hitler." The "Heil Hitler" could be as harmless as the English expression "God save the king" or as sinister as "Salvation is from Hitler."

THE REIGN AND THE WORSHIP OF THE BEAST (13:5–10)

The beast will speak arrogantly and mouth blasphemies. Verse 13:5 is clearly built on Daniel 7:8,20,25 where the "little horn" speaks boastfully and wars against God's people for three and one-half years. So the beast reigns forty-two months and starts a great persecution in which many are killed for the faith. This satanically empowered person will become a world ruler as the devil's vice-regent (John 12:31; 14:30; 16:11). He will achieve what no tyrant has been able to accomplish—a universal dominion with universal worship. All will bow in submission to this person and his rule except God's elect ones. The refusal to go along with this world system will cost the lives of those who take a stand for God and his Messiah (cp. 15:2; 12:11; 7:14).

The solemn warning, "If anyone has ears to hear, let him listen" (13:9), is a call to spiritual perception for all to heed. God's people are to understand that the bitter persecution from the evil one is within the loving providence of the Father. For those who side with Satan, they are warned of the certainty of God's judgment which is to come soon. Patient endurance and faithfulness on the part of the Christian are necessary (cp. Gal 5:22; Rom 5:3,4; Rev 14:12).

Section Summary

The antichrist will rule and be worshiped around the world. Christians will die rather than worship the false god.

THE BEAST FROM THE LAND (13:11–18)

Satan is a counterfeit in many of his ways. Here we see a satanic trinity: the dragon, the beast, and the false prophet. John sees a second beast similar but subservient to the first. He comes from the "earth," which may mean Israel. This beast parodies the Lamb who was slain (Rev 5:6) as well as the Holy Spirit, for he is a false prophet (Rev 20:10) who guides and directs the end-time false worship. This false prophet is analogous to the emperor in the emperor cult of the Roman Empire. People were forced to sacrifice to an image of the emperor.

The false prophet uses wondrous signs which deceive people into thinking that this is the true religion. Long ago Moses warned of false prophets with signs who would try to turn people away from the true

God (Deut 13:1–3). Paul said that the "lawless one is based on Satan's working, with every kind of miracle, both signs and wonders serving the lie, and with every wicked deception among those who are perishing" (2 Thess 2:9–10).

Just as the magicians of Egypt could imitate some of Moses's signs, so this false prophet will simulate impressive signs much as the true witnesses did during the first three and one-half years of the tribulation (Rev 11:5–6). In a spectacular event, this prophet will imitate Elijah and bring down fire from heaven in "front of people" (Rev 13:13). In a world plugged into television and the internet, the world will be mesmerized by this display of power and seduced by this false prophet. Undoubtedly, he will prepare the way for the satanic messiah. Jesus himself predicted the coming of "false messiahs and false prophets," and they "perform great signs and wonders to lead astray, if possible, even the elect" (Matt 24:24).

Once the antichrist has gained power, all tolerance will disappear. The false prophet will require a mark on the right hand or the forehead which will be a sign of ownership and of allegiance to the beast. The opposite will be the "seal" of the 144,000 (Rev 7:4–8), which is the mark of the Father's ownership (Rev 14:1–3). The one without the beast's mark will be unable to "buy or sell." The antichrist will have effective economic control of the world.

The "number" of the beast is a mystery. Many languages, including Hebrew, Aramaic, and Greek, used the letters of the alphabet for numerals (before the Arabic numbers). So every name would have a numerical calculation. Thus, 666 = "Nero Caesar" in Hebrew but not in Greek, which is the language Revelation was written in. Many attempts have been made to link 666 with a great variety of persons: Nimrod (Gen 10:8) the founder of Babylon, Napoleon, Mussolini, and many contemporaries, including Henry Kissinger and Social Security numbers! As the time approaches, the mark of allegiance to the beast will become obvious.

OLD TESTAMENT REFERENCE

"If a prophet or someone who has dreams arises among you and proclaims a sign or wonder to you, and that sign or wonder he has promised you comes about, but he says, 'Let's follow other gods,' which you have not known, 'and let's worship them,' do not listen to that prophet's words or to that dreamer. For the LORD your God is testing you to know whether you love the LORD your God with all your heart and all your soul" (Deut 13:1–3).

QUESTIONS TO GUIDE YOUR STUDY

1. Why is the antichrist called a "beast"?
2. How does the beast of Revelation 13:1–4 relate to Daniel 7?
3. Where do we see deification of the state and its ruler in the world today?
4. How important is it for the Christian to be a nonconformist in the world (Rom 12:1–2)?
5. How will the antichrist win universal rule?
6. How can persecution of believers fit with Romans 8:28?
7. What are the signs of true prophets and of false prophets?
8. How could a "sign" be seen around the world (13:13)?

9. Early Christians faced a simple test: burn incense to Caesar or die. How important is it for you to live? Which sign will you live under or die for?

Section Summary

A satanic trinity will deceive the whole world and dominate it in economics and in religion. Opposition to these evil forces will mean death.

REVELATION 14

THE SONG OF THE 144,000 (14:1–5)

In stark contrast to the satanic trinity of chapter 13, this vision shows the true Messiah and his people. In Ps 2, God laughs at the insolence of those who oppose his people (Ps 2:4). And then in his anger he announces his resolve: "I have installed my king on Zion, my holy mountain" (Ps 2:6). The Lamb is a symbol of Jesus the Messiah (John 1:29; Rev 5:6,12,13; Isa 53:7). The 144,000 (see notes on 7:1–8) are the same group seen in chapter 7, and they share in the victory of the Lord along with the great multitude (7:9–14). These come out of the great tribulation and have been redeemed. Their deliverance is marked out in a new song that Israel sang when they experienced salvation (Exod 15:1; Pss 40:1–3; 98:1–9).

OLD TESTAMENT REFERENCE

Both the Old and New Testament point out the significance of Mount Zion, which is the holy temple mountain in Jerusalem. "Zion" appears to include Mount Moriah, the temple site. Zion is the place of salvation of the Lord (cp. Joel 2:1; 3:16; Mic 4:1–2; Zech 1:14; 14:1–21; Ps 132:13–14, 17–18; Heb 12:22; Gal 4:25–26; Isa 2:2–4; 24:21–23).

The 144,000 are special soldiers of the Lamb who are committed to purity. This purity may be a symbol of abstinence from fornication with the prostitute Babylon (cp. 17:1–2,4; 18:3,9). It could also be literal celibacy during the end time when even marriage might be ill-advised because of the rampant corruption. Most Protestants react against any form of celibacy as a Roman Catholic teaching and a violation of God's plan (Gen 2:18) and his apostle's warning ("They forbid marriage"; 1 Tim 4:3). Yet, in times of crisis such as holy war (Deut 23:9; 1 Sam 21:5; 2 Sam 11:11), celibacy may be necessary. John the Baptist, Jesus, and Paul were unmarried because of a more important commitment (cp. 1 Cor 7:1,8,26–40) or the crisis of the times.

The discipleship of the 144,000 is unconditional and comprehensive. They are model Christians with unblemished character. They have "no lie" in them while the mass of humanity will embrace "the lie" (2 Thess 2:9–11). They will be special "firstfruits" of the great harvest of salvation which will take place during the tribulation (cp. Rev 7:9–13).

PERSONAL APPLICATION

How is your "song life"? Our salvation should bring forth songs of joy and of praise!

ANGELIC ANNOUNCEMENTS (14:6–12)

In rapid succession, John sees three angels flying one after another making announcements. The first tells everyone on earth the sovereign Creator is about to judge the world. Man's day is over and the day of the

Lord has come. This message is not exactly the good news of the grace of God in Jesus's death and resurrection (cp. 1 Cor 15:3–5). By this time, the special ministry of the two witnesses and of the 144,000 will have made the issue clear. Also, the world will have faced the decision about God's mark or Satan's mark. God's judgment is good news, for his justice will be manifested on earth.

The second angel announced the doom of Babylon. This is the first mention of "Babylon" in this book, but in the coming chapters much will be said. The doom of Babylon will be explained in the detailed visions of chapters 17 and 18.

The third messenger proclaims doom on the antichrist and his followers. Babylon has given a cup of stupefying wine to the world, and they are drunk from its false teachings. The angel shouts with a loud voice to awaken humanity from its stupor. Those who worship the beast will have another cup to drink—God's wrath. The issues have eternal outcomes: the saints who are amid the tribulation are called to endurance and faith in Jesus.

OLD TESTAMENT REFERENCE

Babylon

"Babel" or "Babylon" was one of the cities founded by Nimrod (Gen 10:10). It became a symbol of man's pride and of his fall. Babylon was one of the major enemies of Israel, and they destroyed the Jerusalem temple in 586 BC. Zechariah 5:5–11 sees the land of Shinar (Babylon) as the site for wickedness. Daniel also lived in Babylon and experienced its oppression (chaps. 1–4). Interpreters of Revelation differ on whether "Babylon" will be rebuilt or if John is speaking of Rome or "a revived Rome."

Section Summary

The great tribulation will come to an end with the return of Jesus to Zion and the destruction of the kingdom of the antichrist. Rewards and judgment will be given.

THE VISION OF THE GREAT HARVEST AND GOD'S WINEPRESS (14:13–20)

Prior to the vision is the second "beatitude" of this book. Commitment to Jesus will result in death. But death for the believer is to be with the Lord and to be rewarded. It will also bring the end to toil in the tribulation period.

In the vision, Jesus "the Son of Man" receives word from an angel that everything is ready for the harvest judgment. The first reaping is the grain, and the second is the grapes. The picture of the reaping or the harvest is a common biblical figure for the final judgment of the earth (Hos 6:11; Joel 3:13; Jer 51:33). After the grape harvest, the grapes would go into a winepress. People would trample the grapes in a winepress, and the juice would flow out into a lower vat.

In this picture of judgment, human blood instead of grape juice flows out. Both Isaiah and Joel develop this terrible figure (Isa 63:1–7; Joel 3:13). The flow of blood is beyond our imagination. It covers the entire land of Palestine to the depth of four feet! Some commentators spend too much time in literal calculations. This is a vision. We should not expect the beast to have seven literal heads, nor should we expect to see Satan as an enormous red dragon. In a similar way, the winepress

HISTORICAL BACKGROUND

Megiddo was a famous ancient city at the southern edge of the plain of Jezreel where many bloody battles were fought.

PERSONAL APPLICATION

What Happens at Death?

1. We will be with the Lord (Phil 1:23).
2. We will be rewarded (Rev 14:13).
3. We will be freed from earthly pain and problems (Rev 7:17).

judgment will be part of the great final bloody battle known as Armageddon or Megiddo (cp. Rev 16:14–16).

Section Summary

Jesus with his angels will judge the rebellious nations in a final great battle.

QUESTIONS TO GUIDE YOUR STUDY

1. What are the characteristics of a disciple today?
2. Is Christian discipleship an optional activity?
3. How does discipleship relate to salvation?
4. Why do you think God uses the figures of the harvest and the winepress to describe the judgment of the nations?
5. In Isaiah 63, who is coming in judgment?
6. How should this passage motivate Christians today?

REVELATION 15

THE PRELUDE TO THE SEVEN BOWL JUDGMENTS (15:1–8)

The book of Revelation now moves to detailed descriptions of the judgments. Chapter 15 is a prelude. Chapter 16 unfolds the seven bowl judgments. Chapters 17 and 18 are visions of the doom of "Babylon the Great" and of the beast. Chapter 19 reveals the return of the Lord to defeat the hosts of the beast and the kings of the earth in the last battle.

The final series of judgments are called the "bowl judgments" because in the vision John sees seven angels with "bowls." These bowls are full of the last plagues or judgments which will be poured out upon the rebellious nations and the world system. The bowl judgments are similar to the plagues of the Exodus that were poured out on the nation of Egypt. The "sea of glass mixed with fire" (v. 2) that the victors stand on seems to have some analogy to Israel's exodus deliverance. The victors have gone through this into heaven. The cost of their victory has been their earthly lives, but like Israel's crossing of the sea they now have a song of deliverance. The song is called the song of Moses and the Lamb. It unites the people of God in the worship of God.

WORD PICTURE

Bowl

The Greek word *philaē* for "bowl" is specifically a bowl used in offerings. God's judgments are righteous and holy. They are seen to come from the heavenly temple (cp. Rev 5:8; 15:6; 16:1).

The song celebrates the rightness or justice of God as well as his holiness in the coming judgments. Sin and evil need to be destroyed. In the forbearance of God, he has not immediately punished human sin (cp. Rom 3:25–26; 2 Pet 3:9). A long period elapsed before Jesus came the first time to die for our sin (2 Cor 5:17–21). Another long period has passed in which Jesus's sacrifice has been ignored or rejected, and evil has seemed to have free reign. Nevertheless, God will judge the *world* in righteousness.

The holiness and justice of God in his judgments is pictured in several details. First is the content of the song (vv. 3–4). The second is the opening of the heavenly sanctuary, which normally, by analogy, only the high priest entered on earth. Third, the angels are wearing the marks of royal dignity and holiness. Fourth, the sanctuary is filled with smoke. The smoke pictures the awesome power of the glory of God (cp. Exod 19:18; Isa 6:4). At the giving of the law, Mount Sinai quaked and was covered in smoke in the presence of Yahweh. Isaiah had a similar revelation in his commission with the temple shaking and filling with smoke. The high priests could not enter the inner sanctuary without a concealing cloud of smoke of the incense from the altar covering the mercy seat. Violation meant death (Lev 16:12–13).

WORD PICTURE

The World

Although John's favorite term for our world is *kosmos*, the actual word occurs only three times (Rev 11:15; 13:8; 17:8). In contrast, the word *kosmos* occurs ninety-four times in his Gospel and twenty-four times in his epistles. Of the 186 usages of *kosmos* in the New Testament, John uses it 121 times. A common theological definition for this word is "that organized system that leaves God out." Today that includes governments, laws, economic systems, the entertainment industry, and our educational system. In Rev 11:15 the kingdom of the kosmos comes to the rightful ruler—Jesus Christ.

Section Summary

God will judge the world system because of his holiness and righteousness.

QUESTIONS TO GUIDE YOUR STUDY

1. How do God's people conquer the beast?
2. How do songs function in the book of Revelation?
3. What is the role of the "four living creatures" in the book of Revelation?

REVELATION 16

THE SEVEN ANGELS WITH THE SEVEN LAST PLAGUES—THE BOWL JUDGMENTS (16:1–21)

The first bowl judgment is a plague of sores on those who worship the beast. In the sixth plague on Egypt (Exod 9:10–11), "festering boils" broke out on both humans and animals. The Egyptian magicians could not stand before Moses because of their boils. So all those with the mark of the beast now have additional distinguishing marks! God also announced to his people in the Old Testament (Deut 28:58–61) that the rejection of his revelation would be visited by "severe and lasting plagues, and terrible and chronic sicknesses." While this first plague is exceedingly painful, it is not fatal. It is a warning to the world to repent.

The second plague is on the sea, and it corresponds to the first Egyptian plague in which the Nile River "was turned to blood" (Exod 7:20). The fish in the Nile died, and it began to stink. Its water was unfit to drink. So in this judgment the water becomes like the putrefaction of a dead person's blood. No viler object exists for a Jewish observer like

John. He sees the deadly stench of corruption spreading and life in the sea dying. If this is a universal judgment upon all the oceans, the human suffering will be enormous, for humans are dependent on the oceans for food.

The third bowl is poured out on the inland waters or the fresh water supplies. Without fresh water, human life comes quickly to an end. Rejection of the blood of the Lamb—rejection of Jesus's death for sin—results in God's just judgment. The angel in charge of the waters proclaims God's righteous retribution—blood for blood (v. 6). A response comes from the altar: "Yes, Lord God, the Almighty, true and just are your judgments" (v. 7; cp. 6:9).

The fourth bowl is poured on the sun, resulting in intensification of its heat, in contrast to the redeemed who come out of the great tribulation with the promise: "The sun will no longer strike them, nor will any scorching heat" (7:16).

The earth dwellers in their rebellion are scorched, and they scream out in hatred against God. As painful as all these judgments have been, God takes no delight in sin or death. He desires people to trust his salvation (Ezek 18:30–32). Yet the terrible picture in this section is of people so hardened in their ways and so committed to false religions that they will not repent (or change their thinking).

OLD TESTAMENT REFERENCE

"'Throw off all the transgressions you have committed, and get yourselves a new heart and a new spirit. Why should you die, house of Israel? For I take no pleasure in anyone's death.' This is the declaration of the Lord GOD. 'So repent and live!'" (Ezek 18:31–32).

The fifth bowl is poured out on the kingdom of the beast, which is plunged into darkness, much like the ninth Egyptian plague (Exod 10:22) and the fourth trumpet (Rev 8:12). In Egyptian religion, Re (Ra) was the sun god. This was the primary deity whose worship was centered in the city of Heliopolis. The pharaoh was named after Re and called the son of god. Thus, the plague of darkness was a judgment on the Egyptian false religion and its leader. In a similar way, the fifth bowl judgment falls upon the king and his kingdom. Satan, who is also called "Lucifer" (Lat., "light-bearer"), is the false god behind the beast. Satan, who transforms himself into an angel of light (2 Cor 11:14) and who blinds people so they cannot see the light of the glorious gospel, has his kingdom shown for what it is. It is the kingdom of darkness (Col 1:13; cp. Rev 8:12; 9:2; 18:23; Exod 10:22; Isa 8:19–22; Amos 5:18,20; Zeph 1:15; Matt 25:30).

Despite the revelation of God in the judgments and of the false god and his kingdom, the world remains in its rebellion. They blaspheme God and refuse to repent.

The sixth bowl judgment differs from the previous bowls in that it is a preparation for the final battle. The great river Euphrates was the ideal boundary of the Holy Land. Beyond it, world empires and their troops (Assyrians and Babylonians) went forth to conquer. Babylon, the fountain of rebellion against God, was there. The sixth trumpet judgment (9:13–21) also describes part of the process for the end-time

JUDGMENTS IN EXODUS AND REVELATION

	PLAGUES	"SEALS"	"TRUMPETS"	"BOWLS"
Num	Exodus 7:1–12:29	Revelation 6:1–17	Revelation 8:1–9:21	Revelation 15:1–16:16
1.	Water (7:20) becomes blood	Conquest	Vegetation judged	Loathsome sores
2.	Frogs (8:6)	World war	Seas struck	Seas to blood
3.	Gnats (8:17)	Scarcity/famine	Inland waters struck	Inland waters to blood
4.	Flies (8:24)	Death of one-fourth	Cosmic signs	Solar flares
5.	Cattle (9:6) destroyed	Cry of martyrs	Demonic locusts	Darkness on Satan's kingdom
6.	Boils (9:10)	Cosmic signs	Angels from Euphrates	Demonic forces from the Euphrates
7.	Hail (9:23)	—	—	Great cosmic and earthly disturbances
8.	Locusts (10:13)			
9.	Darkness (10:22)			
10.	Firstborn killed (12:29)			

world battle. In this vision, the "kings from the east" (any nation east of the Euphrates River) are led by Satan's demons. The frog was an unclean animal to the Jews, and it was also a symbol of Persian and Egyptian gods or goddesses. Thus, it was doubly unclean and an apt description for satanic spirits.

The focal assembly for the kings of the east is "Harmagedon" (Armageddon). Many (some say two hundred!) great battles have been fought on the plains of Megiddo, and so this is a fitting place for the final great battle. In verse 15 a call from Jesus Christ warns of his unexpected coming (cp. 3:3; Matt 24:43; Luke 12:39; 1 Thess 5:2; 2 Pet 3:10), and he also pronounces a blessing on those who stay away. No one has been able to give a good explanation of the origin of the name "Harmagedon" (Mount of Megiddo) since Megiddo is a city in a great plain. The meaning of the term is the eschatological battle between Jesus Christ and Satan and his forces.

The seventh bowl is the culmination of the plagues. From God's throne and his temple one Greek word sounds (*"Gegonen!"*—"It is done!"). With this the judgment of Babylon will be accomplished. This is the pronouncement, and the details come in the next visions (chaps. 17–19). A shaking of the worlds kingdoms occur because of a great earthquake. John tells us that this is the most violent earthquake ever. Apocalyptic signs and sounds occur with one-hundred-pound hailstones crashing onto the earth.

Section Summary

The final series of judgments ends with the doom of Babylon and the return of Jesus the Messiah to rule.

QUESTIONS TO GUIDE YOUR STUDY

1. Why do we have trouble understanding the justice and holiness of God in judgment?
2. How does Satan work in world governments?
3. How should Christians prepare for the Lord's coming?

REVELATION 17

THE VISION OF THE GREAT PROSTITUTE SITTING UPON THE SCARLET BEAST (17:1–6)

If this division is followed, then a major division begins with chapter 17. The angelic guide shows John a new strange vision of a great prostitute who is seated on many waters. Pictures in "ancient art show cities as their patron goddess, often enthroned on the shore of a river" (Keener, *IVP Bible Background Commentary, New Testament,* 1993, 805). Rome is on the water as is almost every major ancient city. So either Rome or Babylon could be in view here, either standing for the literal Rome or Babylon or as a symbol for the last great capital city. Favoring the view that Babylon is in view is Jer 51:7 and 51:13: "You who reside by abundant water, rich in treasures."

This prostitute has shared her vices and corruption with the world powers (cp. Jer 51:7). John is carried into a desert (v. 3), and the woman is with the beast (Rev 13:1; cp. Isa 14:23; 21:1). The color shows the connection to the great red dragon (Satan). The cup in her hand is like a vision of Jeremiah (51:6–7) where the nations are drunk with Babylon's filth. The woman is also a "mystery" in that she is the mother of idolatrous filth and of persecutions of the righteous.

PERSONAL APPLICATION

The Four Major Visions

The book of Revelation in the Greek text has been divided into as many as 102 segments or paragraphs. Attempts to divide the material into larger units based on phrases in Greek such as "after this I saw" (4:1; 7:1; 7:9; 15:5; 18:1; etc.) as indicating major breaks, and minor or subordinate visions, are not successful in this writer's view. However, four major visions can be isolated based on content:

1. The Glorified Christ and His Church (1:9–3:22)
2. Christ the Lamb and His Judgments (4:1–16:21)
3. The Conquering Christ (17:1–21:8)
4. Christ and His Bride in Consummation: The New Jerusalem (21:9–22:5)

THE INTERPRETATION OF THE PROSTITUTE AND BEAST VISION (17:7–17)

John is amazed at the great personification and embodiment of evil in the woman and the beast. An interpreting angel begins to explain some of the features of the vision to John. The beast is a world empire as in

Dan 7. This world empire had a past existence but ceased to exist. However, it will come back as a manifestation of Satan ("up from the abyss"). The whole world will be amazed at the startling recovery of this empire.

In verses 9 and 10, the beast is connected to the city of Rome which sits on seven hills. But the angel says that the seven hills are also seven kings. "Hills" or "mountains" are often symbols for kings or kingdoms (Isa 2:2; Jer 51:25; Dan 2:35). Kings and their kingdoms are often interchanged in prophetic literature. So the beast seems to be the final form of past world empires. Five world empires were past, Rome was in existence then, and a final form will arise. If this is correct, the five world empires are Egypt, Assyria, Babylon, Medo-Persia, and Greece. Rome in John's days (about AD 96) was the contemporary form of the beast's kingdom. A seventh kingdom will arise which will transmute into the eighth. The eighth will be Satan's masterwork with total domination of the world.

The horns are also interpreted by the angel (v. 12). They are ten kings, and their kingdoms are not yet in existence. But they will arise with the same satanic empowerment as the beast. These ten kingdoms will be united in purpose with the beast and make war against Jesus Christ, who is the Lamb. The angel assured John that the Lamb has complete sovereign power. He will be victorious, and all his followers will share in that victory. The interpretation is similar to Daniel's night vision of the Son of Man (7:13–14). Daniel also has an angel who interprets for him.

It is impossible to predict where and when these ten kingdoms (Dan 7:24,26) will come on the scene of world history. Most interpreters who venture a guess favor the nations in a revived Rome, that is, Europe. But they could come from anywhere in the Mediterranean area or the Middle East.

In verses 15–18, a satanic civil war takes place. The beast and the ten horns (ten kings or kingdoms) destroy the position and power of the great prostitute. Modern history has many examples of political alliances being formed to gain power only to result in betrayal and death once the power is achieved. Both Lenin and Hitler turned on their former allies and killed them. Something similar will happen between the beast and the prostitute. Again, the prostitute is identified in language taken from Jer 51:13 concerning Babylon and from John's contemporary history under the Roman Empire. In verse 18 the prostitute is the city of Rome. The anti-God spirit in ancient Babylon and in first-century Rome is the woman. Her destruction is spelled out in terms taken from the book of Ezekiel (23:11–35).

WORD PICTURE

Angels

Angels in the Bible are seen in many roles. The angels of God carry out his will in judgments; in the protection of his people (Isa 37:36); in the worship of God (Rev 5:11–12); and in revelation. The interpreting angel is often found in the Bible where he makes clear or makes known God's visions (Zech 1–6; Rev 17:7; 21:9–15). The book of Hebrews compares and contrasts Jesus with the angels (1:1–14).

Section Summary

John is shown a vision which is interpreted by an angel. A final world empire will arise and achieve total domination. Political rivals like the great prostitute will be annihilated.

QUESTIONS TO GUIDE YOUR STUDY

1. Why is the sin of adultery used in the Bible to describe apostate religion?
2. How does the study of Daniel 7 help in the interpretation of this vision?
3. How does the study of Zechariah 1 help in the interpretation of this vision?

PERSONAL APPLICATION

Christians should have confidence as they look at history. While evil seems so powerful, appearances are not reality. The Lamb is all-powerful and evil will be conquered. The evil kingdom is full of lies, hatred, and dissension. It will not stand.

REVELATION 18

THE FALL OF BABYLON THE GREAT (18:1–8)

Chapter 18 continues the description of the judgment of the great prostitute or the great city "that has royal power over the kings of the earth" (17:18). Some interpreters (e.g., Walvoord) see chapter 17 as the judgment on religious Babylon and chapter 18 as the judgment on commercial Babylon. It may be that the final form of religious syncretism will achieve a temporary dominance over the final political system. But the political system will overthrow the tyranny in favor of its own deification.

Chapter 18 contains more detail on the destruction of the prostitute, while the political system meets its doom in chapter 19. Often, Israel's enemies were political city-states. These cities were centers of idolatrous religions and vast cruelty.

In 18:2 the angel with power announces that "Babylon the Great has fallen!" This large prosperous city is doomed to be a home for the demons. The cause is its corruption and seduction in leading the world away from God. Prediction is hazardous as to where this center of religion and economics will be located. Who can guess what city will be the final one?

Another angelic voice warns God's people to separate from the system. God will always have his people, even in the worst part of the great tribulation. Many believers will be martyred, but some will escape and live through that period (cp. Matt 24:22).

REACTIONS TO THE FALL OF BABYLON (18:9–24)

The major part of this section is a series of laments by the kings of the earth (vv. 9–10), the merchants (vv. 11–17a), and the seafarers (vv. 17b–19). More and more the economic system of the world is being unified.

Commerce, banking, and computers are tying nations and companies together. Fewer and fewer individual companies will be left. When the great consolidation takes place, a total economic stranglehold will occur—"no one can buy or sell" (13:17) without the mark of the beast. When the center of this system is suddenly destroyed, everyone plugged into the system will be left in total chaos. Commerce, banking, and computers will come to a halt. Today, with weapons of mass destruction, an entire city can be destroyed in an instant.

So it will be with Babylon. The laments are self-centered because they did not love the prostitute, but her judgment is their ruin. The list of cargo is like the judgment on Tyre (Ezek 16:9–13; 27:5–24). Of particular interest is the cargo in "slaves—human lives."

A great outburst of praise takes place in heaven. Saints, apostles, and prophets join together in joy that God has judged the great prostitute and that the return of the Lord is at hand. God's justice is demonstrated in the punishment of those who persecuted God's people and filled the earth with their blood (Rev 17:6).

In a symbolic act, an angel pictures the suddenness and the complete disappearance of Babylon by throwing a huge boulder into the sea. All normal activities (18:22–23) of the great city will cease.

HISTORICAL BACKGROUND

The great tyrannies of the twentieth century (Nazi Germany, Bolshevik Russia) are examples of empires using enslaved peoples. The final tyranny will be far worse.

Section Summary

Babylon will disappear forever in God's righteous judgment. Economic chaos will take place.

QUESTIONS TO GUIDE YOUR STUD1

1. What does the angel announce in verse 22?
2. Another voice calls to God's people (v. 4). What is the command3?
3. Who reacts strongly to the fall of Babylon?

REVELATION 19

THE HALLELUJAHS IN HEAVEN OVER HIS JUDGING (19:1–5)

A great celebration takes place in heaven because God has judged the great prostitute and vindicated his servants. The singers who praise God for his righteous action include a "vast multitude," which is probably the same group seen in Rev 7:9–10. These are the redeemed from every nation. Joining them are various ranks of angelic beings—the twenty-four elders and the four living creatures.

WORD PICTURE

Hebrew Words in English

A number of Hebrew words have been transliterated in our Bibles. Some have become so common that they are part of our normal vocabulary. *Hallelujah* is a word meaning "praise you (pl.) Yahweh." *Yahweh* is one way of writing the name of our God YHWH. Jewish people did not pronounce the vowels of God's name. "Yahweh" and "Jehovah" are two other ways of writing the divine name in the English language. The word *amen* occurs 126 times in the New Testament and eight times in the book of Revelation. It is from a Hebrew word meaning "to be firm." It is used to give solemn assent to a statement or a prayer. In Rev 19:4 it expresses assent to the praise of God. In Rev 3:14 it is used as a title for Jesus as the faithful and true witness.

PERSONAL APPLICATION

Christians should not be surprised by the return of the Lord but should he watching and waiting while working (cp. Matt 25:1–13; 2 Thess 3:6–9; 1 Thess 5:4–11).

NEW TESTAMENT REFERENCE

The Return of the Lord

Both the Old Testament and the New Testament speak of the coming of the Lord to finish the redemption of God's people and to judge the world in righteousness. Jesus often told his people to be ready (Matt 24:44).

THE MARRIAGE OF THE LAMB (19:6–10)

Marriages are almost always significant events in every culture. In the Bible, the unique relationship between man and woman in marriage is often a picture of the Lord with his people (Jer 3:1–14; Ezek 16:1–63; Hos 1:1–3:5; Eph 5:22–33). John in his Gospel begins the ministry of Jesus with his first miracle at a wedding in Cana of Galilee (John 2:1–11). In the book of Revelation, Jesus returns to earth to consummate the redemption of his people and celebrate the marriage supper. The church is the bride and is clothed with fine linen which is interpreted as "the righteous acts of the saints" (v. 8).

A Christian is one who is saved by grace and then is "right" in God's sight because Christ's righteousness has been credited to the believer (Eph 2:8–9; Rom 3:21–26; 4:6–8; 5:1). But one purpose of this salvation is that the believer will live a different kind of life. The new life is for "good works" (Eph 2:10). So the church is adorned with beautiful deeds in the sight of her husband. The pure white garment stands in stark contrast to the luxurious purple and scarlet garments of the great prostitute (Rev 17:1–6). Her deeds are bloody, blasphemous, and foul.

John was so moved by the vision and the interpretation that he fell at the feet of an angel to do homage to him. He is quickly rebuked. The worship of any created being or thing is forbidden. Only God is to be worshiped (19:10). In the early church there was a tendency to worship angels (Col 2:18) or to put too high a valuation on them (cp. Heb 1:1–2:16). Although angels have great power and privilege today, they will be judged by humans (1 Cor 6:3), and they do not participate in the great salvation which humans enjoy. Humans are sons of God by adoption and coheirs with Jesus Christ (Rom 8:14–18). The fact that Jesus Christ is to be worshiped reveals his deity (Heb 1:6; Rev 5:13–14; Matt 14:33; Phil 2:9–11).

Angels are only fellow servants with humans who bear witness to Jesus. The angel also reminded John that the testimony to Jesus is the common theme of prophecy. Jesus told his disciples that the Old Testament Scriptures speak of a suffering Messiah (Isa 53) and of his glorious reign (cp. Dan 7:13–14).

Section Summary

Jesus will return as the glorious King to claim his bride. Heaven and earth rejoice at the prospect.

THE MESSIANIC WARRIOR COMES (19:11–16)

John sees heaven open and a rider on a white horse. This vision is different in subject and content from the rider on a white horse in 6:2. There the person begins the warfare of the great tribulation. Here the vision is of Jesus Christ in triumph. Kings often rode on a donkey or a mule (1 Kgs 1:33; Zech 9:9) as a sign of peace or humility. The Jewish people longed for God to come and judge the nations. As the Old Testament progressively unfolded the details of God's coming, the hope became clearer that the warrior Messiah would come. Paul in 2 Thess 1:7–8 said, "The Lord Jesus" would come from heaven "with his powerful angels, when he takes vengeance with flaming fire on those who don't know God and on those who don't obey the gospel of our Lord Jesus."

The Lamb of 5:5–6 and the exalted priest of 1:13 are now revealed in his role as the messianic warrior. He is the righteous One who will rule in righteousness (cp. 16:5–7; 19:2; Ps 96:13). Jesus is given a number of titles: "Faithful and True," "the Word of God," a secret name, and "KING OF KINGS AND LORD OF LORDS." His eyes penetrate into the hearts of people (1:14; 2:18), and he wears "many crowns." The beast and the dragon also had crowns (12:3; 13:1), but they are usurpers and false leaders. The true or real Sovereign is shown. He comes with armies but not because he needs help in this holy war. All he needs to do is speak, and the reign of Satan is over. The white horse is the symbol of the coming victory. The heavenly hosts come to celebrate his triumph.

His robe is "dipped in blood" (19:13) because of the enemies he has slain in battle (cp. Isa 63:1–6). "A sharp sword came from his mouth" (v. 15) symbolizes the power to kill with his words (cp. Heb 4:12). As in creation, God spoke and it took place (cp. Gen 1:3), so Jesus could still a storm with a word (Matt 8:26) or heal (Matt 9:5) or forgive sins (Matt 9:5–7). Paul wrote, "Then the lawless one will be revealed. The Lord Jesus will destroy him with the breath of his mouth and will bring him to nothing at the appearance of his coming" (2 Thess 2:8). Isaiah also described the victory of the Messiah over his foes in the same language (Isa 11:1–5). The phrase "He will rule them with an iron rod" is also a messianic prediction of his victory over the rebellious nations (Ps 2:1–9).

The figure of "trampl[ing] the winepress" was a common metaphor in an agricultural society where grapes were put in a press or vat and a person trampled the grapes with his or her feet and the red grape juice flowed out. The figure was applied to the warrior Messiah who would trample his enemies under his feet like grapes:

> Who is this coming from Edom
> in crimson-stained garments from Bozrah— . . .
> Why are your clothes red,
> and your garments like one who treads a winepress? . . .
> I trampled them in my anger
> and ground them underfoot in my fury;
> their blood spattered my garments,
> and all my clothes were stained. . . .
> I crushed nations in my anger (Isa 63:1–6).

OLD TESTAMENT REFERENCE

The Coming of God/the Lord (Old Testament)

In the Old Testament are many prophecies that look forward to a new day. Sometimes it is called "the day of the LORD" (Amos 5:18–20), but often there are shorter expressions such as "the day" or "in that day." The day of Yahweh is the occasion when he intervenes in human history to purify Israel, punish sin, and judge the nations. Key texts on this concept are Isa 2:12–22; Joel 1:15–2:2; Zeph 1:7–18; and Zech 14:1–9. Man's day will be over, and the day of Yahweh's reign on earth will begin. The clearest Old Testament passage on the return of the Lord is Zech 14:1–4: "Look, a day belonging to the LORD is coming. . . . I will gather all the nations against Jerusalem for battle. . . . On that day his feet will stand on the Mount of Olives" (cp. Acts 1:10–11; Rev 1:7–8).

THE GREAT VICTORY (19:17–21)

PERSONALALICATION

It is more pleasant to think of heaven than hell; of Jesus as the Lamb of God who takes our sin than of the warrior Jesus who judges the world in righteousness. But both parts of the Revelation are biblical, and both are to be believed and taught. Humanity has a choice about how it will meet God.

In this vision, only the end of the great battle between the messianic warrior—Jesus Christ—and the antichrist and his allies is shown. The vision starts with an angel in the splendor of the sun announcing the victory. After the great battles of history, a bloody carnage fills the fields. In World War I, from 1914–1918, millions of men were slaughtered. The British lost 400 thousand in one battle to gain five miles of mud! The Russians lost more than a million men in a short period on the eastern front. The grisly aftermath is a feast for the carrion eaters such as the vultures. So here the angel calls for the vultures to gather and feast at this "supper." The "great supper of God" (v. 17) is a total contrast to the "marriage feast of the Lamb" (v. 9).

The picture of the kings of the earth and their armies lying dead and unburied is horrible. For ancient people, not to have a decent burial was the final humiliation. To die was bad, but to have one's body eaten by a predator was total ignominy. The battle of Armageddon (16:16) is over and the demonic leaders are cast into "the lake of fire that burns with sulfur" (v. 20). Their armies are quickly destroyed, and the victory is total.

Section Summary

Jesus returns as the messianic warrior who defeats the antichrist and his allies.

QUESTIONS TO GUIDE YOUR STUDY

1. What does the heavenly "Hallelujah Chorus" rejoice over?
2. How should Christians prepare for the wedding?
3. Who are the people invited to the wedding supper?
4. What is the significance of clothing and colors in this vision?
5. If the sword coming out of the mouth of the warrior Messiah is a symbol, what is it a symbol of?
6. How does this vision of Jesus change your conception of him?

THE QUESTION OF THE MILLENNIUM

Revelation 20:1–7 speaks of a thousand-year period of Christ's reign. Three major views have been common in the church: (1) premillennialism, (2) amillennialism, and (3) postmillennialism. The premillennial view has been popular in many evangelical churches of America in two forms: (a) historic premillennialism and (b) dispensational premillennialism. The following chart outlines the major features of each view.

The premillennial view seems to have been the first interpretation of Rev 20:1–7 in the early church. For the first three centuries it was the dominant view and was held by Papias, Irenaeus, Justin Martyr,

Tertullian, Hippolytus, Methodius, Commodianus, and Lactantius. This view looks for a literal kingdom of God on earth ruled by Jesus Christ as King.

The amillennial view denies that there will be a future, literal kingdom on earth ruled by Jesus as King. Instead, Christ is now ruling in heaven and Satan's kingdom (the city of the world) will be destroyed at Christ's return. The allegorical understanding of Origen (ca 185–ca 254) and of Augustine (354–430) of Hippo became the dominant view of the church of the medieval period. Revelation 20 is interpreted as the reign of the dead believers with Christ in heaven.

The postmillennial view believes in the triumph of the gospel in this world. The millennium will come through Christian preaching and teaching. The popularization of this view came from D. Whitby (1638–1726) and during the periods of optimism in England and America.

The pretribulation premillennial view has been popular with evangelicals in England and America. It is based on a fairly literal interpretation of the book of Revelation as well as the Old Testament prophetic books. The major difference between it and "classic" premillennialism is the emphasis on the tribulation and the role of the nation of Israel in the plan of God. It also has two phases in the second advent. First, the rapture occurs in which all believers arise to be with Christ in the heavens. Following the rapture of the church, the great tribulation of Rev 6–19 then takes place with Christ returning to earth to rule (Rev 19–20).

WORD PICTURE

Millennialism

Sometimes this is called *chiliasm* from the Greek word for "thousand." But the usual term is millenarianism or millennialism from the Latin word for "thousand."

Millennial Perspectives on Revelation

POINT OF INTERPRETATION	AMILLENNIAL	HISTORICAL PREMILLENNIAL	DISPENSATIONAL PREMILLENNIAL	POSTMILLENNIAL
DESCRIPTION OF VIEW	Viewpoint that the present age of Christ's rule in the Church is the millennium; holds to one resurrection and judgment marking the end of history as we know it and the beginning of life eternal.	Viewpoint that Christ will reign on earth for a thousand years following His second coming; saints will be resurrected at the beginning of the millennium, nonbelievers at the end, followed by judgment.	Viewpoint that after the Battle of Armageddon, Christ will rule through the Jews for a literal thousand years accompanied by two resurrections and at least three judgments.	Viewpoint that Christ will return after a long period of expansion and spiritual prosperity for the Church, brought about by the preaching of the gospel; the Spirit's blessing; and the Church's work toward righteousness, justice, and peace. The period is not a literal thousand years but an extended time of spiritual prosperity.
BOOK OF REVELATION	Current history written in code to confound enemies and encourage Asian Christians; message applies to all Christians.	Immediate application to Asian Christians; applies to all Christians throughout the ages, but the visions also apply to a great future event.	"Unveiling" of theme of Christ among churches in present dispensation, also as Judge and King in dispensations to come.	Written to encourage Christians of all ages, but the visions also apply to a great future event.
SEVEN CANDLESTICKS (1:13)	Churches		Churches, plus end-time application	Churches

Millennial Perspectives on Revelation (cond.)

POINT OF INTERPRETATION	AMILLENNIAL	HISTORICAL PREMILLENNIAL	DISPENSATIONAL PREMILLENNIAL	POSTMILLENNIAL
CHURCHES ADDRESSED (CHAPS. 2–3)	Specific historical situations, truths apply to churches throughout the ages; do not represent periods of church history.		Specific historical situations and to all churches throughout the ages; shows progress of churches' spiritual state until end of church age.	Specific historical situations, truths apply to churches throughout the ages; do not necessarily represent periods of church history.
TWENTY-FOUR ELDERS (4:4, 10; 5:8, 14)	Twelve patriarchs and twelve apostles; together symbolize all the redeemed.	Company of angels who help execute God's rule (or elders represent twenty-four priestly and Levitical orders).	The rewarded church also represents twelve patriarchs and twelve apostles.	Symbolizes all the redeemed.
SEALED BOOK (5:1–9)	Scroll of history; shows God carrying out His redemptive purpose in history.	Contains prophecy of endtime events of chapters 7–22	Title deed to the world	Portrays God carrying out His redemptive purpose in history.
144,000 (7:4–8)	Redeemed on earth who will be protected against God's wrath.	Church on threshold of the Great Tribulation	Jewish converts of tribulation period who witness to Gentiles (same as 14:1).	Redeemed people of God

Millennial Perspectives on Revelation (con'd.)

POINT OF INTERPRETATION	AMILLENNIAL	HISTORICAL PREMILLENNIAL	DISPENSATIONAL PREMILLENNIAL	POSTMILLENNIAL
GREAT TRIBULATION (FIRST REFERENCE IN 7:4)	Persecution faced by Asian Christians of John's time; symbolic of tribulation that occurs throughout history.	Period at end time of unexplained trouble, before Christ's return; Church will go through it; begins with seventh seal (18:1) which includes trumpets 1–6 (8:2–14:20).	Period at end time of unexplained trouble referred to in 7:14 and described in chapters 11–18; lasts three and a half years, the latter half of a seven-year period between rapture and millennium.	Symbolic of tribulation that occurs throughout history.
FORTY-TWO MONTHS (11:2); 1,260 DAYS (11:3)	Indefinite duration of pagan desolation.	A symbolic number representing period of evil with reference to last days of age.	Half of seven-year tribulation period.	A symbolic number representing an indefinite time and evil influence.
WOMAN (12:1–6)	True people of God under Old and New Covenants (true Israel)		Indicates Israel, not church; key is comparison with Genesis 37:9.	True people of God under Old and New Covenants.
GREAT RED DRAGON (12:3)	All views identify as Satan.			
MAN-CHILD (12:4–5)	Christ at His birth, life events, and crucifixion, whom Satan sought to kill.	Christ, whose work Satan seeks to destroy.	Christ but also the Church (head and body); caught up on throne indicates rapture of Church.	Christ at His birth, life events, and crucifixion, whom Satan sought to destroy.
1,260 DAYS (12:6)	Indefinite time	Symbolic number representing period of evil with special reference to last days of age.	First half of Great Tribulation; Church is raptured.	Indefinite time

Millennial Perspectives on Revelation (con'd.)

POINT OF INTERPRETATION	AMILLENNIAL	HISTORICAL PREMILLENNIAL	DISPENSATIONAL PREMILLENNIAL	POSTMILLENNIAL
SEA BEAST (13:1)	Emperor Domitian, personification of Roman Empire (same as in chap. 17)	Antichrist, here shown as embodiment of the four beasts in Daniel 7.	A new Rome, satanic federation of nations that come out of old Roman Empire.	Roman Empire
SEVEN HEADS (13:1)	Roman emperors	Great power, showing kinship with dragon.	Seven stages of Roman Empire; sixth was imperial Rome (John's day); last will be federation of nations.	Roman Emperors
TEN HORNS (13:1)	Symbolize power	Kings, represent limited crowns (ten) against Christ's many.	Ten powers that will combine to make the federation of nations of a new Rome.	Symbol of power
666 (13:18)	Imperfection, evil; personified as Domitian	Symbolic of evil, short of 777; if a personage meant, he is unknown but will be known at the proper time.	Not know, but will be known when time comes.	Symbol of evil
144,000 ON MOUNT ZION (14:1)	Total body of redeemed in heaven		Redeemed Jews gathered in earthly Jerusalem during millennial kingdom.	Redeemed people of God
RIVER OF BLOOD (14:20)	Symbol of infinite punishment for the wicked	Means God's radical judgment crushes evil thoroughly.	Scene of wrath and carnage that will occur in Palestine.	Symbol of judgment on the wicked
BABYLON (WOMAN-17:5)	Historical Rome	Capital city of future Antichrist.	Apostate church of the future	Symbol of evil

Millennial Perspectives on Revelation (con'd.)

POINT OF INTERPRETATION	AMILLENNIAL	HISTORICAL PREMILLENNIAL	DISPENSATIONAL PREMILLENNIAL	POSTMILLENNIAL
SEVEN MOUNTAINS (17:9)	Pagan Rome, which was built on seven hills	Indicate power, so here means a succession of empires, last of which is end-time Babylon.	Rome, revived at end time	Pagan Rome
SEVEN HEADS (17:7) AND TEN KINGS (17:12)	Roman Emperors From Augustus To Titus, Excluding Three Brief Rules	Five past godless kingdoms; sixth was Rome; seventh would arise in end time.	Five distinct forms of Roman government prior to John; sixth was imperial Rome; seventh will be revived Roman Empire.	Roman emperors
TEN HORNS (17:7) AND TEN KINGS (17:12)	Vassal kings who ruled with Rome's permission	Symbolic of earthly powers that will be subservient to Antichrist.	Ten kingdoms arising in future out of revived Roman Empire.	Symbolic of earthly powers
BRIDE, WIFE (19:7)	Total of all the redeemed		The Church; does not include Old Testament saints or tribulation saints. Total of all the redeemed	Total of all the redeemed
MARRIAGE SUPPER(19:9)	Climax of the age; symbolizes complete union of Christ with His people.	Union of Christ with His people at His coming.	Union of Christ with His church accompanied by Old Testament saints and tribulation saints.	Union of Christ with His people
ONE ON WHITE HORSE (19:11–16)	Vision of Christ's victory over pagan Rome; return of Christ occurs in connection with events of 20:7–10.	Second Coming of Christ		Vision of Christ's victory

Millennial Perspectives on Revelation (con'd.)

POINT OF INTERPRETATION	AMILLENNIAL	HISTORICAL PREMILLENNIAL	DISPENSATIONAL PREMILLENNIAL	POSTMILLENNIAL
BATTLE OF ARMAGEDDON (19:19–21; SEE 16:16)	Not literally at end of time but symbolizes power of God's world overcoming evil; principle applies to all ages.	Literal event of some kind at end time but not literal battle with military weapons; occurs at Christ's return at beginning of millennium.	Literal bloody battle at Armageddon (Valley of Megiddo) at end of great tribulation between kings of the East and federation of nations of new Rome; they are all defeated by blast from Christ's mouth and then millennium begins.	Symbolizes power of God's Word overcoming evil forces.
GREAT SUPPER (19:17)	Stands in contrast to marriage supper	Stands in contrast to marriage supper	Concludes series of judgments and opens way for kingdom to be established.	Stands in contrast to marriage supper.
BINDING OF SATAN (20:2)	Symbolic of Christ's resurrection victory over Satan.	Curbing of Satan's power during the millennium	Curbing of Satan's power during the millennium	Symbolic of Christ's victory over Satan.
MILLENNIUM (20:2–6)	Symbolic reference to period from Christ's first coming to His second.	A historical event, though length of one thousand years may be symbolic, after Armageddon during which Christ rules with His people.	A literal thousand-year period after the church age during which Christ rules with His people but especially through the Jews.	A lengthy period of expansion and spiritual prosperity brought about by the preaching of the gospel.

Millennial Perspectives on Revelation (con'd.)

POINT OF INTERPRETATION	AMILLENNIAL	HISTORICAL PREMILLENNIAL	DISPENSATIONAL PREMILLENNIAL	POSTMILLENNIAL
THOSE ON THRONES (20:4)	Martyrs in heaven; their presence with God is a judgment on those who killed them.	Saints and martyrs who rule with Christ in the millennium.	The redeemed ruling with Christ, appearing and disappearing on earth at will to oversee life on earth.	Saints and martyrs who rule with Christ.
FIRST RESURRECTION (20:5–6)	The spiritual presence with Christ of the redeemed that occurs after physical death.	Resurrection of saints at beginning of millennium when Christ returns.	Includes three groups: (1) those raptured with church (4:1); (2) Jewish tribulation saints during tribulation (11:11); (3) other Jewish believers at beginning of millennium (20:5–6).	The spiritual presence of the redeemed with Christ.
SECOND DEATH (20:6)	Spiritual death, eternal separation from God			
NEW HEAVENS AND EARTH (21:1)	A new order; redeemed earth			
NEW JERUSALEM (21:2–5)	God dwelling with His saints in the new age after all other end-time events.			

REVELATION 20

THE MILLENNIUM (20:1–6)

Why God has permitted sin and rebellion is a much-discussed question. The Bible is clear as to God's sovereignty and his power. In this vision, John sees an angel binding Satan for one thousand years and then his final destiny in the lake of fire (v. 10). One angel is all it takes—not even an archangel or Christ is needed to do the task. Satan's confinement is in the abyss so he cannot deceive the world and lead people into false worship and opposition to God. But in verse 3 a sobering note is sounded: "After that [one thousand years], he must be released for a short time." The release of Satan to test humanity once again is revealed.

At the start of the one-thousand-year period, there is the first resurrection (Dan 7:9,22,27; 12:2–9; 1 Cor 15:22–23; 1 Thess 4:14,16) and the reign with Christ. John does not reveal anything about the actual conditions of the millennium. The Bible speaks little about the conditions of a the resurrection body or of heaven. The emphasis in this passage is the resurrection of the martyrs of the tribulation period. But in other places, we know that every believer will participate in the reign of Christ (Rev 2:26–28; 3:12,21; 5:10) and thus in the first resurrection (cp. John 5:29; 1 Cor 15:12; 1 Thess 4:13). The remainder of the dead are raised to the great white throne judgment (20:11–15).

Section Summary

Jesus, the Messiah, will take over the rule of the earth. Satan will be bound, and a golden age of the fulfillment of the prophecies will take place.

THE DOOM OF SATAN (20:7–10)

In the book of Revelation, Satan is continually defeated: in 12:9 he is cast out of heaven to earth; in 20:1–3 he is cast into the pit or abyss; and now he is thrown into the lake of fire. A strange thing happens at the end of the one-thousand-year reign. Satan is released, nations are again deceived, and a final assault is made against the beloved city of Jerusalem. Satan has completed his task in revealing the hidden sin of the hearts of humanity and now reaches his final doom.

OLD TESTAMENT REFERENCE

The background for this vision is Ezek 38–39 where "Gog and Magog" attack Israel only to be destroyed by God. So here fire falls from heaven, and the hostile armies perish.

WHAT IS THE PURPOSE OF THIS 1,000-YEAR PERIOD?
1. It is the answer to prayers of Christians in every age who have prayed: "Your kingdom come, Your will be done on earth as in heaven."
2. It is the fulfillment of the many prophecies given to the nation of Israel. For example, Isaiah wrote of the days in which "the wolf will dwell with the lamb" (11:1–10), and when "they will beat their swords into plows" and "nation will not take up the sword against nation" (2:1–4, cp. Jer 31:31–34; Ezek 36:22–28; Zech 14:9–21; Luke 1:32–33).

WHAT IS THE PURPOSE OF THIS 1,000-YEAR PERIOD?
3. It is the demonstration of how man should live on earth. The last Adam will overcome the failure of the first Adam.
4. It is the period for rewards for God's servants and especially the martyrs (Matt 19:28–29; 2 Tim 4:8; Rev 20:4).
5. It will be a further revelation of the glories of the Messiah as people and angels come to see him without the limitations of a sinful environment.
6. It will also *reveal* the deep-seated problem in the human heart. Man's problem is not primarily Satan or a sinful environment. Evidently at the return of Christ, only believers will enter the millennium. Those still living on earth will have "normal" lives—marriages and children. So, at the end of the period, there will be a sifting of humanity by Satan.
7. It will also become an interim phase into the eternal reign of God (1 Cor 15:23–25) and preparation for the new heavens and new earth (Rev 21:1; 2 Pet 3:13).

Section Summary

Even in a perfect environment, when all people have an opportunity to know the Lord personally, some will use their freedom to rebel against God.

THE LAST JUDGMENT (20:11–15)

Because of sin, we incur guilt. Objective (in contrast to subjective "guilt feelings") guilt is the liability to be punished. The condemnation or pronouncement of guilt results in sentence or punishment. In the Bible, God is the Judge. Unless a person turns to Christ and trusts his work on the cross, he or she will be condemned (John 3:18; Rom 8:33–34).

In Christian theology, many people have used the term *general judgment* to describe the scene in Rev 20:11–15. Premillennials usually teach that there are at least three distinct judgments:

The *bēma*—or judgment seat for believers for the evaluation of their stewardship (Rom 14:10; 1 Cor 3:12–15; 2 Cor 5:10). The issue is rewards, not salvation.

The judgment of the nations (Joel 3:1–3; Isa 2:4; Matt 25:31–46). The issue is the treatment of the Jewish people.

The great white throne (Rev 20:11–15). All unbelievers stand before God to be finally judged.

The Christian will not be condemned because Jesus bore the guilt, the sin, the punishment on the cross (Ps 1:4–6; John 5:22–24; 2 Cor 5:21; Heb 9:27; 12:23).

A large part of the book of Revelation (chaps. 6–19) is about God's judgment within human history. This vision is of the throne of God who is the judge of all (Heb 12:23). God is visible and his splendor radiates holiness. Earth and sky pass away in his majesty. All of humanity who are unsaved stand before him. Christians are exempt because Jesus Christ has already been judged in our place and has taken our hell.

The judgment is based on the "books." That is, it is objective. Everything men and women have done is recorded. All of the secrets of the mind and heart are known. No one will be saved by works or deeds (Rom 2:1–16; 3:20; 4:1–4). The "book of life" belongs to Jesus the Lamb (21:27), and all who are conquerors (believers in Jesus; 1 John 5:5) are promised his salvation (Rev 3:5).

In the last judgment, the Father has delegated the authority to pronounce judgment to the Son (John 5:26–27). Jesus as the Son of Man (Dan 7:13–14) knows the hearts of people and is the One to whom "the Ancient of Days" (Dan 7:9,13) has given the dominion and the kingship. The text is emphatic that all the rest of humanity will be raised up (the believers were raised in the first resurrection before the millennium). It does not matter when or where a person died—all will be brought up for judgment (Rev 20:12–14). The Bible is clearly against any teaching of reincarnation or annihilation (cp. 14:10–11). A person dies once and then is raised. The issue is clear and the results decisive (20:15). Without Jesus's righteousness, there is no hope.

NEW TESTAMENT REFERENCE

The picture or vision of the final state of the unbeliever is terrible. It is a separation from God and a lake of fire. Scientists tell us our universe is literally full of lakes of fire receding outward in an expanding universe. So the confinement of the lost could be like being placed on a star, receding from God into "outer darkness" (Matt 25:30)—"where there will be weeping and gnashing of teeth" (cp. Jude 13).

Section Summary

Jesus Christ as the Son of Man will judge the unbelievers according to truth, righteousness, and works. All who are not in the "book of life" will experience the "second death."

QUESTIONS TO GUIDE YOUR STUDY

1. How will rewards be apportioned in the millennium (cp. Matt 19:27–30)?
2. What do you think is the most important reason for a millennium?
3. How should we live in the light of the coming kingdom (2 Pet 3:11–13)?
4. Why can a person not be saved by works?
5. How can the three judgments be distinguished?
6. What is wrong with the belief in a general judgment consisting of both saved and unsaved?

REVELATION 21

THE NEW CREATION (21:1–8)

More than fifty times in this book, John is said "to see" (usually a vision), or else an angel is explaining to him what "he saw." Now in verses 1 and

2, the last vision is seen. The remainder of the book is a description of the details of the new Jerusalem and the implications of the revelations given to John. More than seven hundred years before John, Isaiah had a vision of God creating a new heaven and a new earth. Isaiah also saw the new Jerusalem filled with joy and blessing (cp. Isa 65:17–25; 66:22–23).

John saw "a new heaven and a new earth." Peter had previously written about the "day of God" in which the existing cosmos would be dissolved and that Christians were waiting for "new heavens and a new earth" (2 Pet 3:7,12–13) in which righteousness dwells. From Peter's words, there was an order before the flood which perished. The present order will be renovated and purified by fire. The globe or earth will still exist, but there will be a new order of cosmos.

John declared, "The sea was no more." Life as we now know it is built on the "seas." If the earth were perfectly spherical, water would cover it all to a depth of one-half mile. But John is not speaking primarily about the physical state of the new cosmos. To the Hebrews, the sea was always ominous and the place where monsters lived. The "beast" of Rev 13 comes out of the sea (13:1, cp. Job 38:3–11; Ps 89:9–10; Isa 57:20). What John saw was the disappearance of evil and death (cp. 20:13).

It would have seemed natural for the final state of mankind to be "heaven" or else at least a garden like the lost Eden (Gen 2:8–3:24). It comes as a bit of shock that the redeemed are going to be in a city on earth! John sees a new Jerusalem as coming out of heaven to earth. The city has, so often, been the place of rebellion and the center of corruption. Just to name "Babylon, Erech, Accad" (Gen 10:10) starts the long line of "Nineveh," "Babylon," "Tyre," "Sodom," "Gomorrah," "Damascus," "Samaria," "Rome" and the old Jerusalem where our Lord was crucified (Rev 11:8). The book of Revelation speaks of the final great city of "Babylon the Great" in which all the evil is concentrated into one center. Both John and Augustine (*The City of God*, AD 422) have written the story of two cities.

WORD PICTURE

Utopia

Mankind has always sought the ideal city or the ideal state. *Utopia* is a name for the perfect society or environment. But *utopia* means "no place" from two Greek words *ou* "no" + *topos* "place."

Finally, the hopes and dreams of humanity will be fulfilled. There will be a real city built by God himself (Heb 11:10; 12:22; 13:14). The author of the book of Hebrews wrote, "For we do not have an enduring city here; instead, we seek the one to come" (13:14). The new city is "holy" in contrast to today's cities, which are filled with crime and corruption. Old Jerusalem was defiled by the murder of Jesus; the new city has no sin or death. John gives us no physical description of the new earth, but a limited picture of the new city is revealed in 21:9–22:5. Here, he only says she is like a bride adorned for her husband. Brides are always a picture of beauty.

A "loud voice" comes from the throne (v. 3) and announces that God's purpose to be with his people is achieved. God made man to be with him and to enjoy fellowship together. In the incarnation, the Son took on humanity so that humanity is joined to the Godhead as a pledge of the future destiny of all Christians. The destiny is now reached. God, as the good Shepherd, wipes all the tears away from his people. There is no pain, sorrow, war, disappointment, disease, or death. Since sin is finally abolished and the devil is in the lake of fire, all of the terrible misery caused by sin and rebellion are over.

Now God himself speaks. He, as the Creator, who began all things by his words (Gen 1:3), now states he is making a new creation. He is the source and origin of everything. He is also the goal and consummation of all things (cp. 2 Cor 5:17; Rom 11:36). As John was commissioned by Jesus to write (Rev 1:19), so also the Father commands him to write (v. 5). The content of the vision is the eternal blessedness of God's people, and it is utterly reliable so people can stake their lives on it.

"It is done!" means there is no doubt about God's plans. To the thirsty, God meets their needs (cp. John 4:10–14; 7:38–39). The promises are to the conquerors (cp. 1 John 5:5; Rev 2:7,11,17,26; 3:5,12,21).

Verse 8 is a contrast to the overcomers of John's churches. Excluded from the wondrous city are eight classes of people who have not overcome the world system but rather have embraced it.

WORD PICTURE

Alpha and Omega

Alpha and omega are the first and last letters of the Greek alphabet. They are used as a title of God to describe his eternity and his infinity. They are used in Rev 1:8 and 21:6 of God the Father and also of God the Son (Christ) in 22:13. The Hebrew word for "truth" is *'emet*, whose first letter is the first letter of the Hebrew alphabet and whose last letter is the last letter of the Hebrew alphabet. Many scholars think the Greek alpha and omega go back to this origin.

THE NEW JERUSALEM (21:9–27)

John is now shown the new Jerusalem in some detail by an angel. Perhaps it is the same one who showed him the nature and destiny of the great evil city (17:1,3). This city stands in opposition to everything about Babylon-Rome. Indeed, it is different from ancient cities. Most cities in the ancient world were small, crowded, dirty, dark places with a temple dominating the center.

This city is huge! It is a cube shape (or possibly a pyramid) that measures fourteen hundred miles in width and length and height. The highest skyscrapers of today are about two thousand feet high. The Burj Khalifa is over twenty-seven hundred feet high. The Japanese developed plans for a mile-high skyscraper. So a city fourteen hundred miles high is stupendous! No more cramped and crowded little cities.

This city has a splendor from the glory of God and the Lamb (v. 24). God himself "lives in unapproachable light" (1 Tim 6:16), and when Jesus revealed himself to Paul on the Damascus Road (Acts 9:3; 26:13), it was with a light brighter than the midday sun. God illumines this city so there is no darkness and no night (21:23; 22:5). Because there is no night and no crime, there is no need to close the gates of the city. The gates of the city are inscribed with the names of the twelve tribes of Israel, and the foundations have the names of the twelve apostles. In the new city, the separation of Jew and Gentile, and Israel and the church, is overcome. Both peoples dwell together.

HISTORICAL BACKGROUND

Ancient cities were small, crowded, dirty, and dark. Animal and human waste littered the streets. After dark, people locked their doors and bolted the city gates. Lighting was primitive.

Ancient building materials were wood and stone. Cement was just beginning to be used in New Testament times. Modern buildings still use the same materials, but they also add steel and glass. These materials are used mainly because they are plentiful and relatively inexpensive. In contrast, the new Jerusalem is constructed from precious and splendid materials. A transparent gold is the paving of the streets. Immense pearls are the gates of the city. The wall is made of jasper. Foundation stones are adorned with jewels. Ancient brides on their wedding days would wear special clothing adorned with coins and all sorts of fine embroidery. This city (v. 9) as the home for the "bride, the wife of the Lamb" is glorious and extravagant.

In the center of ancient cities stood a temple. Over one-fifth of the area of Jerusalem was devoted to the temple and its courts. In medieval Europe, the center of the town or city was the great church or cathedral. The new city has no temple and no sacrifice. God is the center, and the whole city is holy. The long pilgrimage began with God meeting with Adam and Eve; then after the fall, fellowship in prayer and sacrifice, and then God tabernacling among Israel in a tent. Then came the temple followed by the incarnation and the indwelling of believers. The great goal of creation and redemption is achieved in direct communion and fellowship between God and his people. The new city will be the home for all—angels and mankind, Israel and the church, and God himself.

HISTORICAL BACKGROUND

In the center of modern American cities stands the skyscraper. The skyscraper is often the symbol of commerce and consumerism—the god Mammon.

John sees an additional feature of the city as the place from which the knowledge of God is spread. God had revealed that "in the last days" (Isa 2:2–5) the city of Jerusalem would be a center of holiness and revelation. Justice and the knowledge of God would come from the city to the nations of the earth. In similar language (Rev 21:24–27), John sees the function of the new Jerusalem. Some interpreters see this as a flashback to the function of the millennial Jerusalem. But perhaps what is hinted at is that the revelation of God and his redemption will be spread throughout the universe. At least, Paul sees into the future when "things in heaven and things on earth" are brought "together in Christ" (Eph 1:10). In the future, "God's multi-faceted wisdom may now be made known through the church to the rulers and authorities in the heavens" (Eph 3:10).

Section Summary

The Jerusalem from God will appear like an immense diamond. It will be the place of fellowship with God himself.

QUESTIONS TO GUIDE YOUR STUDY

1. How does one become a citizen of this city?

2. What is the function of the buildings in the center of your city?
3. What does architecture reveal about our interests and our priorities?

REVELATION 22

JOHN IS SHOWN THE RIVER OF LIFE (22:1–5)

John Milton (1608–1674) wrote two great epic poems—*Paradise Lost* and *Paradise Regained*. In a way, this section of John's vision shows paradise regained, but because of Christ, we have far more than just a paradise regained. We are now joined to God as a family (Rom 8:15–17), and we have received the righteousness of God in Jesus Christ (Rom 4:6; 1 Cor 1:30; 2 Cor 5:21).

LOST	GAINED
1. Tree of Life, Genesis 2:7; 3:22, 24	Tree of Life, Revelation 22:2
2. Under a Curse, Genesis 3:14–19	No More Curse, Revelation 22:3
3. Banished, Genesis 3:23	Access to God, Revelation 22:3–4
4. In the Dark (cp. Matt 8:12; 27:45; John 3:19; Eph 5:8)	In the Light, Revelation 22:5 (cp. Eph 5:8; 1 Pet 2:9)

In a semidesert land, water is precious. Without water, death comes quickly for plants, animals, and humans. So water is used as a symbol for spiritual life (Ezek 47:1,12; Zech 14:8; John 4:10,14). In this beautiful picture, a river flows from the throne of God. Our rivers are often brackish, polluted, and discolored. This river speaks of the Holy Spirit who gives life. It flows down the center of the great street and gives life to the tree of life. It seems that there is only one tree, but this vision is built on Ezek 47:1–12, which has a bank of trees bearing fruit. Perhaps John used the one tree as a collective for all that comes from the life-giving Spirit of God. Jericho is an ancient oasis city by the Judean desert where, because of its springs, travelers enjoy beautiful fruit. This is also true in the spiritual realm (cp. Ps 1:3; Gal 5:22). Not only does this tree provide fruit, but even its leaves provide "healing."

Children often ask, "What will we do in heaven?" This passage gives some answers. There will be "worship" (Rev 22:3). There will be fellowship and growing in the knowledge of God. The perfected church will have perfect service accompanied by perfect sovereignty. The rule of God extends throughout the expanding universe, and his people will rule with him forever (22:5).

Section Summary

In God's presence, his people will enjoy life to the maximum forever.

GOD'S FINAL WORDS TO MANKIND: THE EPILOGUE (22:6–21)

The Bible is a library with many kinds of literature—law, prophecy, hymns, proverbs, history, gospels, letters, and poetry. It is a library written by many different people over the course of fifteen hundred years—kings, statesmen, judges, lawgivers, musicians, historians, generals, evangelists, and teachers. In each case, God was at work in the writer's life, so that without violating their personality or literary style, his own word and message were communicated through their words.

John was chosen by Jesus the Messiah to be one of the twelve disciples and apostles (Matt 4:21–22). He was also chosen to be one of the inner three (Matt 17:1), suffer, and have a great revelation given to him (Rev 1:1,9,10,19). The revelation was of Jesus Christ and his role as Judge and Ruler. What remains to be said? The last section of the last book of the Bible contains warnings, applications, affirmations, and exhortations. In this final section, the speakers are varied—angel, Jesus, John, the Spirit, and the bride (the church). Sometimes the speaker cannot be identified, but this does not matter because the whole of the book is God's Word to us.

NEW TESTAMENT REFERENCE

Peter describes the process: "No prophecy ever came by the will of man; instead, men spoke from God as they were carried along by the Holy Spirit" (2 Pet 1:21). Paul was conscious of God's authority: "What I write to you is the Lord's command" (1 Cor 14:37; cp. 2 Tim 3:16–17).

An angel affirms that this book is a reliable revelation from God. It is intended to teach us about the future. It is not an inscrutable mystery but God's message (v. 6).

Jesus affirms his certain return (cp. 1:17). The sixth blessing of the book is given to the one who keeps or observes the instruction given in this book (v. 7).

John, for a second time, almost worships the angel who is interpreting (v. 8).

The angel warns that only God is to be worshiped. It is surprising that John twice could almost make this terrible error. Perhaps this is to warn against the satanic worship of the last days. Satan, an angel, will deceive the world (cp. 20:3; 13:2,4).

The angel tells John not to "seal up" the vision. Ancient books were mainly scrolls, and some were sealed so no one could read them (cp. Rev 5:1,2,4,5; 6:1). The book of Daniel was sealed "But you, Daniel, keep these words secret and seal the book until the time of the end" (Dan 12:4). John's revelation is for us now! (v. 10).

Jesus for a second time in the epilogue promises to return and reward each believer. What will your reward be? (v. 12).

Jesus reveals his absolute deity (v. 13).

The speaker pronounces the seventh and final blessing. It comes to those who "wash their robes" (v. 14; cp. 3:4; 7:14; 1 Cor 6:11).

Outside the city are the "unwashed"—those who reject Jesus and his sacrifice (v. 15).

Jesus authenticates the words of the interpreting angel. He also reveals himself as the fulfillment of the messianic hope. He, in his incarnation, came in the line of David (cp. Isa 11:10; 53:2), and he fulfills the Balaam prophecy (Num 24:17): "A star will come from Jacob."

The church (the bride of Christ), moved by the Holy Spirit, cries out "Come!" As this book is read, the hearer joins in: "Come!" "Come, Lord Jesus" and to the world—come to him. In spite of the sovereign plan of the God who knows the end from the beginning, there is a universal offer of salvation to everyone. God has no delight in the death of the wicked. "Come!" "Be zealous and repent" declares the sovereign Lord (v. 17; 3:19).

PERSONAL APPLICATION

Because the time is short and because people do not change quickly, people need to repent now. Otherwise, they will be fixed in their sins and their destinies (cp. Dan 12:10; Ezek 3:27).

John, knowing his authority was from God, warned against any change in this word by addition or subtraction (vv. 18–19).

Jesus for a third and final time promises his return (v. 20a).

John responds—"Amen!" Yes! "Come, Lord Jesus" (v. 20b).

John's benediction ends his epistle to the churches (cp. 1:4; Heb 13:25) since he was commissioned to write to them. The benediction is also John's final word to the church: "The grace of the Lord Jesus Christ be with everyone" (v. 21).

Section Summary

God's Word through John is the promise of Jesus to come back soon and to complete his plan.

QUESTIONS TO GUIDE YOUR STUDY

1. What is the goal of your life?
2. What do "water" and "light" symbolize?
3. Why do they make good symbols?
4. How does a person wash his or her robes (v. 14)?
5. How can a person's destiny be changed?
6. If Jesus returns today, what will your destiny be? Why?

REFERENCE SOURCES

The following list is a collection of the sources used for this volume. All are from Broadman & Holman's list of published reference resources. They are designed to accommodate the reader's need for more specific information and for an expanded treatment of each New Testament book. All of these works will greatly aid in the reader's study, teaching, and presentation. The accompanying annotations can be helpful in guiding the reader to the proper resources.

MATTHEW

Blair, Joe. *Introducing the New Testament*, pp. 55–67. A high-level overview of Matthew's Gospel that contains outlines of books, special graphics, maps and photos, and summary questions.

Blomberg, Craig. *Matthew* (The New American Commentary 22). A more scholarly treatment of the text of Matthew that provides emphases on the text itself, background, and theological considerations.

Crissey, Clair M., *Matthew* (Layman's Bible Book Commentary15). A popular-level treatment of Matthew's Gospel. This easy-to-use volume provides a relevant and practical perspective.

Holman Bible Dictionary. An exhaustive, alphabetically arranged resource of Bible-related subjects. An excellent tool of definitions and other information on the people, places, things, and events of the Bible.

Holman Bible Handbook, pp. 541–567. A comprehensive treatment of Matthew that offers outlines, commentary on key themes and sections, and full-color photos, illustrations, charts, and maps. Provides an emphasis on the broader theological teachings of Matthew.

Holman Book of Biblical Charts, Maps, and Reconstructions, pp. 86–87, 95–97. A colorful, visual collection of charts, maps, and reconstructions, these well-designed tools are invaluable to the study of the Bible.

Lea, Thomas D. *The New Testament: Its Background and Message*, pp. 167–280. An excellent resource for background material—political, cultural, historical, and religious. Provides background information in broad strokes on specific books, including the Gospels.

Robertson, A. T. *Word Pictures in the New Testament.* vol. 1, "Matthew and Mark," pp. 3–246. Insights into the Greek language of the New Testament. Provides word studies as well as grammatical and background insights into Matthew's text.

Robertson, A. T. A *Grammar of the Greek New Testament in the Light of Historical Research.* An exhaustive scholarly work on the underlying language of the New Testament. Provides advanced insights into the grammatical, syntactical, and lexical aspects of the New Testament.

MARK

Adams, J. McKee, revised by Joseph A. Callaway, *Biblical Backgrounds.* This work provides valuable information on the physical and geographical settings of the New Testament. Its many color maps and other features add depth and understanding.

Blair, Joe, *Introducing the New Testament,* pp. 71–80. Designed as a core textbook for New Testament survey courses, this volume helps the reader in understanding the content and principles of the New Testament. Its features include special maps and photos, outlines, and discussion questions.

Brooks, James A., *Mark* (The New American Commentary 23). A theological commentary on Mark.

Cate, Robert L., *A History of the New Testament and Its Times.* An excellent and thorough survey of the birth and growth of the Christian faith in the first-century world.

Godwin, Johnnie C., *Mark* (Layman's Bible Book Commentary 16). A popular-level treatment of Mark. This easy-to-use volume provides a relevant and practical perspective for the reader.

Holman Bible Dictionary. An exhaustive, alphabetically arranged resource of Bible-related subjects. An excellent tool of definitions and other information on the people, places, things, and events of the Bible.

Holman Bible Handbook, pp. 568–584. A comprehensive treatment that offers outlines, commentary on key themes and sections, and full-color photos, illustrations, charts, and maps Provides an accent on the broader theological teachings of the Gospel of Mark.

Holman Book of Biblical Charts, Maps, and Reconstructions. A colorful, visual collection of charts, maps, and reconstructions, these well–designed tools are invaluable to the study of the Bible.

Robertson, A. T., *Word Pictures in the New Testament,* "Matthew and Mark," vol. 1. This six-volume series provides insights into the language of New Testament Greek. Provides word studies as well as grammatical and background insights into Mark's Gospel.

LUKE

Adams, J. McKee, revised by Joseph A. Callaway, *Biblical Backgrounds*. This work provides valuable information on the physical and geographical settings of the New Testament. Its four-color maps and other features add depth and understanding.

Blair, Joe, *Introducing the New Testament*, pp. 81–90. Designed as a core textbook for New Testament survey courses, this volume helps the reader in understanding the content and principles of the New Testament. Its features include maps and photos, outlines, and discussion questions.

Cate, Robert L., *A History of the New Testament and Its Times*. An excellent and thorough survey of the birth and growth of the Christian faith in the first-century world.

Dean, Robert J., *Luke* (Layman's Bible Book Commentary 17). A popular-level treatment of Luke. This easy-to-use volume provides a relevant and practical perspective for the reader.

Holman Bible Dictionary. An exhaustive, alphabetically arranged resource of Bible-related subjects. An excellent tool of definitions and other information on the people, places, things, and events.

Holman Bible Handbook, pp. 585–605. A comprehensive treatment that offers outlines, commentary on key themes and sections, and full-color photos, illustrations, charts, and maps. Provides an accent on the broader theological teachings.

Holman Book of Biblical Charts, Maps, and Reconstructions, pp. 95–97, 101. A colorful, visual collection of charts, maps, and reconstructions. These well-designed tools are invaluable to the study of the Bible.

Stein, Robert H., *Luke* (The New American Commentary 24). A more scholarly treatment focused on theological commentary and the message of Luke's Gospel.

Lea, Thomas D., *The New Testament: Its Background and Message*, pp. 143–280. An excellent resource for background material—political, cultural, historical, and religious. Provides background information in broad strokes on specific books, including the Gospels.

Robertson, A. T., *A Grammar of the Greek New Testament in the Light of Historical Research*. An exhaustive, scholarly work on the underlying language of the New Testament. Provides advanced insights into the grammatical, syntactical, and lexical aspects of the New Testament.

Robertson, A. T., *Word Pictures in the New Testament*, "Luke," vol. 2. This six-volume series provides insights into the language of New Testament Greek. Provides word studies as well as grammatical and background insights into Luke.

JOHN

Adams, J. McKee, revised by Joseph A. Callaway, *Biblical Backgrounds*. This work provides valuable information on the physical and geographical settings of the New Testament. Its four-color maps and other features add depth and understanding.

Blair, Joe, *Introducing the New Testament*, pp. 91–101. Designed as a core text for New Testament survey courses, this volume helps the reader understand the content and principles of the New Testament. Its features include maps and photos, outlines, and discussion questions.

Borchert, Gerald L., *John* (The New American Commentary 25A). A scholarly treatment of the Gospel of John that provides emphases on the text, background, and theological considerations.

Cate, Robert L., *A History of the New Testament and Its Times*. An excellent and thorough survey of the birth and growth of the Christian faith in the first-century world.

Carter, James E., *John* (Layman's Bible Book Commentary 18). A popular-level treatment of John. This easy-to-use volume provides a relevant and practical perspective for the reader.

Holman Bible Dictionary. An exhaustive, alphabetically arranged resource of Bible-related subjects. An excellent tool of definitions and other information on the people, places, things, and events of the Bible.

Holman Bible Handbook, pp. 606–631. A comprehensive treatment that offers outlines, commentary on key themes and sections, and full-color photos, illustrations, charts, and maps. The content provides an accent on the broader theological teachings of the Bible.

Holman Book of Biblical Charts, Maps, and Reconstructions, pp. 86, 99. A colorful, visual collection of charts, maps, and reconstructions. These well-designed tools are invaluable for study of the Bible.

Lea, Thomas D., *The New Testament: Its Background and Message*, pp. 153–280. An excellent resource for background material—political, cultural, historical, and religious. Provides background information in broad strokes on specific books, including the Gospels.

Robertson, A. T., A *Grammar of the Greek New Testament in the Light of Historical Research*. An exhaustive, scholarly work on the underlying language of the New Testament. Provides advanced insights into the grammatical, syntactical, and lexical aspects of the New Testament.

Robertson, A. T., *Word Pictures in the New Testament,* "The Fourth Gospel," vol. 5. This six-volume series provides insights into the language of New Testament Greek. Provides word studies as well as grammatical and background insights into the Gospel of John.

ACTS

Adams, J. McKee, revised by Joseph A. Callaway, *Biblical Backgrounds.* This work provides valuable information on the physical and geographical settings of Acts. Its full-color maps and other features add depth and understanding to Luke's narrative.

Cate, Robert L., *A History of the New Testament and Its Times.* An excellent and thorough survey of the birth and growth of the Christian faith in the first-century world.

Holman Bible Dictionary. An exhaustive, alphabetically arranged resource of Bible-related subjects. An excellent tool of definitions and other information on the people, places, things, and events of the Bible.

Holman Bible Handbook, pp. 632–672. A comprehensive treatment of the Acts of the Apostles that offers outlines, commentary on key themes and sections, and full-color photos, illustrations, charts, and maps. Provides an accent on the broader theological teachings. Various selections were used throughout the commentary of Acts.

Holman Book of Biblical Charts, Maps, and Reconstructions, pp. 99, 100. A colorful, visual collection of charts, maps, and reconstructions, these well-designed tools are invaluable for study of the Bible.

Lea, Thomas D., *The New Testament: Its Background and Message,* pp. 281–329. An excellent resource for background material—political, cultural, historical, and religious. Provides background information in broad strokes on specific books, including the Gospels.

Maddox, Robert L., Jr., *Acts,* (Layman's Bible Book Commentary 19). A popular-level treatment of the book of Acts. This easy-to-use volume provides a relevant and practical perspective for the reader.

Polhill, John B., *Acts,* (New American Commentary 26). A more scholarly treatment of the text of Acts that provides emphases on the text itself, background, and theological considerations.

Robertson, A. T., *A Grammar of the Greek New Testament in the Light of Historical Research.* An exhaustive, scholarly work on the underlying language of the New Testament. Provides advanced insights into the grammatical, syntactical, and lexical aspects of the New Testament.

ROMANS

Adams, J. McKee, revised by Joseph A. Callaway, *Biblical Backgrounds.* This work provides valuable information on the physical and geographical settings of the New Testament. Its many color maps and other features add depth and understanding.

Blair, Joe, *Introducing the New Testament,* pp. 123–131. Designed as a core text for New Testament survey courses, this volume helps the reader in understanding the content and principles of the New Testament. Its features include special maps and photos, outlines, and discussion questions.

Cate, Robert L., *A History of the New Testament and Its Times.* An excellent and thorough survey of the birth and growth of the Christian faith in the first-century world.

Holman Bible Dictionary. An exhaustive, alphabetically arranged resource of Bible-related subjects. An excellent tool of definitions and other information on the people, places, things, and events of the Bible.

Holman Bible Handbook, pp. 671–685. A comprehensive treatment that offers outlines, commentary on key themes and sections, full-color photos, illustrations, charts, and maps. Provides an accent on the broader theological teachings of the Bible.

Lea, Thomas D., *The New Testament: Its Background and Message,* pp. 393–407. An excellent resource for background material—political, cultural, historical, and religious. Provides background information in both broad strokes on specific books, including Romans.

MacGorman, J. W., *Romans, 1 Corinthians,* (Layman's Bible Book Commentary 20), pp. 15–95. A popular-level treatment of Paul's epistle to the Romans. This easy-to-use volume provides a relevant and practical perspective for the reader.

McQuay, Earl P., *Keys to Interpreting the Bible.* This work provides a fine introduction to the study of the Bible that is invaluable for home Bible studies, lay members of a local church, or students.

McQuay, Earl P., *Learning to Study the Bible.* This study guide presents a helpful procedure that uses the principles basic to effective and thorough Bible study. Using Philippians as a model, the various methods of Bible study are applied. Excellent for home Bible studies, lay members of a local church, and students.

Mounce, Robert H., *Romans,* (The New American Commentary 27). A scholarly treatment of the text of Romans provides emphases on the text itself, background, and theological considerations.

Robertson, A. T., A *Grammar of the Greek New Testament in the Light of Historical Research.* An exhaustive, scholarly work on the underlying language of the New Testament that provides advanced insights into the grammatical, syntactical, and lexical aspects of the New Testament.

Robertson, A. T., *Word Pictures in the New Testament,* "The Epistles of Paul," vol. 4, pp. 323–430. This six-volume series provides insights into the language of New Testament Greek. Provides word studies as well as grammatical and background insights into the book of Romans.

1 CORINTHIANS

Adams, J. McKee, revised by Joseph A. Callaway, *Biblical Backgrounds.* This work provides valuable information on the physical and geographical settings of the New Testament. Its many color maps and other features add depth and understanding.

Blair, Joe, *Introducing the New Testament,* pp. 133–140. Designed as a core textbook for New Testament survey courses, this volume helps the reader in understanding the content and principles of the New Testament. Its features include special maps and photos, outlines, and discussion questions.

Cate, Robert L., A History *of the New Testament and Its Times.* An excellent and thorough survey of the birth and growth of the Christian faith in the first-century world.

Holman Bible Dictionary. An exhaustive, alphabetically arranged resource of Bible-related subjects. An excellent tool of definitions and other information on the people, places, things, and events of the Bible.

Holman Bible Handbook, pp. 686–695. A comprehensive treatment that offers outlines, commentary on key themes and sections, and full-color photos, illustrations, charts, and maps. Provides an accent on the broader theological teachings.

Holman Book of Biblical Charts, Maps, and Reconstructions, p. 98. A colorful, visual collection of charts, maps, and reconstructions, these well-designed tools are invaluable for study of the Bible.

Lea, Thomas D., *The New Testament: Its Background and Message,* pp. 408–424. An excellent resource for background material—political, cultural, historical, and religious. Provides background information in broad strokes on specific books, including 1 Corinthians.

MacGorman, J. W., *Romans, 1 Corinthians,* (Layman's Bible Book Commentary 20), pp. 96–153. A popular-level treatment of the book of 1 Corinthians. This easy-to-use volume provides a relevant and practical perspective for the reader.

McQuay, Earl P., *Keys to Interpreting the Bible.* This work provides a fine introduction to the study of the Bible that is invaluable for home Bible studies, lay members of a local church, or students.

McQuay, Earl P., *Learning to Study the Bible*. This study guide presents a helpful procedure that employs the principles basic to effective and thorough Bible study. Using Philippians as a model, the various methods of Bible study are applied. Excellent for home Bible studies, lay members of a local church, and students.

Robertson, A. T., A *Grammar of the Greek New Testament in the Light of Historical Research*. An exhaustive, scholarly work on the underlying language of the New Testament. Provides advanced insights into the grammatical, syntactical, and lexical aspects of the New Testament.

Robertson, A. T., *Word Pictures in the New Testament*, "Epistles of Paul," vol. 4, pp. 68–204. This six-volume series provides insights into the language of New Testament Greek. Provides word studies as well as grammatical and background insights into the epistles of Paul.

2 CORINTHIANS

Adams, J. McKee, revised by Joseph A. Callaway, *Biblical Backgrounds*. This work provides valuable information on the physical and geographical settings of the New Testament. Its many color maps and other features add depth and understanding.

Blair, Joe, *Introducing the New Testament*, pp. 140–142. Designed as a core textbook for New Testament survey courses, this volume helps the reader in understanding the content and principles of the New Testament. Its features include special maps and photos, outlines, and discussion questions.

Cate, Robert L., *A History of the New Testament and Its Times*. An excellent and thorough survey of the birth and growth of the Christian faith in the first–century world.

George, David C., 2 *Corinthians, Galatians, Ephesians*, (Layman's Bible Book Commentary 21), pp. 13–49. A popular-level treatment of 2 Corinthians. This easy-to-use volume provides a relevant and practical perspective for the reader.

Holman Bible Dictionary. An exhaustive, alphabetically arranged resource of Bible-related subjects. An excellent tool of definitions and other information on the people, places, things, and events of the Bible.

Holman Bible Handbook, pp. 696–700. A comprehensive treatment that offers outlines, commentary on key themes and sections, and full–color photos, illustrations, charts, and maps. Provides an accent on the broader theological teachings.

Holman Book of Biblical Charts, Maps, and Reconstructions. A colorful, visual collection of charts, maps, and reconstructions, These well-designed tools are invaluable to the study of the Bible.

Lea, Thomas D., *The New Testament: Its Background and Message,* pp. 425–436. An excellent resource for background material—political, cultural, historical, and religious. Provides background information in broad strokes on specific books, including the 2 Corinthians.

McQuay, Earl P., *Keys to Interpreting the Bible.* This work provides a fine introduction to the study of the Bible that is invaluable for home Bible studies, lay members of a local church, or students.

McQuay, Earl P., *Learning to Study the Bible.* This study guide presents a helpful procedure that employs the principles basic to effective and thorough Bible study. Using Philippians as a model, the various methods of Bible study are applied. Excellent for home Bible studies, lay members of a local church, and students.

Robertson, A. T., *A Grammar of the Greek New Testament in the Light of Historical Research.* An exhaustive, scholarly work on the underlying language of the New Testament. Provides advanced insights into the grammatical, syntactical, and lexical aspects of the New Testament.

Robertson, A. T., *Word Pictures in the New Testament,* "Epistles of Paul," vol. 4, pp. 205–271. This six-volume series provides insights into the language of New Testament Greek. Provides word studies as well as grammatical and background insights into the epistles of Paul.

GALATIANS

Cate, Robert L., *A History of the New Testament and Its Times.* An excellent and thorough survey of the birth and growth of the Christian faith in the first-century world.

Holman Bible Dictionary. An exhaustive, alphabetically arranged resource of Bible-related subjects. An excellent tool of definitions and other information on the people, places, things, and events of the Bible.

Holman Bible Handbook, pp. 701–710. A comprehensive treatment of Galatians that offers outlines and commentary on key themes and sections. Provides an accent on the broader theological teachings of Galatians.

George, David., *Galatians,* (Layman's Bible Book Commentary 21). A popular-level treatment of Paul's epistle to the Galatians. This easy-to-use volume provides a relevant and practical perspective for the reader.

George, Timothy., *Galatians,* (New American Commentary 30). A scholarly treatment of the text of Galatians that provides emphases on the text itself, background, and theological considerations.

Lea, Thomas D., *The New Testament: Its Background and Message,* pp. 281–329. An excellent resource for background material—political, cultural, historical, and religious. Provides background information and broad overview of Galatians.

McQuay, Earl P., *Keys to Interpreting the Bible.* This work provides a fine introduction to the study of the Bible that is invaluable for home Bible studies, lay members of a local church, or students.

McQuay, Earl P.,, *Learning to Study the Bible.* This study guide presents a helpful procedure that employs the principles basic to effective and thorough Bible study. The various methods of Bible study are applied to the book of Philippians. Excellent for home Bible studies, lay members of a local church, and students.

Robertson, A. T., *A Grammar of the Greek New Testament in the Light of Historical Research.* An exhaustive, scholarly work on the underlying language of the New Testament. Provides advanced insights into the grammatical, syntactical, and lexical aspects of the New Testament.

Robertson, A. T., *Word Pictures in the New Testament,* "The Epistles of Paul," vol. 4, pp. 272–319. Insights into the language of New Testament Greek. Provides word studies as well as grammatical and background insights into Paul's epistle to the Galatians.

EPHESIANS

Adams, J. McKee., revised by Joseph A. Callaway, *Biblical Backgrounds.* This work provides valuable information on the physical and geographical settings of the New Testament. Its many color maps and other features add depth and understanding.

Blair, Joe, *Introducing the New Testament,* pp. 151–156. Designed as a core text for New Testament survey courses, this volume helps the reader understand the content and principles of the New Testament. Its features include special maps and photos, outlines, and discussion questions.

Cate, Robert L., *A History of the New Testament and Its Times.* An excellent and thorough survey of the birth and growth of the Christian faith in the first-century world.

George, David C., *2 Corinthians, Galatians, Ephesians* (Layman's Bible Book Commentary 21), pp. 91–140. A popular-level treatment of several of Paul's epistles, including Ephesians. This easy-to-use volume provides a relevant and practical perspective for the reader.

Holman Bible Dictionary. An exhaustive, alphabetically arranged resource of Bible-related subjects. An excellent tool of definitions and other information on the people, places, things, and events of the Bible.

Holman Bible Handbook, pp. 711–718. A comprehensive treatment that offers outlines; commentary on key themes and sections; and full-color photos, illustrations, charts, and maps. Provides an accent on the broader theological teachings of the Bible.

Lea, Thomas D., *The New Testament: Its Background and Message*, pp. 437–447. An excellent resource for background material—political, cultural, historical, and religious. Provides background information in broad strokes on specific books, including Ephesians.

McQuay, Earl P., *Keys to Interpreting the Bible*. This work provides a fine introduction to the study of the Bible that is invaluable for home Bible studies, lay members of a local church, or students.

McQuay, Earl P., *Learning to Study the Bible*. This study guide presents a helpful procedure that employs the principles basic to effective and thorough Bible study. Using Philippians as a model, the various methods of Bible study are applied. Excellent for home Bible studies, lay members of a local church, and students.

Robertson, A. T., A *Grammar of the Greek New Testament in the Light of Historical Research*. An exhaustive, scholarly work on the underlying language of the New Testament. Provides advanced insights into the grammatical, syntactical, and lexical aspects of the New Testament.

Robertson, A. T., *Word Pictures in the New Testament*, "The Epistles of Paul," vol. 4, pp. 516–552. This six-volume series provides insights into the language of New Testament Greek. Provides word studies as well as grammatical and background insights into the epistles of Paul, including Ephesians.

PHILIPPIANS, COLOSSIANS, AND PHILEMON

Adams, J. McKee, revised by Joseph A. Callaway, *Biblical Backgrounds*. This work provides valuable information on the physical and geographical settings of the book of Acts and the apostle Paul's missionary journeys. Its many color maps and other features add depth and understanding to Luke's narrative.

Blair, Joe, *Introducing the New Testament*, pp. 157–169. Designed as a core text for New Testament survey courses, this volume helps the reader in understanding the content and principles of the New Testament. Its features include special, maps and photos, outlines, and discussion questions.

Cate, Robert L., *A History of the New Testament and Its Times*. An excellent and thorough survey of the birth and growth of the Christian faith in the first-century world.

Holman Bible Dictionary. An exhaustive, alphabetically arranged resource of Bible-related subjects. An excellent tool of definitions and other information on the people, places, things, and events.

Holman Bible Handbook, pp. 719–728, 744–746. A comprehensive treatment that offers outlines, commentary on key themes and sections, full-color photos, illustrations, charts, and maps. Provides an accent on the broader theological teachings. A scholarly treatment of the text of Philippians, Colossians, and Philemon that provides emphases on the text itself, background, and theological considerations.

Lea, Thomas D., *The New Testament: Its Background and Message*, pp. 437–468. An excellent resource for background material—political, cultural, historical, and religious. Provides background information in broad strokes on specific books, including the Gospels.

McQuay, Earl P., *Keys to Interpreting the Bible*. This work provides a fine introduction to the study of the Bible that is invaluable for home Bible studies, lay members of a local church, or students.

McQuay, Earl P., *Learning to Study the Bible*. This study guide presents a helpful procedure that employs the principles basic to effective and thorough Bible study. The various methods of Bible study are applied to the Book of Philippians. Excellent for home Bible studies, lay members of a local church, and students.

Melick, Richard R. Jr., *Philippians, Colossians, Philemon* (The New American Commentary 32). A scholarly treatment of the text of Philippians, Colossians, and Philemon that provides emphases on the text itself, background, and theological considerations.

Robertson, A. T., A *Grammar of the Greek New Testament in the Light of Historical Research*. An exhaustive, scholarly work on the underlying language of the New Testament. Provides advanced insights into the grammatical, syntactical, and lexical aspects of the New Testament.

Robertson, A. T., *Word Pictures in the New Testament*, "The Epistles of Paul," vol. 4, pp. 433–513. Gives insights into the language of New Testament Greek. Provides word studies as well as grammatical and background insights into the Prison Epistles.

Tolbert, Malcolm O., *Philippians, Colossians, 1 & 2 Thessalonians, 1 & 2 Timothy, Titus, Philemon* (Layman's Bible Book Commentary 22). A popular-level treatment of the Books of Philippians, Colossians, and Philemon. This easy-to-use volume provides a relevant and practical perspective for the reader.

1–2 THESSALONIANS

Adams, J. McKee, revised by Joseph A. Callaway, *Biblical Backgrounds*. This work provides valuable information on the physical and geographical settings of the New Testament. Its many color maps and other features add depth and understanding.

Blair, Joe, *Introducing the New Testament*, pp. 171–176. Designed as a core text for New Testament survey courses, this volume helps the reader in understanding the content and principles of the New Testament. Its features include special maps and photos, outlines, and discussion questions.

Cate, Robert L., *A History of the New Testament and Its Times*. An excellent and thorough survey of the birth and growth of the Christian faith in the first-century world.

Holman Bible Dictionary. An exhaustive, alphabetically arranged resource of Bible-related subjects. An excellent tool of definitions and other information on the people, places, things, and events of the Bible.

Holman Bible Handbook, pp. 729–735. A comprehensive treatment that offers outlines, commentary on key themes and sections, and full-color photos, illustrations, charts, and maps. Provides an accent on the broader theological teachings of the Bible.

Lea, Thomas D., *The New Testament: Its Background and Message*, pp. 379–391. An excellent resource for background material—political, cultural, historical, and religious. Provides background information in both broad strokes on specific books, including the books of 1 and 2 Thessalonians.

Tolbert, Malcolm O., *Philippians, Colossians, 1 & 2 Thessalonians, 1 & 2 Timothy, Titus, Philemon* (Layman's Bible Book Commentary 22), pp. 65–96. A popular-level treatment of several of Paul's Epistles, including 1, 2 Thessalonians. This easy-to-use volume provides a relevant and practical perspective for the reader.

McQuay, Earl P., *Keys to Interpreting the Bible*. This work provides a fine introduction to the study of a Bible that is invaluable for home Bible studies, lay members of a local church, or students.

McQuay, Earl P.,*Learning to Study the Bible*. This study guide presents a helpful procedure that employs the principles basic to effective and thorough Bible study. Using Philippians as a model, the various methods of Bible study are applied. Excellent for home Bible studies, lay members of a local church, and students.

Martin, D. Michael, *1,2 Thessalonians* (The New American Commentary 33). A scholarly treatment of the text of 1 and 2 Thessalonians that provides emphases on the text itself, background, and theological considerations.

Robertson, A. T., A *Grammar of the Greek New Testament in the Light of Historical Research*. An exhaustive, scholarly work on the underlying language of the New Testament. Provides advanced insights into the grammatical, syntactical, and lexical aspects of the New Testament.

Robertson, A. T., *Word Pictures in the New Testament*, "The Epistles of Paul," vol. 4, pp. 5–61. This six-volume series provides insights into

New Testament Greek. Provides word studies and well as grammatical and background insights into the epistles of Paul.

1–2 TIMOTHY, TITUS

Adams, J. McKee, revised by Joseph A. Callaway, *Biblical Backgrounds.* This work provides valuable information on the physical and geographical settings of the New Testament. Its many color maps and other features add depth and understanding.

Blair, Joe, *Introducing the New Testament,* pp. 177–184. Designed as a core text for New Testament survey courses, this volume helps the reader understand the content and principles of the New Testament. Its features include many maps and photos, outlines, and discussion questions.

Cate, Robert L., A *History of the New Testament and Its Time.* An excellent and thorough survey of the birth and growth of the Christian faith in the first-century world.

Holman Bible Dictionary. An exhaustive, alphabetically arranged resource of Bible-related subjects. An excellent tool of definitions and other information on the people, places, things, and events of the Bible.

Holman Bible Handbook, pp. 736–743. A comprehensive treatment that offers outlines, commentary on key themes and sections, and full-color photos, illustrations, charts, and maps. Provides an emphasis on the broader theological teachings.

Lea, Thomas D. and Hayne P. Griffin Jr., *1, 2 Timothy, Titus* (The New American Commentary 34). A scholarly treatment of the text of 1 and 2 Timothy, Titus that provides emphases on the text itself, background, and theological considerations.

Lea, Thomas D., *The New Testament: Its Background and Message,* pp. 469–499. An excellent resource for background material—political, cultural, historical, and religious. Provides background information in broad strokes on specific books, including the Gospels. Includes a scholarly treatment of the text of the Pastoral Epistles that provides emphases on the text itself, background, and theological considerations.

McQuay, Earl P., *Keys to Interpreting the Bible.* This work provides a fine introduction to the study of the Bible that is invaluable for home Bible studies, lay members of a local church, or students.

McQuay, Earl P., *Learning to Study the Bible.* This study guide presents a helpful procedure that uses the principles basic to effective and thorough Bible study. Using Philippians as a model, the various methods of Bible study are applied. Excellent for home Bible studies, lay members of a local church, and students.

Robertson, A. T., A *Grammar of the Greek New Testament in the Light of Historical Research*. An exhaustive, scholarly work on the underlying language of the New Testament. Provides advanced insights into the grammatical, syntactical, and lexical aspects of the New Testament.

Robertson, A. T., *Word Pictures in the New Testament*, "The Epistles of Paul," vol. 4, pp. 559–634. This six-volume series provides insights into the language of New Testament Greek. Provides word studies as well as grammatical and background insights into the Pastoral Epistles.

Tolbert, Malcolm O., *Philippians, Colossians, 1 & 2 Thessalonians, 1 & 2 Timothy, Titus, Philemon* (Layman's Bible Book Commentary 22), pp. 97–163. A popular-level treatment of the Pastoral Epistles, this easy-to-use volume provides a relevant and practical perspective for the reader.

HEBREWS

Adams, J. McKee, revised byJoseph A. Callaway, *Biblical Backgrounds*. This work provides valuable information on the physical and geographical settings of the New Testament. Its many colorful maps and other features add depth and understanding.

Blair, Joe, *Introducing the New Testament*, pp. 185–189. Designed as a core text for New Testament survey courses, this volume helps the reader in understanding the content and principles of the New Testament. Its features include special maps and photos, outlines, and discussion questions.

Cate, Robert L., *A History of the New Testament and Its Times*. An excellent and thorough survey of the birth and growth of the Christian faith in the first-century world.

Holman Bible Dictionary. An exhaustive, alphabetically arranged resource of Bible-related subjects. An excellent tool of definitions and other information on the people, places, things, and events.

Holman Bible Handbook, pp. 749–756. A comprehensive treatment that offers outlines, commentary on key themes and sections, and full-color photos, illustrations, charts, and maps. Provides an accent on the broader theological teachings.

Holman Book of Biblical Charts, Maps, and Reconstructions. A colorful, visual collection of charts, maps, and reconstructions, these well-designed tools are invaluable to the study of the Bible.

Lea, Thomas D., *The New Testament: Its Background and Message*, pp. 501–517. An excellent resource for background material—political, cultural, historical, and religious. Provides background information in broad strokes on specific books, including the Gospels.

McQuay, Earl P., *Keys to Interpreting the Bible*. This work provides a fine introduction to the study of the Bible that is invaluable for home Bible studies, lay members of a local church, or students.

McQuay, Earl P., *Learning to Study the Bible*. This study guide presents a helpful procedure that employs the principles basic to effective and thorough Bible study. Using Philippians as a model, the various methods of Bible study are applied. Excellent for home Bible studies, lay members of a local church, and students.

Robertson, A. T., *A Grammar of the Greek New Testament in the Light of Historical Research*. An exhaustive, scholarly work on the underlying language of the New Testament. Provides advanced insights into the grammatical, syntactical, and lexical aspects of the New Testament.

Robertson, A. T., *Word Pictures in the New Testament*, "The Epistle of Hebrews," vol. 5, 325–451. This six-volume series provides insights into the language of New Testament Greek. Provides word studies as well as grammatical and background insights into the epistles of Paul.

Valentine, Foy, *Hebrews, James, 1,2 Peter* (Layman's Bible Book Commentary 23), pp. 13–65. A popular-level treatment of the book of Hebrews. This easy-to-use volume provides a relevant and practical perspective for the reader.

JAMES

Adams, J. McKee, revised by Joseph A. Callaway, *Biblical Backgrounds*. This work provides valuable information on the physical and geographical settings of the New Testament. Its many color maps and other features add depth and understanding.

Blair, Joe, *Introducing the New Testament*, pp. 191–195. Designed as a core textbook for New Testament survey courses, this volume helps the reader in understanding the content and principles of the New Testament. Its features include special maps and photos, outlines, and discussion questions.

Cate, Robert L., *A History of the New Testament and Its Times*. An excellent and thorough survey of the birth and growth of the Christian faith in the first-century world.

Holman Bible Dictionary. An exhaustive, alphabetically arranged resource of Bible-related subjects. An excellent tool of definitions and other information on the people, places, things, and events of the Bible.

Holman Bible Handbook, pp. 757–761. A comprehensive treatment that offers outlines, commentary on key themes and sections, and full-color photos, illustrations, charts, and maps. Provides an accent on the broader theological teachings of the Bible.

Lea, Thomas D., *The New Testament: Its Background and Message*, pp. 519–531. An excellent resource for background material—political, cultural, historical, and religious. Provides background information in broad strokes on specific books, including the Gospels.

Richardson, Kurt A., *James* (The New American Commentary 36). A more scholarly treatment of the text of James that provides emphases on the text itself, background, and theological considerations.

Robertson, A. T., A *Grammar of the Greek New Testament in the Light of Historical Research*. An exhaustive, scholarly work on the underlying language of the New Testament. Provides advanced insights into the grammatical, syntactical, and lexical aspects of the New Testament.

Robertson, A. T., *Word Pictures in the New Testament*, vol. 6, "The General Epistles and The Revelation of John," pp. 1–68. This six-volume series provides insights into the Greek language of the New Testament. It provides word studies as well as grammatical and background insights into the epistles of Paul.

Valentine, Foy, *Hebrews, James, 1 & 2 Peter* (Layman's Bible Book Commentary 23), pp. 43–49. A popular-level treatment of the book of James. This easy-to-use volume provides a relevant and practical perspective for the reader.

1–2 PETER, JUDE

Adams, J. McKee., revised by Joseph A. Callaway. *Biblical Backgrounds*. This work provides valuable information on the physical and geographical settings of the New Testament. Its many colorful maps and other features add depth and understanding.

Blair, Joe, *Introducing the New Testament*, pp.197–204. Designed as a core text for New Testament survey courses, this volume helps the reader in understanding the content and principles of the New Testament. Its features include, maps and photos, outlines, and discussion questions.

Cate, Robert L., *A History of the New Testament and Its Times*. An excellent and thorough survey of the birth and growth of the Christian faith in the first-century world.

Holman Bible Dictionary. An exhaustive, alphabetically arranged resource of Bible-related subjects. An excellent tool of definitions and other information on people, places, things, and events.

Holman Bible Handbook, pp.762–770, 781–782. A comprehensive treatment that offers outlines, commentary on key themes and sections, and full-color photos, illustrations, charts, and maps. Provides an accent on broader theological teachings.

Howard, Fred D., *1, 2, 3 John, Jude, Revelation,* (Layman's Bible Book Commentary 24), pp. 43–49. A popular-level treatment of several general epistles, including Jude. This easy-to-use volume provides a relevant and practical perspective for the reader.

Lea, Thomas D., *The New Testament: Its Background and Message,* pp.533–557, 575–583. An excellent resource for background material—political, cultural, historical, and religious. Provides background information in broad strokes on specific books, including the General epistles.

McQuay, Earl P., *Keys to Interpreting the Bible.* This work provides a fine introduction to the study of the Bible that is invaluable for home Bible studies, lay members of a local church, or students.

McQuay, Earl P., *Learning to Study the Bible.* This study guide presents a helpful procedure that employs the principles basic to effective and thorough Bible study. Using Philippians as a model, the various methods of Bible study are applied. Excellent for home Bible studies, lay members of a local church, and students.

Robertson, A. T., A *Grammar of the Greek New Testament in the Light of Historical Research.* An exhaustive, scholarly work on the underlying language of the New Testament. Provides advanced insights into the grammatical, syntactical, and lexical aspects of the New Testament.

Valentine, Foy, *Hebrews, James, 1, 2 Peter,* (Layman's Bible Book Commentary 23), pp. 43–49. A popular treatment of several epistles, including 1, 2 Peter. This easy-to-use volume provides a relevant and practical perspective for the reader.

1–3 JOHN

Adams, J. McKee, revised by Joseph A. Callaway, *Biblical Backgrounds.* This work provides valuable information on the physical and geographical settings of the New Testament. Its many color maps and other features add depth and understanding.

Akin, Daniel L., *1, 2, 3 John* (The New American Commentary 38). A scholarly exposition of the epistles of John that provides emphases on the text itself, background, and theological considerations.

Blair, Joe, *Introducing the New Testament,* pp. 205–210. Designed as a core text for New Testament survey courses, this volume helps the reader understand the content and principles of the New Testament. Its features include maps and photos, outlines, and discussion questions.

Howard, Fred D., *1, 2, 3 John, Jude, Revelation* (Layman's Bible Book Commentary 24). A popular-level treatment of the epistles of John.

This easy-to-use volume provides a relevant and practical perspective for the reader.

Holman Bible Dictionary. An exhaustive, alphabetically arranged resource of Bible-related subjects. An excellent tool of definitions and other information on the people, places, things, and events of the Bible.

Holman Bible Handbook. A comprehensive treatment that offers outlines, commentary on key themes and sections, and full-color photos, illustrations, charts, and maps. Provides an emphasis on the broader theological teachings of the Bible.

Lea, Thomas D., *The New Testament: Its Background and Message, pp. 559–574.* An excellent resource for background material—political, cultural, historical, and religious. Provides background information in both broad strokes on specific books, including the Gospels.

Robertson, A. T., *A Grammar of the Greek New Testament in the Light of Historical Research.* An exhaustive, scholarly work on the underlying language of the New Testament. Provides advanced insights into the grammatical, syntactical, and lexical aspects of the New Testament.

Robertson, A. T., *Word Pictures in the New Testament,* "The General Epistles," vol. 6, pp. 197–266. This six-volume series provides insights into the language of New Testament Greek. Provides word studies as well as grammatical and background insights into the epistles of John.

REVELATION

Adams, J. McKee, revised by Joseph A. Callaway, *Biblical Backgrounds.* This work provides valuable information on the physical and geographical settings of the New Testament. Its many color maps and other features add depth and understanding.

Blair, Joe, *Introducing the New Testament,* pp. 211–218. Designed as a core text for New Testament survey courses, this volume helps the reader in understanding the content and principles of the New Testament. Its features include special maps and photos, outlines, and discussion questions.

Holman Bible Dictionary. An exhaustive, alphabetically arranged resource of Bible-related subjects. An excellent tool of definitions and other information on the people, places, things, and events of the Bible.

Holman Bible Handbook, pp. 783–804. A comprehensive treatment that offers outlines, commentary on key themes and sections, and full-color photos, illustrations, charts, and maps. Provides an emphasis on the broader theological teachings of the Bible.

Howard, Fred D., *1, 2, 3 John, Jude, Revelation* (Layman's Bible Book Commentary 24), pp. 51–150. A popular treatment of Revelation.

Lea, Thomas D., *The New Testament: Its Background and Message*, pp. 585–613. An excellent resource for background material—political, cultural, historical, and religious. Provides background information in broad strokes on specific books, including Revelation.

Robertson, A. T., *Word Pictures in the New Testament*, "The General Epistles and The Revelation of John," vol. 6, pp. 269–488. This six-volume series provides insights into the language of the Greek New Testament. Provides word studies as well as grammatical and background insights into the book of Revelation.

HARMONY OF THE GOSPELS

	MATT	MARK	LUKE	JOHN
PART I. INTRODUCTORY STATEMENTS				
1.Luke's Historical Introduction			1:1–4	
2. John's Theological Introduction				1:1–18
3. Matthew's and Luke's Genealogical Introductions	1:1–17		3:23–58	
PART II. THE BIRTH AND YOUTH OF JOHN THE BAPTIST AND JESUS				
4. The Annunciation to Zechariah Place: Jerusalem			1:5–25	
5.The Annunciation to the Virgin Mary Place: Nazareth			1:26–38	
6. Songs of Elizabeth and Mary Place: Judea			1:39–56	
7. Birth and Youth of John the Baptist Place: Judea			1:57–80	
8. The Angel's Announcement to Joseph Place: Nazareth	1:18–25			
9. The Birth of Jesus Place: Bethlehem			2:1–7	
10. The Angel and Shepherds Place: Near Bethlehem			2:8–20	
11. Circumcision and Naming of Jesus Place: Bethlehem			2:21	
12. The Presentation in the Temple Place: Jerusalem			2:22–38	
13. The Visit of the Wise Men Places: Jerusalem, Bethlehem	2:1–12			
14. Flight to Egypt and Return to Nazareth Places: Nazareth, Egypt	2:13–23		2:39	
15. His Youth in Nazareth and Visit to Jerusalem Places: Nazareth, Jerusalem			2:40–52	
PART III. MINISTRY OF JOHN THE BAPTIST				
16. The Coming of the Word Place: Wilderness		1:1	3:1–2	
17. Response of John in the Wilderness Place: Wilderness	3:1–6	1:26	3:3–6	
18. The Boldness of His Preaching Place: Wilderness	3:7–10		3:7–14	

HARMONY OF THE GOSPELS

	MATT	MARK	LUKE	JOHN
19. John's Idea of the Messiah	3:11, 12	1:7,8	3:15–18	
PART IV EARLY MINISTRY OF JESUS				
20. The Baptism in the Jordan Place: Jordan	3:13–17	1:9–11	3:21–23	
21. The Temptation of Jesus by Satan Place: Judean wilderness	4:1–11	1:12, 13	4: 1–13	
22. Testimony of John and Disciples Place: Bethany				1: 19–51
23. The First Miracle Place: Cana				2:1–11
24. The First Stay in Capernaum Place: Capernaum				2:12
25. First Passover and Cleansing of Temple Place: Jerusalem				2:13–3:21
26. Closing Ministry and Arrest of John Place: Aenon			3:19, 20	3:22–36; 4:1–3
27. Jesus at Jacob's Well and Sychar Place: Samaria				4:4–42
28. Jesus Returns to Galilee Place: Galilee	4:12	1:14	4:14	4:43–45
PART V. THE MINISTRY IN GALILEE				
29. The Message of Jesus—Repentance Place: Galilee	4:17	1:14–15	4:14–15	
30. Healing the Centurion's Son Place: Capernaum				4:46–54
31. Jesus Rejected by the People Place: Nazareth	4:13–16		4:16–31	
32. Calling the Four Fishermen Place: Capernaum	4:18–22	1:16–20	5:1–11	
33. A Busy Sabbath in Capernaum Place: Capernaum	8:14–17	1:21–34	4:32–41	
34. The First Tour of Galilee Place: Galilee	4:23–25	1:35–39	4:42–44	
35. The Healing of a Leper Place: Galilee	8:2–4	1:40–45	5:12–16	
36. Healing the Paralytic in Peter's Home Place: Capernaum	9:1–8	2:1–2	5:17–26	
37. The Call of Matthew (Levi) Place: Sea of Galilee	9:9–13	2:13–17	5:27–32	

HARMONY OF THE GOSPELS

	MATT	MARK	LUKE	JOHN
38. Three Parables About Fasting Place: The Seaside	9:14–17	2:18–22	5:33–39	
39. First Sabbath Controversy in Jerusalem Place: Jerusalem				5:1–47
40. Further Controversies in Galilee Place: Galilee	12:1–14	2:23–3:6	6:1–11	
41. Choosing the Twelve and Sermon on the Mount Place: Near Capernaum	10:1–5; 5:1–8:1	3:14–19	6:12–49	
42. Healing the Centurion's Servant Place: Capernaum	8:5–13		7:1–10	
43. Raising the Son of a Widow Place: Nain			7:11–17	
44. Doubt of John and Praise of Jesus Place: Nain	11:2–19		7:18–35	
45. The Cities of Opportunity Place: Capernaum	11:20–30			
46. The Sinful Woman in House of Simon Place: Capernaum			7:36–50	
47. Jesus and Disciples Go to Galilee			8:1–3	
48. Jesus Accused of Blasphemy Place: Galilee	12:15–45	3:19–30		
49. The Mother of Jesus Calls Him	12:46–50	3:31–35	8:19–21	
50. The First Extended Group of Parables Place: Sea of Galilee	13:1–53	4:1–34	8:4–18	
51. Jesus Stills the Storm and Heals Demoniac Places: Sea of Galilee; Gadara	8:23–34	4:35–5:20	8:22–39	
52. Healing Jairus's – Jairus's Daughter and Woman with Issue of Blood Place: Capernaum	9:18–26	5:21–43	8:40–56	
53. Two Blind Men and Demoniac Healed Place: Capernaum	9:27–34			
54. Last Rejection at Nazareth Place: Nazareth	13:54–58	6:1–6		
55. The Disciples Given Power to Heal Place: Capernaum	10:1–42	6:7–13	9:1–6	
56. Herod Fears John and Jesus	14:1–12	6:14–29	9:7–9	

HARMONY OF THE GOSPELS

	MATT	MARK	LUKE	JOHN
PART VI. THE WITHDRAWAL FROM GALILEE				
57. Feeding of the Five Thousand	14:13–21	6:30–44	9:10–17	6:1–13
58. The Return to Gennesaret Place: Lake of Gennesaret	14:22–36	6:45–56		6:14–21
59. Rejection of Christ in the Synagogue Place: Capernaum				6:22–71
60. Criticism of the Pharisees Concerning Unwashed Hands Place: Capernaum	15:1–20	7:1–23		7:1
61. Healing Daughter of Syrophoenecian Place: Phoenicia	15:21–28	7:24–30		
62. Jesus Departs to Sea of Galilee	15:29–38	7:31–8:9		
63. Pharisees and Sadducees Attack Jesus, Again Asking a Sign Place: Dalmanutha or Magadan	15:39–16:4	8:10–12		
64. Jesus Again Withdraws to Bethsaida-Julias Place: Bethsaida	16:5–12	8:13–26		
65. The Great Confession of Peter Place: Caesarea-Philippi	16:13–20	8:27–30	9:18–21	
66. Jesus Predicts His Death and Resurrection Place: Galilee	16:21–28	8:31–38; 9:1	9:22–27	
67. The Transfiguration of Jesus Place: Mt. Tabor	17:1–13	9:2–13	9:28–36	
68. Disciples Unable to Cast Out Evil Spirit	17:14–21	9:14–29	9:37–42	
69. Further Reference to His Death and Resurrection Place: Galilee	17:22–23	9:30–32	9:42–45	
70. Jesus Pays Tax by Miracle Place: Capernaum	17:24–27			
71. Disciples Contending Who Is Greatest Place: Capernaum	18:1–5	9:33–37	9:46–48	
72. Jesus Rebukes the Narrowness of John Place: Capernaum	18:6–14	9:38–50	9:49–50	
73. On Forgiving a Brother Place: Capernaum	18:15–35			
74. Christ Requires Full Consecration Place: Capernaum	8:19–22		9:57–62	

HARMONY OF THE GOSPELS

	MATT	MARK	LUKE	JOHN
75. His Unbelieving Brothers Rebuked Place: Capernaum				7:2–10
76. James and John Rebuked for Anger Place: Samaria			9:51–56	
PART VII. THE MINISTRY IN JUDEA				
77. At the Feast of Shelters Place: Jerusalem				7:11–8:11
78. Jesus the Light of the World Place: Jerusalem				8:12–59
79. Opened Eyes of Man Born Blind Place: Jerusalem				9:1–41
80. Parable of the Good Shepherd Place: Jerusalem				10:1–21
81. The Seventy Sent Out			10:1–24	
82. Parable of the Good Samaritan Place: Jerusalem			10:25–37	
83. Jesus Received by Martha and Mary Place: Bethany			10:38–42	
84. The Disciples Taught How to Pray	6:9–13		11:1–13	
85. Accused of Healing Through Beelzebul			11:14–36	
86. The Criticism of Pharisee and Lawyer			11:37–54	
87. Warning the Disciples Against the Leaven of the Pharisees			12:1–12	
88. Covetousness and Parable of Rich Man			12:13–21	
89. The Ravens and Lilies			12:22–34	
90. The Second Coming Referred to by Jesus.			12:35–48	
91. Christ's Eagerness for His Baptism of Death on the Cross			12:49–59	
92. Repentance and Parable of Fig Tree			13:1–9	
93. The Infirm Woman Healed on Sabbath			13:10–21	
94. Jesus at Festival of Dedication Place: Jerusalem				10:22–39
PART VIII. THE MINISTRY IN PEREA				
95. Many Believe on Jesus Place: Bethany				10:40–42
96. Asked Concerning Number of the Saved Place: Perea			13:22–35	

HARMONY OF THE GOSPELS

	MATT	MARK	LUKE	JOHN
97. Jesus Teaches Humility and Service Place: Near Jerusalem			14:1–24	
98. To Be Christ's Disciple Requires Forsaking All Place: Jerusalem			14:25–35	
99. Christ Justifies Himself in Receiving Sinners			15:1–32	
100. Parables Concerning Stewardship			16:1–17:10	
101. The Raising of Lazarus Place: Bethany				11:1–54
102. Jesus Goes to Jerusalem for the Passover Places: Samaria, Galilee			17:11–37	
103. Parables on Prayer on Way to Jerusalem	19:1–2	10:1	18:1–14	
104. Pharisees Tempt Jesus Concerning Divorce	19:3–12	10:2–12		
105. Christ Welcoming Little Children Place: Perea	19:13–15	10:13–16	18:15–17	
106. Parable of the Rich Young Ruler	19:16–29	10:17–30	18:18–30	
107. Parable of the Laborers in Vineyard	20:1–16	10:31		
108. Jesus Again Refers to Death and Resurrection	20:17–19	10:32–34	18:31–34	
109. Selfishness of James and John	20:20–28	10:35–45		
110. Blind Bartimaeus Receives His Sight	20:29–34	10:46–52	18:35–43	
111. Zaccheus and Parable of the Pounds Place: Jericho			19:1–28	
PART IX. THE LAST JERUSALEM MINISTRY				
112. The Interest in Jesus and Lazarus Place: Bethany				11:55–57; 12:1, 9–11
113. The Challenge to the Sanhedrin Place: Jerusalem	21:1–17	11:1–11	19:29–44	12:12–19
114. Cursing the Fig Tree—Cleansing Temple Place: Jerusalem	21:18–19, 12–13	11:12–18	19:45–48	
115. The Greeks Seek Jesus While He Is in Agony of Soul Place: Jerusalem				12:20–50

HARMONY OF THE GOSPELS

	MATT	MARK	LUKE	JOHN
116. The Withered Fig Tree and the Power of Faith Place: Jerusalem	21:19–22	11:19–26	21:37–38	
117.Sanhedrin Questions the Authority of Jesus Place: Jerusalem	21:23–46; 22:1–14	11:27–12:12	20:1–19	
118. An Attempt to Trap Jesus Concerning Tribute to Caesar Place: Jerusalem	22:15–22	12:13–17	20:20–26	
119. A Further Attempt to Confuse Jesus Place: Jerusalem	22:23–33	12:18–27	20:27–40	
120. The Legal Problem of a Lawyer Place: Jerusalem	22:34–40	12:28–34		
121. Jesus Silences Enemies by Appeal to David Place: Jerusalem	22:41–46	12:35–37	20:41–44	
122. A Denunciation of Scribes and Pharisees Place: Jerusalem	23:1–39	12:38–40	20:45–47	
123. The Widow's Two Tiny Coins Place: Jerusalem		12:41–44	21:1–4	
PART X. JESUS COUNSELS HIS DISCIPLES LEADING UP TO HIS SACRIFICE				
124. Jesus's Olivet Discourse Place: Jerusalem	24:1–25:46	13:1–37	21:5–36	
125. Jesus Predicts His Arrest Place: Jerusalem	26:1–5	14:1–2	22:1–2	
126. Jesus Anointed by Mary Place: Bethany	26:6–13	14:3–9		12:2–8
127.The Act of Judas Iscariot Place: Jerusalem	26:14–16	14:10–11	22:3–6	
128.Preparation for Passover and Jealousy of the Disciples Place: Jerusalem	26:17–20	14:12–17	22:7–16, 24–30	
129. Jesus Washes the Apostles' Feet Place: Jerusalem				13:1–20
130. Judas Named as the Betrayer Place: Jerusalem	26:21–25	14:18–21	22:21–23	13:21–30

HARMONY OF THE GOSPELS

	MATT	MARK	LUKE	JOHN
131. Steadfastness of the Disciples Questioned Place: Jerusalem	26:31–35	14:27–31	22:17–20	13:34–38
132. The Memorial Supper Instituted Place: Jerusalem (see also 1 Cor 11:23–26)	26:26–29	14:22–25	22:17–20	
133. Jesus Opens His Heart to the Disciples Concerning His Departure Place: Upper Room and on Way to Gethsemane				14:1–16:33
134. The Intercessory Prayer Place: Near Gethsemane				17:1–26
135. The Agony in Gethsemane	26:36–46	14:32–42	22:39–46	18:1
PART XI. THE CONDEMNATION AND THE CROSS				
136. The Betrayal, Arrest, and Desertion by the Disciples Place: Gethsemane	26:47–56	14:43–52	22:47–53	18:2–12
137.The Examination by Annas Place: Jerusalem				18:13–14, 19–23
138. Condemned on Perjured Testimony Place: Jerusalem	26:57–68	14:53–65	22:54, 63–65	18:24
139. Peter's Three Denials Place: Jerusalem	26:58, 69–75	14:54, 66–72	22:54–62	18:15–18, 25–27
140. An Attempt to Make the Trial Legal Place: Jerusalem	27:1	15:1	22:66–71	
141. Judas Realizes His Sin Place: Jerusalem (See Ac 1:18–19)	27:3–10			
142. Jesus Before Pilate Place: Jerusalem	27:2, 11–14	15:2–5	23:1–5	18:28–38
143. Jesus Is Sent to Herod Place: Jerusalem			23:6–12	
144. Herod Returns Jesus to Pilate Place: Jerusalem	27:15–26	15:6–15	23:13–25	18:39–19:16
145. Jesus Is Mocked by Soldiers Place: Jerusalem	27:27–30	15:16–19		
146. Simon Bears the Cross Place: On Way to Calvary	27:31–34	15:20–23	23:26–33	19:16–17

HARMONY OF THE GOSPELS

	MATT	MARK	LUKE	JOHN
147. Jesus Is Crucified Place: Calvary	27:95–50	15:24–37	23:33–46	19:18–30
148. Events Accompanying Jesus's Death Place: Jerusalem	27:51–56	15:38–41	23:45–49	
149. Burial in Joseph's Tomb Place: Gethsemane	27:57–60	15:42–46	23:50–54	19:31–42
150. The Women by the Tomb	27:61–66	15:47	23:55–56	
PART XII. THE RESURRECTION AND ASCENSION				
151. At the Tomb on the Sabbath Place: Gethsemane	28:1			
152. Anointing with Spices		16:1		
153. The Tomb Is Opened	28:2–4			
154. Women Find the Empty Tomb and Angels	28:5–8	16:2–8	24:1–8	20:1
155. The Women Report to the Apostles Place: Jerusalem			24:9–12	20:2–10
156. Jesus Appears to Mary Magdalene Place: Jerusalem		16:9–11		20:11–18
157. Then Other Women See Him	28:9–10			
158. The Watchmen Bribed to Claim the Body Taken by the Disciples	28:11–15			
159. Jesus Appears on Way to Emmaus		16:12–13	24:13–32	
160. Simon Peter Sees Jesus (see also 1 Cor 15:5)			24:33–35	
161. Entire Group, Except Thomas, See Him, and He Eats Before Them Place: Jerusalem		16:14	24:36–43	20:19–25
162. Entire Group, with Thomas, See Him, Finally Believing				20:26–31
163. Jesus Appears by Sea of Galilee				21:1–25
164. The Apostles Commissioned to Preach Place: Galilee (see also 1 Cor 15:6)	28:16–20	16:15–18		
165. James the Brother of Jesus Sees Him (see also 1 Cor 15:7)				
166. Jesus and Disciples Counsel for the Last Time and Jesus Ascends Place: Olivet (see also Ac 1:3–12)		16:19–20	24:44–53	